The Complete History of

American Slavery

Other Books in
The Complete History of Series:

Ancient Greece
The Death Penalty
The Holocaust

The Complete History of

American Slavery

James Miller, *Book Editor*

Bonnie Szumski, *Editorial Director*
Stuart B. Miller, *Managing Editor*

Greenhaven Press, Inc., San Diego, California

Every effort has been made to trace the owners of copyrighted material. The articles in this volume may have been edited for content, length, and/or reading level. The titles have been changed to enhance the editorial purpose.

No part of this book may be reproduced or used in any form or by any means, electrical, mechanical, or otherwise, including, but not limited to, photocopy, recording, or any information storage and retrieval system, without prior permission from the publisher.

Library of Congress Cataloging-in-Publication Data

American slavery / James Miller, book editor.
        p.   cm. — (Complete history of)
    Includes bibliographical references and index.
    ISBN 0-7377-0424-1 (lib. : alk. paper)
    1. Slavery—United States—History. 2. Afro-Americans—History—To 1863.
I. Miller, James, 1943–   II. Series.

    E441 .A579 2001
    973.04'96—dc21   00-039332
                                                                            CIP

Cover photo: Archive Photos

Copyright © 2001 by Greenhaven Press, Inc.
P.O. Box 289009 San Diego, CA 92198-9009

Printed in the U.S.A.

Contents

Commercial trade in the Chesapeake region of the eighteenth century possessed special characteristics that made it ideal for trading slaves.

CHAPTER 2: BEGINNINGS OF SLAVERY IN ENGLISH NORTH AMERICA

CHAPTER 3: SLAVERY IN EIGHTEENTH-CENTURY NORTH AMERICA

The Stono Rebellion in 1739 was the largest uprising of African slaves in the history of British North America.

Kn... ...ht disperse families forever, slaves built wide
ne... ...ould act as surrogate parents to
th...

The underground railroad by which large numbers of slaves supposedly fled the slave states was largely a figment of antislavery whites' imaginations. Most of the help that fugitive slaves received came from their fellow blacks.

CHAPTER 14: BLACK ABOLITIONISTS

CHAPTER 15: SLAVERY AND THE COMING OF THE CIVIL WAR

Introduction

The two greatest flaws that disfigure America's historical record are the displacement—many would say the genocide—of North America's native population and the importation of Africans to build a slave society, whose institutions survived until 1865 and whose long-range effects still endure. This volume of *The Complete History of* series explores the second of these two great national scars.

Slavery was not simply a tragedy for the approximately 3.9 million black people who were serving in bondage at the time of the Civil War (1861–1865) and for their numberless ancestors who had been brought to America's shores in chains since the early seventeenth century. Slavery has been a lasting tragedy for this nation because it—like the uprooting of the Native American peoples and cultures—stands as the great exception to the hopes and struggles of the peoples of European and Asian ancestry who came here *voluntarily,* seeking freedom in the political and religious spheres and renewed opportunity in their social and economic lives. Until the twentieth century (when a substantial immigration from the West Indies began), all Americans of African ancestry came here *involuntarily,* devoid of hope, freedom, and opportunity. "What to the slave is the Fourth of July?" asked the greatest black leader of the nineteenth century, Frederick Douglass, himself an escaped slave, in 1852. His answer was that the Fourth—to white Americans an occasion for celebrating the nation's promise of personal dignity and a better life—was to African Americans a galling reminder of their lack of freedom. A century and a half later, slavery is but a historical memory, yet the power of that memory still divides our nation. "Fondly do we hope, fervently do we pray, that this mighty scourge of war may speedily pass away," Abraham Lincoln told the nation in his second inaugural address on March 4, 1865. "Yet, if God wills that it continue until all the wealth piled up by the bondsman's two hundred and fifty years of unrequited toil shall be sunk, and until every drop of blood drawn with the lash shall be paid by another drawn with the sword, as it was said three thousand years ago, so still it must be said, 'The judgments of the Lord are true and righteous altogether.'" The immediate occasion of Lincoln's words ("some of the grimmest words ever publicly spoken by an American president," according to his recent biographer) was the appalling cost in blood and property of the Civil War. Yet many would argue that the price for slavery is still being paid, in the form of a heavy shadow of guilt that separates those Americans whose forebears came here to achieve freedom from those whose ancestors arrived in chains.

The central fact of slavery is that its victims were *unfree,* regardless of the variations in the kind of treatment they received. To be unfree meant that slaves were utterly dependent on a master, whose life-and-death powers over his slaves were limited only by his self-interest in preserving the capital investment that his bondspeople represented. Slaves were *chattels,* a legal term that meant that they were property just as the owner's animals, machinery, and furniture were. As such, slaves could be bought and sold, mortgaged or otherwise used to satisfy debts, rented out, and bequeathed to heirs. The law guaranteed absolutely no rights to slaves. They had no defense against sexual abuse or sadistic punishment. Slaves' marriages had no legal standing, for the owner could separate families by sale at any time. Slaves could not testify in court against free people, for the law assumed that whatever a slave said would be controlled by his or her master. If a slave earned any money, it legally belonged to the master, for slaves had no right to own property. Slaves could not legally learn to read and write, or go anywhere without the master's permission. Slaves of course had no right to vote—even though the U.S. Constitution provided that each slave would count as three-fifths of a person to determine how many seats each state should be allocated in the House of Representatives (or how many electoral votes in presidential elections). And even if a slave was murdered, the legal concern with the matter was almost entirely limited to the loss that the slave's *owner* had suffered.

White defenders of slavery always insisted that how slave society actually functioned in the United States could not be inferred solely from the letter of the slave states' laws. They were right: In practice, local custom and the tangled webs of master-slave dependency were more important than the harsh, formal words of the law. Intelligent, experienced masters knew that there were limits beyond which it was not prudent to push slaves in demanding labor and obedience. Most slaves were accorded a minimum of personal "space"—a hut in which couples could live and raise their children, some spare time in which to raise food and perhaps hunt or fish to supplement whatever the master fed them, and occasional holidays on which to relax. Sometimes—primarily in cities—slaves were even permitted to live away from the master's household and to work at an artisan trade, on the condition that they turned over a specified amount of their earnings to their master. But such personal "space" was the master's gift, a privilege that could be withdrawn or enlarged as it suited the master's interest. The key words here are *were permitted*. No slave had a free person's right to do as he or she pleased. The terrible irony of American history is that, in places where slavery existed, free people defined their freedom in terms of having rights that everyone could see were dramatically denied to slaves.

One of the essential ingredients of freedom was the right to own and exploit a slave, and the one attribute that even the poorest, most ignorant, and most disreputable white person could take pride in was the fact of *not* being a slave. These fundamental inequalities help explain the paradox that, beginning in the late seventeenth century, American slavery and American freedom developed in a parallel, interlocking relationship. And in the slaveholding states, the years between the 1820s and the Civil War saw the *simultaneous* spread of democracy for whites and the entrenchment of slavery for blacks.

American Slavery: A Chronological Overview

The varieties of treatment that were accorded slaves and the complex, evolving relationship between American slavery and American freedom underscore the fact that the history of human bondage in this country passed through five distinct phases.

The *first phase* of American slavery began with the arrival of the first cargo of Africans in Virginia in 1619 and ended sometime in the late 1600s. During this phase the legal and economic foundations for a slave society were laid, but slavery in the full sense of the word did not yet exist. Historians do not even know whether those first Africans brought to Virginia on a Dutch vessel in 1619 were treated as slaves—people held to lifelong bondage—or were servants who owed service for a term of years to the person who bought them but thereafter were freed from bondage. We know that some Africans did achieve freedom in early Virginia and Maryland, even acquiring servants and slaves of their own. But life was very hard for everyone in the first few generations of colonial America: Disease was rampant, death often came early, housing was primitive, and economic prospects were highly uncertain. Not surprising, the number of Old World settlers, both white and black, in England's seventeenth-century mainland colonies was very low. Slowly, these struggling communities worked out the legal definitions of slavery and consciously chose to confine slavery to Africans (and occasionally to Indians). But until the last decades of the seventeenth century, everything was tentative.

The *second phase* of American slavery began roughly in the late seventeenth century and lasted until the eve of the American Revolution—that is, roughly until about the 1760s or early 1770s. This period coincided with the rapid rise in population in the colonies and with a dramatic surge in colonial prosperity. The worst ravages of disease were overcome as settlers acquired immunities, improved their hygiene, and avoided the breeding grounds of malaria. Infant mortality declined and families grew larger, with more chance of remaining intact. European immigrants flocked in, attracted by improving opportunities. And tobacco, which from the beginning colonists in Maryland and Virginia had raised (not always profitably) with slave labor as an export crop, now was joined by a second lucrative plantation staple: rice, which by 1690 the English found could be grown with tremendous success in coastal South Carolina and Georgia. To meet the demand for labor, large numbers of slaves were shipped from Africa and the West Indies.

With the institutions of slavery now fixed, the economic incentives to develop a slave society came into focus in the southern colonies. A "slave society" is not simply a society that allows slavery; rather, it is one whose fundamental relationships rest on slavery. And a slave society the South became, in which *all* whites shared the distinction of being free and *all* blacks were trapped in lifelong bondage. Imported either directly from Africa or via a relatively short stay in the West Indies, slaves were sharply isolated both from whites and from each other by differences of language, culture, and religion. Savage discipline, brutally hard and monotonous work, and an utter lack of sympathy from the whites who lorded over them characterized the slave regime of this phase.

Eighteenth-century slavery was certainly not confined to the southern colonies. New England and the so-called Middle Colonies (New York, New Jersey, and Pennsylvania) also tolerated the

institution, but with one crucial difference: Nowhere north of Maryland did colonial slaves constitute the bulk of the labor force, as they did on the South's tobacco and rice plantations. In the northern colonies, white families bought slaves as adjunct labor, to supplement the work that household members and apprentices were performing in the home, in the shop, or on the farm. Seldom if ever did whites north of the Chesapeake depend on slaves for their livelihood. The northern colonies, in short, did not follow the path of the southern ones in becoming slave societies.

The *third phase* of the history of American slavery extended from the beginning of the Revolutionary era to the early 1830s. During this phase, several significant things happened. First, a distinctive African American culture was beginning to form as black people who had lived in North America for several decades, or who had been born here to enslaved parents, learned enough English to communicate effectively with each other and with their masters. Second, the emergence of this African American culture was powerfully affected by a widespread conversion to Christianity. Earlier, masters had tended either to ignore their slaves' religious beliefs and practices or to discourage conversion out of fear that this might encourage insubordination. But beginning in the 1740s (somewhat later in the South), white Americans "got religion" in a massive outburst of evangelical fervor that historians call the First Great Awakening. As preachers of new denominations advocating a more emotional style of Christianity spread through the land, slaves (now more apt to understand English) got the message, too. By the beginning of the nineteenth century, most blacks considered themselves Christians, although they interpreted and practiced their faith differently than whites.

The third fundamental change that affected the nature of American slavery during this phase was the Revolution. The Declaration of Independence's pronouncement that "all men are created equal" challenged the justification for some men enslaving others. Certainly not all the

American revolutionaries subscribed to such a radical interpretation of "equality." Thomas Jefferson, for example, who wrote the Declaration in 1776, would remain a slave owner to the end of his life, exactly fifty years later. But Jefferson and many other white Americans now had a conscious struggle about the morality of slavery; before the Revolution, only a few Quakers had felt any doubts about it. So strongly, in fact, did opinion turn against slavery that all states north of Delaware either officially freed their bondspeople (usually by a gradual process) or allowed slavery unofficially to wither away.

But the Revolution did not end slavery south of the Chesapeake. The southern states, which had become slave societies, were economically too dependent on human bondage to do away with the institution. Occasionally slavery was criticized, even deplored, in the South, but only a relatively few slave owners there actually emancipated their slaves. (One who did, by his last will, was George Washington.) A series of threatened slave uprisings in the South after 1800, as well as the frighteningly successful slave revolt in Haiti, further contributed to slavery's endurance in the South. A growing number of southerners believed that they would be safe only if the institution was vigorously preserved. Slavery may no longer have been an unquestioned fact of life, but it was coming to be regarded in the South as a "necessary evil." Thomas Jefferson spoke for many southerners in 1820 when he wrote "we have the wolf by the ears"—it was too dangerous, he meant, to let go. North and South were, in short, becoming two different societies with respect to slavery, despite the political union that they had formed. When Jefferson wrote his "wolf by the ears" letter, the Union was indeed in crisis over the question of whether slavery should be allowed to expand west of the Mississippi River. That crisis was, Jefferson wrote in the same letter, "a fire bell in the night," which he feared sounded "the death-knell of the union." Congress patched together a compromise, but slavery and the sectional tensions it generated did not disappear.

The *fourth phase* of American slavery can be dated quite precisely: It extended from 1831 to 1861. The dominant theme of this thirty-year period was a steadily worsening sectional quarrel over slavery, culminating in the Civil War. Two events signaled the onset of this dangerous new phase: the appearance on January 1, 1831, of a radical antislavery newspaper in the North called *The Liberator,* and the massacre of some slaveholding families in Virginia by a band of slaves led by the charismatic slave preacher Nat Turner in August 1831. The toll of Nat Turner's Rebellion was fifty-five dead whites, and the rampage was confined to a single county.

Only a few white northerners (and only a handful of white southerners) considered themselves abolitionists, even by 1861, and the vast majority of whites still harbored racist views about blacks. The Civil War did not break out because the North decided that the time had come to abolish slavery by force if necessary. Furthermore, after 1831 almost all white southerners moved rapidly from reluctantly defending their "peculiar institution" as a "necessary evil" to proudly asserting that it was a "positive good." Meanwhile, despite a crescendo of abolitionist exposés of slavery as a horrific institution, what moved northern opinion decisively against slavery was fear that slave owners and their supporters—the so-called Slave Power— were gaining control of the federal government and were preparing to seize control of the West, excluding free white farmers and laborers who could not compete with slave labor. In 1860, Abraham Lincoln's election to the presidency by *northern* voters (he was not even on the ballot in the South) on a platform of excluding slavery from the West finally precipitated the explosion. Fearful that the North was ready to encourage slave uprisings and a race war in their section, most of the slaveholding southern states left the Union.

The *fifth phase* of the history of American slavery was the shortest: It comprised the four years of the Civil War (1861–1865). During this period slavery was destroyed, through processes that reveal much about the nature of the "peculiar institution." For example, the slave insurrections that the white South had always dreaded never occurred, even when a large number of southern adult white males serving in the Confederate army had to leave the supervision of slaves to their wives and daughters. Discipline among slaves on southern plantations and farms sometimes eroded, and often master-slave relationships changed in subtle ways, but in general slaves watched and waited rather than revolt against their owners. Only in places where Union troops approached did slaves tend to flee to the Yankee lines, and their treatment there was often marred by the northern soldiers' racist attitudes. The Union government also did not immediately declare the slaves in the rebel states free, as northern abolitionists ardently urged it to do. Knowing that he had to retain the loyalty of the slaveholding border states, President Lincoln declared that his paramount intention was to save the Union, not to free the slaves. Only when it became apparent that the Confederacy was not going to be quickly defeated on the battlefield did Lincoln decide to strike at the South by undermining the "peculiar institution." The Emancipation Proclamation that he issued on January 1, 1863, declared "forever free" only those slaves in areas actively rebelling against the U.S. government; slaves in Union states like Maryland and Kentucky, as well as in Union-occupied rebel territories, would have to be freed by other legal means.

News that they would be emancipated if the Union won spread quickly among the Confederacy's slaves, but again most of them remained quiet, waiting to see what would happen. Only the actual approach of Union troops precipitated mass flights. The slaves' major contribution to winning their freedom—and it was an enormously important contribution—was the service of about 186,000 black men in the Union army, constituting one-tenth of all the "blue bellies." As war weariness took its toll in the North during the conflict's last year, and as conscription replaced volunteering as the main source of military manpower, the willing service of black troops in the Union ranks became a vital component of victory. African American Yankee sol-

diers included both prewar free blacks and ex-slaves who had fled their masters during the war. So potent was this "sable arm" and so desperate did the Confederate cause seem in the war's last months that Confederate leaders toward the end were thinking thoughts that would have seemed unimaginable in 1861: that slaves should be offered freedom as a reward for fighting to defend the South's independence. Although some black rebel troops were actually enlisted, the war ended before their willingness to fight for the Confederacy could be tested in action.

And so slavery died as a result of slave owners' decision to leave the Union and fight for southern independence, a decision made not in response to abolitionists' determination to *destroy* slavery but merely because the northern public wished to *contain* slavery and reserve the West for free whites. After the slave owners' rebellion was quelled on the battlefield and their slaves were declared freed as a military measure, the Union states ratified the Thirteenth Amendment to the Constitution, which abolished slavery everywhere in the United States. Two other amendments, the Fourteenth and Fifteenth, promised former slaves their basic civil liberties, including the right (of black men) to vote. But it would take almost a century, until the civil rights movement of the 1950s through the early 1970s, before legal and political obstacles to African Americans' exercise of their hard-won freedom were overthrown. Yet still the subtle barriers of racism, exclusion, and dependency, legacies of centuries of American slavery, remain to haunt the land.

The Diversity of Southern Slave Society

American slavery, as we have seen, was not an unchanging institution during the two and a half centuries of its existence. But we must also remember that southern society was not uniform and that different categories of whites and blacks participated in the southern slave society.

At no time were all slave owners masters of large plantations with many slaves. In fact, from early colonial times until the Civil War, the majority of slave owners were white families who possessed between one and five slaves. In 1860, moreover, the U.S. census revealed that the majority of southern whites owned no slaves at all. The majority of slaves lived on large plantations with populations of fifty or more bondspeople.

These statistical disparities underscore several important realities of southern society. First, in the decades before the outbreak of the Civil War, the region's wealth was becoming concentrated into relatively fewer white hands, as the minority of large plantation owners substantially increased their investment in land and slaves and as the ranks also increased of those white southerners who owned only a few slaves or none at all. Second, the majority of black people grew up in fairly large slave communities, rather than being isolated as the only bondsperson in a white household or on a white farm. Third, even though the majority of whites owned no slaves at all, they tended to identify with the values of the great planters, for virtually all whites shared a common disdain for blacks, mingled with a fear of what would happen should the bonds of slavery cease to control them.

Historians have differed in their judgments of whether blacks were relatively worse off if they lived on a big plantation. Slaves' well-documented fears of being "sold down the river" to some big plantation owner, as well as images of the plantations as impersonal forced-labor camps, have persuaded many modern readers that, if one had to be a slave, at least it was better not to have been a plantation slave. Yet the more we learn about slavery and the Old South's slave society, the more it seems that there were certain drawbacks to being an isolated slave in a relatively modest household. Plantation life at least offered slaves the possibility of being able to develop an autonomous life "in the quarters." Whites could not supervise every minute of their time. Living in a slave community gave slaves the opportunity to marry (although there is evidence that many black men preferred not to marry women on their own plantation so that they would not have to endure the humiliation

of seeing their wives and children abused by the master without being able to protect them). Slave communities accorded blacks the chance to have their own religious services, albeit sometimes in secret, and occasionally to relax together. Being the only black—or one of a handful of blacks—in a white household meant having to endure a life of little or no privacy. And if such a slave wanted to marry or even to have a social life, he or she would need the master's permission to be absent occasionally. Moreover, the economic fortunes of an individual owner were more likely to be uncertain than were those of a big plantation owner, increasing the risk that if bad times struck, the slave would have to endure real privation and might well be sold. And, of course, the closer a slave had to live to his or her master, the more occasion there was for irritation, sexual abuse, or even calculated sadism—instances of which ex-slaves' reminiscences give ample, graphic testimony.

No discussion of slavery in pre–Civil War America should ignore the presence of free blacks, who were a significant part of both southern and northern society. The proportion of free blacks relative to slaves was probably greatest in the late eighteenth and early nineteenth centuries, when a fair number of slave owners voluntarily manumitted (that is, legally freed) their slaves out of a distaste for slavery. Some blacks gained their freedom by striking bargains with their owners: They could work independently, save their money, and eventually turn over an agreed-upon sum in order to purchase their liberty. Later, as the slave population multiplied by natural increase (that is, there were more births than deaths), the free black element in southern society grew proportionally smaller.

In the North and South, the great majority of free blacks lived in urban areas, and with a handful of exceptions they were poor. They worked relatively humble crafts or did odd jobs, but they also maintained close-knit communities centered on black church congregations and self-help groups (such as funeral societies). Interactions did occur between free blacks and slaves, particularly those slaves who served in urban households or workshops, but southern free blacks had to be cautious in their relations with rural slaves so that they would not arouse slave owners' suspicions. With good reason, southern whites always worried that local free blacks might be conduits of abolitionist propaganda or that they might harbor runaways.

The 1820s saw the height of the so-called colonization movement, a white-sponsored effort to eject free blacks and manumitted slaves from southern society by resettling them in Liberia. The number of blacks who were actually colonized, however, never amounted to more than the proverbial "drop in the bucket" compared with the growing population of enslaved African Americans. And most free blacks did not show any enthusiasm about being deported (for that is how they saw the matter). Later, as tensions mounted with the approach of the Civil War, white extremists proposed expelling the free blacks entirely or even re-enslaving them, but neither scheme was ever tried.

The geographic distribution of white and black populations in the Old South changed drastically over time. In the seventeenth century, new arrivals of both races from the Old World were clustered along the Atlantic Coast, the so-called Tidewater region. In the eighteenth century, white farmers spread into the Piedmont, the rolling uplands that extend to just east of the Blue Ridge and Allegheny mountains. But the big planters with their export-oriented tobacco or rice plantations tended to remain in the Tidewater, where they could easily load their cargoes onto oceangoing vessels.

The coming of "King Cotton" changed this distribution once again. In the 1790s, Connecticut tinkerer Eli Whitney invented the cotton gin, a crank-driven machine that removed the sticky seeds from the variety of cotton that grows in inland North America. (So-called long-fiber or green-seed cotton, from which the seeds are easily removed, flourishes along the South Carolina and Georgia coasts, but it cannot withstand interior conditions.) When possibilities for settling the interior finally opened after the defeat of the Indian nations in the War of 1812, the Old South's Cotton Kingdom rapidly took shape.

White planters and their slaves poured into the interior, hacking cotton plantations out of the wooded countryside. In the late 1830s, the removal of the "Five Civilized Tribes" of Native Americans opened still more rich southern land—often called the "Black Belt" because of its dark, fertile soil—to cotton cultivation.

Although initially the southern frontier was rather egalitarian (for whites, not for blacks), some whites either had or gained the financial resources to invest more lavishly in slaves, a relatively expensive "start-up cost." Over the course of the years 1820 to 1860, these economic differences widened, leading to the concentration of wealth in the hands of the big planters. Poor whites who could not afford slaves at all tended to migrate to marginal areas like the Appalachians or the infertile piney woods. There they could eke out a basically subsistence living, largely or even wholly independent of the market economy. On the other hand, whites who could afford a few slaves could be found widely interspersed through the fertile parts of the South. Some were young men who added to their slave property as they grew older and prospered. Others, victims of bad luck, bad health, or bad management, fell by the economic wayside. For most aspiring southern whites, slave ownership was the natural road to success, and they viewed their right to invest in bondspeople as proudly as they asserted themselves as free citizens of a democracy. This was the age of "the self-made man," of Jacksonian democracy. southern whites boasted of their democracy, and they meant it. But democracy was for whites only, and in the South it rested on the enslavement of blacks. Little wonder that from the early 1830s on, southern whites overwhelmingly agreed that slavery was a "positive good."

The Study of American Slavery

Serious historical research on slavery dates back to the early twentieth century. The leading authority on the subject in the 1920s was Ulrich B. Phillips, a southern-born white scholar who taught at such prestigious northern schools as the University of Wisconsin and Yale University, where he trained many graduate students. Phillips was a diligent researcher who uncovered a wealth of factual details about the Old South and slavery, and his books can still be mined for information. Unfortunately, however, Phillips was a racist, and his books to some extent downplay the suffering that slavery inflicted on its black victims. He also viewed sympathetically the traditional southern claim that slave owners were paternalistic rather than capitalistic in their outlook. Overall, his picture of slavery stressed a benevolent, gracious, and rather impractical side. In his view, slavery would probably not have withstood competition from the brisk, industrializing, capitalistic North for much longer had the Civil War regrettably not intervened. More recently, Phillips's interpretations have been rejected by almost all historians.

Much of the groundwork for challenging Phillips's work was laid by two African American scholars of the early twentieth century, W.E.B. Du Bois and Carter G. Woodson. Their attention focused mainly on the life and culture of black people under slavery and in the years after slavery ended. During the 1930s, a rich new resource was prepared for scholars. The New Deal's Works Progress Administration conducted oral-history interviews with hundreds of ex-slaves (by then in their eighties and nineties). For the first time, men and women who had lived in slavery—who had worked as field laborers and house servants, who had had parents and siblings torn away by sale, and who had both seen and experienced the terrible lashings that were regularly inflicted to "correct" slaves—were able to have their stories recorded for posterity. Historians still make great use of these interviews, and some appear as documents in this book.

The civil rights movement of the 1950s and 1960s greatly stimulated the study of slavery and the Old South. Supporting African Americans' drive for equality and justice, many white historians such as Kenneth Stampp, Winthrop Jordan, and Eric McKitrick viewed black history far more sympathetically than had Phillips and his students. Their books tended to indict white racism as the cornerstone of slavery, and they took care to document the full extent of the injustice and pain that slavery had wrought. Paralleling their efforts, African American historians led by John Hope Franklin of Duke University created a comprehensive scholarly interpretation of the black experience from slavery times.

Since the 1970s, scholarly work on the history of slavery has somewhat shifted its approach. Whereas earlier the urgent need was to correct racist misconceptions about the severity of the slave experience, now scholars paid greater attention to the lives that black people had built for themselves *despite* enslavement. In other words, slaves were being interpreted not merely as *victims* but also as active *creators*. Several important books pioneered this new approach: Marxist historian Eugene Genovese's *Roll, Jordan, Roll: The World the Slaves Made* (1974); economists Robert Fogel and Stanley Engerman's *Time on the Cross: The Economics of American Negro Slavery* (1976); *The Black Family in Slavery and Freedom* (1975) by Herbert Gutman, a social historian who led a team of researchers; and African American historian John Blassingame's *The Slave Community* (1979). These scholars, and others who shared their approaches, did not necessarily agree with each other, but they had in common a desire to examine and to celebrate the psychological strength of the people who overcame the conditions of servitude to create viable lives and societies for themselves in America.

This *Complete History of* volume is designed to help readers begin to explore the history of slavery in America. Arranged partly chronologically and partly topically, it has sixteen chapters that survey important aspects of the subject. Each chapter offers between four and ten articles of varying length, and each article consists of either an authoritative historical analysis or an important document. The historians whose work is represented in these articles include some of the important scholars mentioned above, and among the documents are transcripts of ex-slaves' oral-history interviews. At the end, a chronology lists significant events, a set of biographical sketches summarizes the lives of significant persons whose names appear in the articles, and a list of suggested readings invites you to investigate other important and reliable sources of information.

Editor's Note

The documents (especially the oral-history interviews with ex-slaves) and the source quotations included in this book often use the word *nigger* in referring to blacks or to slaves. This word, today properly regarded as derogatory and an insult, was routinely used in the past—by whites often with a belittling intent, but also by African Americans as a neutral self-description. For example, when being interviewed, elderly ex-slaves very often spoke of themselves as "the niggers" rather than as "we slaves." Offensive as this word is to modern readers, it cannot be removed from documents without damaging their value as historical sources. Needless to say, by retaining this word in the historical sources that are included in this volume, neither the editor of this volume nor the publisher means to convey any disrespect to African Americans.

The Complete History of

The Atlantic Slave Trade

Chapter 1

Introduction

The intercontinental slave trade was one of the oldest and most durable links in the far-flung commercial markets that historians call the Atlantic economy. Europeans' exports of slaves from West Africa to supply sugar plantations on Atlantic islands, such as Madeira, dated from the mid–fifteenth century, and in the first years of the sixteenth century the first African slaves brought to the New World landed on Spain's West Indian islands. There they filled the places of Native American laborers, whom the Spanish from the outset had put to work growing crops and mining for precious metals, but who were also dying in droves both from overwork and from infectious Old World microorganisms to which their bodies had no natural resistance.

Slave trading in the Atlantic was a profitable, large-scale business dependent on government support. Indeed, Portugal at first attempted to monopolize the commerce, only to have the Spanish force their way in during the sixteenth century. Later, the Dutch, the French, and the English governments forcibly grabbed shares of it and allocated the right to trade in slaves to chartered companies that had been assured of monopoly rights.

Like the slave trade, the plantations that Europeans established in the New World were basically business enterprises, too. The commodities they produced—sugar, tobacco, and rice—were in high demand as luxuries on European markets, and they required a considerable capital investment. Plantation labor was intensive, monotonous, often dangerous, and always exhausting, and it was virtually impossible to find workers willing to do it for wages. Slavery was the obvious solution, although the English experimented with indentured servants who were bound to labor only for a specified period of years. This experiment did not work, leading the English inexorably to slavery.

The human cost of establishing and maintaining a slave-labor plantation economy was immense. Modern historians estimate that 7 to 15 million Africans were brought across the sea to serve in slavery between the time when America was discovered and when slavery came to an end in the second half of the nineteenth century. Most of these people were brought to South America (especially Brazil) and the Caribbean; North America accounted for only a relatively small number, some 600,000. Always, however, the conditions in which these suffering people were transported were appalling. Before embarking, they were usually branded. Then, bent on maximizing profits, the captains of slave ships would pack their human cargoes as tightly as possible; slaves had no room to stand up and were forced to spend most of the passage lying below the deck amid indescribable filth. If the ship caught favorable winds and made a quick passage, captains calculated that enough slaves would arrive alive to fetch a good price, but if the ship was becalmed or blown off course, most or all of the Africans would probably perish.

The Triangle Trade: The Origins of the Slave Trade

James L. Stokesbury

By the middle of the seventeenth century, the Dutch had established thriving slave-labor sugar plantations on various West Indian islands and in parts of Brazil. In addition, trans-Atlantic shipping was on the rise from some of the English colonies on the mainland of North America. The slave trade would endure until the early nineteenth century, and it continued illegally until the time of the American Civil War.

The first leg of the Atlantic slave trade consisted of European or North American merchant vessels sailing to the west coast of Africa, where they would exchange iron bars (a valuable commodity in many West African societies), rum (made from distilled molasses), or manufactured goods for slaves.

In the second leg, slaves would be brought to the New World—primarily to Brazil or the West Indies, but, after 1700, increasingly to North America as well. The third leg was formed by west European or North American shippers sailing from the ports where slaves had been sold, laden with colonial goods (often produced by slave labor) such as sugar, tobacco, and rice for sale in European mar-

Excerpted from James L. Stokesbury, "The Triangle Trade," *American History Illustrated*, April 1973. This article is reprinted from *American History Illustrated* magazine with the permission of PRIMEDIA Special Interest Publications (History Group), copyright American History Illustrated magazine.

kets. In the final stage in the commercial system, goods manufactured in the colonies' mother countries were shipped back to colonial consumers.

Not every ship engaged in the Triangle Trade made a triangular voyage, of course. Many ship captains specialized in back-and-forth voyages across the Atlantic; others sailed at will from one port to another, looking for the best opportunities. However, conveying slave cargoes across the Atlantic Ocean was an essential part of the larger commercial system of the era. It was highly profitable. And, of course, it created immense human suffering.

In this selection, historian James L. Stokesbury vividly describes the history of the Triangle Trade. It is a story essential for understanding how American slavery developed. Stokesbury's account was originally published in American History Illustrated *magazine.*

*D*uring its lifetime the slave trade brought an estimated fourteen million human beings to the New World, and killed perhaps another forty million in the process. It was one of the greatest folk migrations in history, and certainly the most terrible. It made a human desert of the Guinea coast of Africa, a civilization on the lands bordering the Caribbean, and fortunes in Bristol, Liverpool, and Newport. It left a legacy of fear, hate, and racial tension that has yet to be exorcised. No thinking person today would conceivably condone the crimes that made up the trade—yet at the time slavery seemed perfectly logical, and for centuries few thinking persons opposed it. The slave trade simply was a fact of life.

The glory of Greece and the grandeur of Rome were built on the backs of slaves; it is our conceit to remember the temples of the Acropolis and forget the silver mines of Laurium. It was only in the very recent past that slavery came to have new connotations, the ugly overtones of racism on the one hand, on the other the enlightened idea that every man should be born free.

When Europeans first made their way down the coast of Africa towards the east, and discovered the New World to the west, they still believed in slavery as an institution. Some men were free, some were slaves; God had made it that way. When the Spanish therefore enslaved the Indians, it was not to them a reprehensible act; the Church put limitations on what could be done, and attempted to prevent abuses in a social situation that was not itself regarded as an abuse. The first Negro slaves were actually imported for humanitarian reasons. Bishop Las Casas in the West Indies realized that the Indians made poor slaves and soon died off, so he recommended they be replaced by Negroes, who seemed to be more adaptable. His suggestion was taken up with such alacrity that he was soon appalled by it, and died regretting his actions. But within the first generation of settlement of the New World, the slave trade was a going thing, and there was no stopping it.

It was 1619 before the trade hit the newly founded English colonies. A year before the Pilgrim Fathers landed at Plymouth, Paul Rolfe of Virginia reported that in August "came a Dutch man-of-warre that sold us twenty negars." Five years later another batch was sold in New Amsterdam, but the early importation was slow. There were plenty of white indentured bondsmen—and plenty of transported criminals—to do the work of clearing the woods; these were

slaves in all but name and the fact that eventually they would be free men. The British colonies that would become the United States were a hundred years old before the slave trade really got going. The 18th century and the early part of the 19th would be its heyday.

For the trade became peculiarly tied to economics and technology. Slaves became important as a commodity only in the South, which grew the kinds of crops that required much hand cultivation and cheap labor. Then they became vastly more important when the first impact of the Industrial Revolution hit the cotton industry. Ironically, labor-saving devices such as the water frame and more especially the cotton gin caused a tremendous demand for cheap labor—for more slaves. It is even more ironic to think, as many authorities do, that it was the profits from the slave trade that enabled England to get the lead in industrialization to begin with. By that time Liverpool was the world's slaving capital, and fortunes made on the banks of the Niger were spent on cotton mills in the English Midlands. When the famous actor George Cooke appeared drunk in Liverpool and was hooted on the stage, he roared back, "I have not come here to be insulted by a set of wretches every brick of whose infernal town is cemented with an African's blood!"

By the late 18th century the winds of abolition were beginning to gather strength, but it was not until 1807 that Britain outlawed the trade, and not until 1832 that she abolished slavery in the Empire. Even then it was an uphill fight to get other states to agree, and the transAtlantic trade lasted right up until the American Civil War.

Liverpool may have been the world's capital of slavery, but it was by no means the only center. It had pre-empted the primacy of Bristol, an early leader; there was still, however, plenty of competition.

In British North America, if the southern colonies were the center of slavery, New England and New York were the leaders in the trade. Southerners would later take great delight in pointing out to abolitionists from the North that it was the Northerners, after all, who had generally brought the slaves to America.

How the New Englanders and New Yorkers got involved in the trade, when it had little direct relevance to their own local conditions, is a peculiar story. The first New England vessel to take a cargo of slaves was the *Nancey*, of Rhode Island, in 1649. But it was only slowly that the Yankee shipowners became interested in Africa.

The connection grew gradually from the fact that New England was the poor relation of the British Empire; she did not fit into the imperial scheme as it was envisaged in the 17th and 18th centuries. Statesmen then considered that an empire ought to be made up of several complementary entities: a strong mother-country to provide manufactured goods and defense; tropical or semi-tropical colonies to produce agricultural goods not grown at home; and African stations to furnish slaves for the tropics. Colonies in a temperate climate, similar to that of the home country, were a very poor last on the list. If you had to have them, it was better that they be like French Canada, sparsely populated and producing naval stores or furs.

But New England was too far north for tobacco, sugar, or indigo; too far south for much fur. It had been settled by dissidents, and economically and particularly socially continued to be a sore spot in the British scheme of things. It did produce a lot of dried fish, and that was a useful product to sell to Catholic Europe. Then in 1651 the British passed their Navigation Acts, designed to further their vision of a closed empire, and though they made some concessions to local problems, the New Englanders were hit by these new restrictions. To make a living, the Yankees were forced into various byways. Many of them became carriers for imperial products. Little New England vessels became the colonial period's version of the tramp steamer. They became very adept at smuggling, to avoid the restrictions of the Navigation Acts, but even that was not sufficient to restore their fortunes. Finally, since it suffered no particular stigma at the time, they came to slaving.

In its early stages, the New England trade to the southward was a simple back-and-forth af-fair. A local merchant—and most traders were small businessmen—would load up a schooner or a sloop with his products, usually dried fish and lumber, and send the vessel south to the West Indies. It is difficult today to realize how small these enterprises were, the vessels often little larger than a modern sailboat, the crew three or four men and a dog. They would be gone for months. If they were lucky, and avoided storms, calms, sickness, pirates, Spaniards, or Frenchmen, they would return with a cargo of sugar and indigo. Maybe they would have gone from the islands to the southern colonies to pick up tobacco. Sometimes they would come home with a few slaves as deck cargo; that was how most of the slaves imported into New England got there.

It took only the barest acquaintance with the West Indies to realize that what was most in demand there was slaves. If a captain, often the owner of his vessel, was looking for a quick cargo, he could always delay his return to New England. He could take aboard a load of rum, nip across to Africa, exchange his rum for slaves, and run back to the West Indies. His slaves would make him a far greater profit than a straight run to and from New England.

The next logical step was easy to see, and no one has ever accused Yankee businessmen of not being able to see very far. It took a captain no more than a couple of voyages, if he lived through them, to make enough money to set up a regular three-cornered trade. By the mid-18th century the Triangle Trade was well established.

The voyage began with a cargo of rum; in 1750 there were over sixty distilleries in Massachusetts making rum for the slave trade. There were possibly thirty more in Rhode Island, and more in eastern Connecticut and southern New Hampshire. Even so they were unable to keep up with the demand. A vessel would load with hogsheads of rum, and then make its voyage southeast across the Atlantic to the Gulf of Guinea. There were various areas where slaves might be obtained, and the slaving coast stretched almost 4,000 miles from the mouth of the Senegal down past the equator. The Yankees usually traded on the near end of the coast, the Gold Coast or the

Windward Coast as it was called. The farther end was monopolized by the Liverpool slavers, big money men could buy cargoes wholesale; the Yankees were small traders, and amassed their cargoes one slave at a time, dickering with the native chiefs and choosing carefully.

They might, because of this, be on the coast for months before getting a cargo. Once they were filled they stood away for the West Indies. This second leg of the voyage was called the "middle passage," and if the ship ran into storms or became becalmed, or had sickness aboard, was probably the closest thing to hell that living human beings ever saw before the Nazis put 20th century technology to work on their victims. The passage could take anything from a couple of weeks to three or four months.

Once in the West Indies, the surviving slaves were taken ashore and sold. Those who hadn't made it had been thrown overboard; those who lived through the voyage but were so weakened they would die soon after were simply left on the wharves to expire. The ship would then load with molasses for the last leg of her voyage back to New England. The molasses would be transformed into rum, and the whole process would begin over again.

In a callous age—and this was a time when people paid good money for seats at a hanging, and took their children with them—all this made sense; better, it made money. Rum was cheap in New England, but dear on the coast of Africa; slaves were cheap in Africa but dear in the West Indies, and molasses was cheap in the islands but vital in New England. It was a three-way voyage with a three-way profit.

And the profit was indeed tremendous though it fluctuated so greatly that few definitive figures can be given. At the very start of the trade slaves could be bought in Africa for a handful of beads. On his first voyage John Hawkins, the earliest Englishman in the trade, made himself the richest man in Plymouth; that was in the 1560's. His second voyage made him the richest man in England. Two centuries later the native traders had become more sophisticated; they would trade a man for a musket. In some places a prime slave

would bring 200 gallons of rum. Then in the West Indies or the American South the prices varied even more, not only as the trade progressed from one period to another, but also depending on local supply and demand factors. At one point slaves would be a glut on the market, at another they would bring premium prices. A slave who sold for a few dollars in the late 1700's, when the trade was still legal, would bring four or five hundred in the early 19th century after it was outlawed. For all these reasons no hard figures can be given, but it was not unusual for a voyage, if successful, to return a 100 percent profit, and it might bring as much as 300 percent. Many ships paid for themselves in their first voyage; they became so foul that they were often burned after three trips.

Such high profits in the trade compensated so many risks to the vessel, to its crew, and especially to its cargo on the middle passage. To begin with, there were all the normal hazards of wind and water. Sailing vessels may have been among the highest examples of pre-industrial technology, but the best of them was still frail before the elements. It was with some justice during this period that Dr. Johnson remarked, "No man would go to sea who had sense enough to buy a rope and hang himself." And the vessels employed in the trade were by no means the best available. There was very high wastage of them, and through the 17th and 18th centuries they varied enormously.

The practical Dutch had developed special ships for the slave trade, with high holds and 'tween decks, and ventilating ports so that air could be circulated. The British, and particularly the Liverpool merchants during the height of the trade, used large ships, some almost the size of the famous East Indiamen, but there was no hard and fast rule about the type employed. Big slaving companies used large, well-found ships, but smaller private ventures used whatever was at hand.

Most of the New Englanders fell in this latter category, and they had a preference for topsail schooners or brigs, smaller ships that were easily handled by a small crew. Often the boats

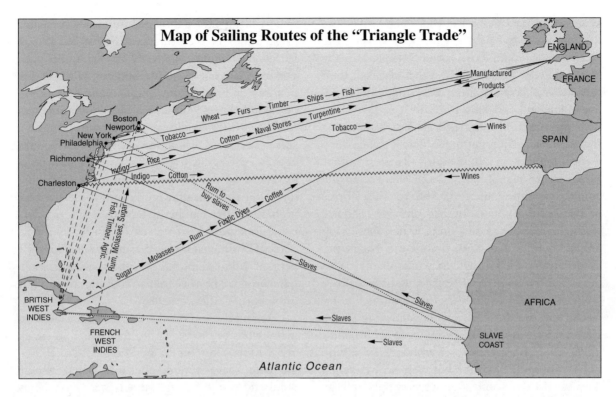

Map of Sailing Routes of the "Triangle Trade"

were in poor condition, and the great Scottish explorer, Mungo Park, who served as a surgeon on a slaver in 1797, reported that he could go up inside the bow and look out at daylight all around her. His ship, the Massachusetts vessel *Charlestown*, made a very poor passage, and at one time began taking so much water that some of the stronger slaves had to be brought up to man the pumps. Even so the *Charlestown* nearly foundered, and at last her crew by a sitdown strike that was a bloodless mutiny forced the captain to put in to Antigua; the vessel was condemned as unfit and the slaves sold. She still made a profit.

The ship on which Park served was a sizeable one—though unseaworthy—by New England standards. In 1789 the largest vessel to sail from Rhode Island for the trade was the sloop *Nancey*, of only sixty tons, one-third the size, that is, of either the *Mayflower* or the schooner yacht *America*. The *Nancey* had a crew of seven. Coincidentally, the smallest vessel that year was named *Nancey*, too, this time a schooner of twenty tons and a crew of four.

One customarily thinks of the slavers as fast, sleek vessels, built on Baltimore clipper lines for great speed. These came later, in the last years when the trade had been made illegal and it was necessary to outrun British cruisers off Africa or, occasionally, the all but nonexistent revenue cutters of the United States. These vessels were so beautifully designed they belied their ugly purpose, but they appeared only after the days of the "legitimate" triangle trade.

Aside from the perils of the elements and the parsimony of the owners, there was the coast of Africa itself to be survived. For three centuries it was known as "the white man's grave," and few men expected to survive there for long. Tropical diseases of all kinds were endemic, yellow fever, dengue fever, malaria, and assorted kinds of dysentery. The white man succumbed to the natives' diseases, and the native to the white man's. Thousands of potential slaves died of measles either in compounds on the coast or on the trip across, and hundreds of white men died in local plagues. In the 1790's British officials could produce figures to show that the slave trade took a greater toll, proportionally, of British merchant seamen than it did of Africans.

Sometimes it would take a slaver months to fill her holds, and it was not unknown for her crew to die off before the task was completed. There were always derelict sailors on the beach looking for a ship, their own having been destroyed by fire, natives, or accidents. But sailors on other ships died so fast that new berths were easy to find as soon as another slaver appeared over the horizon.

Aside from sickness, the sailors were terribly ill-treated. As often as not they had been crimped—shanghaied—and were subject to the most brutal treatment from their officers, with no hope of redress. It was in fact the practice on some British ships to make conditions progressively worse as the vessel neared the West Indies. Fewer hands were needed to get the ship from there to Britain, and men who could be driven to desert need not be paid. One tends to think now that anyone who went slaving deserved what he got, but the common sailor of the 18th century had little more choice than the slave. Jack Tar got dysentery or dengue fever; it was his captain or the ship's owner who ate off silver and made his fortune.

Even the horrors of being a crew member paled beside the agonies of being a slave, however. As time went by, attitudes changed. With the slow growth of humanitarian impulses in Europe and America came the contrary idea that Negroes were sub-human, and were therefore beyond consideration. Perhaps the most appalling thing that strikes one in reading about the trade is the attitude that the slavers were dealing dispassionately in a species of livestock. The abolitionists in England used as their seal a picture of a Negro in chains with the caption, "Am I not a man and brother?" The slavers answered that poignant question with a resounding "No!"

So captains could argue dispassionately the benefits of "loose packing"—giving the slaves breathing room so more would survive the trip—as opposed to "tight packing"—giving no breathing room but cramming the slaves in so numbers would compensate for the ones who died. One of the most famous slavers of all, for example, was John Newton, who spent twenty years in the trade. He eventually got religion and left it, but was still an active slaver when he became noted as a hymn-writer, and he saw nothing incongruous in this. His famous hymn, "How Sweet the Name of Jesus Sounds," was written while he was off the Guinea Coast, waiting to fill the holds of his ship with slaves. But he was one of the very few who ever did become conscience-stricken about the trade.

Of the second leg of the triangle—the infamous "middle passage"—stories are told so horrible that it takes a conscious effort to think oneself back into the context of the time. Perhaps to an age that would maim its children so they would be more effective beggars, or that would work 4-year-olds to death in mines and factories, the middle passage was nothing extraordinary. To us the stories of it are like something out of Dante's *Inferno*.

The slaves were closely packed. Most slavers had special platforms built in their holds, called 'tween decks, to take more slaves. The natives were ironed together, two by two, with either leg irons or handcuffs or both. They were made to lie spoon fashion in some ships, all on their backs in others. Some slavers were crowded to the extent that a man lying on his back had the next above him so close he could not even roll over, and as a rule of thumb it was estimated that a full-grown man needed a space sixteen inches by twenty-two inches by five and a half feet. Women and children were separated, not from any delicacy, but because they could be packed in smaller spaces.

If the weather were fair on the passage, the slaves were brought up on deck each day and exercised. It was thought good for them to "dance"; slaves were subject to extreme melancholia, as well as other diseases, and dancing was supposed to make them happy. Usually they were flogged with a cat or a rope's end to make them jump about. This was the reality behind the picture painted by pro-slavery propagandists of happy Africans dancing and singing their way across the Atlantic to their new homes. By the time they finished the trip, the irons had often worn away the flesh down to the bone and left them with festering, pus- or mucus-covered sores; so the dancing must have been less than pleasurable. Often the slaves would try to jump overboard, in the belief that the moment they died they would go back to Africa.

If the weather was bad, the slaves could not be allowed on deck and the hatches were kept battened down, except for the times in the day, usually twice, when they were fed. In this case they might have no fresh air, and no chance to move around and exercise, for up to several weeks. Often unable to move, they would simply lie there in their own filth until they began to sicken and die. The larger ships carried doctors, or men professing to be such, and their memoirs tell of crawling into the holds—there was no more than crawl space—and hauling out dead bodies while the bottoms of the holds slopped with blood, vomit, mucus, and excreta. Sailors maintained that any ship that had ever carried slaves could be smelled five miles to windward.

All these conditions prevailed if a ship were fairly healthy; if disease got aboard, she was infinitely worse. A ship might lose half her cargo to sickness, and leave a trail of corpses behind her all the way across the Atlantic. Sharks fattened on the slave coast, where the ships had to be loaded through heavy surf and often had their first losses, and then followed the ships across to America feasting off discarded corpses all the way. Disease struck down black and white indiscriminately, and there are records of ghost ships being found, gear adrift, sails flapping and tattered, with the entire crew and cargo dead long since.

Occasionally the crews got careless and the slaves would rise. They were usually soon beaten back below decks, but once in a while they would seize the ship. It did them little good; none of them had the slightest knowledge of how to sail or navigate, and they would simply drift aimlessly about until all were dead, another ship lost without a trace. Such incidents were of course rare. Usually the Negroes were too well-guarded, and the crews too alert. But they did happen.

As the ships neared the West Indies, they met other perils. The 17th century was the great era of piracy; in the 18th, as the wars between the colonial powers reached their peak, foreign privateers and men-of-war were a constant danger. War was so endemic that anyone could procure a privateer's commission or a letter-of-marque from some government. To the peril of disease and the sea was added further danger from one's fellow men. The laws of nations and of warfare were so loosely defined that slavers and more legitimate traders alike slipped easily back and forth over the bounds of legality.

One of the most famous slaver captains was Billy Boates—he got his name because as a baby he had been found abandoned in a ship's boat—and he survived a great many fights and voyages. In 1758, during the Seven Years' War, he was attacked by a large French privateer. Several times the French managed to board his much smaller ship, the *Knight*, and he later happily related that "never a Dago that got over the rail lived to return." He eventually retired with a fortune and took to fitting out privateers, one of which was lucky enough to take a Spanish treasure ship.

Capture by a privateer of course did not mean rescue for the slaves; it merely meant that they would be sold in a different market. There was no release for them; but they tended to be both resigned and resilient, and this may account for the curious fact that on occasion captains armed their slaves to help beat off an enemy ship. Then after the fight they would clap the blacks back in irons again. Some captains were so well-known that the slaves would come down to the docks to cheer them in, cherishing memories of the time when they themselves had come across on such a famous man's ship. The idea seems incomprehensible, but is well-enough documented; probably the captains were no worse than the chiefs who had sold them, or the masters who had bought them, and they may have represented a link, however tenuous, with the longed-for Africa.

As the ships neared the end of the middle passage, the crews would make some attempt to repair the ravages of the voyage. The slaves would be given extra rations, hosed down with sea water, and before they got ashore would be oiled, a way of making their bodies look better, and of covering up, however ineffectually, their sores and wounds. The trade was not remarkable for business honesty; every ship carried a supply of soot and lamp blacking with which to disguise grey hairs. One slaver was noted for hiding the fact that slaves were afflicted with dysentery by stuffing oakum up their rectums. It worked long enough to effect a sale. The earthier humor of the 18th century thought this trick was highly amusing.

Once the middle passage was finished and the slaves sold, the trip home to New England with a cargo of molasses or tropical foodstuffs must have seemed like Heaven. It was a relatively short run, with not too much trouble anticipated. Tying up or dropping anchor in Salem, Newport, Boston, or New London was a world away from the steamy tropics of Africa or the West Indies. The ship would be clean again now—as clean as she would ever be—and the stench of slaves and sickness covered if not hidden by the more pleasant odor of molasses. The crew would be paid off—slavers were usually run on shares, like whalers—and the voyage finished with a final accounting to the owners.

Some famous New England names were involved in the trade. Peter Faneuil, who gave the citizens of Boston the hall named after him, the "cradle of liberty," once took a flyer in slaving; he went halves on a ship also named in his honor, the *Jolly Bachelor*. A well-known Rhode Island slaver was Esek Hopkins, brother of the province's governor. But he was not very successful, and on his record alone would never have become the first commander in chief of the Continental Navy. He was a failure at that, too.

The American Revolution brought changes in the slave trade but not many. Even before it, the West Indies was being replaced by the American South as the prime market. Basically the triangular trade pattern was too efficient to be substantially altered by political upheaval. South America, the islands, and the southern states all continued to need slaves too much for mercantile restrictions to be firmly enforced. But there were some differences. The British occupation of Rhode Island for several years during the war, plus the blockade, temporarily ruined her seaborne trade, and reduced the people "to making a living by taking in each other's washing." It would be some years before she recovered.

In the 19th century the triangle trade began slowly to break down. Britain's outlawing of the slave trade in 1807 at first had little effect. American laws prohibiting the importation of slaves were ignored for years by government and citizens alike. The British patrols on the African coast were ineffectual for a long time. Gradually, however, the triangle trade—though not the slave trade—was broken by the cumulative effect of these things. The price of slaves in the West Indies and the South rose remarkably, and it was less and less worthwhile to bother with the northern legs of the trade. Slavers would carry to Africa specie or any cargo the native chiefs would buy, then get their slaves and run to the west. It was in this period that the specialized slaving vessels were developed.

Eventually Britain did chivvy the other nations into cooperating to end the trade. It was a profitless and uphill fight. The United States with its firmly entrenched "peculiar institution" was one of the last to give in. American officials loudly declared the inviolability of the Stars and Stripes, while slavers flaunted that protection to collect their cargoes.

In its last stages the slave trade moved around to the East African coast, where the Sultan of Zanzibar became fabulously rich by making his island the slave-trading capital of the world. He collected a tax on every slave imported and exported. Slaves by the thousands were brought over from the mainland; as they neared harbor the sickly who would bring a low price were thrown overboard to drown, so there would be no tax on them. Years later, through the clear water, tourists could see the harbor bottom in Zanzibar covered with what they thought were round white stones—the skulls of thousands of unfortunates.

But the humanitarian tide continued to rise, and that, coupled with the American Civil War and emancipation, finally brought an end to the trade. There were many different triangle trades, but by mid-19th century the most infamous of them was finished. Its heyday lasted from about 1675 to perhaps 1825; it may be some measure of progress that we now recognize it, only two long lifetimes later, as one of history's great monuments to human greed and suffering. Its residual effects still wait to be resolved.

Selection 2

An Account of a Slaver's Successful Voyage

John Newton

All kinds of people were involved in the Atlantic slave trade, and a few of them left records of their experiences. One of these was the English sea captain John Newton who kept a journal describing his activities from 1750–1754.

Newton, a pious man who in his spare time composed hymns, never betrayed any thought that the trade in which he was engaged might have been morally questionable. In the mid–eighteenth century, however, few if any Europeans or white Americans questioned the morality of slavery.

In the extracts from Newton's journal that follow, Newton engages in hard bargaining with the African kings who sold their human merchandise, and carefully selects his victims. He preferred to export mainly boys and young men, who would command the highest prices in the West Indies. It is also obvious that his slaves did not passively accept

their lot, but instead had to be controlled by brute force.

L aus Deo [Praise God]

Journal of a voyage intended (by God's permission) in the African, *snow* [sailing ship], *from Liverpool to the windward coast of Africa, etc., 1752. . . .*

Tuesday 30th June. At daylight this morning unmored, and at 11, being high water, weighed from the Black Rock, in company with the *Adlington,* John Perkins, for windward and Gold Coast. . . .

Wednesday 12th August. . . . At 9 saw the looming of the land, and at 10 breakers . . . soon after, clearing up, perceived we had Cape Sierra Leon eastward about 3 miles and that the breakers were upon the rock. . . .

Thursday 13th August. . . . In the morning King Peter of Whiteman's bay sent for his duty, but having heard yesterday that he had been very lately deposed, I put them off till the morrow, and at noon an embassy arrived from his new majesty Seignor Don Pedro de Case upon the same errand, with a written testimonial from Seignor Don de Lopez, the undoubted king-

Excerpted from John Newton, "On Board the *African*," in *The Journal of a Slave Trader*, edited by Bernard Martin and Mark Spurrell (London: Epworth Press, 1962).

maker of Sierra Leon. Upon consideration I found reason to recognize his title preferably to the former, and paid his demand of 16 bars [of iron], which, by the bye, is 4 more than was required by any of his predecessors; but with new kings there will be new laws. I have the honour to be second upon his list. . . .

Saturday 15th August. . . . King Peter came on board . . . brought a fine man slave with him, but had not time to pay for him, being busy with Mr Steele who came in last night from Kissy Kissy, bought 4 men slaves off him. I find the price is established at 70 bars amongst the whites. . . .

Sunday 16th August. . . . Paid King Peter for his man and lent him goods for 3 slaves, likewise made him a present in lieu of his former duty which had a good effect, for in the afternoon he brought off 2 very good boys. . . .

Monday 17th August. . . . At daylight went to the King's town. He shewed me 2 fine men, which I brought on board with me. Refused a woman. . . .

Sunday 24th September. . . . I have refused 7 slaves yesterday and today, being either lame, old or blind. The frenchmen [commanded by M. Gervaizeau] drives a great trade, and it is reported has bought near 40 since he came in, but I beleive many if not most are some of the above qualities. . . .

Tuesday 14th November. [At Mana.] At daylight perceived the longboat in the offing. At 8 a.m. she came on board, brought with her the *Mercy Gee's* punt with 4 hands and the doctor, their vessel having left them at the Gallina's. We are informed by them that the ship we saw here was the *Ellis and Robert,* Jackson; that the *Addlington* is down at or about Bassa with near 200 slaves on board, and that there [has] been an insurrection in her, in which the cheif mate and 19 slaves were killed. The longboat brought a letter and 4 men slaves from Mr Clow, and left goods with him for about 4 more. Had a canoo from the shoar with 4 slaves, refused them all, 2 being too old, and 2 too young. Lent Jemmy Cole goods for 4 slaves. Sent the yaul in shoar with them and some of Mr Tucker's people, and she did not come on board all night. Have the boatswain and 3 more people ill of a fever.

Wednesday 15th November. . . . The yaul returned at 9 a.m. . . . Her long stay, making me very uneasy, gave occasion to the discovering a plot some of our people had been concerned in, which I can suppose to be no less than seizing the ship. William Coney, the informer, told me he had been solicited by Richard Swain to sign what he called a round robin, a term which I was before stranger to. I cannot but acknowledge a visible interposition of Divine Providence, for tho I cannot yet find the bottom of it, I have reason to think this sickness we have had on board within these 3 days has prevented a black design when it was almost ripe for execution, and the unexpected stay of the boat brought it to light. I thought myself very secure from any danger of this kind, as every body has behaved very quiet the whole voyage and I do not remember the least complaint or grievance. Richard Swain was then in the yaul; as soon as she came on board I put him in double irons. He seemed to be much surprized and pretends he knows nothing of the matter. The others [of] whom I have suspicion are at present too ill to bear examining. . . .

Saturday 18th November. . . . I find slaves have been very plenty to leeward for he has 23 in the longboat and Bryan says, when the ship went from here she had 240 on board, but the prices, unless he deceives me, are more extravagant there than ever: 7 guns, 7 cags of powder, 4 whole and 5 cut cloths, 4 pans and basons, 2 or 3 kettles, 2 large cases and from 4 to 10 iron bars upon every slave, besides knives, beads and other small articles which together can be little less than 90 ship's bars, besides a double risque; so that upon the whole I beleive I shall determine to stay to windward, because, if by any means I can compleat a cargo this voyage, I shall always [have] a fixed trade for the future. I hear the *Adlington* had near 200 slaves at the time of the insurrection, and that besides the mate, there were 3 or 4 whites killed.

Sunday 19th November. . . . Just about noon departed this life Peter Mackdonald after a week's illness. . . . [He]was in a continual delirium. . . . Buried him at sunsett. I hope every body else that were sick are recovering fast. . . .

Wednesday 22nd November. . . . Arrived the *Brittannia,* Pemberton, from Liverpool, by whom I had a letter from Mr Manesty, directing me not to call at Antigua, but to sail directly for St Christophers when I leave the coast. . . .

Monday 11th December. . . . By the favour of Divine Providence made a timely discovery to day that the slaves were forming a plot for an insurrection. Surprized 2 of them attempting to get off their irons, and upon farther search in their rooms, upon the information of 3 of the boys, found some knives, stones, shot, etc., and a cold chissel. Upon enquiry there appeared 8 principally concerned to move in projecting the mischeif and 4 boys in supplying them with the above instruments. Put the boys in irons and slightly in the thumbscrews to urge them to a full confession. We have already 36 men out of our small number.

Tuesday 12th December. . . . In the morning examined the men slaves and punished 6 of the principal, put 4 of them in collars.

Thursday 14th December. . . . Weighed at daylight, soon after saw a ship to windward, came fast up with us. At 10 I went on board, proved the *Earl of Halifax,* Daniel Thomson, of London, with an engineer, Mr Apperley, and materials for building a new fort at Annamboe. I wrote a letter in form to the captain requesting that, as he had a large and clear ship, he would take charge of my 2 prisoners, Swain and Forrester, and deliver them to the first man of war that offered. With a good deal of persuasion I at last prevailed, sent them on board, and gave bills on the owners for their wages; wrote a letter to the captain of the man of war (whoever it should be) and inclosed the depositions made by Sadler and Coonery. I am very glad to have them out of the ship, for tho I must say they behaved quietly in their confinement, I could not but be in constant alarms, as such a mark of division amongst us was a great encouragement to the slaves to be troublesome, and for ought I know, had it ever come to extremity, they might have joyned hands. . . .

Fryday 15th December. . . . Shipped the bal-

ance of the *Duke of Argyle's* account on board the *E. of Hallifax* in 13 men and a man boy slave, upon the following considerations: 1st, because as I propose to take no slaves under 4 feet 2 inches there is a probability of getting an overproportion of men for our number and perhaps more than we could stow in the room with convenience or look after with safety for we are but weak handed—only 20, myself and boys included, to take care of the ship and man both boats. 2ndly, upon account of the late intended insurrection, in which as they showed their disposition very early, so I took the opportunity to remove the ringleaders out of the ship. 3rdly, to keep the account of the *D. of A.* entirely separate from our present cargoe. And 4thly, I was induced by the best opportunity that could happen, the *Earl of Hallifax* being a very large, roomy vessel, not intended for slaves, and well manned. They promise to keep them all out of irons the whole passage, which I expect will improve them almost to the difference of the freight, which I agreed at 6£ sterling per head, consigned either to Mr Francis Guichard at St Christophers, or to Messrs Thomas Hibbert & Co. in Jamaica as it shall happen. . . . Captain Thomson is going directly to Anamboo where he is to discharge his cargoe, and will then proceed without stop to the West Indies. . . .

Saturday 16th December. . . . The *Ellis and Robert,* Jackson, have full slaved excepting a debt he is waiting for from Bryan and his brethren, so think not to stay longer than to write home by him, for we shall but hinder each other and it will be setting an ill example against myself to attempt buying slaves they ought to pay, lest it should become my own case when I come to collect from them in my turn. . . .

Monday 18th December. . . . Found *Ellis* here and understood soon that he has made a breach in the King's promise to me and got 14 slaves from him. However when I went on shoar he gave me a better reception than is common with him, and towards evening showed me 8 slaves out of which I picked 5, viz. 3 girls and 2 boys, all sizeable, and brought them off. Spent the evening on board *Ellis.* He threatens a hard competition, the event of which time will show. I am sure he cannot be much better assorted for them than I am. . . .

Thursday 25th January. . . . 6 of our white people and about 5 slaves ill with the flux, but none, I hope, without a prospect of recovery. For these 3 days have omitted giving the slaves pease for breakfast and try them for a while with rice twice a day. . . .

Wednesday 31st January. . . . Buryed a girl slave (No. 92). In the afternoon while we were off the deck, William Cooney seduced a woman slave down into the room and lay with her brute-like in view of the whole quarter deck, for which I put him in irons. I hope this has been the first affair of the kind on board and I am determined to keep them quiet if possible. If anything happens to the woman I shall impute it to him, for she was big with child. Her number is 83. . . .

Fryday 9th February. . . . When we were putting the slaves down in the evening, one that was sick jumped overboard. Got him in again but he dyed immediately between his weakness and the salt water he had swallowed, tho I imagine he would have lived but a little while being quite worn out. . . .

Saturday 17th February. . . . Came down the *Thistle,* Bray, from Gambia. He has about 70 slaves on board in 11 months on the coast. I was informed with a good deal of concern, that Joseph Fellowes, who I shipped second mate with him at Sierra Leon, the 23rd August, deceased in Gambia river. . . .

Fryday 23rd February. . . . The boy slaves impeached the men of an intention to rise upon us. [That is, confessed that the adult male slaves were plotting a revolt.] Found 4 principally concerned, punished them with the thumb screws and afterwards put them in neck yokes. . . .

Saturday 24th February. . . . Mr Tucker sent me word by his canoo that Monsieur Gervaizeau, commander of a french snow at the Bonanaes, had attacked his shallop [a sailing ship] on her return from the Susa's, killed one of his people, drove the shallop and the rest on shoar, and plundered her of 5 slaves and 7 cwt of ivory and my punt. . . . Accordingly put the ship in Mr.

Welch's charge with orders to proceed for Sierra Leon in 10 days if he did not hear from me, and get the ship ready for the sea. At 2 p.m. put off in the yaul and got safe on shoar in a very small, dangerous canoo, the other being stove. Halled the longboat on shoar directly (she being watering), cleaned her, and ballasted her with iron and camwood, put 4 swivel guns in her and supplied myself with small arms and amunition from Mr Tucker, manned with 6 whites and 2 blacks, being not without apprehension Monsieur might be troublesome. On Sunday morning set out with the flood and that evening reached Jamaica, where I met the shallop and understood my voyage was needless and the Frenchman sailed. . . .

Thursday 29th March. . . . Sold the longboat to the factory for 4 tons rice, an article I am in absolute necessity of, and not to be got here without difficulty. I am to deliver the boat upon my return from Sherbro, where I propose to go in a day or two, to try to dispose of my perishable goods, for there is such a universal stagnation of trade here, and so many pre-engagements, that I cannot expect to get a single slave, tho very well assorted for the place.

Fryday 30th March. Were employed all day in fitting out the longboat, loaded her as deep as she could swim, yet could not put in her all that must be either sold, left behind, or quite spoiled and lost.

Saturday 31st March. This morning set out early in the longboat for Rio Sherbro. (Left directions with Mr Welch to lay the ship on shoar on the spring and clean her, and afterwards make the best dispatch in wooding, watering and preparing for the sea till my return.) Sunday afternoon reached the Plantanes, staid there 2 days and with some trouble perswaded Mr Clow to take such goods as he liked best. . . . April the 5th got to Shebar and put all the rest of the goods on shoar with Mr Tucker, good and bad, whether in demand or not. . . . Before I left him I agreed to run the ship down to the Plantanes from Sierraleon, which I must have done likewise on Mr Clow's account. He promises to send the shallop in 7 days to meet me there with what ever he picks up in that time. . . . Fryday the 13th in the afternoon came into Sierra leon, and at 8 p.m. got safe on board the *African*. Found every body well, by God's blessing, and the ship in greater forwardness and order than I could have expected; top, bottom and sides cleaned, the rice from the factory on board, and all the water, being about 60 buts and puncheons [containers of liquid], filled and stowed. Have little now to wait here for but firewood. . . .

Tuesday 24th April. At sunrise weighed . . . at sunset came too . . . about a mile and a half from the Plantanes. . . .

Wednesday 25th April. Found Mr Tucker's shallop here, received from her one ton of wood, which paid for in cloth according to promise, he complaining when I was at Shebar, that it was hard to take such an odd mixture of spoiling goods without a peice of cloth to assort them. Delivered him likewise a small boy slave (No. 158), which he told me he would send one to redeem, but he now sends word that he has not received a slave since I left him, and he then stripped himself of all to furnish me. Upon the whole I did not think it either grateful or prudent to carry the boy away, which I knew would be a great disadvantage; otherwise I was very loth to part with a slave, tho but a small one, when just upon sailing.

Thursday 26th April. . . . At 2 p.m. weighed with a fresh brease at SW., bound by God's permission for St Christophers [in the West Indies]. . . .

Tuesday 22 May. . . . [At sea.] Have lost 6 whole lines and about twice the number of logs within these few days, the lines being all dry rotten. Are forced now to use fishing lines with a log proportionally smaller. . . .

Wednesday 23rd May. . . . Washed the slaves which the weather has not allowed us to do this fortnight nearly. . . .

Thursday 24th May. . . . Shaved the slaves' fore heads. Buryed a man boy (No. 192) of a pleurisy. . . .

Fryday 1st June. [At sea.] . . . At 6 p.m. saw the land to the SSW., tho could hardly be certain that it was land. Run under easy sail all night . . . and at daylight made the East part of Guadelupa [Guadeloupe, in the French West Indies] distance about 4 leagues, and Deseada [Désirade], which I suppose was what we saw in the evening, SE. 7 leagues. . . . At 8 saw Antigua and at 10 Monserrat. . . .

Saturday 2nd June. . . . By 1 p.m. stretched close in with the land about half way between Bas-terre [Bassee-Terre, the main port on Guadeloupe] and the old road, and at 4 anchored in Sandy point bay in 15 fathoms. Went on shoar, waited on Mr Guichard. Find we came too in foul ground, sent Mr Welsh word to new birth.

Sunday 3rd June. . . . In the morning Mr Guichard went off with me to view the slaves. When came on shoar again, after comparing orders and intelligence, he judged it best for the concern to sell here, if I approved it, without which, he was pleased to say, he would do nothing, tho my letters from the owners referred me wholly to his direction. It seems by all I can learn that this is likely to prove as good a market as any of the neighbouring islands; and as for Jamaica or America, I should be extremely loth to venture so far, for we have had the men slaves so long on board that their patience is just worn out, and I am certain they would drop fast had we another passage to make. Wednesday is appointed for the sale.

Monday 4th June. Fair weather, new birthed a second time. Went to Basse terre. Entered the ship in the secretary's and naval office, and waited upon the Lieutenant General.

Tuesday 5th June. Entered in the custom house at Sandy point. Busy in preparations for landing the slaves.

Wednesday 6th June. Landed the slaves. Sold all to about 20.

Fryday 8th June. Buryed one of the remaining slaves, a man (No. 52). . . .

Thursday 14th June. Began to take in sugar.

Saturday 16th June. Went to Basse-terre to buy a cable. . . .

Wednesday 20th June. Finished the sale of the slaves, in all 167, on the ship's account. . . .

Monday 9th July. Received on board the last of our homeward cargoe, in all 74 hogsheads, 4 tierces sugar; 23 bags of cotton.

Wednesday 11th July. . . . At 4 p.m. weighed, bound by God's permission for Liverpoole. . . .

Wednesday 29th August. . . . At 1 p.m. got a pilot, steered NE. for Formby Channel. At 3 made the marks, at 5 entered upon the flats, and about 8 anchored at the Black rock with the best bower in 9 fathoms.

Soli Deo Gloria [Glory to God Alone]

Selection 3

The Middle Passage: A Slave's Narrative

Olaudah Equiano

Of the untold millions of Africans forced to endure "the Middle Passage"—the horrible crossing of the Atlantic Ocean in a slave ship—virtually none could record their experience in writing. But we do not have to rely on our imaginations to understand a slave's perspective on the traumatic transportation to the New World. Olaudah Equiano's narrative remains to record exactly what it was like.

Olaudah Equiano was a chief's son born about 1745 in the interior of what is today the West African country of Benin. Equiano was about 11 years old when he was captured by African marauders and eventually sold to Europeans. Surviving the Atlantic voyage in the West Indies he was enslaved as a personal servant to a master who eventually took him to England. In the end he managed to buy his freedom, which only a handful of eighteenth-century slaves were able to achieve. He converted to Christianity and took the European name Gustavus Vassa. Joining the small abolitionist movement that by the 1780s was taking shape among members of the English public, he foreshadowed the career of the great nineteenth-century American black leader Frederick Douglass. He became a prominent antislavery orator and wrote an autobiography that vividly and eloquently told the story of his harrowing younger days. It was published in 1789 under the title The Interesting Narrative of the Life of Olaudah Equiano, or Gustavus Vassa, the African. *He died in 1797.*

In this excerpt from his Interesting Narrative, *Equiano describes what he saw and felt when he learned that he was to be sold to a European slaver.*

The first object which saluted my eyes when I arrived on the coast, was the sea, and a slave ship, which was then riding at anchor, and waiting for its cargo. These filled me with astonishment, which was soon converted into terror, when I was carried on board. I was immediately handled, and tossed up to see if I were sound, by some of the crew; and I was

Excerpted from Olaudah Equiano, *The Life of Olaudah Equiano; or Gustavus Vassa the African* (Boston: Isaac Knapp, 1837).

now persuaded that I had gotten into a world of bad spirits, and that they were going to kill me. Their complexions, too, differing so much from ours, their long hair, and the language they spoke, (which was very different from any I had ever heard) united to confirm me in this belief. Indeed, such were the horrors of my views and fears at the moment, that, if ten thousand worlds had been my own, I would have freely parted with them all to have exchanged my condition with that of the meanest slave in my own country. When I looked round the ship too, and saw a large furnace of copper boiling, and a multitude of black people of every description chained together, every one of their countenances expressing dejection and sorrow, I no longer doubted of my fate; and, quite overpowered with horror and anguish, I fell motionless on the deck and fainted. When I recovered a little, I found some black people about me, who I believed were some of those who had brought me on board, and had been receiving their pay; they talked to me in order to cheer me, but all in vain. I asked them if we were not to be eaten by those white men with horrible looks, red faces, and long hair. They told me I was not: and one of the crew brought me a small portion of spirituous liquor in a wine glass, but, being afraid of him, I would not take it out of his hand. One of the blacks, therefore, took it from him and gave it to me, and I took a little down my palate, which, instead of reviving me, as they thought it would, threw me into the greatest consternation at the strange feeling it produced, having never tasted any such liquor before. Soon after this, the blacks who brought me on board went off, and left me abandoned to despair.

I now saw myself deprived of all chance of returning to my native country, or even the least glimpse of hope of gaining the shore, which I now considered as friendly; and I even wished for my former slavery in preference to my present situation, which was filled with horrors of every kind, still heightened by my ignorance of what I was to undergo. I was not long suffered to indulge my grief; I was soon put down under the decks, and there I received such a salutation in my nostrils as I had never experienced in my life: so that, with the loathsomeness of the stench, and crying together, I became so sick and low that I was not able to eat, nor had I the least desire to taste any thing. I now wished for the last friend, death, to relieve me; but soon, to my grief, two of the white men offered me eatables; and, on my refusing to eat, one of them held me fast by the hands, and laid me across, I think the windlass, and tied my feet, while the other flogged me severely. I had never experienced any thing of this kind before, and although not being used to the water, I naturally feared that element the first time I saw it, yet, nevertheless, could I have got over the nettings, I would have jumped over the side, but I could not; and besides, the crew used to watch us very closely who were not chained down to the decks, lest we should leap into the water; and I have seen some of these poor African prisoners most severely cut, for attempting to do so, and hourly whipped for not eating. This indeed was often the case with myself. In a little time after, amongst the poor chained men, I found some of my own nation, which in a small degree gave ease to my mind. I inquired of these what was to be done with us? they gave me to understand, we were to be carried to these white people's country to work for them. I then was a little revived, and thought, if it were no worse than working, my situation was not so desperate; but still I feared I should be put to death, the white people looked and acted, as I thought, in so savage a manner; for I had never seen among any people such instances of brutal cruelty; and this not only shown towards us blacks, but also to some of the whites themselves. One white man in particular I saw, when we were permitted to be on deck, flogged so unmercifully with a large rope near the foremast, that he died in consequence of it; and they tossed him over the side as they would have done a brute. This made me fear these people the more; and I expected nothing less than to be treated in the same manner. I could not help expressing my fears and apprehensions to some of my countrymen; I asked them if these people had no country, but lived in this hollow place? (the ship) they told me they did not, but came from a distant one. 'Then,' said I, 'how comes it in all our country we never heard of them?' They told me because they lived so very far off. I then asked where were their women? had they any like themselves? I was told they had. 'And why,' said I, 'do we not see them?' They answered, because they were left behind. I asked how the vessel could go? they told me they could not tell; but that there was cloth put upon the masts by the help of the ropes I saw, and then the vessel went on; and the white men had some spell or magic they put in the water when they liked, in order to stop the vessel. I was exceedingly amazed at this account, and really thought they were spirits. I therefore wished much to be from amongst them, for I expected they would sacrifice me; but my wishes were vain—for we were so quartered that it was impossible for any of us to make our escape.

While we stayed on the coast I was mostly on deck; and one day, to my great astonishment, I saw one of these vessels coming in with the sails up. As soon as the whites saw it, they gave a great shout, at which we were amazed; and the more so, as the vessel appeared larger by approaching nearer. At last, she came to an anchor in my sight, and when the anchor was let go, I and my countrymen who saw it, were lost in astonishment to observe the vessel stop—and were now convinced it was done by magic. Soon after this the other ship got her boats out, and they came on board of us, and the people of both ships seemed very glad to see each other.—Several of the strangers also shook hands with us black people, and made motions with their hands, signifying I suppose, we were to go to their country, but we did not understand them.

At last, when the ship we were in, had got in all her cargo, they made ready with many fearful noises, and we were all put under deck, so that we could not see how they managed the vessel. But this disappointment was the least of my sorrow. The stench of the hold while we were on the coast was so intolerably loathsome, that it was dangerous to remain there for any time, and some of us had been permitted to stay on the

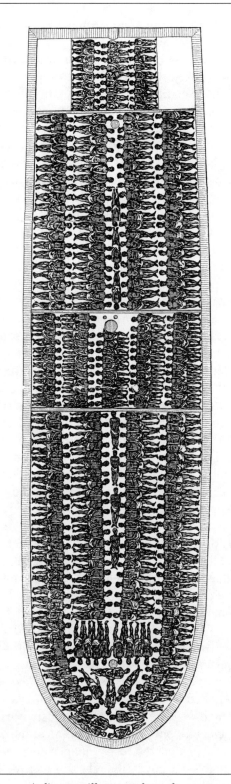

A diagram illustrates how slaves were crowded into ships.

deck for the fresh air; but now that the whole ship's cargo were confined together, it became absolutely pestilential. The closeness of the place, and the heat of the climate, added to the number in the ship, which was so crowded that each had scarcely room to turn himself, almost suffocated us. This produced copious perspirations, so that the air soon became unfit for respiration, from a variety of loathsome smells, and brought on a sickness among the slaves, of which many died—thus falling victims to the improvident avarice, as I may call it, of their purchasers. This wretched situation was again aggravated by the galling of the chains, now became insupportable; and the filth of the necessary tubs, into which the children often fell, and were almost suffocated. The shrieks of the women, and the groans of the dying, rendered the whole a scene of horror almost inconceivable. Happily perhaps, for myself, I was soon reduced so low here that it was thought necessary to keep me almost always on deck; and from my extreme youth I was not put in fetters. In this situation I expected every hour to share the fate of my companions, some of whom were almost daily brought upon deck at the point of death, which I began to hope would soon put an end to my miseries. Often did I think many of the inhabitants of the deep much more happy than myself. I envied them the freedom they enjoyed, and as often wished I could change my condition for theirs. Every circumstance I met with, served only to render my state more painful, and heightened my apprehensions, and my opinion of the cruelty of the whites.

One day they had taken a number of fishes; and when they had killed and satisfied themselves with as many as they thought fit, to our astonishment who were on deck, rather than give any of them to us to eat, as we expected, they tossed the remaining fish into the sea again, although we begged and prayed for some as well as we could, but in vain; and some of my countrymen, being pressed by hunger, took an opportunity, when they thought no one saw them, of trying to get a little privately; but they were discovered, and the attempt procured them some very severe floggings. One day, when we had a smooth sea and moderate wind, two of my wearied countrymen who were chained together, (I was near them at the time,) preferring death to such a life of misery, somehow made through the nettings and jumped into the sea: immediately, another quite dejected fellow, who, on account of his illness, was suffered to be out of irons, also followed their example; and I believe many more would very soon have done the same, if they had not been prevented by the ship's crew, who were instantly alarmed. Those of us that were the most active, were in a moment put down under the deck, and there was such a noise and confusion amongst the people of the ship as I never heard before, to stop her, and get the boat out to go after the slaves. However, two of the wretches were drowned, but they got the other, and afterwards flogged him unmercifully, for thus attempting to prefer death to slavery. In this manner we continued to undergo more hardships than I can now relate, hardships which are inseparable from this accursed trade. Many a time we were near suffocation from the want of fresh air, which we were often without for whole days together. This, and the stench of the necessary tubs, carried off many.

During our passage, I first saw flying fishes, which surprised me very much; they used frequently to fly across the ship, and many of them fell on the deck. I also now first saw the use of the quadrant; I had often with astonishment seen the mariners make observations with it, and I could not think what it meant. They at last took notice of my surprise; and one of them, willing to increase it, as well as to gratify my curiosity, made me one day look through it. The clouds appeared to me to be land, which disappeared as they passed along. This heightened my wonder; and I was now more persuaded than ever, that I was in another world, and that every thing about me was magic. At last, we came in sight of the island of Barbadoes, at which the whites on board gave a great shout, and made many signs of joy to us. We did not know what to think of this; but as the vessel drew nearer, we plainly saw the harbor, and other ships of different kinds and sizes, and we soon anchored amongst them, off Bridgetown. Many merchants and planters now came on board, though it was in the evening. They put us in separate parcels, and examined us attentively. They also made us jump, and pointed to the land, signifying we were to go there. We thought by this, we should be eaten by these ugly men, as they appeared to us; and, when soon after we were all put down under the deck again, there was much dread and trembling among us, and nothing but bitter cries to be heard all the night from these apprehensions, insomuch, that at last the white people got some old slaves from the land to pacify us. They told us we were not to be eaten, but to work, and were soon to go on land, where we should see many of our country people. This report eased us much. And sure enough, soon after we were landed, there came to us Africans of all languages.

We were conducted immediately to the merchant's yard, where we were all pent up together, like so many sheep in a fold, without regard to sex or age. As every object was new to me, every thing I saw filled me with surprise. What struck me first, was, that the houses were built with bricks and stories, and in every other respect different from those I had seen in Africa; but I was still more astonished on seeing people on horseback. I did not know what this could mean; and, indeed, I thought these people were full of nothing but magical arts. While I was in this astonishment, one of my fellow-prisoners spoke to a countryman of his, about the horses, who said they were the same kind they had in their country. I understood them, though they were from a distant part of Africa; and I thought it odd I had not seen any horses there; but afterwards, when I came to converse with different Africans, I found they had many horses amongst

them, and much larger than those I then saw.

We were not many days in the merchant's custody, before we were sold after their usual manner, which is this:—On a signal given, (as the beat of a drum,) the buyers rush at once into the yard where the slaves are confined, and make choice of that parcel they like best. The noise and clamor with which this is attended, and the eagerness visible in the countenances of the buyers, serve not a little to increase the apprehension of terrified Africans, who may well be supposed to consider them as the ministers of that destruction to which they think themselves devoted. In this manner, without scruple, are relations and friends separated, most of them never to see each other again. I remember, in the vessel in which I was brought over, in the men's apartment, there were several brothers, who, in the sale, were sold in different lots; and it was very moving on this occasion, to see and hear their cries at parting. O, ye nominal Christians! might not an African ask you—Learned you this from your God, who says unto you, Do unto all men as you would men should do unto you? Is it not enough that we are torn from our country and friends, to toil for your luxury and lust of gain? Must every tender feeling be likewise sacrificed to your avarice? Are the dearest friends and relations, now rendered more dear by their separation from their kindred, still to be parted from each other, and thus prevented from cheering the gloom of slavery, with the small comfort of being together, and mingling their sufferings and sorrows? Why are parents to lose their children, brothers their sisters, or husbands their wives? Surely, this is a new refinement in cruelty, which, while it has no advantage to atone for it, thus aggravates distress, and adds fresh horrors even to the wretchedness of slavery.

The Life of Olaudah Equiano

E.V. Francis

In 1981, historian E.V. Francis published the following short account of Olaudah Equiano's life in the scholarly journal Negro History Bulletin.

*O*laudah Equiano's autobiography reads like an epic. He served as a slave on three continents and experienced the bitterness of slavery at the hands of both blacks and whites. From a slave he rose to be an accomplished sailor and experienced world traveller.

Olaudah was born in 1745 in Esaka in the kingdom of Benin in the district of Eboe. The kingdom of Benin was a part of Guinea and it touched the boundaries of Abyssinia at that time. Esaka was one of the most fertile parts of Benin and it was mainly ruled by chiefs and less by the King of Benin. Olaudah's father was a chief who was styled "Embrenche", a term used to show the highest distinction. As a sign of his position, his father had the traditional mark across his forehead coming down each of his eye brows. Olaudah's father was one of the chiefs who usually settled disputes and matters of moral incursions. Olaudah remembers how one day a man was brought before his father for

Excerpted from E.V. Francis, "Olaudah Equiano: A Profile," *Negro History Bulletin*, vol. 44, April–June 1981. Reprinted with permission from The Association for the Study of African-American Life and History, Inc.

kidnapping a boy. Even though the culprit was the son of a chief, Olaudah's father and fellow judges ordered him to make recompense by giving a slave to the aggrieved party. On another occasion his father and other judges sentenced to death a woman accused of committing adultery. Aside from these recollections, we do not know much about Olaudah's father.

Olaudah, meaning fortunate and having a loud voice, lived in a community which was sufficient in all things. The land was fertile and the people had abundance to eat. They had plenty of bullocks, goats, poultry, and wide varieties of plantains, yams, beans and corn. Olaudah had six brothers and a sister. Since he was the youngest son, his mother took more attention and care in moulding his character. He was trained very well in the art of warfare at an early age. His mother often adorned him with emblems when he did excellently in his daily exercise of shooting arrows and throwing javelins. Until age 11 Olaudah had a happy life, especially filled with parental love and care.

When he was eleven, Olaudah was taken forcefully away from his home. He writes:

> One day, when all our people were gone out to their works as usual, and only I and my dear sister were left to mind the house, two men and a woman got over our walls, and in a moment seized us both and without giving

us time to cry out, or make resistance, they stuffed our mouths, and ran off with us into the nearest wood.

From there on started the untold miseries for Olaudah. A mere boy, he was sold as a slave several times and moved from one strange place to another where often he had to face a fate of inexplicable sorrow and frustration. The day after his capture he and his sister separated, and that was one of the most unbearable incidents in his life. He spent days and nights in tears and sorrow forgoing even any food. Finally, he was sold to a goldsmith for whom he worked as an aide, especially in working the bellows. His life there was not bad, and he had the liberty to move and one day he tried to escape from there. He hid himself in a bush with the hope of escaping but he soon returned to his master because the way back was quite unknown to him and intricate where more dangers lurked.

Olaudah was again sold and was transferred from place to place. Interestingly enough, though a young boy, Olaudah quickly learned three languages of the places he passed through. Always burdened by hardships, Olaudah never forgot his sister and in an unexpected manner he met his sister brought to the very house he lived. He writes: "As soon as she saw me, she gave a loud shriek, and ran into my arms—I was quite overpowered; neither of us could speak; but, for a considerable time, clung to each other in mutual embrace, unable to do anything but weep."

Olaudah's joy at meeting his sister was short lived and the hand of fate again parted them. The intensity of his sorrow at her parting and the fond memories, he depicts in a highly poetic way: "Yes, thou dear partner of all my childish sports! thou sharer of my joys an sorrows! happy should I have ever esteemed myself to encounter every misery for you and to procure your freedom by the sacrifice of my own." He was again sold to a place called Tinmah. There he was brought by a wealthy person and he became the companion of his master's young son. Life there was easeful and as he was beginning to like the atmosphere, he was again sold. This time the people who bought him were entirely different from the Africans he had seen. These people were partially westernized in their ways of eating meat and drinking liquor. For six months these people carried Olaudah with them as they moved in canoes toward the sea, their final destination. Olaudah was in miserable condition yet he had a keen eye for observation and he gives a vivid account of the place, the people, and their manners which he encountered. One who reads his autobiography can see how talented he was even as a boy in observing the people who were selling him as a chattel!

Finally, he was sold to the slave ship from England. The very sight and behavior of the white stunned and shocked him. He writes: "the white people looked and acted, as I thought, in so savage a manner; for I had never seen among any people such instances of brutal cruelty; and this not only shown towards us blacks, but also to some of whites themselves."

Though a boy Olaudah could not forget the pitiable predicament and the slaves who were hurdled in the hollow of this ship. The closeness of the place of the heat produced suffocated the poor slaves, and he describes:

> This wretched situation was again aggravated by the galling of the chains, now became insupportable; and the filth of the necessary tubs, into which the children often fell, and were almost suffocated. The shrieks of woman, and the groans of dying, rendered the whole a scene of horror almost inconceivable.

Since he was only a boy, he was not chained and often allowed to move to the deck and enjoy the fresh air. Finally, the slave ship reached Barbadoes and many were sold there. Olaudah, being one of the nonsaleable, was taken back to the ship from Barbadoes where he stayed about two weeks.

The slave ship finally came to Virginia, and Olaudah, who had borne the name Michael, was renamed Jacob by the plantation owner who bought him. Soon Olaudah was sold to Michael Henry Pascal, the captain of an English trading ship. When the ship reached England, Pascal changed Olaudah's name to Gustavus Vassa. When Olaudah desired to be called

Jacob, his cruel master beat him until he accepted this new name.

In this ship Olaudah met Richard Baker, a white American, who became his lifelong friend until Baker died in 1759. Of all the beings he met it was only Baker who took Olaudah as his own equal and a friend. In 1757 when Pascal's ship reached England, Olaudah was only 12 years old. A little later Pascal became a lieutenant on a British warship, and Olaudah became his valet. For three years he participated in the Anglo-French war.

Olaudah could speak English very well by this time and showed a keen interest in learning to read and write. When Pascal returned to England, Olaudah had the opportunity of meeting Miss Guerin, the sister of the captain's mate and friend. Though not aware of the teachings in Christianity, Olaudah, who had some faint idea about heaven, knew that he would not go to heaven until baptized. Olaudah requested Miss Guerin to have him baptized and he was baptized in St. Margaret's Church, as Gustavus Vassa. He had a brief period of schooling under Miss Guerin.

Soon Captain Pascal was sent to the Mediterranean to fight against the French and Olaudah accompanied his master. There were several occasions on which he could have lost his life but he had developed a faith in his destiny. He writes: "Cheering myself with the reflection that there was a time allotted for me to die as well as to be born, I instantly cast off all fear or thought of death, and went through the whole of my duty with alacrity." Hardly sixteen years old, he soon became the steward of Pascal. . . .

Olaudah kept an unshaking faith in God: "I began to raise my fear from man to him alone, and to call daily in his holy name with fear and reverence." His interest in learning was still aflame and while in this warship, he improved his skill in writing and in arithmetic. Once Olaudah was able to read, the first book he read was the Bible and was surprised to see in it the rules of his own society in Africa. He comments: "I was wonderfully surprised to see the laws and rules of my own country written almost exactly

here; a circumstance which I believe tended to impress our manners and customs more deeply on my memory." Olaudah's life was suddenly jolted when Captain Pascal who had taken all his prize money and given him only six pence for his service, sold Olaudah to one Captain James Doran of a merchant ship plying between England and the West Indies. He writes: "The only coat I had with me my master took away with him."

Olaudah, by this time, began to think about God and His ways and found fault with himself for his misfortunes. He saw God as a stern taskmaster and thought God was punishing him for he had sworn to indulge in gambling and sport as soon as he got time. Later Olaudah regained his composure and put deep trust in God. He states:

> I considered that trials and disappointments are sometimes for our good, and I thought God might perhaps have permitted this in order to teach me wisdom and resignation; for he had hitherto shadowed me with the wings of mercy, and by his visible but powerful hand brought me the way I knew not.

On February 13, 1763, Olaudah arrived in Montserrat where he was sold to Robert King, a Quaker merchant from Philadelphia. The next three years were the hardest in his life even though King treated him fairly well. He was frequently pained by the atrocities done to other slaves by their owners. Moved by the utter ruthlessness with which black people were treated, Olaudah raised his hands to God with a sense of doubt in God's justice: "He tells us the oppressor and the oppressed are both in his hands; and if these are not the poor, the broken-hearted, the blind, the captive, the bruised, which our Savior speaks of, who are they?" Olaudah could find no answer to the question while white people tortured the poor, unarmed, and defenceless slaves.

Within this period Olaudah had become an experienced sailor. Besides working as the captain's aide and steward, he began to make some money through careful trading of small items like glass wares, limes, and other tropical fruits.

Olaudah always believed that honesty is the best policy. . . . Often he slid back to his own belief in fate: "If ever it were my lot to be freed, nothing could prevent me, although I should at present see no means or hope to obtain my freedom; on the other hand, if it were my fate not be freed, I never should be so, and all my endeavors for that purpose would be fruitless." In one of his trips to Philadelphia he met Mrs. Davis, a clairvoyant, who predicted that he would soon gain his freedom which gave him great consolation.

On July 10, 1766, at the age of 21, Olaudah paid Robert King forty pounds and gained his freedom. He then worked for King on a salary for a short while, and decided later to go to London. Since he had no money, he had to continue working in a merchant ship. At this time he also improved his salary by trading small items in the various West Indian Islands. More than a trader, Olaudah, now as a free man, displayed his foresight and courage especially in times of danger. In one of his trips to Georgia from the West Indies, their ship came across another ship. The captain, an irrascible and headstrong person, mistook the other ship for a pirate ship and at the same time he could not take any decision as what to do. Olaudah wisely told the captain: "We must board her even if we were to die by it; and if they should not receive us kindly, we must oppose them as well as we could, for there was no alternative between their perishing and ours." This counsel was immediately taken; to their surprise, they found in it people from a wretched whaling schooner looking for help.

As a free man Olaudah visited Georgia several times and each time he was harassed by white people. Once two white men tried to kidnap him and he scared them off very well. Before he left Georgia in his last trip, he saw a Black woman who had a child lying dead, wanting a parson for the child's burial. Since no white parson helped the woman, Olaudah offered his service and he performed the funeral ceremony. Once the burden of slavery was cast off, he began to think and act his own ways.

In May 1768 he returned to sea and for about five years Olaudah as a free man gained wide and varied experience visiting different parts of the world. In his journey he visited Turkey and was very much astonished by the humane treatment he got there. He writes: "In general I believe they are fond of black people; and several of them gave me pressing invitations to stay amongst them." In May 1769 he visited Portugal and Italy. In April 1771 he went as a steward in a ship going to the West Indies. While in this ship, he also traded things and earned some more money. Most often the whites who bought his goods refused to pay him and when he complained to the white justice of peace, he always met with threats. Once he lost 25 pounds to a treacherous white merchant in Jamaica who refused to pay for his goods.

In 1773 he joined the expedition of Lord Mulgrave to go to the north pole to explore a northwest passage in India. The expedition lasted four months. Though it failed to accomplish the mission, Olaudah and the expedition reached the pole at 81 degrees north and 20 degrees east longitude.

After the arctic expedition, he returned to Dr. Irving and worked for him. At this time Olaudah experienced the greatest spiritual crisis in his life and he went to different religious sects and groups to get the inner peace he was looking for and met with no satisfaction. He states:

> First I went among the Quakers, where the word of god was neither read nor preached so that I remained as much in the dark as ever. I then searched into the Roman Catholic principles, but was not in the least edified. I at length had recourse to the Jews, which availed me nothing, as the fear of eternity daily harassed my mind, and I knew not where to seek shelter from the wrath to come.

Having seen the Turks and their honesty and finding no satisfaction in Christianity, he set sail again to Turkey in 1774.

His spiritual tension was enhanced by an unfortunate incident. He had a Black friend by name of John Annis whom he had recommended as a cook to one Capt. John Hughes. Later Annis was taken forcefully by one William Kirkpatrick from St. Kitts. Olaudah tried all his

Olaudah Equiano

means to get him relieved; even he hired a lawyer, who turned out to be a scoundrel. Olaudah was disillusioned and began to blaspheme and wished often to be anything but a human being. Olaudah did not fall completely; he continued to read the Bible and finally received the grace from God and ever since that he never deflected from his faith in Christ as God. He saw with pain how Christians deviated from the teaching of Christ and he determined to live as a true follower of Christ, but shortly afterwards Olaudah was again spiritually agitated and even thought of comitting suicide. He continued with his prayer to Jesus and finally he had a vision of Christ. From then on Olaudah was reborn spiritually, and kept a calm and serene mind built on an unwavering faith in God.

In 1775 he sailed again to Spain and visited places like Barcelona and Cadiz. In that trip his ship hit a rock and every hand in the ship was shaken with fear, but Olaudah was calm and showed no fear because such was his joy in meeting the Lord through death. On his return from Spain in 1776, he joined Dr. Irving in developing a plantation in Jamaica and returned to London after a year.

From 1774 to 1784 he stayed in England and visited various parts of the country. In 1784 he went to sea and this time he visited New York. In 1785 he returned to Philadelphia. He gives an account of that visit: "I was very glad to see this favorite old town once more; and my pleasure was much increased in seeing the worthy Quakers freeing and easing the burdens of many of my oppressed African brethren." In October 1785 Olaudah and some of the black people in Philadelphia gave an address of thanks to the Quakers in Grace Church-Court, Lombard Street, where he also signed his name in the register.

When he returned to England, preparations were being made to send the blacks to Sierra Leone. In 1786 he was asked by the British government to superintend part of the undertaking to go with the black poor to Africa. He was made Commisary of Provisions and Stores for the "Black Poor going to Sierra Leone." In February, he set sail in *Nautilus* carrying 426 black persons to Africa and he did his task excellently. On March 21, 1787, he presented to the Queen a petition in behalf of Africans in which he wrote: "I do not solicit your royal pity for my own disaster; my sufferings, although numerous, are in a measure forgotten. I supplicate your Majesty's compassion for millions of my African countrymen, who groan under the lash of tyranny."

Olaudah urges, at the end of his autobiography, to the Europeans to stop enslaving Blacks. He pointed out the benefit of both Africa and Europe if the latter developed a commercial intercourse with Africa. He said that abolishing slavery, England could develop industries which in turn would create markets in Africa. What Olaudah suggested Britain did in its colonies in Africa and Asia by exploiting their resources and selling the finished goods back to the colonies at an inflated price! Though England abolished slavery, it still kept nations as slaves for a long time.

Olaudah's sufferings are numerous, but his perseverance and hard work in improving himself and helping his own people will never be forgotten. Though not born a Christian, the way he realized spiritual truth through his own reading and reflection indeed tells of the tumult that passes through every human mind in distress. Olaudah conquered not only the slavery of his body but also that of his spirit. He is one of the unsung heroes of the unexplored and unnoticed black people who helped to build the European civilization.

Rationalizing African Slavery: Attitudes Toward Native Americans and Blacks

David Brion Davis

Few Europeans or whites settling in the Americas (English, Dutch, French, Spanish, or Portuguese) felt any qualms about enslaving Africans until late in the eighteenth century.

The eminent American historian David Brion Davis, who until his recent retirement was a professor at Yale University, devoted years of his career to writing a multivolume history of attitudes toward slavery in Western civilization. This excerpt is taken from the first volume of that study, The Problem of Slavery in Western Culture, *originally published in 1966. Davis emphasizes that people justified slavery on religious grounds.*

At the time of America's conquest, the Christian view of slavery accommodated a series of balanced dualisms. Slavery was contrary to the ideal realm of nature, but was a necessary part of the world of sin; the bondsman was inwardly free and spiritually equal to his master, but in things external he was a mere chattel; Christians were brothers, whether slave or free, but pagans deserved in some sense to be slaves. There was a further division in thought between the troublesome question of the origin and legitimacy of a slaveholder's power, and the ideal of the servant in a Christian family where spiritual equality harmonized with outward obedience and authority to provide a model of the fraternal relationship of unequals. Such amiable servitude, originating perhaps in a benign serfdom, could easily be dissociated from the violent act of enslavement. Jurists and theologians might continue to endorse the abstract theory of enslaving prisoners of war, but the crime of manstealing they universally condemned. To make a man a slave always involved the possibility of sin, especially if the act seemed to break the order and balance of nature; but to hold a bondservant was to exercise an ordinance that was part of the governing structure of the world. . . .

Prior to 1514, Bartolomé de Las Casas had worked Indian slaves on his estates in Hispaniola, but in that year he experienced one of those crises of conscience that are so indefinable and yet so common in the history of religion. The lives of many future abolitionists would be transformed by a similar upheaval of soul and change of vision. Henceforth, Las Casas's religious life would be given new meaning and direction by his crusade to protect the native American from bondage and extermination. As an alternative to the harsh *encomienda* system, which gave Spanish *encomenderos* rights to the labor and produce of entire Indian villages, he suggested that Indians and Europeans be settled in model communities that would provide the basis for a peaceful Christianization of the New World. If Christian civilization could not establish such harmonious points of contact with American nature, it would fail in its supreme test. Las Casas did fail in his efforts to plant a utopian colony on the coast of South America, but he later succeeded, in his *Very Brief Account of the Destruction of the Indies,* in providing Europe with an enduring image of Spanish cruelty and the rape of innocent America.

But meanwhile Las Casas himself had become involved in the moral ambiguities of America's conquest. Along with his original plan for model Christian communities, he had recommended that forced labor in the mines be confined to Negro slaves, who could tolerate such rigorous conditions better than the Indians. About the year 1518 he made his famous proposal to the Spanish Crown for replacing Indian laborers with Negroes purchased in Iberia. In his *Historia de las Indias,* which was not published for more than three hundred years, Las Casas said that "not long afterwards" he discovered that the enslavement of Negroes was apparently as unjust as that of Indians; and he confessed he

was not certain whether his ignorance and good intention of liberating the Indians would excuse him before the bar of divine justice. But beyond this brief acknowledgment of guilt, there is no indication that the "protector of the Indians" publicly condemned the enslavement of Negroes or advocated their emancipation. He apparently owned slaves himself as late as 1544.

The changing policies of the Spanish and Portuguese governments revealed a similar double standard with respect to Indians and Negroes, which derived in part from the traditional inclination to associate the Africans with Moors, and thus with a menacing infidelity. Even when Negroes had not been tainted by Islam, they were of the Old World, the world of antiquity and of the Bible, which at least had been exposed for many centuries to the word of God. But when Spanish explorers and conquistadores enslaved thousands of helpless Indians, it was difficult to say this was a vindication of the true faith. Hence in 1537 Pope Paul III declared that the sacraments should be withheld from any colonist who, disregarding the truth that Indians were rational beings capable of Christianity, deprived them of their natural liberty. On various occasions the rulers of Spain and Portugal forbade the enslavement of native Americans, even in a supposedly just war. In 1542 the *Nuevas Leyes de las Indias* ruled that owners who lacked proof of a just title must liberate their Indian slaves.

Slaveholders have never taken kindly to moralistic interference, and such laws and edicts provoked colonial insurrections in New Spain, Peru, and New Granada. On various occasions Brazilian colonists expelled the Jesuits for their activities in favor of Indian workers, and in 1652 the inhabitants of Maranhão revolted when a governor arrived with orders from the king of Portugal to emancipate Indian slaves. Paulo da Silva Nunes, who represented Maranhão in Lisbon early in the eighteenth century, argued that Indians were more like beasts than like human beings; constructing a defense of slavery from Biblical and classical sources, he also suggested the possibility that Indians bore the curse of

Cain. Such views were common among slave-holding colonists throughout Latin America, where a humane Indian policy continued to be vitiated by stubborn resistance, jurisdictional disputes, and a recognized need for forced labor.

But despite the cruelties of the *encomienda* system, despite the slaving raids into the interior, the separation of families, and the frightful mortality in the mines, Spanish and Portuguese authorities succeeded in liberating thousands of Indian slaves and in preventing the enslavement of thousands more. Over a period of three centuries a vast body of legislation was created to segregate and protect the native American from the exploitive forces of colonization. Unfortunately, the erosion of Indian slavery simply contributed to the growing demand for Negroes, who were often regarded as a *mala raza,* and who were not protected by a great network of imperial edicts and laws. And some of the leading advocates of the Indian, such as Bishop Landa of Mexico, were the strongest defenders of Negro slavery. This discrimination between the two colored races led quite naturally to a view that Negroes were born to be slaves and were inherently inferior to both Indians and whites. In 1771, for example, the viceroy of Brazil ordered the degradation of an Indian chief who had "sunk so low as to marry a Negress, staining his blood with this alliance.". . .

In spite of a widespread tendency to differentiate the Negro from the Indian and to associate the latter with the freedom of nature, Negro slavery was in actuality imposed on top of a preexisting Indian slavery; in North America, at least, the two never diverged as distinct institutions. Nevertheless, the practical circumstances of colonial settlement afforded the Indian some protection. From Canada to South America colonists took the enslavement of hostile savages as a matter of course; but they knew that their trade, and sometimes their very survival, depended on alliances with friendly tribes.

During the Pequoit War and King Philip's War, New Englanders shipped captured Indians to Bermuda and the West Indies, and at other times used the same punishment as a means of disciplining neighboring tribes. But this meant that "praying Indians," and those who cooperated with the colonists, were usually exempt from the danger of enslavement. A few colonists, such as John Eliot and Roger Williams, who had established intimate relations with the natives, were willing to question the wisdom or justice of condemning even hostile savages to perpetual bondage. In Virginia, on the other hand, Nathaniel Bacon bitterly attacked Governor Berkeley's policy of protecting friendly tribes, and in 1676 the rebel leader secured a law authorizing the enslavement of all Indians captured in war. But notwithstanding Bacon's success in arousing racial hatred and in plundering and enslaving friendly tribes, Virginians tended to make a sharp distinction between domestic allies and foreign enemies. Yet to the purchaser of Negroes, there was no political difference between Mandingo and Dahomean. Removed from the sources of African slavery, he was concerned with tribal origin only as an indication of probable character and stamina.

While North American colonists continued to hold Indian slaves through the eighteenth century, they at least assumed that the majority of Indians were rightfully free and that every bondsman was a legitimate captive, or the descendant of such a captive. They were also alert to the dangers of antagonizing neighboring tribes or of filling their communities with enemy warriors who might easily escape to the nearby forests. As a consequence, colonial legislation gradually revealed a double standard toward Indians and Negroes which was analogous to the distinctions made by Spanish law and by such writers as Las Casas and Du Tertre.

For reasons of expediency, a number of colonies flatly prohibited the importation of Indian slaves. From 1712 to 1714 this was done by Massachusetts, Connecticut, and Rhode Island, in order to stop the influx of large numbers of captives taken in the Tuscarora War in Carolina. Fearing that the shipment of Indian slaves from the continent was detrimental to other commerce, Jamaica passed a law in 1741 which forbade all future purchases of imported Indians, and which granted liberty to those brought illegally into the island. The law did not affect Indians already in the colony, but it is significant that an attempt was made to outlaw the Indian slave trade at a time when Negroes were demanded in ever-increasing numbers.

Although the British and French colonies gave the same legal status to Indian and Negro slaves, they showed a marked tendency, by the eighteenth century, to restrict the bondage of Indians to certain tribes. In South Carolina, Indian slavery was closely linked with the western fur trade; and in the struggle with France and Spain for control of the southwest, the institution became an important weapon for securing alliances and punishing enemies. Carolina traders had no scruples about buying Indians from the *coureurs de bois* at the mouth of the Mississippi, and selling them ultimately in the West Indies. But the Proprietors of the colony always promised protection to their Indian allies. And after 1740, the courts of South Carolina held that the color of an Indian, unlike that of a Negro, was not *prima facie* evidence of slavery, since it could not be presumed that any given Indian or his ancestors had been legitimately captured in war. The distinction would appear to have been an outgrowth of the practical demands of trade and diplomacy.

The French Canadians adopted a somewhat similar policy. From the late seventeenth century the settlements in the Saint Lawrence valley had provided a regular market for Pawnee slaves who were captured in the West by other Indians and eventually sold to the French. But a law of 1709 all *Panis* and Negroes were legally classed as slaves, and in 1760, in the Treaty of Montreal, England formally recognized the legitimacy of Negro and Pawnee slavery in Canada. If it was extraordinary to single out a particular western tribe for enslavement, it is all the more significant that the French called the Pawnees "the Negroes of America." Like the Africans, the Pawnees came from an area so remote that one could ignore the mode and justice of their enslavement. And as Governor La Jonquière ruled, with respect to Negroes who escaped to Canada from the British colonies, ["every black is a slave, wherever he is found"]. But since the ordinance of 1709 confined slavery to these two groups, the question soon arose whether other Indians could legitimately be held as slaves. It was the judgment of Louis XV that the matter should be determined by the established usage of the colony, which gave full rights of French citizenship to converted Indians, with the exception of the unfortunate Pawnees. Although Indians from various western tribes were sometimes classed as Panis, which justified their being held as slaves, the French colonists had no wish to jeopardize vital commercial relationships by enslaving Indians from the lake and forest regions. They did seize or purchase a number of Eskimos, but Eskimos proved to be very poor slaves.

Selection 6

The Myth of Jewish Slave Traders

David Brion Davis

In recent years, various American anti-Semites have claimed that Jews played a particularly large role in the trans-Atlantic slave trade. No reputable historian, regardless of religion or race, accepts that judgment. Guilt for conducting—and for profiting from—the slave trade must fall upon gentile Europeans of practically every nation washed by the Atlantic Ocean. In this selection, which was originally published in 1944, David Brion Davis draws upon a life-time's intensive study of slavery to absolve Jews from responsibility for the slave trade.

*T*he ghastly slave trade from Africa to the Atlantic sugar islands such as Madeira and Säo Tomé and then to the Western Hemisphere began in the mid-1400s and flourished for four centuries. Though historians continue to debate the numbers, it now seems probable that from twelve to fifteen million Africans were forcibly shipped out from their continent by sea. Millions more perished in African wars or raids for enslavement and in the deadly transport of captives from the interior to slave markets on the coast.

Reprinted from David Brion Davis, "The Slave Trade and the Jews," *The New York Review of Books*, December 22, 1994. Copyright © 1994 NYREV, Inc. Reprinted with permission from *The New York Review of Books*. Footnotes in the original have been omitted from this reprint, but can be obtained by application to Raymond Shapiro at the NYREV.

The participants in the Atlantic slave system included Arabs, Berbers, scores of African ethnic groups, Italians, Portuguese, Spaniards, Dutch, Jews, Germans, Swedes, French, English, Danes, white Americans, Native Americans, and even thousands of New World blacks who had been emancipated or were descended from freed slaves but who then became slaveholding farmers or planters themselves. Responsibility, in short, radiated outward to peoples of every sort who had access to the immense profits generated from the world's first system of multinational production for a mass market—production of sugar, tobacco, coffee, chocolate, rum, dye-stuffs, rice, spices, hemp, and cotton.

Today it is both remarkable and deeply disturbing to discover that this Atlantic slave system evoked little if any meaningful protest until the late eighteenth century. When it did finally appear, the Anglo-American antislavery movement was overwhelmingly religious in character, and drew on developments in sectarian and evangelical Protestantism. Yet the world's religions had long given slavery its ultimate sanction. Catholic popes enthusiastically blessed and authorized the first Portuguese slave traders in West Africa. For centuries Muslim *jihads* justified the enslavement of untold numbers of sub-Saharan infidels. In eighteenth-century Barbados the Church of England acquired possession of hundreds of slaves whose chests were branded with the letters "SOCIETY" to signify ownership by the Society for the Propagation of the Gospel. As late as the 1750s many devout British and American Quakers were actively involved in the slave trade. The small number of Jews who lived in the Atlantic community took black slavery as much for granted as did the Catholics, Muslims, Lutherans, Huguenots, Calvinists, and Anglicans. And while at least one Jewish merchant joined New York's first antislavery society in the 1790s, Judaism was as resistant as other tradition-oriented religions to such intellectual and moral innovations.

For four centuries the African slave trade was an integral and indispensable part of European expansion and settlement of the New World. Until the 1830s the flow of coerced African labor exceeded all the smaller streams of indentured white servants and voluntary white immigrants willing to endure the risks of life in the Western Hemisphere. The demand for labor was especially acute in the tropical and semitropical zones that produced the staples and thus the wealth most desired by Europeans. In the mid-1700s the value of exports to Britain from the British West Indies was more than ten times that of exports from colonies north of the Chesapeake. And the economy of the northern colonies depended in large measure on trade with Caribbean markets, which depended in turn on the continuing importation of African labor to replenish a population that never came close to sustaining itself by natural increase.

Fortunately for the planters, merchants, consumers, and other beneficiaries of this lethal system, West Africa offered a cheap and seemingly unlimited supply of slave labor, and the efforts of African kings to stop the ruinous sale of subjects were few and ineffective. Long before the Portuguese African voyages of the fifteenth century, Arab and Berber merchants had perfected the trans-Saharan slave trade and had delivered hundreds of thousands of black slaves to regions extending from the Persian Gulf (via a seaborne trade from East Africa) to Egypt, Sicily, Morocco, and Spain. Sharply divided by tribal rival-

ries, black Africans never looked upon one another as a homogeneous African "race." Most tribes and kingdoms were accustomed to a variety of forms of servitude, and developed highly sophisticated methods for recruiting captives and bartering slaves for coveted commodities, eventually including firearms, which Arabs or the Portuguese could bring from distant lands. The political power and commercial networks of the Sokoto caliphate, the Asante, and the Yoruba states, to name only three examples, were wholly at odds with the popular picture of "primitive" peoples over-awed and dominated by European military might.

Though first monopolized by the Portuguese, the Atlantic slave trade attracted ships from the Netherlands, France, Britain, Denmark, Spain, Sweden, and the English mainland colonies. Even the northern German ports sought to cash in on the lucrative traffic. How did Jews fit into this picture? To keep matters in perspective, we should keep in mind that in 1290 England expelled its entire Jewish population; only a scattering of migrants began to return in the latter half of the seventeenth century. In France a series of expulsions and massacres in the fourteenth century virtually demolished the medieval Jewish communities. In Spain, beginning in the mid-fourteenth century, a much larger Jewish population was subjected to periodic massacres, forced conversion, mob attacks, and final expulsion in 1492. Most of the refugees fled to Turkey and other Muslim lands. The estimated 100,000 Jews who escaped into Portugal were soon compelled to accept Christianity. Large numbers of these "New Christians" intermixed with the "Old Christian" population and lost any Jewish identity, although the Inquisition continued to search for the signs of secret Jewish rituals that could bring arrest, torture, and death.

By the 1570s, during the beginning of Brazil's sugar boom, which depended on African slave labor, Judaism as a religion had been virtually wiped out in England, France, the Germanies, Spain, Portugal, the Low Countries, and most of Italy; the great mass of Jewish survivors had emigrated to Poland, Lithuania, and Ottoman lands in the Balkans and Turkey. No professing Jews were allowed to contaminate the Spanish or Portuguese colonies of the New World; in the 1680s they were also banned from the French West Indies and restricted in British Barbados. These sustained anti-Semitic measures clearly reduced the opportunity Jews might have had for participating in the Atlantic slave system and certainly precluded any Jewish "initiation," "domination," or "control" of the slave trade. Yet the continuing persecution and exclusion, especially of the "New Christians" or Marranos, did lead to a desperate search for new commercial opportunities in the New World, where there was less surveillance by the Inquisition, and in the rebellious Spanish province of the Netherlands, which struggled from 1568 to 1648 to win independence.

At this point one must emphasize that Jews, partly because of their remarkable success in a variety of hostile environments, have long been feared as the power behind otherwise inexplicable evils. For many centuries they were the only non-Christian minority in nations dedicated to the Christianization and thus the salvation of the world. Signifying an antithetical Other, individual Jews were homogenized and reified as a "race"—a race responsible for crucifying the Savior, for resisting the dissemination of God's word, for manipulating kings and world markets, for drinking the blood of Christian children, and, in modern times, for spreading the evils of both capitalism and communistic revolution. Responsibility for the African slave trade (and even for creating and spreading AIDS) has recently been added to this long list of crimes.

Such fantasies were long nourished by the achievements of a very small number of Jews who, barred from landholding, the army, and traditional crafts and professions, took advantage of their cosmopolitan knowledge and personal connections that favored access to markets, credit, and such highly desired commodities as diamonds, spices, wool, and sugar. Much of the historical evidence regarding alleged Jewish or New Christian involvement in the slave system was biased by deliberate Spanish efforts to blame Jewish refugees for fostering Dutch commercial expansion at the expense of Spain. Given this long history of conspiratorial fantasy and collective scapegoating, a selective search for Jewish slave traders becomes inherently anti-Semitic unless one keeps in view the larger context and the very marginal place of Jews in the history of the overall system. It is easy enough to point to a few Jewish slave traders in Amsterdam, Bordeaux, or Newport, Rhode Island. But far from suggesting that Jews constituted a major force behind the exploitation of Africa, closer investigation shows that these were highly exceptional merchants, far outnumbered by thousands of Catholics and Protestants who flocked to share in the great bonanza.

I should add that in trying to determine who was or was not a covert Jew, the historian comes perilously close to acting like the Inquisition. In the early eighteenth century a large number of Brazilian planters, said to be Marranos, were arrested by the Inquisition, extradited, and taken to Lisbon for trial. By any modern definition, excluding the racial definition of the Nazis, these planters were not Jews. Yet various historians have counted such Marranos as Jews and have assumed that an earlier Brazilian planter, Jorge Homen Pinto, who owned six sugar mills, 370 slaves, and a thousand oxen, was a Jew. More careful investigation, however, reveals that Pinto passed the most stringent racial tests as an Old Christian.

Jews and Jewish names are virtually absent from the texts and indexes of all the scholarly works on the Atlantic slave trade and from recent monographs on the British, French, Dutch, and Portuguese branches of the commerce in slaves. To expose the supposedly "secret relationship" between Jews and slavery, anti-Semites have therefore turned to histories of the Jews in such regions as Amsterdam, Brazil, and Curaçao. These works provide material that can easily be misquoted, distorted, and put in totally misleading contexts.

To give only two examples, *The Secret Relationship* asserts that "Dr. Wiznitzer claims that Jews 'dominated the slave trade,' then the most profitable enterprise in that part of the world."

The footnote refers to a book review by Herbert I. Bloom which in no way supports this statement. The Nation of Islam authors never acknowledge that Arnold Wiznitzer, whose *Jews in Colonial Brazil* is frequently cited, writes that "[I]t cannot be said that Jews played a dominant role in Dutch Brazil as 'senhores de engenho,'" or sugar planters—he estimates that Jews made up about six percent of the planters—or that he adds that historians have tended to exaggerate the number of Jews in colonial Dutch Brazil from 1630 to 1654.

From Columbus to Jean Lafitte, the slave-dealing New Orleans pirate, the authors pounce on the most far-fetched claims of "crypto-Jewish" identity. Florida's Senator David Yulee renounced his Jewish origins, converted to Christianity, and even claimed he was descended from a Moroccan prince. But since Yulee took a strongly pro-slavery position in the Senate, the Nation of Islam authors count him as a Jew. Such techniques hardly conform to the standards of fairness, justice, and "great sensitivity" set forth at the beginning of the book in a remarkably hypocritical "Editor's Note." But more insidious than the misquotations and slipshod documentation is the total lack of historical context. Even if every purported "fact" presented in *The Secret Relationship* were true, the uninformed reader would never suspect that for every Jew involved in the Atlantic slave system there were scores or even hundreds of Catholics and Protestants.

In actuality, Jews had no important role in the British Royal African Company or in the British slave trade of the eighteenth century, which transported by far the largest share of Africans to the New World. According to the Dutch historians Pieter C. Emmer and Johanes Menne Postma, Jews had a very limited and subordinate role even at the height of the Dutch slave trade in the seventeenth century: "They did not serve on the *Heren X,* the directorate of the Dutch West India Company. Their investment share amounted to only 0.5 (or one two-hundredth) of the company's capital." I should add that between 1658 and 1674 the Jewish investment in the slave-trading West India Company seems to have risen to 6 or even 10 percent. Keeping in mind that the Dutch share of the trade accounted for only 16 percent of the total, one sees how small the involvement was, and it is as close as Jews ever came to "dominating" the nefarious Atlantic traffic.

If we expand the issue beyond the slave trade itself, small numbers of Sephardi Jews and Marranos were crucial to the process of refining and marketing sugar and then in shifting transatlantic commerce, including the slave trade, from Portugal to Northern Europe. Throughout the Mediterranean, Jews had acquired expertise in refining and marketing sugar, which until the eighteenth century was a much-desired luxury only the well-to-do could afford. Marranos and Italians were prominent in the international sugar trade of the fifteenth and sixteenth centuries. Some of them helped to establish sugar plantations in Madeira and Säo Tomé, in the Gulf of Guinea. Indeed, in 1493, when Portugal was flooded with Jewish refugees from Spain, the government forcibly baptized their children, large numbers of whom were separated from their parents, and shipped off to Säo Tomé as colonists. Most of these Marrano children died, but some survived to become sugar planters, an occupation that was hardly a matter of choice.

The Marranos who moved to Brazil took with them the technical skills of artisans, foremen, and merchants, and took a leading part in developing the sugar export industry. Other Marranos, who sailed with Portuguese expeditions to the Kongo Kingdom and Angola, became expert at contracting for cargoes of slave labor. There can be no doubt that these New Christians contributed much to transform Portugal into Europe's first major supplier of slave-grown sugar. Yet given the extent of intermarriage and loss of Jewish identity, most Marranos were "Jewish" only in their vulnerability to suspicion, persecution, and anti-Semitic fantasies of conspiracy. Ironically, the Inquisition's anti-Semitic crusade, which "fabricated Jews like the mint coined money," as one cynical Inquisitor observed, convinced other Europeans that "Portugal was a nation of crypto-Jews, as exemplified by the coarse Castilian proverb: 'A Portuguese was born of a Jew's fart.'"

Fears of Jewish power were greatly stimulated by the leadership Marranos and professing Jews took in marketing Portuguese East Indian spices and then sugar throughout northern Europe, especially after they became allied with the rebellious Dutch and heretical Protestants. Although the Dutch barred professing Jews from many trades and occupations—it was apparently not until 1655 that two Jewish merchants received permission from the Amsterdam government to establish a sugar refinery—the Netherlands presented a climate of relative religious toleration that encouraged the founding of synagogues and the revival of a small Jewish religious community. The Twelve Years' Truce with the then united Spain and Portugal, from 1608 to 1621, helped the Dutch Sephardi merchants expand various branches of trade with the Iberian Peninsula, Brazil, and Africa. Their knowledge of Spanish and Portuguese, as well as the intricacies of international finance, gave them a particular advantage in procuring and marketing sugar.

Even though Jewish merchants suffered from the resumption of the war with Spain and from Europe's Thirty Years' War, they retained temporary control of sugar and its distribution, which should not be confused with control of the Dutch slave trade. This involvement with sugar was largely the result of the Dutch conquest of north-eastern Brazil in the early 1630s. By 1645 some 1,450 Jews made up about one-half of the white civilian population of Dutch Brazil and owned about 6 percent of its sugar mills. Jewish merchants bought a large share of the slaves transported by the Dutch West India Company and then retailed them to Portuguese planters on credit, arousing complaints of high prices and interest rates. A few Amsterdam Jews, such as Diego Dias Querido, originally a native of Portugal, challenged the [West India Company's] monopoly and chartered their own ships to transport slaves from Africa to Brazil or the Spanish Caribbean. But the Jewish presence in Brazil was short-lived. In the early 1650s, with the collapse of the Dutch occupation and the impending return of the Portuguese, Jews faced the choice of emigration or death.

Some of the émigrés from Brazil moved northwestward to the Caribbean, where they were soon joined by Jewish and Marrano entrepreneurs from Holland. There were a number of reasons for the upsurge of interest in the Caribbean. By the 1650s the British island of Barbados had made a decisive conversion from tobacco to sugar, as African slaves and a new class of large planters replaced a population of white indentured servants. In 1662 Spain awarded an *asiento* (monopoly contract) to the Dutch West Indian Company, seeking a non-Portuguese source of African slaves for the Spanish Caribbean colonies. The main *asientista*, or monopoly contractor, was the Protestant banker Balthazar Coymans, and Jews had little to do with the WIC shipments of slaves from Africa. Still, in 1664 the king of Spain appointed don Manuel de Belmonte, a Jew of Spanish origin, his Agent-General in Amsterdam for the procurement of slaves. And it was in Curaçao, which Marranos had helped to establish in 1651, that Jews found their main outlet for selling slaves and Dutch manufactured goods along the Spanish Main.

For a time Curaçao became the great entrepôt of the Caribbean, trading legally and illegally with Barbados and other rising British and French colonies as well as with the Spanish mainland. In the eighteenth century Jews made up about half the population of Curaçao—as opposed to one percent of the population of New York City—and seem to have been involved mainly in the transshipment of commodities other than slaves to the Spanish colonies. The mainland Spanish colonies never developed true plantation systems; their demand for slaves declined abruptly in the eighteenth century, since they could not begin to compete with colonies like Jamaica, St. Domingue, and Brazil, which constituted the heart of the Atlantic slave system and which imported their labor directly from Africa.

The one colony where a significant number of Jews took up plantation agriculture was Suriname, or what later became Dutch Guiana. The religious freedom of the Dutch colonies allowed Jews to establish their own self-governing town, Joden Savanne (Jewish Savannah) in the interior jungle. There in the late seventeenth and early eighteenth centuries the Sephardim lived the life of sugar planters, extracting labor from African slaves in one of the most deadly and oppressive environments in the New World. Suriname, however, never became a major sugar-producing region.

The significant point is not that a few Jewish slave dealers changed the course of history, which would have been the same without Jewish slave traders and planters. The significant point is that Jews found the threshold of liberation from second-class status or worse, in a region dependent on black slavery. Before turning to the sobering and depressing part of this message, I should stress that even with regard to the Dutch Sephardi sugar trade, we're dealing with a few hundred families. By the 1670s the Dutch sugar boom had ended and Britain would soon emerge as the world's greatest sugar importer and slave-trading nation. In Barbados, to be sure, there were fifty-four Jewish households in 1680. But these were not great slave traders or planters; they were mostly the managers of retail shops and moneylending firms who owned fewer slaves per household (three) than the non-Jewish residents of Bridgetown.

To keep matters in perspective, we should note that in the American South, in 1830, there were only 120 Jews among the 45,000 slaveholders owning twenty or more slaves and only twenty Jews among the 12,000 slaveholders owning fifty or more slaves. Even if each member of this Jewish slaveholding elite had owned 714 slaves—a ridiculously high figure in the American South—the total number would only equal the 100,000 slaves owned by black and colored planters in St. Domingue in 1789, on the eve of the Haitian Revolution.

In actuality, so far as ownership of slaves is concerned, the free people of color in the Caribbean greatly surpassed the much smaller number of Jews. Even in Charleston, South Carolina, the percentage of free African Americans who owned slaves increased from one half to three quarters as one moved up the socio-economic scale as indicated by the ownership of real estate. The thousands of Southern black slave owners included freedpeople who had simply purchased family members or relatives. But there were also colored planters, especially in Louisiana, who owned more than fifty or even one hundred slaves. The allure of profits and power transcended all distinctions of race, ethnicity, and religion.

No one should defend the small number of Jews who bought and sold slaves, or who forced slaves to cut cane on the estates of Joden Savanne. No one should defend the infinitely larger number of Catholics and Protestants who built the Atlantic slave system, or defend the Muslims who initiated the process of shipping black African slaves to distant markets, or defend the Africans who captured and enslaved perhaps twenty million other Africans in order to sell them to European traders for valuable and empowering goods. But while posterity has the right and even duty to judge the past, we must emphatically renounce the dangerous though often seductive belief in a collective guilt that descends through time to every present and future generation.

While insisting that no group is responsible for the sins of its ancestors, I find it deeply disturbing that many Jews, including those who established the first synagogue in Curaçao, found a path to their own liberation and affluence by participating in a system of commerce that subjected another people to contempt, dishonor, coerced labor, and degradation. It has even been said that the more enlightened rulers of eighteenth-century Europe were much swayed by the early achievements of enfranchised Jews in Dutch Brazil, the Caribbean, and North America. This is one side or aspect of the dismal truth that our New World—conceived as a land of limitless opportunity, breaking the crust of old restraints, traditions, and prejudices—was made possible only by the near extinction of indigenous populations and by the dehumanizing subjugation of the so-called African race.

The Slave Trade to Eighteenth-Century Virginia

Herbert S. Klein

Between the sixteenth and the early eighteenth centuries most of the victims of the trans-Atlantic slave trade were brought to either the West Indies or to South America. Very few slaves were carried directly from Africa to the British colonies on the mainland of North America until well into the eighteenth century. Compared to the Caribbean area or to Brazil, the market for slaves in North America was small, and the long voyage from West Africa made it difficult to keep the human cargo alive and well. The African slaves who trickled into seventeenth-century North America in constantly increasing numbers were generally re-exported from the West Indies.

In 1978 historian Herbert S. Klein, who teaches at Columbia University, published a painstaking study, The Middle Passage, *comparing the trans-Atlantic slave trade to all important markets in the New World. This excerpt offers an abridged version (omitting*

much of his detailed statistics) of his account of the export of slaves to eighteenth-century Virginia.

The three most important North American zones of importation throughout most of the 18th century were Virginia, South Carolina, and Georgia. Although Virginia was the largest of the continental slave societies, it ranked second in importance to South Carolina as an importer of slaves. Nevertheless, the abundance and quality of the available data make this colony the best with which to begin a comprehensive study of the dynamics of the slave trade to the region that would form the United States. . . .

Until the end of the 17th century, the slave trade to Virginia remained small, with the majority of slaves coming directly from the British West Indies. With the ending of the Royal African Company's monopoly of African sources after 1698, the number of direct shipments of slaves from Africa to Virginia began to rise rapidly. By the period 1710 to 1718, 42 percent of all of the slaves imported into Virginia were coming directly from Africa, though West Indian sources still accounted for 53 percent of the totals. There-

A ship leaves its cargo of Africans in Jamestown, Virginia. Most of the slaves in seventeenth-century Virginia were imported from the West Indies.

after, direct African slaving expanded rapidly.

Whereas in the 1710–1718 period the average annual importation from Africa was 236 slaves, compared with 300 from the British West Indies, the number of slaves of African origin rose to 1,228 per annum in the period from 25 March 1718 to 25 March 1727. By the third decade of the 18th century, African slavers were monopolizing the trade, and the basic patterns, which remained constant for the rest of the century, had been fully established. . . .

The total number of slave arrivals in any given year was relatively small. The largest annual importation was, in fact, only 3,116 slaves in 1736. Even more impressive is the large number of ships used to transport this relatively small number of slaves. In 1736, for example, it took 40 ships to bring the total number of slaves, or 78 slaves per vessel. In the entire period from 1727 to 1769, some 39,679 slaves were imported in 644 ships, for an average of 62 slaves per vessel.

But this high volume of shipping and low average number of slaves carried was more a function of the intervention of continental coastwise and West Indian shippers in bringing in slaves than of the nature of the direct Africa slave trade. Actually, the bulk of the slaves came from Africa in relatively few vessels. The Virginia slave trade can thus be conceived of as at least two, if not three, essentially different trades. The Africa-to-Virginia route with its 199 slaves per vessel accounted for only 25 percent of the ships, but 81 percent of the slaves who arrived. This was almost exclusively a slave importation system, with little other commercial activity involved. The British West Indian and coastal North American shippers, on the other hand, were much less specialized slave traders, and probably engaged in the transportation of slaves as just one part of a general import trade involving a whole range of goods, including people. This is clearly reflected in their average numbers of 12 and 22 slaves per voyage respectively. Thus, although the British West Indian traders accounted for 64 percent of the slave ships, they brought in only 12 percent of the slaves delivered to Virginia ports. The coastal shippers, for their part, brought in just 4 percent of the slaves but accounted for 10 percent of the shipping.

Not only were the three trading zones different in total numbers of slaves and in average number carried, but they also differed in average tonnage employed. Here again, the African shippers had both a higher average tonnage and also a much higher ratio of slaves per ton than those in the other two major routes.

This sharp difference in average numbers of slaves landed between the direct Africa-to-Virginia and the West Indies-to-Virginia trades seems to be similar to the pattern observed in the Cuban slave trade at the end of the 18th century. Both these trades, which might be termed modified Caribbean systems, contrast sharply with the Brazilian experience, which represents the other extreme. Involved exclusively in an Africa-to-America trade, Brazilian slavers in the early and mid-18th century were landing on average a minimum of 316 slaves per trip, a figure that rose to 440 slaves landed per vessel by the end of the century.

Before we deal further with the contrast between the Africa-Virginia and Africa-Brazil trades, it is essential to determine if the Africa-Virginia route was representative of the entire English Atlantic slave trade. From all available evidence it is obvious that the capacity of English slave shipping in the 18th century was far higher than the landed figures for Virginia. Thus, the 103 ships that left the port of Liverpool to engage in the African slave trade in 1771 carried an average of 274 slaves per vessel. Even as early as the beginning of the century, some 45 English ships sailing from England to Africa estimated that they would carry 252 slaves per vessel. But . . . until the end of the 1770s English shipping did not begin to reach its limits. Thus, in the decade of 1761 to 1770, the English slave trade involved an estimated 1,341 ships going to

Africa, with an average of 112.3 tons per vessel and landing 209 slaves per voyage in America, figures that closely resemble Virginia's for this period. These magnitudes remained constant in the decade of the 1770s, but then rose dramatically in the following two decades. By the 1780s, the averages were 295 slaves landed from ships of 160 tons. By the 1790s, with the introduction of restrictive British legislation, the corresponding figures were 297 slaves landed from an average ship of 207 tons. . . .

Within the British continental North American slave-importing zone, Virginia was the second most important market for slaves after South Carolina prior to the American Revolution. In many respects, the two trades were quite similar. From 1735 to 1769, when there are comparable statistics for the two regions, both obtained the bulk of their slaves directly from Africa (86 percent for South Carolina and 83 percent for Virginia). Both also had slaves arriving on a large number of vessels from the British West Indies and from continental North American ports. . . . The only major difference between the two trades, aside from volume (with South Carolina in this period importing 32 percent more slaves than Virginia), was the relatively higher slaves-carried-from-Africa figure for Virginia (some 203 slaves per vessel) compared with the low 155-slaves-per-vessel for the South Carolina trade.

Although the Africa-Virginia route involved full-time slavers carrying slaves as their only item, on the other two routes of the Virginia slave trade, slaves formed only one part of a diverse collection of imports coming to the colony. Though tonnage figures indicate that shipping from the West Indies or coastwise could have easily carried ten times the number of slaves, they did not do so. With its 0.2 slaves per ton and its 51 ton averages (higher than the coastwise trade), the voluminous Caribbean shipping was importing molasses, sugar, and other West Indian products into Virginia along with a few slaves on every voyage. . . . In this coastwise trade, the prime imports by the 1760s were not slaves but, interestingly enough, re-exports and processed commodities that came from the West Indies. Rum, molasses, and refined and brown sugar made up 95 percent of the total value of goods imported into Virginia from northern ports in the period from 1760–1769.

Although the West Indian and African routes, which brought in 95 percent of slaves, differed radically in their pattern of delivering slaves, both were quite similar in their seasonal patterns. There was a sharp peaking of slave imports from these two regions in the summer months, with the Caribbean trade reaching its maximum in June and the African trade in July. Although both trades are almost parallel in their seasonal fluctuation, for the African trade there is the added factor of no imports whatsoever in the three winter months of December, January, and February. This seasonality seems highly correlated with planter demands and cropping season, which made the period from late April through early November the prime time for the demand for slaves.

Just as the time of arrivals of slaves was influenced by American factors, so also the unique features of the Chesapeake Bay area created the unusual situation of several market regions for slaves, with no one port or site controlling the trade. The ability of so many Tidewater plantations to dock oceangoing vessels on their lands meant that the ships tended to move into many different reaches of the Chesapeake River system. The Upper and Lower James River, the York River, and the Rappahannock districts were obviously the key zones for landing slaves. Within this general movement, there appears some important variation, with the larger direct African ships going inland to the York, Upper James, and Rappahannock, while the West Indian and inter-coastal ships were using Hampton in the Lower James as their prime port of call.

Given the unusually detailed recordings of the British colonial naval lists, a whole range of questions can be answered about the nature of the vessels involved in this trade. Because of the provisions of the Navigation Acts, ship's origin and port of registration were prime items of concern to port officials; thus, detailed information

is available on ship construction, ownership, and even age for each of the major trade routes. Along with these facts, the names of ships, their masters, owners, and tonnage provide enough information to construct frequency tables for the sailings of the ships involved in the Virginia trade, giving key data by which the overall specialization of this trade can be compared with other Atlantic routes.

Most of the ships involved in the trade were built in America. The combination of the New England, Middle Atlantic, Southern, and generic "plantations" (meaning New World British colonies) production accounts for over 84 percent of the shipping. This means that American-built ships not only dominated the West Indian and Coastwise trades, where they accounted respectively for 96 percent and 93 percent of the ships, but were even important in the shipping coming directly from Africa. On this route, they accounted for 44 percent of the ships, with English-built ships making up the rest. That the tonnage of these American-built vessels was equal to that of the English-built ships is indicated by the fact that the latter accounted for 56 percent of the total number of ships and 58 percent of the gross tonnage involved in this route. But on the whole, English-built ships, compared with all of the colonial-built vessels, were much larger and, although they accounted for only 16 percent of the total ships built, they made up 28 percent of the gross tonnage, and carried 58 percent of the slaves coming from Africa.

In a comparison of construction with ownership, the dominance of American-built shipping is again impressive. Fully 100 percent of the ships owned by Southern and West Indian merchants, and 93 percent of the Northern and Middle Atlantic colonial-owned ships, were colonial-built. Of the shipping owned by English merchants, 40 percent was American-made.

Although ship construction may have been primarily a colonial affair, ownership was another matter. In those areas where large profits were to be made, or where English imports were involved, English capital predominated. In the overall trade, English capital brought 79 percent of all slaves to Virginia, even though only 28 percent of the ships were English-owned.

Of the total number of ships coming from Africa, English merchants owned 87 percent, and these ships carried 89 percent of the slaves coming from this region. But even the 6 percent that English merchants owned of the shipping that went between the West Indies and Virginia accounted for 29 percent of the slaves coming from that zone, which indicates English specialization in the slave trade in this area as well. In the New England and Middle Atlantic trade to Virginia, English participation was less than 1 percent, though it dominated the Southern-originated shipping. . . . Thus, the English essentially dominated the slave trade, if not the overall shipping, that came to Virginia in the 18th century.

Although the English owned the majority of the real slavers, the inter-coastal and West Indian trades were controlled by the British North American merchants. . . . Most of that trade was owned, except for the unique case of Bermuda, by continental merchants. In the case of the ships bringing slaves, this meant that 64 percent of West-Indian-originated traders were owned by North American merchants.

As for the inter-coastal traders, the pattern of ownership markedly favored the port from which the ship sailed. Thus, of the ships that arrived in Virginia from the Northern and Middle Atlantic colonies, 80 percent were directly owned in the exporting ports. Although the sample of ships coming from southern ports is extremely small, it would appear that Southerners also owned the bulk of their own shipping. . . .

From the above evidence it would appear that colonials were barely keeping pace with the British in this particular trade in slaves. Although 75 percent of the gross tonnage engaged in the slave trade had been built in England's New World possessions, only 57 percent of that tonnage was owned by the colonists. The British metropolitan merchants owned fully 43 percent. The British home merchants controlled the African slave trade, just as they controlled the largest ships and those longest in service. The West Indian merchants, in turn, owned only

a minor share (13 percent) of the total trade, even though fully 55 percent of the total tonnage was arriving from their islands. In terms of the Continental Colonies, both their share of construction and of ownership was relatively high and about equal, that is, 42 percent of the tonnage was owned by them. . . .

Of the ships with the highest multiple voyage, the most typical sailing was that between Virginia and the West Indies. Of the 9 ships that made 5 voyages or more, all but one were directly engaged in the West Indies–Virginia route. Of these 8 vessels, all but 2 were primarily from Bermuda and the others came from several different Caribbean ports, including Barbados. The ship that completed the most voyages from Africa was the *Liverpool Merchant* out of England. Built in Liverpool, this 80-ton vessel was typical in both its tonnage and slaves-landed figures. In 5 sailings, it carried 130–193 slaves, averaging 166 slaves landed, which was only slightly below the African-originated slavers' mean.

One further item, incidentally revealed by the registration and construction information, is the impact of privateering on the continental West Indian and British merchant shipping. The records show that there were 21 ships (or 4 percent of the total) originally built in foreign countries that had been made prizes by the British and sold to private English and colonial merchants. These 21 ships had made 23 voyages to Virginia in this 42-year period, averaging about 114.0 tons per vessel, and accounted for 4 percent of the voyages. The majority (14) of these vessels came from the French merchant marine.

To place the Virginia slave trade in its broadest context, several major comparisons are in order. First is the relative importance of the Virginia slave trade in the context of the total British North American slave trade. Unfortunately, complete comparative data for North America currently are available only for the later 1760s and early 1770s. But broad comparisons with the South Carolina figures do suggest some relative trends before this period. Although the two were roughly equal as importers in the 1735–1740 period, the relative importance of Virginia declined to the point whereby 1760–1769 South Carolina was importing almost three times as many slaves. It could be argued from this limited data that earlier in the century Virginia weighed more heavily within the total British North American slave trade than it did by the second half of the 18th century. By then, Virginia was only a small part of the trade. . . . Considering that the imports for the upper South also contained Maryland's, which may have made up at least half of the total, it could be estimated that by the decades of the 1760s and 1770s, the Virginia slave trade was entering a period of decline, and accounted for only 10–20 percent of the total number of slaves arriving in the continent. Even in its most expansive stage in the earlier years of the century, Virginia probably never absorbed more than half of the total arrivals, and was most likely in the range of a third of the total numbers of slaves coming into British North America. . . .

In the context of England's overseas trade, the slave trade to Virginia formed a part of what was the largest single trading route: that is, the West Indies and plantation continental American zone. In 1771–1773, for example, of 375,000 tons of English shipping engaged in overseas trade, the largest single route was to the West Indies and America, which absorbed 153,000 tons, or 40 percent of total tonnage. Most of this shipping was involved, of course, in bringing back the sugar, tobacco, and rice that was being exported by the West Indies and Southern colonies respectively. In this trade, the merchants of London were dominant. But in the slave trade, which formed a rather specialized sub-group of this large commerce, the outports of Liverpool and Bristol played a more prominent role. Especially in the early part of the 18th century, Bristol ships dominated the slave trade over London and Liverpool. This is reflected in the Virginia trade. Here, Bristol slavers accounted for 50 percent of

the British-owned tonnage, with Liverpool controlling a third, and London only 12 percent.

In sum, three routes brought slaves to Virginia: a direct African trade that involved shipments of native Africans to the New World; a Caribbean route that brought in both Africans and West Indian creoles; and, finally, a coastwise trade that probably brought in a majority of creole slaves. Of these three trades, only the direct African route was exclusively a slave trade. On the other two routes, the general shippers seem to have included greater or lesser numbers of slaves as the opportunity offered, but their primary concern was with general merchandise. This specialization by the African traders, as opposed to non-specialization of the others, meant that the direct African trade accounted for the majority of slave arrivals, though only a minor part of total shipping. Also, this was the route totally dominated by metropolitan merchants. Although British North Americans dominated the coastwise and the general West-Indian-to-continental-North-American trade, the English controlled the direct Africa-to-Virginia route. Their ships were the biggest and the oldest and brought in the most slaves. Theirs were also the only ones that so systematically specialized in the slave trade.

Finally, in evaluating the Virginia slave trade in the general context of the Atlantic slave trade, we find that we are dealing with one end of a continuum. For Virginia, with its three slave producing streams, its relatively low numbers of arriving slaves, and its low average figures of slaves carried directly from Africa, stands in sharp contrast to the Brazilian extreme of high annual imports, direct African trade, and high average-carried numbers. For the majority of large slave plantation societies, their slave trades probably fell between these two extremes, with those of the West Indies variously sharing elements of both.

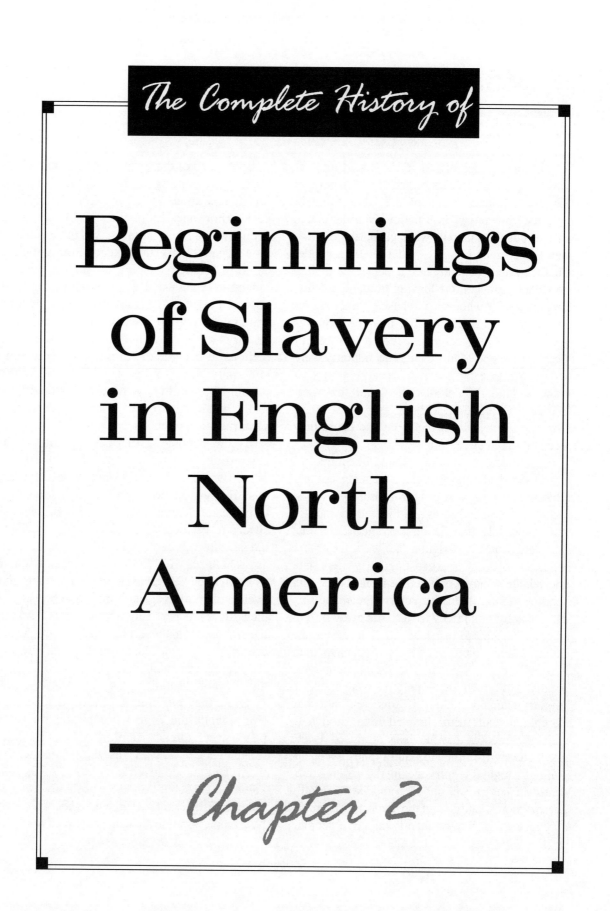

The Complete History of

Beginnings of Slavery in English North America

Chapter 2

Introduction

Slavery got off to a slow start in England's colonies on the North American mainland. Much of the labor force in seventeenth-century Virginia and Maryland was unfree, but the laborers were primarily English men and women bound to indentured servitude. An indentured servant was a person who had signed a contract before leaving England promising to work for whoever purchased him or her on arrival in North America, but their service was only to be for a certain specified number of years. At the end of this term, they not only were to become free but were to receive a modest grant of land. Essentially, the labor they performed was supposed to be a repayment of the cost of passage and for the room and board they received in America.

Indentured servitude may sound like a reasonably good deal (the practice is vaguely comparable to hiring *au pair* girls from Europe), but in reality life frequently was a living hell for the servants who sold their labor. Servants found that they had virtually no rights. The work they were expected to do was exhausting; they were fed, housed, and clothed only as their master thought appropriate; they were frequently beaten and sexually abused; and if they tried to run away or otherwise offer serious resistance to their master, the courts would routinely add more years to their term of service. Women who found themselves pregnant (often by their masters) were liable to similar extensions. And if this was not bad enough, few of them survived long enough to claim the freedom they had been promised. Death rates, chiefly from malaria and typhus, were appallingly high for everyone in the seventeenth-century Chesapeake, and servants, who usually got the poorest rations and the hardest work, probably died even more frequently than free people.

By the end of the seventeenth century, the English were coming to realize that indentured servitude was not going to work in the Chesapeake. For one thing, the supply of English people willing to sell themselves into such servitude began to dry up as economic conditions eased in England. (Going to America under an indenture was usually something people did only if they faced virtual starvation at home, which was common early in the seventeenth century.) Moreover, English servants became rebellious. It became too difficult to treat them as temporary slaves. Why not bring in *real* slaves, people who would have no expectation of eventually regaining their liberties as freeborn English men and women?

By the 1660s, the English authorities in the Chesapeake had a ready model of how a slave system would work: the slave codes of Barbados. Today a favorite tourist destination in the Caribbean, blessed with beautiful beaches and swank resort hotels, the island of Barbados in the seventeenth century could best be described as a hellhole. Its forest cover had been destroyed, and every acre of arable land was given over to plantation agriculture—first tobacco and then sugar. At first English indentured servants had labored on these plantations, but by mid-century they had been mostly replaced by African slaves, who were treated with almost unbelievable brutality.

When they began to shift toward a slave system of labor, the English colonists in the Chesapeake were already familiar with Africans. A relatively few *negars* (as the source defined them) had landed in Virginia in 1619. We do not know for sure, but they were probably treated as indentured servants—for what *that* was worth. Nevertheless, some Africans managed to survive, and became free, even prosperous, men and women. But in the 1660s and 1670s, these relatively fluid arrangements were changing. By 1690, full-fledged slavery was in place in Virginia and Maryland, and it was a status confined to Africans. The first phase of the history of slavery in America was over, and the second phase was at hand.

Selection 1

Slavery in the English Caribbean

Richard S. Dunn

To understand slavery as it developed in the colonies that became the United States, we must first look at the institutions, practices, laws, and attitudes associated with human bondage in the West Indies. On islands such as Barbados and Jamaica in the mid–seventeenth century, Englishmen learned how to develop large-scale plantation agriculture producing a profitable cash crop—sugar—for European markets with a labor force consisting entirely of enslaved Africans. Here were created the models that at the end of the seventeenth century and the beginning of the eighteenth century were transplanted to the North American mainland, especially to South Carolina (a colony first settled by planters from overcrowded Barbados).

In 1972 Richard S. Dunn, a professor of history at the University of Pennsylvania, published Sugar and Slaves: The Rise of the Planter Class in the English West Indies, 1624–1713. *In this excerpt, condensed from*

a chapter in his book, Dunn draws on all the available evidence to describe the steps by which English planters moved toward a brutal form of slavery on seventeenth-century Barbados.

*T*he initial difference between slavery in the two sectors of English America is that the island colonists plunged into the slaveholding business and the mainland colonists inched into it. The first Barbados settlers brought ten Negroes with them in 1627. The English on Tortuga and Providence acquired their first slaves in 1633, and five years later the blacks on Providence Island staged the first slave revolt in English America. When the Spaniards captured this island in 1641 they found four hundred Englishmen and six hundred slaves. The colonists in the eastern Caribbees owned fewer slaves than this during the tobacco years, but with the beginnings of sugar production, five hundred Negroes reportedly arrived at Barbados in 1642 and a thousand in 1645. By 1660, as we have seen, there were about twenty thousand blacks in Barbados, two thousand in the Leewards, and five hundred in Jamaica—as against a thousand in Virginia. . . .

The testimony of Capt. Henry Powell, who brought the first shipload of English settlers to Barbados in 1627, is pertinent here. Powell says he proceeded from Barbados to Surinam, where he persuaded thirty-two Indians to accompany him to Barbados "as free people" to plant tropical produce. The Indians asked "that I should allow them a piece of land, the which I did, and they would manure those fruits, and bring up their children to Christianite, and that we might drive a constant trade between the Island and the Mayne." But after Powell left Barbados his countrymen "hath taken [the Indians] by force and made them slaves" and kept them "long in Bondage." The ten Negroes who were brought to Barbados in 1627 were also called slaves, like the Indians. Henry Winthrop, who arrived with Powell, wrote home that the infant colony contained only "Inglishe men save a matter of 50 slaves of Indyenes and blacks." He varied his language slightly in a second letter: the Barbados population "is but 3 score of christyanes and fortye slaves of negeres and Indyenes." Winthrop was hazy about the exact number of slaves, but keenly aware of their difference from Christian Europeans. In a couple of artless phrases he managed to discriminate between Englishmen and Africans on the basis of race, color, religion, and class. . . .

It took a few years for the problem of interracial sex to develop, since practically all of the first inhabitants—black and white—were males. But in 1644 the Antigua Assembly composed a law against miscegenation, doubtless after the discovery of a mulatto baby. In forbidding "Carnall Coppullation between Christian and Heathen," the Antiguans defined "heathens" as Negroes and Indians and devised a sliding scale of punishments. A freeman or freewoman who fornicated with a black was fined, a servant had his or her term of indenture extended, and the offending heathen was branded and whipped. But to sleep with a black woman was at least held preferable to sleeping with your sister; in this same year the Antiguans passed another law punishing incest with death.

By 1650 certainly, and probably a good bit earlier, slavery in Barbados had become more than a lifetime condition. It extended through the slave's children to posterity. Richard Ligon, who thought the Negroes were treated better than white servants, sharply distinguished between the two categories of servitude:

> The Iland is divided into three sorts of men, viz. Masters, Servants, and slaves. The slaves and their posterity, being subject to their Masters for ever, are kept and preserv'd with greater care than the servants, who are theirs but for five years, according to the law of the Iland.

The blacks in these early days of sugar production probably did receive better treatment than later. But they were already clearly construed as articles of private property.

How many slaves were imported from Africa into the English sugar islands during the seventeenth century? Philip D. Curtin is the latest and best authority on this subject. Estimating that some 9.5 million Africans were landed in America during the entire four hundred years of the trade, he figures that about 42 percent of the cargoes went to the Caribbean Islands and 38 percent to Brazil. Jamaica, Barbados and the Leeward Islands were among the major Caribbean importers; they received roughly 1,480,000 slaves during the seventeenth and eighteenth centuries, or 15 percent of the grand total. The English planters, like their French rivals in St. Domingue, Martinique, and Guadeloupe, bought the bulk of their slaves in the eighteenth century when English and French sugar production reached maximum proportions. Yet the seventeenth-century English slave trade was very sizable. Curtin estimates that a quarter of a million slaves were landed in the English islands at an ever-accelerating rate between 1640 and 1700. . . .

English slaving records from the late seventeenth century enable us to tell pretty well what regions of Africa the traders drew upon. Over 70 percent of the slaves imported by the Royal African Company from 1673 to 1689 came from the Guinea coast, with the rest fairly equally divided between the Senegambia region further north and Angola further south. Thus the first forced black migrants to the English islands were chiefly inhabitants of the Windward Coast (modern Liberia), the Gold Coast (Ghana), and the Slave Coast (Togoland, Dahomey, and western Nigeria). These people lived in small and shifting political units and spoke a hundred different languages. They came from the part of Africa that most closely resembles the Caribbean islands in climate and ecology. The Guinea coast is a region of steaming coastal rain forest and interior grassland. The weather is always hot and humid, with the temperature averaging close to eighty degrees year-round and very heavy rainfall and violent storms, especially on the jungled coast. Plant growth is rapid and insect life is teeming. The West African people in the seventeenth century practiced settled, intensive agriculture. They grew food crops much like the Caribbean staples: plantains, yams, beans, cassava, and corn—the latter two borrowed from America. They ate little meat, a special merit from the English slave master's viewpoint. They

were used to hand labor in the fields, cultivating their crops with iron hoes, but not draft animals, for horses and cattle in West Africa were destroyed by sleeping sickness carried by the tsetse fly. Above all West African kinship and tribal structure inculcated the values of community cooperation and community discipline.

The English supposed, probably correctly, that the great variety of languages and intense tribal rivalries among the Guinea-coast peoples hindered these blacks, once enslaved, from combining against their masters. A writer of 1694 remarked that "the safety of the Plantations depends upon having Negroes from all parts of *Guiny*, who not understanding each others languages and Customs, do not, and cannot agree to Rebel, as they would do . . . when there are too many Negroes from one Country." The West Indian planters were always profoundly ignorant of and indifferent to the cultural attributes of the West Africans. They contented themselves with a simple set of prejudices, such as that Papaws from the Slave Coast made the most docile and agreeable slaves, the Cormantins

Slaves labor on a sugar mill in the West Indies. The number of slaves in the West Indies soared as English settlers began to produce sugar.

from the Gold Coast were proud, brave, and rebellious, and the Ibos from the Niger delta were timorous and despondent. All of these West African Negroes were considered preferable to the Bantu-speaking Angolans, who had the reputation of being not merely rebellious but—unforgivable sin—lazy as well.

The black cargoes assembled on the Guinea coast by the English slave traders in the seventeenth century were, on the whole, selected more carefully than the shiploads of white servants sent out to the West Indies from Britain. When the English traders dealt with African kings and merchants for slaves, they tried to buy as many healthy, young adult males as possible; young women, boys, and girls over the age of twelve were considered acceptable; adults over forty, infants, and sickly persons were rejected when possible. The price of slaves in West Africa rose steadily with the demand. In the 1670s and 1680s the Royal African Company typically paid about £3 in trade goods for a slave. By 1710 the purchase rate had quadrupled. This increase was of course transferred to the West Indies. Before the Glorious Revolution the company policy, broadly adhered to, was to charge £15 for slaves in Barbados, £16 in the Leewards, £17 in Jamaica, and £18 in Virginia. Interlopers sold their slaves rather more cheaply. But the rising African costs, coupled with the risks of the French wars, led the English traders, both company and private, to double their prices in the Indies. After 1700 a newly arrived African slave fetched £25 or £30 in the English islands. This increased market value of the slave had one beneficial effect: it persuaded the slave trader to take better care of his human cargo during the sea passage to America. Mortality on the middle passage was always frightfully high, but it did drop very considerably between 1680 and 1734. In the nine years between 1680 and 1688 the Royal African Company shipped 60,783 Negroes to the West Indies and delivered only 46,396—a loss of 23.5 percent. By 1734 company ships had reduced the loss of slaves in transit to 10 percent, and this seems to be about the average level of loss throughout the eighteenth century.

Thanks to the volume of the slave trade, the sugar planters were soon heavily outnumbered by their slaves. The black population surpassed the white population in Barbados around 1660, in Jamaica soon after 1670, and in the Leeward Islands soon after 1680. By 1713 there were four Negroes for every white man in the English sugar islands. The ratio in the mainland colonies was of course quite the reverse: six whites for every Negro in 1713. Even when the North American slave trade became large in the eighteenth century, South Carolina was the only mainland colony with more black than white inhabitants. A slave system in which the slaves greatly outnumber their masters naturally differs in many respects from a system in which the slaves constitute a minority. The West Indian slave masters could not expect to assimilate or acculturate such a huge alien population. If they wished to preserve their own identity, they had to segregate themselves socially and culturally from the blacks. And if they wished to preserve control, they had to devise a plantation regimen to make the slaves docile and dull and a policing system to keep them disciplined and intimidated.

The slave laws enacted by the island legislatures in the seventeenth century tell us a good deal about the treatment of Negroes and the character of slavery in the Caribbean colonies. These laws set formal standards, to be sure, which were not necessarily enforced. But it was the big planters on the islands who sat in the assemblies and composed these laws, which is to say that in the statute books the chief slaveholders articulated their views on how to handle Negroes. . . .

By 1661 . . . Barbados had a comprehensive slave code. The act passed in 1661 by the Barbados Assembly "for the better ordering and governing of Negroes" is the most important surviving piece of legislation issued in the English islands during the seventeenth century. It was reenacted with slight modifications by later Barbados assemblies in 1676, 1682, and 1688, was copied by the assemblies of Jamaica, in 1664, South Carolina, in 1696, and Antigua, in 1702. The preamble to this document implies that Negro slaves are chattels, for it undertakes "to protect them as wee doe men's other goods and Chattles." It explicitly characterizes Negroes as "an heathenish, brutish and an uncertaine, dangerous kinde of people," unfit to be governed by English law. Yet "the right rule of reason and order" tells the Barbadians that slaves cannot be left "to the Arbitrary, cruell and outragious wills of every evill disposed person." They require somewhat fuller protection than other forms of property, "as being created Men, though without the knowledge of God in the world." Thus the Barbados code aimed to protect the masters from the brutish slaves and the slaves from their bloody-minded masters. But in fact the masters were offered far fuller protection than the slaves.

The Barbados code of 1661 accorded masters, servants, and slaves carefully differentiated rights and obligations. The master had almost total authority over his slaves and markedly less power over his servants. He was obliged to give his Negroes new clothing once a year—a pair of drawers and a cap for every male, a petticoat and cap for every female—but no rules were laid down about slave food or slave working conditions. The master could correct his slaves in any way he liked, and if while beating a Negro for a misdemeanor he happened to maim or kill him ("which seldom happens"), he suffered no penalty. To be sure, the master could be stiffly fined (three thousand pounds of sugar or about £25) for wantonly killing his slave; the fine was a good deal stiffer for wantonly killing someone else's slave. But since the master could always claim to be correcting a slave for a misdemeanor, this fine was easy to evade. By contrast, in legislating for servants, the colony government fixed minimum food allotments as well as clothing allotments and permitted servants to sue in court or appeal to the magistrates if mistreated. The master could be fined for failing to take proper care of a sick servant, and he could be charged with murder should a servant die at his hands. Servants' corpses were routinely checked for signs of lash marks or starvation.

Slave crimes were judged and punished by a different standard than servant crimes. The guilty servant was given an extended term of indenture: one year of extra servitude for laying violent hands on his master, two years for theft, three years for running away or getting a female servant pregnant, seven years for entertaining a fugitive slave. A Negro found guilty of these same offenses was whipped, branded, or had his nose slit. Though castration appears to have been a favorite slave punishment, it was not officially incorporated into the Barbados code. Murder, rape, arson, assault, and theft of anything beyond a shilling in value were all capital crimes for Negroes. A key difference between servant and slave justice is that servants were entitled to jury trial, whereas "brutish slaves deserve not for the baseness of their Conditions to bee tryed by the legall tryall of twelve Men of their appeares [i.e., peers] or Neighborhood. So the Negro was tried by his master for petty offences and by two justices of the peace and three freeholders for major crimes. The most heinous Negro crime was rebellion or conspiracy against the white ruling order, tried by court-martial. The master of a rebel slave received compensation from the island treasury when his Negro was executed. But should a black man fight and hurt a fellow black, he might be merely whipped while his master paid compensation to the owner of the injured slave.

The Barbados slave act of 1661 was in large part a policing measure, designed to control the restive black population on the island. Within each plantation the overseers were expected to keep the Negro cabins under close surveillance, searching twice a month for stolen goods, clubs, and wooden swords. Six days a week the overseers kept the slaves busy at their tasks, but Sundays were free and therefore worrisome days for the whites. The Negroes tended to wander to neighboring plantations and hold markets. The act of 1661 stipulated that a slave who left his plantation on Sunday must carry a ticket stating the hour his master expected him back. The white man who found an unticketed Negro wandering loose was encouraged to give him a "moderate whipping." A French visitor to Barbados in 1654 saw slaves given fifty lashes for walking off limits on Sunday, which shows what "moderate" could mean. To punish a more serious offence, he says, the master sometimes applied a firebrand all over the slave's body, "which makes them shriek with despair." The Barbadians were particularly concerned about stolen and fugitive slaves in 1661. They established a registry of runaway slaves and organized a posse of twenty men to scout the island fastnesses and capture them dead or alive. Evidently some whites in Barbados were suspected of entertaining fugitive slaves, for the colony government promised immediate freedom to any servant who revealed that his master was keeping a runaway and fined the guilty master £80. Note that the fine for adopting a fugitive was much heavier than for murdering a slave. The Negro who caught a fugitive slave was rewarded with a fancy new set of clothes adorned "with a Badge of a Red crosse on his right Arme, whereby hee may be knowne and cherished by all good people"—the archetype of Uncle Tom.

The Barbados slave code was modified in one important respect in 1668, when the Assembly decided to classify Negroes as real estate instead of chattels, so that a slave could be legally tied to a given plantation. The purpose of this measure was to prevent executors from dismantling plantations in probate settlements. Sometimes creditors attached and sold all the slaves on an estate, leaving the heirs with "bare land without Negroes to manure the same," and the Assembly wanted to keep the island plantations as viable working units. What effect, if any, this legislation had upon the slave himself is a moot point. Eugene Sirmans has argued that the Barbados Negro, enjoying the status of freehold property, became a species of serf, and that his master, bereft of absolute ownership, had a right only to his services, not to his person. In practice, however, the Barbados slave certainly enjoyed no new freedom. If anything, the slave laws of the later seventeenth century further restricted his opportunities.

The Barbados Assembly betrayed a growing sense of alarm as the black population rose and the white population fell. In 1676 Barbados Ne-

groes were prohibited from entering such skilled crafts as cooper, smith, carpenter, tailor, or boatman, so as to reserve these occupations for Christian artisans, which might encourage freed servants to remain on the island. An act of 1682 berated the Negroes for driving the small white planters away by their insolent carriage. Policing measures to deal with slaves who prowled and stole at night were tightened up. Another measure of 1685 tried to shut down the Sunday markets by prohibiting white persons from trading with Negroes for pots of sugar and jars of molasses filched from their masters. The last major Barbados slave act of the century, in 1688, mainly echoed the provisions and language of 1661, with greater emphasis than before on the wickedness of Negro "Disorder, Rapines and Inhumanities to which they are naturally prone and inclined." For the first time, however, the Assembly admitted that some Negroes stole food because they were starving. The master who failed to provide his slaves with enough to live on was "in some measure guilty of their Crimes" and could not expect compensation from the island treasury when his Negroes were executed. . . .

Thus the English sugar planters rapidly evolved a legal system of chattel slavery. By the 1660s, if not before, they erected a comprehensive slave code that became the basic social and economic law of the islands. Not surprisingly the island colonists worked out their slave laws more quickly than the mainland planters. Virginia, for example, did not draw up a code comparable to the Barbados statute of 1661 until 1705. The seventeenth-century island laws proved to be remarkably durable; they continued in force with only minor modifications for 150 years. As in any slave-based society, the West Indian laws disciplined and regimented the masters as well as the slaves. The chief planters, speaking through the island assemblies, required each slave owner to act as a policeman, to suppress his humanitarian instincts, and to deal with his Negroes lash in hand. The slave laws legitimized a state of war between blacks and whites, sanctified rigid segregation, and institutionalized an early warning system against slave revolts. After all, the price of tyranny is eternal vigilance.

The three white witnesses who have most to say about early slave life in the English islands are Richard Ligon, John Taylor, and Hans Sloane. . . . They told how, when a slave ship docked, the blacks were greased with palm oil to improve their appearance and paraded naked into the auction hall so that prospective buyers could look into their mouths and test their joints, paying top prices for "the strongest, youthfullest, and most beautiful." New-slaves, says Taylor, lamented their captivity and sang mournful songs about their loss of freedom. Carried to the plantation, the new arrivals were branded with their owner's mark (a silver branding iron for the Negroes is a common artifact in seventeenth-century Jamaican inventories). If they tried to run away they were tracked down by dogs (John Helyar ordered two bloodhounds for Bybrook in 1686). Generally the planter housed his slaves in a row of little oblong huts, built out of sticks and cane trash, facing onto a Negro yard. Each hut was furnished with a mat for sleeping, a pot for cooking, and a calabash gourd or two, cut open to make cups and spoons. One Barbados planter in the 1680s installed his Negroes and his cattle in two sheds of the same size and valuation. The slaves ate a monotonous, meager, and starchy diet of corn, plantains, beans, and yams, supplemented by rum on Saturdays and meat whenever a bullock died of disease on the plantation. The manager of Bybrook claimed unusual benevolence in giving his one hundred slaves a barrel of herring per month. Most planters spent considerably less than £2 per annum to feed and clothe a slave.

The slave's work schedule was long and monotonous. Six days a week the Negroes were roused before daylight when the overseer sounded his conch-shell horn. They labored from about six o'clock to noon and, after an hour's recess for dinner, returned to their jobs until dark. The standard work day was ten or eleven hours. At crop time the Negroes labored in shifts around the clock, sometimes seven days a week. Plantation labor was purposely made more debilitating than diffi-

cult. The slave was locked into a week-long routine that kept him out of mischief (on the same principle as the modern boarding school), was underfed to break his resistance, was given childish tasks to numb his intelligence. The deadening round of simple, repetitive plantation chores, totally bereft of challenge or responsibility, promoted what Stanley Elkins calls the "Sambo" and Orlando Patterson calls the "Quashee" slave personality: docile, stultified, and infantile.

A striking characteristic of Negro slavery in the sugar islands, at least initially, was the planters' determination to keep their blacks at arm's length. Ligon tells us that in his day very few Negroes were permitted inside their masters' houses. Before the close of the century this changed, as the wealthy islanders employed large retinues of house slaves dressed in livery. But even in Bridgetown and Port Royal these domestics lived segregated in huts behind their masters' houses. The humble field hands continued to dwell apart, work apart, dress and eat differently from white men, and of course they remained heathens. Only the Quakers tried to convert their slaves to Christianity, and as we have seen, this activity profoundly upset the colony leaders in Barbados, who fined the Quakers thousands of pounds for bringing their Negroes to meeting.

In refusing to admit slaves into their churches the English planters differed markedly from contemporary French, Spanish, and Portuguese slave owners. The difference can largely be explained by Protestant versus Catholic conversion techniques. The Catholics could baptize their slaves into the church without requiring extensive preparation from the initiates. The Quakers, likewise, in their mystical quest for the Inner Light, could work with the blacks without worrying about book learning and catechizing. But for other forms of English Protestantism, mission work was valueless without some modicum of formal religious instruction, and here was the sticking point for the English planters. Ligon and Taylor both remarked on the planters' adamant refusal to instruct or educate the most intelligent slaves in anything beyond plantation crafts. In 1681 the Barbados Assembly declared that the Negroes' "Savage Brutishness renders them wholly uncapable" of conversion to Christianity. When the Jamaica Assembly reversed this position in 1696 and called upon the slave masters to instruct and baptize "all such as they can make sensible of a Deity and the Christian Faith," the lawmakers added reassuringly that no slave should become free by becoming Christian. But the planters knew better. They sensed the danger of "civilizing" the Negro to the point where he might have to be reckoned with as a man with human rights.

The West Indian slave, barred from the essentials of European civility, was free to retain as much as he wished of his West African cultural heritage. Here he differed from the Negro in Virginia or New England, who was not only uprooted from his familiar tropical environment but thrown into close association with white people and their European ways. It is not surprising, therefore, that blacks in the sugar islands preserved more of their native culture than blacks in North America. The West Indian slaves learned enough broken English to communicate with their overlords, but they were always bilingual and retained their tribal dialects. The large number of West African languages prevented easy communication among the slaves, so they evolved a common creole patois, compounded of English and African elements, which was unintelligible to their masters. At night and on weekends they sang and danced. The English disliked the racket they made with trumpets and African hollow-log drums and banned the drums for another reason, because they could be used to signal island-wide revolts. So the slaves made music with calabash gourds fitted out with twine or horsehair strings. The dancers tied rattles to their legs and wrists and cow tails to their rumps, while the onlookers clapped hands rhythmically and chanted "Alla, Alla." Sloane, who recorded the words and music of several African songs, says their content was always bawdy. Taylor says they howled and bellowed "in an Antique manner, as if they were all madd."

Neither Sloane, Taylor, nor Ligon showed any understanding of West African religion. Unable to fathom their slaves' mode of invoking and propitiating the gods through magical practices, the English put them down simply as devil worshippers. Sloane and Taylor did notice that the blacks staged elaborate and mournful funeral rites at slave burials. The peoples of West Africa believed that their ancestors would help and protect them from the other world; hence it was essential to honor the dead in the best way possible. For African tribesmen the funeral was the true climax to life. At a Caribbean slave funeral the mourners placed cassava bread, roast fowl (if they could get any), sugar, rum, tobacco, and lighted pipes into the grave to sustain the dead man on his journey to the pleasant mountains in Africa where he would dwell after life. This belief in a happy afterlife in Africa tempted many slaves to suicide. Ligon tells a grizzly tale of how Colonel Walrond in Barbados checked a rash of suicides on his plantation. He had one of his Negroes decapitated and stuck his head on a pole to show the other slaves that their companion's body had not traveled home after all and that they could not escape back to their own country through death. . . .

Keeping the Negroes at arm's length did not mean keeping hands off. The English sugar planters, like slave masters everywhere in America, slept with their slave women and sired mulatto children. At least occasionally, white women in the islands cohabited with black men. How much interracial sex play occurred we can only guess, but it is certain that the English planters in the West Indies sanctioned the practice more frankly than their cousins in the mainland colonies. As far as I can discover, Antigua was the only Caribbean colony to legislate against miscegenation in the seventeenth century. The Barbados and Jamaica slave codes, savage in their punishment of every other black peccadillo, are silent on the subject of blacks who fornicate with whites. For obvious reasons. The planters who drafted these codes had no desire to prohibit their extramarital liaisons with black prostitutes and mistresses. Many of the planters, merchants, managers, and overseers who operated the sugar industry were young bachelors or married men who left their wives and children in England. There were always fewer white women than white men living in the islands in the seventeenth century. But this was perhaps not the key consideration. The master enjoyed commandeering his prettiest slave girl and exacting his presumed rights from her. Many planters whose wives and children lived with them in the islands openly kept black concubines. . . .

The acid test of any slave system is the frequency and ferocity of resistance by the slaves. How many major Negro uprisings took place in the English sugar islands during the course of the seventeenth century? The planters hated to talk about this subject, but it is possible to identify seven separate slave revolts in the English islands between 1640 and 1713 in which fifty or more Negroes participated and in which blacks and whites were killed. Another half-dozen major slave conspiracies were nipped in the bud. These early revolts followed a curious pattern. The Negroes took many years to gear themselves for combat with the white man; no major black revolt occurred, no serious black plot was uncovered, in any of the English islands until 1673, a full generation after the start of the slave trade. Then, during the closing quarter of the century, black risings or rumored risings were frequent. When trouble did come nearly all of it was confined to Jamaica. There were several plots in Barbados and the Leewards, but only one small rising; the black slaves on these islands were by every standard more constrained than the white servants.

One might expect Barbados to be the center of slave revolts. The island was compact, the plantations close together, and the slaves heavily outnumbered their masters from 1660 onwards. But the big problem in Barbados was that the island offered no opportunity for halfway measures; black rebels could not simply seize a few guns, kill a few whites, burn a plantation or two, and disappear into the woods. Since the island was fully settled, their only chance for success was to stage a colony-wide conspiracy and take

over the entire island. The white servants on Barbados had tried to do this in 1649 and failed. The slave masters, alerted by this past experience, kept guard inside their fortified houses as though they lived under a state of siege. Through the Barbados slave law of 1661 they policed the blacks as systematically as possible. Each planter took care to buy new slaves a few at a time, from a variety of West African regions, on the theory that tribal animosities and linguistic barriers would keep the blacks divided and confused. Perhaps this theory was correct. It would help explain why the Barbados Negroes did not mount a conspiracy against the English until 1675, by which time many blacks had lived long enough on the island to forget African animosities and to speak in creole patois with Negroes from alien tribes. Gov. William Willoughby in 1668 feared that the "Creolian generation" of young slaves then growing up in Barbados would soon strike against their masters. It is likely also that slave conditions deteriorated on the island between 1650 and 1675. At first, when the blacks worked side by side with large numbers of white servants, they were protected by the whites' refusal to work too long or hard. By the 1670s, with the white field laborers gone and sugar profits narrowing, the Barbados planters were more tempted to take shortcuts by feeding their slaves less and working them harder. Finally, the slave masters grew a bit overconfident and careless. In 1673 they even armed some of their Negroes in order to bolster the militia. All this set the stage for Barbados's biggest fright of the century.

In June 1675 a house slave named Fortuna heard that a ring of Cormantin Negroes from the Gold Coast was plotting a general rising. The aim was to murder all of the whites (except for the fairest white women) and install an ancient Cormantin named Cuffee as king of Barbados. The rising was scheduled for two weeks hence. Fortuna dutifully warned her master, Capt. Giles Hall, a leading planter, who alerted Governor Atkins, who hastily commissioned a dozen militia officers to examine the alleged ringleaders secretly. This court-martial sentenced six Negroes to be burned alive and eleven others to be beheaded and dragged through the streets of Speightstown, the rebel center. One brave black named Tony, who was condemned to be burned, stoutly refused to tell all he knew about the plot. "If you Roast me today," he taunted the provost marshal, "you cannot Roast me tomorrow." The Barbados authorities executed thirty-five Negroes before they felt satisfied that they had snuffed out the conspiracy. They rewarded the faithful Fortuna by granting her freedom. . . .

In Jamaica black unrest was a far more serious matter. During the first dozen years of English occupation, the colonists were constantly fighting the fugitive Spanish Maroons, and once plantation slavery took hold on the island, they had to cope with six sizable slave revolts between 1673 and 1694 and smaller ones thereafter. The first two rebellions, in 1673 and 1675, took place on the remote north coast; in both cases slaves on isolated plantations seized arms and killed their masters. A St. Mary planter named Charles Atkinson reported privately in 1675 that the rebels had been made desperate "by the ill government of their Master." Atkinson's own slaves, though tempted to join, remained faithful to him and disclosed the plot to their overseer. A posse of twenty militiamen, which chased the rebels for three months, caught and killed only eight or nine of them. The others vanished into the wilds or joined the Maroons.

The next Jamaican revolt broke out within five miles of Spanish Town in 1678. Slaves from various plantations plotted this rising when they were brought together to build a fort. Some of the conspirators, interestingly enough, had known each other in Barbados. The revolt started on Capt. Edmund Duck's plantation, where the slaves killed their mistress and several other whites. Martha Duck's weathered tombstone in the yard of Spanish Town cathedral tells the story: "UNDER THIS STONE LYETH THE BODYS OF EDMON DUCKE ESQ. AND MARTHA HIS WIFE, SHE BEING MOST BARBAROUSLY MURTHERED BY SOME OF THEIR OWNE NEGRO SLAVES DEPARTED THIS LIFE THE 28 DAY OF APRIL 1678." Some of Duck's slaves were quickly caught and executed, but thirty of

them slipped into Sixteen Mile Walk in the vicinity of Bybrook plantation and gathered fresh recruits from Sir Thomas Modyford's and William Helyar's Negroes. A loyal slave of Modyford's spied the rebels tossing water into the air from bowls "to see by their witchcraft whither they should be fortunate in their proceedings or not." Some twenty Negroes from Helyar's and Modyford's plantations were implicated and executed. The Jamaica records do not reveal how many Negroes were killed altogether in the process of stamping out this rebellion. The overseer at Bybrook witnessed one execution, and his description amply details the sadistic torture employed upon this unfortunate man:

> His leggs and armes was first brocken in peeces with stakes, after which he was fasten'd upon his back to the Ground—a fire was made first to his feete and burn'd uppe by degrees; I heard him speake severall words when the fire consum'd all his lower parts as far as his Navill. The fire was upon his breast (he was burning neere 3 hours) before he dy'd.

Worse was still to come. In 1685–1686 Jamaica suffered a yearlong slave revolt. About 150 Negroes started the rebellion on the north side in July 1685, when they obtained twenty-five guns, killed eleven whites, and hid out in the mountains. Governor Molesworth proclaimed martial law and sent out patrols of militiamen and dogs, but the rebels eluded capture for many months while inflicting a great deal of damage to the north-coast settlements. The rebellion spread south in March 1686 when 105 slaves at Madam Guy's plantation seized arms in the night "through the faults of the white servants, who were gotten drunk and therefore unable to Quell them." Madam Guy herself leaped out of a window and was hidden by a loyal house slave, but fifteen of the seventeen whites on this plantation were murdered. As the Negroes continued to burn and plunder, John Helyar braced himself for an attack on Bybrook. "Wee will give them such reception," he wrote his father, "as the strength of the house will afford." Every Negro caught during this rebellion was killed—burned alive, torn by dogs, or drawn and quartered. Eventually the colony government restored order, at a total cost of £3,203. Five years later the 400 slaves of Thomas Sutton, the speaker of the Assembly, rose en masse. Sutton's plantation had been considered the largest and finest in Jamaica, but 200 of his Negroes were killed within three weeks in this revolt. Further, smaller revolts occurred in 1694, 1702, and 1704, mainly on the north coast, with the rebels slipping off to join the other slave fugitives hiding in the mountains, setting the stage for the Maroon Wars of 1720 to 1739.

Why were the Jamaica Negroes so much more rebellious than in the other islands? Slave conditions were no worse here. On the contrary, Jamaican slaves had more to eat than in Barbados, for the planters had enough land to spare so that they could give each Negro couple a half acre for provision ground and often a pig, cock, and hen. The Jamaica slave laws, as we have seen, were slightly less repressive than the Barbados code. The plantations that blew up—Edmund Duck's, Madam Guy's, Thomas Sutton's—were not absentee operations. These owners lived on the premises and probably treated their Negroes more humanely than a salaried overseer or manager would tend to. Surely the explanation is that the Jamaican Negroes saw they had a better chance for successful rebellion than in the other islands. The Jamaican revolts started in the largest plantations because the slaves felt safety in numbers. Action centered on the north coast because the plantations were widely scattered there and escape to the mountains and the Maroons was relatively easy. It was not necessary in Jamaica to try to take over the entire island, as in Barbados; all the rebels had to do was cut and run.

The Jamaican slaves rebelled more vigorously and frequently, than the blacks in most other American colonies; their uprisings were decidedly bigger affairs than the slave revolts in colonial North America. The Jamaican slaves put the lie to the planters' contention that Africans were really happy in their bondage; on the only island where rebellion had a chance of success, it happened often. Yet even in Jamaica the blacks were rather ineffectual rebels, a key reason being that in nearly every conspiracy some loyal slave betrayed the secret to his master. Here is the supreme irony. The English planters, who treated their slaves with such contemptuous inhumanity, were rescued time and again from disaster by the compassionate generosity of the Negroes. In consequence the slave uprisings—even in Jamaica—caused less damage to the planters than hurricanes, earthquakes, malaria epidemics, and French raids. It turned out to be true that a small number of Englishmen could manage a horde of black slaves more easily than white servants. The most telling point about the black protest movement in the seventeenth century is that it never began to challenge the vicious slave system in the English islands head on.

Slavery Reaches the Chesapeake

Winthrop D. Jordan

Indentured servants in seventeenth-century Virginia and Maryland were overwhelmingly English men or women, usually young and desperate to escape a homeland ravaged by chronic economic crisis. But a few were also Africans. In 1619 a Dutch vessel deposited in Virginia a cargo that included a number of blacks (whose status as either slaves or indentured servants is unclear), and in subsequent years other African people were also brought to the Chesapeake colonies. Did most or all of them become indentured servants, or were they treated as slaves who could never hope for freedom? We will never know for sure. Not until the 1660s did Virginia's free whites begin to enact laws that rigidly defined black people and their offspring as lifelong slaves.

Historian Winthrop D. Jordan published a groundbreaking study entitled White over Black: American Attitudes Toward the Negro, 1550–1812, *in 1968. In it, Jordan analyzed how whites in North America came to regard blacks as an inferior race who could legitimately be enslaved. Jordan believes that the English (and other Europeans) evolved*

negative stereotypes about Africans almost from the first time that the two races encountered each other in the fifteenth century. Nevertheless, he also believes that the formal institutions of slavery grew only slowly in early Virginia and Maryland, as this excerpt, taken from White over Black, *explains.*

In Virginia and Maryland . . . geographic conditions and the intentions of the settlers quickly combined to produce a successful agricultural staple. The deep tidal rivers, the long growing season, the fertile soil, and the absence of strong communal spirit among the settlers opened the way. Ten years after settlers first landed at Jamestown they were on the way to proving, in the face of assertions to the contrary, that it was possible "to found an empire upon smoke." More than the miscellaneous productions of New England, tobacco required labor which was cheap but not temporary, mobile but not independent, and tireless rather than skilled. In the Chesapeake area more than anywhere to the northward, the shortage of labor and the abundance of land—the "frontier"—placed a premium on involuntary labor.

This need for labor played more directly upon these settlers' ideas about freedom and bondage than it did either in the West Indies or in New England. Perhaps it would be more accurate to say that settlers in Virginia (and in Maryland after settlement in 1634) made their decisions concerning Negroes while relatively virginal, relatively free from external influences and from firm preconceptions. Of all the important early English settlements, Virginia had the least contact with the Spanish, Portuguese, Dutch, and other English colonies. At the same time, the settlers of Virginia did not possess either the legal or Scriptural learning of the New England Puritans whose conception of the just war had opened the way to the enslavement of Indians. Slavery in the tobacco colonies did not begin as an adjunct of captivity; in marked contrast to the Puritan response to the Pequot War the settlers of Virginia did not generally react to the Indian massacre of 1622 with propositions for taking captives and selling them as "slaves." It was perhaps a correct measure of the conceptual atmosphere in Virginia that there was only one such proposition after the 1622 disaster and that that one was defective in precision as to how exactly one treated captive Indians.

In the absence, then, of these influences which obtained in other English colonies, slavery as it developed in Virginia and Maryland assumes a special interest and importance over and above the fact that Negro slavery was to become a vitally important institution there and, later, to the southwards. In the tobacco colonies it is possible to watch Negro slavery *develop,* not pop up full-grown overnight, and it is therefore possible to trace, very imperfectly, the development of the shadowy, unexamined rationale which supported it. The concept of Negro slavery there was neither borrowed from foreigners, nor extracted from books, nor invented out of whole cloth, nor extrapolated from servitude, nor generated by English reaction to Negroes as such, nor necessitated by the exigencies of the New World. Not any one of these made the Negro a slave, but all.

In rough outline, slavery's development in the tobacco colonies seems to have undergone three stages. Negroes first arrived in 1619, only a few days late for the meeting of the first representative assembly in America. John Rolfe described

Dutch traders bring the first Africans to Virginia in 1619. It is unknown whether the first black people in Virginia were slaves or indentured servants.

the event with the utmost unconcern: "About the last of August came in a dutch man of warre that sold us twenty Negars." Negroes continued to trickle in slowly for the next half century; one report in 1649 estimated that there were three hundred among Virginia's population of fifteen thousand—about 2 per cent. Long before there were more appreciable numbers, the development of slavery had, so far as we can tell, shifted gears. Prior to about 1640, there is very little evidence to show how Negroes were treated—though we will need to return to those first twenty years in a moment. After 1640 there is mounting evidence that some Negroes were in fact being treated as slaves, at least that they were being held in hereditary lifetime service. This is to say that the twin essences of slavery—the two kinds of perpetuity—first become evident during the twenty years prior to the beginning of legal formulation. After 1660 slavery was written into statute law. Negroes began to flood into the two colonies at the end of the seventeenth century. In 1705 Virginia produced a codification of laws applying to slaves.

Concerning the first of these stages, there is only one major historical certainty, and unfortunately it is the sort which historians find hardest to bear. There simply is not enough evidence to indicate with any certainty whether Negroes were treated like white servants or not. At least we can be confident, therefore, that the two most common assertions about the first Negroes—that they were slaves and that they were servants—are *unfounded,* though not necessarily incorrect. And what of the positive evidence?

Some of the first group bore Spanish names and presumably had been baptized, which would mean they were at least nominally Christian, though of the Papist sort. They had been "sold" to the English; so had other Englishmen but not by the Dutch. Certainly these Negroes were not fully free, but many Englishmen were not. It can be said, though, that from the first in Virginia Negroes were set apart from white men by the word *Negroes.* The earliest Virginia census reports plainly distinguished Negroes from white men, often giving Negroes no personal name; in 1629 every commander of the several plantations was ordered to "take a generall muster of all the inhabitants men woemen and Children as well *Englishe* as Negroes." A distinct name is not attached to a group unless it is regarded as distinct. It seems logical to suppose that this perception of the Negro as being distinct from the Englishman must have operated to debase his status rather than to raise it, for in the absence of countervailing social factors, the need for labor in the colonies usually told in the direction of non-freedom. There were few countervailing factors present, surely, in such instances as in 1629 when a group of Negroes were brought to Virginia freshly captured from a Portuguese vessel which had snatched them from Angola a few weeks earlier. Given the context of English thought and experience sketched in this chapter, it seems probable that the Negro's status was not ever the same as that accorded the white servant. But we do not know for sure.

When the first fragmentary evidence appears about 1640 it becomes clear that *some* Negroes in both Virginia and Maryland were serving for life and some Negro children inheriting the same obligation. Not all Negroes, certainly, for Nathaniel Littleton had released a Negro named Anthony Longoe from all service whatsoever in 1635, and after the mid-1640's the court records show that other Negroes were incontestably free and were accumulating property of their own. At least one Negro freeman, Anthony Johnson, himself owned a Negro. Some Negroes served only terms of usual length, but others were held for terms far longer than custom and statute permitted with white servants. The first fairly clear indication that slavery was practiced in the tobacco colonies appears in 1639, when a Maryland statute declared that "all the Inhabitants of this Province being Christians (Slaves excepted) Shall have and enjoy all such rights liberties immunities priviledges and free customs within this Province as any naturall born subject of England." Another Maryland law passed the same year provided that "all persons being Christians (Slaves excepted)" over eighteen who were imported without indentures would serve for four years. These laws make very little sense unless the term *slaves* meant Negroes and perhaps Indians.

The next year, 1640, the first definite indication of outright enslavement appears in Virginia. The General Court pronounced sentence on three servants who had been retaken after absconding to Maryland. Two of them, a Dutchman and a Scot, were ordered to serve their masters for one additional year and then the colony for three more, but "the third being a negro named John Punch shall serve his said master or his assigns for the time of his natural life here or else where." No white servant in any English colony, so far as is known, ever received a like sentence. Later the same month a Negro (possibly the same enterprising fellow) was again singled out from a group of recaptured runaways; six of the seven culprits were assigned additional time while the Negro was given none, presumably because he was already serving for life.

After 1640, when surviving Virginia county

court records began to mention Negroes, sales for life, often including any future progeny, were recorded in unmistakable language. In 1646 Francis Pott sold a Negro woman and boy to Stephen Charlton, "to the use of him . . . forever." Similarly, six years later William Whittington sold to John Pott "one Negro girle named Jowan; aged about Ten yeares and with her Issue and produce duringe her (or either of them) for their Life tyme. And their Successors forever"; and a Maryland man in 1649 deeded two Negro men and a woman "and all their issue both male and Female." The executors of a York County estate in 1647 disposed of eight Negroes—four men, two women, and two children—to Captain John Chisman "to have hold occupy posesse and injoy and every one of the afforementioned Negroes forever." The will of Rowland Burnham of "Rapahanocke," made in 1657, dispensed his considerable number of Negroes and white servants in language which clearly differentiated between the two by specifying that the whites were to serve for their "full terme of tyme" and the Negroes "for ever." Nothing in the will indicated that this distinction was exceptional or novel.

Further evidence that some Negroes were serving for life in this period lies in the prices paid for them. In many instances the valuations placed on Negroes (in estate inventories and bills of sale) were far higher than for white servants, even those servants with full terms yet to serve. Higher prices must have meant that Negroes were more highly valued because of their greater length of service. Negro women may have been especially prized, moreover, because their progeny could also be held perpetually. In 1643, for example, William Burdett's inventory listed eight servants, with the time each had still to serve, at valuations ranging from 400 to 1,100 pounds of tobacco, while a "very anntient" Negro was valued at 3,000 and an eight-year-old Negro girl at 2,000 pounds, with no time remaining indicated for either. In the late 1650's an inventory of Thomas Ludlow's estate evaluated a white servant with six years to serve at less than an elderly Negro man and only one half of a Ne-

gro woman. Similarly, the labor owned by James Stone in 1648 was evaluated as follows:

	lb tobo
Thomas Groves, 4 yeares to serve	1300
Francis Bomley for 6 yeares	1500
John Thackstone for 3 yeares	1300
Susan Davis for 3 yeares	1000
Emaniell a Negro man	2000
Roger Stone 3 yeares	1300
Mingo a Negro man	2000

The 1655 inventory of Argoll Yeardley's estate provides clear evidence of a distinction between perpetual and limited service for Negroes. Under the heading "Servants" were listed "Towe Negro men, towe Negro women (their wifes) one Negro girle aged 15 yeares, Item One Negro girle aged about teen yeares and one Negro child aged about sixe moneths," valued at 12,000 pounds, and under the heading "Corne" were "Servants, towe men their tyme three months," valued at 300 pounds, and "one Negro boye ["about three yeares old"] (which by witness of his godfather) is to bee free att twenty foure yeares of age and then to have towe cowes given him," valued at 600 pounds. Besides setting a higher value on Negroes, these inventories failed to indicate the number of years they had still to serve, presumably because their service was for an unlimited time.

Where Negro women were involved, higher valuations probably reflected the facts that their issue were valuable and that they could be used for field work while white women generally were not. This latter discrimination between Negro and white women did not necessarily involve perpetual service, but it meant that Negroes were set apart in a way clearly not to their advantage. This was not the only instance in which Negroes were subjected to degrading distinctions not immediately and necessarily attached to the concept of slavery. Negroes were singled out for special treatment in several ways which suggest a generalized debasement of Negroes as a group. Significantly, the first indications of this debasement appeared at about the same time as the first indications of actual enslavement.

The distinction concerning field work is a case in point. It first appears on the written record in 1643, when Virginia almost pointedly endorsed it in a tax law. Previously, in 1629, tithable persons had been defined as "all those that worke in the ground of what qualitie or condition soever." The new law provided that *all* adult men were tithable and, in addition, *Negro* women. The same distinction was made twice again before 1660. Maryland adopted a similar policy beginning in 1654. This official discrimination between Negro and other women was made by men who were accustomed to thinking of field work as being ordinarily the work of men rather than women. As John Hammond wrote in a 1656 tract defending the tobacco colonies, servant women were not put to work in the fields but in domestic employments, "yet som wenches that are nasty, and beastly and not fit to be so employed are put into the ground." The essentially racial character of this discrimination stood out clearly in a law passed in 1668 at the time slavery was taking shape in the statute books:

> Whereas some doubts, have arisen whether negro women set free were still to be accompted tithable according to a former act, *It is declared by this grand assembly* that negro women, though permitted to enjoy their Freedome yet ought not in all respects to be admitted to a full fruition of the exemptions and impunities of the English, and are still lyable to payment of taxes.

Virginia law set Negroes apart from all other groups in a second way by denying them the important right and obligation to bear arms. Few restraints could indicate more clearly the denial to Negroes of membership in the white community. This first foreshadowing of the slave codes came in 1640, at just the time when other indications first appeared that Negroes were subject to special treatment.

Finally, an even more compelling sense of the separateness of Negroes was revealed in early reactions to sexual union between the races. Prior to 1660 the evidence concerning these reactions is equivocal, and it is not possible to tell whether repugnance for intermixture preceded legislative enactment of slavery. In 1630 an angry Virginia court sentenced "Hugh Davis to be soundly whipped, before an assembly of Negroes and others for abusing himself to the dishonor of God and shame of Christians, by defiling his body in lying with a negro," but it is possible that the "negro" may not have been female. With other instances of punishment for interracial union in the ensuing years, fornication rather than miscegenation may well have been the primary offense, though in 1651 a Maryland man sued someone who he claimed had said "that he had a black bastard in Virginia." (The court recognized the legitimacy of his complaint, but thought his claim for £20,000 sterling somewhat overvalued his reputation and awarded him 1500 pounds "of Tobacco and Cask.") There may have been no racial feeling involved when in 1640 Robert Sweet, a gentleman, was compelled "to do penance in church according to laws of England, for getting a negroe woman with child and the woman whipt." About 1650 a white man and a Negro woman were required to stand clad in white sheets before a congregation in lower Norfolk County for having had relations, but this punishment was sometimes used in cases of fornication between two whites. A quarter century later in 1676, however, the emergence of distaste for racial intermixture was unmistakable. A contemporary account of Bacon's Rebellion caustically described one of the ringleaders, Richard Lawrence, as a person who had eclipsed his learning and abilities "in the darke imbraces of a Blackamoore, his slave: And that in so fond a Maner, . . . to the noe meane Scandle and affrunt of all the Vottrisses in or about towne."

Such condemnation was not confined to polemics. In the early 1660's when slavery was gaining statutory recognition, the assemblies acted with full-throated indignation against miscegenation. These acts aimed at more than merely avoiding confusion of status. In 1662 Virginia declared that "if any christian shall committ Fornication with a negro man or woman, hee or shee soe offending" should pay double the usual fine. (The next year Bermuda prohibited all sexual relations between whites and Negroes.) Two years later Maryland banned interracial marriages:

> forasmuch as divers freeborne English women forgettfull of their free Condicion and to the disgrace of our Nation doe intermarry with Negro Slaves by which alsoe divers suites may arise touching the Issue of such woemen and a great damage doth befall the Masters of such Negros for prevention whereof for deterring such freeborne women from such shamefull Matches,

strong language indeed if "divers suites" had been the only problem. A Maryland act of 1681 described marriages of white women with Negroes as, among other things, "always to the Satisfaccion of theire Lascivious and Lustfull desires, and to the disgrace not only of the English butt allso of many other Christian Nations." When Virginia finally prohibited all interracial liaisons in 1691, the Assembly vigorously denounced miscegenation and its fruits as "that abominable mixture and spurious issue."

From the surviving evidence, it appears that outright enslavement and these other forms of debasement appeared at about the same time in Maryland and Virginia. Indications of perpetual service, the very nub of slavery, coincided with indications that English settlers discriminated against Negro women, withheld arms from Negroes, and—though the timing is far less certain—reacted unfavorably to interracial sexual union. The coincidence suggests a mutual relationship between slavery and unfavorable assessment of Negroes. Rather than slavery causing "prejudice," or vice versa, they seem rather to have generated each other. Both were, after all, twin aspects of a general debasement of the Negro. Slavery and "prejudice" may have been equally cause and effect, continuously reacting upon each other, dynamically joining hands to hustle the Negro down the road to complete degradation. Much more than with the other English colonies, where the enslavement of Negroes was to some extent a borrowed practice, the available evidence for Maryland and Virginia points to less borrowing and to this kind of process: a mutually interactive growth of slavery and unfavorable assessment, with no cause for either which did not cause the other as well. If slavery caused prejudice, then invidious distinctions concerning working in the fields, bearing arms, and sexual union should have appeared *after* slavery's firm establishment. If prejudice caused slavery, then one would expect to find these lesser discriminations preceding the greater discrimination of outright enslavement. Taken as a whole, the evidence reveals a process of debasement of which hereditary lifetime service was an important but not the only part.

White servants did not suffer this debasement. Rather, their position improved, partly for the reason that they were not Negroes. By the early 1660's white men were loudly protesting against being made "slaves" in terms which strongly suggest that they considered slavery not as wrong but as inapplicable to themselves. The father of a Maryland apprentice petitioned in 1663 that "he Craves that his daughter may not be made a Slave a tearme soe Scandalous that if admitted to be the Condicon or tytle of the Apprentices in this Province will be soe distructive as noe free borne Christians will ever be induced to come over servants." An Irish youth complained to a Maryland court in 1661 that he had been kidnapped and forced to sign for fifteen years, that he had already served six and a half years and was now twenty-one, and that eight and a half more years of service was "contrary to the lawes of God and man that a Christian Subject should be made a Slave." (The jury blandly compromised the dispute by deciding that he should serve only until age twenty-one, but that he was now only nineteen.) Free Negro servants were generally increasingly less able to defend themselves against this insidious kind of encroachment. Increasingly, white men were more clearly free because Negroes had become so clearly slave.

Certainly it was the case in Maryland and Virginia that the legal enactment of Negro slavery followed social practice, rather than vice versa, and also that the assemblies were slower than in other English colonies to declare how Negroes could or should be treated. These two patterns in themselves suggest that slavery was less a matter of previous conception or external example in Maryland and Virginia than elsewhere.

The Virginia Assembly first showed itself incontrovertibly aware that Negroes were not serving in the same manner as English servants in 1660 when it declared "that for the future no servant comeing into the country without indentures, of what christian nation soever, shall serve longer then those of our own country, of the like age." In 1661 the Assembly indirectly provided statutory recognition that some Negroes served for life: "That in case any English servant shall run away in company with any negroes who are incapable of making satisfaction by addition of time," he must serve for the Negroes' lost time as well as his own. Maryland enacted a closely similar law in 1663 (possibly modeled on Virginia's) and in the following year, on the initiative of the lower house, came out with the categorical declaration that Negroes were to serve "Durante Vita." During the next twenty-odd years a succession of acts in both colonies defined with increasing precision what sorts of persons might be treated as slaves. Other acts dealt with the growing problem of slave control, and especially after 1690 slavery began to assume its now familiar character as a complete deprivation of all rights. As early as 1669 the Virginia Assembly unabashedly enacted a brutal law which showed where the logic of perpetual servitude was inevitably tending. Unruly servants could be chastened by sentences to additional terms, but "WHEREAS the only law in force for the punishment of refractory servants resisting their master, mistris or overseer cannot be inflicted upon negroes, nor the obstinacy of many of them by other then violent meanes supprest," if a slave "by the extremity of the correction should chance to die" his master was not to be adjudged guilty of felony "since it cannot be presumed that prepensed malice (which alone makes murther Felony) should induce any man to destroy his owne estate." Virginia planters felt they acted out of mounting necessity: there were disturbances among slaves in several areas in the early 1670's.

By about 1700 the slave ships began spilling forth their black cargoes in greater and greater numbers. By that time, racial slavery and the necessary police powers had been written into law. By that time, too, slavery had lost all resemblance to a perpetual and hereditary version of English servitude, though service for life still seemed to contemporaries its most essential feature. In the last quarter of the seventeenth century the trend was to treat Negroes more like property and less like men, to send them to the fields at younger ages, to deny them automatic existence as inherent members of the community, to tighten the bonds on their personal and civil freedom, and correspondingly to loosen the traditional restraints on the master's freedom to deal with his human property as he saw fit. In 1705 Virginia gathered up the random statutes of a whole generation and baled them into a "slave code" which would not have been out of place in the nineteenth century.

Selection 3

Slavery Takes Root in Virginia

Edmund S. Morgan

How is it possible that white Americans, whose historical tradition idealizes freedom, could also justify enslaving other human beings? Yale University historian Edmund S. Morgan, one of the United States' most distinguished authorities on colonial New England and Virginia, set out to explain this apparent paradox in his classic book American Slavery, American Freedom: The Ordeal of Colonial Virginia (1975). *Morgan's research showed that by the 1670s Virginia's white indentured-servant class, as well as former servants who had received small land grants, were becoming assertive and unruly—so much so that in the 1676 revolt known as Bacon's Rebellion they came near to driving from power Virginia's royal governor and the clique of large landowners who supported him. In the aftermath of this revolt, members of Virginia's emerging upper class realized that they should reduce their reliance on disgruntled white servants and should depend more on the labor of black slaves. Talk began to be heard of a common white interest in keeping blacks in permanent bondage, the terms of which grew steadily more harsh and*

Excerpted from Edmund S. Morgan, *American Slavery, American Freedom: The Ordeal of Colonial Virginia.* Copyright © 1975 W.W. Norton & Company, Inc. Reprinted with permission from W.W. Norton & Company, Inc.

more rigid with the enactment of formal slave codes. Whatever their varying economic status—and the disparities were now growing, not diminishing—all whites at least had in common the fact that they were free or could aspire to freedom, which was denied to Virginians of African descent.

Virginians of the late seventeenth century seemed to be plagued by the same kind of restless, roistering rogues who had wandered through Elizabethan England. England had kept them down by the workhouse, by the gallows, by whipping them back to the parish they came from, by sending them off on military expeditions—and by shipping them to Virginia. . . . Although Virginians were not all happy about it, throughout the century they kept crying for more. They wanted men. They could not get enough of them. The problem was not, as in England, to find work for them but simply to keep them working for their betters. . . .

Slavery is a mode of compulsion that has often prevailed where land is abundant, and Virginians had been drifting toward it from the time when they first found something profitable to work at. Servitude in Virginia's tobacco fields approached closer to slavery than anything known at the time in England. Men served longer, were subjected to more rigorous punish-

Plantation owner Nathaniel Bacon (left) presents his demands to Sir William Berkeley, governor of Virginia, during Bacon's 1676 revolt of former indentured servants.

ments, were traded about as commodities already in the 1620s.

That Virginia's labor barons of the 1620s or her land and labor barons of the 1660s and 1670s did not transform their servants into slaves was probably not owing to any moral squeamishness or to any failure to perceive the advantages of doing so. Although slavery did not exist in England, Englishmen were not so unfamiliar with it that they had to be told what it was. They knew that the Spaniards' gold and silver were dug by slave labor, and they themselves had even toyed with temporary "slavery" as a punishment for crime in the sixteenth century. But for Virginians to have pressed their servants or their indigent neighbors into slavery might have been, initially at least, more perilous than exploiting them in the ways that eventuated in the plundering parties of Bacon's Rebellion. Slavery, once established, offered incomparable advantages in keeping labor docile, but the transformation of free men into slaves would have been a tricky business. It would have had to proceed by stages, each carefully calculated to

stop short of provoking rebellion. And if successful it would have reduced, if it did not end, the flow of potential slaves from England and Europe. Moreover, it would have required a conscious, deliberate, public decision. It would have had to be done, even if in stages, by action of the assembly, and the English government would have had to approve it. If it had been possible for the men at the top in Virginia to arrive at such a decision or series of decisions, the home government would almost certainly have vetoed the move, for fear of a rebellion or of an exodus from the colony that would prove costly to the crown's tobacco revenues.

But to establish slavery in Virginia it was not necessary to enslave anyone. Virginians had only to buy men who were already enslaved, after the initial risks of the transformation had been sustained by others elsewhere. They converted to slavery simply by buying slaves instead of servants. The process seems so simple, the advantages of slave labor so obvious, and their system of production and attitude toward workers so receptive that it seems surprising they did not convert sooner. African slaves were present in Virginia, as we have seen, almost from the beginning (probably the first known Negroes to arrive, in 1619, were slaves). The courts clearly recognized property in men and women and their unborn progeny at least as early as the 1640s, and there was no law to prevent any planter from bringing in as many as he wished. Why, then, did Virginians not furnish themselves with slaves as soon as they began to grow tobacco? Why did they wait so long?

The answer lies in the fact that slave labor, in spite of its seeming superiority, was actually not as advantageous as indentured labor during the first half of the century. Because of the high mortality among immigrants to Virginia, there could be no great advantage in owning a man for a lifetime rather than a period of years, especially since a slave cost roughly twice as much as an indentured servant. If the chances of a man's dying during his first five years in Virginia were better than fifty-fifty—and it seems apparent that they were—and if English servants could be made to work as hard as slaves, English servants for a five-year term were the better buy.

If Virginians had been willing to pay the price, it seems likely that they could have obtained Negro slaves in larger numbers than they did. During the first half of the century the Dutch were busy dismantling the Portuguese empire and, in the process, taking over the African slave trade. They promoted the development of English sugar plantations in the West Indies and supplied those plantations with enough slaves to give Barbados (founded twenty years after Virginia) a black population of 5,000 by 1645 and 20,000 by 1660. Virginia could scarcely have had a tenth the number at either date. Yet the Dutch were heavily engaged in the purchase of Virginia tobacco. They would surely, in the course of that trade, have supplied Virginians with slaves if the Virginians had been ready to pay.

That Virginia's tobacco planters would not pay, while Barbados' sugar planters would, requires explanation, for mortality was evidently as heavy in Barbados as in Virginia. If servants for a term were a better buy for Virginians, why not for Barbadians?

Up until the 1640s, when the principal crop in Barbados was, as in Virginia, tobacco, the labor force was mainly composed, as in Virginia, of white servants. But a shift from tobacco to cotton and then to sugar in the early 1640s made the islands less attractive than the mainland for servants who crossed the ocean voluntarily. Sugar production required such strenuous labor that men would not willingly undertake it. Sugar planters, in order to get their crops grown, harvested, and processed had to drive their workers much harder than tobacco planters did. Richard Ligon in the late 1640s was scandalized to see how the Barbados planters beat their servants in order to get the work out of them. Moreover, when a servant turned free, he found land much scarcer than in Virginia or Maryland. And even if he could hire a plot, at high rents, sugar production (unlike tobacco) required a larger outlay of capital for equipment than he could likely lay hands on. For these reasons, when Barbados servants became free, they frequently headed for Virginia or other mainland colonies. The sugar planters may thus have bought slaves partly because they could not buy servants unless the servants were shanghaied, or "barbadosed" as the word was at the time, or unless they were sent as prisoners, like the captured Scottish and Irish soldiers whom Cromwell shipped over. A dwindling supply of willing servants may have forced a switch to slaves.

It is possible that the conversion to slavery in Virginia was helped, as it was in Barbados, by a decline in the number of servants coming to the colony. The conditions that produced Bacon's Rebellion and the continuing discontent thereafter did not enhance the colony's reputation. Moreover, by the third quarter of the century there was less pressure on Englishmen to leave home. Complaints of overpopulation in England had ceased, as statesmen and political thinkers sought ways of putting the poor to work. Certainly the number of white immigrants to Virginia does seem to have declined. But if this was a factor in the conversion process, another, probably of greater consequence, was the decline of heavy mortality toward midcentury, for as life expectancy rose, the slave became a better buy than the servant.

The point at which it became more advantageous for Virginians to buy slaves was probably reached by 1660. In that year the assembly offered exemption from local duties to Dutch ships bringing Negroes. But in the same year Parliament passed the Navigation Acts, interdicting both the export of tobacco from the colonies to the Netherlands and any trade by Dutch ships in the colonies. The result was to delay Virginia's conversion to slavery. The mother country attempted to compensate for the severing of the Dutch slave trade through a royally sponsored English trading company, the Royal Adventurers, which was reorganized and rechartered in 1672 as the Royal African Company. These companies enjoyed a monopoly of supplying all the colonies with African slaves until 1698; but the men who ran them never gained sufficient familiarity with Africa or the slave trade to conduct the business successfully. And even though their monopoly could not be effectively enforced, especially against knowledgeable private traders, both tobacco and sugar planters complained that it prevented them from getting the number of workers they needed. Virginia thus began to change to slave labor at a time when she had to compete with the sugar planters for a smaller supply of slaves than would have been available had the freer conditions of trade still existed under which Barbados had made the conversion.

In the competition for slaves after 1660 the sugar planters still enjoyed some advantages. Although sugar and tobacco were both "enumerated" commodities that must be shipped only to England or to another English colony, England did not collect nearly so heavy an import tax on sugar as on tobacco. Consequently, a larger percentage of the price paid by the consumer went to the grower. Moreover, the price of slaves in the West Indies was less than in Virginia, because the islands were closer to Africa, so that costs of transportation and risk of loss on the "Middle Passage" were therefore less. The figures for slave imports into Barbados, Jamaica, and the Leeward Islands in the last quarter of the century are all far above those for Virginia. That Virginia was able to get any at all was owing to the fact that while slaves had become a profitable investment for tobacco growers, the profitability of growing sugar had declined. . . .

It is clear . . . that by the end of the seventeenth century and probably by the third quarter of it the tobacco growers had one strong advantage in the longevity of their laborers. A smaller proportion of their profits had to go into labor replacement and was available to meet the higher initial cost of a slave. Life expectancy in Barbados, especially for the black population, continued to be low throughout the seventeenth and most of the eighteenth century. The slaves on Barbados plantations had to be replaced at the rate of about 6 percent a year. It is estimated that between 1640 and 1700 264,000 slaves were imported into the British West Indies. The total black population in 1700 was about 100,000. In the next century, be-

tween 1712 and 1762 the importation of 150,000 slaves increased the Barbados black population by only 28,000. By contrast, while Virginia imported roughly 45,000 slaves between 1700 and 1750 (figures from the seventeenth century are sporadic), the black population increased from perhaps 8,000 or 10,000 to over 100,000. In Virginia not only had the rate of mortality from disease gone down, but the less strenuous work of cultivating tobacco, as opposed to sugar, enabled slaves to retain their health and multiply. To make a profit, sugar planters worked their slaves to death; tobacco planters did not have to. A slave consequently had a longer period of usefulness in Virginia than in the West Indies. The return on the investment might be less in the short run, but more in the long run.

The gap between the ability of Virginia and West Indies planters to pay for slaves was also narrowed in the course of the century by changes in the market price of their respective crops. . . .

What these prices meant in profits for the planters depended in large measure on the comparative productivity of sugar and tobacco workers; and, in the absence of actual records of production, that is less easy to determine. No significant innovations in technology occurred in the growth or processing of either crop before the nineteenth century, and by 1660 both sugar and tobacco planters were thoroughly familiar with their respective crops and with ways of maximizing production. . . . It is likely . . . that by the 1660s a man would make less than 1,000 pounds of tobacco in a lean year, but more than 2,000, perhaps much more, in a good year. In the long run a man's labor for a year would probably make about the same weight of tobacco in Virginia as of sugar in the islands. But the tobacco worker could at the same time grow enough corn to sustain himself. And in the most favorable locations, especially on the York and, to a lesser degree, the Rappahannock, he could grow a variety of tobacco (known as sweet-scented) which brought a higher price and weighed more in relation to bulk (reducing freight costs) than the ordinary Orinoco.

In addition, tobacco continued to enjoy the advantage, which it had always had, of requiring a smaller outlay of capital for production equipment. And land, if scarcer than it had been, was still much cheaper in Virginia than in the islands. The far greater number of slaves delivered to the sugar islanders indicates that sugar remained the more attractive risk to English capital investment. Nevertheless, tobacco was so close a competitor that before the 1680s slaves were being shipped from Barbados for sale in Virginia.

In financing the extra cost of slaves, Virginians were not wholly dependent on upswings in the tobacco market. They could draw on capital accumulated during the first half century. Their earnings from tobacco (apart from any they returned to England) had been invested, as we saw earlier, in cattle and hogs and servants. When they wanted to buy slaves in Barbados, they could send cattle and hogs in exchange. Land in the West Indies was too valuable to be devoted to food products, and sugar planters were eager to buy live cattle as well as barreled beef and pork. They needed live cattle not only to turn their mills but also to dung their land as the canes exhausted it. Virginia joined with New England in supplying the need; and though no figures exist to show the volume of the trade, there is a good deal of evidence in county court records of contact between Virginia and Barbados in the seventeenth century. But the extra capital to buy slaves came not only from livestock. In spite of the low profits of tobacco growing after 1660, there were the entrepreneurial profits of the merchant planters and the substantial amounts accumulated by the judicious use of government office.

More important perhaps than the capital generated locally was that attracted from England by the new competitive position of tobacco. Substantial men who might earlier have headed for Barbados now came to Virginia, supplied with funds to purchase or rent land and labor. And men with small amounts of capital, insufficient for the initial outlay of a sugar plantation, could make a good start in Virginia. Though the colony had ceased to be, if it ever was, a land of opportunity for the servant who came with nothing, it offered much to the man with £300 or £400 sterling. With half of it put into buying a well-located plantation, he would have enough left over for eight or ten slaves, and "a handsom, gentile and sure subsistence," as William Fitzhugh said, who had done it. Ten slaves might make 20,000 pounds of tobacco in a good year, which at the time Fitzhugh wrote would be worth from £100 to £200 sterling. The cost of feeding them would be nothing and of clothing them little. The return on the investment would be accordingly a good deal more than could be expected from any agricultural enterprise in England.

Englishmen with spare cash came to Virginia also because the prestige and power that a man with any capital could expect in Virginia was comparatively much greater than he was likely to attain in England, where men of landed wealth and gentle birth abounded. Well-to-do immigrants and their sons, who came to Virginia after midcentury, dominated the colony's politics, probably in default of male survivors of earlier successful immigrants. But the fortunes gathered by those early immigrants during the deadly first half century were not necessarily lost or dispersed. Capital still accumulated in the hands of widows and joined in profitable wedlock the sums that well-heeled immigrants brought with them. The Ludwells, Byrds, Carters, Spencers, Wormeleys, Corbins, and a host of others not only shared the spoils of office among themselves, but also by well-planned marriages shared the savings gathered by their predecessors. In Lancaster County, of the twelve persons who were listed for more than twenty tithables between 1653 and 1679, one was a widow and nine of the remaining eleven married widows.

These were the men who brought slavery to Virginia, simply by buying slaves instead of servants. Since a slave cost more than a servant, the man with only a small sum to invest was likely to buy a servant. In 1699 the House of Burgesses noted that the servants who worked for "the poorer sort" of planters were still "for the most part Christian." But the man who could afford to operate on a larger scale, looking to the long run, bought slaves as they became more profitable and as they became available.

How rapidly they became available and how rapidly, therefore, Virginia made the switch to slave labor is difficult to determine, partly because the Royal African Company monopoly made it necessary to conceal purchases from illicit traders. During the period of the monopoly (1663–98), slaves could presumably still be purchased legally from Barbados, but few records of trade between the two colonies have survived. Nevertheless, from stray bits of evidence we do know that Virginians were getting slaves from other sources than the company and what prices they were willing to pay for them. . . .

There is no way of telling how many slaves were brought to Virginia by interlopers and how many came legally from Barbados. Edmund Jennings, inquiring into the subject in 1708, was told by "some ancient Inhabitants conversant in that Trade . . . that before the year 1680 what negros were brought to Virginia were imported generally from Barbados." It may be that many continued to come by that route. Although the Royal African Company had promised at its founding in 1672 to supply Virginia and Maryland as well as the islands, it sent only a few shiploads before the end of the century. During the 1670s somewhat more than 1,000 may have been landed, and in the 1680s perhaps another 1,000 or 1,500—if the seven or eight captains instructed to go to Virginia actually went there. In the 1690s, however, a list of fifty-four ships sent out between October 25, 1693, and February 15, 1698/9, shows only one consigned to Virginia. . . .

The extent to which slaves were replacing servants during the last decades of the century can be estimated . . . from the lists of tithables for Surry, the only county where the names of all the tithables survive (rather than the mere number of tithables per household). Of Surry tithables who belonged to another man's household, slaves amounted to 20 percent in 1674, 33 percent in 1686, 48 percent in 1694, and 48 percent in 1703. Surry, as we have seen, was one of the poorer regions of Virginia. In the rich counties on the York the proportion must have been

larger. To achieve such a large slave labor force by the end of the seventeenth century Virginians must have been buying at least as many slaves from interlopers and from Barbados as they got from the Royal African Company. And with the end of the company monopoly in 1698, private traders immediately began to bring many more.

If half the labor force was already enslaved by the end of the seventeenth century, much more than half must have been in that position by 1708, for official records show that in the preceding ten years 5,928 slaves were brought by private traders and 679 by the company. And the company's papers testify to a great demand for slaves that raised the Virginia price far enough above the West Indies price to outweigh the costs of the longer voyage. The company's letters to captains in 1701 began advising them to head for Virginia rather than Jamaica, if they could get there in May, June, or July when the demand was greatest. In 1704 they noted that Virginians were paying £30 to £35 a head as against £23 to £27 in Jamaica.

But the planters in Virginia, as in the West Indies, were more eager to buy slaves than to pay for them. During the first five years of the new century, they overextended their credit, and the company was faced with a multitude of protested bills of exchange. By 1705 the Virginia assembly was so disturbed by the rising indebtedness that it tried to slow down the traffic, dropping an import duty on servants while retaining one on slaves. But by then the conversion to slave labor had already been made. . . . This was not the end of white servitude in Virginia, but henceforth white servants were as much the exception in the tobacco fields as slaves had been earlier. Between 1708 and 1750 Virginia recorded the entry of 38,418 slaves into the colony.

Virginia had developed her plantation system without slaves, and slavery introduced no novelties to methods of production. Though no seventeenth-century plantation had a work force as large as that owned by some eighteenth-century planters, the mode of operation was the same. The seventeenth-century plantation already had its separate quartering house or houses for the servants. Their labor was already supervised in groups of eight or ten by an overseer. They were already subject to "correction" by the whip. They were already often underfed and underclothed. Their masters already lived in fear of their rebelling. But no servant rebellion in Virginia ever got off the ground.

The plantation system operated by servants worked. It made many Virginians rich and England's merchants and kings richer. But it had one insuperable disadvantage. Every year it poured a host of new freemen into a society where the opportunities for advancement were limited. The freedmen were Virginia's dangerous men. They erupted in 1676 in the largest rebellion known in any American colony before the Revolution, and in 1682 they carried even the plant-cutting rebellion further than any servant rebellion had ever gone. The substitution of slaves for servants gradually eased and eventually ended the threat that the freedmen posed: as the annual number of imported servants dropped, so did the number of men turning free.

The planters who bought slaves instead of servants did not do so with any apparent consciousness of the social stability to be gained thereby. Indeed, insofar as Virginians expressed themselves on the subject of slavery, they feared that it would magnify the danger of insurrection in the colony. They often blamed and pitied themselves for taking into their families men and women who had every reason to hate them. William Byrd told the Earl of Egmont in July, 1736, that "in case there shoud arise a Man of desperate courage amongst us, exasperated by a desperate fortune, he might with more advantage than Cataline kindle a Servile War," and make Virginia's broad rivers run with blood. But the danger never materialized. From time to time the planters were alarmed by the discovery of a conspiracy among the slaves; but, as had happened earlier when servants plotted rebellion, some conspirator always leaked the plan in time to spoil it. No white person was killed in a slave rebellion in colonial Virginia. Slaves proved, in fact, less dangerous than free or semi-free laborers. They had none of the rising ex-pectations that have so often prompted rebellion in human history. They were not armed and did not have to be armed. They were without hope and did not have to be given hope. William Byrd himself probably did not take the danger from them seriously. Only seven months before his letter to Egmont, he assured Peter Beckford of Jamaica that "our negroes are not so numerous or so enterprizeing as to give us any apprehension or uneasiness."

With slavery Virginians could exceed all their previous efforts to maximize productivity. In the first half of the century, as they sought to bring stability to their volatile society, they had identified work as wealth, time as money, but there were limits to the amount of both work and time that could be extracted from a servant. There was no limit to the work or time that a master could command from his slaves, beyond his need to allow them enough for eating and sleeping to enable them to keep working. Even on that he might skimp. . . .

Demographically, too, the conversion to slavery enhanced Virginia's capacity for maximum productivity. Earlier the heavy concentration in the population of men of working age had been achieved by the small number of women and children among the immigrants and by the heavy mortality. But with women outliving men, the segment of women and their children grew; and as mortality declined the segment of men beyond working age grew. There was, in other words, an increase in the non-productive proportion of the population. Slavery made possible the restoration and maintenance of a highly productive population. Masters had no hesitation about putting slave women to work in the tobacco fields, although servant women were not normally so employed. And they probably made slave children start work earlier than free children did. There was no need to keep them from work for purposes of education. Nor was it necessary to divert productive energy to the support of ministers for spiritual guidance to them and their parents. The slave population could thus be more productive than a free population with the same age and sex structure would have been. It could also be more reproductive than a free population that grew mainly from the importation of servants, because slave traders generally carried about two women for every three men, a larger proportion of women by far than had been the case with servants. Slave women while employed in tobacco could still raise children and thus contribute to the growth of the productive proportion of the population. Moreover, the children became the property of the master. Thus slaves offered the planter a way of disposing his profits that combined the advantages of cattle and of servants, and these had always been the most attractive investments in Virginia.

The only obvious disadvantage that slavery presented to Virginia masters was a simple one: slaves had no incentive to work. The difference, however, between the incentive of a slave and that of a servant bound for a term of years was not great. The servant had already received his reward in the form of the ocean passage which he, unlike the slave, had been so eager to make that he was willing to bind his labor for a term of years for it. Having received his payment in advance, he could not be compelled by threats of withholding it. Virginia masters had accordingly been obliged to make freer use of the lash than had been common in England. Before they obtained slaves, they had already had practice in extracting work from the unwilling. Yet there was a difference. If a servant failed to perform consistently or ran away, if he damaged his master's property either by omission or commission, the master could get the courts to extend the term of his servitude. That recourse was not open to the slaveowner. If the servant had received his reward in advance, the slave had received the ultimate punishment in advance: his term had already been extended.

Masters therefore needed some substitute for the extended term, some sanction to protect themselves against the stubbornness of those whom conventional "correction" did not reach. Their first attempt in this direction was an act, passed in 1661, that is sometimes cited as the first official recognition of slavery in Virginia. In it the assembly tried to handle the most common

form of servile intractability, by making a servant who ran away with a slave responsible for the loss incurred to the master by the absence of the slave. . . .

Though this measure tells us something about the relationship between servants and slaves in these early years, it was a deterrent more to servants than to slaves. And it did nothing for the master who could not get what he considered an adequate amount of work out of his slave by the methods that had sufficed for servants. One way might have been to offer rewards, to hold out the carrot rather than the stick. A few masters tried this in the early years, as we have seen, offering slaves freedom in return for working hard for a few years, or assigning them plots of land and allowing them time to grow tobacco or corn crops for themselves. But to offer rewards of this kind was to lose the whole advantage of slavery. In the end, Virginians had to face the fact that masters of slaves must inflict pain at a higher level than masters of servants. Slaves could not be made to work for fear of losing liberty, so they had to be made to fear for their lives. Not that any master wanted to lose his slave by killing him, but in order to get an equal or greater amount of work, it was necessary to beat slaves harder than servants, so hard, in fact, that there was a much larger chance of killing them than had been the case with servants. Unless a master could correct his slaves in this way without running afoul of the law if he misjudged the weight of his blows, slaveowning would be legally hazardous. So in 1669 the assembly faced the facts and passed an act that dealt with them forthrightly:

An act about the casuall killing of slaves.

Whereas the only law in force for the punishment of refractory servants resisting their master, mistris or overseer cannot be inflicted upon negroes [because the punishment was extension of time], nor the obstinacy of many of them by other than violent meanes supprest, *Be it enacted and declared by this grand assembly*, if any slave resist his master (or other by his masters order correcting him) and by the extremity of the correction should chance to die, that his death shall not be accompted Felony, but the master (or that other person appointed by the master to punish him) be acquit from molestation, since it cannot be presumed that prepensed malice (which alone makes murther Felony) should induce any man to destroy his own estate.

With this act already on the books in 1669, Virginia was prepared to make the most of slavery when slaves began to arrive in quantity. Later legislation only extended the principles here recognized, that correction of slaves might legally be carried to the point of killing them. The most important extensions had to do with runaways. As the numbers of slaves increased and the plantation quarters were placed farther from the house of the master, runaway slaves would frequently hide out in the woods, visiting the quarters by night, where their friends or families would shelter and share food with them. To eliminate this problem, the assembly provided that the names of such outlying slaves should be proclaimed at the door of every church in the county, after divine worship, and then if the runaways did not turn themselves in, it would "be lawful for any person or persons whatsoever, to kill and destroy such slaves by such ways and means as he, she, or they shall think fit, without accusation or impeachment of any crime for the same." The public would compensate the master for the loss of slaves thus killed. If one was captured alive, the owner might apply to the county court "to order such punishment to the said slave, either by dismembring, or any other way, not touching his life, as they in their discretion shall think fit, for the reclaiming any such incorrigible slave, and terrifying others from the like practices."

This was no idle threat. Though the words of the law—"reclaiming," "dismembering," "discretion"—seem to soften the shock, the law authorizes not merely an open season on outlying slaves, but also the deliberate maiming of captured slaves, by judicial order. One gets a glimpse of the law in action in the records of the Lancaster County court for March 10, 1707/8:

Because slaves were property, the killing of a slave by his or her owner was not considered murder.

Robert Carter Esq. Complaining to this Court against two Incorrigible negroes of his named Bambarra Harry and Dinah and praying the order of this Court for punishing the said Negroes by dismembring them It is therefore ordered That for the better reclaiming the said negroes and deterring others from ill practices That the said Robert Carter Esq. have full power according to Law to dismember the said negroes or Either of them by cutting of[f] their toes."

Such was the price of slavery, and Virginia masters were prepared to pay it. In order to get work out of men and women who had nothing to gain but absence of pain, you had to be willing to beat, maim, and kill. And society had to be ready to back you even to the point of footing the bill for the property you killed.

It has been possible thus far to describe Virginia's conversion to slavery without mentioning race. It has required a little restraint to do so, but only a little, because the actions that produced slavery in Virginia, the individual purchase of slaves instead of servants, and the public protection of masters in their coercion of unwilling labor, had no necessary connection with race. Virginians did not enslave the persons brought there by the Royal African Company or by the private traders. The only decision that Virginians had to make was to keep them as slaves. Keeping them as slaves did require some decisions about what masters could legally do to make them work. But such decisions did not necessarily relate to race.

Or did they? As one reads the record of the Lancaster court authorizing Robert Carter to chop off the toes of his slaves, one begins to wonder. Would the court, could the court, could the general assembly have authorized such a punishment for an incorrigible English servant? It seems unlikely that the English government would have allowed it. But Virginians could be confident that England would condone their slave laws, even though those laws were contrary to the laws of England.

The English government had considered the problem in 1679, when presented with the laws of Barbados, in which masters were similarly authorized to inflict punishment that would not have been allowed by English law. A legal adviser, upon reviewing the laws for the Lords of Trade, found that he could approve them, because, he said

> although Negros in that Island are punishable in a different and more severe manner than other Subjects are for Offences of the like nature; yet I humbly conceive that the Laws there concerning Negros are reasonable Laws, for by reason of their numbers they become dangerous, and being a brutish sort of People

and reckoned as goods and chattels in that Island, it is of necessity or at least convenient to have Laws for the Government of them different from the Laws of England, to prevent the great mischief that otherwise may happen to the Planters and Inhabitants in that Island.

It was not necessary to extend the rights of Englishmen to Africans, because Africans were "a brutish sort of people." And because they were "brutish" it was necessary "or at least convenient" to kill or maim them in order to make them work.

The killing and maiming of slaves was not common in Virginia. Incidents like Robert Carter's application to dismember his two slaves are rare in the records. But it is hard to read in diaries and letters of the everyday beating of slaves without feeling that the casual, matter-of-fact acceptance of it is related to a feeling on the part of masters that they were dealing with "a brutish sort of people." Thomas Jones, of Williamsburg, was almost affectionate about it in writing his wife, away on a visit, about her household slaves. Daphne and Nancy were doing well, "But Juliet is the same still, tho I do assure you she has not wanted correction very often. I chear'd her with thirty lashes a Saturday last and as many more a Tuesday again and to-day I hear she's sick."

Possibly a master could have written thus about a white maidservant. Certainly there are many instances of servants being severely beaten, even to death. But whether or not race was a necessary ingredient of slavery, it *was* an ingredient. If slavery might have come to Virginia without racism, it did not. The only slaves in Virginia belonged to alien races from the English. And the new social order that Virginians created after they changed to slave labor was determined as much by race as by slavery.

Selection 4

Anthony Johnson: A Free Black Landowner in Seventeenth-Century Virginia

T.H. Breen and Stephen Innes

Before the late seventeenth century, when slavery was defined by law as the normal condition of every black person in Virginia, some Africans survived their original status of temporary servitude and became, like fellow white ex-servants, small landowners. A few even managed to acquire servants and slaves of their own. One such man was Anthony Johnson, who settled on Virginia's eastern shore.

Using old court records, historians T.H. Breen of Northwestern University and Stephen Innes of the University of Virginia pieced together a short history of Anthony Johnson and his family. The ability of the Johnson clan to prosper as free men and women in early Virginia underscores the tragedy and waste of human talent that was a direct consequence of slavery. Breen and Innes's account appears at the begin-ning of their 1980 book "Myne Owne Ground": Race and Freedom on Virginia's Eastern Shore, 1640–1676.

*a*nthony Johnson would have been a success no matter where he lived. He possessed immense energy and ingenuity. His parents doubtless never imagined that their son would find himself a slave in a struggling, frontier settlement called Virginia. Over his original bondage, of course, Johnson had no control. He did not allow his low status in the New World to discourage him, however, and in his lifetime he managed to achieve that goal so illusive to immigrants of all races, the American dream. By the time Johnson died he had become a freeman, formed a large and secure family, built up a sizable estate, and in the words of one admiring historian, established himself as the "black patriarch" of Pungoteague Creek, a small inlet on the western side of Northampton County. . . .

Johnson arrived in Virginia sometime in 1621 aboard the *James*. People referred to him at this time simply as "Antonio a Negro," and the over-seers of the Bennett or Warresquioake (Wariscoyack) plantation located on the south side of the James River purchased him to work in their tobacco fields. In a general muster of the inhabitants of Virginia made in 1625, Anthony appeared as a "servant," and while some historians argue that many early blacks were indentured servants rather than slaves, Anthony seems to have been a slave. Like other unfree blacks in seventeenth-century Virginia, he possessed no surname. Had he been able to document his conversion to Christianity—preferably by providing evidence of baptism—he might have sued for freedom, but there is no record that he attempted to do so. He settled on Bennett's plantation, no doubt more concerned about surviving from day to day than about his legal status.

The 1620s in Virginia were a time of great expectations and even greater despair. The colony has been described as "the first American boom country," and so it was for a very few men with money and power enough to purchase gangs of dependent laborers. For the servants and slaves, however, the colony was a hell. Young men, most of them in their teens, placed on isolated tobacco plantations, exposed constantly to early, possibly violent, death, and denied the comforts and security of family life because of the scarcity of women, seemed more like soldiers pressed into dangerous military service than agricultural workers. . . .

Immediately before Johnson arrived at Warresquioake, the Virginia Company of London launched an aggressive, albeit belated, program to turn a profit on its American holdings. Sir Edwin Sandys, the man who shaped company policy, dreamed of producing an impressive array of new commodities, silk and potash, iron and glass, and he persuaded wealthy Englishmen to finance his vision. One such person was Edward Bennett, possibly a man of Puritan leanings, who won Sandys's affection by writing a timely treatise "touching the inconvenience that the importacon of Tobacco out of Spaine had brought into this land [England]." Sandys dispatched thousands of settlers to the Chesapeake to work

for the company, but favored individuals like Bennett received special patents to establish "particular plantations," semi-autonomous economic enterprises in which the adventurers risked their own capital for laborers and equipment and, in exchange, obtained a chance to collect immense returns. Bennett evidently sent his brother Robert and his nephew Richard to Virginia to oversee the family plantation. At one time, the Bennetts owned or employed over sixty persons.

On Good Friday, March 22, 1622, the Indians of Tidewater Virginia put an end to Sandys's dream. In a carefully coordinated attack, they killed over three hundred and fifty colonists in a single morning. Fifty-two of these people fell at the Bennett plantation, and in the muster of 1625 only twelve servants were reported living at Warresquioake, which perhaps to erase the memory of the attack was now renamed Bennett's Welcome. One of the survivors was Anthony. Somehow he and four other men had managed to live through the Indian assault; the other seven individuals listed in 1625 had settled in Virginia after the Indian uprising. Johnson revealed even at this early date one essential ingredient for success in Virginia: good luck. In 1622 the *Margrett and John* brought "Mary a Negro Woman" to Warresquioake. She was the only woman living at Bennett's plantation in 1625, and at some point—we do not know when—she became Anthony's wife. He was a very fortunate man. Because of an exceedingly unequal sex ratio in early Virginia, few males, black or white, had the opportunity to form a family. Mary bore Anthony at least four children, and still managed to outlive her husband by several years. In a society in which marriages were routinely broken by early death, Mary and Anthony lived together for over forty years. The documents reveal little about the quality of their relationship, but one infers that they helped each other in myriad ways that we can never recapture. In 1653 Anthony Johnson and Mary "his wife" asked for tax relief from the Northampton County court. The local justices observed that the two blacks "have lived Inhabitants in Virginia (above thirty yeares)" and had achieved widespread respect for their "hard labor and known service." The interesting point is that both Mary and Anthony received recognition; both contributed to the life of their community.

Johnson's movements between 1625 and 1650 remain a mystery. Court records from a later period provide tantalizing clues about his life during these years, but they are silent on how "Antonio a Negro" became Anthony Johnson. Presumably someone named Johnson helped Anthony and Mary to gain freedom, but the details of that agreement have been lost. In 1635 John Upton, living "in the county of Warresquioake," petitioned for 1,650 acres of land based on thirty-three headrights. Included on his list were "Antho, a negro, Mary, a negro." While these two blacks were probably the Johnsons, we have no reason to conclude that they were still slaves in 1635. Men like Upton saved or purchased headrights until they could make a sizable claim, and the headrights for Anthony and Mary may have circulated in the area for a decade.

We do not know when or under what circumstances Johnson transferred to Northampton. His former master, Richard Bennett, developed complex ties with the Virginia Eastern Shore. Between 1652 and 1655 he spent a good deal of time there keeping watch on suspected royalists. Bennett's daughter Elizabeth married Edmund Scarborough's eldest son, Charles. The Scarboroughs were the dominant family in Northampton County, and by 1652 Charles had already patented 3,050 acres on Pungoteague Creek. Like his father, he became a leader in local and colony politics. Bennett may have brought the Johnsons to Northampton and then, as governor, looked after their legal and economic interests. The Johnsons may even have named their son after Bennett. There is no firm evidence that this occurred, but it is curious that the Johnsons appeared in the Eastern Shore records at precisely the time that Bennett became a major political force in the area.

During the 1640s the Johnsons acquired a modest estate. Raising livestock provided a reliable source of income, and at mid-century, espe-cially on the Eastern Shore, breeding cattle and hogs was as important to the local economy as growing tobacco. To judge by the extent of Johnson's livestock operations in the 1650s, he probably began to build up his herds during the 1640s. In any case, in July 1651 Johnson claimed that 250 acres of land were due him for five headrights. The names listed in his petition were Thomas Bembrose, Peter Bughby, Anthony Cripps, John Gesororo, and Richard Johnson. Whether Anthony Johnson actually imported these five persons into the colony is impossible to ascertain. None of them, with the exception of Richard Johnson, his son, appeared in later Northampton tax lists. Like John Upton, Anthony may have purchased headright certificates from other planters. Two hundred and fifty acres was a considerable piece of land by Eastern Shore standards, and though the great planters controlled far more acreage, many people owned smaller tracts or no land at all. Johnson's 250 acres were located on Pungoteague Creek.

In February 1653 Johnson's luck appeared to have run out. A fire destroyed much of his plantation. This event—the Northampton Court called it "an unfortunate fire"—set off in turn a complicated series of legal actions that sorely tested Anthony's standing within the Pungoteague community, and at one point even jeopardized much of his remaining property. The blaze itself had been devastating. After the county justices viewed the damage, they concluded that without some assistance the Johnsons would have difficulty in the "obtayneing of their Livelyhood," and when Anthony and Mary formally petitioned for relief, the court excused Mary and the Johnsons' two daughters from paying "Taxes and Charges in Northampton County for public use" for "their naturall lives." The court's decision represented an extraordinary concession. The reduction of annual taxes obviously helped Johnson to reestablish himself, and the fact that he was a "Negro" and so described during the proceedings seems to have played no discernible part in the deliberations of the local justices. Moreover, the court did more than simply lighten the Johnsons' taxes. By specifically excusing the three black women from public levies, the justices made it clear that, for tax purposes at least, Mary and her daughters were the equals of any white woman in Northampton County. Taxes in seventeenth-century Virginia were assessed on people, not on land or livestock. The definition of a tithable—someone obliged to pay taxes—changed from time to time. In the 1620s the Burgesses had included "all those that worke in the grounde." The Virginia legislators apparently intended to exempt the wives of white planters. Such women, it was assumed, busied themselves with domestic chores and therefore, did not participate directly in income-producing activities. Indeed, it was commonly believed that only "wenches that are nasty, and beastly" would actually cultivate tobacco. Black women, alone, in other words, demeaned themselves by engaging in hard physical labor. In a 1645 act concerning tithables the colonial legislators declared: "And because there shall be no scruple or evasion who are and who are not tithable, It is resolved by this Grand Assembly, That *all negro men and women,* and all other men from the age of 16 to 60 shall be adjudged tithable." Why the Northampton Court made a gratuitous exception to statute law is not clear. Perhaps the Johnsons' economic success coupled with their "hard labor and known service" pointed up the need for local discretion in enforcing racial boundaries.

Anthony Johnson's next court appearance came on October 8, 1653. This time his testimony "concerned a cowe" over which he and Lieutenant John Neale had had a difference of opinion. The court records unfortunately provide no information about the nature of the conflict. The Northampton justices ordered two men familiar with the affairs of Pungoteague Creek, Captain Samuel Gouldsmith and Robert Parker, to make an "examination and finall determination" of the case. Since the Neales were a powerful family on the Eastern Shore, the decision of the justices reveals the high regard in which Johnson was held. Had he been a less important person in that society, they might have immediately found for Neale. Of greater significance, however, was the involvement of Gouldsmith

and Parker in Johnson's personal business. Neither of them was a great planter; but both were ambitious men, who apparently concluded after their investigation that Johnson's fire losses had left him vulnerable to outside harassment.

A year after this litigation had been resolved, Captain Gouldsmith visited the Johnson plantation to pick up a hogshead of tobacco. Gouldsmith presumably expected nothing unusual to happen on this particular day. Like other white planters on the Eastern Shore, he carried on regular business transactions with Anthony Johnson. Gouldsmith was surprised, however, for soon after he arrived, "a Negro called John Casor" threw himself upon the merchant's mercy. He declared with seemingly no prompting that he was not a slave as Johnson claimed in public. He asserted that the Johnsons held him illegally and had done so for at least seven years. Casor insisted that he entered Virginia as an indentured servant, and that moreover he could verify his story. An astonished Johnson assured Gouldsmith that he had never seen the indenture. Whether Casor liked it or not, he was Johnson's "Negro for life."

Robert Parker and his brother George took Casor's side in the dispute. They informed the now somewhat confused Gouldsmith that the black laborer had signed an indenture with a certain Mr. Sandys, who lived "on the other side of the Baye." Nothing further was said about Sandys, and he may have been invented conveniently to lend credibility to Casor's allegations. Whatever the truth was, Robert Parker led Casor off to his own farm, "under pretense that the said John Casor is a freeman," noting as he went that if Johnson resisted, Casor "would recover most of his Cows from him the said Johnson."

The transfer involved a carefully calculated gamble. Parker was tampering with another man's laborer, a serious but not uncommon practice in mid-century Virginia. Like other enterprising tobacco planters, Parker needed field-hands and he was not overly scrupulous about the means he used to obtain them. The House of Burgesses regularly passed statutes outlawing the harboring of runaway servants, explaining, no doubt with people like Parker in mind, that "complaints are at every quarter court exhibitted against divers persons who entertain and enter into covenants with runaway servants . . . to the great prejudice if not the utter undoeing of divers poor men." Regardless of the letter of the law, Gouldsmith reported that Johnson "was in a great feare." In this crisis Anthony called a family conference and, after considerable discussion about the Parkers' threats, "Anthony Johnson's sonne-in-law, his wife and his owne twoe sonnes persuaded the old Negro Anthony Johnson to set the said John Casor free now." The word "old" stands out in this passage. In seventeenth-century Virginia, few men lived long enough to be called old. When they did so, they enjoyed special status as "old planters" or "Antient Livers," people who were respected if for no other reason than they had managed to survive.

This dramatic conference revealed the strong kinship ties that bound the Johnsons together. The group functioned as a modified extended family. The members of each generation lived in separate homes, but in certain economic matters they worked as a unit. Indeed, they thought of themselves as a clan. The bonds between Anthony and his sons were especially important. In 1652 John Johnson patented 450 acres next to his father's lands. Two years later, Richard Johnson laid out a 100-acre tract adjacent to the holdings of his father and brother. Both sons were married and had children of their own. In family government, Mary had a voice, as did the son-in-law, but as all the Johnsons understood, Anthony was the patriarch. The arguments advanced at the family meeting, however, impressed Anthony. Perhaps he was just an "old" man who had allowed anger to cloud his better judgment. In any case, he yielded as gracefully as possible to the wishes of the clan. In a formal statement he discharged "John Casor Negro from all service, claims and demands . . . And doe promise accordinge to the custome of servants to paye unto the Said John Casor corne and leather." The inclusion of freedom dues gives us some sense of the extent of Johnson's fear. Colony law obliged a master to provide his indentured servants with

certain items, usually food and clothes, at the end of their contracts, but it was a rare planter who paid the "custom of the country" without wringing some extra concession out of the servant. Johnson, however, was in no position to haggle.

But the decision did not sit well with Johnson. After brooding over his misfortune for three and one-half months, Johnson asked the Northampton County court to punish Robert Parker for meddling with his slave and to reverse what now appeared a precipitant decision to free Casor. The strategy worked. On March 8, 1655, "complaint was this daye made to the Court by the humble petition of Anthony Johnson Negro; agt Mr. Robert Parker that he detayneth one Jno Casor a Negro the plaintiffs servant under pretense that the said Jno Casor is a free man." After "seriously consideringe and maturely weighinge" the evidence, including a deposition from Gouldsmith, the members of court ruled that "the said Mr. Robert Parker most unjustly kept the said . . . Negro (Jno Casor) from his master Anthony Johnson . . . [and] the said Jno Casor Negro shall forthwith bee returned unto the service of his master Anthony Johnson." As a final vindication of Johnson's position, the justices ordered Parker to "make payment of all charges in the suite." Johnson was elated. Casor was reenslaved and remained the property of the Johnson family. In the 1660s he accompanied the clan when it moved to Maryland. George Parker, who had taken an early interest in the controversy, managed to divorce himself from the last round of legal proceedings. His brother, Robert, of course, lost face. A few years later Robert returned to England, wiser perhaps but not richer for his experiences on the Eastern Shore.

It is important to recognize the cultural significance of this case. Throughout the entire affair the various participants made assumptions not only about the social organization of Northampton County and their place within that organization but also about the value orientations of the other actors. This sort of gambling can be dangerous, as Casor discovered. He wagered that he could forge patronage links stronger than those which his master had built up over the years. In other words, he viewed the controversy largely in terms of patron-client relations. Johnson, however, was much more alert to the dynamics of the situation than was his slave. Anthony realized that he and the local justices shared certain basic beliefs about the sanctity of property before the law. None of the parties involved, not even Casor, questioned the legitimacy of slavery nor the propriety of a black man owning a black slave. Tensions were generated because of conflicting personal ambitions, because tough-minded individuals were testing their standing within the community. In this particular formal, limited sphere of interaction, the values of a free black slaveowner coincided with those of the white gentry. In other spheres of action—as we shall discover—this value congruence did not exist. Johnson owed his victory to an accurate assessment of the appropriate actions within this particular institutional forum.

In the mid-1660s the Johnson clan moved north to Somerset County, Maryland. The Johnsons, like many other people who left Virginia's Eastern Shore during this period, were in search of fresh, more productive land. As in the Casor affair, everyone in the family participated in the decision to relocate. None of the Johnsons remained at Pungoteague. In 1665 Anthony and Mary sold 200 acres to two planters, Morris Matthews and John Rowles. The remaining fifty acres were transferred to Richard, a gift that may have been intended to help their youngest son and his growing family establish themselves in Maryland. Whatever the motive, Richard soon sold the land, his buyer being none other than George Parker. John Johnson, the eldest son, also went to Somerset. He had already acquired 450 acres in Northampton and thus, apparently did not require his parents' financial assistance. A paternity suit, however, clouded John's departure from Virginia. He fathered an illegitimate child, and the local authorities, fearful of having to maintain the young mother and child at public expense, placed John in custody, where he stayed until his wife, Susanna, petitioned for his release. John pledged good behavior and child support and hurried off to Mary-

land, where he resumed his successful career.

For reasons that are unclear, the Johnsons closely coordinated their plans with those of Ann Toft and Randall Revell, two wealthy planters from Virginia's Eastern Shore. When Toft and Revell arrived in Maryland, they claimed 2,350 acres and listed Anthony, Mary, and John Casor as headrights. Whatever the nature of this agreement may have been, the Johnsons remained free. Anthony leased a 300-acre plantation which he appropriately named "Tonies Vineyard." Within a short time, the family patriarch died, but Mary renegotiated the lease for ninety-nine years. For the use of the land she paid colony taxes and an annual rent of one ear of Indian corn.

Anthony's death did not alter the structure of the family. John assumed his father's place at the head of the clan. He and Susanna had two children, John, junior, and Anthony. Richard named his boys Francis and Richard. In both families we see a self-conscious naming pattern that reflected the passing of patriarchal authority from one generation to the next. Another hint of the tight bonds that united the Johnsons was Mary's will written in 1672. She ordered that at her death three cows with calves be given to three of her grandchildren, Anthony, Francis, and Richard. She apparently assumed that John, junior, the patriarch's son, would do well enough without her livestock. The Johnsons' financial situation remained secure. John increased his holdings. In one document he was described as a "planter," a sign that his property had brought him some economic standing within the community. One of his neighbors, a white man named Richard Ackworth, asked John to give testimony in a suit which Ackworth had filed against a white Marylander. The Somerset justices balked at first. They were reluctant to allow a black man to testify in legal proceedings involving whites, but when they discovered that John had been baptized and understood the meaning of an oath, they accepted his statement. Even Casor prospered in Maryland. He raised a few animals of his own, and in 1672 recorded a livestock brand "With the Said Marys Consent." No doubt, Casor had learned an important lesson from his dealings with Anthony. Property, even a few cows or pigs, provided legal and social identity in this society; it confirmed individuality.

The story of the Johnson family concludes strangely. Around the turn of the century, the clan simply dropped out of the records. We have no explanation for the disappearance. Perhaps Anthony's grandchildren left Somerset in search of new opportunities. Perhaps as a result of social and demographic changes in the eighteenth century they lost their freedom. Or perhaps the records themselves are incomplete. All we know is that in 1677 John, junior, purchased a 44-acre tract which he significantly called "Angola." The last mention of this small Somerset plantation occurred in 1706 when John—a third-generation free black—died without heir. And with the passing of "Angola" may have died the memory of Anthony's homeland, which he left a century earlier.

After reading the history of the Johnson family, one can understand why scholars have had such difficulty interpreting it. Traditional categories of analysis fail to comprehend the experiences of people like Anthony, Mary, and John Johnson. On one level, of course, it is tempting to view them as black Englishmen, migrants who adopted the culture of their white neighbors, who learned to handle complex legal procedures and market transactions, and who amassed estates that impressed even their contemporaries. From this perspective we can make sense out of Anthony's victory over Robert Parker in the Northampton County court. Indeed, once the surprise of discovering that Johnson owned a black slave has worn off, we realize that in matters of personal property Casor's race counted for very little. Anthony was in competition with white planters who regularly exploited laborers, black, red, and white, for immediate economic returns. In this world, Anthony more than held his own, and the story of the Pungoteague patriarch and his sons becomes an early chapter in the saga of Old World immigrants "making it" in America.

Somehow this analysis seems incomplete. Pieces of the puzzle remain unaccounted for, and we know from a growing body of historical literature that European and African migrants reacted creatively to their new environments, preserving some traditions, dropping others, but in all cases, resisting assimilation except on their own terms. If the Johnsons were merely English colonists with black skins, then why did John, junior, name his small farm "Angola"? His action, admittedly a small shred of evidence, suggests the existence of a deeply rooted separate culture. Moreover, there is the family itself. The Johnsons formed extraordinarily close ties. The clan was composed entirely of black men and women, and while one might argue that the Johnsons were constrained by external social forces to marry people of their own race, they appear in their most intimate relations to have maintained a conscious black identity.

The Johnsons knew they were "different" from their white neighbors. Their origins, the exclusive monopoly of slave status for blacks (dramatized by Casor's case), the *ordinary* presumption against blacks testifying unless there were countervailing circumstances of a highly unusual nature, all underscored on a daily basis their continual deprivation. But within this circumscribed environment, as the Johnsons' story vividly suggests, possibilities for advancement existed in 1650 that by 1705 were only a memory.

The Complete History of

Slavery in Eighteenth- Century North America

Chapter 3

Introduction

*T*his chapter covers the second phase of the history of American slavery, from the end of the seventeenth century to the beginning of the American Revolutionary era.

Slavery is always a horrible fate to have to endure, but from the standpoint of its victims, this was probably the worst period of all. Carving plantations in Carolina's swampy low country or opening up new tobacco land in the Chesapeake must have been extremely arduous work. In these rough-and-tumble times, slave owners—impatient to start making a profit—drove their slaves as hard as possible. The slaves arrived in America disoriented, bewildered, and (unless they had spent time in the Caribbean) probably unable to converse with anyone. Whites felt no more pangs of doubt or guilt about keeping slaves than about owning work animals. Slavery also became an established, almost wholly unquestioned, institution in all the colonies farther north, and especially in New York and New Jersey. In the North, too, the conditions of servitude were often quite harsh.

As this second phase gave way to the third phase—that of the Revolutionary era—a few changes were in the air. Slaves learned to communicate with each other using a distinctive version of English. They also became acculturated enough to understand the lively preaching that was going on in the white world, and increasing numbers of them became Christians. Although conversion did not affect their status as slaves, it did undermine white assumptions that slaves were simply heathen savages. Meanwhile, some whites began to question the institution of slavery. Baptist preachers, whose message at the time was usually directed exclusively to poor, backcountry whites, often criticized slave owners as arrogant and materialistic abusers of their human property. And a Quaker missionary named John Woolman traveled widely through Pennsylvania, New Jersey, and the Upper South, warning his fellow Friends that they risked damnation if they continued to hold slaves. Apparently he had some success in persuading Quakers to emancipate their chattels. Equally important, he and Friends who thought like him were setting in motion the germ of an abolitionist movement that would grow in strength and fervor in the nineteenth century.

Selection 1

A Black Majority in South Carolina

Peter H. Wood

The colony originally known as Carolina was founded in 1663 by a group of influential politicians at the court of England's King Charles II, and was first settled in 1670 primarily by planters relocating from Barbados in the West Indies. The colony experienced a hard struggle in its early years as the first generation of whites experimented to find a profitable commodity to export. But by 1690 they had found the answer: rice. Ironically, the people who brought the crop on which Carolina's prosperity was destined to rest were African slaves, accustomed to cultivating rice in their homeland. Hitherto slaves had not been numerous in Carolina; masters used them mainly to help clear homestead land, often swinging axes alongside their bondsmen. But the discovery that rice could be grown profitably in Carolina's swampy, mosquito- and snake-infested lowlands and exported to a growing market in England radically changed matters. During the first decade of the eighteenth century Carolina's slave population skyrocketed as whites established a network of rice plantations. Initial costs were high, for slaves were not cheap

whether they were brought from the West Indies or directly from Africa, and the time-consuming work of digging drainage ditches and preparing rice fields delayed the moment of commercial payoff. But for those planters who could absorb the startup costs, the eventual profits were very large. The southern part of Carolina proved, from its white settlers' point of view, a roaring success, and in 1729 it was separated from the slower-growing northern settlements and turned into a separate royal colony, South Carolina. So large was its slave population that, in eighteenth-century British North America, it was the only colony in which blacks outnumbered whites. The presence of this black majority, whom the whites knew must be kept in constant submission, would leave a deep mark on South Carolina's social and political outlook for as long as slavery endured there.

In 1974 historian Peter H. Wood, who teaches at Duke University, published an engrossing account of the rise of South Carolina's slave society, Black Majority: Negroes in Colonial South Carolina from 1670 Through the Stono Rebellion, *from which this selection is excerpted.*

*T*he exact moment at which black inhabitants exceeded white appears to have fallen around the year 1708, for data collected at that time showed the two groups almost even, with just over four thousand in each. This census report, although rough, provides a valuable profile of the colony, for the governor and council broke the survey into distinct categories by age, sex, and race, and indicated the change in each group over the five years since 1703. . . . Due to commerce in war captives, Indian slaves can be seen as the fastest-growing segment of the population between 1703 and 1708. This was a short-term trend that contributed directly to the frontier wars of the ensuing decade, after which the Indian presence would diminish rapidly. Among whites, the number of adults declined by nearly 6 per cent during the five-year span, despite the arrival of newcomers. By contrast, the number of Negro adults rose more than 20 per cent in the same period, due to natural increase as well as importation. The high proportion of children among the whites (42 per cent) suggests a populace with a high rate of mortality. Among black slaves the proportion of children is lower (29 per cent), but their total number of children doubled in the course of five years, arguing a high rate of natural population growth among Africans. These different growth rates continued through the ensuing decade. . . .

Epidemics, Indian wars, and emigration meant that the white population rose by scarcely 2,500 between 1708 and 1721 inclusive, while the Negro population added over 4,000 by natural increase and above 3,600 more through imports during this same period. . . . The annual rate of black population increase in excess of the number of immigrants was a surprising 5.6 per cent during the thirteen years before 1721. Support for these numerical calculations can be found in a 1714 statute which raised the duty on Negro slaves in hopes of reducing their importation. The legislators observed that "the number of negroes do extremely increase in this Province, and through the afflicting providence of God, the white persons do not proportionably multiply."

By the time the Crown assumed control in 1720 it was apparent to all contemporaries that South Carolina, unlike the other mainland English colonies, was dominated demographically by migrants from West Africa. They predominated in terms of total numbers, pace of immigration, and rate of natural increase.

In 1720 the rough population figures accepted in London for the new royal colony were 9,000 whites and 12,000 Negroes, and as is often the case with colonial statistics the figure for Africans was notably more precise than that for Europeans. But it was not until the following March, when census data from each parish were delivered under oath to the tax commissioners in Charlestown, that a detailed picture was available. The interim governor, James Moore, Jr., promptly forwarded to England "An Exact account of the Number of Inhabitants who pay Tax in the Settlement of South Carolina for the yeare 1720 with the Number of Acres and Number of Slaves in each parish." Moore's account . . . places the slave population at 11,828, or within 1 per cent of the estimated figure of 12,000. . . .

During the 1720s the white population may have risen by as much as 50 per cent to roughly ten thousand people, since one estimate at the end of the decade put the number fit to bear arms at "2500 Men or thereabouts," and another reckoned the taxable inhabitants "to be two thousand Whitemen." But the numbers of the unfree climbed fully twice as fast, approximately doubling within the decade. By 1729 there were "above Twenty Thousand Tythable Negroes," presumably between the ages of seven and sixty. The export of both pitch and tar nearly doubled during the first half of the decade, and confident producers bought slaves on credit before the bottom fell from under the naval stores market in 1727. The drop accelerated the transition to rice already under way, and this shift intensified the demand for labor. Where the colony had imported fifteen hundred slaves in the first four years of the decade, it imported four times as many during the last four years.

The white population, benefiting from the clearing of the land and the gradual improvement of food, clothing, and housing, probably owed more of its increase to natural growth than in previous decades. But the same economic growth which improved the lot of free settlers worsened the condition of the unfree. Among slaves the rate of natural increase appears to have declined as the rate of importation swept upward. All told, nearly nine thousand newcomers arrived from Africa during the 1720s . . . , an immigration which was almost equal to the net increase in the slave population. A slight rise in the death rate and decline in the birthrate of the black population would not be surprising. In many European colonies of the South Atlantic the drive to secure profits or remove debts by increasing the production of a plantation economy created a willingness to buy Negroes on credit, a callousness toward the conditions of resident slaves, and a general sense of the expendability of black labor. All these tendencies worsened the prospects for natural population growth among slaves and simultaneously heightened the demand for slave imports. A vicious circle was thereby established in which it appeared advantageous to stress the importation of "salt-water" slaves rather than the survival of those at hand. On some Caribbean sugar islands the natural rate of increase fell below zero for generations with the advent of intensive staple agriculture.

Somewhat the same phenomenon seems to have occurred in South Carolina during the decades after 1720, as rice rose from the status of a competing export to become the colony's central preoccupation. White colonists who responded to the opportunity for profit by investing in labor and expanding the production of staples soon faced declining prices which in turn intensified the urge to broaden production further. Pressures to expand cultivation, increase crop yield, raise efficiency, and reduce overhead all worked directly to depress the lot of the slave. Intensification of the plantation system may have reduced life expectancy and impaired the comparative family stability usually associated with a high birthrate, for the Negro population scarcely sustained itself for several decades. Only because of expanded importation did the

When slave birthrates in South Carolina fell, large numbers of slaves were imported from Africa.

total number of blacks rise more rapidly than ever. Guesses made in 1734 as to the number of slaves range from 22,000 to 30,000, with the proper total probably falling almost halfway between. Assuming the correct figure to be around 26,000, it is notable that even though roughly 15,000 new slaves were imported from Africa over the next six years, the colony's black population was tabulated at only 39,155 in 1740.

The arrival of great numbers of new slaves in increasingly large shipments, directly from Africa, inevitably affected the black demography of every parish. Fewer than 15 per cent of the newcomers at this time were ten years of age or younger, and an equally small proportion were elderly. One South Carolina inventory, drawn up for the estate of John Cawood in 1726, is especially valuable in showing this distribution, since it lists age as well as value for each of thirty-nine slaves. Youth predominates, for almost half (nineteen of thirty-nine) are eighteen or under, while only six are over forty. For the younger slaves exact ages are given, and most were probably born on Cawood's estate. But among the sixteen who were born before 1700 ages are rounded off, and it is interesting to speculate about their origins. Most, like Angola Phillis, whose age was estimated at thirty, were undoubtedly born in Africa and imported after the turn of the century, although Indian Jane (also thirty) was clearly an American by birth. The two most elderly slaves, Old Cate born in 1662 and Old Betty born in 1666, probably began life in the West Indies, since their exact ages were known to the appraisers.

If the slave trade helped shape age distribution, it also played a part in determining the sex ratio among slaves. Rising imports reflected a consistent preference for men over women, which perpetuated the imbalance of earlier years and limited the prospects for a high birthrate which could restore a more even ratio between the sexes. A Charlestown merchant wrote to the owner of a schooner in Barbados that ideal slave cargoes for Carolina would include "especially Boys & Girls of abo^t 15 or 16 y^{rs} of Age . . . ⅔ Boys & ⅓ Girls." An analysis of the twenty-three inventories filed in the eighteen months after January 1, 1730, for estates with more than ten slaves yields a sample of 714 slave names. Of the 663 persons who can be identified by sex, 64.2 per cent (426) are men and only 35.8 per cent (237) are women. In the future, even broader statistical samples taken from import and inventory records over a longer time span may yield a more precise and continuous demographic picture.

Selection 2

Gullah: An African-Based Language

Ruth A. Lee

One of the distinctive characteristics of African American culture in the coastal parts of South Carolina and Georgia is the local speech, called Gullah. Linguists classify Gullah neither as a separate language nor as a dialect of English, but instead call it a pidgin. A pidgin is a means of oral communication that is created by people from different linguistic backgrounds who have to find some way of making themselves mutually understood. Gullah began to take shape in the early eighteenth century as large numbers of Africans, coming from many different nations, arrived in the rice-growing areas of the American southeast. Much of the vocabulary of Gullah is a simplified version of the English that the slaves' masters spoke to them, but there are significant additions of words that can be traced to various African languages, and both the grammar and the syntax give strong evidence of African roots.

Reprinted from Ruth A. Lee, "Gullah Roots in the Sea Islands," *Encore American & Worldwide News*, October 16, 1978.

In this selection, Ruth A. Lee writes about the origins of Gullah and the people who still speak it. This piece was originally broadcast on National Public Radio, and is reprinted from Encore, *the magazine of the Corporation for Public Broadcasting.*

*F*or millions of Black Americans, Alex Haley's *Roots* touched off an awareness of African ancestral ties that could be traced far beyond the shared variations of skin color and hair texture. After *Roots*, the infamous "middle passage" across the Atlantic Ocean was reversed as thousands of African descendants returned to visit a more distant homeland.

But although travel to Africa may be rewarding, the quest for African ties can begin at home, along the coastal shores of South Carolina, Georgia, and Florida. Here in the Sea Islands, the Gullah people and their culture and language form a bridge through time to the point at which Africa first encountered America.

The Sea Islands begin just north of Georgetown, South Carolina, forming a chain south to the Florida border. They range in size from the very small and uninhabited to Johns Island, six miles out from Charleston, the second largest island in the United States. Separated from the mainland by a labyrinth of rivers, salt creeks, and marshes, many of the islands are celebrated as recreation spots; Hilton Head and St. Simon are two of the most popular. Others, such as Jekyll, Blackbeard, and Cumberland, are state and national parks preserved for the study of plant, animal, and sea life that maintain an ecological balance centuries old.

The Gullah people who live on many of the islands are separated from mainstream America by more than water. Black Americans will find a distinctive cultural reservoir in their history. The colonial era is especially significant, since during the 18th century Blacks, who were the majority of the population, constituted the backbone of the economy in South Carolina.

One hundred years before the pilgrims landed at Plymouth, the first Africans arrived on the southeastern shores as members of a Spanish ex-

pedition from the West Indies. Searching for habitable land and a passageway to the Orient, the party of 500 Spanish-speaking Indians, Africans, and Europeans landed at Fort Royal Sound off South Carolina and named the surrounding country Santa Elena (now St. Helena). But the colony was doomed by food shortages, inclement weather, and disease. Within several months the survivors returned to the West Indies.

For the next hundred years, the Spanish and French fought to survive the elements, the Indians, and one another to claim the land. There was no permanent settlement of White men on the southeastern coast until 1670, when English settlers and African slaves from Barbados established a colony near Charleston.

During those early years, as the settlers struggled simply to survive, they began to develop a staple economy, the first economic boost coming from raising livestock. At first the English followed the European custom of raising small herds confined to pastures. But African slaves from the Gambia River region—expert horsemen and herdsmen—tended the livestock and adopted African husbandry patterns of open-grazing and large herds that made practical use of abundant land and a limited labor force.

The livestock economy freed manpower for clearing the land and offered a means of acquiring capital, but the settlers were anxious to pursue their own dream—the development of a plantation economy. In *Black Majority* Peter H. Wood reveals the Englishmen's initial resentment of the livestock economy: "our designe [is] to have Planters there and not Grazers."

During the first 50 years of settlement, rice became the mainstay of the lowland economy and dominated Carolina life for most of the 18th century. The settlers' earlier experiments with rice planting were unsuccessful until the late 17th century. The topography and the climate were ideal for growing rice, but the Europeans lacked the know-how to develop a substantial crop yield. But in Africa, rice had been a staple for centuries. With African slaves as the cultivators and processors, rice emerged as the staple crop.

In the years prior to the rice-dominated economy, Blacks had an active and more diverse involvement in the colony's growth. The severe slavery codes of the plantations had not yet evolved and the distinctions along racial lines were not so clearly drawn. The crude realities of frontier life demanded that servants and masters work and live more intimately than they would in later years.

African slaves cleared the forests and processed timber and wood products for exportation. In the fur trade, the slaves were the interpreters between White settlers and Indians. Slaves expanded the food supply with African techniques of fishing, and hollowed and carved the cypress logs for dugout boats, the central mode of transportation for half a century. And in some of the most crucial struggles for survival, Black "pioneers" fought beside White settlers against the invasion attempts of the French and Spanish and in the frontier wars with the Indians.

The West African slaves possessed skills and strengths suited to life in the South Carolina lowlands. Frontier life demanded survival skills that were integral to African life—managing boats, clearing land, herding cattle, hunting, fishing, working wood, and cultivating the land. For generations West African cultures had stressed harmony with nature and extensive knowledge of the land. The similarities in West African and Carolinian subtropical climates facilitated an easy transfer of knowledge.

Wood reveals two major factors which contributed to the Africans' gradual transition from unfree laborers to chattel slaves: a familiarity with rice cultivation, and a high incidence of the sickle-cell trait. The negative effects of this trait were at least balanced by a positive contribution—it increased the resistance to malaria. The infectious mosquitoes that transmitted the disease bred in the earliest location of rice cultivation, the fresh water marshes between the mainland coast and the Sea Islands.

The African slaves' primary role in the rice-growing economy was paralleled by a rapid increase in the Black population. Slave imports had grown to more than 1,000 per year by the early 1700s. A prohibitive duty was imposed on slave importation in 1741, but the colony's racial demographics already were set in place. Wood notes the comments of one Swiss newcomer: "Carolina looks more like a Negro country than like a country settled by White people."

The high concentration of Blacks in the population and the geographical and cultural isolation of the Sea Islands enabled the Africans to retain many traditions.

The development of the Gullah language, a pidginized English, was as essential to their survival as the skills and knowledge transferred to the new environment.

Once the slaves had been kidnapped from their homeland and separated from their families, the first challenge to their survival was development of a common language. The initial stages of this process began in the slave baracoons along the coast of West Africa. Slaves from various regions, speaking different African languages and dialects, experimented to find common denominators in speech patterns. The pidginization of languages extended to the trading language overheard in African trading ports and throughout the journey across the Atlantic Ocean.

Although the initial pidginization process often was a blending of African languages and English, the slaves encountered other European languages once they arrived in the New World. Slaves living in the Huguenot settlement, north of the Carolina province, spoke French but little or no English. Slaves who had been transported to settlements in Florida spoke only Spanish. Still others had acquired Portuguese and German. The most frequent solution was to resort to some common African speech pattern.

In establishing communication links, the Africans would often rely on traditional dress, hairstyles, or tribal facial markings. When appearances offered no clue to the language spoken, trial and error would reveal similarities in grammar and vocabulary. The White slave owners were aware of African national distinctions and manipulated the differences in languages and tribal rivalries in an attempt to alienate and further disorient the Black newcomers. Ironically, the slave owners' policy of mixing slaves of different backgrounds and tongues resulted in the creation of a common pidgin language.

The simplicity of the early pidgin dialect gradually gave way to a more elaborate creolized language. Through intensive use, the language known as Gullah became more self-contained, with an expanded structure and vocabulary. The distinctiveness of Gullah was reinforced by the increasing number of slaves imported directly from Africa, who in turn learned the language from the native speakers of Gullah.

After the Civil War, the Gullah language changed considerably from that used by earlier speakers. Many African elements, word meanings, and constructions were lost or dropped as the Gullahs continued to decreolize their language. The influence of early public education and social pressures from Blacks and Whites convinced the Gullahs they should "correct" their speech and acquire national norms of English.

Today's Gullah culture and language reflects even more the influence of modern technology and social change, but the evidence of African roots remains strong. Birth and naming practices, motor movements, religious rituals, fishing practices, styles of dress among women, the use of gourds and shells, and local crafts reveal distinct patterns of an African heritage that survives in the Sea Islands.

For Black Americans the essence of the Gullah culture lies not only within its ties to the past but in its reflection of hope for the future. In the words of one elderly resident of Johns Island:

> More light is shining. Can see more. Likewise you can do more and think more, 'cause I believe that more light is shining now than was shining in the past. And so help me God, I so glad that I can see some light. And I know there's more light for me. There is a bright light somewhere and I'm going to find it.

(Carawan and Carawan, "Ain't You Got A Right to the Tree of Life").

Selection 3

The Stono Rebellion

Peter H. Wood

Always restive, the slave population of South Carolina was swept by a brief but violent uprising in 1739, known as the Stono River Rebellion. It was one of the largest slave revolts in American history, and the frightened whites of the colony suppressed it ferociously. This selection, which is drawn from Peter H. Wood's book Black Majority, *describes the rebellion's causes, course, and consequences.*

A brewing war between Britain and Spain helped precipitate African resistance in South Carolina, for the Spanish were actively encouraging South Carolina slaves to seek refuge at a settlement called Mose, near St. Augustine in their colony of Florida. (Rightly fearing that a restive slave population would render white settlers vulnerable, the leaders of Britain's recently founded colony of Georgia at this time banned slavery altogether.) Secret Spanish agents among South Carolina's blacks are thought to have had an important role in stimulating the uprising.

The Stono Rebellion frightened South Carolina's whites, who were outnumbered by their black slaves. Slave codes—the regulations governing the treatment of slaves—were tightened even more severely after the uprising was crushed. For more than a hundred years, until the Civil War, South Carolina whites would be extraordinarily edgy about maintaining strict control over their bondspeople. This heightened nervousness helps explain much of South Carolina's subsequent history, including its leadership in the secession movement in the mid–nineteenth century.

*T*he year 1739 did not begin auspiciously for the [British] settlement [in South Carolina]. The smallpox epidemic which had plagued the town in the previous autumn was still lingering on when the council and commons convened in Charlestown in January. Therefore, Lt. Gov. William Bull, in his opening remarks to the initial session, recommended that the legislature consider "only what is absolutely necessary to be dispatched for the Service of the Province." The primary issue confronting them, Bull suggested, was the desertion of their slaves, who represented such a huge proportion of the investments of white colonists. The Assembly agreed that the matter was urgent, and a committee was immediately established to consider what measures should be taken in response to "the Encouragement lately given by the Spaniards for the Desertion of Negroes from this Government to the Garrison of St. Augustine."

Even as the legislators deliberated, the indications of unrest multiplied. In Georgia William Stephens, the secretary for the trustees of that colony, recorded on February 8, 1739, "what we heard told us by several newly come from Carolina, was not to be disregarded, viz. that a Conspiracy was formed by the Negroes in Carolina, to rise and forcibly make their Way out of

Excerpted from Peter H. Wood, *Black Majority.* Copyright © 1974 Peter H. Wood. Reprinted with permission from Alfred A. Knopf, a division of Random House, Inc.

the Province" in an effort to reach the protection of the Spanish. It had been learned, Stephens wrote in his journal, that this plot was first discovered in Winyaw in the northern part of the province, "from whence, as they were to bend their Course South, it argued, that the other Parts of the Province must be privy to it, and that the Rising was to be universal; whereupon the whole Province were all upon their Guard." If there were rumblings in the northernmost counties, Granville County on the southern edge of the province probably faced a greater prospect of disorder. Stephens' journal for February 20 reports word of a conspiracy among the slaves on the Montaigut and de Beaufain plantations bordering on the Savannah River just below the town of Purrysburg. Two days later the Upper House in Charlestown passed on to the Assembly a petition and several affidavits from "Inhabitants of Granville County relating to the Desertion of their Slaves to the Castle of St. Augustine."

That same week the commons expressed its distress over information that several runaways heading for St. Augustine had been taken up but then suffered to go at large without questioning. An inquiry was ordered, but it was not until early April that the Assembly heard concrete recommendations upon the problem of desertions. The first suggestion was for a petition to the English king requesting relief and assistance in this matter. Secondly, since many felt that the dozens of slaves escaping in November had eluded authorities because of a lack of scout boats, it was voted to employ two boats of eight men each in patrolling the southern coastal passages for the next nine months. Finally, to cut off Negroes escaping by land, large bounties were recommended for slaves taken up in the all-white colony of Georgia. Men, women, and children under twelve were to bring £40, £25, and £10, respectively, if brought back from beyond the Savannah River, and each adult scalp "with the two Ears" would command £20.

In the midst of these deliberations, four slaves, apparently good riders who knew the terrain through hunting stray cattle, stole some horses and headed for Florida, accompanied by an Irish Catholic servant. Since they killed one white and wounded another in making their escape, a large posse was organized which pursued them unsuccessfully. Indian allies succeeded in killing one of the runaways, but the rest reached St. Augustine, where they were warmly received. Spurred by such an incident, the Assembly completed work April 11 on legislation undertaken the previous month to prevent slave insurrections. The next day a public display was made of the punishment of two captured runaways, convicted of attempting to leave the province in the company of several other Negroes. One man was whipped and the other, after a contrite speech before the assembled slaves, "was executed at the usual Place, and afterwards hung in Chains at Hangman's Point opposite to this Town, in sight of all Negroes passing and repassing by Water.". . .

A letter the same month from Lt. Gov. Bull to the Duke of Newcastle, summarizing the situation, reflected the anxiety of the white populace:

My Lord,

I beg leave to lay before Your Grace an Affair, which may greatly distress if not entirely ruin this His Majesty's Province of South Carolina.

His Catholick Majesty's Edict having been published at St. Augustine declaring Freedom to all Negroes, and other slaves, that shall Desert from the English Colonies, Has occasioned several Parties to desert from this Province both by Land and Water, which notwithstanding They were pursued by the People of Carolina as well as the Indians, & People in Georgia, by General Oglethorpes Directions, have been able to make their escape.

Bull repeated the blunt refusal which the Spanish governor had given to deputies visiting St. Augustine to seek the return of fugitives, and he reported that "This Answer has occasioned great disatisfaction & Concern to the Inhabitants of this Province, to find their property now become so very precarious and uncertain." There was a growing awareness among whites, Bull concluded, "that their Negroes which were their chief support may in little time become their Enemies, if not their Masters, and that this Government is unable to withstand or prevent it."

Developments during the summer months did little to lessen tensions. In July the *Gazette* printed an account from Jamaica of the truce which the English governor there had felt compelled to negotiate with an armed and independent force of runaways. During the same month a Spanish Captain of the Horse from St. Augustine named Don Piedro sailed into Charlestown in a launch with twenty or thirty men, supposedly to deliver a letter to Gen. Oglethorpe. Since Oglethorpe was residing in Frederica far down the coast, the visit seemed suspicious, and it was later recalled, in the wake of the Stono incident, that there had been a Negro aboard who spoke excellent English and that the vessel had put into numerous inlets south of Charlestown while making its return. Whether men were sent ashore was unclear, but in September the Georgians took into custody a priest thought to be "employed by the Spaniards to procure a general Insurrection of the Negroes."

Another enemy, yellow fever, reappeared in Charlestown during the late summer for the first time since 1732. The epidemic "destroyed many, who had got thro' the Small-pox" of the previous year, and as usual, it was remarked to be "very fatal to Strangers & Europeans especially." September proved a particularly sultry month. A series of philosophical lectures was discontinued "by Reason of the Sickness and Heat"; a school to teach embroidery, lacework, and French to young ladies was closed down; and the *Gazette* ceased publication for a month when the printer fell sick. Lt. Gov. Bull, citing "the Sickness with which it hath pleased God to visit this Province," prorogued the Assembly which attempted to convene on September 12. The session was postponed again on October 18 and did not get under way until October 30. By then cool weather had killed the mosquitoes which carried the disease, and the contagion had subsided, but it had taken the lives of the chief justice, the judge of the Vice-Admiralty Court, the surveyor of customs, the clerk of the Assembly, and the clerk of the Court of Admiralty, along with scores of other residents.

The confusion created by this sickness in Charlestown, where residents were dying at a rate of more than half a dozen per day, may have been a factor in the timing of the Stono Rebellion, but calculations might also have been influenced by the newspaper publication, in mid-August, of the Security Act which required all white men to carry firearms to church on Sunday or submit to a stiff fine, beginning on September 29. It had long been recognized that the free hours at the end of the week afforded the slaves their best opportunity for cabals [conspiracies], particularly when whites were engaged in communal activities of their own. In 1724 Gov. Nicholson had expressed to the Lords of Trade his hope that new legislation would "Cause people to Travel better Armed in Times of Publick meetings when Negroes might take the better opportunity against Great Numbers of Unarmed men." Later the same year the Assembly had complained that the recent statute requiring white men "to ride Arm'd on every Sunday" had not been announced sufficiently to be effective, and in 1727 the Committee of Grievances had objected that "the Law [which] obliged people to go arm'd to Church [etc.]: wants strengthening." Ten years later the presentments of the Grand Jury in Charlestown stressed the fact that Negroes were still permitted to cabal together during the hours of divine service, "which if not timely prevented may be of fatal Consequence to this Province." Since the Stono Uprising, which caught planters at church, occurred only weeks before the published statute of 1739 went into effect, slaves may have considered that within the near future their masters would be even more heavily armed on Sundays.

One other factor seems to be more than coincidental to the timing of the insurrection. Official word of hostilities between England and Spain, which both whites and blacks in the colony had been anticipating for some time, appears to have reached Charlestown the very weekend that the uprising began. Such news would have been a logical trigger for rebellion.

If it did furnish the sudden spark, this would help explain how the Stono scheme, unlike so many others, was put into immediate execution without hesitancy or betrayal, and why the rebels marched southward toward Spanish St. Augustine with an air of particular confidence.

During the early hours of Sunday, September 9, 1739, some twenty slaves gathered near the western branch of Stono River in St. Paul's Parish, within twenty miles of Charlestown. Many of the conspirators were Angolans, and their acknowledged leader was a slave named Jemmy. The group proceeded to Stono Bridge and broke into Hutchenson's store, where small arms and powder were on sale. The storekeepers, Robert Bathurst and Mr. Gibbs, were executed and their heads left upon the front steps.

Equipped with guns, the band moved on to the house of Mr. Godfrey, which they plundered and burned, killing the owner and his son and daughter. They then turned southward along the main road to Georgia and St. Augustine and reached Wallace's Tavern before dawn. The innkeeper was spared, "for he was a good man and kind to his slaves," but a neighbor, Mr. Lemy, was killed with his wife and child and his house was sacked. "They burnt Colonel Hext's house and killed his Overseer and his Wife. They then burnt Mr Sprye's house, then Mr Sacheverell's, and then Mr Nash's house, all lying upon the Pons Pons Road, and killed all the white People they found in them." A man named Bullock eluded the rebels, but they burned his house. When they advanced upon the home of Thomas Rose with the intention of killing him, several of his slaves succeeded in hiding him, for which they were later rewarded. But by now reluctant slaves were being forced to join the company to keep the alarm from being spread. Others were joining voluntarily, and as the numbers grew, confidence rose and discipline diminished. Two drums appeared; a standard was raised; and there were shouts of "Liberty!" from the marchers. The few whites whom they encountered were pursued and killed.

By extreme coincidence, Lt. Gov. Bull was returning northward from Granville County to

Charlestown at this time for the beginning of the legislative session. At about eleven in the morning, riding in the company of four other men, Bull came directly in view of the rebel troop, which must have numbered more than fifty by then. Comprehending the situation, he wheeled about, "and with much difficulty escaped & raised the Countrey." The same account states that Bull "was pursued," and it seems clear that if the lieutenant governor had not been on horseback he might never have escaped alive. Bull's death or capture would have had incalculable psychological and tactical significance. As it was, the rebels probably never knew the identity of the fleeing horseman or sensed the crucial nature of this chance encounter. Instead they proceeded through the Ponpon district, terrorizing and recruiting. According to a contemporary account, their numbers were being "increased every minute by new Negroes coming to them, so that they were above Sixty, some say a hundred, on which they halted in a field and set to dancing, Singing and beating Drums to draw more Negroes to them."

The decision to halt came late on Sunday afternoon. Having marched more than ten miles without opposition, the troop drew up in a field on the north side of the road, not far from the site of the Jacksonburough ferry. Some of the recruits were undoubtedly tired or uncertain; others were said to be intoxicated on stolen liquor. Many must have felt unduly confident over the fact that they had already struck a more successful overt blow for resistance than any previous group of slaves in the colony, and as their ranks grew, the likelihood of a successful exodus increased. It has been suggested that the additional confidence needed to make such a large group of slaves pause in an open field in broad daylight may have been derived from the colors which they displayed before them. Whatever the validity of this suggestion, the main reason for not crossing the Edisto River was probably the realistic expectation that by remaining stationary after such an initial show of force, enough other slaves could join them to make their troop nearly invincible by morning.

But such was not to be the case, for by Sunday noon some of the nearest white colonists had been alerted. Whether Bull himself was the first to raise the alarm is unclear. According to one tradition Rev. Stobo's Presbyterian congregation at Wiltown on the east bank of the Edisto was summoned directly from church, and since this would have been the first community which Bull and his fellow riders could reach, the detail is probably valid. By about four in the afternoon a contingent of armed and mounted planters, variously numbered from twenty to one hundred, moved in upon the rebels' location (long after known as "the battlefield").

Caught off guard, the Negroes hesitated as to whether to attack or flee. Those with weapons fired two quick but ineffective rounds; they were described later in white reports as having "behaved boldly." Seeing that some slaves were loading their guns and others were escaping, a number of whites dismounted and fired a volley into the group, killing or wounding at least fourteen. Other rebels were surrounded, questioned briefly, and then shot.

White sources considered it notable that the planters "did not torture one Negroe, but only put them to an easy death," and several slaves who proved they had been forced to join the band were actually released. Those who sought to return to their plantations, hoping they had not yet been missed, were seized and shot, and one account claimed that the planters "Cutt off their heads and set them up at every Mile Post they came to." Whether the riders used drink to fortify their courage or to celebrate their victory, a bill of more than £90 was drawn up the next day for "Liquors &c" which had been consumed by the local militia company.

Although secondary accounts have suggested that the Stono Uprising was suppressed by nightfall, contemporary sources reveal a decidedly different story. By Sunday evening more than twenty white settlers had already been killed. Initial messages from the area put the number twice as high and reported "the Country thereabout was full of Flames." The fact that black deaths scarcely exceeded white during the first twenty-four hours was not likely to reassure the planters or intimidate the slave majority. Moreover, at least thirty Negroes (or roughly one third of the rebel force) were known to have escaped from Sunday's skirmish in several groups, and their presence in the countryside provided an invitation to wider rebellion. Roughly as many more had scattered individually, hoping to rejoin the rebels or return to their plantations as conditions dictated.

During the ensuing days, therefore, a desperate and intensive manhunt was staged. The entire white colony was ordered under arms, and guards were posted at key ferry passages. The Ashley River militia company, its ranks thinned by yellow fever, set out from Charlestown in pursuit. Some of the militia captains turned out Indian recruits as well, who, if paid in cash, were willing to serve as slave-catchers. A white resident wrote several weeks later that within the first two days these forces "kill'd twenty odd more, and took about 40; who were immediately some shot, some hang'd, and some Gibbeted alive. A Number came in and were seized and discharged." Even if these executions were as numerous, rapid, and brutal as claimed, the prospect of a sustained insurrection continued. It was not until the following Saturday, almost a week after the initial violence, that a white militia company caught up with the largest remnant of the rebel force. This band, undoubtedly short on provisions and arms, had made its way thirty miles closer to the colony's southern border. A pitched battle ensued, and at length (according to a note sent the following January) "[the] Rebels [were] So entirely defeated & dispersed [that] there never were Seen above 6 or 7 together Since."

It was not until a full month later, however, that a correspondent in South Carolina could report that "the Rebellious Negros are quite stopt from doing any further Mischief, many of them having been put to the most cruel Death." And even then, white fears were by no means allayed. The Purrysburg militia company had remained on guard at the southern edge of the colony, and in Georgia Gen. Oglethorpe, upon receiving Lt. Gov. Bull's report of the insurrection, had called out rangers and Indians and issued a proclamation, "cautioning all Persons in this Province, to have a watchful Eye upon any Negroes, who might attempt to set a Foot in it." He had also garrisoned soldiers at Palachicolas, the abandoned fort which guarded the only point for almost one hundred miles where horses could swim the Savannah River and where Negro fugitives had previously crossed. Security in South Carolina itself was made tight enough, however, so that few if any rebels reached Georgia. But this only increased the anxiety of whites in the neighborhood of the uprising.

In November several planters around Stono deserted their homes and moved their wives and children in with other families, "at particular Places, for their better Security and Defence against those Negroes which were concerned in that Insurrection who were not yet taken." And in January the minister of St. Paul's Parish protested that some of his leading parishioners, "being apprehensive of Danger from [the] Rebels Still outstanding," had "carried their Families to Town for Safety, & if [the] Humour [inclination] of moving continues a little longer, I shall have but a Small Congregation at Church." The Assembly placed a special patrol on duty along the Stono River and expended more than £1,500 on rewards for Negroes and Indians who had acted in the white interest during the insurrection. Outlying fugitives were still being brought in for execution the following spring, and one ringleader remained at large for three full years. He was finally taken up in a swamp by two Negro runaways hopeful of a reward, tried by authorities at Stono, and immediately hanged.

"Seasoning" in Virginia

Lorena S. Walsh

Seasoning was the slave owners' expression for breaking in slaves newly arrived from Africa. Seasoning involved teaching them work routines and discipline, forcing them to learn enough English to understand and obey simple commands, and making them accustomed to the local environment—if indeed they survived being uprooted and forcibly resettled in North America.

Using the unusually full records maintained by the family of Robert "King" Carter and his descendants, who were among the largest landowners in eighteenth-century Virginia, historian Lorena S. Walsh re-creates the process of seasoning that African-born slaves experienced when they arrived at the plantation known as Carter's Grove. This selection is excerpted from her 1997 book From Calabar to Carter's Grove: The History of a Virginia Slave Community.

S hortly after a slave ship dropped anchor in the York or Rappahannock River, Robert Carter boarded the vessel and picked out some of the most promising captives for Merchant's Hundred. Those debarking on the Rappahannock went first to his home plantation, Corotoman, while those coming ashore on

the York probably were taken first to Fairfield where Carter or the Burwell manager immediately issued them clothing and bedding. Within a few days Carter evaluated the slaves and chose an English name by which each was to be known thereafter. As he explained the process in 1727, "I nam'd them here & by their names we can always know what sizes they are of & I am sure we repeated them so often to them that every one knew their names & would readily answer to them." Quarter overseers were then to "take care that the negros both men & women I sent you up last always go by ye names we gave them" and not allow them to revert to their African names. Another Carter letter makes clear that he did not turn over the initial name training to underlings. Either Carter or one of his sons repeated the newly assigned names until the slaves responded, and meanwhile the whites committed to memory at least a superficial perception of the individual. . . .

Weakened and traumatized by the Middle Passage and unaccustomed to the Chesapeake disease environment, many of the slaves immediately fell sick or never recovered their health. Some suffered from "scurveys, swellings, and other disorders," likely the result of months of short and bad rations, others were "lame" in their knees, and still others were sick with undiagnosable "strange distempers"; some died within a few days. Many new hands who arrived in the spring also fell sick by early fall from the strains of malaria endemic in the region. In October 1729, for example, Carter reported: "My new Hands are all down in their Seasoning Except one. I must wait with Patience till they recover their strength before I can send them [to a distant quarter]." Carter hoped that adequate food and warm clothes and bedding would speed their recovery. Unfortunately, many of those who survived the spring and summer did not live through their first winter in a colder climate, a season in which both whites and blacks often succumbed to respiratory diseases. Carter blamed "the carelessness and cruelty of the overseers in turning the people out in hard and bitter weather."

The winter of 1726–27 was especially deadly. "I have had prodigeous loss in my Slaves this winter and have bin forced to recruit by purchasing a large number of new Negroes," Carter wrote one correspondent in May. At least seventy adult slaves perished that winter, including several at Merchant's Hundred, and in April 1727 Carter bought eighty more Africans. Because most quarters were short of working hands, Carter especially wanted prime male workers—"the choice of ye Ship, three men to one woman."

Some of the strongest Africans immediately tried to escape their captors, as did seven men who took off from Corotoman in a slave's canoe five days after their ship arrived and managed to elude recapture for a week. Others, once they had regained some strength and found an opportunity, took off into the woods. By the 1720s Carter had had enough experience with newly arrived Africans to expect this, and for the first few months he ordered his overseers "to be kind to all the negros but especially to the new ones." Of one new slave woman who had been hiding out in the neighborhood of one of the quarters, Carter observed that "now she hath tasted of the hardship of ye woods she will go near to stay at home where she can have her belly full." Carter undoubtedly hoped that "kind" treatment would minimize early deaths occasioned by "seasoning" or sheer despair.

Eventually, however, Carter ran out of patience with Africans who refused to adapt to their

Owners sometimes punished runaway slaves by cutting off their toes.

new situation. Then he turned to brutal measures. When, for example, in 1727, Carter decided that chronic runaway Ballazore was an "incorrigeble rogue" he ordered the overseer to have the man's toes cut off; "nothing less than dismembring will reclaim him." This was not an isolated act of brutality, for Carter asserted, "I have cured many a negro of running away by this means." Lancaster County court records for 1710 and a private diary entry for 1722 show at least three other instances of a similar cure. Other slaves who resisted in unspecified ways were whipped and branded. Slaves who repeatedly challenged their new owners paid a heavy price.

One of Carter's strategies for forcing new Africans to become productive workers and reconciling them to bondage was to encourage them to form families as soon as possible. Married slaves were much less likely to try to run away than were unattached individuals. Like most other period slaveholders, Carter was unwilling to sacrifice short-term returns from expanded tobacco crops for the possibility of longer-term returns in the form of slave children. He generally bought nearly twice as many men as women, but he did encourage those men who could find mates to enter into regular unions. By 1733 almost no adult women on Carter quarters lived by themselves; most either were married according to whatever understanding they and their husbands had negotiated between themselves and with Carter or else were part of a household consisting of two or three other apparently unrelated men and women. Wherever possible, Carter kept husbands and wives together on the same plantation and allotted them a house to themselves. When spouses lived on another quarter or had died, mothers and their children or, less often, fathers and their children lived together. Unattached and probably recently arrived men usually shared a cabin with one to three other males. . . . Because no more than fifteen to twenty-five slaves resided at any individual quarter, there were no large concentrations of men living in barrackslike housing for any length of time.

Carter's encouragement of slave marriages highlights emerging differences in planters' strategies for controlling bound laborers. Indentured servants were expected to abstain from sexual relations during their term of service, and those whose transgressions resulted in the conception of an out-of-wedlock child were severely punished. Lifelong service was a different matter, but since the institution of slavery evolved piecemeal in the Chesapeake, so did slave owners' policies regarding slaves' sexual and reproductive behavior. A few masters who, like Carter, were familiar with the wider slave trade may have known that West African slave owners used the creation of domestic units as a strategy for integrating male slaves into the local society and motivating them to work harder. (In all the slave systems, slave women had much less control over their situations.) An additional incentive to marry for both men and women was the chance to acquire "securable and separate domestic environments," a privilege usually reserved only for married couples or women with one or more children. The greater privacy a house of one's own afforded also offered greater control over most aspects of private life.

Another of Carter's strategies for extracting work from the slaves was regimented gang labor. Rather than assigning slaves individual tasks, overseers put all the laborers to work on one job at a time, keeping watch over all and forcing all to work at a similar pace. Carter's letters include repeated references to slave gangs. Whether it was planting, weeding, or harvesting corn or tobacco, gathering corn fodder, or digging a millrace, his slaves usually worked as a single unit. And indeed, there was just one unit, for the total labor force on any one of Carter's quarters averaged only nine able-bodied men, women, and older children. On the quarters inventoried in 1733, the range was two to twenty-three laborers; however, there were more than fifteen potential workers on only three quarters. The overseers were "always to be with the people to keep them to their work." Very likely Carter had hit upon this solution as the only way to control the many new African slaves he added to his workforce, most of whom understood little or no English and whose main goal was to escape their captors. Slaves too young, old, or sick to keep up with the other laborers were assigned light tasks with little or no supervision. Such marginal workers largely were left to do whatever they could, and, in effect, as they would.

Carter usually mixed more acclimated slaves with the "new Negroes" on the various quarters, probably hoping to speed the assimilation process but also aiming to gain more control over the recent arrivals through the mediation of the more acculturated slaves. With the exception of artisans on his home plantation, by 1733 Carter owned few white indentured servants. In earlier years such servants might have served as an intermediating group; now their presence, on outlying quarters at least, would likely have complicated the imposition of radically un-English work regimens.

Slaves who had a much longer history in Virginia and likely had appropriated some of the customary privileges of white indentured servants probably suffered deteriorating work conditions as Carter added numbers of new, less-acculturated workers. Work rules for blacks and whites quickly diverged, and old hands soon were subjected to the increased regimentation that planters thought the continued influx of new arrivals required. Skilled white indentured servants—by this time almost always adult men—did what they could to distance themselves from the increasingly disprivileged blacks. Those arriving in the 1720s and 1730s refused to work and did little but press complaints until they extracted current "customary" English workers' privileges, which exceeded those allowed unskilled indentured servants at the turn of the century. And, unlike some of the mostly unskilled white men servants who had arrived a few years earlier, the later ones seem usually to have avoided contact with black women.

Carter's third strategy for extracting work from new arrivals was to appoint a slave man on each quarter as foreman. These men must have demonstrated superior skills in raising tobacco and corn and managing livestock and probably were among the most influential quarter residents. Carter advanced each man certain privileges, likely including the "provisions Equall to an overseer (vizt) halfe a middleing beefe[,] one barrow Hogg for bacon and one small hogg for Pork and such other things as [are] . . . reasonable for such a trusty negro" enumerated by a contemporary Virginia planter. Carter provided each slave supervisor a house to himself, even if he was single; on one quarter, one of the foremen had two wives, a common custom in Africa but unusual in the Chesapeake. In return Carter presumably made the foreman responsible for keeping the other slaves in line and working at an acceptable pace. Some of the foremen had been enslaved for some time (several are described as "old"), and a few were creoles. There were not enough such men to go around, however, and Carter selected a number of more recently arrived Africans as foremen including Ebo George at Totuskey, another Ebo George at Head of the River, and likely King Tom at Ham-

stead and George at Forrest with the two wives.

Regular use of slave foremen—working as drivers under the supervision of a white overseer—was something of an innovation for the region. In the early eighteenth century, Virginia and Maryland quarters were not uncommonly run by a trusted slave with no overseer present, despite laws that mandated a resident white supervisor. Later in the century slaves less often officially headed quarters, but planters did continue on occasion to dispense with white supervisors for a year or so, appointing one of the slaves as de facto interim overseer. Designated drivers, on the other hand, common on larger West Indian and South Carolina plantations, were much less frequently part of the formal management structure on Chesapeake plantations. There is little discussion in planter records of what Chesapeake foremen were expected to do aside from setting the work pace and advising about the best techniques for managing the crops and coping with adverse growing conditions occasioned by unfavorable seasonal variations in temperature and precipitation. Unlike many of their lower South counterparts, Chesapeake drivers seem not to have formally disciplined other slaves. Some of King Carter's children and grandchildren continued to appoint slave foremen on most of their farms, as did a few other very large slave owners, but there is no direct evidence of drivers on later Burwell quarters.

In contrast to the Burwell farms, there is little evidence of a color-based occupational hierarchy on the Carter plantations. For one thing, Africans greatly outnumbered any creoles whom Carter may have bought or who reached working age early in the century, and for another, so far as we can tell, only a handful of the Carter slaves were of mixed race. The family apparently put little stock in country of birth or mixed blood; with recent arrivals predominating, the Carters distinguished only between old and new hands. In addition, not many of the Carter slaves worked as craftsmen or domestics. For artisans, Carter relied primarily on white indentured servants; most of the scattering of slave carpenters and coopers were creoles, but only one was identified as a mulatto. Most of the privileged slaves were either foremen or sailors, and many of these were Africans. Given the unprecedented scale of the Carter operations in a Chesapeake context, contemporary Caribbean plantations may provide the best models for better understanding conditions on the Carter plantations in the 1720s and 1730s.

We can get some impression of the living conditions at Merchant's Hundred from the detailed inventories of forty-seven of Robert Carter's quarters taken in 1733. By that time the Merchant's Hundred slaves likely numbered between fifteen and twenty-five. Fifteen was both the mean and median number of people on the inventoried quarters, and Carter considered this the optimal-size workforce for seating outlying units. Indeed, the largest of Carter's quarters (with the exception of his home quarter) housed no more than twenty-six men, women, and children. Carter also judged eighteen to twenty-five workers a suitable dowry for two of his daughters. Ten to fifteen hands were apparently the most workers that ordinary overseers could effectively supervise in raising tobacco and grain, and twenty-five the maximum assigned to even the most experienced supervisors. A workforce of fifteen to twenty hands is also confirmed by the size of the tobacco crops—between ten and seventeen hogsheads a year from 1723 to 1731— that the Merchant's Hundred slaves raised. . . .

If the composition of the Merchant's Hundred workforce in the early 1730s was like that on other Carter quarters, there were almost twice as many men as women. Young adults would have predominated as well. . . . Only 4 percent of the inventoried slaves had survived long enough to be classified as old. The African-born women were slow to bear children. Only half of the slave households on Carter's quarters included any children at all. . . . Children under six were less numerous than children aged six to fifteen, hardly a normal pattern. Almost certainly some of the older children were also recently captured Africans. Most of the larger families were those of long-resident or creole slaves; the ages of the children indicate that most mothers with three or

more surviving offspring in 1733 had been in the colony for a minimum of twelve years. Even these women did not bear children as regularly as did contemporary white mothers; many had long gaps in their childbearing histories, likely evidence of unions disrupted by separation or death of the father.

Other quarter households would have consisted of single men living together, of apparently unrelated households containing both sexes, or of only a husband and wife. . . . The seemingly unrelated households may have consisted of people bound by ties important to the slaves but not noticed by the inventory takers. These slaves could have been shipmates who had recently survived the Middle Passage together or members of the same national group. Overall, most of the slaves on Robert Carter's quarters had had time to establish at best only rudimentary family connections and were likely less healthy and more alienated than African Americans who arrived earlier in Virginia.

The Carter letter books and inventory also suggest something of the material conditions at Merchant's Hundred in the 1730s. Each slave was issued a new suit of winter clothing annually as well as some lighter summer wear including, for the men, shirts, fustian jackets, and linen breeches and, for the women, shifts, petticoats, and aprons. Children got only a frock. To complete their outfits, the adults also had a pair of imported shoes, Irish stockings or plaid hose, and Kilmarnock mined caps. Bed rugs and blankets or hair coverlets were replaced only when those first issued became threadbare. The Carters shipped new bedding to the quarters with "the names of every negro they are for" attached. The Merchant's Hundred overseer probably collected the winter clothing at Fairfield each fall, checked the bundles to "see that everything is right," and then distributed the individually labeled garments. He had orders not to give out the winter clothes until the weather turned cold, as "some of ym would destroy [or, perhaps, trade] them before."

The weekly rations Carter supplied consisted primarily of ground or unground maize. Meat rations were less frequent, with the overseers only occasionally killing an old steer or giving out some preserved pork "that they may have a bit now and then and the fat to grease their Homony." In summer months the slaves were expected to get by without meat; if poor whites could make do in hot weather with "Good Milk & Homony & Milk & Mush," Carter was sure the slaves could do so as well. However, when some Merchant's Hundred laborers were sent to dig a millrace on another Carter plantation in York County in August 1729, they got more regular issues of fresh pork or beef: "I would allow ye people (it is hard work if they follow it close) a pound a meat a man, one day if not two days in a week."

Carter took some pains with housing the slaves, wanting "very good Cabbins to be made for my people that their beds may lye a foot and a half from ye ground." Even a good, new cabin was of course a tiny, crude log shelter with a dirt floor, wood chimney, and unglazed windows. Other owner-supplied domestic equipment was scanty: wooden pails and other containers, an iron pestle, iron pots and pothooks, and, if there was no gristmill nearby, a handmill for grinding corn. The main agricultural tools were hoes and axes, wedges for splitting timber, and a grindstone for sharpening tool edges. There might also have been some equipment for pressing cider if someone had gotten around to planting fruit trees at the quarter. Otherwise, Carter supplied the white overseer with little more in the way of domestic goods than he did the slaves: nothing more than basic bedding, cooking pots, and usually a gun. The quarter livestock would have consisted almost entirely of cattle and hogs, about fifty of each, and perhaps a horse for the overseer's use. . . .

Carter hired doctors on annual contracts to tend to the slaves on the various quarters. Unfortunately there was little white physicians could do to cure the most serious ailments. One of the doctors, in Carter's opinion, neglected his charges, refusing to visit sick slaves when sent for. The man may well have been reaping a profit at the expense of the slaves, administering "pokes and other unwarrantable potions of his own Con-

trivance that cost him nothing in good and laudable medicines that comes out of England." But perhaps the doctor was instead collaborating with the slaves in using herbal remedies.

To supply other needs, the slaves had to rely largely on craft skills acquired in Africa, at least until they learned the lay of the neighborhood and developed contacts with other local slaves with whom they might barter goods. And there are glimpses of the Carter slaves using traditional skills; on one plantation they made "hollow gumbs" to store corn and salt. Even bartering may have been rather limited at first, because it likely took time for the slaves to find or fashion tradables. Most transportees were relatively young, and they may not have perfected the higher levels of artisanal skill that often only older African specialists had mastered. In addition, the raw materials available in tidewater Virginia differed from those found in West Africa. Some time might have been required for the Africans to learn where to obtain raw materials and to master the use of unfamiliar woods, fibers, and clays. Similarly, while experienced fishermen could more readily transfer their skins from one environment to another, hunters probably needed more time to learn the habits and habitats of local animals, some of which, like the opossum and the raccoon, were unfamiliar.

On outlying quarters like Merchant's Hundred, with the overseer the only white on the plantation, and he probably a poor, single man, there were few castoffs or hand-me-downs to be had and fewer goods that might be pilfered than were at hand on some house plantations. Slave artisans, however, many of whom were probably creoles and who periodically came to the quarters to put up or fix cabins and tobacco barns, seem quickly to have taken advantage of the smallest openings that the underdeveloped local economy, both white and black, afforded. In 1731 the Carters suspected that a team of black carpenters and coopers, ostensibly building a barn and making containers and tools for an outlying quarter, "must spend a great deal of their Time in making pails & piggins & churns for merchandising," and that a slave blacksmith was working on the side and on his own account for neighboring whites.

Almost all the work the Carter slaves were forced to do was physically demanding and entirely manual. By 1729 Carter was encouraging some of his overseers to train oxen to help with heavy hauling. However, in the 1733 inventory there is evidence of working oxen on only six of the forty-seven quarters. Likely there were none at Merchant's Hundred. By Carter's own account most of the slaves had to carry all fencing materials from the woods to the fields, tote firewood from wherever they cut it to their cabins, and haul corn and tobacco from field to barn either on their backs or, African style, on their heads. Robert's son Landon recollected in 1776 that his father had used no plows and had no more than twelve draft oxen on all the quarters. On quarters where Carter raised wheat, the slaves leveled the ground and chopped in the seed with hoes. They also rolled tobacco hogsheads to landings and loaded ships with thousands of bushels of wheat and corn entirely by hand. The Merchant's Hundred Africans, then, almost certainly were forced to do extremely hard physical labor on scanty and monotonous fare and had the comfort of few nonessential material goods during their first years in Virginia.

Carter's practices represented in part simply the easiest and cheapest method for extracting labor in the Chesapeake in the early eighteenth century. But, while Carter surely demanded more intense labor over a longer portion of the growing season than Africans customarily required of themselves, he and fellow Chesapeake slave owners succeeded in large measure because they incorporated, knowingly or unknowingly, many of the highly efficient African farming practices. Coming largely from areas infested with the tsetse fly, African-born slaves were unaccustomed to the use of plows and draft animals. West African farmers instead were skilled in the bush fallow, hoe-and-hill agriculture that European tobacco and maize farmers had quickly adopted from Native Americans. John Barbot, traveling in West Africa around 1680, had noted that there "two men will dig as much land in a day, as one plow can turn over in England." Two men required less food than did one man and a horse. The technology, then, was essentially the same, and while tobacco and maize were not staple West African crops, most slaves were well versed in raising them.

African Slaves' Reactions to Captivity

Gerald W. Mullin

Historian Gerald W. Mullin discusses another dimension of the "seasoning" process in colonial Virginia: the ways in which newly arrived (and often strongly resistant) Africans learned to speak some English and became integrated into a community of fellow bonds-

people. In addition to analyzing the work routines and living conditions of recently arrived Africans, Mullin considers the contrasting behaviors displayed by that of new slaves and seasoned "new Negroes" when they ran away from or otherwise resisted their masters. This article is condensed from Professor Mullin's important 1972 book Flight and Rebellion: Slave Resistance in Eighteenth-Century Virginia.

*T*he acculturative process whereby Africans came to be "new Negroes," and a much smaller number assimilated slaves, was marked by three stages. First, the "outlandish" Africans reacted to slavery on the basis of the communal lives they had been living when enslaved. As their prior cultural directives proved unworkable, they began as best they could to bend such elements of the new culture as the English language, and in rare instances, technical skills to their advantage. Nearly all Africans became field laborers, "new Negroes," who represented the second level of assimilation. Since there seemed to be a "fit," or degree of congruence, between their cultural background and the plantation's communal norms, few Africans ever became more than "new Negroes." But those who did, the more educable and thoroughly assimilated Africans, were representative of the third level of acculturation. The latter were usually artisans, whose imaginative exploits as fugitives dramatized the reciprocal relationship between the acquisition of skills and more advanced assimilation. Artisanship and acculturation made blacks individuals while enhancing their ability to cope creatively with slavery. And individualism, already a basic ideal in colonial American society, was not, as we shall see, a very highly developed phenomenon in African tribes. Thus for the planter the acculturated slave's altered perception of himself and

slavery had some unforeseen and undesirable consequences.

Newspaper advertisements for fugitive slaves are the most useful and reliable source for demonstrating the effectiveness of the acculturation argument. The advertisements are fairly objective. . . . Slaveowners who used them were neither explaining nor defending slavery, they simply—in sparse, graphic phrases—listed their runaway's most noticeable physical and psychological characteristics, while commenting on his origin, work, and use of English. Since the notices also lend themselves well to a quantitative analysis of such characteristics as height, posture, skin color, habits of grooming and dress, and emotional peculiarities—for example, speech defects and uncontrollable movements of hands and face—they are indispensable for studying the change of physical norms, demographic make-up, and acculturation levels in the colonial slave population. For example:

> RUN AWAY about the First Day of *June* last from the Subscriber, living on *Chickahominy* River, *James City* County. A Negroe Man, short and well-set, aged between 30 and 40 Years, but looks younger, having no Beard, is smooth-fac'd, and has some Scars on his Temples, being the Marks of his Country; talks pretty good *English*; is a cunning, subtile Fellow, and pretends to be a Doctor. It is likely, as he has a great Acquaintance, he may have procur'd a false Pass. Whoever brings him to me at my House aforesaid, shall have two Pistoles Reward, besides what the Law allows.
>
> Michael Sherman

Approximately 1,500 notices in newspapers published from 1736 to 1801 in Williamsburg, Richmond, and Fredericksburg were analyzed, including all notices in all of the various editions of the *Virginia Gazette* that are extant. These described 1,138 men and 142 women. Another 400 people were advertised as runaways taken up by constables or jailers. In this period only 138 fugitives, about 1 in 8, were advertised as born in Africa. These exceptions were usually two kinds: "outlandish" Africans, and the relatively acculturated slaves who were longtime residents in Virginia. "New Negroes," isolated on the quarters and in a phase of acculturation between the new arrivals and the assimilated slaves, are conspicuously absent from the notices.

Since the new arrivals and their masters had talked informally about Africa—an intriguing insight into the nature of procurement for both sides—the notices are filled with information about what Africans chose to tell whites about their lives before enslavement. Bonnaund told his master that he was from "the Ibo Country," where he "served in the Capacity of a Canoe Man." Charles and Frank were also Ibo runaways, whose identities were conspicuous even though they were unable to tell their jailer whether or not they were Africans: their teeth were filed and chipped and their foreheads carved with ritual scars. While Frank's filed teeth were described as "sharp," Charles, who had "lost or broke off one or two of his fore Teeth," presumably tried to explain his ritual mutilations in what he already perceived to be a socially acceptable manner, said it was "done by a Cow in his country."

Ritual scars were dramatic testimony to the West Africans' life before slavery. To see how these men may have stood out among all others in colonial America, compare reproductions of an Ife brass head and an eighteenth-century portrait painted, say, by Benjamin West or John Durand. On the one side, blacks have faces marked from ear to ear, hairline to throat, by deep striations proclaiming a heritage that was based on a fully ritualized cultural existence, and which sustained a society that functioned on a corporate and traditional basis. On the other side, whites are without scars or with "scars" outside themselves of velvet and lace at cuff and throat, feather fans and open books—symbols of a European culture which centuries earlier had reduced its ceremonies of human and social renewal to compartmentalized activities as neat as the sitting rooms in which they posed. Symbols too of a society—at least beyond the plantation—that functioned on an impersonal, civil, and individual basis.

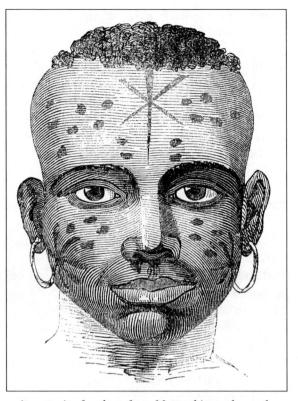

A portrait of a slave from Mozambique shows the ritual facial scars obtained in his home country.

Many slaveowners had closely observed the Africans' scars and could describe them in minute detail. "He is marked in the manner of his country with dots under both eyes, and on the right side of his neck with something resembling a ladder." "He has a very noted mark carved on his forehead resembling a diamond, and some marks of his country on his temples"; or this variation: "he has a Flower in his Forehead made in the Form of a Diamond with Specks down to the End of his Nose." And "he has six rings of his country marks round his neck, his ears full of holes."

These slaves had received their marks in ceremonies of pain, mystery, and celebration, which inculcated a distinctive sense of history (e.g. of reckoning time) and a sense of community, and made their initial adjustments unique among slaves. On the personal level the rite was an unforgettable ordeal in which the emotional ties of a group of young adults were reoriented from their families to their village society. The ceremonies, calculated to burn the lesson of companionship and community into the very souls of the young participants, also left indelible scars that were visible. These "country-marks" announced: "I am because we are, and since we are, I am." The West African scholar, John Mbiti, further explains that the rites united the celebrants with the rest of the community both living and dead, and "humanly speaking nothing can separate him from this corporate society."

Thus, on the community level, the rites were a matter of survival. Most colonial slaves came from small-scale, technologically simple societies that lived in a precarious relationship with their environment. The facts of individual differences, of varied and uneven rates of growth among their young men of the same age, constituted a grave threat to the basic ordering of society, particularly during the grim and perilous days of the international slave trade. Individual preference and initiative, unnatural thoughts of self-improvement at the community's expense, all had to be redirected; thus the schema of the rites of passage. "The individual person or [age] group is cut off, isolated and then restored," writes the anthropologist David F. Pocock, "but never again to be the same; in this restoration individual distinctions and differences are translated into social ones."

Philosophically, the coming of age ceremony was an integral part of the tribesman's conception of time. And the way the African slave marked time was at the core of how he made the world intelligible. Time in western technological society is a predictable and uniform movement; it is a commodity, too, that is utilized, measured in units, and so often bought and sold. For the African, however, time was created: it was based either on the major events of his life, such as coming of age, or at another level, on certain repetitive cyclic natural events, such as phases of the moon and the harvest seasons.

The essentials of this non-western folk ethos, man-in-community and discontinuous time-reckoning, survived enslavement and became an integral part of the African's behavior as a slave.

But only for a while. When his heritage proved unworkable, his job and other factors became reference points for his adjustment. Those Africans who initially reacted to slavery as runaways, and their later activities as learners of English, provide an opportunity to evaluate both their adjustment and the usefulness of the acculturation model itself for future studies of American Negro slavery.

"Outlandish" slaves, still to become "new Negroes," were unique among runaways in the colonial period. Whatever the precise meaning of procurement for the African as a person, his fellowship or affectivity, a core area of human behavior, remained intact as a slave. Africans, assuming that resistance was a group activity, ran off with their own countrymen, and American-born slaves including mulattoes. In all of the advertisements there were only a very few groups of American-born slaves and these were made up of not more than three men. But there were five larger groups, all composed of Africans. A sixth group included two African men and their American-born wives, and another pair, an African and a white indentured servant. Africans were also the only fugitives in eighteenth-century Virginia reported to be in even larger groups, pursuing cooperative ventures (usually in their determination to return "home," as they said) or to be in the more remote areas of the colony. Step, for example, left Petersburg with a twelve-year-old girl. "He went off with several others," his master wrote, "being persuaded that they could find the Way back to their own Country." Six weeks later this group was discovered in Mecklenburg County on the colony's frontier.

In at least one instance such a group was clearly organized to form a settlement of runaways. In a 1727 report to the Board of Trade, the governor, Sir William Gooch, mentioned fifteen Africans who left a "new" plantation at the falls of the James River to settle near the present site of Lexington, Virginia. Here they attempted to reconstruct familiar social and political arrangements. But shortly after building huts and sowing crops they were recaptured.

In South Carolina recently imported Africans

were even more active. What were merely tendencies among Africans in Virginia were definite patterns of behavior in South Carolina, where slaves made up about 60 per cent (as opposed to 40 per cent in Virginia) of the population. In sample runs of the South Carolina *Gazette* in the early 1750's and 1771 there was clear evidence of tribal cooperation in advertisements for the return of four "new Gambia men"; three Angolans, "all short fellows"; six other Angolans, purchased in the summer of 1771 and runaways by November, "so they cannot as yet speak English"; and four men from the "Fullah Country." There were also several family groups that were advertised; one included an African husband and wife, a "country-born man and woman," and Jack, a young "mustee" man. An advertiser for three men, an African from "Guinea," a slave from Angola ("a very good sawyer"), and a native American, said "they would either be on the Santee River, or higher up in the Black Settlements." These Black Settlements, and Ponpon, an area about forty miles south of Charleston, attracted a number of fugitives. While Virginia runaways seldom burdened themselves with anything more than the clothes on their back and ran away just to escape, South Carolina Africans ran off with their hoes, axes, bedding, and other equipment in order to replicate the community life they lived before slavery, or to join the Indians, or the Spanish in St. Augustine, Florida.

If runaways were recaptured but not reclaimed their jailers published notices such as the following:

COMMITTED to the gaol of *Westmoreland,* on *Monday,* the 21st of *October* [1771] two Negro Men, the one a yellow fellow, with a remarkable flat nose, the other black, with filed teeth, about 4 feet 8 or 9 inches high eac[h]. They are both *Africans,* and speak very little *English,* so they are not able to tell their master's name. They had with them two muskets, and two small books, in one of which is wrote *Elijah Worden.* They are supposed to have run from *Maryland,* as there was a strange canoe found near the place they were taken. The owner is desired to take them away and pay charges the law directs.

Edward Ransdell, jun. D.S.

The majority of Virginia slaves advertised as "taken up" had evidently fled soon after their enslavement. Fugitive Africans who were recaptured—often cold and frost-bitten, nearly naked after long treks and weeks in the wilds of the colonial South—could at most usually only speak a few words of English: they are "all in rags"; he has "nothing on but a blanket"; they are "entirely naked . . . and by lying in the cold, their feet and legs have swelled very much, so that they are not able to be sent to the [Charleston] work house." "He speaks very bad English, but says his master's name is *William Cook,* as plain as he can."

The jailers listened carefully to the Africans' replies, and were sometimes sufficiently interested to record and print literally what they were told. Consequently this data provides invaluable insights into how Africans thought in their own languages while conversing in English. Their responses also suggest that they looked upon slavery as a temporary misfortune, that perhaps the jailer might help them return "across grandywater" to their real homes in Africa. For example, when asked where they came from they took this to mean Africa, not the colonies. He "only calls himself Peter [and] says he is of the Bumbarozo Country." Or, he "calls his Country Mundingo," part of the Western Sudan. Most of the Africans who responded in this way, in fact, were from this area. Sarah, for example (one of the very few African women who ran away in eighteenth-century Virginia and was later described in a newspaper advertisement), was a 14-year-old with severe "choaking fits." She spoke English so poorly that she could not tell her master's name. She did, however, identify herself as a Mundingo. But Africans who were long time residents in slavery soon learned the proper cues. Dick, a small fellow about 50 years of age, had roamed about the Stafford County seat for months before he was taken up, and was described this way: "by what little English he talks and by signs he makes, he belongs to one *William Helm,* as he expressed it, in *Maryland."*

The Africans' efforts to talk about what their new masters meant to them are perhaps also more understandable when seen in connection with their upbringing. In going from old to new authorities, Africans obviously made various adjustments; but one type of authority relationship which the African considered no longer valid when his master died is persistently alluded to in the advertisements. For example: the jailer of a South Carolina runaway advertised: he "says master dead"; an Angolan, also taken up in South Carolina, made the revealing statement that his master was one William Anderson, "but [he] being dead, he cannot live with the family"; James, with filed teeth and the slave of a Richard Adams, said that his master was dead "and his widow ha[d] gone out of the country"; and a notice for two fugitives, who spoke "little English," said "their father's name is Davis but he is now dead."

These two runaways had traveled a great distance for a considerable time. But their jailer had to estimate where they were from (he said either the Carolinas or Georgia), because he had to superimpose his reckoning of time on theirs. The Africans knew the proper words but still reacted to their old cultural directives. They had been, they said, "ten Moons from home."

Occasionally in such conversations the two cultures' mythic paradigms for explaining location in time and space were set side by side. Sandy with filed teeth was asked how long he had been in the colony. He had, he replied, "made two crops for his master," and had been "absent from his service [for] two moons." "All I can learn from her," wrote another jailer, "is that she belongs to one Mr. Ruff, who lives in a great town, by a grandywater." Another African, who spoke "much broken," said he lived near "one Mr. Burley's where long leaf pine grows." Although data of this type is fragmentary—as is so often the case with historical reality for the "inarticulate"—it suggests that even though the African had partially adopted a new set of language symbols, his frame of reference had not changed. The "outlandish" slave's initial reaction to slavery as a runaway and his reluctance or inability to learn English demonstrate that at the dynamic level of his behavior, the level of philosophical orientation, he had remained an African.

But in a year or so the "outlandish" African changed. As he became a "new Negro" he acquired English and new work routines which transformed his communal and outward style of rebelliousness. For the African, learning English was the key to this process of cultural change, for the norms of the slave society were mediated through his captor's language. In acquiring English the "new Negro" learned about slavery, and how whites expected field hands to act.

A record of runaway notices that included comments on the slave's proficiency in English indicates that the African's acquisition of his second language fell into two periods. During the first few months after procurement, while some were trying to form settlements or return "home," Africans were unable to learn even a word of English. But after about six months, knowledge of the language increased sharply; and within another two or two and a half years most Africans were conversant in English. There are few notices of this type, however, because most runaways were not Africans and those who were represented either end of the acculturation scale: they were either new arrivals who spoke no English whatsoever, or assimilated Africans who spoke English fluently. For example, an October 1752 notice stated matter-of-factly, "they were imported in August and can't speak any English." Another mentioned that five months after Charles's arrival he could only "call himself Charles which is every word of English he can speak." Three runaways from an ironworks were "all new Negroes who had not been above 8 Months in the Country." Nonetheless one of them, Sambo, a small, thin, 30-year-old man, could speak English "so as to be understood." Tom, a Mungingo, had been "in this Country about eighteen Months," his master reported. "He lived this Year under the direction of Mr. *Edward Giles,* and if he should be strictly questioned can tell either Mr. *Giles'* name or my

Name." Proficiency came after about three years of residence.

Age at time of importation, location (in or outside the plantation world), and job, in that order, were the most important variables with regard to the rate at which the African learned English. If the slave had been imported as a youth or had worked in an urban setting, for example, it was expected that he would speak "sensibly." A Fredericksburg merchant wrote a slave trader in surprise, that "although [Dobbo] has been constantly in Town [he] cannot yet speak a word of English," and was therefore an exceptional case. Another master noted that his 30-year-old *"Angola* fellow" spoke "very good *English,* as he was imported young."

The Field Slaves' Adjustment to Slavery

Dobbo was an exceptional African; virtually all new arrivals were forced into field labor on the up-country quarters. These small, specialized plantations were a world of their own. Large planters divided their lands into small tracts called quarters. Usually from 500 to 1,500 acres in size, the quarters were economically specialized and isolated—separated from the activity and diversity of the home plantation, and surrounded by woods, swamps, rivers, and reserve land. There was a subtle compatibility among the quarter's essential components: the field slaves and overseer, the small flocks of fowl, herds of cattle and pigs, the coarse, makeshift slave huts and crude outbuildings amidst fields of tobacco, corn, small grain, and sometimes hemp. . . .

The field slave "is called up in the morning at daybreak, scarcely allowed time to swallow three mouthfuls of homminy," wrote the English traveler J.F.D. Smyth. Brief notations like this in travelers' and plantation accounts and record books must suffice for data on the field slave's material condition. Although the records are sketchy, his diet, although probably adequate in bulk, was scarcely nourishing. "Homminy," Indian corn, was the slaves' staple food.

Random accounts of quantities of corn allotted suggest that provisions were sometimes based on the worker's productivity. During the Revolutionary War, "Councillor" Carter asked that "the stronger Shears [shares] men & women" be given one peck of corn per week, "the Remainder of the Black People they to have ¼ Peck per Week each." By 1787 Carter, who was one of the least oppressive slave masters, increased this slightly. He ordered 44 pecks of shelled Indian corn as two weeks' allowance for 26 slaves, less than a full peck per week per laborer. (One peck equals 14 lbs. of Indian corn.)

Meat was seldom given to slaves. Smyth said slaves ate hoecakes and little else; unless their master "be a man of humanity the slave eats a little fat, skimmed milk, and rusty bacon." La Rochefoucauld-Liancourt said that on large plantations the slave subsisted on corn and sometimes on buttermilk. They were given meat 6 times a year. Robert "Councillor" Carter estimated that the common allowance for wheat per hand per year was 15 bushels for those "negroes, who are not fed with animal food" (e.g. meat). These slaves only received meat on special occasions. Joseph Ball wrote his steward that slaves were to "have ffresh meat when they are sick, if the time of the year will allow it." The cuts were to be the least desirable, although not necessarily the least nutritious. When calves were slaughtered, Ball ordered him to give the field hands the "head and Pluck"; the "ffat backs, necks, and other Coarse pieces" of hogs were also to be reserved for the slaves. James Mercer directed his steward to give the slaves the innards of chickens unless he sold them to the local Negro chicken merchants.

Plantation slaves wore clothing usually cut from a heavy, coarse cloth of flax and tow originally manufactured in Osnabrück, Germany. Following the non-importation agreements of the late 1760's, coarse-textured cotton wool weave, "Virginia plains," "country linen," replaced "Osnabrugs." Unlike the colorful variety of many of the artisan's clothing, the notices for runaways after 1770 indicate that field laborers wore uniform pants and trousers. "They are well clothed in the usual manner for Negroes";

"clothed as usual" and "the usual winter clothing for corn field negroes" are representative descriptions from advertisements of that period.

Black women who worked on the quarter wore clothing of the same weight and texture as the men. They usually dressed in a loose-fitting smock or shift, often tied at the waist; a short waistcoat was fitted over this dress. A Dutch blanket used for a sleeping robe and shoes and stockings completed the plantation Negroes' clothing allowance.

Housing for slaves varied widely. But there are frequent references in travelers' accounts to clusters of slave cabins that looked like small villages, and, in plantation records, numerous directions from masters indicating a concern for warm, dry houses with floors, lofted roofs, and on occasion, fireplaces. Slave quarters, however, may have been a late development. Subscribers who used advertisements to sell plantations frequently mentioned "negro quarters," but usually only in those notices published in the last quarter of the century. The plantation's size, location, and wealth were not factors; nearly all had slave quarters. It is likely that the smaller planter's field hands may have slept in the lofts of barns, in tobacco houses, and other outbuildings before the war. Joseph Ball told his nephew that the slaves "must ly in the Tobacco house" while their quarters, 15 by 20 feet with fireplace and chimney, were "lathed & fitted." However several planters, including George Washington, used a less substantial, pre-fab arrangement. These shacks were small, temporary, and were moved from quarter to quarter following the seasonal crop.

J.F.D. Smyth was forced to take shelter one evening in a "miserable shell" inhabited by six slaves and their overseer. Unlike many slaves' houses "it was not lathed nor plaistered, neither ceiled nor lofted above . . . one window, but no glass in it, not even a brick chimney, and, as it stood on blocks about a foot above the ground, the hogs lay constantly under the floor, which made it swarm with flies."

On the home plantations, "servants," like the crop hands, usually slept in their own quarters. A planter who moved to the valley in 1781 asked his steward to place the "house Servants for they have been more indulged than the rest" with the overseer and his family, "till Such Time as Warehouses can be provided for them." Slaves evidently rarely slept in the great house. A letter dated 1823 written to Dr. A.D. Galt of Williamsburg, mentioned that the writer's father could not find a house, "and the ones he has seen have not had separate quarters for the servants." They would then "have to stay in the basement or the garret rooms." This, she concluded, "[as] you know cannot be very agreeable to Virginians."

Some idea of a slave's yearly expenses is provided by James Madison's remark to a British visitor earlier in the nineteenth century. "Every negro earns annually, all expenses being deducted, about $257," wrote John Foster. "The expense of a negro including duty, board, clothing, and medicines, he [Madison] estimates from $12–13."

The lean, spare character of the field slave's material condition was a function of his place in the servile work hierarchy. Most plantation slaves worked in the fields where their tasks were tedious, sometimes strenuous, and usually uninspiring. Although tobacco is a difficult and challenging crop, field laborers—especially the "new Negroes"—were forced into the most routine tasks of transplanting seedlings, weeding, suckering, and worming. Following the harvest their work days extended into the night, when they sorted, bundled, and pressed the tobacco into hogsheads for shipment.

The slave jobber's work assignments were not as routine as the field laborer's chores. Armistead was hired out by his master to "act as a jobber, viz. to cut firewood, go to [the] Mill, work in your garden, and occasionally to work in your Corn-field." Jobbers also mended stone and wood fences, patched and whitewashed the plantation's outbuildings, dug irrigation and drainage ditches, and the like. . . .

But jobbers were scarcely better off than the field laborers, because they too did not travel outside the plantation. Nor did their menial tasks spur assimilation and a corresponding change in their view of slavery. Regardless of the specific nature of their tasks, the horizons and expectations of most plantation slaves were sharply limited by the plantation environment.

Their tiresome routines in the meager setting of reserve land, in meadow and woods, monotonous rows of tobacco, and temporary, ramshackle buildings, made the quarter a world of its own. But the isolation and work routines of the quarter provided slaves with a convenient means of expressing their unhappiness, so it was also a constant, nagging source of trouble for the planter. Blacks and whites alike knew that the plantation's efficiency and profitability could be seriously impaired simply by a "little leaning" on the slaves' part. "My people seem to be quite dead hearted, and either cannot or will not work"; "my people are all out of their senses for I cannot get one of them to do a thing as I would have it and as they do it even with their own time they have it to do again immediately." These words are Landon Carter's. A tough and competent man, Carter did not bend easily, but this note of resignation is heard early in his diary.

Accounts of the field slave's performance are rare, but one of the best can be found in Jack P. Greene's fine edition of Landon Carter's Diary which tells a dreary story of the crop laborers' quiet and persistently non-cooperative actions. Slaves reported ill every day but Sunday when there were no complaints because they considered this "a holy day"; men treading wheat slept while their "boys," left to do the job, "neglected" it; the "crop people," forced to stem tobacco in the evening hours, retaliated "under the guise of semi-darkness [by] throwing away a great deal of the saleable tob[acco]"; men whom Carter harassed about weeding a corn patch feigned stupidity and leveled thousands of hills of corn seedlings. Carter's slaves, in fact, were so rebellious that he came to question the profitability of slavery. . . .

In the familial and domestic world of eighteenth-century plantation society, the location of a slave's job was an important part of his activities as a slave. "Outlandish" Africans often reacted to their new condition by attempting to

escape, either to return to Africa or to form settlements of fugitives to re-create their old life in the new land. These activities were not predicated upon the Africans' experience of plantation life, but on a total rejection of their lot.

Most Africans who did not run off at this point were placed on the isolated, up-country quarters, where they remained for the rest of their lives, slowly learning the ways of their captors. This task assignment affected "new Negroes" in two ways. First, the quarter limited their contact with persons who spoke good English and possessed job skills, thus reducing the possibilities that they would readily acquire skills that would widen horizons and move them out of the plantation circuit. Second, since the quarter was isolated, it directed the slaves' rebelliousness toward the plantation itself, rather than toward the less accessible outer world. The field laborers' acts of defiance produced a satisfaction which, though often short-lived, was direct, and brought a quick and visible relief to immediate pressures.

This inward-directed rebelliousness included attacks on crops, stores, tools, and overseers, as well as deliberate laziness, feigned illness, and truancy. While this type of behavior on the part of one slave was ineffectual, slaves understood that if together they did a "little leaning," the overall effect on the plantation's efficiency could be considerable. Only rarely did the quarter slaves reject slavery completely by resisting it outwardly.

A few Africans and many of their children did gain the requisite linguistic and occupational skills to make the move from the quarter to the slightly larger world of the great planter's house, or, rarely, into an even larger arena by way of literate and technical skills. For the house servants, most rebelliousness was still manifested in inward-directed ways: in games with the master, drunkenness, and "laziness." Unlike the crop hands, house servants were also subjected to frequent and often frightening confrontations with the master himself; some of them exhibited neurotic symptoms during these encounters. For the artisans and waitingmen, who—because they traveled extensively—were more able to see their relatively "privileged" positions in relationship to the possibilities of life outside the plantation, rebelliousness became a matter of escaping from slavery itself, of turning their hostilities away from themselves and the plantation. Both their jobs and their facility in speaking English gave them an assurance that they did not need the paternalistic protection of their masters or the plantation environment to survive within the society. On reaching a high level of understanding of their masters' ways, artisans too desired an "independence on every one but Providence"; and although they also sometimes exhibited fear reactions when confronting their masters, they were resourceful runaways, and by the end of the century, had become insurrectionists.

New York: Slavery in an Eighteenth-Century Northern Society

Edgar J. McManus

Slavery is usually thought of as an institution confined to the American South, but in colonial times this was not true. Slavery was allowed in every mainland British colony, and it played a fairly important economic role in the middle colonies: New York, New Jersey, and Pennsylvania. Slave-trading also enriched many sea captains and merchants in maritime New England.

There were, however, important differences between the plantation slave systems of the Chesapeake, the Carolinas, and Georgia, and the slave labor that was used on farms and in households and workshops in the middle colonies and New England. Some of these differences, and how they affected the enslaved population, are discussed in this article, excerpted from a 1973 book by Edgar J. McManus, Black Bondage in the North.

Excerpted from Edgar J. McManus, *Black Bondage in the North* (Syracuse, NY: Syracuse University Press, 1973). Reprinted with permission.

*a*s the Northern economy became more complex, with industry and commerce playing larger roles in most of the colonies, employers were willing to pay high prices for slaves capable of productive labor. Generally the bondsmen most in demand were young adults from whom the buyer could expect many years of service. Besides having a larger proportion of their lives to live, young slaves were more active and also likelier to learn new tasks and skills. Writing to a business associate in 1715, Jonathan Dickinson reported that Pennsylvania employers were reluctant to buy any slaves "except boys or girls." Many of the slave cargoes landed at Northern ports were almost exclusively blacks between the ages of fourteen and twenty. Buyers naturally wanted slaves who were in a good state of general health, but particularly those with an immunity to smallpox since there would be no danger that an immune slave might contract that dread disease and perhaps communicate it to his master. Sales advertisements make it clear that smallpox immunity greatly enhanced the market value of a slave.

So much emphasis on youth and good health naturally undercut the market for older blacks. Slaves older than forty were rarely sold but generally remained with the master for whom they had worked during their more productive years. . . .

Some masters tried to get rid of their slave women at the first sign of pregnancy. One woman in Philadelphia was advertised for sale in the *Pennsylvania Gazette,* May 21, 1767, because she was "big with child," her owner noting that she was being sold "for no other fault but that she breeds fast.". . .

Since productivity largely determined the demand for slaves, men rather than women made up most of the working force. Relegated to household chores and domestic service, women did not play a significant role in the slave economy. The preference for males was reflected in the instructions carried by a slave ship bound for Africa in 1759 to "buy no girls and few women . . . buy some prime boys and young men." So heavy was the demand for men that a marked disproportion between the sexes developed in the North's black population. By 1755 the ratio of adult males to females in Massachusetts was nearly two to one. Men were in the majority everywhere, though in some colonies the disproportion was less. In New Hampshire male slaves outnumbered women by four to three, and in Connecticut the ratio was three to two. A New York census taken in 1756 listed over 7,500 male slaves and fewer than 6,000 women.

The average slaveowner needed only one or two men to supplement his own labor, plus a woman for domestic service. Larger holdings tended to be inconvenient, particularly for small farmers and artisans who often had to share their living space with slaves. The average holding in New England was about two slaves per family, though in eastern Connecticut and the Narragansett region of Rhode Island larger holdings were common. The same pattern of small-scale slaveholding existed in the Middle colonies. In Pennsylvania masters seldom owned more than four blacks, and the average holding was no more than one or two per family. A partial census taken in New York in 1755 showed that 2,456 adult slaves were divided among 1,137 different owners. . . .

Newspaper advertisements reveal that a large proportion of the slaves worked in various phases of agriculture. Besides producing food crops and raising livestock, they also grew such staples as flax, hemp, and tobacco. Since farming was on a small scale, slaves generally worked side by side with the master and shared the same living quarters. Their labor followed the usual routine of duties on a Northern farm— planting, harvesting, and the care of buildings, animals, and land. Moreover, the task system was employed, so slaves were usually free to manage their own time and rate of work. The system encouraged qualities of independence that distinguished Northern slaves from their plantation counterparts in the South. Frequently they were highly versatile workers, with proficiency as blacksmiths, carpenters, and shoemakers in addition to their agricultural skills.

The largest slaveholders were naturally the great landowners. . . . The same land-slave pattern prevailed in the Middle colonies. . . .

Slaveholding reflected social as well as economic standing, for in colonial times servants and retainers were visible symbols of rank and distinction. The leading families of Massachusetts and Connecticut used slaves as domestic servants, and in Rhode Island no prominent household was complete without a large staff of black retainers. New York's rural gentry regarded the possession of black coachmen and footmen as an unmistakable sign of social standing. In

A household slave in New York. Black servants were a status symbol in the northern colonies.

Boston, Philadelphia, and New York City the mercantile elite kept retinues of household slaves. Their example was followed by tradesmen and small retailers until most houses of substance had at least one or two domestics. Probably the largest urban staff was kept by William Smith of New York City, who had a retinue of twelve blacks to keep his household in order.

The wide diffusion of slaveholdings brought blacks into every phase of the economy. Learning virtually every trade and skill, slaves became assistants and apprentices to established craftsmen. In Philadelphia, New York, and Boston, blacks worked as bakers, tailors, weavers, coopers, tanners, blacksmiths, bolters, millers, masons, goldsmiths, cabinetmakers, naval carpenters, shoemakers, brushmakers, and glaziers. These industrial slaves matched the finest skills of the best white artisans. In the artistic crafts blacks also performed as ably as whites. Thomas Fleet of Boston employed three slaves in his printing shop to set type and cut wooden blocks for engravings. One of these black engravers was responsible for most of the illustrations turned out by Fleet. Some slaves who served as apprentices to doctors eventually became medical practitioners on their own account.

The colonial iron industry depended heavily upon black labor. In 1727 the ironmasters of Pennsylvania petitioned the assembly to reduce the import duty on slaves on the grounds that the supply of white workers was not sufficient to keep their mills working. The need for forced labor increased as production grew, for the hard conditions that prevailed in the bloomeries and mills repelled free workers. Reporting on Pennsylvania's iron manufactories in 1750, Israel Acrelius noted that "the laborers are generally composed partly of Negroes (slaves), partly of servants from Germany or Ireland brought for a term of years." Firms like Morriss, Shreltee, and Company and Bennett's Iron Works used slaves in every phase of production. Besides performing heavy labor as hammermen, attenders, and refiners, slaves also became proficient in the iron crafts. Black ironworkers in Andover, New Jersey, produced finished goods of such high quality that their wares were accepted on the basis of the brand name alone.

Slaves were also indispensable in the maritime industry upon which so much of the North's economy depended. The shipbuilding trades relied heavily on blacks as sailmakers, ropemakers, caulkers, shipwrights, and anchormakers. Slaves provided manpower for the fishing and trading ships of every colony. A black sailor belonging to Peter Cross of Massachusetts became so skillful at his calling that he was eventually placed in charge of a sloop. New England's whaling industry made heavy use of slaves, and in some cases half the men of a whaling crew were black. Not only were Negroes common on regular fishing and trading ships, but some served on privateers and even slave ships. So great was the demand for their services that every colony had laws specifically forbidding ship officers to sign on blacks without first obtaining their master's consent.

The versatility of slave labor brought blacks into competition with white workers. As early as 1660, a Boston town meeting tried to protect white mechanics by forbidding the use of slaves in the skilled crafts. In 1686 workers in the market houses of New York City complained that the employment of blacks had caused "discouragement and loss to the sworn porters." To protect the whites, an ordinance was passed providing that "no slave be suffered to work . . . as a porter about any goods either imported or exported from or into this city." These measures brought almost no relief, for slaves continued to be used for whatever work suited their masters. By 1691 New York's free porters complained that slave competition had "so impoverished them that they could not by their labors get a competency for the maintenance of themselves and families."

Slaves trained in the industrial arts were particularly ruinous competitors. In 1707 Philadelphia's white artisans petitioned the assembly against "the want of employment and lowness of wages occasioned by the number of *Negroes* . . . who being hired out to work by the day, take away the employment of the petitioners." Again, in 1737, they protested the assembly's failure to pass laws protecting them against black competitors. The rising tide of slave competition brought a protest from New York's coopers in 1737 against the "great numbers of Negroes" entering their trade. They petitioned the assembly for protection against "the pernicious custom of breeding slaves to trades whereby the honest and industrious tradesmen are reduced to poverty for want of employ." In support of the petition Lieutenant Governor Clarke denounced slave competition for having "forced many to leave us to seek their living in other countries." No protective legislation was enacted, however, for the wide diffusion of slave property made such restrictions politically inexpedient.

Since large numbers of slaves were generally available for hire, non-slaveholders could draw upon the slave force to meet their labor needs. Some masters made a business of hiring slaves out, and others, without enough work of their own, did so to obtain some return on their investment. Newspaper notices of slaves being sought or offered for hire attest to the prevalence of the practice. Sometimes slaves were rented along with a business so that the tenants could take over with no interruption of production. Slave-hiring was particularly common among craftsmen and artisans who needed labor but who did not want the responsibilities of outright ownership. Iron manufacturers also used hired slaves when other labor was scarce or production was unusually heavy. One Pennsylvania employer advertised for two months trying to hire a slave "that fully understands managing a bloomery." Though less common outside the towns, many farmers also found it convenient to rent slaves in order to meet seasonal labor needs.

Slave-hiring combined the economic flexibility of wage labor with the compulsory advantages of slavery. The system enabled employers to increase or reduce their labor force without paying the higher wages demanded by free workers and without tying up substantial capital in the purchase of slaves. That the wage savings alone could be considerable is revealed in the bitter resistance of the white mechanics to slave competition. Black workers could be hired from their masters with all the flexibility of free labor whether the period of service was for days, months, or even years. When the hiring was for longer than a week, a formal contract was usually signed specifying the period of service, the work to be performed, the wages to be paid, and the hirer's responsibility for the slave. Long-term hirers usually provided the slave with room and board, while the owner was responsible for his clothing. To allow the hirer to deduct the cost of clothing from the wages only invited dispute. One master who made such an agreement discovered to his chagrin that the alleged cost of the clothing exceeded the slave's annual wages.

The hiring system owed its success to the ability of slaves to compete effectively with all types of free labor. Slaves became so skillful and versatile that employers found it profitable to rent their services rather than bid for the labor of free workers who were both difficult to obtain and expensive to retain. Moreover, the services of slaves were easily available, for owners who did not have enough work for their bondsmen often preferred to hire them out instead of selling them. Even when slaves were rented for long or indefinite periods, some masters preferred to retain ownership. . . .

Slaveholders who hired out their bondsmen

for long-term service ran obvious risks. If the hirer failed to provide adequate food and shelter, or if he overworked the slave and used him for dangerous tasks, the owner might suffer a loss of capital. If the slave rebelled against the conditions of his employment by running away, the hirer had no obligation to reimburse the owner. Moreover, hiring had a corrosive effect on discipline, for it underscored for the slave that he was working for the benefit of another. As slaves served under successive hirers, bonds of personal loyalty tended to weaken and discipline became more difficult to maintain. Even seemingly docile slaves turned sullen and defiant after a term of service with another master.

Another problem was the possibility of collusion between slaves and employers. Once slave-hiring became commonplace, it was relatively easy for slaves to sell their services to anyone who needed cheap labor. Many employers found it profitable to hire slaves directly at bargain rates without dealing with their masters. Slaves were so eager to work for their own benefit that many neglected their regular duties; some even ran away in order to work for themselves on a full-time basis. Clandestine hiring caused slaveholders such heavy losses that every colony had stringent laws against such practices. In 1711 New York City's Common Council tried to bring the problem under control by restricting slave-hiring to a single market house "whereby all persons may know where to hire slaves . . . and also masters discover when their slaves are so hired." The need to reenact the ordinance in 1731, and again in 1738, attests to the difficulty of preventing hiring abuses.

Hired slaves played such an important role in the working force that some employers would have been hard-pressed without them. Small farmers and artisans who were unable to use slaves economically on a full-time basis found the hiring system particularly suitable for their seasonal needs. Jonathan Dickinson of Philadelphia observed that so many masters made their slaves available for hire that the "tradesmen cannot fail of constant employment." There was a heavy demand for household slaves by persons who preferred to hire rather than purchase their domestic retainers. Cooks, coachmen, gardeners, and laundresses passed from employer to employer as easily and certainly less expensively than free workers. There was virtually no labor need that hired bondsmen did not fill. The system worked so well that even owners who had hired out their own slaves could usually hire replacements if the need unexpectedly arose.

Selection 7

An Account by an Early Quaker Abolitionist

John Woolman

The Society of Friends, whose members are generally known as Quakers, have been a small but highly distinctive element in American society ever since William Penn, a wealthy English member of the sect, used his influence at the court of Charles II (1660–1685) to found Pennsylvania as a refuge for these and other people who were being persecuted for their unorthodox religious ideas. Quaker beliefs included pacifism, a refusal to maintain a clergy, and a rejection of all religious dogma. Instead, their doctrine of the "inner light" stressed the capacity of all believers to be directly inspired by the Holy Spirit, and in their religious services, called meetings, it was their custom for all to remain silent until one or more felt called upon by the Holy Spirit to speak. Quaker communities tended to be earnest, moral, and close-knit. In their social lives, Quakers stressed personal humility, rejected all forms of personal ostentation, and encouraged hard work and thrift. All these qualities helped many Quakers to thrive in the parts of North America where they generally settled—chiefly Pennsylvania, adjacent parts of New Jersey and Maryland, and Rhode Island. By the mid–eighteenth century, some Quakers had grown quite rich and worldly, and not a few of them became slave owners or even slave traders.

John Woolman (1720–1772), a New Jersey–born Quaker, always lived an extremely modest life. Following an intense religious experience in his early twenties, he dedicated himself to the vocation of traveling (usually on foot) to visit far-flung Quaker communities and sharing his spiritual insights, supporting himself by working as a tailor. Eventually his missionary impulse led him to England, where he died.

Almost from the beginning of his career, Woolman's faith led him to condemn slavery. No human being, he believed, could be trusted with the power of ownership over another person. And the more he saw of slavery as he moved about the middle colonies, Maryland, and northern Virginia, the more convinced he became that the institution was not only sinful but fraught with abuses. His method of opposing slavery was to meet one-on-one with Quaker slave owners and persuade them to free their slaves or face damnation. Often he was successful. His journal, excerpted here, contains many refer-

Excerpted from John Woolman, *The Journal of John Woolman*, edited by Charles W. Eliot (New York: Collier, 1909).

ences to the sad conditions of slavery that he frequently encountered.

Thanks in significant part to Woolman's efforts, the Society of Friends was the first major religious group in America to take a stand against slavery. Numerous Quaker meetings insisted that their members either free their slaves or leave the Society. Quakers were in the forefront of successful efforts to abolish slavery in Pennsylvania after the American Revolution, and in the early nineteenth century members of the Society were among the first leaders of the abolitionist movement.

Scrupling to do writings relative to keeping slaves has been a means of sundry small trials to me, in which I have so evidently felt my own will set aside that I think it good to mention a few of them. Tradesmen and retailers of goods, who depend on their business for a living, are naturally inclined to keep the good-will of their customers; nor is it a pleasant thing for young men to be under any necessity to question the judgment or honesty of elderly men, and more especially of such as have a fair reputation. Deep-rooted customs, though wrong, are not easily altered; but it is the duty of all to be firm in that which they certainly know is right for them. A charitable, benevolent man, well acquainted with a negro, may, I believe, under some circumstances, keep him in his family as a servant, on no other motives than the negro's good; but man, as man, knows not what shall be after him, nor hath he any assurance that his children will attain to that perfection in wisdom and goodness necessary rightly to exercise such power; hence it is clear to me, that I ought not to be the scribe where wills are drawn in which some children are made ales masters over others during life.

About this time [1756] an ancient man of good esteem in the neighborhood came to my house to get his will written. He had young negroes, and I asked him privately how he purposed to dispose of them. He told me; I then said, "I cannot write thy will without breaking my own peace," and respectfully gave him my reasons for it. He signified that he had a choice that I should have written it, but as I could not, consistently with my conscience, he did not desire it, and so he got it written by some other person. A few years after, there being great alterations in his family, he came again to get me to write his will. His negroes were yet young, and his son, to whom he intended to give them, was, since he first spoke to me, from a libertine become a sober young man, and he supposed that I would have been free on that account to write it. We had much friendly talk on the subject, and then deferred it. A few days after he came again and directed their freedom, and I then wrote his will.

Near the time that the last-mentioned Friend first spoke to me, a neighbor received a bad bruise in his body and sent for me to bleed him, which having done, he desired me to write his will. I took notes, and amongst other things he told me to which of his children he gave his young negro. I considered the pain and distress he was in, and knew not how it would end, so I wrote his will, save only that part concerning his slave, and carrying it to his bedside read it to him. I then told him in a friendly way that I could not write any instruments by which my fellow-creatures were made slaves, without bringing trouble on my own mind. I let him know that I charged nothing for what I had done, and desired to be excused from doing the other part in the way he proposed. We then had a serious conference on the subject; at length, he agreeing to set her free, I finished his will.

Having found drawings in my mind to visit Friends on Long Island, after obtaining a certificate from our Monthly Meeting, I set off 12th of fifth month, 1756. When I reached the island, I lodged the first night at the house of my dear friend, Richard Hallett. The next day being the first of the week, I was at the meeting in New Town, in which we experienced the renewed manifestations of the love of Jesus Christ to the comfort of the honest-hearted. I went that night to Flushing, and the next day I and my beloved friend, Matthew Franklin, crossed the ferry at White Stone; were at three meetings on the main, and then returned to the island, where I spent the remainder of the week in visiting meetings. The Lord, I believe, hath a people in those parts who are honestly inclined to serve him; but many I fear, are too much clogged with the things of this life, and do not come forward bearing the cross in such faithfulness as he calls for.

My mind was deeply engaged in this visit, both in public and private, and at several places where I was, on observing that they had slaves, I found myself under a necessity, in a friendly way, to labor with them on that subject; expressing, as way opened, the inconsistency of that practice with the purity of the Christian religion, and the ill effects of it manifested amongst us. . . .

Ninth of fifth month [1757].—A Friend at whose house we breakfasted setting us a little on our way, I had conversation with him, in the fear of the Lord, concerning his slaves, in which my heart was tender; I used much plainness of speech with him, and he appeared to take it kindly. We pursued our journey without appointing meetings, being pressed in my mind to be at the Yearly Meeting in Virginia. In my travelling on the road, I often felt a cry rise from the centre of my mind, thus: "O Lord, I am a stranger on the earth, hide not thy face from me." On the 11th, we crossed the rivers Patowmack and Rapahannock, and lodged at Port Royal. On the way we had the company of a colonel of the militia, who appeared to be a thoughtful man. I took occasion to remark on the difference in general betwixt a people used to labor moderately for their living, training up their children in frugality and business, and those who live on the labor of slaves; the former, in my view, being the most happy life. He concurred in the remark, and mentioned the trouble arising from the untoward, slothful disposition of the negroes, adding that one of our laborers would do as much in a day as two of their slaves. I replied, that free men, whose minds were properly on their business, found a satisfaction in improving, cultivating, and providing for their families; but negroes, laboring to support others

who claim them as their property, and expecting nothing but slavery during life, had not the like inducement to be industrious.

After some further conversation I said, that men having power too often misapplied it; that though we made slaves of the negroes, and the Turks made slaves of the Christians, I believed that liberty was the natural right of all men equally. This he did not deny, but said the lives of the negroes were so wretched in their own country that many of them lived better here than there. I replied, "There is great odds in regard to us on what principle we act"; and so the conversation on that subject ended. I may here add that another person, some time afterwards, mentioned the wretchedness of the negroes, occasioned by their intestine wars, as an argument in favor of our fetching them away for slaves. To which I replied, if compassion for the Africans, on account of their domestic troubles, was the real motive of our purchasing them, that spirit of tenderness being attended to, would incite us to use them kindly that, as strangers brought out of affliction, their lives might be happy among us. And as they are human creatures, whose souls are as precious as ours, and who may receive the same help and comfort from the Holy Scriptures as we do, we could not omit suitable endeavors to instruct them therein; but that while we manifest by our conduct that our views in purchasing them are to advance ourselves, and while our buying captives taken in war animates those parties to push on the war, and increase desolation amongst them, to say they live unhappily in Africa is far from being an argument in our favor. I further said, the present circumstances of these provinces to me appear difficult; the slaves look like a burdensome stone to such as burden themselves with them; and that if the white people retain a resolution to prefer their outward prospects of gain to all other considerations, and do not act conscientiously toward them as fellow-creatures, I believe that burden will grow heavier and heavier, until times change in a way disagreeable to us. The person appeared very serious, and owned that in considering their condition and the manner of their treatment in these provinces he had sometimes thought it might be just in the Almighty so to order it.

Having travelled through Maryland, we came amongst Friends at Cedar Creek in Virginia, on the 12th; and the next day rode, in company with several of them, a day's journey to Camp Creek. As I was riding along in the morning, my mind was deeply affected in a sense I had of the need of Divine aid to support me in the various difficulties which attended me, and in uncommon distress of mind I cried in secret to the Most High, "O Lord be merciful, I beseech thee, to thy poor afflicted creature!" After some time, I felt inward relief, and, soon after, a Friend in company began to talk in support of the slave-trade, and said the negroes were understood to be the offspring of Cain, their blackness being the mark which God set upon him after he murdered Abel his brother; that it was the design of Providence they should be slaves, as a condition proper to the race of so wicked a man as Cain was. Then another spake in support of what had been said. To all which I replied in substance as follows: that Noah and his family were all who survived the flood, according to Scripture; and as Noah was of Seth's race, the family of Cain was wholly destroyed. One of them said that after the flood Ham went to the land of Nod and took a wife; that Nod was a land far distant, inhabited by Cain's race, and that the flood did not reach it; and as Ham was sentenced to be a servant of servants to his brethren, these two families, being thus joined, were undoubtedly fit only for slaves. I replied, the flood was a judgment upon the world for their abominations, and it was granted that Cain's stock was the most wicked, and therefore unreasonable to suppose that they were spared. As to Ham's going to the land of Nod for a wife, no time being fixed, Nod might be inhabited by some of Noah's family before Ham married a second time; moreover the text saith "That all flesh died that moved upon the earth." (Gen. vii. 21.) I further reminded them how the prophets repeatedly declare "that the son shall not suffer for the iniquity of the father, but every one be answerable for his own sins." I was troubled to perceive the darkness of their imaginations, and in some pressure of spirit said,

> The love of ease and gain are the motives in general of keeping slaves, and men are wont to take hold of weak arguments to support a cause which is unreasonable. I have no interest on either side, save only the interest which I desire to have in the truth. I believe liberty is their right, and as I see they are not only deprived of it, but treated in other respects with inhumanity in many places, I believe He who is a refuge for the oppressed will, in his own time, plead their cause, and happy will it be for such as walk in uprightness before him.

And thus our conversation ended. . . .

The prospect of a way being open to the same degeneracy, in some parts of this newly settled land of America, in respect to our conduct towards the negroes, hath deeply bowed my mind in this journey, and though briefly to relate how these people are treated is no agreeable work yet, after often reading over the notes I made as I travelled, I find my mind engaged to preserve them. Many of the white people in those provinces take little or no care of negro marriages; and when negroes marry after their own way, some make so little account of those marriages that with views of outward interest they often part men from their wives by selling them far asunder, which is common when estates are sold by executors at vendue. Many whose labor is heavy being followed at their business in the field by a man with a whip, hired for that purpose, have in common little else allowed but one peck of Indian corn and some salt, for one week, with a few potatoes; the potatoes they commonly raise by their labor on the first day of the week. The correction ensuing on their disobedience to overseers, or slothfulness in business, is often very severe, and sometimes desperate.

Men and women have many times scarcely clothes sufficient to hide their nakedness, and boys and girls ten and twelve years old are often quite naked amongst their master's children. Some of our Society, and some of the society called Newlights, use some endeavors to instruct those they have in reading; but in common this is not only neglected, but disapproved. These are the people by whose labor the other inhabitants are in a great measure supported, and many of them in the luxuries of life. These are the people who have made no agreement to serve us, and who have not forfeited their liberty that we know of. These are the souls for whom Christ died, and for our conduct towards them we must answer before Him who is no respecter of persons. They who know the only true God, and Jesus Christ whom he hath sent, and are thus acquainted with the merciful, benevolent, gospel spirit, will therein perceive that the indignation of God is kindled against oppression and cruelty, and in beholding the great distress of so numerous a people will find cause for mourning.

From my lodgings I went to Burleigh Meeting, where I felt my mind drawn in a quiet, resigned state. After a long silence I felt an engagement to stand up, and through the powerful operation of Divine love we were favored with an edifying meeting. The next meeting we had was at BlackWater, and from thence went to the Yearly Meeting at the Western Branch. When business began, some queries were introduced by some of their members for consideration, and, if approved, they were to be answered hereafter by their respective Monthly Meetings. They were the Pennsylvania queries, which had been examined by a committee of Virginia Yearly Meeting appointed the last year, who made some alterations in them, one of which alterations was made in favor of a custom which troubled me. The query was, "Are there any concerned in the importation of negroes, or in buying them after imported?" which was thus altered, "Are there any concerned in the importation of negroes, or buying them to trade in?" As one query admitted with unanimity was, "Are any concerned in buying or vending goods unlawfully imported, or prize goods?" I found my mind engaged to say that as we profess the truth, and were there assembled to support the testimony of it, it was necessary for us to dwell deep and act in that wisdom which is pure, or otherwise we could not prosper. I then men-

tioned their alteration, and referring to the last-mentioned query, added, that as purchasing any merchandise taken by the sword was always allowed to be inconsistent with our principles, so negroes being captives of war, or taken by stealth, it was inconsistent with our testimony to buy them; and their being our fellow-creatures, and sold as slaves, added greatly to the iniquity. Friends appeared attentive to what was said; some expressed a care and concern about their negroes; none made any objection, by way of reply to what I said, but the query was admitted as they had altered it.

As some of their members have heretofore traded in negroes, as in other merchandise, this query being admitted will be one step further than they have hitherto gone, and I did not see it my duty to press for an alteration, but felt easy to leave it all to Him who alone is able to turn the hearts of the mighty, and make way for the spreading of truth on the earth, by means agreeable to his infinite wisdom. In regard to those they already had, I felt my mind engaged to labor with them, and said that as we believe the Scriptures were given forth by holy men, as they were moved by the Holy Ghost, and many of us know by experience that they are often helpful and comfortable, and believe ourselves bound in duty to teach our children to read them; I believed that if we were divested of all selfish views, the same good spirit that gave them forth would engage us to teach the negroes to read, that they might have the benefit of them. Some present manifested a concern to take more care in the education of their negroes.

Twenty-ninth fifth month.—At the house where I lodged was a meeting of ministers and elders. I found an engagement to speak freely and plainly to them concerning their slaves; mentioning how they as the first rank in the society, whose conduct in that case was much noticed by others, were under the stronger obligations to look carefully to themselves. Expressing how needful it was for them in that situation to be thoroughly divested of all selfish views; that, living in the pure truth, and acting conscientiously towards those people in their education and otherwise, they might be instrumental in helping forward a work so exceedingly necessary, and so much neglected amongst them. At the twelfth hour the meeting of worship began, which was a solid meeting.

The next day, about the tenth hour, Friends met to finish their business, and then the meeting for worship ensued, which to me was a laborious time; but through the goodness of the Lord, truth, I believed, gained some ground, and it was a strengthening opportunity to the honest-hearted. . . .

The Monthly Meeting of Philadelphia having been under a concern on account of some Friends who this summer (1758) had bought negro slaves, proposed to their Quarterly Meeting to have the minute reconsidered in the Yearly Meeting, which was made last on that subject, and the said Quarterly Meeting appointed a committee to consider it, and to report to their next. This committee having met once and adjourned, and I, going to Philadelphia to meet a committee of the Yearly Meeting, was in town the evening on which the Quarterly Meeting's committee met the second time, and finding an inclination to sit with them, I, with some others, was admitted, and Friends had a weighty conference on the subject. Soon after their next Quarterly meeting I heard that the case was coming to our Yearly Meeting. This brought a weighty exercise upon me, and under a sense of my own infirmities, and the great danger I felt of turning aside from perfect purity, my mind was often drawn to retire alone, and put up my prayers to the Lord that he would be graciously pleased to strengthen me; that setting aside all view's of self-interest and the friendship of this world, I might stand fully resigned to his holy will.

In this Yearly Meeting several weighty matters were considered, and toward the last that in relation to dealing with persons who purchase slaves. During the several sittings of the said meeting, my mind was frequently covered with inward prayer, and I could say with David, "that tears were my meat day and night." The case of slave-keeping lay heavy upon me, nor did I find any engagement to speak directly to any other matter before the meeting. Now when this case was opened several faithful Friends spake weightily thereto, with which I was comforted; and feeling a concern to cast in my mite, I said in substance as follows:—

> In the difficulties attending us in this life nothing is more precious than the mind of truth inwardly manifested; and it is my earnest desire that in this weighty matter we may be so truly humbled as to be favored with a clear understanding of the mind of truth, and follow it; this would be of more advantage to the Society than any medium not in the clearness of Divine wisdom. The case is difficult to some who have slaves, but if such set aside all self-interest, and come to be weaned from the desire of getting estates, or even from holding them together, when truth requires the contrary, I believe way will so open that they will know how to steer through those difficulties.

Many Friends appeared to be deeply bowed under the weight of the work, and manifested much firmness in their love to the cause of truth and universal righteousness on the earth. And though none did openly justify the practice of slave-keeping in general, yet some appeared concerned lest the meeting should go into such measures as might give uneasiness to many brethren, alleging that if Friends patiently continued under the exercise the Lord in his time might open a way for the deliverance of these people. Finding an engagement to speak, I said,

> My mind is often led to consider the purity of the Divine Being, and the justice of his judgments; and herein my soul is covered with awfulness. I cannot omit to hint of some cases where people have not been treated with the purity of justice, and the event hath been lamentable. Many slaves on this continent are oppressed, and their cries have reached the ears of the Most High. Such are the purity and certainty of his judgments, that he cannot be partial in our favor. In infinite love and goodness he hath opened our understanding from one time to another concerning our duty towards this people, and it is not a time for de-

lay. Should we now be sensible of what he requires of us, and through a respect to the private interest of some persons, or through a regard to some friendships which do not stand on an immutable foundation, neglect to do our duty in firmness and constancy, still waiting for some extraordinary means to bring about their deliverance. God may by terrible things in righteousness answer us in this matter.

Many faithful brethren labored with great firmness, and the love of truth in a good degree prevailed. Several who had negroes expressed their desire that a rule might be made to deal with such Friends as offenders who bought slaves in future. To this it was answered that the root of this evil would never be effectually struck at until a thorough search was made in the circumstances of such Friends as kept negroes, with respect to the righteousness of their motives in keeping them, that impartial justice might be administered throughout. Several Friends expressed their desire that a visit might be made to such Friends as kept slaves, and many others said that they believed liberty was the negro's right; to which, at length, no opposition was publicly made. A minute was made more full on that subject than any heretofore; and the names of several Friends entered who were free to join in a visit to such as kept slaves.

The Complete History of

Slavery, the Revolution, and the Constitution, 1760–1787

Chapter 4

Introduction

*C*hapter 4 begins the third phase of the history of American slavery. The most significant event that occurred during this phase began to unfold in June 1776 when the Second Continental Congress, deliberating in Philadelphia while the early battles of the American Revolution were raging, asked one of its youngest members, Virginia's Thomas Jefferson, to draft a statement telling the world why American patriots were declaring their country independent. "We hold these truths to be self-evident," Jefferson wrote, in ringing phrases that every American has come to cherish, "that all men are created equal; that they are endowed by their creator with certain inalienable rights; that among these are life, liberty, and the pursuit of happiness."

Formal adoption of the Declaration of Independence in July 1776 framed the issue even more dramatically. At that time, about 20 percent of the American population were slaves. How would the new nation live up to its founding principles with regard to them? Americans heard the gibes of foreigners such as that of England's man of letters Samuel Johnson, who asked how it could be that "the loudest *yelps* for liberty come from the drivers of Negroes," and they found it more difficult to justify the continued existence of slavery. In colonial times, almost no Americans had questioned slavery, regardless of whether they owned slaves themselves. From now until the Civil War, slavery was to be either attacked or defended; it could not be ignored.

In very concrete terms, in fact, Virginians were brought face-to-face with the implications of slavery even before independence was declared. On November 1, 1775, the colony's British governor, Lord Dunmore, challenged the foundations of Virginia society by promising freedom to any slave who left a rebellious master and enlisted under the king's banner. The move backfired: Very few slaves dared to act on his offer, and wavering planters almost unanimously rallied to the patriot camp, outraged that the British should be so dastardly as to threaten them with a "servile uprising." Even so, Dunmore had shown that there was a "slave card" to be played. The tactic was tried again in 1779 when the British army invaded the Deep South, and again most slaves reacted cautiously, rightly trusting neither the redcoats nor their own masters.

About five thousand blacks did enlist in the fight for American independence. Aside from the personal body servants of various patriot military leaders, the black troops were either northern free blacks or slaves serving with their masters' consent. More African Americans ended up serving on the British side, either as auxiliary troops or as laborers. Many of these "black Tories" were evacuated with the British army at the end of the war. The lucky ones were resettled in Canada or the West African colony of Sierra Leone (where their descendants still live) or were allowed to continue serving as colonial British troops in the West Indies. The unlucky ones found themselves sold back into slavery.

But the idea of emancipation was now in the air. During or immediately after the war, Pennsylvania and most of the New England states enacted laws that freed the slaves within their borders, usually within a specific number of years or as slaves reached a certain age. In New Hampshire, where no emancipation act was formally passed, slavery simply died out informally. New York and New Jersey, where slavery had been more deeply entrenched in colonial times, acted somewhat later, passing emancipation laws in 1799 and 1804, respectively. These state actions are directly traceable to the victorious revolutionaries' conviction that the principles they had espoused in fighting for liberty made it impossible to deny liberty to others. Slaves contributed directly to the campaign by petitioning the state legislatures—demanding (as bondspeople in Portsmouth, New Hampshire, put it) liberty "to dispose of our lives, freedom, and property."

No state south of Pennsylvania emancipated its slaves, but even here the spirit of liberty was stirring. Most southern states did pass laws making it easier for individual owners to manumit (free) their slaves voluntarily. In Maryland and Virginia, enough owners granted their slaves freedom to raise the proportion of free blacks to about 5 percent of all African Americans living in these states.

In the Deep South states of South Carolina and Georgia, slavery was both essential to the local economy and badly damaged by the war. Plantations and their laboriously constructed rice fields were in ruins; slave-labor forces were depleted by wartime flight and the British army's seizure of patriots' bondspeople as war booty. White leaders in these states adamantly insisted that they must rebuild the infrastructure of the plantation economy, including stocks of unfree laborers. There was no thought of emancipation. When representatives of these states came to the Constitutional Convention in 1787, they made it clear that the proposed federal union must offer no challenge to slavery; otherwise their states would not join. Slavery was a contentious issue at the convention, as certain northern representatives pointedly criticized human bondage as disgraceful and unproductive. But in the end, the framers of the Constitution compromised by granting the Deep South delegations almost everything they wanted.

The United States emerged from the Revolutionary era with slavery abolished in some states, criticized in others, and more deeply entrenched than ever in still other states. Several time bombs were buried in the new federal Constitution, including the "three-fifths clause," which gave slaveholding states partial representation for their slave inhabitants even though these bondspeople did not vote; a requirement that states "deliver up" slaves who fled into their jurisdiction; and the unanswered question of whether Congress might someday claim the power to abolish slavery. (Even before the Constitution was adopted, Congress under the Articles of Confederation had banned slavery forever from the Northwest Territory, encompassing all the lands north of the Ohio River.) Yet another time bomb also ticked beneath what the southern states would later call their "peculiar institution": the Declaration of Independence's statement that "all men are created equal" and entitled to "life, liberty, and the pursuit of happiness."

Selection 1

South Carolina Slaves During the Revolutionary War

Sylvia R. Frey

The American Revolution was the first civil war for the United States, pitting American Patriots who aimed at independence against American Loyalists who refused to reject British supreme authority—and who, of course, were supported by British military and naval forces. Like all civil wars, this was a bloody conflict, in many locales pitting neighbor against neighbor, even brother against brother. Stakes were high, atrocities were committed on both sides, justice was apt to be summary, and vengeance was exacted whenever possible.

In the South, where the civil war was especially bitter, slaves were pawns caught in the middle. Patriot (or "whig") planters constantly feared that the British would incite their slaves to desert or revolt. Sometimes, indeed, British military leaders like General Sir Henry Clinton tried to persuade slaves to turn against rebel Patriot masters; more often, they treated Patriots' slaves who fell into their hands as prizes of war, and either put

the slaves to work for the redcoats or gave them as rewards to Loyalist planters. What happened in Georgia and the Carolinas during the Revolutionary War foreshadowed what was to come in the American Civil War, when Union armies would have to deal with fleeing slaves ("contrabands") and would weigh the military advantages of emancipating rebels' human property.

Historian Sylvia R. Frey, who teaches at Tulane University, has studied how South Carolina slaves weighed their options and tried to survive while their masters fought it out under the Patriot and Loyalist banners. This excerpt is taken from her 1991 book, Water from the Rock: Black Resistance in a Revolutionary Age.

Before mounting the Southern campaign, General Clinton issued from his headquarters in Philipsburg, New York, the carefully worded proclamation of June 30, 1779. In it he warned that all blacks taken in rebel service by British armies would be sold for the benefit of their captors. Those who deserted the rebels for British service were, however, promised "full security to follow within these Lines, any Occupation which [they] shall think proper." Like Dunmore's proclamation before it and Lincoln's after, Clinton's Philipsburg proclamation embodied no moral or philosophical convictions. It was foremost a military measure whose stated purpose was to counteract the American "practice of enrolling Negroes Among their Troops." The tacit purpose was to weaken and demoralize southern rebels by depriving them of their labor force and of their resources; to accommodate Britain's perennial needs for pioneers and military laborers in North America and for recruits for service in the West Indies; and to cement their local alliances and to keep the loyalty of their troops by distributing captured slaves after military victories. Although it did not directly alter the legal status of slaves, even those belonging to rebels, the proclamation did raise the specter of emancipation. In so doing it inspirited instead of intimidated white rebels, embittered instead of demoralized them. The predatory conduct of the army condoned by the proclamation antagonized citizens and, in many cases, created prorebel sympathies. In South Carolina it prompted a successful insurgency that turned the state into a battle-

ground and plunged it into the most savage civil war fought in America during the Revolution. The marches and countermarches of the armies and the savage underwar that soon blazed out of control left South Carolina's once-rich plantations in ruins, the fields laid in waste, the livestock gone, and the system of labor nearly destroyed.

Slaveholders, who saw the Philipsburg proclamation as an attack on property and on the labor system of the South and an invitation to anarchy, were incensed rather than lulled by its equivocation. Blacks took every conceivable political posture in response to it, which demonstrates not that they were divided in their attitudes toward slavery but that they were pragmatic in their quest for freedom. The flight of white families following the surrender of Charleston left blacks alone on the plantations, without supervision or control for perhaps the first time in their lives. That situation presented them with an opportunity to make the hard decision to accept slavery or to resist. The choice for most was not clearcut. Lacking either the will or the means to realize their dreams, some remained apparently loyal. Some were probably dissuaded from ac-

Slaves unload rice barges in South Carolina. During the Revolutionary War,
South Carolina slaves were caught between battling Patriots and Loyalists.

tion by the recollection of the fate of earlier protest movements. Many had family; some owned property. Like most whites, they took a wait-and-see attitude. In many, perhaps in most, cases their inactivity was a form of passive resistance.

Although the case is by no means typical, of the two hundred slaves owned by whig General William Moultrie "not one of them left me during the war," Moultrie proudly boasted, "although they had had great offers, nay, some were carried down to work on the British lines, yet they always contrived to make their escapes and return home." When after being exchanged as a prisoner of war Moultrie returned to his plantation for a brief visit, he was greeted by his slaves singing an African war song, "welcome the war home." Some slaves, like those belonging to the Reverend Archibald Simpson, pastor of the Independent Presbyterian church of Stoney Creek, apparently shared their master's distrust of the British. When Simpson returned home at the end of the war, he found his slaves at work in the woods. "They saw me," Simpson recalled in his journal, "and ran with transports of joy, holding me by the knees as I sat on horseback, and directly ran off to the plantation to give notice to Mr. Lambert." Like Moultrie's slaves, they had refused a British invitation to follow the army: "They asked me if I was going to leave them when they had stayed on the plantation when the British wanted them to go away," Simpson continued, and they "abused the two who had left me and gone with Colonel Moncrieff."

Left to their own devices, slaves on many plantations conceivably ceased to be slaves. When a British army commanded by General Prevost overran most of the coastal area between Savannah and Charleston in the spring of 1779, the troops and their Indian allies raided coastal plantations and some further inland, including one belonging to Thomas Pinckney. In his account of the raid, Pinckney told how the British "took" nineteen of his slaves, leaving only "the sick women, and the young children, and about five fellows who are now perfectly free and live on the best produce of the plantation." After the British departed for Georgia, Pinckney's over-

seer, who had been hiding in the swamps, returned to the plantation. "I hope," Pinckney fretted, "he will be able to keep the remaining property in some order, though the Negroes pay no attention to his orders." Fewer than half of the slaves of Wadboo Barony, the ancestral home of Sir John Colleton, one of the original proprietors of South Carolina, remained on the plantation, and in the breakdown of authority that followed the surrender of Charleston, they acknowledged "no subjection to the Overseers."

The conditions of war made it increasingly difficult for most slaves to decide to leave the plantations. According to William Richardson Davie, the cavalry commander who served as commissary general under Nathanael Greene, as they swept through the state, "the troops of both armies took what they wanted without ceremony or accountability and used it without measure or economy." Tory and British forces and later some whig militia brigades were thorough and even wanton in their destruction. Anthony Allaire, a twenty-five-year-old loyalist officer who served with the tory forces that captured Charleston, boasted that the army foraged "by destroying furniture, breaking windows, etc., taking all their [rebel] horned cattle, horses, mules, sheep, fowls, etc. and their negroes to drive them.". . .

The surpassing cruelty that was the hallmark of the war in South Carolina constituted a compelling reason why many slaves viewed the British offer of freedom with caution. Severe punishment, and often death, was a virtual certainty for an unsuccessful escape. A case in point was the capture by whig forces of four men, two of them white, one a mulatto, and the fourth a black, all suspected of deserting to the enemy. Governor John Rutledge, happening by at the time, was asked what should be done with the alleged fugitives. Rutledge's reply was to "Hang them up to the beam of the gate" by which they were standing. The governor's orders were promptly carried out and the four hung there all day, a gruesome reminder of the chilling brutality of war. Their choices seemingly limited to the relative security of the slave or freedom in the grave, thousands of slaves stayed on the farms and plantations. These were not, as they were later made out to be, necessarily loyal slaves. Rather they were, like thousands of whites, neutral; neutrality for them was a survival mechanism. Under the circumstances, the refusal of many slaves to join the British might also be seen as a form of resistance to exploitation. Inspired by the well-established colonial tradition of freedom in return for military service, a small minority of slaves decided to throw in their lot with the Revolution and served alongside their owners.

For the vast majority of slaves who actively participated in the Revolution, the arrival of the British army was a liberating moment. Although Clinton's Philipsburg proclamation was but a pale likeness of the sweeping measure it was later made out to be, thousands of South Carolina's slaves chose to interpret his offer of freedom to "enemy Negroes" as a general emancipation. Presuming themselves to be "Absolved from all respect to their American masters, and entirely released from servitude" by it, men, women and children streamed to British lines, usually fleeing alone or in pairs. Despite the greater risks of detection, some runaways traveled in groups made up of family members or friends from the same plantation, which suggests both the significance of community bonds and kinship ties and the depth of commitment to the dream of freedom. . . .

Young and old, male and female, skilled and unskilled, creole and African, alone and in groups, they streamed in like a tidal flood, their sheer numbers overwhelming the army. Although Clinton had tried to limit the effects of the Philipsburg proclamation, the magnitude of the slave response to it threatened to transcend the proclamation's carefully constructed confines and to become a mass resistance movement in which African-American resentments and aspirations could become overtly expressed in more militant form. The British response to the massive self-liberation movement was shaped by conflicting pressures and ambitions: the urge to exploit slave labor for military purposes, and the virtual impossibility of subsisting the numbers of deserters,

which was, in any event, far in excess of what the army could profitably use as military laborers or train and discipline as soldiers; the urge to deprive the enemy of its most vital resource without precipitating violent and radical changes in the economic and social structures; the urge, in short, to stabilize and upset the delicate balance of southern society for British political and military advantage. Operating in the dynamic context of war, those conflicting pressures and ambitions produced an anomalous situation and in the end, an ambiguous compromise. . . .

It was, however, the disruption of the plantation system caused by the war and by the unprecedented number of slave desertions to the British that proved most vexing to the political and military plans of civil and military authorities. To prevent the collapse of the labor system and to reassure at the same time white loyal slaveholders that the Philipsburg proclamation did not constitute a general attack on property rights, the military command quickly approved a plan proposed by the Board of Police for the immediate restoration of all slaves belonging to loyalists and to slaveholders who agreed to take the oath of allegiance, on condition only that the latter compensate the army for their maintenance at the rate of one shilling sterling per day. Three prominent loyalists, William Carson, Robert Ballingall, and Thomas Inglis, were appointed commissioners of claims to supervise the delivery of runaways to claimants able to certify ownership. Early in June the commissioners called upon the various departments of the army to hand into their custody all slaves fitting the above description in anticipation of returning them to those masters "who by a public avowal of their Loyalty and Attachment to His Majesty's Government have a Right to them."

The efforts of the British army to maintain the plantocracy and the slave system were only partially inspired by political considerations. The army also looked upon slaves as a labor reservoir to satisfy its chronic need for military and agricultural laborers and to satiate its appetite for booty. Army slave policy as expressed in the Philipsburg proclamation had distinguished between slaves who fled to British protection and those taken captive during military operations or on rebel plantations. The former were accepted for military service. Although nominally free once they entered British lines, the majority of blacks enrolled in the army usually served in a variety of noncombatant but vital supporting roles. Because slaves ordinarily had no training in European military skills and were, moreover, neither acquired nor trained for regular service by the British army, they were often assigned duties that allowed them to use the civilian skills they already possessed.

Both men and women served in all of the civil departments of the army. Next to engineering the Royal Artillery was the largest employer of blacks. Artificers—carpenters, wheelers, smiths, sawyers, and collar makers—repaired and built wagons, mended equipment and arms, made platforms and attended to numerous other tasks associated with the artillery. Men and women made musket cartridges for ordnance. The quartermaster and barrackmaster departments employed hundreds of black artificers and laborers in constructing barracks and in building and repairing boats and wagons. Commissaries used black workers to butcher livestock and to pickle, barrel, and store meat for the use of the troops. The hospital department also used black men and women in a variety of capacities. Men served as orderlies, women as nurses in hospitals. The hospital frames were made in England and were then fitted and assembled by black carpenters for use as temporary hospitals in America.

Black pioneers, attached either to individual regiments or organized as autonomous units under white officers, performed an assortment of garrison duties, thereby freeing white troops for field service. Paid at the rate of six pence a day, they served as guides or baggage carriers. They assisted the artificers in building and repairing bridges. They cleared the roads of stones or fallen trees, and they cleaned up the encampments. They did the heavy work of loading and hauling. When not employed on other service, they made fascines and carried out countless other noncombatant duties. Scores of blacks were employed as officers' servants. Army regulations allowed field officers of the infantry two blacks, subalterns and staff, one. The regulations were routinely ignored, however, and even common soldiers occasionally had black servants.

In keeping with ancient military practice, the army regarded slaves who were taken captive in war as prizes of war, title to which it claimed "as to any other acquisition or article of prize." Reduced to practice this meant that captured slaves could be sold, hired out, or employed for the benefit of their captors. In the months before the surrender of Charleston, the British army in South Carolina collected vast quantities of goods, principally indigo and livestock, and several thousand slaves from deserted estates. The British navy, in the meantime, confiscated ships and their cargoes, plus large amounts of cordage and gunpowder. Following the practice common among preindustrial empires, Clinton promised that the proceeds of victory would be distributed among the men who had served on the expedition. Indifferent to the moral side of slavery, he had originally planned to treat all captured slaves as booty. Political expediency forced him instead to remand those belonging to loyalists. The rest were treated as contraband of war. Whether they were sold with the other spoils of war is subject for debate. David Ramsay, the South Carolina historian of the Revolution, claimed that over two thousand "plundered Negroes" were shipped off at a single embarkation. Although it does not constitute proof, Clinton's memorandum to the commandant of Charleston seems to corroborate the substance of Ramsay's charge. In his instructions concerning the disposition of slaves, Clinton ordered

> That of the Negroes who shall go with the Army to the Northward (except such as described in my orders, and those who have been brought away without their own consent) those belonging to Friends and persons under protection of Government shall be hired as was done at Savannah and in case of death paid for. . . .

The organization of slave labor by the British army helped to defuse the potential for rebellion by drawing into the army the most courageous slaves, who had the greatest potential for revolutionary leadership and employing them at noncombatant duties. The condition of their lives once in the army further militated against a slave uprising. Although British slave policy was rooted in a clear belief in the racial inferiority of blacks, army treatment of them was restrained somewhat by conventional British morality and by the personal standards of decency of some of the officers. The well-being of army blacks was, however, frankly subordinate to purely military needs. Reasoning that military expediency justified it, the army maintained strict racial distinctions between black and white soldiers. Black soldiers were quartered in separate encampments and given inferior food. When supplies ran short, their rations were the first to be cut. Whereas many white owners recognized the potential hazards of overexertion and exposure and eased their slaves' tasks at certain times of the year, the British army, driven by the dangers and necessities of war, made excessive demands of its military laborers. Overworked and undernourished, they fell easy prey to disease, for which the army provided no effective protection or cure. . . .

The final irony, perhaps, is that when the imperatives of war seemed to require it, the army openly abandoned its pose as liberator by selling some of its captives and using the proceeds to buy supplies for the army. When recommending the sale of some of the blacks captured at Camden, Colonel Balfour stressed to Cornwallis the practical advantages: "Will it not be worthwhile," he reasoned, "to convince *Blacke* that he must not fight against us—to sell them and buy shoes for your corps?" It is clear from his instructions to Lieutenant Colonel Charles Grey, a provincial officer in Colonel William Henry Mills's company, to "sell a Negro to help provide for yourself," that Cornwallis felt no moral compunction about the practice.

By resorting to the burning of houses and the confiscation of crops and slaves belonging to the disaffected, Cornwallis had hoped to pacify the country. Instead, he created havoc, leaving a wide swath of bitter enemies and disappointed friends, black and white alike. Far from being intimidated, many of the disaffected were reinspirited. Paul Trapier, who sustained losses totalling almost £5,000, including crops, livestock, plantations, and fifteen slaves whose value he estimated at over £1,000, became actively rebellious and served as captain of the artillery company at Georgetown. When John Postell protested the loss of some of his slaves to the British at Camden, he was told that "my property was in the hands of such as were friends to government, who had the best right to them." When in mid-October Tarleton's dragoons returned to Postell's plantation and "invited all my negroes to come to Camden, promising them rewards if they would and that I would never get them again," Postell broke his parole and joined Marion's brigade. . . .

Half-starved and half-naked, slaves on the devastated plantations had also to live with the constant fear of abduction by a roving partisan band or by one of the belligerents. Throughout the war, slaves were stolen back and forth by both sides. Beginning in 1781, Sumter and Pickens systematized plundering operations as part of the pay and recruitment procedure of the whig militia. Under "Sumter's Law," slaves and goods seized from backcountry farms and plantations were used to attract recruits and to pay officers and men. For ten months of service, each lieutenant colonel was promised three grown slaves and one small one; each major, three adult slaves, and so on, diminishing by rank so that each private received one adult slave. To form a body of state cavalry, Sumter seized some four hundred slaves from loyalist estates along the Congaree River; similar seizures were made in Sumter's name along the Black River. By such methods Sumter alone raised eleven hundred men, a substantial number of whom were from as far away as Virginia and North Carolina. In lieu of payment, two-thirds of all of the goods taken from tories were divided among the officers and men raised by Sumter's system. Although some whig partisans, among them Francis Marion, declined to use "Sumter's Law," countless slaves on low-country plantations shared a similar fate. . . .

During the final bitter months of British occupation, General Alexander Leslie broke away from the conventions of warfare and began forming black troops. The first reports that several black companies were being raised began circulating soon after Leslie's arrival in Charleston. By the spring of 1782 some seven hundred black soldiers were reportedly under arms. There is no evidence that they fought in an organized fashion, but sometimes battle came to them. On April 21 a Captain Neil of the Partisan Legion reported falling in "with one of ye British negro Captains and his Troop." Charged by the patriots, the black troops broke and fled, which suggests perhaps that they were outnumbered or that they had not undergone much training. In the last engagement between the partisan leader Francis Marion and a British force, known as "the affair at Wadboo," Marion's force was attacked by a hundred British horse and "some Coloured Dragoons" led by Major Thomas Fraser. When the rapidly charging horse approached within thirty yards, Marion's force opened fire and the British troop retreated. Armed blacks also did battle in less important contests, such as Fort Dreadnought near Augusta. Among the prisoners taken when the fort capitulated in May 1781, were sixty-one slaves, "principally armed," according to one patriot report.

During the last six months of British occupation, Leslie's Black Dragoons terrorized the inhabitants of the Goose Creek area north of Charleston by "daily committing the most horrible depredations and murders on the defenceless parts of our Country." Although few in numbers, their nightly raids through Goose Creek and down the Cooper River haunted the imagination of whites. Despite the efforts of state authorities to track them down, the black soldiers managed to maintain an "infamous traffic" in livestock, which kept the British markets at Charleston "daily supplied with the greatest plenty of everything they want." From the patriot point of view, the knowledge that hundreds of self-liberated slaves were in possession of weapons was, as General Sumter put it, "sufficient to rouse and fix the resentment and detestation of every American who possesses common feelings." Belatedly, the British army came to a different conclusion.

Impressed by the conduct of his black dragoons in South Carolina, General Leslie formed them into autonomous units for service in Florida and the West Indies, where Leslie observed "their past services will engage the grateful attention of Government to which they will continue to be useful." Their experience with black troops in the American Revolution also convinced other officers that the best solution to British military problems in the West Indies was to enlist slaves by offering them freedom in exchange for military service. As military governor of Jamaica, Archibald Campbell sent recruiters to Charleston shortly before the evacuation to raise a battalion from among free blacks and "people of color" to aid regular troops in the defense of Jamaica. General John Vaughan also advocated the addition of black regiments to the regular British army for service in Saint Domingue during the French Revolution and Napoleonic Wars. Ultimately black troops such as these became part of the standing professional slave army upon which Britain relied increasingly after 1790 for support of its military establishment in the West Indies.

Selection 2

Slavery at the Constitutional Convention

James Madison

Extraordinary political talent was assembled in Philadelphia during the long, hot summer of 1787, at which a federal constitution was drafted to replace the weak and cumbersome union of states under the Articles of Confederation. The meetings were held in strict secrecy (for example, the windows of Independence Hall were nailed shut to prevent people outside from hearing what was being debated inside). The convention drew up a plan for a relatively centralized and much invigorated government that went far beyond the series of modest amendments to the Articles that the group had been mandated to produce. One state, Rhode Island, was so opposed to changing the Articles that it refused to send representatives to Philadelphia. Other state delegations were badly split during the contentious deliberations. And when the new Constitution was announced and put to a state-by-state vote, opposition was so strong that in several key states the new system of government was accepted by only the slimmest of margins— sometimes with the help of unscrupulous political maneuvering. In short, the federal Consti-

tution that Americans today revere almost failed to be written and then came close to being rejected.

Even though the men in Independence Hall basically shared a common political viewpoint—most wanted to put loyalty to the United States above loyalty to their states, most wanted a strong central government with a vigorous executive, and none wanted to give too much power to ordinary citizens— drafting the Constitution and getting it through the convention required many compromises. Some of the most basic, and fateful, compromises involved slavery. In the northern and middle colonies, public sentiment was running strongly enough against slavery for serious steps toward emancipation to have either been already taken or to be under way. In Virginia and Maryland, influential men including Thomas Jefferson believed that slavery was a disgrace and a threat to public order (for slaves might one day rebel), and they hoped that somehow slavery could be eliminated. But in the Carolinas and Georgia, the white upper class knew that the plantation economy had been badly damaged by the war and felt that only a rapid reinvestment in slaves could save their region from disaster—and they refused even to discuss emancipating their bondsmen

Excerpted from *Notes of Debates of the Federal Convention of 1787*, reported by James Madison, with an introduction by Adrienne Koch (Ohio University Press, 1985). Reprinted with permission of Ohio University Press, Athens, Ohio.

or curtailing the trans-Atlantic slave trade. Moreover, there was the question of runaway slaves: Would the new federal government permit masters to recover fugitives who escaped across state lines?

James Madison, the young Virginian who is often (and rightly) called "the father of the Constitution" on account of his intellectual leadership of the Philadelphia Convention, recorded the debates in a journal that was not published for more than a generation. On a number of occasions he took note of extended discussions of the problem of slavery. Members like Pennsylvania's Gouverneur Morris and Virginia's George Mason expressed a profound dislike of slavery, but representatives from South Carolina such as Charles Pinckney, his cousin Charles Cotesworth Pinckney, and John Rutledge countered by making it clear that if any antislavery provisions were written into the Constitution, the states of the Deep South would simply refuse to join the Union.

To placate slaveholding interests such as these, it was agreed that for purposes of representation each slave would be counted as three-fifths of a free person—a provision that gave the slaveholding states disproportionate political power. Slaveholders were also promised that Congress would not interfere with the trans-Atlantic slave trade for at least twenty years and that runaway slaves would be returned even if they fled to a free state. To spare everyone embarrassment, the ugly word slave *was never even mentioned.*

"Great as the evil [that is, slavery] is," wrote James Madison, "dismemberment of the union would be worse." Fifty years later, in the 1830s, abolitionist William Lloyd Garrison would publicly burn the Constitution as a "compact with hell" because it made these compromises with slavery. Reading these extracts from Madison's journal, and having the benefit of historical hindsight (including knowledge that a civil war would be fought between slaveholding and free states), raises the question of whether

the men in Philadelphia were justified in compromising with slavery. Some historians argue that the United States would have been better off not to have included states that were prepared to fight in order to maintain slavery.

*a*ugust 8, 1787:
Mr. Gouverneur MORRIS [of Pennsylvania] moved to insert "free" before the word inhabitants. Much, he said, would depend on this point. He never would concur in upholding domestic slavery. It was a nefarious institution. Compare the free regions of the middle states, where a rich and noble cultivation marks the prosperity and happiness of the people, with the misery and poverty which overspread the barren wastes of Virginia, Maryland, and the other states having slaves. Travel through the whole continent and you behold the prospect continually varying with the appearance and disappearance of slavery. The moment you leave the eastern states [New England] and enter New York, the effects of the institution become visible, passing through the Jerseys and entering Pennsylvania every criterion of superior improvement witnesses the change. Proceed southwardly and every step you take through the great region of slaves presents a desert increasing, with the increasing proportion of these wretched beings. Upon what principle is it that the slaves shall be computed in the representation? Are they men? Then make them citizens and let them vote. Are they property? Why then is no other property included? The houses in this city [Philadelphia] are worth more than all the wretched slaves which cover the rice swamps of South Carolina. The admission of slaves into the representation when fairly explained comes to this: that the inhabitant of Georgia and South Carolina who goes to the coast of Africa, and in defiance of the most sacred laws of humanity tears away his fellow creatures from their dearest connections and damns them to the most cruel bondages, shall have more votes in a government instituted for protection of the rights of mankind, than the citizen of Pennsylvania or

New Jersey who views with a laudable horror so nefarious a practice. He would add that domestic slavery is the most prominent feature in the aristocratic countenance of the proposed constitution. The vassalage of the poor has ever been the favorite offspring of aristocracy. And what is the proposed compensation to the northern states for a sacrifice of every principle of right, of every impulse of humanity[?] They are to bind themselves to march their militia for the defense of the southern states; for their defense against those very slaves of whom they complain. They must supply vessels and seamen in case of foreign attack. The legislature will have indefinite power to tax them by excises and duties on imports; both of which will fall heavier on them than on the southern inhabitants; for the [imported] tea used by a northern freeman will pay more tax than the whole consumption of the miserable slave, which consists of nothing more than his physical subsistence and the rag that covers his nakedness. On the other side the southern states are not to be restrained from importing fresh supplies of wretched Africans, at once to increase the danger of attack and the difficulty of defense; nay, they are to be encouraged to it by an assurance of having their votes in the national government increased in proportion, and are at the same time to have their exports and their slaves exempt from all contributions for the public service. Let it not be said that direct taxation is to be proportioned to representation. It is idle to suppose that the general [i.e., federal] government can stretch its hand directly into the pockets of the people scattered over so vast a county. They [i.e., the federal government] can do it only through the medium of exports, imports, and excises. For what then are all these sacrifices to be made? He [Morris] would sooner submit himself to a tax for paying for all the Negroes in the United States, than saddle posterity with such a Constitution.

. . . [The motion was seconded by Jonathan Dayton of New Jersey.]

Mr. [Roger] SHERMAN [of Connecticut], did not regard the admission of the Negroes into the ratio of representation as liable to such insu-perable objections. It was the freemen of the southern states who were in fact to be represented according to the taxes paid by them, and the Negroes are only included in the estimate of the taxes. This was his idea of the matter.

Mr. [Charles Cotesworth] PINCKNEY [of South Carolina], considered the fisheries and the western frontier as more burdensome to the U.S. than the slaves. He thought this could be demonstrated if the occasion were a proper one.

Mr. [James] WILSON [of Pennsylvania] thought the motion premature. An agreement to the clause would be no bar to the object of it.

Question on the motion to insert "free" before "inhabitants." New Hampshire no. Massachusetts no. Connecticut no. New Jersey aye. Pennsylvania no. Delaware no. Maryland no. Virginia no. North Carolina no. South Carolina no. Georgia no. . . .

August 21, 1787

[Debate over Congress's power to regulate imports, including slaves, and possibly to ban the slave trade.]

Mr. L[uther] MARTIN [of Maryland] proposed to vary the section 4, Article VII* so as to allow a prohibition or tax on the importation of slaves. In the first place, as five slaves are to be counted as 3 free men in the apportionment of Representatives: such a clause would leave an encouragement to this traffic. In the second place, slaves weakened one part of the Union which the other parts were bound to protect: the privilege of importing them was therefore unreasonable. And in the third place, it was inconsistent with the principles of the revolution and dishonorable to the American character to have such a feature in the Constitution.

Mr. [John] RUTLEDGE [of South Carolina] did not see how the importation of slaves could be encouraged by this Section. He was not apprehensive of insurrections and would readily exempt the other States from the obligation to protect the Southern against them. Religion and

* Numbered according to the draft document that members of the convention were debating. In the Constitution as it was finally adopted (and as it exists today), this corresponds to Article I, sections 8 and 9.

humanity had nothing to do with this question. Interest alone is the governing principle with nations. The true question at present is whether the southern states shall or shall not be parties to the Union. If the northern states consult their interest, they will not oppose the increase of slaves, which will increase the commodities of which they will become the carriers.

Mr. [Oliver] ELLSWORTH [of Connecticut] was for leaving the clause as it stands. Let every state import what it pleases. The morality or wisdom of slavery are considerations belonging to the states themselves. What enriches a part enriches the whole, and the states are the best judges of their particular interest. The old confederation [the Articles of Confederation] had not meddled with this point, and he did not see any greater necessity for bringing it within the policy of the new one.

Mr. [Charles] PINCKNEY. South Carolina can never receive the plan if it prohibits the slave trade. In every proposed extension of the powers of the Congress, that state has expressly and watchfully excepted that of meddling with the importation of Negroes. If the states be all left at liberty on this subject, South Carolina may perhaps by degrees do of herself what is wished [that is, abolish the slave trade], as Virginia and Maryland have already done.

August 22, 1787

[The previous day's debate continued.]

[Draft] Article VII, section 4 resumed. Mr. SHERMAN was for leaving the clause as it stands. He disapproved of the slave trade; yet as the states were now possessed of the right to import slaves, as the public good did not require it to be taken from them, and as it was expedient to have as few objections as possible to the proposed scheme of government, he thought it best to leave the matter as we find it. He observed that the abolition of slavery seemed to be going on in the U.S. and that the good sense of the several states would probably by degrees complete it. He urged on the convention the necessity of dispatching its business.

Col. [George] MASON [of Virginia]. This infernal traffic originated in the avarice of British merchants. The British government constantly checked the attempts of Virginia to put a stop to it. The present question concerns not the importing states alone but the whole union. The evil of having slaves was experienced during the late war. Had slaves been treated as they might have been by the enemy, they would have proved dangerous instruments in their hands. But their folly dealt by the slaves, as it did by the Tories. He mentioned the dangerous insurrections of the slaves in [ancient] Greece and Sicily; and the instructions given by Cromwell to the commissioners sent to Virginia [in the 1650s], to arm the servants and slaves in case other means of obtaining its [Virginia's] submission should fail. Maryland and Virginia, he said, had already prohibited the importation of slaves expressly. North Carolina had done the same in substance. All this would be in vain if South Carolina and Georgia be at liberty to import. The western people are already calling out for slaves for their new lands, and will fill that country with slaves if they can be got through South Carolina and Georgia. Slavery discourages arts and manufactures. The poor despise labor when performed by slaves. They prevent the immigration of whites, who really enrich and strengthen a country. They produce the most pernicious effect on manners. Every master of slaves is born a petty tyrant. They bring the judgment of heaven on a country. As nations cannot be rewarded or punished in the next world they must be in this. By an inevitable chain of causes and effects providence punishes national sins by national calamities. He lamented that some of our eastern [i.e., New England] brethren had from a lust of gain embarked in this nefarious traffic. As to the states being in possession of the right to import, this was the case with many other rights, now to be properly given up. He held it essential in every point of view that the general [that is, the federal] government should have power to prevent the increase of slavery.

Mr. [Oliver] ELLSWORTH [of Connecticut]. As he had never owned a slave [he] could not judge of the effects of slavery on character. He said however that if it was to be considered in a

George Washington (standing, right) presides over the Constitutional Convention of 1787. The convention delegates debated whether slavery should be allowed in the Union and, if so, under what circumstances.

moral light we ought to go farther and free those already in the country. As slaves also multiply so fast in Virginia and Maryland that it is cheaper to raise than import them, whilst in the sickly rice swamps foreign supplies are necessary, if we go no farther than is urged, we shall be unjust towards South Carolina and Georgia. Let us not intermeddle. As population increases, poor laborers will be so plenty as to render slaves useless. Slavery in time will not be a speck in our country. Provision is already made in Connecticut for abolishing it. And the abolition has already taken place in Massachusetts. As to the danger of insurrections from foreign influence, that will become a motive to kind treatment of the slaves.

Mr. [Charles] PINCKNEY. If slavery be wrong, it is justified by the example of all the world. He cited the case of Greece and Rome and other ancient states; the sanction given by France, England, Holland, and other modern states. In all ages one half of mankind have been slaves. If the southern states were let alone they will probably of themselves stop importations. He would himself as a citizen of South Carolina vote for it. An attempt to take away the right as proposed will produce serious objections to the constitution which he wished to see adopted.

General [Charles Coatesworth] PINCKNEY declared it to be his firm opinion that if himself and all his colleagues were to sign the constitution and use their personal influence, it would be of no avail towards obtaining the assent of their constituents. South Carolina and Georgia cannot do without slaves. As to Virginia, she will gain by stopping the importations. Her slaves will rise in value, and she has more than she wants. It would be unequal to require South Carolina and Georgia to confederate [i.e., join the Union] on such unequal terms. He said the royal assent [that is, veto power] before the Revolution had never been refused to South Carolina as to Virginia. He contended that the importation of slaves would be for the interest of the whole union. The more slaves, the more produce to employ the carrying trade; the more consumption also, and the more of this, the more of revenue for the common treasury. He admitted it to be reasonable that slaves should be [subject to] duties like other imports, but should consider a rejection of the clause as an exclusion of South Carolina from the Union.

Mr. [Abraham] BALDWIN [of Georgia] had conceived national objects alone to be before the convention, not such as like the present were of a local nature. Georgia was decided on this point. That state has always hitherto supposed a general [that is, federal] government to be the pursuit of the central states who wished to have a vortex for every thing—that her distance would preclude her from equal advantage—and that she could not prudently purchase it by yielding national powers. From this it might be understood in what light she would view an attempt to abridge one of her favorite prerogatives. If left to herself, she may probably put a stop to the evil. As one ground for this conjecture, he took notice of the sect of [blank], which he said was a respectable class of people, who carried their ethics beyond the mere *equality of men*, extending their humanity to the claims of the whole animal creation.

Mr. WILSON observed that if South Carolina and Georgia were themselves disposed to get rid of the importation of slaves in a short time as had been suggested, they would never refuse to unite because the importation might be abolished. As the section now stands, all articles imported are to be taxed. Slaves alone are exempt. This is in fact a bounty on that article.

Mr. [Elbridge] GERRY [of Massachusetts] thought we had nothing to do with the conduct of the states as to slaves, but ought to be careful not to give any sanction to it.

Mr. [John] DICKINSON [of Delaware] considered it as inadmissible on every principle of honor and safety that the importation of slaves should be authorized to the states by the Constitution. The true question was whether the na-

tional happiness would be promoted or impeded by the importation, and this question ought to be left to the national government, not to the states particularly interested. If England and France permit slavery, slaves are at the same time excluded from both these kingdoms. Greece and Rome were made unhappy by their slaves. He could not believe that the southern states would refuse to confederate on the account apprehended; especially as the power was not likely to be immediately exercised by the general [that is, federal] government.

Mr. [Hugh] WILLIAMSON [of North Carolina] stated the law of North Carolina on the subject, to wit that it did not directly prohibit the importation of slaves. It imposed a duty of £5 on each slave imported from Africa, £10 on each from elsewhere, and £50 on each from a state licensing manumission. He thought the southern states could not be members of the Union if the clause should be rejected, and that it was wrong to force any thing down, not absolutely necessary, and which any state must disagree to.

Mr. [Rufus] KING [of Massachusetts] thought the subject should be considered in a political light only. If two states will not agree to the Constitution as stated on one side, he could affirm with equal belief on the other, that great and equal opposition would be experienced from the other states. He remarked on the exemption of slaves from duty whilst every other import was subjected to it, as an inequality that could not fail to strike the commercial sagacity of the northern and middle states.

Mr. [John] LANGDON [of New Hampshire] was strenuous for giving the power to the general [that is, federal] government. He could not with a good conscience leave it with the states who could then go on with the traffic [i.e., the slave trade], without being restrained by the opinions here given that they will themselves cease to import slaves.

General [Charles Coatesworth] PINCKNEY thought himself bound to declare candidly that he did not think South Carolina would stop her importations of slaves in any short time, but only stop them occasionally as she now does.

He moved to commit the clause that slaves might be made liable to an equal tax with other imports which he thought right and which would remove one difficulty that had been started.

Mr. [John] RUTLEDGE [of South Carolina]. If the convention thinks that North Carolina, South Carolina, and Georgia will ever agree to the plan, unless their right to import slaves be untouched, the expectation is vain. The people of those states will never be such fools as to give up so important an interest. He was strenuous against striking out the section, and seconded the motion of General Pinkney for a commitment [that is, for adoption of the section as drafted].

Mr. Gouverneur MORRIS wished the whole subject to be committed [adopted] including the clauses relating to taxes on exports and to a navigation act. These things may form a bargain among the northern and southern states.

Mr. [Pierce] BUTLER [of South Carolina] declared that he never would agree to the power of taxing imports.

Mr. SHERMAN said it was better to let the southern states import slaves than to part with them, if they made that a *sine qua non* [an absolute condition of agreement]. He was opposed to a tax on slaves imported as making the matter worse, because it implied they were *property*. He acknowledged that if the power of prohibiting the importation should be given to the general [that is, federal] government it would be exercised. He thought it would be its duty to exercise the power. . . .

Mr. [John] RANDOLPH [of Virginia] was for committing in order that some middle ground might, if possible, be found. He could never agree to the clause as it stands. He would sooner risk the constitution. He dwelt on the dilemma to which the convention was exposed. By agreeing to the clause, it would revolt the Quakers, the Methodists, and many others in the states having no slaves. On the other hand, two states might be lost to the Union. Let us then, he said, try the chance of a commitment.

On the question for committing the remaining part of Section 4 and 5 of Article VII[†]. New Hampshire no. Massachusetts abstained. Connecticut aye. New Jersey aye. Pennsylvania no. Delaware no. Maryland aye. Virginia aye. North Carolina aye. South Carolina aye. Georgia aye. . . .

August 28, 1787:

[Debate over what is today Article IV, section 2 of the Constitution, providing for the return of fugitives, including slaves, who flee across state lines.]

. . . Article XIV was taken up.[§]

General PINCKNEY was not satisfied with it. He seemed to wish some provision should be included in favor of property in slaves.

On the question on Article XIV: New Hampshire aye. Massachusetts aye. Connecticut aye. New Jersey aye. Delaware aye. Maryland aye. Virginia aye. North Carolina aye. South Carolina no. Georgia divided.

Article XV being taken up, the words "high misdemeanor" were struck out, and "other crime" inserted, in order to comprehend [include] all proper cases: it being doubtful whether "high misdemeanor" had not a technical meaning too limited.

Mr. BUTLER and Mr. PINCKNEY moved "to require fugitive slaves and servants to be delivered up like criminals."

Mr. WILSON. This would oblige the executive of the state to do it at the public expense.

Mr. SHERMAN saw no more propriety in the public seizing and surrendering a slave or servant, than a horse.

Mr. BUTLER withdrew his proposition in order that some provision might be made apart from this article.

Article XV as amended was then agreed to [without discussion].

Adjourned.

August 29, 1787

[Continued debate over the requirement that states be obliged to return fugitives, including runaway slaves.]

. . . Mr. BUTLER moved to insert after Article

† Now Article I, sections 8 and 9.
§ Now Article IV, sections 1 and 2.

XV: "If any person bound to service or labor in any part of the United States shall escape into another state, he or she shall not be discharged from such service or labor, in consequence of any regulations subsisting in the state to which they escape, but shall be delivered up to the person justly claiming their service or labor," which was agreed to [without discussion]. . . .

September 8, 1787 [Debate over the Amendment process]:

. . . Mr. [James] MADISON [of Virginia] moved to . . . take up the following:

"The legislature of the U.S., whenever two thirds of both houses shall deem necessary, or on the application of two thirds of the legislatures of the several states, shall propose amendments to this Constitution, which shall be valid to all intents and purposes as part thereof, when the same shall have been ratified by three fourths at least of the legislatures of the several states, or by conventions in three fourths thereof, as one or the other mode of ratification may be proposed by the legislature of the U.S."

Mr. [Alexander] HAMILTON [of New York] seconded the motion.

Mr. RUTLEDGE said he never could agree to give a power by which the articles relating to slaves might be altered by the states not interested in that property and prejudiced against it. In order to obviate this objection, these words were added to the proposition: "provided that no amendments which may be made prior to the year 1808 shall in any manner affect the fourth and fifth sections of the VII article."[¶] . . .

On the question on the proposition of Mr. Madison and Mr. Hamilton as amended: New Hampshire divided. Massachusetts aye. Connecticut aye. New Jersey aye. Pennsylvania aye. Delaware no. Maryland aye. Virginia aye. North Carolina aye. South Carolina aye. Georgia aye.

¶ Now Article V.

Selection 3

Celebrating the Constitution: A Dissent

Thurgood Marshall

During 1987, the year commemorating the two-hundredth anniversary of the Philadelphia Convention, public discussion in the media centered on the long-term historical signifi-

Reprinted from Thurgood Marshall, "Celebrating the Constitution: A Dissent," a speech delivered May 6, 1987, to a conference of the San Francisco Patent and Trademark Law Association, Maui, Hawaii.

cance of the framing of the U.S. Constitution. Most commentators praised what had been done at Philadelphia as a step toward building a stable, law-abiding democracy.

One prominent American who dissented from this congratulatory chorus was Thurgood Marshall, who as a lawyer in the 1950s led the legal challenge to segregation that resulted in the Brown *school desegre-*

gation case and who in 1965 became the first African American Supreme Court justice. In a speech given on May 6, 1987, and reprinted here, Marshall found the Constitution deeply flawed in everything that pertained to slavery.

*n*ineteen eighty-seven marks the two-hundredth anniversary of the United States Constitution. A commission has been established to coordinate the celebration. The official meetings, essay contests, and various festivities have begun.

Like many anniversary celebrations, this one takes particular events and holds them up as the source of all the very best that has followed. Patriotic feelings will surely swell, prompting proud proclamations of the wisdom, foresight, and sense of justice shared by the Framers and reflected in a written document now yellowed with age. This is unfortunate—not the patriotism itself but the tendency to oversimplify, to overlook the many other events that have been instrumental to our achievements as a nation. The focus of this celebration invites a complacent belief that the vision of those who debated and compromised in Philadelphia yielded the "more perfect Union" it is said we now enjoy.

I cannot accept this invitation, for I do not believe that the meaning of the Constitution was forever "fixed" at the Philadelphia Convention. Nor do I find the wisdom, foresight, and sense of justice exhibited by the Framers particularly profound. To the contrary, the government they devised was defective from the start, requiring several amendments, a Civil War, and momentous social transformation to attain the system of constitutional government—and its respect for the individual freedoms and human rights—that we hold as fundamental today. When contemporary Americans cite the Constitution, they invoke a concept that is vastly different from what the Framers barely began to construct two centuries ago.

For a sense of the evolving nature of the Constitution we need look no further than the first three words of the document's preamble: "We the people." When the Founding Fathers used this phrase in 1787, they did not have in mind the majority of America's citizens. "We the people" included, in the words of the Framers, "the whole Number of free Persons." On a matter so basic as the right to vote, Negro slaves were excluded, although they were counted for representational purposes—each as three-fifths of a person. Women did not gain the right to vote for over a hundred and thirty years.

These omissions were intentional. The record of the Framers' debates on the slave question is especially clear: the Southern states acceded to the demands of the New England states for giving Congress broad power to regulate commerce, in exchange for the right to continue the slave trade. The economic interests of the regions coalesced: New Englanders engaged in the "carrying trade" would profit from transporting slaves from Africa as well as goods produced in America by slave labor. The perpetuation of slavery preserved the primary source of wealth in the Southern states.

Despite this clear understanding of the role slavery would play in the new republic, use of the words *slaves* and *slavery* was carefully avoided in the original document. Political representation in the House was to be based on the population of "free Persons" in each state, plus three-fifths of all "other Persons." Moral principles against slavery, for those who had them, were compromised, with no explanation of the conflicting principles for which the American Revolutionary War had ostensibly been fought: the self-evident truths that "all men are created equal, that they are endowed by their Creator with certain inalienable Rights, that among these are Life, Liberty and the pursuit of Happiness."

At the Constitutional Convention, eloquent objections to the institution of slavery went unheeded, and its opponents eventually consented to a document that laid a foundation for the tragic events that were to follow. Pennsylvania's Gouverneur Morris provides an example. At the Convention he objected that the inhabitant of Georgia [or] South Carolina who goes to the coast of Africa, and in defiance of the most sacred laws of humanity tears away his fellow creatures from their dearest connections and damns them to the most cruel bondages, shall have more votes in a Government instituted for protection of the rights of mankind, than the Citizen of Pennsylvania or New Jersey who views with a laudable horror, so nefarious a practice.

And yet Morris eventually accepted the three-fifths accommodation. In fact, he wrote the final draft of the Constitution.

No doubt it will be said, when the unpleasant truth of the history of slavery in America is mentioned during this bicentennial year, that the Constitution was a product of its times, and embodied a compromise that, under other circumstances, would not have been made. But the effects of the Framers' compromise have remained for generations. They arose from the contradiction between guaranteeing liberty and justice to all, and denying both to Negroes.

The original intent of the phrase "We the people" was far too clear for any ameliorating construction. Writing for the Supreme Court in 1857, Chief Justice Roger Taney penned the following passage in the *Dred Scott* case on the issue of whether, in the eyes of the Framers, slaves were "constituent members of the sovereignty" and were to be included among "We the people":

> We think they are not, and that they are not included, and were not intended to be included. . . . They had for more than a century before been regarded as beings of an inferior order . . . altogether unfit to associate with the white race . . .; and so far inferior, that they had no rights which the white man was bound to respect; and that the negro might justly and lawfully be reduced to slavery for his benefit. . . . Accordingly, a negro of the African race was regarded . . . as an article of property, and held, and bought and sold as such. . . . No one seems to have doubted the correctness of the prevailing opinion of the time.

And so, nearly seven decades after the Constitutional Convention, the Supreme Court reaffirmed the prevailing opinion among the Framers regarding the rights of Negroes in America. It took a bloody Civil War before the Thirteenth Amendment could be adopted to abolish slavery—though not the consequences slavery would have for future Americans.

While the Union survived the Civil War, the Constitution did not. In its place arose a new, more promising basis for justice and equality: the Fourteenth Amendment, ensuring protection of the life, liberty, and property of all persons against deprivations without due process, and guaranteeing equal protection under the laws. Yet almost another century would pass before any significant recognition was obtained of the rights of black Americans to share equally even in such basic opportunities as education, housing, and employment, and to have their votes counted, and counted equally. In the meantime, blacks joined America's military to fight its wars and invested untold hours working in its factories and on its farms, contributing to the development of this country's magnificent wealth and waiting to share in its prosperity.

What is striking is the role legal principles have played throughout America's history in determining the condition of Negroes. They were enslaved by law, emancipated by law, disenfranchised and segregated by law, and, finally, they have begun to win equality by law. Along the way, new constitutional principles have emerged to meet the challenges of a changing society. The progress has been dramatic, and it will continue.

The men who gathered in Philadelphia in 1787 could not have envisioned these changes. They could not have imagined, nor would they have accepted, that the document they were drafting would one day be subject to interpretation by a Supreme Court to which had been appointed a woman and the descendent of an African slave. "We the people" no longer enslave, but the credit does not belong to the Framers. It belongs to those who refused to acquiesce to outdated notions of liberty, justice, and equality, and who strived to better them.

And so we must be careful, when focusing on

the events that took place in Philadelphia two centuries ago, that we not overlook the momentous events that followed, and thereby lose our proper sense of perspective. Otherwise, the odds are that for many Americans the bicentennial celebration will be little more than a blind pilgrimage to the shrine of the original document now stored in a vault in the National Archives. If we seek instead a sensitive understanding of the Constitution's inherent defects—and its promising evolution through two hundred years of history—the celebration of the "miracle at Philadelphia" will be a far more meaningful and humbling experience. We will see that the true miracle was not the birth of the Constitution but its life, a life nurtured through two turbulent centuries of our own making, and embodying much good fortune that was not.

Thus, we may not all participate in the festivities with flag-waving fervor. Some may more quietly commemorate the suffering, struggle, and sacrifice that triumphed over much of what was wrong with the original document, may observe the anniversary with hopes not realized and promises not fulfilled. I plan to celebrate the bicentennial of the Constitution as a living document, including the Bill of Rights and the other amendments protecting individual freedoms and human rights.

Selection 4

Post-Revolutionary Antislavery Impulses

David Brion Davis

In the 1975 book that forms the sequel to his history of early modern attitudes toward slavery in Western civilization, David Brion Davis carefully studied the rising sentiment against slavery that accompanied the American, French, and Latin American revolutions of the late eighteenth and early nineteenth centuries. Some of these feelings emerged at the Philadelphia Convention of 1787 and helped fuel the decisions of the New England and Mid-Atlantic states to abolish slavery. This excerpt, taken from Davis's *The Problem of Slavery in the Age of Revolution, 1770–1823, analyzes the dilemmas that would-be opponents of slavery faced.*

Excerpted from David Brion Davis, *The Problem of Slavery in the Age of Revolution, 1770–1823.* Copyright © 1975 Cornell University. Reprinted with permission from the author. New edition published by Oxford University Press, 1999.

*D*uring the 1780s . . . signs were highly encouraging to the reformers, who worked from Delaware to Rhode Island to secure laws prohibiting slave importations and providing for gradual emancipation. Interstate communication gave them a sense of united effort in overcoming powerful interests, in implementing the principles of the Revolution, and thus in preventing any historical validation of America's inconsistency. Early in 1784

[Rhode Island reformer] Moses Brown passed on the news that Congress had proposed the year 1800 as the terminal date for slavery in the new states and perhaps even in the existing states. In 1785, it appeared that even political squabbles could not prevent New York from joining the three other northern states that had adopted laws for gradual emancipation. In 1791, Jonathan Edwards, Jr., predicted that, at the present rate of progress, within fifty years it would "be as shameful for a man to hold a Negro slave, as to be guilty of common robbery or theft." Many Northerners were heartened by reports, especially from Virginia and Maryland, that Southerners were beginning to doubt the profitability of slave labor. The Upper South's hostility to the slave trade could easily be interpreted as the first step toward general emancipation. Benjamin Rush hoped that even South Carolina would respond to the idealism of the Revolution and refuse to import further slaves.

Above all, the years immediately following the Revolution brought a mood of self-congratulation. For the first time, numerous writers began to review the history not only of slavery, but of anti-slavery sentiment. To their astonishment, they found that except for a few isolated voices Negro slavery had been virtually unopposed prior to the imperial crisis. Such research gave a new self-consciousness to anti-slavery leaders. It also led to two conclusions that would have contradictory consequences: first, it appeared that the exertions of a few dedicated individuals could transform the public consciousness; second, since so much had been accomplished in so brief a time, it seemed that post-Revolutionary Americans should marvel less at their own remnants of inconsistency than at the incredible progress of antislavery sentiment.

These themes provided a formula for evasion, or for what the American Convention in 1794 termed "our consolation and encouragement." Recent history showed that one could count on "the irresistible, though silent progress of the principles of true philosophy." "Let us remember," the Convention urged its constituent abolition societies, "although interest and prejudice may oppose, yet the fundamental principles of our government, as well as the progressive and rapid influence of reason and religion, are in our favour." The more that reformers praised American institutions and congratulated themselves on living in an enlightened age, the more prepared they were to postpone the Revolution's goal to future centuries. Thus William Griffith, addressing the New Jersey Abolition Society in 1804, expressed "wonder and gratification" over the immense progress America had made in eradicating slavery and assimilating Negroes to the standards of their superiors. Much was still to be done, especially before "riches increase, and corruption (as it will) gains on the public morals." It was imperative to act while "individual and national feelings are alive to sentiments of charity and justice." Yet Griffith cautioned: "Nor is it to be wished, much less expected, that sudden and general emancipation should take place. A century may and probably will elapse, though every fair exertion shall be made, before it can be eradicated from our country."

In 1793, Noah Webster was not quite so optimistic, although he had no rival in celebrating the glories and promise of American life. His predictions about slavery must be comprehended in juxtaposition with his introductory paean to the new republic:

Here the equalizing genius of the laws distributes property to every citizen . . . here no tithes, no rack rents, no lordly exactions of gratuities and fines for alienation, no arbitrary impositions of taxes, harass the cultivator of the soil and repress his exertions. Here no beggarly monks and fryars, no princely ecclesiastics with their annual income of millions, no idle court-pensioners and titled mendicants, no spies to watch and betray the unsuspecting citizen, no tyrant with his train of hounds, bastards and mistresses. . . . Here no commercial or corporation monopolies give exclusive advantages to favored individuals . . . no sacramental test bars the conscientious sectary from places of trust and emolument . . . here no monasteries, convents and nunneries, the retreats of idleness and the nurseries of superstition and debauchery. . . . Here every man finds employment, and the road is open for the poorest citizen to amass wealth by labor and economy, and by his talents and virtue to raise himself to the highest offices of State.

And so on and so on, to the vista of wealth, manufacturing, and commerce: "and in the short period of 170 years, since our ancestors landed on these shores, a trackless wilderness, inhabited only by savages and wild beasts, is converted into fruitful fields and meadows, more highly cultivated than one half of Europe."

During his travels Webster had seen how the fields were cultivated in South Carolina, and he reminded his readers that the proportion of slaves in the American population was "a circumstance which cannot fail to allay the joy, that the prosperous state of the country would otherwise inspire in every patriotic bosom." In Webster's view this circumstance was an unfortunate accident, the product of the misguided policy of an unenlightened age. Oddly enough, however, his model for emancipation had nothing to do with the brave new world where "the mind of man, as free as the air he breathes, may exert all its energy, and by expanding its powers to distant and various objects, its faculties may be enlarged to a degree hitherto unknown." Rather, when Webster thought of emancipation his mind turned to the gradual elevation of serfs, which had presumably taken place in the depraved environment that Americans had escaped: "Indeed if we judge from the fate of villanage [sic: serfdom] in many parts of Europe, it is no ill-founded prediction, that slavery in this country will be utterly extirpated in the course of two centuries, perhaps in a much shorter period, without any extraordinary efforts to abolish it."

Webster recognized that such progress would be too slow to satisfy "the friends of humanity, in this enlightened period of the world," and he called for efforts, both public and private, "to accelerate the progress of freedom, with all convenient speed." Nevertheless, the whole point of his argument was the peril of any sudden abolition. Negro emancipation would come inevitably,

without extraordinary effort, although the task might take as long as had America's slow emancipation from Europe. Webster was not alone in seeing the post-Revolutionary years as a midpoint between the origins of North American slavery (and colonization), and a terminal date of about 1960. Nor was he alone in screening out any perceptions that might cast doubt on his belief in irresistible progress. Like various other antislavery writers of the time, Webster found himself in the anomalous position of exclaiming over the "improved" condition of southern slaves. Masters had been touched by the benevolent spirit of the age, and had also come to appreciate that kindness was good policy. American slaves already enjoyed many of the privileges of English villeins [medieval serfs], and could never again be forced, for example, to dig more than a quarter of an acre of land in a day or to work on the days they called their own! Indicating a similar frame of mind, the American Convention urged in 1798 that slaves should be quietly submissive to their masters, since this would lead to better treatment and might also help persuade masters of the injustice of human bondage.

But however sanguine Americans might be about the distant future, they could not escape the idea of declension, since virtually any statute on slavery was bound to compromise the "higher law" principle of natural rights. It was clear that union required the postponement of emancipation, not only in the South, but in most of the northern states as well. Yet the Revolution had been rooted in the "higher law" doctrine, as quoted by Benezet, that "No Legislature on Earth . . . can alter the Nature of things, or make that to be lawful, which is contrary to the Law of God." The success of the Revolution presumably showed the danger as well as the illegitimacy of laws based on expediency, of laws like those of Parliament which had sanctioned the Guinea trade, and which, as Benezet put it, had brought "under hard Bondage a people over whom the Parliament had not the least shadow of Rights." In 1783, Benezet exhorted British Quakers to begin pressing the king and Parliament to abolish the iniquitous traffic. At the same time, however, he wrote to Benjamin Franklin, then in Paris, observing that it was "sorrowfully astonishing that after the declaration so strongly and clearly made of the value & right of liberty on this continent, no state but that of Pennsylvania & that imperfectly, have yet taken a step towards the total abolition of slavery."

Hugh Henry Brackenridge mockingly praised Pennsylvania's act on the grounds of expediency which, he said, should be extended still further:

On this principle, I have always thought a defect in the criminal codes of most nations, not giving license to the perpetrators of offences, to proceed, for a limited time, in larcenies, burglaries, &c. until they get their hands out of use to these pursuits, and in use to others. For it must be greatly inconvenient to thieves and cut-throats, who have engaged in this way of life, and run great risks in acquiring skill in their employment, to be obliged all at once to withdraw their hands, and lay aside picking locks, and apply themselves to industry in other ways, for a livelihood.

Legislators, he warned, should never confuse the slavery issue with moral doubts regarding the original right of capturing or subjugating Africans, since that would raise difficulties over the *"natural right to hold a slave for a moment, even whether the law sanctioned it or not; in which case we should find it necessary to go as far as the fanatics in religion, and set our slaves free altogether."*

This was the "higher law" doctrine advanced by George Wallace, by the French Encyclopedists, and by a scattering of American Quakers and Calvinists. In America the state constitutions supposedly embodied the "higher law" of natural rights. Yet David Cooper expressed dismay over the constitutions which showed such extraordinary care in guarding the rights and privileges of white citizens, but which gave "no gleam of notice" to the oppressed Africans. The Vermont constitution of 1777 specifically outlawed slavery. Several Massachusetts towns objected to the lack of such a clause in the Massachusetts constitution of 1778. But the framers of the new

1780 constitution contented themselves with a general declaration that "all men are born free and equal, and have certain natural, essential, and unalienable rights." Jeremy Belknap later wrote that this bill of rights, which roughly followed the wording of the Virginia Convention of 1776, had been inserted "with a particular view to establishing the liberty of the negroes on a general principle, and so it was understood by the people at large; but some doubted whether this was sufficient." Moses Brown, for one, was convinced by 1784 that the Massachusetts constitution had put an end to slavery, and that Negroes had been adjudged to be free. Various historians have . . . reached little agreement on the actual process of emancipation in Massachusetts. Here it is sufficient to say that by the early 1780s Massachusetts slaveholders had little confidence in their legal claims to proprietorship, in part because of the actions of town governments; that an attorney like Levi Lincoln was prepared to write an eloquent brief condemning slavery on religious and "higher law" principles, but with little reference to the constitution; and that while individual slaves were freed by jury decisions—or by their boldness in simply leaving their masters—no court specifically and clearly ruled that slavery was unconstitutional, although Chief Justice William Cushing instructed a jury in 1783 that slavery was inconsistent with the constitution. Regardless of popular opinion in Massachusetts, there was no publicized case that encouraged constitutional emancipation in other states with similar bills of rights. In 1794, for example, the counsel of the Pennsylvania Abolition Society was evenly divided on whether the 1790 state declaration of rights had outlawed slavery. Though the Society pursued the question in court, the High Court of Errors and Appeals judged that slavery had existed legally in the state prior to the 1790 constitution, and was unaffected by the declaration of rights.

Encouraged by signs of unmistakable progress, abolitionists also fell within the yawning gap between Revolutionary expectations and political realities. In 1776, Samuel Hopkins could assure the honorable members of the Continental Congress that their resolution against the slave trade "leaves in our minds no doubt of your being sensible of the equal unrighteousness and oppression, as well as inconsistence with ourselves, in holding so many hundreds of thousands of blacks in slavery, who have equal right to freedom with ourselves." He could express confidence that they would apply their wisdom "to bring about the total abolition of slavery." By 1787 he was reporting to Moses Brown that various Rhode Island clergymen objected to petitioning the state assembly on the subject of the slave trade, since "the present ruling part in the Assembly, have appeared to be so destitute of all principles of justice, or regard to it . . . that there is an impropriety in applying to them for justice." No doubt Hopkins was surprised when the assembly, in that very year, voted to prohibit the slave trade!

But in 1787 Hopkins was well aware of the debates in a larger political arena. Along with other antislavery leaders, he felt that the Constitutional Convention should be bound by the precedents of the Revolution, particularly the 1774 slave-trade resolution and the Declaration of Independence. There is fragmentary evidence of organized attempts on the part of abolitionists to influence the Philadelphia delegates. Since 1783 the Quakers, especially, had gained experience from their lobbying campaigns with state assemblies, with the Continental Congress, and, via their British connections, with Parliament. In petitioning the Constitutional Convention, the Pennsylvania Abolition Society appealed to the Revolutionary resolutions against the slave trade, to Europe as a judge of hypocrisy, and to the certainty of divine judgment. Tench Coxe, a member of the Society and one of the earliest champions of the Constitution, later confided to James Madison that it had required tremendous efforts to suppress the pleas of overzealous but honest men. "A very strong paper was drawn & put into my hands," he wrote, "to procure the signature of Dr. Franklin to be presented to the federal convention—I enclosed to the Dr. with my opinion that it would be a very improper season & place to hazard the Application."

At this time Coxe was in correspondence with prominent British abolitionists who were eager for information on the achievements of emancipated Negroes. Coxe, an ardent Federalist and proponent of industrial progress, shared with the more progressive British reformers a common set of values. What separated them—and what proved to be a liability to American antislavery—was the different meaning of rising "establishments." In 1787, even in 1792, England could hardly match America in the number of prominent citizens who theoretically embraced the antislavery cause: statesmen of international rank, legislators, lawyers, clergymen, merchants, bankers, manufacturers, and prophets of the new age. But the leading English spokesmen for abolition were not faced with a constitutional convention, the success of which depended on the compliance of West Indian delegates.

One may object that accommodation is the fulcrum of politics, that British antislavery leaders could bend when the occasion demanded, and that the weaknesses of antislavery principles cannot be gauged by what legislators did or left undone. In America, however, it was the Revolutionary expectations that made the difference. Nor could Europe offer examples of virgin states, such as Kentucky, where colonizers were re-enacting the drama of separation and self-determination. As David Rice exhorted the Danville convention (which did not heed his words): "Holding men in slavery is the national vice of Virginia; and, while a part of that state, we were partakers of the guilt. As a separate state, we are just now come to the birth; and it depends upon our free choice whether we shall be born in this sin, or innocent of it."

The logic of the Revolution suggested that such principles might have prevailed at the Constitutional Convention. For a time it was by no means clear exactly which principles had prevailed. The text, like that of the King James Bible, scrupulously avoided the word "slave." On November 8, 1787, an anonymous Pennsylvanian complained that "the words, dark and ambiguous, such as no plain man of common sense would have used, are evidently chosen to conceal from Europe, that in this enlightened century, the practice of slavery has its advocates among men in the highest stations."

Luther Martin, who as a disgruntled delegate had walked out of the Convention and had refused to sign the Constitution, explained what lay behind the dark and ambiguous words. Leading a campaign in Maryland to oppose ratification, he exposed the deal within the committee, of which he was a member, whereby the New England states had agreed to give the slave trade a twenty-year immunity from federal restriction in exchange for southern votes to eliminate any restrictions on navigation acts. To the rest of the world, Martin wrote, it must appear "absurd and disgraceful to the last degree, that we should *except* from the exercise of that power [to regulate commerce], the *only branch* of *commerce* which is *unjustifiable in its nature,* and *contrary* to the rights of *mankind."* Moreover, the authors had been so anxious to avoid a word "which might be odious in the ears of Americans" that they had inadvertently authorized Congress to impose a duty of ten dollars on any free immigrant who entered the United States.

Martin, who had graduated from the Presbyterian College of New Jersey in the afterglow of the Great Awakening, expanded eloquently on the themes and inconsistency, apostasy, and divine judgment. The slave-trade and three-fifths compromises "ought to be considered as a *solemn mockery of,* and *insult to that God* whose protection we had then implored, and could not fail to hold us up in *detestation,* and render us *contemptible* to every *true friend* of liberty in the world." It ought to be considered, Martin warned,

that national *crimes* can only be, and *frequently are punished* in this world, by national punishments; and that the *continuance* of the slave-trade, and thus giving it a *national sanction* and *encouragement,* ought to be considered as *justly exposing* us to the *displeasure* and *vengeance* of *Him*, who is equally Lord of all, and who views with equal eye the poor *African slave* and his *American master.*

At the Convention, a number of delegates made such arguments, but were seldom free from the suspicion of ulterior motives. George Mason, for example, who also refused to sign the Constitution, had much to say about the evils of slavery and the dangers of divine judgment. Like Martin, he was outraged by the coalition

The writers of the Constitution purposely avoided using the word slave *in an effort to make the document more palatable to the public.*

between the states of New England and the Deep South, a coalition which had shattered the expected alignment of agrarian interests. Yet in opposing ratification in Virginia, Mason qualified his antislavery principles by arguing that "though this infamous traffic be continued, we have no security for the property of that kind which we have already. There is no clause in this Constitution to secure it; . . . so that 'they have done what they ought not to have done, and have left undone what they ought to have done.'"

During the Convention debates Charles Cotesworth Pinckney, of South Carolina, explained that Virginians could afford a specious humanitarianism: "S. Carolina & Georgia cannot do without slaves. As to Virginia she will gain by stopping the importations. Her slaves will rise in value, & she has more than she wants." Oliver Ellsworth, of Connecticut, pointed out that if slavery were to be considered in a moral light, "we ought to go farther and free those already in the Country." This was a gibe at Mason. In justice to Georgia and South Carolina, Ellsworth argued, the delegates should remember that slaves "multiply so fast in Virginia & Maryland that it is cheaper to raise than import them, whilest in the sickly rice swamps foreign supplies are necessary." He was confident, in any event, that poor laborers would soon become so plentiful "as to render slaves useless. Slavery in time will not be a speck in our Country. Provision is already made in Connecticut for abolishing it." Pinckney, on the other hand, held "that the importation of slaves would be for the interest of the whole Union. The more slaves, the more produce to employ in carrying trade; the more consumption also, and the more of this, the more of revenue for the common treasury."

It is not surprising that the Constitution was subject to a variety of interpretations or that its defenders helped to popularize conflicting expectations. General William Heath assured the Massachusetts ratifying convention that "the federal convention went as far as they could; the migration or importation, &c. is confined to the states, now *existing only,* new states cannot claim it." Congress, he promised, had already

prohibited slavery in the new states. William Dawes added "that although slavery is not smitted by an apoplexy, yet it has received a mortal wound and will die of a consumption." With these judgments James Wilson entirely agreed. Speaking to the Pennsylvania convention, as one of the framers of the Constitution, he interpreted the slave-trade clause "as laying the foundation for banishing slavery out of this country; and though the period is more distant than I could wish, yet it will produce the same kind of gradual change which was pursued in Pennsylvania." Wilson also expressed confidence that Congress would never allow the introduction of slaves in the new states.

In Virginia, however, Governor Edmund Randolph, also one of the framers, hinted at undisclosed understandings which convinced even South Carolina that slavery would be secure: "I believe, whatever we may think here, that there was not a member of the Virginia delegation who had the smallest suspicion of the abolition of slavery." Farther to the south, Charles Cotesworth Pinckney had to meet objections that South Carolina had conceded too much. Unfortunately, he explained, "your delegates had to contend with the religious and political prejudices of the Eastern and Middle States, and with the interested and inconsistent opinion of Virginia, who was warmly opposed to our importing more slaves." Yet the Constitution in no way ruled that the slave trade must cease in 1808; it provided security that the general government could never emancipate slaves in the states; it guaranteed the right "to recover our slaves in whatever part of America they may take refuge, which is a right we had not before." All things considered, Pinckney said, "we have made the best terms for the security of this species of property it was in our power to make. We would have made better if we could; but, on the whole, I do not think them bad." Robert Barnwell was even more sanguine. By 1808, he predicted, the New England states would be the main carriers of slaves cargoes, and it would thus be in their interest to encourage the trade as long as possible. "I am of opinion," he concluded, "that, without we ourselves put a stop to them, the traffic in negroes will continue forever."

A few of the antislavery leaders appreciated that a fundamental law which satisfied so many interests could only be interpreted as the ultimate and fatal betrayal of the Revolution. In a letter to Moses Brown, William Rotch anticipated the view of [William Lloyd] Garrison: the Constitution was "founded on *Slavery* and that is on *Blood.*" But the sharpest public attacks on the Constitution came from men like Luther Martin and George Mason, who opposed ratification on a variety of grounds. And as Benjamin Rush informed Jeremy Belknap, the vast majority of Quakers were "highly Federal": "The appeals, therefore, that have been made to the humane & laudable prejudices of our Quakers by our Antifederal writers upon the subject of negro slavery, have been greeted by that prudent society with silence and contempt."

By 1789 the Pennsylvania Abolition Society could assure the British abolitionists that no apostasy had occurred. The large number of Negroes in some states simply prevented "making a general arrangement *at this moment,* that should carry the American principles on this subject to their full length." Nevertheless, the Constitution should be considered as a testimonial against the slave trade, which would doubtless be abolished by the individual states in the near future. Then, in a classic use of projection, the Pennsylvanians added: "We are very sensible of the difficulties, that must arise to you in Great Britain from the prejudices & arts of interested men. But similar prejudices have been *removed,* & similar arts have been *defeated* in this country."

Selection 5

Slavery and Emancipation in New York

Shane White

Today American slavery is considered an exclusively southern historical problem, but in New York State at the end of the eighteenth century it was neither a mild institution nor easy to abolish. Historian Shane White has provided a well-researched account of how *slavery functioned in New York City and nearby rural areas, and of the steps that the local upper class took to extinguish it gradually. This excerpt is taken from White's book* Somewhat More Independent: The End of Slavery in New York City, 1770–1810.

Excerpted from Shane White, *Somewhat More Independent: The End of Slavery in New York City, 1770–1810.* Copyright © 1991 University of Georgia Press. Reprinted with permission of the University of Georgia Press.

Perhaps the best known of these slaveholders was John Jay, chief justice of the United States, governor of New York, and for many years president of the New

York Manumission Society. Despite his oft-quoted comment that should America fail to introduce an abolition measure her "Prayers to Heaven for Liberty" during the Revolutionary war would be "impious," Jay was listed in both the 1790 and 1800 censuses as owning five slaves. . . . Jay claimed, "I purchase slaves and manumit them when their faithful services shall have afforded a reasonable retribution."

To the modern reader the attitude of Jay and other slaveholders in the New York Manumission Society smacks of little more than hypocrisy. Even if Jay's version of his activities is accepted at face value, all that he was really doing was receiving most of the benefits of slavery while avoiding the moral opprobrium with which transatlantic opinion was increasingly regarding slaveholders. It is doubtful whether Jay's philanthropy caused him any financial inconvenience; indeed, judging from the length of time [one of his slaves] was kept enslaved, Jay may well have made a profit. The bottom line, as far as these New York gentlemen were concerned, was that the man made the institution. Not only were their own motives beyond reproach, but slavery, under the firm but caring hand of slaveholders such as themselves, was the most suitable preparation for the eventual freedom of the blacks. Southern or even more particularly West Indian slavery, however, was another matter. There slavery was not going to end in the foreseeable future, and more important, the moral caliber of many slaveholders was, at the very least, questionable. Not for the first time, or for the last, the South was suffering from an image problem in New York. The members of the city's Manumission Society had believed their own propaganda, disseminated so widely in the magazines of the North. For them and other New Yorkers, the urgent problem lay not in their city but farther to the south.

Toleration of slaveholding members in a society ostensibly concerned with ending the practice provides a starting point for a reconsideration of the New York Manumission Society's role. Over the years historians have treated the organization very gently. . . . The reason for such a favorable assessment is the apparently obvious association of the society with the eventual passage of the Gradual Manumission Act in 1799. As a result of the Revolution, so runs the usual story, many New Yorkers realized that slaveholding was immoral, an attitude often illustrated by quoting Jay's comment about the "impious prayers" of the Revolutionaries. As a consequence the New York Manumission Society was founded. Despite early failures its members persevered, struggling against the entrenched interests of slaveholders, until by the late 1790s they had managed to convince most New Yorkers of the merits of their case—here reference is almost invariably made to William Dunlap's 1797 assertion that "within 20 years the opinion of the injustice of slaveholding has become almost universal." In 1799 the act finally went through. In this interpretation, the New York Manumission Society is seen as the instrument of Revolutionary ideology, and one of the few laudable moments in race relations in the first two and a half centuries of white settlement on the American continent is securely tied to the American Revolution.

Such an interpretation may say more about the mythology of the American Revolution than about the actual course of events in New York. Even a cursory perusal of the New York Manumission Society's papers makes suspect any notion that it was the driving force behind the New York legislation. For a start it was very much a city organization, with little impact in the rest of the state; yet it was not New York City that passed the abolition legislation. In 1799, the legislature did not even meet in the city, assembling in Albany instead. The attitude of the country, not the city, was crucial in securing the 1799 legislation. Here a number of factors—the electoral redistribution of 1796 that gave more weight to country areas, the massive migration of New Englanders into the western parts of the state, and some sort of crisis of identity among the inhabitants of Dutch origin—appear to have been much more important than anything the New York Manumission Society did.

What the society's records further show is

that the appropriate context within which to view its activities is not the abolitionist crusade of the 1830s, but the genteel and paternalistic reform movements of the 1790s and of the early years of the nineteenth century. Humanitarian and benevolent organizations proliferated in New York City after the Revolution. In the years to 1825 . . . over one hundred such groups existed, not counting the special ad hoc committees set up to combat the regular crises caused by fire, harsh winters, and outbreaks of disease. The frequently overlapping membership of these organizations was drawn from a pool of merchants, lawyers, physicians, and other professionals. Civic-minded, well-to-do, influential, and above all patrician, these men wished to control and minimize the disruptive impact of helter-skelter expansion.

Probably the main achievement of the New York Manumission Society, and certainly the activity that absorbed most of its members' energies in the last decade and a half of the eighteenth century, was the African Free School. Illustrating well the concerns of these genteel reformers, the school aimed to instill virtue into New York's free blacks and to prevent them "from running into practices of immorality or Sinking into Habits of Idleness." In this way the school would help negate the argument that blacks were unfit for freedom. Yet the African Free School reflected also the more general desire of the elite involved in this and similar humanitarian organizations to order the behavior of New York's lower classes.

In the face of strong resistance to emancipation and no doubt inhibited by the continued presence of slaveholders among its members, the New York Manumission Society scrupulously refrained from directly attacking slavery in New York. A petition organized by the society in 1786, a year after its founding, calling on the legislature to prevent the exportation of slaves from New York signaled the future course of antislavery in the state. In language redolent of antislavery imaginative literature, the petitioners declared themselves to be "deeply affected" by the nefarious practice of "exporting them like cattle" to the West Indies and the southern states, a practice that frequently resulted in "very affecting instances of husbands being torn from their wives, wives from husbands, parents from their children, children from their parents." But the effect of such language was dissipated by the limited intent of the proposed legislation, which could hardly have offended, let alone threatened, the slaveholders of New York. Although the petition began in a mildly critical vein by affirming that New York blacks were "free by the laws of GOD" even if "held in slavery by the laws of this state," the rest of the document was conciliatory to local slaveholders, agreeing with them that "it is well known that the condition of slaves in this state is *far more tolerable and easy* than in many other countries." The proposed legislation was designed to protect both New York slaves from the slave system thought to exist in the rest of the New World and New York slaveholders from their consciences. In short, the New York Manumission Society was employing the language and rhetoric of antislavery not to end the system itself but to reform it.

To a large extent New Yorkers were successful in maintaining this distance between themselves and other slave societies. . . . The New York Manumission Society was always at its most effective if the quarantine protecting New York from the South and the West Indies was threatened. When suspicious vessels arrived in the harbor, members organized watches and even placed advertisements in the newspapers warning blacks to be wary of kidnappers. Slaveholders who tried to sell slaves to the South were pursued vigorously and brought before the courts. In 1806, for example, the society obtained a court writ to prevent a sloop leaving the port with three free blacks on board. A Frenchman had allegedly gotten them drunk and tricked them into going on to the vessel. Similarly, when characteristics associated with slavery in the South or the West Indies—such as violence and cruelty—surfaced in New York, the society mobilized to try to eradicate them. The standing committee that investigated these incidents became the vehicle by which the members of the New York Manumission Society sought to impose their own higher standards of behavior on local slaveholders.

The society attempted to regulate and control both the free black population and the local slaveholders and to ensure that the eventual end of slavery occurred with the minimum of disruption. Little wonder, then, that it received substantial encouragement from local slaveowners. An analysis of the 1786 petition to prevent the exportation of New York slaves, the first major activity of the fledgling society, further reveals the conservative nature of the organization. The 132 signatories, a veritable who's who of the city's social, economic, and political elite in the decades following the Revolution, included John Jay, Alexander Hamilton, John Lamb, James Duane, and no fewer than eight Livingstons. A majority were also slaveholders. Although it is not possible to establish how many of these men owned slaves when they signed the petition in 1786, a minimum of 63 out of the 132 possessed slaves at the time of the 1790 census. A further 6, who either owned no slaves in 1790 or could not be found in that census, had acquired slaves by the next census in 1800. Not only did more than one in two of the supporters of the New York Manumission Society's petition of 1786 own slaves at some time in the ensuing decade and a half, but by New York City's standards they were also heavy users of slave labor. The mean slaveholding in the city in 1790 was 2 slaves, but these men owned on average 2.9 slaves each, an increase of almost 50 percent on the city norm. In fact, had the signatories to this document manumitted their own slaves in 1790 they would have freed not far short of one in ten of the slaves in the city.

If even the society ostensibly devoted to the task of ending slavery conceded that the condition of local slaves was "far more tolerable and easy" than elsewhere, it is hardly surprising that most New Yorkers agreed. New Yorkers could fearlessly condemn the barbarities of slavery in the West Indies, or even in the South, yet remain indifferent to the continued existence of the institution in their city. Material from contemporary

newspapers illustrates this point well. In 1788, for example, the *Daily Advertiser* reprinted from a British newspaper an account of a number of runaway advertisements presented as evidence before the inquiry into the African slave trade. All the runaways had been scarred by whips and had suffered further mutilation. The piece ended by suggesting that readers could easily confirm such barbarous treatment "by looking over the West Indian newspapers in the city coffee houses." But subscribers to New York's *Daily Advertiser* had no need to consult such a source: over the ensuing two decades their own newspaper printed close to a thousand runaway advertisements, quite a few from Virginia and South Carolina, but the majority of which were from the immediate vicinity. Not a few of the runaways described in them were mutilated in some way or other. . . .

Ever willing to differentiate themselves from the South, New Yorkers displayed a remarkable myopia about the continued existence of slavery in and around their city. In the face of ample evidence suggesting that slaveowners in New York were hardly less capable of brutality than were southerners, New Yorkers managed to hold tenaciously to their ideas about the local institution's benevolent nature. Although the sources are far from perfect, the historian of slavery in New York does not have to search very far to find examples of New Yorkers behaving in a cruel and barbarous fashion. In 1792, for example, the *New Jersey Journal,* reporting on the inquest of a female slave who had died a few hours after "a most barbarous and inhuman whipping," quoted the coroner's observation that "a more painful death than she must have suffered can scarcely be possible." Moreau de St. Méry saw an apothecary repeatedly whip a "little mulatto," who was chained in an attic and kept alive on a diet of bread and water for the crime of stealing some drugs. Another traveler, after noting that "shocking cruelties" occurred even in the "enlightened state of New York," recounted the case of a seven-year-old child who was flogged, given salt to make him thirsty, and then confined in a room with nothing to drink. The records of the Standing Committee of the Manumission Society, too, are filled with details of less sensational, almost mundane, cruelties committed by New Yorkers. Assaults, beatings, and attempts to sell slaves illegally to the South occurred with depressing regularity.

Comparisons of the level of physical treatment in different slave regimes are difficult, if not impossible, to make. But if, on the whole, there was some truth in the New Yorkers' assertion that day-to-day living conditions for their slaves were better than those in the South and the West Indies, the distance between slave regimes was less than they cared to admit, and certainly not large enough to justify any claims that theirs was a benevolent regime. The city's slaves, too, rejected any such self-serving comparison. [T]hey were probably an even more restive property than their counterparts in the South.

On another level of treatment, however, New York and New Jersey slaves did not fare nearly so well. In terms of . . . the "conditions of life," including family security and opportunities for an independent social and religious life, slaves from around New York were considerably worse off than those in the South. In fact, the ethnocentric assumption that the wholesale adoption of white values and mores was both inevitable and beneficial, a crucial element in the New Yorkers' favorable comparison of themselves with the South, specifically denied the importance of this aspect of black life. The very factors that were believed to promote the well-being of the slaves—in particular, the small holdings and familial nature of slavery—combined to fragment the slave family and to hinder the development of a slave culture.

. . . Although New York was the heaviest user of slave labor north of the Mason-Dixon line, slaves were still only about 10 percent of the total population and slaveholdings were almost miniscule by southern standards. In 1790, the year of the first federal census, the average holding in New York City was two slaves. More than half of the city slaveholders owned only one slave, and three out of every four owned either one or two. Consequently, almost one in two of the city slaves either lived by themselves or with only one other slave in the white household. More than eight in every ten slaves were owned by masters with fewer than five slaves. Further, there were only three slaveowners with ten or more slaves, and the largest slaveholding was thirteen.

Although the size of holdings was larger in the city's hinterland—the average in Kings, Queens, Richmond, and Manhattan Island north of the city was 3.4 slaves—contact between slaves on farms was made relatively difficult by the low density of settlement. The greatest concentration of slaves in the North was on the western end of Long Island and on Staten Island. In Richmond County and the rural part of Kings County in 1790 more than a quarter of the total population were slaves, and in marked contrast to the city, only about one in seven of the slaves in this area was owned by a master with either one or two slaves. Conversely, more than six in ten of the slaves lived on farms where there were five or more slaves, and slightly more than 15 percent of the slaves were owned by the one in twenty slaveholders possessing ten or more slaves.

Under these circumstances, the slave family in and around New York was, at best, a fragile creation. Not only was there an unbalanced sex ratio among the slaves in the city, with females significantly outnumbering males, making the search for a sexual partner difficult, but the small size of slaveholdings also resulted in few slave families having the opportunity to live together under the same roof. Furthermore, for some slaveowners living in cramped quarters and with only limited labor requirements a married slave was an unnecessary encumbrance: occasionally buyers of slaves advertising in the papers made it clear that married slaves were unacceptable. . . . Although at least some urban slaveowners actively discouraged their slaves from marrying and having children, many New York slaves attempted to overcome the exigencies of their position and establish a family. But the usual result was a split household: typically the male slave was owned by one master and the female and any children by another.

Some owners . . . appear to have been particularly intolerant of the presence of slave children within the confined space of urban housing. "For sale" notices in the press often noted that female slaves were being sold only on account of their children: in 1774, one owner offered to sell his female slave and three children because "it is inconvenient to the owner to keep a breeding wench." A few years later, another grumbled that he was selling his slave wench and her one-year-old male child because the "present proprietor does not like noise." In at least one case the seeming inability to have a child was listed as one of a slave woman's attributes: a twenty-two-year-old "likely handy negro wench" advertised for sale had had "the small pox and measles and has been married several years without having a child."

Even if New York slaves managed to overcome the odds and establish a family the existence of that family was always under threat. . . . [S]lavery in New York City was characterized by a very high rate of turnover among the slaveholders: only a minority of slaveowners in 1800, for example, had been listed in the 1790 census as having slaves. This feature appears to have been particularly disruptive of the slave family, as given labor demands in New York, buyers seldom wanted to purchase families. Although only a fraction of this turnover of slaves is now visible—mainly in wills and for sale notices in the press—what is most striking is the very high number of slaves who were sold or bequeathed as individuals. In the vast majority of cases there is no indication that the slaves were members of a family. Further, when such links clearly did exist, New York and New Jersey slaveowners had little, if any, compunction about sundering them. In 1773, for example, an owner advertised for sale a family consisting of a "very valuable negro man, wench and several children," who were sold for "no fault" and could be bought "either together or separate." Owners were seemingly untroubled by similarly separating very young children from their mothers: in 1772 one owner offered a thirty-year old female slave

for sale either with or without a female child of two years and eight months, and a decade later Samuel Minor of Middlesex County, New Jersey, advertised a twenty-six-year-old woman and her boy of eight and girl of two "either together or separate, as best suits the purchasers.". . .

Very occasionally slaveowners selling slaves demonstrated a certain amount of concern for the future welfare of their slaves and at least attempted to facilitate the continuance of some semblance of family life. When John Bray of Raritan Landing advertised for sale his thirty-two-year-old male slave, a twenty-four-year-old female slave, and her child of fifteen months, he noted that they "being man and wife would make it most agreeable to sell them together." Nevertheless he ended the notice by commenting that "a few miles separation will not prevent the sale." In 1774 John Broome, a New York merchant, went to considerable trouble in order to help his twenty-nine-year-old slave. Reversing the usual practice, Broome insisted that the reputation of the potential buyer, rather than the slave, should be beyond reproach: the purchaser "must be of known sobriety and good character who lives not above ten miles from Staten Island." Broome went on to explain that his slave's wife "now lives there and after many attempts he has failed in getting her brought nearer to his present residence" in New York City and that offering the slave for sale was "an act of humanity in his master on that account." But even had Broome been successful in finding a suitable purchaser, his slave could probably have visited his wife at most once a week, so that even in such atypical cases mildly concerned masters were able to offer little practical assistance to their slaves. . . .

The reality of life for a slave in a peripheral slave society such as New York was that sooner or later one partner would be sold and moved even farther away. Although the New York Manumission Society managed, at least partially, to prop up the law and prevent many owners from selling slaves to the South or the West Indies, internal sales continued unhindered, inevitably separating husbands from wives and parents from children. William Dunlap, a member of the Manumission Society, witnessed a scene in Perth Amboy in 1797 that must have been repeated frequently: Andrew Bell "seperated a child from its mother, his slave, the Mother by her cries has made the town reecho & has continued her exclamations for 2 hours incessantly & still continues them." Dunlap recorded in his diary, "I am sick, at oppression," but, of course, he had merely observed the spectacle. It was the slaves and the slave family who took the full brunt of this emotionally devastating feature of New York and New Jersey slave life. Only when slavery ended could the black family establish a firm footing in and around New York.

But in spite of the considerable obstacles in their path, New York slaves were never simply victims of the white institution. Although there were not many slaves in the city and holdings were so small that family life was narrowly circumscribed, New Yorkers still managed to forge a distinctive black culture. In large part this was due to the compact urban environment. Close supervision of slaves in these densely settled areas was almost impossible. On their way to fetch water from the pump or, in the evening, wending their way to the river to dispose of sewage, slaves were able to mix with their compatriots. Furthermore, unlike the situation in southern cities, where the enclosed courtyard style of architecture allowed (theoretically at least) some control of slaves' movements, the design of New York City residences fostered a certain amount of slave autonomy. Typically, slaves lived in cellars or cellar kitchens located partially underground and had separate access to the street, a situation that encouraged the development of networks of kin, friends, and acquaintances among the city blacks. One day in 1804, for example, Jake sought out Ben by going to the cellar kitchen where Ben lived, knocking on the window, and persuading one of the female slaves to pass on the message.

This urban culture can occasionally be glimpsed through the disapproving and distorting prism of white commentary. For example, one detailed advertisement for the sale of a slave in 1775 noted that the man was a very good cook, with "many excellent good qualities and some superlatively bad ones." These detrimental attributes were closely associated with elements of city life that were virtually impossible to regulate and control. In this case an unusual candor compelled the owner "to declare that he is a slave unfit for a town resident but as his vices are chiefly local he would suit a family in the country extremely well." In another advertisement a young slave woman offered for sale in 1770 was described by her owner as having "Foibles that cannot be guarded against in town.". . . [A]s far as the slaves generally were concerned, these owners were offering the reverse image as reality: "gadding about" and indulging in vices of a "chiefly local" nature were, regardless of white opinion, major attractions of city life for most slaves.

The situation in the surrounding countryside was rather different. . . . Although slaves in this area made up twice as high a proportion of the total population as did slaves in the city and slaveholdings were larger, the low density of rural settlement effectively negated these advantages. In their day-to-day lives rural slaves came in contact with a much smaller number of compatriots than did their urban counterparts, which inevitably limited development of the networks that were so extensive and important for city slaves. While the larger size of rural slaveholdings may have increased marginally the chances of having a spouse resident on the same farm, the problem for the majority who did not live with their sexual partner was only exacerbated. In New York City couples were unlikely to be separated by more than a fifteen-minute walk, but in rural areas the distance could easily have been many miles.

Occasionally, blacks tried to overcome the tyranny of rural distances by using their master's horse. Sambo, an ingenious slave belonging to a Mount Pleasant doctor, devised his own solution to the problem by constructing a small sled for use in the winter months. His owner's wife noted that the sled "would have Answered to carry a bag of grain to mill & some other little purposes," but Sambo, who had had less utilitarian intentions in mind, converted it into a "pleasure Sled." One evening the restive slave "borrowed" a neighbor's horse, visited friends, and was able to return home by a "desent bed time." Generally, however, rural slaves lived an isolated existence, narrowly bounded by the rigors of work on the small farms that dotted the city's hinterland. . . .

In the slack between agricultural tasks complaisant masters allowed their slaves short periods of free time, and some took advantage of this latitude to visit the metropolis. During the day the black population of the city was swelled considerably by slaves from the surrounding area. Some slaves secured their owner's permission: Andrew Powlis, who lived seven miles from the Brooklyn ferry, was allowed by his master to go to New York for a few days to see his friends. Others doubtless slipped away, risking punishment by failing to obtain the required pass. Nor was it uncommon for slaves to make regular trips, either with or without their masters, to the city markets to buy and sell produce. While waiting for the tide to turn, they could often enjoy a few free hours. . . .

Although material on black rural life is extraordinarily hard to come by, it appears that at various times of the year country blacks attended organized gatherings as well. The most important institution here was the church. Slaves generally had Sundays off, and blacks came from miles around to attend religious services. In 1800 Samuel Thompson noted in his diary that "the black man Paul" preached two sermons to a large assembly in the meetinghouse and that a contribution was collected for him. Secular holidays were also observed; Thompson recorded that his slaves had celebrated the new year. Runaway advertisements furnish examples of slaves who had permission to stay away for holidays but did not return. In 1796, for instance, Jack had his master's "consent to keep the late holidays," but "as he has been away for a longer time than he had permission it is supposed that he intends not returning." At various times in the year the rural gentry engaged in a round of "frolics," sledding, and turkey shoots, and to a more limited extent so did the slaves. In June 1803 Thompson allowed his slave Killis to attend a "strawberry frolic." Pierre Van Cortlandt, whose family seat was on the east bank of the Hudson, wrote in 1799 to James Mandiville in nearby Peekskill claiming that "my Negro man Ishmael is one of the Fiddlers that frequents you[r] house at frolicking times." In future, Van Cortlandt intended to "prosicute any person that Encourages, or Suffer him to play the fiddle at Night in their houses."

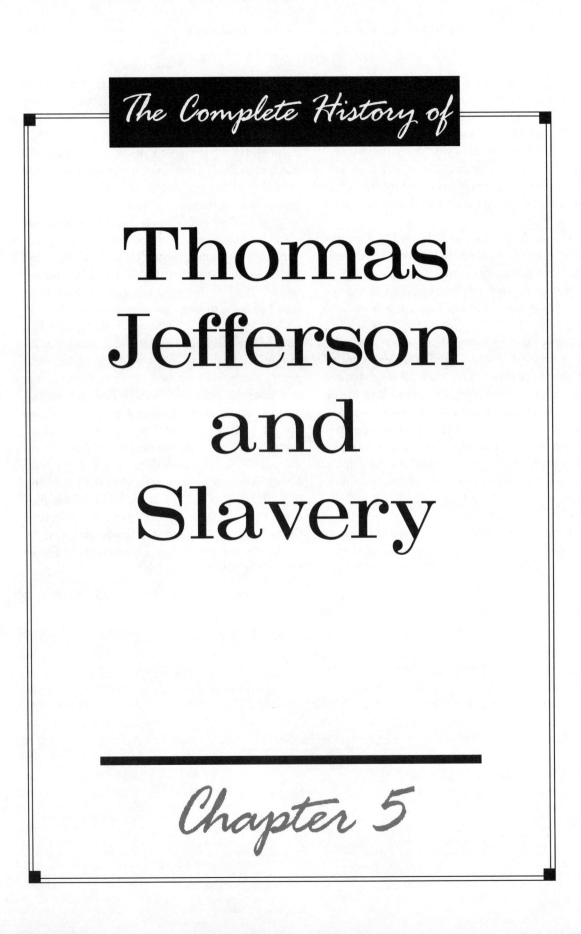

The Complete History of

Thomas Jefferson and Slavery

Chapter 5

Introduction

Of all the leaders of the American Revolution and founders of the new nation, none is as controversial as Thomas Jefferson. It is impossible not to be impressed by, and at the same time deeply disturbed about, the man. He was one of the most brilliant and versatile intellects who ever lived in this country. He drafted the Declaration of Independence and Virginia's Statute on Religious Liberty. He knew many languages, including ancient Greek and Anglo-Saxon. He was conversant with the cutting-edge science of his day. He founded the University of Virginia—planning its curriculum, designing its buildings, hiring its faculty, and lobbying the state legislature for its funding. He was one of America's greatest architects, the creator of a beautiful Virginia home called Monticello, and an accomplished amateur violinist. He invented practical devices and experimented with raising new crops. He was a polished diplomat and a shrewd politician. He served with distinction as the nation's first secretary of state and as its third president, and he doubled the nation's size by the Louisiana Purchase. He launched the Democratic Republican Party and eloquently expounded the cause of liberty, limited government, and human rights. He wrote many thousands of letters and could converse on topics as diverse as meteorology and theology. And he had the time to do all these things during his long life (1743–1826) because he was a wealthy slave owner. One thing he did *not* accomplish; he did not free his slaves. After his death, most of his bondspeople had to be sold to pay off his debts.

Always a center of controversy during his lifetime—his conservative political enemies detested him as "atheistical" and "Mad Tom the democrat"—"Mr. Jefferson" has recently returned to the spotlight of public scrutiny. Stories had continuously circulated among African Americans that Jefferson had fathered children by one of his slaves, a woman named Sally Hemings. In 1998, DNA evidence was used to show that these stories were probably true, though absolute certainty is still elusive.

The Jefferson-Hemings case has implications far beyond the spectacle of one more president being implicated in a sex scandal. Since Jefferson is so central a figure in our national heritage, and since slavery is so painful an issue for all Americans to confront, whatever we think of Mr. Jefferson's record on slavery says a great deal about how we regard American history and race relations.

Selection 1

Sally Hemings: Jefferson's Mistress?

Bernard A. Weisberger

Today, virtually all Americans know that there is strong evidence that Thomas Jefferson had an ongoing sexual relationship with one of his slaves, Sally Hemings—a relationship that may have begun when Jefferson, whose wife Martha had recently died, took the teenage Sally with him to France in the 1780s to be his daughter's personal servant. To complicate matters still further, Sally was Martha's half-sister, and apparently bore a striking physical resemblance to Jefferson's dead wife.

In this selection, historical writer Bernard A. Weisberger gives details of the Jefferson-Hemings relationship and speculates about the motives of the individuals involved. The story is complex, and many of the details are surprising. Weisberger's article was published in American Heritage *magazine in November 1997, a year before it was announced that DNA evidence had been found linking either Jefferson or one of his male kin to a known descendant of Sally Hemings.*

 hen the Supreme Court ruled that President Clinton was not immune during his term of office from Paula

Jones's suit charging alleged sexual harassment, I thought at once of writing a column about the accusations of sexual misconduct brought against previous Presidents. But I discarded the idea largely because the major stories were probably overfamiliar to those even passingly acquainted with presidential history. They begin with Thomas Jefferson's supposed fathering of children by his slave Sally Hemings and run on through various alleged or actual cases of bastardy and adultery involving some half-dozen other Chief Executives.

Instead I began a more sober essay on other cases in which the Supreme Court ruled on the extent of a sitting President's immunity from the legal obligations of ordinary citizens. But Sally Hemings kept coming back into my mind and would not go away.

I think I know why. First of all, because a bit of my personal history and that of *American Heritage* is involved in this particular episode. Second, because the story was recently revived by a 1995 movie, *Jefferson in Paris,* which was justly criticized in these pages by Geoffrey C. Ward for presenting the affair as unchallenged fact rather than speculation. And, third, because a new book, *Thomas Jefferson and Sally Hemings: An American Controversy*, by Annette Gordon-Reed, has just made its appearance and generated a fair amount of coverage. Gordon-

Reed, an African-American professor of law, makes a very potent case for the genuineness of the story. Sally Hemings is indisputably "in the news" again, and what is more, I have for a long time felt (as does Gordon-Reed) that the whole episode is no mere racy footnote to a great life.

Thomas Jefferson

The charge that Jefferson "kept as a concubine one of his slaves," by whom he had at least one son who resembled him, was first publicly made in 1802 by a hostile Richmond newspaperman (a renegade ex–Jefferson supporter) named James Callender. Callender is pretty generally agreed to have been a venal slanderer, and Jefferson's biographers lumped this assertion with other campaign calumnies that they dismissed as unworthy of refutation. I hardly recall being aware of it before 1971.

That year, however, *American Heritage* sent me to a meeting of the Organization of American Historians to scout for likely articles. There I heard the late Fawn Brodie, then teaching at

UCLA, deliver an eye-opening paper on the subject. I personally learned for the first time that Sally Hemings was not just any slave but the half-sister of Jefferson's beloved dead wife, Martha. Martha's father, John Wayles, was also Sally's father, by Betty Hemings, whom he owned, and Betty was herself the daughter of a white man and a slave woman. Three of Sally's grandparents, in short, were white. It came as news to me, too, that Madison Hemings, one of Sally's own sons, had at least confirmed Callender's essential point (but not his lurid details) in an interview in an Ohio newspaper in 1873. He said that Sally, then long dead, had told him that she had become Jefferson's concubine (his exact wording) when Jefferson (a widower since 1782) was ambassador to France and she was the maidservant of his small daughter Polly. In 1789, when she was sixteen, she had become pregnant with a son. Madison Hemings said that Sally, who could have been free by French law, consented to come back only on Jefferson's promise to grant her "extraordinary privileges" and to emancipate her children at the age of twenty-one. She went on to bear three more sons and a daughter to the master of Monticello and no children to anyone else.

Brodie believed this account and made a strong circumstantial (and plausible) case for it, which can be found in *American Heritage* for January 1972, for I brought the paperback with me and presented it to the editor in chief, Oliver Jensen. Jensen, no man to trifle with the reputation of a Thomas Jefferson, nonetheless saw it as a moving and attention-worthy piece of work and printed it, even departing from the magazine's custom to include footnotes.

Brodie's arguments are based on scrutiny of plantation records and rest essentially on three props: the special lifelong treatment accorded to Sally Hemings and her children, Jefferson's presence at Monticello whenever those children were conceived, and no solid evidence of any other paternity. Brodie believed that Sally was Jefferson's long-time secret mistress, that he could neither liberate nor acknowledge her and the children (as some slaveholders in such liaisons did) without destroying his career and lifework, and that his concealment of the connection compounded his guilt and ambivalence about his role as a slaveholder. You can find the thesis fully laid out in her 1974 book, *Thomas Jefferson: An Intimate Portrait*. That volume generated sharp rebuttals, which have been repeated in reviews of the movie and in recent studies of Jefferson.

Most of these simply say we can never know, which is the only sure truth, but I believe they then protest Jefferson's innocence too much. They don't always specify the blood relationship between Sally and Mrs. Jefferson or give much weight to Madison Hemings's testimony. Jefferson in his lifetime chose neither to rebut nor to affirm, but his legitimate daughters by Martha Wayles Jefferson and their children in turn were strenuous in denial. They explained the uncontested fact of a Jefferson look-alike among Sally's sons by saying that the father must have been one of the President's cousins. What we are left with, then, is the word of her black family against his white family. Who can be surprised that the almost universal judgment of white male historians is in favor of the latter?

Black historians of both sexes are more likely to think otherwise. This is not, I think, a mere matter of closing racial ranks. It's simply that African-Americans are not unfamiliar with such happenings. That John Wayles would keep his black daughter as a slave, that she should upon his death become the slave of his white daughter and thereafter the property of that daughter's husband, who might sleep with her—well, what would be so surprising about that? Dozens, hundreds of such sagas are recorded, not merely in abolitionist propaganda but in legal documents and black family memories.

Like it or not, we have to recognize that some things are refracted differently through the prisms of different collective experiences. Race does matter in how we see "our" past as well as the present. I am in no way suggesting that we can't have some form of shared and unifying American history, and I decidedly reject the proposition that there are only "identity group"

histories, each one "true" for members exclusively. All historians can find common ground in respect for rules of evidence and for the egalitarian strivings as well as failures of the American people. But the case of Sally Hemings reminds me that in some areas historians of differing ethnic backgrounds are likely to have differing but equally sustainable viewpoints. We need to recognize, not fight, that reality.

The storm over Brodie's book led me to other thoughts on the nature of history that have stayed with me. She made free use of the techniques of so-called psychobiography, which accepts a key premise of modern psychoanalysis—to wit, that within all of us are unconscious impulses and feelings that we repress when they are painful or problematic but that betray themselves in our words and behavior, to which they furnish a hidden key. For example, Brodie studied Jefferson's journals and letters for the summer of 1788 and found "evidence" of a burgeoning forbidden attraction for the adolescent slave girl in his household both in his frequent use of the word *mulatto* to describe the color of certain soils and in his burst of envious admiration for the patriarch Abraham in a painting of him and his concubine, Hagar, who was also his wife's servant. Critics insisted that one cannot put dead people on the couch so cavalierly.

With that last point I agree. Nonetheless, I question the wisdom of any historians too quick to discard what twentieth-century psychology, sociology, biology, and anthropology have taught us about the intricate workings of human consciousness. The question is not whether to use psychological insights but how. Otherwise we seem to say that people of the past must be assessed entirely on their own terms as "rational beings." I, for one, find it perfectly plausible that a forty-five-year-old Jefferson in Paris had sexual feelings even if he did not express them with the openness of a Benjamin Franklin, nor am I outraged by attempts to know the whole complex man better by searching for them. In fact he himself left a charming record of a clearly romantic Parisian involvement with Maria Cosway, the wife of an English painter.

Of course it was a different matter with Sally. If the story is true, he unambiguously exploited her dependent status. That brings up the general question of how to deal with the moral failings of our heroes, and here I can only offer my individual judgment and invite you to consult yours. Jefferson remains heroic to me for his superb utterances on freedom. Would I be dismayed if positive proof surfaced that Callender was right? No more so than I already am by Jefferson's slaveholding. Exploitation was what slavery was all about; you can't prettify it, and Jefferson himself knew that. Do I then reject his ideas? Of course not. Inspiring works of the mind do not, alas, always come from spotless beings. They may actually owe their existence to the inner conflicts and outer circumstances of their creators. But once born, they soar on wings of their own. Slaveholder Jefferson's hymns to liberty belong in the long run to all of us—to Sally Hemings's descendants as much as to Martha Jefferson's, and to yours and mine too.

What the DNA Evidence Suggests About Jefferson's Character

Ken Ringle

In late 1998, the prestigious British journal Science *announced that a team of experts had concluded that one known descendant of Sally Hemings carried DNA identical with that of the descendants of Thomas Jefferson. The American press generally treated this news as virtual certain proof that the long-rumored story of Thomas Jefferson having a slave mistress was true, and a powerful blow was struck at Jefferson's historical reputation. This selection is taken from reporter* Ken Ringle's story in the Washington Post, *reporting the news on November 7, 1998.*

Perhaps the most fascinating aspect of the story of Thomas Jefferson and his house slave Sally Hemings is the way it becomes a litmus test for our individual beliefs about this country.

Those who see the nation as a caldron of racism and hypocrisy can take the story as proof of white denial of the abusive racial sins of our forefathers.

Those who see the United States as the wellspring of liberty can view the relationship as one of human desire dwarfed by Jefferson's soaring vision of the rights of man.

Cynics can find cynicism, romantics can find romance, and others can find everything in between. And little of that is likely to change in the wake of apparent genetic proof that Jefferson fathered at least one of Hemings's children. Somebody or other has been making that charge for nearly 200 years.

What is likely to change is our view of the third president. Now in addition to weighing his accomplishments as a politician, statesman, writer, farmer, violinist, philosopher, mathematician, astronomer, architect, oenophile, linguist, inventor, ethnographer, classicist and author of perhaps the most influential document of the millennium—the Declaration of Independence—we'll be called on to debate yet another of his dimensions. But the label each of us puts on that dimension (backstairs lover? child-raping slave owner?) will say as much about us as it does about Thomas Jefferson.

Four years ago, Edward L. Ayers, co-author of "The Strange Case of Thomas Jefferson: Race and Slavery in American Memory," discovered in studying documents debating the Jefferson-Hemings relationship over the years that writers and scholars "who believe it do so for different reasons. White liberals, for example, tend to think of it as a rape—as the exploitation by power of a white slave owner on a helpless black slave." Black writers, on the other hand, have tended to "view it as a love story—as a triumph of the human heart over racial prejudice which whites don't want to consider possible."

In 1977, for example, the late John Chester Miller, in his classic study of Jefferson and slavery "Wolf by the Ears," wrote that if the Sally Hemings story were true, Jefferson

> deserves to be regarded as one of the most profligate liars and consummate hypocrites ever to occupy the presidency. To give credence to the Sally Hemings story . . . is to infer that there were no principles to which he was inviolably committed, that what he acclaimed as morality was no more than a rhetorical facade for self-indulgence, and that he was always prepared to make exceptions in his own case when it suited his purpose.

This week, Annette Gordon-Reed, an African American associate professor at the New York School of Law and author of "Thomas Jefferson and Sally Hemings, an American Controversy," declared the DNA findings will make Jefferson more accessible to all Americans, particularly blacks. "It makes him more human," she said. "We're not two separate people, blacks and whites. We're related by culture and by blood. And the nuances of that relationship" of which the Jefferson-Hemings story is an example "need to be understood. Slavery was not monolithic. And it demeans the lives of individual slaves not to give justice to those nuances."

If the public has taken to the Jefferson-Hemings relationship in recent years, historians until now almost universally dismissed it as unfounded hearsay, largely because it seemed so out of character for Jefferson. It was not that anyone thought him without flaws or ignored his continued employment of slavery while preaching against it, or even because they knew he decried miscegenation as an evil. After all, he ran a plantation where everyday evidence of it was inescapable: literally working in the fields and playing in the yard. He clearly accepted race-mixing in reality, however much he disapproved of it in theory.

But while his feelings about race and slavery were complex and often contradictory, his attitudes about females and family and his own personal rectitude appeared clear. He was overwhelmingly devoted to and protective of his daughters, so grief-stricken by his wife's death that he carried her last letter until the end of his days, so personally disciplined he rose every day before sunrise and washed in ice water. He tolerated weaknesses in others but seemed bent on obliterating them in himself.

"To me the story would be no more credible (and no more creditable) if the supposed object of Mr. Jefferson's amours had been white," wrote Jefferson biographer Dumas Malone in 1975. "From my understanding of his character, temperament, and judgment I do not believe that he would have done that with a woman of any sort."

Furthermore, ever since a dissolute and frustrated political office seeker named James

Thomson Callender first charged Jefferson in 1802 with maintaining Hemings as a mistress, the story has borne the taint of a partisan attack. Parts of it just didn't add up.

For example, Callender charged that Jefferson had fathered by Hemings a boy named Tom who at that point Callender wrote was 10 years old. Yet no such child was ever listed among Sally Hemings's children in the exhaustive plantation records that covered every aspect of Monticello.

In recent years descendants of a former slave named Thomas Woodson have maintained that their family oral history identified Woodson as Jefferson's son by Hemings. He was said to have been sent away—presumably in an effort to disguise his paternity—to grow up on a nearby plantation. But if Jefferson was fathering children by Hemings and trying to hide it, why would he send one away and not the rest?

In 1974, author Fawn Brodie dusted off an 1873 article published by an abolitionist journalist in a small Ohio paper called the Pike County Republican. In it, Madison Hemings, a child of Hemings who was homesteading in the area, detailed stories of his years in slavery, claiming in the process to be Jefferson's son. But few took that claim seriously.

In the mid–19th century, Jefferson's grandson Thomas J. Randolph had identified the father of Hemings's children as Peter Carr, Jefferson's nephew, whose association with Hemings was described as "perfectly notorious" at Monticello.

That might have accounted for the Jeffersonian resemblance apparent in Hemings's four children who survived infancy. But even as they noted an absence of any credible documentation for the Hemings-Jefferson relationship, scholars have been haunted by one great circumstantial question mark: Jefferson was away from Monticello for much of his life. Yet, whenever Sally Hemings conceived a child, including two who died in infancy, Jefferson was in residence.

Now comes the bombshell article in the highly respected scientific journal *Nature*. In scarcely a page-and-a-half it appears to cut through all the circumstantial knots in the case. Whoever Thomas Woodson was, DNA testing

shows, he was not the son of Thomas Jefferson. Thus Callender's original scenario was wrong. But Hemings's youngest son, Eston, apparently was Jefferson's child, barring some unlikely still-to-be-discovered other link between a Hemings descendant and a male Jefferson. The testing ruled out both Peter Carr and his brother, Samuel, though not apparently Jefferson's younger brother, Randolph, who visited Monticello on occasion.

"Nothing in [the DNA] study and nothing in the vast historical literature sheds any light on the character of the relationship between Jefferson and Sally Hemings," said an accompanying essay in *Nature* by Eric S. Lander and Joseph J. Ellis. "Was it . . . lust and rape? Was it . . . a love story? Or was it something in between? These questions are open to endless interpretation but . . . give blacks and whites alike an opportunity to confront a largely secret, shared history."

The biggest enigma of all, of course, is Sally Hemings. We know little about her, except that she was part of a family Jefferson inherited from his wife's father, John Wayles, who according to historians at Monticello, had been directly involved in the importation of slaves into Virginia.

Her mother, Betty, who had at least 10 children, was the daughter of an African slave and an English sea captain, and at least seven of her children were fathered by white men. Various contemporary stories, though no surviving documents, identify Wayles as Sally's father. There are only two known descriptions of Sally Hemings by contemporaries, one from a fellow slave and one from Jefferson's grandson. Both describe her as quite beautiful and so light-skinned she was almost white. She was 3 when she and her family arrived at Monticello, and within about five years had been enlisted to help care for Jefferson's youngest daughter, Mary, six years her junior.

From the time of their arrival, the Hemings family held a relatively privileged position among the slaves at Monticello. As house servants, they worked high on the plantation pecking order, with duties that demanded both tact and responsibility, rather than the harsher physical labors of the field. For example, according to historian Lucia C. Stanton, who has spent the past eight years researching slavery at Monticello, the Hemings women were the only slaves on the plantation regularly exempted from participation in the grueling wheat harvest.

When Sally was 14, she was sent with 8-year-old Mary to Paris, where Jefferson was ambassador. In Paris, according to Stanton, she would have received training in needlework and care of clothing to equip her as a lady's maid. In addition, Jefferson's account books note increasing expenses for clothing for both Sally and Jefferson's older daughter Martha (Patsy) when the latter began stepping out as a young lady in French society, with Sally as an attendant. Sally also occasionally received a monthly wage equivalent to about two dollars.

As Patsy's attendant, Sally also was exposed to the social refinements she would be expected to help impart to Mary in the absence of Jefferson's wife, Martha, who had died five years before. There is at least some evidence that she spoke French and may have played the harpsichord as well.

According to Madison Hemings's account, Sally and Jefferson began their relationship in Paris, and she returned with him in 1789, pregnant with a child that died in infancy. That part of the story has always been highly problematic for scholars, partly because of Sally's youth at the time, partly because no record of such child has ever been found. But it also seemed curious because during much of his time in France, Jefferson was obsessed with a British-Italian artist named Maria Cosway, the only woman after his wife's death for whom he ever evidenced any public attraction.

Paris offered no shortage of other beautiful and willing women as well. Why would he turn instead to his daughter's maid? One possible explanation offered by some historians is the connection between Sally Hemings and the wife Jefferson so adored. At his wife's deathbed, the third president took an oath never to marry again and place a stepmother between himself and his daughters.

Perhaps he saw in her a resemblance or a surrogate. Perhaps he came to desire her for her own beauty, unrelated to his wife. But how did she look on him? As an exploiter? As a molester? As a protector?

Historian Gordon-Bennett believes the relationship was "at least consensual."

"Obviously as his property Sally was potentially subject to any sort of treatment including rape," she said. But she cites two reasons for her belief that it was more than that—the apparent length of the relationship (at least nine years if Madison Hemings's story is believed) and the likelihood that Hemings could have easily escaped to freedom in France.

"She returned with Jefferson voluntarily, so there had to be some feeling there," Gordon-Bennett said, "however difficult that is for many to believe.

"I certainly don't romanticize slavery," which she said is "difficult both intellectually and emotionally" for people to deal with more than a century later, particularly African Americans like her. "But master-slave relationships were far more intricate and contradictory than most people realize."

As an example, she puts forward the case of Sally's sister Mary, who was leased to a Charlottesville man named Thomas Bell before Jefferson left for Paris.

"When Jefferson returned from France," Gordon-Bennett said, "Mary asked to be sold to Bell, and as he usually did for such requests, Jefferson agreed. Mary Hemings and Bell lived together for something like 15 years, had two children and when Bell died he left her his house" on Charlottesville's Main Street where Hemings descendants continued to live for a century.

"Now, I don't want to make that sound typical. Slavery was such a varied and complex situation there is no such thing as a 'typical' slave story. But things like this happened."

According to Jefferson's records, Stanton says, Sally Hemings had four surviving children. Beverly, born in 1798, was a carpenter and fiddler who was permitted to leave the plantation in the early 1820s and, according to Madison Hemings, passed into white society in Washington, D.C. He appears to have been accompanied by his sister Harriet, born in 1801. Madison Hemings, a carpenter, was freed in Jefferson's will and settled in Ohio. Eston Hemings, born in 1808 and also trained as a carpenter, moved to Chillicothe, Ohio, in the 1830s where he was a well-known musician. He later moved to Wisconsin and changed both his name and racial identification.

Sally Hemings was never freed by Thomas Jefferson. Apparently, in lieu of legal emancipation, his daughter Martha gave Hemings virtual freedom under an arrangement that allowed her to remain in Virginia, instead of leaving the state as the law required freed slaves to do. She lived in Charlottesville for nine years after his death in 1826.

No portrait of her is known to exist.

The DNA Evidence: Unanswered Questions

Leef Smith

Much of the American public (including most hitherto-skeptical American historians) was convinced that DNA evidence that linked Jefferson to Sally Hemings proved Jefferson had an affair with his maid. DNA evidence could not rule out, however, the possibility that one of Jefferson's male relatives may have carried the genetic markers that were identified in Hemings's descendants. Other factors complicate this matter: The child whose descendant's DNA apparently proved a link between Jefferson and Hemings was born when Jefferson was a rather elderly man. The other child whose descendant's DNA was tested and who Hemings bore earlier was not

shown to be related to her master. The mystery of whether Jefferson was Hemings's lover (or sexual exploiter) may still not be resolved to everyone's satisfaction. Historians have noted, however, that the times at which Hemings conceived all five of her children coincided with times when Jefferson was known to have been staying at Monticello.

This selection is reporter Leef Smith's Washington Post *story on January 6, 1999, about two months after the initial news broke that a DNA link had been established between Jefferson and Hemings.*

Some critics of a scientific study that found Thomas Jefferson probably fathered a child with his slave Sally Hemings have mounted a campaign to challenge the study's conclusions.

Although the group has not contested the results of genetic tests performed on descendants of Hemings and the Jefferson family, members argue that the report that appeared in the journal *Nature* in November was misleading, particularly in its headline: "Jefferson fathered slave's last child."

The critics say the headline caused some news organizations to oversimplify the study and report that DNA showed conclusively that Jefferson was the father of Hemings's son Eston. In fact, the study concluded that the scientific evidence, combined with historical evidence, showed Jefferson to be the likely father. It is theoretically possible, though unlikely, that another Jefferson male could have been the father, the authors of the study said.

Editors at *Nature* have acknowledged that the headline was unintentionally misleading and have suggested that their article could have included more alternative explanations of the children's paternity. But they said this week that they stand by the accuracy of the study and its conclusion that Jefferson was the likely father.

The coalition of Jefferson buffs and scholars scheduled a news conference in the District to publicize its criticism of the study. The group is led by Herbert Barger, who has studied Jefferson genealogy for more than 25 years and helped recruit Jefferson descendants for the genetic study. Also scheduled to attend is historian Willard S. Randall, author of "Thomas Jefferson: A Life," and members of the God and Country Foundation, a group that states one of its aims as being a watchdog against attacks on the reputations of the Founding Fathers.

Barger and others say there is credible and overlooked historical evidence to suggest that Jefferson's cousin George Jefferson Jr., Jefferson's brother Randolph or one of Randolph's five sons could have been the father of Hemings's children.

"There are eight people who could have been the father," Barger said. "That's all we want the public to know. . . . We're holding a press conference to get out the truth. I want it correct so that our children's history books are not incorrect. So that Thomas Jefferson is not branded a hypocrite.

That's the feeling of certain people today."

Nature will publish two letters from critics and a response from the study's authors in tomorrow's edition of the journal.

"This is not a correction or a retraction," said Laura Garwin, *Nature*'s North American editor. "The study still stands. It wasn't made perhaps as clear as it could have been . . . in hindsight, we could have done a better job."

The clarification, as Garwin has termed it, is contained in the published response from Eugene A. Foster, the retired University of Virginia pathologist who coordinated the DNA study with European scientists. In his letter, Foster reiterates that the genetic results do not rule out other Jefferson males with the same marker on their Y chromosome, saying that space constraints prevented the study authors from naming all other possible candidates.

Foster's letter also criticizes the headline on the study as "misleading." He said the headline represented only the simplest explanation of the group's findings: that the DNA match with descendants of Eston Hemings was made with Jefferson's family descendants, rather than with descendants of Jefferson's nephews Samuel and Peter Carr, whom many historians had cited as the best alternative candidates for fathering Eston.

Still, Foster defended the conclusions of the study. "We know from the historical and the DNA data that Thomas Jefferson can neither be definitely excluded nor solely implicated in the paternity of illegitimate children with his slave Sally Hemings," he wrote.

> When we embarked on this study we knew that the results could not be conclusive, but we hoped to obtain some objective data that would tilt the weight of the evidence in one direction or another. We think we have provided such data and that the modest, probabilistic interpretations we have made are tenable at present.

Historian Joseph J. Ellis, who won the National Book Award in 1997 for "American Sphinx: The Character of Thomas Jefferson," had long dismissed the possibility of a sexual relationship between Jefferson and Hemings. He said the DNA study changed his mind because the scientific evidence gave weight to the historical evidence linking the couple.

"The burden of proof has dramatically shifted," said Ellis, who co-wrote a companion piece to the *Nature* study. "If you want to argue Thomas Jefferson is not the father, you now have a tough case to make. . . . You have to be on a crusade to rescue Thomas Jefferson to not believe it."

But Randall, who spent five years writing his 1993 biography of Jefferson, said he remains unmoved by scientific or historical evidence suggesting a liaison.

"There were 25 men within 20 miles of Monticello who were all Jeffersons and had the same Y chromosome," said Randall, who will be the main speaker at today's news conference. "And 23 of them were younger than Jefferson, who was 65 years old, at that time a very advanced age, when Eston was conceived. . . . There's too much circumstantial evidence and Jefferson's explicit denial" that he fathered children with Hemings.

Selection 4

The Testimony of Jefferson's Slave

Brian McGinty

Aside from the sensational Sally Hemings story, what else is known about Thomas Jefferson's treatment of the slaves at Monticello? Long after Jefferson's death, one of his slaves told an interviewer what he remembered about "the old master's" character and habits, and how he treated his bondspeople. The slave, Isaac Jefferson (who, like many ex-slaves, had adopted his master's last name but who has never been suspected of being Jefferson's offspring), generally had good memories of "the Sage of Monticello," and some of what he said is consistent with other evidence of Jefferson's life and interests. Nevertheless, when interviewed, Isaac Jefferson was still a slave, he was speaking to a white man, and he might have said things that he knew his interviewer wanted to hear. Isaac Jefferson's stories must, therefore, be treated with a certain amount of caution.

This article originally appeared in 1987 as an essay by California lawyer Brian McGinty in the magazine American History Illustrated.

Reprinted from Brian McGinty, "Isaac Jefferson: The Slave Who Remembered," *American History Illustrated*, 1987. This article is reprinted from *American History Illustrated* magazine with the permission of PRIMEDIA Special Interest Publications (History Group), copyright American History Illustrated magazine.

S ome men are remembered after they die for the empires they built, the fortunes they acquired or spent, or the books they wrote. Others are remembered only for the ways in which their lives touched the lives of other men. Isaac Jefferson is remembered today for a man who once owned him—and for the extraordinary memories he left of that owner.

Isaac was past seventy years old and working

The slave quarters at Thomas Jefferson's
Monticello home in Virginia

in a blacksmith shop in Petersburg, Virginia, when he met a schoolmaster, author, and historian named Charles Campbell in 1847. Campbell's attention had been drawn to the old slave by a Petersburg resident who had often heard Isaac talk about his "old master," Thomas Jefferson. The slave was pleased by the attention Campbell showed him, and, as the historian asked him questions and took careful notes, Isaac talked freely and enthusiastically. He swore that every word of his story was true, "of course according to the best of my knowledge & belief."

As recorded by Campbell, Isaac's recollections had the unmistakable ring of truth. He had been born at Jefferson's Monticello in 1775, the son of a slave named George and his slave wife, "Usler" (Ursula). George was known on the Jefferson lands as "Great" or "King" George, his wife as "Queen." These regal appellations probably had more to do with the couple's commanding physical presences and personalities than to any privileges they enjoyed, for their "quarters" at Monticello were as humble as any. Ursula was, in the words of one of Jefferson's

overseers, a "big fat woman" who was in charge of all the children on the plantation when they were not in school. By occupation, she was a washerwoman and cook. Among Isaac's earliest memories of life at Monticello were visions of Mrs. Jefferson visiting his mother in "the quarters" where, with cookbook in hand, she gave instructions for making cakes, tarts, and other baked goods. Isaac "toted" wood for his mother and made her fires.

When Isaac was about four years old, the "old master" (he was then only thirty-six) took Isaac and some of the other slaves from Monticello to live at Williamsburg, where Jefferson had gone to serve as governor of Virginia. When, a short time later, the capital moved from Williamsburg to Richmond, the Jefferson entourage moved with it. Isaac was in Richmond when word reached the new capital that Benedict Arnold was approaching at the head of a British army. He saw Jefferson climb up into the skylight of the governor's house with a spyglass in hand and look searchingly toward the east. Isaac had "larnt to beat drum" in Richmond, and the skill stood him in good stead when, a short time later, Arnold's troops invaded the city and sent all the white people (Jefferson included) fleeing into the hills. "[I]t was an awful sight," Isaac told Charles Campbell: "seemed like the day of judgment was come."

Isaac's father was in front of the governor's house when a British officer rode up and demanded (as Isaac recalled later), "Where is the Governor?"

"He's gone to the mountains," George replied.

"Where are the keys of the house?"

George gave the officer the keys Jefferson had left with him.

"Where is the silver?" the officer continued.

"It was all sent up to the mountains," George lied, hoping the invaders would not discover that he had hidden Jefferson's silver in the house. His deception was not discovered, and, when Jefferson found out about it, he was so grateful that he rewarded George with his freedom.

Isaac's memories of life at Monticello were full. He said the big house on the plantation "was pulled down in part & built up again some six or seven times. . . . They was forty years at work upon that house before Mr. Jefferson stopped building."

"Old master had abundance of books," Isaac continued: "sometimes would have twenty of 'em down on the floor at once: read fust one, then tother. . . . [W]hen they go to him to ax him anything, he go right straight to the book & tell you all about it."

Isaac remembered Jefferson's love of music—the "fiddles" he played in the big house in the afternoons and sometimes after supper; the spinet his daughter played; and the pianoforte and guitar that French visitors sometimes used to entertain the family. "Mr. Jefferson always singing when ridin or walkin," Isaac explained: "hardly seen him anywhar out doors but what he was a-singin."

When Jefferson went to Philadelphia in 1790 as George Washington's secretary of state, Isaac (then fifteen years old) went with him. He was apprenticed for a couple of years to a Philadelphia tinsmith. After a while, Jefferson summoned the slave and, as he recalled nearly sixty years later, said: "Isaac you are larnin mighty fast: I bleeve I must send you back to Virginny to car on the tin-business. You is growing too big: no use for you to stay here no longer."

And so Isaac returned to Monticello to establish a tin shop and, later, to work in the large nailery on Jefferson's property. For a period of years, Isaac lived with Jefferson's son-in-law, Thomas Mann Randolph. But he was back at Monticello in 1822, when Jefferson's health (the great man was then seventy-nine years old) began to fail. "[H]e was took with a swelling in his legs," Isaac explained: "used to bathe 'em & bandage 'em: said it was settin too much: when he'd git up & walk it wouldn't hurt him." Isaac and another slave nursed the old man for two months, during which time they had to "car him about on a hanbarrow."

The will that Jefferson left after his death in 1826 granted freedom to five slaves, but Isaac was not one of them. Little is known of Isaac's life after Jefferson died, but a historian who made an exhaustive search of the records could find no evidence that he ever achieved the status of a free man.

If Isaac bore any ill will toward the man who could have freed him but did not, he did not hint at it in his talks with Charles Campbell. His comments on the "old master" were uniformly complimentary. "Mr. Jefferson was a tall straight-bodied man as ever you see," Isaac said: "right square-shouldered: nary man in this town walked so straight as my old master. . . ."

"Old master very kind to servants," Isaac said. "Gave the boys in the nail-factory a pound of meat a week, a dozen herrings, a quart of molasses & peck of meal. Give them that wukked the best a suit of red or blue: encouraged them mightily."

The handwritten manuscript that Charles Campbell titled "Life of Isaac Jefferson of Petersburg, Virginia, Blacksmith, . . . the whole taken down from his own words" was not published until 1951, almost a century after the slave's death in about 1853. In it Campbell noted that Isaac was "sensible, intelligent pleasant" and that he "bore a good character." He might have added: "And he remembered well."

Jefferson the Idealist

Douglas L. Wilson

Should we judge Thomas Jefferson—author of the Declaration of Independence, slave owner, and perhaps sexual abuser of a slave woman—by the standards by which a contemporary man of his stature would be judged? Or should our judgment of a man who lived two hundred years ago take into account the enormous changes in political, social, and cultural standards that have occurred between his time and ours? These are some of the issues addressed by Douglas L. Wilson in an article published in the Atlantic Monthly *in November 1992, at a time when controversies surrounding Bill Clinton's character were first becoming the subject of intense public debate.*

"*T*oday, makes yesterday mean."
Emily Dickinson's gnomic utterance contains at least one undoubted truth—that the perspectives of the present invariably color the meanings we ascribe to the past. Nothing confirms this so readily as the changing reputations of historical figures, whose status often appears indexed to present-day preoccupations. It may be inevitable that every age should refashion its historical heroes in a contemporary idiom, but doing so carries with it an obvious and

Reprinted from Douglas L. Wilson, "Thomas Jefferson and the Character Issue," *The Atlantic Monthly*, November 1992. Reprinted with permission from the author.

inherent danger. In imposing Today's meanings on Yesterday, we run the risk of distorting it—whether willfully, to suit our own purposes, or unintentionally, by unwarranted assumptions and because of meager information. In this way we lose track of what might be considered the obverse of Emily Dickinson's remark: that Yesterday has meanings of its own that are prior to and necessarily independent of Today's.

Thomas Jefferson is one of the few historical Americans who need no introduction. Even the most abbreviated knowledge of American history, at home or abroad, includes the author of the Declaration of Independence. Identified around the world with democracy and human rights, Jefferson's name and words have been invoked for two hundred years in the cause of freedom and political reform. But here in his own country, where the name synonymous with democracy is exhibited everywhere—on counties, cities, schools, streets, and every imaginable form of institution, business, and product—it sometimes seems that the man himself is receding from view, and that what is commonly thought and said about him gets harder and harder to reconcile with the great national hero. With the approach of the two hundred and fiftieth anniversary of his birth, in 1743, it seems appropriate to note some of the ways in which Thomas Jefferson is remembered by the American public and to examine the historical lens through which the man and his contributions are seen.

Only a generation ago Jefferson was still considered to be and treated as an object of veneration, so closely identified with the spirit of America as to constitute a problem for the historian. In 1960 Merrill D. Peterson confronted this problem in one of the most revealing works of Jefferson scholarship, *The Jefferson Image in the American Mind,* which surveys what Jefferson has meant to succeeding generations of Americans. "Where the object is Jefferson," Peterson wrote,

> the historian's obligation to historical truth is compromised, in some degree, by his sense of obligation to the Jefferson symbol. Jefferson occupies such an important place in the symbolical architecture of this nation that the search for the elusive *himself* from the vaunted summit, Objectivity, must not be allowed to empty the symbol of meaning for "Jefferson's children."

It is a measure of the change that has occurred in the past thirty years that the one thing Jefferson's children nowadays are most likely to associate with him, apart from his authorship of the Declaration of Independence, is a sexual liaison with one of his slaves, Sally Hemings. College teachers are often dismayed to discover that many if not most of their students now regard this as an accepted fact. But this is not all. In the prevailing ethos of the sexual revolution, Jefferson's supposed liaison is widely received with equanimity and seems to earn him nothing more reproachful than a knowing smile. For most, such a liaison is apparently not objectionable, and for some, its presumed reality actually seems to work in his favor, showing him to have been not a stuffy moralist but a man who cleverly managed to appear respectable while secretly carrying on an illicit relationship. In effect, something that before the 1960s would have been universally considered a shameful blot on Jefferson's character has become almost an asset. Confirming this state of affairs is the case of a prominent black civil-rights leader who complained not long ago that Jefferson's alleged relationship with Hemings is not forthrightly acknowledged by the proprietors of Monticello, Jefferson's residence, and who frankly confessed that this liaison had for him a positive effect in showing that, though a slaveholder, Jefferson was well disposed toward black people.

Although the charge that Jefferson had fathered several children by one of his slaves was first made public in his lifetime, by a vindictive journalist and office-seeker, James Callender, it was believed mainly by those who disparaged Jefferson for political reasons and was not credited by Jefferson scholars or the public at large. But that began to change in 1974, when Fawn M. Brodie published a widely read book on Jefferson in which she attempted to establish the truth of Callender's charge as a prime biographical fact. Brodie's thesis about Jefferson and Hemings is an embellished and controversial reading of the evidence, but what is more significant in the present context is that her story was well geared to the dispositions of her audience. She insisted that her object was not to pillory Jefferson or to make him out as a moral monster but merely to depict him as a man. If, as a widower, he fell in love with a beautiful slave girl and took her as a mistress when she was fourteen years old, it was "not scandalous debauchery with an innocent slave victim," she assured us, "but rather a serious passion that brought Jefferson and the slave woman much private happiness over a period lasting thirty-eight years." Brodie's benign version of the story has proved persuasive, and where previous versions had depicted such behavior as scandalous, hypocritical, or shameful, Jefferson and Hemings are represented as a pair of happy lovers, bravely defying the conventions of a sexually puritanical and racist society.

Compelling as this picture has proved to the American public, most Jefferson scholars and historians have remained unpersuaded. It is true that Jefferson was extremely protective of his personal life and went to considerable lengths to keep it private, but it does not follow, as Brodie would have us believe, that he must therefore have had something to hide. In accounting for Jefferson's behavior in the context of his own time, rather than ours, it is difficult for knowledgeable authorities to reconcile a liaison with Hemings with much else that is known about him. Jefferson implicitly denied the charge, and such evidence as exists about the paternity of Hemings's children points not to Jefferson but to his nephews. It is, of course, impossible to prove a negative, but the real problem with Brodie's interpretation is that it doesn't fit Jefferson. If he did take advantage of Hemings and father her children over a period of twenty years, he was acting completely out of character and violating his own standards of honor and decency. For a man who took questions of morality and honor very seriously, such a hypocritical liaison would have been a constant source of shame and guilt. For his close-knit family, who worshipped him and lived too near to him to have been ignorant of such an arrangement, it would have been a moral tragedy of no small dimensions.

But haunted as he was by other troubles and difficulties, there is no sign of this sort of shame or guilt in Jefferson's life. That is why Brodie must present Jefferson and Hemings as a happy couple and their supposed life together as giving satisfaction and lasting pleasure. And whereas there are grounds for suspecting a liaison, such as the terms of Jefferson's will and the testimony of Hemings's son Madison, there are no grounds whatever for believing in what Brodie called the "private happiness" enjoyed by Jefferson and Hemings. That is pure speculation. Because Brodie's thesis deals in such unwarranted assumptions, the great Jefferson biographer Dumas Malone regarded it as "without historical foundation." But what makes it possible for the American public to take the Sally Hemings story to heart, even more than the suspicious circumstances, seems to be a prevailing presentism.

"Presentism" is the term that historians use for applying contemporary or otherwise inappropriate standards to the past. An awkward term at best, it nevertheless names a malaise that currently plagues American discussions of anything and everything concerning the past: the widespread inability to make appropriate allowances for prevailing historical conditions.

The issue of presentism is hardly new, but it has perhaps been amplified of late by the debunking and revisionist spirit of the times and the effect this has had on public perceptions. As the uncritically positive and unabashedly patriotic approach that for so long characterized the teaching of American history in the public schools has abated, the emphasis has steadily shifted to the problems and failures of the past. The saga of the glories of the old West has thus given way to a saga of exploitation and greed. Pride in conquering the wilderness has yielded to the shame of despoiling the land and dispossessing the indigenous peoples. What seems to have happened is that a laudably corrective trend has predominated to such an extent that the emphasis seems somehow reversed, and parents complain that they scarcely recognize the history their children are taught.

With a built-in emphasis on what had previously been ignored or suppressed, it is hardly surprising that almost all the revisionist news, at least where traditional American heroes are concerned, is bad. A question that was once reasonably clear has become a muddle: How should we remember the leading figures of our history? By their greatest achievements and most important contributions or by their personal failures and peccadilloes? Can one category cancel out the other? In a sense these reversals of fortune are inevitable, inasmuch as nothing ever keeps its place in a world of incessant change. It is perhaps an instance of what the historian Henry Adams called the law of acceleration—the tendency of change to come faster and faster—that John F. Kennedy and Martin Luther King Jr., whose murders elevated them to martyrdom, should both come in for reappraisal while their memories and legacies are still fresh. Do the revelations about such things as Kennedy's womanizing, his not-so-heroic war record, and his nonauthorship of a book for which he accepted the Pulitzer Prize detract from his positive accomplishments as President? Do the revelations about King's philandering and his plagiarism as a graduate student have any bearing on his conspicuous achievements as a civil-rights leader?

Or is this a case of asking the question backward? Is it perhaps more appropriate and revealing to ask, Are the significant contributions of Kennedy and King, which affected the lives of millions of Americans, in any way diminished by subsequent revelations about their shortcomings and failings in other areas? In this climate the difficulties of judging a figure like Thomas Jefferson by an appropriate standard are considerably compounded. One who writes voluminously over a long time may easily have his own words quoted against him or cited to prove that he held views later modified or abandoned. Jefferson was pre-eminently such a person. On this point Merrill D. Peterson has observed,

> His speculative and practical sides were frequently confused. Few men took into account that Jefferson's private self, as expressed in his letters, might not coincide with his public self. Or that his opinion at one time might not represent his opinion under different circumstances. Or that a man of his intellectual temperament did not often bother to qualify felicitous generalizations.

In some ways that are little recognized, Jefferson is surprisingly modern and accessible to the present age. His pronounced notions about health, for example, which seemed somewhat odd to previous generations, appear nowadays in an entirely different light. He believed strongly that regular exercise was essential to physical and mental well-being. As a college student he developed a regimen of daily running to keep himself fit, and he came to believe in later life that walking was the most salutary form of exercise for the ordinary person. On the subject of diet he also held strong views, which minimized meat and animal products and emphasized instead the prime importance of vegetables. For our own time, at least, Jefferson turns out to have been something of a health-food prophet.

Whether his leading ideas on politics and government will prove as resilient remains to be seen. In spite of his great reputation as a statesman, many of these have proved as counter to the prevailing currents of American history as his prejudice against large cities and manufacturing. He could never reconcile himself, for example, to the Supreme Court's deciding the constitutionality of laws and acts of the executive—a development he regarded as unwarranted and disastrous. His preference for a small central government and his insistence on the prerogatives of the States have been strongly rebuffed, if not virtually obliterated, by decisive turns in our national development. Although history cannot be reversed, the relative size and power of the central government is once more (or still) at issue, as is the proper scope and authority of the Supreme Court. Even Jefferson's views on the disadvantages of large cities have today a resonance that was unheard or unheeded by previous generations.

Because he was attracted to laborsaving devices and was an ingenious adopter and adapter of new gadgets, Jefferson has gained a reputation as an inventor, but aside from a few items— an innovative moldboard for a plough, a revolving book stand—he probably invented little. Though he used and enthusiastically promoted the polygraph, a machine for making simultaneous copies of a written document, he did not invent it, and could not even keep his own in repair. But the fact that Jefferson is perceived as an inventor tells us something about the way he is valued. Abraham Lincoln was much interested in inventions and even went so far as to have one of his own patented, but this fact has made little impression on his admirers and is entirely absent from the legend.

President Kennedy paid a famous tribute to the multiplicity of Jefferson's talents, but they have always been regarded as astonishing. James Parton, one of Jefferson's nineteenth-century biographers, gave his dazzling range of abilities a dramatic accent when he characterized his subject as a man who "could calculate an eclipse, survey an estate, tie an artery, plan an edifice, try a cause, break a horse, dance a minuet, and play the violin." And Parton was describing a young Jefferson who had not yet written the Declaration. When the world's leading scientist and explorer, Alexander von Humboldt, came to visit Jefferson in Washington in 1804, he came to see not the President of the United States so much as the president of the American Philosophical Society and the author of *Notes on the State of Virginia* (1785). Had he visited the President at his home in Virginia, he would have seen what was perhaps the finest private library in America, which later became the foundation of the Library of Congress.

Not all of Jefferson's extraordinary talents are fully recognized by the public at large. One that is not is his great achievement as an architect. Self-taught from books and, until he went abroad, almost without worthy architectural models to observe, Jefferson managed to design a number of memorable structures. The residence of his that crowns (and names) a small mountain in the Virginia Piedmont has become one of the most familiar objects in American iconography. And Jefferson can claim credit for not just one Monticello but two: the domed structure represented on the back of the nickel is his second version of the house, which superseded the first one on the same site, and is dramatically different.

Part of the evidence for Jefferson's distinction as an architect is found in his beautifully detailed drawings, some of which reveal fanciful structures that were never built. But his most original and most imaginative design, and the one recognized by professional architects as among the greatest of all American architectural achievements, is his "academical village"—the campus of the University of Virginia. In forming his conception Jefferson effectively reinvented the idea of the university, from the innovative curriculum to the unique arrangement and design of the buildings. Here those seeking his monument have only to look about them.

Although he was a many-sided and multi-talented man who left a lasting imprint on a number of endeavors, there seems to be little doubt that Jefferson's pre-eminent contribution to the world was the Declaration of Independence— particularly its enduring affirmations of liberty and equality. In the prologue of the Declaration these affirmations were made the axioms from which the rights of revolution and self-government could confidently be deduced. The idea of individual liberty was not, of course, original with Jefferson, or exclusively an American invention. It was fostered in Western Europe by philosophers, religious dissidents, and political rebels, but it took root tenaciously among transplanted Europeans in the New World and, with the founding of the American republic, received its most durable expression in the Declaration of Independence. To the Declaration's studious and deeply learned author, many of what had passed in the history of the world for the prerogatives of governmental power were arbitrary and intolerable restraints on individual freedom. In fact, it is not too much to say that Jefferson's reigning political passion was a hatred of tyranny. And although his fear of the tyrannous abuse of power has sometimes been judged excessive, it is hard to argue that tyranny has ever been, or is even now, in short supply.

If it is possible to reduce so complex an issue to its simplest terms, one might venture that for Jefferson the paramount political issue in the American Revolution was what he called liberty and what we now call personal freedom, or choice. It was and remains the virtual sine qua non of American culture, something that Americans from the first have been strongly conscious of and willing to fight for. But what has become the most familiar and the most quoted phrase in the Declaration—"all men are created equal"—is about something else. It is an intriguing fact that although Americans generally understand that the prologue to the Declaration is their charter of freedom, even more indelibly impressed upon their imagination is its affirmation of the ideal of human equality.

How could the man who wrote that "all men are created equal" own slaves? This, in essence, is the question most persistently asked of those who write about Thomas Jefferson, and by all indications it is the thing that contemporary Americans find most vexing about him. In a recent series of some two dozen radio talk shows, I was asked this question on virtually every program, either by the host or by a caller. Most often, those who point to this problem admire Jefferson, and they appear as reluctant to give up their admiration as they would be to give up the principle of equality itself. But they are genuinely baffled by the seeming contradiction.

The question carries a silent assumption that because he practiced slaveholding, Jefferson must have somehow believed in it, and must therefore have been a hypocrite. My belief is that this way of asking the question, as in the cases of Kennedy and King, is essentially backward, and reflects the pervasive presentism of our time. Consider, for example, how different the question appears when inverted and framed in more historical terms: How did a man who was born into a slaveholding society, whose family and admired friends owned slaves, who inherited a fortune that was dependent on slaves and slave labor, decide at an early age that slavery was morally wrong and forcefully declare that it ought to be abolished?

Though stating the same case, these are obviously different questions, focusing on different things, but one is framed in a historical context and the other ignores historical circumstances. The rephrased question reveals that what is truly remarkable is that Jefferson went against his society and his own self-interest to denounce slavery and urge its abolition. And, crucially, there is no hidden assumption that he must in some way have believed in or tacitly accepted the morality of slavery.

But when the question is explained in this way, another invariably follows: If Jefferson came to believe that holding slaves was wrong, why did he continue to hold them? This question, because of its underlying assumptions, is both harder and easier than the first. It is harder because we are at such a great remove from the conditions of eighteenth-century Virginia that no satisfactory explanation can be given in a nutshell. To come to terms with the tangle of legal restrictions and other obstacles faced by the eighteenth-century Virginia slaveholder who might have wished freedom for his slaves, together with the extraordinary difficulties of finding them viable places of residence and means

of livelihood, requires a short course in early American history. But the question is easier in that there is no doubt that these obstacles to emancipation in Jefferson's Virginia were formidable, and the risk was demonstrably great that emancipated slaves would enjoy little, if any, real freedom and would, unless they could pass as white, be more likely to come to grief in a hostile environment. In short, the master whose concern extended beyond his own morality to the well-being of his slaves was caught on the horns of a dilemma. Thus the question of why Jefferson didn't free his slaves only serves to illustrate how presentism involves us in mistaken assumptions about historical conditions—in this case that an eighteenth-century slaveholder wanting to get out from under the moral stigma of slavery and improve the lot of his slaves had only to set them free.

The inevitable question about slavery and equality partly reflects the fact that most Americans are only vaguely familiar with the historical Jefferson, but delving into his writings and attempting to come to terms with the character of his thought, though illuminating, can create further consternation. The college student confronting Jefferson's one published book, *Notes on the State of Virginia*, is nowadays unprepared for and often appalled at what the author of the Declaration of Independence had to say about race. Thirty years ago college students were shocked to find Jefferson referring to the slave population as "blacks," a term that to them suggested racial insensitivity. But to those born after the civil-rights acts of the 1960s, it comes as a shock to discover that Jefferson, while firmly in favor of general emancipation, held out no hope for racial integration. Believing that an amalgamation of the races was not desirable and would not work, he advocated a plan of gradual emancipation and resettlement. Present-day students are even more shocked to find Jefferson concluding, albeit as "a suspicion only," that the blacks he had observed were "inferior to the whites in the endowments both of body and mind." Even his positive finding that blacks appeared to be superior to whites in musical ability rankles, for it comes through to students of the current generation as an early version of a familiar stereotype.

At a time like the present, when relations between the races are in the forefront of public discussion and desegregation is the law of the land, it is not surprising that college students should be sensitive to discrepancies between what they understand to be the prevailing ideals of their country and the views of its most prominent Founding Father. National ideals, however, spring not only from the beliefs and aspirations of founders but also, as this essay attempts to show, from the experience and efforts of subsequent generations. Though he foresaw that slavery could not prevail ("Nothing is more certainly written in the book of fate than that these people are to be free"), Jefferson can hardly be counted bigoted or backward for seriously doubting that a racially integrated society of white Europeans and black Africans was truly feasible. As the Harvard historian Bernard Bailyn has written, "It took a vast leap of the imagination in the eighteenth century to consider integrating into the political community the existing slave population, whose very 'nature' was the subject of puzzled inquiry and who had hitherto been politically non-existent." Interestingly, the reasons that Jefferson gave for doubting the possibility of integration—"deep rooted prejudices entertained by the whites; ten thousand recollections, by the blacks, of the injuries they have sustained; new provocations; [and] the real distinctions which nature has made"—are the same reasons often cited by black separatists, who entertain the same misgivings.

But if Jefferson's being a separatist can be accounted for, what can be said about his invidious comparison of the natural endowments of blacks with those of whites, or with those of American Indians, whom he found to be on a par with whites? His own testimony suggests an answer, for he admitted that his acquaintance with blacks did not extend to the African continent and embraced only black people who had been born in and forced to live under the degrading conditions of slavery. "It will be right to make great allowances for the difference of condition, of education, of conversation, of the sphere in which they move," Jefferson wrote, but it is evident in the hindsight of two hundred years that his estimate of the capabilities of blacks failed to make sufficient allowances, particularly for the things he himself named. It is perhaps poetic justice that posterity should be liable to the same kind of mistake in judging him.

But if Jefferson's beliefs add up to a kind of racism, we must specify two important qualifications. First, that Jefferson offered his conclusions as a hypothesis only, acknowledging that his own experience was not a sufficient basis on which to judge an entire race. Had he lived long enough to meet the ex-slave Frederick Douglass or hear the searing eloquence of his oratory, he would have recognized intellectual gifts in a black man that were superior to those of most whites. Douglass's oratory brings us to the second qualification, which is a telling one. Attacking the justifications for slavery in 1854, Douglass observed,

> Ignorance and depravity, and the inability to rise from degradation to civilization and respectability, are the most usual allegations against the oppressed. The evils most fostered by slavery and oppression are precisely those which slaveholders and oppressors would transfer from their system to the inherent character of their victims. Thus the very crimes of slavery become slavery's best defence. By making the enslaved a character fit only for slavery, they excuse themselves for refusing to make the slave a freeman.

Although we may find Jefferson guilty of failing to make adequate allowance for the conditions in which blacks were forced to live, Jefferson did not take the next step of concluding that blacks were fit only for slavery. This rationalization of slavery was indeed the common coin of slaveholders and other whites who condoned or tolerated the "peculiar" institution, but it formed no part of Jefferson's thinking. In fact, he took the opposite position: that having imposed the depredations of slavery on blacks, white Americans should not only emancipate them but also educate and train them to be self-sufficient, provide them with necessary materials, and establish a colony in which they could live as free and independent people.

But if going back to original sources and historical contexts is essential in discerning the meanings that Today has imposed on Yesterday, it is equally important in determining how Yesterday's meanings have colored Today's. The concept of equality that is universally recognized in our own time as a fundamental principle of American society only had its beginnings in the eighteenth century; it did not emerge full-blown from the Declaration of Independence.

Whenever he sent correspondents a copy of the Declaration, Jefferson transcribed the text in such a way as to show what the Continental Congress had added to his draft and what it had cut out. The process of congressional emendation was clearly a painful memory for him, and the deletion about which he probably felt the most regret was also the most radical of the passages, for it undertook to blame the King of England directly for the African slave trade. It begins,

> He has waged cruel war against human nature itself, violating it's most sacred rights of life and liberty in the persons of a distant people who never offended him, captivating & carrying them into slavery in another hemisphere, or to incur miserable death in their transportation thither. . . . Determined to keep open a market where MEN should be bought & sold, he has prostituted his negative for suppressing every legislative attempt to prohibit or to restrain this execrable commerce.

Had this passage been ratified as part of the official Declaration, then a question often raised in the nineteenth century—Did Jefferson mean to include blacks in the language of the Declaration?—would have been susceptible of a clear-cut and demonstrable answer. For, as the political scientist Jean Yarbrough has recently pointed out, this passage says unmistakably that the Africans captured into slavery were not a separate category of beings but men, with the sacred rights of life and liberty that are said in the pro-

logue of the Declaration to be the natural endowments of all men. It is precisely in having these same rights that the prologue asserts that all men are created equal.

This deleted passage also provides an answer to a question often raised in the twentieth century: Did Jefferson mean to include women in the phrase "all men are created equal"? Implicit in the passage is that "men" is being used in the broader sense of "mankind," for those who were cruelly transported to be "bought & sold" on the slave market were certainly female as well as male.

That blacks and women were meant to be included in the affirmations of Jefferson's Declaration at a time when they enjoyed nothing remotely like political and social equality underscores a source of continuing confusion for contemporary Americans—the difference between a philosophical conception of natural rights and a working system of laws and societal values which allows for the fullest expression of those rights. In our own time the stubbornly persistent disparity between these two is often a source of cynicism and despair, but a Jeffersonian perspective would put more emphasis on the considerable progress made in closing the gap. Jefferson himself was sustained by a profound belief in progress. His unshakable conviction that the world was steadily advancing, not only in the material but also in the moral sphere, is abundantly evident in his writings. Though sometimes criticized as being naive in this regard, he was fully aware that his belief embraced the prospect of recurrent political and social transformations. Writing from retirement at the age of seventy-three, he told a correspondent that "laws and institutions must go hand in hand with the progress of the human mind."

> As that becomes more developed, more enlightened, as new discoveries are made, new truths disclosed, and manners and opinions change with the change of circumstances, institutions must advance also, and keep pace with the times. We might as well require a man to wear still the coat which fitted him when a boy, as civilized society to remain ever under the regimen of their barbarous ancestors.

Historians question whether Jefferson meant for the ideals in the Declaration of Independence to apply to black Americans.

One way of looking at American history from Jefferson's day down to our own is as the series of changes and adjustments in our laws and institutions necessitated by the ideals implicit in Jefferson's Declaration. Sometimes the effect of these ideals has been simply to prevent other, incompatible ideals from gaining ascendancy, as in the case of Social Darwinism, whose notions of the natural inferiority of certain racial and social groups were impeded by the prevalence and familiarity of the Declaration's precepts. But without doubt the most important event in the development of the American ideal of equality, after Jefferson's Declaration, was Abraham Lincoln's address at Gettysburg. Without any warrant from the founders themselves or from subsequent interpreters or historians, Lincoln declared that not only the essential meaning of the Civil War but also the national purpose itself was epitomized in Jefferson's phrase "all men are created equal.". . .

Lincoln at Gettysburg was practicing not presentism but futurism. In the most stunning act of statesmanship in our history, he invested Jefferson's eighteenth-century notion of equality with an essentially new meaning and projected it onto the future of the nation. Transfigured in the context of civil war, and transformed by Lincoln into a larger and more consequential ideal, Jefferson's formulation would never be the same. Thanks in large part to Lincoln, Americans no longer understand the prologue of the Declaration as a philosophical expression of natural rights, but rather take it to be a statement about the social and political conditions that ought to prevail.

Jefferson's Declaration is thus remarkable not only for its durability—its ability to remain meaningful and relevant—but also for its adaptability to changing conditions. At a time when natural rights are widely proclaimed a nullity, the language of the Declaration is universally understood as affirming human rights, and is resorted to even by those who do not consciously associate their ideas or aspirations with Jefferson. When the black separatist Malcolm X underwent a change of heart about white people and publicly renounced the "sweeping indictments of one race," he told an audience in Chicago, "I am not a racist and do not subscribe to any of the tenets of racism. In all honesty and sincerity it can be stated that I wish nothing but freedom, justice, and equality; life, liberty, and the pursuit of happiness—for all people." Simply to name the most basic American ideals is to invoke the words of Jefferson.

"Today, makes Yesterday mean." In the light of the foregoing at least one more meaning for Emily Dickinson's evocative phrase emerges: that the constantly shifting conditions of the present serve to revivify the past, offering it up as a subject for renewed exploration. Thus we can never hope to say the last word about our history—about Thomas Jefferson, for example—because we are continually having to re-open the past and consider its transactions anew in the light of an unforeseen and unforeseeable present.

The Complete History of

Revolts and Colonization, 1791–1831

Chapter 6

Introduction

Despite hopeful signs that the Revolutionary era might clear the way for eventually ridding the new nation of human bondage, the third phase in the history of American slavery ended in a downward slide toward entrenching the "peculiar institution" more deeply than ever. Jefferson's gloomy thoughts in 1820 about whether it would ever be possible to cease gripping "the wolf by the ears" show the direction in which intelligent southern slave owners were moving.

Two factors help explain what was happening. First, a "slave society"—a set of complex social and economic relationships rooted in slavery—was entrenched in the Deep South and was clearly taking shape in the Chesapeake region. Second, white southerners were being driven to the conclusion that slavery must be tolerated as a "necessary evil" because the institution was too dangerous to abolish.

Ideas of liberty were in the air as the eighteenth century was giving way to the nineteenth; slaves knew this. They now had a common language in which they could speak, and they understood what their masters were saying among themselves. Christianity was giving them a shared vision of human dignity and a belief that the same God white people worshiped intended that they themselves should be free. Many of them heard that in the French Caribbean colony of Saint Domingue, between 1791 and 1804, enslaved blacks had thrown off slavery, killed or driven out their masters, and created an independent republic called Haiti. White slave owners knew this, too, for French refugees had fled to the United States from Saint Domingue with horrifying stories of whites being hacked to death or buried alive by their rebellious slaves.

The Haitian revolution quickly became North American slave owners' ultimate nightmare, and there were ominous signs that the same thing might happen in the United States. An apparently widespread slave conspiracy to seize Richmond and other cities in the state, and then to incite a rebellion of rural bondspeople, was uncovered in the nick of time in 1800. A similar conspiracy whose ringleader was a local free black man came to light in Charleston, South Carolina, in 1822. In 1829, a free black in faraway Boston, Massachusetts, named David Walker published a long, inflammatory pamphlet calling on black people to strike for freedom and warning whites that, unless slavery was quickly abolished, they would suffer divinely inspired vengeance at the hands of the blacks they so despised. Copies of Walker's *Appeal* turned up in the hands of many southern blacks. Then, in 1831, a seemingly docile slave preacher named Nat Turner, whose master was not known to have been especially abusive, led a band of Virginia slaves on a bloody rampage through rural Southampton County that left fifty-five whites axed to death. Jefferson's metaphor of whites holding an angry wolf by the ears seemed apt.

What to do? One solution was to deport blacks from the country, preferably back to their native Africa. Doing so would "rid" the nation of what most whites considered an inferior, dangerous, and unassimilable presence in their midst. At the same time, this would continue the Revolution's legacy of extending human freedom and repaying whatever moral debt whites owed to blacks for having enslaved them in the first place. In 1816, well-meaning but still essentially racist whites founded the American Colonization Society with the aim of promoting the resettlement of emancipated blacks abroad. Thomas Jefferson and many other important men of the day commended its aims and methods. The society raised enough money to sponsor the emigration of about fourteen hundred ex-slaves to what is now the Republic of Liberia.

But colonization would never work. Accomplishing its stated goals would have cost far more money than white America was ever prepared to spend. For every black person it dispatched to Liberia, dozens of enslaved and free black children were being born in America. In addition, few blacks wanted to go. Overwhelmingly, free blacks now considered themselves African Americans and wanted to stay in this country, working to better their own lives and to bring freedom as soon as possible to their enslaved brothers and sisters. To send meaningful numbers of blacks back to Africa would have required force; it would have amounted to what today is called "ethnic cleansing." And, of course, most slave owners knew that they could not dispense with their human property. Black people were here to stay; the burning question was, Was slavery also here to stay? In 1831, the year of Nat Turner's Rebellion, that question was being posed with unusual starkness.

Selection 1

The Slave Owners' Nightmare: The Haitian Revolution

Philip D. Curtin

In the eighteenth century, French-ruled Saint Domingue, occupying the western third of the island of Hispaniola, was the wealthiest sugar-producing colony in the West Indies, with a population (in 1789) of about 550,000—all but 50,000 of them black slaves. (About half of the remainder were whites, the rest being free blacks and persons of mixed race.) In 1791, the bondspeople be-

gan a bloody rebellion against the brutal slave system. Not wanting to lose the colony, France's revolutionary government fought to retain its rule over Saint Domingue while, in 1794, formally abolishing slavery. The next year, France annexed from Spain the eastern two-thirds of the island (the area then called Santo Domingo and today known as the Dominican Republic), but for almost a decade the French government exercised no effective control over the colony. During this period the ex-slave Toussaint L'Ouverture, a man of great ability and magnetic character, was the island's de facto ruler, though still under

Excerpted from Philip D. Curtin, *The Rise and Fall of the Plantation Complex.* Copyright © 1990, 1998 Cambridge University Press. Reprinted with permission from Cambridge University Press.

nominal French sovereignty. But in 1801 relations deteriorated after France's new ruler, Napoléon Bonaparte, sent an army to restore more direct control. Toussaint was arrested, deported, and died in a French prison, but other black leaders precipitated a new revolt. By the end of 1803, the French were defeated, and on January 1, 1804, the blacks declared the island's independence, reviving its old Native American name: Haiti.

The Haitian revolution horrified white Americans. Soon after it got under way, refugee French planters began streaming into the United States with tales of the savagery of the black rebels. Fears of a similar uprising in the United States contributed heavily to the decline of post-revolutionary talk of abolishing slavery, especially in the Chesapeake states. Not until 1862, after representatives of most of the slaveholding states were no longer present in Congress to block the action, did the United States muster the political will to recognize Haiti.

In this selection, Philip D. Curtin, a well-known authority on African and world history who teaches at Johns Hopkins University, analyzes the Haitian revolution. It marked, he finds, the beginning of the end of the slave-labor plantation system in the New World, which had originated in the seventeenth century.

*T*he slave rebellion that began in 1791 and led to the independence of Haiti in 1804 was the key revolution in the fall of the plantation complex. It not only ended the slave regime on the French half of the island; it also made Haiti the first European colony with a non-European population to achieve independence and formal, if somewhat grudging, recognition as a member of the community of Western nations.

The Haitian revolution was also the most violent step toward the end of the plantation complex. Its only rival in violence was the American Civil War some seventy years later; but North American plantations were marginal to the complex, and the American Civil War was fought

about other issues as well as slavery. The French Antilles, on the other hand, were central to the slave regime in the Caribbean, and the Caribbean was central to the whole plantation complex in the late eighteenth century.

Geography of the French Antilles

The large colony of Saint Domingue was the heart of the French Caribbean as of the 1780s, even more so than Jamaica was in the British Caribbean. But Saint Domingue was not a single social and economic unit in the same way Jamaica was. It was divided into three separate provinces that communicated with France and with one another by sea. Each province was socially and economically distinct; each was focused on its own urban center or centers. The provinces were just as much separate entities as were the two island colonies of Guadeloupe and Martinique. In that sense, the French Caribbean consisted of five island colonial units, plus Cayenne, or French Guiana.

The geography of Saint Domingue was largely responsible for the division of the colony into three separate units. The western end of the islands is shaped like a U with its top to the west—the two arms of the U being long peninsulas formed by mountain ranges that take off from the central massif along the French-Spanish border. The colony could therefore be approached from the north coast, the south coast, or the central bay.

The North Province included the northern peninsula stretching to the west, but it centered on the lowlands of the north coast. The *plaine du nord* was the best sugar land on the island, with the largest concentration of estates and the most valuable estates. Cap Français was its metropolis, the largest town in the whole colony, and the capital.

The West Province was not west at all, but central. Unlike the north, it was split topographically into three areas of good sugar land, each with its own small town centers. These were the Valley of the Artibonite, shipping through the ports of Saint Marc and Gonaïves; the valley of the cul-de-sac, shipping through Port-au-Prince, capital of the province; and the coastal plain around Léogane.

The South Province was mainly the southern peninsula stretching to the west, rugged and mountainous, with only pockets of good sugar land along the coasts. Its main product was coffee, grown in the mountains on many comparatively small estates. With smaller estates, the proprietors were less wealthy than the sugar planters of the coastal plains; more of the proprietors were men of color; and the provincial society was less tightly stratified, though a tense rivalry existed between the colored and white castes. The only urban centers were small and scattered port towns—Jérémie, Aux Cayes, and Jacmel.

Below the provincial level was the parish—as in Jamaica or Louisiana—equivalent to a North American county. The parishes were the basic units of local government and militia organization, and the first rung for the formation of planter opinion or political action of any kind. . . .

Social Structure and Social Tensions

The social structure of Saint Domingue was much like that of other West Indian colonies of the period; but class and caste divisions were more aggravated here than elsewhere, and the conflict with the metropolis was more serious. In caste terms, the numerical breakdown in the late 1780s was 40,000 whites, 28,000 free colored, and 452,000 slaves—8, 5, and 87 percent, respectively.

Caste relations had been deteriorating in the 1770s and 1780s. Growing demand for Saint Domingue sugar had increased slave imports, whereas the white population had been stable for several decades. The planters drove the slaves harder to meet the increased demand for their products. Saint Domingue had more proprietors and wealthy whites in residence than was common on most British Caribbean islands. Resident owners used slaves as domestics,

which increased the proportion of house to field slaves, and the division between house and field slaves was drawn more tightly than it was elsewhere. This, in turn, increased resentment when planters sent house slaves to the fields as punishment, and the number of runaways increased.

The colored caste was also restive. As the children, and often the recognized children, of French fathers, they claimed equality with other children of Frenchmen. Indeed, the *code noire* [black code], the general slave code promulgated many decades earlier, bestowed a technical equality, but new legislation took it away. French laws of the 1770s prohibited marriage of coloreds with free whites and the practice of the privileged professions, even in France.

Within the white caste, class divisions were particularly strong and class relations were bad. The planters of Saint Domingue were, more generally than elsewhere, related to the French nobility, and they were trying to raise themselves to a special privileged order equivalent to that nobility. In law, however, all colonial land was unprivileged, and colonial landowners were members of the third estate of commoners. The growing separation between the most aristocratic of the whites, called the *grands blancs* [great whites], and the others was accentuated by the bitterness of those whites who had come to the Caribbean at great personal risk to try to make a fortune but had failed. The majority of whites were still *petits blancs* [little whites]—small planters, clerks, merchants' agents, shopkeepers, and skilled workers.

Relations between the colony and the metropolis created another kind of division. Officials, army officers, and merchants all had strong interests in metropolitan France; they were fully aware that their presence in the colony was temporary. The absentee planters also wanted the island to stay within the French Empire, and so did some of the *petits blancs*. But the wealthy planters as a class found the metropolitan controls galling and would have preferred independence—all things being equal.

In the Lesser Antilles, all of these social stresses and strains were repeated, but with slightly different twists. The colonies were smaller, of course—about 85,000 slaves for each of Martinique and Guadeloupe—but with larger proportions of whites than in Saint Domingue. Economically, these islands were no longer growing rapidly. The slave trade still went on, but only to rectify the excess of deaths over births. The big growth, and the big plantations within the French sphere, were in Saint Domingue. Martinique came next in social prestige and Guadeloupe last. An eighteenth-century commentator on the French Antilles epitomized these gradations by referring to the *grands seigneurs* [great lords] of Saint Domingue, the *gentilshommes* [gentlemen] of Martinique, and the *bonnes gens* [good men] of Guadeloupe. White planters in Martinique would sometimes tell visitors, behind the hand, that all the so-called whites of Guadeloupe were really light colored people, not pure French at all.

Other social differences had economic roots. French merchants did not usually buy directly from the planters through their agents in the colonial port towns. Instead, a local class of merchants bought from individual planters, bulked the product, and sold to the French merchants. The existence of this class of brokers, or *commissaires*, helped to reduce the tension between the planters on the islands and the merchants of France, and it helped to increase the tension between the planting class on their rural estates and the townsmen and merchants with whom they dealt.

As of 1788, differences between these social tensions in the islands and those in France are immediately striking. In France, the peasantry wanted to remove the remnants of their feudal obligations. In Saint Domingue there were no peasants, only slaves; no nobles, only planters. In France the bourgeoisie resented the legal privilege of the noble estate. In Saint Domingue there was no privileged estate, only a privileged racial caste of whites who were, incidentally, members of the French third estate. In France, many wanted reform and the rationalization of government to make it more efficient, remove outworn abuses, and provide equality before the law. In the colony, the most vocal and powerful minorities demanded relaxation of government control, but certainly not equality—not even within the white caste, much less between white and colored. If slavery were to be considered an outworn abuse, as many people in France were beginning to believe, white colonial opinion wanted it continued as long as possible.

It is hard to see how these different social tensions would mesh together if and when revolution came in either France or Saint Domingue. Actually, they meshed in a very peculiar way. When French agitators demanded change, they tended to put their particular and specific grievances in general terms. They talked about "liberty, equality, and fraternity" or about the "rights of man." The colonists saw the generalizations and read into them their own specific grievances, however different.

The *grands blancs* generally justified their attempt at separatism and their own control of the colony in terms of liberty. Clearly, they said, the general will should rule, and who, better than they, represented the general will of the colony. The *petits blancs* justified themselves in terms of fraternity, or continued union with France, the indivisible nation, in which all citizens should have an equal say. The colored people stood by the idea of equality: Were not all men (except slaves) born free and equal in their rights? Clearly they were entitled to participate as well.

The Revolution on Saint Domingue

The revolution on Saint Domingue began to take form in 1788, with the first French call for a meeting of the Estates General, and it ended with Haitian independence in 1804. The events in between were most complex. One way through the maze is to envisage a drama in three acts, and with three major questions at stake: How would the colony be related to France? Who would emerge as the dominant group within the colony? What relations would that group have with the workers?

The first act of the play ran from 1788 to 1791.

It was a period in which each social group with a grievance—and every social group on the island had one—entered in turn into active participation in open rebellion against someone else. The first revolt was that of the *grands blancs.* When the French government called for a meeting of the Estates General for 1789, it had not intended the colonies to be represented, but the *grands blancs* saw an opening. Here was a chance to win out over their enemies, the merchants and officials—against what they regarded as ministerial despotism and stifling trade restrictions.

They therefore elected representatives to the Estates General and sent them to France, invited or not. The representatives were mostly nobles or pseudonobles, mostly wealthy planters, and mostly from the North Province. They hung around Paris, scrapping with the absentee planters (who wanted to represent the islands themselves), and finally, by the middle of 1789, gained admission to the National Assembly. Once in Paris, curiously enough, they tended to vote with the moderate revolutionaires of the third estate.

Meanwhile, back in the colony, the same group that had sent the representatives to Paris went on to elect a set of local assemblies—one for the whole colony and one for each province. They kept the *petits blancs* out of power by limiting the franchise to those who owned twenty or more slaves, and, once elected, the assemblies began moving toward autonomy of some sort, perhaps full independence following the North American precedent.

The second revolt (the second scene in the first act of the drama) was that of the *petits blancs,* the officials, and the merchants—all of whom either believed that they were being excluded from local political power or were disturbed at the prospect of colonial independence. Throughout the latter part of 1789 and early 1790, these people became increasingly agitated. Finally, in the spring of 1790, the agitation turned to civil war, though a civil war confined to the white caste; the colored people and the slaves simply looked on. The *petits blancs* were generally successful in a number of small engagements. Finally, in August 1790,

the *grand blanc* Assembly of Saint Marc (in theory, the central assembly for the entire colony) captured a ship and sailed for France. The *petits blancs* had won that round, but was it a victory for the revolution or the counter-revolution? Nobody really knew. Both factions claimed to represent the revolution that was going on in France. Neither actually represented anyone but themselves—but the white civil war prepared the way for a new rising.

A third revolt, the third scene of the first act, came from the *gens de couleur* [people of color], who had not yet moved. The colored people were in a good position in France, where they could claim their equality under the rights of man. They worked through their own self-appointed representatives in Paris, cooperated with the French antislavery society—the Société des Amis des Noirs [Society of Friends of the Blacks]—and finally got an act passed giving them complete equality with whites throughout the French Empire. This agitation, however, took time and was not achieved until May 1791.

Meanwhile, some of the colored people preferred not to wait. One leader, Vincent Ogé, went from France to the United States, bought some arms, and landed secretly on the north coast of Saint Domingue in October 1790. He hoped to raise the colored people in a general revolt against the whites. He failed and was executed, along with several hundred others. In the end, all he accomplished was to bring about a wave of racial repression throughout the northern part of the island. That was the final revolt of the first act of the drama. By the summer of 1791, all the possible white and colored factions had entered the revolution. All claimed to be revolutionary and against the Old Regime. All claimed to represent the ideals of the revolution in France.

The second act began when the slaves moved. They had done nothing significant during the three years of disputation that had begun in mid-1788. Small-scale slave rebellions had occurred throughout the seventeenth and early eighteenth centuries. Runaway bands of maroons were already in the hills, especially the mountain chain separating the French from the Spanish part of the islands. All they needed was an opportunity, and the struggles between the white and colored factions supplied one.

The rebellion broke out in August 1791. Within ten days the whole North Province was in revolt, leaving the whites only a weak hold on the city of Cap Français itself. Within the first month about 200 sugar estates had been burned, along with many more coffee and other small plantations. About 1,000 whites were caught in rural areas and killed. The rest escaped to the towns, and many left the island.

The successful surprise of the revolt shows the organizational ability of the leadership. It was one thing to organize a revolt in secret that could carry one or two plantations. This one carried the greater part of the North Province at one time. The exact nature of that organization is unknown and unknowable at this distance in time. Given the size of the operation, the leaders must have been drawn from among the existing leaders of the slave society. On eighteenth-century plantations, slave leaders were either trained, skilled slaves who had learned a good deal about European culture—slave drivers whom the others were already accustomed to obey—or people with significant roles in the traditional religion.

The original leader of the North Province revolt of 1791, for example, was a *commandeur de plantation*, the equivalent of a head driver. He was also a cult leader in a non-Christian religious sect of a type ancestral to the modern Haitian vodun. The French records report his name as Boukman. *Boukman* was the title of a quasi-religious, quasi-political officer in some Mande or Malinké states in West Africa at that time. The coincidence may not indicate that the leader was himself African born, but it suggests that his leadership had religious roots in Haitian creole culture. Boukman may have been his title rather than his name.

This second act of the drama of revolution lasted from August 1791 well into 1794. It was marked by generalized anarchy, civil war, and swift changes in the fortunes of those wars. It was, in essence, a four-sided civil war among the two white factions, the colored, and the slaves acting in various combinations. In 1793, Spanish forces from the other half of the island and British forces from Jamaica also joined in, so that the fighting became six-sided. A six-sided war is hard to fight consistently; temporary alliances and combinations tend to emerge; chance and circumstance made for strange bedfellows.

As an example, toward the end of 1791, three different forms of alliance existed simultaneously in the three provinces. In the North Province, the slave rising posed such a threat that the whites and coloreds forgot their differences and joined forces to protect Cap Français. In the West Province there was still no slave rising, but the planting class as a whole (both white and colored) was so unfriendly to the officials, *petits blancs*, and merchants of Port-au-Prince that the struggle became a rural-urban conflict— caste and race aside. In the South Province, coffee planters had better relations with their slaves than was the case elsewhere in the island but the white-colored conflict was very bitter. In this area, some of the white and colored planters armed their slaves and fought each other in a war between the two upper castes, the slaves taking part on both sides. Here the townsmen, who were few in any case, played only a minor part.

But none of these situations could be permanent. During 1792 the slave revolt spread to the two southern provinces. Anarchy became general. From then on, the only overall leadership came from the commissioners sent out from France. These commissioners, in effect governors, were the representatives of revolutionary France. They tried to decide which, if any, of the various groups in the colonial society were the true equivalents of the *sans culottes*, the lower ranks of the bourgeoisie, who were becoming more powerful in the National Assembly throughout 1793 and 1794.

They tried, at first, to form an alliance of *petits blancs* and colored people, since neither the big planters nor the slaves seemed much like good French bourgeois. This alliance was never strong, but it could work as long as the slaves

*Toussaint L'Ouverture was the ex-slave
who led the Haitian revolution.*

were the greatest threat to any part of the old order. But the course of military affairs brought about some important shifts. The slave forces weakened, and the British and Spanish invaders became more of a threat. In this situation, some *grands blancs* in 1793 thought they saw the opportunity for a cout d'etat against the French officials. In response, the officials were forced to seek support further down in the colonial class structure. They responded by arming some 12,000 slaves, who became their main fighting force, capable of holding whatever part of the island France held at all.

Then, in 1794, the National Assembly in France shifted further to the left. It proclaimed the emancipation of the slaves in all the colonies. With this, the leaders of the ex-slaves in rebellion against France on Saint Domingue changed sides. The French commissioners could then rally the support of the ex-slaves as a group. That ended the second act with a victory for the slaves (in the struggle for local superiority) and for France (in the struggle between the colony and the metropolis).

The third act occupied the entire decade of 1794 to 1804. It was an equally confused period in which the slave victory was mainly assured; but the French victory was nullified, and Haiti emerged as an independent state. This shift in Haitian affairs was mainly the work of Toussaint L'Ouverture. He was one of the many slave leaders who had fought on one side, then another. The Emancipation Act brought him to the side of France in the summer of 1794. From then on, he built a growing following among the black group as a whole. With this unity he was able to defeat first the British and Spanish invaders, then the remaining *gens de couleur,* and finally the governor-general sent from France to take control of the newly won colony. By 1801, Toussaint was in actual control, and he was recognized by France as the official representative of French power.

Perhaps this really is the end of the drama, but with an epilogue. In 1802 and 1803 the French tried to reconquer the colony, but failed. They captured Toussaint L'Ouverture and sent him to France. The final defense of his work was left to his lieutenants, Jean-Jacques Desallines and Henri Christophe. By 1803, they had driven out the French. On January 1, 1804, they proclaimed the independence of Haiti.

Gabriel's Insurrection

Virginius Dabney

The year 1800 was a time of great political tension in the United States. The conflict between Federalists who deeply distrusted democracy and Republicans who wanted more democracy climaxed in a battle for control of Congress and the presidency, pitting Federalist president John Adams against Republican vice-president Thomas Jefferson. Under Federalist-sponsored legislation, free speech was seriously curtailed, and there was talk of using the country's small standing army to quell the opposition. Republicans in Virginia and Kentucky threatened to nullify federal laws that they thought endangered freedom. Just in case, President Adams kept a cache of arms in the presidential mansion (which was not yet called the White House). The balloting for president led to a tie between Jefferson and his ambitious, tricky running mate, Aaron Burr. (Under the constitutional rules then in force, such a bizarre outcome was possible.) As the year ended, the deadlock deepened.

Such were the ominous circumstances under which a plot was revealed during the summer of 1800. It became known that slaves were planning to seize Virginia's capital, Richmond, to kill as many whites as they could, and then set in motion uprisings elsewhere in

Reprinted from Virginius Dabney, "Gabriel's Insurrection," *American History Illustrated*, July 1976. This article is reprinted from *American History Illustrated* magazine with the permission of PRI-MEDIA Special Interest Publications (History Group), copyright American History Illustrated magazine.

the state. Whites had fresh memories of the slave uprising in Saint Domingue. Blacks, too, had memories not only of the suffering they had to endure as slaves but also of overhearing their masters' conversations about "inalienable rights" and "the right of revolution"; nor were Virginia slaves unaware of what had been happening in the land soon to be known as Haiti. The leader of the conspiracy, the slave Gabriel Prosser (generally known simply as "Gabriel"), was well informed and highly articulate. Professor Virginius Dabney, a well-known historian of Virginia, tells the story of Gabriel's planned insurrection in the following selection.

*n*at Turner's Insurrection of 1831 in Southampton County, Virginia, is widely believed to have been the greatest and most significant slave conspiracy in the history of the United States. Yet a slave plot that occurred nearly a third of a century earlier, centering in the Richmond area and extending throughout much of the commonwealth, was even more alarming. Led by a slave named Gabriel Prosser, it was known as Gabriel's Insurrection. Most Americans have never heard of it.

Thousands of blacks were involved in the Gabriel affair—which took place in 1800—and in the events that followed during the ensuing two years. The large number of participants contrasts with the small band of about sixty slaves who followed Nat Turner. The attempted rebellion under Gabriel was designed to bring about a wholesale massacre of the whites, not only in Richmond but throughout the slave-holding areas of Virginia and beyond. In 1801 and 1802 there were other planned insurrections and intended massacres in half a dozen Virginia counties and several cities, as well as in a comparable number of counties just over the border in North Carolina.

The significance of Gabriel's planned uprising lies not so much in the failure of these efforts to butcher the slave owners as in the fact that so much deep-seated hostility toward them was revealed.

The slaves did not hesitate to risk their lives in these desperate adventures. Even after Gabriel and some thirty-five of his followers had been hanged, further plots were hatched in both Virginia and North Carolina. All these schemes were thwarted, several of them as a result of timely information furnished by bondsmen loyal to their owners—evidence that there were slaves who felt genuine affection for their masters and mistresses. At the same time, antagonism toward many slaveowners was shown to be great.

Rumors of impending insurrection had been heard off and on since the American Revolution, during which much emphasis had been placed on the "rights of man." Dr. William P. Palmer, a scholarly Richmond physician who was vice president of the Virginia Historical Society noted in a series of articles for the Richmond *Times* in the late 19th century that after the Revolution "a vague idea of future freedom seemed to permeate the entire slave community" of Virginia. He added that "at one time there was scarcely a quarter of the state in which there was not a feeling of insecurity. . . . Richmond itself seemed to be quaking with apprehension." Appeals to the governor for arms as protection against possible uprisings were received by the executive from various directions.

The frightful massacres by the slaves of their often cruel French masters in Santo Domingo (now Haiti) beginning in 1791 caused rumblings of revolt in various parts of Virginia and as far south as Louisiana. In July 1793 one hundred thirty-seven square-rigged vessels, loaded with terrified and destitute French refugees and escorted by French warships, arrived at Norfolk. A considerable number moved on to Richmond and other cities.

The manner in which the blacks had taken over in Santo Domingo by liquidating the whites caused apprehension in Virginia and other slave states. As one historian put it: "The fame of Toussaint L'Ouverture had spread to every corner of the Old Dominion. Around the cabin fires of slave-quarters excited Negro voices repeated again the saga of the black hero who had defied Napoleon himself to free his people."

Richmonders asked themselves: If the blacks had managed this coup in a Caribbean island, what was to prevent their attempting to do the same in Virginia or elsewhere?

A prominent Richmond citizen wrote Governor "Light Horse Harry" Lee on July 21, 1793, that he had heard two Negroes talking of insurrection. He had gone quietly to a window in the darkness and had listened as one black told another of a plot "to kill the white people . . . between this and the fifteenth of October." The Negro called attention to the manner in which the blacks had slain the whites "in the French island and took it a little while ago."

John Marshall, the future chief justice, wrote Governor Lee in September and enclosed a communication concerning the situation in nearby Powhatan County. The letter stated that about 300 slaves had met shortly before in the county, several Negro foremen "had run away," and the writer believed "the intended rising is true." As for Richmond, Mr. New, captain of the guard, had "a few men and guns" but not a "pound of shot," in case of trouble.

Other reports of a like nature came from the Eastern Shore, from Cumberland, Mathews, Elizabeth City, and Warwick counties, and from Yorktown, Petersburg, and Portsmouth. In the last-named place, four Negroes were found hanging from a cedar tree in the center of town. The Portsmouth citizen who communicated this news to the governor said the men had been executed by other Negroes, which may or may not have been correct.

The authorities were largely indifferent to these reports until an awareness of the realities roused then to action. In many areas the militia were armed and held in readiness, other whites were supplied with weapons, and volunteer guards and patrols watched the movements of the slaves. The presence in Virginia of some 5,000 veterans of the Revolution also had its effect.

"The summer and autumn of 1793 was long remembered as one of the most trying periods of the state's history," Dr. Palmer wrote a century later. The unrest among the slaves occurred despite the fact that after the Revolution their treatment had been markedly better. They were given more freedom to move about, and punishments inflicted on them were less severe.

After the rumblings of 1792 and 1793 were quelled, the slave population in Virginia was almost entirely quiet for seven years. Then, in the midst of this treacherous calm, pent-up resentments exploded in the most far-reaching plot for massacre that has ever occurred within the borders of the United States.

Although hundreds, if not thousands, of blacks were scheming for months to kill the whites, hardly a hint reached the ears of the latter until a few hours before the murders were to begin. The plans were laid in the Richmond area by slaves who were allowed to attend religious gatherings and barbecues, and were free to roam after nightfall.

The leader of this widely ramified plot was a powerfully built, 24-year-old slave named Gabriel Prosser, the property of Thomas H. Prosser, who had a large plantation a few miles north of Richmond in a well cultivated section of Henrico County. There were various other extensive plantations in this attractive region, owned by such families as the Winstons, Prices, Seldens, Mosbys, Sheppards, Youngs, and Williamsons. Prosser's house, Brookfield, was less than a quarter of a mile from, and on the eastern side of, what was later called Brook Turnpike. It was just beyond the bridge over the Brook, or Brook Run.

Brookfield has vanished and only two residences from that period are standing today in the area. One is Meadow Farm, the Sheppard home near Glen Allen, owned in 1800 by Mosby Sheppard who had an important role in thwarting the uprising. A century and a half later it was occupied by his descendant, Major General Sheppard Crump, Adjutant General of Virginia. The other dwelling surviving from that era is Brook Hill, home at that time of the Williamsons, and situated just across the Brook from the Prosser plantation where Gabriel planned the rebellion. It was lived in for generations by the Stewart family, descendants of the Williamsons. On the death of the last of the Stewart ladies it became the home of their great-nephew, Joseph Bryan III, a current author.

Gabriel was Prosser's most trusted slave. His brothers, Solomon and Martin, also were on the Prosser plantation. The killing was to begin with the Prosser family and spread to nearby plantations, and then to much of the state.

Preparations had been careful and extensive through out the whole Richmond-Petersburg region, and in Louisa and Caroline counties, the Charlottesville area, and portions of the lower Tidewater. James River watermen spread the word up and down that stream. A post rider whose route extended from Richmond to Amherst County enlisted recruits along the way. He also was active in the vicinity of the state arsenal at Point of Fork. A preacher in Gloucester County was a part of the plot.

All the foregoing participants were black, but there are excellent reasons for believing that at least one Frenchman—and probably two—were important to the enterprise. The slaves steadfastly refused to give the names of these men. However, Gabriel was known to have declared that a Frenchman "who was at the siege of Yorktown" would meet him at the Brook and serve as commander on the first day of the revolt, after which he himself would take over. This Frenchman may well have been Charles Quersey, who had lived at the home of Francis Corbin in Caroline County a few years prior to the Gabriel plot. Gilbert, another slave who was a leader in the intended rebellion, was quoted as stating that

Quersey frequently urged him and other blacks to rise and murder the whites. Quersey said he would help them and show them how to fight. Gilbert was informed that Quersey had been active in fomenting the Gabriel uprising.

The feeling was widespread that certain refugees from the island of Santo Domingo, both white and black, had important roles in planting the idea of insurrection in the minds of Virginia slaves. A number of free Negroes also are said to have been active in aiding with the plans.

Gabriel's right-hand man was a huge slave named Jack Bowler, 6 feet 5 inches tall, "straight made and perhaps as strong a man as any in the state." He had long hair, worn in a queue and twisted at the sides. The 28-year-old Bowler sought to lead the rebellion, but when a vote was called for, Gabriel was elected "general" by a large majority.

The slave, Gilbert, a thoughtful man, was determined to go through with the plot, but said he could not bring himself to kill his master and mistress, William Young and his wife, since they had "raised him." He agreed, however, that they should be put to death.

Principal places of rendezvous for the plotters in those hot summer months of 1800 were at Young's Spring in the vicinity of Westbrook, at Prosser's blacksmith shop, and at Half Sink, the Winston plantation on the Chickahominy River.

Antagonism, even hatred, toward the whites was revealed at various parlays. Several slaves said they would have no hesitation in killing white people. One was quoted as saying that he could kill them "as free as eat."

Nothing less than revolution was envisioned. The first blow would fall on Saturday night, August 30. Martin, Gabriel's brother, pointed out that the country was at peace, the soldiers discharged, their "arms all put away," and "there are no patrols in the county." It seemed an ideal time to strike. "I can no longer bear what I have borne," Martin declared.

The number of slaves who had enrolled for the massacre cannot be determined with any exactitude. Gabriel claimed "nearly ten thousand" at one point, but this extravagant figure was apparently used to impress the slaves to whom he was speaking. That number, and many more, were expected to join him when the plot succeeded, but it seems certain that nothing like so many had enlisted at the outset. The secret nature of the plans, the absence of written records, the wide area over which the participating slaves were scattered, all combined to preclude accurate estimates of the number involved. Dr. Palmer held it to be "abundantly proved" that the plot's "ramifications extended over most of the slave-holding parts of the state."

Weapons were fashioned by the slaves in anticipation of the coup. There were frighteningly lethal swords made from scythes, as well as pikes, spears, knives, cross-bows, clubs and bullets, plus stolen muskets and powder. The plan was to seize many additional arms at the capitol in Richmond and others at the magazine, to release the convicts from the penitentiary, commandeer the treasury, and gain control of the city. Gabriel or one of his agents had somehow managed to enter the capitol on Sunday, when it was supposedly closed, and had found where the arms were stored.

Crucial to the success of the conspirators was the ingenious plan to move in the middle of the night and set fire to the wooden buildings along Richmond's waterfront at Rocketts. The whites would rush en masse from Shockoe Hill and Church Hill down to the river to put out the flames. Once they were fully occupied, slaves numbering perhaps a thousand would enter the city from the north. When the whites returned exhausted from fighting the conflagration, the blacks would engage them and wipe them out if possible. The insurrectionists also planned to kidnap Governor James Monroe.

Vague rumors of impending trouble were heard in Richmond during August, but nobody was able to pinpoint them. Dr. James McClurg, Richmond's mayor, ordered temporary patrols, but the whites by and large remained in blissful ignorance of what was impending.

On Saturday, August 30, a strange phenomenon was noted. Whereas on Saturdays the slaves were accustomed to leave the surrounding areas for diversion in Richmond, it was observed that nearly all of them seemed to be going in the opposite direction. They were heading for Gabriel's pre-arranged meeting place just north of the Brook.

Mosby Sheppard, one of the leading Henrico County planters, was sitting in his counting room on that day when two slaves, Pharoah and Tom, came in and nervously shut the door. They told him that the blacks planned to rise that night and kill him and all the other white people in the area. They would then proceed to Richmond and attempt to seize the city and murder its white population.

Sheppard got this alarming word to Governor Monroe at once. The latter called out all the Militiamen who could be reached. He ordered them to guard the capitol, the magazine, and the penitentiary, and to patrol the roads leading into Richmond.

That afternoon dark clouds gathered in the west, thunder rolled, and jagged lightning stabbed the sky. Rain fell in sheets. It was a storm such as Virginia had seldom experienced. Roads were turned into quagmires, streams into roaring cataracts. The brook rose far out of its banks and became a foaming torrent. If the blacks had tried to cross it in either direction, they could not have done so. Disheartened by the rushing water and bottomless mud, and viewing the storm as a heavenly portent, Gabriel postponed the uprising until the next night. By then, the governor's patrols were covering the city and its environs so thoroughly that there was no chance for a successful uprising. The entire plan was abandoned and the leaders fled.

Most of them were rounded up promptly. No efforts were made by the whites to take the law into their own hands, and though some accounts claim the opposite, the men were apparently tried in strict accordance with legal procedures. The Henrico defendants, who constituted the great majority, were furnished with counsel. There was no disorder in any of the counties or cities where the hearings were held.

The dimensions of the plot unfolded as various slaves turned state's evidence against their fellows. There were some conflicts as to details,

but the general outlines of the conspiracy were clear. All agreed that the whites in a large area of Henrico were to be massacred, after which the slaves would march on Richmond and carry out their plan for wholesale arson and slaughter. There was some disagreement as to exactly what would happen once Richmond was in the hands of the black insurgents. Gabriel was aware that unless his plan achieved almost instant success, with the whites defeated and the city seized, there would be no mass uprising of the slaves. But if the city surrendered and the whites agreed to free their chattels, Gabriel planned to raise a white flag as a signal to blacks in the countryside to rise and join him. He would also "dine and drink with the merchants of the city." Whites whose lives were spared would "lose an arm," according to one version. Methodists, Quakers, and Frenchmen would not be harmed, according to another. The prominent Mrs. David Meade Randolph, it was further reported, would be made Gabriel's "queen" because of her virtuosity as a cook.

Whatever the precise details of the plot, those who studied the evidence had no doubt as to its main outlines. Governor Monroe spoke positively to the General Assembly on December 5, 1800, four months after the scheme had been smashed:

> It was distinctly seen that it [the conspiracy] embraced most of the slaves in this city and neighborhood, and that the combination extended to several of the adjacent counties, Hanover, Caroline, Louisa, Chesterfield, and to the neighborhood of Point of Fork; and there was good cause to believe that the knowledge of such a project pervaded other parts, if not the whole, of the state.

> The probability was if their first effort succeeded, we should see the town in flames, its inhabitants butchered and a scene of horror extending through the country.

The governor also believed that someone other than the slaves had instigated the plot. He deemed it "strange that the slaves should embark in this novel and unexampled enterprise of their own accord." He suspected that they were "prompted to it by others who were invisible."

Most of the slaves who had been active in the plot were arrested within a few days of the conspiracy's collapse, but the two principal leaders, Gabriel and Jack Bowler, remained at large for weeks. Bowler was the first to be apprehended, but Gabriel managed to elude his pursuers until September 24. He hid in the swamps along the James below Richmond until the three-masted schooner *Mary* came down the river. Gabriel hailed the ship and was taken aboard by Captain Richardson Taylor. Isham and Billy, two slaves who were serving in the crew, told Captain Taylor that they believed this was the man for whose capture a $300 reward had been offered. But Taylor, an antislavery Methodist, made no move to arrest his newly acquired passenger. When the ship arrived at Norfolk, Billy managed to get word of his suspicions to an acquaintance, and Gabriel was taken into custody by constables. Captain Taylor evidently had realized the slave's identity, but had been unwilling to turn him in.

Gabriel remained almost totally silent after his capture. He refused to tell Governor Monroe or anyone else details of the plot. He was tried and condemned to death.

While about thirty-five slaves were executed, this was a relatively small number, considering the hundreds if not thousands, who were involved in the conspiracy. Not only so, but at least twelve were acquitted and several more were pardoned. Several pardons were granted on the petition of persons whom the condemned men admitted they had planned to kill. The clemency was on condition that those who received it be sold into slavery in the far South or the West Indies. Owners of executed slaves had to be compensated financially by the state for their loss. This may have tended to hold down the number of convictions.

John Randolph of Roanoke, who witnessed some of the trials, wrote a friend that "the executions have not been so numerous as might under such circumstances have been expected," but added these pregnant words: "The accused have exhibited a spirit which, if it becomes general,

must deluge the Southern country in blood. They manifested a sense of their rights and contempt of danger, and a thirst for revenge which portend the most unhappy consequences." A Richmond resident wrote one of the local newspapers that the condemned men "uniformly met death with fortitude."

The hangings were carried out at various points in Henrico, and also in Caroline and elsewhere, but the great majority were held in Richmond at the usual place of execution. This was a small clearing, surrounded by pines and undergrowth, just north of the intersection of today's Fifteenth and Broad streets. Crowds attended the hangings, and the doomed men went to their deaths "amid the singing of hymns and the wails of their fellow-slaves and friends."

Richmonders were profoundly affected by these tragic events, and for years thereafter they avoided passing by the place where the gibbets stood.

Governor Monroe's conduct throughout the crisis was exemplary. He leaned over backward to be fair, and was careful not to issue inflammatory statements. He resisted the appeals of citizens who were inclined to take the law into their own hands among whom Joseph Jones of Petersburg was conspicuous. Jones, one of the leading citizens of Virginia, wrote the governor that "where there is any reason to believe that any person is concerned, they ought immediately to be hanged, quartered and hung upon trees on every road as a terror to the rest." He urged that trials be under martial law, since "if they are tryed by the Civil Law, perhaps there will not be one condemned; it will not do to be too scrupulous now." Monroe paid no attention to such hysterical appeals.

His friend, Thomas Jefferson, was a calming influence throughout. Like Monroe, Jefferson was opposed to slavery. He replied to Monroe's request for advice as follows: "The other states & the world at large will forever condemn us if we indulge a principle of revenge, or go one step beyond absolute necessity. They cannot lose sight of the rights of the two parties, & the object of the unsuccessful one."

Governor Monroe was determined to prevent Gabriel's desperate design from being revived. He ordered a "respectable force" to parade "Daily on the Capitol Square . . . that our strength might be known to the conspirators." The move was temporarily successful, but in his message to the General Assembly four months later the governor said: "What has happened may occur again at any time, with more fatal consequences, unless suitable measures are taken to prevent it."

George Tucker, youthful cousin of the famous St. George Tucker, was so concerned that he published a pamphlet. "The late extraordinary conspiracy . . . has waked those who were asleep," he wrote, and he went on to describe the situation in Virginia as "an eating sore" that was rapidly becoming worse.

The alarm was so general that a permanent guard was stationed at the capitol. It remained there until the Civil War.

Governor Monroe's forebodings of further trouble were soon borne out. Despite the execution of Gabriel and his fellow-conspirators, the fires of revolt had by no means been quenched.

There were definite evidences in late 1801 that all was far from serene in the cities and on the plantations. Monroe described some of the happenings in a message to the General Assembly in January 1802. He stated that "an alarm of a threatened insurrection among the slaves took place lately in Nottoway County which soon reached Petersburg. . . . The publick danger proceeding from this . . . is daily increasing." Monroe expressed the view that "a variety of causes" were responsible, including "the contrast in the condition of the free Negroes and slaves, the growing sentiment of liberty existing in the minds of the latter, and the inadequacy of existing patrol laws."

The interception of a letter from a Negro named Frank Goode to a man named Roling Pointer in Powhatan County caused further apprehension. "We have agreed to begin at Jude's Ferry and put to death every man on both sides of the river to Richmond," said this missive. It declared further that "our traveling friend has got ten thousand in readiness to the night." Nothing of this magnitude developed, but there was decided slave unrest in that area, as well as in much of lower Tidewater and especially in the Southside.

Two slaves were executed in Brunswick County and another in Halifax for involvement in plots to murder the whites. A third was hanged in Hanover County on a similar charge. Two slaves were sentenced to die in Norfolk when a plot to burn the city and massacre the white population was discovered. Governor Monroe granted the men a temporary reprieve, which brought a remonstrance from the mayor and 227 citizens of Norfolk, who signed a petition urging no further clemency. One of the men was hanged soon thereafter, but the other was transported out of the state.

In Williamsburg and Suffolk there was much unrest among the slaves. Across the border in North Carolina there were threats of an uprising. From Hertford County came a letter "to the citizens of Nansemond County," Virginia that "a horrid plot has been discovered amongst the Negroes of this county and the county of Bertie, which has for its object the total destruction of the whites . . . there is not a doubt remaining that such a plan does exist." A letter giving details had been found "in a cotton barrel in one of their cabins."

There were repercussions from these events in the Carolina counties of Camden, Currituck, Martin, Halifax, and Pasquotank. Historians have estimated, on the basis of incomplete newspaper accounts, that at least five slaves were executed in North Carolina, with others lashed, branded, and cropped. This last refers to the cropping of ears. It appears probable that the total number hanged was nearer fifteen than five.

Participation of white men in some of the Virginia slave plots of 1802 is apparently established. Documents from Halifax, Nottoway, and Henrico counties seem to bear out this suspicion. Arthur, a slave on the plantation of William Farrar of Henrico, is supposed to have referred to "eight or ten white men" who were cooperating with him.

A certain amount of hysteria was involved in several of the above-mentioned alarms over the years in both Virginia and North Carolina, and some of the reports of planned insurrections were undoubtedly exaggerated. On the other hand, there was enough evidence of genuine conspiracy in both states, especially Virginia, to cause widespread and justifiable uneasiness.

This uneasiness was aroused only spasmodically in the years after 1802, until the Nat Turner outbreak of 1831. There were specific developments in 1808 and 1809, and Richmond seems to have been the center of these. Lieutenant Governor Alexander McRae informed the military on December 19 of the former year that he had satisfactory evidence, verbal and written, of an impending uprising to take place during the following week. Samuel Pleasants Jr. of Richmond published a circular "respecting insurrection of Negroes." The military was called out in the capital and remained on the alert until January 1. There were other similar warnings in Chesterfield County, as well as in Norfolk and the counties of Nelson and Albemarle.

Richmond was the center of further alarms in 1813. Mayor Robert Greenhow wrote that there were insurrectionary movements among the blacks, at the instigation of the British, with whom we were fighting the War of 1812. The mayor called out patrols and urged removal of the powder magazine to a safer place.

A conspiracy with greater potentialities was formed in 1815 and 1816 in Spotsylvania, Louisa, and Orange counties. It was the work of a weird character named George Boxley, a white man who kept a country store. Boxley declared that a little white bird had brought him a holy message, directing him to deliver his fellow man from bondage. He persuaded many slaves to join him in a planned revolt, which was to involve an attack on Fredericksburg and then a march on Richmond. As had happened with several previous attempts at insurrection, a loyal slave informed her master of the plot. Many were arrested, including Boxley. He escaped and was never recaptured, but six slaves were hanged. Six others were sentenced to the same fate, but many whites appealed for clemency, and the blacks were reprieved and banished.

All this unrest among the slaves, especially that evidenced in Gabriel's attempted insurrection, caused a marked lessening of efforts by the whites to abolish chattel servitude. Such efforts had been actively pursued in the years following the Revolution, albeit without tangible results. But after 1800 the trend was the other way, and the Virginia Abolition Society ceased to function, as did all other such societies in the South. Not only so, but Virginia passed a law in 1806 providing that any slave who was freed had to leave the state within twelve months. This law was later modified to permit local courts to give certain manumitted slaves permission to remain, but passage of the harsh statute showed the tenor of the time.

A melancholy ballad, set to music, entitled "Gabriel's Defeat," is said to have been composed by a black, following the collapse of Gabriel's epochal rebellion. A reporter claimed to have heard it "at the dances of the whites and in the huts of the slaves." The song soon faded away and has not been heard for many years. Its mournful notes may well have provided an appropriate requiem for the revolt that failed.

Selection 3

A Warning to White America: 1829

David Walker

The insurrection that Gabriel planned in Richmond, Virginia, in 1800 was not the only tremor that frightened American slave owners, their nerves already set on edge by the Haitian revolution. In 1822, another slave conspiracy was uncovered in Charleston, South Carolina, organized by a free black named Denmark Vesey. Like Gabriel, he was tried and hanged, along with a considerable number of co-conspirators and other blacks who may well have been uninvolved in the plot.

Remembering these bids for freedom, in 1829 a free black in Boston named David Walker published a long Appeal . . . to the Colored Citizens of the World *(as the title read in part). Walker eked out a living as a dealer in old clothes—the kind of humble occupation that blacks in northern cities often found was the only way they could earn a living. Yet his powerful imagination was fired by his knowledge of the suffering that slaves endured, by his resentment over discrimination against northern free blacks, and by his close study of the Bible, which convinced him that God would soon inflict severe punishment on whites unless they learned to treat*

Excerpted from David Walker, *Appeal, in Four Articles; Together with a Preamble, to the Coloured Citizens of the World, but in Particular, and Very Expressly, to Those of the United States of America* (Boston: n.p., 1829).

blacks with justice. Walker was, moreover, moved to indignation by reading the patronizing assessment of blacks' innate abilities that Thomas Jefferson had seen fit to include in Notes on the State of Virginia. *If this was the view of white Americans, Walker reasoned, what hope was there for people of African descent in America? Walker's* Appeal *was, in fact, a call to revolt, all the more eloquent because of the deep religious feeling that it embodied.*

Soon after Walker published his tract, he died under mysterious circumstances that have never been explained. He was still a young man, not known to have been suffering from ill health, and foul play cannot be ruled out.

Beloved brethren—here let me tell you, and believe it, that the Lord our God, as true as be sits on his throne in heaven, and as true as our Saviour died to redeem the world, will give you a Hannibal, and when the Lord shall have raised him up, and given him to you for your possession, O my suffering brethren! remember the divisions and consequent sufferings of *Carthage* and of *Hayti*. Read the history particularly of Hayti, and see how they were butchered by the whites, and do you take warning. The person whom God shall give you, give him your support and let him go his length, and behold in him the salvation of your God. God will indeed, deliver you through him from your deplorable and wretched condition under the Christians of America. I charge you this day before my God to lay no obstacle in his way, but let him go.

The whites want slaves, and want us for their slaves, but some of them will curse the day they ever saw us. As true as the sun ever shone in its meridian splendor, my colour will root some of them out of the very face of the earth. They shall have enough of making slaves of, and butchering, and murdering us in the manner which they have. No doubt some may say that I write with a bad spirit, and that I being a black, wish these things to occur. Whether I write with a bad or a good spirit, I say if these things do not occur in their proper time, it is because the world in which we live does not exist, and we are deceived with regard to its existence.—It is immaterial however to me, who believe, or who refuse—though I should like to see the whites repent peradventure God may have mercy on them, some however, have gone so far that their cup must be filled.

But what need have I to refer to antiquity, when Hayti, the glory of the blacks and terror of tyrants, is enough to convince the most avaricious and stupid of wretches—which is at this time, and I am sorry to say it, plagued with that scourge of nations, the Catholic religion; but I hope and pray God that she may yet rid herself of it, and adopt in its stead the Protestant faith; also, I hope that she may keep peace within her borders and be united, keeping a strict look out for tyrants, for if they get the least chance to injure her, they will avail themselves of it, as true as the Lord lives in heaven. But one thing which gives me joy is, that they are men who would be cut off to a man, before they would yield to the combined forces of the whole world—in fact, if the whole world was combined against them, it could not do any thing with them, unless the Lord delivers them up. . . .

Addition.—I will give here a very imperfect list of the cruelties inflicted on us by the enlightened Christians of America.—First, no trifling portion of them will beat us nearly to death, if they find us on our knees praying to God,—They hinder us from going to hear the word of God—they keep us sunk in ignorance, and will not let us learn to read the word of God, nor write—If they find us with a book of any description in our hand, they will beat us nearly to death—they are so afraid we will learn to read, and enlighten our dark and benighted minds—They will not suffer us to meet together to worship the God who made us—they brand us with hot iron—they cram bolts of fire down our throats—they cut us as they do horses, bulls, or hogs—they crop our ears and sometimes cut off bits of our tongues—they chain and hand-cuff us, and while in that miserable and wretched condition, beat us with cow-hides and clubs—they keep us half naked and starve us sometimes nearly to death under their infernal whips or lashes (which some of them shall have enough of yet)—They put on us fifty-sixes and chains, and make us work in that cruel situation, and in sickness, under lashes to support them and their families.—They keep us three or four hundred feet under ground working in their mines, night and day to dig up gold and silver to enrich them and their children.—They keep us in the most death-like ignorance by keeping us from all source of information, and call us, who are free men and next to the Angels of God, their property!!!!!! . . .

Do the colonizationists think to send us off without first being reconciled to us? Do they think to bundle us up like brutes and send us off, as they did our brethren of the State of Ohio? Have they not to be reconciled to us, or reconcile us to them, for the cruelties with which they have afflicted our fathers and us? Methinks colonizationists think they have a set of brutes to deal with, sure enough. Do they think to drive us from our country and homes, after having enriched it with our blood and tears, and keep back millions of our dear brethren, sunk in the most barbarous wretchedness, to dig up gold and silver for them and their children? Surely, the Americans must think that we are brutes, as some of them have represented us to be. They think that we do not feel for our brethren, whom they are murdering by the inches, but they are dreadfully deceived. I acknowledge that there are some deceitful and hypocritical wretches among us, who will tell us one thing while they mean another, and thus they go on aiding our enemies to oppress themselves and us. But I declare this day before my Lord and Master, that I believe there are some true-hearted sons of Africa, in this land of oppression, but pretended *liberty!!!!!*—who do in reality feel for their suffering brethren, who are held in bondage by tyrants. Some of the advocates of this cunningly devised plot of Satan represent us to be the greatest set of cut-throats in the world, as though God wants us to take his work out of his hand before he is ready. Does not vengeance belong to the Lord? Is he not able to repay the Americans for their cruelties, with which they have afflicted Africa's sons and daughters, without our interference, unless we are ordered? It is surprising to think that the Americans, having the Bible in their hands, do not believe it. Are not the hearts of all men in the hands of the God of battles? And does he not suffer some, in consequence of cruelties, to go on until they are irrecoverably lost? Now, what can be more aggravating, than for the Americans, after having treated us so bad, to hold us up to the world as such great throat-cutters? It appears to me as though they are resolved to assail us with every species of affliction that their ingenuity can invent. . . .

The Americans may say or do as they please, but they have to raise us from the condition of brutes to that of respectable men, and to make a national acknowledgement to us for the wrongs they have inflicted on us. As unexpected, strange, and wild as these propositions may to some appear, it is no less a fact, that unless they are complied with, the Americans of the United States, though they may for a little while escape, God will yet weigh them in a balance, and if they are not superior to other men, as they have represented themselves to be, he will give them wretchedness to their very heart's content.

And now brethren, having concluded these four Articles, I submit them, together with my Preamble, dedicated to the Lord, for your inspection, in language so very simple, that the most ignorant, who can read at all, may easily understand—of which you may make the best you possibly can. Should tyrants take it into their heads to emancipate any of you, remember that your freedom is your natural right. You are men, as well as they, and instead of returning thanks to them for your freedom, return it to the Holy Ghost, who is our rightful owner. If they do not want to part with your labours, which have enriched them, let them keep you, and my word for it, that God Almighty, will break their strong band. Do you believe this, my brethren?—See my Address, delivered before the General Coloured Association of Massachusetts, which may be found in Freedom's Journal, for Dec. 20, 1828.—See the last clause of that Address. Whether you believe it or not, I tell you that God will dash tyrants, in combination with devils, into atoms, and will bring you out from your wretchedness and miseries under these *Christian People!!!!!!*

Selection 4

A Confession: 1831

Nat Turner

Although copies of David Walker's Appeal *occasionally turned up in the hands of southern slaves, no evidence exists that the book was known to the most formidable black rebel of the nineteenth century, Nat Turner. The son of an African-born mother, Turner was a self-taught visionary who blended Judeo-Christian ideas of divine justice with African religious traditions. In rural Southampton County, Virginia, where he lived his entire life, he became well known as a charismatic preacher.*

Turner apparently had no reason to resent his master, who treated him leniently—except for the fact, that as a slave, he had no freedom. In fixing on this unjust foundation of a slave society, Turner realized that there could be little difference between a "good" and a "bad" master: Simply having a master and being a slave were evil enough. This was the message that he spread, in secret, to his fellow bondspeople. Then a series of natural phenomena—spotting various markings on vegetation, seeing a lunar eclipse—that his African heritage told him were significant inspired Turner and the slaves under his influence to launch a desperate, bloody uprising. After hacking to death fifty-five slave-owning whites (men, women, and children), Turner's band was dispersed, and when he was finally tracked down, he was put on trial, convicted, and hung.

Thomas Gray, the court-appointed white lawyer who defended Turner, was a firm believer in slavery and white supremacy, and he had no sympathy for his client's aims. He attributed Turner's ability to lead a violent uprising to his "fanatical" character, yet he was evidently fascinated by his magnetic qualities. Turner, who probably realized that talking to Gray offered him his last and best chance of explaining his motives to the world, may not have said all that was on his mind. Certainly the "Confession" that Gray attributed to Turner, and that he published (to his considerable profit) after Turner's execution, has many signs of white rather than black authorship. Nevertheless, the document, most of which appears here, is treated by historians as an important source, but one that (like all historical sources) must be read critically.

*a*greeable to his own appointment, on the evening he was committed to prison, with permission of the jailer, I visited NAT on Tuesday the 1st November, when, without being questioned at all, he commenced his narrative in the following words:—

SIR,—You have asked me to give a history of the motives which induced me to undertake the late insurrection, as you call it—To do so I must go back to the days of my infancy, and even be-

Excerpted from Nat Turner, *The Confessions of Nat Turner and Related Documents*, edited by Kenneth S. Greenberg (Boston: Bedford Books of St. Martin's Press, 1996).

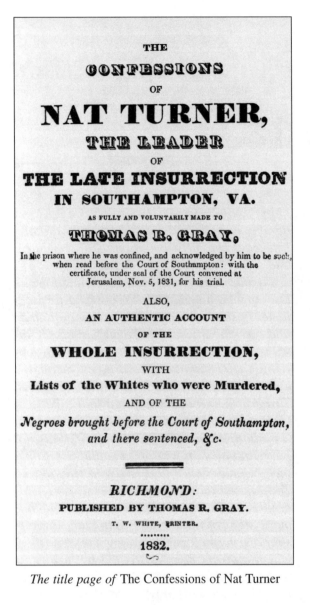

THE

CONFESSIONS

OF

NAT TURNER,

THE LEADER

OF

THE LATE INSURRECTION

IN SOUTHAMPTON, VA.

AS FULLY AND VOLUNTARILY MADE TO

THOMAS R. GRAY,

In the prison where he was confined, and acknowledged by him to be such,
when read before the Court of Southampton: with the
certificate, under seal of the Court convened at
Jerusalem, Nov. 5, 1831, for his trial.

ALSO,

AN AUTHENTIC ACCOUNT

OF THE

WHOLE INSURRECTION,

WITH

Lists of the Whites who were Murdered,

AND OF THE

*Negroes brought before the Court of Southampton,
and there sentenced, &c.*

———

RICHMOND:

PUBLISHED BY THOMAS R. GRAY.

T. W. WHITE, PRINTER.

....

1832.

The title page of The Confessions of Nat Turner

fore I was born. I was thirty-one years of age the 2nd of October last, and born the property of Benj. Turner, of this county. In my childhood a circumstance occurred which made an indelible impression on my mind, and laid the ground work of that enthusiasm, which has terminated so fatally to many, both white and black, and for which I am about to atone at the gallows. It is here necessary to relate this circumstance—trifling as it may seem, it was the commencement of that belief which has grown with time, and even now, sir, in this dungeon, helpless and for-

saken as I am, I cannot divest myself of. Being at play with other children, when three or fours years old, I was telling them something, which my mother overhearing, said it had happened before I was born—I stuck to my story, however, and related somethings which went, in her opinion, to confirm it—others being called on were greatly astonished, knowing that these things had happened, and caused them to say in my hearing, I surely would be a prophet, as the Lord had shewn me things that had happened before my birth. And my father and mother strengthened me in this my first impression, saying in my presence, I was intended for some great purpose, which they had always thought from certain marks on my head and breast—[a parcel of excrescences which I believe are not at all uncommon, particularly among negroes, as I have seen several with the same. In this case he has either cut them off or they have nearly disappeared]—My grandmother, who was very religious, and to whom I was much attached—my master, who belonged to the church, and other religious persons who visited the house, and whom I often saw at prayers, noticing the singularity of my manners, I suppose, and my uncommon intelligence for a child, remarked I had too much sense to be raised, and if I was, I would never be of any service to any one as a slave—To a mind like mine, restless, inquisitive, and observant of every thing that was passing, it is easy to suppose that religion was the subject to which it would be directed, and although this subject principally occupied my thoughts—there was nothing that I saw or heard of to which my attention was not directed—The manner in which I learned to read and write, not only had great influence on my own mind, as I acquired it with the most perfect ease, so much so, that I have no recollection whatever of learning the alphabet—but to the astonishment of the family, one day, when a book was shewn me to keep me from crying, I began spelling the names of different objects—this was a source of wonder to all in the neighborhood, particularly the blacks—and this learning was constantly improved at all opportunities—when I got large enough to go to work, while employed, I was reflecting on many things that would present themselves to my imagination, and whenever an opportunity occurred of looking at a book, when the school children were getting their lessons, I would find many things that the fertility of my own imagination had depicted to me before; all my time, not devoted to my master's service, was spent either in prayer, or in making experiments in casting different things in moulds made of earth, in attempting to make paper, gunpowder, and many other experiments, that although I could not perfect, yet convinced me of its practicability if I had the means.* I was not addicted to stealing in my youth, nor have ever been—Yet such was the confidence of the negroes in the neighborhood, even at this early period of my life, in my superior judgment, that they would often carry me with them when they were going on any roguery, to plan for them. Growing up among them, with this confidence in my superior judgment, and when this, in their opinions, was perfected by Divine inspiration, from the circumstances already alluded to in my infancy, and which belief was ever afterwards zealously inculcated by the austerity of my life and manners, which became the subject of remark by white and black.—Having soon discovered to be great, I must appear so, and therefore studiously avoided mixing in society, and wrapped myself in mystery, devoting my time to fasting and prayer—By this time, having arrived to man's estate, and hearing the scriptures commented on at meetings, I was struck with that particular passage which says: "Seek ye the kingdom of Heaven and all things shall be added unto you." I reflected much on this passage, and prayed daily for light on this subject— As I was praying one day at my plough, the spirit spoke to me, saying "Seek ye the kingdom of Heaven and all things shall be added unto you." *Question*—what do you mean by the Spirit. *Ans.* The Spirit that spoke to the prophets in former days—and I was greatly astonished, and for two years prayed continually, whenever my duty would permit—and then again I had the same revelation, which fully confirmed me in the impression that I was ordained for some great purpose in the hands of the Almighty. Several years rolled round, in which many events occurred to strengthen me in this my belief. At this time I reverted in my mind to the remarks made of me in my childhood, and the things that had been shewn me—and as it had been said of me in my childhood by those by whom I had been taught to pray, both white and black, and in whom I had the greatest confidence, that I had too much sense to be raised, and if I was, I would never be of any use to any one as a slave. Now finding I had arrived to man's estate, and was a slave, and these revelations being made known to me, I began to direct my attention to this great object, to fulfil the purpose for which, by this time, I felt assured I was intended. Knowing the influence I had obtained over the minds of my fellow servants, (not by the means of conjuring and such like tricks—for to them I always spoke of such things with contempt) but by the communion of the Spirit whose revelations I often communicated to them, and they believed and said my wisdom came from God. I now began to prepare them for my purpose, by telling them something was about to happen that would terminate in fulfilling the great promise that had been made to me—About this time I was placed under an overseer, from whom I ran away—and after remaining in the woods thirty days, I returned, to the astonishment of the negroes on the plantation, who thought I had made my escape to some other part of the country, as my father had done before. But the reason of my return was, that the Spirit appeared to me and said I had my wishes directed to the things of this world, and not to the kingdom of Heaven, and that I should return to the service of my earthly master—"For he who knoweth his Master's will, and doeth it not, shall be beaten with many stripes, and thus have I chastened you." And the negroes found fault, and murmured against me, saying that if they had my sense they would not serve any master in the world. And about this time I had a vision—and I saw white spirits and black spirits engaged in

---

*When questioned as to the manner of manufacturing those different articles, he was found well informed on the subject.

battle, and the sun was darkened—the thunder rolled in the Heavens, and blood flowed in streams—and I heard a voice saying, "Such is your luck, such you are called to see, and let it come rough or smooth, you must surely bare it." I now withdrew myself as much as my situation would permit, from the intercourse of my fellow servants, for the avowed purpose of serving the Spirit more fully—and it appeared to me, and reminded me of the things it had already shown me, and that it would then reveal to me the knowledge of the elements, the revolution of the planets, the operation of tides, and changes of the seasons. After this revelation in the year 1825, and the knowledge of the elements being made known to me, I sought more than ever to obtain true holiness before the great day of judgment should appear, and then I began to receive the true knowledge of faith. And from the first steps of righteousness until the last, was I made perfect; and the Holy Ghost was with me, and said, "Behold me as I stand in the Heavens"— and I looked and saw the forms of men in different attitudes—and there were lights in the sky to which the children of darkness gave other names than what they really were—for they were the lights of the Saviour's hands, stretched forth from east to west, even as they were extended on the cross on Calvary for the redemption of sinners. And I wondered greatly at these miracles, and prayed to be informed of a certainty of the meaning thereof—and shortly afterwards, while laboring in the field, I discovered drops of blood on the corn as though it were dew from heaven— and I communicated it to many, both white and black, in the neighborhood—and I then found on the leaves in the woods hieroglyphic characters, and numbers, with the forms of men in different attitudes, portrayed in blood, and representing the figures I had seen before in the heavens. And now the Holy Ghost had revealed itself to me, and made plain the miracles it had shown me— For as the blood of Christ had been shed on this earth, and had ascended to heaven for the salvation of sinners, and was now returning to earth again in the form of dew—and as the leaves on the trees bore the impression of the figures I had

seen in the heavens, it was plain to me that the Saviour was about to lay down the yoke he had borne for the sins of men, and the great day of judgment was at hand. About this time I told these things to a white man, (Etheldred T. Brantley) on whom it had a wonderful effect—and he ceased from his wickedness, and was attacked immediately with a cutaneous eruption, and blood ozed from the pores of his skin, and after praying and fasting nine days, he was healed, and the Spirit appeared to me again, and said, as the Saviour had been baptised so should we be also—and when the white people would not let us be baptised by the church, we went down into the water together, in the sight of many who reviled us, and were baptised by the Spirit—After this I rejoiced greatly, and gave thanks to God. And on the 12th of May, 1828, I heard a loud noise in the heavens, and the Spirit instantly appeared to me and said the Serpent was loosened, and Christ had laid down the yoke he had borne for the sins of men, and that I should take it on and fight against the Serpent, for the time was fast approaching when the first should be last and the last should be first. *Ques.* Do you not find yourself mistaken now? *Ans.* Was not Christ crucified. And by signs in the heavens that it would make known to me when I should commence the great work—and until the first sign appeared, I should conceal it from the knowledge of men—And on the appearance of the sign, (the eclipse of the sun last February) I should arise and prepare myself, and slay my enemies with their own weapons. And immediately on the sign appearing in the heavens, the seal was removed from my lips, and I communicated the great work laid out for me to do, to four in whom I had the greatest confidence. (Henry, Hark, Nelson, and Sam)—It was intended by us to have begun the work of death on the 4th July last—Many were the plans formed and rejected by us, and it affected my mind to such a degree, that I fell sick, and the time passed without our coming to any determination how to commence—Still forming new schemes and rejecting them, when the sign appeared again, which determined me not to wait longer.

Since the commencement of 1830, I had been living with Mr. Joseph Travis, who was to me a kind master, and placed the greatest confidence in me; in fact, I had no cause to complain of his treatment of me. On Saturday evening, the 20th of August, it was agreed between Henry, Hark and myself, to prepare a dinner the next day for the men we expected, and then to concert a plan, as we had not yet determined on any. Hark, on the following morning, brought a pig, and Henry brandy, and being joined by Sam, Nelson, Will and Jack, they prepared in the woods a dinner, where, about three o'clock, I joined them.

Q. Why were you so backward in joining them.

A. The same reason that had caused me not to mix with them for years before.

I saluted them on coming up, and asked Will how came he there, he answered, his life was worth no more than others, and his liberty as dear to him. I asked him if he thought to obtain it? He said he would, or loose his life. This was enough to put him in full confidence. Jack, I knew, was only a tool in the hands of Hark, it was quickly agreed we should commence at home (Mr. J. Travis') on that night, and until we had armed and equipped ourselves, and gathered sufficient force, neither age nor sex was to be spared, (which was invariably adhered to.) We remained at the feast, until about two hours in the night, when we went to the house and found Austin; they all went to the cider press and drank, except myself. On returning to the house, Hark went to the door with an axe, for the purpose of breaking it open, as we knew we were strong enough to murder the family, if they were awaked by the noise; but reflecting that it might create an alarm in the neighborhood, we determined to enter the house secretly, and murder them whilst sleeping. Hark got a ladder and set it against the chimney, on which I ascended, and hoisting a window, entered and came down stairs, unbarred the door, and removed the guns from their places. It was then observed that I must spill the first blood. On which, armed with a hatchet, and accompanied by Will, I entered my master's chamber, it being dark, I could not

give a death blow, the hatchet glanced from his head, he sprang from the bed and called his wife, it was his last word, Will laid him dead, with a blow of his axe, and Mrs. Travis shared the same fate, as she lay in bed. The murder of this family, five in number, was the work of a moment, not one of them awoke; there was a little infant sleeping in a cradle, that was forgotten, until we had left the house and gone some distance, when Henry and Will returned and killed it; we got here, four guns that would shoot, and several old muskets, with a pound or two of powder. We remained some time at the barn, where we paraded; I formed them in a line as soldiers, and after carrying them through all the manoevres I was master of, marched them off to Mr. Salathul Francis', about six hundred yards distant. Sam and Will went to the door and knocked. Mr. Francis asked who was there, Sam replied it was him, and he had a letter for him, on which he got up and came to the door; they immediately seized him, and dragging him out a little from the door, he was dispatched by repeated blows on the head; there was no other white person in the family. We started from there for Mrs. Reese's, maintaining the most perfect silence on our march, where finding the door unlocked, we entered, and murdered Mrs. Reese in her bed, while sleeping; her son awoke, but it was only to sleep the sleep of death, he had only time to say who is that, and he was no more. From Mrs. Reese's we went to Mrs. Turner's, a mile distant, which we reached about sunrise, on Monday morning. Henry, Austin, and Sam, went to the still, where, finding Mr. Peebles, Austin shot him, and the rest of us went to the house; as we approached, the family discovered us, and shut the door. Vain hope! Will, with one stroke of his axe, opened it, and we entered and found Mrs. Turner and Mrs. Newsome in the middle of a room, almost frightened to death. Will immediately killed Mrs. Turner, with one blow of his axe. I took Mrs. Newsome by the hand, and with the sword I had when I was apprehended, I struck her several blows over the head, but not being able to kill her, as the sword was dull. Will turning around and discovering it, despatched her also. A general destruction of property and search for money and ammunition, always succeeded the murders. By this time my company amounted to fifteen, and nine men mounted, who started for Mrs. Whitehead's, (the other six were to go through a by way to Mr. Bryant's, and rejoin us at Mrs. Whitehead's,) as we approached the house we discovered Mr. Richard Whitehead standing in the cotton patch, near the lane fence; we called him over into the lane, and Will, the executioner, was near at hand, with his fatal axe, to send him to an untimely grave. As we pushed on to the house, I discovered some one run round the garden, and thinking it was some of the white family, I pursued them, but finding it was a servant girl belonging to the house, I returned to commence the work of death, but they whom I left, had not been idle; all the family were already murdered, but Mrs. Whitehead and her daughter Margaret. As I came round to the door I saw Will pulling Mrs. Whitehead out of the house, and at the step he nearly severed her head from her body, with his broad axe. Miss Margaret, when I discovered her, had concealed herself in the corner, formed by the projection of the cellar cap from the house; on my approach she fled, but was soon overtaken, and after repeated blows with a sword, I killed her by a blow on the head, with a fence rail. By this time, the six who had gone by Mr. Bryant's, rejoined us, and informed me they had done the work of death assigned them. We again divided, part going to Mr. Richard Porter's, and from thence to Nathaniel Francis', the others to Mr. Howell Harris', and Mr. T. Doyles. On my reaching Mr. Porter's, he had escaped with his family. I understood there, that the alarm had already spread, and I immediately returned to bring up those sent to Mr. Doyles, and Mr. Howell Harris'; the party I left going on to Mr. Francis', having told them I would join them in that neighborhood. I met these sent to Mr. Doyles' and Mr. Harris' returning, having met Mr. Doyle on the road and killed him; and learning from some who joined them, that Mr. Harris was from home, I immediately pursued the course taken by the party gone on before; but knowing they would complete the work of death and pillage, at Mr. Francis' before I could get there, I went to Mr. Peter Edwards', expecting to find them there, but they had been here also. I then went to Mr. John T. Barrow's, they had been here and murdered him. I pursued on their track to Capt. Newit Harris', where I found the greater part mounted, and ready to start; the men now amounting to about forty, shouted and hurraed as I rode up, some were in the yard, loading their guns, others drinking. They said Captain Harris and his family had escaped, the property in the house they destroyed, robbing him of money and other valuables. I ordered them to mount and march instantly, this was about nine or ten o'clock, Monday morning. I proceeded to Mr. Levi Waller's, two or three miles distant. I took my station in the rear, and as it 'twas my object to carry terror and devastation wherever we went, I placed fifteen or twenty of the best armed and most to be relied on, in front, who generally approached the house as fast as their horses could run; this was for two purposes, to prevent their escape and strike terror to the inhabitants—on this account I never got to the houses, after leaving Mrs. Whitehead's, until the murders were committed, except in one case. I sometimes got in sight in time to see the work of death completed, viewed the mangled bodies as they lay, in silent satisfaction, and immediately started in quest of other victims—Having murdered Mrs. Waller and ten children, we started for Mr. William Williams'—having killed him and two little boys that were there; while engaged in this, Mrs. Williams fled and got some distance from the house, but she was pursued, overtaken, and compelled to get up behind one of the company, who brought her back, and after showing her the mangled body of her lifeless husband, she was told to get down and lay by his side, where she was shot dead. I then started for Mr. Jacob Williams, where the family were murdered—Here we found a young man named Drury, who had come on business with Mr. Williams—he was pursued, overtaken, and shot. Mrs. Vaughan was the next place we visited—and after murdering the family here, I determined on starting for Jerusalem—Our number amounted now to fifty or sixty, all mounted and armed with guns, axes, swords and clubs—On reaching Mr. James W. Parker's gate, immediately on the road leading to Jerusalem, and about three miles distant, it was proposed to me to call there, but I objected, as I knew he was gone to Jerusalem, and my object was to reach there as soon as possible; but some of the men having relations at Mr. Parker's it was agreed that they might call and get his people. I remained at the gate on the road, with seven or eight; the others going across the field to the house, about half a mile off. After waiting some time for them, I became impatient, and started to the house for them, and on our return we were met by a party of white men, who had pursued our blood-stained track, and who had fired on those at the gate, and dispersed them, which I knew nothing of, not having been at that time rejoined by any of them—Immediately on discovering the whites, I ordered my men to halt and form, as they appeared to be alarmed—The white men, eighteen in number, approached us in about one hundred yards, when one of them fired, (this was against the positive orders of Captain Alexander P. Peete, who commanded, and who had directed the men to reserve their fire until within thirty paces.) And I discovered about half of them retreating, I then ordered my men to fire and rush on them; the few remaining stood their ground until we approached within fifty yards, when they fired and retreated. We pursued and overtook some of them who we thought we left dead; (they were not killed) after pursuing them about two hundred yards, and rising a little hill, I discovered they were met by another party, and had haulted, and were reloading their guns, (this was a small party from Jerusalem who knew the negroes were in the field, and had just tied their horses to await their return to the road, knowing that Mr. Parker and family were in Jerusalem, but knew nothing of the party that had gone in with Captain Peete; on hearing the firing they immediately rushed to the spot and arrived just in time to arrest the progress of these barbarous villians, and save the lives of their friends and fellow citizens.) Thinking that those who retreated first, and the party who fired on us at fifty or sixty yards distant, had all only fallen back to meet others with amunition. As I saw them re-loading their guns, and more coming up than I saw at first, and several of my bravest men being wounded, the others became panick struck and squandered over the field; the white men pursued and fired on us several times. Hark had his horse shot under him, and I caught another for him as it was running by me; five or six of my men were wounded, but none left on the field; finding myself defeated here I instantly determined to go through a private way, and cross the Nottoway river at the Cypress Bridge, three miles below Jerusalem, and attack that place in the rear, as I expected they would look for me on the other road, and I had a great desire to get there to procure arms and amunition. After going a short distance in this private way, accompanied by about twenty men, I overtook two or three who told me the others were dispersed in every direction. After tyring [sic] in vain to collect a sufficient force to proceed to Jerusalem, I determined to return, as I was sure they would make back to their old neighborhood, where they would rejoin me, make new recruits, and come down again. On my way back, I called at Mrs. Thomas's, Mrs. Spencer's, and several other places, the white families having fled, we found no more victims to gratify our thirst for blood, we stopped at Majr. Ridley's quarter for the night, and being joined by four of his men, with the recruits made since my defeat, we mustered now about forty strong. After placing out sentinels, I laid down to sleep, but was quickly roused by a great racket; starting up, I found some mounted, and others in great confusion; one of the sentinels having given the alarm that we were about to be attacked, I ordered some to ride round and reconnoitre, and on their return the others being more alarmed, not knowing who they were, fled in different ways, so that I was reduced to about twenty again; with this I determined to attempt to recruit, and proceed on to rally in the neighborhood, I had left. Dr.

Blunt's was the nearest house, which we reached just before day; on riding up the yard, Hark fired a gun. We expected Dr. Blunt and his family were at Majr. Ridley's, as I knew there was a company of men there; the gun fired to ascertain if any of the family were at home; we were immediately fired upon and retreated, leaving several of my men. I do not know what became of them, as I never saw them afterwards. Pursuing our course back and coming in sight of Captain Harris', where we had been the day before, we discovered a party of white men at the house, on which all deserted but two, (Jacob and Nat,) we concealed ourselves in the woods until near night, when I sent them in search of Henry, Sam, Nelson, and Hark, and directed them to rally all they could, at the place we had had our dinner the Sunday before, where they would find me, and I accordingly returned there as soon as it was dark and remained until Wednesday evening, when discovering white men riding around the place as though they were looking for some one, and none of my men joining me, I concluded Jacob and Nat had been taken, and compelled to betray me. On this I gave up all hope for the present; and on Thursday night after having supplied myself with provisions from Mr. Travis's, I scratched a hole under a pile of fence rails in a field, where I concealed myself for six weeks, never leaving my hiding place but for a few minutes in the dead of night to get water which was very near; thinking by this time I could venture out, I began to go about in the night and eaves drop the houses in the neighborhood; pursuing this course for about a fort-night and gathering little or no intelligence, afraid of speaking to any human being, and returning every morning to my cave before the dawn of day. I know not how long I might have led this life, if accident had not betrayed me, a dog in the neighborhood passing by my hiding place one night while I was out, was attracted by some meat I had in my cave, and crawled in and stole it, and was coming out just as I returned. A few nights after, two negroes having started to go hunting with the same dog, and passed that way, the dog came again to the place, and having just gone out to

walk about, discovered me and barked, on which thinking myself discovered, I spoke to them to beg concealment. On making myself known they fled from me. Knowing then they would betray me, I immediately left my hiding place, and was pursued almost incessantly until I was taken a fortnight afterwards by Mr. Benjamin Phipps, in a little hole I had dug out with my sword, for the purpose of concealment, under the top of a fallen tree. On Mr. Phipps' discovering the place of my concealment, he cocked his gun and aimed at me. I requested him not to shoot and I would give up, upon which he demanded my sword. I delivered it to him, and he brought me to prison. During the time I was pursued, I had many hair breadth escapes, which your time will not permit you to relate. I am here loaded with chains, and willing to suffer the fate that awaits me.

I here proceeded to make some inquiries of him, after assuring him of the certain death that awaited him, and that concealment would only bring destruction on the innocent as well as guilty, of his own color, if he knew of any extensive or concerted plan. His answer was, I do not. When I questioned him as to the insurrection in North Carolina happening about the same time, he denied any knowledge of it; and when I looked him in the face as though I would search his inmost thoughts, he replied, "I see sir, you doubt my word; but can you not think the same ideas, and strange appearances about this time in the heaven's might prompt others, as well as myself, to this undertaking." I now had much conversation with and asked him many questions, having forborne to do so previously, except in the cases noted in parenthesis; but during his statement, I had, unnoticed by him, taken notes as to some particular circumstances, and having the advantage of his statement before me in writing, on the evening of the third day that I had been with him, I began a cross examination, and found his statement corroborated by every circumstance coming within my own knowledge or the confessions of others whom had been either killed or executed, and whom he had not seen nor had any knowledge since 22nd of Au-

*Nat Turner is discovered after his August 21, 1831, slave
uprising, in which he and his followers killed fifty-five people.*

gust last, he expressed himself fully satisfied as to the impracticability of his attempt. It has been said he was ignorant and cowardly, and that his object was to murder and rob for the purpose of obtaining money to make his escape. It is notorious, that he was never known to have a dollar in his life; to swear an oath, or drink a drop of spirits. As to his ignorance, he certainly never had the advantages of education, but he can read and write, (it was taught him by his parents,) and for natural intelligence and quickness of apprehension, is surpassed by few men I have ever seen. As to his being a coward, his reason as given for not resisting Mr. Phipps, shews the decision of his character. When he saw Mr. Phipps present his gun, he said he knew it was impossible for him to escape as the woods were full of men; he therefore thought it was better to surrender, and trust to fortune for his escape. He is a complete fanatic, or plays his part most admirably. On other subjects he possesses an uncommon share of intelligence, with a mind capable of attaining any thing; but warped and perverted by the influence of early impressions.

He is below the ordinary stature, though strong and active, having the true negro face, every feature of which is strongly marked. I shall not attempt to describe the effect of his narrative, as told and commented on by himself, in the condemned hole of the prison. The calm, deliberate composure with which he spoke of his late deeds and intentions, the expression of his fiend-like face when excited by enthusiasm, still bearing the stains of the blood of helpless innocence about him; clothed with rags and covered with chains; yet daring to raise his manacled hands to heaven, with a spirit soaring above the attributes of man; I looked on him and my blood curdled in my veins.

I will not shock the feelings of humanity, nor wound afresh the bosoms of the disconsolate sufferers in this unparalleled and inhuman massacre, by detailing the deeds of their fiend-like barbarity. There were two or three who were in the power of these wretches, had they known it, and who escaped in the most providential manner. There were two whom they thought they left dead on the field at Mr. Parker's, but who were only stunned by the blows of their guns, as they did not take time to re-load when they charged on them. The escape of a little girl who went to school at Mr. Waller's, and where the children were collecting for that purpose, excited general sympathy. As their teacher had not arrived, they were at play in the yard, and seeing the negroes approach, she ran up on a dirt chimney, (such as are common to log houses,) and remained there unnoticed during the massacre of the eleven that were killed at this place. She remained on her hiding place till just before the arrival of a party, who were in pursuit of the murderers, when she came down and fled to a swamp, where, a mere child as she was, with the horrors of the late scene before her, she lay concealed until the next day, when seeing a party go up to the house, she came up, and on being asked how she escaped, replied with the utmost simplicity, "The Lord helped her." She was taken up behind a gentleman of the party, and returned to the arms of her weeping mother. Miss Whitehead concealed herself between the bed and the mat that supported it, while they murdered her sister in the same room, without discovering her. She was afterwards carried off, and concealed for protection by a slave of the family, who gave evidence against several of them on their trial. Mrs. Nathaniel Francis, while concealed in a closet heard their blows, and the shrieks of the victims of these ruthless savages; they then entered the closet where she was concealed, and went out without discovering her. While in this hiding place, she heard two of her women in a quarrel about the division of her clothes. Mr. John T. Baron, discovering them approaching his house, told his wife to make her escape, and scorning to fly, fell fighting on his own threshold. After firing his rifle, he discharged his gun at them, and then broke it over the villain who first approached him, but he was overpowered, and slain. His bravery, however, saved from the hands of these monsters, his lovely and amiable wife, who will long lament a husband so deserving of her love. As directed by him, she attempted to escape through the garden, when she was caught and held by one of her servant girls, but another coming to her rescue, she fled to the woods, and concealed herself. Few indeed, were those who escaped their work of death. But fortunate for society, the hand of retributive justice has overtaken them; and not one that was known to be concerned has escaped.

The Commonwealth, vs. *Nat Turner*} Charged with making insurrection, and plotting to take away the lives of divers free white persons, &c. on the 22nd of August, 1831.

The court composed of ——, having met for the trial of Nat Turner, the prisoner was brought in and arraigned, and upon his arraignment pleaded *Not guilty;* saying to his counsel, that he did not feel so.

On the part of the Commonwealth, Levi Waller was introduced, who being sworn, deposed as follows: *(agreeably to Nat's own Confession.)* Col. Trezvant* was then introduced, who being sworn, narrated Nat's Confession to him, as follows: *(his Confession as given to Mr.*

*The committing Magistrate

Gray.) The prisoner introduced no evidence, and the case was submitted without argument to the court, who having found him guilty, Jeremiah Cobb, Esq. Chairman, pronounced the sentence of the court, in the following words: "Nat Turner! Stand up. Have you any thing to say why sentence of death should not be pronounced against you?

Ans. I have not. I have made a full confession to Mr. Gray, and I have nothing more to say.

Attend then to the sentence of the Court. You have been arraigned and tried before this court, and convicted of one of the highest crimes in our criminal code. You must have been convicted of plotting in cold blood, the indiscriminate destruction of men, of helpless women, and of infant children. The evidence before us leaves not a shadow of doubt, but that your hands were often imbrued in the blood of the innocent; and your own confession tells us that they were stained with the blood of a master; in your own language, "too indulgent." Could I stop here, your crime would be sufficiently aggravated. But the original contriver of a plan, deep and deadly, one that never can be effected, you managed so far to put it into execution, as to deprive us of many of our most valuable citizens; and this was done when they were asleep, and defenceless; under circumstances shocking to humanity. And while upon this part of the subject, I cannot but call your attention to the poor misguided wretches who have gone before you. They are not few in number—they were your bosom associates; and the blood of all cries aloud, and calls upon you, as the author of their misfortune. Yes! You forced them unprepared, from Time to Eternity. Borne down by this load of guilt, your only justification is, that you were led away by fanaticism. If this be true, from my soul I pity you; and while you have my sympathies, I am, nevertheless called upon to pass the sentence of the court. The time between this and your execution, will necessarily be very short; and your only hope must be in another world. The judgment of the court is, that you be taken hence to the jail from whence you came, thence to the place of execution, and on Friday next, between the hours of 10 A.M. and 2 P.M. be hung by the neck until you are dead! dead! dead and may the Lord have mercy upon your soul.

A LIST OF PERSONS MURDERED IN THE INSURRECTION, ON THE 21ST AND 22ND OF AUGUST, 1831.

Joseph Travers and wife and three children, Mrs. Elizabeth Turner, Hartwell Prebles, Sarah Newsome, Mrs. P. Reese and son William, Trajan Doyle, Henry Bryant and wife and child, and wife's mother, Mrs. Catharine Whitehead, son Richard and four daughters and grand-child, Salathiel Francis, Nathaniel Francis' overseer and two children, John T. Barrow, George Vaughan, Mrs. Levi Waller and ten children, William Williams, wife and two boys, Mrs. Caswell Worrell and child, Mrs. Rebecca Vaughan, Ann Eliza Vaughan, and son Arthur, Mrs. John K. Williams and child, Mrs. Jacob Williams and three children, and Edwin Drury—amounting to fifty-five.

Why Both Abolition and Colonization Will Fail

Thomas R. Dew

In 1832, soon after the defeat of Nat Turner's Rebellion, white Virginians seriously debated the question of whether slavery was too dangerous an institution to maintain. Governor John Floyd was among those who thought that the only safe course was to abolish slavery and expel the ex-slaves.

Thomas R. Dew, a thirty-year-old professor at the College of William and Mary, intently followed the debates on this momentous subject in the Virginia Assembly and published the pamphlet excerpted here. His conclusions were stark: Emancipation would ruin the state's agriculture and impoverish slave owners; colonization would be far too expensive an undertaking for the state to afford; in short, slavery cannot safely be abolished. The pamphlet made Dew's reputation as a hardheaded spokesman for the South's interests.

Dew's pamphlet sounds cold today, and its racist assumption that blacks would never be "civilized" is offensive. But Dew was right to conclude that colonization was impractical. Whites would not pay the price, and most blacks did not want to be "colonized." White taxpayers would never have accepted the burden of compensated emancipation; more-

over, after 1831 southern whites came to feel that slavery had to be defended at all costs. Even so, the eventual price of abolishing slavery—a Civil War that killed six hundred thousand Americans and devastated the South physically and economically—would be higher than Dew or any of his contemporaries could have imagined.

Excerpted from Thomas R. Dew, "Abolition of Negro Slavery," in *The Confessions of Nat Turner and Related Documents*, edited by Kenneth S. Greenberg. (Boston: Bedford Books of St. Martin's Press, 1996).

In looking to the texture of the population of our country, there is nothing so well calculated to arrest the attention of the observer as the existence of negro slavery throughout a large portion of the confederacy [union]; a race of people differing from us in colour and in habits, and vastly inferior in the scale of civilization, have been increasing and spreading—"growing with our growth and strengthening with our strength"—until they have become intertwined with every fibre of society. Go through our southern states, and every where you see the negro slave by the side of the white man, you will find him alike in the mansion of the rich, the cabin of the poor, the workshop of the mechanic, and the field of the planter. Upon the contemplation of a population framed like this, a curious and interesting question readily suggests itself to the inquiring mind. Can these two distinct races of people, now living together as master and servant, be ever separated? Can the black be sent back to his African home? or will the day ever arrive when he can be liberated from this thraldom, and mount in the scale of civilization and rights to an equality with the white? This is a question of truly momentous character: it involves the whole framework of society, contemplates a separation of its elements, or a radical change in their relation, and requires for its adequate investigation the most complete and profound knowledge of the nature and sources of national wealth and political aggrandizement, an acquaintance with the elastic and powerful spring of population, and the causes which invigorate or paralyze its energies. It requires a clear perception of the varying rights of man amid all the changing circumstances by which he may be surrounded, and a profound knowledge of all the principles, passions, and susceptibilities, which make up the moral nature of our species, and according as they are acted upon by adventitious circumstances, alter our condition, and produce all that wonderful variety of character which so strongly marks and characterizes the human family. Well, then, does it behoove even the wisest statesman to approach this august subject with the utmost circumspection and diffidence; its wanton agitation even is pregnant with mischief, but rash and hasty action threatens, in our opinion, the whole southern country with irremediable ruin. The evil of *yesterday's* growth may be extirpated *to-day,* and the vigour of society may heal the wound; but that which is the growth of *ages* may require *ages* to remove. . . .

If ever there was a question debated in a deliberative body, which called for the most exalted talent, the longest and most tried experience, the utmost circumspection and caution, a complete exemption from prejudice and undue excitement where both are apt to prevail, an ardent and patriotic desire to advance the vital interests of the state, uncombined with all mere desire for vain and ostentatious display, and with no view to party or geographical divisions, that question was the question of the *abolition* of *slavery* in the Virginia legislature. . . .

We are very ready to admit, that in point of ability and eloquence, the debate transcended our expectations. One of the leading political papers in the state remarked—"We have never heard any debate so eloquent, so sustained, and in which so great a number of speakers had appeared, and commanded the attention of so numerous and intelligent an audience. Day after day multitudes throng to the capital, and have been compensated by eloquence which would have illustrated Rome or Athens." But however fine might have been the rhetorical display, however ably some isolated points might have been discussed, still we affirm, with confidence, that no enlarged, wise, and practical plan of operations, was proposed by the abolitionists. . . .

We have not formed our opinion lightly upon this subject; we have given to the vital question of abolition the most mature and intense consideration which we are capable of bestowing, and we have come to the conclusion—a conclusion which seems to be sustained by facts and reasoning as irresistible as the demonstration of the mathematician—that every plan of emancipation and deportation which we can possibly conceive, is *totally* impracticable. . . .

It is almost useless to inquire whether this deportation of slaves to Africa would, as some seem most strangely to anticipate, invite the whites of other states into the commonwealth. Who would be disposed to enter a state with worn out soil and a black population mortgaged to the payment of millions per annum, for the purpose of emancipation and deportation, when in the West the most luxuriant soils, unencumbered with heavy exactions, could be purchased for the paltry sum of $1.25 per acre?

Where, then, is that multitude of whites to come from, which the glowing fancy of orators has sketched out as flowing into and filling up the vacuum created by the removal of slaves? The fact is—throughout the whole debate in the Virginia legislature, the speakers seemed to consider the increase of population as a sort of fixed quantity, which would remain the same under the endless change of circumstance, and consequently that every man exported from among the blacks, lessened *pro tanto* exactly the black population, and that the whites, moving on with their usual speed, would fill the void; which certainly was an erroneous supposition, and manifested an almost unpardonable inattention to the wonderful *elasticity* of the powerful spring of population. The removal of inhabitants, accompanied with great loss of productive labour and capital, so far from leaving the residue in a better situation, and disposing them to increase and multiply, produces the directly opposite effect; it deteriorates the condition of society, and deadens the spring of population. . . .

Against most of the great difficulties attendant on the plan of emancipation above examined, it was impossible for the abolitionists entirely to close their eyes; and it is really curious to pause a moment and examine some of the reflections and schemes by which Virginia was to be reconciled to the plan. We have been told that it would not be necessary to purchase all the slaves sent away—that many would be surrendered by their owners without an equivalent. "There are a number of slave-holders," (said one who has all the lofty feeling and devoted patriotism which have hitherto so proudly characterized Virginia,) "at this very time, I do not speak from vain conjecture, but from what I know from the best information, and this number would continue to increase, who would voluntarily surrender their slaves, if the state would provide the means of colonizing them elsewhere. And there would be again another class, I have already heard of many, while they could not afford to sacrifice the entire value of their slaves, would cheerfully compromise with the state for half of their value." In the first place, we would remark that the gentleman's anticipation would certainly prove delusive—the surrender of a very few slaves would enhance the importance and value of the residue, and make the owner much more reluctant to part with them. Let any farmer in Lower Virginia ask himself how many he can spare from his plantation—and he will be surprised to see how few can be dispensed with. If that intelligent gentleman, from the storehouse of his knowledge, would but call up the history of the past, he would see that *mere philanthropy,* with all her splendid boastings, has never yet accomplished one great scheme; he would find the remark of that great judge of human nature, the illustrious author of the Wealth of Nations [Adam Smith], that no people had the generosity to liberate their slaves until it became their interest to do so, but too true; and the philosophic page of Hume, Robertson, Stuart, and Sismondi [important eighteenth-century historians], would inform him that the serfs of Europe have been only gradually emancipated through the operation of *self interest* and not *philanthropy:* and we shall soon see that it was fortunate for both parties that this was the cause.

But it is strange indeed that gentlemen have never reflected, that the pecuniary loss to the state, will be precisely the same, whether the negroes be purchased or gratuitously surrendered. In the latter case the burthen is only shifted from the whole state to that portion where the surrender is made—thus if we own $10,000 worth of this property, and surrender the whole to the government, it is evident that we lose the amount of $10,000; and if the whole of Lower Virginia could at once be induced to give up all this property, and it could be sent away, the only effect of this generosity and self devotion would be to inflict the *blow* of *desolation* more exclusively on this portion of the state—the aggregate loss would be the same, the burthen would only be shifted from the whole to a part—the West would dodge the blow, and perhaps every candid citizen of Lower Virginia would confess that he is devoid of that refined incomprehensible patriotism which would call for self immolation on the shrine of folly, and would most conscientiously advise the eastern Virginians never to surrender their slaves to the government without a fair equivalent. Can it be genuine philanthropy to persuade them *alone* to step forward and bear the whole burthen?

Again; some have attempted to evade the difficulties by seizing on the increase of the negroes after a certain time. Thus Mr. Randolph's plan proposed that all born after the year 1840, should be raised by their masters to the age of eighteen for the female and twenty-one for the male, and then hired out, until the neat sum arising therefrom amounted to enough to send them away. Scarcely any one in the legislature—we believe not even the author himself—entirely approved of this plan.* It is obnoxious to the objections we have just been stating against voluntary surrender. It proposes to saddle the slaveholder with the whole burthen; it infringes directly the rights of property; it converts the fee simple possession of this kind of property into an estate for years; and it only puts off the great sacrifice required of the state to 1840, when most of the evils will occur that have already been described. In the mean time it destroys the value of slaves, and with it all landed possessions—checks the productions of the state, imposes (when 1840 arrives) upon the master the intolerable and grievous burthen of raising his young slaves to the ages of eighteen and twenty-one, and then liberating them to be hired out under the superintendence of government (the most miserable of all managers,) until the proceeds arising therefrom shall be sufficient to send them away. If any man at all conversant with political economy should ever anticipate the day when this shall happen, we can only say that his faith is great indeed, enough to remove mountains, and that he has studied in a totally different school from ourselves.

Again; we entirely agree with the assertion of Mr. Brown, one of the ablest and most promising of Virginia's sons, that the ingenuity of man, if exerted for the purpose, could not devise a more efficient mode of producing discontent among our slaves, and thus endangering the peace of the community. There are born annually of this population about 20,000 children. Those which are born before the year 1840 are to be slaves; those which are born after that period are to be free at a certain age. These two classes will be reared together; they will labour together, and commune together. It cannot escape the observation of him who is doomed to servitude, that although of the same colour and born of the same parents, a far different destiny awaits his more fortunate brother—as his thoughts again and again revert to the subject, he begins to regard himself as the victim of injustice. Cheerfulness and contentment will flee from his bosom, and the most harmless and happy creature that lives on earth, will be transformed into a dark designing and desperate rebel. . . .

There are some again who exhaust their ingenuity in devising schemes for taking off the breeding portion of the slaves to Africa, or carrying away the sexes in such disproportions as will in a measure prevent those left behind from breeding. All of these plans merit nothing more than the appellation of *vain juggling legislative conceits,* unworthy of a wise statesman and a moral man. If our slaves are ever to be sent away in any systematic manner, *humanity* demands that they should be carried in families. The voice of the world would condemn Virginia if she sanctioned any plan of deportation by which the male and female, husband and wife, parent and child, were systematically and relentlessly separated. If we are to indulge in this kind of regulating vice, why not cure the ill at once, by following the counsel of Xenophon in his Economics, and the practice of Old Cato the Censor [Xenophon and Old Cato were an ancient Greek and an ancient Roman writer on slavery and related matters.]? Let us keep the male and female separate* in *Ergastula,* or dungeons, if it be necessary, and the one generation will pass away, and the evil will be removed to the heart's content of our humane philanthropists! But all these puerile conceits fall far short of surmounting the great difficulty which . . . is eternally present and cannot be removed. . . .

There is $100,000,000 of slave property in the state of Virginia, and it matters but little how you destroy it, whether by the slow process of the cautious *practitioner,* or with the frightful despatch of the self confident *quack*; when it is gone, no matter how, the deed will be done, and Virginia will be a desert.

*The difficulty of falling upon any definite plan which can for a moment command the approbation of even a few of the most intelligent abolitionists, is an unerring symptom of the difficulty and impracticability of the whole.

*See Hume's Essay on the populousness of Ancient Nations, where he ascribes this practice to Cato and others, to prevent their slaves from breeding.

Colonizing Liberia: One Solution to Revolt

David Lindsay

One of the most difficult questions facing early nineteenth-century American whites who wished to see slavery abolished was: What is to become of the freed slaves? Even most whites who opposed or deplored slavery believed that blacks were inherently inferior, and many thought that the best solution would be to send emancipated slaves out of the country—perhaps back to Africa. Colonization was ostensibly a humanitarian objective, and most whites who supported it thought that they were doing blacks a service, but its motivation was basically racist.

In the following selection, historian David Lindsay discusses the rise of the chief white organization that sponsored colonization—the American Colonization Society—and shows how it organized the settlement of a few former slaves in what became the African republic of Liberia. Bear in mind, however, that compared to the ever-increasing number of slaves in the United States before the Civil War (rising from some 1.2 million in 1810 to almost 4 million in 1860), the approximately 1,400 who went to Liberia were negligible. A serious effort to send meaningful numbers of

Reprinted from David Lindsay, "'The Land of Their Fathers,' Liberia," *American History Illustrated*, May 1972. This article is reprinted from *American History Illustrated* magazine with the permission of PRIMEDIA Special Interest Publications (History Group), copyright American History Illustrated magazine.

African Americans back to "the land of their fathers" would have meant an immense outlay of money—and also force, because very few African Americans wanted to go. Hard as conditions were in America, this was now their country; they wanted freedom and justice here, not a white-sponsored "homeland" in Africa. Nor did the native people of Liberia welcome returning American blacks: The subsequent history of that country has been marred by deep resentment between descendants of former American slaves and the indigenous people.

*T*he republic of Liberia was launched in Washington, D.C. The time: December 21, 1816. The place: the elegant Davis Hotel where a group of eminent gentlemen met for talk and planning. Presiding at the meeting Speaker of the House of Representatives, affable Henry Clay, appealed warmly to the assembled dignitaries—lawyers, clergymen, landowning gentry, Congressmen, Senators, and businessmen. Noting the depressed status of free Negroes in America, Clay urged undertaking efforts to colonize them in Africa, in his phrase, to restore them "to the land of their fathers." Other speakers followed in much the same vein as Clay—Elias Caldwell, chief clerk of the United States Supreme Court, and Virginian John Randolph of Roanoke among them. The meeting responded by voting to establish a society to plan and launch a colony of free American Negroes in Africa.

A week later a second meeting, convened in the hall of the House of Representatives in the Capitol, formally created the American Society for Colonizing the Free People of Color. A constitution was approved and officers elected. Justice Bushrod Washington of the Supreme Court, nephew of George Washington, was named president, while the thirteen vice presidents included Henry Clay, Secretary of the Treasury William Crawford of Georgia, General Andrew Jackson of Tennessee, Richard Rush of Pennsylvania, John Taylor of Virginia, and the Reverend Robert Finley of New Jersey.

It was Finley who had sparked the movement. While many had earlier talked of creating a colony in Africa to which American Negroes could migrate, Finley, a graduate of the College of New Jersey—later Princeton University— and Presbyterian minister and teacher of Basking Ridge, New Jersey, acted. Connected by marriage with the wealthy, influential Boudinot family of New Jersey, the young Finley was caught up in the stirrings of the reform and social betterment drive sweeping the country in the wake of the War of 1812. A rash of benevolent societies sprang up in the postwar years— the American Peace Society, American Bible Society, American Temperance Union, Board of Foreign Missions, American Education Society. As part of a broad evangelical crusade, infused with missionary zeal, each of these voluntary associations aimed to eliminate some abuse or evil in American society. War, drunkenness, illiteracy, ignorance, and heathen darkness would have to yield before the benevolent crusade. Preachers exhorted their congregations to rise up and strike a blow for the "good causes."

In developing a colonization plan, Finley consulted, among others, Paul Cuffee, a remarkable Negro Quaker shipowner operating out of Massachusetts ports. In 1811 Cuffee had visited Sierra Leone, the British-sponsored haven and colony on Africa's west coast for kidnapped

Africans rescued from slave trading ships by the Royal Navy. Declaring that "The travail of my soul is that Africa's inhabitants may be favored with reformation," Cuffee transported thirty-eight American Negroes to Sierra Leone and planned a larger operation. Hope for the colonizing project, dimmed by Cuffee's untimely death, was revived by Finley.

In the fall of 1816 Finley revealed his plan, rallied support among Presbyterians at the College of New Jersey and won endorsement by the New Jersey Legislature. Arguing that "the sons of Africa" should in justice by returned to "the land of their fathers," Finley asserted that his colonization scheme would save free Negroes from the "entrenched prejudice" and inferior status they faced, would offer a "happy and progressive" means for ending slavery in America and would implant Christianity and civilization in the "benighted regions" of Africa. Crucial to carrying out the plan was financial support from the Federal Government. Because a Federal law of 1807 outlawed the slaved trade, Congress, Finley contended, should help establish a colony since an African station would provide a refuge for Africans rescued from illegal slave-running ships.

Arriving in Washington in December 1816, Finley brought letters of introduction to President James Madison, a fellow College of New Jersey alumnus, and other leaders. His most helpful contact was his brother-in-law, Elias B. Caldwell, who as a lawyer and chief clerk of the Supreme Court for sixteen years knew the leading attorneys and politicians in the Capitol. Already active in benevolent society affairs, Caldwell eagerly agreed to help and enlisted the aid of attorney Francis Scott Key, author of "The Star Spangled Banner." Caldwell and Finley pumped out colonization publicity through the Washington *National Intelligencer*. Caldwell persuaded Justice Washington and Speaker Clay to endorse the proposal, while Key won John Randolph's approval. From these efforts, as December 1816 drew to a close, came the formal creation of the American Colonization Society with Washington as president and Caldwell as secretary. Finley would soon move on to become president of the University of Georgia, leaving the colonization crusade in other hands.

Public reaction to the new society was mixed. Philadelphia Negroes led by sailmaker James Forten protested that the scheme did nothing to speed the end of slavery and was designed to force blacks out of the country. Some Pennsylvania Quakers also objected. But other church groups, notably Presbyterians and Methodists, hailed the new organization. Ex-President Thomas Jefferson sent his endorsement from Monticello. Virginia's legislature adopted approving resolutions and urged Federal sponsorship of colonization in Africa. In January 1817 John Randolph submitted to the House of Representatives a memorial signed by Bushrod Washington urging Congress to create a free Negro colony in Africa. The House committee on the slave trade, after considering the memorial, suggested an alternative of cooperating with England in the colony at Sierra Leone.

Shortly President James Monroe, in a message noting that the British Navy maintained a strong anti-slave ship patrol off the West African coast, urged Congress to take similar action against the continuing, illegal slave trade. While Congress procrastinated over such a measure, Society spokesmen beat the drums throughout the country to stimulate support for the colonization drive. Again the *National Intelligencer* churned out items supplied by Secretary Caldwell. Agents canvassed the country for donations. Auxiliaries sprang up in New York, Philadelphia, Baltimore, and elsewhere. Financial support began to trickle in.

On March 3, 1819, Congress adopted the Anti-Slave Trade Act authorizing the President to maintain a Navy patrol against slavers off the African coast and to "effect arrangements" for supporting and resettling in Africa any Africans rescued by the patrol. A $100,000 appropriation was approved. In response to an inquiry in London, British antislavery leaders suggested a site for a colony down the west African coast from Sierra Leone.

To seek out a site the Colonization Society dispatched a "mission of inquiry," composed of the Reverend Samuel J. Mills, a young Massa-

chusetts preacher and fund raiser for the Society, and Professor Ebenezer Burgess of Burlington College in Vermont. After a month in England, the pair sailed to Sierra Leone. There they consulted with John Kizell, who years before had been freed from slavery in South Carolina by the British in the American Revolution and transported to Nova Scotia. Later he had migrated to Sierra Leone where he became Paul Cuffee's partner. With Kizell as interpreter-guide, Mills and Burgess examined the coast. Nearby Sherbro Island impressed them as suitable, and they described it glowingly in their report to the Colonization Society in which they urged establishing a colony there.

With the Society's recommendation in hand, President Monroe consulted his Cabinet and got conflicting advice. Secretary of State John Quincy Adams contended that the 1819 law did not authorize the President to purchase land for a colony. But Attorney General William Wirt, after initial doubts, held the President did have such authority. When a shipload of Africans, captured at sea by the Navy and landed in Georgia, was about to be auctioned, a new urgency demanded a decision. Monroe then announced he would welcome the assistance of the Colonization Society, which promptly recommended the Reverend Samuel Bacon of Sturbridge, Massachusetts as director for the projected colony. Under combined government-society sponsorship, Bacon proceeded to charter the ship *Elizabeth*, engage sixteen Negro carpenters, masons, and blacksmiths, and purchase provisions to support 300 people for a year. He also secured tools, carts, implements, wagons, 100 muskets, several cannon, and a dozen barrels of gunpowder. But six months of the Society's recruiting efforts yielded only eighty-six Negro volunteers, twenty-eight men among them, to go to Africa.

On January 31, 1820, the brig *Elizabeth*, labeled the "Black Mayflower" by the press, sailed out of New York harbor and headed east across the Atlantic. On board the colonists looked hopefully eastward, reassured by the escorting presence of the U.S. Navy sloop *Cyane*.

Three months and 6,000 miles later, the party landed at Sherbro Island. There they discovered that John Kizell had secured land from local chiefs and built temporary huts and a warehouse for the colonists' use. It was the last stroke of good fortune the expedition would have.

Inexperienced and unacclimated as they were, the colonists faced a hostile environment in a battle to survive. Lack of a drinkable water supply was discouraging enough, but the task of clearing stubborn tropical vegetation to prepare tillable fields proved even tougher. Health problems erupted at once. Dr. John Crozier, who as a Norfolk slave had learned medicine from his doctor-master, developed malaria and died within a few weeks. By the end of September 1820, a dozen others including director Bacon died. Into his post stepped the Reverend Daniel Coker, a teacher-preacher of Baltimore's free Negro community who had helped organize the African Methodist Church and declined appointment as a bishop in order to go to Africa. Coker's first step as leader was to move the colony from Sherbro to a temporary location on Fourah Bay near Freetown, Sierra Leone. Urgent reports were sent to Washington, requesting instructions and aid.

President Monroe responded by making available the Navy brig *Nautilus*. A new expedition of thirty-five black recruits was fitted out with the Colonization Society appointing as leaders the Reverend Ephraim Bacon, brother of Samuel, and Joseph Andrus, a Baltimore Negro minister. When the *Nautilus* sailed from Norfolk on January 21, 1821, escorting her was the Navy schooner *Alligator* commanded by Lieutenant Robert F. Stockton (who earlier had attended Finley's academy in New Jersey and who later would achieve fame in the conquest of California). Monroe's personal envoy, Navy surgeon Dr. Eli Ayres, accompanied Stockton.

This second expedition reached Fourah Bay in mid-March, much to the relief of the waiting, original voyagers. Within a few months directors Andrus and Bacon both died of fever. Scouting expeditions, led by Stockton and Navy Lieutenant Matthew Perry (later to lead the celebrated sortie to open Japan) searched the coast to

the south for a suitable site for the colony. After several false starts, Stockton and Perry selected a spot on thirty-mile-long Cape Mesurado near the mouth of Mesurado River.

After negotiations with King Peter and other Bassa and Dey tribal chiefs, who accepted $300 worth of beads, muskets, tobacco, mirrors, rum, and other goods in payment, the area was deeded to the colony. In January 1822 the colonists landed and began clearing land, building huts, laying out a public square, and planting crops. A fire in the colony storehouse put the entire group under strict rationing of supplies. Surgeon Ayres, after making repeated pleas to Washington for new provisions, sailed for America. In his absence, leadership was assumed by Daniel Coker and Elisha Johnson, Negro artilleryman veteran of the War of 1812. They were joined in carrying the colony and saving it from repeated Bassa harassments by Lott Cary, who as a slave had risen to foreman of a Richmond tobacco warehouse, purchased his own freedom, and became a preacher. Swept up in the colonization excitement, Cary declared: "I am an African. I wish to go to a country where I shall be estimated by my merits, not by my complexion; and I feel bound to labor for my suffering race." A member of the second expedition, he would soon prove his talent for leadership in the struggling community.

Six months passed before an American merchantman arrived bringing fifty-five free Negro volunteers, together with supplies, medicine, clothing, and tools. Arriving also as assistant director, under Dr. Ayres, was 28-year-old Yankee Jehudi Ashmun, a Middlebury graduate and preacher who had been editing a Baltimore religious paper. His 21-year-old wife, who accompanied him, died of fever within a few weeks of arrival. By late fall a new crisis almost destroyed the colony. Of the 200 American Negroes who made the crossing to Africa, only 141 remained alive. Of these more than thirty were sick, leaving only thirty-six able-bodied men. With this handful, Johnson and Cary in charge of defense had to meet a full scale assault by Bassa tribal warriors on the settlement. The attackers' numbers were estimated at 800. Johnson and Cary placed their cannon at strategic spots along the earthworks before a sturdy log stockade, but they had little hope of staving off the massed attackers. When the assault came on November 30, 1822, the Bassas knifed easily through the outer defenses and charged the stockade. Temporarily repulsed by musket fire, they were regrouping near an outer cannon for the inevitable final attack when elderly, husky Matilda Newport, carrying a life coal in her pipe, shouldered her way through the startled Bassas, dropped the coal in the cannon's powder chamber and quickly withdrew. The resulting explosion, killing and wounding many nearby, so shocked the attackers that they left the field. In relief Ashmun declared "a day of thanksgiving" in which all colonists, even the sick, heartily joined.

The struggle for survival continued as settlers planted gardens, built additional houses for newcomers, and established their first public market place at their major town Christopolis, later renamed Monrovia to honor the American President. The name Liberia, "land of freedom," was coined in 1824 by Robert G. Harper, an active sponsor of the Maryland Colonization Society for whom a Liberian town was later named.

Fund raising in the United States was almost as difficult for the Colonization Society as crop raising for Liberian settlers. The Panic of 1819, coupled with competition from other benevolent societies for donations, created difficulty in winning support, which after dropping to a discouraging $800 in 1822 ran at about $4,000 annually through the 1820's.

In America motives behind the colonization drive were mixed from the start. Some backers supported it from humanitarian feelings that free Negroes were blocked by insurmountable white prejudice from a fair chance to compete in American society. Hence, the reasoning went, they would be better off among their own kind in Africa. Others saw colonization as a means of nibbling away at slavery to bring an eventual end to the "peculiar institution" by making it possible for a slaveowner to manumit his slaves, a step prohibited by law in most Southern states

unless at the same time the owner arranged emigration from the state. Still others viewed colonization as a channel for draining off freed blacks whom they considered an "undesirable, even dangerous," element. Others, unconcerned with moral or humane considerations, visualized the movement as opening a vast, valuable trade with the African continent, with Liberia serving as a commercial station.

Jehudi Ashmun, for example, went to Africa not only as a humanitarian but as a representative of the Baltimore Trading Company intending to become a rich merchant handling ivory, palm oil, cam wood, and gold dust. Before going, he attempted in vain to get the Colonization Society to give his firm a monopoly of the colony's trade. Upon becoming colonial resident agent, Ashmun shifted position. He now championed agriculture over commerce, but he found the colonists little inclined to plant staple crops. Few attempted large farming operations. Even the small farming efforts at the outset were hampered by poor soil near Monrovia, unfamiliar pests, and 200 inches of rain a year. Besides, farming was heavy labor compared to the commercial road to profits. Many colonists early turned to local trade, bartering cloth, rum, and beads with native tribes for ivory, cam wood, and palm oil. Others engaged in import-export trading and prospered in time. Lott Cary became Liberian representative of a Richmond commercial firm. Reverend Colston Waring formed a trading partnership with a Virginia Negro that grossed $70,000 in 1830. The commercial firm of Roberts, Colson and Company, organized by colonist Joseph J. Roberts and a Petersburg, Virginia friend, ran its own schooner in a regular America-Africa trading operation.

As the Society's agent in Liberia, Ashmun proceeded to knock out slavers' efforts along the nearby coast. He also eliminated French, Spanish, and English trading posts as potential rivals in Liberia's sphere. To make this policy stick, he engaged in annexing territory. In 1825–26 he managed to acquire 150 miles along the coast and major rivers near Monrovia. King Peter, former owner of Cape Masurado, now gave up Cape

Mount, a sizeable area above Monrovia, and an island renamed Bushrod Island upon annexation to Liberia. Up the St. Paul's River, tribesmen were pressed into ceding a large tract on which Ashmun built a log trading post to garner the interior trade. Native tribes came to fear the colony's power, looked upon Liberian colonists as "white men," and many remained alienated and resentful of the dominant Americo-Liberians well into the 20th century.

Within the colony itself harmony did not always prevail. Many settlers resented the arbitrary rule imposed by the Colonization Society. When Ashmun threatened to cut off rations from persons he charged with malingering, open defiance sprouted. A gathering of discontented colonists issued a "Remonstrance of December 5, 1823," demanding a greater share in running the colony. They complained that land distribution was slow and stingy and that resident agents were seeking personal gain in dividing town lots. When Ashmun tried to crack down, Lott Cary led a revolt, seizing weapons from the colonial arsenal and taking over the food stores. Ashmun, pleading ill health, was actually forced to flee to the Cape Verde Islands.

The Colonization Society in Washington responded by getting President Monroe to send the USS *Porpoise* carrying Ralph R. Gurley as government agent. Gurley, a 25-year-old Yale graduate, was already serving energetically as the Society's secretary, having replaced Caldwell. Gurley brought with him to Monrovia a tentative constitution, which he submitted to the colony's voters. Approval given, colonists now could assemble and elect an advisory council of five members as a legislature to aid Ashmun, who was now restored as resident agent.

The colony was slowly getting its feet on solid ground. With an annual increase of more than 100 immigrants from America, plus periodic arrivals of Africans taken from slave ships by the Navy, population expanded steadily. Liberia occupied several hundred square miles, and new communities like New Georgia sprouted in the late 1820's. Farming was beginning to produce a local food supply, although colonists still preferred foodstuffs brought from America. Under Lott Cary's lead, new lands produced rice, millet, root crops like cassava, tarot, and yams, peppers, peanuts, eggplants, along with native bananas, pineapples, and palm kernels. Local resources also yielded "trader goods" like dye woods, palm oil, ivory, and leopard skins, the last shortly becoming the leading commercial export.

Reports that slavers were operating to the southeast in the Grand Bassa area reached the colony in 1826. In response, Lott Cary organized an armed force, which with Navy aid drove out the slavers and released the captured Africans in Liberia's first war of liberation. The following year the USS *Sharp* brought additional arms and with help from the colonists built Fort Norris near Cape Mesurado to forestall future slaving and check passing ships. Cary and Ashmun got local chiefs to boycott white traders suspected of collusion with slavers. A year later poor health required Ashmun to resign as colonial agent. Shortly after returning to America, he died in New Haven, hailed as "the great martyr to Africa's salvation."

A curious affair focused attention on the Colonization Society in 1828. In Mississippi, an aged Negro known as Prince and emancipated after years of slavery by owner Thomas Foster of Natchez, declared that his real name was Abdul Rahahman, that he had been born and educated in the palace of his grandfather, king of Timbuctu, and that his father founded the city of Teembo in Footah Jalloh kingdom. The State Department under Henry Clay certified his story as authentic. He wished to return to his home from which forty years earlier he had been snatched by slave traders and shipped to America. Needing money to buy his wife's freedom, he was sponsored by the Colonization Society on a speaking tour that produced substantial donations. In February 1829 prince Abdul sailed with his wife aboard the brig *Harriet*, along with 160 other emigrants. Within weeks of his arrival in Liberia he died of malarial fever.

As the colony enlarged and gained strength, local revenues from excise taxes produced funds for public projects. Added to money received from the United States Treasury, they made possible the building of a "government house" as a haven for new arrivals, and two schools. Children of friendly tribespeople were invited to attend, opening the way for a trade and friendship treaty with the Bosporo tribe, the first of a long series of such pacts.

As the colony neared the end of its first decade, changes were clearly in the air. Five Negro missionaries arrived from America to establish additional evangelical churches, added to the original Methodist and Baptist efforts, and to work among tribesmen. In agriculture, livestock imported from America did not survive the tsetse fly, but animals from neighboring Sierra Leone fared better. Upon Ashmun's departure Cary's role as leader, with Elisha Johnson assisting, increased.

The year 1829 saw 200 rescued Africans and 600 American Negroes land in Liberia, now spreading along Africa's "Pepper Coast." Among the new arrivals that year and the following ones, were several remarkable men. Anthony Williams, son of South Carolina slaves, taught himself to read and write after reaching Liberia and rose later to be acting governor. John Russwurm, hailed as America's first Negro graduate of a college (Bowdoin 1826), who had earlier as editor of *Freedom's Journal* in New York opposed colonization, migrated to Liberia with his printing press and revived the *Liberia Herald* newspaper; later he would be governor of Maryland in Liberia. Joseph J. Roberts of Petersburg, Virginia, at age 19 persuaded his mother and two brothers to accompany him to Liberia, where seventeen years later he would become the country's first president.

The colony's progress, limited though it was, produced a renewal of interest in America. The American Colonization Society's periodical, the *African Repository,* began regular publication in 1825 under editor Ralph Gurley, also the Society's secretary. Launching a drive for further Federal aid, Gurley and other Society spokesmen argued that private and state funds were not sufficient to achieve the object of colonizing free Negroes and that only Congress could supply sufficient "national means" to solve a national problem. In 1825 Thomas Jefferson seconded the move, urging that proceeds from Federal land sales be used to support colonization. Seven state legislatures passed resolutions endorsing this proposal. In 1831 Nat Turner's uprising aroused new interest in Virginia. Ex-President Madison, noting that the "spirit of private manumission" was rising and that Liberia was thriving "in a highly encouraging degree," gave a $100 contribution. In 1833 Virginia's legislature approved a bill appropriating $18,000 a year for five years to aid voluntary emigration by free blacks. In Washington, Henry Clay, longtime colonization advocate, pushed through Congress a bill to distribute to the states Federal surplus funds from land sales to be used for education, internal improvements, or colonization, as each state chose. But President Jackson vetoed the measure. In 1836 Clay succeeded Madison as Colonization Society president and served until 1849.

Blocked from Federal aid, the Society won support in other quarters during the 1830's and 40's. Its rallies in major cities and on college campuses yielded increased donations, the yearly average rising to $12,000. The Maryland Colonization Society, breaking off from the national organization, won a grant from the state legislature of $10,000 a year for ten years to finance its own colonizing scheme. In 1832 it sent a ship with 144 colonists to Liberia and two years later established its own colony at Cape Palmas some 300 miles down the coast from Monrovia. Named "Maryland in Liberia," a smaller replica of the earlier Mesurado settlement developed here with Dr. James Hall, a physician, bringing settlers from Monrovia and serving as Maryland Society agent.

Others followed suit. The Philadelphia Society, in collaboration with the New York Society, bought its own ship for transporting settlers. In 1835 it established its own colony along the St. John's River at Bassa Cove, which under the lead of men devoted to Quaker principles of peace and temperance was almost wiped out by a native attack in its first year. The Mississippi

Fleeing Jim Crow, a few African Americans moved to Liberia after the Civil War, such as these sailing from Savannah, Georgia, on March 19, 1895.

Society, too, launched its own colony under the name "Mississippi in Liberia," centering around Greenville on the Sinou River 130 miles southeast of Monrovia. Encountering many problems, it barely managed to survive.

Something of Liberia's growth was revealed in an informal census of 1838, which showed 2,500 American Negro residents, a slightly smaller number of rescued Africans and roughly an estimated 28,000 tribespeople in loose cooperation with the newcomers. With twenty-eight trading firms and eight ships operating regu-

larly, Liberia exported $250,000 worth of goods and received $150,000 of imports. A new constitution, drafted by a Harvard professor and approved by the voters in 1839, provided a larger measure of autonomy for what was now called the Commonwealth of Liberia.

Philadelphia Quaker Thomas Buchanan (whose brother James would later become United States President) was chosen governor, with Joseph Roberts as vice governor. The first problem to claim the new administration's attention was the outbreak of inter-tribal warfare between the Deys and the Golas that impinged upon outlying settlements of colonists. Buchanan gave Roberts command of the militia. In a swift military strike Roberts subdued the Golas, forced them to repair the damage they had done in the settlements and then concluded a trade-friendship treaty with them, setting thereby a pattern for many such treaties in the future. When Buchanan died of fever in 1841, Roberts succeeded him as governor.

In the next few years Liberia encountered increasing external problems. French colonialism, spilling over from neighboring Ivory Coast began nibbling at territory claimed by Liberia. British merchants refused to pay Liberian customs, the British foreign office dismissing Liberia as "no more than a commercial experiment of a philanthropic society" and not a sovereign government. Roberts appealed to the American Government and the Colonization Society but got no support. He then undertook a speaking tour in the United States which succeeded in raising needed funds but won no official notice in Washington.

After returning to Monrovia, Roberts called the legislature into session and urged "the Government of Liberia, by formal act, to announce its independence . . . [as] a sovereign independent state." In a subsequent referendum voters approved 801–356 the calling of a constitutional convention that met at Monrovia July 3–23, 1847, and approved a national constitution. On July 26, 1847, following a morning of church services, Roberts and other dignitaries and citizens listened as the convention's secretary read the Declaration that ". . . we the People . . . hereby solemnly associate and constitute ourselves a Free and Sovereign and Independent State by the name of the Republic of Liberia . . ."

The convention had already established emblems for the infant republic. The great national seal portrayed a dove, a sailing ship before a rising sun, together with a palm tree, plow and spade, under the national motto, "The love of liberty brought us here." The nation's flag bore six red and five white stripes, symbolizing the eleven signers of the Declaration of Independence, and a blue corner square with one white star representing Africa with Liberia "lighting its way."

In October elections voters ratified the constitution and formally elected Joseph Roberts as President of the Republic. On January 3, 1848, Roberts took the oath of office and in his inaugural address urged Liberians to work for Africa and the cause of the black race and "to lay our shoulders to the wheel and resist manfully every obstacle which may oppose our progress in the great work which lies before us." Thirty years after the original meeting in Washington, Liberia was now launched as an independent republic among the nations of the world.

The Complete History of

Slave Owners and the Economics of Slavery

Chapter 7

Introduction

In the pre–Civil War South, slave owners varied, from masters of great plantations with large gangs of slaves, to individuals who owned just a single black man or woman for personal service or farm help. Some southeastern Indians also owned slaves (and proved themselves highly capable at running cotton plantations), and there was even a handful of free African Americans who owned members of their own race.

All slave owners faced similar economic problems, although the nature of these problems varied tremendously depending on the scale of operations and on whether they were using their slaves for agricultural labor. The central concern for all slave owners was that slavery yielded them a profit. In calculating profits, owners had to reckon the income that a healthy adult slave could produce for them, minus whatever had to be spent to feed, clothe, and house that slave. The owner also had to consider the "overhead" cost of maintaining an unproductive slave child or an underproductive elderly, sick, injured, or pregnant slave. If the slave owner ran a farm or plantation (as most slave owners did), those costs and profits had to be balanced against the uncertainties of a volatile market for cotton, sugar, tobacco, rice, or whatever other staples were being produced. Overproduction, a crop failure, or a drop in demand could be disastrous, especially if the slave owner was deeply in debt—as many were after having bought their slaves. If the owner rented out his slaves' labor to a factory owner, a railroad, or some other industrial enterprise, he had to be concerned with his human property's physical well-being (for if the slave was seriously injured or abused, this would in turn affect the owner's production) and ensure that the slave could not escape.

Nineteenth-century defenders of slavery sometimes argued that slave owners were not like the grasping industrial capitalists of the North or of Great Britain. Unlike these heartless businessmen, so the argument ran, patriarchal southern planters would not fire their labor force in hard times or abandon sick or elderly workers to shift for themselves. And it is true that masters usually found some kind of productive work for slaves to do, whatever their age or physical condition. But they, like industrial capitalists, had to keep a close eye on the bottom line, and on their debit and credit ledgers. In a bad year, or if they contracted debt that they could not otherwise repay, the solution usually was to sell some of the slaves. Likewise, if they found themselves with more slaves than they could support while still turning a profit, the same solution presented itself. They also were often tempted by the high prices that certain kinds of slaves—field hands or housemaids, for example—commanded at the moment, and thus would find a slave dealer's offer irresistible. Finally, there was the question of what to do when an owner died and heirs had to divide the assets. Again, splitting slave families was often the only way to settle up.

As cogs in a larger economic enterprise, slaves had to pay the price for their owners' uncertain prospects. It is estimated that about one-third of all slaves living on the eve of the Civil War were directly affected by the breakup of their families. Their fate was the equivalent of the sufferings that working people in the North sometimes had to pay in a boom-and-bust economy, with its periodic bouts of unemployment without the protections that we expect today. Yet the cost of being sundered from one's parents, spouse, children, and siblings, which slave owners routinely and unthinkingly inflicted on their human chattels, far outweighed the privations that even the poorest free workers had to face in a market economy when unemployment struck.

Selection 1

Slavery Was Profitable

Robert William Fogel and Stanley L. Engerman

By the time of the Civil War, some scholars argue that slavery had become economically outmoded; a backward-looking institution that tied up capital in an unfree labor force and thus blocked investment in more productive ventures. The argument extends further, with historians contending that slavery trapped the South in backwardness as the North was industrializing and developing a modern capitalist society.

Ulrich B. Phillips, the leading historian of slavery in the first half of the twentieth century, was one who argued the above position. For two generations, other historians followed Phillips's lead on this matter, even though most of them rejected the racist assumptions that had marred his work. But in 1974 two scholars trained in both history and technical economic analysis, Robert William Fogel of the University of Chicago and Stanley L. Engerman of the University of Rochester, published a book called Time on the Cross: The Economics of American Negro Slavery *that boldly argued that in the middle of the nineteenth century American slavery was* not *on its way to economic collapse. In particular, they maintained, the large-scale slave owners had to be hard-headed businessmen who understood the*

markets for which they produced and the most productive ways to use the capital they had invested in human beings. Slavery, Fogel and Engerman concluded, was profitable and showed no signs of fading away.

Fogel and Engerman did not win over all their critics. Marxist scholars such as Eugene D. Genovese continued to insist that slavery was a pre-capitalist economic institution, and many who read the book superficially objected to Time on the Cross *on the grounds that it "justified" slavery. (Fogel and Engerman did no such thing. They fully recognized that slavery was a terribly cruel system. Their point was that slave workers were in fact highly productive.) Excerpted here,* Time on the Cross *remains a controversial book, but it is essential reading for anyone who wants to understand American slavery in the years before the Civil War.*

*T*he source and the magnitude of the profit of slaveowners has been something of a mystery. The absence of hard data touched off a debate on these issues among professional historians that has extended for nearly three quarters of a century. Until recently, the debate was dominated by the views of Ulrich B. Phillips. A Southerner by birth, and a professor of history at the Universities of Wisconsin, Michigan, and Yale, Phillips was for many years the doyen of those writing on the antebellum South. His interpretation of the economics of slavery was first set forth in an essay published in 1905 and later elaborated in books published in 1918 and 1929. Phillips scoured southern archives for both quantitative and qualitative information bearing on the operation of slave plantations. His search was more thorough than that of any scholar who preceded him and most of those who followed him. Still, the evidence he turned up was insufficient for the calculation of representative profit margins. In the end, he based his argument largely on data he collected with respect to the prices of slaves and prices of cotton.

In Phillips's view, the inefficiency of slave labor made it a profitable investment only when there was a conjunction of three conditions. These conditions were: 1, an extreme scarcity of, and a high price for, free labor; 2, a system of agricultural organization and a set of crops that permitted the strict supervision of slaves in simple routines; and 3, a low price for slaves. Phillips argued that all of these conditions existed in the southern colonies prior to the American Revolution and that is why slavery took root and prospered there.

He also argued that these propitious conditions for slavery began to give way during the decade following the peace treaty of 1783. In particular, the eroding of world markets for plantation crops undermined the second condition. The price of tobacco, said Phillips, had fallen to such low levels "that the opening of each new tract for its culture was offset by the abandonment of an old one." "Indigo production was decadent," he added, "and rice culture was in painful transition." Without the development of the cotton gin, slavery might have disappeared. However, the rise of the cotton culture gave a new impetus to black bondage. The booming world market for cotton stimulated the domestic demand for slaves and reinvigorated the slave trade.

A new threat to the continuation of slavery arose, said Phillips, when the congressional ban against further importations of Africans was put into force in 1808. It took some time for the effects of this action to be felt in the marketplace. Finally, the low and relatively steady slave prices of earlier years gave way to an era in which slave prices bounded upward. Phillips stressed the fact that the rise in slave prices was far more rapid than the rise in cotton prices. To him, the ratio of cotton to slave prices was as crucial in evaluating the wisdom of an investment in slaves as the price-to-earnings ratio was for evaluating the wisdom of an investment in corporate stocks.

The data assembled by Phillips showed that the ratio of slave to cotton prices rose by over sixfold between 1805 and 1860. A change of this magnitude clearly indicated to Phillips that, by the last decade of the antebellum era, slaves were overvalued—that is, priced too high to permit an investor to earn a normal rate of profit.

What caused the rise in the ratio of slave to cotton prices? According to Phillips, it could not be explained by a decline in the cost of maintaining slaves. Nor could it be explained by an increase in the productivity of slaves since, "in his capacity for work, a prime negro in 1800 was worth nearly or quite as much as a similar slave in 1860."

The rise, Phillips concluded, was primarily the consequence of speculation. The supply of slaves had been "cornered" as a consequence of the closing of the slave trade. Hence "it was unavoidable that the price should be bid up to the point of overvaluation." This speculative pressure was reinforced by two other tendencies. First, there were economies of scale in cotton production. Thus, plantation owners were constantly trying to increase the size of their slave force in order to reap the benefits of large-scale operations. Second, slaves were desired not only for productive purposes but also as symbols of social status and wealth.

It should be stressed that Phillips never provided evidence that speculation, economies of scale, and conspicuous consumption were responsible for the rise in the slave-cotton price ratio. He merely asserted that these were the true explanatory factors.

The proposition that slavery was unprofitable to most planters suggests that the slave system was dying, or at least declining, due to internal economic contradictions. Phillips did not himself propound this thesis, but it was forcefully developed by a number of historians who fall into what might be called, "the Phillips school." These scholars attempted to ferret out the economic forces which would eventually have led to the self-strangulation of slavery. Three features of the slave economy were singled out.

First, it was asserted that southern planters were beset by an irresistible tendency toward the overproduction of cotton. The chief author of this thesis was Charles W. Ramsdell of the University of Texas. Ramsdell argued that the tendency toward overproduction was clearly evident in the rapid expansion of the cotton culture after 1858, and in the subsequent decline in the price of cotton. . . .

What caused this sudden rise in output? It was due, said Ramsdell, "in part to the rapid building of railroads throughout the South toward the end of the decade, which brought new lands within reach of markets and increased the cotton acreage; but part of the increase was due to the new fields in Texas." To Ramsdell, prevailing circumstances clearly indicated that the future course of output was up, while that of prices was down. "Had not the war intervened," he continued, "there is every reason to believe that there would have been a continuous overproduction and very low prices throughout the sixties and seventies."

But what precisely was the "every reason" for Ramsdell's belief? It was merely his conviction that the virgin lands of Texas would have been brought into cotton production and that the increased output of cotton would have led to a decline in its price. Ramsdell presented no evidence to back up his prediction.

The second argument for the economic self-strangulation of slavery has come to be known as the "natural limits" thesis. This thesis was derived from two subsidiary propositions. The first asserts that climate and soil set a limit to the geographic extension of the cotton culture and, hence, of slave agriculture. Charles Ramsdell, who was also one of the principal authors of this view, contended that this natural limit had in fact been reached by 1860. The other proposition asserts that slavery required continuous territorial expansion in order to remain profitable. Since slavery led to rapid soil exhaustion, an adequate level of slave productivity could be maintained only by continuously bringing new land into production. Consequently, if expansion was ruled out by the natural limits of soil and climate, the level of slave productivity would soon have fallen to levels too low to permit the survival of the system.

The third argument for the existence of fatal internal economic contradictions rests on an asserted incompatibility between slavery and urban society. . . . Some writers based this view on the racist contention that the slave was "too primitive" to successfully adapt to the complexities of urban production and life. Others saw the threat as arising from the difficulty of controlling slaves in an urban environment. Strikes, attacks on property, other forms of crime, and the greater ease of escape all added greatly to the cost of policing slaves. It has also been asserted that as the density of cities increased, the cost of control rose at a disproportionate rate: the "peculiar institution" was bound to be squeezed between the unprofitability of urban slavery and the relentless tendency toward the urbanization of society.

Some writers found evidence of the corrosive effects of urbanization on slavery in the decennial censuses. Population reports showed a marked and accelerating decline in the proportion of slaves living in the ten largest southern cities between 1820 and 1860. Indeed, during the last decade of the antebellum era the decline was absolute.

Not all members of the Phillips school leaped from the proposition that slavery was unprofitable to the conclusion that slavery was bound to fall of its own weight. The most notable exception is Eugene Genovese. A scholar of Marxist persuasion, Genovese sought to free Phillips's analysis of its racist aspects and bring to the fore what he considered to be the true class relationship implied by Phillips's research and discoveries.

Like other members of the Phillips school, Genovese agreed that slavery was economically inefficient, that it exhausted the soil, that it restricted the development of manufacturing, that it conflicted with urbanization, and that it generated a relentless drive for territorial expansion. He was, however, ambivalent on the issue of profitability, at times agreeing that on a strict commercial basis an investment in slaves may not have been profitable, and at other times arguing that it probably was. Nor did Genovese regard this as a matter that had to be resolved. Quite the contrary—he lashed out against the preoccupation of his predecessors with the issue of profitability, a preoccupation which blinded them to the central, overriding characteristics of the slave system and the slaveowning class.

Planters, said Genovese, were "precapitalist" aristocrats imbued with an "antibourgeois spirit," with values and mores which subordinated the drive for profit to honor, luxury, ease, accom-plishment, and family. "Whereas in the North people followed the lure of business and money for their own sake, in the South specific forms of property carried the badges of honor, prestige, and power." Because of these noneconomic objectives, slaveowners were prepared to shun the greater profits of industry, to maintain their wealth in slaves, even though physical capital offered higher rates of return.

Consequently, the notion that planters would have abandoned slavery simply because of declining profits was absurd, said Genovese. While slaveholders were not unconcerned about profit, they were more concerned about maintenance of their power, their moral values, their social milieu. Given such an outlook, there was no reason to assume that planters would "divest themselves of slaves as easily as a northern capitalist sold his holdings of railroad stock or of

Scholars debate whether slavery was an unprofitable, dying institution or a lucrative, firmly ingrained way of life in the South.

corporate bonds when the earnings on such securities faltered." Genovese believed that in the face of declining profits slaveholders would seek a political solution to their economic plight. In his view, the Civil War was the solution of the master class to the growing crisis that confronted it toward the end of the antebellum era. The slavocracy hoped in one "bold stroke to complete their political independence and to use it to provide an expansionist solution for their economic and social problems."

In contrast to the formidable legions that made up the Phillips school, those who believed that slaveholders earned high rates of return were until recently a beleaguered minority. This small group of scholars viewed slavery as an economically viable system and rejected the view that economic forces by themselves would have soon undermined the system. Agreement on these points did not, however, lead to a common view on the efficiency of slave labor or on the relative importance of the various sources from which masters derived income from their bondsmen. . . .

The Level of Profits and the Capitalist Character of Slavery

Strange as it may seem, the *systematic* investigation of the average rate of profit on investments in slaves did not begin until more than half a century after U.B. Phillips launched the issue. There were some casual attacks on the problem in the 1930s and 1940s, but for various reasons they were wanting. In general, the authors of these early efforts failed to appreciate the complexity of the problem of calculating profit rates. They gave little thought to the nature of the equations to be used in the calculation, failed to take account of the multiplicity of revenues and costs that had to be estimated, and did little to probe the representativeness of the scattered and incomplete records on which their estimates were based.

The study by Alfred H. Conrad and John R. Meyer marked a decisive turning point in the effort to deal with the question of profits. "From the standpoint of the entrepreneur making an investment in slaves," they wrote, "the basic problems involved in determining profitability are analytically the same as those met in determining the returns from any other kind of capital investment." In posing the problem in this way, Conrad and Meyer were, of course, merely taking up one of Phillips's suggestions. For it was Phillips who originally stressed the similarity between the slave and stock markets. However, while Phillips did not know how to pass from his conceptualization of the problem to the measurement of the rate of return on an investment in slaves, these two economists did.

Conrad and Meyer produced separate estimates of the rates of return on males and females. The computation of the return on male slaves was the simpler case. They first derived the average capital cost per slave, including not only the price of a slave, but also the average value of the land, animals, and equipment used by a slave. Estimates of gross annual earnings were then built up from data on the price of cotton and the physical productivity of slaves. The net figure was obtained by subtracting the maintenance and supervisory costs for slaves from gross earnings. The average length of the stream of net earnings was determined from mortality tables. With these estimates Conrad and Meyer computed rates of return on male slaves and found that for the majority of antebellum plantations the return varied between 5 and 8 percent, depending on the physical yield per hand and the prevailing farm price of cotton. On the farms in poor upland pine country or in the exhausted lands of the eastern seaboard, the range of rates was merely 2 to 5 percent. However, in the "best lands of the new Southwest, the Mississippi alluvium, and the better South Carolina and Alabama plantations" rates ran as high as 10 to 13 percent.

The computation of the rate of return on female slaves was somewhat more complicated. Conrad and Meyer had to take account not only of the productivity of a female in the field, but of such additional matters as the productivity of her offspring between their birth and the time of their sale; maternity, nursery, and rearing costs;

and the average number of offspring. Contending that very few females produced less than five or more than ten children that survived to be sold, Conrad and Meyer computed lower and upper limits on the rate of return. These turned out to be 7.1 and 8.1 percent respectively. Thus, planters in the exhausted lands of the upper South who earned only 4 or 5 percent on male slaves, still were able to achieve a return on their total operation equal to alternative opportunities. They did so by selling the offspring of females to planters in the West, thus earning rates of 7 to 8 percent on the other half of their slave force. Proof of such a trade was found not only in the descriptions of contemporaries, but also in the age structure of the slave population. The selling states had a significantly larger proportion of persons under fifteen and over fifty, while the buying states predominated in slaves of the prime working ages.

Rather than ending the controversy on profitability, the study of Conrad and Meyer intensified it. However, because of their work, the debate became much more sharply focused than before. They had clearly identified the crucial variables pertinent to the calculation, and the type of equations on which the calculation had to be based. Subsequent work by over a score of scholars was aimed at correcting their estimates of the values of the relevant variables and at refining their computational equations.

It is interesting that the first wave of criticisms of Conrad and Meyer turned up errors running almost exclusively in one direction—errors that made their estimate of the rate of profit too high. Thus, it was pointed out that their assumption that all slaves lived the average length of life biased the estimated rate of profit upward. They also greatly overestimated the number of slave children per female who lived to reach age eighteen. And they underestimated the amount of capital equipment required for slaves, as well as such varied costs as medical care, the employment of managerial personnel, food, and clothing.

As the debate developed, it became clear that Conrad and Meyer had also erred on the other side. They greatly underestimated the average productivity of a prime hand (a healthy slave between the ages of eighteen and thirty) as well as the productivity of females relative to males. At the same time they overestimated such items as maternity costs and the amount of land, equipment, and livestock required for young and old field hands. They also made the erroneous assumption that the land and physical capital employed by each slave died when he or she died.

To trace the twists and turns of this highly technical debate is beyond the scope of this book. . . . At this point we wish merely to stress that the net result of the various corrections has been to raise, not lower, the Conrad and Meyer estimate of the rate of return. On average, slaveowners earned about 10 percent on the market price of their bondsmen. Rates of return were approximately the same for investments in males and females. They were also approximately the same across geographic regions. . . .

The computations yielded average rates of return equal to, or in excess of, the averages which obtained in a variety of nonagricultural enterprises. For example, the average rate of return earned by nine of the most successful New England textile firms over the period from 1844 through 1853 was 10.1 percent. And a group of twelve southern railroads averaged 8.5 percent for the decade 1850–1860.

The finding that the rate of return on slaves was quite high does not rule out the possibility that some planters were willing to pay a premium to buy slaves, or that some planters held excessive numbers of slaves at prevailing prices. However, it does show that the aggregate demand of this category of slaveowners was too limited to raise the market price of slaves above the level dictated by normal business standards; that is, the demand of those slaveowners who desired to hold slaves for conspicuous consumption was quite small relative to the total demand for slaves. . . .

The demonstration that an investment in slaves was highly profitable not only undermines the case for conspicuous consumption; it also throws into doubt the contention that southern slaveholders were a "precapitalist," "uncommercial" class which subordinated profit to considerations of power, lifestyle, and "patriarchal commitments." The point at issue is not whether the slavocracy valued its power, lifestyle, and patriarchal commitments, but whether the pursuit of these objectives generally conflicted with, or significantly undermined, the pursuit of profit.

Paternalism is not intrinsically antagonistic to capitalist enterprise. Nor is it necessarily a barrier to profit maximization. Such well-known and spectacularly profitable firms as the International Business Machines Corporation and Eastman Kodak practice paternalism. Their experience suggests that patriarchal commitments may actually raise profits by inducing labor to be more efficient than it would have been under a less benevolent management. There is no reason to rule out the possibility that paternalism operated in this way for slaveowners. No one has shown that masters who practiced paternalism had lower rates of return on the average than those who were unconcerned or heartless with respect to the welfare of their bondsmen.

On the other hand, there is considerable evidence that slaveowners were hard, calculating businessmen who priced slaves, and their other assets, with as much shrewdness as could be expected of any northern capitalist. . . . While there was variation in price [of male slaves] at each age (as one would expect of slaves who differed in health, attitudes, and capacities); the distribution displays a quite definite pattern. On average, prices rose until the late twenties and then declined. The decline was slow at first but then became more rapid, until advanced ages were reached. . . .

What explains the age pattern of prices? Conspicuous consumption and other nonpecuniary arguments offered to explain the trend in slave prices over time clearly fail here. It seems hardly likely that twenty-six-year-olds were priced twice as high as ten-year-olds because twice as much honor and prestige were attached to the owners of the older than of the younger slaves.

The age-price profile is better explained by the pattern of earnings over the life cycle of slaves. Indeed, the age-price profile implies a corresponding earnings profile. . . . About the year 1850, [n]et earnings were negative until age eight. Then they became positive and rose to a peak at age thirty-five. It is interesting to note that earnings of sixty-five-year-olds were still positive and, on average, brought an owner as much net income as a slave in the mid-teens. This does not mean that every slave aged sixty-five produced a positive net income for his owner. Some of the elderly were a net loss. However, the income earned by the able-bodied among the elderly was more than enough to compensate for the burden imposed by the incapacitated. The average net income from slaves remained positive until they reached their late seventies. Even after that age the average burden was quite low, since a fair share of the slaves who survived into their eighties still produced positive net incomes.

Thus, the frequent contention that slaveowners preferred to work slaves to death at early ages, in order to avoid the burden of maintenance at late ages, is unfounded. Slaveowners were generally able to employ their bondsmen profitably throughout the life cycle. Planters solved the problem of old age by varying tasks according to the capacities of slaves. There were many occupations on plantations for which the elderly were suited. Women too old to labor in the fields could, for example, be made responsible for the care of slave children or serve as nurses to the sick. They could also be employed as seamstresses, or in spinning cotton and weaving. Elderly men were put in charge of the livestock, or were made responsible for the care of implements. Some became gardeners or household servants. This capacity to utilize the labor of the elderly was probably not so much a feature of slavery *per se* but of the predominantly agrarian nature of slavery. The rise of the problem of what to do with the elderly coincides with the emergence of urbanized, industrial societies. It is a problem that is rarely encountered in the countryside.

. . . The prices of males and females . . . were virtually identical until age nine, after which female prices rose less rapidly than those of males. At age twenty-seven the female price was about 80 percent of the male price. The ratio fell to 60 percent at age fifty and to less than half at age seventy.

Again, the explanation of this pattern is found in the life cycles of the net earnings of males and females. . . . For most of the years of their lives, female earnings were below those of males by 20 to 40 percent. Interestingly, prior to age eighteen, female earnings exceeded those of males. This differential is not explained by income produced from children borne by teen-age mothers. As will be shown, earnings from childbearing were quite small during these years. The early advantage in female earnings appears to have been due primarily to a more rapid rate of maturity among women than among men.

In the absence of evidence on the market behavior of slaveowners, it was easy for historians inclined to the romantic to postulate a dichotomy between paternalism and profit-seeking. They took evidence of paternalism to imply that slaveowners must have sacrificed profits to other objectives. Now that the profitability of slavery and the overwhelming dominance of business considerations in the market behavior of slaveowners are firmly established, should we assume that paternalism was an invention of apologists for slavery? That conclusion would be as romantic and naïve as the one we have rejected. There is too much evidence of deep personal attachments between owners and their bondsmen to deny that this was a facet of the slave system. "Now my heart is nearly broke," wrote a Louisiana planter on the occasion of the death of the principal slave manager. "I have lost poor *Leven,* one of the most faithful black men [that] ever lived. [H]e was truth and honesty, and without a fault that I ever discovered. He has oversed the plantation nearly three years, and [has] done much better than any white man [had] ever done here, and I lived a quiet life."

Would this expression of affection have been quite so deep if Leven had been inefficient, dishonest, and troublesome? While we do not mean to imply that affection for slaves was purely a function of their earning capacity, we do mean to suggest that it was more usual for affection and productivity to reinforce each other than to conflict with each other. Both cruelty and affection had their place on southern plantations. . . .

The Economic Viability of Slavery After the Revolution and on the Eve of the Civil War

Two episodes during the antebellum era have been singled out as proof that underlying economic forces were working toward the destruction of the slave system. Phillips located one of these episodes in the decade following the close of the American Revolution. Ramsdell located the other in the decade preceding the Civil War.

Phillips based his case on scattered reports by planters who spoke of hard times. "Slave prices everywhere . . . ," he wrote, "were declining in so disquieting a manner that as late as the end of 1794 George Washington advised a friend to convert his slaves into other forms of property. . . ." However, Phillips was not able to use the series on slave prices that he so laboriously constructed to test these assertions, since his series only extended back to 1795. He simply accepted the scattered reports of distress as proof that "the peace of 1783 brought depression in all the plantation districts," which lasted for more than a decade and which converted the previously profitable investment in slaves into a heavy burden.

As it turns out, slave prices showed some weakness after the Revolution, but there was not a sustained, severe depression. While slave prices were acutely depressed during the last years of the Revolution, they rebounded to roughly the pre-Revolutionary level by the mid-1780s and remained on a fairly high plateau for the rest of that decade. Between 1784 and 1794 slave prices averaged 89 percent of their pre-Revolutionary level. There was an additional drop of about 5 percent between 1794 and 1795. But this slide was abruptly reversed in 1798.

Furthermore, neither the softening of prices during the early 1790s nor the brief plunge later in the decade necessarily implies that the demand for slaves was declining. It may only show that the supply of slaves was increasing more rapidly than the demand for them. This appears to have been the case. . . . [T]he decade of the 1790s was marked by an unprecedented increase in the size of the slave population. Not only was the natural increase large, but slave imports—which exceeded 79,000—were greater than in any previous decade. Indeed, the decade rate of imports during the 1790s was nearly twice as high as that which prevailed during the previous half century.

Despite the post-Revolutionary softness in prices, the trend in the demand for slaves was strongly upward from 1781 on. . . . George Washington's apparent gloom was not generally shared by other slaveowners. As a group, slaveowners wanted to increase, not reduce, their holdings of slaves. Even in 1796, when prices were at the lowest point of the post-Revolutionary era, the demand for slaves was over 50 percent higher than it had been in 1772.

The hesitation in the growth of demand for a few years after 1791 may have been due to fear created by the Haitian slave revolt, as well as reactions to the various emancipation laws in northern states. On the other hand, the Haitian revolution could have been responsible for a sudden increase in the supply of slaves in the United States during these years. There are reports which indicate that large numbers of slaveowners from the West Indies sold their slaves to American buyers or fled with them to establish new plantations on the mainland. Southern supply may have been swelled also by the attempt of northern slaveowners to avoid the consequences of emancipation.

In any case, the heavy flow of slaves into the United States clearly contradicts the thesis that slavery was rescued from its deathbed by the rise of the cotton culture. If slavery had become generally unprofitable during the 1780s and 1790s, one would have observed a cessation of slave imports. If the crises had been of substantial proportions, the flow of slaves would have reversed. The United States would have turned from a net importer to a net exporter of slaves, as American planters strove to limit their losses

by selling their chattel to areas where slavery was still profitable.

The episode singled out by Ramsdell turns, not on the movement of slave prices, but on the movement of cotton production and cotton prices. He knew very well that slave prices were rising throughout the 1850s. Nevertheless, Ramsdell believed that planters were being irresistibly driven toward the overproduction of cotton and that this undefinable force was tolling the death knell of slavery. He saw clear evidence of the tendency to overproduction in the unprecedented rise in the output of cotton between 1850 and 1860. The increase in production during this decade was greater than the increase over the entire previous century. Moreover, the rate of increase in cotton production accelerated as the decade wore on. Between 1857 and 1860 alone, cotton production increased by 1,500,000 bales. This spectacular rise was more than had been achieved during the four decades stretching from the invention of the cotton gin to the close of the Jacksonian administration.

To Ramsdell, the implication of this compulsion to shift resources into cotton was obvious. The price of cotton was bound to decline—would, indeed, eventually decline to levels so low that slavery would become unprofitable. The signs of the future were already evident, for the leap in output between 1858 and 1860 had initiated the predicted decline in prices. Thus "those who wished it [slavery] destroyed," concluded Ramsdell, "had only to wait a little while—perhaps a generation, probably less."

While one cannot deny that the rise in cotton production during the decade of the 1850s was spectacular, the conclusion that this increase reflected irrational, uncommercial behavior *is* disputable. Neither an extremely rapid growth in output, nor a fall in price are *per se* evidence of overproduction. The output of cotton *cloth*, for example, tripled between 1822 and 1827. At the same time the price of cloth declined by 35 percent. Yet no one has ever accused these northern cloth manufacturers of an irresistible tendency to overproduction. Quite the contrary, their dynamism in responding to the booming market for cloth has been celebrated far and wide. And the capacity of cloth manufacturers to bring down their prices has been taken as a mark of the vitality of the factory system.

There was nothing unusual about the slight decline in cotton prices that occurred between 1857 and 1860. The fact is that the general trend of raw cotton prices was downward from 1802 on. . . . Although there were fluctuations about this trend, the average annual rate of decrease was 0.7 percent. The basic cause of this long-term decline was the steady increase in productivity. Among the developments which made cotton farming increasingly more efficient were the improvements in the varieties of cotton-seeds, the introduction of the cotton gin, the reduction in transportation and other marketing costs, and the relocation of cotton production in the more fertile lands of the New South.

It was, therefore, to be expected that increases in production would generally be associated with declining prices. Since advances in productivity caused costs to fall, profits of planters may have been rising despite declining cotton prices. What is crucial, then, is not the absolute level of prices, but the level of profits. An approximation to the movement of profits may be obtained by examining the deviation of cotton prices from their long-term trend. When cotton prices were above their long-term trend value, profits of planters were likely to have been above normal. When prices were below their trend values, profits on cotton production were likely to have been below normal.

Figure 27 indicates that the 1850s constituted a period of sustained boom in profits for cotton planters. It was an era that outstripped even the fabled prosperity of the 1830s. Nearly every year of the decade was one of above-normal profit. What is more, profits remained high during the last four years of the decade, with prices averaging about 15 percent above their trend values. No wonder cotton production doubled between 1850 and 1860. It was clearly a rational economic response to increase cotton production by over 50 percent between 1857 and 1860. If planters erred, it was not in expanding cotton production

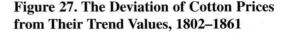

Figure 27. The Deviation of Cotton Prices from Their Trend Values, 1802–1861

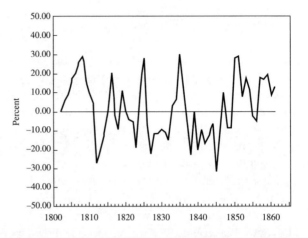

by too much. Quite the contrary—they were too conservative. Their expansion had not been adequate to bring prices down to their trend values and profits back to normal (equilibrium) levels.

What was responsible for making the 1850s so prosperous for cotton planters? . . . The worldwide demand for cotton began to increase rapidly beginning in 1846. Over the next fifteen years, the average annual rate of change in demand was about 7 percent per annum. . . . Changes in the supply of cotton generally lagged behind changes in demand. As a consequence, prices and profits tended to be above normal in periods when demand was increasing, and below normal when demand was decreasing or stagnating.

To summarize: The unprecedented increase in cotton production after 1857 was due to a rapid advance in the world demand for U.S. cotton. The lag of cotton supply behind demand caused the price of cotton to rise well above normal levels, creating unusually large profits for planters. While planters responded to this incentive, they did not increase output rapidly enough to return cotton prices and profits to a normal level.

Thus, the tale about the uncommercial planter who was gripped by an irresistible tendency to the overproduction of cotton is sheer fantasy. It is to those who romanticize the antebellum South what the story of the slave-breeding planter was to abolitionist critics—a convenient invention.

Selection 2

Slave Owners and Non–Slave Owners: The Economics of Slave-Labor Cotton Production

Gavin Wright

Cotton was not the only crop that slaves raised for their masters in the pre–Civil War South. Sugar was grown on plantations in Louisiana, rice in South Carolina, tobacco in Virginia, and hemp (used to make rope for cotton bales) in Kentucky. But cotton was "king" in a wide band of fertile southern country stretching from the uplands of central South Carolina to East Texas, and the spectacular rise of cotton as a cash crop greatly expanded the area in which slavery held sway.

In this selection, Stanford University economist and economic historian Gavin Wright analyzes the economic choices facing slave owners who produced cotton in the Old South.

*T*he western expansion of the cotton belt proceeded with remarkable speed and persistence down to the Civil War. The pace was not altogether uniform, the major deviations from the trend coming with the demand-initiated boom of the 1830s and the subsequent slump of the early 1840s. But on the whole, antebellum cotton demand was ebullient, and migration continued even in slack times. Typically, small slaveless farmers were the first to move, but the movement of the slave population into the richest cotton areas of the Southwest was also rapid. The strong momentum is largely explained by the natural superiority of cotton land in the old Southwest. The . . . character of the process, from inferior to superior soil, has given rise to greatly exaggerated conceptions of the extent of soil exhaustion and erosion in the Southeast. Cotton is not in fact a highly exhaustive crop, and the gutted, windswept hills of the Piedmont . . . were as much the result of abandonment as its cause. The migration of cotton and slaves was not a mindless east-west movement from exhausted to virgin soils, but a rational process of geographical expansion and relocation which continued along similar lines well after the war.

By the mid–nineteenth century, the Cotton Kingdom stretched from the Carolinas to east Texas, from northwest Florida to central and western Tennessee, and was expanding rapidly into Arkansas and the Texas plain. . . .

Despite the distinctness, the Cotton South was not at all homogeneous in many respects. Within the South, regions differed markedly in soils, fertility, numbers of slaves, and average farm size. . . . A brief survey of these regions will convey a sense of the diverse cross section which comprised the Cotton South in 1860.

The *Piedmont* of the Carolinas and Georgia (reaching into eastern Alabama) was the first area of rapid expansion of cotton and slavery. Upland cotton takes its name from the irregular terrain of granite and metamorphic rock in this region. Despite its primacy, the Piedmont was by no means the most fertile cotton land in the country, but its decline from the early nineteenth century was only in relative, not absolute, terms. The Piedmont contained roughly one-fifth of the cotton-county farms in 1860, but produced only one-tenth of the cotton.

Between the *Piedmont* and the coast, from North Carolina to Mississippi, lies a gently sloping plain, which we divide into the inner *Central Plain* . . . and outer *Coastal Plain*. . . . These soils are mainly sands and sandy loams, generally of below-average fertility, with the *Coastal Plain* the poorer of the two. The fall line between Piedmont and plain is marked by a smaller *Sand Hills* region of still lower fertility.

Southwest of the Piedmont and above the Coastal Plain lies the *Black Prairie* region of central Alabama and Mississippi. These stiff black calcareous soils are extremely fertile. Population and production grew rapidly in the 1830s and 1840s, and the region was second only to the alluvial lowlands in cotton productivity and in the dominance of large plantations. In northern Alabama and south central Tennessee lies another concentration of cotton and slaves, the *Valley* lands of red calcareous soil along the Tennessee River.

The richest of the cotton regions were the *Alluvial* river bottoms along the Mississippi in Louisiana, Mississippi, and Arkansas, and along the Red River in Louisiana. This delta region, in which we include three Texas counties at the mouth of the Brazos, was easily the most naturally fertile in the South. It contained the largest plantations and the highest concentration of slave population in 1860. East of the delta in Mississippi and Tennessee lies the *Brown Loam,* or "loess", region of mellow, siliceous loams. It is also fertile, but its soils are easily eroded, and it contained a much more balanced mixture of farm sizes than the alluvium. Both regions developed earlier than less fertile areas to the east, but the alluvium was still rapidly expanding its cotton output in the 1850s.

Above the delta on either side of the Mississippi is the *Western Upland* region. Reaching from western Alabama into east Texas, this so-called shortleaf pine hills region was predominantly a small-farm area with relatively few concentrations of slaves. However, the soil of this region is as good or better for cotton-growing than the Piedmont, and the growth of population, cotton output, and slaves was rapid in the 1850s. In Texas and Arkansas, this region contained the western frontier of the Cotton South in the late antebellum period. . . .

It is equally important not to lose sight of the essential unity of the Cotton South, of the relationship of these parts to each other. In every part of the Cotton South one could find slave-using cotton farms, and in every section one could find small slaveless farms, many of which grew little or no cotton. In every region, concentrations of slaves gravitated toward the best and best-located cotton land. . . . It is some exaggeration, but not much, to say that the Cotton South was like a stick of Brighton Rock—bite it off anywhere and the character of the economic cross section was much the same.

For the slaveholders, much of this regional unity extended to the non-cotton areas as well. The essential unifying element was the fact that cotton determined the value of slaves, and slave property was the predominant form of wealth in the South. The importance of slaves as a form of wealth emerges from a study of wealth holdings in 1850 and 1860.

The Distribution of Wealth in the Cotton South

The structure of antebellum Southern society has been described very differently by different writers at different times. . . . The simplest way to characterize these differing views is to say that the [one group of scholars] focuses on the numerical majority of the small- and medium-scale farmers, while the critics stress the disproportionate shares of land and wealth held by the large planters. . . . [But] if we compare the median improved acreage of farms in the cotton belt with that of farms in the Northern United States, we find surprisingly little difference. In an older state like Ohio, the typical farm was actually somewhat larger than the typical farm in the small-farm regions of the Cotton South. However, the average farm size in the Cotton South is double that of the Northwest. The overall degree of concentration in landholdings . . . is substantially greater in *every one* of the cotton regions than in any of the Northern states. . . . The distribution is not actually very different between the two regions in the lower range of farm sizes, but Northern farms faced an upper limit which did not exist in the South. Less than three-tenths of 1 percent of farms exceeded 500 improved acres in the North, and virtually none were as large as 1,000 improved acres. In the South, some farms, though by no means most, were able to expand to a large scale. . . .

This does not of course mean that slavery as an institution had nothing to do with the observed pattern of concentration. If slavery is the explanation, however, it must be because of the economic effects of slavery, and not simply because accounting practices regarding property were different North and South. That slavery contributed to the high degree of inequality is suggested by the fact . . . that slaveholdings were significantly more concentrated than other forms of wealth. Half of the farms in the Cotton South did not own slaves. Before jumping to a "slavery" interpretation of the wealth distribution, however, one should note that the same table could support a "cotton" interpretation: the distribution of cotton output is just as concentrated as slaveholdings, and indeed the two distributions are remarkably similar. . . .

What is the nature of this connection between cotton, slavery, and the scale of production? Was it the efficiency of cotton-growing using slave labor that caused the concentrations of slaves, or was it the existence of large slaveholdings that explains the pattern of cotton-growing? These alternatives may sound too simple, but this is fundamentally what the choice comes to. . . . It would be difficult to find any indication of scale economies in cotton production. . . . The high degree of concentration in slaveholding is primarily associated with the high percentage of nonslaveowners. . . .

Wealth Distribution in Historical Perspective

We can get some additional hints by asking whether the pattern of concentration had emerged anew during the cotton-boom decade of the 1850s, or whether it had existed beforehand. On the whole, the evidence suggests that a high degree of concentration existed well before the late antebellum period. . . .

The same conclusion applies to the ownership of slaves. . . . Despite a very marked increase in the dominance of large slaveholders in the alluvial areas and a lesser increase in the Piedmont, it simply is not true that this trend characterizes the Cotton South as a whole. The rise in prominence of slaveholdings of modest size is clearly the dominant trend in the Valley, Black Prairie, and Brown Loam regions. These divergent regional structures and regional trends help to explain how [one historian] could write that "the great mass of negroes [*sic*] lived on small farms," while another found that "the vast majority of colored people . . . were on large plantations." By varying the area and the cutoff between "large" and "small," either conclusion can be supported. A truer characterization would be that the distribution of slaveholding sizes was remarkably smooth and remarkably stable.

Can this description be extended back earlier than 1850? . . . The average size of slaveholding did drift upward over time but not drastically (from about eight slaves per holder in 1790 to ten in 1860). . . . Studies of colonial wealth holdings going as far back as the seventeenth century show greater inequality in slaveholding regions than in free-farm agricultural areas. While there are indications that inequality in the tobacco regions became significantly greater during the eighteenth century, it appears that the cotton era largely maintained a distribution of land and wealth which had been established before the nineteenth century.

Slaves sit in front of a gin house preparing cotton for the gin on a South Carolina plantation.

But these essential elements of stability should not be taken to indicate that Southern society was static or stagnant. The available evidence does not allow us to identify the membership of the different wealth-holding classes at different times, nor to trace the lifetime careers of typical individuals. Nonetheless, some suggestions of important long-run changes may be found. It is important to note, for example, that the stability of land and slaveholding is an aggregate phenomenon: in the oldest cotton area of the Piedmont and the most valuable cotton areas of the alluvium a decided trend toward consolidation in large holdings is evident in the 1850s. . . . One might infer that the overall pattern of stability depended on continued access to good cotton land in the newer regions. Such an interpretation is supported by the few studies available which attempt to locate the same farm operator in both the 1850 and 1860 census. [A] study of Hancock County, Georgia, found that very few of the poorest farmers in 1850 had improved their position by 1860: most of the landless had become farm laborers or emigrated from the county. In contrast, the small farmers identified in both years in a study of Mississippi had almost all improved their economic position. In both cases the essential missing information is what happened to the emigrants. But it is well-established that small and usually slaveless farmers led the westward migration, and their opportunities in the east could only have been more restricted if this alternative had not been open to them.

There is another important change in the character of Southern wealth in the 1850s: . . . a striking increase in the percentage of farm operators with no slaves, from less than 40 percent in 1850 to approximately one-half in 1860. In contrast to the previous picture of regional diversity, and in contrast to the general stability of the distribution of slaves among slaveholders, this decline in the percentage of slaveowning farms occurs in almost all regions and in the aggregate. Furthermore, the evidence is that this is not merely a development of the 1850s but is instead an observable trend of at least thirty years. The fraction of all Southern families who were slaveowners declined from .36 in 1830 to .31 in 1850 to .25 in 1860. . . .

The changing fractions of slaveowners and nonslaveowners is important because of the rise in slave values, especially during the last antebellum decade. Whereas the average slaveholding rose by about 10 percent between 1850 and 1860, the average value of slaveholdings rose by about 100 percent, from about $4,800 to about $9,400 per slaveowner. Slaveowners constituted the wealthiest class in the country by far. The average slaveowner was more than five times as wealthy as the average Northerner, more than ten times as wealthy as the average nonslaveholding Southern farmer. A man who owned two slaves and nothing else was as rich as the average man in the North.

This division was growing [rapidly]. Slaveholders controlled between 90 and 95 percent of agricultural wealth in both 1850 and 1860. Since the fraction of slaveholders in the farm operator population was declining, this share was not in fact rising. But relative to their share in the population, slaveholder wealth was growing rapidly. . . . The Cotton South was approaching a situation in which a little less than half the farm operators held almost twice their numerical weight in wealth. . . . [Moreover,] the wealth of the average slaveholder was growing more rapidly than that of the average nonslaveholder: hence, the ratio of the two was rising, and the absolute differential was increasingly staggering. Nothing . . . argues that nonslaveholders were being squeezed or damaged or immiserated by slavery: but the economic distance between the two kinds of free Southerners was rapidly widening.

The social importance of these changes cannot be underestimated. . . . Slaveownership was by many standards broadly distributed in the South—compared, for example, to stock ownership in modern America. . . . this was no tiny elite enjoying these capital gains, but a substantial minority of farmers, particularly in the states that became the Confederacy. But is it safe to minimize the increasing barriers to slaveownership and the growing gap between owners and nonowners in a slave society concerned about its political future? The . . . fact that the percentage of slaveowners was much higher in the Confederacy than in all slave states . . . suggests otherwise, because the weakening political supports for slavery in the border states was, quite appropri-

ately, a matter of grave concern to Southern leaders in the 1850s.

Slaves, Wealth, and Political Economy: The Paradoxes of Southern Society

The significance of these various statistics depends upon an assessment of the significance of wealth itself. Wealth is no measure of living standards, and many economists regard the calculation of wealth distributions as arbitrary and misleading, because, to list only the primary objections, it omits the many nontangible sources of income such as strength, experience, schooling, entrepreneurial talent, and other forms of "human capital." This objection is only telling, however, if the distribution of wealth is viewed as a proxy for the income distribution. But this is not its essential significance. Contemporaries of the early nineteenth century viewed wealth holdings as fundamentally important because of the instrumental role of wealth in human relations. A family's wealth position could determine its bargaining power, its ability to wait and examine competing alternatives, and its capacity to resist arbitrary actions by outsiders. Wealth represented wherewithal in economic affairs, the power to take risks of likely profitability without risking destitution. This strategic importance of wealth was particularly critical in an era when such modern substitutes as credit markets, insurance, and collective-action groups were poorly developed. The social divisions of antebellum America were essentially wealth-holding categories—planters, small slaveowners, yeoman farmers, tenants, and landless wage earners. In a word, wealth was a basic defining characteristic of social class.

If wealth is important because of its instrumental role, it should not be assumed that a very close relationship existed between power and the market value of real and personal property. The ability to survive indefinitely on a backwoods subsistence farm may have strategic importance far beyond that indicated by the market value of the farm. One assumes that power and value are correlated, but they are surely not identical.

The market value of an asset is important in its own right, however, as an object of political and economic behavior. This is really quite a different point. Property values can be strongly affected by political decisions, and basic political groupings and loyalties can be heavily influenced by the lineup of how the values are affected by political alternatives. Because the value of durable assets like land and slaves reflects an expected stream of returns over a long period, this capital-values effect may have a political impact many times greater than any effect on current earnings. These considerations loomed very large in developmental issues such as canals, railroads, and land sales policies, and the same is true for slavery. Thus, the wealth distribution is significant for a second reason as well: its effect on the incentives and logic of political coalitions.

What conclusions can we draw about antebellum Southern society in light of these two dimensions of wealth holding? A review of the evidence makes it plain that simple categories like "planter dominance" or "economic democracy" are not adequate to describe the several dimensions of the Cotton South. Instead we have a series of apparent paradoxes which cry out for explanation.

We have established that holdings of land and other forms of wealth were, and had been for some time, substantially more concentrated among free farm operators in the South than in other farming areas. This conclusion would not be altered if the comparison were extended to the entire population of agricultural areas. . . . It is surely an exaggeration to describe the rural North as a homogeneous, egalitarian society of freeholding farmers, but that region was much closer to such an ideal than was the South. So much for "economic democracy."

But there is nothing in this evidence to justify a claim of planter domination of the small farmers in the sense of the exercise of power or control. As we have seen, the pattern of concentration in land is attributable to the existence of some very large holdings, and not to the existence of disproportionate numbers of very small

farms. Most of the small farmers were landowners, (80 to 90 percent . . .) and there is nothing to indicate that they stood in any direct relation of intimidation or threat to the planter. . . . The small farms were highly self-sufficient and had comparatively few direct economic relations with the plantations—certainly nothing comparable to the relationship of employer and worker in the North.

To press the point further, note that Southern wealth holdings were not substantially more concentrated than those of the Northern economy as a whole—*less* so than wealth holdings in cities, where large numbers of individuals held virtually no nonhuman wealth. Now of course, this kind of comparison would look very different if the slaves were included as members of the population—by treating slave and slave values in various hypothetical ways, one can duplicate the urban distributions. But it is not news that slaves were a submerged, exploited, and largely powerless class. What is noteworthy for our purposes is the point that the degree of inequality among free households in the South, though greater than that of Northern agriculture, was by no means unprecedented or even extreme by comparison with other historical cases.

The same ambiguity is found in the political history. Many political writers focusing on slavery issues and the Civil War have had the decided impression that large slaveholders were dominant in Southern politics. . . . But . . . circumstantial evidence tells about the personnel of government, not the exercise of power by constituent groups. Many writers have called attention to the fact that Southern politics went through the same process of "democratization" as the rest of the country in the 1820s and 1830s, from which it emerged with some of the most democratic state constitutions in the country. Some political accounts describe significant involvement and activity on the part of small and nonslaveholding farmers, and it has not been shown that slaveowners were able to extract resources from small farmers by political means, nor, with the possible exception of secession itself, enact any program to which there was significant small-farm opposition. Even on an issue like the relatively backward state of Southern public education—which some writers view as the essential proof of the undemocratic South—it is not clear that small farmers favored an expansion. As Genovese has argued, the case comes down to a claim that nonslaveholding whites did not understand and pursue their own interests. This is a much more fragile, *post hoc* sort of argument than one based on concentrated wealth and power.

On the other hand, the statistical evidence does clearly show the overriding and increasing importance of the value of slave property. Even on issues such as secession, and others in which slavery was directly involved, however, there is little in the evidence to suggest the exercise of power by an elite, as opposed to the intense mobilization of a substantial minority which felt its vital interests were at stake. As we have seen, the concentration of slaves among slaveowners was not extreme and was not increasing. On issues involving the value of slave property, it is difficult to find an important difference in interests between "large" and "small" holders: even a few slaves would dominate the portfolio of all

but the wealthiest capitalist or landlord. And the minority owning slaves was by no means a tiny one—roughly half in the Cotton South, better than one-fourth of all families in the slave states.

Nonetheless, the evidence does contain a suggestion that the rising values of slave property in the 1850s had their ominous side, not because they threatened to make slavery unprofitable, but because they were making slaves too expensive for most Southern farmers to gain a share of the profits. The very forces that were strengthening the economic incentives for slaveowners to retain slavery were slowly weakening the political supports for the institution. Slaveowners as a fraction of Southern families had been declining for some time, and the increasing geographic concentration of slavery meant that in many of the border states the relative numbers of slaveholders were becoming quite small indeed. . . . The point that emerges now is that it was not the division of wealth between planter and farmer, but the division of slave property values between owners and non-owners that formed the cutting edge of Southern political economy in the 1850s.

The Leasing of Slaves Ensured the Institution's Continuance

Robert S. Starobin

It is usually assumed today that slaves worked only on agricultural plantations and in their masters' households. But an overlooked—and disturbing—aspect of slavery was the ability of owners to put their human property to work in industrial settings, usually by leasing slaves to a factory owner, a railroad company, or some other employer. Had slavery not been ended by the Confederacy's defeat in the Civil War, it is quite possible that slave owners would have increasingly found ways to adapt human bondage to the process of industrialization, thereby ensuring slavery's survival into the twentieth century.

In his 1970 book Industrial Slavery in the Old South, *excerpted here, historian Robert S. Starobin discusses the ways in which masters looked after their own self-interest when they leased their slaves for use in industrial labor.*

To discourage mistreatment of their slaves, some masters carefully stipulated working conditions in their hiring agree-

ments. A few expressly forbade their blacks to be worked in such hazardous occupations as railroad, turnpike, or waterway construction, as well as mining, sawmilling, steamboating, or turpentine distilling. Other masters required employers to "feed and clothe well and treat hands with the utmost degree of humanity in every other respect." Still other owners requested hirers to rent slaves in groups, "in order to have my hands all together," and preferred to hire to the same employer year after year, "rather than be moving from one to another." One master even asked a renter to keep his slave "from running about at night. Don't let him become disapated."

Masters became most concerned for the well-being of their slave property during epidemics. "I am much concerned about my Boys & I should be extremely glad to have them near me during the present alarm, and would make any arrangement you might require as to allowance &c," a slaveowner informed a Petersburg tobacco manufacturer, as the cholera scourge of 1832 swept up from the Virginia Tidewater. "The amount of hire is of small consideration to the value of the negro and risk of life unless you will take the risk and responsibility upon your selves. . . . I should suppose the risk would be very great to the owners of such property," he concluded, "by allowing negroes to remain exposed to the consequences, as it would be hardly possible for the owners of the Factories to give suitable attention to the sick, and [I] think they would be safer with their masters." Similarly, hiring bonds occasionally required employers to furnish extra clothing or shoes when slaves worked in industries that were hard on their apparel.

By the 1850's, many slaveowners had become reluctant to rent their Negoes to certain dangerous industries. "Servants who have once worked in tobacco factories are in a measure disqualified for other employments," publicly warned a "Farmer." "At least it takes some time to make them efficient laborers for other purposes, after they have been cooped up in the unwholesome and destructive atmosphere of a tobacco factory." A hiring agent repeatedly reported that he was doing everything in his power "to do away with the existing prejudices now existing against hands being put on public works." Within the space of two years, two masters independently objected to the abuse of their bondsmen at a Virginia iron works. "Davy Says that working in the furnace is Injurious to his eyes," complained one of the slaveowners. "Therefore I do not wish him to work there against his Will." A traveler observed that masters only grudgingly hired slaves to iron furnaces, because

> they were worked hard, and had too much liberty, and were acquiring bad habits. They earned money by overwork, and spent it for whiskey, and got a habit of roaming about and *taking care of themselves*; because when they were not at work in the furnace, nobody looked out for them.

Other masters were reluctant to rent slaves for work in distant or dangerous places. One Carolinian feared that his hirelings at a railroad would "be exposed in the mud and water and it is too far from home, for if they were to get sick they might die before I could have an opportunity to do anything for them." A Virginian decided not to rent his Negro to an iron works, because the slave had "left no doubt on my mind, but he

would make an effort to reach the State of Ohio, and by being placed at your Works it would greatly facillitate his Object." A Georgia rice miller refused to let his black carpenters leave the county, because "they are away from their families—generally uncomfortably lodged—away from restraints and exposed to temptations of various kinds—are much upon the road going and returning home on visits—& consequently in the way of colds & sicknesses—and if they are *taken sick*—we cannot be with them—they are left to strangers—and Doctors' Bills consume all they make."

Despite such apprehensions, most masters rented slaves to industrial enterprises with little apparent concern for their well-being. Only a few hiring contracts actually stipulated precise working conditions; only a minority of masters refused to permit their slaves to work in certain hazardous occupations. Indeed, in the 1850's, many slaveowners anxiously solicited employers to hire their bondsmen, and the slave hiring system seemed to be expanding and flourishing. "I am quite willing that you should take my hands for another year and that they should remain with you during the Christmas holidays," ran a typical letter from an owner to a turpentine manufacturer in 1851.

That the slave hiring system emerged only as the South industrialized, and that slave hiring (like incentive payments) was leading to the breakdown of the institution of slavery has been argued by some historians. "There had been ceaselessly at work for at least two decades a slow and subtle erosion of the base of the institution," declares one scholar. "The growing practice of obtaining the service of slave labor by hire in stead or by purchase was invisibly loosening the bonds of an archaic system." The slave hiring system was expanding because of the growth of industry, he continues, "and as industry . . . increased in the South the rigidities of slavery were forced to yield. The hiring system contributed to this result by giving greater freedom and higher status to the hired slave. Indeed," he concludes, "the industrial occupations were the very points at which slavery was showing signs of breaking down."

Actually, the evidence indicates that slave hiring dates from the early beginnings of slavery, and throughout the slave period it was nearly as common on plantations and farms, and in domestic servitude, as it was in industries. Southern industrialization may have accelerated slave hiring, but slave hiring antedated the emergence of industries. More important, slave hiring (like rewards) gave little promise of transforming slavery into freedom. The divorce of management from ownership inherent in the slave hiring system did not necessarily mean that the hireling was less a slave. That slave hirelings "bargained" with their employers or chose their masters freely is an exaggeration, and there is little evidence that most hirelings obtained any more freedom than those employed directly by their owners. In general, as one authority has concluded, "the hired slave stood the greatest chance of subjection to cruel punishments as well as to overwork," and slave hiring remained essentially "a systematic method of controlling and exploiting labor."

Since many slaveowners eagerly sought to rent their slaves to industries in the last antebellum decades, the theory that slave hiring was transforming the institution of slavery into a wage labor system seems doubtful. Instead, such evidence demonstrates that slave hiring was profitable and convenient both to slave owners and to slave hirers. The dramatic rise in prices paid for slave hirelings in the 1850's also confirms that the demand for, and popularity of, hired slaves was increasing. If anything, slave hiring permitted employers to obtain labor without making heavy investments in Negroes. Slave hiring thus extended the benefits of bondage to non-slaveowners and thereby strengthened the institution of slavery as a whole. Slave hiring suggests how an allegedly rigid institution—slavery—could adapt to the needs of southern society.

Selection 4

Being Hired Out: An Interview with Ex-Slave Baily Cunningham

Charles L. Perdue Jr., Thomas E. Barden, and Robert K. Phillips

Excerpted from *Weevils in the Wheat: Interviews with Virginia Ex-Slaves*, edited by Charles L. Perdue Jr., Thomas E. Barden, and Robert K. Phillips. Copyright © 1976 by the Rector and Visitors of the University of Virginia. Reprinted with permission from the University Press of Virginia.

Slaves, of course, were never consulted when their masters decided to lease them as laborers. How they felt about it is suggested by the following Virginia ex-slave's reminiscence of having been hired out as a hotel servant.

*B*aily Cunningham (Colored) was born in Franklin County, Va., he claims, December 25, 1837 [*must mean 1827*], however, I am of the opinion that he is mistaken, as he says his master sold (hired him out) him to a man running a hotel in Lynchburg when he was twenty years old and he remembers seeing the soldiers march through Lynchburg at the first of the war which was, more than likely, 1862, this would make him about 99 years old, however his daughter, who is about 60 years old says he was 110 years old Dec. 25, Christmas day, 1937. His mind is fairly clear and he can readily recall incidences of his boyhood days. He never attended school nor can he read or write. His eyesight is good and he has never used glasses. He owns and lives on a little plot of land he bought near Starkey, six miles south of Roanoke, Va., on which he built a one story two-room log house seventy years ago.

In reply to a question regarding his parents he said, "My grandfather Cunningham was a white man. He came from the old country, Germany, and brought my grandmother, a colored woman, with him. My father was a Cunningham and a white man, my mother was a Silvers, and was colored." His appearance indicates the possession of caucasian blood.

My mother and my grandmother were slaves. My mother belonged to Bemis English who had a large plantation about eleven miles from Rocky Mount, Va., in Franklin County. He moved to another plantation on Roanoke River in Bedford County soon after the war. When I was a boy he had about seventy five slaves, including the children. The children were considered free until they were twenty years old and did not have to work. After they were twenty they had to work on the plantation or be sold (hired) out by our master. I was sold to a hotel man in Lynchburg soon after I was twenty for one year for $125.00. I remember well as I had never had on "britches" or a suit of clothes until I went to Lynchburg. All the boys and girls wore "shirt tails" until we were twenty. I never had a hat or shoes until I was twenty. All under twenty were treated the same as the stock on the plantation.

What do you mean by "shirt tails?" "It was a long garment that came down to the knees. The boys and girls never wore but one garment even in the winter time. It was made large and out of cotton, flax, or wool on the old loom which was kept going all the year."

How did the boys and girls spend their time until they were twenty, if they did no work? "We played around the quarters, and played 'Hide the Switch' most of the time. I did not work in the field until I came home from Lynchburg."

What kind of rations did you have?

We ate twice a day, about sunup and at sundown. All the work hands ate in the cabins and all the children took their *cymblin* [squash] *soup bowl* to the big kitchen and got it full of cabbage soup, then we were allowed to go [to] the table where the white folks ate and get the crumbs from the table. We sat on the ground around the quarters to eat with wooden spoons. Rations were given to the field hands every Monday morning. They would go to the smokehouse and the misses would give us some meal and meat in our sack. We were allowed to go to the garden or field and get cabbage, potatoes and corn or any other vegetables and cook in our shanties. We had plenty to eat. We had a large iron baker with a lid to bake bread and potatoes and a large iron kettle to boil things in. On Saturday morning we would go to the smokehouse and get some flour and a piece of meat with a bone so we could have a hoe-cake for dinner on Sunday. Sometimes we had plenty of milk and coffee.

What kind of cabins did you have?

They were log cabins, some had one room and some had two rooms, and board floors. Our master was a rich man. He had a store and a sawmill on the creek. The cabins were covered with boards, nailed on and had stick-and-mud chimneys. We had home-made beds, corded, with mattresses made of linen filled with straw, and pillows the same and a woolen or cotton blanket. We had home-made tables and chairs with wooden bottoms. The field hands had wooden sole shoes, the wooden bottom was made of maple, the size of the foot, one half inch thick or thicker and the leather nailed to the wood. Our master had lots of sheep and the wool was made into yarn and we had yarn socks in the winter. The cabins were built in two rows not very far from the misses big house. My mother kept house for our misses and looked after the quarters and reported anything going wrong to the misses.

What kind of amusements did the grown folks have?

They had big dances at night, sometimes. Somebody would play the fiddles and some the banjo and sometimes had a drum. We did the 'buck dance.' A boy and girl would hold hands and jump up and down and swing around keeping time with the music. We would dance awhile then go to the other room and drink coffee, corn whisky or apple brandy, sometimes some of us would get drunk. We would dance and play all night but had to be ready to work next day. We had to get a pass from our master or misses to go to the dance, as we were afraid the 'Patty Rolers' (patty roler—a corruption of the word patrol) would get us. The master would have eight or ten men on horses watching and any one caught without a pass was taken up and punished, sometimes whipped. The boys and girls were not allowed to play together, any violation was a serious matter.

Did you have any holidays?

We didn't know but one holiday, that was Christmas day, and it was not much different from any other day. The field hands did not have to work on Christmas day. We didn't have any Christmas presents. We never went to school or to church. All the field hands our master did not need on the plantation were sold (hired out) to the tobacco factories at Lynchburg. The stray slaves wandering about were taken up by the 'traders' and held until he had about a hundred then they were sold and taken to the southern cotton fields. They were chained together, a chain fastened to the arm of each one and they went afoot to North Carolina, South Carolina, or Georgia driven by their new master.

How were you treated when you were sick?

A sick slave was reported to the misses. She had three kinds of medicine that would cure everything.

What were these medicines?

One was vinegar nail, one rosin pills and the other was tar. When we had aches or pains in the stomach or the back she would make us drink 'vinegar nail' which was made by getting about a pound of square cut iron nails and put them in a jug with a lot of vinegar, then at night we had to take two rosin pills. These pills were made of raw pine rosin. When we had the tooth ache or the ear ache she would fill the tooth or ear full of tar. We never had a doctor.

Uncle Baily, what was the most eventful day of your life?

The day the stars fell. I was eight years old but I remember it as well as if it was yesterday. They began to fall about sundown and fell all night. They fell like rain. They looked like little balls about as big as marbles with a long streak of fire to them. They fell everywhere but you couldn't hear them. They did not hit the ground, or the house. We were all scared and did not go out of the house but could see them everywhere. A few days later it began to snow and snowed three days and nights, the snow piled up over some of the houses, some people froze and some starved.

Note: You will observe that the customs and slave life under Baily's master, Bemis English, who was of German descent, is somewhat different from the usual Virginia slave owners. The foregoing continuity is in the language of Baily Cunningham just as he related it, in the most part. He does not use any of the usual slave broge [brogue], in fact talks very well.

Selection 5

Rationalizing the Breakup of Slave Families

Michael Tadman

Selling slaves in the same family to different buyers thus breaking up families was perhaps the most notorious aspect of slave owners' freedom to act in their own economic self-interest. Slave families could be broken up for many reasons: because a young slave had grown up and could fetch a high price as a field hand; because the owner had died and his or her heirs had to divide the assets; because an owner had fallen into debt or suffered business losses; or simply because a speculator (a professional slave dealer) made an attractive offer. No matter how averse a slave owner might be to family breakup, such owners were not immune to death or business failure. Thus, no slave family was assured that they would remain together and it has been estimated at least one-third of all nineteenth-century slaves were personally affected by this cruel practice at least once in their lives.

Historian Michael Tadman made a thorough study of the business of "speculating" in the Old South in his 1989 book Speculators and Slaves: Masters, Traders, and Slaves in the Old South, *which is excerpted here. He*

discusses the ways in which slave owners justified (to themselves, at least) the practice of selling off members of the same family, which might well result in the permanent separation of husbands from wives, children from parents, or brothers from sisters.

Speculative sales and family separations emerge as having been central both to the realities of the Old South and to the mythmaking in which its white citizens so lavishly indulged. Such sales tell us much about the attitudes of antebellum masters to their slaves, and about the paternal self-image which, despite those sales, the slaveholding class maintained. And speculation seems to be of central importance, too, in considering slave mentalities. . . . The evidence of the massive interregional traffic suggests that that context was usually one of deep distrust of masters and of a profound separation between the values of slaves and masters.

Trading . . . accounted from the 1810s or 1820s onward for at least 60 percent of the overall interregional movement; and those sales occurred, not because of crippling debt or the death of owners, but overwhelmingly for speculative reasons. In the antebellum South, the slaveowning class was generally willing, simply for reasons of financial advantage, to separate black families. The scale of those separations

A child is separated from his mother as she is sold to a new owner. An estimated one-third of all slaves in the nineteenth century experienced painful family breakups such as this one.

was such that one out of every five marriages of Upper South slaves would have been prematurely terminated by the trade; if other interventions by masters are added, the proportion rises to about one in three. Furthermore, the trade would have separated about one in three of the exporting region's slave children (under fourteen years) from their parents; again, local sales and other actions by masters would have raised this proportion to about one in two. And, with very intensive rates of importation into many Lower South states throughout the antebellum period, the impact on the importing states was similarly profound. Remember that the proportions forcibly separated would not have been fundamentally different if only 50 or even 45 percent of movements, not 60 percent, been allocated to the trade. And the evidence suggests that 60 percent, if anything, is an undercount rather than an overcount.

Proslavery literature and the magazines and prints of the antebellum South generally were overwhelmingly racist or protoracist—persistently arguing for innate black laziness, inferior intellectual capacity, and natural promiscuity

and instability in family and sexual matters. This almost universal racism could theoretically have led to one of two main outcomes—a tendency to protect "innately weak" black families and institutions, or, on the other hand, a tendency for the majority to exploit the myth that only "temporary hardships" occurred when families were wrecked or arbitrarily disturbed by masters. Despite the layers of myth which the Old South generated to make itself comfortable at home and acceptable abroad, the trade shows that the second tendency was clearly dominant. In effect, the vast bulk of the Old South's literary output on black "character," family, and "amalgamation" ingeniously constructed a framework of fable whereby masters could both separate families whenever they wished and regard themselves as paternalists whatever they did.

Again and again, the white South's view of black character and potential began with the black's supposed natural tendency toward promiscuity and innate inability, unless under the strictest white supervision, to form lasting and loving family relationships. The journals of the South abounded with "guides for the supervision of Negroes," and "Negro Amalgamation" formed a constant theme. A guide published in *De Bow's Review* and considered by the editor as "a practical and valuable paper for the planters" observed that on the contributor's plantation,

> beds with ample clothing are provided for them [the slaves], and in them they are *made to sleep*. As to their habits of amalgamation and intercourse, I know of no means whereby to regulate them, or to restrain them; I attempted it for many years by preaching virtue and decency, encouraging marriages, and by punishing, with some severity, departures from marital obligations; but it was all in vain.

A few months later, "A Small Farmer" wrote in the same journal: "'Habits of amalgamation' I cannot stop; I can check it, but only in the name. I am willing to be taught, for I have tried everything I know."

James H. Hammond sometimes found it inconvenient to let slaves choose their own marriage partners and provided his overseer with detailed instruction on the marriages of slaves. At the same time, as we know, he was a past master at forcible family separation—and, as his wife, to her intense annoyance, knew, he had several children by at least one slave mistress (the latter being forbidden a slave husband). Even so, he could happily write in *De Bow* that family separations were rare among slaves. Those which did occur, he assured his readers, tended to be because of the slave's "perverse tendency" to link with a partner on another plantation, or came about because slaves generally preferred to be separated from their spouse rather than be parted from a master who might be migrating or changing his circumstances. And Hammond added that, of course, slave senses were "dull," but if pleasure was the absence of pain, then American slaves were very happy.

Despite the massive extent of interregional trading and of other causes of forced separation, the procedure of southern writers was almost always to open with the claim that separations were rare, and then to emphasize that separations in any case brought little hardship for blacks.

Chancellor Harper of South Carolina argued that blacks always lacked any real capability for domestic affection and showed "insensibility to ties of kindred." In Africa, he maintained, there had been fear of parents but no love of children. And with American slaves, he went on, separations were far less keenly felt than were those of whites. In any case, the small chance of blacks being separated was as nothing compared with the risk of their being unemployed and unable to cope in a free society. . . .

Thomas R. Cobb managed to recruit black "love of dance" into the medley of special pleading. He opened, following tradition, with the view that "the unnecessary and wanton separation of persons standing in the relation of husband and wife" was found "rarely if ever" under slavery. But where masters did for some reason lapse from their generations of good practice, Cobb was still ready to preempt any sympathy for the slave for, he wrote,

> The dance will allay his most poignant grief, and a few days blot out the memory of his most bitter bereavement. His natural affection is not strong, and consequently he is cruel to his own offspring, and suffers little by separation from them. . . .

In John H. Van Evrie's *Negroes and Negro "Slavery"* (1853), so many of the traditional propaganda pieces were deployed that we have a more or less complete manual for the misrepresentation of the slave family. Whites, we are told, because of "the elevated intellectualism of the race," displayed lofty values and a deep love of family. As for slaves, "the mother has a similar love of her offspring at an early period of its existence, possibly stronger." This intense attachment, however, arose because the black woman's "maternal instincts are more imperative, more closely approximated to the animal." Slavery, we are informed, was ordained by God and, in family capabilities, as elsewhere, was said perfectly to fit the "black temperament." A natural process of attachment and distancing was, therefore—and following God's plan—said to have evolved. "The Negro mother," Van

Evrie tells us, "has always control and direction of her offspring at the South so long as that is needed by the latter." Of course, he adds, the master was the "supreme ruler, . . . the very providence of these simple and subordinate people, . . . [protecting] them in all of their rights"; but mother and child were not disturbed. We next are asked to believe, however, that slave children "like a dog or calf" quickly grew independent of their mother, and were as mature as they ever would be by age twelve to fifteen. They were still "boys," he said, but added that they would remain "intellectually boys forever."

A convenient process then unfolds in Van Evrie's fable: the mother once had "boundless affection for her infants," but that attachment "grows feebler as the capacities of the child are developed; at 12 or 15 she is relatively indifferent," and eventually she "barely recognizes it." And, we are told "all of these phases . . . are in accord with the specific nature and purpose assigned . . . by the Almighty Creator." As for the husband, he mattered little, showing "a feeble and capricious love of his wife and indifference to his offspring." So far as marriage separations were concerned, then,

> Where the white husband, and certainly the white wife, might despair or die, the negro and the negress, with new partners and another marriage, are quite as happy as if they had never been separated.

After all of this, we find of course, that family separations were extremely rare, and were far less common, for example, than among "the lower orders in England." And throughout the whole process, the one person who consistently mattered for the slave was the master—since "the strongest affection the negro nature is capable of feeling is love of his master, his guide, protector, friend, and indeed Providence.". . .

The . . . opinions just outlined represented a deeply embedded white racist view of blacks and the black family connection. With such views, all things were possible. Owners could discipline slaves by threatening to sell them from their families, could look to recover run-

aways by searching close to the fugitive's old family, and yet could still find it possible to see black family attachments as fickle and transitory. They could separate families and still see themselves as paternalists—since they could deceive and flatter themselves with the view that only they, the whites, really worried about black families. They could readily persuade themselves that they *were* paternalists, and that separations were only incidental to the system—for in their view the whole relationship of slavery was of primary benefit to the slaves, any temporary "hardships" of separation easily being overcome. And, in any case, as J.H. Hammond told himself, a great satisfaction was that his slaves "loved and appreciated him." The chief and only lasting loyalty of slaves was, supposedly, to the master and not the slave family. To have believed that the black family was really anything like as important as the white family would have meant permanent moral crisis for whites. Without that belief, the system was infinitely capable of combining a vicious program of speculation and separation with a comforting, paternal self-image for masters.

For those operating a racist system, a paternal self-image, whatever the realities of their actions, would hardly be surprising. Day-to-day racist practice might vary greatly in its manifestations and level of brutality, but racism when set down in legitimizing theory, or when consciously rationalized, tends often to speak the language of paternalism. . . .

The evidence of the slave trade, however, makes it possible to talk specifically, not just in entirely general terms, about paternalism and the practical limitations to it. One can distinguish three or four general types of slaveholder attitudes. A first category is that of the "broad paternalists" who took a wide view of their role, including in it a firmly held belief that the emotional and family welfare of slaves was more important than the convenience of masters. A second group consists of the "narrow paternalists," for whom the protection of the slave family was secondary to white convenience, but who made some effort to provide for physical needs and perhaps to limit work loads somewhat. The third and fourth categories would, for the slaves, be little different, but they can be termed "theoretical paternalists" and "supremacy policemen." By "theoretical paternalists" I mean to identify a group who used the language of paternalism as far as it occurred in proslavery arguments, but who in practice took from that framework only the idea of race hierarchy and innate white "superiority." The final category includes those not greatly inclined to trouble with self-legitimizing theory, but simply inclined toward a tough day-to-day assertion of white power. Of the categories just sketched, the first three views can perhaps be considered consensus theories based on some idea of a stable "natural order," whereas the last has stronger elements of conflict theory (with a constant need directly to assert strength so as to preserve order).

These categories are not intended to be exhaustive and represent no more than a few very general types. The evidence of the trade, however, helps to make sense of them. "Broad paternalists," although figuring so prominently in the proslavery argument and in the long-sustained tradition of the plantation legend—were a distinct minority. Individual slaves, perhaps especially some domestics, might have been indulged by some owners from category two (and perhaps even categories three and four), but genuine paternalistic sacrifice seems to have been a rarity. Slaveholder and slaves were not intimately linked in a sort of extended family; for the great majority, relationships seem to have been much more distant, jarring, and lacking in mutual trust. The actions of masters in wrecking families and the low priority given to the deepest of slave emotions do not suggest a system based on positive incentives, diligent workers, high morale, and accommodation within a joint economic enterprise. Slaveholder priorities and attitudes suggest, instead, a system based much more crudely on arbitrary power, distrust, and fear. It is true there was, to some extent, interpenetration of white and slave culture—particularly in the outer form which slave religion took—but the general context of planter as spec-

ulator suggests only a severely limited interaction and sharing. Essentially, speculators—meaning in this case slaveholders as well as traders—did not know and did not want to know enough of slave values for profound interactions to take place.

A fundamental yardstick by which slaves could judge masters—and, indeed, the whole system of slavery—was the black family and white attitudes toward it. As an old former slave, Jennie Hill, told her interviewer:

> Some people think that slaves had no feeling—that they bore their children as animals bear their young and that there was no heartbreak when the children were torn from their parents or the mother taken from her brood to toil for a master in another state. But that isn't so. The slaves loved their families even as the Negroes love their own today and the happiest time of their lives was when they could sit at their cabin doors when the day's work was done and sing the old slave songs, 'Swing Low Sweet Chariot', 'Massa's in the Cold, Cold Ground', and 'Nobody Knows What Trouble I've Seen'. Children learned these songs and sang them only as a Negro child could. That was the slave's only happiness, a happiness that for many of them did not last.

The former slave explained that she got married when she was twenty years old, and

> then came my little babies and just before the war broke out I had three. How well I remember how I would sit in my room with the little ones on my lap and the tears would roll down my cheeks as I would ponder the right and wrong of bringing them into the world. What was I bringing them into the world for? To be slaves and go from morning to night. They couldn't be educated and maybe they couldn't even live with their families. They would just be slaves. All that time I wasn't even living with my husband. He belonged to another man. He had to stay on his farm and I on mine. That wasn't living—that was slavery.

Despite all of this, however, she added that her master "was the best man that ever owned a nigger," and that "in all the 27 years I served my master as a slave I got but two whippings. That in itself speaks for the kindness of the master even though both of these whippings were for little things."

Jennie Hill's story was not at all unusual. A great many ex-slaves reported that they had had "good" masters, but nevertheless clearly showed their hatred of slavery. Such ex-slaves tended to judge masters on a relative scale—given that they had been slaves and had had to have masters, their master was not the worst class of master. In a sense such slaves had accommodated to the system, but this was only an accommodation through the violence of the system to them or to others. They might judge masters, for example, on something like the four-category scale outlined a little earlier. A few "good" masters might have come from category one (the "broad paternalist," who made the slave family the dominant priority), but most would no doubt have come from category two. "Bad" masters would no doubt have come from categories three and four. Even those whose own masters happened to be "broad paternalists" would most probably have been aware of the prevailing culture of speculation among masters generally, so that acceptance of the slavery system as a whole would have been only a little more likely than with other slaves. Some slaves with "broad paternalist"

masters might have felt themselves genuinely to have been a part of the master's extended family, and might therefore have shown deep-rooted loyalty and affection. The great majority of "deeply loyal slaves" though, like those who "loved and appreciated" James H. Hammond, would have been a fictive white creation arising out of the needs of the slaveholder's self-image.

In the antebellum period, those specialist dealers, variously called slave traders, "soul drivers," "nigger drovers," and the like, were not the only "Negro speculators" in the South, and the slaves knew it! The predominantly speculative character of slaveholder attitudes lent itself to an underground slave culture of satirical songs and folk tales. Sale and family separation facilitated the geographical growth of slavery in America and the development of economic fortunes for slaveholders, but they carried penalties for the master class too. Few economic systems actually broke up families so arbitrarily and on such a scale, so that despite the terrible power of masters, their authority, with most slaves, was only accepted conditionally. Black and white values relating to the slave family kept masters and slaves largely in separate, segregated worlds. The years of segregation began long before the age of "Jim Crow" and the ugly laws of the late nineteenth century.

Selection 6

Being Sold: An Ex-Slave's Narrative

Delia Garlic

What it meant to be sold off and separated from one's family is best learned from the narratives of slaves who suffered such a tragedy. Here is one of many such personal accounts, told by an aged former slave named Delia Garlic to an interviewer in the 1930s. Compare her story with the assertion frequently made by slave owners that blacks had little emotional attachment to other members of their families and quickly got over whatever "momentary" regrets the parting caused.

*D*elia Garlic lives at 43 Stone Street, Montgomery, and insists she is 100 years old. Unlike many of the old Negroes of the South, she has no good words for slavery days or the old masters, declaring: "Dem days was hell."

She sat on her front porch and assailed the taking of young children from mothers and selling them in different parts of the country.

"I was growed up when de war come," she said, "an' I was a mother befo' it closed. Babies was snatched from dere mother's breas' an' sold to speculators. Chilluns was separated from sis-

ters an' brothers an' never saw each other ag'in.

"Course dey cry; you think dey not cry when dey was sold lak cattle? I could tell you 'bout it all day, but even den you couldn't guess de awfulness of it.

"It's bad to belong to folks dat own you soul an' body; dat can tie you up to a tree, wid yo' face to de tree an' yo' arms fastened tight aroun' it; who take a long curlin' whip an' cut de blood ever' lick.

"Folks a mile away could hear dem awful whippings. Dey was a turrible part of livin'."

Delia said she was born at Powhatan, Virginia, and was the youngest of thirteen children.

"I never seed none of my brothers an' sisters 'cept brother William," she said. "Him an' my mother an' me was brought in a speculator's drove to Richmon' an' put in a warehouse wid a drove of other niggers. Den we was all put on a block an' sol' to de highes' bidder.

"I never seed brother William ag'in. Mammy an' me was sold to a man by de name of Carter, who was de sheriff of de county.

"No'm, dey warn't no good times at his house. He was a widower an' his daughter kept house for him. I nursed for her, an' one day I was playin' wid de baby. It hurt its li'l han' an' commenced to cry, an' she whirl on me, pick up a hot iron an' run it all down my arm an' han'. It took off de flesh when she done it.

Excerpted from Delia Garlic, "The Faces of Power," in *Remembering Slavery: African Americans Talk About Their Personal Experiences of Slavery and Freedom*, edited by Ira Berlin, Marc Favreau, and Steven F. Miller. Copyright © 1998 Ira Berlin, Marc Favreau, and Steven F. Miller. Reprinted with permission from The New Press.

"Atter awhile, marster married ag'in; but things warn't no better. I seed his wife blackin' her eyebrows wid smut one day, so I thought I'd black mine jes' for fun. I rubbed some smut on my eyebrows an' forgot to rub it off, an' she kotched me. She was powerful mad an' yelled: 'You black devil, I'll show you how to mock your betters.'

"Den she pick up a stick of stovewood an' flails it ag'in' my head. I didn't know nothin' more 'till I come to, lyin' on de floor. I heard de mistus say to one of de girls: 'I thought her thick skull and cap of wool could take it better than that.'

A slave pen (lower right corner) sits outside of a slave dealer's building in Alexandria, Virginia.

"I kept on stayin' dere, an' one night de marster come in drunk an' set at de table wid his head lollin' aroun'. I was waitin' on de table, an' he look up an' see me. I was skeered, an' dat made him awful mad. He called an overseer an' tol' him: 'Take her out an' beat some sense in her.'

"I begin to cry an' run an' run in de night; but finally I run back by de quarters an' heard mammy callin' me. I went in, an' raght away dey come for me. A horse was standin' in front of de house, an' I was took dat very night to Richmon' an' sold to a speculator ag'in. I never seed my mammy any more.

"I has thought many times through all dese years how mammy looked dat night. She pressed my han' in bofe of hers an' said: 'Be good an' trus' in de Lawd.'

"Trustin' was de only hope of de pore black critters in dem days. Us jest prayed for strength to endure it to de end. We didn't 'spect nothin' but to stay in bondage 'till we died.

"I was sol' by de speculator to a man in McDonough, Georgia. I don't ricollect his name, but he was openin' a big hotel at McDonough an' bought me to wait on tables. But when de time come aroun' to pay for me, his hotel done fail. Den de Atlanta man dat bought de hotel bought me, too. 'Fo' long, dough, I was sol' to a man by de name of Garlic, down in Louisiana, an' I stayed wid him 'till I was freed. I was a regular fiel' han', plowin' an' hoein' an' choppin' cotton.

"Us heard talk 'bout de war, but us didn't pay no 'tention. Us never dreamed dat freedom would ever come."

Delia was asked if the slaves ever had any parties or dances on her plantation.

"No'm," she replied, "us didn't have no parties; nothin' lak dat. Us didn't have no clothes for goin' 'roun. I never had a undershirt until jest befo' my first chil' was borned. I never had nothin' but a shimmy an' a slip for a dress, an' it was made out'en de cheapes' cloth dat could be bought; unbleached cloth, coarse, but made to las'.

"Us didn't know nothin' 'cept to work. Us was up by three or four in de mornin' an' everybody got dey somethin' to eat in de kitchen. Dey didn't give us no way to cook, nor nothin' to cook in our cabins. Soon as us dressed us went by de kitchen an' got our piece of cornbread. Dey wan't even no salt in dem las' years. Dat piece of cornbread was all us had for breakfus', an' for supper, us had de same.

"For dinner us had boiled vittles; greens, peas an' sometimes beans. Coffee? No'm, us never knowed nothin' 'bout coffee.

"One mornin' I 'members I had started to de fiel', an' on de way I los' my piece of bread. I didn't know what to do. I started back to try to fin' it, an' it was too dark to see. But I walk back raght slow, an' had a dog dat walked wid me. He went on ahead, an' atter awhile I come on him lyin' dere guardin' dat piece of bread. He never touched it, so I gived him some of it.

"Jus' befo' de war I married a man named Chatfield from another plantation; but he was took off to war an' I never seed him ag'in. Atter awhile I married a boy on de plantation named Miles Garlic.

"Yas'm, Massa Garlic had two boys in de war. When dey went off de Massa an' missis cried, but it made us glad to see dem cry. Dey made us cry so much.

"When we knowed we was free, everybody wanted to git out. De rule was dat if you stayed in yo' cabin you could keep it, but if you lef', you los' it. Miles was workin' at Wetumpka, an' he slipped in an' out so us could keep on livin' in de cabin.

"My secon' baby soon come, an' raght den I made up my min' to go to Wetumpka where Miles was workin' for de railroad. I went on down dere an' us settled down.

"Atter Miles died, I lived dere long as I could an' den come to Montgomery to live wid my son. I'se eatin' white bread now an' havin' de best time of my life. But when de Lawd say, 'Delia, well done: come up higher,' I'll be glad to go."

Selection 7

Cherokee Slaveholders

R. Halliburton Jr.

Many people do not know that some Indian tribes in the Old South were also slave owners. Before their own harrowing removal to what is now Oklahoma in the 1830s, a number of Cherokee Indians of northern Georgia and western North Carolina were substantial owners of black slaves. These slaves accompanied their Indian masters on the infamous "Trail of Tears," and the survivors and their descendants continued to serve in slavery until the Civil War. Indeed, one reason why southern whites (including President Andrew Jackson) were so anxious to see "the Five Civilized [Indian] Nations" driven from their

ancestral lands was how deftly these native Americans successfully adopted white ways, including slave-labor plantation agriculture.

In this selection, historical writer R. Halliburton Jr. explores this dimension of the history of American slavery.

Slavery, as the term is usually understood, did not exist among the Cherokee Indians before the arrival of Europeans. Although there are accounts of black slaves escaping from De Soto's expedition of 1540, black slavery was introduced into the Cherokee Nation by English traders. These traders frequently hunted and fought with their Indian customers, learned their language, married Cherokee women, fathered children, amassed property, and worked toward cultural assimilation. Some traders developed plantations that soon rivaled those of

Excerpted from R. Halliburton Jr., "Black Slavery Among the Cherokees," *American History Illustrated*, vol. 11, no. 6 (1976). Reprinted by permission of the author.

the Carolinas in size. They purchased black slaves and other properties and left them as an inheritance to their Cherokee children. Other traders brought black slaves into the Cherokee Nation and sold them to tribal members.

As the white colonization of the country progressed, the Cherokees came into possession of runaway blacks from the frontier settlements. This posed a serious problem for the colonists and brought about the Treaty of Dover. In 1730 a delegation of seven Cherokees journeyed to England, were received by King George II, and subsequently "signed" the Treaty of Dover in Whitehall.

The treaty stipulated in part:

> That if any Negroe Slaves shall run away into the woods from their English Masters, the Cherokee Indians shall endeavour to apprehend them, and either bring them back to the Plantation from whence they run-away, or to the Governor. . . .

Slave Catcher became a common Cherokee name. Cherokee women immediately approved black slavery. It lightened their tasks of tilling the communal fields. But the colonists had no desire for the Cherokees to adopt black slavery. They correctly foresaw Indians raiding their settlements for "hair and horses" and slaves. Consequently they enacted laws that prohibited traders from keeping or taking blacks into the Cherokee Nation. Traders circumvented the law, however, by purchasing slaves in the names of their Indian wives or other persons. Simultaneously, the British Government was presenting slaves to influential Indians and calling them "Kings Gifts."

The establishment of black slavery in the Cherokee Nation, as in the United States, was an evolutionary process. The tribe exhibited a strong color consciousness at an early date, and black slavery became a part of tribal common law long before it was given statutory sanction. The constant encroachment by colonial frontiersmen coupled with the good will efforts of the British caused the Cherokees to aid England during the American Revolution. Some slave-owning Tories sought refuge among the Cherokees and brought their property with them. The subsequent destruction of Cherokee towns by colonial forces and the cession of much of their lands provided additional incentive to abandon the towns and communal fields for individual farming units.

By 1790 black slavery was an established institution throughout the Cherokee Nation. Such names as Ross, Vann, Foreman, Alberty, Scales, Boudinot, Lowrey, Rogers, McNair, Ridge, Downing, Drew, Martin, Nave, Jolly, Hildebrand, Webber, Adair, and numerous others became slaveholders. In 1799 Moravian [Church] missionaries reported seeing "many plantations with large fenced fields of corn, wheat, cotton, vegetables and orchards." The clerics also reported that "Our hosts had, also, negro slaves that were well clothed, bright, lively and appeared to be happy and well cared for. These slaves conducted themselves towards the Indians, with all courtesy."

The Ridge (Kah-nung-da-cla-geh), later known as "Major" Ridge for his exploits in the Battle of Horseshoe Bend [against Andrew Jackson's forces in 1814], was the first Cherokee plantation owner of magnitude. Sometime before 1800 the fullblood Indian warrior—who remained illiterate throughout life—and his bride, forsaking the tradition of their people, began chopping, plowing, knitting, and weaving. He also began to acquire black slaves "to do the harder work about the premises."

Major Ridge's plantation, known as "Chieftains," grew rapidly. His orchard eventually contained more than 1,500 trees. Eight fields containing nearly 300 acres were soon under cultivation. The principal crop was corn, but cotton, tobacco, wheat, oats, indigo, and sweet and Irish potatoes were also cultivated. There were also a vineyard, a nursery, and a garden which contained a large variety of ornamental shrubs as well as vegetables. By the early 1820's Major Ridge had accumulated thirty black slaves.

Major Ridge sent his son John to the Cornwall School in Connecticut. In 1819 he visited his son and caused considerable comment. He arrived in Cornwall "in the most splendid carriage that had ever entered the town," wearing a coat trimmed in "gold lace" and enjoyed "waiters in great style." During John's years at Cornwall he met and courted Sarah Bird Northup, the daughter of a prominent, local white family. When John later asked for Sarah's hand in matrimony, her parents refused. They objected strongly to the proposed union ostensibly because "John suffered from a hip disease" or "scrofulous complaint." Finally, it was agreed that if John would go home and return after one year—entirely well—the parents would consent to the marriage. John agreed to the stipulated conditions. After the lapse of a year, he reappeared in Cornwall riding in a magnificent coach drawn by four beautiful white horses and driven by a black coachman in livery.

James Vann was another early Cherokee planter. He was a rich man and operated a trading post near Spring Place, Georgia. Vann was far-famed, little loved, and greatly feared. He owned considerable cattle and farmed many acres of rich land. His black slaves labored under the supervision of a white overseer. Vann enjoyed the luxury of two Cherokee wives and was extremely fond of strong drink. He maintained his own private distilling apparatus and kept "gargantuan supplies of brandy and whiskey and delt [sic] drinks like a lord to his followers." But, "drunk or sober, he ruled his slaves with a rod of iron. He shot one whom he caught plotting against his life; another who had robbed him he burned at the stake." Vann's epitaph read:

Here lies the body of James Vann.
He killed many a white man.
At last by a rifle ball he fell,
And devils dragged him off to hell.

John Ross (Cooseescoowee) was a large slaveholder. He was a merchant and a planter and owned a fine two-story home where black slaves waited upon him and his fullblood wife, Quatie. Peacocks "strutted about the grounds" and the house contained a small but well-organized library. The Ross slaves worked five fields ranging in size from fourteen to seventy-five acres

and totaling nearly 170 acres. By the early 1830's Ross possessed nearly twenty black slaves who labored under an overseer.

Lewis Ross, brother of John Ross, also owned about twenty slaves. A visitor in 1829 described the Ross home as "an elegant white house near the bank of a river, as neatly furnished as almost any house . . . and has Negroes enough to wait on us." It was also reported that David McNair had "a beautiful white house, and about six or seven hundred acres of the best land you ever saw and Negroes enough to tend it and clear as much more as he pleases."

John Martin, who served as Treasurer and the first Chief Justice of the Supreme Court of the Cherokee Nation, reportedly owned 100 black slaves. Martin had two wives and owned an "elegant" home known for its marble mantels and hand-carved stairways. One of his plantations was on the Federal Road near the Coosawattee River. After removal, his property became the possession of a family named Carter. "From the great productiveness of the land, the . . . colloquialism has arisen: 'He has as much money as Carter has oats.'"

Another large slaveowner was Peter Hildebrand. He farmed a large plantation with many black slaves. Hildebrand employed an architect and constructed a magnificent mansion that took seven years to build. After his house was finished, he decided that it was too handsome to use and built a log cabin nearby to live in so he could really enjoy life.

In 1810 the *Christian Observer* reported that there were 538 black slaves in the Cherokee Nation. In 1811 the population of the Cherokee Nation was reported to have been 12,395, excluding 341 whites living within the Nation. Cherokees reportedly possessed 538 slaves at that date.

Slaveholders were among the earliest converts, staunchest supporters, and closest friends of the missionaries and the church. This relationship continued throughout the era of black slavery. The Cherokees called Moravians "The Ravens" because of their black dress. The Methodists were called "Loud Talkers," the Presbyterians were the "Soft Talkers," and the Baptists were known as "The Baptizers."

The increased numbers of black slaves in the Nation brought about a rash of legislation. Miscegenation and intermarriage between Cherokees and blacks had been repugnant from their earliest contacts. The first known marriage of a Cherokee to a Negro was that of Chief Shoe Boots. After his white wife left him, he married her black servant Lucy, who was his property. Lucy bore him two children. The chief petitioned the Council seeking free status for his children, who were his black slave property, according to common law. The request was granted, but the Council warned Chief Shoe Boots that interracial marriages between Cherokees and blacks were not socially acceptable. The Council made its position unequivocally clear with the passage of the following act:

New Town Cherokee Nation, November 11th, 1824

Resolved by the National Committee and Council,

That intermarriages between negro slaves and Indians, or whites, shall not be lawful, and any person or persons, permitting and approbating his, her or their negro slaves, to intermarry with Indians or whites, he, she, or they, so offending, shall pay a fine of fifty dollars, one half for the benefit of the Cherokee Nation; and

Be it further resolved, That any male Indian or white man marrying a negro woman slave, he or they shall be punished with fifty-nine stripes on her or their bare back.

By order of the National Committee
Jno. Ross, Pres't N. Com.
Approved—Path Killer

The Cherokees did not experience the inner conflict between black slavery and conscience that permeated much of the United States. They never felt the need to justify slavery and never expressed the opinion that slavery was in the best interest of the blacks. Neither did they give voice to the "positive benefits" of Christianizing and civilizing their slaves. Slavery was evidently justified solely on the basis of the benefits which accrued to the master. Yet—unlike the white community—there appear to be few or no guilt feelings among the Cherokees today.

The Cherokee Phoenix reported that there were 1,038 black slaves in the Nation in 1824. There were 20 gristmills, 14 sawmills, 56 blacksmith shops, and 6 cotton gins in operation at that time. In 1825 it was reported that a total of 13,563 native Cherokees resided in the East. They possessed 1,217 black slaves. Elias Boudinot conducted a survey in 1825 and determined that Cherokees owned 22,531 black cattle, 7,683 horses, 46,732 hogs, 2,566 sheep, 330 goats, 172 wagons, 2,843 plows, 762 looms, 2,486 spinning wheels, 10 sawmills, 31 gristmills, 1 powder mill, 62 blacksmith shops, 2 tanneries and 8 cotton gins.

Chief John Jolly (Oo-loo-te-ka), Walter Webber, Captain John Rogers, and John Drew were among the more affluent slaveowners in the West. They engaged in commercial farming and hastened to claim large tracts of fertile land. They cultivated cotton and corn which were tended by blacks under the supervision of overseers. The rich bottomland was ideal for growing crops which were transported to market by Arkansas River steamers. "At one time in the Cherokee Nation there was more than one slave for every ten Indians, and several Indians owned as many as one hundred slaves." The poorer and less educated Cherokees usually sought the back country hills which reminded them of their eastern home. They usually tilled only small garden plots, lived in simple structures, and had little need for large numbers of slaves.

Sam Houston had been a slaveowner in Tennessee and reportedly was accompanied by a slave when he began his famous journey to the Cherokee Nation. The slave was supposedly "lost" in a poker game on board a steamboat in route. Houston owned black slaves while he resided at "Wigwam Neosho" near Skin Bayou Bluff on the Arkansas River. There was peace and tranquility for the troubled Houston at Wigwam Neosho, where he established his Cherokee bride in a large log house, set out an apple orchard, and "lived in style," transacting his affairs and entertaining friends. Houston's wife Diana or Tiana Rogers was the niece of John Jolly and was also a black slaveholder. Late in 1832 Sam Houston left his Cherokee wife, his plantation, and his black slaves and rode off to Texas.

[In 1837–1838, d]espite the heroic efforts of such champions of their cause as Henry Clay, Davy Crockett, Ralph Waldo Emerson, Edward Everett, Theodore Frelinhuysen, Sam Houston, John Howard Payne, and Daniel Webster, the Cherokees were forced to emigrate en masse to the West. The hardships suffered during that migration are well known. Principal Chief John Ross's wife Quatie died at Little Rock, Arkansas during the journey. The Cherokees refer to the trek as *Nuna-da-ut sun'y*, "The Trail Where They Cried," and commonly known as the "Trail of Tears." It is not commonly known that many black slaves also tramped that trail and it has been estimated that 125 to 175 of them perished during the journey.

After removal, hunting continued to consume less and less of the time of the Cherokees. Cultivation of the land and herding continued to grow in importance. The plantation became a more important unit of production as it had long been in the southern United States. Plantation agriculture demanded an abundant labor supply for "gang system" cultivation. Capital was borrowed from banks in neighboring states to develop plantations and cattle ranches. Range cattle were purchased in Texas. Dairy cattle were purchased in Wisconsin and transported to the Nation by water. Cotton, wheat, and other seed-grains were obtained at New Orleans. Additional black slaves were purchased in slave markets as far away as Mobile and New Orleans.

The Cherokees enacted a comprehensive slave code which was comparable in harshness with the laws of the Southern states. The motives for these laws were identical. They were designed to preserve the slave mentality, to protect against insurrection, control free blacks, prevent miscegenation, and control virtually all personal and group activities of slaves.

When John Ross arrived in the West he settled at Park Hill and erected a house which he called "Rose Cottage." In 1840 John Howard Payne—the composer of "Home Sweet Home"—visited Ross at Park Hill for several months. Payne reported that there were many black slaves at Rose Cottage at that time. As Ross's economic circumstances improved, the modest house was replaced by a magnificent mansion. It was furnished with rosewood and mahogany, silver plate, and imported china. The great house was surrounded by native trees and was approached by a half-mile long driveway bordered with exotic roses. "Rose Cottage" could accommodate forty guests in comfort. The ample interior included guest rooms, family rooms, a library, and a parlor. The spacious grounds surrounding the house were enhanced by shrubbery and flowers. The orchards (the apple orchard contained a thousand trees) and vegetable gardens supplied the family table, which usually included guests and a retinue of house and field servants.

Rose Cottage grew to a thousand acres or more by 1844 and had its own blacksmith shop, brick kiln, laundry, smokehouse, dairy, and ". . . Negro cabins galore." Ross married Mary Bryan Stapler of Wilmington, Delaware, in September of 1844 and he and his wife lived and entertained in opulent style. He and his beautifully gowned young wife traveled in a handsome Victoria carriage with a black driver and footman in livery.

Rose Cottage was operated in the same manner as any large Southern plantation and was immensely profitable. All food, clothing, and implements were grown or manufactured on the premises. Only the luxuries of the great house were imported. In 1852 a visitor to Ross's plantation reported seeing about forty black slaves at work in the fields. Rose Cottage was burned by General Stand Watie during the Civil War.

The work performed by Cherokee slaves varied little from that done by slaves in the Southern states. Agriculture consumed the time and energy of most slaves. Blacks cleared and improved land, split rails, built fences, plowed ground, planted, cultivated, and harvested crops of cotton, corn, and other commodities. They also tended livestock, milked, and provided domestic service by cooking meals, waiting tables, cleaning, washing, gardening, and grooming horses. Female slaves sometimes served as "mammies" and taught their mistresses the operation of the card and spinning wheel. A small minority of slaves were highly skilled artisans, wheelrights, blacksmiths, midwives, millrights, millers, carpenters, tanners, cobblers, physicians, and masons, since domestic manufacture was frequently an important slave activity. Beginning with raw materials, blacks produced tools, cotton and woolen cloth, knitted stockings, gloves, and scarfs. Slaves also operated several salt works. Old slaves were given the customary title "Uncle" and "Aunt."

"Hunter's Home" was the Park Hill plantation of George Michael Murrell. It was a spacious, two-story frame mansion built with slave labor and with furnishings imported from France and Italy. The furniture was mahogany and "red plush," and imported curtains surrounded the beds. "Hunter's Home," built in 1844–45, typified antebellum Southern-style architecture. The mansion contained a parlor, library, dining room, entrance hall, kitchen, four spacious bedrooms, and large porches at the front and rear. There were also a smokehouse, spring house, barns, a mill, and slave quarters. Robert E. Lee was once a guest at "Hunter's Home" when he was at Fort Gibson in November 1855. Alice Robertson—a future member of the United States House of Representatives from Oklahoma—said that it was always a thrill to see the Murrell coach with its liveried black coachman and footman "with a high cocked hat" arrive at her Grandfather Steven A. Worchester's church at Park Hill.

Joseph Vann (Teaultle), the son of James Vann, became the largest slaveowner in the Cherokee Nation. He had inherited the bulk of his father's estate and was considered to be the wealthiest man in the Nation. He was known throughout the Indian country as "Rich Joe" Vann. "Rich Joe" was also one of the most colorful Cherokees; he stood 6 feet 6 inches tall, was fond of blooded horses, racing, and strong drink.

After removal, he settled a few miles downstream from Muskogee where he lived in a three-story brick mansion at Webbers Falls on the Arkansas River. He operated a plantation of 500 or 600 acres and reportedly owned 300 to 400 slaves. In addition to his plantation, Vann possessed other interests, including the steam-

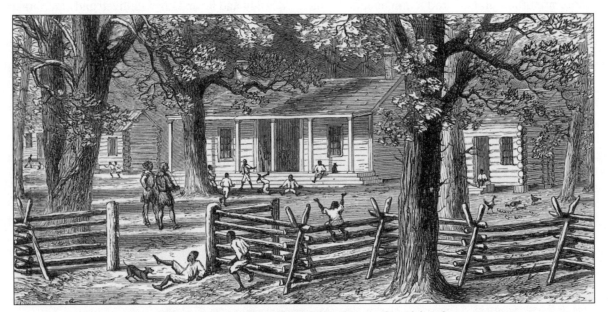

The Cherokee quickly adopted the white settlers' lifestyle,
including plantation farming and using slaves for labor.

boat *Lucy Walker.* He operated the side-wheeler on the Arkansas, Mississippi, Ohio, and Tennessee rivers. Louisville, Memphis, and New Orleans were regular ports of call. Slaves constituted the majority of the *Lucy Walker's* crew.

When the Civil War erupted in the United States, John Ross announced a position of neutrality for the Cherokee Nation. The Civil War polarized the Cherokees in much the same way as it did the United States. The powerful anti-Ross, proslavery faction which had evolved under the leadership of Stand Watie was openly Southern in sentiment. The withdrawal of Federal troops from Indian Territory, the early military succe[...] Confederacy, Confederate treaties w[...] Tribes," pressure [...] pressure [...] Cherokees ca[...] John Ross to agree to form an alliance [...] the Confederacy [...]

On July 15, 1862, Ross was captured by Union forces and removed from the Nation. The subsequent factionalism among the Indians resulted in a rump group of pro-Union, non-slaveowning Cherokees repudiating the Confederate treaty and emancipating Cherokee slaves. The "Southern Wing" of the Cherokees contained most of the slaveowners. They recognized Stand Watie as principal chief and refused to recognize the Emancipation Proclamation.

The peace treaty formulated and signed in Washington on July 19, 1866, recognized the validity of Cherokee emancipation and further stipulated ". . . never hereafter shall either slavery or involuntary servitude exist in their nation. . . ." Finally, on November 28, 1866, a convention of the Cherokee people, meeting at Tahlequah, amended their Constitution to comply with the peace treaty.

Selection 8

Black Slave Owners

Philip Burnham

A few slave owners in the Old South were black. Some were free blacks who had purchased spouses or other family members to get them out of slavery. But in some atypical cases free African Americans accumulated enough wealth to acquire businesses, farms, or plantations that exploited slave labor. The behavior of such black slave owners does not seem to have differed much from whites who owned slaves, and some bizarre situations could result. On one occasion, a Louisiana black who traveled to the Richmond, Virginia, slavemarket to buy slaves found himself barred, as a black man, from returning home on the railroad; he had to go back by sea!

In this selection, freelance journalist Philip Burnham explores the ironic history of blacks who owned fellow blacks.

Reprinted from Philip Burnham, "Selling Poor Steven," *American Heritage*, February/March 1993. Reprinted by permission of *American Heritage* magazine, a division of Forbes, Inc., © Forbes, Inc., 1993.

*I*n the 1640s John Casor was brought from Africa to America, were he toiled as a servant for a Virginia landowner. In 1654

Casor filed a complaint in Northampton County Court, claiming that his master, Anthony Johnson, had unjustly extended the terms of his indenture with the intention of keeping Casor his slave for life. Johnson, insisting he knew nothing of any indenture, fought hard to retain what he regarded as his personal property. After much wrangling, on March 8, 1655, the court ruled that "the said Jno Casor Negro shall forthwith bee returned unto the service of his master Anthony Johnson," consigning him to a lifetime of bondage. Given the vulnerable legal status of servants—black and white—in colonial America, the decision was not surprising. But the documents reveal one additional fact of interest: Anthony Johnson, like his chattel, Casor, was black.

Johnson's life in America has something in it of a rags-to-riches tale. He appears to have arrived in Virginia in 1621 and is noted in the early records simply as "Antonio, a Negro." Though the general-muster rolls of 1625 list his occupation as "servant," twenty-five years later he had somehow accumulated a respectable surname and two hundred and fifty acres of land on Virginia's Eastern Shore. Surviving both a fire that damaged their plantation and the protracted legal tiff with Casor, Anthony and his wife, Mary, moved to the Eastern Shore of Maryland in the early 1660s, their contentious slave in tow. In 1666 Johnson leased a lot of three hundred acres, on which the prosperous landowner remained until his death. As for Casor, he stayed on as a "servant," witnessing Mary Johnson's will of 1672 and registering his own livestock brand in the same year, apparently something of a colonial success story himself.

By the early eighteenth century the Johnson family had disappeared from the historical record. But in the hundred and fifty years that followed, many other black slaveowners imitated Johnson's example, and for a variety of reasons. According to 1830 U.S. census records, 3,775 free blacks—living mostly in the South—owned a total of 12,760 slaves. Though the vast majority of these owned no more than a few slaves, some in Louisiana and South Carolina held as many as seventy or eighty. Nor was the South the only region to know black slaveowners. Their presence was recorded in Boston by 1724 and in Connecticut by 1783. As late as 1830 some blacks still owned slaves in Rhode Island, Connecticut, Illinois, New Jersey, and New York, as well as in the border states and the District of Columbia.

The motives that guided black slaveowners were many and complex. Most of them appear to have "owned" slaves for the benevolent purpose of protecting family members from a society that habitually regarded free black people with deep suspicion. But a significant minority did so for the same reasons that motivated white slaveowners: commercial profit and prestige. Slaveowning on the part of this latter group was a strategy for assimilation in a mistrustful and potentially explosive social atmosphere. Not only were black slaveowners sometimes reviled by other blacks, but they were equally feared by the white middle class as potential usurpers. Whatever our stereotype of the American master in the antebellum era, neither the commercial nor the humanitarian black slaveowner easily fits it.

A crucial prerequisite for slaveowning was, of course, freedom. At the time of the 1830 census, nearly one out of eight blacks in the United States was a "free person of color," whether by birthright, manumission, or the purchase of his or her freedom. Whatever their improved legal status, free people of color still experienced many of the same difficulties that slaves did. The laws differed according to period and region, but free blacks of the antebellum era were generally forbidden the right to vote, to bear arms, and to testify against whites in a court of law. They were often denied credit, consigned to segregated churches, prevented from establishing permanent residences, and even denied licenses to sell liquor. They often lived side by side with slaves—on occasion marrying them— and their white neighbors tended to see them as a potentially disruptive force. Most free people of color were poor. They lived, as the historian John Hope Franklin has put it, in a state of "quasi-freedom."

There was often deep mistrust between free

and enslaved black people. Free blacks only rarely expressed open sympathy for slaves. Most tended to guard jealously the few privileges they had secured; generally, the higher they rose, the more advantages they hoped to protect. And though free people of color might embrace racial equality as a worthy ideal, many used their intermediate status to exploit those at the bottom. What's more, such tensions, as the historian Ira Berlin has noted, in *Slaves Without Masters*, "often divided free Negroes from one another as much as it divided them from whites."

In absolute terms the number of slaveowning blacks was always small. In antebellum North Carolina, for example, only about 10 percent of free blacks owned any kind of property at all, let alone slaves. In the America of 1830 more than three hundred thousand people of color were free; of these, about 2 percent were slaveholders. One scholar has estimated that from 1790 to 1860 just one in eighty free blacks was a slaveowner. Blacks who owned slaves were thus a tiny minority within a minority. Of course, white slaveowners were a minority too—though a much larger one—composing about a third of white families in the first half of the nineteenth century. Booker T. Washington, born to slavery in Virginia, revealed in 1905 that he did not even know black slaveowners had existed. Perhaps he did not want to, for black masters, though few, were widespread, their presence, as John Russell wrote in his 1916 history of early Virginia, "so common in the period of the Commonwealth as to pass unnoticed and without criticism by those who consciously recorded events of the times."

It is not unusual to find that people of color who owned slaves did so for humanitarian motives. In the 1830s John Barry Meachum, a St. Louis minister, bought bondsmen and then invited them to purchase their freedom on easy terms. A woman from Charleston, South Carolina, sold a slave in 1828 on the condition that "he is kindly treated and is never sold, he being an unfortunate individual and requiring much attention." In one extraordinary case a Baptist Negro church in Lexington, Kentucky, is said to

have gained a slave preacher by paying for him on the installment plan, passing the Sunday collection plate to pay the deacons of a local white congregation who had purchased him.

Most often black slaveowners were men who had bought their own family members. For instance, Mosby Shepherd, manumitted by the Virginia legislature for giving information concerning the Gabriel insurrection of 1800, bought his own son with the express purpose of later freeing him. Owning blood relatives could be a convenient legal fiction to protect them from the hostility that free blacks attracted. Often it was a way to evade stringent laws requiring newly freed slaves to leave the state within a certain period. Sometimes free blacks married slaves and raised families. If the slave in such a union was owned by a third party and "threatened" with freedom, the spouse could purchase him or her. Some laws even made it easier for blacks to own family members than to manumit them.

Frequently terrible decisions would have to be made, as when children had to be sold off to purchase a spouse. Rose Petepher of New Bern, North Carolina, bought her husband, Richard Gasken, a runaway who had spent several years roaming the woods. They raised several children later hired out as slaves, presumably to keep family finances afloat. Daniel Brown of Norfolk, Virginia, purchased his freedom through hard work and was sold to his wife, Ann, to avoid the law requiring newly manumitted slaves to leave Virginia. When Brown decided he wanted to emigrate to Liberia, his wife balked, not only refusing him permission to go but threatening to sell him. After great effort he persuaded her to manumit him, and he shipped out for Liberia. In 1854 Brown wrote from Monrovia pleading that "Liberia is the place for us and our children, and no where else but here." Later that year Ann finally decided to join him.

Ownership could, of course, add a strange dimension to ordinary family squabbles. Dilsey Pope of Columbus, Georgia, a free woman of color, owned her husband. After they quarreled, she sold him to a white slaveowner; he refused to sell him back once the couple had reconciled.

Carter Woodson, the historian who in the 1920s published the research on black slaveholders in the 1830 census, recalled an acquaintance whose mother had been purchased out of slavery by her husband, himself a former slave. When later she grew enamored of another man—a slave, it turned out—and secretly bestowed upon him her husband's manumission papers, the police, thinking the husband had conspired to give up his papers, arrested him and brought him to trial. To cover his legal expenses, the angry husband sold his wife for five hundred dollars.

Black slaveowners, like white ones, sometimes bid for their charges on the open market. Many, however, did not actively seek to obtain slaves but inherited them from family members or white neighbors. In the latter case the person inherited often appears to have been the product of a secret sexual liaison. Henry Lipscomb, a white slaveowner from Cumberland County, Virginia, willed several slaves—probably his own children—to a black family by the same name, headed by Nancy Lipscomb, a "free woman of color." Another black woman, Priscilla Ivey of Mecklenburg County, Virginia, inherited several slaves from a white man in 1821 and held them for thirty-five years, eventually willing them to her children.

Humanitarian motives didn't always play a part in the black slaveowner's trade. Nat Butler, of Aberdeen, Maryland, obtained slaves by a gambit worthy of Simon Legree. Something of a rarity, Butler specialized in turning high hopes to abject misery. He was known to help runaways, providing them with a hiding place while they waited to escape North. At the same time, posing as a slave catcher, he would offer to resell the runaways to their original owners. If the price offered was too low, Butler would sell the slaves to a third party for a neat profit.

Like their white counterparts, black slaveowners advertised for runaways. Sarah Johnson, a seamstress from Charleston, South Carolina, placed an ad in a local paper in August 1836 to locate a servant of "small stature a little pitted with small pox her front teeth much decayed had on when she went away a striped blue frock. It is suspected that she will try and go into the country. . . . I will pay any reasonable reward." In 1859 Eliza McNellage offered a reward of twenty dollars in the Charleston *Mercury* for a sixteen-year-old named Mary who was "well known in the vicinity of Market and Archdale Streets."

Some owners mingled their more generous instincts with economic self-interest. Samuel Smith of Chesterfield, Virginia, willed his slave family to his daughter-in-law "to hold the above-mentioned slaves during her natural life, and at the death of the above named Betsy Smith, I desire that they shall be free." Smith had earlier used a child as collateral for a loan, stipulating that should he not repay the outstanding debt, his creditor should "expose the said Negro boy for sale." The evidence suggests that the child was Smith's own son.

In 1845 Ricksum Webb, of Caroline County, Maryland, willed to his son a slave named Jerry, to be kept for ten years and then freed. The will provided good incentive for the bondsman to accept his lot. "Should Jerry abscond from service and be taken," the document read, he was "to be sold for life to the highest bidder." Richard Parsons, a farmer and boatman of Campbell County, Virginia, set free his slave children in a will of 1842 but made no such provisions for nine other slaves he considered simply to be property. In a particularly complex case Judith Angus of Petersburg, Virginia, willed her estate to her sons, George, Moses, and Frank. Moses was free at the time; the other two were slaves. The 1832 will stipulated that George was to be freed—unless Moses returned to Petersburg, in which case the former was to be "at his disposal." If George did remain a slave, he was to be hired out, the funds from his labor to be used to buy free the third son, Frank, owned by another party. Among black slaveowners, family hierarchy could have its harsh prerogatives.

The legal complications encountered by families part slave and part free were nothing short of Byzantine, and in many cases Solomon himself would have been hard pressed to mete out justice. A slave named Miles took a slave wife in

North Carolina. He was freed by his master and then purchased his wife, whom he in turn freed. One of their children was born when the mother was a slave, the others when she was free. When the mother died, Miles remarried a free woman of color by whom he had several more children. In 1857 Miles died intestate; the children of both mothers disputed the division of property. The North Carolina Supreme Court reasoned that the children of the first marriage had no claim to the estate since slaves could not make contracts that were legally binding. Thus Miles's original marriage was a "fiction," the children not recognized as legal heirs. He had, in short, failed to legitimize the marriage once he and his wife had become free.

Many black slaveowners lived in cities, where they freely mixed with local slaves and occasionally bought and sold them. Urban slaveowners engaged in a variety of occupations: they were barbers, livery stable men, blacksmiths, mechanics, grocers, even prostitutes. In South Carolina and Louisiana a powerful mulatto caste developed in the large cities, comprising lighter-skinned people of color who separated themselves at all costs from the lowly slaves who worked the plantations. The slaveowners among them amassed considerable commercial power, often parlaying it into greater social acceptance and educational advancement.

Like slaves, most free blacks were illiterate. But along the lower Mississippi some obtained more than a rudimentary education and left letters and diaries that offer fascinating glimpses into the lives of antebellum black slaveowners. Among these was William Johnson, a slave turned free man of color in Natchez, Mississippi. Granted his freedom in 1830, Johnson set up business in Natchez as a barber and moneylender until he purchased a nearby farm. At the time of his death in 1851 he owned fifteen slaves, with an eye to turning a profit. And yet, his diary indicates, some of them evoked in him a turbulent mixture of emotions. "To day has been to me a very Sad Day," he wrote on December 31, 1843. "Many tears were in my Eyes to day On acct. of my Selling poor Steven. I

went under the hill this Evening to See him of[f] but the Boat did not Cross over again and Steven got drunk in a few minutes and I took him Home & made him Sleep in the garret and Kept him Safe." Johnson, who had bought Steven in 1832 for $455, had just sold him for $600. The next day the former slave still grappled with his conscience: "I felt hurt but Liquor is the Cause of his troubles; I would not have parted with Him if he had Only have Let Liquor alone but he Cannot do it I believe."

As a black slaveholder Johnson was caught in a tangle of ironies. His diaries reveal the rancor he felt toward the arrogant white slaveowners of his area, though he was cautious to keep his resentment under wraps. While he expressed considerable compassion for his slaves, the only one who ever escaped from him was helped to freedom by a man he called "a white scoundrel." Johnson was murdered in 1851, apparently by a mulatto whose race the courts had difficulty ascertaining. Baylor Winn—who claimed Indian and white ancestry—was never found guilty of murdering Johnson because it could not be proved that Winn was a "Negro." Mississippi law forbade the testimony of black witnesses against white people, and as the only witnesses for the prosecution were people of color, Winn was never convicted.

Andrew Durnford, a free man of color in nearby Louisiana, was a sugar planter who owned seventy-seven slaves at his death in 1859. In his correspondence Durnford describes his 1835 visit to a slave auction in Richmond, Virginia. "I went to see a family of four children, father & mother for 1800$ of yellow complexion," he wrote to a Louisiana friend. "I acted and played the indifferent saying they were too high. An other family of a father & mother with two children for 1200$. I was requested to make an offer, butt would nott do it as I find that some of the farmers . . . don't like to sell to Negro traders butt will, to anybody that buys for their own use."

In fact, Durnford *was* buying for his own use on the sugar plantation he called St. Rosalie, thirty miles south of New Orleans. A man of business, he lamented the high cost of slaves, complaining that Alabamians had bid too high and driven up the market price. "I could have bought some cheaper but, they are what I call rotten people." After buying twenty-five slaves, he encountered some difficulty getting them home. "I wrote in Baltimore to get a passage on board of the brig Harriet cleared for New Orleans, but the captain would not agree to take Blacks."

Durnford's correspondence is richly revealing of the complicated lives led by antebellum mulatto planters. His letters from Richmond are addressed to John McDonogh of New Orleans, a white friend and creditor who later served as a vice president to the American Colonization Society, which resettled freed slaves in Liberia. McDonogh, an unusual master by any standards, sent eighty-five of his slaves to this African republic and later provided in his will for the manumission of many others. Durnford was not so sanguine about the prospects of manumission, though he did free four slaves during his life. "Self interest is too strongly rooted in the bosom of all that breathes the American atmosphere," he wrote in 1843. "Self interest is al la mode." Paternalism and cruelty went hand in hand at Durnford's plantation. "Jackson has just left here," he wrote of a runaway in 1836. "I ordered five rounds to be given him yesterday for cutting my cane and corn. He is a wicked fellow. Was he not a relic I would gett clear of him."

As the Civil War approached, more restrictions were imposed on black slaveowners, and the abolitionist press made white Southerners warier still of this unusual group in their midst. As Northern cries for manumission grew stronger, certain states denied free blacks property rights. In 1860 the North Carolina legislature formally forbade blacks to "buy, purchase, or hire for any length of time any slave or slaves, or to have any slave or slaves bound as apprentice or apprentices."

As public opinion turned against free blacks, William Ellison, Jr., a free mulatto whose father owned dozens of slaves, attempted to leave South Carolina in 1860. The agents for a Philadelphia steamer refused Ellison and his children passage, claiming that if they turned out to be escaped slaves, anyone found guilty of helping them leave the South could be executed. They suggested instead that Ellison declare his children slaves—though they were not—and put them in the charge of a white passenger. Sensing danger, he obtained passage for them on another ship by using his influence and financial resources. Clearly even the wealthy mulatto caste had come to feel threatened by the eve of the Civil War.

Elsewhere in the Deep South the landowning mulatto caste was anxious to prove its loyalty to the cause. Several black slaveowners in the Delta region wrote jointly to the New Orleans *Daily Delta* in December 1860 that "the free colored population (native) of Louisiana . . . own slaves, and they are dearly attached to their native land . . . and they are ready to shed their blood for her defence. They have no sympathy for abolitionism; no love for the North, but they have plenty for Louisiana." Thus the Emancipation Proclamation of 1863 struck as much of a blow to commercial black slaveowners—like the descendants of William Johnson and Andrew Durnford—as it did to their white counterparts. And where owners were compensated for their losses, even those with benevolent motives profited, providing a windfall for people who had been protecting family members. In the District of Columbia, for example, where slavery was abolished in 1862 in advance of the Proclamation, Robert Gunnell received three hundred dollars each for his wife, children, and grandchildren, eighteen people in all.

That black people could have owned slaves at all is a strange irony of American history, one that has led to all manner of theorizing, much of it untenable. It would be a mistake, for example, to think that black slaveholders turned the entire institution of slavery on its head, for even the most powerful black planters could own only people of color, not whites. Though whites were commonly employed as indentured servants in the colonial era, they were never held as slaves as the term is normally used. It is true that free people of color sometimes hired white laborers for temporary work. "I send Noel up to let you know that I will do without dutch people this year," wrote Andrew Durnford to John Mc-

Donogh. But as a Virginia statute from 1670 proclaims: "No negro or Indian though baptized and enjoyed their own freedome shall be capable of any purchase of Christians but yet not debarred from buying any of their owne nation." The existence of the statute seems to suggest that holding white "slaves"—or servants—was conceivable for a black only in the early years of colonial Virginia. Such a practice, had it endured, would have undermined the entire social foundation of slavery, resting as it did on the oppression of people of color.

Over the years a number of unconvincing apologies have been offered on behalf of the black slaveholder. The historian Luther Porter Jackson has argued that the 1830 census figures for black slaveowners were inflated, since some of those who appear on the rolls were people of color who had *hired* slaves, not purchased them. Even so, it's difficult to claim that people who "hired" others from their owners were not profiting participants in the peculiar institution. It has rightly been noted that many black slaveholders were, at least in their intentions, benevolent, but it's also clear that not all slaves owned by family members—ostensibly sympathetic masters—were treated with much compassion. Benevolent slaveowning in the Northern states is even more difficult to rationalize, since the act of manumission there was less fraught with legal difficulties. Examined in all its variety, the story of black slaveowners gives powerful evidence that slavery was just as complex an institution for them—as they grappled with economic forces and social realities—as it was for whites.

Anthony Johnson and his spiritual descendants remind us that however much we may generalize, the experience of individuals ranges from the heights of human compassion to the depths of profound greed—and all variations therein. As Andrew Durnford wrote in his will, "I also hereby emancipate and order to be emancipated, the boy of my servant Wainy born the 2d of January 1857 and when the Said boy shall be ten years old I hereby give him two thousand dollars to contribute to give Said boy a good education." The boy, it turns out, wasn't just anyone: He was Durnford's son by a slave mistress. Even after death Durnford was looking out for his own. As the planter himself had once put it in a letter to McDonogh, "self interest is al la mode."

The Complete History of

A "Positive Good"

Chapter 8

Introduction

It may seem incomprehensible to us today, but in the mid–nineteenth century almost all slave owners, as well as the majority of southern whites, firmly believed that slavery was a "positive good." The phrase "positive good" was apparently coined by South Carolina's formidable senator John C. Calhoun in 1837, and its appearance marked an important turning point in the nation's contentious debate over slavery.

Intending his defense of slavery as part of his larger strategy of promoting his section's interests, Calhoun was both swimming with the tide and helping to direct it. In 1831 Nat Turner had shown how dangerous a slave rebellion could be, and that same year the Yankee abolitionist William Lloyd Garrison had begun denouncing slavery as a national sin. Economically, the rise of "King Cotton" filled white southerners with self-confident pride. Calhoun's 1837 Senate speech set the tone of the South's defiant response to changing times. (The immediate occasion of his speech was a controversy over whether Congress should refuse even to read abolitionists' antislavery petitions. With the aid of northern Democrats who were indifferent to slavery, Calhoun and his fellow southern lawmakers won the argument, enacting the so-called gag rule.)

Led by the grim, rigid ideologue Calhoun ("that cast-iron man," a visiting Englishwoman called him), southern whites from the 1830s to 1860 told the world that they were proud to be slave owners. Slavery, they insisted, was not only in the South's and the nation's best interests; it was even beneficial to blacks, who otherwise would be mired in Africa's hopeless backwardness. (Blacks, of course, were not asked their opinion.)

Southern clergy joined the chorus. In the decades before the Civil War, the Baptists, Methodists, and Presbyterians all split into northern and southern organizations, with slavery as the main issue separating them. With very few exceptions, southern ministers found it prudent to tell their white parishioners that slavery, far from being sinful, was God's will, and the means by which "heathen" Africans were to be saved. (Clergy who disagreed did not remain in the South.) The Bible was ransacked for evidence that would sanction slavery, and many favorable references indeed were found.

The more acceptance that the doctrine of "positive good" gained among southern whites, the less chance there was that the South would ever agree to abolish slavery voluntarily. Although very few northern whites agreed with the abolitionists that slavery should be ended whether the South consented or not, few northerners wanted to see slavery expand either. The stage was being set for a dangerous sectional conflict, and slavery was at the root of it all.

It is important to realize that the southern defenders of slavery were not speaking only to the owners of slaves. After the Virginia state legislature debated whether to abolish slavery in 1831–1832, the southern white mind closed on the subject. Both public opinion and southern state laws did everything possible to stifle discussion of whether slavery might be wrong. Antislavery publications were barred from the mails. Non-slaveholding whites were constantly reminded of the economic benefits of slave ownership, and were told that the only way to ensure that blacks were kept "in their place" was by enslaving them. Although whites who owned no slaves often felt resentment against the wealthy planters who dominated southern society and politics, their resentment rarely took the form of wishing that slavery could be done away with. Non-slaveholding whites, particularly if they were young men, generally looked forward to the day when they could afford to invest in slaves.

Overt white racism, latent white fear of black violence, white pride in being free citizens with equal rights, and white dreams of personal prosperity all combined to produce a fierce southern determination to preserve the South as a slave society. We cannot understand either American slavery or the political crisis that led to the Civil War without appreciating the strength of white solidarity in the Old South.

Selection 1

Slavery Is a "Positive Good"

John C. Calhoun

The slave South and its "peculiar institution" had no stronger defender in American public life than South Carolina's influential senator John C. Calhoun (1782–1850). Originally an American nationalist, Calhoun became the primary advocate of the South's sectional interests in the late 1820s. His political shift coincided with his state's economic decline, as South Carolina began losing population and capital to the more fertile slave states farther west, such as Alabama and Mississippi. South Carolina was adversely affected by the tariffs on foreign imports that the industrializing North favored: Such tariffs drove up the price of foreign manufactured goods that South Carolinians had to buy, while America's trading partners, especially Great Britain, retaliated by rais-

ing the duty on South Carolina's rice exports. Finally, the state's black majority population kept its white population particularly on edge over the danger of a slave uprising. Intensely aware of all this, Calhoun embraced ever more extreme political positions. In 1828, about to become Andrew Jackson's vice president, he anonymously published a pamphlet asserting that the South Carolina state legislature had the right to nullify (that is, make inapplicable within its borders) any federal law that it felt threatened the state's vital interests—such as a tariff or any measure interfering with slavery. When South Carolina was forced by Jackson to back down from pursuing such a policy in the so-called Nullification Crisis of 1832–1833, Calhoun's chances of winning the presidency were dashed. From this point until his death in 1850, Calhoun was the South's most outspoken defender in Congress. Always insisting that he wanted to maintain the Union, he warned that a means must be found to give

Excerpted from John C. Calhoun, "Speech on the Reception of Abolition Petitions," delivered to the U.S. Senate, February 6, 1837.

the South veto power over hostile actions by the non-slaveholding majority—otherwise his state's only defense would be secession.

By the necessary course of events, if left to themselves, we must become, finally, two people. It is impossible under the deadly hatred which must spring up between the two great sections, if the present causes are permitted to operate unchecked, that we should continue under the same political system. The conflicting elements would burst the Union asunder, powerful as are the links which hold it together. Abolition and the Union cannot co-exist. As the friend of the Union I openly proclaim it,—and the sooner it is known the better. The former may now be controlled, but in a short time it will be beyond the power of man to arrest the course of events. We of the South will not, cannot surrender our institutions. To maintain the existing relations between the two races, inhabiting that section of the Union, is indispensable to the peace and happiness of both. It cannot be subverted without drenching the country in blood, and extirpating one or the other of the races. Be it good or bad, it has grown up with our society and institutions, and is so interwoven with them, that to destroy it would be to destroy us as a people. But let me not be understood as admitting, even by implication, that the existing relations between the two races in the slaveholding States is an evil:—far otherwise; I hold it to be a good, as it has thus far proved itself to be to both, and will continue to prove so if not disturbed by the fell spirit of abolition. I appeal to facts. Never before has the black race of Central Africa, from the dawn of history to the present day, attained a condition so civilized and so improved, not only physically, but morally and intellectually. It came among us in a low, degraded, and savage condition, and in the course of a few generations it has grown up under the fostering care of our institutions, reviled as they have been, to its present comparatively civilized condition. This, with the rapid increase of numbers, is conclusive proof of the general happiness of the race, in spite of all the exaggerated tales to the contrary. . . .

In one thing only are we [southern whites] inferior—the arts of gain; we acknowledge that we are less wealthy than the Northern section of this Union, but I trace this mainly to the fiscal action of this Government, which has extracted much from, and spent little among us. Had it been the reverse,—if the exaction had been from the other section, and the expenditure with us, this point of superiority would not be against us now, as it was not at the formation of this Government.

But I take higher ground. I hold that in the present state of civilization, where two races of different origin, and distinguished by color, and other physical differences, as well as intellectual, are brought together, the relation now existing in the slaveholding States between the two, is, instead of an evil, a good—a positive good. I feel myself called upon to speak freely upon the subject where the honor and interests of those I represent are involved. I hold then, that there never has yet existed a wealthy and civilized society in which one portion of the community did not, in point of fact, live on the labor of the other. Broad and general as is this assertion, it is fully borne out by history. This is not the proper occasion, but if it were, it would not be difficult to trace the various devices by which the wealth of all civilized communities has been so unequally divided, and to show by what means so small a share has been allotted to those by whose labor it was produced, and so large a share given to the non-producing classes. The devices are almost innumerable, from the brute force and gross superstition of ancient times, to the subtle and artful fiscal contrivances of modern. I might well challenge a comparison between them and the more direct, simple, and patriarchal mode by which the labor of the African race is, among us, commanded by the European. I may say with truth, that in few countries so much is left to the share of the laborer, and so little exacted from him, or where there is more kind attention paid to him in sickness or infirmities of age. Compare his condition with the tenants of the poor houses in the more civilized portions of Europe—look at the sick, and the old and infirm slave, on one hand, in the midst of his family and friends, under the kind superintending care of his master and mistress, and compare it with the forlorn and wretched condition of the pauper in the poor house. But I will not dwell on this aspect of the question; I turn to the political; and here I fearlessly assert that the existing relation between the two races in the South, against which these blind fanatics are waging war, forms the most solid and durable foundation on which to rear free and stable political institutions. It is useless to disguise the fact. There is and always has been in an advanced stage of wealth and civilization, a conflict between labor and capital. The condition of society in the South exempts us from the disorders and dangers resulting from this conflict; and which explains why it is that the political condition of the slaveholding States has been so much more stable and quiet than that of the North. The advantages of the former, in this respect, will become more and more manifest if left undisturbed by interference from without, as the country advances in wealth and numbers. We have, in fact, but just entered that condition of society where the strength and durability of our political institutions are to be tested; and I venture nothing in predicting that the experience of the next generation will fully test how vastly more favorable our condition of society is to that of other sections for free and stable institutions, provided we are not disturbed by the interference of others, or shall have sufficient intelligence and spirit to resist promptly and successfully such interference. It rests with ourselves to meet and repel them. I look not for aid to this Government, or to the other States; not but there are kind feelings towards us on the part of the great body of the non-slaveholding States; but as kind as their feelings may be, we may rest assured that no political party in these States will risk their ascendency for our safety. If we do not defend ourselves none will defend us; if we yield we will be more and more pressed as we recede; and if we submit we will be trampled under foot. Be assured that emancipation itself would not satisfy these fanatics:—that gained, the next step would be to raise the negroes to a social and political equality with the whites; and that being effected, we would soon find the present condition of the two races reversed. They and their northern allies would be the masters, and we the slaves; the condition of the white race in the British West India Islands, bad as it is, would be happiness to ours.

Selection 2

Proslavery Arguments

Larry E. Tise

Excerpted from Larry E. Tise, *Proslavery: A History of the Defense of Slavery in America, 1701–1840.* Copyright © 1987 The University of Georgia Press. Reprinted with permission from The University of Georgia Press.

Although most of slavery's defenders before the Civil War were southerners, some were northern whites, particularly those with an economic interest in the South's cotton exports.

In his book Proslavery: A History of the

Defense of Slavery in America, 1701–1840, *excerpted here, historian Larry E. Tise studied the range of proslavery arguments in the United States.*

*a*mong the possible definitions of slavery that a proslavery writer might select, three were most common in all six groups. Three-fourths of the defenses portrayed slavery either as a state in which man is governed without his consent, as the "slavery principle" implied by all government (for government to exist there must be some restraint placed on citizens), or as a status in society with corresponding rights and duties. Only a few writers (mainly West Indians) opted for the harsher choice of slavery as the absolute control of the master over a slave. . . . Among the three major definitions there was an even distribution among all groups, except for northern proslavery men living in the South who revealed a nearly unanimous preference for the slavery principle of

government. Nevertheless, in general, the majority of writers in all groups preferred definitions devoid of a moral content that placed the guilt for slavery upon society or civilization. Yet, a large number selected the morally laden classical definition of a state in which man is governed without his consent.

When the authors of these defenses attempted to account for the origin of slavery, one-third revealed a desire to place the brunt of responsibility on society. They believed that slavery resulted naturally from the need of man to organize functioning societies. Two considerably less popular causes for slavery were God's curse on Ham and the inequality of men. While a third of the southern writers held that slavery resulted from inequality, numerous writers in each of the remaining six groups argued similarly. . . .

The overwhelming majority of proslavery writers believed that slavery either should or would be a perpetual institution. More than half of them argued either that circumstances re-

Proponents of slavery maintained that the institution was an inevitable result of the need to form a functioning society, and it was the nature of this society to perpetuate slavery in one form or another.

quired an endless perpetuation or that the nature of society demanded the presence of slavery in some form. About one-third (most of them in the North or South after 1831) felt that slavery might some day be ended either at the will of masters, by the preparation of slaves for freedom, or through the removal of the Negro from American society. As in the case of other proslavery comments on the institution, at least a few representatives of each group supported these contentions. Since all groups shared a common heritage, however, it is not surprising that their general notions on slavery should be similar.

The Negro

Of the five categories of argument relating to the Negro and to the question of race, a significant number of proslavery writers chose to apply arguments from only two. Under the heading of Negro physiology only twenty-four of the ninety-one writers mentioned that blackness was a physiological mark of inferiority, that resistance to heat prepared the Negro for burdensome work in the tropics, or that immunity to certain diseases indicated a natural inclination for tropical toil. Similarly, only half of them appealed to ethnological arguments on racial unity or diversity. Thirty-five writers, evenly distributed among all six groups, argued that the Negro was an inferior species of man; but only one writer followed the American School of Ethnology, which became popular in the 1850s, in contending that the Negro was a separate species. The fact that only fourteen used arguments for racial unity (all except one were dated in the 1840s or 1850s) indicates that detailed questions about race did not become important until after the appearance of what most proslavery thinkers called an unbiblical doctrine of racial diversity.

However, about two-thirds of the writers used extensively two categories of arguments on the Negro. They related to the Negro past in Africa and the Negro character. . . .

A similar nonracist pattern appears in the distribution of arguments on the Negro character. . . . Except for British and West Indian writers one-third to one-half of the writers in each group made no mention of Negro character in their defenses. Once again West Indian proslavery authors showed a greater tendency to apply racist arguments, particularly in their demand for strict regimentation of Negroes. In striking contrast, all American writers after 1831 attested to the ability of the Negro to enjoy some improvement, even though they did not think he could become the white man's equal. Of all the groups, early American writers mentioned the Negro character less frequently (in part because the available defenses from that period are much briefer). Nevertheless, none of the other groups held a monopoly on the use of racist argumentation.

Slave Society

Whereas little measurable variation can be detected among the various groups in their application of racist arguments to defend slavery, the distribution of arguments on slave society reflects definite tendencies. Under the heading of social classes all groups stressed the fact that slave society provided the only sure protection of property against the propertyless in the presence of an alien race. All American writers after 1831 contended that slave society is perfectly ordered with each class fulfilling a role or function. But only southerners and northern writers living in the South went on to argue that slave society produces the truest republicanism and liberty for all citizens and that it creates the wisest and best rulers. Furthermore, only in the South (including transplanted northerners) did they make the case that slave society fosters equality and a common interest among nonslaves. But, in view of the nature of these latter arguments, it is possible that their popularity in the South indicated more about southern nationalism than any unique propensity in the defense of slavery. . . .

A similar pattern emerges in the distribution of arguments comparing slave and free society. All proslavery writers after about 1800 turned to comparative political economy to bolster their defenses of slavery. . . . Extending their views on capital and labor, they depicted slave society as a self-contained unit able to handle reforms, deal with social ills, and protect its poorest members. In contrast to arguments on the status and value of slave labor, northern writers shared with southern writers organismic views of slave society for they, too, were intimately involved in stamping out abolitionism as a troublesome reform movement. . . .

American Slavery

Even though proslavery writers generally agreed on the nature of slave society, when they came to consider the nature of American slavery, significant variations in their arguments began to appear. Those most intimately involved in slavery were the most vocal in accusing others for introducing slavery to America. All writers believed that colonists in America or the West Indies had little choice in the form of labor adopted. But earlier writers frequently blamed slavery's origin on Africans who fought intertribal wars to enslave other Africans and who sold their captives to slave traders. Yet southerners and northern writers living in the South were quick to point their fingers at British imperial policy or the greed of New England and British merchants. Southern-based proslavery writers also examined colonists' attempts to abolish the slave trade, declaring that the continued practice even after those protests made emancipation impossible. The tendency of southern writers to score Britain and New England rather than Africans indicated the pleasure southerners took in highlighting the moral inconsistencies of the North.

Even greater variation appeared in assessments of the character of American and West Indian slavery. All proslavery writers . . . believed the system of slavery they defended to be the mildest in history. Whereas only West Indians argued that slavery was an appropriate practice in a mercantile system, almost all later defenders characterized slavery as a missionary institution. However, certain other arguments became popular primarily in North America and the Old South. The southern argument that slavery was a divine trust complemented the view that slavery was a missionary institution, while the belief that slavery was an essential ingredient in the

American experiment proceeded from the teachings of political economy that the South provided the lion's share of governmental capital through the massive exportation of cotton.

The universal contention among American proslavery writers and some West Indians that American slavery was the same as that practiced in the Bible testifies to the nature of the slavery debate in its last phases in both Britain and America. Ignoring the teachings of political economy, abolitionists charged that slavery was an immoral, unchristian institution. In response to this attack, proslavery writers turned increasingly from arguments of political economy popular in the 1820s to concepts related to morality and religion. Hence, they characterized slavery as a missionary institution, a divine trust, and a practice encouraged by Scripture. From the perspective of moral science no argument was more important for the proslavery case than proving the biblical authorization for American slavery.

In terms of the history of American slavery, nearly half of the writers in all groups argued that slavery and slave society reached the greatest degree of perfection in America (or the West Indies). They also declared that considerations of public policy and benevolence required the continuation of slavery for the foreseeable future. American writers more than West Indians believed that slavery would come to an end only when the Negro was returned to Africa. Yet, as the Civil War approached, southern-based writers frequently stated that either the United States or the South had a mission to maintain perfected republicanism through the perpetuation of slavery. As in the case of the West Indies, when the crisis grew in intensity, the possible alternatives diminished in number and appeal until proslavery writers could speak only in terms of perpetual slave society.

Slavery in American Government

Although there was some variation in the application of arguments on the abstract nature of American slavery, when proslavery writers discussed the legal and constitutional problems relating to slavery they spoke with one voice (except colonial writers and West Indians who lived in different legal settings). Following the American Revolution, proslavery writers everywhere and at all times argued that bills of rights and the dogma of equalitarianism applied only abstractly to man in nature. They held that slaves, a species of property, were protected by statute and the Constitution, and that they could not be taken away without the destruction of law and order. These writers also agreed that slaves were chattel protected by the law of property, but subject to laws on persons for their conduct. States could reform circumstantial evils connected with the practice of slavery, but neither the state nor the federal government could remove the institution.

Most proslavery advocates went even further in their legal justifications. In a republican government, they said, slavery was necessary to protect the rights of freemen. In fact, slavery ensured American republicanism by protecting property, fostering equality, and guaranteeing liberty to nonslaves. Therefore, not only did the Constitution permit the continuation of slavery, but it also permitted restrictions on the rights of free Negroes and required the return of fugitive slaves to their masters. Since slavery was demonstrably an essential feature of American republicanism, many proslavery writers argued that no amendment could be added to the Constitution that altered the nature of government or the character of society by abolishing slavery. While proslavery writers did not generally discuss the constitutional question in detail, whenever and wherever they did, they were agreed on these points. Southern-based writers stressed them more often and with greater vehemence. But they were not alone in their contentions.

The Morality of Slavery

Following the rise of abolitionism in the 1830s, the debate focused primarily on the morality of slavery. Despite their previous research into political economy and their desire to sell slavery on the grounds of policy and economy, proslavery writers in antebellum America were forced to confront the morality of their institution. But this shift in focus did not lead to the creation of new arguments. It merely meant that, for the first time since the debate on slavery began in the eighteenth century, every writer who favored its perpetuation found it necessary to discuss the manner in which slavery could be viewed as a moral (at least not immoral) institution.

Scripture proved the most important source for establishing the morality of slavery. Arguments based on Scripture had been an integral feature of proslavery literature in early America, the West Indies, and the United States before 1831. . . . It only became more significant after 1831. In their use of Scripture to defend slavery, proslavery writers could follow one of several courses. The most positive and racist approach looked upon the curse on Ham as a divine decree that set the Negro race apart as an inferior and servile people. The second most positive approach discovered a divine sanction for slavery (irrespective of the enslaved people) in the Old Testament, a negative approval in the Gospels, and the sanction of the Apostles in the Epistles. And the third least positive approach found no condemnation of slavery in Scripture. These three approaches were represented about equally among all groups. The bulk of writers selected the median position.

From the time of the American Revolution the words *reason, humanity,* and *nature* appeared frequently in proslavery literature and became epistemological tools in religion and philosophy. They also developed into authorities for morality. Although few proslavery writers dwelt on them extensively, almost all at some point affirmed the compatibility of slavery with reason, nature, and humanity. . . . No group (except perhaps northern writers) stressed the reasonableness and humanity of slavery over any other argument. And in this case, unlike that of Scripture, West Indians were in agreement.

A similar pattern emerged in the use of religious tradition as an authority for the morality of slavery. Whether or not they entered into a detailed examination of the role of slavery in church history, both West Indian and American writers appealed to classical and traditional Christian justifications. Another much older belief accepted by Christians from ancient times centered on the right of the faithful to enslave heathen peoples. Based on tradition, the argument was sometimes used in the nineteenth century to justify the enslavement of heathen Africans. Although few applied it, the argument remained current among all groups (except early American) to some extent.

Proslavery writers also appealed to theology to substantiate the morality of slavery. American writers, in particular, drew upon theological affirmations. . . . Christian theologians believed that certain institutions—family, government, and the church—had been ordained by God as permanent features of society. In the process of developing images of the slave society, proslavery writers in America often included the relation of master and slave. Many saw slavery as a part of God's historic scheme for bringing all men to salvation and argued negatively that if slavery were indeed evil God would not have given it sanction in Scripture. American writers were more likely to attempt to justify slavery theologically, but among the various groups of American proslavery thinkers there was little variation.

Moral science developed as a branch of theology and philosophy in the United States during the first half of the nineteenth century. Hence, it was not surprising that Christian proslavery writers should apply the procedures and insights of their ethical thinking to slavery. They unanimously chanted that reason and conscience were inadequate rules for morality and that Scripture or revelation embodied the only plenary rule for man. After investigating their basic authority, American proslavery writers concluded that the slave was an individual with the rights of a human being according to his station in life. But he was by no means entitled to some abstract and unscriptural natural rights. More than half of all proslavery writers after 1800 in the United States easily armed this position.

Another source of proslavery argumentation integrally related to the problem of the morality of slavery revolved around the proper place of the church in slave society. Particularly in America where clergymen played a major role in the day-to-day combat over slavery, debates on the functions and powers of the church in dealing with social problems sometimes overshadowed the central question of the morality of slavery. American proslavery writers after 1831 universally placed strictures on the powers of the church to deal with slavery. Moreover, they spoke with a single voice in affirming that the church's function was to perfect not to challenge slave society. While these arguments did not directly justify slavery as a moral practice, they did codify the perpetuation of slavery. And what is more, the unanimity of proslavery writers on this point suggests that proslavery writers, wherever they were located in antebellum America, may have shared other convictions on societal arrangements as they impinged upon the overarching issue of slavery.

Master and Slave

Proslavery writers generally articulated the duty of masters to treat slaves justly, and they frequently urged more particularized obligations relating to the slave's comfort and religious instruction. . . . More than for early writers and West Indians, religious duties were important to American writers. In terms of reforming slavery, they tended to stress the need to foster and protect marriage and family structures among slaves. Despite the fact that slave codes did not recognize slave marriages and families, after 1831 proslavery writers increasingly called upon masters to institute unwritten laws of their own. Some of them even petitioned legislatures to enact laws barring the separation of slave families.

If they enforced the duties of masters, proslavery writers (at least in America) also expounded the obligations of slaves. More than British and West Indian proslavery thinkers, American writers discussed the social and religious foundations for servile obedience always in the context of their larger defense of slavery. While it is not strange that they should be willing and able to argue the case of slave obedience, it is remarkable that proslavery writers not connected in any way with slavery as an institution should have included such discussions in their defenses. That they did is suggestive of the socially holistic and prescriptive nature of proslavery writings wherever they appeared in America. Far from being mere racist defenses of slavery, proslavery writings generally exhibited an inclusive system of social thought.

It can be concluded that proslavery argumentation (the basic arguments and their formulations) remains relatively constant over time and place. Wherever and whenever one encounters a defense of slavery (assuming that it is more than an isolated thrust), the arguments adduced will conform with those of proslavery literature in other slave societies and with those in the same society at other periods of time. Although there will be variations in the selection of arguments and in the number and scope of defenses, the species of argumentation will remain largely unchanged. Depending upon the circumstances and the nature of attacks upon slavery, particular types of arguments may be more frequently employed (such as racist arguments in the West Indies and comparative economy in the United States in the 1820s). But on the whole, all types of argumentation are available and will be applied at least to some extent wherever proslavery literature appears. Consequently when one attempts to understand and assess the history of proslavery thought, argumentation is not and cannot be used as sole index of change.

If argumentation remains essentially constant over time and locality, such demonstrably synthetic delimiters as the positive good argument or political economy are false indices of variations. Similarly, because of the universality of arguments on Negro racial inferiority in both slave and free, American and European societies, any analysis that deals exclusively or even primarily with racist argumentation in proslavery literature and thought will reveal neither the crucial changes in nor the unique character of proslavery in a particular society. Hence, in examining racist arguments in proslavery literature, one will learn more about alterations in theories of race than about the nature of proslavery. This is not to say that proslavery literature is not a repository and thereby an appropriate body of source material for the study of race and racism. But it is to say that racist argumentation that seeks to demonstrate that the Negro was an appropriate subject for enslavement was a constant in proslavery literature.

Selection 3

The Biblical Justification of Slavery

Thornton Stringfellow

North and South, the United States in the nineteenth century was a deeply religious, Bible-reading nation. Firmly believing that

God was directing the nation's destiny, Americans felt a strong need for religious guidance on every important issue in private or public life, and a religious justification for every action and every institution. Slavery was no exception. Abolitionists assailed slavery as sin, but slavery's defenders sought biblical evidence that God not only allowed the institution but even favored it. Besides the familiar message to slaves that they should humbly obey their masters, southern pulpits also resounded with staunch defenses of slavery as an institution that God had permitted in the Old Testament. Many a tract likewise rolled off southern presses proving that "the peculiar institution" was divinely blessed. This excerpt from an 1856 book by a Virginia Baptist minister named Thornton Stringfellow is an example of how southern clergy found biblical proof of slavery's legitimacy. It is also a testimony to how far southern white Baptist clergy had moved from the sharp criticism of slavery that their predecessors had advanced in the late eighteenth century.

*T*he first recorded language which was ever uttered in relation to slavery, is the inspired language of Noah. In God's stead he says, "Cursed be Canaan;" "a servant of servants shall he be to his brethren." "Blessed be the Lord God of Shem; and Canaan shall be his servant." "God shall enlarge Japheth, and he shall dwell in the tents of Shem; and Canaan shall be his servant."—Gen. ix: 25, 26, 27. Here, language is used, showing the *favor* which God would exercise to the posterity of Shem and Japheth, while they were holding the posterity of Ham in a state of *abject bondage.* May it not be said in truth, that God decreed this institution before it existed; and has he not connected its *existence* with prophetic tokens of special favor, to those who should be slave owners or masters? . . .

But, says the spirit of abolition, with which the Bible has to contend, you are building your house upon the sand, for these were nothing but hired servants; and their servitude designates no such state, condition, or relation, as that, in which one person is made the property of another, to be bought, sold, or transferred forever. To this, we have two answers in reference to the subject, *before giving the law.* In the first place, the term servant, in the schedules of property among the patriarchs, *does designate* the state, condition, or relation in which one person is the legal property of another, as in Gen. xxiv: 35, 36. Here Abraham's servant, who had been sent by his master to get a wife for his son Isaac, in order to prevail with the woman and her family, states, that the man for whom he sought a bride, was the son of a man whom God had greatly blessed with riches; which he goes on to enumerate thus, in the 35th verse: "He hath given him flocks, and herds, and silver, and gold, and men-servants, and maid-servants, and camels, and asses;" then in verse 36th, he states the disposition his master had made of his estate: "My master's wife bare a son to my master when she was old, and unto him he hath given all that he hath." Here, servants are enumerated with silver and gold as part of the patrimony. And, reader, bear it in mind; as if to rebuke the doctrine of abolition, servants are not only inventoried as property, but as property which *God had given to Abraham.* After the death of Abraham, we have a view of Isaac at Gerar, when he had come into the possession of this estate; and this is the description given of him: "And the man waxed great, and went forward, and grew until he became very great; for he had possession of flocks, and possession of herds, and *great store of servants.*"—Gen. xxvi: 13, 14. This state in which servants are made chattels, he received as an inheritance from his father, and passed to his son Jacob. . . .

For the fifteen hundred years, during which these laws [of Moses] were in force, God raised up a succession of prophets to reprove that people [the ancient Jews] for the various sins into which they fell; yet there is not a reproof uttered against the institution of *involuntary slavery,* for any species of abuse that ever grew out of it. A severe judgment is pronounced by Jeremiah, (chapter xxxiv: see from the 8th to the 22d

Excerpted from Thornton Stringfellow, *Scriptural and Statistical Views in Favor of Slavery* (Richmond, VA: Randolph, 1856).

verse,) for an abuse or violation of the law, concerning the *voluntary* servitude of Hebrews; but the prophet pens it with caution, as if to show that it had no reference to any abuse that had taken place under the system of *involuntary slavery*, which existed by law among that people; the sin consisted in making hereditary bond-men and bond-women of Hebrews, which was positively forbidden by the law, and not for buying and holding one of another nation in hereditary bondage, which was as positively allowed by the law. And really, in view of what is passing in our country, and elsewhere, among men who profess to reverence the Bible, it would seem that these must be dreams of a distempered brain, and not the solemn truths of that sacred book.

Well, I will now proceed to make them good to the letter, see Levit. xxv: 44, 45, 46; "Thy bond-men and thy bond-maids which thou shalt have, shall be of the heathen that are round about you; of them shall ye buy bond-men and bond-maids. Moreover, of the children of the strangers that do sojourn among you, of them shall ye buy, and of their families that are with you, which they begat in your land. And they shall be your possession. And ye shall take them as an inheritance for your children after you, to inherit them for a possession they shall be your bond-men forever." I ask any candid man, if the words of this institution could be more explicit? It is from God himself; it authorizes that people, to whom he had become *king and law-giver,* to purchase men and women as property; to hold them and their posterity in bondage; and to will them to their children as a possession forever; and more, it allows *foreign slaveholders to settle and live among them; to breed slaves and sell them.* Now, it is important to a correct understanding of this subject, to connect with the right to *buy* and *possess,* as property, the amount of authority *to govern,* which is granted by the *law-giver*; this amount of authority is implied, in the first place, in the law which prohibits the exercise of rigid authority upon the Hebrews, who are allowed to sell themselves for limited times. "If thy brother be waxen poor, and be sold unto thee, thou shalt not *compel him* to serve as a *bond servant,* but as a *hired servant*, and as a *sojourner* he shall be with thee, and shall serve thee until the year of jubilee—*they shall not be sold as bond-men;* thou *shalt not rule over them with rigor.*"—Levit. xxv: 39, 40, 41, 42, 43. It will be evident to all, that here are *two states* of servitude; in reference to *one* of which, *rigid* or *compulsory* authority, is *prohibited,* and that its *exercise is authorized in the other. . . .*

I affirm then, first, (and no man denies,) that Jesus Christ has not abolished slavery by a prohibitory command: and second, I affirm, he has introduced no new moral principle which can work its destruction, under the gospel dispensation; and that the principle relied on for this purpose, is a fundamental principle of the Mosaic law, under which slavery was instituted by Jehovah himself: and third, with this absence of positive prohibition, and this absence of principle, to work its ruin, I affirm, that in all the Roman provinces, where churches were planted by the apostles, hereditary slavery existed, as it did among the Jews, and as it does now among us, (which admits of proof from history that no man will dispute who knows any thing of the matter,) and that in instructing such churches, the Holy Ghost by the apostles, has recognized the institution, as one *legally existing* among them, to be perpetuated in the church, and that its duties are prescribed.

Now for the proof: To the church planted at Ephesus, the capital of the lesser Asia, Paul ordains by letter, subordination in the fear of God,—first between wife and husband; second, child and parent; third, servant and master; *all, as states, or conditions, existing among the members.*

The relative duties of each state are pointed out; those between the servant and master in these words: "Servants be obedient to them who are your masters, according to the flesh, with fear and trembling, in singleness of your heart as unto Christ; not with eye service as men pleasers, but as the servants of Christ, doing the will of God from the heart, with good-will, doing service, as to the Lord, and not to men, knowing that whatsoever good thing any man doeth, the same shall he receive of the Lord, whether he be bond or free. And ye masters do the same things to them, forbearing threatening, knowing that your master is also in heaven, neither is there respect of persons with him." Here, by the Roman law, the servant was property, and the control of the master unlimited, as we shall presently prove. . . .

We will remark, in closing under this head, that we have shown from the text of the sacred volume, that when God entered into covenant with Abraham, it was with him as a slaveholder; that when he took his posterity by the hand in Egypt, five hundred years afterward to confirm the promise made to Abraham, it was done with them as slaveholders; that when he gave them a constitution of government, he gave them the right to perpetuate hereditary slavery; and that he did not for the fifteen hundred years of their national existence, express disapprobation toward the institution.

We have also shown from authentic history that the institution of slavery existed in every family, and in every province of the Roman Empire, at the time the gospel was published to them.

We have also shown from the New Testament, that all the churches are recognized as composed of masters and servants; and that they are instructed by Christ how to discharge their relative duties; and finally that in reference to the question which was then started, whether Christianity did not abolish the institution, or the right of one Christian to hold another Christian in bondage, we have shown, that "the words of our Lord Jesus Christ" are, that so far from this being the case, it adds to the obligation of the servant to render service with good-will to his master, and that gospel fellowship is not to be entertained with persons who will not consent to it!

Selection 4

The White South's Commitment to Slavery

David M. Potter

In 1860, less than half of southern white households owned slaves, and most slave owners owned only one or two slaves. The big slave owners, on whose plantations fifty or more slaves labored, were a distinct minority in southern society—rarer than millionaires are in today's America.

How, then, did the minority of white southerners who were slave owners, and the tiny minority of large-scale slave owners who formed the region's political elite and led the South into secession, persuade the majority of southern whites to follow them? Historian David M. Potter posed this question in his classic book The Impending Crisis, *which is excerpted here.*

*W*hat were the factors of affinity making for cohesion within the South in 1860, and what were the factors of repulsion between the South and the rest of the Union which gave negative reinforcement to southern unity?

The vast and varied region extending from the Mason-Dixon line to the Rio Grande and from the Ozarks to the Florida Keys certainly did not constitute a unity, either physiographic or cultural. But the whole area lay within what may be called the gravitational field of an agricultural economy specializing in staple crops for which plantations had proved to be effective units of production and for which Negro slaves had become the most important source of labor. This, of course, did not mean that all white southerners engaged in plantation agriculture and owned slaves—indeed only a small but very influential minority did so. It did not even mean that all of the states were heavy producers of staple crops, for the cotton states were only in the lower South. But it did mean that the economy of all of these states was tied, sometimes in secondary or tertiary ways, to a system of plantation agriculture.

Agricultural societies tend to be conservative and orthodox, with strong emphasis on kinship ties and on the observance of established customs. If land is held in great estates, such societies tend to be hierarchical and deferential. Thus, even without slavery, the southern states would have shared certain attributes to a high degree. But the presence of slavery had dictated conditions of its own, and these too were shared very widely throughout the South. Indeed they became the criteria for determining what constituted the South.

A slave system, since it means the involuntary subordination of a significant part of the population, requires a social apparatus distinctively adapted in all its parts to imposing and to maintaining such subordination. In the South, this subordination was also racial, involving not only the control of slaves by their masters but also the control of a population of 4 million blacks by 8 million whites. Such a system cannot be maintained simply by putting laws on the statute books and making formal records that one individual has acquired legal ownership of another. It is axiomatic that the enslaved will tend to resist their servitude and that the slaveowners must devise effective, practical means of control. The first requisite is that the system shall be able to deal with the contingency of insurrection. This alters the priorities, for though the system of subordination may have originated as a means to an end—to assure a permanent labor supply for the cultivation of the staple crops—the immediacy of the hazard of insurrection soon makes the subordination of the slaves an end in itself. This was what Thomas Jefferson meant when he said, "We have a wolf by the ears."

The question of the extent to which the South stood in real danger of slave insurrection is a most difficult one, complicated by the fact that the white South could never for a moment rid itself of the fear of insurrection, yet at the same time could never admit even to itself, much less to others, that its "civilized," "contented," and "loyal" slaves might some day massacre their masters. The fear was probably out of proportion to the actual danger. But the point is that white southerners shared, subjectively, a fear of what the slaves might do, and, objectively, a social system designed to prevent them from doing it.

From the time of Spartacus,* all slaveholding societies had lived with the danger of slave revolt. But for the South, no reminders from antiquity were needed. On the island of Santo Domingo, between 1791 and 1804, black insurrectionists under a series of leaders including Toussaint L'Ouverture and Jean Jacques Dessalines had risen in revolt, virtually exterminating the entire white population of the island and committing frightful atrocities, such as burying people alive and sawing them in two. Survivors had fled to New Orleans, Norfolk, and other places in the United States, and southerners could hear from their own lips the stories of their ordeal. Santo Domingo lived as a nightmare in the mind of the South. Within the South itself, of course, there

*A rebel slave gladiator in ancient Rome.

were also revolts or attempted revolts. Gabriel Prosser led one at Richmond in 1800. Some sort of conspiracy under the leadership of Denmark Vesey apparently came near to hatching at Charleston in 1822. Nat Turner led his famous insurrection in Southampton County, Virginia, in 1831. All of these were negligible compared with Santo Domingo or even with revolts in Brazil, but, each one hit an exposed nerve in the southern psyche. Also there were local disturbances. Altogether, one historian has collected more than two hundred instances of "revolts," and while there is reason to believe that some of these were wholly imaginary and that many others did not amount to much, still every one is a proof of the reality of southern apprehensions if not of the actual prevalence of the danger. On isolated plantations, and in districts where blacks heavily outnumbered whites, the peril seemed a constant one. Every sign of restlessness in the slave quarters, every stranger seen along a lonely road, every withdrawn or cryptic look on a slave face, even the omission of some customary gesture of deference, might be the forewarning of nameless horrors lurking just beneath the placid surface of life.

This pervasive apprehension explains much, of course, about southern reaction to the antislavery movement. The southerners were not deeply concerned with what the abolitionists might persuade Congress or the northern public to do—indeed the whole elaborate territorial controversy had many of the aspects of a charade—but with what they might persuade the slaves to do. Southerners were acutely sensitized to direct abolitionist efforts at incitation, such as Henry H. [Garnet's] speech at a national Negro convention in 1843 in which he urged slaves to kill any master who refused to set them free. It was seldom difficult to make an equation between abolitionist exhortation and slave violence. Thus southerners tried to link Nat Turner's revolt in August 1831 with the first appearance of the *Liberator* eight months previously, but in truth it appears likely that Turner was more influenced by an eclipse of the sun in February than by William Lloyd Garrison in January. Twenty-eight years later, however, John Brown made the equation explicit: a white abolitionist was caught trying to rouse the slaves to revolt. Brown's tying of the bond between abolition and slave revolt gave electrifying importance to what might otherwise have been dismissed as an act of suicidal folly.

This concern about antislavery propaganda as a potential cause of slave unrest also explains in part why white southerners seemed so oblivious to the great difference between the moderate attitude of an "ultimate extinctionist" like Lincoln and the flaming abolitionism of an "immediatist" like Garrison. When southerners thought of extinction it was in terms of Santo Domingo and not in terms of a gradualist reform to be completed, maybe, in the twentieth century. From their standpoint, the election to the presidency of a man who stated flatly that slavery was morally wrong might have a more inciting effect upon the slaves than denunciatory rhetoric from the editor of an abolitionist weekly in Boston.

Since the determination to keep blacks in subordination took priority over other goals of southern society, the entire socio-economic system had to be conducted in a way that would maximize the effectiveness of racial control. This went far beyond the adoption of slave codes and the establishment of night patrols in times of alarm. It meant also that the entire structure of society must be congruent with the objective, and no institutional arrangements should be countenanced which would weaken control. The blacks should live on plantations not only because plantations were efficient units for cotton production, but because in an era prior to electronic and bureaucratic surveillance, the plantation was a notably effective unit of supervision and control. Also, it provided maximum isolation from potentially subversive strangers. Slaves should be illiterate, unskilled, rural workers not only because the cotton economy needed unskilled rural workers for tasks in which literacy would not increase their usefulness, but also because unskilled rural workers were limited in their access to unsupervised contacts with strangers, and because the illiterate could neither read seditious literature nor exchange surreptitious written communication. In fact, the conditions of employment in the cotton culture seemed to fit the needs of a slave system as neatly as the conditions of slavery fitted the needs of employment in the cotton culture, and if cotton fastened slavery upon the South, it is also true that slavery fastened cotton upon the South.

Even beyond these broad relationships, the system of subordination reached out still further to require a certain kind of society, one in which certain questions were not publicly discussed. It must give blacks no hope of cultivating dissension among the whites. It must commit the non-slaveholders to the unquestioning support of racial subordination, even though they might suffer certain disadvantages from a slave system in which they had no economic stake. This meant that books . . . [critical of slavery] must not circulate, and, indeed, universal education, extending literacy indiscriminately to all lower-class whites, need not be encouraged. In a mobile society it would be harder to keep slaves firmly fixed in their prescribed positions; therefore, the society must be relatively static, without the economic flexibility and dynamism of a money economy and a wage system. The more speculative a society became in its social thought, the more readily it might challenge the tenets of the established order. Therefore the South tended toward a religion which laid major emphasis on personal salvation and on a

A planter's house on the Mississippi River. Plantation owners with a large number of slaves were a small minority among southerners.

Bible-based orthodoxy; toward an educational system which stressed classical learning; and toward reforms of a pragmatic kind, such as better care for the blind, rather than reforms associated with ideology. In short, the South became increasingly a closed society, distrustful of isms from outside and unsympathetic toward dissenters. Such were the pervasive consequences giving top priority to the maintenance of a system of racial subordination.

By 1860, southern society had arrived at the full development of a plantation-oriented, slave-holding system with conservative values, hierarchical relationships, and authoritarian controls. No society is complete, of course, without an ethos appropriate to its social arrangements, and the South had developed one, beginning with a conviction of the superior virtues of rural life. At one level, this conviction embodied a Jeffersonian agrarianism which regarded landowning cultivators of the soil as the best kind of citizens, because their landownership and their production for use gave them self-sufficiency and independence, uncorrupted by commercial avarice—and also because their labor had dignity and diversity suitable to well-rounded men. But at another level, the commitment to rural values had led to a glorification of plantation life, in which even slavery was idealized by the argument that the dependence of the slave developed in the master a sense of responsibility for the welfare of the slaves and in the slaves a sense of loyalty and attachment to the master. This relationship, southerners argued, was far better than the impersonal, dehumanized irresponsibility of "wage slavery," which treated labor as a commodity.

From an idyllic image of slavery and plantation conditions, it was but a short step to the creation of a similar image of the planter as a man of distinctive qualities. Thus, the plantation virtues of magnanimity, hospitality, personal courage, and loyalty to men rather than to ideas held a social premium, and even the plantation vices of arrogance, quick temper, and self-indulgence were regarded with tolerance. From materials such as these, in an era of uninhibited romanticism and sentimentality, the southern upper class built a

fully elaborated cult of chivalry, inspired by the novels of Sir Walter Scott and including tournaments, castellated architecture, a code of honor, and the enshrinement of women. Thus, with a mixture of self-deception and idealism, the South adopted an image of itself which some men used as a fiction to avoid confronting sordid reality, while others used it as a standard toward which to strive in order to develop, as far as they were able, the better aspects of human behavior that were latent even in a slaveholding society.

One other belief shared by the men of the South in 1860 was especially important because they felt just uncertain and insecure enough about it to be almost obsessively insistent and aggressive in asserting it. This was the doctrine of the inherent superiority of whites over Negroes. The idea was not distinctively southern, but it did have a distinctive significance in the South, for it served to rationalize slavery and also to unite slaveholders and nonslaveholders in defense of the institution as a system, primarily, of racial subordination, in which all members of the dominant race had the same stake.

This racial prejudice against Negroes cannot, of course, be dismissed as nothing but a rationalization to justify their subordination of the blacks, for in fact it was in part just such prejudice which had originally made blacks and Indians subject to enslavement, while servants of other races were not. Initially, the prejudice may have stemmed from the superiority which technologically advanced societies feel over less advanced societies; it may have reflected something of the attitude of Christians toward the "heathen"; it may have reflected the universal antagonism of in-groups and out-groups or the universal distrust of the unfamiliar. In these aspects, prejudice may even be regarded as a relatively innocent form of ethnocentrism, uncorrupted by consideration of self-interest. But once it became firmly tied to slavery, prejudice began to have certain functional uses which added immeasurably both to the strength of slavery and also to its brutalizing quality. Racial prejudice and slavery together created a vicious circle in which the assumed inferiority of the blacks was used as justification for their en-slavement, and then their subordination as slaves was used to justify the belief that they were inferior. The stigma of race increased the degradation of slavery, and servile status, in turn, reinforced the stigma of race.

Doctrines of race not only served to minimize the potentially serious economic divisions be-tween slaveholders and nonslaveholders, but also furnished southerners with a way to avoid confronting an intolerable paradox: that they were committed to human equality in principle but to human servitude in practice. The paradox was a genuine one, not a case of hypocrisy, for though southerners were more prone to accept social hierarchy than men of other regions, still they responded very positively to the ideal of equality as exemplified by Jefferson of Virginia and Jackson of Tennessee. In their politics, they had moved steadily toward democratic practices for whites, and in fact it was argued, with a cer-tain plausibility, that the system of slavery made for a greater degree of democracy within that part of the society which was free, just as it had made for democracy among the freemen of an-cient, slaveholding Athens. Still, this only made the paradox more glaringly evident, and no doubt it was partly because of the psychological stress arising from their awareness of the para-dox that southern leaders of the late eighteenth and early nineteenth centuries had played with the idea of some day eliminating slavery. That was, in part, why the South had acceded to the exclusion of slavery from the Northwest Terri-tory in 1787 and to the abolition of the African slave trade in 1808. It was why a limited num-ber of southerners had emancipated their slaves, especially during the half-century after the Dec-laration of Independence, and why a greater number had indulged themselves in a rhetoric which deplored slavery without exactly con-demning it. Some had even joined antislavery societies, and southerners had taken the lead in emancipating slaves and colonizing them in Liberia. Thus, for a generation, the great para-dox had been masked by the vague and pious notion that at some remote future, in the fullness of time and God's infinite wisdom, slavery would pass away.

By the 1830s, however, this notion had begun to lose its plausibility, for even the most self-deceiving of wishful thinkers could not com-pletely ignore the changes under way. In the lower South the great cotton boom was extend-ing slavery westward across Georgia, Alabama, Mississippi, and Louisiana, and into Arkansas and Missouri. Texas had set up as an indepen-dent slaveholding republic. The traffic in slaves between these new states and the older centers of slavery was probably greater in magnitude than the traffic from Africa to the thirteen colonies had ever been. Compared to the birth rate of new slaves, the rate of emancipation was as nothing. Meanwhile, the New England states, New York, Pennsylvania, and New Jersey had abolished slavery. Concurrently, northern anti-slavery men had begun to abandon their tone of gentle, persuasive reproachfulness in discussing slavery and had fallen not only to denouncing slavery as a monstrous sin, but also to castigat-ing slaveholders, as hideous sinners. One should not accept the apologia that the South would it-self have got rid of slavery if this indiscriminate onslaught had not compromised the position of the southern emancipationists, but it does seem valid to say that, in the face of such bitter con-demnation, white southerners lost their willing-ness to concede that slavery was an evil—even an inherited one, for which Yankee slave sellers and the southern slave buyers of the eighteenth century shared responsibility. Instead they re-sponded by defending slavery as a positive good. But this made all the more stark the con-tradiction between equality in theory and servi-tude in practice, and their only escape was to deny that the blacks were qualified for equality on the same basis as other men. Some theoreti-cians of race even denied that blacks were the descendants of Adam, which was a long step to-ward their exclusion not only from equality but also from the brotherhood of man.

With the theory of race thus firmly linked to the theory of slavery, the belief in Negro inferi-ority was as functional and advantageous psychologically as slavery itself was economically. The belief could be used to justify a certain amount of ill treatment of the blacks and even hostility toward them, since, lacking full humanity, they did not deserve fully human treatment and might justifiably be despised for their inherent deficiencies. By maintaining slavery, the South had violated its own ideal of equality, but by adopting racist doctrine it had both perverted and rejected the ideal, as the only way, other than emancipation, to escape from their dilemma.

All these shared institutions, practices, attitudes, values, and beliefs gave to southern society a degree of homogeneity and to southerners a sense of kinship. But a sense of kinship is one thing, and an impulse toward political unity is another. If one searches for explicit evidence of efforts to unify the South politically because of cultural homogeneity, common values, and other positive influences, rather than as a common negative response to the North, one finds relatively little of it.

Selection 5

Expanding Slavery

Eugene D. Genovese

In The Political Economy of Slavery: Studies in the Economy and Society of the Slave South, *excerpted here, Eugene D. Genovese demolished the view that American slavery had been "walled off" in the Old South. Particularly in the 1850s, slave owners were aggressively seeking to expand the boundaries of slavery, and it was by no means clear that their plans were unrealistic.*

The Contradictory Nature of the "Natural Limits" Thesis

*T*he "natural limits" thesis is self-contradictory—and, in one important sense, irrelevant—for it simultaneously asserts that slavery was nonexpansionist and

that it would have perished without room to expand. The only way to avoid judging the thesis to be self-contradictory is to read it so as to state that slavery needed room to expand but that, first, it needed room only in the long run and, second, that it had no room. This reading removes the contradiction but destroys the thesis.

If the slave states would eventually need room to expand, they had to set aside new territory when they could get it or face a disaster in a few years or decades. Hence, wisdom dictated a fight for the right to take slaves into the territories, for ultimately that right would be transformed from an abstraction into a matter of life and death. W. Burwell of Virginia wrote in 1856 that the South needed no more territory at the moment and faced no immediate danger of a redundant slave population. "Yet statesmen," he concluded, "like provident farmers, look to the prospective demands of those who rely upon their forethought for protection and employment. Though, therefore, there may be no need of Southern territory for many years, yet it is important to provide for its acquisition when needed. . . ."

To establish that slavery had no room to expand is not to refute the theory of slavery expansionism. If it could be firmly established that slavery needed room to expand but had none, then we should have described a society entering a period of internal convulsion. The decision of most slaveholders to stake everything on a desperate gamble for a political independence that would have freed them to push their system southward emerges as a rational, if dangerous, course of action.

The Territorial Question

One of the most puzzling features of [the "natural limits" thesis] is the virtual equation of cotton and slavery. Only occasionally and never carefully does [the leading historical advocate of this thesis] glance at the prospects for using slave labor outside the cotton fields. To identify any social system with a single commodity is indefensible, and in any case, Southern slavery had much greater flexibility. [His] essay is puzzling with respect to these general considerations but even more so with respect to his specific contention that contemporary Southerners viewed the territorial question as a cotton question. They did not.

When the more intelligent and informed Southerners demanded the West for slavery they often, perhaps most often, spoke of minerals, not cotton or even hemp. Slavery, from ancient times to modern, had proved itself splendidly adaptable to mining. Mining constituted one of the more important industries of the Negroes of preconquest Africa, and slave labor had a long history there. The Berbers, for example, used Negro slaves in West Africa, where the salt mines provided one of the great impetuses to the development of commercial, as opposed to traditional and patriarchal, forms of slavery. Closer in time and place to the South, Brazil afforded an impressive example of the successful use of slave labor in mining. In the middle of the eighteenth century diamond mining supplemented gold mining in Minas Gerais and accounted for a massive transfer of masters and slaves from the northeastern sugar region. Southern leaders knew a good deal about this experience. "The mines of Brazil," reported *De Bow's Review* in 1848, "are most prolific of iron, gold, and diamonds. . . . The operation is performed by negroes . . . 30,000 negroes have been so employed." The eastern slave states had had experience with gold mining, and although the results were mixed, the potentialities of slave labor had been demonstrated. Planters in the Southwestern states expressed interest in gold mines in Arkansas and hopefully looked further west. "If mines of such temporary value should, as they may, be found in the territories, and slaves could be excluded from these," wrote A. F. Hopkins of Mobile in 1860, "it would present a case of monstrous injustice."

During the Congressional debates of 1850, Representative Jacob Thompson of Mississippi, later to become Secretary of the Interior under Buchanan, expressed great concern over the fate of the public domain of California if she were to be hastily admitted to the Union and expressed special concern over the fate of the gold mines. Ten years later, after a decade of similar warnings, pleas, hopes, and threats, S.D. Moore of Alabama wrote that the South was "excluded from California, not pretendedly even by 'isothermal lines,' or want of employment for slave labor, for in regard to climate and mining purposes the country was admirably adapted to the institution of African slavery." Had it not been for the anti-slavery agitation, Representative Clingman told the House in 1850, Southerners would have used slaves in the mines of California and transformed it into a slave state. Albert Gallatin Brown, one of the most fiery and belligerent of the pro-slavery extremists, wrote his constituents that slave labor was admirably suited to mining and that California could and should be made into a slave state. Even as a free state California demonstrated the usefulness of slave labor. In 1852 the state legislature passed a mischievous fugitive slave law that could be and was interpreted to allow slaveholders to bring slaves into the state to work in the mines and then send them home.

Similarly, a Texan wrote in 1852 that a Mississippi and Pacific railroad would secure the New Mexico territory for the South by opening the mining districts to slave labor. During the War for Southern Independence, Jefferson Davis received a communication from his Southwestern field commander that a successful drive to California would add "the most valuable agriculture and grazing lands, and the richest mineral region in the world."

Southerners had long cast eyes toward Mexico and looked forward to additional annexations. "I want Cuba," roared Albert Gallatin Brown. "I want Tamaulipas, Potosí, and one or two other Mexican states; and I want them all for the same reason—for the planting or spreading of slavery." Throughout the 1850s, *De Bow's Review* printed articles about Mexico and particularly about Mexican mines. In 1846, Joel R. Poinsett reviewed Waddy Thompson's *Reflexions on Mexico* and noted the extensive mineral wealth in an article that struck no bellicose note. During the same year Gustavus Schmidt, in a humane, nonracist, nonchauvinist account, wrote of Mexico's "inexhaustible deposits of gold and silver." In 1850, Brantz Mayer of Baltimore estimated that one-fifth of Mexican territory contained excellent mineral resources. Covetous eyes and bellicose projects appeared soon enough.

> The mineral resources of Mexico are unquestionably immense. . . . The moment Mexico falls into the hands of the Anglo-Saxon race, every inch of her territory will be explored. . . . The mines of Mexico, which have now been worked near three hundred years, are inexhaustible; and they only need the protection of a good government and the skill of an intelligent and industrious people, to render them productive of the most astonishing quantities of the precious metals.

George Frederick Holmes, in a long, rambling article on gold and silver mines, wrote glowingly of Chile as well as Mexico. H. Yoakum ended an article on Mexico with the warning, "*You must make progress, or you will be absorbed by a more energetic race.*" Southerners and Mexicans

took these designs seriously. Confederate troops marched into New Mexico with the intention of proceeding to Tucson and then swinging south to take Sonora, Chihuahua, Durango, and Tamaulipas. The Confederate government tried to deal with Santiago Vidaurri, the strong man of Coahuila and Nuevo León, to bring northern Mexico into the Confederacy, and Juárez was so alarmed that he was ready to go to great lengths to help the Union put down the rebellion.

It is one thing to note that Southerners sought to expand slavery into Mexico's mining districts or that they lamented the political barriers to the expansion of slavery into New Mexico's; it is another for us to conclude that their hopes and desires were more than wishful thinking. Allan Nevins has presented a formidable case to suggest that slavery had little room even in the mining districts of the Southwest and Mexico. He shows that even in the Gadsden Purchase the economic exigencies of mining brought about the quick suppression of the enterprising individual by the corporation. Western mining, as well as transportation, lumbering, and some forms of agriculture, required much capital and became fields for big business. High labor costs led to a rising demand for labor-saving machinery, but Nevins does not consider that this very condition might, under certain circumstances, have spurred the introduction of slave labor. He writes:

> For three salient facts stood out in any survey of the Far West. First, this land of plain and peak was natural soil for a free-spirited and highly competitive society, demanding of every resident skill and intelligence. It was, therefore, even in that Gadsden Purchase country which had been bought at the behest of the slave states, a country naturally inhospitable to slavery. Second, when so much energy was steadily flowing into western expansion, and such wide outlets for more effort existed there, it was impossible to think of the country turning to Caribbean areas for a heavy thrust southward. Its main forces moved naturally toward the sunset, where rich opportunities were hardly yet sampled. The cotton kingdom, which realized that the West gave little

scope for its peculiar culture, might plan grandiose Latin American adventures; but it would get little support from other regions. And in the third place, conditions in the West demanded capital and organization on a broad scale; if it was a land for individualists, it was even more a land for corporate enterprise—a land for the businessman. Those who pondered these three facts could see that they held an ominous meaning for the South. The nearer Northwest had already done much to upset the old sectional balance, and the Far West, as it filled up, would do still more.

On economic grounds Nevin's analysis has much to offer, but his remarks on the competitive struggle in the Southwest and on the inability of Southerners to get national support for Caribbean adventures do not prove nearly so much as he thinks. At most, they suggest that the North was strong enough to block slavery expansionism into the Southwest and frustrate Southern ambitions elsewhere. If so, the case for secession, from the proslavery viewpoint, was unanswerable.

Nevin's remarks illustrate the wisdom of other Southern arguments—that the South had to secure new land politically, not by economic advance, and that the South had to have guarantees of positive federal protection for slavery in the territories. The *Charleston Mercury,* climaxing a decade of Southern complaints, insisted in 1860 that slavery would have triumphed in California's gold-mining areas if Southerners had had assurances of protection for their property. It singled out the mineral wealth of New Mexico as beckoning the South and even saw possibilities for slave-worked mining in Kansas. With fewer exaggerations De Bow, a decade earlier, had pointed to the political aspect of the problem:

"Such is the strength and power of the Northern opposition that property, which is ever timid, and will seek no hazards, is excluded from the country in the person of the slave, and Southerners are forced, willingly or not, to remain at home. Emigrants, meanwhile, crowd from the North." During the bitter debate in Congress over the admission of California, Senator Jeremiah Clemens of Alabama replied heatedly to Clay in words similar to those used by De Bow. Free-soil agitation, he said, had kept slavery from the territories. "Property is proverbially timid. The slaveholder would not carry his property there with a threat hanging over him that it was to be taken away by operation of law the moment he landed." Representative Joseph M. Root of Ohio, Whig and later Republican, commented on such charges by boasting that if the Wilmot Proviso had accomplished nothing more than to create a political climate inimical to slavery expansion, it had accomplished its purpose.

The Southern demand for federal guarantees made sense, but even that did not go far enough. Ultimately, the South needed not equal protection for slave property but complete political control. If a given territory could be organized by a proslavery party, then slaveholders would feel free to migrate. Time would be needed to allow the slave population to catch up; meanwhile, free-soil farmers had to be kept out in favor of men who looked forward to becoming slaveholders. Under such circumstances the territory's population might grow very slowly, and the exploitation of its resources might lag far behind that of the free territories. Nothing essential would be lost to the South by underdevelopment; the South as a whole was underdeveloped. In short, the question of political power necessarily had priority over the strictly economic questions.

The Complete History of

Slaves' Work

Chapter 9

Introduction

One topic that has long interested historians of American slavery has been the work that slaves performed. Because documents from slavery times—plantation records, correspondence and diaries, comments by visitors, and former slaves' oral testimonies—give a wealth of references to the work that slaves did or were expected to do, this was one of the first subjects to be given intensive scholarly attention.

Selection 1

Field Work

Kenneth M. Stampp

Few have ever doubted the rigors of working in the fields as a slave. Kenneth M. Stampp, one of this country's leading authorities on the history of slavery, documents what it was like to be a field slave in his well-known 1956 book The Peculiar Institution: Slavery in the Ante-Bellum South.

The day's toil began just before sunrise. A visitor on a Mississippi plantation was regularly awakened by a bell which was rung to call the slaves up. "I soon hear the tramp of the laborers passing along the avenue. . . . All is soon again still as midnight. . . . I believe that I am the only one in the house that the bell disturbs; yet I do not begrudge the few minutes' loss

of sleep it causes me, it sounds so pleasantly in the half dreamy morning." On James H. Hammond's South Carolina plantation a horn was blown an hour before daylight. "All work-hands are [then] required to rise and prepare their cooking, etc. for the day. The second horn is blown just at good day-light, when it is the duty of the driver to visit every house and see that all have left for the field." At dusk the slaves put away their tools and returned to their quarters.

The working day was shorter in winter than in summer, but chiefly because there was less daylight, not because there was much less to do. Seldom at any time of the year was the master at a loss to find essential work to keep his hands busy. Those who planned the routine carefully saved indoor tasks for rainy days. An Alabama planter told his father in Connecticut that cotton picking continued until January, "and after that [we] gathered our corn which ripened last August. We then went to work with the waggons ha[u]ling rails and repairing and rebuilding fences, say two weeks, we then knocked down cotton stalks and pulled up corn stalks and commenced plowing. There is no lying by, no leisure, no long sleeping season such as you have in New England." The terse plantation records of the year-round routine of slaves whose principal work was growing cotton usually ran something like this:

January–February: Finished picking, ginning, and pressing cotton and hauling it in wagons to the point of shipment; killed hogs and cut and salted the meat; cut and hauled wood; cut and mauled fence rails; repaired buildings and tools; spread manure; cleaned and repaired ditches; cleared new ground by rolling and burning logs and grubbing stumps; knocked down corn and cotton stalks and burned trash; plowed and "bedded up" corn and cotton fields; planted vegetables.

March–April: Opened "drills," or light furrows, in the corn and cotton beds; sowed corn and cotton seeds in the drills and covered them by hand or with a harrow; replanted where necessary; cultivated the vegetable garden; plowed and hoed in the corn fields.

May–August: "Barred" cotton by scraping dirt away from it with plows; "chopped" cotton with hoes to kill weeds and grass and to thin it to a "stand"; "molded" cotton by "throwing dirt" to it with plows; cultivated corn and cotton until it was large enough to be "laid by"; made repairs; cleared new ground; "pulled fodder," i.e., stripped the blades from corn stalks; cleaned the gin house.

September–December: Picked, ginned, pressed, and shipped cotton; gathered peas; hauled corn and fodder; dug potatoes; shucked corn; cleaned and repaired ditches; repaired fences; cut and hauled wood; cleared new ground.

Thus the operations of one growing cycle overlapped those of the next. There were, of course, variations from planter to planter and differences in the time of planting crops in the upper and lower parts of the cotton belt. Slaves who grew long-staple, or sea-island, cotton in the coastal areas of South Carolina and Georgia had to exercise greater care in picking, ginning, and packing this finer and more expensive variety. But these were differences only in detail. The routine work of cotton growers was essentially the same everywhere, and their basic tools were always the hoe and the plow.

Slaves who cultivated sugar, rice, tobacco, or hemp were involved in a similar year-round routine. They used the same basic tools and much of the time performed the same kinds of supplementary tasks. But each of the staples required special techniques in planting, cultivating, harvesting, and preparing for market.

Some slaves in Texas, Florida, Georgia, and other scattered places in the Deep South produced a little sugar, but those who worked on plantations lining the rivers and bayous of southern Louisiana produced ninety-five per cent of this crop. Most of them were attached to large estates whose owners had heavy investments in land, labor, and machinery. On sugar plantations in the late fall and winter the slaves prepared the land with plows and harrows; before the end of February they planted the seed cane in deep furrows. The shoots grew from eyes at the joints of the seed cane, or ratooned from the stubble of the previous crop. Then came months of cultivation with hoes and plows until the crop was laid by in July. Meanwhile, other slaves cut huge quantities of wood and hauled it to the sugar house, and coopers made sugar hogsheads and molasses barrels. Much heavy labor also went into ditching to provide drainage for these lands which sloped gently from the rivers toward the swamps.

The first cane cut in October was "matalayed" (laid on the ground and covered with a little dirt) to be used as the next year's seed cane. During the frantic weeks from then until December most of the slaves worked at cutting the cane and stripping the leaves from the stalks, loading it into carts, and hauling it to the sugar house. At the mill other slaves fed the cane through the rollers, tended the open kettles or vacuum pans, kept the fires burning, hauled wood, and packed the unrefined sugar into hogsheads. When the last juice was boiled, usually around Christmas, it was almost time to begin planting the next crop.

Soon after the Revolution South Carolina planters abandoned the cultivation of one of their staples—indigo. But to the end of the antebellum period rice continued to be the favorite crop of the great planters along the rivers of the South Carolina and Georgia Low Country. Slaves had turned the tidal swamps into fertile rice fields by constructing an intricate system of banks, "trunks" (sluices), and ditches which made possible periodic flooding and draining with the rising and falling tides. Throughout the year slaves on rice plantations devoted much of their time to cleaning the ditches, repairing the banks and trunks, and keeping the tide-flow irrigation system in efficient operation.

In winter the slaves raked the rice fields and burned the stubble. After the ground was broken and "trenched" into drills, the seeds were planted in March and early April. During the first flooding (the "sprout flow") other crops on higher ground were cultivated. When the rice fields were drained and dried they were hoed to loosen the ground and to kill grass and weeds. The next flooding (the "stretch flow") was followed by a long period of "dry growth" during which hoeing went on constantly. Then came the final flooding (the "harvest flow") which lasted until September when the rice was ready to be cut. The slaves cut the rice with sickles, tied it into sheaves, and stacked it to dry. After it had dried they carried the rice to the plantation mill to be threshed, "pounded" to remove the husks from the kernels, winnowed, screened, and packed in barrels. The other crops grown on lands above the swamps were gathered in time to begin preparations for the next year's planting.

The Tobacco Kingdom stretched into the border states of Maryland, Kentucky, and Missouri, but in the ante-bellum period its heart was still the "Virginia District." This district embraced the piedmont south of Fredericksburg, including the northern tier of counties in North Carolina. Here the plantations were smaller than in the Lower South, because each hand could cultivate fewer acres and because the crop had to be handled

with great care. The unique aspects of tobacco culture included the preparing of beds in which the tiny seeds were sown during the winter, the transplanting of the shoots in May, and the worming, topping, and suckering of the plants during the summer months. In the late summer the tobacco stalks were split, cut, and left in the fields to wilt. Then they were carried to the tobacco houses to be hung and cured during the fall and winter. The following year, when work had already begun on the next crop, the leaves were stripped from the stalks, sorted, tied into bundles, and "prized" into hogsheads.

The Bluegrass counties of Kentucky and the Missouri River Valley were the chief hemp producing regions of the Old South. Slaves were almost always the working force on hemp farms, because free labor avoided the strenuous, disagreeable labor required to prepare a crop for market. After the ground was prepared, the seeds were sown broadcast in April and May and covered lightly with a harrow or shovel plow. Unlike the other staples, hemp required no cultivation during the growing season, and slaves were free to tend other crops. In late summer the hemp was cut, laid on the ground to dry, and then tied in sheaves and stacked. In November or December it was again spread out in the fields for "dew rotting" to loosen the fiber. A month or so later the hemp was stacked once more, and the lint was laboriously separated from the wood with a hand "brake." The fiber was taken to the hemp house where it was hackled or sold immediately to manufacturers.

In 1850, the Superintendent of the Census estimated that 2,500,000 slaves of all ages were directly employed in agriculture. Of these, he guessed that 60,000 were engaged in the production of hemp, 125,000 in the production of rice, 150,000 in the production of sugar, 350,000 in the production of tobacco, and 1,815,000 in the production of cotton. Somewhat casually he observed that these slaves also produced "large quantities of breadstuffs." This was scarcely adequate recognition of the amount of time they devoted to such crops, even on many of the plantations which gave chief attention to one of the five staples.

To be sure, some planters in the Lower South were so preoccupied with staple production that they grew almost nothing else—not even enough corn and pork to feed their slaves. This pattern was common in the Louisiana sugar district. One planter explained that when sugar sold for fifty dollars a hogshead, "it is cheaper to buy pork[,] for it is utterly impossible to raise hogs here without green pastures and plenty of corn[,] and all lands here fit for pasturage will make a hogshead [of] sugar pr acre—The great curse of this country is that we are all planters and no farmers." An Alabama cotton planter was alarmed when pork failed to arrive from Tennessee: "All of our towns and most of our large Planters are dependent on Drovers for their meat." Even some of the cotton and tobacco planters in North Carolina bought food supplies for their slaves. Such planters were convinced that it was most profitable to concentrate on the production of a single cash crop.

Most planters, however, did not share this point of view. Almost all of the hemp and tobacco growers of the Upper South planted many acres of food crops to supply their own needs—and frequently additional acres to produce surpluses for sale. A major feature of the agricultural revival in ante-bellum Virginia was an improved system of crop rotation with increased emphasis upon corn, wheat, and clover. Many of the tobacco planters gave enough attention to these and other crops to approximate a system of diversified farming. Their field-hands often devoted less than half of their time to tobacco.

Few planters in the Deep South approached such levels of diversification, but most of them produced sizeable food crops for their families and slaves. In southern agricultural periodicals they constantly admonished each other to strive for self-sufficiency. They instructed their overseers to produce adequate supplies of corn, sweet potatoes, peas, and beans, and to give proper attention to the poultry, hogs, and cattle. A Mississippi planter warned his overseer "that a failure to make a bountiful supply of corn and meat for the use of the plantation, will be considered as notice that his services will not be required for the succeeding year." The average planter, however, was tempted to forgive a great deal if his overseer managed to make enough cotton. Interest in other crops tended to vary with fluctuations in cotton prices. Even so, most of the field-hands on cotton plantations were at least familiar with the routine of corn cultivation. . . .

In cotton production those with modest slaveholdings faced no overwhelming competitive disadvantage. Some of the smaller cotton growers were as preoccupied with this staple as were their neighbors on the large plantations. Some even depended upon outside supplies of food. Many of them reported astonishing cotton-production records to the census takers, the number of bales per hand easily matching the records of the planters.

Nevertheless, the majority of small slaveholders did engage in a more diversified type of agriculture than most of the large planters. Slavery could be, and was, adapted to diversified agriculture and to the labor needs of small farms. It did not necessarily depend upon large plantations or staple crops for its survival.

For the owner of a few slaves, labor management was a problem of direct personal relationships between individuals. For the owner of many, the problem was more difficult and required greater ingenuity. Both classes of masters desired a steady and efficient performance of the work assigned each day. They could not expect much cooperation from their slaves, who had little reason to care how much was produced. Masters measured the success of their methods by the extent to which their interest in a maximum of work of good quality prevailed over the slaves' predilection for a minimum of work of indifferent quality. Often neither side won a clear victory.

Slaveowners developed numerous variations of two basic methods of managing their laborers: the "gang system" and the "task system." Under the first of these systems, which was the one most commonly used, the field-hands were divided into gangs commanded by drivers who were to work them at a brisk pace. Competent masters gave some thought to the capacities of individual slaves and to the amount of labor that a gang could reasonably be expected to perform in one day. But the purpose of the gang system was to force every hand to continue his labor until all were discharged from the field in the evening.

Under the task system, each hand was given a specific daily work assignment. He could then set his own pace and quit when his task was completed. The driver's job was to inspect the work and to see that it was performed satisfactorily before the slave left the field. "The advantages of this system,"according to a Georgia rice planter, "are encouragement to the laborers, by equalizing the work of each agreeable to strength, and the avoidance of watchful superintendence and incessant driving. As . . . the task of each [slave] is separate, imperfect work can readily be traced to the neglectful worker."

The task system was best adapted to the rice plantation, with its fields divided into small segments by the network of drainage ditches. Outside the Low Country of South Carolina and Georgia planters occasionally used this system or at least experimented with it, but many of them found it to be unsatisfactory. For one thing, they could get no more work out of their stronger slaves than out of their weaker ones, since the tasks were usually standardized. The planters also found that the eagerness of slaves to finish their tasks as early as possible led to careless work. After using the task system for twenty years, an Alabama planter abandoned it because of evils "too numerous to mention." A South Carolina cotton planter, who also gave it up, noted with satisfaction that under the gang system his slaves did "much more" and were "not so apt to strain themselves."

Actually, most planters used a combination of the two systems. Cotton planters often worked plow-hands in gangs but gave hoe-hands specific tasks of a certain number of cotton rows to hoe each day. Each hand was expected to pick as much cotton as he could, but he might be given a minimum quota that had to be met. Sugar, rice, and tobacco planters applied the task system to their coopers, and hemp growers used it with hands engaged in breaking or hackling hemp. Masters generally tasked their hands for digging ditches, cutting wood, or mauling rails.

Selection 2

A Slave's Work: An Ex-Slave's Narrative

George Fleming

Excerpted from George Fleming, "Work and Slave Life," in *Remembering Slavery: African Americans Talk About Their Personal Experiences of Slavery and Freedom*, edited by Ira Berlin, Marc Favreau, and Steven F. Miller. Copyright © 1998 Ira Berlin, Marc Favreau, and Steven F. Miller. Reprinted with permission from The New Press.

Aged former slaves had grim memories of their experiences as plantation workers when they were young. Here is one of many such narratives, in the words of George Fleming, a South Carolina slave born in 1854.

Born in 1854, George Fleming grew up on an estate in upcountry South Carolina he described as "de biggest plantation . . . I is ever seed or heard tell of." Decades later, Fleming depicted a regimen in which every slave who could work did so, either at raising cotton and other crops, maintaining the owner's house, or performing one of the innumerable other tasks necessary for the operation of a great plantation.

Some of de women dat didn't have a passel of lil' brats was 'signed to de job of cooking fer de field hands. Some of 'em come home to eat, but mostly dey stayed in de fields. De dinner horn blow'd 'zactly at 12 o'clock and dey know'd it was time fer grub. Everybody drapped what dey was doing and compiled demselves in groups. Dey could see de buckets coming over de hill. Dar was more dan one group, fer de fields was so big dat dey couldn't all come to one place. Cose all dat was planned out by de overseers. Had lots of overseers and dey had certain groups to look out fer.

Most of de food was brung to de fields in buckets, but sometimes de beans and de like of dat come in de same pots dey was cooked in. It took two big niggers to tote de big pots. Dar was no want of food fer de hands. Marse know'd if dey worked dey had to eat. Dey had collards, turnips and other good vegetables wid cornbread. Chunks of meat was wid de greens, too, and us had lots of buttermilk.

Women worked in de field same as de men. Some of dem plowed jes' like de men and boys. Couldn't tell 'em apart in de field, as dey wore pantelets or breeches. Dey tied strings 'round de bottom of de legs so de loose dirt wouldn't git in deir shoes. De horn blow'd to start work and to quit. In de morning when de signal blow'd, dey all tried to see who could git to de field first. Dey had a good time and dey liked to do deir work. Us didn't pay much mind to de clock. We worked frum sun to sun. All de slaves had to keep on de job, but dey didn't have to work so hard. Marse allus said dey could do better and last longer by keeping 'em steady and not overworking 'em.

Dar was all kinds of work 'sides de field work dat went on all de time. Everybody had de work dat he could do de best. My daddy worked wid leather. He was de best harness maker on de place, and he could make shoes. Dey had a place whar dey tanned cow-hides. Dat was called de tannos. Dey didn't do much spinning and weaving in de home quarters; most of it was done in one special place Marse had made fer dat purpose. Some of de slaves didn't do nothing but spin and weave, and dey sho was good at it, too. Dey was trained up jes' fer dat particular work.

I don't know how many spinning wheels and looms and dem things Marse had, but he sho had lots of 'em. Dat business making cloth had lots to it and I don't know much 'bout it, but it was sort of dis way. Dey picked de seeds out of de cotton; den put de cotton in piles and carded it. Dey kept brushing it over and over on de cards till it was in lil' rolls. It was den ready fer de spinning wheels whar it was spun in thread. Dis was called de filling. I don't know much 'bout de warp, dat is de part dat run long ways.

Dem spinning wheels sho did go on de fly. Dey connected up wid de spindle and it go lots faster dan de wheel. Dey hold one end of de cotton roll wid de hand and 'tach de other to de spindle. It keep drawing and twisting de roll till it make a small thread. Sometimes dey would run de thread frum de spindle to a cornshuck or anything dat would serve de purpose. Dat was called de broach. Some of den didn't go any further dan dat, dey had to make sech and sech broaches a day. Dis was deir task. Dat's de reason some of dem had to work atter dark, dat is, if dey didn't git de task done befo' dat.

Dey run de thread off de broach on to reels, and some of it was dyed on de reels. Dey made deir own dyes, too. Some of it was made frum copperas, and some frum barks and berries. Atter while, de thread was put back on de spinning wheel and wound on lil' old cane quills. It was den ready fer de looms. Don't know nothing, de looms—boom! boom! sho could travel. Dey put de quills, atter de thread was wound on dem, in de shettle and knocked it back and forth twixt de long threads what was on de beams. Can't see de thread fly out of dat shettle it come so fast. Dey sho could sheckle it through dar. Day peddled dem looms, zip! zap! making de thread rise and drap while de shettle zoom twixt it. Hear dem looms booming all day long 'round de weaving shop. De weaving and spinning was done in de same place.

Overseers lived on de plantation. No, dey wasn't poor whites. All Marse Sam's overseers was good men. Dey lived wid deir families, and Marse's folks 'sociated wid dem, too. Dey had good houses to live in. Dey built better dan ours was. Marse didn't 'low dem to whip de slaves, but dey made us keep straight. If any whipping had to be done, Marse done it, but he didn't have to do much. He didn't hurt 'em bad, den, jes' git a big hickry and lay on a few. He would say if dat nigger didn't walk de chalk, he would put him on de block and settle him. Dat was usually enough, 'cause Marse mean't dat thing and all de niggers know'd it. . . .

Slaves started to work by de time dey was old enough to tote water and pick up chips to start fires wid. Some of dem started to work in de fields when dey about ten, but most of 'em was older. Lawd, Marse Sam must have had more dan a dozen house niggers. It took a lot of work to keep things in and 'round de house in good shape. Cose most of de slaves was jes' field hands, but some of dem was picked out fer special duties. Slaves didn't get any pay in money fer work, but Marse give 'em a lil' change sometimes.

Everybody have plenty to eat. Lots of times

A slave owner's daughter brings a gift of food to slaves on Christmas.
Though some slaves were well fed, others were given a poor, limited diet.

we had fish, rabbits, possums and stuff like dat; lots of fishing and hunting in dem days. Some slaves have lil' gardens of deir own, but most de vegetables come frum de big garden. Missus was in charge de big garden, but cose she didn't have to do no work. She sho seed atter us too. Even de poor white trash had plenty to eat back in dem times. Marse have a hundred head of hogs in de smokehouse at one time. Never seen so much pork in my life. We sho lived in fine fashion in hog killing time, cose de meats was cured and us had some all de year. Yes sir, Marse ration out everybody some every week. Watermelons grow awful big, some of 'em weigh a hundred pounds. Dey big stripes ones, called "rattlesnakes," so big you can't tote it no piece. All de baking and biling was done over de big fireplaces.

Didn't wear much clothes in summer 'cause we didn't need much, but all de grown niggers had shoes. Lawd, I wore many pair of Marse Lyntt's boots, I means sho 'nuff good boots. Marse had his own shoemakers, so twan't no use us gwine widout. Had better clothes fer Sunday. Most de washing was done on Saturday afternoons, and we be all setting purty fer Sunday. Cold weather we was dressed warm, and we had plenty bed kivvers, too. Cose all slaves didn't have it as good as Marse Sam's did. Lawd, I is seed lil' naked niggers setting on de rail fences like pa'cel of buzzards; but Marse Sam's niggers never had to go dat way. . . .

When de slaves come from de field, deir day's work was done. Fact is, everybody's work was done 'cept maybe some of de spinners or weavers dat didn't quite finish deir task. Dey was de onliest ones dat had to ever work atter dark, and dat not often. Sometimes on Saturdays we didn't have to work a-tall, dat is in de fields, and sometimes we had to work till 12 o'clock. Lots of de men went fishing and hunting, and mostly de women washed. Saturday nights some groups would git together and sing. I can still hear dem old songs in my mind, but I doesn't recalls de words.

Selection 3

The Slaves' Work Ethic

Eugene D. Genovese

In his book Roll, Jordan, Roll, *Eugene D. Genovese offered the insightful analysis of the slaves' attitude toward their work in this selection. As evidence Genovese uses the accounts of Frederick Law Olmsted, a famous landscape architect (he designed New York's Central Park) who traveled extensively in the South in the 1850s. In his analysis, Genovese associates the slaves' sense of how to regulate the intensity of their work with patterns common among all people in traditional societies. Working "by the clock," he believes, is an attitude fostered by modern industrial society.*

*O*lmsted reported that the slaves could be and often were driven into hard, unremitting toil but that they responded with a dull, stupid, plodding effort which severely reduced their productive contribution. The slaves, he added, "are far less adapted for steady, uninterrupted labor than we are, but excel us in feats demanding agility and tempestuous energy." Olmsted's argument became standard among postbellum employers who were trying to rebuild with a labor force of freedmen. As one farmer in North Carolina told John Richard Dennett in 1865, "You know how it is with them—for about three days it's work as if they'd break everything to pieces; but after that it's go out late and come in soon." Ironically, this distinction parallels precisely the one made by proslavery ideologues who wished to describe the cultural differences between themselves and the Yankees. It is also the distinction made by scholars in describing the position of southern blacks who went north to cities like Chicago during the twentieth century.

What did the blacks themselves say? Isaac Adams, who had been a slave on a big plantation in Louisiana, recalled that most of the blacks remained there when the Yankees emancipated them. "But," he added, "they didn't do very much work. Just enough to take care of themselves and their white folks." Frank Smith, an ex-slave who went north from Alabama to Illinois, complained: "I didn't lak de Yankees. Dey wanted you to wuk *all de time,* and dat's sump'n I hadn't been brung up to do.". . .

The slaves' willingness to work extraordinarily hard and yet to resist the discipline of regularity accompanied certain desires and expectations. During Reconstruction the blacks sought their own land; worked it conscientiously when they could get it; resisted being forced back into anything resembling gang labor for the white man; and had to be terrorized, swindled, and murdered to prevent their working for themselves. This story was prefigured in antebellum times when slaves were often allowed garden plots for their families and willingly worked them late at night or on Sundays in order to provide extra food or clothing. The men did not generally let their families subsist on the usual allotments of pork and corn. In addition to working with their wives in the gardens, they fished and hunted and trapped animals. In these and other ways they demonstrated considerable concern for the welfare of their families and a strong desire to take care of them. But in such instances they were working for themselves and at their own pace. Less frequently, slaves received permission to hire out their own time after having completed the week's assigned tasks. They were lured, not by some internal pressure to work steadily, but by the opportunity to work for themselves and their families in their own way.

Many slaves voluntarily worked for their masters on Sundays or holidays in return for money or goods. This arrangement demonstrated how far the notion of the slaves' "right" to a certain amount of time had been accepted by the masters; how readily the slaves would work for themselves; and how far the notion of reciprocity had entered the thinking of both masters and slaves.

The slaves responded to moral as well as economic incentives. They often took pride in their work, but not necessarily in the ways most important to their masters. Solomon Northup designed a better way to transport lumber only to find himself ridiculed by the overseer. In this case it was in the master's interest to intervene, and he did. He praised Northup and adopted the plan. Northup comments: "I was not insensible to the praise bestowed upon me, and enjoyed especially, my triumph over Taydem [the overseer], whose half-malicious ridicule had stung my pride."

From colonial days onward plantation slaves, as well as those in industry, mining, and town services, received payments in money and goods as part of a wider system of social control. These payments served either as incentive bonuses designed to stimulate productivity, or more frequently, as a return for work done during the time recognized as the slaves' own. Many planters, including those who most clearly got the best results, used such incentives. Bennet H. Barrow of Louisiana provides a noteworthy illustration, for he was not a man to spare the whip. Yet his system of rewards included frequent holidays and dinners, as well as cash bonuses and presents for outstanding work. In Hinds County, Mississippi, Thomas Dabney gave small cash prizes—a few cents, really—to his best pickers and then smaller prizes to others who worked diligently even if they could not match the output of the leaders. In Perry County, Alabama, Hugh Davis divided his workers into rival teams and had them compete for prizes. He supplemented this collective competition with individual contests. In North Carolina at the end of the eighteenth century Charles Pettigrew, like many others before and after him, paid slaves for superior or extra work.

The amounts sometimes reached substantial proportions. Captain Frederick Marryat complained that in Lexington, Kentucky, during the late 1830s a gentleman could not rent a carriage on Sundays because slaves with ready money invariably rented them first for their own pleasure. Occasionally, plantation records reported surprising figures. One slave in Georgia earned fifty to sixty dollars per year by attending to pine trees in his off hours. Others earned money by applying particular skills or by doing jobs that had to be done individually and carefully without supervision. Amounts in the tens and even hundreds of dollars, although not common, caused no astonishment.

The more significant feature of these practices, for the society as a whole if not for the economy in particular, was the regularity—almost the institutionalization—of payments for work on Sundays or holidays. Apart from occasional assignments of Sunday or holiday work as punishment and apart from self-defeating greed, not to say stupidity, which led a few masters to violate the social norm, Sunday was the slaves' day by custom as well as law. The collective agreement of the slaveholders on these measures had its origin in a concern for social peace and reflected a sensible attitude toward economic efficiency. But once the practice took root, with or without legal sanction, the slaves transformed it into a "right." So successfully did they do so that the Supreme Court of Louisiana ruled in 1836: "According to . . . law, slaves are entitled to the produce of their labor on Sunday; even the master is bound to remunerate them, if he employs them." Here again the slaves turned the paternalist doctrine of reciprocity to advantage while demonstrating the extent to which that doctrine dominated the lives of both masters and slaves.

Ralph Ellison writes of his experience as a boy: "Those trips to the cotton patch seemed to me an enviable experience because the kids came back with such wonderful stories. And it wasn't the hard work which they stressed, but the communion, the playing, the eating, the dancing and the singing." A leading theme in the blues tradition of black "soul" music is "Do your best." The emphasis in both performance and lyrics rests not on the degree of success but on the extent and especially the sincerity of effort. Underlying black resistance to prevailing white values, then, has been a set of particular ideas concerning individual and community responsibility. It is often asserted that blacks spend rather than save as someone else thinks they should. But the considerable evidence for this assertion must be qualified by the no less considerable evidence of the heartbreaking scraping together of nickels and dimes to pay for such things as the education of children, which will generally draw Anglo-Saxon applause, and the provision of elaborate funerals, which generally will not but which for many peoples besides blacks constitutes a necessary measure of respect for the living as well as the dead.

The slaves could, when they chose, astonish the whites by their worktime élan and expenditure of energy. The demands of corn shucking, hog killing, logrolling, cotton picking, and especially sugar grinding confronted the slaves with particularly heavy burdens and yet drew from them particularly positive responses.

With the exception of the Christmas holiday—and not always that—former slaves recalled having looked forward to corn shucking most of all. Sam Colquitt of Alabama explained:

> Next to our dances, de most fun was corn-shucking. Marsa would have de corn hauled up to de crib, and piled as a house. Den he would invite de hands 'round to come and

hope shuck it. Us had two leaders or generals and choose up two sides. Den us see which side would win first and holler and sing. . . . Marsa would pass de jug around too. Den dey sho' could work and dat pile'd just vanish.

Some ex-slaves remembered corn shuckings as their only good time, but many more said simply that they were the best. Occasionally a sour note appeared, as when Jenny Proctor of Alabama said, "We had some co'n shuckin's sometimes but de white folks gits de fun and de nigger gits de work." For the vast majority, however, they were "de big times."

The descriptions that have been preserved provide essential clues for an understanding of plantation life and its work rhythms. According to Robert Shepherd of Kentucky:

Dem corn shuckin's was sure 'nough big times. When us got all de corn gathered up and put in great long piles, den de gettin' ready started. Why, dem womans cooked for days, and de mens would get de shoats ready to barbecue. Master would send us out to get de slaves from de farms round about dere. De place was all lit up with light-wood knot torches and bonfires, and dere was 'citement aplenty when all niggers get to singin' and shoutin' as dey made de shucks fly.

An ex-slave from Georgia recalled:

In corn shucking time no padderollers would ever bother you. We would have a big time at corn shuckings. They would call up the crowd and line the men up and give them a drink. I was a corn general—would stand out high above everybody, giving out corn songs and throwing down corn to them. There would be two sides of them, one side trying to outshuck the other. Such times we have. . . .

Certainly, the slaves had some material in-centives. The best shuckers would get a dollar or a suit of clothes, as might those who found a red ear. But these incentives do not look impressive and do not loom large in the testimony. Those plantations on which the prize for finding a red ear consisted of a dollar do not seem to have done any better than those on which the prize consisted of an extra swig of whiskey or a chance to kiss the prettiest girl. The shucking was generally night work—overtime, as it were—and one might have expected the slaves to resent it and to consider the modest material incentives, which came to a special dinner and dance and a lot of whiskey, to be inadequate.

The most important feature of these occasions and the most important incentive to these long hours of extra work was the community life they called forth. They were gala affairs. The jug passed freely, although drunkenness was discouraged; the work went on amidst singing and dancing; friends and acquaintances congregated from several plantations and farms; the house slaves joined the field slaves in common labor; and the work was followed by an all-night dinner and ball at which inhibitions, especially those of class and race, were lowered as far as anyone dared.

Slavery, a particularly savage system of oppression and exploitation, made its slaves victims. But the human beings it made victims did not consent to be just that; they struggled to make life bearable and to find as much joy in it as they could. Up to a point even the harshest of masters had to help them do so. The logic of slavery pushed the masters to try to break their slaves' spirit and to reconstruct it as an unthinking and unfeeling extension of their own will, but the slaves' own resistance to dehumanization compelled the masters to compromise in order to get an adequate level of work out of them.

Selection 4

The Work Day: An Ex-Slave's Narrative

Charley Williams

Charley Williams, who had been a slave in Louisiana, recalled the slaves' work day in this interview during the 1930s.

When de day began to crack de whole plantation break out wid all kinds of noises, and you could tell what going on by de kind of noise you hear.

Come de daybreak you hear de guinea fowls start potracking down at de edge of de woods lot, and den de roosters all start up 'round de barn and de ducks finally wake up and jine in. You can smell de sow belly frying down at the cabins in de "row," to go wid de hoecake and de buttermilk.

Den purty soon de wind rise a little, and you can hear a old bell donging way on some plantation a mile or two off, and den more bells at other places and maybe a horn, and purty soon younder go old Master's old ram horn wid a long toot and den some short toots, and here come de overseer down de row of cabins, hollering right and left, and picking de ham out'n his teeth wid a long shiny goose quill pick.

Bells and horns! Bells for dis and horns for

dat! All we knowed was go and come by de bells and horns!

Old ram horn blow to send us all to de field. We all line up, about seventy-five field niggers, and go by de tool shed and git our hoes, or maybe go hitch up de mules to de plows and lay de plows out on de side so de overseer can see iffen de points is sharp. Any plow gits broke or de point gits bungled up on de rocks it goes to de blacksmith nigger, den we all git on down in de field.

Den de anvil start dangling in de blacksmith shop: Tank! Deling-ding! Tank! Deling-ding!", and dat ole bull tongue gitting straightened out!

Course you can't hear de shoemaker awling and pegging, and de card spinners, and de ole mammy sewing by hand, but maybe you can hear de ole loom going "frump, frump," and you know it all right iffen your clothes do be wearing out, 'cause you gwine git new britches purty soon!

We had about a hundred niggers on dat place, young and old, and about twenty on de little place down below. We could make about every kind of thing but coffee and gunpowder dat our whitefolks and us needed.

When we needs a hat we gits inside cornshucks and weave one out, and makes horse collars de same way. Jest tie two little soft shucks together and begin plaiting.

All de cloth 'cepting a de Mistress' Sunday dresses come from de sheep to de carders and de

Excerpted from Charley Williams, "Work and Slave Life," in *Remembering Slavery: African Americans Talk About Their Personal Experiences of Slavery and Freedom*, edited by Ira Berlin, Marc Favreau, and Steven F. Miller. Copyright © 1998 Ira Berlin, Marc Favreau, and Steven F. Miller. Reprinted with permission from The New Press.

spinners and de weaver, den we dye it wid "butternut" and hickory bark and indigo and other things and set it wid copperas. Leather tanned on de place made de shoes, and I never see a store boughten wagon wheel 'cepting among de stages and de freighters along de big road.

We made purty, long back-combs out'n cow horn, and knitting neddles out'n second hickory. Split a young hickory and put in a big wedge to prize it open, then cut it down and let it season, and you got good bent grain for wagon hames and chair rockers and such.

Selection 5

The Slave Driver

Randall M. Miller

One of the most complex positions on a larger slave-labor plantation was that of the slave driver. His job must not be confused with that of the overseer, a supervisor who was invariably a white man hired by the master. The slave driver was a black man, drawn from the ranks of the bondspeople, and it was his responsibility to get the slaves going every day, to set the rhythms of work, and to punish laggards. He was the intermediary between the white authorities (master and overseer) and the field hands. Because he had to discipline the slaves and at the same time lead them, his was a difficult job. Sometimes drivers abused their power; sometimes they did all they could to ease the burden of their fellow slaves. Truly the driver was "the man in the middle," as historian Randall M. Miller describes him in this selection.

Reprinted from Randall M. Miller, "The Man in the Middle," *American Heritage*, 1979. Reprinted by permission of *American Heritage* magazine, a division of Forbes, Inc., © Forbes, Inc., 1979.

*W*ise planters of the ante-bellum South never relaxed their search for talent among their slaves. The ambitious, intelligent, and proficient were winnowed out and recruited for positions of trust and responsibility. These privileged bondsmen—artisans, house servants, foremen—served as intermediaries between the master and the slave community; they exercised considerable power; they learned vital skills of survival in a complex, often hostile world. Knowing, as they did, the master's needs and vulnerabilities, they were the most dangerous of slaves; but they were also the most necessary.

None of these men in the middle has been more misunderstood than the slave driver, policeman of the fields and the quarters. To enforce discipline and guarantee performance in the fields, planters enlisted slave foremen or drivers. On large plantations they worked as assistants to the white overseers; on smaller units they served immediately under the master. Generally, they were of an imposing physical presence capable of commanding respect from the other slaves. Ex-slaves described the drivers as, for example, "a great, big cullud man," "a large tall, black man," "a burly fellow . . . severe in the extreme." Armed with a whip and outfitted in high leather boots and greatcoat, all emblematic of plantation authority, the driver exuded an aura of power.

The English traveler, Basil Hall, thought the driver had power more symbolic than real. The slaves knew better. With hardly repressed anger, ex-slave Adelaine Marshall condemned the black foremen at the Brevard plantation in Texas for "all de time whippin' and stroppin' de niggers to make dem work harder." Many other former slaves echoed this theme of driver brutality; accounts of mutilations, lacerations, burnings, and whippings fill the pages of the slave narratives. But physical coercion alone never moved slaves to industry. The drivers, therefore, were selected as men able to bargain, bribe, cajole, flatter, and only as a last resort, to flog the slaves to perform their tasks and refrain from acts destructive of order in the quarters.

Masters often conferred with their black slave drivers on matters of farming, or on social arrangements in the quarters, and often deferred to their advice. As the driver matured and became more knowledgeable, his relationship with his master became one of mutual regard, in sharp contrast to the master's less settled and more transient relationship with white overseers.

White overseers as well were frequently governed by the driver's counsel, although the relationship between these two species of foreman was sometimes strained. The overseer's insistence on steady work from the slaves, and the driver's interest in protecting his people from white abuses, placed the driver in the agonizing dilemma of torn loyalties and interest. In this conflict the driver often appealed to the master and won his support. A chorus of complaints from white Southern overseers alleged that planters trusted the black driver more than the overseer. The charge seems to have been justified. John Hartwell Cocke of Virginia regarded his driver as his "humble friend," but held overseers at arm's length. The astute agricultural reformer and planter, James H. Hammond, unabashedly acknowledged that he disregarded his overseer's testimony in many instances and instead heeded his driver, whom Hammond considered a "confidential servant" especially

enjoined to guard against "any excesses or omissions of the overseer." Planters dismissed overseers as an expendable breed, and, indeed, overseers rarely lasted more than two or three seasons with any single master. The driver, however, stayed on indefinitely as the master's man, and some masters came to depend on him to an extraordinary degree.

Through the driver, the planter sought to inculcate the "proper" standards of work and behavior in his slaves. A few carefully enumerated the driver's duties, leaving him little discretion; but for most, formal rules were unknown, and broad policy areas were left to the driver's judgment. Although an overseer reviewed his work on large farms, the driver made many of the day-to-day decisions on farming as well as meting out rewards and punishments. By blowing on a bugle or horn, he woke up the slaves each morning. He determined the work pace; he directed the marling, plowing, terracing, planting, hoeing, picking, and innumerable other farming operations; he encouraged the slaves in their religious instruction and sometimes led devotions; he mediated family disputes. His duties varied from disciplinarian to family counselor or hygienist. The quick-witted driver who amputated the finger of a woman slave who had been bitten by a rattlesnake saved her life. More than this, he took over the function of the master as protector by making slaves instinctively look to him for aid in times of crisis. So, too, did the driver who held the keys to the plantation stores and parceled out the weekly rations to the slaves. Whatever changes might occur in white management, the basic daily functions of the plantation routine continued unbroken under the driver.

The slave driver had power. For favorites he might sneak extra rations or wink at minor indiscretions; for recalcitrants he might ruthlessly pursue every violation of the plantation code of conduct. But he wielded power only to a point, for when the driver's regime became tyrannical or overly dependent on brute force, he ceased to serve his purpose for the master or the slaves. Planters wanted stability and profits, not discord. Slaves wanted peace in the quarters and a minimum of white intrusion into their lives. A factious slave population sabotaged farming arrangements, ran off, or dissembled in countless ways. To ensure his continued rule, the driver had to curry favor in both camps, black and white. His justice must remain evenhanded, and his discipline rooted in something more enduring than the lash—namely community approbation.

In exchange for the driver's services, the planter compensated him with privileges, even offers of freedom. More immediately, planters tried to encourage the driver in a variety of small ways—with bits of praise, pats on the back, presents. They gave material rewards such as double rations, superior housing, and gifts for the driver's family. Some masters allowed their drivers to marry women "off the plantation," and a few drivers had more than one wife. Planters often set aside extra land for the driver's personal use, and allowed him to draft other slaves to tend his garden and cotton patch. He was usually permitted to sell the produce of his own garden in town for cash. Drivers also went to town to purchase supplies for the master, to do errands, and to transact business for the slaves. They often received cash payments of ten to several hundred dollars a year as gifts, or even wages. During winter months some drivers hired themselves out to earn extra money, and others learned trades with which to build personal estates. Conspicuous consumption heightened the driver's standing and gave sanction to his authority.

Who were these men, and how did they rise in the plantation hierarchy? A collective portrait of the slave driver drawn from slave narratives and planters' accounts yields little support for the generalized charge that drivers were brutish and isolated from their fellow slaves. Although some were kinfolks of other privileged bondsmen, many came from more humble origins. Few slaves were bred to be drivers, and fewer still were purchased for that reason. Most important, no pronounced sense of caste developed in the South to set off drivers from the rest of the slave community.

The awkward attempts of some planters to put distance between slave elites and field hands, by means of special clothes and indulgences, fooled no one. Drivers, after all, took their meals in the quarters, married and raised their families there, worshiped there, and frolicked there. The location of the driver's cabin at the head of the row, midway between the Big House and the quarters, placed the driver closest to the master symbolically, but his place remained in the quarters. Rather than suffer a driver with a puffed-up ego who had little rapport with the slaves, a master might even administer a whipping to him in front of the others. Lashings, demotions, and other humiliations provided ample reminders that the driver was more slave than free.

Drivers were generally in their late thirties or early forties when appointed, and they usually held long tenures. Yet there were a few in their twenties and at least one in his teens. If the candidate was, as one planter wrote, "honest, industrious, not too talkative (which is a necessary qualification), a man of good sense, a good hand himself, and has been heretofore faithful in the discharge of whatever may have been committed to his care," he would do nicely. Whatever the strictures on verbosity, planters chose articulate men capable of communicating the master's wishes and values to the slaves with a minimum of distortion and at the same time able to relay accurately the messages and impulses of the slaves to the master. Thus one planter sent the driver along with a boatload of slaves divided from the rest by sale so that the driver could "jolly the negroes and give them confidence" and explain the master's side.

In reading black and white accounts of bondage, one is struck by the repeated references to the master's confidence in his black slave driver. He left his family alone with the driver, entrusted his comfort and well-being to his care, and gave the driver free rein in ordering the private affairs of his other slaves. One rice planter, R.F.W. Allston, a shrewd student of slave psychology, confirmed his driver in an impressive, formal ceremony of investiture blessed by a clergyman. William S. Pettigrew of North Carolina often reminded his drivers that their good "credit" depended on their faithful duty during his absence. This call for reciprocity worked in subtle ways to compel the driver to uphold the master's interest. Former driver Archer Alexander described his entrapment. He justified his loyalty to his master, who once sold two of his children away from him, by explaining that the master "trusted me every way, and I couldn't do no other than what was right."

Ambiguities of the driver's relationship with the master and the slaves are best illustrated in the one area he could not readily conceal from the overseer or the master—work. All masters demanded frequent performance reports from their drivers. Masters knew the slaves' minimal capacities, and they could corroborate the driver's testimony with private inspections of the field and with their own crop tallies after harvest. Aware of these facts, slaves conceded the driver's need to keep them moving, and forgave occasional excesses of zeal.

In assigning tasks or setting the work pace, the driver could push the slaves relentlessly to impress the master, apply the slaves' time to his private purposes, or manipulate the system to reward favorites and punish enemies. Those members of the driver's family who toiled in the fields usually drew light chores; as a rule they also escaped the lash. So did lovers. A slave woman who spurned a driver's advances, however, might find herself isolated in a remote section of the field, and thus vulnerable to the driver's amorous assaults, or assigned impossible tasks so that the vengeful driver could punish her under the guise of sound labor management.

In the face of driver abuses, however, no slave was wholly defenseless. If the driver unduly imposed on him, he might run to the master or overseer for relief. Enlightened planters advised against punishing a slave beyond the limits of reasonable service, because hard treatment brought forth scant improvement and much dissatisfaction. Drivers usually marked out tasks for each slave according to ability, and remained on the ground until everyone finished. Even the cruel driver had little personal interest in overmeasuring tasks, since unfinished work kept

him in the fields. Moreover, unrealistic work demands might prompt a general flight to the swamps, sabotage, or worse.

As the lead man in the gang labor system, a thoughtful driver would set a steady pace—singing, shouting, cracking his whip, or working at the head of the gang. In this way the slaves could do their work in a manner that would both satisfy the master and reduce the driver's need to whip or embarrass the weaker, slower slaves. Slave accounts tell of men like Moses Bell, a driver on a wheat farm in Virginia, who helped one woman "cause she wasn't very strong"; or like the driver who countermanded his master's orders and sent a nursing mother back to her cabin because she was "too sick to work." Like any champion of the weak, the driver acquired stature in the eyes of the oppressed. Young slaves appreciated drivers like July Gist, who eased their transition to fieldwork and taught them how to avoid punishment. Gist stressed careful husbandry and never rushed the young slaves as they adapted to the rigors of plowing, hoeing, and picking from sunup to sundown.

Unwritten rules governed the driver's conduct. He must not whip with malice or without cause, for example. The driver who exceeded his authority and surpassed whites in viciousness produced bitterness and recalcitrance. Jane Johnson of South Carolina considered the driver "de devil settin' cross-legged for de rest of us on de plantation," and she could not believe that her master intended "for dat nigger to treat us like he did. He took 'vantage of his [the master] bein' 'way and talk soft when he come again." Slaves reserved special enmity for such drivers. After witnessing a driver lash his mother and aunt, Henry Cheatem swore "to kill dat nigger iffen it was de las' thing I eber done." Mary Reynolds despised Solomon for his savage whippings, and even more because he disrupted the slaves' "frolickin'" and religious meetings in the quarters. In her old age she consoled herself with the assurance that the driver was "burnin' in hell today, and it pleasures me to know it."

If masters or informal community pressures did not check abusive drivers, the slaves resorted to more direct remedies. For example, a host of Florida slaves plotted a mass escape from the driver Prince's blows. When discovered, several of the conspirators preferred incarceration to further subservience to Prince. Some slaves refused to be whipped or to have their families mistreated in any manner, and a driver who challenged them risked violent resistance. According to an Alabama driver who tried to correct an alleged shirker, the slave "flong down his cradle and made a oath and said that he had as live [lief] die as to live and he then tried to take the whip out of my hand." The slaves could return cruelty with cruelty. One group of Louisiana slaves murdered a driver by placing crushed glass in his food, and another killed their driver and cut him into small pieces to conceal the crime.

Many slaves, however, recognized that the driver whipped out of duty rather than desire. Moses Grandy, for example, refused to condemn harsh drivers because he understood that they must whip with "sufficient severity" to retain their posts and keep the lash off their own backs. Slaves would grant the driver that much provided that he showed no taste for it and did not whip when he was not obligated to do so. Many drivers deluded their masters by putting on grand exhibitions of zeal in the white men's presence. Some developed the art, as driver Solomon Northup described it, of "throwing the lash within a hair's breadth of the back, the ear, the nose, without, however, touching either of them." When his master was out of sight, "Ole" Gabe of Virginia whipped a post instead of the slaves while the ostensible victims howled for the master's benefit. He once cracked the post so loudly that his master yelled for him to desist lest he kill the slave, who then bolted screaming from the barn with berry juice streaming down his back. This so horrified the master that he threatened Gabe with a thrashing equal to the one he gave the slave.

The successful driver did not tattle on his people and he kept the white folks out of the slaves' private lives as much as possible. In the letters written by literate drivers to their masters, the drivers remained remarkably reticent on life

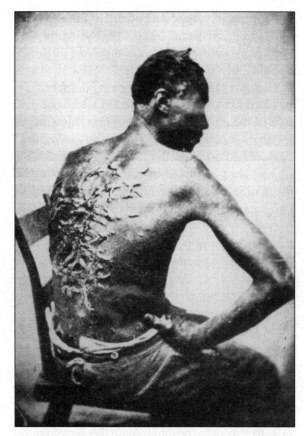

Whip scars crisscross the back of a freed slave from Baton Rouge, Louisiana, in this 1863 photo.

in the quarters: the masters knew little about what went on there from sundown to sunup because the drivers, their principal agents, did not tell them. To be sure, severe fighting among the slaves and egregious crimes were impossible to conceal. By and large, however, the drivers successfully contained the breakdowns of plantation authority, and received sufficient cooperation from the slaves so that they would not be called upon to explain and to punish.

The conscientious driver widened his circle of friends by doing favors, overlooking faults, never breaking a promise, avoiding confrontations whenever possible, and working through the informal group structure to resolve disputes and problems. If clashes occurred—and they were inevitable in the elemental world of the plantation—the driver gave his opponents an opportunity to save face rather than shaming them.

Sometimes he fattened the slaves' larder by pilfering for them from the plantation smokehouse, or arranged passes for them, ostensibly to attend religious meetings or to do chores, but in fact to visit relatives and friends on other plantations. In the quarters he left the correction of a wayward child to the child's parents, respected the slaves' religious leaders, mediated marital squabbles, and protected the weak from thieves and bullies. Slaves applauded the driver who broke up a boisterous, quarrelsome couple by placing them in separate cabins, thus restoring quiet to the quarters and saving the couple from sale at the hands of an irritated master. In brief, the driver acted the way any responsible community leader would act to keep his community intact and safe. He earned the slaves' trust. Ex-slave Billy Stammper summed up the feelings of many slaves toward the driver: "Cullud folks don' min' bein' bossed by er cullud man if he's smart an' good to em," which is to say, if he was smart enough to be good to them.

More than any other event, the Civil War tested the driver's loyalty and expanded his opportunities for self-aggrandizement and to help his people. With the menfolk away during the war, the Southern white lady and the black slave drivers assumed control of the plantations. Frustrated in their efforts to engage white overseers, masters ignored the laws and left their plantations in the hands of house servants, older privileged bondsmen, or drivers of long service—men they could trust not to ravage their land or their women during their absence. In their diaries and later in their histories, planters congratulated themselves that they had not misplaced their trust. However romanticized, the stories of faithful retainers hiding the family silver and shielding the planter's family and homestead from Yankee depredations are legion.

But planters who wanted universal, unfeigned loyalty from their drivers asked for too much. In the midst of unraveling planter hegemony, slave foremen looked to their own interest. Some, like Edmund Ruffin's "faithful and intelligent" Jem Sykes, simply absconded. Some went alone; others inspired a general stampede. If they remained

on the plantations, they sometimes took part in raids on the master's cellar and storehouse. In the absence of a strong white power the slaves neglected the upkeep of the farm and equipment and idled away their days as much as possible. Apparently, drivers could not or would not push their people under such circumstances. The worst excesses occurred in the sugar parishes of Louisiana, where drivers had commanded unusually harsh regimes. The Union advance in 1863 excited many slaves to flee the plantations, but not before they murdered some of their overseers and masters. One Rapides Parish planter wrote that the presence of Federal troops "turned the negroes crazy . . . and everything like subordination and restraint was at an end." The slaves slaughtered livestock and plundered furiously. In this, the drivers "everywhere have proved the worst negroes," perhaps in a bid to retain their leadership through exaggerated displays of violence.

Most drivers, however, remained calm. Conservative men by temperament, they were not about to launch a premature, perhaps suicidal, revolution. On the Chesnut plantation, for example, the drivers early expressed enthusiasm for the Confederate side, thus satisfying their master of their loyalty. In 1864, however, they declined an offer to fight for the Confederacy in exchange for freedom because, as Mrs. Chesnut sagely observed, "they are pretty sure of having it anyway."

Many masters found their drivers "much changed" by emancipation. An embittered Mary Jones of Georgia wrote of the metamorphosis of the driver Cato who headed up a black delegation demanding land: "Cato has been to me a most insolent, indolent, and dishonest man; I have not a shadow of confidence in him, and will not wish to retain him on the place." The Edmonstons of South Carolina found that with freedom their Henry, for fifteen years the master's "right hand man," dropped his "affection and cheerful simplicity" and became "grasping" in his "exorbitant demands" for land. Where they remained as foremen over hired gangs of freedmen, they ingratiated themselves with their charges by easing up on work requirements and stealing for the hands. Much of their authority disappeared with emancipation. When Mrs. R.F.W. Allston visited the plantation of her brother-in-law in April, 1865, she confronted a sullen and insolent group of former slaves who had recently completed their plunder of the plantation provision houses. Mrs. Allston called for Jacob, the head man and sole manager of the estate during the war, and ordered him to give the keys to her. A "huge man" then stepped forward to warn Jacob that if he complied, "blood'll flow." Mrs. Allston departed without the keys.

The paternalistic order of the past was rapidly disrupted by impersonal economic forces in the prostrate postwar South. Planters attempted to lock their former slaves into long-term labor contracts, and looked to the drivers to hold the people on the farms. But neither drivers nor slaves would stay under such conditions. Some owners, short of capital, divided their holdings into tenant parcels and installed a black family on each, sharing the crops of each parcel with the tenant after the harvest. There was, however, no room in this arrangement for the driver.

But with the possible exception of the former slave artisans, the former driver was the most qualified freedman to survive on his own. Indeed, for devotees of Horatio Alger, some former drivers provided inspiring, if somewhat scaled-down, models of success. The story of Limus, a former driver on the sea islands of South Carolina, is a case in point. A "black Yankee" in habits and values, the fifty-year-old freedman started with his one-half acre plot and a beaten-down horse, and raised vegetables and poultry for the Hilton Head market nearby. He also hunted and fished to supplement his income and his family's diet. With two wives and two families to support, he could hardly afford to relax. He worked fourteen acres of cotton on abandoned land to the three to six acres of his fellow freedmen. He also purchased a large boat on which he transported passengers and produce to Hilton Head. His prior marketing experience as a driver stood him in good stead as he negotiated contracts with whites and blacks alike, and he established himself as the principal supplier for the Union troops stationed in the area. By

practicing ruthless underconsumption and efficient management, he saved almost five hundred dollars in his first year of freedom, money which he plowed back into his enterprises.

Some drivers had received gifts of cash and land during slavery from which they could build their estates in freedom; they were able to exploit old relationships for credit; they had learned marketing skills and how to deal with whites in a cash economy, so that they were not so easily cheated or overawed by whites after the war; they understood every level of farm management and practice; and with the artisans they were the slaves most likely to have imbibed the Protestant work ethic of self-denial and persevering labor. If alert and lucky, they could turn the limited opportunities of freedom to their pecuniary gain, provided they did not alienate their benefactors. Recognizing this continued dependence on white aid, one driver warned his fellow freedmen to ignore carpetbagger blandishments, for the "outsiders" would "start a graveyard" if they persuaded blacks to "sass" whites. Even in freedom the former driver straddled two worlds.

The experience of the slave driver should remind us that slavery affected each slave differently—that to fathom the complexities and subtleties of the peculiar institution and those trapped within it, we must take into account each slave's occupational role, his place in the slave and plantation hierarchy, his manner of interaction with the white and black communities, his self-image, to name the most obvious factors. Slave drivers have not fared well in our histories of American Negro slavery. The prevailing neo-abolitionist historiography has limned a portrait of the driver as an unscrupulous, brutal, even sadistic betrayer of his race. He was nothing of the sort. While the driver's behavior was sometimes extreme, it strikingly exemplified the ambiguities and paradoxes of the slave system. Drivers did not brood in self-pity or guilt over their miserable condition and the heavy demands made on them from above and below. They took their world for granted and made the best out of a bad situation. They had to do so. Both white and black depended on the man in the middle.

Slave Girls' Training

Elizabeth Fox-Genovese

Slave women worked at many jobs—house servant, nurse, spinner and seamstress, field hand—not to speak of all that they had to do (in the time their masters allotted) for their own families. One of the topics that historian Elizabeth Fox-Genovese discusses in her book Within the Plantation Household: Black and White Women of the Old South, *excerpted here, is how young slave girls were prepared for the working lives they would face when they left childhood behind, a transition that for many of them came early.*

*E*ven with improvements, slave cabins hardly offered a solid foundation for an independent domestic sphere over which the mother of the family could preside. Primarily places to sleep, take shelter, and eat the last meal of the day, they did not harbor the real life of slave families, much less of the slave community. Harrison Beckett's mother, for example, came in from the fields at nine or ten o'clock at night, often too tired to cook for her husband and children—although she had to if they were to eat. "But lots of times she's so tired she go to bed without eatin' nothin' herself."

However crude and uncomfortable, the cabins bore the mark of their role as extensions of the big house. Like the kitchen, the smokehouse and other outbuildings, they embodied the features of household life that slaveholders preferred to keep at some remove, if also under supervision. Care for her cabin did not normally figure at the core of a slave woman's identity. Especially in the villages of the larger plantations, the slaves could enjoy some sense of their own domestic space, but even there the nearby overseer's house reminded them of the master's observation and control. As often as not, cabins were built and maintained as a responsibility of the household rather than the individual. Many planters would have all the cabins whitewashed by the hands on one occasion and perhaps the floors limed on another. They issued thin cotton blankets that served as the slaves' standard bed coverings. Slaves frequently made an effort to add personal touches here and there. The women contributed quilts to cover the wood beds that slave men often made, and they accumulated small items to make life more comfortable. But there is no evidence that they placed a premium on cleaning or that they could have been especially successful at it if they had. Between the infestations of bugs and the ubiquitous poultry and small animals, not to mention the rigors of field labor, they faced overwhelming odds.

The daughters of specialized nurses, cooks, or textile workers might spend the major part of their time with their own mothers. Mattie Logan's mother was much prized by her mistress, "Miss Jennie" (Mrs. John B. Lewis), all of whose children she nursed. Since Mattie and her siblings and Miss Jennie's children were all conveniently born at about the same time, Mattie's mother just raised "the whole kaboodle of them" together. Mattie Logan "was born about the same time as the baby Jennie. They say I nursed on one breast while that white child, Jennie, pulled away at the other!" Mattie wryly noted that the arrangement served the mistress well, "for it didn't keep her tied to the place and she could visit around with her friends most any time she wanted 'thout having to worry if the babies would be fed or not." Phyllis Petite "just played around" until, at about age six, she was sent to the big house to work with her mother. "She done all the cording and spinning and weaving, and I done a whole lot of sweeping and minding the baby," who was only about six months old. She "used to stand by the cradle and rock it all day, and when I quit I would go to sleep right by the cradle sometimes before mammy would come and get me." Slave mothers, nonetheless, left a strong impression on their daughters, who, after emancipation, variously recalled their mothers' love, discipline, cooking, and occupations. But if slave girls were assigned to general work in the big house, they might not begin their training under their own mothers' direction, and their early years of service might even, to their mothers' distress, remove them from immediate maternal influence.

Slave girls between the ages of six and twelve were frequently enlisted for service in the big house. Nurses might easily be obliged to sleep in their charges' rooms or in the rooms of other white family members in order to be on call during the night and to make the morning fire. Mistresses liked to have a young servant sleep on the floor of their rooms, and even when the girl did not sleep in the room, she would be expected to appear early to make the fire. One slave woman recalled that during her childhood she slept in the bed of her widowed mistress. Another recalled that she slept with her mistress "till I was too big and used to kick her," and that she thereafter slept on the floor. Yet another slept at the foot of her master and mistress's bed.

Some advantages, such as special food and pampering, may have accompanied the move, but they were frequently bought at the price of her everyday relations with her own mother. Sarah Debro, the daughter of a field hand, recalled that when her mistress took her to the big house for training, her own mother cried because she would no longer be living with her.

Other slave girls simply had to be on hand in the big house, "pickin' up chips, sweepin' de yard an' such as dat." Alice Shaw's job as a child was "to fan the flies off the table while the white folks eat and to tote the dishes to the kitchen." Should she drop one, "Miss cracked me on the head." According to Harriet Benton, who had performed the same tasks, "de kitchen wuz way out from de big house," but when it rained "dey had a kin o' cover to put over de trays an' dey jes' come on in de house." The food stayed dry. "Cose, de slaves, dey always got drenched to de bone." When Joanne Draper was six she was taken into the big house "to learn to be a house woman, and they show me how to cook and clean up and take care of babies." Charity Anderson's first job "was lookin' atter de corner table whar nothin' but de desserts set." Initially, young slave girls did not have highly specialized tasks in the house, but, if their nursing sometimes escaped close supervision, their behavior around the mistress did not. Ida Adkins's mistress had snapping black eyes "an' dey seed everythin." "She could turn her head so quick dat she'd ketch you every time you tried to steal a lump of sugar." Ida Adkins preferred her master, whom all "us little chillun" called "Big Pappy. And every time he come back he brung us niggers back some candy."

Convenience alone did not account for the slaveholders' propensity to absorb slave girls into the big house. It was widely believed that the best way to develop good house servants, who were notoriously difficult to come by, was to raise them. In effect the mistress, ably seconded if not outclassed by the cook or mammy, presided over a kind of primary school for servants. Not all of the slave girls who passed through this preliminary training went on to become house servants. Some proved so unpromising that they were assigned to field work as soon as they were considered strong enough to be useful, at about the age of twelve. Others were kept on for more specific training, but, especially in the older regions of labor surplus, they were sold once they had acquired the skills that would net their masters a good return. A few progressed through their apprenticeship to full status as regular house servants, at which point they might have spent their formative years in closer contact with the white family than with the black. At least, the whites hoped so, for the further these black women distanced themselves from the mass of the field slaves, the less likely they would be to spy in the big house. In the many cases in which planters and their families lived much of the year in villages, towns, or cities, the house girls, even if they were with their mothers, grew up well removed from the immediate influence of the slave community.

Within the big house, slave girls received their first introduction to the conditions of their future lives. Even the youngest could become the object of the mistress's flash of anger. The odd piece of sugar was difficult to resist, and the mistress's eagle eye and quick hand did not serve as effective deterrents against repeated attempts. Yet odd tokens of kindness may have had a more lasting effect. As a child, Sally Brown was responsible for carrying food from the kitchen to the big house. The temptations were considerable, for even house slaves were not allowed to eat the delicacies prepared for the white family. One morning, she "wuz carryin' the breakfast to the big house" and there were waffles "that wuz a pretty golden brown and pipin' hot. They wuz a picture to look at and I jest couldn't keep from takin' one." Never was a waffle so hard to eat, especially because she had to get it down before arriving at the big house, but the real difficulty, she claimed years later, came from her own conscience. "I jest couldn't git that waffle down 'cause my conscience whipped me so." More commonly, the white folks rather than conscience administered the whippings. For the slave girl, the quick blows

and occasional whippings rapidly became an expected feature of everyday life. If she could drop a baby without being observed, it is safe to assume that older white children could tease and hit her without adult intervention or even observation. Random cruelty and violence were part of what whites did—part of what they were. Even the kindnesses that singled out particular whites as good masters and mistresses were interpreted as the result of their own basic characters or passing whims, rather than as a response to the slave girl's good efforts.

The early years in the big house could, as intended, frequently develop a slave girl's familiarity with the ways of the house and even a sense of attachment to the white family, but they did not readily foster the kind of systematic training that would have developed a firm sense of the relation between performance and reward. Cicely Cawthon started young in the big house, where her mother had been a house servant since childhood. She had no clearly defined tasks, but "just staid around the house with the Mistis. I was just, you might say, her little keeper." She waited on the mistress, "handed her water, fanned her, kept the flies off her, pulled up her pillow, and done anything she'd tell me to do." Her mother combed the mistress's hair and dressed her. Cicely Cawthon remembered that hair as being so long that her mistress could sit on it, light in color, and "so pretty! I'd call it silver." Fanny Smith Hodges recalled an early master and mistress as "good people." When she began working for them, she was "big enough to draw water, an' put it in a tub an' wash Miss Mary, Miss Annie, an Miss July." Her job was to keep them clean. "I had to comb dey hair an' dey would holler an' say I pulled. I was tol' not to let anything hurt dem chilluns." Fanny Smith Hodges had no mother to monitor her performance or to set an example, for she and her mother lived on different plantations. Just when she had become big enough to dress and wash little children in the household, the master had sold her.

For some slave girls, early association with the white family in the big house provided lasting lessons in what they themselves came to see as "de quality," and occasionally with the roots of what developed into genuine attachment for the white family. If they occasionally bore the brunt of the white children's temper and impertinence, they also shared games and a feeling of childhood camaraderie. Queen Elizabeth Bunts, who owed her name to her young mistress's admiration for the intelligence of that monarch, had a first job of playing with the white children and keeping them entertained. She credited her close association with her master's family for many of her attitudes. "I was never very superstitious, as I was reared by white people and they were never as superstitious as the colored people." Other slave girls played with the white children for fun. Harriet Benton played "hide and seek" and "stealing bases" with the white children. "I looked up to my white folks, of course, but thought of us all, white and black as belonging to one family." As a girl, Mary Anderson visited other plantations with her mistress and looked after the baby girl, Carrie. As Carrie grew up, Mary Anderson remained her special attendant and companion. "She taught me how to talk low and how to act in company. My association with white folks and my training while I was a slave is why I talk like white folks." When Thomas Bayne removed his family from New Orleans to a cottage in Mississippi to avoid the summer heat, he took along four nurses. At the same ages at which the white and black girls were playing together, the white and black boys began to develop special ties through the hunting and fishing that they shared and from which the girls were largely excluded. But even young slaves exercised their own influence on the members of the white family. Virginia Clay-Clopton retained a vivid impression of the "ghastly ghost stories" that she had been told by a house servant, who threatened the white children that if they did not go to sleep immediately, "evil spirits would descend on them."

For slave as for slaveholding girls, the mixed play of early childhood gave way, by early adolescence at the latest, to preparation for their adult roles, at least for those who remained in the big house. Those who were dispatched to the fields also felt the influence of white and black attitudes toward appropriate gender roles, but not so much in their work, which could include many of the tasks normally ascribed to men. Those who stayed on in the big house increasingly found their working lives, however physically demanding, defined by the same expectations about gender roles that governed the lives of slaveholding women.

Slave codes rigorously prohibited teaching slaves to read and write, and well over 90 percent of the slaves remained illiterate. Slave girls' training rarely included the instruction in letters so important for slaveholders' daughters, although continued service in the big house slightly increased their chances of learning to read. As the white girls began to learn to read and write from their mothers, they in turn might try to teach their favorite slaves, who might—but might not—be interested in learning. Many mistresses as well as their daughters frequently avowed their commitment to teaching the female house slaves religious principles and read to them from the Bible or tried to draw them into family prayers. These well-meaning mistresses rarely recognized the slave mother's role in raising her daughter with religious principles. Eliza Clitherall purchased a young maid toward whom she hoped to do her religious duty only to learn, from a letter from the slave girl's mother, "that she has been religiously brought up."

Many slaves passed their girlhoods in the big house, and many more had easy access to it. In any case, they enjoyed light work loads and an appreciable amount of time for play. Elsie Moreland was "a little gal, 'bout six or eight years old, when they put me ter sweepin' yards." When that was done, she would drive cows to pasture and, when she was somewhat older, she "toted water ter the field hands an when they's ginnin' cotton I driv' the gin with fo' mules hitched ter it." During the same period, her sister was a waitress in the big house. Boys as well as girls were regularly assigned to carry water to the field hands and fetch wood for the kitchen. Even girls who worked in the house could be called upon for farm labor. Lily Perry remembered having been a "house gal, pickin' up chips, mindin' de table an' feedin' de hogs." Feeding the hogs taxed her strength, because "de slop buckets wus heavy an' I had a heap of wuck dat wus hard ter do." She did her very best, "but often I got whipped jest de same." One woman, when very young, had accompanied her mother to the fields to tend the baby, her younger sibling. She "tote it down to de fiel' for her to nuss. Den de baby would go to sleep and we'd lay it down 'twixt de cotton rows and ma would make me help her." But working with her mother did not spare her the threat of discipline, for her mother, who had permission to leave the fields when she had completed a specified amount of work, expected her daughter to work at a rapid pace. Mother had a "long switch and iffen I didn't wuk fast enuf, she switch me." More often than not they would finish by noon and return to the quarters, where, if it was "fruit time," mother "put up some fruit for mistis."

Between the ages of six and twelve, slave girls who did not go to the big house spent much of their time in the yard, where they would work with old slaves and other slave children in the trash gang. Caroline Ates "never did no house work 'till after freedom," although one of her aunts was a cook for the master, another his house maid, and her mother the cook for all of the slaves. "When I wuz 'bout leben, I began totin' water ter the field han's. Then, they started learnin' me ter chop cotton an' I soon began workin' there, too." Gradually the girls were eased into field work, where—at least initially, perhaps even more than in the big house—they might be introduced to their working lives by their own mothers, who could teach them such basic tasks as picking cotton and perhaps protect them from the impatience of the overseer. Fannie Moore's mother was whipped by the overseer for fighting him when he whipped her children. As their work in the fields became a regular responsibility, slave girls, like slave boys, were treated as half-hands and worked with other children at the lighter tasks. Jim Allen remembered that he and a girl worked in the

field, "carrying one row" since it "took two chillens to make one hand." During the picking season on cotton plantations, children joined the women in picking. Nicholas Massenburg noted that in September, while the women were spinning, the "small hands" were pulling peas and doing other light tasks. By their mid-teens, young slave women would be assuming their adult work loads.

Neither slaves nor mistresses provided clear accounts of how young slave women were trained for their adult responsibilities, although occasionally a mistress noted that she was training or would have to train a young maid. Such passing remarks do not clarify whether the mistress herself would do the training or whether, as in so many other instances, she would delegate the task to one of her house slaves. Masters showed even less interest in training the young female field hands, although their notations on the work of mature women demonstrate that the women who worked in the fields developed distinct skills from plowing to spinning. Young slave women learned primarily from older slave women, in some instances their own mothers. Picking cotton is the clearest example, but there are others. The slave girls who worked in the big house had more supervisors than they wanted, from the mistress and her daughters to the established house servants. When there was a meal to prepare, an experienced cook expected swift obedience from her helpers, especially from her own daughter, however easygoing she might be under more relaxed circumstances. Few had patience with dropped dishes or flies in the dessert. But there remained a gap between the expectation of performance and the acquisition of skills.

Slave nurses, more commonly than other slaves, reported that they had been "trained up" for their occupation. Mistresses frequently wrote of nurses who, like Sarah Gayle's Rose, had been nursing since their earliest years. Among the many baby-minders, some showed an aptitude for their work and continued in it as more babies came. By the time they had nursed three, four, or more of their mistresses' children, they had reached womanhood with an established identity as a nurse, and by then the mistress's oldest daughter might be needing a nurse for her own firstborn. Amos Gadsden's grandmother had nursed all the children and grandchildren on the plantation, but her own daughter, instead of following in her mother's path, had become a laundress. Margaret Thornton had been brought up to nurse and believed that she had done her share. She reckoned that she had nursed 'bout two thousand babies." More modestly, Maggie Black, who was also raised to be a nurse, only claimed that she probably had more children than any sixty-year-old in the vicinity. No, she had no children of her own: "Aw my chillun white lak yuh." But Liza Strickland, who also began by tending her mistress's children, went on to become a "waiting maid," who did just about everything around the house. Amanda McDaniel, who also spent her early years nursing, went on to field work. During her early years in the fields she planted peas and corn and picked cotton, but "never had to hoe and do the heavy work like my mother and sisters did."

Young slave women had to acquire a variety of skills, for although the cooks and other specialized house servants spent most of their lives in their craft, others were drawn into whatever tasks required pressing attention. On the largest plantations, especially the more pretentious ones, a woman was more likely to be sent from the house to help out in the fields than the reverse. Lucy McCullough was raised in the kitchen, where her mother was cook, and in the backyard. "Ah wuz tuh be uh maid fer de ladies in de big house. De house servants hold that dey is uh step better den de field niggers. House servants wuz hiyyah quality folks." Her mother had high standards for her daughter's "quality" behavior. When she was little more than four years old, Lucy McCullough listened to her mistress "scold my mammy 'bout de sorry way mammy done clean de chitlins." She had never heard any-

one berate her mother before. In turn, she drew herself up and rebuked her mistress, "Doan you know Mammy is boss ef dis hyar kitchen. You can't come a fussin' in hyar." Lucy's mother grabbed a switch "en gin ticklin' my laigs." "Miss Millie" laughed. Only her intervention saved little Lucy from a serious whipping.

Lucy McCullough and her mother both grasped an important feature of the status of the most experienced and responsible house servants. Even as a tot, Lucy McCullough had learned that her mother reigned supreme in the kitchen, into which Miss Millie would not normally venture. Doubtless her mother enjoyed wielding her authority, which the other servants had—at least up to a point—to respect. She had doubtless already told her daughter that Miss Millie did not know anything worth knowing about the secrets of cooking. But Lucy's mother knew that Miss Millie ranked higher than her accomplished and indispensable cook in the hierarchy that emanated from the master. No, Miss Millie did not know much about the cleaning of "chitlins," but in practice as well as in theory she had the right to meddle. If she, as mistress, was in one of those moods, the cook had to wait for a more appropriate moment to remind her that they both worked for a higher authority. The assertiveness of cooks and so many other skilled slaves suggests that, in their own scale of values, competence had its own hierarchy, as even the master himself should appreciate. In extreme cases, the reminders—as mistresses knew but did their best to repress—could take the form of poison. Lucy's mother could not afford to raise her daughter in the illusion that it was permissible to defy Miss Millie's position as mistress, even if she was already privately teaching her to mock Miss Millie's pretensions to culinary expertise. She could—as did more than a few others—instruct her in the most powerful weapons at her disposal.

Slave Women as Field Workers

Jacqueline Jones

Field work, never easy even for physically fit male slaves, laid an especially heavy burden on slave women. Often the overseers and drivers made no allowance for the lesser strength of female slaves, or for the differences in productivity that age, pregnancy, or the presence of small children could make. Women, too, were subject to the same brutal discipline as were men. In this selection, historian Jacqueline Jones discusses what it meant for slave women to do field work in this excerpt from her 1995 book Labor of Love, Labor of Sorrow: Black Women, Work, and the Family from Slavery to the Present.

The drive for cotton profits induced slaveowners to squeeze every bit of strength from black women as a group. According to some estimates, in the 1850s at least 90 percent of all female slaves over sixteen years of age labored more than 261 days per year, eleven to thirteen hours each day. Few overseers or masters had any patience with women whose movements in the field were persistently "clumsy, awkward, gross, [and] elephantine" for whatever reasons—malnutrition, exhaustion, recalcitrance.

As [ex-slave] Hannah Davidson said: "If you had something to do, you did it or got whipped." The enforced pace of work more nearly resembled that of a factory than a farm; [Fanny] Kemble* referred to female field hands as "human hoeing machines." The bitter memories of former slaves merely suggest the extent to which the physical strength of women was exploited. Eliza Scantling of South Carolina, only sixteen years old at the end of the Civil War, plowed with a mule during the coldest months of the year: "Sometimes me hands get so cold I jes' cry." Matilda Perry of Virginia "use to wuk fum sun to sun in dat ole terbaccy field. Wuk till my back felt lak it ready to pop in two."

Although pregnant and nursing women suffered from temporary lapses in productivity, most slaveholders apparently agreed with the . . . "well-known, intelligent and benevolent" Mississippi planter who declared that "Labor is conducive to health; a healthy woman will rear most children." (They obviously did not have the benefit of modern medical knowledge that links the overwork of pregnant mothers not only with a consequent decline in their reproductive capacity but also with Sudden Infant Death Syndrome affecting primarily children under six months of

* An Englishwoman who lived in the South and described slavery vividly.

age.) Still, slaveowners faced a real dilemma when it came to making use of the physical strength of women as field workers and at the same time protecting their investment in women as childbearers. These two objectives—one focused on immediate profit returns and the other on long-term economic considerations—at times clashed, as women who spent long hours picking cotton, toiling in the fields with heavy iron hoes, and walking several miles a day sustained damage to their reproductive systems immediately before and after giving birth. At the regional level, a decline in slave fertility and increase in miscarriage rates during the cotton boom years of 1830 to 1860 reveals the heightened demands made upon women, both in terms of increased workloads in the fields and family breakups associated with the massive, forced migration of slaves from the Upper to the Lower South.

On individual plantations, for financial reasons, slaveholders might have "regarded pregnancy as almost holy," in the words of one medical historian. But they frequently suspected bondswomen, whether pregnant or not, of shamming illness and fatigue—"play[ing] the lady at your expense," as one Virginia planter put it. These fears help to account for the reckless brutality with which owners forced women to work in the fields during and after their "confinement"—a period of time that might last as long as four or six weeks, or might be considerably shortened by masters who had women deliver their children between the cotton rows. Indeed, in the severity of punishment meted out to slaves, little distinction was made between the sexes. Black women attained parity with black men in terms of their productive abilities in the cotton fields; as a result they often received a proportionate share of the whippings. In response to an interviewer's inquiry, a former Virginia slave declared, "Beat women! Why sure he [master] beat women. Beat women jes lak men. Beat women naked an' wash 'em down in brine."

Moreover, it is significant that overseers ordered and supervised much of the punishment in the field, for their disciplinary techniques were calculated to "get as much work out of the slaves as they can possibly perform." Agricultural journalists, travelers in the South, and planters themselves loudly condemned overseers—usually illiterate men of the landless class—for their excessive use of violence. Yet despite the inevitable depletion of their work force from illness and high mortality rates, slaveholders continued to search for overseers who could make the biggest crop. Consequently, many slave women were driven and beaten mercilessly, and some achieved respite only in return for sexual submission. To a white man, a black woman was not only a worker who needed prodding, but also a female capable of fulfilling his sexual or aggressive desires. For this reason, a fine line existed between work-related punishment and rape, and an overseer's lust might yield to sadistic rage. For example, the mother of Minnie Fulkes was suspended from a barn rafter and beaten with a horsewhip "nekkid 'til the blood run down her back to her heels" for fending off the advances of an overseer on a Virginia plantation.

The whipping of pregnant and nursing mothers —"so that blood and milk flew mingled from their breasts"—revealed the myriad impulses that conjoined to make women especially susceptible to physical abuse. The pregnant woman represented the sexuality of the slave community in general, and that of her husband and herself in particular; she thus symbolized a life in the quarters carried on apart from white interference. One particular method of whipping pregnant slaves was used throughout the South; "they were made to lie face down in a specially dug depression in the ground," a practice that provided simultaneously for the protection of the fetus and the abuse of its mother. Slave women's roles as workers and as childbearers came together in these trenches, these graves for the living, in southern cottonfields. The uniformity of procedure suggests that the terrorizing of pregnant women was not uncommon.

Impatient with slow workers and determined to discipline women whom they suspected of feigning illness, masters and overseers at times indulged in rampages of violence that led to the victim's death. Former Mississippi slave Clara

Young told of her seventeen-year-old cousin "in de fambly way fer de fust time" who "couldn' work as hard as de rest." The driver whipped her until she bled; she died the next morning. He had told the other slaves, "if dey said anything 'bout it to de marster, he'd beat them to death, too, so ever'body kep' quiet an' de marster neber knowed." Thus cruelty derived not only from the pathological impulses of a few individuals, but also from a basic premise of the slave system itself: the use of violence to achieve a productive labor force.

Upon first consideration, the frequency with which small boys and girls, pregnant women, mothers of as many as ten children, and grandmothers were beaten bloody seems to indicate that an inexplicable sadism pervaded the Old South. In fact, whites often displaced their anger at particularly unruly blacks onto the most vulnerable members of the slave community. Frederick Douglass, a former slave, argued that "the doctrine that submission to violence is the best cure for violence did not hold good as between slaves and overseers. He was whipped oftener who was whipped easiest." Like the mistress who was "afraid of the grown Negroes" and beat the children "all the time" instead, many whites feared the strong men and women who could defend themselves—or retaliate. Primary sources contain innumerable examples of slaves who overpowered a tormenter and beat him senseless or killed him with his own whip. Referring to a powerful slave who "wouldin' 'low nobody ter whip 'in," one plantation owner told his overseer, "let 'im 'lone[;] he's too strong ter be whup'd." The overseer's hatred of this slave was bound to find some other form of release; by abusing a weaker person, he could unleash his aggression and indirectly punish the menacing relative or friend of his victim.

At times, a woman would rebel in a manner commensurate with the work demands imposed upon her. "She'd git stubborn like a mule and quit." Or she took her hoe and knocked the overseer "plum down" and "chopped him right across his head." When masters and drivers "got rough on her, she got rough on them, and ran away in the woods." She cursed the man who insisted he "owned" her so that he beat her "till she fell" and left her broken body to serve as a warning to others: "Dat's what you git effen you sass me." Nevertheless, a systematic survey of the FWP slave narrative collection reveals that women were more likely than men to engage in "verbal confrontations and striking the master but not running away," probably because of their family responsibilities. A case study of a Georgia plantation indicates that, when women did run away, they usually accompanied or followed spouses already in hiding.

Family members who perceived their mothers or sisters as particularly susceptible to abuse in the fields conspired to lessen their workload. Frank Bell and his four brothers, slaves on a Virginia wheat farm, followed his parents down the long rows of grain during the harvest season. "In dat way one could help de other when dey got behind. All of us would pitch in and help Momma who warn't very strong." The overseer discouraged families from working together because he believed "dey ain't gonna work as fast as when dey all mixed up," but the black driver, Bell's uncle, "always looked out for his kinfolk, especially my mother." James Taliaferro told of his father, who counted the corn rows marked out for Aunt Rebecca, "a short-talking woman that ole Marsa didn't like" and alerted her to the fact that her assignment was almost double that given to the other women. Rebecca indignantly confronted the master, who relented by reducing her task, but not before he threatened to sell James's father for his meddling. On another plantation, the hands surreptitiously added handfuls of cotton to the basket of a young woman who "was small and just couldn't get her proper amount."

No slave woman exercised authority over slave men as part of their work routine, but it is uncertain whether this practice reflected the sensibilities of the slaveowners or of the slaves themselves. Women were assigned to teach children simple tasks in the house and field and to supervise other women in various facets of household industry. A master might "let [a woman] off fo' de buryings 'cause she know how to manage de other niggahs and keep dem quiet at de fu-nerls," but he would not install her as a driver over people in the field. Many strong-willed women demonstrated that they commanded respect among males as well as females, but more often than not masters perceived this as a negative quality to be suppressed. One Louisiana slaveholder complained bitterly about a particularly "rascally set of old negroes"—"the better you treat them the worse they are." He had no difficulty pinpointing the cause of the trouble, for "Big Lucy, the leader, corrupts every young negro in her power." On other plantations women were held responsible for instigating all sorts of undesirable behavior among their husbands and brothers and sisters. On Charles Colcock Jones's Georgia plantation, the slave Cash gave up going to prayer meeting and started swearing as soon as he married Phoebe, well-known for her truculence. Apparently few masters attempted to co-opt high-spirited women by offering them positions of formal power over black men.

Selection 8

Hired-Out Slaves

Kenneth M. Stampp

In this selection, Kenneth M. Stampp analyzes the kinds of work performed by slaves in southern industry, most of them leased for a set term by their owners.

Each year, around the first of January, at southern crossroad stores, on the steps of county courthouses, and in every village and city, large crowds of participants and spectators gathered for "hiring day." At this time masters with bondsmen to spare and employers in search of labor bargained for the rental of slave property. Thus thousands of nonslaveholders managed temporarily to obtain the services of slaves and to enjoy the prestige of tenuous membership in the master class. Thus, too, many bondsmen found it their lot to labor for persons other than their owners. Hired slaves were most numerous in the Upper South; during the 1850's perhaps as many as fifteen thousand were hired out annually in Virginia alone. But slave-hiring was a common practice everywhere.

In December and January southern newspapers were filled with the advertisements of those offering or seeking slaves to hire. Some of the transactions were negotiated privately, some by auctioneers who bid slaves off at public outcry, and some by "general agents" who handled this business for a commission. In Richmond, P.M. Tabb & Son, among many others, advertised that they attended "to the hiring out of negroes and collecting the hires" and promised to give "particular attention . . . through the year to negroes placed under their charge."

Though slaves were occasionally hired for short terms, it was customary to hire them from January until the following Christmas. Written contracts specified the period of the hire, the kind of work in which the slaves were to be engaged, and the hirer's obligation to keep them well clothed. Usually an owner could spare only a few, but occasionally a single master offered as many as fifty and, rarely, as many as a hundred. Though most slaves were hired in the vicinity of their masters' residences, many were sent long distances from home. . . .

A variety of circumstances contributed to this practice. If for some reason the owner was unable to use his slaves profitably, if he was in debt, or if he had a surplus of laborers, he might prefer hiring to selling them. Executors hired out slave property while estates were being settled. Sometimes lands and slaves together were rented to tenants. Heirs who inherited bondsmen for whom they had no employment put them up for hire. Many spinsters, widows, and orphans lived off the income of hired slaves who were handled for them by administrators. Masters often directed in their wills that slaves be hired out for the benefit of their heirs, or that cash be invested in slave property for this purpose. A widow in Missouri hired out most of her slaves, because she found it to be "a better business" than working them on her farm. Occasionally a slaveowner endowed a church or a benevolent institution with slaves whose hire was to aid in its support.

In addition, urban masters often hired out the husbands or children of their female domestics. Both they and planters who had more domestics than they could use or afford disposed of them in this manner. It was also very common for urban and rural owners of skilled slaves to hire them to others at least part of the time. Planters hired their carpenters and blacksmiths to neighbors when they had no work for them and thus substantially augmented their incomes. A master sometimes hired a slave to a white artisan with the understanding that the slave was to be taught his skill. For example, a contract between a North Carolina master and a white blacksmith provided that the hirer was to work a slave "at the Forge during the whole time and learn him or cause him to be learned the arts and mysteries of the Black Smith's trade."

A few Southerners bought slaves as business ventures with the intention of realizing profits solely through hiring them to others. Between 1846 and 1852, Bickerton Lyle Winston, of Hanover County, Virginia, purchased at least fifteen slaves for this purpose. Winston kept careful records of these investments, noting the purchase prices, the annual income from and expenses of each slave, and the net profit. The slaves Randal and Garland were his first speculations. Randal's record ended abruptly in 1853 with the terse notation: "Deduct medical and funeral expenses: $20." Four years later Winston recorded the fact that "Garland came to his end . . . by an explosion in the Black Heath Pits." Some overseers pursued a similar course by investing in slaves whom they hired to their employers. A resident in Mississippi knew families "who possess not an acre of land, but own many slaves, [and] hire them out to different individuals; the wages constituting their only income, which is often very large."

Farmers and planters frequently hired fieldhands to neighbors for short periods of time. Cotton growers who finished their picking early contracted to help others pick their cotton for a fee. When a planter's crop was "in the grass" he tried to borrow hands from neighbors with the understanding that the labor would be repaid in the future. Small slaveholders sometimes made less formal agreements to help each other. A Virginia farmer lent his neighbor two mules and received in return "the labor of one man for the same time." Many masters were generous in lending the labor of their slaves to friends.

The demand for hired slaves came from numerous groups. The shortage of free agricultural labor caused planters to look to this practice as a means of meeting their seasonal needs for additional workers. During the grinding season sugar growers hired hands from Creole farmers or from cotton planters after their crops were picked. Small farmers who could not afford to buy slaves were well represented in the "hiring-day" crowds. Some landowners employed free Negroes, Indians, or poor whites, but they generally preferred to hire slaves when they were available.

The great majority of hired slaves, however, were employed by those who sought a supply of nonagricultural labor. Many urban families hired rather than owned their domestic servants. Advertisements such as these appeared in every southern newspaper. "Wanted immediately, a boy, from 14 to 19 years of age, to do house work. One that can be well recommended from his owner." "Wanted a Black or Colored Servant, to attend on a Gentleman and take care of a Horse." Hotels and watering places hired most of their domestics; laundries, warehouses, shipyards, steamships, cotton presses, turpentine producers, mine operators, lumberers, and drayage companies all made considerable use of hired slaves. Free artisans seldom could afford to own bondsmen and therefore hired them instead. Even a free Negro cooper in Richmond for many years hired a slave assistant.

In most cases southern railroad companies did not own the slaves they employed; rather, they recruited them by promising their owners generous compensation. Railroad builders obtained most of their hands in the neighborhood of their construction work, but they often bid for them in distant places. . . .

An advertisement in a Kentucky newspaper for "twenty-five Negro Boys, from thirteen to fifteen years old, to work in a woolen factory" pointed to another source of the demand for hired slaves. Gristmills, sawmills, cotton factories, hemp factories, iron foundries, and tobacco factories used them extensively, especially the smaller enterprises with limited capital. In 1860, about half of the slave laborers in Virginia tobacco factories were hired.

A small group of slaves obtained from their masters the privilege of "hiring their own time." These bondsmen enjoyed considerable freedom of movement and were permitted to find work for themselves. They were required to pay their masters a stipulated sum of money each year, but whatever they could earn above that amount was theirs to do with as they wished. Almost all of the slaves who hired their own time were skilled artisans; most of them were concentrated in the cities of the Upper South. Though this practice was illegal nearly everywhere and often denounced as dangerous, there were always a few slaves who somehow managed to work in this manner under the most nominal control of their owners.

By permitting a trusted slave artisan to hire his own time the master escaped the burden of feeding and clothing him and of finding employment for him. Then, as long as his slave kept out of trouble, the master's sole concern was getting his payments (which were almost the equivalent of a quitrent) at regular intervals. Frederick Douglass described the terms by which he hired his own time to work as a calker in the Baltimore shipyards: "I was to be allowed all my time; to make all bargains for work; to find my own employment, and to collect my own wages; and, in return for this liberty, I was required, or obliged, to pay . . . three dollars at the end of each week, and to board and clothe myself, and buy my own calking tools. A failure in any of these particulars would put an end to my privilege. This was a hard bargain."

But whatever the terms, most slave artisans eagerly accepted this arrangement when it was offered to them. A Negro blacksmith in Virginia pleaded with his master for the privilege of hiring his own time: "I would . . . be much obliged to you if you would authorize me to open a shop in this county and carry it on. . . . I am satisfied that I can do well and that my profits will amount to a great deal more than any one would be willing to pay for my hire."

This slave had his wish granted, but few others shared his good fortune. It was the lot of the ordinary bondsman to work under the close supervision of his master or of some employer who hired his services. For him bondage was not nominal. It was what it was intended to be: a systematic method of controlling and exploiting labor.

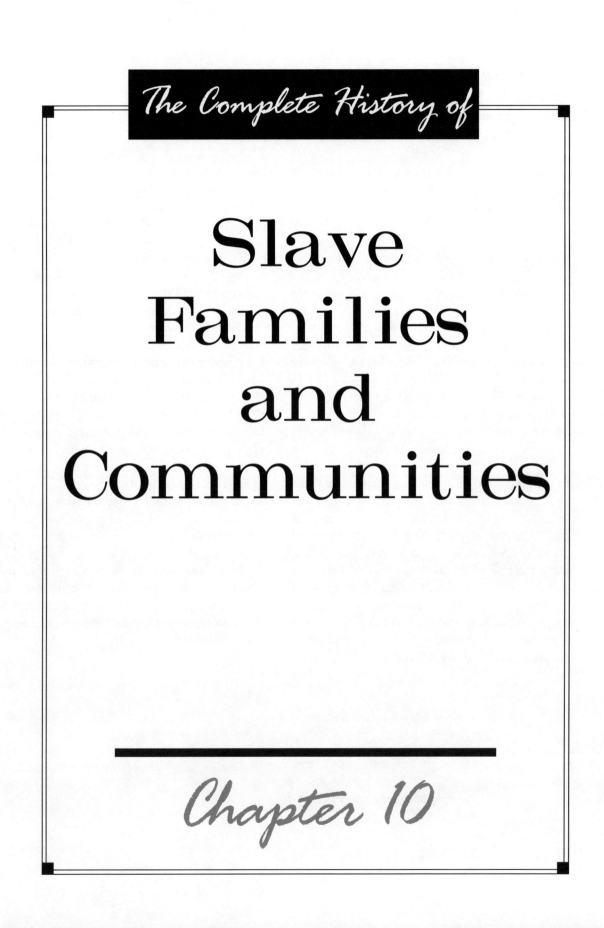

The Complete History of

Slave Families and Communities

Chapter 10

Introduction

The subject of this chapter is elusive: the kind of families and communities that enslaved black people created for themselves despite the hardships of bondage. It also touches on the sensitive topic of sexual abuse by white masters—one of the most painful aspects of enslavement, since it struck directly at the family institutions that African Americans were trying to build.

Until the mid–twentieth century, whites who were studying slavery tended to assume that black family structures were weak. Constantly threatened by their owners' arbitrary power to disrespect them and to break up their families through sale, it seemed unlikely that enslaved blacks stood much chance of developing stable families and communities of their own. One prominent white historian, deeply sympathetic to the slaves' plight, concluded that slavery had been a "total" institution comparable to a prison or even a Nazi concentration camp. Thus, its black victims emerged with severely damaged "Sambo" personalities: They were humiliated, lacked a sense of group solidarity, and were conditioned to try to survive by shirking work when possible and by currying favor with those in authority when necessary. It was not a pretty picture, but it had also incorporated the findings of psychological studies of Holocaust survivors.

Discussions among U.S. government policy-makers in the late 1960s and early 1970s concerning what should be done to repair the perceived "dysfunction" of urban black families drew on such scholarly generalizations about the long-range effects of slavery.

Thus the 1970s work on black social institutions under slavery published by such major historians as John Blassingame, Herbert Gutman, and Eugene Genovese appeared at an important time in American public life. The essence of these and other scholars' findings was that enslaved African Americans formed families and communities that were remarkably cohesive and close-knit despite the obstacles of bondage. Their social institutions, however, differed from white institutions, and therefore they were often difficult for white observers to notice and understand. This was particularly so because enslaved blacks needed as much psychological "space" as they could create to separate themselves from the intrusions of the whites who forced themselves into so many aspects of their lives.

This chapter includes the writings of scholars who have investigated black social institutions under slavery, as well as some documents that touch on the treatment and the sexual abuse of enslaved women.

The Slave Family

John Blassingame

In this selection, Afri... rian John Blassin... University of M... summary of his re... century slave fam... published a full-l... Slave Community... Antebellum South... e a role in determining behavioral patterns, ...als, and values, the slave family ...ed in order to understand slave ...orm of family life in the quarters ...y from that among free Negroes ...does not mean that the institu- ...to perform many of the tradi- ...of the family. The rearing of ...e of the most important of these ...slave parents were primarily re- ...ining their children, they could ...ck of bondage for them, help ...nd their situation, teach them ...om those their masters tried to ...d give them a referent for self- ...their master.

he Southern ... the New Wo... development ... family. In sharp contr... imbalance in the sex r... slaves severely restri... monogamous mating ... ple, in 1860 there wer... very 100 female slaves in Cuba. The physical basis for the monogamous slave family appears clearly in the sex ratio among slaves in the Southern states. The number of females to every 100 male slaves in the United States was 95.1 in 1820, 98.3 in 1830, 99.5 in 1840, 99.9 in 1850, and 99.3 in 1860. When the sex ratio is broken clown by ages, there were 99.8 and 99.1 females for every 100 male slaves over 15 years of age in 1850 and 1860 respectively.

Since childhood is the most crucial era in the development of personality, and parents play so

If he was lucky, the slave belonged to a master who tried to foster the development of strong family ties in the quarters. A number of planters attempted to promote sexual morality in the quarters, punished slaves for licentiousness and adultery, and recognized the male as the head of the family. One planter asserted in 1836 that he particularly enjoined upon his slaves, "the observance of their marriage contracts. In no instance do I suffer any of them to violate these ties; except where I would consider myself justified in doing so." White churches (when slaves attended them) sometimes helped to promote morality in the quarters by excommunicating adulterers and preaching homilies on fidelity. Most slaveholders, however, did not care about the sexual customs of their slaves as long as

Reprinted from John Blassingame, "The Slave Family in America," *American History Illustrated*, 1979. Reprinted with permission from the Estate of John Blassingame.

there was no bickering and fighting. As a result, planters were generally more interested in encouraging monogamy because it was conducive to discipline than because of any interest in encouraging morality in the quarters. Many of the plantations were so large that it was impossible for masters to supervise both the labor and the sex lives of their slaves. Sexual morality, often imperfectly taught (or violated by whites with impunity), drifted down through a heavy veil of ignorance to the quarters. Consequently, for a majority of slaves, sex was a natural urge frequently fulfilled in casual liaisons.

The white man's lust for black women was one of the most serious impediments to the development of morality. Few slave parents could protect their pretty daughters from the sexual advances of white men particularly when the slaves belonged to a white bachelor or lived near white bachelors. Often through "gifts," but usu-

ally through force, white overseers and planters obtained the sexual favors of black women. Generally speaking, the women were literally forced to offer themselves "willingly" and receive a trinket for their compliance rather than a flogging for their refusal and resistance. A number of white men sought more than fleeting relationships with black women. Frequently they purchased comely black women for their concubines. In many cases the master loved his black concubine and treated her as his wife. On innumerable occasions white women also had assignations with black slaves. The evidence from Virginia divorce petitions is conclusive on this point: a Norfolk white man asserted in 1835 that his wife had "lived for the last six or seven years and continues to live in open adultery with a negro man. . . ." A Nansemond County white man declared in 1840 that his wife had given birth to a mulatto child and that she had "recently been

Despite living under the control of their masters and being subject to their owners'
sexual advances, many slaves managed to form stable family relationships.

engaged in illicit intercourse with a negro man at my own house and on my own bed." In many cases the sexual relations between Negro men and white women went undetected because the children resulting from such union were light enough to pass for white. For example, one Virginian testified that when his white wife gave birth to a mulatto he "did not at first doubt [it] to be his, notwithstanding its darkness of color, and its unusual appearance."

One white woman in 18th century Virginia who had a mulatto child convinced her husband that the child was dark because someone had cast a spell on her. (He believed the story for eighteen years.)

Regardless of the actions of the planters, the courtship pattern in the quarters differed, in many respects, from that of whites. Sexual conquest became a highly respected avenue to status in the quarters. The slave caroused with black damsels on his own plantation and slipped away, with or without a pass, to other estates until he was smitten by love. He persistently pursued the one of his choice often over a long period of courtship. He flattered her, exaggerated his prowess, and tried to demonstrate his ambition and especially his ability to provide for her.

Love is no small matter for any man; for a slave it represented one of the major crises in his life. Many slaves vowed early in life never to marry and face separation from loved ones. If they had to marry, the slave men were practically unanimous in their desire to marry women from another plantation. They did not want to marry a woman from their own and be forced to watch as she was beaten, insulted, raped, overworked, or starved without being able to protect her.

Unfortunately for most slaves, the master had the final word in regard to their marriage partners. Most slaveholders, feeling that the children their male slaves had by women belonging to other planters was so much seed spewed on the ground, insisted that they marry women on their own estates. Such a practice placed all of the slave's interests under the control of the master and gave the slave fewer excuses to leave the estate. Some masters brought both of the prospec-

tive mates together and inquired if they understood the seriousness of their undertaking. If they belonged to different masters it was often more difficult for them to obtain the consent of either one. But, if both the lovers persistently spurned prospective partners on their own plantations, the planters, by mutual agreement, might resolve the controversy. Wealthy masters frequently purchased the female slave and thereby won the loyalty of the male. If the matter could not be resolved by the planters, the love might be consummated in spite of their objections. The marriage ceremony in most cases consisted of the slaves' simply getting the master's permission and moving into a cabin together. The masters of domestic servants either had the local white minister or the black plantation preacher perform the marriage ceremony and then gave a sumptuous feast in their own parlors to the slave guests. Afterwards, the slaves had long dances in the quarters in honor of the couple.

In spite of the loose morality in the quarters, in spite of the fact that some men had two wives simultaneously, there was a great deal of respect for the monogamous family. Whether the result of religious teachings, the requirements of the master, or the deep affection between mates, many slaves had only one partner. Henry Box Brown, for instance, refused his master's order to take another mate after his wife was sold because he felt marriage "was a sacred institution binding upon me." Affection, not morality, was apparently the most important factor which kept partners together. This emerges most clearly in the lamentations and resentments which pervade the autobiographies over the separation of family members. Frequently when their mates were sold, slaves ran away in an effort to find them. The fear of causing disaffection forced planters to recognize the strength of the monogamous family; they frequently sold a slave in the neighborhood of his mate when they moved their slaves farther south. Because they were denied all the protection which the law afforded, slaves had an almost mythological respect for legal marriage. Henry Bibb believed that "there are no class of people in the United States who so highly appreciate the legality of marriage as those persons who have been held and treated as property."

After marriage, the slave faced almost insurmountable odds in his efforts to build a strong stable family. First, and most important of all, his authority was restricted by his master. Any decision of his regarding his family could be countermanded by his master. The master determined when both he and his wife would go to work, when or whether his wife cooked his meals, and was often the final arbiter in family disputes. In enforcing discipline, some masters whipped both man and wife when they had loud arguments or fights. Some planters punished males by refusing to let them visit their mates when they lived on other plantations. In any event, these slaves could only visit their mates with their masters' permission. When the slave lived on the same plantation with his mate, he could rarely escape frequent demonstrations of his powerlessness. The master, and not the slave, furnished the cabin, clothes, and the minimal food for his wife and children. Under such a regime slave fathers often had little or no authority.

By all odds, the most brutal aspect of slavery was the separation of families. The callous attitudes frequently held by planters toward slave unions are revealed in the marriage contracts of the Freedmen's Bureau: 32.4 per cent of the unions were dissolved by masters. An overwhelming majority of the couples were separated before they reached their sixth anniversary. The heartlessness of the planters is revealed more clearly in their separation of slaves who had lived together for decades. Several instances of this appeared in Louisiana: Hosea Bidell was separated from his mate of twenty-five years; Valentine Miner from his after thirty years; and, in the most horrifying case of them all, Lucy Robinson was separated from her mate after living with him for forty-three years. Although such separations made the slave family one of the most unstable institutions imaginable, it should be emphasized that there were numerous unions which lasted for several decades. Those enduring for twenty or thirty years were not uncommon, and a few recorded in Tennessee lasted for more than forty years. If only the actions of masters are considered, 67.6 per cent of the slave unions were unbroken. In other words, in spite of their callous attitudes, masters did not separate a majority of the slave couples.

Many slaves were lucky enough to have masters who refused to intercede in family affairs. In order to relieve themselves of responsibility, many planters gave slave parents complete control of their children. Some masters did not punish slave children but instead asked their parents to do so. On Charles Ball's plantation the overseer did nothing to undermine the authority black males had in their families even when they beat their wives. On large plantations and in cities the slaves were so rarely under the constant surveillance of their masters that there the black male faced no obstacle (other than his mate) in exercising authority in his family. While living in Baltimore, for instance, Noah Davis declared that he had "the entire control" of his family.

There were several avenues open to the slave in his effort to gain status in his family. Whenever possible, men added delicacies to their family's monotonous fare of corn meal, fat pork, and molasses by hunting and fishing. If the planter permitted the family to cultivate a garden plot or to raise hogs, the husband led his wife in this family undertaking. The husband could also demonstrate his importance in the family unit by making furniture for the cabin or building partitions between cabins which contained more than one family. The slave who did such things for his family gained not only the approbation of his wife, but he also gained status in the quarters. According to William Green, in the view of the slaves when one tried to provide for his family in this manner: "the man who does this is a great man amongst them." Sometimes, by extra work, slave men earned enough money to buy sugar and coffee for the family or to surprise their wives with scarves or dresses. Often, when masters did not provide adequate clothing for their slaves, black men bought clothes for their children and wives.

Masters, not the black man, determined how much care and attention slave women received when they were pregnant and the treatment that infants received. During her pregnancy a slave wife usually continued her back-breaking labor until a few weeks before her child was born. Solicitous of the health of the new child, the slave owner generally freed the mother of labor for a few days and often for weeks to nurse the infant. If he were especially interested in rearing slave children (and most masters were), he established a definite routine for nursing the child. The mother either carried the infant to the field with her or returned to the cabin at intervals during the day to nurse it. In either case, he was neglected. Fed irregularly or improperly, young black children suffered from a variety of ills. Treated by densely ignorant mothers or little more enlightened planters, they died in droves.

If he survived infancy, the slave child partook, in bountiful measure for a while, of many of the joys of childhood. Slave parents, in spite of their own sufferings, lavished love on their children—fathers regaled their children with fascinating stories and songs and won their affections with little gifts. These were all the more important if the father lived on another plantation. Grandparents, as for all children, loomed large in the life of the slave child. Grandmothers frequently prepared little tidbits for the children, and grandfathers often told them stories about their lives in Africa.

Often assigned as playmates to their young masters, Negro children played in promiscuous equality with white children. Together they roamed the plantation or went hunting, fishing, berry picking, or raiding watermelon and potato patches. Indeed, at first, bondage weighed lightly on the shoulders of the black child. Lunsford Lane, in reflecting on his childhood on a North Carolina plantation, wrote: "I knew no difference between myself and the white children, nor did they seem to know any in turn. Sometime my master would come out and give a biscuit to me and another to one of his white boys; but I did not perceive the difference between us."

Most of the slaves, of course, did not have such idyllic childhoods. Thomas Jones summed up the experience of many slaves when he declared: "I was born a slave. . . . I was made to feel, in my boyhood's first experience, that I was inferior and degraded, and that I must pass through life in a dependent and suffering condition."

Those who were lucky enough to avoid Jones's experience in early childhood knew what he felt by the time they reached their teens. Many began working irregularly at light tasks before they were 10. After that age they usually started working in the fields. Such labor was the first, and irreparable, break in the childhood equality in black-white relations. Most black children learned vicariously what slavery was long before this point. They were often terrified by the violent punishment meted out to the black men around them.

In the face of all of the restrictions, slave parents made every effort humanly possible to shield their children from abuse and teach them how to survive in bondage. Many of the slave parents tried to inculcate a sense of morality in their children. Strict and pious parents not only taught religious principles to their children, they also taught them not to rebel against their masters. The lessons the slave child learned about conformity were complex and contradictory. Recognizing the overwhelming power of the whites, parents taught children obedience as a means of avoiding pain, suffering, and death. At the same time, they did not teach unconditional submission. Instead, children were often taught to fight their masters and overseers to protect their relatives. For instance, W.H. Robinson's father once told him: "I want you to die in defense of your mother. . . ."

The degree to which slaves were able to give their children hope in the midst of adversity is reflected in the attitudes the black autobiographers held toward their parents. Fathers were loved and respected because of their physical strength, courage, and compassion. Austin Steward described his father as "a kind, affectionate husband and a fond, indulgent parent." James Watkins admired his father because he was "a clever, shrewd man." James Mars stood in awe of his father who "was a man of considerable muscular strength, and was not easily frightened into obedience." Although they were not always perfect male models, most slave fathers had the respect of their children. Viewing the little things that they did to make life more pleasant for their children, Charles Ball asserted: "Poor as the slave is, and dependent at all times upon the arbitrary will of his master, or yet more fickle caprice of the overseer, his children look up to him in his little cabin, as their protector and supporter."

Slave mothers, were, of course, held in even greater esteem by their children. Frequently small children fought overseers who were flogging their mothers. Even when they had an opportunity to escape from bondage, many slaves refused to leave their mothers. As a young slave,

William Wells Brown did not run away because he "could not bear the idea" of leaving his mother. He felt that he, "after she had undergone and suffered so much for me would be proving recreant to the duty which I owed to her."

The love the slaves had for their parents reveals clearly the importance of the family. Although it was weak, although it was frequently broken, the slave family provided an important buffer, a refuge from the rigors of slavery. While the slave father could rarely protect the members of his family from abuse, he could often gain their love and respect in other ways. In his family, the slave not only learned how to avoid the blows of the master, but also drew on the love and sympathy of its members to raise his spirits. The family was, in short, an important survival mechanism.

Selection 2

Kin Networks and Surrogate Families

Herbert G. Gutman

The late Herbert G. Gutman, who taught at Columbia University and headed a large group of historical researchers known as the American Social History Project, in 1976 published a very important book entitled The Black Family in Slavery and Freedom, 1750–1925, *excerpted here. Using an enormous*

body of documentary evidence, Gutman refuted the claim—often repeated both by whites sympathetic to black people's interests and by racists looking for proof of black inferiority—that slavery had badly damaged African Americans' ability to create and sustain strong family structures. Gutman found, however, that because of the constant risk of breakup through sale, slaves defined their families in broader terms than whites understood. Slave children were taught to recognize distant relatives as blood kin and to respect all the older people in their community as "aunts" and "uncles"; everyone understood that the time might well come when such surrogates would have to substitute for parents.

K in groups had powerfully influenced nearly all aspects of traditional West African community life, including agricultural and other economic activities, but New World enslavement prevented the replication of such organic relationships. Plantation work patterns, the common gang system and the less frequent task system, apparently failed to take into account enlarged slave kin groups, and further study may show that a central tension between slaves and their owners had its origins in the separation of work and kinship obligations. Evidence suggesting such tension is found over the entire South just after emancipation. The historians Joel T. Williamson and William S. McFeely find a close connection between post-emancipation land use and familial and kin beliefs. Williamson says the South Carolina ex-slaves "evinced a strong desire to get away from their former owners" but "also showed a desire to remain on or near their home plantation." Williamson's research left him with "the distinct impression that even as most freedmen left the slave villages they spent their lives on farms carved out of plantations within a few miles of the place of their previous servitude." Such behavior follows from their slave experiences. If ex-slaves had deep ties only to immediate family members and wanted to quit former owners, only their poverty would have kept them close to the "home plantation." The cost of moving fifty miles in 1865–1866 was not that much greater than moving "a few miles." But the extended kin networks among the plantation blacks were sufficient reason to remain in a local familial and social setting. Moving a few miles allowed an immediate family to cut loose from the symbol of its servitude and yet remain attached to the kin networks that had developed among them as slaves. McFeely emphasizes a different point than Williamson:

> Much of the impetus for the establishment of the tenant farmer and sharecropper systems came from the former slaves themselves. Work in a field gang had been one of the most hated aspects of slavery. . . . In exchange for agreeing to care for the dependents—old people and children—for whom the planter had been responsible . . . the freedman farmer obtained from the planter a plot of land he would work on his own. . . .

Freshly emancipated and descended from three or more generations of slaves , . . . Georgia blacks [soon after emancipation] condemned their old owners for not providing for "our *old and infirm Mothers* and *Fathers* and our *children*," revealing that their obligations moved backward and forward in social time from their families of origin to the families they then headed as rural laborers. That pull in two directions revealed, once again, how extended kin ties had bound the slaves to one another. About the time they filed this petition [to the Freedman's Bureau], other Georgia ex-slaves and wartime refugees returned home from the South Carolina Sea Islands. "Ay!" the northern missionary W.T. Richardson said of them, "to them, that is holy ground; for it has been watered by their tears and blood. Strange as it may seem to us, the freedmen exhibit strong desires to go back to their former homes, if possible, and enjoy the blessings of freedom, with their families. I know of no other class of persons who manifest stronger local ties."

Few contemporaries and later students of Afro-American behavior realized that these strong "local ties" primarily rested on slave kin networks that bound together immediate families. The Yankee William Gannett, who spent the wartime years among the Sea Islanders, was an exception. "On many estates," he wrote in 1865, "the whole population consists of but two or three distinct families. Everyone is aunt or uncle or cousin to everyone else. The latter titles are so common that abbreviations are necessary: At 'Cl' 'Arkles' Uncle Hercules will turn his head; and even in a quarrel with 'Co' Randy,' the cousinship is not denied." What Gannett noticed among the Sea Island blacks and what was so expressively revealed in the naming practices of Virginia,

North and South Carolina, and Louisiana slaves casts fresh light on Melville J. Herskovits's pioneering *The Myth of the Negro Past* (1941). Ten years before its publication, he and two associates studied 639 Monroe County, Mississippi, blacks, and in the later work Herskovits said that these people "represented 171 families . . . the word 'family' in this context signifying those standard primary biological relationships—parents, children, and grandchildren, but not collateral relatives. One group of related immediate families . . . comprised 141 individuals." Such evidence suggested possible continuities with earlier West African cultural practices: "The mere fact that a feeling of kinship as widespread as this exists among a group whose ancestors were carriers of a tradition wherein the larger relationship units are as important as in Africa gives this case importance as a lead for future investigation.". . .

The Good Hope, Stirling, Cedar Vale, and Bennehan-Cameron slaves deserve a place in this significant controversy. It was over them— and their ancestors and their descendants—that Herskovits and [his scholarly critics] disputed. Too little is yet known about *eighteenth-century* West African familial and kin life and about the domestic arrangements and kin networks that developed among first- and second-generation eighteenth-century North American slaves to suggest direct continuities between kinship networks that existed among Afro-American plantation slaves in the 1850s and the 1860s and their West African forebears. But enough is now known about such networks in the 1850s and the 1860s to suggest continuities between slaves in that time and the rural Mississippi blacks Herskovits studied in the third decade of the twentieth century. Herskovits, who knew a great deal about twentieth-century West African and Afro-American communities, did as much to correct distorted views of these peoples as any scholar of his generation, but his failure to study the changing history of enslaved Afro-Americans led him to emphasize direct continuities between discontinuous historical experiences. Yet, a great debt is owed Herskovits for bringing attention to the "extensive relationship groupings" that existed among early-twentieth-century rural southern blacks. That presence convinced him that "African tradition . . . must . . . be held as prominent among those forces which made for the existence of a sense of kinship among Negroes that is active over a far wider range of relationships than among whites." Herskovits's emphasis on a direct continuity with "African tradition" is not essential in weighing the larger implications of such a comparison. . . .

Obligations rooted in kin ties also affected relations between slaves unconnected to one another by either blood or marital ties. That is learned by giving further attention to the slave "aunt" and "uncle." It is well known that calling adult slaves by such collateral titles occurred commonly among southern whites and blacks, but why such terms of address were used and their social meaning have been little studied. When whites regularly began addressing elderly blacks by the titles "aunt" and "uncle" is unknown, but such terms of address were common in the decades prior to the emancipation. No evidence has yet been found indicating that whites did so before 1800, and it is probable that such titles became common in the early nineteenth century. Slaves—and I mean *Africans, not Afro-Americans*—did so before that time. Mintz and Price suggest that African slaves cut off from very different West African social settings "continued to view kinship as the normal idiom of social relations," and on slave ships, according to Orlando Patterson, "it was customary for children to call their parents' shipmates 'uncle' and 'aunt'" and even for adults to "look upon each other's children mutually as their own." ("So strong were the bonds between shipmates," writes Patterson, "that sexual intercourse between them, in the view of one observer, was considered incestuous.")

Nineteenth-century whites used kin terms of address toward slaves for different reasons. They had two purposes: to show their personal attachment and even respect toward adult slaves (usually house servants) and to use a nonreciprocal term of address that defined an essential status difference between a slave and his or her owners. "Uncle" and "Mister" lived in related but very different worlds. The slaves had different reasons for using similar terms of address. The first is simple. On plantations like the Stirling and Good Hope places, children had uncles and aunts nearby, older kin related to them by blood or marriage. *Uncle* Tom was not the product of Harriet Beecher Stowe's imagination: every Good Hope child born after 1830, for example, had at least one real aunt and uncle living there, and the terms of address used by these children reflected nothing more than the realities of actual kin connections. But parents and other adult blacks also taught slave children to use such titles when addressing *older slaves unrelated to them by either blood or marriage.*

Scant but nevertheless suggestive evidence hints that making children address all adult blacks as either "aunt" or "uncle" socialized them into the enlarged slave community and also invested non-kin *slave* relationships with symbolic kin meanings and functions. Only a few antebellum southern blacks remembered the process clearly. The former Eastern Shore, Maryland, free black Levi Coppin, who was born in 1848, said merely that "the white people did not permit us to say 'Mr.' and 'Mrs.' to each other, so, the children, for 'manner's sake,' were taught to call the older people, 'aunt' and 'uncle.'" ("The slave," Coppin also observed, "was not allowed to say 'sister and brother' in the presence of the master. I came near getting a flogging once because I said to the country storekeeper that I came for a package which 'my sister left there.' 'Your sister!' he shouted. 'Do you mean Mary?' And yet that same man would not hesitate to say that the colt he offered for sale was sister to the one hitched at the post.") A woman who was born a Tennessee slave in 1844 remembered that her master owned four slave families, "Aunt Caroline's family, Uncle Tom's family, Uncle Dave's family, and the family of which I was a member." "None of these others," she said, "were related by blood to us." Her father "had several brothers who lived on other places."

Frederick Douglass and the Yankee schoolteacher Lucy Chase offered explicit reasons why young slaves addressed elderly non-kin by collateral kin titles. Douglass said:

"Uncle" Toby was the blacksmith, "Uncle" Harry the cartwright, and "Uncle" Abel the shoemaker, and these had assistants in their several departments. These mechanics were called "Uncles" by all the younger slaves, not because they really sustained that relationship to any, but according to plantation etiquette as a mark of respect, due from the younger to the older slaves. Strange and even ridiculous as it may seem, among a people so uncultivated and with so many stern trials to look in the face, there is not to be found among any people a more rigid enforcement of the law of respect to elders than is maintained among them.

The young had to "approach the company of an older slave with hat in hand. . . . So uniformly are good manners enforced *among the slaves,* that I can easily detect a 'bogus' fugitive by his manners." Lucy Chase made a similar point in 1863: "They show great respect for age as is manifest from one custom of theirs; they always call an older person Aunt or Uncle." The illustration Chase used strengthened her general observation: "We had two servants living with us. One was a boy and the other a girl. The boy who was younger always called the girl Aunt." A kin term of address was even used toward an older youth.

Kin terms of address taught young slaves to respect older ones, kin and non-kin alike, a respect essential to the socialization and enculturation processes in slave communities where older slaves played crucial roles. "It is from the grandparents of both sexes," Meyer Fortes writes of the West African Ashanti, "that children learn of family history, folklore, proverbs, and other traditional lore. The grandparents are felt to be living links with the past." Elderly slaves—fictive aunts and uncles among them—played that role among Afro-American slaves, a role given status within the slave community by investing such persons with symbolic, or fictive, kin titles. A white met an elderly man on a Mississippi plantation and learned from his owner that "Uncle Jacob was a regulator on the plantation; . . . a *word* or a *look* from him, addressed to younger slaves, had more efficiency than a *blow* from the overseer.". . .

Slaves apparently often addressed all capable leaders as quasi kin, but children learned to address all older slave men and women (not just leaders) by kin titles, a practice that perhaps bound them to fictive kinsmen and kinswomen, preparing them in the event that sale or death separated them from parents and blood relatives. Socializing children to respect all elderly blacks also may have taught them to hide slave feelings and beliefs from nonslaves. Asked about the attitudes of children toward their parents, Laura Towne [a northern white teacher in the post–Civil War South] said, "I never saw it equaled anywhere—their love and obedience." That was so even though parents "were exceedingly severe." She remembered only one instance of "anything like indulgence toward children." "I think they . . . will bear pain to any extent," said Towne. "If a boy cries too early because he is suffering they will deride him. He must be stoical under trouble and his parents will not suffer

complainings. Children undergo a regular discipline." In return, adult kin and non-kin did their best to protect children. In the summer of 1865, the teacher Mary Ames lived among the Edisto Island, South Carolina, blacks and "asked the children if some of their fathers could not come and fix the stove. They began, 'I haven't any father'—'I live with Aunty.'"

Further study of the fictive aunt and uncle promises to enlarge understanding of how slave children became slave adults—that is, how the son, brother, and nephew became husband, father, and uncle and how the daughter, sister, and niece became wife, mother, and aunt. But such study needs first to locate fairly precisely in time when kin terms of address toward non-kin adults began to be used regularly by slaves. We shall probably learn that slaveowners called some elderly black men and women "uncle" and "aunt" because as children they had learned that this was the conventional way in which slave children had been taught to address fictive as well as real black adult kin.

Selection 3

A Southern White Woman Deplores Sexual Abuse

Mary Boykin Chesnut

No one knows how frequently masters, their sons, and other male relatives and their overseers used their power to force slave women

into sexual relationships with them. Slaves' memories, anecdotal evidence, and the frequent presence in the Old South of racially mixed children suggest that sexual abuse was very common. So does the obvious fact that slavery gave owners virtually unlimited power over their bondspeople, a power that could all

Excerpted from Mary Boykin Chesnut, *A Diary from Dixie* (New York: Appleton, 1905).

too easily become an occasion for sexual exploitation and even sadism.

Mary Boykin Chesnut (1823–1886) was the wife of a prominent and wealthy South Carolina politician of the Civil War era. The wartime diary that she kept (and heavily reworked for publication after the war) is filled with incisive comments about changing political and military situations; about the foibles and doings of her neighbors, friends, and relatives; about the growing difficulties of wartime life in the Confederacy (of whose chances for survival she was skeptical); and occasionally about slavery. Early in her diary she reflected on the prevalence of white men having sex with black women; it was one of the things that she most came to hate about slavery.

I wonder if it be a sin to think slavery a curse to any land. [Charles] Sumner said not one word of this hated institution which is not true. Men and women are punished when their masters and mistresses are brutes and not when they do wrong—and then we live surrounded by prostitutes. An abandoned woman is sent out of any decent house elsewhere. Who thinks any worse of a negro or mulatto woman for being a thing we can't name? God forgive us, but ours is a *monstrous* system and wrong and iniquity. Perhaps the rest of the world is as bad—this *only* I see. Like the patriarchs of old our men live all in one house with their wives and their concubines, and the mulattoes one sees in every family exactly resemble the white children—and every lady tells you who is the father of all the mulatto children in everybody's household, but those in her own she seems to think drop from the clouds, or pretends so to think. Good women we have, *but* they talk of all *nastiness*—tho' they never do wrong, they talk day and night of [*erasures illegible save for the words* "all unconsciousness"] my disgust sometimes is boiling over—but they are, I believe, in conduct the purest women God ever made. Thank God for my countrywomen—alas for the men! No worse than men everywhere, but the lower their mistresses, the more degraded they must be.

My mother-in-law told me when I was first married not to send my female servants in the street on errands. They were then tempted, led astray—and then she said placidly, so they told *me* when I came here, and I was very particular, *but you see with what result.*

Mr. Harris said it was so patriarchal. So it is—flocks and herds and slaves—and wife Leah does not suffice. Rachel must be *added,* if not *married.* And all the time they seem to think themselves patterns—models of husbands and fathers.

The Sexual Abuse of Slave Women

Jacob Manson

Jacob Manson, who was born in slavery in North Carolina, told his story to a federal interviewer in the 1930s. His experience was severe but certainly not atypical; notice, for example, the prohibition against slave "prayer meetings" but the requirement that they attend church services with the whites, where they could be properly instructed to be obedient. So it should come as no surprise that Manson saw a good deal of evidence of black women being sexually abused by their masters, as well as by other whites. Manson also claims that certain black men were selected as "breeders" and mated with multiple black women, as if they were all so many horses or cattle.

The story that Manson relates of another master's sexual escapades, to which the master's wife reacted so violently, reveals another evil dimension of slavery, which victimized the white families who supposedly benefited from their privileged position.

It has been a long time since I wus born. 'Bout all my people am dead, 'cept my wife an' one son an' two daughters.
I belonged to Colonel Bun Eden. His plantation

Excerpted from "Jacob Manson," in *Bullwhip Days: The Slaves Remember*, edited by James Mellon. Copyright © 1988 James Mellon. Reprinted with permission from Grove/Atlantic, Inc.

wus in Warren County, an' he owned 'bout fifty slaves or more. Dere wus so many of 'em dere he did not know all his own slaves. We got mighty bad treatment, an' I jest wants to tell you a nigger didn't stan' as much show dere as a dog did. Dey whupped fur mos' any little trifle. Dey whupped me—so dey said—jes' to help me git a quicker gait. De patterollers come sneakin' round often an' whupped niggers on Marster's place. Dey nearly killed my uncle. Dey broke his collarbone when dey wus beatin' him, an' Marster made 'em pay for it, 'cause Uncle never did git over it.

Marster would not have any white overseers. He had nigger foremen. Ha, ha—he liked some of de nigger women too good to have any udder white man playin' aroun' wid 'em.

We worked all day an' some of de night, an' a slave who make a week, even atter doin' dat, wus lucky if he got off widout gettin' a beatin'. We had poor food, an' de young slaves wus fed outen troughs. De food wus put in a trough an' de little niggers gathered round an' et. Our cabins wus built of poles an' had stick-an'-dirt chimneys, one door, an' one little winder at de back end of de cabin. Some of de houses had dirt floors. Our clothin' was poor an' homemade.

Many of de slaves went bareheaded and barefooted. Some wore rags roun' deir heads and some wore bonnets. Marster lived in de greathouse. He did not do any work but drank a lot of whiskey, went dressed up all de time, an' had niggers to wash his feet an' comb his hair. He made me scratch his head when he lay down, so he could go to sleep. When he got to sleep I would slip out. If he waked up when I started to leave, I would have to go back an' scratch his head till he went to sleep agin. Sometimes I had to fan de flies 'way from him while he slept.

No prayer meetings wus allowed, but we sometimes went to de white folks church. Dey tole us to obey our marsters an' be obedient at all times.

When bad storms come, dey let us rest, but dey kept us in de fields so long sometimes dat de storm caught us 'fore we could git to de cabins.

Niggers watched de wedder in slavery time, an' de ole ones wus good a' prophesyin' de wedder.

Marster had no chilluns by white women. He had his sweethearts 'mong his slave women. I ain't no man for tellin' false stories. I tells de truth, an' dat is de truth. At dat time it wus a hard job to find a marster dat didn't have women 'mong his slaves. Dat wus a ginerel thing 'mong de slave owners.

One of de slave girls on a plantation near us went to her missus and tole her 'bout her marster forcing her to let him have somethin' to do wid her, and her missus tole her, "Well, go on. You belong to him."

Female slaves who caught the eye of their male owners were often forced to become concubines.

Another marster named Jimmie Shaw owned a purty slave gal, nearly white, an' he kept her. His wife caught 'im in a cabin bed wid her. His wife said somethin' to him 'bout it, an' he cussed his wife. She tole him she had caught 'im in de act. She went back to de greathouse an' got a gun. When de marster come in de greathouse, she tole 'im he must let de slave girls alone, dat he belonged to her. He cussed her agin an' said she would have to tend to her own damn business an' he would tend to his. Dey had a big fuss an' den Marster Shaw started towards her. She grabbed de gun an' let him have it. She shot 'im dead in de hall. Dey had three chillun—two sons an' one married daughter. Missus Shaw took her two sons an' left. De married daughter an' her husband took charge of de place. Missus an' her sons never come back as I knows of.

A lot of de slave owners had certain strong, healthy slave men to serve de slave women. Ginerally, dey give one man four women, an' dat man better not have nothin' to do wid de udder women, an' de women better not have nothin' to do wid udder men. De chillun wus looked after by de ole slave women who were unable to work in de fields, while de mothers of de babies worked. De women plowed an' done udder work as de men did. No books or larnin' of any kind wus allowed.

One mornin', de dogs begun to bark, an' in a few minutes the plantation wus kivvered wid Yankees. Dey tole us we wus free. Dey axed me whar Marster's things wus hid. I tole 'em I could not give up Marster's things. Dey tole me I had no marster, dat dey had fighted four years to free us, an' dat Marster would not whup me no more. Marster sent to de fields an' had all de slaves come home. He told me to tell 'em not to run but to fly to de house at once. All plow hands an' women come running home. De Yankees told all of 'em dey wus free.

Marster offered some of de Yankees somethin' to eat in his house, but dey would not eat cooked food; dey said dey wanted to cook deir own food.

I married Roberta Edwards fifty-one years ago. We had six sons and three daughters. After the War, I farmed around from one plantation to another. I have never owned a home of my own. When I got too ole to work, I come an' lived wid my married daughter, in Raleigh. I been here four years. I think slavery wus a mighty bad thing. It's been no bed of roses since, but den no one can whup me no mo'.

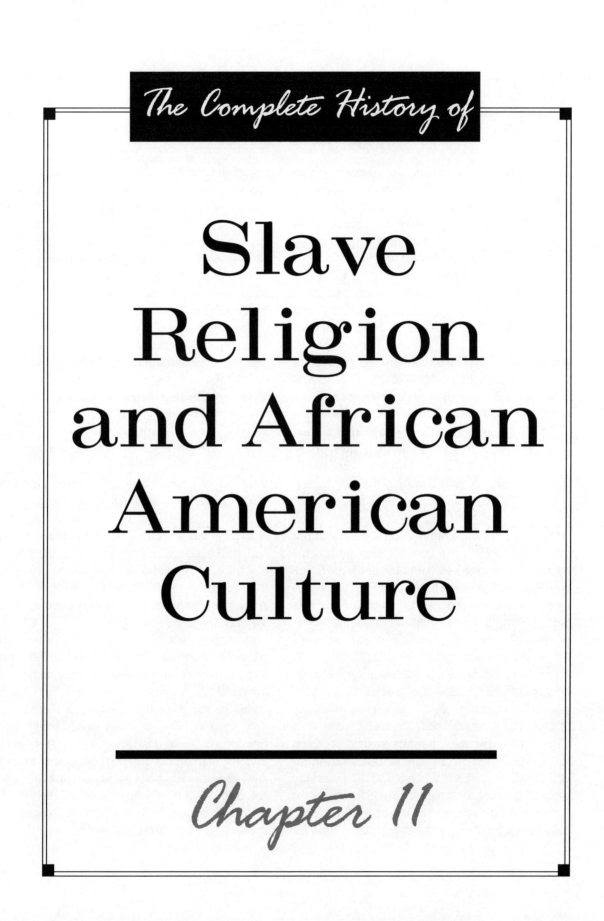

The Complete History of

Slave Religion and African American Culture

Chapter 11

Introduction

*I*n the past, scholars sometimes differed over how much of their heritage their native African slaves were able to preserve in North America. So totally devastating must have been the experience of being forcibly transferred to the New World and made to labor under inhumanly difficult conditions, the argument was often made, that slaves became completely disoriented and lost their old cultural identity, including their art and their religion. More recently, with the advent of contemporary African American efforts to encourage pride in their heritage, scholars have searched systematically for evidence of African influence in the religion and culture of North American slaves.

Today the consensus seems to be that a great deal of their native traditions persisted in the slaves' lives but that these traditions were modified and reshaped into a unique African American culture. For example, slaves evolved "pidgin" languages, like Gullah, that preserved some African words and grammatical forms within a simplified English that could readily be learned by people deprived of formal schooling. Some words appear to have come into modern English by way of slaves' pidgin. For example, linguists believe that *cool,* in its familiar colloquial sense of "good," is the transplanted West African word of the same meaning, *kul.*

Another important example of cultural change concerns religion. By the nineteenth century, African Americans were adopting Christianity readily, but it was not the "sanitized" version of Christianity that their masters wanted to teach them that moved blacks' hearts. Instead of biblical injunctions that "servants" should humbly obey their masters, trusting to the hereafter for their reward (which was the message of the white ministers who preached to them), slaves took in-spiration from the story of Moses, who had led enslaved Israel out of bondage, and of "Massa Jesus," whom God had sent to lead them to freedom. Slavery, they learned on the sly from unlettered but powerful black preachers (themselves fellow slaves), was a trial that God allowed them to suffer. But if they followed God, they would receive eventual freedom in this life and final happiness in heaven, while the masters who had enslaved them would get their appropriate retribution in hell. When they could (that is, outside the church services that the whites provided for them), blacks worshiped with passionate enthusiasm, punctuating their preacher's sermons with "Amens!" and singing, clapping, dancing, and swaying as the spirit moved them. Religious practices descended from their African traditions lived on, often in the form of what whites patronized as "superstitious" habits and what blacks associated with efforts to "read" nature signs and ensure good luck. In short, what was emerging was a synthesis of their native heritage and of chosen elements of Judeo-Christianity that they interpreted to fit their needs—a distinctive religious style that was neither wholly African nor wholly Euro-American but, rather, *African American.*

A similar pattern evolved in the arts. Using whatever materials that they could find in the American environment and that their masters allowed them to have, slaves retained African styles in the basketry, pottery, and woodwork they created for their daily needs (only a tiny fraction of which has survived). Masters generally forbade slaves to own "loud instruments" such as horns and bells, which disturbed whites' rest and could be used to signal an uprising, but they were generally free to fashion string instruments as they pleased and to drum on whatever metal buckets were available. In this way the banjo, for example, became an American musical instrument. It was of purely African origin, though in America fashioned from gourds and hides, and even its name survived intact.

"Slaves sing most when they are most unhappy," wrote Frederick Douglass. "The songs of the slave represent the sorrows of his heart; and he is relieved by them, only as an aching heart is relieved by its tears." To think of black music in slavery times, as most whites did, as harmless entertainment is to miss its point entirely. The chant-and-response (sometimes with satirical overtones), the work song, and the deeply felt "spirituals" all became vehicles for expressing frustration with enslavement and hopes for deliverance. Likewise, black oral tales (the "Uncle Remus" stories, compiled by a white man who overheard them, are a familiar example) had the highly serious purpose of passing on to young people "coded" advice for how to cope with slavery and how to behave toward white authorities. They, too, are essential to understanding how black people shaped their own lives while in bondage.

Selection 1

The Slaves Assimilate Christianity

Eugene D. Genovese

The mass conversion of slaves to Christianity, which began in the second half of the eighteenth century and intensified after 1830, marked an important historical turning point. No longer were slaves simply transplanted Africans, cut off from their native cultures in an alien land; now a widespread African American culture was taking shape, using the same English language that the slaves' masters spoke and rooted in the same Judeo-Christian religion that their masters professed.

In this selection, Eugene D. Genovese continues his exploration of the master-slave relationship by considering what Christianity meant to bondspeople in pre–Civil War America. As he shows, slaves (and in many cases free blacks as well) understood what they learned from the Bible differently than did whites. Enslaved people found in the Judeo-Christian message a compelling means for interpreting their experience in bondage and an inspiration that freedom would eventually come.

*F*olk beliefs might not so easily have passed into the heart of black Christianity had the slaves and free Negroes of the cities not wrested some degree of control of the churches from the whites. Without that degree of autonomy within the structure of formal religion folk belief might have remained an antithesis, and the slaves might have had to make the hard choice between Christianity and an anti-Christianity. Institutional developments and the ability of preachers and the slaves themselves to take advantage of them opened the way toward the absorption of much of the folk culture into the Christian faith.

Whatever the religion of the masters, the slaves, when given a choice, overwhelmingly preferred the Baptists and secondarily the Methodists. By the 1850s the recruitment of blacks to the Episcopal Church in Virginia had virtually ceased. In the South as a whole the Presbyterians had a small following, especially in the up country, and the Catholics scored some success in Louisiana. Melville J. Herskovits has advanced the provocative thesis that the slaves' preference for the Baptists reflected the continued strength of traditional West African religion. Noting the practice of total immersion, he has suggested a connection in the slaves' mind with the powerful river spirits in the West African religions; in particular, he thinks that enslaved priests from Dahomey must have provided leadership and continuity from Africa to Afro-America. E. Franklin Frazier, who has led the attack on Herskovits's thesis, dismisses the argument on the grounds that enslavement and the slave trade had effectively destroyed the social basis of African religion among the blacks and that Herskovits's speculations hardly constitute evidence. He suggests, instead, that the slaves responded to the fiery style and uninhibited emotionalism of the frontier Baptist and Methodist preachers and that the Baptists had the additional advantage of a loose church structure to accommodate slaves more easily. Although Frazier's views have come under withering fire for their extreme formulation of a break with the African past, he clearly has had the better of this particular argument. Herskovits's insistence on links between West African and Afro-American folk religion has merit, but it simply cannot be stretched to account for the slaves' preference for the Baptists.

Arthur Huff Fauset has pointed out that the same blacks who chose the Baptists might have chosen the Methodists, the Baptists' hottest rivals in the plantation districts—and the Methodists' greatest fun in life was ridiculing total immersion and adult baptism.

Methodism, on the face of it, hardly seems a likely candidate for the affections of a high-spirited, life-loving people. Grim, humorless, breathing the fires of damnation—notwithstanding love feasts and some joyful hymns—it was more calculated to associate Jesus with discipline and order than with love. The slaves adjusted Methodism, as they adjusted every other creed, to their own way of life, and they transformed each in the process, as the ring shout may demonstrate. Once converted, the slaves had to stop dancing, for it was sinful. Dutifully, they stopped going to dances and went to the praise-house instead. What they did there looked like dancing to the white uninitiated and still looks like dancing to those who recognize the origin of the Charleston and several other popular dances. But no: it could not have been dancing. Dancing was sinful, and these slaves had been converted. They were not dancing; they were "shouting." Henry George Spaulding, a white Unitarian minister who visited Port Royal, South Carolina, with the United States Sanitary Commission during the war, left us a description of the ring shout, which he insisted was the "religious dance of the Negroes":

> Three or four, standing still, clapping their hands and beating time with their feet, commence singing in unison one of the peculiar shout melodies, while the others walk around in a ring, in single file, joining also in the song. Soon those in the ring leave off their singing, the others keeping it up the while with increased vigor, and strike into the shout step, observing most accurate time with the music. . . . They will often dance to the same song for twenty or thirty minutes. . . .

Whatever Spaulding thought, the blacks convinced themselves that they did not dance the shout, for as everyone knows, you cross your feet when you dance; and since they did not tolerate crossing of feet, they clearly were not dancing.

The slaves' insistence on shouting harked back to Africa in both form and content. The style, which subsequently came to dominate American popular dancing in a variety of versions, could not have been more clearly African. The same might also be said about the insistence that the community worship God in a way that integrated the various forms of human expression—song, dance, and prayer, all with call-and-response, as parts of a single offering the beauty of which pays homage to God. This idea of beauty as deriving from the whole of human expression rather than from its separate manifestations, or even its artifacts, was not entirely new to the Christian tradition. It had originally been as much a part of Euro-Christian tradition as of African but had been lost during the Middle Ages and especially after the Reformation. . . .

The Methodists had in common with the Baptists certain features, beyond those mentioned by Frazier, that did appeal to the slaves. They had retained some interest in ameliorating plantation conditions; their congregations had long been racially mixed and never wholly accepted the white pressures to segregate; and above all, their preachers spoke plainly. Richard Allen, founder of the Bethel African Methodist Episcopal Church of Philadelphia and himself an ex-slave, explained: "I was confident that no religious sect or denomination would suit the capacity of the colored people so well as the Methodists, for the plain simple gospel suits best for any people, for the unlearned can understand, and the learned are sure to understand." But the greatest advantage held by both Baptists and Methodists, with their particular strength in the countryside and in the cities respectively, was that they worked hard to reach the blacks and understood the need to enlist black preachers and "assistants" to work with them. Emotional appeal and organizational flexibility gave the Baptists the edge, but they might have thrown it away had they not undertaken the task of conversion with the vigor they did. The organizational flexibility of the Baptists pro-

vided a particularly good opportunity for the retention of magic and folk belief despite the theological strictures against them. Excommunications for backsliding into paganism occurred, but the loose methods of organization made surveillance difficult; and the black preachers found it easy to look the other way without incurring the wrath of a watchful hierarchy.

The Baptists' efforts to proselytize among slaves and their willingness to rely on, or at least not exclude, black preachers did not prove them less racist or more deeply concerned with the secular fate of the blacks than were others. Whatever advantage they may have derived from their early hostility to slavery and later concern with amelioration faded as the several southern churches closed ranks behind the single reform formula of confirming slavery as a normal condition for blacks and urging more humane treatment. During the last three decades of the antebellum period Baptists, Methodists, Presbyterians, and others accelerated, both by design and simply by taking the path of least resistance, the long-developing trend toward racial separation within the churches.

Even during the eighteenth century a double push for separation had been taking place. Hostile whites steadily tried to push the blacks into separate congregations, especially where the black population was substantial, and blacks often moved to facilitate the split, partly because they felt uncomfortable and wished to practice their religion in their own way, and partly because they resented the inferior position into which they were being thrust within the white churches. For the blacks the move to separate was thus both a positive desire for independent cultural expression and a defense against racism.

The rise of the independent black churches in Philadelphia and other cities of both North and South, often under the leadership of strong personalities, did make the task of the white segregationists all the easier. At the same time the trend toward separation affected the plantation belt itself in less dramatic and less formal ways. By the end of the antebellum period most southern blacks who professed Christianity called themselves Baptists, and so they were. But they had become black Baptists—a category increasingly of their own making. The division had fateful consequences. Ulrich Bonnell Phillips clearly saw the negative implications for both black and white, but especially white:

> In general, the less the cleavage of creed between master and man, the better for both, since every factor conducing to solidarity of sentiment was of advantage in promoting harmony and progress. When the planter went to sit under his rector while the slave stayed at home to hear an exhorter, just so much was lost in the sense of fellowship.

What Phillips did not wish to see was that the consequences for the slaves were not entirely negative, for separation helped them to widen the degree of autonomy they were steadily carving out of their oppressors' regime.

On the plantations and farms the slaves met for services apart from the whites whenever they could. Weekly services on Sunday evenings were common. Where masters were indulgent, additional meetings might take place during the week, and where they were not, they might take place anyway. Masters and overseers often accepted the Sunday meetings but not the others, for the slaves would stay up much of the night praying, singing, and dancing. The next day being a workday, the meetings were bad for business.

The slaves' religious meetings would be held in secret when their masters forbade all such; or when their masters forbade all except Sunday meetings; or when rumors of rebellion or disaffection led even indulgent masters to forbid them so as to protect the people from trigger-happy patrollers; or when the slaves wanted to make sure that no white would hear them. Only during insurrection scares or tense moments occasioned by political turmoil could the laws against such meetings be enforced. Too many planters did not want them enforced. They regarded their slaves as peaceful, respected their religious sensibilities, and considered such interference dangerous to plantation morale and productivity. Others agreed that the slaves presented no threat of ris-

ing and did not care about their meetings. Had the slaves been less determined, the regime probably would have been far more stringent; but so long as they avoided conspiracies and accepted harsh punishment as the price for getting caught by patrols, they raised the price of suppression much too high to make it seem worthwhile to planters with steady nerves.

When the meetings had to be held in secret, the slaves confronted a security problem. They would announce the event by such devices as that of singing "Steal Away to Jesus" at work. To protect the meeting itself, they had an infallible method. They would turn over a pot "to catch the sound" and keep it in the cabin or immediate area of the woods. Almost infallible: "Of course, sometimes they might happen to slip up on them on suspicion.". . . [T]he practice of turning over a pot probably had African origins, and [another scholar] links it to rituals designed to sanctify the ground. The slaves' belief in its efficacy gave them additional confidence to brave the risks, and their success in avoiding detection led some whites to think that there might just be something to the pot technique.

The desire of the slaves for religious privacy took a limited as well as a general form. Eliza Frances Andrews went down to the plantation praise-house after dinner one night to hear the slaves sing. "At their 'praise meetings,'" she commented, "they go through all sorts of motions in connection with their songs, but they won't give way to their wildest gesticulations or engage in their sacred dances before white people for fear of being laughed at." But the slaves had no objection to pleasing curious whites when they expected an appreciative response. They took enormous pride in their singing and in the depth of their religious expression. They resisted being laughed at, but they responded to expressions of respect. Gus Feaster, an ex-slave from Union County, South Carolina, proudly told of such instances:

> At night when the meeting done busted till next day was when the darkies really did have they freedom of spirit. As the wagon be creeping along in the late hours of moonlight, the

darkies would raise a tune. Then the air soon be filled with the sweetest tune as us rid on home and sung all the old hymns that us loved. It was always some big black nigger with a deep bass voice like a frog that'd start up the tune. Then the other mens jine in, followed up by the fine little voices of the gals and the cracked voices of the old womens and the grannies. When us reach near the big house us soften down to a deep hum that the missus like! Sometimes she hist up the window and tell us sing "Swing Low, Sweet Chariot" for her and the visiting guests. That all us want to hear. Us open up, and the niggers near the big house that hadn't been to church would wake up and come out to the cabin door and jine in the refrain. From that we'd swing on into all the old spirituals that us love so well and that us knowed how to sing. Missus often 'low that her darkies could sing with heaven's inspiration. . . .

The blacks did not hide their disdain for white shouters, whom they regarded, as Dr. Du Bois did later, as a plain copy of themselves. Even in the early camp meetings the blacks notoriously outshouted the whites and stayed up singing and praying long after the whites had retired. They made up their own hymns, which drew protests from orthodox whites because they were their own and because they came too close to sound-

A slave prayer meeting. Many slave religious services, especially those occurring on days other than Sunday, were held in secret.

ing like plantation jubilee melodies. Viewing a meeting in Georgia, which attracted even more blacks than whites, Olmsted observed:

> The Negroes kept their place during all the tumult; there may have been a sympathetic groan or exclamation uttered by one or two of them, but generally they expressed only the interest of curiosity. . . . There was generally a self-satisfied smile upon their faces; and I have no doubt they felt they could do it with a great deal more energy and abandon, if they were called upon.

Beneath the similarities and differences of style lay a divergence of meanings, including some divergence in the very meaning of God.

The slaves drew their call-and-response pattern from their African heritage, however important the reinforcing elements from the Europeans. Europeans had also used something like a song-style of preaching and responding, which had somewhat different qualities. Blacks and whites in the South performed in distinct ways. The content of the white responses to a preacher—undoubtedly with many exceptions—consisted of "Amens" and the like. The whites cheered their preacher on or let him know they were moved. The preacher needed that response, craved it, even demanded it. But the black preacher had to evoke it, not for his own satisfaction, subjectively important as that may have been, but because without it the service had no relationship to God. This difference in style betrayed a difference in theological tendency. The whites were fundamentalists to the core, the blacks only apparently so. Both preached the Bible in fiery style, but as the Reverend Henry H. Mitchell suggests, the whites were fiery mad, while the blacks were fiery glad. Or as Martin Ruffin, an ex-slave from Texas, said of a black preacher, Sam Jones, he "preached Hell-fire and judgment like the white preachers.". . .

Despite a few hints to the contrary, the slaves did not view their predicament as punishment for the collective sin of black people. No amount of white propaganda could bring them to accept such an idea. Occasionally, blacks spoke of slav-

ery as a punishment for sin, but even then the precise meaning remained vague. . . .

For the slaves, sin meant wrongdoing—injustice to others and violation of accepted moral codes. Their otherworldly idea of Heaven shared its place with a this-worldly idea that stressed freedom and a community of love for one's brothers and sisters; little room remained for a theology based on original sin. Hence, black theology largely ignored the one doctrine that might have reconciled the slaves to their bondage on a spiritual plane. . . .

The African legacy to Afro-America—that celebrated joy in life which is so often denigrated or explained away—represented a life-affirming faith that stressed shame and minimized guilt. Enslavement might be shameful and an expression of weakness, but it could not easily produce a sense of guilt—of getting what you deserved and of being punished for having offended God. . . .

The ambiguity of the slaves' Heaven and of the limitations on their idea of sin had roots in African ideas of the Soul. Again, it is not possible to know to what extent they stubbornly clung to African ideas and to what extent plantation slave conditions recreated certain patterns of thought. But, clearly, no sharp break occurred. Their life as slaves in the New World, even after conversion to Christianity, did not destroy the traditional sensibility. . . .

A more significant question concerns the relationship of the Soul to the natural order. In the classical Christian tradition man is unique; he alone has a Soul, which establishes his claims to freedom as a matter of responsibility before God. Even in Calvinist theology, in which man's Soul is predestined to salvation or damnation, man himself chose not to obey God in the first place. African ideas place man himself and therefore his Soul within nature. Reincarnation and the return of spirits to the world of the living may occur. Man's Soul is one spirit among many, for all things are infused with spirits. Man himself is one of many material hosts. For traditional Africans, like many non-Christian peoples elsewhere, the Soul came to mean the inner life. . . .

Did the slaves sing of God's Heaven and a life beyond this life? Or of a return to Africa? Or of a Heaven that was anywhere they would be free? Or of an undefined state in which they could love each other without fear? On any given occasion they did any one of these; probably, in most instances they did all at once. Men and women who dare to dream of deliverance from suffering rarely fit their dreams into neat packages. . . .

The image of Moses, the this-worldly leader of his people out of bondage, and Jesus, the otherworldly Redeemer, blended into a pervasive theme of deliverance. A former house slave, who considered himself superior to the field hands, admitted praying with them. "Well, yes'm," he explained, "we would pray the Lord to deliver us." Eliza Frances Andrews waxed indignant over the freedmen's adulation for the abolitionist who had come to teach them during the Union occupation. They think he is Jesus Christ, she protested. "Anyhow," she paraphrased them, "he has done more for them than Jesus Christ ever did." The Reverend C.C. Jones observed that the few remaining Muslim slaves on the Georgia coast identified Muhammed with Jesus, and he might have added, therefore with Moses too.

Selection 2

From Muslim to Christian

Omar ibn Seid

Although most Africans who were brought to America as slaves were products of traditional African belief systems, a minority of slaves came from the Muslim communities of West Africa's interior. It was, however, all but impossible to sustain Islam in the New World under conditions of slavery. Islam is a faith rooted in the study of the Qur'an; it requires Arabic-speaking teachers to pass on its learning. Moreover, the practice of Islam is a community—not just an individual—experience: Awareness and observance of Islamic law are essential if its value-system is to function properly. Neither Qur'anic scholarship nor Islamic communities could survive from one generation to the next among slaves whose masters were both ignorant of Islam and hostile to it.

This selection is a document from the early nineteenth century that was originally written in Arabic by a slave trained in Islamic law in his native West Africa. Omar ibn Seid was thus highly atypical of his fellow bondspeople, and the respect and gentle treatment that he won from the master who purchased him (apparently as a curiosity) also set him apart. The statement of his religious beliefs that he prepared also poignantly testifies to the eventual loss of his ancestral faith and the ways in which he assimilated the Christian ideas that surrounded him as a slave in North America.

Excerpted from "The Narrative of Omar ibn Seid," *American Historical Review*, vol. 30, 1925.

*I*n the name of God, the merciful the gracious.—God grant his blessing upon our Prophet Mohammed. Blessed be He in whose hands is the kingdom and who is Almighty;

who created death and life that he might test you; for he is exalted; he is the forgiver (of sins), who created seven heavens one above the other. Do you discern anything trifling in creation? Bring back your thoughts. Do you see anything worthless? Recall your vision in earnest. Turn your eye inward for it is diseased. God has adorned the heavens and the world with lamps, and has made us missiles for the devils, and given us for them a grievous punishment, and to those who have disbelieved their Lord, the punishment of hell and pains of body. Whoever associates with them shall hear a boiling caldron, and what is cast therein may fitly represent those who suffer under the anger of God.—Ask them if a prophet has not been sent unto them. They say, "Yes; a prophet has come to us, but we have lied to him." We said, "God has not sent us down anything, and you are in grievous error." They say, "If we had listened and been wise we should not now have been suffering the punishment of the Omniscient." So they confess they have sinned in destroying the followers of the Omniscient. Those who fear their Lord and profess his name, they receive pardon and great honor. Guard your words, (ye wicked), make it known that God is all-wise in all his manifestations. Do you not know from the creation that God is full of skill? that He has made for you the way of error, and you have walked therein, and have chosen to live upon what your god Nasûr has furnished you? Believe on Him who dwells in heaven, who has fitted the earth to be your support and it shall give you food. Believe on Him who dwells in Heaven, who has sent you a prophet, and you shall understand what a teacher (He has sent you). Those that were before them deceived them (in regard to their prophet). And how came they to reject him? Did they not see in the heavens above them, how the fowls of the air receive with pleasure that which is sent them? God looks after all. Believe ye: it is He who supplies your wants, that you may take his gifts and enjoy them, and take great pleasure in them. And now will you go on in error, or walk in the path of righteousness. Say to them, "He who regards you with care, and who

has made for you the heavens and the earth and gives you prosperity, Him you think little of. This is He that planted you in the earth, and to whom you are soon to be gathered." But they say, "If you are men of truth, tell us when shall this promise be fulfilled?" Say to them, "Does not God know? and am not I an evident Prophet?" When those who disbelieve shall see the things draw near before their faces, it shall then be told them, "These are the things about which you made inquiry." Have you seen that God has destroyed me or those with me? or rather that He has shewn us mercy? And who will defend the unbeliever from a miserable punishment? Say, "Knowledge is from God." Say; "Have you not seen that your water has become impure? Who will bring you fresh water from the fountain?"

O Sheikh Hunter, I cannot write my life because I have forgotten much of my own language, as well as of the Arabic. Do not be hard upon me, my brother.—To God let many thanks be paid for his great mercy and goodness.

In the name of God, the Gracious, the Merciful.—Thanks be to God, supreme in goodness and kindness and grace, and who is worthy of all honor, who created all things for his service, even man's power of action and of speech.

From Omar to Sheikh Hunter.

You asked me to write my life. I am not able to do this because I have much forgotten my own, as well as the Arabic language. Neither can I write very grammatically or according to the true idiom. And so, my brother, I beg you, in God's name, not to blame me, for I am a man of weak eyes, and of a weak body.

My name is Omar ibn Seid. My birthplace was Fut Tûr, between the two rivers. I sought knowledge under the instruction of a Sheikh called Mohammed Seid, my own brother, and Sheikh Soleiman Kembeh, and Sheikh Gabriel Abdal. I continued my studies twenty-five years, and then returned to my home where I remained six years. Then there came to our place a large army, who killed many men, and took me, and brought me to the great sea, and sold me into the hands of the Christians, who bound me and sent me on board a great ship and we sailed upon the great sea a month and a half, when we came to a place called Charleston in the Christian language. There they sold me to a small, weak, and wicked man, called Johnson, a complete infidel, who had no fear of God at all. Now I am a small man, and unable to do hard work so I fled from the hand of Johnson and after a month came to a place called Fayd-il [Fayetteville, North Carolina]. There I saw some great houses (churches). On the new moon I went into a church to pray. A lad saw me and rode off to the place of his father and informed him that he had seen a black man in the church. A man named Handah (Hunter?) and another man with him on horseback, came attended by a troop of dogs. They took me and made me go with them twelve miles to a place called Fayd-il, where they put me into a great house from which I could not go out. I continued in the great house (which, in the Christian language, they called *jail*) sixteen days and nights. One Friday the jailor came and opened the door of the house and I saw a great many men, all Christians, some of whom called out to me, "What is your name? Is it Omar or Seid?" I did not understand their Christian language. A man called Bob Mumford took me and led me out of the jail, and I was very well pleased to go with them to their place. I stayed at Mumford's four days and nights, and then a man named Jim Owen, son-in-law of Mumford, having married his daughter Betsey, asked me if I was willing to go to a place called Bladen [County, North Carolina]. I said, Yes, I was willing. I went with them and have remained in the place of Jim Owen until now.

Before [after?] I came into the hand of Gen. Owen a man by the name of Mitchell came to buy me. He asked me if I were willing to go to Charleston City. I said *"No, no, no, no, no, no, no,* I not willing to go to Charleston. I stay in the hand of Jim Owen."

O ye people of North Carolina, O ye people of S. Carolina, O ye people of America all of you; have you among you any two such men as Jim Owen and John Owen? These men are good men. What food they eat they give to me to eat. As they clothe themselves they clothe me. They

permit me to read the gospel of God, our Lord, and Saviour, and King; who regulates all our circumstances, our health and wealth, and who bestows his mercies willingly, not by constraint. According to power I open my heart, as to a great light, to receive the true way, the way of the Lord Jesus the Messiah.

Before I came to the Christian country, my religion was the religion of "Mohammed, the Apostle of God—may God have mercy upon him and give him peace." I walked to the mosque before day-break, washed my face and head and hands and feet. I prayed at noon, prayed in the afternoon, prayed at sunset, prayed in the evening. I gave alms every year, gold, silver, seeds, cattle, sheep, goats, rice, wheat, and barley. I gave tithes of all the above-named things. I went every year to the holy war against the infidels. I went on pilgrimage to Mecca, as all did who were able.—My father had six sons and five daughters, and my mother had three sons and one daughter. When I left my country I was thirty-seven years old; I have been in the country of the Christians twenty-four years.— Written A.D. 1831.

O ye people of North Carolina, O ye people of South Carolina, O all ye people of America—

The first son of Jim Owen is called Thomas, and his sister is called Masa-jein (Martha Jane?). This is an excellent family.

Tom Owen and Nell Owen have two sons and a daughter. The first son is called Jim and the second John. The daughter is named Melissa.

Seid Jim Owen and his wife Betsey have two sons and five daughters. Their names are Tom, and John, and Mercy, Miriam, Sophia, Margaret and Eliza. This family is a very nice family. The wife of John Owen is called Lucy and an excellent wife she is. She had five children. Three of them died and two are still living.

O ye Americans, ye people of North Carolina —have you, have you, have you, have you, have you among you a family like this family, having so much love to God as they?

Formerly I, Omar, loved to read the book of the Koran the famous. General Jim Owen and his wife used to read the gospel, and they read it to me very much,—the gospel of God, our Lord, our Creator, our King, He that orders all our circumstances, health and wealth, willingly, not constrainedly, according to his power.—Open thou my heart to the gospel, to the way of uprightness.—Thanks to the Lord of all worlds, thanks in abundance. He is plenteous in mercy and abundant in goodness.

For the law was given by Moses but grace and truth were by Jesus the Messiah.

When I was a Mohammedan I prayed thus: "Thanks be to God, Lord of all worlds, the merciful the gracious, Lord of the day of Judgment, thee we serve, on thee we call for help. Direct us in the right way, the way of those on whom thou hast had mercy, with whom thou hast not been angry and who walk not in error. Amen."—But now I pray "Our Father", etc., in the words of our Lord Jesus the Messiah.

I reside in this our country by reason of great necessity. Wicked men took me by violence and sold me to the Christians. We sailed a month and a half on the great sea to the place called Charleston in the Christian land. I fell into the hands of a small, weak and wicked man, who feared not God at all, nor did he read (the gospel) at all nor pray. I was afraid to remain with a man so depraved and who committed so many crimes and I ran away. After a month our Lord God brought me forward to the hand of a good man, who fears God, and loves to do good, and whose name is Jim Owen and whose brother is called Col. John Owen. These are two excellent men.—I am residing in Bladen County.

I continue in the hand of Jim Owen who never beats me, nor scolds me. I neither go hungry nor naked, and I have no hard work to do. I am not able to do hard work for I am a small man and feeble. During the last twenty years I have known no want in the hand of Jim Owen.

Selection 3

Coping with Slavery: Trickster Tales

Charles Joyner

Modern anthropologists find one element common to folk cultures throughout the world is the "trickster" tale. The "trickster" is usually a clever animal (or occasionally a human) character who survives by outwitting stronger but less intelligent creatures. Such tales are typically used by parents and other elders to teach survival skills to young people, and they also serve as crucial indicators of community values.

This selection is an excerpt from the book by historian Charles Joyner entitled Down by the Riverside: A South Carolina Slave Community. *Joyner's book is an example of what historians call "total history"—a study not only of surface political events and economic relationships but also of the deeper mentality of the people under study. In the part of the book from which the present selection is taken, the author reconstructs the basic values of the enslaved people of a rice plantation in coastal South Carolina. Trickster tales suggested ways in which young people could adjust to the realities of slavery.*

The best known and most widely collected folktales among both Africans and Afro-Americans are the animal tales, and the best known and most widely collected animal tales are trickster tales. In All Saints Parish, too, animal trickster tales constitute the most common type of folk narrative. The most obvious feature of the All Saints animal tales is their emphasis on small but sly creatures, weak but wily animals who continually get the better of their bigger and more powerful adversaries through superior cunning. Despite physical puniness, the tiny trickster's personality is marked by audacity, egotism, and rebellion. Through the symbolic identification of nature with society the animal trickster tales defined the trickster and his actions as both necessary and good. Such symbolic identification served as a means of transforming the unavoidable into the desirable and of giving a certain freedom of individual action despite group restraints.

Uprooted Africans and their descendants did not simply retain their ancestral trickster tales unchanged, either in All Saints Parish or anywhere else. On the contrary, the African narrative tradition itself was creative and innovative both in Africa and in the New World, where it encountered a strikingly different natural and social environment. Afro-American trickster tales exemplify the slaves' response to that new environment and their efforts to manipulate it verbally and symbolically. It would appear, for instance, that wish fulfillment and role inversion played a somewhat more prominent role in slave trickster tales than in African trickster tales. Nor are trickster tales unique to African and African-derived cultures; on the contrary, trickster tales are universal. But they are not universally alike. What they have in common is the hero who lives by his wits. His behavior is at odds with the cultural values—often deeply held—that restrain him. But what those values are and how the trickster gets around them varies from culture to culture. For example, while the Afro-American slave trickster figure and the Native American trickster figure are both rabbits (and are historically related), they exhibit important differences. The slave trickster, while he may fail or even be repaid in kind for his swindles, is neither a clown nor a self-devourer, as in the Native American trickster.

The intricate combination of realism and fantasy in the animal trickster tales made it possible for them to carry more complex and subtle meanings than simple, unambiguous plots—a trickster tries to deceive another animal and either succeeds or is himself tricked. These tales of thoroughly humanized animals exemplified the process of symboling. The animals think like humans, they behave like humans, they experience human emotions, and they live in a realistic world that is clearly like that of their narrators. But they also remain recognizably animals. The big animals are usually strong and powerful but not very bright; they are constantly being duped by the less powerful trickster figures. This combination of realism and fantasy made it possible for storytellers and audiences in Africa and America alike to identify with the animal characteristics without the identification becoming rigid or allegorical. To miss that identification is to miss perhaps the central meaning of the trickster tales to the slaves; but to magnify that identification out of proportion—to take the trickster tales *merely* as vicarious protest tales—is to miss other levels of their meaning completely. That the animal trickster tales provided slaves with a satirical depiction of the society in which they lived has been somewhat obscured by an overemphasis on similarities between the trickster and the slave. A people's perception of their social and economic system grows out of an identification of the people with nature and their perception of nature in terms of social relations. Thus the struggle between Buh Rabbit (the slave) and Buh Bear (the "maussa") could be perceived as founded in nature and thus inevitable.

The animal trickster appears in many guises in black folktales in Africa and in the New World. On the rice plantations of the Waccamaw he is usually Buh Rabbit (or Buddah Rabbit), although he also appears as Buh Cootah (Cooter, a small turtle), Buh Squel (Squirrel), and Buh Pa'tridge (Partridge). Buh Rabbit is not always the trickster; in his encounters with Buh Pa'tridge he is himself tricked. This shifting of roles in the tales is important, for it underlines the educative function of folktale narration in the slave community. From such role switching, slaves learned not merely how to emulate the trickster but also how to avoid being tricked.

The central theme of the animal trickster tales is the struggle for mastery between the trickster and his adversary, as expressed in possession of the two most basic signs of status—food and sex. An ironic inversion of the cultural notion of food-sharing as a hallmark of community runs through a number of the tales. For example, in "Duh Rabbit, Fox, an' Goose," Buh Rabbit has been stealing food from a garden owned by an absentee owner. The owner leaves word with his "lil gal" to watch out for the next time Buh Rabbit breaks into the garden and not let him out. She does so while the man tells Buh Fox to go eat Buh Rabbit. But Rabbit tells Fox he will show him some tasty geese if he won't eat him. Fox goes off after the geese, Rabbit tells him a bear is chasing him, Fox runs away, and Rabbit is free. He has taken his fill from the garden without suffering the consequences. In the universe of the trickster tales there is no food-sharing, merely a continuing struggle among the animals over control of the food supply. In such an environment, as this story and others like it make clear, the slaves were aware of the positive advantages of role playing.

Not the least of the lessons for the slaves embedded in their folktales was that values which are appropriate in some situations may not be useful in others. Friendship and altruism were held up as positive values within the slave community, but such traits were not exhibited by the tricksters in their social relations with the powerful. In the story "Buddah Bear's Fish," Buddah Bear is walking through the woods with some freshly caught fish when he sees what appears to be a dead rabbit in the path. It is Buddah Rabbit playing dead. Scampering ahead after Buddah Bear passes by, Buddah Rabbit repeats this trick three more times. Finally, Buddah Bear sets down his fish and goes back to retrieve the four "dead rabbits." When he returns, he finds Buddah Rabbit already cooking up a fish stew. Bear reclaims the fish, but Rabbit escapes unpunished. In this tale the trickster is unsuccessful, but in many others he succeeds. The lesson is clear—when dealing with the powerful, one has everything to gain and little if anything to lose by adopting the value system of the trickster.

While the possession of food is a common symbol of status and power, significantly the trickster found his greatest satisfaction not in the mere possession of food, but in *taking* it from the more powerful animals. In "De Buttah Tree," Buh Woof and Buh Rabbit are joint owners of a butter tree. While Wolf and Rabbit are hoeing rice one day, Rabbit keeps slipping off and eating some of the butter until he has eaten it all. Not only does he deny having eaten the butter, but also he rubs butter on Wolf's mouth while he is sleeping and accuses him of eating the butter. Were mere survival perceived by the narrators to be the theme of the stories, it is unlikely that the final episode would have remained part of the emotional core of the story. Clearly this story is not about food as a symbol of survival, but food as a symbol of power. . . .

Storytelling sessions in the slave community functioned as sources for inspiration and education and transformed pure rhetoric into quasi-religious ritual. The verbal action of the narratives . . . evoked a behavioral response in the hearers. The storytellers' stylistic techniques of acceleration and retard, their subtle use of verbal dynamics and vocal imitations of the animals, and the audience's laughter and interjected comments on the action—matching what they heard in the story with what they already knew and felt—all exemplified the social relations that generated the audience's emotional response to the narrative and the narrative's dependence on the spontaneous cooperation between the story-teller and the slave community in the narration. In the mutually revealing relationships between a society and its folktales, the interplay of per-sonality and social relations was one of the prime movers of such symbolic action as story-telling. But the social situations of storytelling had distinctive structures of their own, which were not necessarily like those of social struc-tures of the society at large. It is perhaps less ac-curate to think of storytelling in the slave com-munity as a narrator's performance before an audience than to regard it as a mutual perfor-mance. Granting that, as stories were told time and again, they were reshaped with each telling, and conceding that with changes in context came subtle changes in meaning, one is never-theless struck, after all, more with the major continuities than with the minor variations.

Slave storytelling, then, may be regarded in some sense as a ritual—an everyday symbolic enactment—that provides both a condensed rep-resentation of cultural ideas and social necessi-ties, and a frame for experience. . . .

Speculation on the extent to which slave sto-rytellers and their listeners considered their sto-ries to be educational is presumptuous, probably impossible, and perhaps useless. Clearly folk-tales have functions, but precisely what their function may be is easier to assume than to demonstrate. One of the uses—as distinguished from functions—of trickster tales on the Wacca-maw was sheer entertainment, no insignificant contribution in the House of Bondage. Many of the animal tales were seen as light-hearted nar-ratives of the amusing antics of various animals in a wide range of situations. A tally of the cast of characters—alligators, bears, buzzards, coot-ers, cows, crows, deer, dogs, fish, foxes, frogs, geese, goats, guineas, hawks, hogs, opossums, owls, partridges, rabbits, raccoons, squirrels, turkeys, wolves, and an occasional human be-ing—reveals that the animals depicted were

common in All Saints Parish and were well known to the audience. In this regard slave sto-rytellers followed the practice of their African ancestors, as they did when they added to the fun with such paralinguistic features as imita-tions of the appearance, voices, and demeanor of the animals.

No matter how entertaining, some tales end with a kind of moral, sometimes in the form of a proverb's informing the listeners that they can learn a lesson from the experiences of the char-acters in the narrative. Some tales depicted the fate of those who failed to acknowledge their dependence on God. In the story "Buzzard and Hawk," a hawk and a buzzard meet and discuss their methods of procuring food. It is clear from the tone of their discussion that Buh Hawk plans on showing off. In the process he impales him-self on a sharp fence post. The tale ends with the buzzard's making a statement that specifies the moral of the tale: "Hit good to wait on de Lawd." Many slave folktales, on the Waccamaw and elsewhere in the slave South, were implic-itly or explicitly didactic. Such tales were widely used in Africa as part of the education of children. Their descendants on the slave planta-tions of the New World continued the tradition of education through folktales.

The educative function of folktales in All Saints Parish was primarily oriented toward a model that stressed how to act and how to sur-vive, rather than one that explained how things came to be. There are no examples of the kinds of cosmological myths found in some cultures that purport to explain all kinds of natural and supernatural phenomena. The nearest thing on the Waccamaw to such myths were the etiologi-cal tales, which ostensibly explained to the slaves the origin of some observable characteris-tic of some member of the animal kingdom. This they usually did humorously. Etiological themes in the African prototypes of such tales were not confined to animal tales (as they were on the Waccamaw); but the tradition of explaining, in amusing stories, striking animal characteristics already known to the audience was especially strong in African animal tales. One such etiological tale from All Saints is "Buddah Woof Fool Buddah Rabbit." Rabbit meets Wolf one day after Wolf has caught many fish. Rabbit asks how he caught so many. Wolf says he caught them with his tail. Rabbit goes to the creek and dips his tail in the ice-cold water, in which it freezes fast. But Owl, responding to Rabbit's cries for help, grabs him by the ears and tries to pull his tail out of the creek. Not only does he stretch Rabbit's ears and eyes in the process, he also breaks off Rabbit's frozen tail. Thus, because of Wolf's trickery, Rabbit winds up with no fish; but he has big eyes, long ears, and no tail.

The slaves' folktales also served the important psychological function of projecting personal hopes and fears, frailties and weaknesses onto a surrogate (usually a weaker animal), which is then made to defeat his stronger and larger adversaries (usually big but not very smart animals such as Buh Bear and Buh Wolf). This trickster-surrogate steals his adversaries' food and women, cheats them in races, shifts the blame for his own misdeeds onto them, and even tricks them into fratricide and homicide. It is significant that Buh Rabbit and John do not merely defeat their adversaries; they do so while flaunting a jaunty sassiness and cool imperturbability that slaves were under pressure to conceal from their masters. The trickster shares with the slaves the cynical view of a social order as it is observed from the bottom up. Life in the universe of the trickster tales, as in the House of Bondage, is a constant struggle. These tales make it clear that the struggle is not merely for food and sex for their own sake, but as symbols of mastery over the powerful. The trickster's victories represent projections of the slaves' most acutely frustrated desire—status in a highly status-conscious time and place. These symbolic attacks upon power itself clearly reveal the slaves' irreverence toward the power arrangements of the slavery system, and the trickster's victories over the powerful served to enhance the slaves' self-image.

It is important that one look beyond the surface themes of the trickster tales. The enhancement of self-image, of identity, was an important function of the All Saints trickster tales, however elusive it may be to examine. Like Buh Rabbit, slaves too had to make do with their natural resources and learn to maneuver with what they had. Encompassed within the definition of a situation was a strategy for dealing with its reality. The importance of self-reliance, as indicated in the trickster tales, was underscored in the proverb of one of the All Saints slaves, Hagar Brown, who noted, "Each tub stand on its own bottom." Survival in the slave system depended upon the slaves' ability always to remember who and where they were and upon their ability to "put yuh bess foot fo moss" (put your best foot foremost) in any crisis.

The trickster was an inspiration as well as a projection of frustrations, and he occasionally served as a role model as well. But it is important to note that the trickster was portrayed by slave storytellers in ambivalent terms. In his single-minded pursuit of mastery he becomes as merciless as the master. The slave folktales were full of aggressive humor, perhaps the most useful of humanity's numerous aggressive implements. The trickster's aggressive brutality and destructive cruelty served less as role models for slaves to emulate than as outlets for repressed antisocial hostilities engendered by the slave system. Trickster tales to some extent served as object lessons in the tactics of day-to-day resistance to slavery. A tally of the tactics actually used by slaves in All Saints Parish and in other slave societies reads like a motif-index of slave trickster tales—lying, cheating, theft, "accidental" destruction of property, feigned sickness, and the like. It is clear that such tactics as these ran counter to the values of their African heritage and of their creolized form of Christianity. If the slaves suffered any pangs of conscience over the adoption of patterns of behavior at variance with their deepest values, these trickster tales served as a release valve. These stories provided a rationale for adopting such behavior patterns in particular situations without necessarily regarding them as normal or socially approved behavior patterns. By such situational ethics, theft from a fellow slave was wrong; but theft from the master was not really theft, as the masters were already thieves because they were masters. That slaves perceived the relationship between master and slave to be one of "thief" and "stolen property" is indicated in the Gullah proverb, "Ef bukra [white man] neber tief, how come neggar yer?"

Thus the trickster tales served as an inspiration for and justification of some forms of antisocial behavior and simultaneously served as a release valve for even more aggressive and antisocial repressed desires. In so doing they both promoted day-to-day resistance to slavery and at the same time lessened the likelihood that a large-scale slave rebellion might overthrow the system. Not the least important part of the slaves' deft blend of accommodation and resistance, the trickster tales were in fact a crucial element in the development of an adaptive Afro-American culture. That culture was the most significant form of resistance against the spiritual and psychological, if not the physical, effects of slavery.

Selection 4

Songs of Work and Sorrow

Dena J. Epstein

In the days of slavery, whites usually convinced themselves that slaves were happy-go-lucky folk who amused themselves with singing and other forms of highly rhythmic music. The "minstrel show" song-and-dance routines by which whites in blackface entertained white audiences helped sustain stereotypes—usually belittling ones—about African American life.

Authentic black music in pre–Civil War America was seldom carefree or lighthearted. Often its content was satirical or ironic, although the message was not always apparent to whites who happened to be within earshot. Blacks sang or chanted work songs to help them keep up the pace of heavy labor. Spirituals were religious songs expressing longing for freedom. And many songs were sung to release the tension, apprehension, or sorrow that were always part of the burden of life under slavery.

Dena J. Epstein's 1977 book Sinful Tunes and Spirituals: Black Folk Music to the Civil War, *excerpted here, surveyed all aspects of African American music in slavery times.*

*a*fter 1800, descriptions of worksongs became more numerous, associated with a variety of different occupations ranging from field labor through domestic chores such as flailing rice, grinding hominy, spinning, and making baskets, to more industrial employments such as loading cargo, processing hemp or tobacco, and firing engines. Most common among contemporary reports were boat songs to regulate rowing, and corn or other harvest songs. Some of these songs provided rhythmic regulation of the rate of labor; others passed the time and relieved boredom, but all of them provided fuel for the perennial argument about whether the slaves were happy. Apologists for the "peculiar institution" seemed compelled to convince the world that the slaves were not only well fed and healthy, but the happiest people in the world. . . .

There is evidence that slave masters regarded the singing of their slaves as an inducement to greater exertion. In an essay entitled "Management of Negroes" and signed Agricola, the author wrote: "When at work I have no objection to their whistling or singing some lively tune, but no *drawling* tunes are allowed in the field, for their motions are almost certain to keep time with the music." This would seem to confirm Fanny Kemble's statement, although she was anathema to slaveholders:

> I have heard that many of the masters and overseers on these plantations prohibit melancholy tunes or words, and encourage nothing but cheerful music and senseless words, deprecating the effect of sadder strains upon the slaves, whose peculiar musical sensibility might be expected to make them especially excitable by any songs of a plaintive character, and having any reference to their particular hardships. If it is true, I think it a judicious precaution enough. . . .

Frederick Douglass summed up his view of the matter:

> Slaves are generally expected to sing as well as to work. A silent slave is not liked by masters or overseers. *"Make a noise," "make a noise,"* and *"bear a hand,"* are the words usually addressed to the slaves when there is silence amongst them. This may account for the almost constant singing heard in the southern states. There was, generally, more or less singing among the teamsters, as it was one means of letting the overseer know where they were, and that they were moving on with the work.

A former slave recalled that not all the songs were nonsensical. "Boss like for de slaves to sing while workin'. We had a jackleg slave preacher who's hist de tunes. Some was spirituals."

Not many descriptions of field hands singing at work have been found, possibly because the travelers who wrote so many of the accounts rarely saw them at work. But a description written by a planter in the Leeward Islands would have been equally appropriate for the mainland: "The slaves then work in a long string, and follow each other in regular order. Some one takes the lead and breaks out with a song, to which there is always a chorus. In this they all join, and the union of such a number of voices, produces a very animated and pleasing effect." Only one description has been found of slaves singing in the cotton fields, although no movie of plantation life would have been considered complete without such music:

> From Branchville we took the direct route to Charleston by way of the South Carolina Railroad. . . . We saw cotton fields stretching away on either side as we passed. . . . The negroes were at work in the fields, picking cotton and stowing it in long baskets. [Most accounts mentioned long bags tied to the pickers' waists.] They worked in gangs, or companies. . . . While at work in the cotton fields, the slaves often sing some wild, simple melody, by way of mutual cheer, which usually ends in a chorus, in which all join with a right hearty good will, in a key so loud as to be heard from one plantation to another, and the welkin is made to ring for miles with musical echoes. . . . I could not comprehend the words of the songs or choruses. . . .

Grinding grain, spinning and weaving, basket-making, and nursing children all were accompanied with songs. A northern teacher, stationed at Beaufort, South Carolina, during the war, described the process of grinding hominy:

> This hominy was ground between two flat stones, one of which was stationary and the other was moved by hand by means of an upright stick inserted in a groove in the stone. It was a slow and tedious process, but always enlivened by the songs and jokes of the colored people, when grinding. Two or three always came together, as one could not move the stone alone. . . . There were people grinding corn . . . every hour, day and night. Boys

*In addition to singing at prayer meetings, slaves sang while
working in the fields, doing household chores, and nursing children.*

and girls would come in procession with their "fanners" filled with corn perched on the top of their heads. Singing and laughing and joking they would wait for hours for a turn to grind. . . . At night the older people came. . . . All night long I could hear the whizzing of the wheel and the shouts of the people. . . . All kept time by clapping their hands and stamping their feet. . . .

The South was primarily an agricultural region, but some industries closely allied to staple crops flourished. As early as 1830 hemp factories were thriving in Lexington, Kentucky:

At one of the principal bagging and balerope establishments, there are employed from 60 to 100 negroes, of all ages . . . some of whom contrive to . . . drown the noise of the machinery by their own melody. . . . The leader would commence singing in a low tone— "Ho! Ho! Ho! Master's gone away." To which the rest replied with rapidity, "Ho! Ho!— chicken-pie for supper, Ho! Ho!—Ho! Ho!". . . When they get tired of this, anyone who had a little fancy—and precious little would answer the purpose, would start something equally as

sentimental; to which the rest again responded, at the same time walking backward and forward about their spinning, with great regularity, and in some measure keeping time with their steps. . . .

The hemp spinners did not attract as much attention from tourists as did the tobacco workers in Richmond. William Cullen Bryant saw them in 1843 and quoted his guide on the repertory: "Their taste is exclusively for sacred music; they will sing nothing else." Fredrika Bremer, who was in Richmond in June, 1851, became ecstatic:

I heard the slaves, about a hundred in number, singing at their work in large rooms; they sung quartettes, choruses, and anthems, and that so purely, and in such perfect harmony, and with such exquisite feeling, that it was difficult to believe them self-taught. . . . The slaves were all Baptists, and sung only hymns. . . .

The occasions on which slaves could have been said to march were carefully regulated by the authorities, for nothing was more feared than large groups of slaves moving about on their own. Movements within the plantation included the "marching" of labor gangs out to the fields, or up to the "big house" to receive weekly allotments of rations. Under the conditions of slavery, there were very few group expeditions into the world outside the plantation, and those few were usually unpleasant. With the end of the overseas slave traffic in 1808, the domestic slave trade took on new importance, as slaves from the overpopulated states like Virginia were moved to the fresh cotton territories in Alabama, Louisiana, Mississippi, Arkansas, and Texas. Some migrations were organized by planters moving their entire households and working farces, but other coffles were led by slave traders transporting groups of slaves to better markets. The means of travel could be by water, by wagon, or later by railroad, but the cheapest was on foot. The earliest description of such a slave coffle, singing as it walked, came from Portsmouth, Virginia. As George Tucker stood on the courthouse steps, he saw

> a group of about thirty Negroes, of different ages and sizes, following a rough looking white man. . . . They came along singing a little wild hymn of sweet and mournful melody.
> . . . "It's nothing at all but a parcel of Negroes, sold to Carolina, and that man is their driver, who has bought them."

One Thomas Shillitoe wrote of an incident he observed near Mount Vernon, Kentucky, in 1829:

> This morning we were met by a company of slaves, some of them heavily loaded with irons, singing as they passed along; this, we were informed, was an effort to drown the suffering of mind they were brought into, by leaving behind them wives, children, or other near connexions and never likely to meet them again in this world.

The coffle gang was a sight that even proslavery Southerners found distressing and unpleasant, while abolitionists featured it as a standard item in their propaganda. The "Song of the Coffle Gang" appeared in several antislavery songsters with "Words by the Slaves":

> This song is said to be sung by Slaves, as they are chained in gangs when parted from

friends for the far South—children taken from parents, husbands from wives, and brothers from sisters:

> See these poor souls from Africa
> Transported to America:
> We are stolen, and sold to Georgia, will you go along with me?
> We are stolen and sold to Georgia, go sound the jubilee. . . .

Peter Bruner, who was born a slave in Winchester, Clark County, Kentucky, in 1845, described slave coffles traveling by riverboat:

> The slave traders would buy the slaves at market and take them down the river on a boat. Then he would tell them to start up a song, and then I would hear them begin to sing:
>
> > "O Come and let us go where pleasure never dies,
> > Jesus my all to Heaven is gone,
> > He who I fix my hopes upon.
> > His track I see and I'll pursue
> > The narrow road till him I view
> > O come and let us go,
> > O come and let us go where pleasure never dies."
>
> . . . Those that refused to sing they would throw that big whip in among them and make them sing.

This text, derived from an English hymn attributed to John Cennick (1718–55), with interpolations, was possibly atypical of songs sung under these conditions. Since Bruner's account is undated, all that can be fixed about it is that he was describing events late in the antebellum period. Besides singing, slave traders also used fiddles to raise the spirits of their coffles. . . .

Nehemiah Caulkins described singing under more pleasant conditions in southeastern North Carolina sometime before 1839:

> When the slaves get a permit to leave the plantation, they sometimes make all ring again by singing the following significant ditty, which shows that after all there is a flow of spirits . . . [that] enables them to forget their wretchedness.

Hurra, for good ole Massa,
  He giv me de pass to go to de city
Hurra, for good ole Missis,
  She bile de pot, and giv me de licker.
    Hurra, I'm goin to de city.

Frederick Douglass described similar singing in eastern Maryland before 1845, when he escaped:

Slaves are generally expected to sing as well as to work. A silent slave is not liked by masters or overseers. . . . This may account for the almost constant singing heard in the southern states. . . . On allowance day, those who visited the great house farm were peculiarly excited and noisy. While on their way, they would make the dense old woods, for miles around, reverberate with their wild notes. . . . In all the songs of the slaves, there was ever some expression of praise of the great house farm; something which would flatter the pride of the owner, and, possibly, draw a favorable glance from him.

"I am going away to the great house farm,
  O yea! O yea! O yea!
My old master is a good old master,
  O yea! O yea! O yea!"

This they would sing, with other words of their own improvising—jargon to others, but full of meaning to themselves.

Douglass's impassioned interpretation of the meaning of these songs to the men who sang them far exceeds in eloquence and sensitivity any other comparable statement in the literature.

I did not, when a slave, understand the deep meaning of those rude and apparently incoherent songs. I was myself within the circle; so that I neither saw nor heard as those without might see and hear. They told a tale of woe which was then altogether beyond my feeble comprehension; they were tones loud, long and deep; they breathed the prayer and complaint of souls boiling over with the bitterest anguish. . . .

I have often been utterly astonished, since I came to the north, to find persons who could speak of the singing, among slaves, as evidence of their contentment and happiness. It is impossible to conceive of a greater mistake. Slaves sing most when they are most unhappy. The songs of the slave represent the sorrows of his heart; and he is relieved by them, only as an aching heart is relieved by its tears. At least, such is my experience.

John Dixon Long, a Philadelphia clergyman, was less personally involved in these songs, but his interpretation complements Douglass's.

Listen to his songs while seated on his ox-cart hauling wood, or splitting rails. . . . his holiday songs and his self-made hymns. His songs do not always indicate a happy state of mind. He resorts to them in order to divert his thoughts from dwelling on his condition. . . . The songs of a slave are word-pictures of every thing he sees, or hears, or feels. The tunes once fixed in his memory, words descriptive of any and every thing are applied to them, as occasion requires. . . . Imagine a colored man seated on the front part of an ox-cart, in an old field, unobserved by any white man, and in a clear loud voice, ringing out these words. . .

"William Rino sold Henry Silvers;
  Hilo! Hilo!
Sold him to de Georgy trader;
  Hilo! Hilo!
His wife she cried, and children bawled,
  Hilo! Hilo!
Sold him to de Georgy trader;
  Hilo! Hilo!"

Selection 5

Singing: An Ex-Slave's Narrative

Vinnie Brunson

Through the words of Vinnie Brunson, an elderly ex-slave interviewed in the 1930s, this selection conveys something of how African Americans understood what their singing was meant to convey.

De Bible tells how de angels shouted in heaven, so dat is where dey get de scriptures fer de dance dat is called de "Shout." De ones dat do dis does not sing, dey jes dance, dey songs are sung by de congregashun. In most cases de "shout" is done at de end of de services.

In de shoutin' song de best singers git to gether an start de song, hit moves slow at fust den gits faster an louder, as dey sing dey jine hands an make a circle, den somebody git happy an jumps out in de middle of de circles an goes to dance to de time of de singing an de clappin' of hands and feet, others jine her as de spirit moves dem, till dey all make a ring dat circles roun' an roun'. De folks in de congregashun jine de singin' an keepin' de time by pattin' de hands an feet an' hit makes a big noise an praise service.

As one crowd git's tired an quits, another

starts up 'till dey all has a chance to take part in de praise service of de dance shout. De spiritual songs is sung in time to de kind of service hit is efn hit is a meetin song hit is sung fast an if hit is a funeral hit is sung slow. Dey sing "Swing Low Sweet Chariot" a heap at de praise song, an' at de funerals bof.   (Praise song fast.)

> Swing low, Sweet chariot, Comin' fer ter carry me home.
> Swing low, sweet chariot, comin' fer ter carry me home.
> I looked over Jordan an' what did I see, Comin' fer to carry me home?
> A band of angels comin' after me, Comin' fer to carry me home.
>   (Funeral slow)
> Swing-low, sweet chariot, coming fer to carry me home,
> Swing l-o-w, s-w-e-e-t–char-iot, C'omin' fer to carry me home.

Yes'm de nigger used to sing to nearly everything he did. Hit wuz des de way he 'spressed his feelin's an hit made him relieved, if he wuz happy, hit made him happy, if he wuz sad hit made him feel better, an so he des natcherly sings his feelin's.

De timber nigger he sings as he cuts de logs an keeps de time wid his axe. De wimmen sing as dey bend over de washtub, de cotton choppers sing as he chops de cotton. De mother sing as she rocks her baby to sleep. De cotton picker sing as he picks de cotton, an dey all sing in de meetin's an at de baptizin' an' at de funerals.

Hit is de niggers mos' joy, an his mos comfort w'en he needs all dese things. Dey sing 'bout de joys in de nex' world an de trouble in dis. Dey first jes sung de 'ligious songs, den dey commenced to sing 'bout de life here an w'en dey sang of bof' dey called dem de "Spirituals." De ole way to sing dem wuz to keep time wid the clappin of de han's an pattin' of de feet.

Dey sing dem in different ways for different occasions, at a meetin' w'en dey shouts dey sing hit joyful, an w'en they sing de same song at a funeral dey sing it slow an moanful, w'en dey sing de same song in de fiel's hit is sung, if dey work fas', quick, if dey is tired hit is sung slow. If hit is sung at Chrismas, den hit is sung gay an happy.

De days of slavery made de nigger live his life over in de "spirituals," most of de real ole time slaves are gone, jes a few maybe who were boys den, but dar song lives on wif bof' de white an de black folks, we forgets de sorrows an remembers de happy days jes like in de songs.

The Complete History of

Resistance After 1831

Chapter 12

Introduction

Why was Nat Turner's Rebellion the last attempt at a massive slave uprising, something that was not emulated even in the tense times of the Civil War? Certainly not because blacks were thoroughly cowed by their masters and lost their spirit to resist. In little ways, bondspeople did what they could to gain more personal "space" and to avoid abuse. But they seem to have understood the futility of fighting back on a large scale. White power could be too quickly mobilized and concentrated for poorly armed blacks to have hopes for more than momentary success, and there were few remote backcountry places where rebels could retreat to wage a guerrilla resistance (as had happened in Brazil, for example, or as Indians did in the West).

There are many documented instances of slaves refusing personally or as a community to submit to indignities, or in subtle ways letting their masters know what were the limits. The readings in this chapter illustrate scholars' findings on this topic. They also point to the factors that were both inhibiting slaves from offering overt resistance and according them some community protections. These included slaves' efforts to strengthen their own family bonds and their realization that working moderately hard at keeping their masters' plantations prosperous could also be in their own interests.

Selection 1

A Slave Tries to Run Away

John Brown

Fleeing was for most slaves a desperate act that could have serious consequences, especially if the goal was permanent escape from slavery. The risk of capture was high; if caught, the punishment was usually drastic (a severe beating or even sale); and if successful, the price was a permanent separation from family and community bonds. So most slaves, when they fled, intended to hide out temporarily in nearby woods (where friends might periodically bring them food) or to visit a spouse held in slavery on a neighboring plantation. Motives for such flight might be to escape an impending punishment, or to protest unusual demands, or

Excerpted from John Brown, *Slave Life in Georgia: A Narrative of the Life, Sufferings, and Escape of John Brown, a Fugitive Slave, Now in England* (London: Watt, 1855).

simply to spend more time with a loved one. So frequent was such flight that masters usually did not advertise for the recapture of a slave until a considerable time had passed and it became apparent that the slave had indeed run away permanently.

The Georgia slave John Brown—not to be confused with the white abolitionist of the same name who tried to start a slave rebellion at Harpers Ferry, Virginia, in 1859—was a slave whose first flight was impelled simply by fear of a brutal punishment. His treatment after his recapture, however, drove him to plan a second, ultimately successful escape to permanent freedom. In 1855 he told his story in a book, published in England, that was well known in antislavery circles. In the excerpt quoted here, he describes his first flight and its consequences.

I began to ponder on what means I should employ to ensure the success of my next attempt to escape; for I was still bent upon accomplishing my object. I determined to do all that I could to delude my master into the belief that I was cured of running off, and by appearing very humble and submissive, first gain his confidence. I dare say the good people who read this confession will think I was very wicked, and I do not mean to say it is not wrong to deceive; but I do not think any one should judge me too harshly for following the example that was set by everybody around me. My master was always deceiving us slaves. If he promised us any thing we never got it, except it happened to be a flogging; and I must say he always kept his word in that. We used to know we were cheated, when having done our best, he swore we had skulked, and cowhided us for it. His dealings with everybody were all on the same principle of trying to over-reach them. Then we could not help seeing many things we knew to be wrong, and which we could have set right if our evidence had been taken; but whenever it suited our master's purpose to require us to lie, we were obliged to do as he wished, or take the consequences. In fact, we felt we were living under a system of cheating, and lying, and deceit; and being taught no better, we grew up in it, and did not see the wrong of it, so long as we were not acting against one another. I am sure that, as a rule, any one of us who would have thought nothing of stealing a hog, or a sack of corn, from our master, would have allowed himself to be cut to pieces rather than betray the confidence of his fellow-slave; and, perhaps, my mentioning this fact may be taken as a set-off against the systematic deception we practised, in self-defence, on our master.

Having made up my mind now to cheat Stevens into a good opinion of me, I took to answering him very humbly, and pretended to be frightened of him. Every thing he bade me do, I did, until at length he got to think the last flogging he had given me, had done me good, and made me submissive. Then he would chuckle and crow over me, thinking it a great victory to have succeeded, as he thought, in breaking down my spirit. Indeed, the experiment in my case seemed so satisfactory, that he thought he would try it on two rather unruly "boys" named Alfred and Harry. One day he sent them to catch four mules which were loose in the stable. This was only a pretext, for he beckoned me to him, and we followed them in. When we were in, he set his back against the door, and, drawing a bit of cord from under his coat, told me to catch the "boys," as he intended to flog them. As soon as they saw what he was after, they began dodging round and under the mules, I trying my hardest to lay hold of them. The mules, in running, rubbed against Decatur, and pushed him away from the door, which was no sooner open, than boys and mules bolted, master swearing at me for letting them get away, and declaring that I had done so for the purpose. I told him I had done just the contrary; but in spite of all I could say, he got into a towering rage and as I was going out at the door, leaped on my back, holding me fast round the neck, and calling out to Aunt Sally—one of the old negro women—to bring him down his gun. Aunt Sally ran into the house, and presently I saw her come out of it, holding up the gun that my master's father had shot poor

Morgan with. I do not know whether Decatur intended to shoot me, but I know I became dreadfully alarmed, and without being scarcely aware of what I did, I tipped him down off my shoulders, and he fell to the ground, severely hurting his neck. I immediately took to my heels and escaped into the wood near the plantation. I staid here all day, in fear and trembling, thinking of the law which punishes, with the loss of his right arm, any slave who shall inflict injury on or raise his arm against his master. By the time night had fallen I became so miserable, that I resolved to drown myself, and proceeded to the river for that purpose. When I got there, however, and saw the water looked so cold and so deep, my resolution was shaken. I candidly confess I did not like the prospect, even though death seemed preferable to the life I was leading, with its hourly miseries, and almost daily punishments. But I reflected that so long as I had life, there was hope; so I turned my back upon the river, and made my way to our old apple-orchard, where I laid down, and dozed till morning.

I wandered about here three days, eating berries—for there was no fruit—until, at the end of that time, I was well nigh famished. I then concluded to return to my master, and to meet the consequences of his displeasure. I went round to where the coloured people were at work, who advised me to make for the house by the way of the spring, and I should see what was going on, and what was in store for me. Accordingly I bent my steps in that direction, until I came to a little knoll or rising ground, from which I could overlook the plantation and buildings. I saw two posts set upright in the ground, and a cross-beam reaching from one to the other, to which a block and a rope were attached. I concluded Stevens was going to hang me, so I set off running. I had, however, been perceived, and I soon found that I was being hunted down with dogs. I looked behind, and saw my master and a good many strange people, some on horses and some on foot, who were exciting the hounds to follow me. These were gaining fast upon me, but I observed that they minded the strange people, or any one who urged them on,

so I determined I would give them the slip if I could. As they came up, I began to halloo and shout to them as lustily as any body, all the while running as fast as I could.

"Catch him, fellow," said I, urging the dogs on; "catch him; hey, fellow, hey, fellow; catch him."

The poor animals wagged their tails, and, excited by me, ran right ahead, quite fooled, and jumping and looking about, as though they sought to find out what we were all after. But at this moment, Billy Curtis, a planter, who was one of the party, and who was well mounted, rode up and struck me on the head with a dogwood club. The blow felled me, as though I had been shot, completely stunning me. When I recovered, I found myself stretched on the ground, my head bleeding fearfully, and my master standing over me, with his foot on my forehead. The scar that blow made, I retain to this day.

I was now forced to get up, when they drove me to where I had seen the posts. Here they tied my hands and feet together, and passing the rope through the block and pulleys, hoisted me up and began to swing me backwards and forwards. Billy Curtis stood on one side, with a bull-whip in his hand, and David Barrett on the other, with a cowhide. My master stood a little further off, laughing, and as Curtis and Barrett could not whip and swing me too, a negro was set to keep me going. As I swung past them, these men hit me each a lick with their whips, and they continued doing so until I fainted, when I was taken down.

But I was not done with yet.

Many people say that half of what Mrs. Stowe and others have written about the punishments inflicted on slaves is untrue. I wish, for the sake of those who are now in bonds, that it were so. Unfortunately it is too true; and I believe half of what is done to them never comes to light. This is what happened to me next.

To prevent my running away any more, Stevens fixed bells and horns on my head. This is not by any means an uncommon punishment. I have seen many slaves wearing them. A circle of iron, having a hinge behind, with a staple and padlock before, which hang under the chin, is fastened round the neck. Another circle of iron fits quite close round the crown of the head. The two are held together in this position by three rods of iron, which are fixed in each circle. These rods, or horns, stick out three feet above the head, and have a bell attached to each. The bells and horns do not weigh less than from twelve to fourteen pounds. When Stevens had fixed this ornament on my head, he turned me loose, and told me I might run off now if I liked.

I wore the bells and horns, day and night, for three months, and I do not think any description I could give of my sufferings during this time would convey any thing approaching to a faint idea of them. Let alone that their weight made my head and neck ache dreadfully, especially when I stooped to my work, at night I could not lie down to rest, because the horns prevented my stretching myself, or even curling myself up; so I was obliged to sleep crouching. Of course it was impossible for me to attempt to remove them, or to get away, though I still held to my resolution to make another venture as soon as I could see my way of doing it. Indeed, during those three long months, I thought more of John Glasgow, and getting off to England, than I had ever done all the time before, with such a firm purpose. I collected and arranged in my mind all the scraps of information I had been able to procure from others, or that I had acquired myself; and concealed, in the trunk of an old tree, a bundle of clothes and a flint and steel and tinderhorn: for though my case seemed desperate, I clung to hope, with a tenacity which now surprises me. It was a blessed consolation, and only for it I must have died.

Selection 2

Fighting Back

Frederick Douglass

By common consent, the greatest black leader in nineteenth-century America was Frederick Douglass (1817–1895), whose biography is sketched in this selection. Behind his imposing physical presence and his powerful command of written and spoken English lay an assurance of moral superiority over his adversaries that he had honed during his young days as a slave in Maryland. Quite literally, Douglass had to fight physically to gain this self-assurance. In his autobiography, Narrative of the Life of Frederick Douglass, An American Slave, *one of the most important of all pre–Civil War antislavery books, Douglass included an episode that has become famous, not only for its realistic depiction of life under slavery but also for what it says about the shaping of Douglass's character and for what it symbolizes about African American resistance to enslavement.*

The incident narrated in this selection took place when Douglass, in his late teens, was turned over by his master to a "slave breaker," a certain Mr. Covey, whose speciality was reducing recalcitrant young slaves to

Excerpted from Frederick Douglass, *The Life and Times of Frederick Douglass* (Hartford, Park, 1881).

abject obedience—"breaking" them. After several months under Covey's "care," consisting of hard labor and brutal discipline, Douglass tried to escape, but failed. Back at Covey's place on Maryland's Eastern Shore, his will was indeed almost broken, and he found himself about to be given a severe lashing. At that point he realized that to save himself both physical punishment and psychological degradation, he must fight back— and in an exhausting fistfight with Covey, he discovered that he himself could break the will and undermine the authority of the white man who had held power over him.

I had not gone far before my little strength again failed me. I could go no farther. I fell down, and lay for a considerable time. The blood was yet oozing from the wound on my head. For a time I thought I should bleed to death; and think now that I should have done so, but that the blood so matted my hair as to stop the wound. After lying there about three quarters of an hour, I nerved myself up again, and started on my way, through bogs and briers, barefooted and bareheaded, tearing my feet sometimes at nearly every step; and after a journey of about seven miles, occupying some five hours to perform it, I arrived at master's store. I then presented an appearance enough to affect any but a heart of iron. From the crown of my head to my feet, I was covered with blood. My hair was all clotted with dust and blood; my shirt was stiff with blood. My legs and feet were torn in sundry places with briers and thorns, and were also covered with blood. I suppose I looked like a man who had escaped a den of wild beasts, and barely escaped them.

In this state I appeared before my master, humbly entreating him to interpose his authority for my protection. I told him all the circumstances as well as I could, and it seemed, as I spoke, at times to affect him. He would then walk the floor, and seek to justify Covey by saying he expected I deserved it. He asked me what I wanted. I told him, to let me get a new home; that as sure as I lived with Mr. Covey again, I

should live with but to die with him; that Covey would surely kill me; he was in a fair way for it. Master Thomas ridiculed the idea that there was any danger of Mr. Covey's killing me, and said that he knew Mr. Covey; that he was a good man, and that he could not think of taking me from him; that, should he do so, he would lose the whole year's wages; that I belonged to Mr. Covey for one year, and that I must go back to him, come what might; and that I must not trouble him with any more stories, or that he would himself *get hold of me.* After threatening me thus, he gave me a very large dose of salts, telling me that I might remain in St. Michael's that night, (it being quite late,) but that I must be off back to Mr. Covey's early in the morning; and that if I did not, he would *get hold of me,* which meant that he would whip me.

I remained all night, and, according to his orders, I started off to Covey's in the morning, (Saturday morning,) wearied in body and broken in spirit. I got no supper that night, or breakfast that morning. I reached Covey's about nine o'clock; and just as I was getting over the fence that divided Mrs. Kemp's fields from ours, out ran Covey with his cowskin, to give me another whipping. Before he could reach me, I succeeded in getting to the cornfield; and as the corn was very high, it afforded me the means of hiding. He seemed very angry, and searched for me a long time. My behavior was altogether unaccountable. He finally gave up the chase, thinking, I suppose, that I must come home for something to eat; he would give himself no further trouble in looking for me. I spent that day mostly in the woods, having the alternative before me,—to go home and be whipped to death, or stay in the woods and be starved to death.

That night, I fell in with Sandy Jenkins, a slave with whom I was somewhat acquainted. Sandy had a free wife who lived about four miles from Mr. Covey's; and it being Saturday, he was on his way to see her. I told him my circumstances, and he very kindly invited me to go home with him. I went home with him, and talked this whole matter over, and got his advice as to what course it was best for me to pursue. I found Sandy an old adviser. He told me, with great solemnity, I must go back to Covey; but that before I went, I must go with him into another part of the woods, where there was a certain *root,* which, if I would take some of it with me, carrying it *always on my right side,* would render it impossible for Mr. Covey, or any other white man, to whip me. He said he had carried it for years; and since he had done so, he had never received a blow, and never expected to while he carried it. I at first rejected the idea, that the simple carrying of a root in my pocket would have any such effect as he had said, and was not disposed to take it; but Sandy impressed the necessity with much earnestness, telling me it could do no harm, if it did no good. To please him, I at length took the root, and, according to his direction, carried it upon my right side.

This was Sunday morning. I immediately started for home; and upon entering the yard gate, out came Mr. Covey on his way to meeting. He spoke to me very kindly, bade me drive the pigs from a lot near by, and passed on towards the church. Now, this singular conduct of Mr. Covey really made me begin to think that there was something in the *root* which Sandy had given me; and had it been on any other day than Sunday, I could have attributed the conduct to no other cause than the influence of that root; and as it was, I was half inclined to think the *root* to be something more than I at first had taken it to be.

All went well till Monday morning. On this morning, the virtue of the *root* was fully tested. Long before daylight, I was called to go and rub, curry, and feed, the horses. I obeyed, and was glad to obey. But whilst thus engaged, whilst in the act of throwing down some blades from the loft, Mr. Covey entered the stable with a long rope; and just as I was half out of the loft, he caught hold of my legs, and was about tying me. As soon as I found what he was up to, I gave a sudden spring, and as I did so, he holding to my legs, I was brought sprawling on the stable floor.

Mr. Covey seemed now to think he had me, and could do what he pleased; but at this moment—from whence came the spirit I don't know—I resolved to fight; and, suiting my action to the resolution, I seized Covey hard by the throat; and as I did so, I rose. He held on to me, and I to him. My resistance was so entirely unexpected, that Covey seemed taken all aback. He trembled like a leaf. This gave me assurance, and I held him uneasy, causing the blood to run where I touched him with the ends of my fingers. Mr. Covey soon called out to Hughes for help. Hughes came, and, while Covey held me, attempted to tie my right hand. While he was in the act of doing so, I watched my chance, and gave him a heavy kick close under the ribs. This kick fairly sickened Hughes, so that he left me in the hands of Mr. Covey. This kick had the effect of not only weakening Hughes, but Covey also. When he saw Hughes bending over with pain, his courage quailed. He asked me if I meant to persist in my resistance. I told him I did, come what might; that he had used me like a brute for six months, and that I was determined to be used so no longer. With that, he strove to drag me to a stick that was lying just out of the stable door. He meant to knock me down. But just as he was leaning over to get the stick, I seized him with both hands by his collar, and brought him by a sudden snatch to the ground. By this time, Bill came. Covey called upon him for assistance. Bill wanted to know what he could do. Covey said, "Take hold of him, take hold of him!" Bill said his master hired him out to work, and not to help to whip me; so he left Covey and myself to fight our own battle out. We were at it for nearly two hours. Covey at length let me go, puffing and blowing at a great rate, saying that if I had not resisted, he would not have whipped me half so much. The truth was, that he had not whipped me at all. I considered him as getting entirely the worst end of the bargain; for he had drawn no blood from me, but I had from him. The whole six months afterwards, that I spent with Mr. Covey, he never laid the weight of his finger upon me in anger. He would occasionally say, he didn't want to get hold of me again. "No," thought I, "you need not; for you will come off worse than you did before."

This battle with Mr. Covey was the turning-point in my career as a slave. It rekindled the few expiring embers of freedom, and revived within me a sense of my own manhood. It recalled the departed self-confidence, and inspired me again with a determination to be free. The gratification afforded by the triumph was a full compensation for whatever else might follow, even death itself. He only can understand the deep satisfaction which I experienced, who has himself repelled by force the bloody arm of slavery. I felt as I never felt before. It was a glorious resurrection, from the tomb of slavery, to the heaven of freedom. My long-crushed spirit rose, cowardice departed, bold defiance took its place; and I now resolved that, however long I might remain a slave in form, the day had passed forever when I could be a slave in fact. I did not hesitate to let it be known of me, that the white man who expected to succeed in whipping, must also succeed in killing me.

From this time I was never again what might be called fairly whipped, though I remained a slave four years afterwards. I had several fights, but was never whipped.

It was for a long time a matter of surprise to me why Mr. Covey did not immediately have me taken by the constable to the whipping-post, and there regularly whipped for the crime of raising my hand against a white man in defence of myself. And the only explanation I can now think of does not entirely satisfy me; but such as it is, I will give it. Mr. Covey enjoyed the most unbounded reputation for being a first-rate overseer and negro-breaker. It was of considerable importance to him. That reputation was at stake; and had he sent me—a boy about sixteen years old—to the public whipping-post, his reputation would have been lost; so, to save his reputation, he suffered me to go unpunished.

Selection 3

The *Amistad* Mutiny

Helen Kromer

One of the most spectacular acts of resistance to slavery in the nineteenth century took place at sea. In 1839 a group of Africans who had just been brought to Cuba (until 1898 a Spanish colony) rebelled as they were being transported by sea along the Cuban coast to the plantation of the man who had purchased them at the Havana slave market. (Slavery still flourished in Cuba, although the British navy was trying to enforce a ban on the trans-Atlantic slave trade.) Led by an intrepid man named Singbe (or Cinqué), the slaves seized control of their ship, the Amistad *(which in Spanish means "friendship") and tried to sail back to Africa. But being untrained in navigation, they wound up drifting in the Atlantic, slowly starving until they ran ashore on the U.S. coast. Interned and in serious danger of being returned to Cuba to face charges of murder and mutiny, the slaves were befriended by American antislavery groups. For-*

Excerpted from Helen Kromer, *Amistad: The Slave Uprising Aboard the Spanish Schooner.* Copyright © 1997 Helen Kromer. Reprinted with permission from The Pilgrim Press.

mer president John Quincy Adams (now an outspoken antislavery Congressman) argued on their behalf before the U.S. Supreme Court, demanding their freedom not only because the international slave trade was now illegal but also on broad human rights grounds. In 1841 they were freed and allowed to return to their homeland, in what is now Sierra Leone. Their case attracted enormous attention in the United States, and its dramatic power still remains potent, as a recent, heavily fictionalized film version of their story attests.

This selection, excerpted from historian Helen Kromer's book Amistad: The Slave Uprising Aboard the Spanish Schooner, *narrates the events of the actual mutiny.*

*I*n late March 1839, two months after Singbe was brought into Lomboko, the schooner *Teçora* came into port to trade, and several hundred slaves were herded on board. The Atlantic passage was stormy, and the Africans rolled about until parts of their bodies were rubbed raw. When the ocean grew calm, the heat increased their thirst and discomfort. They did indeed suffer terribly, as they later told reporters.

Finally, in June, they sighted land. They were put ashore and thrown into the slave pen at Havana. This time, the wait was short. After ten days a young Spaniard named Jose Ruiz came to buy. He selected forty-nine slaves; Singbe, Fawni, and their companions were among them. Ruiz paid $450.00 for each of them, then he went to the office of Governor-General Espeleta and paid $10.00 apiece for a pass that gave him permission to ship the slaves to his plantation at Puerto Principe, in Cuba.

No one asked Ruiz where the slaves had come from. No one asked him if these were Cuban slaves. Yet in 1820 the Spanish Crown had made it a crime to import slaves from Africa. Only slaves who had been in Cuba since *before* 1820 could be legally shipped. But the governor-general ignored the law, signed the passes, and pocketed the money.

That night, Ruiz marched his forty-nine slaves through the streets of Havana to the harbor, where the coastal schooner *Amistad* was anchored. The Spanish word *amistad* means "friendship," but the Africans could not read Spanish. What they could understand was the whip and the gun that forced them to board the schooner.

An elderly Spanish gentleman, Pedro Montes, also bound for Puerto Principe, had arrived earlier and was settled in with his purchases—the three little girls and the boy Ka-li.

At dawn on June 28, 1839, the "long, low black schooner" topped with a headful of billowing white sail got under way briskly. Puerto Principe was only three hundred miles down the coast and Captain Ramon Ferrer expected the trip to take no more than two days. But their fast start proved deceptive, for the winds shifted. So little headway had been made by the second day that the captain realized the passage might take as long as two weeks. On board he had only enough food and water for five days, so he ordered a cut in the blacks' rations, giving them only "half eat and half drink."

Cutting food and drink proved to be a foolish measure. The blacks were not chained on this trip as securely as they had been on the Atlantic passage. Their heavy neck irons were still used at night, but during the day they were chained only by the wrists and ankles and they were allowed up from the hold in groups of ten to eat and to exercise on deck. When they began to suffer from thirst, two of them who were on deck stole to the water cask and helped themselves. Members of the crew caught them at it, and Captain Ferrer had Fuli whipped. Then he was whipped again four times during the night. The next day, Kimbo, Pie, Moru, and Fawni were beaten, and their wounds were treated according to the painful custom of the time, by rubbing them with salt, gunpowder, and rum.

The floggings drove the Africans to fury. They had endured the sufferings of the Atlantic voyage and their patience was at an end. To make matters worse, Singbe, by "talking with his fingers," had asked Celestino, the mulatto cook, what was going to happen to them. Celestino made a cruel joke. He "told" them they would be killed, chopped into pieces, and salted down for meat for the Spaniards.

The Africans did not find the joke funny. None of them were cannibals and the idea of white men feasting on their flesh filled them with horror. They began to talk and plan among themselves. Though they spoke different dialects, most were Mendis, and certain words they all knew were similar. They turned to Singbe, their natural leader, who urged them to revolt. "We may as well die in trying to be free as to be killed and eaten," he said.

The slaves knew that among the cargo were boxes of the large, sharp knives used in Cuba for cutting sugarcane. These could be turned into weapons; though they had no guns, the slaves were forty-nine adults against the Spanish captain, his two crewmen, Ruiz, Montes, and the two mulatto slaves—Celestino and the cabin boy Antonio.

To get to the weapons, however, the Africans needed freedom from their chains and favorable weather conditions. When Singbe was called on deck to exercise and felt a loose nail beneath his foot, he picked it up and hid it in his armpit. Then, on the fifth night, it rained very hard. All crew hands were called on deck to manage the ship, and the sound of the downpour hid the noise of the slaves working in the hold. While the children were asleep, Singbe went to work to pry open the padlock anchoring the chain threaded through the Africans' neck irons and fastened to a ringbolt on the deck. When the padlock snapped, the men turned in a frenzy to rid one another of the smaller chains. The first men free rushed to the cargo and broke open the boxes of cane knives. The children awakened and Singbe ordered Ka-li to keep them quiet.

The rain had begun to peter out and the Africans waited silently belowdecks while the captain and the passengers settled down to sleep; Celestino lay down beside his master on a mattress on the deck. The slaves waited until it grew very late, and then, while the clouds still covered the moon, they ripped off the grating of the hold and rushed for the deck.

Singbe found Celestino and killed him with a single blow. The captain fought back until Singbe and some of the others overpowered him; then he, too, was mortally wounded Montes was attacked, but managed to break free, rush below, and wrap himself in a sail. The children were now on deck, screaming with fright. In the confusion the two Spanish sailors lowered a boat and slipped away.

Singbe found Montes and wanted to kill him, but the others prevented it. The Africans would need the Spaniards—especially Montes, who had once been master of a vessel—to help them sail the ship back to Africa. Antonio also was spared because he was the only one on board who could act as interpreter for the Africans and the Spaniards.

Montes and Ruiz were now lashed together while the Africans ransacked the cabin and the cargo, which included everything from glass doorknobs to Spanish shawls, from gingham umbrellas to a trunkful of gold doubloons. They broke open the casks and boxes of food, eating as they hunted, strewing food and goods about the decks—dishes and clothing and raisins and jewelry and beef and medicines and wines. They ate and drank their fill, mixing the medicines with the beef and raisins and washing it all down with wine. While the ship blew with the wind they celebrated their victory. They threw the dead overboard—including two of their fellow Africans who had been killed in the struggle along with Celestino and the captain—and they washed down the decks. They danced and shouted until some fell down drunk. Some became sick from the medicines, and two more died.

In the morning, Singbe appeared on deck dressed in a pair of white pantaloons, with a red scarf at his neck and the captain's sword fixed at his belt. He made it clear that he would be in command of the ship. He had Montes brought up from below and ordered him to steer the *Amistad* back to Sierra Leone. Montes understood the cane knives flashing above his head and he turned the ship east, straight into the rising sun. Singbe now ordered those Africans still able to walk to set the sails as Montes directed. But they knew nothing at all of sailing; the flapping canvas jerked out of their hands and the ropes danced away in the wind. The Africans soon climbed down from the rigging, leaving only the jib and the topsails to catch the wind.

The weather had begun to turn cooler. The Africans had been naked in the hold, and they began rummaging about in the cargo for odd bits of clothing and bright-colored silks and satins, to dress themselves as Singbe had done.

Thus fantastically dressed and sailing their strangely appointed ship, the Africans began the voyage that would make them famous throughout the world. . . .

None of the ships sent to hunt down the *Amistad* found her, and those that came upon her by chance steered clear and left her to pursue her aimless course alone.

Taken Captive Again!

Singbe finally dropped anchor off Culloden Point near the tip of Long Island, and on August 26 he and a group of the Africans rowed ashore to get food and water.

While some of them were loading water casks on a cart they had borrowed from a farmer and while Singbe was bargaining for food supplies, two ship captains—Henry Green and Peletiah Fordham, who were out hunting that day—saw them. They joined the bargaining group, but they offered more than the meat, bread, and gin that the Africans had collected. Captain Green took one look at the gold doubloons that Singbe carried. If Singbe could produce enough of that gold, he managed to make the African understand, he would sail the strangers back to Sierra Leone. Singbe had the trunk brought from the ship and rattled it before the captain.

But even as Singbe was bargaining to get his countrymen back to Africa, the *Amistad* was being seized by officers of a United States government vessel. From the moment Lieutenant Commander Thomas R. Gedney and his first officer, Lieutenant Richard W. Meade, standing on the deck of the surveying brig *Washington,* had seen this tattered ship with its black crew, they had realized that she might be the much-publicized "mystery ship." If she was and they captured her, they knew they might claim prize money or salvage.

That they chanced upon her when Singbe was not aboard was their good fortune, for it was Singbe who had so managed the blacks that they frightened off other ships. It was Singbe who had kept the Spaniards out of sight. Now, without Singbe on board, the blacks gave up easily and the Spaniards burst from the hold, with Ruiz crying out for United States protection and Montes falling upon the neck of Lieutenant Meade in such hysterical relief that Meade thought he was mad.

Uncertain of what was happening, Singbe and his men started back for the ship. They were quickly taken prisoner, but Singbe, like a fly in a web, kept working to escape. His efforts were later described by a reporter from the *New York Sun.*

As soon as the ropes were made fast from the *Washington* to the *Amistad,* Singbe grew frantic. He "went below, and tying some gold about his person, he leapt out of the main hatch and at one bound was over the side." He had packed too much in the money belt and sank like a stone, but managed to work himself free.

> [He] came up about 100 yards from the vessel, having been under water at least 5 minutes. The boat was instantly manned and sent in chase of him. When the boat neared him he would stop, but just as it came within reach he would dive down and come up again some yards behind her stern. He thus employed them about 40 minutes, when seeing further attempts useless, he gave himself up.

He was taken to the *Washington,* but appeared to be so uneasy and anxious that the crew returned him to the *Amistad.* There "the poor wretches clustered about him, making the most extravagant demonstrations of joy. Some laughed, some screamed, some danced, and some wept." Singbe faced them grimly. He told them he preferred death to serving the white man: "You had better be killed than live many moons in misery."

The Africans began uttering piercing yells, and Gedney ordered Singbe back to the *Washington,* where he was manacled all night to prevent his leaping overboard. The next morning he convinced Gedney by sign language that if he were returned to the *Amistad,* he would give the commander a handkerchief of gold, which he had hidden away. He was put back aboard the schooner and sent below, but Antonio was sent along with him to watch and to listen. Singbe quickly collected his countrymen around him, saying:

> My brothers . . . you have only one chance for death and none for liberty. I am sure you prefer death as I do. You can, by killing the white men now on board—and I will help you—make the people here kill you. It is better for you to do this, and then you will not only avert bondage yourselves, but prevent . . . unnumbered wrongs on your children.

Antonio, seeing "how the Negroes yelled and . . . leapt about and seemed . . . under some talismanic power," quickly signaled the Americans, who dragged Singbe from the hold. While

Singbe led the 1839 revolt on the slave ship Amistad.

his comrades moaned and cried, Singbe rode back in the cutter, moving not a muscle, his eye fixed on the schooner. On board the *Washington,* he would not rest until the crew had taken him on deck, where he stood all night staring fixedly at the *Amistad.* "He evinces no emotion," the *Sun* reported, ". . . and had he lived in the days of Greece or Rome, his name would have been handed down to posterity as one who had practiced those most sublime of all virtues—disinterested patriotism and unshrinking courage."

The *New York Sun* reporter concluded his description by expressing an admiration and respect for the rebel leader that many people would feel in the months ahead. . . .

The *Washington* now towed the *Amistad* across Long Island Sound and into the port of New London, Connecticut. All up and down the shore, people saw her coming and ran for the docks. They were curious for several reasons: the two Spaniards who had gone over the side the night of the uprising and who the Africans believed "could not catch land, they must have swum to the bottom of the seas" had instead reached Cuba and reported the uprising. That news had filtered into the United States and the crowd now gathered thought this vessel might be not only the famed "ghost ship," but also the mutinous one. . . .

The inquiry began with a complaint filed by Ruiz and Montes against Singbe and the other adult Africans who were still alive. Then Singbe was brought in to hear the charges against him, though he understood not a word. He was kept standing through the rest of the proceedings while the court considered the evidence and heard the testimony of Ruiz and Montes. Among Captain Ferrer's papers were found the two passes issued by the governor-general of Cuba. One gave permission for Ruiz to transport forty-nine slaves; the other gave Montes permission to transport the three girls. There was no pass at all for Ka-li; this strange oversight meant that Montes could not claim him in a court of law.

Ruiz and Montes told about the events of the night of the mutiny. Although they could not name the murderers of the captain and the cook, for there had been too much confusion, Antonio could, for he had been awake through it all. So the court moved to the *Amistad* and Antonio went below to pick out the two slaves who he said had committed the murder along with Singbe and a fourth man who had died on the voyage.

The judge now decided that Singbe and the others should stand trial before the next circuit court, which would meet in Hartford, Connecticut, on September 17. The three girls, Ka-li, and Antonio were also to appear and give evidence. In the meantime, all the Africans were to be taken to New Haven and held in the county jail.

The Absence of Large-Scale Slave Revolts

John B. Boles

Gabriel's Insurrection of 1800, Denmark Vesey's conspiracy in 1822, and Nat Turner's Rebellion of 1831 all failed, and the later Amistad *mutiny was an isolated incident in an atypical setting. Why were there so few American slave revolts, and nothing on the scale of the massive uprisings of bondspeople that erupted in nineteenth-century Jamaica and Brazil? Historian John B. Boles, who teaches at Rice University and edits* The Journal of Southern History, *explains why slave resistance in the United States almost always took the form of individual acts, and why a large insurrection—as slaves seemed to understand—never had a chance.*

*T*he one overriding fact about slave rebellion in the Old South was the almost complete absence of large-scale armed insurrection such as occurred in Latin America and the Caribbean and lay like a horrible specter in the back of the minds of countless southern planters. Explaining nonoccurrences is always difficult, and this case is no exception. But even a partial explanation does shed light on two important components of any historical analysis, the comparative and the temporal. The situation in the South after about 1800 was significantly different from that elsewhere in the Americas. Moreover, one must remember the wide variety of rebellious acts that stopped short of insurrection, rebellious acts as diverse and individualized as the planter-slave confrontations themselves. Yet during the heyday of the Old South, in the final decades before the Civil War when cotton was king and the slave population was at its highest, the broad surface of the plantation society was remarkably smooth and stable despite the many small eddies of unrest and the strong, deep current of slaves' cultural and psychological rejection of enslavement. That apparent calm, experienced even by those acute observers who suspected the swirling torrents underneath, has helped perpetuate many myths about the Old South and its two peoples, black and white.

Many factors mitigated against successful armed insurrection by slaves in the Old South. Unlike the situation in Latin America, in the Old South as a whole whites far outnumbered slaves, and of course totally controlled the police power of the states. . . . In certain regions like the sea islands of South Carolina and Georgia and the sugar districts of Louisiana, blacks were in a significant majority, yet even there the distance between individual plantations and the maze of unbridged estuaries, rivers, bayous, sloughs, and swamps made communication and travel between plantations difficult. The geography of the Old South conspired with demography to complicate still further slave attempts at rebellion and escape. Slaves in Brazil and in the Guiana region of northeastern South America, for example, had the huge, unexplored jungle fastness of the Amazon River basin in which to escape; similarly, plantations were located on the perimeters of the West Indian islands, whose interiors offered sure havens for runaways. In both regions slaves escaped to the interior and in maroon settlements often managed to survive for years, occasionally fighting white authorities to a standstill and achieving treaty recognition of their status (often in exchange for returning newly escaped slaves).

This kind of escape from slavery was never possible for the overwhelming majority of bondsmen in the Old South. Except for those few who lived near the Dismal Swamp on the eastern Virginia–North Carolina boundary, and some in Florida and Georgia near the Okefenokee Swamp and the trackless Everglades, there was no safe hinterland where maroons could survive. Moreover, cold winters, particularly in the Upper South, made the prospect of hiding out in the woods uninviting. In the early decades of plantation development, the Indians in the backcountry quickly learned they would be rewarded for capturing and returning slave runaways. The Indians were replaced in later decades by yeoman farmers who either returned the runaways for the reward or kept them. For most slaves the freedom territory north of the Mason-Dixon line or the Ohio River was simply too far away, and while several thousand bondsmen in the last half-century of slavery did escape by way of the Underground Railroad, most of them came from the border states of Maryland and Kentucky.

In Latin America and the Caribbean Islands, where hundreds of slaves lived on huge plantations, the owners were absent, and the working conditions were far more harsh than those typical in the South, desperate slaves, often plagued with famine as well as overwork, occasionally struck out against their brutal oppression and escaped to preexisting maroon communities. The working conditions on the tropical sugar plantations drove slaves to rebellion, and the example of successful escape offered by the maroon settlements in the backcountry emboldened otherwise hesitant bondsmen to act. There was, in other words, a heritage of insurrection in the Caribbean and Latin America that offered slaves not only incentive to rebel but the expectation of success. No such vital spark of hope was possible in the Old South. The few insurrections were small, localized, and quickly and brutally suppressed, with many innocent slaves usually punished and the general restrictions against all slaves made temporarily more harsh.

After 1808 the foreign slave trade to the United States ended, but in the slave societies to the south the transatlantic trade in humans continued. As always, the African imports were disproportionately young males, maintaining the highly unequal slave sex ratios in Latin America and the Caribbean. This, combined with the rigorous work routines, the cruelty of managers on absentee plantations, and the disease-induced high death rates produced a degree of despair that seldom obtained in the Old South. A work force of mostly young males, with neither wives nor families to be concerned about, with expectations of a life that could only be "nasty, brutal, and short," with an almost impenetrable backcountry beckoning them and the ever-present example of successful maroons suggesting that escape was possible, and with the number of superintending whites tiny in proportion to the black population—there is no wonder that out of this unstable situation slave resistance and insurrection were constant realities. Yet by the time there were significant numbers of blacks in the antebellum South, the demographic situation was so different as to provide in effect a check on potential slave unrest.

During the era of the cotton kingdom most slaves were American born, the sex ratio was practically equal (more so than the white ratio), and slaves typically lived in family groupings. As a result the slave family became the single most important bond holding members together, and as we have seen, naming practices and kinship systems evolved to cement relationships made fragile by the possibility of sale or removal. This demographic development also prevented slave insurrection.

While a population composed mostly of unattached young males can be very explosive (especially when faced with harsh conditions and the possibility of escape), a population where males and females are equally present, family relationships have been formed and there are small children to love and care for, is far more conservative. The possibility of an entire family escaping was practically nil, and parents were loath to forsake their children to save themselves. Likewise few men would leave their loved ones for an escape attempt with little chance of success. If family attachments lessened runaway efforts, so much more did the ties of family affection reduce the possibilities of insurrection. Few male slaves would risk almost sure death when to do so would leave their families fatherless. Moreover, the knowledge that family members and innocent bystanders would be pitilessly punished and their rights severely circumscribed in the aftermath of a rebellion attempt must have restrained many discontented slaves.

In the Old South, where family structures, leisure time, and fairly good living conditions prevented most slaves from being driven into utter desperation, slaves usually found less risky avenues of countering the dehumanization of chattel bondage. Because hunger and abject hopelessness were less common in the Old South, slaves calculated their options more carefully, waiting—sometimes all their lives—for good chances for successful rebellion. Thousands did not find the right moment to strike until the Civil War and the presence of Union troops profoundly changed the balance. Then no one was more shocked than complacent planters when droves of their seemingly most devoted, most responsible slaves "deserted" and chose freedom.

The realities of power and geography in the Old South also minimized the kind of slave rebellion that often occurred in the other New World plantation societies. In the antebellum South, slaves were very seldom driven to mindless, suicidal acts of outrage and rebellion. Fully aware of their situation, they learned, socialized, and passed on to their children a wide range of behavior—voice intonations, facial expressions, feigned illness, purposeful laziness and slowness of motion, dumb-like-a-fox incomprehension—that combined equal portions of insubordination and minor rebellion to produce a constant undercurrent of resistance to psychological bondage. Although never completely giving in to authority, most slaves were able, at least in the eyes of their master, to acquiesce in their state of servitude and thus survive with their essential humanity intact. In the most fundamental sense, racial slavery as it existed in the Old South was premised on the assumption by whites that blacks were inferior, either a subhuman or a permanently childlike race. Planters' everyday experience, of course, gave the lie to this assumption, and therein may have been the cause of the guilt that some historians believe troubled many whites, particularly those who constructed elaborate proslavery defenses. Had slaves in general accepted this racial subordination and aspired to be only what the white man prescribed, then blacks would have been total slaves, and all resistance—except occasional outbursts of violence—would have disappeared. But the rich panoply of Afro-American culture, their tales, music, art, and religion protected bondsmen from complete capitulation. Out of the inner reserves of their humanity slaves in measured ways resisted servitude and defended the limited rights that had become, through mutual accommodation, accepted by whites. The black community evolved a culture from which proceeded all forms of slave resistance other than rebellion.

Owners were most concerned with their slaves' labor output, and for that reason bondsmen developed a repertoire of techniques to gain a modicum of control over the amount of work required of them. While some slaves were downright lazy, a low-incentive labor system like slavery obviously gave them few reasons to overexert themselves. Even the application of force soon became counterproductive. Slaves realized they had to work at a moderate pace, for their physical well-being and the stability of their family relationships depended on the success of the plantation. While there was never enough incentive or mobility to turn bondsmen into competitive men-on-the-make, they did accept a responsibility to work at a productivity level that eventually came to be accepted by master and slave alike. Often there was a perpetual low-grade war of wills between the two, with masters cajoling, threatening, and occasionally whipping and slaves complaining, moving at a deliberate pace (though the nature of the crop culture required careful labor that outside observers apparently misunderstood at times for indolence), and even practicing minor agricultural sabotage like breaking tools, "accidentally" plowing up crops, "carelessly" letting the teams get out of the barn-lot, and so on. To what extent owners realized what was going on is problematical; usually they ascribed such behavior to the accepted irresponsibility and childishness of slaves, but surely they at times must have comprehended the guerilla resistance under way. (It should be said that such sabotage had a negligible effect on the total agricultural system.) Slaves frequently acted dumb, carefully "misunderstood," and—in earlier days—confessed ignorance of English as effective ways to minimize the demands placed on them.

When a master or overseer tried to force slaves to work harder, or longer hours, than convention had come to establish as the norm, slaves were quick to protest. Not only did the war of the wills heat up, but slaves were sometimes quite bold in their insistence against being pushed beyond endurance or general practice. Particularly if an overseer was the offending taskmaster, slaves did not hesitate to take their case to their masters. Whether the overseer was the culprit or not, aggrieved and protesting slaves complained and shuffled along, slowed their pace, and feigned illness. On any plantation at any given moment there were always several laid up for sickness, real and pretended, a tactic planters were ultimately helpless to counteract. If conditions persisted, or when personal relations between a slave and his owner or overseer became extremely strained—as when a slave felt himself unjustly punished—bondsmen often ran away.

Slave runaways were a perennial problem for southern planters. Over the course of the slave-plantation system in the South the nature of runaways and their destinations changed, but in the antebellum period, after the spread of cotton and sugar cultivation, bondsmen ran away for three general reasons. Probably most common and of least worry to owners were those who in response to a real or felt injustice ran away for a short period simply to deprive the owner of a portion of the slave's labor. After all, here was a way for a slave to exert himself, to thwart his owner's intentions, to make a statement about his rights even if it came at some eventual cost to himself. Periodically when an owner or overseer forced slaves to work too hard or on the accepted weekend off (usually Saturday afternoon and Sunday), punished one unjustly, blamed one unfairly, or insulted a specially favored or skilled slave, the offended bondsman would disappear for several days or for three or four weeks.

Masters sometimes came to accept with a shrug this type of protest, knowing the absent slave would soon reappear, having in the meantime been living probably on the fringes of the plantation, maybe even slipping back to the quarters at night for food. Usually when the runaway did return he would receive a whipping or some other punishment, but occasionally owners disregarded the infraction of their rules and welcomed the runaway's return without disciplinary measures. This kind of commonplace running away was not a threat to the institution of slavery. The runaways themselves were protesting less the institution itself than invasions of their perceived rights as slaves. Owners seldom hunted for, probably never advertised for, such absent—not escaped—slaves. Because such limited running away was an accepted if unconscious method for aggrieved or angered slaves to work out their feelings in a bold but, from the owner's view, safe and harmless form, it no doubt relieved tensions, allowed resentments on both sides to cool, and incidentally reduced the possibility that hidden or suppressed rage might build to explosive levels.

While temporary running away was in effect a safety valve, a second common reason for running away represented a longer-term threat to slavery. The separation of slave families caused many bondsmen to leave their plantations in an effort to reunite with loved ones. Even if runaways of this kind eventually returned to their owners, the absence was often long enough to persuade the owner to place advertisements for their return in local newspapers. These advertisements, written as accurately as possible in hopes that the described slave would be located, frequently included hints that the runaway had joined his spouse or children at a certain location. Perhaps there is no stronger indication of the strength and resiliency of family ties among bondsmen than these efforts against all obstacles to see once again kin separated by distance. Even when runaways like these were recaptured and returned to their owners, the more realistic owners frequently would sell them to someone living in the vicinity of the loved one, knowing full well that the bonds of affection were stronger than discipline. Certainly many callous sellers and buyers of men disdained any human sympathies, but just as many—for reasons of practicality if not humanity—tried not to separate families unless in their view economic necessity required them to do so. Slavery's defenders as well as its critics recognized that the separation of families was a moral sore spot in the theoretical justification of bondage, and for that reason very seldom were small children parted from their mothers. Nevertheless, the trauma associated with sales of whatever nature forced many slaves to risk great danger and even greater hardships to see once more the faces of dear ones stolen away from them.

Despite the various factors that minimized slave rebellion and running away, there were nonetheless always situations, personality clashes, misunderstandings that drove slaves to cast aside their doubts and fears and escape to freedom. Often slaves who could not endure their bondage any longer but recognized the futility of individual violence or the inhospitableness of the countryside simply ran away to southern cities where they blended into the sizable free black population and disappeared. Skilled, articulate slaves, well-versed in the ways and expectations of their masters, were at the same time those most able to direct a potential slave insurrection and those most able, and likely, to succeed and even prosper as free blacks in Richmond, Charleston, or New Orleans. In yet another way southern cities, by offering a refuge to highly skilled slave runaways, helped defuse the potential for rebellion that might destroy the institution of bondage. Permanent slave escapees, then, whether they fled north or to southern cities to gain their freedom, had the ironic effect of making the existing system of slavery more stable by depriving the larger population of bondsmen of their most vocal, most able leaders.

While slave owners often convinced themselves that the possibilities of large-scale slave insurrection were remote and failed to recognize the intent of resistance present in malingering and short-term running away, they realized that there were lethal individualistic ways of rebelling. Slaves were often suspected of arson and poisoning, in part because the causes of destructive fires and fatal diseases were so often mysterious. There are of course recorded instances of bondsmen using either of these to strike back at their owners, and surely both were successfully employed occasionally without raising undue suspicions. Contemporaries seem sometimes to have become almost hysterical over the imagined presence of vindictive slaves behind every unexplained fire or death. It would be a mistake, however, to follow the lead of overwrought, guilt-ridden slave owners. Sparks from fireplaces, poorly constructed chimneys, accidents associated with the smoking of meat or drying of tobacco, spontaneous combustion, and a lengthy list of barely understood and misdiagnosed diseases were probably more often at the bottom of sudden fires and unexplained illnesses.

The absence of a tradition of armed slave uprisings in the Old South in no way supports the old myth of Sambo, the contented slave. Certainly there were passive, fawning, irresponsible, childlike Sambos, but they must have been but a fraction of the slave population. Far more common were the realistic slaves, men and women who knew they had to accept at least the physical constraints of bondage, who had a healthy sense of the possible and for whom family concerns were restraints against self-destructive rage. Whether it was understood or not, the vital Afro-American culture protected realistic slaves from being dehumanized; their culture provided them alternative ways of viewing life and did not allow the white man to control their inner world of values and dreams. By having something of their own to hold to, most bondsmen survived slavery, bending when survival dictated but not letting their spirit be broken.

They learned by necessity to cope with their existence, being by turns passive and assertive; knowing when to fawn and dissemble and when to protest; knowing how to get by guile what they had to have and how to avoid punishment. This indispensable know-how was transmitted from parents to children in a variety of ways. Whites, who seldom could see beyond their slaves' black faces, comprehended them all as Sambos, but

again and again, when pushed too far, slaves resisted with a firmness and forthrightness that surprised their masters. To suppress their guilt over slaveholding, most southern whites tried desperately to convince themselves that blacks were a permanent child-race who needed and preferred slavery. When time after time slaves reacted with a maturity and boldness that should have called the racial stereotype into question, whites instead suspected outside forces—abolitionists, the example of free blacks, emancipationist literature—at work.

These realistic slaves represented the huge middle range of character types; at the opposite end of the spectrum from true Sambos were an equally small number of true rebels who with every fiber of their being rejected enslavement. Slave parents, knowing the consequence of attitudes of this kind, would try to dissuade their children from conspicuous rebellion. If the warnings were of no avail, sooner or later rebels were usually killed or suffered such brutality that their spirit was permanently broken, with suicide or self-mutilation sometimes the ultimate result. Too much attention has been focused on Sambos and rebels; most slaves were neither, though they could be a little of both as the occasion required.

With the invention of the cotton gin in 1793, the closing of the foreign slave trade in 1808, and the opening of the Old Southwest to the expansion of slavery after 1815, the political and economic foundations of the cotton kingdom were laid. The Revolutionary era imperceptibly merged into the Old South, with the institution of slavery like a giant black glacier inexorably spreading across the land, grinding down the rocks of resistance along the way and changing the entire social and cultural landscape in its wake. Nothing and no one remained untouched across the face of the South. Only a cataclysmic civil war could wrench blacks out of bondage and transform even incompletely a land so marked by natural beauty and human tragedy.

The Complete History of

White Abolitionists

Chapter 13

Introduction

a movement to abolish slavery entirely gained strength in parts of the English-speaking world in the early nineteenth century. Great Britain, not the United States, was the most important center of antislavery action. With its mighty navy, Great Britain took generally (but not completely) effective steps to suppress the Atlantic slave trade after 1815. In 1833, the British antislavery movement reached its climax when Parliament voted to abolish human bondage throughout the empire, giving some compensation to slave owners for their losses. Because British slave owners tended to be wealthy "nabobs" living in luxury in England off the profits that their West Indian sugar plantations generated, they constituted an isolated and unpopular target in the home country. Abolishing slavery at the national level in Britain required the summoning of much less political will than a comparable action would demand in the United States, where slave owners were a widespread and highly vocal element in the electorate. Because of its strongly British cast, many Americans rejected antislavery as one more of John Bull's clever tricks to hamper U.S. progress.

But strongly moralistic Americans, usually with a family background in New England Puritanism or Pennsylvania Quakerism, found antislavery a cause to which they could devote intense energy. Around 1830, abolitionism began to attract passionate and highly articulate advocates.

Why then? With the presidential campaign of 1828, electoral politics was becoming exciting, as property-ownership requirements for voting were dropped in state after state, opening political participation to virtually all adult white males. A newly energized Democratic Party shouted for the popular Old Hero, Andrew Jackson, and by 1840 the new Whig Party answered with its raucous rallies for William Henry Harrison. Throughout the North after the 1820s, moralistic crusades had been constantly competing for public attention. The Protestant revivalism of the era, which historians call the Second Great Awakening, kept the North in a state of constant religious enthusiasm. Religiously inspired movements to curb Americans' enormous thirst for alcohol, to enforce strict Sabbath observance, and to ban the Sunday delivery of the mails attracted middle-class, Bible-reading men—and even more so women, for whom rough-and-tumble, hard-drinking, male-dominated electoral politics was not an option. Indeed, now that politics was open to the enthusiastic participation of the common man, rather than being a "gentlemanly" pursuit for the educated and prosperous elite (as had been the rule in the early republic), many upstanding citizens took alarm. If the "common man" was now to rule, he had better be taught how to behave himself, and his energies should be channeled toward morally acceptable ends. The result was a proliferation of reform societies during the 1830s and 1840s, often spearheaded by women. Campaigns to promote public schooling, to ensure that lawbreakers were induced to repent and reform, to discourage all forms of "vice," and to promote self-improvement among the down-and-out all joined the existing temperance crusade as parts of the so-called Benevolent Empire, as the informal coalition of the era's do-good organizations was called. The most prominent spokesman for all this reform activity was the Reverend Lyman Beecher, a Congregationalist minister and the father of the future author of *Uncle Tom's Cabin,* Harriet Beecher Stowe.

Antislavery became one of the many outposts of the Benevolent Empire. What more obvious blemish on America's democratic promise than the "peculiar institution" that brutalized and degraded its victims and its perpetrators alike? What more glaring occasion for lust than the subjugation of bondswomen to the unchecked power of male masters and overseers? What more crass example of materialism and greed run wild than the buying and selling of human beings so that more money could be made by raising and selling cotton, rice, and molasses? What worthier cause for good Christians than that of delivering slaves from suffering?

Not all reformers became abolitionists, and the movement often aroused ridicule—or worse—among the general public. Compared with the campaigns for public schools and temperance, abolitionism struck most northern whites as cranky. Racism was a basic fact of nineteenth-century American life, and democracy was something only for white people. The Democratic Party of Andrew Jackson, a wealthy slave owner, was frankly racist; Jackson said that abolitionists should be hanged, and he probably meant it. It was one thing for upper-crust members of the American Colonization Society to talk of resettling freed slaves in Africa, but abolitionist calls for emancipating bondspeople without deporting them frightened average white Americans with the specter of losing their jobs to ex-slaves. Even the thought of having to live side-by-side with dark-skinned people, who presumably would flood into northern cities if ever they were released from southern plantations, unnerved northern whites.

To abolitionists, none of these concerns mattered. Not all of them personally managed to overcome their racist attitudes toward blacks, nor did their movement make allowances for nonabolitionists' racism. For men and women who supported antislavery, all that counted was that slavery was evil, that slave owners were sinners, that the defenders of slavery were an affront to American freedom in general. Was not "the Slave Power," a supposed conspiracy of proslavery interests much talked about before the Civil War, responsible for curtailing Americans' freedom to receive abolitionist newspapers through the mails? Did not slavery's advocates stifle free speech in the South and, with the "gag rule," prevent Congress from receiving abolitionist petitions? Most abolitionists angrily rejected the older colonization movement's proposals to send ex-slaves to Africa; they demanded freedom now, and usually disdained the thought of compensating slave owners who had already extracted filthy profits from the ownership of human flesh. Abolitionism was not practical politics, and practical politicians who were also antislavery, like Abraham Lincoln, carefully distanced themselves from the cause and disavowed the label.

Abolitionism did not remain a single, unified movement. By the end of the 1830s, William Lloyd Garrison, one of the most prominent abolitionists, veered off on an ultra-radical course that included denouncing the U.S. Constitution, advocating pacifism and "nonresistance," and embracing a utopian religious viewpoint called "Christian perfectionism." Just as the civil rights and antiwar movements of the 1960s helped generate women's liberation and feminist "consciousness raising" in the early 1970s, so abolitionism was the starting point for significant numbers of American women to become women's rights advocates in the 1840s. (Many abolitionist women came to realize that laws restricting their rights held them in a bondage that they compared to slavery. They were also spurred into activism by the patronizing attitudes of some male abolitionists.) Garrison supported the broadening of abolitionism, but many other antislavery men did not. After 1839, the abolitionists' main organization, the American Anti-Slavery Society, split over various issues, including feminism.

Abolitionists remained a small minority in the North, even at the time of the Civil War. Their role in bringing about the destruction of the "peculiar institution" was secondary and supporting. But their moral outrage pricked the nation's conscience, and it is doubtful whether secession and the Civil War—through which slave owners ultimately dug slavery's grave—would have happened without their earnest, strident voices being part of the American debate over race and bondage.

Selection 1

A White Eyewitness to Slavery

Sarah Grimké

Sarah Grimké (1792–1873) and her younger sister Angelina were born into a wealthy, slave-owning family in Charleston, South Carolina. But in the 1820s they became Quakers, moved to Philadelphia, and soon became vehement abolitionists. (Later, stirred to action by the patronizing attitudes of many male antislavery activists, they also became notable advocates of women's rights.) Angelina became the wife of the prominent abolitionist Theodore Weld and did much of the work of editing American Slavery As It Is *(1839), a widely distributed book consisting of hundreds of eyewitness accounts that graphically described the outrages that masters inflicted on their human property. One of the many harrowing selections in this book, excerpted here, was contributed by Sarah Grimké, relating the kind of experience that had turned these sisters into tireless crusaders against slavery.*

*a*s I left my native state on account of slavery, and deserted the home of my fathers to escape the sound of the lash and the shrieks of tortured victims, I would gladly bury in oblivion the recollection of those scenes

Reprinted from Sarah Grimké, "Narrative and Testimony of Sarah M. Grimké," in *American Slavery As It Is* (n.p., 1839).

with which I have been familiar; but this may not, cannot be; they come over my memory like gory spectres, and implore me with resistless power, in the name of a God of mercy, in the name of a crucified Savior, in the name of humanity; for the sake of the slaveholder, as well as the slave, to bear witness to the horrors of the southern prison house. I feel impelled by a sacred sense of duty, by my obligations to my country, by sympathy for the bleeding victims of tyranny and lust, to give my testimony respecting the system of American slavery,—to detail a few facts, most of which came under my *personal observation*. And here I may premise, that the actors in these tragedies were all men and women of the highest respectability, and of the first families in South Carolina, and, with one exception, citizens of Charleston; and that their cruelties did not in the slightest degree affect their standing in society.

A handsome mulatto woman, about 18 or 20 years of age, whose independent spirit could not brook the degradation of slavery, was in the habit of running away: for this offence she had been repeatedly sent by her master and mistress to be whipped by the keeper of the Charleston workhouse. This had been done with such inhuman severity, as to lacerate her back in a most shocking manner; a finger could not be laid between the cuts. But the love of liberty was too strong to be annihilated by torture; and, as a last resort, she was whipped at several different times, and kept a close prisoner. A heavy iron collar, with three long prongs projecting from it, was placed round her neck, and a strong and sound front tooth was extracted, to serve as a mark to describe her, in case of escape. Her sufferings at this time were agonizing; she could lie in no position but on her back, which was sore from scourgings, as I can testify, from personal inspection, and her only place of rest was the floor, on a blanket. These outrages were committed in a family where the mistress daily read the scriptures, and assembled her children for family worship. She was accounted, and was really, so far as alms-giving was concerned, a charitable woman, and tender hearted to the poor; and yet this suffering slave, who was the seamstress of the family, was continually in her presence, sitting in her chamber to sew, or engaged in her other household work, with her lacerated and bleeding back, her mutilated mouth, and heavy iron collar, without, so far as appeared, exciting any feelings of compassion.

A highly intelligent slave, who panted after freedom with ceaseless longings, made many attempts to get possession of himself. For every offence he was punished with extreme severity. At one time he was tied up by his hands to a tree, and whipped until his back was one gore of blood. To this terrible infliction he was subjected at intervals for several weeks, and kept heavily ironed while at his work. His master one day accused him of a fault, in the usual terms dictated by passion and arbitrary power; the man protested his innocence, but was not credited. He again repelled the charge with honest indignation. His master's temper rose almost to frenzy; and seizing a fork, he made a deadly plunge at the breast of the slave. The man being far his superior in strength, caught his arm, and dashed the weapon on the floor. His master grasped at his throat, but the slave disengaged himself, and rushed from the apartment. Having made his escape, he fled to the woods; and after wandering about for many months, living on roots and berries, and enduring every hardship,

he was arrested and committed to jail. Here he lay for a considerable time, allowed scarcely food enough to sustain life, whipped in the most shocking manner, and confined in a cell so loathsome, that when his master visited him, he said the stench was enough to knock a man down. The filth had never been removed from the apartment since the poor creature had been immured in it. Although a black man, such had been the effect of starvation and suffering, that his master declared he hardly recognized him— his complexion was so yellow, and his hair, naturally thick and black, had become red and scanty; an infallible sign of long continued living on bad and insufficient food. Stripes, imprisonment, and the gnawings of hunger, had broken his lofty spirit for a season; and, to use his master's own exulting expression, he was "as humble as a dog." After a time he made another attempt to escape, and was absent so long, that a reward was offered for him, *dead or alive*. He eluded every attempt to take him, and his master, despairing of ever getting him again, offered to pardon him if he would return home. It is always understood that such intelligence will reach the runaway; and accordingly, at the entreaties of his wife and mother, the fugitive once more consented to return to his bitter bondage. I believe this was the last effort to obtain his liberty. His heart became touched with the power of the gospel; and the spirit which no inflictions could subdue, bowed at the cross of Jesus, and with the language on his lips—"the cup that my father hath given me, shall I not drink it?" submitted to the yoke of the oppressor, and wore his chains in unmurmuring patience till death released him. The master who perpetrated these wrongs upon his slave, was one of the most influential and honored citizens of South Carolina, and to his equals was bland, and courteous, and benevolent even to a proverb.

A slave who had been separated from his wife, because it best suited the convenience of his owner, ran away. He was taken up on the plantation where his wife, to whom he was tenderly attached, then lived. His only object in running away was to return to her—no other fault was attributed to him. For this offence he was confined in the stocks *six weeks*, in a miserable hovel, not weather-tight. He received fifty lashes weekly during that time, was allowed food barely sufficient to sustain him, and when released from confinement, was not permitted to return to his wife. His master, although himself a husband and a father, was unmoved by the touching appeals of the slave, who entreated that he might only remain with his wife, promising to discharge his duties faithfully; his master continued inexorable, and he was torn from his wife and family. The owner of this slave was a professing Christian, in full membership with the church, and this circumstance occurred when he was confined to his chamber during his last illness.

A punishment dreaded more by the slaves than whipping, unless it is unusually severe, is one which was invented by a female acquaintance of mine in Charleston—I heard her say so with much satisfaction. It is standing on one foot and holding the other in the hand. Afterwards it was improved upon, and a strap was contrived to fasten around the ankle and pass around the neck; so that the least weight of the foot resting on the strap would choke the person. The pain occasioned by this unnatural position was great; and when continued, as it sometimes was, for an hour or more, produced intense agony. I heard this same woman say, that she had the ears of her waiting maid *slit* for some petty theft. This she told me in the presence of the girl, who was standing in the room. She often had the helpless victims of her cruelty severely whipped, not scrupling herself to wield the instrument of torture, and with her own hands inflict severe chastisement. Her husband was less inhuman than his wife, but he was often goaded on by her to acts of great severity. In his last illness I was sent for, and watched beside his death couch. The girl on whom he had so often inflicted punishment, haunted his dying hours; and when at length the king of terrors approached, he shrieked in utter agony of spirit, "Oh, the blackness of darkness, the black imps, I can see them all around me— take them away!" and amid such exclamations he expired. These persons were of one of the first families in Charleston.

A friend of mine, in whose veracity I have entire confidence, told me that about two years ago, a woman in Charleston with whom I was well acquainted, had starved a female slave to death. She was confined in a solitary apartment, kept constantly tied, and condemned to the slow and horrible death of starvation. This woman was notoriously cruel. To those who have read the narrative of James Williams I need only say, that the character of young Larrimore's wife is an exact description of this female tyrant, whose countenance was ever dressed in smiles when in the presence of strangers, but whose heart was as the nether millstone toward her slaves.

As I was traveling in the lower country in South Carolina, a number of years since, my attention was suddenly arrested by an exclamation of horror from the coachman, who called out, "Look there, Miss Sarah, don't you see?"—I looked in the direction he pointed, and saw a human head stuck up on a high pole. On inquiry, I found that a runaway slave, who was outlawed, had been shot there, his head severed from his body, and put upon the public highway, as a terror to deter slaves from running away.

On a plantation in North Carolina, where I was visiting, I happened one day, in my rambles, to step into a negro cabin; my compassion was instantly called forth by the object which presented itself. A slave, whose head was white with age, was lying in one corner of the hovel; he had under his head a few filthy rags, but the boards were his only bed, it was the depth of winter, and the wind whistled through every part of the dilapidated building—he opened his languid eyes when I spoke, and in reply to my question, "What is the matter?" he said, "I am dying of a cancer in my side."—As he removed the rags which covered the sore, I found that it extended half round the body, and was shockingly neglected. I inquired if he had any nurse, "No, missey," was his answer, "but de people (the slaves) very kind to me, dey often steal time to run and see me and fetch me some ting to eat; if dey did not, I might starve." The master and mistress of this man, who had been worn out in their service, were remarkable for their intelligence, and their hospitality knew no bounds towards those who were of their own grade in society: the master had for some time held the highest military office in North Carolina, and not long previous to the time of which I speak, was the Governor of the State.

On a plantation in South Carolina, I witnessed a similar case of suffering—an aged woman suffering under an incurable disease in the same miserably neglected situation. The "owner" of this

Sarah Moore Grimké

slave was proverbially kind to her negroes; so much so, that the planters in the neighborhood said she spoiled them, and set a bad example, which might produce discontent among the surrounding slaves; yet I have seen this woman tremble with rage, when her slaves displeased her, and heard her use language to them which could only be expected from an inmate of Bridewell; and have known her in a gust of passion send a favorite slave to the workhouse to be severely whipped.

Another fact occurs to me. A young woman about eighteen, stated some circumstances relative to her young master, which were thought derogatory to his character; whether true or false, I am unable to say; she was threatened with punishment, but persisted in affirming that she had only spoken the truth. Finding her incorrigible, it was concluded to send her to the Charleston workhouse and have her whipt; she pleaded in vain for a commutation of her sentence, not so much because she dreaded the actual suffering, as because her delicate mind shrunk from the shocking exposure of her person to the eyes of brutal and licentious men; she declared to me that death would be preferable; but her entreaties were in vain, and as there was no means of escaping but by running away, she resorted to it as a desperate remedy, for her timid nature never could have braved the perils

necessarily encountered by fugitive slaves, had not her mind been thrown into a state of despair.—She was apprehended after a few weeks, by two slave-catchers, in a deserted house, and as it was late in the evening they concluded to spend the night there. What inhuman treatment she received from them has never been revealed. They tied her with cords to their bodies, and supposing they had secured their victim, soon fell into a deep sleep, probably rendered more profound by intoxication and fatigue; but the miserable captive slumbered not; by some means she disengaged herself from her bonds, and again fled through the lone wilderness. After a few days she was discovered in a wretched hut, which seemed to have been long uninhabited; she was speechless; a raging fever consumed her vitals, and when a physician saw her, he said she was dying of a disease brought on by over fatigue; her mother was permitted to visit her, but ere she reached her, the damps of death stood upon her brow, and she had only the sad consolation of looking on the death-struck form and convulsive agonies of her child.

A beloved friend in South Carolina, the wife of a slaveholder, with whom I often mingled my tears, when helpless and hopeless we deplored together the horrors of slavery, related to me some years since the following circumstance.

On the plantation adjoining her husband's, there was a slave of pre-eminent piety. His master was not a professor of religion, but the superior excellence of this disciple of Christ was not unmarked by him, and I believe he was so sensible of the good influence of his piety that he did not deprive him of the few religious privileges within his reach. A planter was one day dining with the owner of this slave, and in the course of conversation observed, that all profession of religion among slaves was mere hypocrisy. The other asserted a contrary opinion, adding, I have a slave who I believe would rather die than deny his Saviour. This was ridiculed, and the master urged to prove the assertion. He accordingly sent for this man of God, and peremptorily ordered him to deny his belief in the Lord Jesus Christ. The slave pleaded to be excused, constantly affirming that he would rather die than deny the Redeemer, whose blood was shed for him. His master, after vainly trying to induce obedience by threats, had him terribly whipped. The fortitude of the sufferer was not to be shaken; he nobly rejected the offer of exemption from further chastisement at the expense of destroying his soul, and this blessed martyr *died in consequence of this severe infliction.* Oh, how bright a gem will this victim of irresponsible power be, in that crown which sparkles on the Redeemer's brow; and that many such will cluster there, I have not the shadow of a doubt.

Selection 2

William Lloyd Garrison Launches *The Liberator*

Henry Mayer

For most Americans in the decades before the Civil War, the most famous (or infamous, depending on one's viewpoint) white abolitionist was William Lloyd Garrison (1805–1879). Bald and bespectacled, as vehement in public as he was kindly and soft-spoken in private, and fanatical in his detestation of slavery as a national sin, Garrison was not a man about whom anyone could hold a neutral opinion. He was deeply religious in the old Puritan tradition of his native Massachusetts, fearless, and ready to draw the most extreme conclusions from his principles. Did the U.S. Constitution implicitly sanction slavery? Then it was "a compact with hell," and he outraged the country by publicly burning a copy and advocating abstaining from civic affairs. Did the legally

powerless position of women in pre–Civil War American society bear parallels to the plight of the slaves? Then he became a radical feminist who attacked the institution of marriage as it was defined by law. (In his personal life, he was a strict monogamist.) Did the New Testament command nonviolence? Then he proclaimed himself a pacifist and nonresister.

During the late 1820s Garrison worked as a printer for a Quaker named Benjamin Lundy, publisher of an antislavery newspaper that rather gently supported the gradual emancipation of slaves. Garrison came to believe that a more forceful approach was needed, and reading David Walker's Appeal *shocked him into realizing that America might be engulfed in a race war if justice was not done immediately for the slaves. On January 1, 1831—at the beginning of the same year that would also see Nat Turner's Rebellion—Garrison launched his own newspaper,* The Liberator, *in Boston. Writing the paper was virtually a one-man job for Garrison (his partner Knapp took care of the business side of the operation), and its finances were always precarious. Most of its subscribers were northern free blacks. The Liberator was, as Garrison promised in his fiery opening editorial, utterly uncompromising. And southerners, unnerved by Nat Turner's Rebellion and by reports that Garrison's paper was turning up in slaves' and southern free blacks' hands, responded in kind. Proslavery politicians in Washington (including Andrew Jackson) made sure that* The Liberator *was barred from the federal mails in the South. southern legislatures offered rewards to anyone who could kidnap Garrison and bring him south for trial on the grounds of inciting slave revolt (a capital crime in every slave state). In 1835, he narrowly escaped lynching by a mob in Boston itself.*

This excerpt from the latest biography of Garrison by Henry Mayer describes how Garrison began publishing The Liberator.

*G*arrison decided to go ahead with a "specimen number"—printer's lingo for a sample—which he intended to publish on New Year's Day, 1831. Relying upon the "truck and dicker" system, he and Knapp gathered their equipment and traded their manual labor for office space and some case and press time at Foster's *Christian Watchman* in Merchants' Hall. Knapp canvassed for supplies: potash and lime for cleaning type, lamp oil, and charcoal for ink, brushes and rollers and blotters, baskets for papers and twine for bundling stacks for the post office. Garrison, who would have sole billing as editor though he shared the publisher's title with Knapp, began the task of typesetting copy and composing the pages. By the end of December 1830, Garrison had made ready an issue of four pages, with four columns laid out neatly on a modest fourteen-by-nine page. He faced only one more obstacle: a lack of paper.

. . . The project seemed stalled until Knapp found another firm that would advance a small quantity of paper on seven days' credit. They went ahead with the press run, assuming that money somehow would turn up in time. On the day the bill was due Garrison went to the post office and found a check for fifty-four dollars from James Forten, the black leader from Philadelphia, who asked the editor to consider the money as advance payment for twenty-seven subscriptions. . . .

On the afternoon of Saturday, January 1, 1831, the first issue came off the press. Block capital letters proclaimed THE LIBERATOR across the banner. The front page offered a poetic salutation, reports on the campaign to abolish slavery in the District of Columbia, and the customary address "To the Public", which Garrison turned into an editorial manifesto. In August he had issued proposals for establishing a journal in Washington, D.C., he said, but the enterprise "was palsied by public indifference." Having become convinced that the free states, especially New England, required "a greater revolution in public sentiment" than he had previously realized, he would now "lift up the standard of emancipation in the eyes of the nation, *within sight of Bunker Hill and in the birth place of liberty.*"

Judging it unnecessary to republish his August manifesto, Garrison emphasized only his reliance on the Declaration of Independence and a nonsectarian intention to enlist all religions and parties in "the great cause of human rights." He would "strenuously contend for the immediate enfranchisement of our slave population," Garrison promised, and he repudiated what he called his "unreflecting" assent to the "popular but pernicious doctrine of *gradual* abolition" that he had expressed at Park Street Church in July, 1829. "I seize this opportunity to make a full and unequivocal recantation," he wrote, "and thus publicly ask pardon of my God, of my country, and of my brethren the poor slaves, for having uttered a sentiment so full of timidity, injustice and absurdity."

The Liberator, he promised, would make slaveholders and their apologists tremble. He would redeem the nation's patriotic creed by making "every statue leap from its pedestal" and rouse the apathetic with a trumpet call that would "hasten the resurrection of the dead." He would speak God's truth "in its simplicity and power," and he would speak severely. He would also speak from the heart, in his own voice and in the first person singular rather than the more distant and aloof editorial plural. "I *will be* as harsh as truth, and as uncompromising as justice," Garrison pledged. "On this subject I do not wish to think or speak, or write, with moderation. No! No! Tell a man whose house is on fire to give a moderate alarm . . . but urge me not to use moderation in a cause like the present." He drove the point home with staccato phrases: "I am in earnest—I will not equivocate—I will not excuse—I will not retreat a single inch." Then he reached into the upper case and added one more promise: "—AND I WILL BE HEARD."

Thus began one of the most remarkable ventures in the history of American journalism. No editor has ever produced a newspaper of agitation for longer than Garrison sustained *The Liberator,* which appeared weekly without interruption for thirty-five years and did not cease publication until the ratification of the Thirteenth Amendment constitutionally abolished slavery in December 1865. . . . With ferocious determination, Garrison broke the silence and made the public listen in a way that his predecessors had not. He employed a writing style of extraordinary physicality—in his columns trumpets blare, statues bleed, hearts melt, apologists tremble, light blazes, nations move— . . . and he made the moral issue of slavery so palpable that it could no longer be evaded. "Surely, no man yet/ Put lever to the heavy world with less," the poet James Russell Lowell wrote in 1848. "What need of help?—He knew how types were set,/ He had a dauntless spirit and a press.". . .

Garrison's life was completely defined by *The Liberator* and the abolitionist cause. He worked at odd jobs by day so that he could produce the newspaper at night. He had his circle of printers and reform-minded friends, but he hardly had a social life beyond church suppers or musicales in the black community and an occasional call upon the few well-to-do families who patronized the paper. No more lounging at the Athenaeum or paying court to his Dulcinea. Garrison never wrote a word about it, but—as he had done in Vermont—he used his newspaper's poetry column to hint at his frustrations with poem after poem about unrequited love. His bouts of self-pity faded, however, as he grew ever more absorbed in the work and attracted a notoriety that pleased the agitator in him if not the swain.

The venture took more time than expected, however, and Garrison regretted not being able to pay more attention to the editorial department. People think that "I have six days each week to cater for it, when, in fact, scarcely six hours are allotted to me, and these at midnight," he lamented to Samuel J. May. The "mechanical part" of the paper required "the most unremitted labor," he added. For every issue Garrison and Knapp composed and distributed one hundred thousand types, performed the presswork, folded, bundled, and mailed the papers, dealt with correspondence, and scanned the exchanges for possible material.

For an editor preoccupied with technical matters Garrison nonetheless displayed great literary facility. For the first four issues of *The Liberator,* he personally wrote enough copy to fill six columns each week: several editorials, many headnotes and pugnacious footnotes, book notices and reviews, innumerable squibs and fillers, and nearly a dozen poems. In the remainder of the paper Garrison provided a lively mixture of excerpts from the religious and temperance press, factual material on slavery, reports of meetings held to protest the slave trade or register opposition to colonization schemes, inspiring verses from Cowper and Byron and the black literary societies, and provocative letters from readers and the editorial fraternity—along with the editor's annotations and rebuttals. Endeavoring "to diversify the contents of the Liberator, as to give an edge to curiosity," Garrison brought all his training in the roles of a country editor—the wry observer, the humorist, the booster, the partisan—to the more complex task of reaching a diverse national audience on the most explosive issue of the times. The first issues of *The Liberator* looked no bigger than a pane of window glass, Garrison liked to say, but they certainly "let in the light," combining high purpose with a zestiness that in retrospect made Garrison's work on the *Genius* seem gray and ponderous. . . .

From the outset, *The Liberator* attacked racial prejudice and political hypocrisy with as much force as it directed toward the peculiar institution itself. Garrison blazoned the front page of his second issue with two dozen "truisms" that mocked the paralyzing contradictions of American society: "All men are born equal, and entitled to protection, excepting those whose skins are black and hair woolly . . ." Garrison's satiric catechism began. "If white men are ignorant and depraved, they ought freely to receive the benefits of education," he continued, "but if black men are in this condition, common sense dictates that they should be held in bondage and never instructed." Yet Garrison could not remain sour for very long. He followed these caustic columns with a paragraph entitled "Our Trust" in which he refused "to give up our country as sealed over to destruction" and declared that "as long as there remains a single copy of the Declaration of Independence, or of the Bible, in our land, we will not despair."

An improvement in the condition of black citizens formed an essential element in Garrison's abolitionist strategy. Advancing the cause of civil rights would further undermine the rationale for slavery and would offer a vision of peaceable emancipation. "The toleration of slavery at the South is the chief cause of the unfortunate situation of free colored persons at the North," *The Liberator* maintained. "It is this institution which brought their color into contempt and still perpetuates the feeling." White people would have to "take our free colored and slave inhabitants as we find them," Garrison said, "[and] . . . respect them as members of one great family, who may be made useful in society, and honorable in reputation." In a series of articles addressed directly to black Americans— perhaps the first ever by a white writer to employ the salutation "countrymen"—Garrison

emphasized the need for united political action to challenge "every law which infringes on your rights as free native citizens." Racial discrimination in the election and judicial codes and in the laws regulating transportation, schooling, the issuance of business permits, and marriage licenses were all "gross and palpable violations" of the U.S. Constitution, the Bill of Rights, and the constitutions of every state, he said. From his second issue onward Garrison campaigned for repeal of an archaic Massachusetts statute that forbade ministers from marrying a white person to a Negro, Indian, or mulatto. The argument that the personal right to marry should not be abridged by the state epitomized Garrison's willingness to stand against the inhumanity of racism even at the explosive frontier of sexual relationships. Despite some editorial sneers at the editor's personal interest in amalgamation and the sanctimonious objection that liberalization in Massachusetts would be an affront to the laws of other states, Garrison's relentless logic carried enough force to secure repeal in the lower house of the legislature.

The editor wanted his newspaper to be a forum for black activists and a vehicle for a biracial political coalition, and he set a militant tone by devoting at least ten column inches over the first few months to notices and correspondence about David Walker's *Appeal*. Though Garrison would not endorse violent resistance, he made sure that the black community understood his regard for forthright expression. "Let your voices be heard," Garrison urged, and he welcomed black writers to *The Liberator*'s pages. His Baltimore friend William Watkins indignantly denounced the timidity of editors of religious papers who ignored the plight of the free black population out of deference to their slaveholding subscribers. The Philadelphia leader James Forten, who had fought in the Continental Navy and whose own family had lived freely in Pennsylvania since the days of William Penn, passionately attacked the colonization principle that "a man is an alien to the country in which he was born." "To separate the blacks from the whites is as impossible as to bale out the

Delaware with a bucket," Forten jibed, and he suggested that if the [American] Colonization Society [ACS] spent its money on offering premiums to master mechanics to take black apprentices, they would do far more to uplift the race and overcome prejudice. (The publishers of *The Liberator* did their part without a cash incentive: they hired the Rev. Thomas Paul's youngest son and namesake as an apprentice in February 1831. The boy, however, did not remain in the trade, but went on to college—Dartmouth '41—and became a teacher.)

His sympathetic vision made Garrison a hero to his black readers. "How sweetly sounds the name of 'Liberator,'" a Bostonian wrote, with a prayer that the editor's mission would "prove as fruitful as the coming of Titus into Macedonia." Black subscribers proved to be the sustaining force of *The Liberator*'s first year, with over five hundred subscriptions sold by midsummer, though the newspaper's readership—given that copies were passed around by hand and posted in reading rooms and barbershops—was considerably greater. Garrison especially took heart from the meetings of black political associations that sprang up to denounce the colonization scheme. *The Liberator* hailed each one with a ritual headline—"A Voice from New Bedford!" "A Voice from Providence!"—and a full report. . . .

Garrison had aimed his newspaper at five constituencies—which he enumerated as the religious, the philanthropic, the patriotic, the tyrannical, and the free people of color—but only the last two had responded, black people affirmatively and slaveholding editors and politicians with abuse. Unlike the *Genius*, which had representatives in the upper South, *The Liberator* had no agents and few subscribers south of Washington, D.C., yet through the medium of newspaper exchange, Southern editors not only saw the paper but reprinted material from it—accompanied by bitter condemnation—which was then picked up by other papers and eventually worked over again by Garrison in a lively cycle that kept his name and cause before the public and enabled *The Liberator* to make a noise out of proportion to its size or subscription base. . . .

Although Garrison had hoped to reach reform-minded benevolent leaders through *The Liberator,* their initial apathy changed into hostility as he increased the tempo of his attacks, especially against the ACS. Lyman Beecher, among others, felt obliged to warn his congregation to disregard the "few foolish whites" who opposed the benevolent plan of repatriation and "recklessly" advocated immediate abolition. (It was the first time, said Garrison, that Dr. Beecher had advised "a gradual abolition of wickedness.") The ACS national secretary, Ralph R. Gurley, who had earlier dismissed Garrison as "a rash and deluded youth," now denounced him as a "mad incendiary . . . scattering firebrands from Boston" and emphasized the point at the lectern by crumpling a folded sheet of *The Liberator* like kindling. Shortly after Gurley's return to Washington, D.C., from a New England tour, anonymous letters advised Southern postmasters that a newspaper called *The Liberator*—published in Boston, or Philadelphia, by a white man, with the avowed purpose of inciting rebellion in the South"—was openly circulated among the free blacks in the capital. No one could prove that the ACS had begun the hostile campaign, but it seemed likely. Garrison himself received a nasty letter from Washington warning that his paper would not be "much longer tolerated" and advising him to "go to Africa" with his "flat-nosed" friends.

Unlike the self-effacing Lundy, Garrison had deliberately chosen to make himself an issue. "There shall be no neutrals; men shall either like or dislike me," he announced. The editor—and the newspaper as an extension of himself— would draw energy, like a lightning rod, to galvanize the cause. His statements poured forth with an intensity that seemed more like a spontaneous eruption than a composed literary style, which was precisely the effect Garrison wanted. He could have been "as smooth and politic as anyone," the editor once observed, but declared that he much preferred "nature to art." It was nonetheless a deliberate decision, not an irresistible impulse, that led him to write as he did. He chose his words, one close friend said, with the care of a pharmacist weighing out a prescription.

Nearly every visitor commented upon the surprising contrast between the private Garrison and the public firebrand. People walked in expecting to find "a stout, rugged, dark-visaged desperado," as one guest put it, and found instead "a pale, delicate, and apparently overtasked gentleman" scurrying from desk to case to imposing stone, making light of the work with an unending series of hymn tunes and jokes, and stopping occasionally to stroke the pussycat stretched out affectionately on the periphery of the work space. Never too busy to talk, it seemed, Garrison stimulated an unending flow of conversation—copious, strong-minded, and fervent—that often turned the printing office into a seminar or Sunday school. . . .

Garrison found himself so busy that he let a milestone go by unremarked: for the first time in his career he had sustained a venture for longer than six months. Yet before the year ended he faced a major effort to suppress his paper as the instigator of slave revolt. At the end of August 1831, the dread words "INSURRECTION IN VIRGINIA!" jumped from the pages of every newspaper in the country. Dispatches from Richmond related the blood-soaked tale: a contingent of slaves in "Southampton County had risen against their masters, killing seventy white people, before being subdued by the state militia." Over the next several weeks the "Southampton Tragedy" deepened as more than one hundred black people died at the hands of soldiers and vigilantes in reprisals across the county. A manhunt for the leader of the uprising—a visionary slave preacher named Nat Turner—kept much of southeastern Virginia and North Carolina in an uproar over the next seven weeks until he was captured and jailed in Jerusalem, the county seat, where he was hanged on November 11, 1831.

"We are horror-struck," Garrison wrote upon receiving the first reports from Virginia. Recalling his prophetic verse in the opening number of *The Liberator* that depicted the slaughter of innocents if emancipation came not peaceably but by the sword, Garrison said gravely, "What was poetry—imagination—in January, is now a bloody reality." As a pacifist who sought "to accomplish the great work of national redemption through the agency of moral power," Garrison would not condone the calamitous massacre, but neither would he ignore its underlying causes. "In his fury against the revolters," the editor asked, "who will remember their wrongs?" He had put the same question to critics of *Walker's Appeal,* but what had been intellectual debate two years earlier now had become the most urgent political question of the generation.

Garrison faced the pacifist's quandary about revolutionary social change. He did not want to condemn the ends because he disapproved of the means, and he especially wanted white Americans to realize that their own political experience sanctioned Turner's course. "The slaves need no incentives at our hands," he pointed out to those who would "slander . . . pacific friends of emancipation" as provocateurs. Scarred backs and endless labor were spurs enough, he argued, as was the credo of liberty espoused by those "patriotic hypocrites" who refused to recognize that oppressed black people "rise to contend—as other 'heroes' have contended—for their lost rights." Yet Garrison had moral reservations about the violent legacy most Americans accepted. "I deny the right of any people to *fight* for liberty, and so far am a Quaker in principle," Garrison told a friend privately. "I do not justify the slaves in their rebellion; yet I do not condemn *them,* and applaud similar conduct in *white men.*" Few editorial writers beyond his immediate circle endorsed Garrison's view of the insurrection as an apocalyptic warning or shared his willingness to sympathize with the oppressed despite their turn to measures he deplored. Although his former sponsor, the *Transcript's* Lynde Walter, found himself shaken enough to urge Virginians to consider a gradual abolition plan, most commentators took the violent affair as a sign of a residual black barbarism that made emancipation a practical impossibility.

Southerners, predictably, saw a conspiratorial dimension in the uprising and directed their anger toward free Negroes, especially peddlers and preachers, whom they suspected of spreading seditious ideas in pamphlets and newspapers. The *Richmond Enquirer* asked its readers to supply information about the circulation of "Garrison's 'Boston Liberator' (or Walker's Appeal)" in the state, and Virginia's governor, John Floyd, established a separate file folder for information on meddling agitators. In the anxious weeks following the bloodshed he rapidly filled it. Floyd received letters from all over the South describing suspicious events and the malign influence of Quakers, itinerants, and "fanatical" Yankee editors. "Much mischief is hatching here," said one informant from Philadelphia; articles from *The Liberator* were being read aloud at conclaves in black churches. One Virginia postmaster after another confiscated copies of *The Liberator* and mailed them to the governor as evidence.

Garrison received abusive and threatening letters from the South (the postage due hurt worse than the warnings, Garrison joked) and not a few hints of assassination from New England. A friendly minister advised the editor that he had overheard men in the Andover stagecoach talking of Garrison being "taken away, and no one be the wiser," a remark, given the mysterious fate of David Walker, that should have given him pause. The editor remained unfazed. "I hold my life at a cheap rate," he replied gratefully to his friend, for "if the assassin take it away, the Lord will raise up another and better advocate in my stead." Upon learning of the death threats, Arthur Tappan sent $100 to Garrison so that he could mail *The Liberator* to national leaders, adding with untoward jocularity, "As I see your life is threatened, I feel anxious to have all the advantage of it while you live. . . ." Some of the free copies Garrison sent to legislators and college presidents wound up in Governor Floyd's dossier.

While the Virginia leader pondered legal moves against "the club of villains" at Boston, public opinion convicted Garrison as the hidden architect of the Southampton Tragedy. The editors of the most influential newspaper in Washington—the *National Intelligencer*—declared in an article destined to be reprinted all over the country that publishing and circulating a paper as "diabolical" as *The Liberator* constituted "a crime as great" as poisoning a community's water supply. They called upon the mayor of Boston and the Massachusetts legislature to suppress the paper and punish the "instigator of human butchery" who produced it. In a blistering reply Garrison laid bare the politics of repression. The clamor against him was intended "to prevent public indignation from resting upon the system of slavery." The institution brewed its own destruction, yet its partisans attributed the explosion to "a foreign and an impossible cause." He employed no secret agents, Garrison jibed, for his paper "courts the light, and not darkness. . . . Tell me not that an evil is cured by covering it up . . . that if nothing be said, more will be done." He conducted *The Liberator,* Garrison emphasized, in order "to *prevent* rebellion" and save lives by overthrowing the blood-drenched slave system "by moral power, by truth and reason." He filled his letter with extracts from his previous editorials and the speeches of British abolitionists in the hope that the editors around the country who had copied the attack would also pick up his rebuttal from the *National Intelligencer* and thus give the material wider circulation. *National Intelligencer* editors Gales and Seaton, however, foiled him by spiking the piece. They judged its language "too severe" for their newspaper and publicly admonished Garrison to cease his "misguided crusade against a relation of society which he does not comprehend and must aggravate by intermeddling." Furious at this departure from journalistic custom, Garrison printed his rebuttal across the width of his own front page, hoping to get other newspapers to copy it directly from him. None did.

The outcry against Garrison continued throughout the fall, but the editor would not let himself be silenced. He had a riposte for each attack, and his confidence swelled with each outburst of hostility. In early October 1831, the town of Georgetown in the District of Columbia passed an extraordinary law prohibiting free Negroes from taking copies of *The Liberator* out of the post office under penalty of a twenty-dollar fine and thirty days in jail, as well as the threat of being sold into slavery for four months if the fines and jail fees went unpaid. ("An outrage," stormed Garrison; the law must be challenged in the U.S. Supreme Court.) In Raleigh, North Carolina, a grand jury indicted Garrison and Knapp for distributing incendiary matter on the strength of a reference to *rumors* of a Carolina insurrection that a postmaster had found in a confiscated copy of the newspaper, and in Columbia, South Carolina, a vigilance association posted a $1,500 reward for the apprehension and conviction of any white person circulating *The Liberator* or other publications of a "seditious tendency." ("A pretty liberal sum," Garrison joked, "but we think we are worth more.") In Georgia the legislature upped the ante by offering a reward of $5,000 for anyone who arrested Garrison and brought him to the state to be tried for seditious libel. (That was not a joking matter. "A bribe to kidnappers," he raged, "a price set upon the head of a citizen from Massachusetts! . . . Where are the immunities secured to us by our Bill of Rights?")

The question was not a rhetorical one. Some Southern officials worked hard to make suppressing *The Liberator* an issue of interstate comity. For the sake of harmony in the Union, they argued, Northerners had to silence the fanatics who would disrupt the social fabric of the Southern states. Whether this was a rhetorical point or an actual legal mandate occasioned much discussion in Richmond, and when it ended inconclusively, Governor Floyd groused that "this Union is at an end [if we are] tied up . . . from doing ourselves justice.". . .

The proximity of Garrison's rise and Turner's rebellion unmasked for a new generation the intransigence of proslavery politicians and their Northern allies and allowed Garrison to dwell upon the darker side of the constitutional compromises Americans accepted as fundamental. It is too much to say—as some commentators do—that Nat Turner made William Lloyd Garrison's reputation, but by making a scapegoat of *The Liberator,* Southern leaders played into Garrison's hands and enhanced his sense of power. The attacks revealed the dynamic that would underlie the tempestuous events of the next three decades. At each challenge Southerners would emphasize that their commitment to the Union was contingent not only upon protection of their property in human beings, but upon protection from criticism of their peculiar institution. As long as Northern public opinion valued the political and commercial stability epitomized by the Union more highly than the moral and spiritual precepts of the abolitionists, it would accede to the slaveholders' demands. When the president of Brown University, Francis Wayland, wrote to Garrison asking that "the paper you very politely sent me" be discontinued, he gave as his reason the need to preserve harmony in the Union. *The Liberator*'s "menacing and vindictive" attitude toward slaveholders, Wayland admonished, "prejudices their minds against a cool discussion of the subject" and, not incidentally, threatened to aggravate the slaves' hard lot. . . .

Here, in essence, lay Garrison's understanding of his task as an agitator. He was determined to put a lurid cast upon the landscape of compromise and concession, to heat up the issue until the public felt ashamed of its connection to slavery and angry at granting political privileges to

William Lloyd Garrison

slaveholders. While public officials spoke glowingly about the harmony of the Union, Garrison encouraged the testimony of religious-minded people who no longer wished to "remain constitutionally involved" in the guilt of slavery, and in defending *their* right to be heard, the editor believed that he was doing no more than meeting his civic obligation. . . .

Garrison . . . understood emancipation as a transfiguring moment—a collective Jubilee—that would bring America into a millennial age. Inescapably, then, emancipation had to be the work of Christianity and the churches. "Nothing but extensive revivals of pure religion can save our country," Garrison wrote in April 1831. "All reformations, whether political, civil, or religious are . . . the result of long accumulating causes [and] are the harvests of the spiritual husbandmen, who have tilled the ground and scattered the good seed. . . ." These were not simply metaphors for agitation. Garrison believed that only by purging itself of the sinful practice of slavery could his society attain the Christian purity its religious leaders advocated. He lovingly called *The Liberator* "a root out of dry ground," an allusion to a striking passage from Isaiah (53:2–4) that is the Old Testament's most vivid evocation of the Messiah, and Garrison felt a kinship with the righteous servant—"despised and rejected of men"—whom the Lord had chosen to bear the transgressions of the heedless and point the way to redemption. Yet the greater the sin, the greater the glory of those who suffer to extirpate it. Garrison could revel at times in the abuse he received because the epithets of the unrighteous confirmed his own sense of moral grandeur. The abolitionists knew themselves to be heroes and looked to the postmillennial day—as a fantasy in an April *Liberator* had it—when Christian principle had overthrown prejudice, a black president ruled the country, the capital had changed its name from the slave-

master Washington to the abolitionist Wilberforce, and "wonder-working time" had at last honored "the noblest efforts of the noblest minds which our country has produced."

In twelve months of unflagging labor and furious controversy, Garrison had taken up the mantle of Walker and tried to make his countrymen understand the message of Turner. Sustained by the hard-earned contributions of hundreds of black people and a handful of well-to-do reformers, *The Liberator* had withstood its enemies and thoroughly defined itself as a radical messenger by the end of its first volume. In December 1831, Garrison promised to enlarge the newspaper and urged each friend of immediate abolition to bring in a new subscriber for the ensuing year and to "agitate the subject on every suitable occasion, and among all classes of people." He now could describe the dynamic of a gathering social movement: "talking will create zeal—zeal, opposition—opposition will drive men to inquiry—inquiry will induce conviction—conviction will lead to action—action will demand union—and then will follow victory." *The Liberator,* he vowed, "shall yet live to hail the day of universal emancipation."

Selection 3

Garrison Faces the Boston Mob

Robert Elliott MacDougall

Abolitionists aroused intense opposition, not only from slave owners and southerners generally, who feared that any challenge to slav- *ery would open the way to a slave revolt and a race war, but also from most northern whites. Racism was rampant in nineteenth-*

century America, with almost all whites convinced that blacks were inherently inferior. Why, northerners asked, should the Union be endangered by agitation on behalf of black slaves? And how would northern workers fare if they suddenly had to compete for jobs with freed slaves?

In 1835, relatively early in his career as a highly unpopular abolitionist, William Lloyd Garrison was threatened by a Boston mob. This selection, written by Robert Elliott Mac-Dougall and originally appearing in 1988 in the magazine American History Illustrated, *attests to the vehemence with which most ordinary Americans rejected the abolitionists' campaign against slavery.*

On the evening of August 21, 1835, Boston Mayor Theodore Lyman presided over a capacity crowd at Faneuil Hall, a produce exchange and one of the city's popular gathering places. Principal among those scheduled to speak were Peleg Sprague, a former senator from Maine; and Harrison Gray Otis, nephew of the great eighteenth-century orator James Otis. Both denounced abolitionists and declared their support for the perpetuation of slavery. Then those in attendance passed a resolution accusing abolitionists of trying to scatter "among our southern friends firebrands and arrows of death."

The resolution also denounced "the intrusion upon our domestic relations of foreign emmisaries [sic]." Otis and others were upset that Boston abolitionist and editor William Lloyd Garrison had invited George Thompson, an English abolitionist, to visit America on a speaking tour. Thompson, a tall, dynamic, and forceful speaker, was now in the United States. The Faneuil Hall crowd disliked the idea of a foreigner disrupting the Union; implied, if not explicit, in the speeches was the message that strong measures should be taken against Thompson and other abolitionists.

Reprinted from Robert Elliott MacDougall, "Mr. Garrison and the Mob," *American History Illustrated*, February 1988. This article is reprinted from *American History Illustrated* magazine with the permission of PRIMEDIA Special Interest Publications (History Group), copyright American History Illustrated magazine.

Rather than fearing any actions that Boston's pro-slavery faction might take, Garrison was delighted with the meeting. The Faneuil Hall speeches provided new fodder for his abolitionist newspaper the *Liberator*. Garrison had been publishing it from a dingy printing office in Merchant's Hall throughout the past four years.

Garrison did not look like the dangerous radical his opponents thought him to be. The twenty-nine-year-old abolitionist was nearly bald, wore round, metal-rimmed spectacles, and spoke in a voice so calm and serene one would suspect he was a poet or a musician. But in 1835 the people of Boston were convinced that his disruptive and outrageous ideas were going to bring economic ruin on the city and quite possibly destroy the Union.

In the *Liberator*'s first edition Garrison had vowed to use strong language in denouncing slavery, slaveholders, and the "abbettors of slavery," including the people of the North who condoned or passively tolerated it. Every weekly edition since then had lived up to its editor's promise, calling slaveowners "manstealers," "thieves," and "murderers," and proclaiming that the people of Massachusetts—because they enjoyed the benefits of slavery—shared fully in slavery's shame.

Although few people subscribed to the *Liberator* and hardly any copies reached the South (where local postmasters habitually burned them), Southerners had grown increasingly furious with Garrison's unrelenting attacks on them and their "peculiar institution." So angry was one group of Mississippi planters that they reportedly offered $20,000 for Garrison's head. Southern newspapers had called on Bostonians to silence the raving fanatic and incendiary. If Garrison continued to publish, they threatened, the South would be forced to sever its profitable commercial relationship with Boston, home to numerous shipping firms, many of which carried cotton, tobacco, and slaves.

Thoroughly alarmed, fifteen hundred of Boston's most prominent and wealthy residents had signed a call for the August 21, 1835, meeting at Faneuil Hall. Former President John Quincy

Adams recorded in his diary, "In Boston there is a call for a town meeting . . . to pass resolutions against the abolitionists, to soothe and conciliate the temper of the southern slaveholders."

Garrison had not been surprised at the furor against him in Boston. He had realized long before that Bostonians were nearly as proslavery in sentiment as were Southerners. In the first edition of the *Liberator* he had stated, "I found contempt in New England more bitter, opposition more active, . . . prejudice more stubborn . . . than among the slaveholders themselves." For this reason he had decided to publish in Boston "to lift up the standard of emancipation within sight of Bunker Hill and in the birthplace of liberty."

After the proslavery meeting, Garrison had taken satisfaction in pointing out in his *Liberator* articles that two names once so closely linked with liberty—Otis and Faneuil Hall—were now linked with slavery. And in a letter to a fellow abolitionist he wrote, "Bostonians have a strong attachment for Faneuil Hall, and we shall raise a blush of shame upon their cheeks, ere long, by dwelling continually upon the disgrace which has been cast upon it by a proslavery meeting."

Garrison expected that a more immediate, active response could result from the proslavery enthusiasm generated at Faneuil Hall. "I assume our principal cities will be visited by assassins," he wrote almost hopefully. "It matters not . . . if we perish, our loss will but hasten the destruction of slavery more certainly." The abolitionist editor was aware that the violent feelings aroused against him might result in his martyrdom, and he was prepared for it, almost welcomed it.

During October 1835 Bostonians learned that Thompson planned to speak on the twenty-first at a meeting of the Female Anti-Slavery Society. The *Boston Commercial Gazette* took the lead in arousing public outrage, and its editor predicted that men "of property and standing" would prohibit the Englishman from speaking.

Two Boston merchants, Isaac Sterns and Isaac Means, commissioned apprentices at the *Gazette* to print handbills informing the public of the Englishman's planned visit and noting that this offered "a fair opportunity for the friends of the Union to snake Thompson out!" The notice went on to offer a $100 reward to the "individual who shall first lay violent hands on Thompson so that he may be brought to the tar kettle before dark."

On the morning of October 21, 1835, these posters appeared on warehouse walls and in shops, hotel lobbies, and bars throughout the commercial district. Hundreds of men, including some of the most prosperous and respected men in the city, made plans to be at the New England Anti-Slavery Society offices at 46 Washington Street in time for the meeting scheduled for three o'clock that afternoon.

Garrison had already decided that Thompson should remain outside the town. During the previous six weeks the Englishman had been assaulted in Concord, New Hampshire, and elsewhere. Garrison, apparently fearing nothing from threats to his own safety, left his home on Brighton Street at two o'clock to attend the meeting. As he approached the door he saw about one hundred people gathered in the street outside. On the stairway leading to the antislavery meeting room he had to squeeze past several more menacing young men.

Inside, society members were trying to hold their meeting despite the jeers of several intruders at the rear of the room. As Garrison took a seat one man shouted, "That's Garrison!"

The abolitionist turned and said, "Gentlemen, perhaps you are not aware that this is a meeting of the Boston *Female* Anti-Slavery Society." He asked them to leave unless, perhaps, some of them were women in disguise, in which case he would introduce them to the rest of their gender and they could be seated. His mocking words quieted the crowd only briefly. Soon more men had forced their way from the stairway into the room.

The society's president, Mary Parker, suggested that Garrison leave to avoid offering the mob any pretext for violence. Garrison agreed and went into an office next to the meeting room. There he sat down to write an account of the incident for the next edition of the *Liberator*.

Meanwhile, the mob outside had grown to several thousand people, filling Washington Street. Shouts of "Thompson! Thompson!" filled the air. Mayor Lyman arrived and tried to explain to the crowd that Thompson was not present, but the crowd pressed forward anyway. Inside, some young men began to kick down the door to Garrison's office. The abolitionist saw them peering through the broken boards and cursing at him, but he continued writing, seemingly unperturbed.

The women continued with their meeting despite the uproar, bowing their heads in prayer, seemingly unmindful of the rampage. But Mayor Lyman, fearing for their safety, beseeched the members of the society to go home. His constables had cleared the stairway and, he said, if the women did not take this opportunity to escape he could not guarantee their safety. The women agreed to leave, but only after they had approved, with proper parliamentary procedure, a motion to adjourn. Then they marched out together, white women paired with black, "thus giving," as society member Maria Chapman later put it, "what protection a white skin could ensure a dark one."

With the women gone and Thompson absent, the mob's attention now focused on the abolitionist editor. "Lynch Garrison!" the men shouted as they pressed toward the door. Some of those in the crowd demanded that the sign reading "ANTI-SLAVERY ROOMS" be torn down. The mayor, in an effort to appease the demonstrators, ordered the sign thrown into their midst where it was promptly broken up and its pieces distributed for souvenirs.

The constables now managed to clear the door to Garrison's office, and the mayor ran in and begged the still-complacent abolitionist to leave through a rear window. Outside, the shouts of "Garrison!" grew louder. Although loathe to show any fear of a mob, Garrison finally submitted and jumped from the window onto a shed roof, almost falling headlong from there to the ground. He ran to a nearby carpenter's shop and tried to cut through it to Wilson's Lane, but

some of the crowd saw him. Although the friendly carpenters attempted to bolt the door and hide Garrison behind lumber on the second floor, the mob soon caught up with him. Garrison's assailants were prepared to hurl him out the window but relented at the last minute and allowed him to climb down a ladder to the throng below.

Fortunately for Garrison, Dan and Aaron Cooley, brothers who ran a teamsters business on India Street, were the first to grab him. Although the Cooleys were well known as opponents of abolition, they shouted "He shan't be hurt!" and protected Garrison as the crowd swept him along. At one point a frenzied man tried to club Garrison, but one of the Cooleys raised his arm to deflect the blow.

The crowd pushed Garrison out Wilson's Lane onto State Street. Along the way Garrison's clothes were torn and he lost his coat, hat, and glasses. He was a sorry sight to onlookers who were nevertheless impressed with his calm serenity and seeming willingness to let the mob do what it would.

The Cooley brothers decided the safest place for Garrison was City Hall (the Old State House). So, with great difficulty, they pushed him through the crowd, into the south door, and up the stairs to the mayor's office. While the mob screamed outside, several men offered Garrison garments to replace those he had lost, giving him an old coat, pantaloons, and a cap. Then Mayor Lyman decided, for safety's sake, to arrest Garrison for disturbing the peace and to lock him up in the Leverett Street jail. Once again Garrison was led through the angry crowd, this time to a horse-drawn coach. Perhaps because the mob did not immediately recognize Garrison in his borrowed clothing, he made his way into the vehicle with little difficulty. But then the throng surged forward, making it almost impossible for the coachman to get the rig moving. Finally the driver frantically whipped the horses, and the carriage lurched ahead before careening awkwardly down Court Street with the mob in hot pursuit.

Some of the crowd tried to grab the horses or

hang onto the carriage wheels; others pounded their fists against the rig's sides. When the mad procession finally reached the jail, the few who had come the whole distance tried to grab Garrison, but he was rushed inside and locked safely in a cell. The men in the street grumbled and cursed, but finally went back to the warehouses, offices, and banks from where they had come.

The mob having receded, Garrison enjoyed a pleasant night. Friends came to talk to him at his cell window. He sat on his bed, musing contentedly on the notoriety he had achieved and the sympathy that was certain to be aroused by this vicious attack. For posterity he wrote on his cell wall: "William Lloyd Garrison was put into this cell on Wednesday afternoon, October 21, 1835, to save him from the violence of a 'respectable and influential' mob who sought to destroy him for preaching the abominable and dangerous doctrine that 'all men are created equal.'"

Garrison was released the next day and never again harmed. But he made the most of what had happened. In the *Liberator* he expressed outrage that *he* should have been arrested for disturbing the peace while every member of the mob went free. He warned that such attacks, which attempted to deny a citizen his right to freedom of speech, were a natural consequence of slavery. The "peculiar institution" could only exist if thinking men and women were forced to be silent.

As Garrison had predicted, sympathy for his cause was aroused. Within a month of the mob attack Garrison was able to write to his wife: "New subscribers to the *Liberator* still continue to come in—not less than a dozen today. Am much obliged to the mob."

For the next thirty years Garrison continued to publish the *Liberator* and to call for emancipation of the slaves. Gradually, as the South continued to react violently and to demand the protection and extension of slavery, the sympathies of Garrison's fellow Bostonians began to change. By the 1850s new mobs were forming in the city, this time to protest the capture of runaway slaves. And by 1861 throngs of young men were enlisting to fight to save the Union and, as many believed, to free the slaves.

When emancipation finally came in 1863, Massachusetts promptly organized black regiments to fight against the South. One lieutenant in the black Massachusetts 55th was Garrison's son, George Thompson Garrison, named for the Englishman so hated by Bostonians in 1835. As this young man marched by with hundreds of black men in uniform, the elder Garrison watched with tears in his eyes; he stood on the corner of Wilson's Lane where, twenty-eight years before, he had been dragged off by the mob.

Selection 4

Elijah Lovejoy: Abolitionist Martyr

David W. Blight

William Garrison was lucky to escape alive after being attacked by a mob in Boston. In this selection, historian David W. Blight describes another such incident in Alton, Illinois, in 1837. Another abolitionist publisher, Elijah Lovejoy, was not as fortunate as Garrison. Notice the strong cultural and economic antipathy between the puritanical Lovejoy and the "upstanding" citizens who lynched him.

During the 1830's, the first full decade of the organized anti-slavery movement in America, the abolitionists faced their most spirited opposition. The vital factors in the abolition movement's growth were the dual causes of freedom for the slaves and freedom of the press. Only by coupling these two moral and legal forces could the abolitionists expand their influence. Out of all the mob violence that erupted in the mid-1830's, the most profound was the assassination of the abolitionist-editor Elijah Parish Lovejoy in November 1837 at Alton, Illinois.

In 1833, Lovejoy, full of frontier zeal, abandoned the East and returned to St. Louis, Missouri, where he had worked as a teacher and editor-publisher of the St. Louis *Times*. He experienced religious conversion in 1832 as the Great Revival spread even beyond the Mississippi River, and his new commitment carried him back to Princeton Theological Seminary and into the Presbyterian ministry. His mission was the editorship of a religious publication, the St. Louis *Observer*. The *Observer* was a typical religious journal, urging its readers to denounce the conventional sins of greed, intemperance, infidelity, Sabbath-breaking, the misguided and erroneous dogmas of "popery," and even slave-holding.

The St. Louis in which Lovejoy settled in 1833 was wild, with saloons full of rowdy fur trappers. When public opinion was not aroused against a specific tribe of Indians, the wicked Mormons would do. Lovejoy's paper, however, remained aloof from this discord and steered a middle path on most controversial issues.

On the subject of slavery, Lovejoy was by no means a true abolitionist at the outset of his editorship of the *Observer*. He was decidedly against all extremist agitation and declared his compassion for the man who was "reared in the midst of slavery." He declared that the slaveholder was sometimes falsely charged, and that his feelings were too often not considered. Lovejoy was convinced that slavery was wrong

Reprinted from David W. Blight, "The Martyrdom of Elijah P. Lovejoy," *American History Illustrated*, November 1977. This article is reprinted from *American History Illustrated* magazine with the permission of PRIMEDIA Special Interest Publications (History Group), copyright American History Illustrated magazine.

and that changes were necessary, but "the danger is in the manner in which that change is to be brought about."

By 1835, Lovejoy's discussions of slavery became more frequent and his attitudes clearer. His position became that of the classic "gradualist," proclaiming: "We only propose, that measures shall now be taken for the abolition of slavery, at such distant period of time as may be thought expedient, and eventually for ridding the country altogether of a coloured population."

In October 1835 the anti-abolitionist storm broke in St. Louis as it had in several places across the nation. Five slaves had escaped into Illinois and a mob of Missourians rushed across the river and recaptured them along with two whites suspected of aiding the Negroes in their escape. The fate of the two whites was a bloody lashing until they confessed guilt. So fierce was the public outrage that it was declared by committees of vigilance that action would be taken against anyone "suspected of preaching" abolition. Lovejoy had received his first serious challenge as an anti-slavery advocate and his days were numbered as a resident and editor in St. Louis.

During the slave-recapturing incident, Lovejoy had been absent from St. Louis on presbytery and synod duties. Upon his return he received a letter from a group of citizens urging the exclusion of anti-slavery material from the pages of the *Observer*. These citizens, who included the proprietors of the paper itself, were asking Lovejoy to "pass over in silence everything connected with the subject of slavery." Furthermore, at a citizens' meeting the following resolution was adopted and forwarded to Lovejoy. It provides an excellent illustration of the sentiments of the anti-abolitionists as a whole.

Resolved, That the right of free discussion and freedom of speech exists under the constitution, but that being a conventional reservation made by the people in their sovereign capacity, does not imply a moral right, on the part of the Abolitionists, to freely discuss the question of Slavery, either orally or through the medium of the press. It is the agitation of a question too nearly allied to the vital interests of the slave-holding states to admit of public disputation; and so far from the fact, that the movements of the Abolitionists are constitutional, they are in the greatest degree seditious, and calculated to incite insurrection and anarchy, and, ultimately, a disseverment of our prosperous Union.

This demonstrates the ease with which basic civil liberties can be forgotten in favor of protection of local institutions. Freedom of speech to this group was not a basic American liberty, but rather a privilege relative to the will of the majority. The abolitionist, whether in St. Louis or Boston, faced this intolerance, but ironically it would be this mode of intolerance, coupled with its violent by-products, which would bring abolition its first martyr, and concurrently, a tremendous boost in public acceptance.

Lovejoy's response to this challenge from the citizenry of St. Louis was spirited and clear. He defended himself and the entire anti-slavery movement against the charge of "amalgamation" and was vehement in his disgust over the use of the Bible as a defense of slavery. Finally, he directly answered the demand of silence on the slavery question with what amounted to a counterchallenge:

I do, therefore, as an American citizen, and Christian patriot, and in the name of Liberty, and Law, and Religion, solemnly protest against all these attempts, howsoever or by whomsoever made, to frown down the liberty of the press, and forbid the free expression of opinion. Under a deep sense of my obligations to my country, the church, and my God, I declare it to be my fixed purpose to submit to no such dictation. And I am prepared to abide the consequences. I have appealed to the Constitution and laws of my country; if they fail to protect me, I appeal to God, and with Him I cheerfully rest my cause.

The battle had been joined and this phase of Lovejoy's struggle to plead the cause of the slave through the free press would not end until he was forced out of St. Louis.

That departure from St. Louis was hastened

by a shameful event in the spring of 1836. A free Negro by the name of Francis McIntosh was burned alive by a mob for the murder of a white man. Lovejoy could not espouse the brutal indifference with which most of the St. Louis populace viewed the episode. He condemned the "mob-spirit" which instigated the tragedy; his criticism of the city produced an editorial outcry from other papers which were concerned about the use that might be made of the McIntosh affair in the Eastern anti-slavery press.

To further fuel the fire, the judge in the case (several people having been brought to trial for McIntosh's murder), ironically Luke E. Lawless, maintained that abolitionists had really stirred up all the trouble anyway. Lawless contended that the acts of an indistinguishable mob were "beyond the reach of human law," and that it was impossible to punish an "electric frenzy." The unscrupulous judge further led the proslavery populace on their witch hunt by clearly holding Lovejoy personally responsible for the McIntosh affair.

Lovejoy's reply to Lawless' charges was filled with venomous anti-Catholic attacks (the judge was an Irish Catholic). Lovejoy resorted to an appeal for prejudice of his own in order to demonstrate the injustice of Lawless' accusations, and thwart the attempt to discredit himself and the *Observer*. This effort was, of course, in vain because the crafty judge had awakened and sparked a key element in the anti-abolitionist strategy. The excesses of the slave system and the pervasive racism which it bred were much easier to rationalize by finding a misguided, fanatical abolitionist to blame. In St. Louis, Lovejoy was, by the summer of 1836, just that person and by July he would be looking for a new home for himself and his *Observer*. By that time the newspaper had suffered several destructive attacks, the press being finally ruined.

On July 21, 1836, Elijah Lovejoy landed his new printing press on the docks at Alton, Illinois, a sleepy but rapidly growing river port town. Alton, located about twenty miles north of St. Louis at the junction of North America's two great rivers, the Missouri and Mississippi, was not, however, to be a peaceful refuge for the beleaguered editor. The press arrived on the Sabbath, so Lovejoy decided to let it rest on the dock until the following morning. By sunrise the press had been demolished, its many pieces hurled into the Mississippi River.

A meeting was shortly convened, attended by many of Alton's most prominent citizens, in order to raise money for a new press. It was later alleged that at this meeting of July 25 Lovejoy made a "solemn pledge" to refrain from all agitation of the slavery question. What he did say was that he did not consider himself an abolitionist according to the generally accepted definition, and that he favored gradual emancipation. The crux of the editor's statement asserted that he was "the uncompromising enemy of slavery." He continued:

> But, gentlemen, as long as I am an American citizen, and as long as American blood runs in these veins, I shall hold myself at liberty to speak, to write, and to publish whatever I please on any subject, being amenable to the laws of my country for the same.

Between the fall of 1836 and the spring of 1837, Lovejoy's anti-slavery sentiments were transformed from gradualism to hard-hitting immediatism. His doctrinal conversion was probably similar to that experienced by many of the leading figures of the abolition movement. He was growing increasingly aware of a sense of personal responsibility as a clergyman, and the promptings and misrepresentations of his violent opposition were particular causes of this drift. Lovejoy had seen the evils of slavery first hand, and to maintain silence any longer would be to defy the dictates of his angry God.

In January 1837 Lovejoy delivered his first real abolitionist speech, arguing for the affirmative in a debate before the Young Men's Lyceum of Upper Alton. The topic was "Does the principle of right require the immediate emancipation of the slave?" In this dissertation he discovered how easily many of the emotional pro-slavery arguments could be refuted. By February Lovejoy was chastising the clergy of Illinois and Mis-

*The abolitionist remarks of Elijah Lovejoy evoked
a hostile response from slavery supporters.*

to Lovejoy—State of Illinoys
Alton Town Jan. 26, 1837

Sir,
I received a papor on the Subject of Slavery
Sir I seprised that you would have had the assurance to presume to sepose I could take it
only as an insult, and no person but a unprin-
siabled man would persume to offer such,
aman that had inguered his Countery as have
and have been trying to Incurage things that
would End in murder and I have good reasons
to believe that was and is your intentions, and
Sir I wish you to keep your self out of my
Sunshine and Sir I have umbled my self to
much in offering to put apen on paper for you

Abraham Byrd

Due to such reactions and the increased violence against abolitionists across the North,
Lovejoy felt compelled to explain his new convictions to the proprietors of the *Observer.*

The economic panic of 1837 brought an increase in anti-abolition hostility in Alton. Lovejoy gave his appraisal of the economic woes of
the nation in a vituperative editorial which tied
the economic question with the evils of slavery.
He found the greed of commercialism and the
pursuit of wealth to be the overriding causes of
the panic: "Men were either too busy in making
money themselves, or too desirous to get a share
of that earned by the forced labour of the poor
slave, to hear his groans." To Lovejoy, the economic plight of the nation, as well as the perpetuation of slavery, was directly attributable to the
licentious "whoring" after wealth and the "accursed love of gold" of Northern businessmen.

These accusations did not settle well with the
business community of Alton. Nothing seemed
to fire the emotions of the anti-abolitionists
quite as much as a direct attack on the moral
motives and social position of the "pillars" of
the Northern business elite. It was, perhaps, this
factor as much as any other that led to the irrepressible hostility that Lovejoy faced in the last
month of his life.

Lovejoy's persistent battle to speak the voice
of emancipation at Alton reached its first major

souri for their lack of concern and perseverance
on the question of slavery. Ministers of the
Gospel who preached against intemperance,
Sabbath-breaking, and covetousness, yet passed
over slavery in silence, were "shunning to declare the whole counsel of God." Finally, by
March, he was ready to declare that the preaching of the Gospel was not even enough to end
slavery because God's words were twisted and
misused by the South. He could no longer accept the limited anti-slavery position against
maltreatment of slaves by owners. Lovejoy's
new stand was:

> The gospel of the Son of God, requires not the
> good treatment of the black man as a slave,
> but as a man, and a moral and accountable be-
> ing; and the very first step in this good treat-
> ment is to set him free!

By the spring of 1837 the *Observer*'s number
of subscribers had grown from just under 1,000
to well over 2,000. The publication had grown
as a religious and farming journal, read widely
throughout the upper Mississippi Valley. But
Lovejoy's increased concern with antislavery
agitation was bound to simulate hostile reactions, as in the following letter from a frontiers-
man in Jefferson City, Missouri:

crisis in July 1837. On the Fourth of July he penned his most aggressive editorial yet. Appealing to the moral introspection and the Independence Day emotions of his readers, Lovejoy went on the attack:

> We assemble to thank God for our own freedom, and to eat and drink with joy and gladness of heart, while our feet are upon the necks of nearly three millions of our fellow men! Not all our shouts of self-congratulation can drown their groans—even that very flag of freedom that waves over our heads is formed from materials cultivated by slaves, on a soil moistened with their blood drawn from them by the whip of a republican taskmaster! . . . Come, then, to the rescue. The voice of three millions of slaves calls upon you to come and 'unloose the heavy burdens, and let the oppressed go free!'

This was too much. On July 8 an anonymous handbill appeared on the streets of Alton, requesting all "dissatisfied readers" of the *Observer* to come to a meeting at the Market House. This congregation of some of Alton's leading citizens produced a series of resolutions that provides another interesting illustration of the dogmas of the anti-abolitionists. Their preamble contended that Lovejoy had broken his "solemn pledge" (one he never made) to keep the *Observer* an exclusively religious journal. The Altonians further feared that Lovejoy's abolition doctrines would bring disfavor from sister states to the South. Finally, the citizens declared that they were merely asserting their independence and liberty, and resolved to send a "polite request" to the editor to halt his incendiary doctrines.

In his reply to the "polite request" Lovejoy declared that he could not consent or he would be compromising the liberty of the press and free speech. He stated that he would refrain from "unwise agitation" and "intemperance of language," but that he could not allow his pen to be dictated by the whims of the citizenry. The editor's response had been inadequate; the battle for a free press in Alton was now in full swing.

Lovejoy's opposition not only included a large portion of the citizenry, but also a very outspoken pro-slavery press, which entered the conflict with force in August 1837. The Missouri *Republican* (published in St. Louis) portrayed Lovejoy's paper as the "minister of mischief" and declared that his abolition doctrines had "forfeited all claims to the protection of that [Alton] or any other community." If the citizens of Alton did not expel him from their midst, the *Republican* maintained that all trade between Missouri and Illinois should cease.

Clearly, this editorial stand against Lovejoy was interpreted as a "call to arms" against the editor, who now became the scapegoat for all society's ills. On August 21 Lovejoy's office was ransacked and his printing press again demolished and cast into the muddy currents of the great river. The voice of anti-abolitionism resounded loud and clear, and where it lacked the power of logic, it substituted the blind force of mob violence. Soon Lovejoy would face the terror of the mob in person.

Lovejoy lived in a wooded area about one-half mile from town. In early September while walking home, Lovejoy encountered a well-organized group of Altonians who were prepared to give him a final message that he had overstayed his welcome in Alton; they planned to tar and feather him. On the brink of imminent death, Lovejoy appealed to the conscience of the crowd, who consented to refrain from their hateful deed.

Before the month of September was over, another press had arrived and was stored in a warehouse. When the constable who had been designated to guard the press went home, about a dozen men disguised with handkerchief masks broke in and smashed the press. By October 1837 Lovejoy had had a total of four of his presses destroyed and thrown into the Mississippi River. He had been the victim of two physical attacks, the second occurring while visiting in St. Charles, Missouri. The home in which he was staying was invaded by a drunken mob and he narrowly escaped by agreeing to leave town the next morning. These events led the beleaguered editor finally to offer his resignation to the proprietors of the *Observer*. Since they could not agree unanimously either to back him or to evict him, the proprietors declined to accept Lovejoy's resignation.

With renewed faith and a stern will Lovejoy resolved to go on, regardless of the fate which might befall him and his family. The following accurately depicts the state of affairs for Lovejoy as he prepared to face anew the persistence of the anti-abolitionists:

> We have no one with us to-night, except the members of our family. A loaded musket is standing at my bed-side, while my two brothers, in an adjoining room, have three others, together with pistols, cartridges & c. And this is the way we live in the city of Alton!

The final episodes of Lovejoy's struggle for the slave and the free press unfolded in late October, as he and several other prominent anti-slavery people called for a convention to meet in Alton to form an Illinois State Anti-Slavery Society. The convention, attended by genuine anti-slavery delegates from all over the state, was also attended by a group calling themselves the "friends of free inquiry." It seems that Lovejoy, in accordance with the wishes of Reverend Edward Beecher (Lovejoy's closest friend) but against his own better judgment, had used the phrase "friends of free inquiry" in his public invitation for the convention, instead of merely inviting all believers in the doctrine of "immediate abolition." This band of pro-slavery disruptionists, under the adept leadership of the Attorney General of Illinois, Usher F. Linder, succeeded in making a sham of the proceedings.

Linder and his cohorts recruited a throng of men who masqueraded as free speech advocates and managed adoption of a resolution which declared man's right to hold human property, therefore making emancipation illegal. The only true abolitionist resolutions adopted were discussed at meetings in the private homes of what Beecher called the "real" members of the convention. Other members and sympathetic supporters were definitely threatened by the mob atmosphere which was created by Linder and his forces. This silence, especially on the part of many uncommitted neutrals, was brought on by the intimidating tactics of the "friends of free inquiry." It was a key factor in the violence that was to come to the streets of Alton.

The imminent arrival of yet another printing press to the docks of Alton increased tensions during the first week of November. The issues were no longer the lofty principles of abolition versus slavery, but rather, the essential question of whether law and order would be maintained in Alton, or Lovejoy's fate and that of the city's reputation would be sacrificed to mob rule.

A crucial meeting convened on November 2, both sides being represented by their leading spokesmen in hopes that a compromise might be negotiated to avert further violence. The pro-Lovejoy faction was led by Beecher who presented nine resolutions, all of which were essentially a plea for the principles of free speech and press, and of the need for peace and understanding. Beecher defended abolitionists as men who were guided by "deep religious principle" and not fanaticism. He appealed to the patriotism of the audience, reminding them that the national and international reputations of Illinois and the United States were at stake in whatever they resolved.

Not a single voice was raised in support of Beecher's resolutions. The anti-abolition forces, again led by Usher Linder and Cyrus Edwards (candidate for governor and member of the Illinois legislature), demanded that Lovejoy cease printing the *Observer* and threatened him with force if he persisted. A committee was formed to draw up a compromise and its report was delivered on the second day of the meeting.

The "compromise" was anything but a *quid pro quo* agreement. Its essential elements were a respect for the Bill of Rights and discountenance of violence on the one hand, and a direct demand that Lovejoy quit as editor of the *Observer* on the other. The resolution had recognized Lovejoy's liberty of expression and then asserted the contradictory premise that he could be denied that right for the good of the community.

Lovejoy himself addressed the meeting and confronted the absurd logic of his opposition in a vain attempt to stir the compassion of the citizenry. He recounted the many offenses which he had suffered at the hands of the people of Alton and concluded:

> And now, if I leave here and go elsewhere, violence may overtake me in my retreat, and I have no more claim upon the protection of any other community than I have upon this; and I have concluded, after consultation with my friends, and earnestly seeking counsel of God, to remain at Alton, and here to insist on protection in the exercise of my rights. If the civil authorities refuse to protect me, I must look to God; and if I die, I have determined to make my grave in Alton.

Several members of the meeting were driven to tears by Lovejoy's remarks, but not Usher Linder. He delivered a violent speech in response, assaulting not only the doctrines of abolitionism, but Lovejoy's personal character as well. The meeting ended in a verbal free-for-all with the "get-Lovejoy" forces shouting the loudest and longest.

The long-awaited fifth press arrived two days after the fateful "compromise" meeting. It was stored in the warehouse of Godfrey and Gilman, the largest and strongest building in Alton.

On the night of November 7, 1837, a mob led by several of Alton's more prominent residents converged at the ill-fated warehouse. Lovejoy and several members of a hastily organized militia (under legal authority of the mayor) were inside the building, having vowed to defend the press. Bricks were thrown, shots were exchanged, and when a young man began to climb a ladder in order to set the building on fire, Lovejoy rushed out to stop him. In a matter of seconds Lovejoy was shot with five bullets, stumbled back into the warehouse, and died. Abolition had its first martyr, and the most would be made of it.

The following poem, "Lovejoy," appeared in the *Liberator* in 1837:

> Thou restest from thy labors, but thy blood
> Hath raised to heaven no unavailing cry;
> It claimeth kindred to that crimson flood,
> Which brought of old glad tidings from on high.
> Its power shall hence inseparably wed
> Good men and angels to the bleeding slave;
> While prejudice and pride, and the base dread
> Of death shall perish in the martyr's grave,
> Love thence shall spring, and conquering truth rejoice
> With thousand, thousand times re-echoed voice.

All over the North press reactions were swift and emotional. The *Emancipator* spoke of the "lines being drawn," and that all Americans would now be compelled to choose between abolition and the pro-slavery mob. The *Herald of Freedom* declared: "The blood of Elijah P. Lovejoy will cry out from the ground in a voice that shall stir the forests and prairies of the west into a living army of abolitionists." In like manner, the Salem *Gazette* proclaimed: "The murder of Lovejoy . . . will do more to drive a nail into the coffin of the patriarchal system than a living Lovejoy could effect in a century of effort." And finally, William Lloyd Garrison in the *Liberator* concluded:

> That his loss will be of incalculable gain to that noble cause which was so precious to his soul, is certain. In destroying his press, the enemies of freedom have compelled a thousand to speak out in its stead. In attempting to gag his lips, they have unloosed the tongues of tens of thousands of indignant souls.

Southern, border-state, and some Northern journals, however, were not so ecstatic in their reactions to the Alton riot. The New York *Observer* called Lovejoy a "mobocrat," and portrayed him as "a martyr to his own folly, insubordination, and independence of the laws." The Louisville *Journal,* Cincinnati *Republican,* and St. Louis *Republican* were equally hostile to Lovejoy, placing blame for the riot directly upon the abolitionist editor himself. The Louisville *Journal* further warned against the consequence of violence committed against abolitionists by stating that it would only "inflame their zeal, enlarge their numbers, and increase the power of their dangerous doctrines." It is indeed true that the murder of Lovejoy produced for the abolition movement a catalyst for popular discussion, and ultimately, the growth in acceptance of anti-slavery ideology.

The warehouse burned and the press destroyed, the mob retired by 2 A.M. that fateful November night in Alton. Lovejoy's two brothers were standing guard at his home a short distance from town. A warning of the awful news arrived when Lovejoy's riderless horse returned in the middle of the night.

In the early morning hours of November 8 a few devoted friends carried the dead minister home. On the following day, Lovejoy's 35th birthday, he was buried in the mud of a nearby field, with only a simple prayer offered—there was yet fear of further mob activity. Celia Ann Lovejoy, wife of the fallen editor, was a widow at the youthful age of 24.

Not since the era of the Revolutionary War, perhaps, had the nation become so aroused over a single event. The death of Lovejoy would echo long in the history of that turbulent era. At an in-

dignation service at Union College in Ohio a young citizen jumped to his feet, raised his right fist to the sky, and announced: "Here, before God, in the presence of these witnesses, from this time I consecrate my life to the destruction of slavery!" His name was John Brown and he would keep his promise. At Illinois College in Jacksonville a young law student named William Herndon was swept up in the anti-slavery sentiment following Lovejoy's assassination. "The murder of Lovejoy filled me with desperation," confessed Herndon, and soon he was encouraging anti-slavery thoughts in his Springfield law partner, Abraham Lincoln.

Perhaps the most famous convert to abolitionism produced by the murder of Lovejoy was the Massachusetts orator, Wendell Phillips:

> I can never forget the quick, sharp agony of that hour which brought us the news of Lovejoy's death. The gun fired at Lovejoy was like that of Sumter—it shattered a world of dreams. How prudently most men creep into nameless graves while now and then one or two forget themselves into immortality.

Selection 5

An Attack on White Racism

Lydia Maria Child

Lydia Maria Child (1802–1880) made her mark in nineteenth-century America as a well-known writer of children's literature, advice books for housewives, and abolition-

Excerpted from Lydia Maria Child, *An Appeal in Favor of That Class of Americans Called Africans* (Boston: Allen & Tichnor, 1833).

ist tracts. Drawn into the antislavery cause after she met William Lloyd Garrison in 1831, Child became best known for her 1833 book An Appeal in Favor of That Class of Americans Called Africans, *of which an excerpt appears here.*

Unlike the vast majority of white Americans and (sad to say) even some abolitionists, Child felt no racial prejudice against blacks. Her Appeal, *in fact, is notable for its indictment of white racism as one of the foundations on which slavery rested. She was far in advance of her time in calling for an end to all forms of discrimination against African Americans, as embodied in the segregationist laws of virtually every northern state. Shocking contemporary opinion, she even condemned legal prohibitions against interracial marriage.*

Child paid a high price for publishing the Appeal. *She was ostracized by the "respectable" white society of Massachusetts, and her once-popular children's magazine lost its subscribers. Because she was the financial mainstay of her family (her husband repeatedly failed in business), these were severe blows. Nevertheless, she persisted, and historians credit her writings with slowly winning more supporters to the antislavery cause.*

While we bestow our earnest disapprobation on the system of slavery, let us not flatter ourselves that we are in reality any better than our brethren of the South. Thanks to our soil and climate, and the early exertions of the Quakers, the *form* of slavery does not exist among us; but the very *spirit* of the hateful and mischievous thing is here in all its strength. The manner in which we use what power we have, gives us ample reason to be grateful that the nature of our institutions does not intrust us with more. Our prejudice against colored people is even more inveterate than it is at the South. The planter is often attached to his negroes, and lavishes caresses and kind words upon them, as he would on a favorite hound: but our cold-hearted, ignoble prejudice admits of no exception—no intermission.

The Southerners have long continued habit, apparent interest and dreaded danger, to palliate the wrong they do; but we stand without excuse. They tell us that Northern ships and Northern capital have been engaged in this wicked business; and the reproach is true. Several fortunes in this city have been made by the sale of negro blood. If these criminal transactions are still car-

ried on, they are done in silence and secrecy, because public opinion has made them disgraceful. But if the free States wished to cherish the system of slavery forever, they could not take a more direct course than they now do. Those who are kind and liberal on all other subjects, unite with the selfish and the proud in their unrelenting efforts to keep the colored population in the lowest state of degradation; and the influence they unconsciously exert over children early infuses into their innocent minds the same strong feelings of contempt.

The intelligent and well informed have the least share of this prejudice; and when their minds can be brought to reflect upon it, I have generally observed that they soon cease to have any at all. But such a general apathy prevails and the subject is so seldom brought into view, that few are really aware how oppressively the influence of society is made to bear upon this injured class of the community. When I have related facts, that came under my own observation, I have often been listened to with surprise, which gradually increased to indignation. In order that my readers may not be ignorant of the extent of this tyrannical prejudice, I will as briefly as possible state the evidence, and leave them to judge of it, as their hearts and consciences may dictate.

In the first place, an unjust law exists in this Commonwealth [Massachusetts] by which marriages between persons of different color is pronounced illegal. I am perfectly aware of the gross ridicule to which I may subject myself by alluding to this particular; but I have lived too long, and observed too much, to be disturbed by the world's mockery. In the first place, the government ought not to be invested with power to control the affections, any more than the consciences of citizens. A man has at least as good a right to choose his wife, as he has to choose his religion. His taste may not suit his neighbors; but so long as his deportment is correct, they have no right to interfere with his concerns. In the second place, this law is a *useless* disgrace to Massachusetts. Under existing circumstances, none but those whose condition in life is too low to be much affected by public opinion, will form such alliances; and they, when they choose to do so, *will* make such marriages, in spite of the law. I know two or three instances where women of the laboring class have been united to reputable, industrious colored men. These husbands regularly bring home their wages, and are kind to their families. If by some of the odd chances, which not unfrequently occur in the world, their wives should become heirs to any property, the children may be wronged out of it, because the law pronounces them illegitimate. And while this injustice exists with regard to *honest,* industrious individuals, who are merely guilty of differing from us in a matter of taste, neither the legislation nor customs of slave-holding States exert their influence against *immoral* connexions.

In one portion of our country this fact is shown in a very peculiar and striking manner. There is a numerous class at New Orleans, called Quateroons, or Quadroons, because their colored blood has for several successive generations been intermingled with the white. The women are much distinguished for personal beauty and gracefulness of motion; and their parents frequently send them to France for the advantages of an elegant education. White gentlemen of the first rank are desirous of being invited to their parties, and often become seriously in love with these fascinating but unfortunate beings. Prejudice forbids matrimony, but universal custom sanctions temporary connexions, to which a certain degree of respectability is allowed, on account of the peculiar situation of the parties. These attachments often continue for years—sometimes for life—and instances are not unfrequent of exemplary constancy and great propriety of deportment.

What eloquent vituperations we should pour forth, if the contending claims of nature and pride produced such a tissue of contradictions in some other country, and not in our own!

There is another Massachusetts law, which an enlightened community would not probably suffer to be carried into execution under any circumstances; but it still remains to disgrace the statutes of this Commonwealth.—It is as follows:

No African or Negro, other than a subject of the Emperor of Morocco, or a citizen of the United States, (proved so by a certificate of the Secretary of the State of which he is a citizen,) shall tarry within this Commonwealth longer than two months; and on complaint a justice shall order him to depart in ten days; and if he do not then, the justice may commit such African or Negro to the House of Correction, there to be kept at hard labor; and at the next term of the Court of C.P., he shall be tried, and if convicted of remaining as aforesaid, shall be whipped not exceeding ten lashes; and if he or she shall not *then* depart such process shall be repeated and punishment inflicted *toties quoties*

Stat. 1788, Ch. 54.

An honorable Haytian or Brazilian, who visited this country for business or information, might come under this law, unless public opinion rendered it a mere dead letter.

Lydia Maria Child

There is among the colored people an increasing desire for information, and a laudable ambition to be respectable in manners and appearance. Are we not foolish as well as sinful, in trying to repress a tendency so salutary to themselves, and so beneficial to the community? Several individuals of this class are very desirous to have persons of their own color qualified to teach something more than mere reading and writing. But in the public schools, colored children are subject to many discouragements and difficulties; and into the private schools they cannot gain admission. A very sensible and well-informed colored woman in a neighboring town, whose family have been brought up in a manner that excited universal remark and approbation, has been extremely desirous to obtain for her eldest daughter the advantages of a private school; but she has been resolutely repulsed, on account of her complexion. The girl is a very light mulatto, with great modesty and propriety of manners; perhaps no young person in the Commonwealth was less likely to have a bad influence on her associates. The clergyman respected the family, and he remonstrated with the instructer; but while the latter admitted the injustice of the thing, he excused himself by saying such a step would occasion the loss of all his white scholars.

In a town adjoining Boston, a well-behaved colored boy was kept out of the public school more than a year, by vote of the trustees. His mother, having some information herself, knew the importance of knowledge, and was anxious to obtain it for her family. She wrote repeatedly and urgently; and the school-master himself told me that the correctness of her spelling, and the neatness of her hand-writing formed a curious contrast with the notes he received from many white parents. At last, this spirited woman appeared before the committee, and reminded them that her husband, having for many years paid taxes as a citizen, had a right to the privileges of a citizen; and if her claim were refused, or longer postponed, she declared her determination to seek justice from a higher source. The trustees were, of course, obliged to yield to the equality of the laws, with the best grace they could. The boy was admitted, and made good progress in his studies. Had his mother been too ignorant to know her rights, or too abject to demand them, the lad would have had a fair chance to get a living out of the State as the occupant of a workhouse, or penitentiary.

The attempt to establish a school for African girls at Canterbury, Connecticut, has made too much noise to need a detailed account in this volume. I do not know the lady who first formed the project, but I am told that she is a benevolent and religious woman. It certainly is difficult to imagine any other motives than good ones, for an undertaking so arduous and unpopular. Yet had the Pope himself attempted to establish his supremacy over that commonwealth, he could hardly have been repelled with more determined and angry resistance.—Town meetings were held, the records of which are not highly creditable to the parties concerned. Petitions were sent to the Legislature, beseeching that no African school might be allowed to admit individuals not residing in the town where said school was established; and strange to relate, this law, which makes it impossible to collect a sufficient number of pupils, was sanctioned by the State. A colored girl, who availed herself of this opportunity to gain instruction, was warned out of town, and fined for not complying; and the instructress was imprisoned for persevering in her benevolent plan.

It is said, in excuse, that Canterbury will be inundated with vicious characters, who will corrupt the morals of the young men; that such a school will break down the distinctions between black and white; and that marriages between people of different colors will be the probable result. Yet they seem to assume the ground that colored people *must* always be an inferior and degraded class—that the prejudice against them *must* be eternal; being deeply founded in the laws of God and nature.—Finally, they endeavored to represent the school as one of the *incendiary* proceedings of the Anti-Slavery Society; and they appeal to the Colonization Society, as an aggrieved child is wont to appeal to its parent.

The objection with regard to the introduction of vicious characters into a village, certainly has some force; but are such persons likely to leave cities for a quiet country town, in search of moral and intellectual improvement? Is it not obvious that the *best* portion of the colored class are the very ones to prize such an opportunity for instruction? Grant that a large proportion of these unfortunate people *are* vicious—is it not our duty, and of course our wisest policy, to try to make them otherwise? And what will so effectually elevate their character and condition, as knowledge? I beseech you, my countrymen, think of these things wisely, and in season.

As for intermarriages, if there be such a repugnance between the two races, founded in the laws of *nature*, methinks there is small reason to dread their frequency.

The breaking down of distinctions in society, by means of extended information, is an objection which appropriately belongs to the Emperor of Austria, or the Sultan of Egypt.

I do not know how the affair at Canterbury is *generally* considered; but I have heard individuals of all parties and all opinions speak of it—and never without merriment or indignation. Fifty years hence, the *black* laws of Connecticut will be a greater source of amusement to the antiquarian, than her famous *blue* laws.

A similar, though less violent opposition arose in consequence of the attempt to establish a college for colored people at New Haven. A young colored man, who tried to obtain education at the Wesleyan college in Middletown, was obliged to relinquish the attempt on account of the persecution of his fellow students. Some collegians from the South objected to a colored associate in their recitations; and those from New England promptly and zealously joined in the hue and cry. A small but firm party were in favor of giving the colored man a chance to pursue his studies without insult or interruption; and I am told that this manly and disinterested band were all Southerners. As for those individuals, who exerted their influence to exclude an unoffending fellow-citizen from privileges which ought to be equally open to all, it is to be hoped that age will make them wiser—and that they will learn, before they die, to be ashamed of a step attended with more important results than usually belong to youthful follies.

It happens that these experiments have all been made in Connecticut; but it is no more than justice to that State to remark that a similar spirit would probably have been manifested in Massachusetts, under like circumstances. At our debating clubs and other places of public discussion, the demon of prejudice girds himself for the battle, the moment negro colleges and high schools are alluded to. Alas, while we carry on our lips that religion which teaches us to "love our neighbor as ourselves," how little do we cherish its blessed influence within our hearts! How much republicanism we have to *speak of,* and how little do we practise!

Let us seriously consider what injury a negro college could possibly do us. It is certainly a fair presumption that the scholars would be from the better portion of the colored population; and it is an equally fair presumption that knowledge would improve their characters. There are already many hundreds of colored people in the city of Boston.—In the street they generally appear neat and respectable; and in our houses they do not "come between the wind and our nobility." Would the addition of one or two hundred more even be perceived? As for giving offence to the Southerners by allowing such establishments—they have no right to interfere with our internal concerns, any more than we have with theirs.—Why should they not give up slavery to please us, by the same rule that we must refrain from educating the negroes to please them? If they are at liberty to do wrong, we certainly ought to be at liberty to do right. They may talk and publish as much about us as they please; and we ask for no other influence over them.

It is a fact not generally known that the brave Kosciusko left a fund for the establishment of a negro college in the United States. Little did he think he had been fighting for a people, who would not grant one rood of their vast territory for the benevolent purpose!

According to present appearances, a college for colored persons will be established in Canada; and thus, by means of our foolish and wicked pride, the credit of this philanthropic enterprise will be transferred to our mother country.

The preceding chapters show that it has been no uncommon thing for colored men to be educated at English, German, Portuguese and Spanish Universities.

In Boston there is an Infant School, three Primary Schools, and a Grammar School. The two last, are I believe supported by the public; and this fact is highly creditable. [A building for the colored Grammar School is not supplied by the city, though such provision is always made for similar institutions for white boys.—The apartment is close and uncomfortable, and many pupils stay away, who would gladly attend under more convenient circumstances. There ought likewise to be a colored teacher instead of a white one. Under the dominion of existing prejudices, it is difficult to find a white man, well qualified to teach such a school, who feels the interest he ought to feel, in these Pariahs* of our republic. The parents would repose more confidence in a colored instructer; and he, both from sympathy and pride, would be better fitted for his task.

It is peculiarly incumbent on the city authorities to supply a commodious building for the colored grammar school, because public prejudice excludes these oppressed people from all lucrative employments, and they cannot therefore be supposed to have ample funds of their own.]**

I was much pleased with the late resolution awarding Franklin medals to the colored pupils of the grammar school; and I was still more pleased with the laudable project, originated by Josiah Holbrook, Esq. for the establishment of a colored Lyceum. Surely a better spirit *is* beginning to work in this cause; and when once begun, the good sense and good feeling of the community will bid it go on and prosper. How much this spirit will have to contend with is illustrated by the following fact. When President Jackson entered this city, the white children of all the schools were sent out in uniform, to do him honor. A member of the Committee proposed that the pupils of the African schools should be invited likewise; but he was the only one who voted for it. He then proposed that the yeas and nays should be recorded; upon which, most of the gentlemen walked off, to prevent the question from being taken. Perhaps they felt an awkward consciousness of the incongeniality of such proceedings with our republican institutions. By order of the Committee the vacation of the African schools did not commence until the day after the procession of the white pupils; and a note to the instructer intimated that the pupils were not expected to appear on the Common. The reason given was because "their numbers were so few;" but in private conversation, fears were expressed lest their sable faces should give offence to our slave-holding President. In all probability the sight of the colored children would have been agreeable to General Jackson, and seemed more like home, than anything he witnessed.

In the theatre, it is not possible for respectable colored people to obtain a decent seat. They must either be excluded, or herd with the vicious.

A fierce excitement prevailed, not long since, because a colored man had bought a pew in one of our churches. I heard a very kindhearted and zealous democrat declare his opinion that "the fellow ought to be turned out by constables, if he dared to occupy the pew he had purchased." Even at the communion-table, the mockery of human pride is mingled with the worship of Jehovah. Again an again have I seen a solitary negro come up to the altar, meekly an timidly, after all the white communicants had retired. One Episcopal clergyman of this city, forms an honorable exception to this remark. When there is room at the altar, Mr—often makes a signal to the colored members of his church to kneel beside their white brethren; and once, when two white infants and one colored one were to be

*The Pariahs are the lowest and most degraded caste in Hindostan. The laws prevent them from ever rising in their condition or mingling with other castes.
**Bracketed passage omitted from the 1836 edition.-Ed.

baptized, and the parents of the latter bashfully lingered far behind the others, he silently rebuked the unchristian spirit of pride, by first administering the holy ordinance to the little dark-skinned child of God.

An instance of prejudice lately occurred, which I should find it hard to believe, did I not positively know it to be a fact. A gallery pew was purchased in one of our churches for two hundred dollars. A few Sabbaths after, an address was delivered at that church, in favor of the Africans. Some colored people, who very naturally wished to hear the discourse, went into the gallery; probably because they thought they should be deemed less intrusive there than elsewhere. The man who had recently bought a pew, found it occupied by colored people, and indignantly retired with his family. The next day, he purchased a pew in another meeting-house, protesting that nothing would tempt him again to make use of seats, that had been occupied by negroes.

A well known country representative, who makes a very loud noise about his democracy, once attended the Catholic church. A pious negro requested him to take off his hat, while he stood in the presence of the Virgin Mary. The white man rudely shoved him aside, saying, "You son of an Ethiopian, do you dare to speak to me!" I more than once heard the hero repeat this story; and he seemed to take peculiar satisfaction in telling it. Had he been less ignorant, he would not have chosen "son of an *Ethiopian*" as an *ignoble* epithet; to have called the African his own equal would have been abundantly more sarcastic. The same republican dismissed a strong, industrious colored man, who had been employed on the farm during his absence. "I am too great a democrat," quoth he, "to have any body in my house, who don't sit at my table; and I'll be hanged, if I ever eat with the son of an Ethiopian."

Men whose education leaves them less excuse for such illiberality, are yet vulgar enough to join in this ridiculous prejudice. The colored woman, whose daughter has been mentioned as excluded from a private school, was once smuggled into a stage, upon the supposition that she was a white woman, with a sallow complexion.

Her manners were modest and prepossessing, and the gentlemen were very polite to her. But when she stopped at her own door, and was handed out by her curly-headed husband, they were at once surprised and angry to find they had been riding with a mulatto—and had, in their ignorance, been really civil to her!

A worthy colored woman, belonging to an adjoining town, wished to come into Boston to attend upon a son, who was ill. She had a trunk with her, and was too feeble to walk. She begged permission to ride in the stage. But the passengers with *noble* indignation, declared they would get out, if she were allowed to get in. After much entreaty, the driver suffered her to sit by him upon the box. When he entered the city, his comrades began to point and sneer. Not having sufficient moral courage to endure this, he left the poor woman, with her trunk, in the middle of the street, far from the place of her destination; telling her, with an oath, that he would not carry her a step further.

A friend of mine lately wished to have a colored girl admitted into the stage with her, to take care of her babe. The girl was very lightly tinged with the sable hue, had handsome Indian features, and very pleasing manners. It was, however, evident that she was not white; and therefore the passengers objected to her company. This of course, produced a good deal of inconvenience on one side, and mortification on the other. My friend repeated the circumstance to a lady, who, as the daughter and wife of a clergyman, might be supposed to have imbibed some liberality. The lady seemed to think the experiment was very preposterous; but when my friend alluded to the mixed parentage of the girl, she exclaimed, with generous enthusiasm, "Oh, that alters the case, *Indians* certainly *have* their rights."

Every year a colored gentleman and scholar is becoming less and less of a rarity—thanks to the existence of the Haytian Republic, and the increasing liberality of the world! Yet if a person of refinement from Hayti, Brazil, or other countries, which we deem less enlightened than our own, should visit us, the very boys of this republic would dog his footsteps with the vulgar outcry of

"Nigger! Nigger!" I have known this to be done, from no other provocation than the sight of a colored man with the dress and deportment of a gentleman. Were it not that republicanism, like Christianity, is often perverted from its true spirit by the bad passions of mankind, such things as these would make every honest mind disgusted with the very name of republics.

I am acquainted with a gentleman from Brazil who is shrewd, enterprising, noble-spirited, and highly respectable in character and manners; yet he has experienced almost every species of indignity on account of his color. Not long since, it became necessary for him to visit the southern shores of Massachusetts, to settle certain accounts connected with his business. His wife was in a feeble state of health, and the physicians had recommended a voyage. For this reason, he took passage for her with himself in the steam-boat; and the captain, as it appears, made no objection to a colored gentleman's money. After remaining on deck some time, Mrs—attempted to pass into the cabin; but the captain prevented her; saying, "You must go down forward."—The Brazilian urged that he had paid the customary price, and therefore his wife and infant had a right to a place in the ladies' cabin. The captain answered, "Your wife a'n't a lady; she is a nigger." The forward cabin was occupied by sailors; was entirely without accommodations for women, and admitted the seawater, so that a person could not sit in it comfortably without keeping the feet raised in a chair. The husband stated that his wife's health would not admit of such exposure; to which the captain still replied, "I don't allow any niggers in my cabin." With natural and honest indignation, the Brazilian exclaimed, "You Americans talk about the Poles! You are a great deal more Russian than the Russians." The affair was concluded by placing the colored gentleman and his invalid wife on the shore, and leaving them to provide for themselves as they could. Had the cabin been full, there would have been some excuse; but it was occupied only by two sailors' wives. The same individual sent for a relative in a distant town on account of illness in his family. After

staying several weeks, it became necessary for her to return; and he procured a seat for her in the stage. The same ridiculous scene occurred; the passengers were afraid of losing their dignity by riding with a neat, respectable person, whose face was darker than their own. No public vehicle could be obtained, by which a colored citizen could be conveyed to her home; it therefore became absolutely necessary for the gentleman to leave his business and hire a chaise at great expense. Such proceedings are really inexcusable. No authority can be found for them in religion, reason, or the laws.

The Bible informs us that "a man of Ethiopia, a eunuch of great authority under Candace, Queen of the Ethiopians, who had charge of all her treasure, came to Jerusalem to worship." Returning in his chariot, he read Esaias, the Prophet; and at his request Philip went up into the chariot and sat with him, explaining the Scriptures. Where should we now find an apostle, who would ride in the same chariot with an Ethiopian!

Will any candid person tell me why respectable colored people should not be allowed to make use of public conveyances, open to all who are able and willing to pay for the privilege? Those who enter a vessel, or a stagecoach, cannot expect to select their companions. If they can afford to take a carriage or boat for themselves, then, and then only, they have a right to be exclusive. I was lately talking with a young gentleman on this subject, who professed to have no prejudice against colored people, except so far as they were ignorant and vulgar; but still he could not tolerate the idea of allowing them to enter stages and steam-boats. "Yet, you allow the same privilege to vulgar and ignorant white men, without a murmur," I replied; "Pray give a good republican reason why a respectable colored citizen should be less favored." For want of a better argument, he said—(pardon me, fastidious reader)—he implied that the presence of colored persons was less agreeable than Otto of Rose, or Eau de Cologne; and this distinction, he urged was made by God himself. I answered, "Whoever takes his chance in a public vehicle, is liable to meet with uncleanly white passengers, whose breath may be redolent with the fumes of American cigars, or American gin. Neither of these articles have a fragrance peculiarly agreeable to nerves of delicate organization. Allowing your argument double the weight it deserves, it is utter nonsense to pretend that the inconvenience in the case I have supposed is not infinitely greater. But what is more to the point, do you dine in a fashionable hotel, do you sail in a fashionable steam-boat, do you sup at a fashionable house, without having negro servants behind your chair. Would they be any more disagreeable, as *passengers* seated in the corner of a stage, or a steam-boat, than as *waiters* in such immediate attendance upon your person?"

Stage-drivers are very much perplexed when they attempt to vindicate the present tyrannical customs; and they usually give up the point, by saying they themselves have no prejudice against colored people—they are merely afraid of the public. But stage-drivers should remember that in a popular government, they, in common with every other citizen, form a part and portion of the dreaded public.

The gold was never coined for which I would barter my individual freedom of acting and thinking upon any subject, or knowingly interfere with the rights of the meanest human being. The only true courage is that which impels us to do right without regard to consequences. To fear a populace is as servile as to fear an emperor. The only salutary restraint is the fear of doing wrong.

Selection 6

Was There Really an Underground Railroad?

Larry Gara

There is no doubt that some antislavery whites (and proportionally greater numbers of northern free blacks) helped runaway slaves escape, particularly after the passage of the tough Fugitive Slave Law of 1850, under which ex-slaves living or passing through the North were in serious danger of being returned to owners who claimed them. Lydia Maria Child, for example, offered her home as a refuge to escaping slaves, some of them bound for Canada.

But the so-called Underground Railroad, described as an elaborate organized network of escape routes and secret hiding places that sometimes is still mentioned in American history textbooks, appears to have been largely a myth, invented long after the Civil War. Historian Larry Gara, who has written a book on the subject, in this selection summarizes the case for regarding the Underground Railroad skeptically. This piece first appeared in the magazine American History Illustrated *in 1978.*

Reprinted from Larry Gara, "The Myth of the Underground Railroad," *American History Illustrated*, January 1978. This article is reprinted from *American History Illustrated* magazine with the permission of PRIMEDIA Special Interest Publications (History Group), copyright American History Illustrated magazine.

*O*f all the legends growing out of the Civil War era and the slavery struggle preceding it, none has taken deeper root in popular thought than that of the underground railroad. Although details are usually indistinct, the term still suggests a widespread, highly secret conspiracy to transport slaves from southern bondage to northern freedom. The railroad operated a very busy line, despite the constant dangers its employees faced. And the abolitionist operators usually outwitted the road's would-be sabateurs with such tricks as secret rooms and passageways, instant disguises, and many other devices based on ingenuity and daring. It was an abolitionist institution and most of its willing passengers would have been helpless without the road's many services.

The underground railroad of legend, like most legendary institutions, is a blend of fiction and fact. Most of the historical source material which provided the basis for the traditional view of the institution was not recorded until long after the events took place, much of it in the post–Civil War era when abolitionists and their descendants wrote their reminiscences or handed down the anecdotes of exciting times by word of mouth. With one major exception, the books published after the Civil War containing first-hand underground railroad accounts view the events from the standpoint of the white abolitionists. As all historical sources reflect the bias of their writers, abolitionist sources tended to view the ante bellum past as a morality play with themselves in the role of righteous crusaders, Southerners as the villains, and the fugitive slaves as helpless, passive recipients of aid. The former antislavery activists were recalling a time of high danger and excitement. When Professor Wilbur H. Siebert contacted hundreds of abolitionists in the 1890's for material for his history of the underground railroad, one wrote him: "There was a peculiar *fascination* about that 'U.G.R.R.' biz., that *fires me up,* even now when I recall the scenes of excitement and danger."

In retrospect, the romance of underground railroad work inevitably led to some exaggeration. There was some organized assistance provided in a few northern communities for fleeing slaves, but there was nothing resembling a nationally organized effort, and much of the aid was rendered on a temporary and haphazard basis. With the passage of time one or two well-known incidents concerning fugitives and those who helped them sometimes created a popular image of a busy underground line in a particular locale. Well-known figures in the anti-slavery movement were often associated with underground railroad activity, whether or not they had actually participated in that phase of the effort. When Professor Siebert contacted the Reverend Joshua Young of Groton, Massachusetts, for his experiences, Young replied that he could tell very little. "Perhaps my connection with the U.G.R.R. has been exaggerated," he explained, "owing to the circumstances of my being the only present and officiating clergyman at John Brown's funeral, which gave me some prominence among abolitionists."

Not all the former abolitionists were as modest as the Reverend Young; in the postwar period individuals and their relatives sometimes expanded on their actual adventures in underground railroad work. Thus family pride contributed to the legend. Among other things, those people who had been scorned and ridiculed in many communities now had their position vindicated. Thrilling stories were recounted at gatherings of northern local historical societies, repeated in hundreds of newspapers, and often found their way into the county histories which were published in the 1880's. Communities as well as individuals claimed an unblemished record of sacrificial service to the victims of slavery who were fleeing from its toils. Hardly a town in the North was without its local legends or a house reputed to have been a major depot on the underground line. Very few such places have had their historical reputations verified, and in some instances even houses built after the Civil War came to share an underground railroad reputation.

One of the more serious distortions caused by the legend of the underground railroad concerns the role of the fugitives themselves. An overemphasis on the amount of assistance rendered by

Some scholars feel that the escaped slaves' success was due more to their own ingenuity and planning than to assistance from abolitionists.

white abolitionists has tended to make the people the railroad was designed to aid—the fugitive slaves—either invisible or passive and helpless without aid from others. In fact, they were anything but passive. The thousands of slaves who left the South usually planned and carried out their own escape plans. They were careful, determined, and imaginative in devising such plans.

Some slaves merely ran off, traveling by night and resting by day, with assistance from other slaves, free black persons, and occasionally sympathetic whites, not necessarily abolitionists. Others made contact with and paid ship captains running from southern to northern ports to hide them among the cargo. When viewed from the perspective of the slave narratives dictated or written by the former slaves themselves, the whole fugitive slave epoch takes on a different emphasis with more attention to the fugitives' own self-help efforts, though credit is ac-

corded abolitionist assistance when it was given.

Often there was no help available, either in planning or carrying out slave escapes, and in light of such circumstances a successful escape was a major accomplishment of the human spirit. In 1838 Charles Ball traveled 1,200 miles from Alabama to New York, unaided by any underground railroad. Ball journeyed at night, living mostly on roots and berries, and contacted abolitionists only after he reached New York. Another slave took an entire year to reach Cincinnati from Alabama. The scant records which are available indicate that many escaping slaves were afraid to trust any outside assistance, preferring to rely as little as possible on others.

Since free blacks were legally obligated to carry certificates of freedom at all times, the fugitives frequently borrowed free papers or had them forged. When Frederick Douglass succeeded in leaving slavery he borrowed the "protection papers" of an American sailor, but it was only in the postwar edition of his autobiography that he revealed his method of escape. Disguise was also commonly used by fugitives. Light-colored slaves sometimes posed as white travelers. When Lewis Clarke left Kentucky slavery, he wore only dark glasses to disguise himself. Clarke stayed in hotels and taverns along the way and reached Ohio safely, later continuing his journey to Canada.

One of the most imaginative and daring of slave escape plans was that devised and carried out by William and Ellen Craft of Macon, Georgia. Ellen, who was the daughter of her own master and of very light complexion, posed as an elderly and infirm southern gentleman with a bandaged head and one arm in a sling. The Crafts used the sling in order to make it impossible for the traveling "master" to sign necessary forms and to register at hotels, a ploy to hide Ellen's illiteracy. William played the part of a loyal personal servant. He was a skilled cabinetmaker who had earned enough of his own money to purchase a railroad ticket from Georgia to Philadelphia. The Crafts played their roles well. Except for a brief moment of near-disaster in Baltimore when a railroad ticket agent wanted Ellen to sign a form and provide a bond for her servant, the couple had no trouble along the way.

A free black fellow passenger gave the Crafts the name of an abolitionist in Philadelphia; this was their first knowledge of any possible aid from such a source. They rested briefly in Philadelphia before going on to Boston, where they made their home until they fled the country to elude agents of their former owner. The Crafts recorded their remarkable escape story in a pamphlet, "Running a Thousand Miles for Freedom, or the Escape of William and Ellen Craft from Slavery," published in England.

Henry Brown, a slave in Richmond, Virginia, used an equally daring method to escape from slavery. He decided to have himself crated and shipped north by railway express. The plan was Brown's, but of course it required an accomplice. Brown contacted Samuel A. Smith, a sympathetic white man, who followed instructions and, for a fee of $40, sent the crate to the Philadelphia Anti-Slavery Office. Brown's safe arrival was hailed as a miracle in the antislavery press. Later he spoke to numerous abolitionist gatherings, exhibiting the box used in his flight from slavery, along with a powerful diorama showing many scenes of southern slave life, painted for him by Benjamin Roberts, a black artist from Boston. Meanwhile, Samuel Smith helped several others to escape and was apprehended and convicted for his efforts, serving eight years in a Virginia prison. Henry "Box" Brown and the Crafts were frequently referred to as "passengers" on the underground railroad, even though their escapes were planned and largely carried out by themselves, certainly not according to the usual transportation service that institution brings to mind.

When fugitive slaves did receive aid it was mostly by chance and after they had succeeded in completing the most dangerous part of their journey through the southern states. There were abolitionists who made the underground railroad a kind of special concern though the aid they provided was on a regional rather than a national basis. Two who were very active in this phase of the antislavery work were Levi Coffin and Thomas Garrett, both Quakers. Coffin lived and worked in Newport, Indiana, for more than twenty years, then moved to Cincinnati, where he added a degree of local organization to the efforts of those who were already helping runaway slaves. Coffin and his friends transported fugitives in wagons from one town to another, on occasion having to elude slave hunters. They also provided the former slaves with clothing and other necessities, and sometimes boarded them until they could be transported or sent by themselves farther north. Much of Levi Coffin's underground railroad work was aboveboard, especially as antislavery sentiment strengthened in the years just preceding the Civil War. He recorded in his memoirs, written many years later, that public opinion in his neighborhood became so strongly antislavery that he kept fugitives at his house "openly, while preparing them for their journey to the North."

Thomas Garrett provided skillful leadership

in assisting fugitive slaves in and around Wilmington, Delaware, working closely with others in Chester County, Pennsylvania, and the Philadelphia area. Garrett spared neither time nor expense in his efforts, which usually involved sheltering fugitives, making arrangements for their transportation, and paying necessary expenses. Several times he assisted Harriet Tubman, who, having escaped herself, made trips into the South to rescue others. Although Delaware was a slave state, Garrett capitalized on its unusual degree of free speech and freedom of the press and he seldom worked in secrecy. Sued for damages by a number of slave owners who won verdicts against him totalling nearly $8,000, Garrett eventually settled for a quarter of that amount, still a considerable sum of money.

Thomas Garrett, Levi Coffin, and other abolitionists involved in the work of assisting fugitive slaves nearly always concentrated their efforts in their own localities. With very few exceptions, such locally organized assistance was unavail-

able in the South, and even the more militant abolitionists declined to entice slaves from their bondage. Levi Coffin made frequent business trips into the South, but never had any trouble while there. Although he spoke openly of his opposition to slavery, he assured his southern acquaintances that it was not his business while in the South "to interfere with their laws or their slaves." Others believed the risk outweighed the benefits. James H. Fairchild, president of Oberlin College, recalled that the majority of Oberlin abolitionists did not consider it "legitimate to go into the Slave States and entice the slaves from their masters." While they denied the master's ownership they looked upon venturing into the South as a "reckless undertaking, involving too much risk, and probably doing more harm than good." It is no wonder then that the former slaves who recorded their escape accounts tell of plans and daring journeys involving only themselves.

All of the prosecutions under the Federal Fugitive Slave Act of 1850 were for acts allegedly

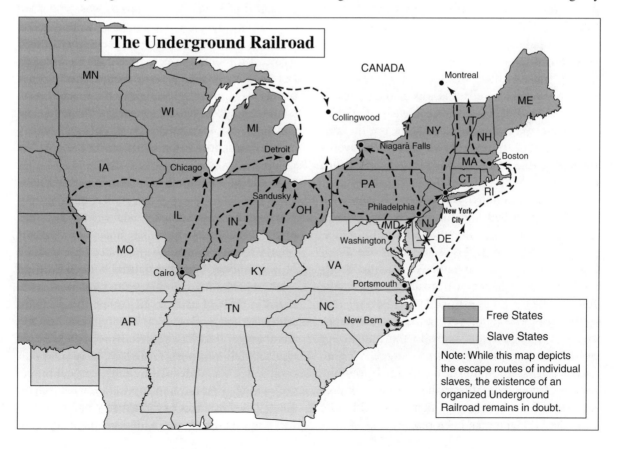

committed in the North. Although only about a dozen cases were prosecuted, they received a great deal of public attention and did much to popularize antislavery and anti-southern sentiment. The act itself met with widespread criticism and opposition in the northern states. As part of the Compromise of 1850 it was designed to mollify the slave interests, but its blatant violation of the rights of anyone accused of being a fugitive slave gave a powerful propaganda weapon to the antislavery forces. They pointed out that there was no provision for a jury trial for alleged fugitives and that in fact the law, which they usually referred to as a "bill," denied the protection of free soil to fleeing slaves and made slavery a national rather than a sectional institution. Many Northerners who had little concern for the slaves themselves resented this intrusion of the slave power into their free society.

When fugitives were captured and returned to slavery the effect on northern public opinion was even stronger. Anthony Burns, a former Virginia slave living in Boston, was arrested on May 24, 1854, only days after the Senate passed the unpopular Kansas-Nebraska Bill opening new territories to slave expansion. A group of people, most of them black, tried to break into the courthouse where Burns was held and rescue him. In the scuffle one officer was killed and later there were arrests for that act, but no conviction. With extraordinary security the Government was able to try Burns and order his return to slavery.

The day Anthony Burns left Boston the church bells tolled and the line of march was draped in mourning crepe. Thousands of disgusted citizens watched while contingents of police, twenty-two companies of Massachusetts soldiers, and a battery of artillery guarded the fugitive. One scholar estimated that Burns's rendition cost $100,000, yet the nationally publicized event converted many to the antislavery point of view. One abolitionist urged William Lloyd Garrison to publish the entire Burns history, believing that "it furnishes far more important materials for History, than it would have furnished had the man been rescued."

Much of the publicity concerning Anthony Burns was promoted by the Boston Vigilance Committee, one of several such committees founded or reactivated in response to the Fugitive Slave Law of 1850. The work of these committees contributed substantially to the popular image of the underground railroad, though much of their work was aboveboard and routine. Some were founded by Negroes and all of them used black sympathizers as contacts and workers. One of the more active was the Philadelphia Vigilance Committee with William Still, a black abolitionist, as chairman. Approximately 100 fugitives a year received assistance from the committee during the eight-year period when William Still kept records of its work. Still and committee members also interviewed each of the former slaves, carefully recorded essential facts, and preserved the organization's financial records and some of its correspondence. William Still later used this and other first-hand material in compiling his important book, *The Underground Rail Road*. As a Negro he was concerned that the fugitives receive credit as well as those whites who risked much to help them. Still wrote, promoted, and sold his book through agents. He hoped the work would inspire other blacks to greater efforts until they could gain wealth and produce literary works of quality. As the only book-length account of the underground railroad written by a black author, Still's volume is unique.

In the years before the Civil War the underground railroad also provided a wealth of propaganda material for the antislavery cause. Incidents concerning fugitives and their rescue, often by black crowds, were frequently reported in the reform press. Abolitionists boasted of their underground railroad activity and published details of escapes to arouse further sympathy for the fugitives and the antislavery cause. Sometimes escaped slaves were exhibited at abolitionist meetings. Available assistance was even listed in some of the antislavery newspapers along with the narratives of former slaves. Nearly every aspect of the activity had potential for winning new free soil or antislavery converts. The fugitives aroused sympathy, for their treatment by southern slave hunters and by the courts violated all sense of decency and respect for civil liberties. All of this contributed to a growing resentment of the encroachments and demands of what Northerners referred to as the slave power.

It was in the years after the Civil War had destroyed the slave power and its hold on the nation that the underground railroad assumed the character of a cherished American legend. Many Northerners viewed the past and the defeated slave interests with a vision distorted by the course of events. The immorality of slavery became obvious with its defeat, and some who had had only marginal connections with free soil or antislavery efforts were prone to exaggerate their contributions. As early as 1864 abolitionist Lydia Maria Child remarked to William Lloyd Garrison that new antislavery friends were "becoming as plenty as roses in June," and she marveled "at their power of keeping a secret so long!" A year later an abolitionist reported that it was "rare to meet one who has ever wished well to slavery, or desired anything but its final abolition."

The romantic nature of underground railroad activity virtually assured its place in Civil War tradition. In the 1890's, when Professor Siebert corresponded with hundreds of abolitionists and their descendants, only a few denied having valid recollections of the institution. Journalists and local historians in many northern communities took for granted an underground railroad record, and to some Northerners the thousands of slaves who escaped became millions.

A pattern of action emerged in these accounts, with emphasis on the role of white abolitionists, a pattern which was repeated in a number of works of fiction as well as in some historical writing. Consequently, the black participants became virtually invisible in the underground railroad of legend. Exposing the distortions and oversimplifications associated with the underground railroad in the years since the Civil War should not denigrate those abolitionists who were actively involved, nor should it minimize the importance of their efforts. The historical picture, however, is much more complex and vastly different from the legendary accounts with their heroes and villains participating in a noble crusade to free helpless victims of slavery. Underground railroad operators did aid some slaves in their escape, but such aid must not overshadow or obliterate the efforts of the slaves to free themselves.

The Complete History of

Black
Abolitionists

Chapter 14

Introduction

Continuing a vocal campaign that had begun in the Revolutionary era, when northern slaves had boldly petitioned the white authorities for liberty, blacks in the North never muted their voices against slavery. (Free blacks in the South always had to be careful of what they said in public.) David Walker should certainly be classed among the early abolitionists, though he died before the movement took shape. In the 1830s, free blacks constituted three-fourths of *The Liberator*'s readership and provided most of its meager financial support.

By the 1840s, however, African Americans in the North were divided over whether they should continue to follow the leadership of white abolitionists or develop their own parallel antislavery movement. The split between white Garrisonian and anti-Garrisonian abolitionists added to the free blacks' dilemma. Black abolitionists keenly felt the condescension that their white allies sometimes expressed, either consciously or unthinkingly. Frederick Douglass, for example, was told that he should confine his public speeches to relating personal experiences as a slave rather than expressing more general thoughts about American society and politics. Above all, black abolitionists felt a deep need to declare their independence, to lead their own cause proudly, and to build the self-esteem of the free black community. They had to become more than stage props for white orators and editorialists.

Frederick Douglass was the greatest of the black abolitionists, and unquestionably one of the foremost thinkers, writers, and political activists of American history. As an abolitionist—in the 1840s under the auspices of the white antislavery movement and in the 1850s as a wholly independent voice—he constantly showed physical courage and psychological strength, qualities that he possessed in abundance. But he was not alone. Women like Sojourner Truth and Harriet Tubman frequently spoke on the abolitionist circuit, and men such as Charles Lenox Remond and Henry Highland Garnet constantly challenged the abolitionist movement to push black claims to dignity and self-determination up to and beyond the limits that white society permitted.

Selection 1

Black Abolitionists and Antislavery Whites

Benjamin Quarles

In a chapter of his 1969 book Black Abolitionists, *excerpted here, African American historian Benjamin Quarles discusses how pre–Civil War free blacks debated whether they should follow the lead of white abolitionists or launch their own antislavery movements. The issue was complicated by divisions that appeared within the white abolitionist movement, notably between supporters of William Lloyd Garrison and more moderate elements.*

One of the reasons so many whites joined the abolitionist movement, wrote a Negro editor, was their belief that it stood for abstract principles to be applied to the South, without requiring them to battle the prejudices in their own hearts. James McCune Smith found it strange that in the constitution of the American Anti-Slavery Society, no mention was made of social equality as one of its aims. The editor of the *Northern Star and Freeman's Advocate* had a terse bit of advice: "Until abolitionists eradicate prejudice from their own hearts, they can never receive the unwavering confidence of the people of color."

There were instances in which white abolitionists attended concerts or recitals at which Negroes were barred or segregated. Moreover, some abolitionists, particularly during the formative 1830's, held that Negroes should not be admitted to antislavery meetings or hold membership in the societies. . . .

Even when they worked side by side, white and Negro abolitionists scarcely sustained a peer relationship. Whites tended to be paternalistic, reflecting a "father knows best" attitude. They tended to praise an above-average Negro almost to the point of eulogy, as if in surprise that he revealed any ability at all. And like the earlier abolitionists they were fond of giving advice to Negroes, their remarks interlarded with beatitudes. The advice might have been good—certainly it was much like that given by Negro leaders themselves. But if one Negro criticized another for patronizing a Dan Rice minstrel show while ignoring a magic lantern exhibition on slavery being held in the same block, the whole thing somehow seemed freer of racial connotations.

The chief criticism against the white abolitionists by their black counterparts was their halfheartedness in carrying out the second of their twin goals—the elevation of the free Negro. Equal rights for Negroes was an essential corollary of abolitionism—improving the lot of the Northerners of color was a clearly stated

*An antislavery meeting. Most abolitionists focused on the fight
to end slavery, and few worked to help freed slaves find jobs.*

goal. The Maine Union in Behalf of the Colored
Race, formed in Portland in 1835, was a reflection of this outlook. Aware of this dual commitment, nearly every abolitionist society had a
special committee on the welfare of the free Negro. But in most instances this is about as far as
it went—such committees, as a rule, simply did
not function.

Hence, in this quarter the abolitionists were
vulnerable. In their strong campaign against
slavery in the South, "they half overlooked slavery in the North," wrote a Negro editor in 1839.
The Negro people needed jobs, as their spokesmen constantly stressed. In 1831 Maria W.
Stewart asked "several women" to hire colored
girls. Abolitionists were asked to give Negro
apprentices and mechanics an equal chance at
least, and a preference if possible—their "being
a neglected people." In an editorial that brought

a flood of approving letters, an Albany weekly
informed the white abolitionists that Negroes
did not expect to ride in their carriages or sup at
their parties, but they did hope that avenues of
employment would be opened up by their alleged friends.

Such thrusts, sharp as they were, brought few
changes. Most white abolitionists simply did not
think in terms of the workingman, white or colored. Men of great understanding in some
things, they never seemed to fully sense that
economic freedom was coequal with, if not basic to, all other freedoms.

To be sure, there were a few gestures by individuals and organizations. In isolated instances
an abolitionist might employ a skilled Negro.
Lewis Tappan, for example, paid Patrick H. Reason $70 to do a steel engraving of his brother,
Benjamin. The Tappans were pleased with the

product, and Lewis thought that the antislavery cause would be advanced if it were known that a Negro was capable of such craftsmanship. But, he added in his letter to Reason, "perhaps it will be best to wait until you have engraved two or three more before the secret is let out."

Abolitionist organizations made some token efforts to help the black workingman. Following an address by Charles Lenox Remond in November 1837, the Rhode Island Anti-Slavery Society voted to aid Negroes to get jobs as clerks. *The Philanthropist,* organ of the Ohio society, made its office into a referral agency at which employers willing to take colored apprentices might leave their names and colored parents with sons to be apprenticed might follow suit.

Perhaps the most futile attempt at helping the Negro by an organization was furnished by the American Union for the Relief and Improvement of the Colored Race. Founded in Boston in 1835 and backed by one hundred men in ten states, it proposed to give elementary schooling to the Negro and to teach him trades. The American Union's membership was of the old-school, pillars-of-society type, men who were given more to reflection than to action. Hoping to resurrect the harmony and forbearance of the old days, they shied away from the word "immediate," favored colonization, and preferred to characterize slavery as a wrong rather than as a sin, a vital distinction then.

As could be expected, the union aroused the scorn and hostility of Garrison. Labeling it "An Anti-Garrison Society," he issued an address to Negroes informing them that the object of the union was to put them down, with him thrown in for good measure. This ended the possibility that the union would obtain the necessary cooperation of the colored people in the 1830's. The union expired within two years. . . .

If elevating the free Negro required money, it also called for common sense. And this too was something missing in the proposals made by the abolitionists. In 1839 the New York City Anti-Slavery Society, in a thirteen-point list of ways to help the colored people, recommended that a book on domestic economy be printed for them and that a joint stock company be organized to trade with the West Indies.

Many white abolitionists, as Negroes had sorrowfully came to learn by 1840, had a tendency to abstraction. Such white coworkers viewed the movement as an ideological warfare, the outcome of which was secondary to the stimulus of the mental jousting. To strike a moral posture was more important than to strike at slavery. Wendell Phillips, although almost without peer in the crusade, voiced something of this sense of disengagement in an informal talk to a gathering of fellow reformers at Cochituate Hall in Boston: "My friends, if we never free a slave, we have at least freed ourselves, in the effort to emancipate our brother man."

Negro abolitionists, with the exception of William Whipper, had no fondness for abstraction. Their interest was more personal. A Negro could scarcely muster enough detachment to live in the realms of pure principle, the world being too much with him. An abolitionist who could say, as did Charles K. Whipple, that the principles of morality and religion remain undisturbed by our private exigency, was likely to be white—that is, a person with a less urgent "private exigency."

In their ranks the abolitionists had some question marks. Like any other reform the crusade had its component of deviant personalities who found in it a release for private devils. The movement also had its universal reformers, men who, like Garrison, embraced several causes concurrently, thus diluting their abolitionism. And finally the movement had its summer soldiers who after a season disappeared in the shadows. Impulses to withdraw from the movement were numerous, ranging from a waning sympathy for the slave to a desire to concentrate on making enough money to put one's sons through college. . . .

Following the national division in 1840, the immediate question facing the Negro leaders was whether to adopt a go-it-alone policy, relying exclusively on all-Negro agencies. The issue came to the fore in May 1840 when a group of Connecticut Negroes, meeting in Hartford, recommended that a national convention of black men be held in New Haven in September. . . .

The argument as to the desirability of all-Negro reform societies did not end in 1840; indeed, it never ended in antebellum America. But as concerns the abolitionist movement, the great majority of Negroes preferred to act in concert with whites. The colored convention of 1848, held in Cleveland, recommended that Negroes join white abolitionist societies wherever possible. If, however, Negroes had no choice other than to organize societies, they should do so "without exclusiveness." Hence after 1840, Negro abolitionists continued to participate in the general societies, in many instances holding high office. In 1847 Frederick Douglass became president of the New England Anti-Slavery Society; Robert Purvis served as president of the Pennsylvania Society from 1845 to 1850, declining a sixth term; and Charles Lenox Remond held similar office in the Essex Anti-Slavery Society for a like length of time.

Fortunately for the abolition crusade, a number of able Negro recruits swelled the ranks around 1840, most of them former slaves. Free-born or slave-born, the Negroes who became active abolitionists were generally the most able men in the group, the cream of the crop. For although the Negroes in general favored the antislavery movement, not all of them took part in it. . . .

Obviously not all Negroes had two of the most essential qualities requisite to a black reformer—the will to activism and a full readiness to risk personal assault. Many Negroes were outwardly apathetic, their indifference a shield against a hostile world. Their bystander behavior was a form of survival insurance in a social order that denied them legal and political equality.

A Negro abolitionist might not be called upon to stop the mouths of lions, but he ran risks exceeding those of his white counterpart. When William Lloyd Garrison and Frederick Douglass appeared at the courthouse in Harrisburg, Pennsylvania, on August 8, 1847, to hold a meeting, no attempt was made to molest Garrison—indeed, he was listened to with marked attention and respect. But when Douglass arose there were loud catcalls, followed by a barrage of rotten eggs and brickbats and an explosion of firecrackers. As Douglass observed later, a hated opinion is not always in sight whereas a hated color is. Lecturing in Buck and Montgomery counties in Pennsylvania in the spring of 1845, Charles Lenox Remond wrote that mobs and rumors of mobs were to be expected. Such disorderly and mischief-bent groups had a penchant for Negro properties; in the outbreak of violence against the abolitionists in New York in July 1834, the more than twenty houses leveled to the ground all belonged to Negroes.

Some light-skinned Negroes, not caring to battle against discrimination, passed for white. Some who were Negroes in the South became white upon crossing the Mason-Dixon line. The "colored white," as James McCune Smith called them, were numerous in New York State; six of Smith's acquaintances at The New York African Free School crossed over in 1826, as did ten of Peter Clark's schoolmates in Cincinnati. Negroes believed that as a rule a swarthy person who was hostile to blacks was likely to be a "passer."

Generally those Negroes who were themselves inactive in the movement held a high regard for those who were. This esteem for black movers and shakers reflected a familiar process of identification re-enforced by one of the universal factors in man's experience—a homage to men of mark. For those who had the wish to be active abolitionists but who lacked the will, one enterprising business firm furnished a substitute of sorts. It produced lithograph portraits of black reformers Delany, Douglass, Garnet, and Remond, advertising the portraits as highly suitable for hanging in the parlor.

The most notable of the hero figures who emerged so providentially in the 1840's were former slaves. In most instances their freedom had been self-won, either by flight or purchase. In fewer cases their freedom came from others, either from relatives or friends who purchased it or from kindly or conscience-stricken masters. . . .

Former slaves proved a godsend to the cause. The Western Anti-Slavery Society reported that volunteer agents Harmon Bealer and his brother,

Halliday, had received their commissions not from the society but from God by virtue of their skin color and their experience of "the depth and damning wickedness of American slavery." Writing in 1850, William Lloyd Garrison ranked such figures as Henry Bibb, William Wells Brown, and Frederick Douglass with the ablest speakers in the movement, and "the best qualified to address the public on the subject of slavery." While not the only black abolitionists emerging in the 1840's, this trio does provide a suggestive portrait of their colleagues of color, illustrating procedures that were commonly employed. . . .

The most influential of the former slaves who joined the abolitionist forces was Frederick Douglass, who ran away from his Maryland master in 1838, settling in New Bedford, Massachusetts. In August 1841, while attending an abolitionist meeting at Nantucket, he was called upon to speak. His sentences were somewhat halting, but William Lloyd Garrison, who followed him, used them as a text for a stirring speech. After the meeting Douglass was approached by John A. Collins, general agent of the Massachusetts Anti-Slavery Society, asking him to become a lecturer. Believing that the public was "itching" to "hear a colored man speak, particularly a slave," Collins had been on the lookout for someone like Douglass.

From the outset Douglass exceeded the highest hopes of his abolitionist employers. He revealed a flair for dramatic utterance: "I appear before the immense assembly this evening as a thief and a robber," ran his opening remarks at a meeting of the Massachusetts Society in January 1842. "I stole this head, these limbs, this body from my master, and ran off with them." Three months later, when Douglass spoke at the annual meeting of the New England Society, a newspaper editor wrote that he had seldom heard a better speech as to language and manner—"the appropriateness of his elocution and gesticulation, and the grammatical accuracy of his sentences."

Fortunately for Douglass, his companions on the reform circuit in his formative years were likely to be good speakers with well-stocked minds. He could learn much from a figure like Wendell Phillips, who had deserted the bar and turned his back on a political career to cast his lot with the reformers. Philips's oratorical abilities were unsurpassed in nineteenth-century America, entitling him to be called "abolition's golden trumpet."

Douglass, however, was not one likely to be overlooked on the public platform, no matter what the company. From his first weeks with Collins, he was a drawing card. His voice struck the ear pleasantly, and as he gained experience he capitalized on it to the fullest. Melodious and strong, it varied in speed and pitch according to its use, whether to convey wit, sarcasm, argument, or invective. A first-rate speaking voice was not Douglass's only asset—he caught the eye, a man people would come to see. Six feet tall, broad-shouldered, his hair long (as was the custom) and neatly parted on the side, his eyes deep-set and steady, nose well formed, lips full, and skin bronze-colored, he looked like someone destined for the platform or pulpit.

Not relying solely on nature, Douglass had something to say. In his first weeks as a traveling agent and lecturer, he devoted himself to a simple narration of his experiences before freedom. From a description of slavery he began to go into a more direct denunciation of it. Gradually in his public appearances he broadened his subject matter, attacking the church for its timidity on slavery, demanding its abolition in the District of Columbia, and criticizing the annexation of Texas.

In 1845 Douglass added to his growing prominence by the publication of a book describing his life as a slave, *Narrative of the Life of Frederick Douglass*. Storytelling in tone, it was of absorbing interest in its sensitive descriptions of persons and places, including a sharply etched portrait of a slave-breaker named Edward Covey. Boosted by good press notices and reviews, the *Narrative* became a best-seller on two continents, over thirty thousand copies being sold in five years.

Douglass's biography was but one of the nearly one hundred such slave narratives published in book form. These autobiographies and biographies of former bondmen loomed large in the campaign literature of abolitionism, furnishing propaganda of considerable proportions. . . .

Slave narratives made a deep impression in the North, most readers finding their testimony quite persuasive. To Giles B. Stebbins the narrative by Douglass was "a voice coming up from the prison-house, speaking like a thousand-voiced psalm." Another reader said that she had wept over *Oliver Twist*, that her tears had moistened whole chapters of Eugene Sue's *Mysteries of Paris*, but that Douglass's narrative had "entered so deep into the chambers of my soul, as to entirely close the safety valve." In December 1855 Lewis Tappan wrote Douglass that his wife had read "your history" over and over again: "Its contents will be laid up in our hearts.". . .

Harriet Beecher Stowe praised slave narratives for the vigor, shrewdness, and originality that their characters exhibited, and for their clear portrayal of the slave's own viewpoint. Well might the author of *Uncle Tom's Cabin* speak such words of commendation. Far more than she could ever sense, the vast audience that responded to her classic tale of Uncle Tom was an audience that had already been conditioned and prepared by the life stories of runaway slaves. For, as the knowledgeable Frederick Law Olmsted pointed out, most Northerners got their impressions of slavery from having read slave narratives. Hence if President Lincoln could greet Mrs. Stowe as "the little lady who made this big war," certainly some of this credit might be shared by those former slaves whose stories had been dinned in the public mind, creating an adverse image of slavery that helped make possible the emergence of a Mrs. Stowe and an Abraham Lincoln.

Selection 2

Frederick Douglass

Richard Conniff

The stirring story of Frederick Douglass is an essential part of the history of American slavery and of those who resisted it. This selection reprints a biographical sketch of Douglass's life by Richard Conniff, which appeared in Smithsonian *magazine in 1995, marking the one-hundredth anniversary of Douglass's death.*

Reprinted from Richard Conniff, "Frederick Douglass Always Knew He Was Meant to Be Free," *Smithsonian*, February 1995. Reprinted with permission from the author.

*T*he "uproarious and happy boy" then known as Frederick Bailey was 6 years old on the morning his grandmother Betsey took his hand and walked him 12 miles into his life as a slave. It was a bright August day on the Eastern Shore of Maryland, hot and humid, he later wrote. At times, his grandmother had to tote him on her shoulders; at times, he walked beside her, imitating her practiced stride. When the dirt road took them into the woods, he clutched her hand at the sight of monstrous, staring figures, which turned out to be tree stumps.

Real terrors lay ahead that day in 1824, but about them his grandmother maintained "the reserve and solemnity of a priestess." She had been through these forced separations too many times before: like the other grandchildren she reared, Frederick had been someone else's property since birth, hers only on loan. In mid-afternoon they arrived at the Chesapeake Bay plantation where "old master" lived, and she set Frederick among the other slave children. Then, not wanting to prolong the sorrow of parting, she slipped away from him without a word. The boy wept himself to sleep that night, torn from "the only home I ever had." It was "my first introduction to the realities of slavery."

By the standards of slavery, Frederick was often to get favored treatment over the next 14 years. But the realities were to include hunger so sharp that he had to vie with the dog for table scraps, and cold so intense that his bare, calloused feet cracked open. Like other slaves, he was systematically denied family, education, even the knowledge of his own birth date. He saw his fellow slaves savagely beaten. He suffered the pencil-thick scars of the whip on his own back. These realities of slavery were an outrage Frederick refused to accept almost from that first day, and the struggle begun then would in time anger and inspire millions of Americans.

He called himself Frederick Douglass after he escaped to freedom at the age of 20, and he soon established himself in the antislavery movement as a fearless enemy of the slave owner and the hypocrite.

"What, to the American slave, is your Fourth of July?" he asked, in one impassioned speech, at a time when more than three million African-Americans remained in bondage. "To him, your celebration is a sham . . . your shouts of liberty and equality, hollow mockery. . . . There is not a nation on the Earth guilty of practices more shocking and bloody than are the people of the United States at this very hour."

White Americans came to his talks by the thousands, sometimes just to gawk or jeer. But they also listened, if only because Douglass shrewdly cast himself in a classic American mold, as an almost miraculously self-made man. To audiences in the decades before the Civil War, it was as if this slave—deemed a "chattel" by law—had leapt to the speaker's podium straight from his grandmother's cabin at Tuckahoe Creek. "*It* could speak," Douglass remarked mordantly. In truth, he spoke with wit, erudition and richness of voice to rival Daniel Webster's.

His physical presence was also commanding. He was more than six feet tall, with olive brown skin, a shock of hair slanting across his broad forehead, and flashing, wounded eyes. The feminist Elizabeth Cady Stanton vividly remembered the first time she heard Douglass speak, at an antislavery meeting in Boston, where he swept his listeners from laughter to tears on the tide of his voice. "All the other speakers seemed tame after Frederick Douglass," Stanton wrote. "He stood there like an African prince, majestic in his wrath."

When the voice was stilled by death 100 years ago, Frederick Douglass vanished for a time from history. Even the estimable Samuel Eliot Morison found no room to include him in his *Oxford History of The American People*, published in 1965. But since then Douglass has been rediscovered in three substantial biographies, and on television and stage. Yale University is methodically publishing the multivolume *Frederick Douglass Papers*, and the Library of America last year issued *Frederick Douglass: Autobiographies*, an annotated collection. To mark the centennial of his death, the Smithsonian's National Portrait Gallery is now presenting the exhibition "Majestic in His Wrath: The Life of Frederick Douglass."

It was an astonishing life. "I feel greatly embarrassed when I attempt to address an audience of white people . . . it makes me tremble," he declared to a group of Massachusetts abolitionists in one of his earliest speeches. But it didn't stop him from adding: "Prejudice against color is stronger North than South; it hangs around my neck like a heavy weight."

Before there was a civil rights movement, before the word "racism" itself existed, Douglass led the movement that desegregated the schools of Rochester, New York, where he and his wife raised their family. Long before Rosa Parks refused to give up her seat to a white man on a segregated bus in Alabama, Douglass had to be dragged bodily from a whites-only railroad car in Massachusetts—and he tore the seat out with him. Before the assassinations of Malcolm X and Martin Luther King Jr., Douglass was repeatedly attacked and beaten by mobs yelling "Kill the damned nigger!" Repeatedly he fought back, and lived.

Nor did the pressing issues of race prevent him from advocating human liberty at large. At the Seneca Falls, New York, convention of 1848, where the feminist movement was born, Frederick Douglass was the only man to vote for women's suffrage. The newspaper he had founded the previous year proudly declared, "Right is of no sex, truth is of no color."

In time, the tireless voice of Frederick Douglass would help lay the groundwork for the emancipation of slaves in the Civil War and for the 15th Amendment to the Constitution, which, on paper, guaranteed black men the right to vote. But he would also live to see the failure of his grand vision that freedom and the vote would win blacks an equal place with whites in American life. He lived to see his own achievements tainted with racial humiliation and sometimes misused not to advance other blacks, as he had dreamed, but to put them down.

The plantation where his grandmother left young Frederick Bailey that afternoon in 1824 was one of Maryland's most prosperous—10,000 acres of flat, fertile land on which the Lloyd family had settled in the 1660s. The "great house" still stands and looks much as it did when Frederick knew it. In the cellar, most of the steel bars have fallen out of the window of a small, dank room. But upstairs, huge tarnished mirrors still hang where they once reflected the face of Jefferson Davis after the fall of the Confederacy, and of Frederick Douglass on his return visit as an elder statesman. Until her death in 1993, a member of the Lloyd family still lived there.

It is a handsome Federal-style house at the end of a long, tree-lined avenue, a few miles outside Easton. The sight of its "solemn grandeur," Douglass later wrote, "was a treat to my young and gradually opening mind." Frederick was already an unusual child. He became the companion and, surreptitiously, a careful student of the Lloyd family's youngest boy. The great house, not the slave quarters, was to be his chosen element.

His mind also opened quickly to the horrific gulf between these worlds. Apart from cold and hunger, Douglass suffered little personal mistreatment on the Lloyd plantation. But in *Narrative of the Life of Frederick Douglass,* published in 1845, he recounted the violence all around him.

One incident burned itself into the child's memory. Frederick was the property not of the Lloyds themselves but of their head manager, Captain Aaron Anthony, the man his grandmother had spoken of as "old master." His modest brick house also still stands, on the plantation farm road, but the site of the kitchen building where Frederick slept is now just a faint depression in the grass.

Just before dawn one morning, from his bed on the rough floor of a pantry there, Frederick heard a noise. Peering out through cracks in the coarse boards of the door, he saw his Aunt Hester with "old master." She was a tall, well-formed 15-year-old, and from motives Douglass later described simply as "abhorrent," "old master" had forbidden her to court a young slave of her own age. She disobeyed, and now "old master" tied her crossed hands to a beam in the kitchen ceiling and tore open her unblemished back with a cowhide whip. Douglass wrote that she screamed "Have mercy! Oh! have mercy!" but "her piercing cries seemed only to increase his fury."

With constrained emotion, Douglass commented that a slave woman was routinely vulnerable to the "caprice and passion of her owner," and that marriage was allowed to have no meaning among slaves. But he did not pursue the tormenting idea that Captain Anthony may have subjected Hester's older sister Harriet to the same monstrous treatment. Harriet was Frederick's mother. For much of his childhood, she was a field hand on a distant farm, and the memory of her infrequent visits remained achingly fresh.

She died before he was 10, without confirming or denying the rumor in the slave quarters that Captain Anthony was his father. Slavery, he wrote, "left me without an intelligible beginning in the world."

Douglass' mother became an almost mythic figure for him. He attributed the love of letters for which he became famous largely to this "unprotected and uncultivated" field hand, who had somehow learned to read. He also credited his grandmother's valuable example. Though illiterate, she had won a measure of independence by her practical skills at farming and at manufacturing the long drift nets used for harvesting shad and herring from the Tuckahoe. Recognizing something special in Frederick, perhaps including kinship, Captain Anthony's family soon spirited him away from the brutality of the plantation to be a house servant for their in-laws in Baltimore.

There, Sophia Auld started to teach the 8-year-old his letters, but her husband quickly stopped her. "Learning would spoil the best nigger in the world," he said, as if Frederick could not hear every word. Education "would forever unfit him to be a slave. . . . If you learn him how to read, he'll want to know how to write; and this accomplished, he'll be running away with himself." Douglass later described it as "the first decidedly antislavery lecture" he ever heard.

The boy set out, against all odds, to educate himself. Put to work in a local shipyard, he noticed that the carpenters chalked each sawed-out timber with initials, like "sf" for "starboard forward," indicating its eventual placement in the ship. Copying these letters on a fence board, he challenged his white playmates to beat his penmanship and thus inveigled them into helping him learn the alphabet.

He also listened as they memorized speeches for school from a standard anthology of the day, *The Columbian Orator.* Words like "emancipation" (albeit of Catholics in Ireland) and "equality" (albeit of white Americans with their European rivals) fired his imagination. When he had accumulated 50 cents from polishing boots, he bought a secondhand copy for himself. There he found the three-page "Dialogue Between A Master and Slave," in which the slave argues that kind treatment can never compensate for depriving a man of liberty. When the master declares that "Providence" has made him a slave, the slave replies that Providence "has also given me legs to escape with."

Frederick would carry with him the message, the rhetorical method and his copy of *The Columbian Orator* when he made his own escape eight years later. Using the borrowed papers of a free black seaman, he took a train north.

By 1841, the fugitive Frederick Bailey had become "Frederick Douglass" (a name borrowed from a poem by Sir Walter Scott). He had married Anna Murray, a free black woman from Baltimore who had helped him escape, and they were living in Massachusetts. He shoveled coal and dug cellars for a living, and stoked his wrath against slavery by reading William Lloyd Garrison's abolitionist newspaper, *The Liberator.* He also preached abolition to other blacks in his local church.

Garrison, the leader of the antislavery movement, heard Douglass speak in Nantucket in 1841; the group that Garrison led immediately hired him as a lecturer. For the struggling antislavery movement of the 1840s, Douglass was, in his own words, a "brand new fact," the first fugitive-slave lecturer: "Up to that time, a colored man was deemed a fool who confessed himself a runaway slave, not only because of the danger to which he exposed himself of being retaken, but because it was a confession of very *low* origin!"

Frederick Douglass was unafraid to say just how low slavery had set him, and he made a virtue of overcoming it. He had spent the years before his escape working both in Baltimore and in the fields of the Eastern Shore. He could recount the horrors of slavery in the most moving language many listeners had ever heard, in a voice that could be conversational one moment, and the next, "roll out full and deep" as organ music. "I have come to tell you something about slavery—what I know of it, as I have felt it," he began. Other abolitionists could not speak "from experience; they cannot refer you to a back covered with scars, as I can; . . . my blood has sprung out as the lash embedded itself in my flesh." And he added, from a deeper vein of emotion, "the whip we can bear without a murmur, compared to the idea of separation . . . the agony of the mother when parting from her children."

When critics doubted the stories he told, Douglass took the extraordinary risk of revealing his true identity and the names of his tormentors in his 1845 *Narrative*. Anyone could now go to the very fields where young Frederick Bailey had been hired out to Edward Covey, a tenant farmer and reputed slave breaker, and ask the truth about what Douglass called "the turning point" in his career as a slave.

Even today, it's possible for a curious visitor to find the farm, where another tenant farmer now grows soybeans and winter wheat, and stand looking out on the same turbid waters of the Chesapeake Bay. Here, in despair at the age of 15, Frederick envied the white sails of ships freely passing by and begged for deliverance: "O God, save me! . . . Let me be free!" Soon afterward, in a barn here, Covey attempted once too often to whip him. Knocked sprawling on the stable floor, Frederick felt his spirit revive: "I resolved to fight; and . . . I seized Covey hard by the throat." They grappled for two hours, and in the end the slave had made it clear "that the white man who expected to succeed in whipping, must also succeed in killing me." He was never whipped again.

The account of his life in slavery was so detailed and accurate that Frederick Douglass faced renewed danger of being kidnapped back to the South. On the advice of his mentors in the antislavery movement, he sailed for Europe— and was nearly heaved overboard en route by proslavery passengers who did not want him to lecture. The incident made headlines on his arrival, and his lectures over the next 21 months enabled him to return to the United States as an international celebrity—and, literally, as his own man. British supporters raised $700 to buy his freedom from the Auld family. They also allowed him for the first time in his life to eat a meal, register at a hotel, go to church or visit a friend free from the dismal American refrain, "We don't allow niggers in here!"

Back in this country, Douglass moved his wife and their children away from Massachusetts, where white abolitionist leaders still regarded him more as a hired performer than as their peer. He established his own newspaper, the *North Star*, in Rochester, New York. He and Anna made their new home a refuge for the steady traffic of runaway slaves who were following the underground railroad to Canada. A white Englishwoman named Julia Griffiths managed the publishing business during his frequent absences on the lecture circuit. She also became his intellectual companion, and their appearance together on the streets of New York City drew obscene shouts and a physical assault. The friendship developed as Douglass and his wife were drifting apart emotionally. As he moved out into the world of politics and letters, Anna Douglass withdrew into child-rearing and her garden. Books were his private passion, but she could read only two words: "Fred" and "Douglass."

The voice of Frederick Douglass grew more powerful through the violent decade leading up to the Civil War. Most abolitionists abhorred the U.S. Constitution, which treated the slave as three-fifths of a human being. But Douglass now declared that the constitutional oath to "secure the Blessings of Liberty to ourselves and our Posterity" was, in fact, an oath to free the slaves. He advocated emancipation within the political system, and despite his sympathies, he refrained from openly advocating a slave rebellion. Better than most abolitionists, he could imagine the bloody consequences for blacks.

Seeing the wild impracticality of the scheme, he refused to join his friend John Brown in a suicidal raid on the federal arsenal at Harpers Ferry in 1859. The raid, of course, failed. One of the martyrs of the event, Shields Green, had traveled with Douglass to meet with Brown before the raid, and when Douglass resolved to leave, Green stayed behind. "I b'lieve I'll go wid de ole man," he said mildly. His death and the others at Harpers Ferry aroused the nation. Douglass later remarked, "I could live for the slave; John Brown could *die* for him." He was soon battering his way to the podium through a crowd of racist hecklers to advocate death to slave-holders, death to slave-catchers, and war.

"I believe in agitation," he declared, and the Civil War did not change that. When President Lincoln found it expedient to wage war to preserve the Union, not to end slavery, Douglass denounced the Administration for "moral blindness . . . and helpless imbecility." He helped maintain the political pressure which, together with military expediency (and moral vision), induced Lincoln to issue the Emancipation Proclamation on January 1, 1863. Douglass called it "a day for poetry and song," wept with fellow abolitionists—and continued to agitate. He set to work recruiting more than a hundred men, including two of his own sons, to make the emancipation of slaves a reality under the banner of the U.S. Army's newly formed 54th Massachusetts, the first black regiment. Then Douglass went to the White House to agitate on behalf of black soldiers.

Lincoln greeted Douglass warmly and listened to his complaints: black soldiers got half the pay of white soldiers, could not become officers and faced the added peril of being put to death if captured by the Confederates.

Some of the soldiers Douglass had recruited had already fought and died at Fort Wagner; prisoners from the 54th had been sold into slavery. Douglass came away impressed with Lincoln's sincerity and convinced he would act—always within the limits of practical politics—to protect the black soldier.

Back on the lecture circuit, Douglass remained the conscience of the war effort, keeping his listeners focused on the high moral ground of freedom versus slavery. "No war but an Abolition war," he declared in 1864, when Lincoln and the Union wavered, "no peace but an Abolition peace; liberty for all, chains for none; the black man a soldier in war; a laborer in peace; a voter at the South as well as at the North. . . . Such, fellow-citizens, is my idea for the mission of this war."

The decades after the war brought Douglass honors but seemed to take away his spirit. He worked tirelessly for the passage in 1870 of the 15th Amendment to the Constitution. Black men now had the vote, but that did not prevent them from being "mobbed, beaten, shot, stabbed, hanged, burnt . . . the target of all that is malignant in the North and all that is murderous in the South." His own home in Rochester was destroyed by arson in 1872. The postwar years saw the use of every imaginable device, legal or otherwise, to keep blacks from exercising their new rights.

Douglass moved his family to Washington, D.C. in search of a public office worthy of his abilities. As a 19-year-old slave he'd had the audacity to dream out loud among his free black friends that he would some day become a U.S. Senator. Now he became president of the Freedman's Bank, just in time to take the blame when it defaulted on the meager savings of its black account holders. He went on to become Marshal of the District of Columbia, a job that gave Douglass status and the power to employ blacks. But this appointment of the most prominent black man in America also served as a screen for the decision of the Hayes Administration to withdraw vital military protection of blacks from some areas of the South.

In 1877 Frederick and Anna Douglass bought a beautiful house on a hilltop in the rural southeastern corner of the city. He had the satisfaction of knowing that a previous owner had tried to prevent the property from ever being owned by blacks or Irish; from his porch, he could look down across the Anacostia River onto the great dome of the Capitol. That same autumn, he went back to the Eastern Shore and located the site of his grandmother's slave cabin, near a familiar-looking cedar tree. Douglass scooped up some of the soil to scatter at his new home, which he called Cedar Hill.

Having triumphed in the great fight over slavery, Douglass could afford to be magnanimous with his white connections on the Eastern Shore—too magnanimous for his critics. He sipped Madeira on the porch of the great house of the Lloyd plantation and spoke of "gratitude" at his reunion with the Lloyd family. He had an emotional meeting with Thomas Auld, one of his former owners, now on his deathbed; he expressed regret that he had publicly accused Auld of "cruel" treatment of his grandmother, whom he had mistakenly thought was one of Auld's slaves. Auld wept and told him in turn that "had I been in your place, I should have done as you did."

Anna Douglass died in 1882, and two years later Douglass married Helen Pitts, a clerk in his office. She was a white woman, and his own family took the marriage as a repudiation of blacks. Her father, who had been an abolitionist, also rejected the marriage, refusing to allow Douglass into his house. Of their outside critics, Douglass inquired with simple dignity, "What business has the world with the color of my wife?" Helen remarked, "I was not afraid to marry the man I loved because of his color." It was a happy marriage, and the criticism did not prevent Douglass from being named Minister to Haiti in 1889.

Near the end of his life, Douglass also formed a vital friendship with another woman. Ida B. Wells, a young black writer in Memphis, had published a detailed account of the extent to which the lynching of blacks had become a form of social control in the South. "What a revelation of existing conditions," Douglass remarked, when he read her work. Like the younger Douglass, Wells fearlessly named names, places and motives. When they met, they would also share intellectual interests and a combative zeal. Wells later recalled going to lunch with him one day after a speech. She mentioned that a nearby restaurant did not serve blacks. "Mr. Douglass, in his vigorous way, grasped my arm and said, 'Come, let's go there' . . . and we sauntered into the Boston Oyster House as if it were an everyday occurrence, cocked and primed for a fight if necessary." Fortunately for the restaurant, Douglass received a hero's welcome.

Another time, when Wells was a guest in the Douglass home, she received an invitation to undertake a lecture tour in Britain. Douglass en-

couraged her to go, saying, "You go my child; you are the one to go, for you have the story to tell." It was, Wells wrote, "like an open door in a stone wall" of public indifference. She passed through it and carried her mentor's struggle for racial equality well into the 20th century.

Douglass himself found a new opening in his protégée's example. In January 1894, full of his old majesty and wrath, he delivered one of his greatest speeches at a church in Washington, D.C. In "The Lessons of the Hour," Douglass carefully dissected the ways prejudice worked to keep blacks down. "A white man has but to blacken his face and commit a crime," he said, "to have some Negro lynched in his stead. An abandoned woman has only to start to cry that she has been insulted by a black man, to have him arrested and summarily murdered by the mob." More than 850 Southern blacks had been executed by officials or lynched by mobs from 1890 to 1892

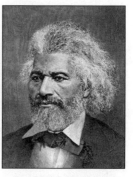

Frederick Douglass

alone. The usual trumped-up charge of sexual assault on white women, he said, was shrewdly calculated to drive from the suspect "all sympathy and all fair play." Moreover, it was a charge not merely against the individual but against all blacks: "When a white man steals, robs or murders, his crime is visited upon his own head alone. . . . When [a black man] commits a crime the whole race is made to suffer."

The so-called race problem, Douglass said,

cannot be solved by keeping the Negro poor, degraded, ignorant and half-starved. . . . It cannot be solved by keeping the wages of the laborer back by fraud. . . . It cannot be done by ballot-box stuffing . . . or by confusing Negro voters by cunning devices. It can, however, be done, and very easily done. . . . Let the white people of the North and South conquer their prejudices. . . .

Time and strength are not equal to the task before me,

he concluded.

> But could I be heard by this great nation, I would call to mind the sublime and glorious truths with which, at its birth, it saluted a listening world. . . . Put away your race prejudice. Banish the idea that one class must rule over another. Recognize . . . that the rights of the humblest citizen are as worthy of protection as are those of the highest, and . . . your Republic will stand and flourish forever.

A little more than a year later, as he recounted for his wife the events of the women's rights rally he had attended that afternoon, Douglass sank to the floor of their home and died. His body was taken to Rochester for burial.

The gravestone is curiously generic for a man whose life was full of well-chosen words, and historians now know that the year of his birth, which eluded him till the end, is wrong. The stone reads: "To the memory of Frederick Douglass— 1817–1895." A visitor paying homage might think, instead, of the newspaper called the *North Star* that a visionary, headstrong young man once published in the city. The title came from a fugitive-slave song. Frederick Douglass could sing the words with a truth matched by few Americans before him or after: "I kept my eye on the bright north star, and thought of liberty."

Sojourner Truth

Elizabeth Shafer

One of the most eloquent and prominent black women to crusade against slavery was Sojourner Truth, who was born into slavery in New York about 1797 and lived through most of the nineteenth century, dying in 1883. Her life was notable for her religious fervor, her tireless fight against slavery (and, after the Civil War, segregation), her advocacy of women's rights, and her goal of promoting human brotherhood. Her story is told in the following biographical sketch by Elizabeth Shafer.

Reprinted from Elizabeth Shafer, "Sojourner Truth: 'A Self-Made Woman,'" *American History Illustrated*, January 1974. This article is reprinted from *American History Illustrated* magazine with the permission of PRIMEDIA Special Interest Publications (History Group), copyright American History Illustrated magazine.

She was over 6 feet tall, rawboned, black, and—for the first forty years of her life—a slave. The next forty-six years she spent becoming, as she said, "a self-made woman."

Sojourner Truth was a powerful and eloquent speaker against slavery and for women's rights, lecturing in twenty-one states and the District of Columbia from 1843 until 1878, when she was 81. She was a friend and co-worker of the great names among the abolitionists and fighters for women's rights. She was a guest of Harriet Beecher Stowe, who celebrated her as "The Libyan Sibyl" in *The Atlantic Monthly*; and she was received at the White House by Abraham Lincoln.

Those who heard her speak and sing in her deep, strong voice never forgot her nor her shrewd wit, simple wisdom, and droll humor.

Mrs. Stowe wrote of the "power and sweetness in that great warm soul and that vigorous frame," adding, " I do not recall ever to have been conversant with anyone who had more of that silent and subtle power which we call personal presence than this woman." From the sister of the famous preacher and spellbinder, Henry Ward Beecher, this was the ultimate compliment.

She was born in 1797 in Ulster County, New York, the twelfth child of Bomefree and Mama Bett, slaves of a Dutchman, Charles Hardenbergh. (New York and New Jersey were the last of the northern states to keep slaves; the other states had abolished slavery following the Revolution.) When Sojourner was about 11, Hardenbergh died, and "Isabella," as she was then called, was sold at an auction of "slaves, horses, and other cattle" to a Yankee storekeeper, John Nealy. Nealy paid a hundred dollars for the gawky child and a herd of sheep.

Years later she was to say, "Now the war begun." For Isabella spoke only Low Dutch, and the Nealys spoke only English. When her father learned how they beat her, he begged a local tavernkeeper to buy her. She lived eighteen months with the Scrivers, working in the house and in the fields and serving customers in the tavern. She was 13 now, and already 6 feet tall.

She was happy those brief months, but in 1810 John J. Dumont of nearby New Paltz bought her for $300. (As a sturdy young woman, her value was going up.) Dumont was a large slaveholder by New York standards, keeping ten slaves. They all lived in a large room behind the kitchen called the slave kitchen.

Isabella was a good worker—too good in the opinion of her fellow slaves, who called her "white man's nigger." She fell in love with "Catlin's Robert," as slaves were identified in those days. But Robert's master beat him terribly and forced him to marry one of the Catlin slaves. Isabella, in turn, was married to old Thomas, one of Dumont's slaves. They were to have five children.

While she was chiefly a house slave for Mrs. Dumont, she also worked in the fields. She would put her latest baby in a basket, tie a rope to the handles, and suspend it in a tree, where a small child was set to swinging it.

Meanwhile, New York State had passed a new law. All slaves born before July 4, 1799, were to be freed on July 4, 1827. All slaves younger than 28 were "free"—but had to work as unpaid servants until the boys were 28, the girls 25. Because she was such a faithful worker, Dumont promised Isabella he would free her a year early. But in the summer of 1826, he refused to fulfill his promise.

Isabella remembered the Quaker, Levi Rowe, who had said to her once, years before, "Thou should not be a slave." She took her youngest child, Sophia, leaving the others at Dumont's with Thomas, and walked to Rowe's farm.

Rowe was dying, but he sent her on to Mr. and Mrs. Isaac S. Van Wagener. When Dumont followed, demanding his property, the Van Wageners agreed to buy Isabella's services for the rest of the year for twenty dollars, and the child's services until she was 25 for five dollars. However, they instructed Isabella not to call them "master" and "mistress," and she was treated as a paid servant.

Once she became homesick and almost agreed to accompany Dumont back to his farm, but as she was heading for the gate she heard a voice: "Not another step!" She quickly returned to her room, where she prayed for strength. Her mother had long ago taught her the Lord's prayer in Low Dutch, and had told her solemnly, "There is a God, who hears and sees you." It was at this crisis in her life that Isabella discovered Jesus. But she was afraid, she said afterwards, that the whites would discover that Jesus was her friend and take him from her as they had taken everything else, so she kept her new friend a secret.

There was a small island in a nearby stream. Here she wove a wall of willows and conducted private talks with God and Jesus. She was to continue this very personal dialog for the rest of her life.

On "freedom day," July 4, 1827, Isaac and Maria Van Wagener conducted a small private ceremony, reading from the Bible. Maria kissed

Isabella on the cheek. "Take thy Sophia, too, into freedom," she said, handing her the child. They agreed upon wages for her labor, and Isabella and the child lived with them for another two years.

Her son, Peter, had disappeared, and Isabella finally learned that Dumont had sold the boy to a family whose daughter had taken Peter south to Alabama. This meant, of course, that he would never be free.

When Isabella spoke to Mrs. Dumont about Peter, the woman jeered at her. Isabella drew herself to her full height and cried in her deep voice, "I'll have my child again!" She was to recall afterwards, "When I spoke to my mistress that way, I felt so tall within. I felt as if the power of a nation was within me."

An abolitionist advised her to go to a certain Quaker for help. She arrived at night, and was given a room of her own with a tall poster bed. She remembered later, "I was scared when she left me alone with that great white bed. I had never been in a real bed in my life. It never came into my mind she could mean me to sleep on it. So I just camped under it, and I slept pretty well there on the floor."

Next morning, she took her case to the grand jury at Kingston. This was the first of many battles she was to undertake and win. The woman who was to become Sojourner Truth believed in the power of the law and used it effectively for herself and her people.

Peter was returned to her, and the two went to New York City in 1829. But the boy fell into bad company and she was forced to send him to sea. He sent her several letters, saying he had received none of her. Then he stopped writing; she never heard from him again.

While in New York she learned English, which she always spoke with a heavy Dutch accent, and worked as a domestic for various families and for a religious group called The Kingdom. But in 1843, she had a vision. She took her clothes, some bread and cheese, and twenty-five cents for the ferry to Brooklyn. "I am no longer Isabella," she said. "I am Sojourner." But Sojourner what? She gave the matter some thought.

Remembering that a slave always took the name of her master, she said, "Oh, God, thou art my last master, and thy name is Truth, so shall Truth be my abiding name until I die."

And so, at 46, Sojourner Truth was born.

The year 1843 was a time of great religious revival. Reform was in the air. Abolitionists were calling for an end to slavery. Talk of women's rights would culminate in the first Women's Rights Convention at Seneca, New York, in 1848. Men and women were setting up religious communities. Camp meetings were held everywhere.

In her wanderings, Sojourner came upon her first camp meeting. She began to speak and sing at many such gatherings. Later, she advertised and conducted meetings of her own. Olive Gilbert, who was the first to help Sojourner put her story into print (*Narrative of Sojourner Truth: A Northern Slave,* 1850) commented, "All who have ever heard her sing . . . will probably remember it as long as they remember her."

At one such camp meeting, a group of rowdies threatened to disrupt the proceedings. Sojourner walked to one side, on a little knoll, and began to sing. The rowdies gathered around her, begging her to sing some more, and became quiet. They even laughed appreciatively when she told them, "Well, there are two congregations on this ground. It is written that the sheep shall be separated from the goats. The other preachers have the sheep, I have the goats. I have a few sheep among my goats, but they are very ragged." Both meetings went on without incident after that.

She met all the great figures of the abolition movement: Samuel Hill, Wendell Phillips, Parker Pillsbury, Frederick Douglass, and William Lloyd Garrison. These men also worked with women in organizing the first women's rights convention.

Sojourner knew Lucretia Mott, Susan B. Anthony, Elizabeth Cady Stanton, and Lucy Stone. She was the only black delegate to the Worcester, Massachusetts, women's rights convention in 1850. Men jeered, newspapers called it the Hen Convention, and one minister even threatened to expel from his congregation any member daring to attend.

It was at this convention that Sojourner, ever the militant, asked, "If women want any rights more'n they've got, why don't they just take 'em and not be talking about it?"

She was a faithful fighter for all women's rights, but she drew the line at the current fad of wearing "bloomers." Recalling her days as a slave who got only a single length of cloth to cover her long frame and so had to stitch up the legs for modesty, she declared, "Tell *you*, I had enough of bloomers in them days!"

With the passage of the Fugitive Slave Act in 1850, the abolitionists redoubled their activities. Sojourner was invited to join them on their speaking tours.

She often traveled alone, in a borrowed buggy loaded with copies of her book, song sheets of her own composing, and copies of her photograph ("I sell the shadow to support the substance.") She would give the horse its head, saying, "God, you drive." It always seemed to turn out right. She would stop at a crossroads or in a village square, unfold the freedom banner which the Akron, Ohio, women's rights convention had given her, and speak and sing.

One of her own songs, eleven stanzas long, began:

> I am pleading for my people—
> A poor, down-trodden race,
> Who dwell in freedom's boasted land
> With no abiding place.
>
> I am pleading that my people
> May have their rights restored,
> For they have long been toiling
> And yet have no reward.

Uncle Tom's Cabin had received instant acclaim in 1852, and, wanting to meet the author, Sojourner appeared at Harriet Beecher Stowe's home in Andover, Massachusetts. Harriet was so taken with her visitor that she invited her to stay for several days.

"An audience was what she wanted," Harriet was to write later. "It mattered not whether high or low, learned or ignorant. She had things to say, and was ready to say them at all times, and to anyone."

In 1857 the *Dred Scott* decision ruled that a slave could not be a citizen, and that Congress had no power to exclude slavery from the western territories. This precipitated new abolitionist activity. Sojourner went into Indiana with Parker Pillsbury. It was during this speaking tour that a hostile doctor rose and demanded that she show her breasts to a group of women from the audience. He said, "Your voice is not the voice of a woman, it is the voice of a man, and we believe you are a man."

Silently, Sojourner Truth, now 60, undid her Quaker kerchief and opened her dress, displaying her breasts to the whole congregation. "It is not my shame but yours that I do this," she said.

Events began moving more swiftly now. In 1859, John Brown raided Harpers Ferry. In 1860, Lincoln was elected President. And by April 1861, Fort Sumter had been fired upon.

Josephine Griffing of Ohio asked Sojourner to accompany her on an anti-slavery lecture tour into Indiana, where Copperheads (pro-slavery forces) controlled the legislature. This was a dangerous undertaking, but Sojourner agreed at once. Two miles across the Ohio-Indiana border, she was arrested. Josephine got a court order for her release. Hecklers broke up their first meeting and they were taken into protective custody by a member of the Union home guard, who escorted them to Angola. Here, the Copperheads threatened to burn the building where Sojourner was to speak.

"Then I will speak upon the ashes," she said firmly.

The women of the town dressed her in a red, white, and blue shawl with a sash and apron to match. She wore a cap with a star, and a star on each shoulder.

Sojourner remembered:

When we were ready to go, they put me into a large, beautiful carriage with the captain and other gentlemen, all of whom were armed. The soldiers walked by our side and a long procession followed. As we neared the court house, looking out of the window I saw that the building was surrounded by a great crowd. I felt as I was going against the Philistines and I prayed the Lord to deliver me out of their hands. But when the rebels saw such a mighty army coming, they fled, and by the time we arrived they were scattered over the fields, looking like a flock of frightened crows, and not one was left but a small boy, who sat upon the fence, crying, "Nigger, nigger!"

The procession marched into the court house, everyone sang, and she spoke without interruption.

The tour was a triumph, but it exhausted her. She was ill for some time, and there were rumors she was dead. But the Emancipation Proclamation of January 1, 1863, heartened her; she declared that she must get well.

Slowly, over the years, she had been gathering her family about her in Battle Creek, Michigan— her daughters and grandsons Sammy and James, who sometimes acted as escorts on her journeys. When she was not lecturing, she earned her living as she always did, cooking, cleaning house, doing laundry, and caring for the sick.

Grandson James Caldwell had joined the Union Army now that they were accepting Negroes. At Thanksgiving in 1863, Sojourner visited the 1st Michigan Colored Infantry at Detroit, taking them donations of good things to eat. She taught them to sing her latest song, to the tune of *John Brown's Body:*

We are the valiant soldiers who've 'listed for
    the war;
We are fighting for the Union, we are fighting
    for the law;
We can shoot a rebel farther than a white man
    ever saw,
As we go marching on. . . .

From Detroit, she went to New York, speaking to Henry Ward Beecher's Brooklyn congregation at Plymouth Church. And on October 29, 1864, she met Abraham Lincoln at the White House. The President signed her "Book of Life," an autograph book containing the signatures of many of the most famous people of her time.

She found plenty to do in Washington. She

Sojourner Truth

spoke to the Colored Soldiers' Aid Society. She worked at Arlington Heights, Virginia as a counselor for the National Freedmen's Relief Association, and that autumn she was asked to help the surgeon in charge of the Freedmen's Hospital to "promote order, cleanliness, industry, and virtue among the patients."

Before the war, the streetcars in Washington had been segregated. After Lincoln signed a law outlawing discrimination in Washington public transportation, many conductors simply refused to stop for black passengers. One day Sojourner

Truth stood in the middle of the street and shouted three times at the top of her lungs, "I WANT TO RIDE!" She nearly panicked the horses, but she managed to get on, then refused to stand on the platform behind the horses, "I am a passenger and shall sit with the other passengers."

In a later incident, an irate conductor slammed her against the door, pushing her shoulder out of joint. Again, she went to court. The Freedmen's Bureau lawyer sued the company, the conductor lost his job, and from then on blacks rode the Washington streetcars.

In 1867, escorted by grandson Sammy, she traveled through western New York, seeking jobs for freed slaves. Journalist Theodore Tilton asked permission to write her life story. She replied, "I am not ready to be writ up yet, for I have still lots to accomplish." And in 1870 she set out on "the last great mission of her life"—petitioning Congress for free land for the former slaves. But Senator Charles Sumner, who had worked for passage of the bill, died. Then grandson Sammy fell ill and died. Sojourner herself suffered a stroke and a lengthy illness. The petition for free land failed, one of the few failures in her long and productive life.

In the nation's centennial year, she celebrated her eightieth birthday. Her paralysis had disappeared, her hair began to grow in black instead of its former gray, and as writers of the period commented, her deep voice had lost none of its power. When she was 81, she spoke in thirty-six different towns in her home state of Michigan. And in July of that year, she was one of three Michigan delegates to the 30th anniversary meeting of the Women's Rights Convention.

While her dream of free land had not been realized, she was to see 60,000 freedmen take up homesteads in Kansas by the end of 1879.

Sojourner Truth died at her home in Battle Creek on November 26, 1883, with her family around her. She was buried at Oak Hill Cemetery. Many of her early friends were dead or too old to attend the services, but Frederick Douglass sent a message, as did Wendell Phillips. A thousand friends and neighbors filed past her coffin. Among the floral offerings was a great sheaf of ripened wheat from the freedmen of Kansas.

Once when a friend had asked, "But Sojourner, what if there is no heaven?" she had replied, "What will I say if I don't get there? Why, I'll say, 'Bless the Lord! I had a good time thinking I would!'"

Selection 4

A Call for Resistance

Henry Highland Garnet

Even more militant than Frederick Douglass was black abolitionist Henry Highland Gar-

Excerpted from Henry Highland Garnet, "An Address to the Slaves of the United States of America," in *Negro Orators and Their Orations*, edited by Carter G. Woodson (Washington, DC: Associated Publishers, 1925).

net (1815–1882). Garnet was born a slave, escaped in 1824, became a Presbyterian minister, and joined the antislavery movement. He electrified a free black antislavery meeting in 1843 by calling for slaves to use any form of resistance, including killing their masters if necessary, to gain freedom. But the meeting refused to endorse his stand.

Eventually Douglass eclipsed Garnet as the best-known black abolitionist, and Garnet dedicated himself primarily to his work as a minister. After the Civil War and the failure of Reconstruction, with African Americans facing an ever-rising tide of discrimination, Garnet re-emerged as an activist by urging blacks to give up faith in ever obtaining justice in the United States and return to Africa. He himself immigrated to Liberia in 1882, but died just two months after arriving.

BRETHREN AND FELLOW CITIZENS: Your brethren of the North, East, and West have been accustomed to meet together in National Conventions, to sympathize with each other, and to weep over your unhappy condition. In these meetings we have addressed all classes of the free, but we have never, until this time, sent a word of consolation and advice to you. . . .

Many of you are bound to us, not only by the ties of a common humanity, but we are connected by the more tender relations of parents, wives, husbands, and sisters, and friends. As such we most affectionately address you.

Slavery has fixed a deep gulf between you and us, and while it shuts out from you the relief and consolation which your friends would willingly render, it afflicts and persecutes you with a fierceness which we might not expect to see in the fiends of hell. But still the Almighty Father of mercies has left to us a glimmering ray of hope, which shines out like a lone star in a cloudy sky. Mankind are becoming wiser, and better—the oppressor's power is fading, and you, every day, are becoming better informed, and more numerous. Your grievances, brethren, are many. We shall not attempt, in this short address, to present to the world all the dark catalogue of the nation's sins, which have been committed upon an innocent people. Nor is it indeed necessary, for you feel them from day to day, and all the civilized world looks upon them with amazement. . . .

Nearly three millions of your fellow-citizens are prohibited by law and public opinion (which in this country is stronger than law) from reading the Book of Life. Your intellect has been destroyed as much as possible, and every ray of light they have attempted to shut out from your minds. The oppressors themselves have become involved in the ruin. They have become weak, sensual, and rapacious—they have cursed you—they have cursed themselves—they have cursed the earth which they have trod. . . .

SLAVERY! How much misery is comprehended in that single word. What mind is there that does not shrink from its direful effects? Unless the image of God be obliterated from the soul, all men cherish the love of liberty. The nice discerning political economist does not regard the sacred right more than the untutored African who roams in the wilds of Congo. Nor has the one more right to the full enjoyment of his freedom than the other. In every man's mind the good seeds of liberty are planted, and he who brings his fellow down so low, as to make him contented with a condition of slavery, commits the highest crime against God and man. Brethren, your oppressors aim to do this. They endeavor to make you as much like brutes as possible. When they have blinded the eyes of your mind—when they have embittered the sweet waters of life—when they have shut out the light which shines from the word of God—then, and not till then, has American slavery done its perfect work.

TO SUCH DEGRADATION IT IS SINFUL IN THE EXTREME FOR YOU TO MAKE VOLUNTARY SUBMISSION. The divine commandments you are in duty bound to reverence and obey. If you do not obey them, you will surely meet with the displeasure of the Almighty. He requires you to love Him supremely, and your neighbor as yourself—to keep the Sabbath day holy—to search the Scriptures—and bring up your children with respect for His laws, and to worship no other God but Him. But Slavery sets all these at nought, and hurls defiance in the face of Jehovah. The forlorn condition in which you are placed does not destroy your obligation to God. You are not certain of heaven, because you allow yourselves to remain in a state of slavery, where you cannot obey the commandments of the Sovereign of the universe. If the ignorance of slavery is a passport to heaven, then it is a blessing, and no curse, and you should rather desire its perpetuity than its abolition. God will not receive slavery, nor ignorance, nor any other state of mind, for love and obedience to Him. Your condition does not absolve you from your moral obligation. The diabolical injustice by which your liberties are cloven down, NEITHER GOD NOR ANGELS, OR JUST MEN, COMMAND YOU TO SUFFER FOR A SINGLE MOMENT. THEREFORE IT IS YOUR SOLEMN AND IMPERATIVE DUTY TO USE EVERY MEANS, BOTH MORAL, INTELLECTUAL, AND PHYSICAL, THAT PROMISES SUCCESS. . . .

Brethren, it is as wrong for your lordly oppressors to keep you in slavery as it was for the man thief to steal our ancestors from the coast of Africa. You should therefore now use the same manner of resistance as would have been just in our ancestors when the bloody foot-prints of the first remorseless soul-thief was placed upon the shores of our fatherland. The humblest peasant is as free in the sight of God as the proudest monarch that ever swayed a sceptre. Liberty is a spirit sent out from God, and like its great Author, is no respecter of persons.

Brethren, the time has come when you must act for yourselves. It is an old and true saying that, "if hereditary bondmen would be free, they must themselves strike the blow." You can plead your own cause, and do the work of emancipation better than any others. The nations of the Old World are moving in the great cause of universal freedom, and some of them at least will, ere long, do you justice. The combined powers of Europe have placed their broad seal of disapprobation upon the African slave-trade. But in the slaveholding parts of the United States the trade is as brisk as ever. They buy and sell you as though you were brute beasts. The North has done much—her opinion of slavery in the abstract is known. But in regard to the South, we adopt the opinion of the *New York Evangelist*— "We have advanced so far, that the cause apparently waits for a more effectual door to be thrown open than has been yet." We are about to point you to that more effectual door. Look around you, and behold the bosoms of your loving wives heaving with untold agonies! Here [sic] the cries of your poor children! Remember the stripes your fathers bore. Think of the torture and disgrace of your noble mothers. Think of your wretched sisters, loving virtue and purity, as they are driven into concubinage and are exposed to the unbridled lusts of incarnate devils. Think of the undying glory that hangs around the ancient name of Africa—and forget not that you are native-born American citizens, and as such you are justly entitled to all the rights that are granted to the freest. Think how many tears you have poured out upon the soil which you have cultivated with unrequited toil and enriched with your blood; and then go to your lordly enslavers and tell them plainly, that you *are determined to be free*. Appeal to their sense of justice, and tell them that they have no more right to oppress you than you have to enslave them. Entreat them to remove the grievous burdens which they have imposed upon you, and to remunerate you for your labor. Promise them renewed diligence in the cultivation of the soil, if they will render to you an equivalent for your services. Point them to the increase of happiness and prosperity in the British West Indies since the Act of Emancipation. Tell them in language which they cannot misunderstand of the exceeding sinfulness of slavery, and of a future judgment, and of the righteous retributions of an indignant God. Inform them that all you desire is FREEDOM, and that nothing else will suffice. Do this, and forever after cease to toil for the heartless tyrants, who give you no other reward but stripes and abuse. If they then commence work of death, they, and not you, will be responsible for the consequences. You had far better all die—*die immediately*, than live slaves, and entail your wretchedness upon your posterity. If you would be free in this generation, here is your only hope. However much you and all of us may desire it, there is not much hope of redemption without the shedding of blood. If you must bleed, let it all come at once—rather *die freemen than live to be the slaves.* It is impossible, like the children of Israel, to make a grand exodus from the land of bondage. The Pharaohs are on both sides of the blood-red waters! You cannot move *en masse* to the dominions of the British Queen— nor can you pass through Florida and overrun Texas, and at last find peace in Mexico. . . .

You will not be compelled to spend much time in order to become inured to hardships. From the first movement that you breathed the air of heaven, you have been accustomed to nothing else but hardships. The heroes of the American Revolution were never put upon harder fare than a peck of corn and few herrings per week. You have not become enervated by the luxuries of life. Your sternest energies have been beaten out upon the anvil of severe trial. Slavery has done this to make you subservient to its own purposes; but it has done more than this, it has prepared you for any emergency. If you receive good treatment, it is what you can hardly expect; if you meet with pain, sorrow, and even death, these are the common lot of the slaves. . . .

In 1822, Denmark Veazie [Vesey], of South Carolina, formed a plan for the liberation of his fellowmen. In the whole history of human efforts to overthrow slavery, a more complicated and tremendous plan was never formed. He was betrayed by the treachery of his own people, and died a martyr to freedom. Many a brave hero fell, but history, faithful to her high trust, will transcribe his name on the same monument with Moses, Hampden, Tell, Bruce, and Wallace, Toussaint L'Ouverture, Lafayette, and Washington. That tremendous movement shook the whole empire of slavery. The guilty soul-thieves were overwhelmed with fear. It is a matter of fact that at this time, and in consequence of the threatened revolution, the slave States talked strongly of emancipation. But they blew but one blast of the trumpet of freedom, and then laid it aside. As these men became quiet, the slaveholders ceased to talk about emancipation: and now behold your condition to-day! Angels sigh over it, and humanity has long since exhausted her tears in weeping on your account!

The patriotic Nathaniel Turner followed Denmark Veazie. He was goaded to desperation by wrong and injustice. By despotism, his name has been recorded on the list of infamy, and future generations will remember him among the noble and brave.

Next arose the immortal Joseph Cinque, the hero of the Amistad. He was a native African, and by the help of God he emancipated a whole ship-load of his fellowmen on the high seas. And he now sings of liberty on the sunny hills of Africa and beneath his native palm-trees, where he hears the lion roar and feels himself as free as the king of the forest.

Next arose Madison Washington, that bright star of freedom, and took his station in the constellation of true heroism. He was a slave on board the brig *Creole*, of Richmond, bound to New Orleans, that great slave mart, with a hundred and four others. Nineteen struck for liberty or death. But one life was taken, and the whole were emancipated, and the vessel was carried into Nassau, New Providence.

Noble men! Those who have fallen in freedom's conflict, their memories will be cherished by the true-hearted and the God-fearing in all future generations; those who are living, their names are surrounded by a halo of glory.

Henry Highland Garnet

Brethren, arise, arise! Strike for your lives and liberties. Now is the day and the hour. Let every slave throughout the land do this, and the days of slavery are numbered. You cannot be more oppressed than you have been—you cannot suffer greater cruelties than you have already. *Rather die freemen than live to be slaves.* Remember that you are FOUR MILLIONS!

It is in your power so to torment the God-cursed slaveholders that they will be glad to let you go free. If the scale was turned, and black men were the masters and white men the slaves, every destructive agent and element would be employed to lay the oppressor low. Danger and death would hang over their heads day and night. Yes, the tyrants would meet with plagues more terrible than those of Pharaoh. But you are a patient people. You act as though you were made for the special use of these devils. You act as though your daughters were born to pamper the lusts of your masters and overseers. And worse than all, you tamely submit while your lords tear your wives from your embraces and defile them before your eyes. In the name of God, we ask, are you men? Where is the blood of your fathers? Has it all run out of your veins?

Awake, awake; millions of voices are calling you! Your dead fathers speak to you from their graves. Heaven, as with a voice of thunder, calls on you to arise from the dust.

Let your motto be resistance! *resistance!* RE-SISTANCE! No oppressed people have ever secured their liberty without resistance. What kind of resistance you had better make you must decide by the circumstances that surround you, and according to the suggestion of expediency. Brethren, adieu! Trust in the living God. Labor for the peace of the human race, and remember that you are FOUR MILLIONS!

Selection 5

"What to the Slave Is the Fourth of July?"

Frederick Douglass

Frederick Douglass was one of the greatest orators in American history. The oration "What to the Slave Is the Fourth of July?" which he delivered at Rochester in 1852, challenged white Americans to rethink their political values to take into account the perspective of blacks who—alone of all the peoples who settled the New World—had not come here voluntarily. His statement tran-

scends even the issues posed by slavery and continues to have relevance today. This is an excerpt from that oration.

Fellow-citizens, pardon me, allow me to ask, why am I called upon to speak here to-day? What have I, or those I represent, to do with your national independence? Are the great principles of political freedom and of natural justice, embodied in that Declaration of Independence, extended to us? and am I, therefore, called upon to bring our humble offering to the national altar, and to confess the benefits and express devout gratitude for the bless-

Excerpted from Frederick Douglass, "What to the Slave Is the Fourth of July?" speech delivered in Rochester, New York, July 5, 1852.

ings resulting from your independence to us?

Would to God, both for your sakes and ours, that an affirmative answer could be truthfully returned to these questions! Then would my task be light, and my burden easy and delightful. For *who* is there so cold, that a nation's sympathy could not warm him? Who so obdurate and dead to the claims of gratitude, that would not thankfully acknowledge such priceless benefits? Who so stolid and selfish, that would not give his voice to swell the hallelujahs of a nation's jubilee, when the chains of servitude had been torn from his limbs? I am not that man. In a case like that, the dumb might eloquently speak, and the "lame man leap as an hart."

But, such is not the state of the case. I say it with a sad sense of the disparity between us. I am not included within the pale of this glorious anniversary! Your high independence only reveals the immeasurable distance between us. The blessings in which you, this day, rejoice, are not enjoyed in common.—The rich inheritance of justice, liberty, prosperity and independence, bequeathed by your fathers, is shared by you, not by me. The sunlight that brought life and healing to you, has brought stripes and death to me. This Fourth [of] July is *yours*, not *mine*. *You* may rejoice, *I* must mourn. To drag a man in fetters into the grand illuminated temple of liberty, and call upon him to join you in joyous anthems, were inhuman mockery and sacrilegious irony. Do you mean, citizens, to mock me, by asking me to speak to-day? If so, there is a parallel to your conduct. And let me warn you that it is dangerous to copy the example of a nation whose crimes, towering up to heaven, were thrown down by the breath of the Almighty, burying that nation in irrecoverable ruin! I can to-day take up the plaintive lament of a peeled and woe-smitten people!

> By the rivers of Babylon, there we sat down. Yea! we wept when we remembered Zion. We hanged our harps upon the willows in the midst thereof. For there, they that carried us away captive, required of us a song; and they who wasted us required of us mirth, saying, Sing us one of the songs of Zion. How can we sing the Lord's song in a strange land? If I for-

get thee, O Jerusalem, let my right hand forget her cunning. If I do not remember thee, let my tongue cleave to the roof of my mouth.

Fellow-citizens; above your national, tumultous joy, I hear the mournful wail of millions! whose chains, heavy and grievous yesterday, are, to-day, rendered more intolerable by the jubilee shouts that reach them. If I do forget, if I do not faithfully remember those bleeding children of sorrow this day, "may my right hand forget her cunning, and may my tongue cleave to the roof of my mouth!" To forget them, to pass lightly over their wrongs, and to chime in with the popular theme, would be treason most scandalous and shocking, and would make me a reproach before God and the world. My subject, then, fellow-citizens, is AMERICAN SLAVERY. I shall see, this day, and its popular characteristics, from the slave's point of view. Standing, there, identified with the American bondman, making his wrongs mine, I do not hesitate to declare, with all my soul, that the character and conduct of this nation never looked blacker to me than on this 4th of July! Whether we turn to the declarations of the past, or to the professions of the present, the conduct of the nation seems equally hideous and revolting. America is false to the past, false to the present, and solemnly binds herself to be false to the future. Standing with God and the crushed and bleeding slave on this occasion, I will, in the name of humanity which is outraged, in the name of liberty which is fettered, in the name of the constitution and the Bible, which are disregarded and trampled upon, dare to call in question and to denounce, with all the emphasis I can command, everything that serves to perpetuate slavery—the great sin and shame of America! "I will not equivocate; I will not excuse;" I will use the severest language I can command; and yet not one word shall escape me that any man, whose judgment is not blinded by prejudice, or who is not at heart a slaveholder, shall not confess to be right and just.

But I fancy I hear some one of my audience say, it is just in this circumstance that you and your brother abolitionists fail to make a favorable impression on the public mind. Would you argue more, and denounce less, would you persuade more, and rebuke less, your cause would be much more likely to succeed. But, I submit, where all is plain there is nothing to be argued. What point in the anti-slavery creed would you have me argue? On what branch of the subject do the people of this country need light? Must I undertake to prove that the slave is a man? That point is conceded already. Nobody doubts it. The slaveholders themselves acknowledge it in the enactment of laws for their government. They acknowledge it when they punish disobedience on the part of the slave. There are seventy-two crimes in the State of Virginia, which, if committed by a black man, (no matter how ignorant he be,) subject him to the punishment of death; while only two of the same crimes will subject a white man to the like punishment.—What is this but the acknowledgement that the slave is a moral, intellectual and responsible being? The manhood of the slave is conceded. It is admitted in the fact that Southern statute books are covered with enactments forbidding, under severe fines and penalties, the teaching of the slave to read or to write.—When you can point to any such laws, in reference to the beasts of the field, then I may consent to argue the manhood of the slave. When the dogs in your streets, when the fowls of the air, when the cattle on your hills, when the fish of the sea, and the reptiles that crawl, shall be unable to distinguish the slave from a brute, *then* will I argue with you that the slave is a man!

For the present, it is enough to affirm the equal manhood of the negro race. Is it not astonishing that, while we are ploughing, planting and reaping, using all kinds of mechanical tools, erecting houses, constructing bridges, building ships, working in metals of brass, iron, copper, silver and gold; that, while we are reading, writing and cyphering, acting as clerks, merchants and secretaries, having among us lawyers, doctors, ministers, poets, authors, editors, orators and teachers; that, while we are engaged in all manner of enterprises common to other men, digging gold in California, capturing the whale

in the Pacific, feeding sheep and cattle on the hill-side, living, moving, acting, thinking, planning, living in families as husbands, wives and children, and, above all, confessing and worshipping the Christian's God, and looking hopefully for life and immortality beyond the grave, we are called upon to prove that we are men!

Would you have me argue that man is entitled to liberty? that he is the rightful owner of his own body? You have already declared it. Must I argue the wrongfulness of slavery? Is that a question for Republicans? Is it to be settled by the rules of logic and argumentation, as a matter beset with great difficulty, involving a doubtful application of the principle of justice, hard to be understood? How should I look today, in the presence of Americans, dividing, and subdividing a discourse, to show that men have a natural right to freedom? speaking of it relatively, and positively, negatively, and affirmatively. To do so, would be to make myself ridiculous, and to offer an insult to your understanding.—There is not a man beneath the canopy of heaven, that does not know that slavery is wrong *for him.*

What, am I to argue that it is wrong to make men brutes, to rob them of their liberty, to work them without wages, to keep them ignorant of their relations to their fellow men, to beat them with sticks, to flay their flesh with the lash, to load their limbs with irons, to hunt them with dogs, to sell them at auction, to sunder their families, to knock out their teeth, to burn their flesh, to starve them into obedience and submission to their masters? Must I argue that a system thus marked with blood, and stained with pollution, is *wrong*? No! I will not. I have better employments for my time and strength, than such arguments would imply.

What, then, remains to be argued? Is it that slavery is not divine; that God did not establish it; that our doctors of divinity are mistaken? There is blasphemy in the thought. That which is inhuman, cannot be divine! *Who* can reason on such a proposition? They that can, may; I cannot. The time for such argument is past.

At a time like this, scorching irony, not convincing argument, is needed. O! had I the ability, and could I reach the nation's ear, I would, to-day, pour out a fiery stream of biting ridicule, blasting reproach, withering sarcasm, and stern rebuke. For it is not light that is needed, but fire; it is not the gentle shower, but thunder. We need the storm, the whirlwind, and the earthquake. The feeling of the nation must be quickened; the conscience of the nation must be roused; the propriety of the nation must be startled; the hypocrisy of the nation must be exposed; and its crimes against God and man must be proclaimed and denounced.

What, to the American slave, is your 4th of July? I answer; a day that reveals to him, more than all other days in the year, the gross injustice and cruelty to which he is the constant victim. To him, your celebration is a sham; your boasted liberty, an unholy license; your national greatness, swelling vanity; your sounds of rejoicing are empty and heartless; your denunciations of tyrants, brass fronted impudence; your shouts of liberty and equality, hollow mockery; your prayers and hymns, your sermons and thanksgivings, with all your religious parade, and solemnity, are, to him, mere bombast, fraud, deception, impiety, and hypocrisy—a thin veil to cover up crimes which would disgrace a nation of savages. There is not a nation on the earth guilty of practices, more shocking and bloody, than are the people of these United States, at this very hour.

Go where you may, search where you will, roam through all the monarchies and despotisms of the old world, travel through South America, search out every abuse, and when you have found the last, lay your facts by the side of the every day practices of this nation, and you will say with me, that, for revolting barbarity and shameless hypocrisy, America reigns without a rival. . . .

The Constitution

But it is answered in reply to all this, that precisely what I have now denounced is, in fact, guaranteed and sanctioned by the Constitution of the United States; that the right to hold, and to hunt slaves is a part of that Constitution framed by the illustrious Fathers of this Republic.

Then, I dare to affirm, notwithstanding all I have said before, your fathers stooped, basely stooped

> "To palter with us in a double sense:
> And keep the word of promise to the ear,
> But break it to the heart."

And instead of being the honest men I have before declared them to be, they were the veriest imposters that ever practised on mankind. *This* is the inevitable conclusion, and from it there is no escape; but I differ from those who charge this baseness on the framers of the Constitution of the United States. *It is a slander upon their memory,* at least, so I believe. There is not time now to argue the constitutional question at length; nor have I the ability to discuss it as it ought to be discussed. The subject has been handled with masterly power by Lysander Spooner, Esq., by William Goodell, by Samuel E. Sewall, Esq., and last, though not least, by Gerritt Smith, Esq. These gentlemen have, as I think, fully and dearly vindicated the Constitution from any design to support slavery for an hour.

Fellow-citizens! there is no matter in respect to which, the people of the North have allowed themselves to be so ruinously imposed upon, as that of the pro-slavery character of the Constitution. In *that* instrument I hold there is neither warrant, license, nor sanction of the hateful thing; but, interpreted, as it *ought* to be interpreted, the Constitution is a GLORIOUS LIBERTY DOCUMENT. Read its preamble, consider its purposes. Is slavery among them? Is it at the gateway? or is it in the temple? it is neither. While I do not intend to argue this question on the present occasion, let me ask, if it be not somewhat singular that, if the Constitution were intended to be, by its framers and adopters, a slave-holding instrument, why neither *slavery, slaveholding,* nor *slave* can anywhere be found in it. What would be thought of an instrument, drawn up, *legally* drawn up, for the purpose of entitling the city of Rochester to a track of land, in which no mention of land was made? Now, there are certain rules of interpretation, for the proper understanding of all legal instruments. These rules are well established. They are plain, common-sense rules, such as you and I, and all of us, can understand and apply, without having passed years in the study of law. I scout the idea that the question of the constitutionality, or unconstitutionality of slavery is not a question for the people. I hold that every American citizen has a right to form an opinion of the Constitution, and to propagate that opinion, and to use all honorable means to make his opinion the prevailing one. Without this right, the liberty of an American citizen would be as insecure as that of a Frenchman.* Ex-Vice-President [George] Dallas tells us that the Constitution is an object to which no American mind can be too attentive, and no American heart too devoted. He further says, the Constitution, in its words, is plain and intelligible, and is meant for the home-bred, unsophisticated understandings of our fellow-citizens. Senator Berrien tells us that the Constitution is the fundamental law, that which controls all others. The charter of our liberties, which every citizen has a personal interest in understanding thoroughly. The testimony of Senator Breese, Lewis Cass, and many others that might be named, who are everywhere esteemed as sound lawyers, so regard the Constitution. I take it, therefore, that it is not presumption in a private citizen to form an opinion of that instrument.

Now, take the Constitution according to its plain reading, and I defy the presentation of a single pro-slavery clause in it. On the other hand it will be found to contain principles and purposes, entirely hostile to the existence of slavery.

I have detained my audience entirely too long already. At some future period I will gladly avail myself of an opportunity to give this subject a full and fair discussion.

Allow me to say, in conclusion, notwithstanding the dark picture I have this day presented, of the state of the nation, I do not despair of this country. There are forces in operation, which must inevitably, work the downfall of slavery. *"The arm of the Lord is not shortened,"* and the doom of slavery is certain. I, therefore, leave off where I began, with *hope.* While drawing encouragement from the Declaration of Independence, the great

principles it contains, and the genius of American Institutions, my spirit is also cheered by the obvious tendencies of the age. Nations do not now stand in the same relation to each other that they did ages ago. No nation can now shut itself up, from the surrounding world, and trot round in the same old path of its fathers without interference. The time *was* when such could be done. Long established customs of hurtful character could formerly fence themselves in, and do their evil work with social impunity. Knowledge was then confined and enjoyed by the privileged few, and the multitude walked on in mental darkness. But a change has now come over the affairs of mankind. Walled cities and empires have become unfashionable. The arm of commerce has borne away the gates of the strong city. Intelligence is penetrating the darkest corners of the globe. It makes its pathway over and under the sea, as well as on the earth. Wind, steam, and lightning are its chartered agents. Oceans no longer divide, but link nations together. From Boston to London is now a holiday excursion. Space is comparatively annihilated.—Thoughts expressed on one side of the Atlantic are distinctly heard on the other.

The far off and almost fabulous Pacific rolls in grandeur at our feet. The Celestial Empire [China], the mystery of ages, is being solved. The fiat of the Almighty, *"Let there be Light,"* has not yet spent its force. No abuse, no outrage whether in taste, sport or avarice, can now hide itself from the all-pervading light. The iron shoe, and crippled foot of China must be seen, in contrast with nature. *Africa must rise and put on her yet unwoven garment. "Ethiopia shall stretch out her hand unto God."* In the fervent aspirations of William Lloyd Garrison, I say, and let every heart join in saying it:

God speed the year of jubilee
    The wide world o'er!
When from their galling chains set free,
Th' oppress'd shall vilely bend the knee,
And wear the yoke of tyranny
    Like brutes no more.
That year will come, and freedom's reign,
To man his plundered rights again
    Restore.

*France had recently (1851) become a dictatorship.

Slavery and the Coming of the Civil War

Chapter 15

Introduction

*T*he two-party system (of Democrats and Whigs) that dominated American politics in the 1830s and 1840s collapsed after 1850, and the resulting realignment of parties worsened the clash of sections so badly that the nation's constitutional structure collapsed. Such is the verdict of most historians today on the coming of the Civil War.

The Civil War, however, did not erupt because inept politicians had blundered. Slavery lay at the root of the sectional clash. The Jacksonian-era two-party system had been built, in large measure, to defuse the issue of slavery, which had shaken the Union in the Missouri Crisis of 1819–1820 and which had driven South Carolina into its Union-threatening nullification posture in 1832–1833. Under the old party system, both the Democrats and the Whigs had strong voter appeal in the North and the South alike, and neither party was antislavery. Bondage was simply an issue that most major-party candidates tried to evade in national campaigns. But the political landscape changed in 1844, a presidential election year. The hot issue in that campaign was whether the United States should annex the slaveholding Republic of Texas. Democratic candidate James K. Polk, a Tennessee slave owner, pushed vigorously for expansion. The veteran Whig nominee, Henry Clay, also a slave owner, knew that many of his northern Whig supporters adamantly opposed adding more slave states to the Union, so he fudged. That gave an opening to the small, abolitionist Liberty Party, which won enough votes in New York to deny that state to Clay—and thus handed the presidency to Polk. Once in office, Polk welcomed Texas into the Union, provoked a war with Mexico (1846–1848), and annexed a huge block of formerly Mexican territory: present-day

California, Arizona, New Mexico, Nevada, Utah, and western Colorado. (By threatening war with Great Britain, he also annexed the Pacific Northwest.) But swallowing so much land from Mexico proved to be, in the words of the antislavery essayist Ralph Waldo Emerson, a dose of "poison." The Union spiraled into one crisis after another, ending in the Civil War.

The issue of what to do with the Mexican booty within a few years broke up the Jacksonian-era two-party system. Northerners of both parties fiercely resisted opening any of the new western lands to slavery—not because they were abolitionists or especially concerned for the fate of slaves but because they feared that allowing slave owners to impose their "peculiar institution" on the Far West would shut free white labor out of the region. Southerners of both parties were outraged that slave owners should be barred from taking their human property into territories for which white southern volunteers had paid with their blood in the Mexican War. By 1850, Congress was deadlocked over the issue, and militant southerners, like the dying John C. Calhoun, talked of secession if their region did not get its way. The two other giants of the Senate, Henry Clay and Daniel Webster (who would also go to their graves within a few years), struggled to find another Union-saving deal. The result was the Compromise of 1850, which gave each section something it wanted—and also something it hated.

According to the Compromise of 1850, California became a free state, and the rest of the Southwest was organized as free territory. Texas had its debts paid by the U.S. government. The buying and selling of slaves (but not slavery itself) was banned in the District of Columbia, ending the spectacle of slaves being auctioned on Capitol Hill. But the North had to accept a stringent Fugitive Slave Law, ensuring that southerners could reclaim slaves who had fled to free states. This law for the first time brought the reality of slavery to many northern citizens. It may not have turned all of them into abolitionists, but many now saw a moral issue where previously they had been indifferent.

Soon the nation's political system unraveled further. Hopelessly divided between northern and southern factions, the Whig Party collapsed after it lost the 1852 elections. Then, in 1854, Illinois's Democratic senator Stephen A. Douglas, in effect, repealed the Missouri Compromise by ramming through Congress a bill that would have permitted Kansas and Nebraska to become slave states if the people who settled there voted to do so. (In return, Douglas won southern votes to subsidize a transcontinental railroad starting in Chicago.) Kansas promptly became the scene of pitched battles as proslavery and antislavery settlers poured in, racing to see which could more quickly establish a territorial government that the federal government would recognize. From 1855 to 1857, "Bleeding Kansas" polarized the nation, as the pro-southern administrations of presidents Franklin Pierce and James Buchanan pulled wires behind the scenes on behalf of slave-owning interests.

As northern politicians scrambled to regroup, a new party emerged that represented a purely sectional interest: the Republican Party, made up of former Whigs and northern Democrats who shared a common interest in thwarting "the Slave Power" and ensuring that the West would become a land of "free soil, free labor, and free men." Without winning a single vote in the South, their presidential candidate in 1856, John C. Frémont, came close to winning the election. At the same time, the Democratic Party was being transformed from a national to a southern institution.

Only days after Democrat James Buchanan ("a northern man with southern principles") was inaugurated president in March 1857, the U.S. Supreme Court dropped a bombshell. It ruled that Dred Scott, a slave who had sued in the federal courts for his liberty, must remain a slave for two reasons, both shocking to northerners: (1) Because of their race, neither he nor other black people had any right to be U.S. citizens, and thus no right to sue in the federal courts; and (2) the Missouri Compromise, by which Congress had barred slavery from the trans-Mississippi West (and on which basis Scott had sued for freedom), was unconstitutional. Here, most northerners felt, was obvious proof that the "Slave Power" conspiracy controlled both the presidency and the Supreme Court—and next would legalize slavery everywhere in the Union. Such was the lesson that the Illinois Republican politician Abraham Lincoln drew from the *Dred Scott* decision, and it was the question of how to safeguard the West for free labor that Lincoln and Douglas debated in their 1858 senatorial campaign. Lincoln, while denying that he was an abolitionist and while making verbal concessions to Illinois whites' blatant racism, insisted in these debates that slavery was "a moral, social, and political evil."

By 1859 the Union was in perpetual crisis. So deep was the sectional impasse that Congress could get virtually no business done. Political parties reflected essentially sectional, not national, interests. White northerners and white southerners each assumed that the other section was bent on subverting American democracy. In this poisonous atmosphere, abolitionist John Brown led a small armed band in seizing the federal arsenal at Harpers Ferry, Virginia, in late 1859, expecting to touch off a slave insurrection. The wildly different perceptions of Brown's action by whites in the North and in the South was a telling gauge of how far apart the two sections had drifted—and of how deep was the South's fear of a slave rebellion.

When northern votes alone elected Abraham Lincoln president of the United States in November 1860, many whites in the South decided that the time had come to seek safety in secession. They feared that with the North in the grip of the "Black Republican Party," it was only a matter of time before the Yankees would move to abolish slavery. Lincoln and most Republicans had no such intention, but they did believe that slavery should be "put on the path of ultimate extinction"—the path, they insisted, that the nation's founding fathers had intended. In December 1860, South Carolina took the fateful step its leaders had threatened for so long to take: It seceded, and this time other slave states, one by one, followed.

As Lincoln declared in one of his most celebrated speeches, the nation had become "a house divided" over slavery, and divided it could not stand—it must become either wholly slave or wholly free. The Civil War was not fought because northerners decided to embark on a crusade to free the slaves. It came because southern whites had grown so obsessive about maintaining a society based on human bondage that they would pay any price to be "let alone."

Boston Defies the Fugitive Slave Act

Henry Mayer

For the first time the Fugitive Slave Law of 1850 brought home to many northern whites the realities of southern slavery. An essential part of the Compromise of 1850, this law guaranteed slave owners that the federal government would do everything in its power to prevent runaway slaves from seeking refuge in the free states. Slave owners or their paid agents were empowered to enter northern communities, to seize the runaway (or some other black person whom they claimed was the runaway) and bring him or her before a federal commissioner, who had the sole power to decide the case—and who received a higher fee if he ruled that the prisoner was a runaway slave. There were no juries and no appeals, and the law charged lo- *cal officials in free states to do everything in their power to aid the "slave catchers." Here, then, was a vivid demonstration of the domination that masters wielded over their human property in the slave states, of the capacity of "the Slave Power" to control the federal government, and of the impotence of northern citizens and local authorities in the face of this massed authority. Little wonder that, for many northerners, memories were kindled of colonial resistance to British imperial power in the 1760s and early 1770s. As one New Englander put it, when the Fugitive Slave Law went into effect, people who had never thought about the slavery controversy before woke up to find themselves abolitionists.*

Boston became the scene of some of the North's bitterest battles over the Fugitive Slave Law. In his recent biography of William Lloyd Garrison, excerpted here, historian Henry Mayer narrates what happened.

*I*f Daniel Webster personified the spirit of compromise, then William Lloyd Garrison made sure that the fugitive slave defined the opposition. Each week's *Liberator* brought a fresh headline about the enforcement of the new law. The first, from New York City in mid-September 1850, resulted in the return of a man named James Hamlet to Maryland as a slave; the next two, in Harrisburg and Bedford, Pennsylvania, returned ten more alleged fugitives to Southern claimants, and by the end of the year, the total had increased to nineteen, with only two dismissals. The beleaguered black communities, roiling with long-settled runaways suddenly rendered vulnerable to summary proceedings, immediately formed new vigilance committees, while hundreds of fugitives scrambled to conceal their whereabouts and flee to Canada. . . .

It was clear to all parties that the 1850 Fugitive Slave Law was not so much a remedy for the South's chronic runaway problem as it was a deliberate condemnation of the abolitionist agitation that had unsettled traditional politics, and its strict enforcement became so passionately contested because, at the very moment that the antislavery tide had turned in Northern public opinion, the South demanded new pledges of fidelity to the old habits of compromise. The controversy over the law thus sharpened the ideological argument Garrison had long waged against the Constitution, underscored the contradictions of the Union, and fostered a period of proto-revolutionary thinking that pointed toward a violent resolution of the national dilemma.

As the measure's text, which Garrison printed in his "Refuge of Oppression" column, made plain, the new law articulated a clear congressional preference for harsh and summary enforcement over the protection of civil liberties. The owner, or his agent, could reclaim a fugitive either by securing a warrant beforehand or arresting the alleged runaway on the spot. The case for removal could be heard either by a federal judge or a court-appointed federal commissioner, who would be paid ten dollars if a certificate of removal was issued, but only five dollars if the claim was denied. Testimony from the fugitive was prohibited, no jury could be called, the commissioner's verdict could not be appealed, and other courts or magistrates were barred from issuing habeas corpus writs or other legal mandates that might postpone or override an order to remand the defendant into slavery. If the claimant persuaded the commissioner that an attempt to liberate or "rescue" the fugitive might occur during the return, moreover, the commissioner was authorized to appoint special deputies, call out a citizen's posse, and allow the arresting officer to hire additional help at federal expense. These provisions called forth denunciation of the law as a "kidnapping" machine, while the stiff penalties—up to six months in jail and a $1,000 fine—mandated for anyone aiding a fugitive or interfering with a return emphasized that the law also sought to suppress dissent and allow the courts wide latitude for harassing the opposition.

Boston seethed for months. The city's streets and squares filled with determined sentinels on the lookout for "slave-hunters"; its elegant homes and back-alley tenements forged a network for concealing, assisting, and relocating fugitives; its law offices busily studied the devices of obstruction and repeal; and its conservative mercantile elite became infuriated at hearing its support for the Union-saving compromise compared to the royalism of the city's Tory government in the Revolutionary crisis of the 1770s. Between October 1850 and April 1851, the city experienced three major confrontations that polarized public opinion and gave Garrisonians their most dramatic forum yet to protest complicity with slavery. Their activities, this time, looked to direct action as well as denunciation.

When two Georgians arrived in the city late in October 1850 with warrants to arrest the popular fugitive lecturers Ellen and William Craft, the vigilance committee hid the Crafts while abolitionist crowds dogged the hunters at every step. They blocked the way to Craft's cabinet shop, milled in the lobby and halls of the Georgians' hotel, set up a ruckus every time the "kidnappers" tried to meet with the local constabulary, and sought to have them arrested instead. A prominent Whig sent word to the Crafts that if they would submit to a peaceable arrest, guarantors would repurchase and free them immediately. The Crafts rejected the offer, saying that they represented hundreds of other fugitives and would not jeopardize their freedom by legitimizing the law's operation. After a fruitless week of maneuvering, with the city in an uproar, the agents gave up their quest as impossible, but taking no chances, the vigilance committee dispatched the Crafts on a speaking tour of Great Britain. . . . The Rev. Theodore Parker, who had married the heroic couple in the formal ceremony denied them in bondage, dared President Fillmore to indict him for aiding his parishioners in defiance of the law.

Fillmore did not rise to the bait, but several months later, a more spectacular act of resistance drew a prompt and energetic presidential response. In February 1851, a waiter in a Cornhill coffeehouse named Frederick Jenkins was suddenly arrested and, still wearing his apron, rushed to court, where he was charged with being an escaped slave known as Shadrach to his Virginia master, whose high-priced Boston attorney now sought a certificate for his return. The vigilance committee hurried several attorneys, including Garrison's old friends Ellis Loring and Samuel Sewall, to the courtroom, while word spread through the streets that another judicial kidnapping was in progress. By the time an anxious crowd arrived at the building, the commissioner had granted the defense a postponement, the hearing room was nearly empty, and the marshal was preoccupied with turning away several newspaper reporters. It proved absurdly easy for a gang of black men to stream through the doors, shout "hurrah" to the startled prisoner, and quick-march out again with the liberated Shadrach safely in their midst "Plucked as a brand from the burning," Garrison said later, evoking the trial of the fugitive's Biblical namesake in the fiery furnace. "Nobody injured, nobody wronged, but simply a chattel transformed into a man by unarmed friends of equal liberty."

The "rescue" of Shadrach, soon resettled in Montreal, severely embarrassed the Boston defenders of the "peace" measures and antagonized the administration. Daniel Webster, now secretary of state, heard the commissioner and the commercial press decry the action as "levying war," and he promptly pronounced the rescue as "strictly speaking, a case of treason." President Fillmore issued a wrathful proclamation—in the traditional phraseology of the riot acts—authorizing federal troops to quell dangerous "combinations" and ordering prosecution of those who aided so "flagitious" an offense. In the Senate, Henry Clay sought a congressional investigation and stiffer penalties for obstructing a fugitive's return. The outrage had been committed by "a band not of our people," said Clay, and therefore it raised the urgent question of whether "the government of white men is to be yielded to a government of blacks." (Clay did not know that Lewis Hayden, the black clothing dealer who had led the Shadrach rescue, had himself fled Kentucky bondage in 1844 with his wife and child and was in fact the son-in-law of one of the senator's own slaves.)

Clay's vicious remarks "threw off the mask," in Garrison's candid phrase; with one foot in the grave, the Kentuckian had made "his damnation doubly sure" by revealing the racist underpinnings of the compromise. Boston's Benjamin R. Curtis, an eminent member of the bar and likely nominee for a vacancy on the U.S. Supreme Court, followed Clay's lead by comparing the return of fugitive slaves to the extradition of criminals and insisted that the law appropriately regarded runaways as foreigners without legal standing in Massachusetts. Whatever the natural rights of black people might be, Curtis told a Unionist rally in Faneuil Hall, he did not consider Massachusetts the place to vindicate them. "This is *our* soil, sacred to *our* peace, on which we intend to perform *our* promises, and work out for the benefit of ourselves . . . the destiny which our creator has assigned to *us*," he said. Ever since the fight against colonization in the early 1830s, Garrison had insisted that the abolition of slavery had to be accompanied by the inclusion of African-Americans in the political community. The callousness with which the Fugitive Slave Law disregarded the rights of black citizens in the North and blurred the distinctions between slave and free, chattel and criminal, revealed both the acuity of his insight and the limits of the abolitionists' achievement. Just as the rise of Free-Soilism exposed the white racism that might coexist with antislavery feelings, so did the defense of the "adjustment" measures reveal the prejudice that lay at the heart of the constitutional compromises. That the mobilization against the law produced an unprecedented degree of interracial cooperation as black and white abolitionists organized vigilance committees, sheltered fugitives, and engaged in public acts of defiance stood, by contrast, as a living demonstration of the radical definition of liberty for which the Garrisonians had long contended.

It also produced, especially in Boston, a close identification with the Revolutionary spirit of '76, with its traditions of a patriotic underground organization and a militant public opinion, that proved both inspiring and problematic. Theodore Parker termed the Shadrach rescue "the most noble deed done in Boston since the destruction of the tea," and in its aftermath Wendell Phillips thought that the Bostonians were experiencing the flavor of the liberal insurgencies of 1848, as well as the city's hallowed defiance of Lord North's edicts and King George III's redcoats. People everywhere used the old phrase "Liberty or Death" with a new ferocity, and Parker had publicly stated that the fugitive had the same natural right to defend himself against the slave-catcher that he had against a murderer or a wolf. Indeed, it was well known that the outspoken Lewis Hayden had barricaded and armed his house, long a major refuge for runaways, and threatened to blow it up if federal troops besieged it. The turn toward arms alarmed Garrison, who told a mass meeting that while each person had to be true to his own principles, as a nonresistant he hoped that the fugitive would be "more indebted to the moral power of public sentiment than to any display of physical resistance." His friends, hoping to distance the editor

from some of the more militant activities, kept his name off the vigilance committee roster, yet Garrison could not help but feel an increasing tension between his conscientious opposition to force and the appeal of the revolutionary examples—from William Tell to George Washington and Toussaint L'Ouverture—that he repeatedly said the nation could not claim for itself and deny to those it enslaved.

The Shadrach rescue and the repressive threats it provoked gave the abolitionists a sense of triumph, but they knew that it would be short-lived. Boston remained filled with Southern agents; "All they want is *one from Boston*," said Phillips, "to show the discontented ones at home that *it can be done. . . .*" The administration, too, felt pressured to put down the agitation in Boston in order to redeem its pledge of "finality." Eight men—four black, including Lewis Hayden, and four white, including Elizur Wright, now the editor of a Free-Soil newspaper—were indicted for abetting the Shadrach affair, but divided juries failed to convict anyone. While the trials wore on, however, yet another fugitive case gave the Fillmore administration an opportunity to make an example of Boston, although the measures it employed corroborated the abolitionists' charge that the law travestied the very liberty for which the Union stood.

Thomas Sims, a runaway bricklayer from Savannah, was arrested by city policemen on a trumped-up charge of disturbing the peace, but once in the courthouse, he was turned over to federal marshals for a hearing before the fugitive slave commissioner. . . . [The] officers confined Sims under close guard in the federal courtroom overnight, but they connived to transform the entire building into a federal prison. When crowds of abolitionists arrived at Court Square in the dawn light of April 4, 1851, they were flabbergasted to discover the courthouse itself girded with iron chains, its doorways fettered with ropes, and the entire city police force—reinforced by special deputies recruited among waterfront hooligans—ringing the building and patrolling the vicinity. The public was barred from entry, and even the attorneys and judges allowed to cross the threshold had to crouch quite low to get beneath the barrier. The spectacle of the state's aged chief justice—proud, stiff-necked Lemuel Shaw . . . —stooping under heavy chains to enter the halls of justice appalled the abolitionists. Garrison termed it "one of the most disgraceful scenes ever witnessed in this city," for it made inescapably vivid how completely the legal system upheld the interests of slaveholders. Even Henry Wadsworth Longfellow, the poet laureate of Union and no friend to agitation, winced at the "degradation" imposed on Shaw and mourned, "Alas for the people who cannot feel an insult."

For an entire week the volunteer attorneys for Sims tried every conceivable device to interrupt the proceedings against the slender, frail mulatto, who looked younger than his twenty-three years and whose unwise but plaintive letter to his freeborn wife had tipped the authorities to his whereabouts. The lawyers filed several habeas corpus motions with Chief Justice Shaw, who refused to intervene, citing both a lack of jurisdiction based on the *Prigg* decision and his predisposition that the Fugitive Slave Law served the constitutional purpose of maintaining comity between the states. While the attorneys maneuvered, the abolitionists rallied, holding daily vigils at the courthouse and an open-air meeting on the Common, at which Wendell Phillips allowed that it would be a disgrace if Sims was deported without crowds blocking the streets and halting the machinery of an oppressive government. The impetuous young minister Thomas Wentworth Higginson talked with a few kindred spirits

about a physical assault on the courthouse or hiring a privateer to intercept any Savannah-bound vessels, but nothing tangible materialized from such desperate fantasies. On Friday afternoon, April 11, 1851, the certificate of removal was issued, and before daylight the next morning a company of three-hundred policemen, armed with U.S. military sabers, formed a hollow square and slowly marched the weeping Sims down State Street to the Long Wharf and the ship hired to return him to bondage.

The *Boston Courier* spoke for the "cotton press" in lauding the city's "sound attachment" to the Union, while the *Mail* sank to minstrel-show vulgarity with what Garrison called the "depraved" fiction that Sims had sung "Carry Me Back to Old Virginny" as the boat's pilot beat a Jim Crow dance tune with castanets. Whittier countered with a lament, "Moloch in State Street," and the city's eldest statesman, Josiah Quincy, mourned that Boston had lost its moral sense and become "a mere shop." With his unwavering hope, Garrison predicted that the return of Sims would agitate the public and prove "a disastrous triumph" for the slave power. One week later, on the seventy-sixth anniversary of the British attack on Lexington and Concord, Massachusetts learned that the United States government had successfully returned Thomas Sims to Savannah, where he was given thirty-nine lashes in the public square. "Let the Heavens weep and Hell be merry!" wrote Frederick Douglass. "Daniel Webster has at last obtained from Boston . . . a living sacrifice to appease the slave god of the American Union."

Uncle Tom's Cabin

Harriet Beecher Stowe

"So you are the little lady who made this great big war," Abraham Lincoln is alleged to have quipped when introduced to Harriet Beecher Stowe (1811–1896) at a White House reception during the Civil War. It was an apt remark, and was certainly not meant to be patronizing. Stowe's 1852 novel Uncle Tom's Cabin, and the many adaptations of it that were presented on northern stages, brought home to northerners—in language they could understand—what slavery was really like.

Today, many people dismiss Stowe's novel as sentimental, and for a black man to be called an "Uncle Tom" means that he has no pride, that he weakly allows himself to be victimized by racism. But if we read Uncle Tom's Cabin with these modern judgments in mind, we miss the book's historical significance, and we cannot possibly understand why the famous Russian writer Leo Tolstoy (the author of War and Peace) called Stowe's work one of the few truly great novels ever written.

It is true that Uncle Tom's Cabin plays on the reader's emotions: That was exactly what Stowe intended. She fully understood the sentimental idiom that dominated novel-writing in the 1850s; without being able to exploit this style, her novel would never have become the best-seller that it was, and thus would have had no influence. Stowe used her command of sentimentalisms to hammer home a series of powerful messages: that slavery struck at the institution that northerners considered the bedrock of all other values, the family; that even well-intentioned, "good" slave owners were trapped in an evil system that forced them to do wrong; that black people were capable of great personal nobility and true Christian goodness; and that any free person who ignored the moral evils of slavery was guilty of helping to perpetuate it. It is easy to forget that Uncle Tom, the saintly old slave who is sold to a vicious owner and eventually beaten to death, is the first black *hero* in American literature—a powerful answer to all the "Zip Coons" and "Sambos" of pre–Civil War popular culture through whom whites derived disrespectful pictures of African Americans. And we should also remember that Stowe skillfully makes the novel's villain, Simon Legree, not a stereotypical southerner but a transplanted Yankee, gone to the South to get rich as a plantation owner. (There were, in fact, real-life Simon Legrees.)

Stowe did careful research in writing Uncle Tom's Cabin. Southern critics were right to complain that she had spent almost no time in slave states and had seen very little of slavery first hand, but this was beside the point. Most of her knowledge of slavery was derived from antislavery newspapers and

Excerpted from Harriet Beecher Stowe, *Uncle Tom's Cabin* (New York: Bantam Books, 1851–52).

lectures, from books like the abolitionist anthology American Slavery As It Is, *and from the personal testimony of free blacks and escaped slaves whom she had met while active in the abolitionist movement. This material was enough to convince her of the fundamental evil of slavery and how it destroyed the character of even "good" whites who were personally involved in it. Together with the impact of the Fugitive Slave Law on northern communities,* Uncle Tom's Cabin *made white people in the free states aware that slavery and those who supported it represented a fundamental danger to the future of American democracy. The chasm between North and South grew ever wider during the 1850s, and in the end the white people of each section saw those of the other as enemies, not as fellow citizens. In that sense Lincoln was right to see Stowe as one of the instigators of the Civil War.*

This selection combines two excerpts from Uncle Tom's Cabin, *both occurring early in the novel. A well-meaning Kentucky slave owner, Mr. Shelby, has unwisely fallen into debt and to satisfy it must sell some of his slaves: the young son of his wife's favorite mixed-race servant Eliza, and old Uncle Tom. Mrs. Shelby protests, for she has taken a strong interest in Eliza, but both must bow to reality, and arrangements are made to deliver the slaves to an uncouth "speculator." Eliza overhears what is in store and escapes with her son, fleeing across the half-frozen Ohio River to freedom —a dramatic episode that always "stopped the show" when presented on stage. Self-sacrificing Uncle Tom submits to fate with what readers at the time would have recognized as a true Christian attitude, and is torn from his children and his wife. Eventually a cruel new master beats him to death.*

Harriet Beecher Stowe

r. and Mrs. Shelby had retired to their apartment for the night. He was lounging in a large easy-chair, looking over some letters that had come in the after-

noon mail, and she was standing before her mirror, brushing out the complicated braids and curls in which Eliza had arranged her hair; for, noticing her pale cheeks and haggard eyes, she had excused her attendance that night, and ordered her to bed. The employment, naturally enough, suggested her conversation with the girl in the morning; and, turning to her husband, she said, carelessly,

"By the bye, Arthur, who was that low-bred fellow that you lugged in to our dinner-table to-day?"

"Haley is his name," said Shelby, turning himself rather uneasily in his chair, and continuing with his eyes fixed on a letter.

"Haley! Who is he, and what may be his business here, pray?"

"Well, he's a man that I transacted some business with, last time I was at Natchez," said Mr. Shelby.

"And he presumed on it to make himself quite at home, and call and dine here, ay?"

"Why, I invited him; I had some accounts with him," said Shelby.

"Is he a negro-trader?" said Mrs. Shelby, noticing a certain embarrassment in her husband's manner.

"Why, my dear, what put that into your head?" said Shelby, looking up.

"Nothing,—only Eliza came in here, after dinner, in a great worry, crying and taking on, and said you were talking with a trader, and that she heard him make an offer for her boy—the ridiculous little goose!"

"She did, hey?" said Mr. Shelby, returning to his paper, which he seemed for a few moments quite intent upon, not perceiving that he was holding it bottom upward.

"It will have to come out," said he, mentally; "as well now as ever."

"I told Eliza," said Mrs. Shelby, as she continued brushing her hair, "that she was a little fool for her pains, and that you never had anything to do with that sort of person. Of course, I knew you never meant to sell any of our people,—least of all, to such a fellow."

"Well, Emily," said her husband, "so I have always felt and said; but the fact is that my business lies so that I cannot get on without. I shall have to sell some of my hands."

"To that creature? Impossible! Mr. Shelby, you cannot be serious."

"I'm sorry to say that I am," said Mr. Shelby. "I've agreed to sell Tom."

"What! our Tom?—that good, faithful creature!—been your faithful servant from a boy! O Mr. Shelby!—and you have promised him his freedom, too,—you and I have spoken to him a hundred times of it. Well, I can believe anything now,—I can believe *now* that you could sell little Harry, poor Eliza's only child!" said Mrs. Shelby, in a tone between grief and indignation.

"Well, since you must know all, it is so. I have agreed to sell Tom and Harry both; and I don't know why I am to be rated, as if I were a monster, for doing what every one does every day."

"But why, of all others, choose these?" said Mrs. Shelby. "Why sell them, of all on the place, if you must sell at all?"

"Because they will bring the highest sum of any,—that's why. I could choose another, if you say so. The fellow made me a high bid on Eliza, if that would suit you any better," said Mr. Shelby.

"The wretch!" said Mrs. Shelby, vehemently.

"Well, I didn't listen to it, a moment,—out of regard to your feelings, I wouldn't;—so give me some credit."

"My dear," said Mrs. Shelby, recollecting herself, "forgive me. I have been hasty. I was surprised, and entirely unprepared for this;—but surely you will allow me to intercede for these poor creatures. Tom is a noble-hearted, faithful fellow, if he is black. I do believe, Mr. Shelby, that if he were put to it, he would lay down his life for you."

"I know it,—I dare say;—but what's the use of all this?—I can't help myself."

"Why not make a pecuniary sacrifice? I'm willing to bear my part of the inconvenience. O Mr. Shelby, I have tried—tried most faithfully, as a Christian woman should—to do my duty to these poor, simple, dependent creatures. I have cared for them, instructed them, watched over them, and known all their little cares and joys, for years; and how can I ever hold up my head again among them, if, for the sake of a little paltry gain, we sell such a faithful, excellent, confiding creature as poor Tom, and tear from him in a moment all we have taught him to love and value? I have taught them the duties of the family, of parent and child, and husband and wife; and how can I bear to have this open acknowledgment that we care for no tie, no duty, no relation, however sacred, compared with money? I have talked with Eliza about her boy—her duty to him as a Christian mother, to watch over him, pray for him, and bring him up in a Christian way; and now what can I say, if you tear him away, and sell him, soul and body, to a profane, unprincipled man, just to save a little money? I have told her that one soul is worth more than all the money in the world; and how will she believe me when she sees us turn round and sell her child?—sell him, perhaps, to certain ruin of body and soul!"

"I'm sorry you feel so about it, Emily,—indeed I am," said Mr. Shelby; "and I respect your feelings, too, though I don't pretend to share them to their full extent; but I tell you now, solemnly, it's of no use—I can't help myself. I didn't mean to tell you this, Emily; but, in plain words, there is no choice between selling these two and selling everything. Either they must go, or *all* must. Haley has come into possession of a mortgage, which, if I don't clear off with him directly, will take everything before it. I've raked, and scraped, and borrowed, and all but begged,—and the price of these two was needed to make up the balance, and I had to give them up. Haley fancied the child; he agreed to settle the matter that way, and no other. I was in his power, and *had* to do it. If you feel so to have them sold, would it be any better to have *all* sold?"

Mrs. Shelby stood like one stricken. Finally, turning to her toilet, she rested her face in her hands, and gave a sort of groan.

"This is God's curse on slavery!—a bitter, bitter, most accursed thing!—a curse to the master and a curse to the slave! I was a fool to think I could make anything good out of such a deadly evil. It is a sin to hold a slave under laws like ours,—I always felt it was,—I always thought so when I was a girl,—I thought so still more after I joined the church; but I thought I could gild it over,—I thought by kindness, and care, and instruction, I could make the condition of mine better than freedom—fool that I was!"

"Why, wife, you are getting to be an abolitionist, quite."

"Abolitionist! if they knew all I know about slavery, they *might* talk! We don't need them to tell us; you know I never thought that slavery was right—never felt willing to own slaves."

"Well, therein you differ from many wise and pious men," said Mr. Shelby. "You remember Mr. B.'s sermon, the other Sunday?"

"I don't want to hear such sermons; I never wish to hear Mr. B. in our church again. Ministers can't help the evil, perhaps,—can't cure it, any more than we can,—but defend it!—it always went against my common sense. And I think you

didn't think much of that sermon, either. "

"Well," said Shelby, "I must say these ministers sometimes carry matters further than we poor sinners would exactly dare to do. We men of the world must wink pretty hard at various things, and get used to a deal that isn't the exact thing. But we don't quite fancy, when women and ministers come out broad and square, and go beyond us in matters of either modesty or morals, that's a fact. But now, my dear, I trust you see the necessity of the thing, and you see that I have done the very best that circumstances would allow."

"O yes, yes!" said Mrs. Shelby, hurriedly and abstractedly fingering her gold watch,—"I haven't any jewelry of any amount," she added, thoughtfully; "but would not this watch do something?—it was an expensive one, when it was bought. If I could only at least save Eliza's child, I would sacrifice anything I have."

"I'm sorry, very sorry, Emily," said Mr. Shelby, "I'm sorry this takes hold of you so; but it will do no good. The fact is, Emily, the thing's done; the bills of sale are already signed, and in Haley's hands; and you must be thankful it's no worse. That man has had it in his power to ruin us all,—and now he is fairly off. If you knew the man as I do, you'd think that we had had a narrow escape."

"Is he so hard, then?"

"Why, not a cruel man, exactly, but a man of leather,—a man alive to nothing but trade and profit,—cool, and unhesitating, and unrelenting, as death and the grave. He'd sell his own mother at a good percentage—not wishing the old woman any harm, either."

"And this wretch owns that good, faithful Tom, and Eliza's child!"

"Well, my dear, the fact is that this goes rather hard with me! it's a thing I hate to think of. Haley wants to drive matters, and take possession to-morrow. I'm going to get out my horse bright and early, and be off. I can't see Tom, that's a fact; and you had better arrange a drive somewhere, and carry Eliza off. Let the thing be done when she is out of sight."

"No, no," said Mrs. Shelby; "I'll be in no sense accomplice or help in this cruel business.

I'll go and see poor old Tom, God help him, in his distress! They shall see, at any rate, that their mistress can feel for and with them. As to Eliza, I dare not think about it. The Lord forgive us! What have we done, that this cruel necessity should come on us?"

There was one listener to this conversation whom Mr. and Mrs. Shelby little suspected.

Communicating with their apartment was a large closet, opening by a door into the outer passage. When Mrs. Shelby had dismissed Eliza for the night, her feverish and excited mind had suggested the idea of this closet; and she had hidden herself there, and, with her ear pressed close against the crack of the door, had lost not a word of the conversation.

When the voices died into silence, she rose and crept stealthily away. Pale, shivering, with rigid features and compressed lips, she looked an entirely altered being from the soft and timid creature she had been hitherto. She moved cautiously along the entry, paused one moment at her mistress' door, and raised her hands in mute appeal to Heaven, and then turned and glided into her own room. It was a quiet, neat apartment, on the same floor with her mistress. There was the pleasant sunny window, where she had often sat singing at her sewing; there a little case of books, and various little fancy articles, ranged by them, the gifts of Christmas holidays; there was her simple wardrobe in the closet and in the drawers:—here was, in short, her home; and, on the whole, a happy one it had been to her. But there, on the bed, lay her slumbering boy, his long curls falling negligently around his unconscious face, his rosy mouth half open, his little fat hands thrown out over the bedclothes, and a smile spread like a sunbeam over his whole face.

"Poor boy! poor fellow!" said Eliza; "they have sold you! but your mother will save you yet!"

No tear dropped over that pillow; in such straits as these, the heart has no tears to give,— it drops only blood, bleeding itself away in silence. She took a piece of paper and a pencil, and wrote, hastily,

"O Missis! dear Missis! don't think me un-grateful,—don't think hard of me, any way,—I heard all you and master said to-night. I am going to try to save my boy—you will not blame me! God bless and reward you for all your kindness!"

Hastily folding and directing this, she went to a drawer and made up a little package of clothing for her boy, which she tied with a handkerchief firmly round her waist; and, so fond is a mother's remembrance, that, even in the terrors of that hour, she did not forget to put in the little package one or two of his favorite toys, reserving a gayly painted parrot to amuse him, when she should be called on to awaken him. It was some trouble to arouse the little sleeper; but, after some effort, he sat up, and was playing with his bird, while his mother was putting on her bonnet and shawl.

"Where are you going, mother?" said he, as she drew near the bed, with his little coat and cap.

His mother drew near, and looked so earnestly into his eyes, that he at once divined that something unusual was the matter.

"Hush, Harry," she said; "mustn't speak loud, or they will hear us. A wicked man was coming to take little Harry away from his mother, and carry him 'way off in the dark; but mother won't let him—she's going to put on her little boy's cap and coat and run off with him, so the ugly man can't catch him."

Saying these words, she had tied and buttoned on the child's simple outfit, and, taking him in her arms, she whispered to him to be to be very still; and, opening a door in her room which led into the outer verandah, she glided noiselessly out.

It was a sparkling, frosty, starlight night, and the mother wrapped the shawl close round her child, as, perfectly quiet with vague terror, he clung round her neck.

Old Bruno, a great Newfoundland, who slept at the end of the porch, rose, with a low growl, as she came near. She gently spoke his name, and the animal, an old pet and playmate of hers, instantly, wagging his tail, prepared to follow her, though apparently revolving much, in his simple dog's head, what such a indiscreet midnight promenade might mean. Some dim ideas of imprudence or impropriety in the measure seemed to embarrass him considerably; for he often stopped, as Eliza glided forward, and looked wistfully, first at her and then at the house, and then, as if reassured by reflection, he pattered along after her again. A few minutes brought them to the window of Uncle Tom's cottage, and Eliza, stopping, tapped lightly on the window-pane.

The prayer-meeting at Uncle Tom's had, in the order of hymn-singing, been protracted to a very late hour; and, as Uncle Tom had indulged himself in a few lengthy solos afterwards, the consequence was, that, although it was now between twelve and one o'clock, he and his worthy help-meet were not yet asleep.

"Good Lord! what's that?" said Aunt Chloe, starting up and hastily drawing the curtain. "My sakes alive, if it ain't 'Lizy! Get on your clothes, old man, quick!—there's old Bruno, too, a-pawin' round; what on airth! I'm gwine to open the door."

And, suiting the action to the word, the door flew open, and the light of the tallow candle, which Tom had hastily lighted, fell on the haggard face and dark, wild eyes of the fugitive.

"Lord bless you!—I'm skeered to look at ye, 'Lizy! Are ye tuck sick, or what's come over ye?"

"I'm running away—Uncle Tom and Aunt Chloe—carrying off my child—Master sold him!"

"Sold him?" echoed both, lifting up their hands in dismay.

"Yes, sold him!" said Eliza firmly; "I crept into the closet by Mistress' door to-night, and I heard Master tell Missis that he had sold my Harry, and you, Uncle Tom, both, to a trader; and that he was going off this morning on his horse, and that the man was to take possession to-day."

Tom had stood, during this speech, with his hands raised, and his eyes dilated, like a man in a dream. Slowly and gradually, as its meaning came over him, he collapsed, rather than seated himself, on his old chair, and sunk his head down upon his knees.

"The good Lord have pity on us'" said Aunt Chloe. "O! it don't seem as if it was true! What

has he done, that Mas'r should sell *him?*"

"He hasn't done anything,—it isn't for that. Master don't want to sell; and Missis—she's always good. I heard her plead and beg for us; but he told her 'twas no use; that he was in this man's debt, and that this man had got the power over him; and that if he didn't pay him off clear, it would end in his having to sell the place and all the people, and move off. Yes, I heard him say there was no choice between selling these two and selling all, the man was driving him so hard. Master said he was sorry; but oh, Missis—you ought to have heard her talk! If she an't a Christian and an angel, there never was one. I'm a wicked girl to leave her so; but, then, I can't help it. She said, herself, one soul was worth more than the world; and this boy has a soul, and if I let him be carried off, who knows what'll become of it? It must be right: but, if it an't right, the Lord forgive me, for I can't help doing it!"

"Well, old man!" said Aunt Chloe, "why don't you go, too? Will you wait to be toted down river, where they kill niggers with hard work and starving? I'd a heap rather die than go there, any day! There's time for ye,—be off with 'Lizy,—you've got a pass to come and go any time. Come, bustle up, and I'll get your things together."

Tom slowly raised his head, and looked sorrowfully but quietly around, and said,

" No , no—I an't going. Let Eliza go—it's her right! I wouldn't be the one to say no—tan't in *natur* for her to stay; but you heard what she said! If I must be sold, or all the people on the place, and everything go to rack, why, let me be sold. I s'pose I can b'ar it as well as any on 'em," he added, while something like a sob and a sigh shook his broad, rough chest convulsively. "Mas'r always found me on the spot—he always will. I never have broke trust, nor used my pass no ways contrary to my word, and I never will. It's better for me alone to go, than to break up the place and sell all. Mas'r ain't to blame, Chloe, an he'll take care of you and the poor—"

Here he turned to the rough trundle-bed full of little woolly heads, and broke fairly down. He leaned over the back of the chair and covered his face with his large hands. Sobs, heavy, hoarse, and loud, shook the chair, and great tears fell through his fingers on the floor: just such tears, sir, as you dropped into the coffin where lay your first-born son; such tears, woman, as you shed when you heard the cries of your dying babe. For, sir, he was a man,—and you are but another man. And, woman, though dressed in silk and jewels, you are but a woman, and, in life's great straits and mighty griefs, ye feel but one sorrow!

"And now," said Eliza, as she stood in the door, "I saw my husband only this afternoon, and I little knew then what was to come. They have pushed him to the very last standing-place, and he told me, to-day, that he was going to run away. Do try, if you can, to get word to him. Tell him how I went, and why I went; and tell him I'm going to try and find Canada. You must give my love to him, and tell him, if I never see him again,"—she turned away, and stood with her back to them for a moment, and then added, in a husky voice, "tell him to be as good as he can, and try and meet me in the kingdom of heaven."

"Call Bruno in there," she added. "Shut the door on him, poor beast! He mustn't go with me!"

A few last words and tears, a few simple adieus and blessings, and, clasping her wondering and affrighted child in her arms, she glided noiselessly away. . . .

It is impossible to conceive of a human creature more wholly desolate and forlorn than Eliza, when she turned her footsteps from Uncle Tom's cabin.

Her husband's suffering and dangers, and the danger of her child, all blended in her mind, with a confused and stunning sense of the risk she was running, in leaving the only home she had ever known, and cutting loose from the protection of a friend whom she loved and revered. Then there was the parting from every familiar object,—the place where she had grown up , the trees under which she had played, the groves where she had walked many an evening in happier days, by the side of her young husband,— everything, as it lay in the clear, frosty starlight, seemed to speak reproachfully to her, and ask her whither could she go from a home like that?

But stronger than all was maternal love, wrought into a paroxysm of frenzy by the near approach of a fearful danger. Her boy was old enough to have walked by her side, and, in an indifferent case, she would only have led him by the hand; but now the bare thought of putting him out of her arms made her shudder, and she strained him to her bosom with a convulsive grasp, as she went rapidly forward. . . .

She was many miles past any neighborhood where she was personally known. If she should chance to meet any who knew her, she reflected that the well-known kindness of the family would be of itself a blind to suspicion, as making it an unlikely supposition that she could be a fugitive. As she was also so white as not to be known as of colored lineage, without a critical survey, and her child was white also, it was much easier for her to pass on unsuspected.

On this presumption, she stopped at noon at a neat farm-house, to rest herself, and buy some dinner for her child and self; for, as the danger decreased with the distance, the supernatural tension of the nervous system lessened, and she found herself both weary and hungry.

The good woman, kindly and gossiping, seemed rather pleased than otherwise with having somebody come in to talk with; and accepted, without examination, Eliza's statement, that she " was going on a little piece, to spend a week with her friends,"—all which she hoped in her heart might prove strictly true.

An hour before sunset, she entered the village of T——, by the Ohio River, weary and footsore, but still strong in heart. Her first glance was at the river, which lay, like Jordan, between her and the Canaan of liberty on the other side.

It was now early spring, and the river was swollen and turbulent; great cakes of floating ice were swinging heavily to and fro in the turbid waters. Owing to the peculiar form of the shore on the Kentucky side, the land bending far out into the water, the ice had been lodged and detained in great quantities, and the narrow channel which swept round the bend was full of ice, piled one cake over another, thus forming a temporary barrier to the descending ice, which lodged, and formed a great, undulating raft, filling up the whole river, and extending almost to the Kentucky shore.

Eliza stood, for a moment, contemplating this unfavorable aspect of things, which she saw at once must prevent the usual ferry-boat from running, and then turned into a small public house on the bank, to make a few inquiries.

The hostess, who was busy in various fizzing and stewing operations over the fire, preparatory to the evening meal, stopped, with a fork in her hand, as Eliza's sweet and plaintive voice arrested her.

"What is it?" she said.

"Isn't there any ferry or boat, that takes people over to B——, now?" she said.

"No, indeed!" said the woman; "the boats has stopped running."

Eliza's look of dismay and disappointment struck the woman, and she said, inquiringly,

"May be you're wanting to get over?—anybody sick? Ye seem mighty anxious?"

"I've got a child that's very dangerous," said Eliza. "I never heard of it till last night, and I've walked quite a piece to-day, in hopes to get to the ferry."

"Well, now, that's onlucky," said the woman, whose motherly sympathies were much aroused; "I'm re'lly consarned for ye. Solomon!" she called, from the window, towards a small back building. A man, in leather apron and very dirty hands, appeared at the door.

"I say, Sol," said the woman, "is that ar man going to tote them bar'ls over to-night?"

"He said he should try, if 'twas any way prudent," said the man.

"There's a man a piece down here, that's going over with some truck this evening, if he dur's to; he'll be in here to supper to-night, so you'd better set down and wait. That's a sweet little fellow," added the woman, offering him a cake.

But the child, wholly exhausted, cried with weariness.

"Poor fellow! he isn't used to walking, and I've hurried him on so," said Eliza.

"Well, take him into this room," said the woman, opening into a small bedroom, where

stood a comfortable bed. Eliza laid the weary boy upon it, and held his hands in hers till he was fast asleep. For her there was no rest. As a fire in her bones, the thought of the pursuer urged her on; and she gazed with longing eyes on the sullen, surging waters that lay between her and liberty. . . .

[The slave trader pursues Eliza to the tavern.] A thousand lives seemed to be concentrated in that one moment to Eliza. Her room opened by a side door to the river. She caught her child, and sprang down the steps towards it. The trader caught a full glimpse of her, just as she was disappearing down the bank; and throwing himself from his horse, calling loudly on Sam and Andy, he was after her like a hound after a deer. In that dizzy moment her feet to her scarce seemed to touch the ground, and a moment brought her to the water's edge. Right on behind they came; and, nerved with strength such as God gives only to the desperate, with one wild cry and flying leap, she vaulted sheer over the turbid current by the shore, on to the raft of ice beyond. It was a desperate leap—impossible to anything but madness and despair; and Haley, Sam, and Andy, instinctively cried out, and lifted up their hands, as she did it.

The huge green fragment of ice on which she alighted pitched and creaked as her weight came on it, but she stayed there not a moment. With wild cries and desperate energy she leaped to another and still another cake;—stumbling—leaping—slipping—springing upwards again! Her shoes are gone—her stockings cut from her feet—while blood marked every step; but she saw nothing, felt nothing, till dimly, as in a dream, she saw the Ohio side, and a man helping her up the bank.

"Yer a brave gal, now, whoever ye ar!" said the man, with an oath.

Eliza recognized the voice and face of a man who owned a farm not far from her old home.

"O Mr. Symmes!—save me—do save me—do hide me!" said Eliza.

"Why, what's this?" said the man. "Why, if 'tan't Shelby's gal!

"My child!—this boy!—he'd sold him! There

is his Mas'r," said she, pointing to the Kentucky shore. "O Mr. Symmes, you've got a little boy!"

"So I have," said the man, as he roughly, but kindly drew her up the steep bank. "Besides, you're a right brave gal. I like grit, wherever I see it."

When they had gained the top of the bank the man paused.

"I'd be glad to do something for ye," said he; "but then thar's nowhar I could take ye. The best I can do is to tell ye to go *thar*," said he, pointing to a large white house which stood by itself, off the main street of the village. "Go thar; they're kind folks. Thar's no kind o' danger but they'll help you,—they're up to all that sort o' thing."

Why Non-Slaveholding Southern Whites Support Slavery

J.D.B De Bow

J.D.B. De Bow (1820–1867) was the most influential southern journalist of the 1850s. His New Orleans–based magazine De Bow's Review, *read by most educated southerners, presented a relentlessly proslavery viewpoint bolstered by heavy reliance on statistics and arguments that appealed to the business side of slave-labor plantation agriculture. De Bow was also in the forefront of those prominent southerners who warned that the South must develop its industrial potential.*

In an 1860 article that he wrote in defense of "peaceful secession," excerpted here, De Bow explains why the big planters (who constituted almost all of his subscribers) were

not the only southern whites who saw slavery as essential to their interests.

When in charge of the national census office, several years since, I found that it had been stated by an abolition Senator from his seat, that the number of slaveholders at the South did not exceed 150,000. Convinced that it was a gross misrepresentation of the facts, I caused a careful examination of the returns to be made, which fixed the actual number at 347,255, and communicated the information, by note, to Senator Cass, who read it in the Senate. I first called attention to the fact that the number embraced slaveholding families, and that to arrive at the actual number of slaveholders, it would be necessary to multiply by the proportion of persons, which the census showed to a family. When this was done, the number

Reprinted from J.D.B. De Bow, "The Non-Slaveholder of the South," in *The Interest in Slavery of the Southern Non-Slaveholder*, by J.D.B. De Bow et al. (Charleston, SC: Evans & Cogswell, 1860).

was swelled to about 2,000,000.

Since these results were made public, I have had reason to think, that the separation of the schedules of the slave and the free, was calculated to lead to omissions of the single properties, and that on this account it would be safe to put the number of families at 375,000, and the number of actual slaveholders at about two million and a quarter.

Assuming the published returns, however, to be correct, it will appear that one-half of the population of South Carolina, Mississippi, and Louisiana, excluding the cities, are slaveholders, and that one-third of the population of the entire South are similarly circumstanced. The average number of slaves is nine to each slaveholding family, and one-half of the whole number of such holders are in possession of less than five slaves.

It will thus appear that the slaveholders of the South, so far from constituting numerically an insignificant portion of its people, as has been malignantly alleged, make up an aggregate, greater in relative proportion than the holders of any other species of property whatever, in any part of the world; and that of no other property can it be said, with equal truthfulness, that it is an interest of the whole community. Whilst every other family in the States I have specially referred to, are slaveholders, but one family in every three and a half families in Maine, New Hampshire, Massachusetts and Connecticut, are holders of agricultural land; and, in European States, the proportion is almost indefinitely less, The proportion which the slaveholders of the South, bear to the entire population is greater than that of the owners of land or houses, agricultural stock, State, bank, or other corporation securities anywhere else. No political economist will deny this. Nor is that all. Even in the States which are among the largest slaveholding, South Carolina, Georgia and Tennessee, the land proprietors outnumber nearly two to one, in relative proportion, the owners of the same property in Maine, Massachusetts and Connecticut, and if the average number of slaves held by each family throughout the South be but nine, and if one-half of the whole number of slaveholders own

under five slaves, it will be seen how preposterous is the allegation of our enemies, that the slaveholding class is an organized wealthy aristocracy. *The poor men of the South are the holders of one to five slaves, and it would be equally consistent with truth and justice, to say that they represent, in reality, its slaveholding interest.*

The fact being conceded that there is a very large class of persons in the slaveholding States, who have no direct ownership in slaves; it may be well asked, upon what principle a greater antagonism can be presumed between them and their fellow-citizens, than exists among the larger class of non-landholders in the free States and the landed interest there? If a conflict of interest exists in one instance, it does in the other, and if patriotism and public spirit are to be measured upon so low a standard, the social fabric at the North is in far greater danger of dissolution than it is here.

Though I protest against the false and degrading standard, to which Northern orators and statesmen have reduced the measure of patriotism, which is to be expected from a free and enlightened people, and in the name of the non-slaveholders of the South, fling back the insolent charge that they are only bound to their country by its "loaves and fishes," and would be found derelict in honor and principle and public virtue in proportion as they are needy in circumstances; I think it but easy to show that the interest of the poorest non-slaveholder among us, is to make common cause with, and die in the last trenches in defence of, the slave property of his more favored neighbor.

The non-slaveholders of the South may be classed as either such as desire and are incapable of purchasing slaves, or such as have the means to purchase and do not because of the absence of the motive, preferring to hire or employ cheaper white labor. A class conscientiously objecting to the ownership of slave-property, does not exist at the South, for all such scruples have long since been silenced by the profound and unanswerable arguments to which Yankee controversy has driven our statesmen, popular orators and clergy. Upon the sure testimony of God's

Holy Book, and upon the principles of universal polity, they have defended and justified the institution. The exceptions which embrace recent importations into Virginia, and into some of the Southern cities from the free States of the North, and some of the crazy, socialistic Germans in Texas, are too unimportant to affect the truth of the proposition. . . .

1. *The non-slaveholder of the South is assured that the remuneration afforded by his labor, over and above the expense of living, is larger than that which is afforded by the same labor in the free States.* To be convinced of this he has only to compare the value of labor in the Southern cities with those of the North, and to take note annually of the large number of laborers who are represented to be out of employment there, and who migrate to our shores, as well as to other sections. No white laborer in return has been forced to leave our midst or remain without employment. Such as have left, have immigrated from States where slavery was less productive. Those who come among us are enabled soon to retire to their homes with a handsome competency. The statement is nearly as true for the agricultural as for other interests, as the statistics will show.

The following table was recently compiled by Senator Johnson, of Tennessee, from information received in reply to a circular letter sent to the points indicated.

Daily wages in New Orleans, Charleston and Nashville:

Bricklayers.	Carpenters.	Laborers.
$2½ to 3½	$2¼ to 2¾	$1 to 1½.

Daily wages in Chicago, Pittsburgh and Lowell, Mass.:

Bricklayers.	Carpenters.	Laborers.
$ 1½ to $2	$ 1½ to 1¾	75c to $1.

The rates of board weekly for laborers as given in the census of 1850, were in Louisiana $2 70, South Carolina $1 75, Tennessee $1 32, in Illinois $1 49, Pennsylvania $1 72, Massachusetts $2 12. The wages of the agricultural classes as given in Parliamentary reports are in France $20 to $30 per annum with board. In Italy $12 to $20 per annum. In the United States agricultural labor is highest in the Southwest, and lowest in the Northwest, the South and North differing very little, by the official returns.

2. *The non-slaveholders, as a class, are not reduced by the necessity of our condition, as is the case in the free States, to find employment in crowded cities and come into competition in close and sickly workshops and factories, with remorseless and untiring machinery.* They have but to compare their condition in this particular with the mining and manufacturing operatives of the North and Europe, to be thankful that God has reserved them for a better fate. Tender women, aged men, delicate children, toil and labor there from early dawn until after candle light, from one year to another, for a miserable pittance, scarcely above the starvation point and without hope of amelioration. The records of British free labor have long exhibited this and those of our own manufacturing States are rapidly reaching it and would have reached it long ago, but for the excessive bounties which in the way of tariffs have been paid to it, without an equivalent by the slaveholding and non-slaveholding laborer of the South. Let this tariff cease to be paid for a single year and the truth of what is stated will be abundantly shown.

3. *The non-slaveholder is not subjected to that competition with foreign pauper labor, which has degraded the free labor of the North and demoralized it to an extent which perhaps can never be estimated.* From whatever cause, it has happened, whether from climate, the nature of our products or of our labor, the South has been enabled to maintain a more homogeneous population and show a less admixture of races than the North. This the statistics show.

RATIO OF FOREIGN TO NATIVE POPULATION.		
Eastern States 12.65	in every 100	
Middle States 19.84	"	"
Southern States 1.86	"	"
South-western States 5.34	"	"
North-western States 12.75	"	"

Our people partake of the true American character, and are mainly the descendants of those who fought the battles of the Revolution, and who understand and appreciate the nature and inestimable value of the liberty which it brought. Adhering to the simple truths of the Gospel and the faith of their fathers, they have not run hither and thither in search of all the absurd and degrading isms which have sprung up in the rank soil of infidelity. They are not Mormons or Spiritualists, they are not Owenites, Fourierites, Agrarians, Socialists, Free-lovers or Millerites. They are not for breaking down all the forms of society and of religion and re-constructing them; but prefer law, order and existing institutions to the chaos which radicalism involves. The competition between native and foreign labor in the Northern States, has already begotten rivalry and heart-burning, and riots; and lead to the formation of political parties there which have been marked by a degree of hostility and proscription to which the present age has not afforded another parallel. At the South we have known none of this, except in two or three of the larger cities, where the relations of slavery and freedom scarcely exist at all. The foreigners that are among us at the South are of a select class, and from education and example approximate very nearly to the native standard.

4. *The non-slaveholder of the South preserves the status of the white man, and is not regarded as an inferior or a dependent.* He is not told that the Declaration of Independence, when it says that all men are born free and equal, refers to the negro equally with himself. It is not proposed to him that the free negro's vote shall weigh equally with his own at the ballot-box, and that the little children of both colors shall be mixed in the classes and benches of the school-house, and embrace each other filially in its outside sports. It never occurs to him, that a white man could be degraded enough to boast in a public assembly, as was recently done in New York, of having actually slept with a negro. And his patriotic ire would crush with a blow the free negro who would dare, in his presence, as is done in the free States, to characterize the father of the country as a "scoundrel." No white man at the South serves another as a body servant, to clean his boots, wait on his table, and perform the menial services of his household. His blood revolts against this, and his necessities never drive him to it. He is a companion and an equal. When in the employ of the slaveholder, or in intercourse with him, he enters his hall, and has a seat at his table. If a distinction exists, it is only that which education and refinement may give, and this is so courteously exhibited as scarcely to strike attention. The poor white laborer at the North is at the bottom of the social ladder, whilst his brother here has ascended several steps and can look down upon those who are beneath him, at an infinite remove.

5. *The non-slaveholder knows that as soon as his savings will admit, he can become a slaveholder, and thus relieve his wife from the necessities of the kitchen and the laundry, and his children from the labors of the field.* This, with ordinary frugality, can, in general, be accomplished in a few years, and is a process continually going on. Perhaps twice the number of poor men at the South own a slave to what owned a slave ten years ago. The universal disposition is to purchase. It is the first use for savings, and the negro purchased is the last possession to be parted with. If a woman, her children become heir-looms and make the nucleus of an estate. It is within my knowledge, that a plantation of fifty or sixty persons has been established, from the descendants of a single female, in the course of the lifetime of the original purchaser.

6. *The large slaveholders and proprietors of the South begin life in great part as non-slaveholders.* It is the nature of property to change hands. Luxury, liberality, extravagance, depreciated land, low prices, debt, distribution among children, are continually breaking up estates. All over the new States of the South-west enormous estates are in the hands of men who began life as overseers or city clerks, traders or merchants. Often the overseer marries the widow. Cheap lands, abundant harvests, high prices, give the poor man soon a negro. His ten bales of cotton bring him another, a second crop increases his purchases, and so he goes on opening land and adding labor until in a few years

his draft for $20,000 upon his merchant becomes a very marketable commodity.

7. *But should such fortune not be in reserve for the non-slaveholder, he will understand that by honesty and industry it may be realized to his children.* More than one generation of poverty in a family is scarcely to be expected at the South, and is against the general experience. It is more unusual here for poverty than wealth to be preserved through several generations in the same family.

8. *The sons of the non-slaveholder are and have always been among the leading and ruling spirits of the South; in industry as well as in politics.* Every man's experience in his own neighborhood will evince this. He has but to task his memory. In this class are the McDuffies, Langdon Cheves, Andrew Jacksons, Henry Clays, and Rusks, of the past; the Hammonds, Yanceys, Orrs, Memmingers, Benaminjs, Stephens, Soulés, Browns of Mississippi, Simms, Porters, Magraths, Aikens, Maunsel Whites, and an innumerable host of the present; and what is to be noted, these men have not been made demagogues for that reason, as in other quarters, but are among the most conservative among us. Nowhere else in the world have intelligence and virtue disconnected from ancestral estates, the same opportunities for advancement, and nowhere else is their triumph more speedy and signal.

9. *Without the institution of slavery, the great staple products of the South would cease to be grown, and the immense annual results, which are distributed among every class of the community, and which give life to every branch of industry, would cease.* The world furnishes no instances of these products being grown upon a large scale by free labor. The English now acknowledge their failure in the East Indies. Brazil, whose slave population nearly equals our own, is the only South American State which has prospered. Cuba, by her slave labor, showers wealth upon old Spain, whilst the British West India Colonies have now ceased to be a source of revenue, and from opulence have been, by emancipation, reduced to beggary. St. Domingo shared the same fate, and the poor whites have been massacred equally with the rich. . . .

10. *If emancipation be brought about as will undoubtedly be the case, unless the encroachments of the fanatical majorities of the North are resisted now the slaveholders, in the main, will escape the degrading equality which must result, by emigration, for which they would have the means, by disposing of their personal chattels: whilst the non-slaveholders, without these resources, would be compelled to remain and endure the degradation.* This is a startling consideration. In Northern communities, where the free negro is one in a hundred of the total population, he is recognized and acknowledged often as a pest, and in many cases even his presence is prohibited by law. What would be the case in many of our States, where every other inhabitant is a negro, or in many of our communities, as for example the parishes around and about Charleston, and in the vicinity of New Orleans where there are from twenty to one hundred negroes to each white inhabitant? Low as would this class of people sink by emancipation in idleness, superstition and vice, the white man compelled to live among them, would by the power exerted over him, sink even lower, unless as is to be supposed he would prefer to suffer death instead.

Dred Scott's Fight for Freedom

Brian McGinty

The famous Dred Scott *case that gripped the nation's attention in early 1857, when the pro-southern Supreme Court ruled that blacks could not be citizens and that the Missouri Compromise had unconstitutionally barred slavery from the West, is so large an issue in American history that we tend to overlook the man who was at the center of it all. Who was Dred Scott? Historical writer Brian McGinty answers this question in a biographical sketch of this illiterate, mild-mannered, but shrewd and persistent African American presented here.*

He was an unlikely figure to be the focal point of one of the most controversial cases in the annals of American justice. A slight man, standing not much over five feet tall, with a dark complexion and a shock of wiry hair, he was past 50 years old and already suffering from the hacking cough that would eventually take his life when circumstances called him to the center stage of history. He could neither read nor write (on legal documents he made his "mark" in lieu of a signature), and he had only

Reprinted from Brian McGinty, "A Heap O' Trouble," *American History Illustrated*, May 1981. This article is reprinted from *American History Illustrated* magazine with the permission of PRIMEDIA Special Interest Publications (History Group), copyright American History Illustrated magazine.

the vaguest understanding of the momentous legal arguments that swirled around him.

But he was neither stupid nor ignorant. He had traveled widely and was a keen observer of people and events. He was willing to accept advice, to listen to his lawyers, and to follow their instructions faithfully. Above all, he trusted in the wisdom and fairness of the judges who would ultimately decide his fate. Many times during his long and discouraging fight for freedom, the slave known as Dred Scott could have run away—escaped from his home in St. Louis into the nearby woods, or slipped across the Mississippi into the free state of Illinois. He chose instead to remain and see his case through to its glorious (or would it be tragic?) conclusion.

There were many who regarded Dred Scott as a mere pawn in the great legal struggle that bore his name. Surely the Supreme Court's opinion in *Scott v. Sandford,* handed down in March 1857, decided many issues that transcended the obscure slave's fight for freedom. It was, in fact, a pivotal case in American judicial history, a turning point in the uneasy national truce that had, for nearly half a century, kept firebrands in the North and South from each other's throats. Chief Justice Roger B. Taney of Maryland, who wrote the majority opinion in the *Dred Scott* case, thought the decision would settle the question of slavery in America for all time. Abraham Lincoln branded it "an astonisher in legal history" and made it a principal issue in his campaign for the Senate in 1858. Far from settling the slavery question, the *Dred Scott* case brought the festering national sore to a spectacular head. It at once enraged the North, hardened the South, divided the nation's Democrats, and fueled the burgeoning cause of the Republicans. Last but not least, it led directly and inexorably to Lincoln's victory in the election of 1860, an election that dramatically changed the nation's attitude toward slavery. "It may fairly be said," constitutional historian Charles Warren has written, "that Chief Justice Taney elected Abraham Lincoln to the Presidency."

However far-reaching its implications, the *Dred Scott* case was also the story of a personal struggle; the story of an illiterate black's dream of escaping from slavery and building a new life for himself and his family outside the iron confines of "the peculiar institution," and the story of a personal battle that became the trumpet call for a race.

It was not easy for a black man in mid-19th-

Dred Scott

century America to break his bonds, however strong his legal claims to freedom. The courts were, in both North and South, controlled by whites, and the whims of juries had fully as much weight in courtrooms as statutes and precedents. If the Constitution did not precisely approve of slavery, it did recognize it, allowing traders to continue to import Africans until 1808, and permitting Southern states to count three-fifths of the slaves within their borders in determining their representation in Congress.

Congress had dealt often with the issue of slavery, though never satisfactorily. In 1787 it banned the institution from the Northwest Territory (the land that comprises Ohio, Indiana, Illinois, Michigan, and Wisconsin); but the ban was interpreted to exclude new slaves only, and not to grant freedom to the old. In 1820, led by Kentucky's Henry Clay, Congress approved the Missouri Compromise, allowing Maine to enter the Union as a free state, admitting Missouri as a slave state, and drawing a line westward from Missouri's southern border, north of which all new states would be free, south of which they would be slave.

Dred Scott was born and lived most of his life in the South, but he had, perhaps a half-dozen times in the 1830s and '40s, crossed into free territory—first into Illinois, later into a part of the Louisiana Purchase that eventually became Iowa, and finally to Fort Snelling, near the site of what ultimately became St. Paul, Minnesota. He did not escape into these territories, like thousands of fugitive slaves before and after. He was voluntarily taken there by his owner, an army surgeon who, in the course of his military duties, traveled frequently from post to post. While living in Illinois, Iowa, and Minnesota, Scott rendered the same services that he customarily rendered in Missouri. It is unlikely that either the slave or his owner appreciated the legal consequences of their sojourns on free soil, though more than a decade later these sojourns were to form the basis of Scott's claim to freedom—and fuel one of the bitterest controversies ever brought before the Supreme Court of the United States.

Dred Scott was born of slave parents in Southampton County, Virginia, around 1800. In 1819 his owner, Peter Blow, moved with his family and slaves (Scott included) to a farm near Huntsville, Alabama. In 1830 the family made a second move, this time to the thriving Mississippi River town of St. Louis. Blow died in 1832, and Scott was sold to John Emerson, an assistant surgeon in the United States Army. In 1833 Dr. Emerson was ordered to Rock Island, Illinois, a state in which slavery had twice been forbidden, first by Congress in 1787 and again by the state constitution of 1818. Scott accompanied Emerson to Illinois and, across the Mississippi near what is now Davenport, Iowa, helped him build a log cabin. In 1836 Dr. Emerson and Scott moved on to Fort Snelling. There the army officer purchased a female slave named Harriet. Scott had been married once, but his wife had died, and he had no children. With Emerson's permission, he now married Harriet. Emerson was briefly transferred to Louisiana in 1837, where the Scotts followed him, but he returned to Fort Snelling again within the year. It was in 1838, on a small river boat somewhere north of the Missouri border, that Harriet Scott gave birth to a daughter named Eliza. Two sons and another daughter were born later, but only the daughters survived infancy.

Emerson died in 1843, and Dred Scott and his family—back once again in Missouri—passed with other assets of the Emerson estate to the doctor's widow. Dred was hired out to an army captain with whom he traveled to Louisiana and Texas, but he returned to St. Louis in 1846. He tried twice to buy his freedom, offering to pay part of the price in cash and give security for the balance, but Mrs. Emerson refused the proposal. Thus rebuffed, Scott sought the assistance of Henry and Taylor Blow, sons of Peter Blow, who had grown up with the slave and still took a brotherly interest in his welfare. The Blows, in turn, consulted lawyers, and in April 1846 Dred Scott filed suit in a St. Louis court to secure his and his family's freedom.

The legal argument was simple: By taking Scott to live in Illinois, Iowa, and Minnesota, Dr.

Emerson had emancipated the slave, and when Scott later returned to Missouri, he did so as a free man. The case was tried twice, the second time resulting in victory for Scott. Following a long line of Missouri state court decisions, the trial judge held that a slaveholder who voluntarily took his slaves into free territory thereby released them from bondage. For the time being, at least, Dred Scott was a free man.

But Mrs. Emerson's lawyers promptly appealed the decision to the Missouri Supreme Court, which decided that it would not take notice of the Illinois laws prohibiting slavery, nor of the Federal statutes that banned the institution from the northern reaches of the Louisiana Purchase. Such laws were hostile to Missouri's own laws on the subject, the court said, and not binding in the slave-holding states. Since the Missouri Supreme Court would not admit that slavery was forbidden in Illinois or Iowa or Minnesota, Dred Scott was told that he must live the rest of his life in slavery.

The decision rankled in the slave's mind, but he was in no position to finance a continuation of his long and increasingly costly battle. He was working in St. Louis now as a household servant, his earnings being held by the sheriff pending a final decision in his case (if he lost, every penny would be paid over to his owner). But he had friends and supporters who were unwilling to see his cause abandoned.

Since 1851 Scott had been working for Charles La Beaume, a St. Louis resident and brother-in-law of Henry Blow. Some years after Scott's first petition was filed, Mrs. Emerson moved to Massachusetts and married a physician named Calvin Chaffee. At about the same time, her brother, John Sanford of New York, became Scott's owner. Field now advised Scott and the Blows that the Federal courts were required to hear cases in which there was "diversity of citizenship"–suits, in the Constitution's words, "between citizens of different States." Since Sanford was a citizen of New York and Scott lived in Missouri, the case seemed open and shut.

Field now drafted a petition in which he alleged that Sanford, wrongfully treating Scott as his slave, had assaulted, threatened, and restrained him and his family, all to their damage in the sum of $9,000. The petition was filed in the U.S. Circuit Court in St. Louis on November 2, 1853. In his answer, Sanford claimed that he had only "gently laid his hands" on the Scotts, "as he had a right to do," because they were his slaves. The case came to trial on May 15, 1854. The judge sustained Scott's right to maintain the suit, but the jury found that he and his family were still slaves and, as such, not entitled to any damages from Sanford.

Field now called on a former St. Louis attorney named Montgomery Blair to take Scott's appeal to the U.S. Supreme Court. Born in Kentucky, Blair had lived in St. Louis for years before leaving for Washington, D.C. in 1853 to practice law in the shadow of the Capitol (during the Civil War he was to serve as Abraham Lincoln's postmaster general). Blair agreed to take Scott's case without fee, though he insisted that others be responsible for the court costs. Henry S. Geyer, newly elected U.S. senator from Missouri, and Reverdy Johnson, former senator from Maryland and onetime U.S. attorney general, were retained to represent Sanford.

The Supreme Court in 1856 enjoyed wide respect, though its views on the subject of slavery were not such as to give opponents of the institution any great cause for hope. Five of the nine justices were from south of the Mason-Dixon line, and only one was known to have strong anti-slavery views. Four members owed their appointments to President Andrew Jackson and, among them, represented nearly ninety years of experience on the high court. Roger Taney of Maryland had served as attorney general and as secretary of the treasury before Jackson elevated him to the chief justiceship in 1836. Now in his twenty-first year on the Court, his somber eyes overhung by a craggy mop of gray hair, Taney looked every bit of his eighty years.

As a young man the chief justice had expressed somewhat liberal views about slavery, but advancing years had stifled any inclination he might once have felt to upset the institution.

He was an intelligent man, an able lawyer, and an energetic, if increasingly sickly, judge, who made no effort to conceal his sympathy for the cause of Southern chivalry.

Arguments in the *Dred Scott* case began on February 11, 1856, and continued for four days. The Court conferred twice on the case without reaching a decision, then recessed for the month of March. Newspapers had carried little news of the case before April, when Horace Greeley's New York *Tribune* began to speculate on the decision, perhaps because the nation was once again in the throes of a great debate over slavery. The admission to the Union of California as a free state in 1850 had aroused the pro-slavery interests to a frenzy of legislative action. Led by Illinois Senator Stephen A. Douglas, Congress had in 1854 passed the Kansas-Nebraska Act, allowing settlers in those territories (both north of the Missouri Compromise line) to establish slavery if such was the will of the majority of their voters. The Republican party, dedicated to the gradual eradication of slavery throughout the nation, had been formed in 1854 and was now preparing to run its first candidate for the presidency. Supreme Court Justice John McLean of Ohio, a long-time opponent of slavery, hoped to become the Republicans' first candidate. Greeley's Washington correspondent, a McLean supporter, expected that the majority of Supreme Court justices would vote against Dred Scott. If they did, he told *Tribune* readers, they could expect a "rousing dissent" from McLean.

The Southern justices were alarmed. If McLean filed a "rousing dissent," the document might catapult him into the White House and irreparably injure the slaveholders' cause. Prudence winning out over vehemence, the justices met in May and, by a vote of 5 to 4, decided to postpone final judgment in the case—and to hear new arguments in December.

Democrat James Buchanan was the president-elect in December 1856 when *Dred Scott* came up for its second hearing in the Supreme Court. By now the case was a national *cause célébre*. It was widely whispered that the Southern majority planned to use the case, not only to seal Dred

Scott's fate, but also to strike down the Missouri Compromise's limitation on slavery in the territories, and thus to open vast reaches of the West to the institution.

Such an all-encompassing decision was far from essential to final disposition of the case. The Court might settle the controversy quietly, deciding simply that the Missouri slave's fate was to be determined by the law of Missouri and, since Missouri had ruled against him, the case was closed. Or it might have based its decision on the question of jurisdiction, holding that a slave was not a "citizen" and thus not entitled to maintain a suit in Federal court. But the United States Supreme Court in December 1856 was not inclined to limit its ruling. The slavery controversy was wracking the nation. If it could be settled by the stroke of a pen (or by the cumulative strokes of nine pens), it might be put to rest forever.

It was Justice James Wayne of Georgia who conceived the idea of issuing a broad decision that would condemn the anti-slavery provisions of the Missouri Compromise. After Wayne convinced Taney and three others of his views, the old chief justice began to draft an opinion.

President-elect Buchanan had been kept abreast of the Court's deliberations by a series of letters written by Justice John Catron of Tennessee. In one of his letters, Catron asked the president-elect to urge his fellow Pennsylvanian, Justice Robert Grier, to join in the Taney opinion. In his inaugural address on March 4, 1857, Buchanan professed not to know how the *Dred Scott* case would be decided, but he urged all citizens to "cheerfully submit" to the ruling, whatever it was.

Two days later, on March 6, 1857, Chief Justice Taney read his opinion. Since the Constitution recognized slavery, Taney wrote, and since at the time of the document's adoption blacks were uniformly regarded as "beings of an inferior order," no black could be deemed a "citizen." Because Dred Scott was not a "citizen," he could not sue in Federal court. Moreover, Congress's attempt to ban slavery from the territories north of the Missouri Compromise line was unconsti-

tutional. Slaves were a form of property, Taney said. The Fifth Amendment provides, among other things, that no person shall be "deprived of . . . property, without due process of law." A law that strips a man of his slaves merely because he crosses a state or territorial boundary, the chief justice said, "could hardly be dignified with the name of due process of law."

Dissenting opinions were filed by McLean and by Justice Benjamin Curtis of Massachusetts. The Missouri Compromise, the dissenters said, was quite constitutional. Slaves were "property" only in states that said they were, and not elsewhere. The idea that the Constitution branded slaves as "property" throughout the Union or prevented them from being considered as citizens was a perversion of the framers' intentions.

The dissents were vigorous, but they failed to carry the day. By a final vote of 7 to 2, the Supreme Court decided that Dred Scott must remain a slave.

The ruling aroused howls of denunciation. "The decision of the Supreme Court," said the New York *Independent,* "is the Moral Assassination of a Race and Cannot be Obeyed." Senator William Seward of New York charged President Buchanan with complicity in a decision "to hang the millstone of slavery on the neck of the people of Kansas." "If epithets and judicial denunciation could sink a judicial body," wrote the New York *Tribune,* "the Supreme Court of the United States would never be heard of again."

Abraham Lincoln, challenging Stephen Douglas's bid for reelection to the Senate, hinted darkly that *Dred Scott* was the result of a conspiracy between Douglas, Taney, Buchanan, and former President Franklin Pierce. Fearing that the Supreme Court's next step would be to make slavery "perpetual and universal" throughout the nation, Lincoln said it was imperative that *Dred Scott* be reversed.

Lincoln did not win the election of 1858, but he was the victor in an even bigger contest in 1860—thanks largely to the political excitement occasioned by *Dred Scott.* If, before *Dred Scott,* opponents of slavery were willing to bide their time, trusting in the gradual evolution of attitudes to phase out the institution, they were, after the decision, increasingly impatient to get on with the work of abolition. If, before *Dred Scott*, Southern slaveholders trusted in the Federal courts to protect them from "meddlesome" Yankees, they were, after the decision, more and more alarmed by the vehemence of Northern attacks. Would the Supreme Court continue to protect them against the Abolitionists? Would the Constitution, as interpreted by the nation's Dixie-dominated Federal judiciary, continue to be their last and best defense against the opponents of slavery? With a man like Abraham Lincoln in the White House—a man determined to seek a reversal of *Dred Scott*—the slaveholders' uneasiness grew quickly into panic.

Dred Scott himself accepted his defeat stoically. John Sanford had died before the Supreme Court's decision was announced, and Mrs. Emerson's husband, now an Abolitionist congressman from Massachusetts, hastened to make amends for the injustice of the case. For a nominal sum, he arranged to have the slave transferred to Taylor Blow who, on May 26, 1857, finally freed him and his family.

Newspaper reporters hurried to St. Louis to interview the celebrated black. Scott laughed about "de fuss dey made dar in Washington 'bout de old nigger," but became serious when he spoke of the long years of litigation and the heavy expense it had entailed. If he had known the case "was gwine to last so long," he would not have started it. It had, he said, given him and his family a "heap o' trouble."

If the Supreme Court's decision was a "heap o' trouble" for the old slave, it was a source of even greater anguish for the slaveholders of the old South. They had won in the Supreme Court, but, as they soon discovered, they could not convert their judicial majority into a popular victory, nor could they muster their forces on the field of battle as effectively as they had in the high court. The law, said the Supreme Court, was on their side—but the moral verdict was far less clear. The great Civil War that was, in large part, precipitated by the *Dred Scott* decision did not end until the South was defeated and slavery finally abolished throughout the nation. Dred Scott died on September 17, 1858, a victim of consumption, hardly aware of the monumental consequences of his brave fight for freedom. For him the case had been a "heap o' trouble." For millions of his fellow blacks, it was a clarion call to freedom.

Selection 5

Dred Scott Remains a Slave

Roger B. Taney

The story of the Dred Scott *decision is complex, involving the politics of the North-South sectional struggle of the 1850s, the ambitions of most contenders for the presidency (including Abraham Lincoln and his Democratic rival, Stephen Douglas), and the racial and political prejudices of the justices of the Supreme Court. Even today, historians*

Excerpted from Roger B. Taney, U.S. Supreme Court decision in *Dred Scott v. Sandford*, March 1857.

have not untangled all the mysteries of the case, including the question of why Chief Justice Roger B. Taney decided to issue a sweeping ruling that declared blacks ineligible for citizenship and the entire West open to slavery.

Taney (1777–1864)—whose name is pronounced "Taw-ney"—was a political associate of Andrew Jackson. He succeeded John Marshall as chief justice in 1836, and as a builder of the American legal tradition he ranks not far below Marshall himself. The descendant of a wealthy Maryland Catholic family, he freed the slaves he had inherited, believed slavery to be evil, and thought that the institution should be gradually abolished. Yet, he insisted, only the states, and not the federal government, should deal with slavery. In the decision that he announced in the Dred Scott case, Taney was speaking only for himself, yet combined with the other southern and pro-southern justices' decisions, the Court ruled 7–2 in favor of keeping Scott a slave.

It is likely that Taney was motivated by a decision to settle, once and for all, the intense national debate over whether slavery could expand into the territories that the United States had bought from France in 1803 and had conquered from Mexico in 1848. He evidently hoped to put the Supreme Court's prestige behind a decision that slave owners could take their human property into any western territory. Instead, the result was to inflame the two opposing groups still more violently.

Taney's decision, excerpted here, has indelibly marred his historical reputation. The contempt with which he regarded black people seems shocking today; it is difficult to believe that such words were written by a chief justice of the United States. Readers should remember that they were unquestioningly shared by southerners of his time, and that what shocked most northerners about his decision was not so much Taney's racial prejudice as his ruling that Congress could not legally bar slavery from the western territories. Most northern whites were unabashed racists, and some (not all) were indifferent to the plight of the slaves, but the vast majority of them had no desire to see the West settled by slave labor, which they feared would inevitably squeeze out free white farmers, workers, and shopkeepers.

The question is simply this: Can a negro, whose ancestors were imported into this country, and sold as slaves, become a member of the political community formed and brought into existence by the Constitution of the United States, and as such become entitled to all the rights, and privileges, and immunities, guarantied by that instrument to the citizen? One of which rights is the privilege of suing in a court of the United States in the cases specified in the Constitution. . . .

The words "people of the United States" and "citizens" are synonymous terms, and mean the same thing. They both describe the political body who . . . form the sovereignty, and who hold the power and conduct the Government through their representatives. . . . The question before us is, whether the class of persons described in the plea in abatement [people of African ancestry] compose a portion of this people, and are constituent members of this sovereignty? We think they are not, and that they are not included, and were not intended to be included, under the word "citizens" in the Constitution, and can therefore claim none of the rights and privileges which that instrument provides for and secures to citizens of the United States. On the contrary, they were at that time considered as a subordinate and inferior class of beings, who had been subjugated by the dominant race, and, whether emancipated or not, yet remained subject to their authority, and had no rights or privileges but such as those who held the power and the Government might choose to grant them.

It is not the province of the court to decide upon the justice or injustice, the policy or impolicy, of these laws. The decision of that question belonged . . . to those who formed the sovereignty and framed the Constitution. The duty of the court is, to interpret the instrument they have framed, with the best lights we can obtain on the subject, and to administer it as we find it, according to its true intent and meaning when it was adopted. . . .

The question then arises, whether the provisions of the Constitution, in relation to the personal rights and privileges to which the citizen of a State should be entitled, embraced the negro African race . . . made free in any State; and to put it in the power of a single State to make him a citizen of the United States, and endue him with the full rights of citizenship in every other State without their consent? Does the Constitution of the United States act upon him whenever he shall be made free under the laws of a State, and raised there to the rank of a citizen, and immediately clothe him with all the privileges of a citizen in every other State, and in its own courts?

The court think the affirmative of these propositions cannot be maintained. And if it cannot, [Dred Scott] could not be a citizen of the State of Missouri, within the meaning of the Constitution of the United States, and, consequently, was not entitled to sue in its courts.

It is true, every person, and every class and description of persons, who were at the time of the adoption of the Constitution recognized as citizens in the several States, became also citizens of this new political body; but none other; it was formed by them, and for them and their posterity, but for no one else. And the personal rights and privileges guaranteed to citizens of this new sovereignty were intended to embrace those only who were then members of the several State communities, or who should afterwards by birthright or otherwise become members, according to the provisions of the Constitution and the principles on which it was founded. . . .

It becomes necessary, therefore, to determine who were citizens of the several States when the Constitution was adopted. . . .

. . . [T]he legislation and histories of the times, and the language used in the Declaration of Independence, show, that neither the class of persons who had been imported as slaves, nor their descendants, whether they had become free or not, were then acknowledged as a part of the people, nor intended to be included in the general words used in that memorable instrument.

It is difficult at this day to realize the state of public opinion in relation to that unfortunate race, which prevailed in the civilized and enlightened portions of the world at the time of the Declaration of Independence, and when the Constitution of the United States was framed and adopted. . . .

They had for more than a century before been regarded as beings of an inferior order, and altogether unfit to associate with the white race, either in social or political relations; and so far inferior, that they had no rights which the white man was bound to respect; and that the negro might justly and lawfully be reduced to slavery. . . . He was bought and sold, and treated as an ordinary article of merchandise and traffic, whenever a profit could be made by it. This opinion was at that time fixed and universal in the civilized portion of the white race. It was regarded as an axiom in morals as well as in politics, which no one thought of disputing, or supposed to be open to dispute; and men in every grade and position in society daily and habitually acted upon it in their private pursuits, as well as in matters of public concern, without doubting for a moment the correctness of this opinion. . . .

The language of the Declaration of Independence is equally Conclusive: . . .

> We hold these truths to be self-evident: that all men are created equal; that they are endowed by their Creator with certain unalienable rights; that among them is life, liberty, and the pursuit of happiness; that to secure these rights, Governments are instituted, deriving their just powers from the consent of the governed.

The general words above quoted would seem to embrace the whole human family, and if they were used in a similar instrument at this day would be so understood. But it is too clear for dispute, that the enslaved African race were not intended to be included, and formed no part of the people who framed and adopted this declaration; for if the language, as understood in that day, would embrace them, the conduct of the distinguished men who framed the Declaration of Independence would have been utterly and flagrantly inconsistent with the principles they asserted; and instead of the sympathy of mankind, to which they so confidently appeared, they would have deserved and received universal rebuke and reprobation.

Yet the men who framed this declaration were great men—high in literary acquirements—high in their sense of honor, and incapable of asserting principles inconsistent with those on which they were acting. They perfectly understood the meaning of the language they used, and how it would be understood by others; and they knew that it would not in any part of the civilized world be supposed to embrace the negro race, which, by common consent, had been excluded from civilized Governments and the family of nations, and doomed to slavery. They spoke and acted according to the then established doctrines and principles, and in the ordinary language of the day, no one misunderstood them. The unhappy black race were separated from the white by indelible marks, and laws long before established, and were never thought of or spoken of except as property, and when the claims of the owner or the profit of the trader were supposed to need protection.

This state of public opinion had undergone no change when the Constitution was adopted, as is equally evident from its provisions and language. . . .

[There] are two clauses in the Constitution which point directly and specifically to the negro race as a separate class of persons, and show clearly that they were not regarded as a portion of the people or citizens of the Government then formed.

One of these clauses reserves to each of the thirteen States the right to import slaves until the year 1808. . . . And by the other provision the States pledge themselves to each other to maintain the right of property of the master, by delivering up to him any slave who may have escaped

from his service, and be found within their respective territories. . . . And these two provisions show, conclusively, that neither the description of persons therein referred to, nor their descendants, were embraced in any of the other provisions of the Constitution; for certainly these two clauses were not intended to confer on them or their posterity the blessings of liberty, or any of the personal rights so carefully provided for the citizen.

No one of that race had ever migrated to the United States voluntarily; all of them had been brought here as articles of merchandise. The number that had been emancipated at that time were but few in comparison with those held in slavery; and they were identified in the public mind with the race to which they belonged, and regarded as a part of the slave population rather than the free. It is obvious that they were not even in the minds of the framers of the Constitution when they were conferring special rights and privileges upon the citizens of a State in every other part of the Union. . . .

. . . The power to expand the territory of the United States by the admission of new States is plainly given; and in the construction of this power . . . it has been held to authorize the acquisition of territory, not fit for admission at the time, but to be admitted as soon as its population and situation would entitle it to admission. It is acquired to become a State, and not to be held as a colony and governed by Congress with absolute authority; and as the propriety of admitting a new State is committed to the sound discretion of Congress, the power to acquire territory for that purpose, to be held by the United States until it is in a suitable condition to become a state upon an equal footing with the other States, must rest upon the same discretion. . . .

Taking this rule to guide us, it may be safely assumed that citizens of the United States who migrate to a Territory belonging to the people of the United States, cannot be ruled as mere colonists, dependent upon the will of the General Government, and to be governed by any laws it may think proper to impose. The principle upon which our Governments rest, and upon which alone they continue to exist, is the union of States, sovereign and independent within their own limits in their internal and domestic concerns, and bound together as one people by a General Government, possessing certain enumerated and restricted powers, delegated to it by the people of the several States, and exercising supreme authority within the scope of the powers granted to it, throughout the dominion of the United States. A power, therefore, in the General Government to obtain and hold colonies and dependent territories, over which they might legislate without restriction, would be inconsistent with its own existence in its present form. . . .

But the power of Congress over the person or property of a citizen . . . [is] regulated and plainly defined by the Constitution itself. And when the Territory becomes a part of the United States, the Federal Government enters . . . upon it with its powers over the citizen strictly defined, and limited by the Constitution. . . . It has no power of any kind beyond it; and it cannot, when it enters a Territory of the United States, put off its character, and assume discretionary or despotic powers which the Constitution has denied to it. . . . [A]nd the Federal Government can exercise no power over his person or property, beyond what that instrument confers, nor lawfully deny any right which it has reserved. . . .

For example, no one, we presume, will contend that Congress can make any law in a Territory respecting the establishment of religion, or the free exercise thereof, or abridging the freedom of speech or of the press, or the right of the people of the Territory peaceably to assemble, and to petition the Government for the redress of grievances.

Nor can Congress deny to the people the right to keep and bear arms, nor the right to trial by jury, nor compel any one to be a witness against himself in a criminal proceeding. . . .

The powers over person and property of which we speak are not only not granted to Congress, but are in express terms denied, and they are forbidden to exercise them. And this prohibition . . . extend[s] to the whole territory over which the Constitution gives it power to legislate. . . . It is a total absence of power everywhere within the dominion of the United States, and places the citizens of a Territory, so far as these rights are concerned, on the same footing with citizens of the States, and guards them as firmly and plainly against any inroads which the General Government might attempt, under the plea of implied or incidental powers. And if Congress itself cannot do this—if it is beyond the powers conferred on the Federal Government—it will be admitted, we presume, that it could not authorize a Territorial Government to exercise them. It could confer no power on any local Government, established by its authority, to violate the provisions of the Constitution.

It seems, however, to be supposed, that there is a difference between property in a slave and other property, and that different rules may be applied to it in expounding the Constitution of the United States. And the laws and usages of nations, and the writings of eminent jurists upon the relation of master and slave and their mutual rights and duties, and the powers which Governments may exercise over it, have been dwelt upon in the argument.

But in considering the question before us, it must be borne in mind that there is no law of nations standing between the people of the United States and their Government, and interfering with their relation to each other. The powers of the Government, and the rights of the citizen under it, are positive and practical regulations plainly written down. . . . It has no power over the person or property of a citizen but what the citizens of the United States have granted. And no laws or usages of other nations, or reasoning of statesmen or jurists upon the relations of master and slave, can enlarge the powers of the Government, or take from the citizens the rights they have reserved. And if the Constitution recognises the right of property of the master in a slave, and makes no distinction between that description of property and other property owned by a citizen, no tribunal, acting under the authority of the United States, whether it be legislative, executive, or judicial, has a right to draw such a distinction, or deny to it the benefit of the provisions and guarantees which have been provided for the protection of private property against the encroachments of the Government.

Now, as we have already said . . . the right of property in a slave is distinctly and expressly affirmed in the Constitution. The right to traffic in it, like an ordinary article of merchandise and property, was guaranteed to the citizens of the United States, in every State that might desire it, for twenty years. And the Government in express terms is pledged to protect it in all future time, if the slave escapes from his owner. This is done in plain words—too plain to be misunderstood. And no word can be found in the Constitution which gives Congress a greater power over slave property, or which entitles property of that kind to less protection than property of any other description. The only power conferred is the power coupled with the duty of guarding and protecting the owner in his rights.

Upon these considerations, it is the opinion of the court that the act of Congress which prohibited a citizen from holding and owning property of this kind in the territory . . . is not warranted by the Constitution, and is therefore void; and that neither Dred Scott himself, nor any of his family, were made free by being carried into this territory; even if they had been carried there by the owner, with the intention of becoming a permanent resident. . . .

But there is another point in the case which depends on State power and State law. And it is contended, on the part of the plaintiff, that he is made free by being taken to Rock Island, in the State of Illinois, independently of his residence in the territory of the United States; and being so made free, he was not again reduced to a state of slavery by being brought back to Missouri.

Our notice of this part of the case will be very brief; for the principle on which it depends was decided in this court, upon much consideration, in the case of *Strader et al. v. Graham* [1850]. In that case, the slaves had been taken from Kentucky to Ohio, with the consent of the owner, and afterwards brought back to Kentucky. And this court held that their *status* or condition, as free or slave, depended upon the laws of Kentucky, when they were brought back into that State, and not of Ohio; and that this court had no jurisdiction to revise the judgment of a State court upon its own laws. This was the point directly before the court, and the decision that this court had no jurisdiction turned upon it, as will be seen by the report of the case.

So in this case. As Scott was a slave when taken into the State of Illinois by his owner, and was there held as such, and brought back in that character, his *status*, as free or slave, depended on the laws of Missouri, and not of Illinois. . . .

Upon the whole, therefore, it is the judgment of this court, that it appears by the record before us that the plaintiff in error is not a citizen of Missouri, in the sense in which that word is used in the Constitution; and that the Circuit Court of the United States, for that reason, had no jurisdiction in the case, and could give no judgment in it. Its judgment for the defendant must, consequently, be reversed, and a mandate issued, directing the suit to be dismissed for want of jurisdiction.

The *Dred Scott* Decision Should Be Condemned

Frederick Douglass

In this excerpt, Frederick Douglass gives his forthright response to the Supreme Court's ruling in the Dred Scott *case. He was one of innumerable abolitionists and northern politicians who denounced the decision (so did Abraham Lincoln, who promised that a way would be found some day to get the Supreme Court to reverse itself), but Douglass's answer to Taney was especially sweeping and eloquent.*

This infamous decision of the slaveholding wing of the Supreme Court maintains that slaves are, within the contemplation of the Constitution of the United States, property; that slaves are property in the same sense that horses, sheep, and swine are property; that the old doctrine that slavery is a creature of local law is false; that the right of the slaveholder to his slave does not depend upon the local law but is secured wherever the Constitution of the United States extends; that Congress has no right to prohibit slavery anywhere; that slavery may go in safety anywhere under the star-spangled banner; that colored persons of African descent have no rights that white men are bound to respect; that colored men of African descent are not and cannot be citizens of the United States.

You will readily ask me how I am affected by this devilish decision—this judicial incarnation of wolfishness? My answer is, and no thanks to the slaveholding wing of the Supreme Court, my hopes were never brighter than now.

I have no fear that the national conscience will be put to sleep by such an open, glaring, and scandalous tissue of lies as that decision is and has been, over and over, shown to be.

The Supreme Court of the United States is not the only power in this world. It is very great, but the Supreme Court of the Almighty is greater. Judge Taney can do many things, but he cannot perform impossibilities. He cannot bail out the ocean, annihilate the firm old earth, or pluck the silvery star of liberty from our northern sky. He may decide, and decide again; but he cannot reverse the decision of the Most High. He cannot change the essential nature of things—making evil good, and good evil.

Happily for the whole human family, their rights have been defined, declared, and decided in a court higher than the Supreme Court. "There is a law," says Brougham, "above all the enactments of human codes, and by that law, unchangeable and eternal, man cannot hold property in man."

Excerpted from Frederick Douglass, "The Infamous Decision," in *Frederick Douglass: Selected Writings*, edited by Philip Foner (New York: International Publishers, 1945).

Your fathers have said that man's right to liberty is self-evident. There is no need of argument to make it clear. The voices of nature, of conscience, of reason, and of revelation, proclaim it as the right of all rights, the foundation of all trust and of all responsibility. Man was born with it. It was his before he comprehended it. The deed conveying it to him is written in the center of his soul and is recorded in Heaven. The sun in the sky is not more palpable to the sight than man's right to liberty is to the moral vision. To decide against this right in the person of Dred Scott, or the humblest and most whip-scarred bondman in the land, is to decide against God. It is an open rebellion against God's government. It is an attempt to undo what God has done, to blot out the broad distinction instituted by the Allwise between men and things, and to change the image and superscription of the ever-living God into a speechless piece of merchandise.

Such a decision cannot stand. God will be true though every man be a liar. We can appeal from this hell-black judgment of the Supreme Court to the court of common sense and common humanity. We can appeal from man to God. If there is no justice on earth, there is yet justice in Heaven. You may close your Supreme Court against the black man's cry for justice, but you cannot, thank God, close against him the ear of a sympathizing world nor shut up the Court of Heaven. All that is merciful and just, on earth and in Heaven, will execrate and despise this edict of Taney.

If it were at all likely that the people of these free states would tamely submit to this demoniacal judgment, I might feel gloomy and sad over it, and possibly it might be necessary for my people to look for a home in some other country. But as the case stands, we have nothing to fear.

In one point of view, we, the abolitionists and colored people, should meet this decision, unlooked for and monstrous as it appears, in a cheerful spirit. This very attempt to blot out forever the hopes of an enslaved people may be one necessary link in the chain of events preparatory to the downfall and complete overthrow of the whole slave system.

The whole history of the antislavery movement is studded with proof that all measures devised and executed with a view to allay and diminish the antislavery agitation have only served to increase, intensify, and embolden that agitation. This wisdom of the crafty has been confounded, and the ungodly brought to nought. It was so with the Fugitive Slave Bill. It was so with the Kansas-Nebraska Bill; and it will be so with this last and most shocking of all pro-slavery devices, this Taney decision.

Selection 7

John Brown's Raid

Allen Keller

Reprinted from Allen Keller, "John Brown's Raid," *American History Illustrated*, August 1976. This article is reprinted from *American History Illustrated* magazine with the permission of PRIMEDIA Special Interest Publications (History Group), copyright American History Illustrated magazine.

John Brown (1800–1859), a militant white abolitionist who already had blood on his hands for having massacred proslavery settlers in Kansas in 1856, was convinced that

God had charged him with leading a mighty slave uprising that would "purge this land in blood." A frustrated and fanatical man who had failed in everything he tried in daily life, Brown has had his sanity questioned by many modern scholars (none of whom, of course, ever had a chance to question him on a psychiatrist's couch). As a strategist, he clearly had his limitations: After seizing the federal arsenal at Harpers Ferry, Virginia (now West Virginia), in October 1859, he and his little band of volunteers did nothing, expecting that slaves would flock to his standard and ignite a revolution. His supreme accomplishment was to become an eloquent martyr when, after most of his band (including his two sons) had been killed, he was arrested, tried for treason by the commonwealth of Virginia, condemned to death, and hung. Although he did not set off a slave uprising, his actions so polarized the nation that it moved rapidly toward civil war. Understanding what Brown hoped to accomplish, why he failed in the short run, and why he helped precipitate the Civil War is an essential part of the history of American slavery. Historical writer Allen Keller discusses John Brown's raid in the following article.

For six miles the little procession moved through the chill night along a dirt road leading to Harpers Ferry—John Brown riding on the seat of a stout wagon filled with rifles, pikes, and wrecking tools, his men plodding along, two by two, guns slung from their shoulders. It was a strange army of liberation: only eighteen men, black and white, bound together in an incredible undertaking to free the South's slaves from bondage, its plans poorly conceived, its members untrained, and its leader confused and unstable.

Yet the echoes of those footsteps were to rise above the noise of bullets and the clash of sword and bayonet into a tidal wave of passion that would sweep away slavery only a few years later.

It was a Sunday night, October 16, 1859, when the bearded fanatic who had won support from Northern abolitionists and churchmen said to his followers: "Men, get on your arms; we will proceed to the Ferry." They would capture the U.S. Arsenal at the confluence of the Potomac and Shenandoah, he hoped, and give the guns to blacks who wanted freedom. He had planned this day for years, and every member of the little armed band was relieved the waiting was over.

A troop of tenderfoot boy scouts would have been better organized. Brown and his men had secret passwords, military-type commissions, orders in their pockets, and lofty dreams of what their expedition could accomplish. But they had no precise plan of operations, no rallying point if things went sour, no mountain retreat selected against possible failure. Years later historians were to liken it to the mismanagement of the Children's Crusade to the Holy Land. But no one has ever doubted the impact this small force exerted upon a nation driven by the curse of human bondage.

In the light of blazing torches held by his men, Brown spoke to the two prisoners, explaining his aims: "I came here from Kansas, and this is a slave state; I want to free all the Negroes in this state; I have possession now of the U.S. Armory, and if the citizens interfere with me I must only burn the town and have blood." It was the first anyone outside his band and a few supporters knew what was in the old man's mind.

A few blocks down on the Shenandoah River side of town a separate rifle factory was captured and John Henry Kagi and John Copeland, a free black, were left to guard it. About the same time a party of six raiders hurried beyond the Ferry and came up to the plantation of Colonel Lewis W. Washington, a great-grandnephew of the first President. One of Brown's lieutenants, John E. Cook, had lived in Harpers Ferry, studying the area, and knew that Colonel Washington possessed a sword given his ancestor by Frederick the Great and a pistol presented the hero by Lafayette.

John Brown, far ahead of his time, understood public relations, and he wanted these weapons for their symbolic value. Colonel

Washington was forced to hand them over to Osborn Anderson, a black, and then accompany the raiding party back to the Ferry. Another planter, John Allstadt, was captured on the way back and a gaggle of slaves from each plantation went along with their owners.

So far, things had not gone badly, but now the dream was evaporating, and the lack of precise plans began to have an effect. Patrick Higgins, night watchman on the Maryland bridge, was slightly wounded by Brown's son, Oliver, when he refused to surrender. Just then the Wheeling to Baltimore night express rolled into the station, and Higgins told the conductor of being attacked by riflemen. Women on the train wept and screamed. Men hid their wallets, expecting robbery. The engineer saw armed men in the dark cavern of the bridge and refused to move on.

Shortly thereafter the baggageman, Shephard Hayward, a free Negro, walked onto the tracks looking for Higgins. A rifle cracked and Hayward fell with a bullet under his heart. It was an evil omen. John Brown's first victim was no heartless slave owner, no evil oppressor of blacks, but a free Negro respected by every man and woman in Harpers Ferry, regardless of color.

John Brown

When daylight came the train pulled out for Baltimore. At Monocacy, a way station, the conductor, A.J. Phelps, wired officials in the head office that armed insurrection had broken out up the Potomac. Messages flashed to President James Buchanan, Governor Henry A. Wise of Virginia, and a handful of military leaders. The jaws of the vise that was to crush John Brown started to close.

As soon as he could see well, Dr. John Starry, a physician at the Ferry, mounted his horse and galloped to Charles Town, spreading word of the raid. Not waiting to don their uniforms, the Jefferson Guards marched toward the scene of violence. Then from Shepherdstown came other militia, and a company from Martinsburg crowded onto flatcars and rode into Harpers Ferry.

Desultory sniping had gone on around the engine house of the arsenal where Brown set up his headquarters. A citizen was shot at dawn and home guards drew closer around the raiders. They drove Oliver Brown, one of the leader's sons, and two others out of the bridge, killing Dangerfield Newby, son of a Scottish man and a black slave woman. Newby had spent the days before the raid reading and re-reading a letter from his wife, begging him to "buy" her freedom and that of their seven children. Now he lay dead in the gutter in front of the saloon.

At 10:30 P.M. the troupe reached the covered bridge across the Potomac. John Henry Kagi and Aaron Stevens, captains in Brown's "Provisional Army," went ahead and made a night watchman, William Williams, their prisoner. The others followed and debouched into a small open space fronting the Baltimore & Ohio Railroad station, the Federal armory, and a saloon called the Galt House. Daniel Whelan, guard at the armory gate, refused to hand over the keys and the raiders broke it open with crowbars.

A strange lassitude seemed to come over John Brown as armed men gathered to put down the insurrection. Kagi sent word from the rifle factory, begging the leader to order a retreat to the hills, but the bearded veteran of struggles in "Bleeding Kansas" made no move. Instead he sent William Thompson, one of his men, and a prisoner to the Galt House to discuss surrender plans. Thompson was captured. Later another white flag covered Aaron Stevens and Watson Brown, another son, as they sallied out to hold a parley. Slugs from heavy rifles cut both men down; Stevens was dragged into an upstairs room in the Wager Hotel, and Watson Brown crawled back into the engine house.

A slave-holder named George Turner came into town carrying a shotgun, but before he could use it one of the raiders shot him dead. Noon came and went, with none of the penned-up raiders or their prisoners bothering to eat in the engine house. There was another lull in the conflict that presaged some hope of a peaceful arrangement, but it was broken when the town's mayor, Fontaine Beckham, was killed by a shot from the raiders' stronghold. After the deed was done there was a dispute as to whether he was only trying to see what was going on or was seeking to find a vantage point from which to fire. What really mattered was the change in the atmosphere in Harpers Ferry.

All thought of peaceful accommodation vanished. Crowds tried to get into the room in the Wager Hotel where the prisoner Thompson was being held. Some succeeded and would have killed the raider there had not Christina Fouke, sister of the hotel owner, thrown herself in front of the prisoner. It was a heroic gesture but a futile one. Drunken, rowdy men bore the raider out of the hotel onto the bridge and shot him so that his body fell into the shallows.

Violence had Harpers Ferry by the throat. Grown men, sated with redeye from the Galt bar, and boys with their squirrel guns in hand spent the next few hours firing at Thompson's body. Others cut off Dangerfield Newby's ears for souvenirs.

All through this wretched day three of the raiders fought for their lives in the isolated rifle factory. Kagi and Copeland had been joined by Lewis Sheridan Leary, a black, and all had been under heavy attack from townsmen and militia. Hoping for a way out, the three stole from a back door and started across the Shenandoah, making for a flat rock in midstream. Kagi died on the way, Leary was mortally wounded, and Copeland captured. Only the intercession of the ubiquitous Dr. Starry saved him for the gallows.

Old John Brown showed no sign of pessimism. Inside the small brick engine house with Colonel Washington, Mr. Allstadt, several other prisoners, and the slaves brought in from the plantations, the bearded revolutionary discussed the evils of slavery, sent out notes to enemy leaders who demanded surrender, and watched his son Watson dying. Colonel Washington testified later that he had never seen a calmer man than Brown. Oliver Brown, shot as he stood in the doorway, died before his brother, but their father held firm—his plans awry, his dream hopelessly

shattered, most of his "provisional army" dead or missing, and militia forces building up rapidly in the town. The troops rode in on horseback or in flat cars: three companies from Frederick, Maryland (the Hamtramck Guards), five from Baltimore, one from Winchester, and finally, five hours late, Company F from Richmond, commanded by Governor Wise.

Despite this massing of militia, no one seemed eager to storm the engine house. All through the bloody afternoon Brown and his little body of supporters stood off hundreds of uniformed and nonuniformed citizen soldiers. The home guards showed an eager desire to keep out of range of the Sharps rifles firing intermittently from the little fortress.

If Brown took comfort from this, it was to no avail. What he didn't know was that regular troops were gathering in Maryland and Virginia and in the nation's Capital, or were already en route to the Ferry. President Buchanan, his aides, in fact everyone in authority were overreacting to the insurrection. Remembering decades of fear of slave uprising, they exaggerated the menace. Headlines in the newspapers had hundreds, even thousands, of slaves rising in revolt, and train crews refused to approach the Ferry for fear of harm.

Federal authorities, although obviously frightened, moved swiftly to put down the insurrection. The President and John B. Floyd, Secretary of War, agreed at once that Regulars were needed. Floyd ordered three companies of artillery to move from Fort Monroe but, wanting men from closer at hand, also sent a small detachment of Marines who were on duty in the Washington Navy Yard.

Who was to command these regular troops? There seems to have been no doubt. It would be Brevet Colonel Robert E. Lee. Looking for a courier to send word to Lee, an army official literally stumbled over the legs of a young cavalry lieutenant, James Ewell Brown Stuart, waiting to see the Secretary. Stuart volunteered to deliver the message and then talked Lee into taking him along as aide.

After they left, riding on an engine with no

cars, pandemonium seized the Capital. Buchanan ordered more militia under arms in Washington and Alexandria and finally sent 200 rifles and ammunition to the city hall to be issued to police and citizens of known good character if the rebellion spread. It was as bad in Richmond. Wise, eager for the fray, had left with his militia company but still other forces were ordered under arms. The populace listened greedily but fearfully as unfounded rumors poured into the Virginia capital telling of armed mobs of blacks rampaging in the mountains and gathering up supporters and prisoners.

Of all this, naturally, John Brown knew nothing. Penned up in the engine house, he neither slept nor ate. He debated issues with his captives, bade his dying son to "die like a man" when Watson pleaded to be put out of his misery, and watched the flimsy enterprise on which he had labored for months disintegrate like a sand castle in the rain. With dead men lying under the afternoon sun in the streets, with one son dead, one dying, and a third beyond reach across the Potomac, John Brown was still as cool as a cod on ice, never too busy to discuss slavery and its evils with anyone who would debate.

He heard the firing when the three defenders of Hall's rifle factory tried to escape and must have sensed its meaning, but it changed nothing. Kagi, the best educated of his lieutenants, had urged a withdrawal before dawn, had had the request denied, and had died for the cause without a whimper.

Bonfires flickered in the streets across from the engine house and in front of the Wager Hotel and the Galt House. At the latter place men gathered up "Dutch courage" by imbibing heavily, but they avoided the vicinity of the raiders' fortress, preferring to pour bullets into the shattered body of William Thompson, lying face up in the backwaters of the Potomac.

All through this long period of fighting two of Brown's men played no vital role. They were Albert Hazlett, a white man, and Osborn Anderson, a black Canadian who had been won to the cause by Brown's eloquence. The leader had stationed them in the armory, where they stayed all through the day of shooting and mayhem. Then, probably while the attention of the militiamen was directed toward the engine house, they stole away in the night and crossed the Potomac to the Maryland side in an old boat discovered by the railroad tracks. Hazlett was captured later in Pennsylvania but Anderson made good his escape.

Before nightfall a Captain Sinn of the Frederick militia had a long talk with Brown in the engine house. Brown complained that his men had been "shot down like dogs" under flags of truce and demanded the right to leave the Ferry. He pointed out that at the outset of the raid he had had the town at his mercy and could have massacred the civilian inhabitants. For this reason he thought he deserved to go free. Sinn patiently explained that Brown had given up any hope of such treatment when he had taken up arms against the government.

After nightfall Harpers Ferry took on some of the characteristics of a carnival town. Sporadic shooting came from all parts of the city. Men, heavily intoxicated, staggered about the streets, singing bawdy songs, and yelling at the men penned in the engine house. Militia officers exerted no control and their own men were little better than the drunks. Then, an hour or so before midnight, the Marines marched across the bridge into town, Robert E. Lee and Jeb Stuart at their head.

Almost at once order prevailed. Lee posted his men so that none of the raiders could possibly escape and cleared the streets near the armory. He testified later that he would have ordered an assault at once except for fear some of the prisoners would be killed in the darkness. So he drew up plans with his aide and waited for the morning.

At first dawn, motivated by military etiquette, Lee offered the honor of storming the enemy stronghold to the militia commanders but they turned it down. Colonel Shriver of the Maryland militia was downright rude to Lee.

"These men of mine have wives and children at home," he said. "I will not expose them to such risks. You are paid for doing this kind of work."

Lee, his face hiding his feelings, turned away

and set the assault in motion. He sent Stuart up to the door of the engine house with a demand for surrender. The man who would one day become Lee's great cavalry leader was told to wave his cap if Brown refused. Lieutenant Israel Green of the Marines, with a detail of twelve men with bayonets fixed awaited the signal. Three other Marines with axes and sledge hammers stood at one side. Green had no weapon except a light dress sword he had snatched up on his way to the railroad station in Washington.

Stuart read Lee's letter to the bearded insurrectionist. Brown debated the points in the demand, saying he had the right to lead his party out of the engine house to safety. The parley dragged on until, sensing that it was getting nowhere, Stuart backed away and waved his cap.

The men with wrecking tools attacked the heavy door but made little progress. Lieutenant Green noticed a ladder nearby and ordered it used as a battering ram. At the second blow the bottom corner of the huge door broke and Marines started in, stooping low to enter. A shot rang out from inside and Private Luke Quinn went down, mortally wounded.

Using the bayonet for fear of wounding prisoners, the others surged inside "like tigers" according to Green. Colonel Washington described the scene in these words:

> Brown was the coolest and firmest man I ever saw in defying danger and death. With one son dead at his side, and another shot through, he felt the pulse of his dying son with one hand and held his rifle with the other, and commanded his men with the utmost composure, encouraging them to be firm and to sell their lives as dearly as they could.

That was the scene that Lieutenant Green saw when he stood erect after crawling through the aperture in the door. He saw Brown working the lever of his Sharps rifle and leaped upon him with his sword. The dress sword bent into a semicircle but Brown went down with a deep gash in his head.

Writing of Brown's raid a half century later, Oswald Garrison Villard said Green had unwittingly done Brown a great favor by not wearing his service sword.

"Men had carved their way to kingdoms by the stoutness of their swords," wrote Villard, "but here was one who by the flimsiness of his blade permitted his enemy to live to thrill half a nation by his spoken and written word."

It was true. Had Brown died there in the little engine house, he might have been saved the bitterness of disappointment and disillusionment. As it was, while he awaited trial and then underwent the trauma of the court procedures, he must have suffered grievously as he thought how things had gone wrong from the very beginning.

Innocent men had died needlessly. Terror had stalked the country and, worst of all, no blacks had rallied to his banner. This must have been a hurt beside which his physical wounds paled. His dream that thousands of slaves would break their chains and join his band had evaporated in the acrid smoke of black powder.

But, had he fallen among the crude hose carts and firefighting apparatus at Harpers Ferry, the trial would have been unnecessary, and the bearded activist would have lost his greatest forum. As it was, during the trial he rallied thousands to the cause of abolition. His words did so much where his bullets had done so little.

Weeks later as he stood on the gallows in the bright sunlight streaming down above the Blue Ridge Mountains, he may have pondered his crimes and the blood he had shed. It is more likely, though, that he sensed that he had altered the conscience of half a nation, and perhaps he could even see, beyond any tangible horizon, the long columns of blue-clad men who would soon be marching out of the North to end the curse of slavery.

Selection 8

A Plea for Captain John Brown

Henry David Thoreau

Henry David Thoreau (1817–1862) is best known for his book Walden, *a meditation on living self-sufficiently and simply with nature. He was also a highly principled opponent of slavery who once went to jail rather than pay a tax that would support the Mexican War, which he believed was part of a slave owners' plot to conquer new territory for slavery. Out of that experience grew his essay "Civil Disobedience," which deeply influenced Dr. Martin Luther King and the civil rights movement. It is a classic expression of why and how people must obey their consciences rather than unjust laws.*

Thoreau was not a pacifist; under some circumstances, he believed, resorting to force was justifiable in the pursuit of a just cause. For that reason he applauded John Brown's attempt to start a slave rebellion in 1859. Thoreau was not one of the abolitionists who had secretly financed Brown's doomed enterprise, but he was sympathetic to what Brown and his backers wanted to accomplish. Nor did he know the full story of Brown's bloody doings in Kansas, where he had hacked to death a group of proslavery men and boys as

Excerpted from Henry David Thoreau, "A Plea for John Brown," a speech delivered to the citizens of Concord, Massachusetts, October 30, 1859.

they lay sleeping. For Thoreau, Brown was simply a heroic soldier of freedom, cast in the mold of the old-time New England Puritans and Yankee Minutemen of 1775. He delivered his address, "A Plea for Captain John Brown," excerpted here, in his hometown of Concord, Massachusetts, between the time of Brown's trial and execution.

One writer says that Brown's peculiar monomania made him to be "dreaded by the Missourians as a supernatural being." Sure enough, a hero in the midst of us cowards is always so dreaded. He is just that thing. He shows himself superior to nature. He has a spark of divinity in him.

> "Unless above himself he can
> Erect himself, how poor a thing is man!"

Newspaper editors argue also that it is a proof of his *insanity* that he thought he was appointed to do this work which he did,—that he did not suspect himself for a moment! They talk as if it were impossible that a man could be "divinely appointed" in these days to do any work whatever; as if vows and religion were out of date as connected with any man's daily work; as if the agent to abolish slavery could only be somebody appointed by the President, or by some political party. They talk as if a man's death were a failure, and his continued life, be it of whatever character, were a success.

When I reflect to what a cause this man devoted himself, and how religiously, and then reflect to what cause his judges and all who condemn him so angrily and fluently devote themselves, I see that they are as far apart as the heavens and earth are asunder.

The amount of it is, our *"leading men"* are a harmless kind of folk, and they know *well enough* that *they* were not divinely appointed, but elected by the votes of their party.

Who is it whose safety requires that Captain Brown be hung? Is it indispensable to any Northern man? Is there no resource but to cast this man also to the Minotaur? If you do not wish it, say so distinctly. While these things are being done, beauty stands veiled and music is a screeching lie. Think of him,—of his rare qualities!—such a man as it takes ages to make, and ages to understand; no mock hero, nor the representative of any party. A man such as the sun may not rise upon again in this benighted land. To whose making went the costliest material, the finest adamant; sent to be the redeemer of those in captivity; and the only use to which you can put him is to hang him at the end of a rope! You who pretend to care for Christ crucified, consider what you are about to do to him who offered himself to be the saviour of four millions of men.

Any man knows when he is justified, and all the wits in the world cannot enlighten him on that point. The murderer always knows that he is justly punished; but when a government takes the life of a man without the consent of his conscience, it is an audacious government, and is taking a step towards its own dissolution. Is it not possible that an individual may be right and a government wrong? Are laws to be enforced simply because they were made? or declared by any number of men to be good, if they are *not* good? Is there any necessity for a man's being a tool to perform a deed of which his better nature disapproves? Is it the intention of lawmakers that *good* men shall be hung ever? Are judges to interpret the law according to the letter, and not the spirit? What right have *you* to enter into a compact with yourself that you *will* do thus or so, against the light within you? Is it for *you* to *make up* your mind,—to form any resolution whatever,—and not accept the convictions that are forced upon you, and which ever pass your understanding? I do not believe in lawyers, in that mode of attacking or defending a man, because you descend to meet the judge on his own ground, and, in cases of the highest importance, it is of no consequence whether a man breaks a human law or not. Let lawyers decide trivial cases. Business men may arrange that among themselves. If they were the interpreters of the everlasting laws which rightfully bind man, that would be another thing. A counterfeiting law-factory, standing half in a slave land and half in a free! What kind of laws for free men can you expect from that?

I am here to plead his cause with you. I plead not for his life, but for his character,—his immortal life; and so it becomes your cause wholly, and is not his in the least. Some eighteen hundred years ago Christ was crucified; this morning, perchance, Captain Brown was hung. These are the two ends of a chain which is not without its links. He is not Old Brown any longer; he is an angel of light.

I see now that it was necessary that the bravest and humanest man in all the country should be hung. Perhaps he saw it himself. I *almost fear* that I may yet hear of his deliverance, doubting if a prolonged life, if *any* life, can do as much good as his death.

"Misguided!" "Garrulous!" "Insane!" "Vindictive!" So ye write in your easy-chairs, and thus he wounded responds from the floor of the Armory, clear as a cloudless sky, true as the voice of nature is: "No man sent me here; it was my own prompting and that of my Maker. I acknowledge no master in human form."

And in what a sweet and noble strain he proceeds, addressing his captors, who stand over him: "I think, my friends, you are guilty of a great wrong against God and humanity, and it would be perfectly right for any one to interfere with you so far as to free those you willfully and wickedly hold in bondage."

And, referring to his movement: "It is, in my opinion, the greatest service a man can render to God."

"I pity the poor in bondage that have none to help them; that is why I am here; not to gratify any personal animosity, revenge, or vindictive spirit. It is my sympathy with the oppressed and the wronged, that are as good as you, and as precious in the sight of God."

You don't know your testament when you see it.

"I want you to understand that I respect the rights of the poorest and weakest of colored people, oppressed by the slave power, just as much as I do those of the most wealthy and powerful."

"I wish to say, furthermore, that you had better, all you people at the South, prepare your-selves for a settlement of that question, that must come up for settlement sooner than you are prepared for it. The sooner you are prepared the better. You may dispose of me very easily. I am nearly disposed of now; but this question is still to be settled,—this negro question, I mean; the end of that is not yet."

I foresee the time when the painter will paint that scene, no longer going to Rome for a subject; the poet will sing it; the historian record it; and, with the Landing of the Pilgrims and the Declaration of Independence, it will be the ornament of some future national gallery, when at least the present form of slavery shall be no more here. We shall then be at liberty to weep for Captain Brown. Then, and not till then, we will take our revenge.

The Republicans and John Brown

Richard H. Sewell

John Brown's raid presented a dilemma for the new Republican Party in 1859. The party took a strong antislavery stand, but its opposition was to slavery's existence into the West; moderate Republicans (including Abraham Lincoln) tried to reassure south-erners that they did not want to interfere with slavery's existence in the southern states. Few Republican politicians wanted to appear to condone violence. Yet Brown's "martyr-dom" made him a hero to many northerners, no matter what his background had been. Historian Richard H. Sewell explores the ways in which Republican politicians attempted to deal with the issue of Brown's raid and its consequences in his book Ballots for Freedom: Antislavery Politics in the United States, 1837–1860.

Excerpted from Richard H. Sewell, *Ballots for Freedom: Antislavery Politics in the United States, 1837–1860.* Copyright © 1976 Oxford University Press, Inc. Reprinted with permission from Oxford University Press, Inc.

*a*s it turned out . . . the John Brown affair did little to soften Republican antislavery attitudes. Far from facilitating a union of all anti-Democratic forces, Harpers Ferry frightened the Southern Opposition so thoroughly that henceforth all talk of intersectional coalition was just so much hot air. Moreover, the Republican response to the Brown episode proved surprisingly aggressive. The attempted insurrection itself, of course, drew nothing but condemnation from Republicans of all types, in and out of Congress. Party prints damned it as an act of treason born of madness, an "utterly repugnant," hopelessly counterproductive act of violence. . . .

Yet even while the 1859 campaign raged (and still more afterward), many Republicans freely praised Brown's motives and most blamed the peculiar institution and proslavery Democrats for the blood spilled at Harpers Ferry. At worst, several party publicists argued, Brown remained less a felon or a traitor than were Southern filibusters and "border ruffians"—and he, at least, had worked to free, not to enslave or oppress. Many spoke favorably of Brown's courage, resolution, and magnanimity. Privately, even conservatives granted the misguided warrior good intentions. . . . Once Brown had gone bravely and serenely to the gallows, Republicans freely expressed respect for the man if not for his deed. Typical, at least of radical opinion, was the response of the Concord, New Hampshire, *Independent Democrat*: "'Old Brown' has gone from earth, and while the enterprise in which he engaged, may be condemned, yet the popular heart recognizes in him a hero—a misguided, perchance, hallucinated, but an honest, fearless, Christian man, who dared do what he thought was right."

More insistently, Republicans contended that the real villain was not poor old John Brown but "the great Monstrosity" at which he had struck—human bondage. The violence in Virginia was of a piece with the bloodshed in Kansas, filibustering in Central America, lynch laws to suppress free speech, and the code duello—all products of the violence inherent in slavery itself. Southerners ought to take a hard look, many Republicans maintained, at an institution at once so monstrous and fragile that a bare handful of fanatics could strike terror throughout an entire region. Goodly numbers of Northerners had already done just that, reported the *Aledo* (Ill.) *Record,* gaining thereby a heightened appreciation "of the inherent wrongfulness of slavery in *itself,* without reference to parallels of latitude." If Brown had been right in forcibly resisting "border-ruffianism" in Kansas, had he been altogether sinful in Virginia? Most Republicans answered this question affirmatively, yet in a way which focused attention on the still-greater sin of slavery.

Republican trimming on the slavery question was most conspicuous within the halls of Congress. During the first few weeks of the Thirty-sixth Congress (which convened on December 5, 1859, only three days after John Brown's body had been cut from the gallows) Republicans in both houses scrambled so hard to dissociate themselves from Harpers Ferry . . . that sometimes their constituents complained. William Herndon, for one, accused his party's representatives of "grinding off the flesh from their knee caps, attempting . . . to convince the Southern men that we are *cowards.*" It was enough to make one ashamed to be a Republican. To Theodore Parker he pungently remarked: "I am like the little girl who accidentally shot off wind in company. She said 'I wish I was in hell a little while.' I feel like I wanted to scorch off the disgrace of our kneeling whining cowardice."

Much to the disgruntlement of Northern radicals, Republicans in the House muted their antislavery remarks while, for two months and forty-four ballots, a battle raged over the speakership (won, ultimately, by William Pennington, a conservative Republican from New Jersey) And in the Senate William Seward sought to rub from his cloak some of the stains of extremism—and thereby improve his presidential "availability"—with a much-publicized speech stressing the basic nationalism and conservatism of Republican doctrines. Denouncing John Brown's abortive insurrection as "an act of sedition and treason" and denying that Republicans contemplated unconstitutional aggression against slavery in the states, the New York leader assured the South that his party already felt "the necessity of being practical in its care of the national health and life." Gone was any hint of the higher law or the irrepressible conflict. . . .

Better than any other Republican politician, Abraham Lincoln caught the prevailing temper of his party. In dozens of speeches during the fall and winter of 1859–60—throughout the Middle West, New York, and New England—Lincoln hammered away at two themes: that slavery was first and foremost a moral question, and that the Republican party must firmly resist all attempts to compromise away its principles. Especially did he fight against the substitution of an amoral, "insidious" popular sovereignty for what he insisted had been the true policy of the Founding Fathers: federal prohibition of slavery expansion. Lincoln's tone was invariably evenhanded and good-tempered, but his message was at all times uncompromising:

> Republicans believe that slavery is wrong [Lincoln told Ohio audiences in 1859]; and they insist, and will continue to insist upon a national policy which recognizes it, and deals with it, *as a wrong*. There *can* be no letting down about this.

Even Lincoln's renowned address at Cooper Institute, New York City, on February 27, 1860, was conciliatory only to a point. To the Southern people and their Northern allies he offered assurances that his party intended no invasion of vested rights, and he denounced as "malicious slander" the charge of Republican complicity in John Brown's raid. To fellow Republicans he counseled forebearance and understanding whenever possible. Yet in sharp distinction to Seward's speech of two days later, Lincoln repeatedly reminded his audience of slavery's moral dimension.

> All they ask [he observed in closing], we could readily grant, if we thought slavery right; all we ask, they could as readily grant, if they thought it wrong. Their thinking it right, and our thinking it wrong, is the precise fact upon which depends the whole controversy. Thinking it right, as they do, they are not to blame for desiring its full recognition, as being right; but, thinking it wrong, as we do, can we yield to them? . . . Wrong as we think slavery is, we can yet afford to let it alone where it is, because that much is due to the necessity arising from its actual presence in the nation; but can we, while our votes will prevent it, allow it to spread into the National Territories, and to overrun us here in these Free States? If our sense of duty forbids this, then let us stand by our duty, fearlessly and effectively.

Instead of trying to paper over sectional differences, as Seward had done, Lincoln faced them head on, urging Republicans to stand firmly by their original creed. In this, and in his insistence on recognizing the black man's humanity and on treating slavery as a moral wrong, Lincoln won favor with party radicals. At the same time, his manifest humility, reasonableness, and sense of fair play appealed to more conservative Republicans. As one perceptive New Yorker wrote to Lincoln soon after the Cooper Institute address: "It has produced a greater effect here than any other single speech. It is the real platform in the eastern states and must carry the conservative element in New York, New Jersey, and Pennsylvania." Already the Illinoisian's name was beginning to crop up in presidential speculations.

Selection 10

White Georgians Respond to John Brown's Raid

Clarence L. Mohr

To understand why Brown contributed to igniting not a slave revolt but the Civil War that would in the end destroy slavery, readers should examine the Harpers Ferry episode from the southern point of view. Historian Clarence L. Mohr in 1986 published an absorbing book entitled On the Threshold of Freedom: Masters and Slaves in Civil War Georgia. *The book, excerpted here, opens by analyzing the deep fears that news of Brown's raid kindled among white Georgians. The realization that so many northerners applauded Brown convinced countless southern whites—whether or not they owned slaves—that northern "abolitionists" and "Black Republicans" (as they called all adherents of the Republican Party) were prepared to unleash a "servile insurrection" and a race war in the South, and that the only way the South could protect itself was to secede.*

*D*espite the mounting tensions of the 1850s, Georgia was hardly a garrison state in mid-October 1859 when the telegraph clicked out the shocking news of a "Terrible Insurrection at Harpers Ferry." The

first reports, although garbled and inaccurate, still gave ample cause for alarm. From the very outset, newspaper accounts gave the raid racial overtones and accorded abolitionists a leading role. Even before accurate reports were available an editor in Columbus, Georgia, described the event as an "outbreak and insurrection," stressing that the "insurgents" were composed "partly of negroes" undoubtedly "incited by abolitionists." Two days later the same editor confirmed what he had previously surmised; not only had abolitionists incited the rebellion but the ringleaders were widely known as "blatant 'freedom shriekers.'" To any white Georgian who read the papers or listened to street rumors during these tense few days, the signals were clear. The long familiar, almost stylized scenario was commencing. Inexorably and ominously, the cycle of terror had begun to build.

Within a week the facts concerning the Brown raid were available. John Brown himself was wounded and captured, and the majority of his followers were killed, wounded, or taken prisoner. Their plan for bringing immediate liberation to Virginia bondsmen had been thwarted. In theory at least, the immediate cause of alarm was removed, but neither the swift suppression of the Harpers Ferry raid nor the subsequent trial and execution of its instigator brought calm to the troubled minds of white Georgians. On October 22, 1859, the Savannah *Morning News* in a lengthy editorial sounded the theme which would be echoed by citizens from all walks of life during the months ahead. After attributing guilt for the Brown raid to Northern abolitionists and linking the outbreak directly to the doctrines of the major leaders of the Republican Party, the editor stressed the need for swift action to safeguard the slave regime's internal security. His argument had the ring of a call to arms:

> What these insane abolitionists have accomplished . . . , the blood that they have caused to be shed, and the frightful scheme of insurrection, murder, and rapine which they have developed will, we trust, serve to convince the people of the South of the necessity of greater watchfulness, and of some concerted and effective means of protecting themselves from similar demonstrations of modern philanthropy.

Although most slaveholders would probably have offered a fervent "amen" to the above sentiments, not all planters agreed that events in Virginia posed an immediate danger. From the beginning some white Georgians sought to preserve the important psychological crutch inherent in reaffirmation of black contentment under slavery. The Reverend Charles C. Jones of Liberty County found it easier to admit the existence of a monolithic sectional conspiracy against the South than to face the terrifying prospect of black unrest at home. Jones admitted that the Brown raid was more serious than he had originally thought—"not in reference to the Negro population, for that had nothing to do with it; but in reference to the hostility of . . . men of all classes in the free states." The young Savannah aristocrat George A. Mercer echoed these sentiments, while sprinkling the prose in his diary with disquieting images of violence: "The most remarkable feature of the [John Brown] affair is

Marines burst into the federal arsenal at Harpers Ferry
to capture John Brown and his remaining rebels.

the refusal of the slaves to accept their freedom, and impale their masters upon the pikes furnished to them; not a single slave is implicated." In a similar vein, a woman from Charlton County sent newspaper accounts of the raid to her parents and stressed "how very anxious (I speak ironically) the slaves are to be liberated."

Belief in the innate docility of local bondsmen died hard among Georgia planters, many of whom would continue to deny that slavery was in jeopardy even as the system crumbled around them during the Civil War. Yet optimists were probably always a minority in Georgia, and during the tension-filled months after Harpers Ferry most whites were ready to believe the worst about any strange person or questionable situation. As during previous insurrection panics, Yankee peddlers and traveling salesmen were especially vulnerable. Being both strangers and Northerners they were doubly suspect, and an idle remark was often sufficient to link them directly to the John Brown raid. In mid-November Columbus, Georgia, was thrown into a state of "considerable excitement" by the "arrest" of one Charles Scott, who represented a New York firm dealing in embroideries and linens. Although "mild and inoffensive in appearance," Scott aroused suspicion by showing "more interest in the 'nigger question' than in the . . . object of his visit" and reportedly expressed "great sympathy for 'Old Brown.'" After being ejected from a local merchant's shop for undue "boldness," he tried to leave town but was "taken, brought back and examined by a committee of citizens." They discovered nothing new, but remained convinced that Scott "was an abolitionist 'dyed in the wool,' and an unsafe man for any Southern community." Understandably, Scott took the next train north. . . .

As whites grew more tense, the specter of John Brown seemed to lurk everywhere. Unexplained events and local calamities immediately assumed a sinister character. The burning of numerous cotton gins throughout the state in the month of November produced wild rumors and some actual violence. Accidental fires were common during the busy fall ginning season and in normal years would scarcely have caused comment. But to panic-stricken editors the fires now became clear evidence of "Kansas Work in Georgia." When some seventeen Talbot County structures were destroyed within two weeks a Savannah newspaper observed pointedly that "incendiarism was one of the plans of 'Old Brown,' and that particular region was specifically designated on his map." During this same period a wildly exaggerated letter reached Milledgeville announcing that a "squad of Brown's emissaries" were hidden near Pine Mountain in Meriwether County, waiting to give battle to a force sent from the county seat to "secure that region." In other parts of the state where no "emissaries" were reported, Brown's influence seemed to be at work among the slaves. Near Forsyth a slave reportedly burned twelve bales of his master's cotton, and in Jasper County a local planter shot and killed one of his own Negroes whom he discovered applying a lighted match to his gin house. As far north as Elbert and Floyd counties, "incendiary" fires were also reported.

Within a few weeks the apocalyptic vision of John Brown's army burning its way through Georgia and inciting black violence began to take a psychological toll. Heeding earlier calls for "concerted and effective" resistance, many white Georgians adopted the traditional expedient of extralegal vigilance committees. These grass-roots organizations bore a variety of names but shared common goals. Their primary concerns were to ferret out "abolition emissaries," enforce racial orthodoxy among whites, and suppress unrest among blacks.

The way in which local communities gave semiofficial sanction to lynch law is clearly illustrated by events in the southeast Georgia county of Effingham. On December 17, 1859, a crowd assembled at the county seat of Springfield to adopt measures for "common vigilance and security" against the "supposed presence" of Yankee abolitionists. The meeting authorized two principal committees of "citizen vigilants" to supervise the work of four subcommittees operating in separate militia districts. Since this organization encompassed only a portion of the county, a second group met in January 1860 to form a "Committee of Safety." This group claimed authority in a precisely defined neighborhood bounded on the "North by Hudson's Ferry Road, East by the Savannah River, South by the district line, and West by the Middle Ground road." With equal precision, committee members spelled out their motivation and objectives. They were convinced by the Harpers Ferry raid that "Commotions of an incendiary character" were increasing throughout the North and that "thousands of emissaries" were overrunning the South "infusing" slaves with their "baneful opinions." Committee members resolved to exclude drummers, peddlers, or "other suspicious characters" from the area and to arm and equip themselves for instant response to any emergency. They were especially determined to rid the area of all free Negroes within a month's time and to "put down" all establishments where liquor could be obtained.

The same racial anxiety which motivated Effingham County citizens stirred many other white Georgians to action. Throughout the state whites met to organize and take protective measures. In Rome a company of one hundred "minute men" armed with shotguns and revolvers stood ready to march to the aid of Virginia if "Northern fanatics" should attempt to rescue John Brown from the hangman. The Savannah Vigilance Association threatened "condign punishment" for anyone attempting to excite insurrection or insubordination among local blacks. White residents of Liberty County formed a "rifle corps and Vigilance Committee" to apprehend suspected abolitionists and "inflict such punishment as the nature of the case may require." From Columbus, Augusta, Americus, Fort Valley, and elsewhere the summons was repeated again and again. John Brown's body might be mouldering in the grave, but to Georgia whites his spirit seemed only too alive.

Although the Georgia response to Harpers Ferry followed familiar and well-established patterns, it far exceeded most previous insurrection scares in duration and intensity. As time passed and whites began to ponder the raid's broad implications, initial panic and hysteria solidified into cold fear. Instead of evaporating, the crisis mentality deepened and secured a firmer grip on the minds of many whites. "Never has the country been so excited before," wrote a Savannah resident in late December 1859. "[T]here was great feeling in 1820," he continued, "but not like the present. The South is deeply stirred." Similar reports came from Augusta, where pressure for racial solidarity among whites had thrown even the conservative American Colonization Society into disrepute. "Every day public affairs in this part of the country are getting more confused," reported a wealthy slaveholder seeking to manumit his bondsmen in Liberia. If his emancipation plans became public knowledge it would be "nearly impossible" to carry them out and the freedom promised to his slaves would be in "extremest jeopardy."

The Complete History of

The Civil War and the End of Slavery

Chapter 16

Introduction

When Abraham Lincoln was inaugurated on March 4, 1861, only abolitionists on the political fringe were prepared to support freeing the slaves. Less than two years later, Lincoln issued the Emancipation Proclamation, with widespread (yet certainly not universal) public support.

The Civil War did not put an end to slavery because the North embraced abolitionism or ideas of racial equality. The Lincoln administration turned the war into a crusade for human freedom because attacking slavery seemed the best way of undermining rebel morale, because it was essential to avert European intervention on the slaveholding Confederacy's side, and because a policy of emancipation was inescapable if the Union army was to tap the growing ranks of free blacks and runaway slaves.

The complex story of how the Confederacy managed to keep slavery alive through four years of invasion and privation, and of how President Lincoln reached his decision to make emancipation part of his war strategy, is told in Chapter 16.

Selection 1

Maintaining Slavery in Wartime Georgia

Clarence L. Mohr

Contrary to southerners' fears at the time of John Brown's raid on Harpers Ferry, the outbreak of civil war did not incite the slaves to rebel. In fact, no slave rebellions occurred during the Civil War. But master-slave relations were affected by the war in subtle ways. Often, for example, day-to-day management of plantations passed into the hands of the masters' wives and daughters. Tempers and discipline sometimes frayed. Privation increased, as whites and blacks alike felt the effects of the northern blockade and of the Confederate army's need to requisition food and supplies. In areas close to military operations, slaves sometimes fled to the Union lines

Excerpted from Clarence L. Mohr, *On the Threshold of Freedom: Masters and Slaves in Civil War Georgia.* Copyright © 1986 University of Georgia Press. Reprinted with permission from the author.

(with their masters often fleeing in the other direction). Slaves were aware of what was happening, and by 1863 they understood that a Union victory would bring them freedom. Masters' anxieties about how—or whether— they could maintain control mounted steadily. These and other dimensions of day-to-day life for masters and slaves in wartime Georgia are explored in this excerpt from Clarence L. Mohr's book On the Threshold of Freedom: Masters and Slaves in Civil War Georgia.

B etween 1861 and 1865 blacks who left the countryside as runaways, industrial workers, or displaced refugees found increasing freedom in Georgia's cities and towns. Slavery, however, remained a predominantly rural institution which kept most bondsmen isolated on remote farms and plantations throughout the greater part of the war. Change of any sort occurred slowly in the state's agricultural heartland where custom and fixed routine imparted a timeless continuity to the rhythms of daily life. Yet even in Georgia's most secure interior counties the foundations of chattel bondage eventually began to crumble under the pressure of the war environment.

In a purely physical sense, the already meager living standard of most slaves deteriorated even further during the war, particularly after 1861 when the Federal blockade tightened around Southern ports and local merchants exhausted stocks of Northern goods. . . .

On some farms and plantations, increases in the stringency of daily life led to a gradual modification of the tenor of master-slave relationships. As in the case of the coastal refugees discussed earlier, wartime economic pressures caused many up-country slaveowners to abandon any normal proclivities toward patriarchal benevolence. . . .

Across the entire spectrum of slave life the meager fruits of selectively bestowed paternalistic indulgence withered and died in the arid soil of economic self-interest and racial exploitation. Blacks accustomed to planting small cotton crops after working hours to sell for their own benefit found this privilege abruptly curtailed in

1863 when the state legislature limited cotton acreage on all plantations to three acres per hand. "I cut the negroes crop off one half as theirs has to be included in the amount planted on each place," wrote the son of a wealthy slaveowner with plantations in four Georgia counties. For some blacks the shift from cotton to food crop production simply meant an increased burden of toil and drudgery at the hands of profitminded planters determined to salvage everything possible from their agricultural endeavors. "I never done much field work till de war come on," recalled Nicey Kinney, a former slave housemaid in Jackson County:

> Marster was too old to go to de war, so he had to stay home and he sho seed dat us done our wuk raisin' somepin t'eat He had us plant all our cleared ground, and I sho has done some hard wuk down in dem old bottom lands, plowin', hoein', pullin' corn and fodder, and Ise even cut cordwood and split rails. Dem was hard times.

Numerous blacks found that in addition to heavier work loads the war also brought basic dietary restrictions to the slave quarters. Emma Hurley, who had been a slave in Oglethorpe County during the war, was explicit on this point: "Them wuz the hardest an' saddest days I ever knowed. . . ."

In the opinion of one veteran white overseer, the deliberate stinting of slave rations was likely to be no more successful on large plantations than on small ones. . . . Perhaps the most revealing insight into how Georgia bondsmen perceived masters who reduced slave rations in order to save money came from ex-slave Nancy Boudry, who spent the war on a small farm in Columbia County. "We done de bes' we could," she said, referring to herself and the two other blacks owned by her master. "We et what we could get, sometimes didn' have nothin to eat but piece of cornbread, but de white folks allus had chicken."

Black resentment over Civil War food shortages occurred at a time when the traditional lines of authority in agricultural society had been weakened by demographic change. Prior to secession, masters or overseers resided on virtually all Georgia plantations, secure in the knowledge that neighboring whites stood ready to offer prompt assistance in matters of slave discipline. Bondsmen might enjoy numerical superiority in a particular locale, but night-riding patrol squads of planters and yeomen provided ample proof that slaveowners could, if necessary, marshal overwhelming power in defense of the racial status quo. Secession changed all of that. In Georgia and throughout the South the war years witnessed a wholesale exodus of white adult males from the countryside, as men of all social classes volunteered or, after April 1862, were conscripted into military service.

The Confederacy's massive redeployment of white manpower had both immediate and long-term effects upon the stability of rural bondage. Male absenteeism struck first and most directly at the state's newly revised slave policing system. Grand jury complaints that patrol laws were "entirely neglected" or "utterly disregarded" became commonplace during the last two years of the war and were echoed frequently by apprehensive whites in their private correspondence. . . .

Although wartime slave patrols lost much of their effectiveness, it would be misleading to say that bondsmen went entirely unsupervised. Policing arrangements for blacks in rural districts changed frequently during the war as legislators and other officials sought ways to offset the ongoing drain of civilian manpower. Late in 1862 the upper age limit of persons subject to patrol duty was raised from forty-five to sixty years, and a few months later the legislature passed a comprehensive bill "to suppress insurrection and organize a home guard militia." Governor Brown vetoed the measure because it weakened his ability to fight Confederate conscription, but on May 26, 1863, he issued a proclamation urging the formation of local defense companies in all Georgia counties. . . .

The 1864 Atlanta campaign strained conventional methods of slave supervision almost to the breaking point as more and more white Georgians were pressed into emergency combat service. But even in the last desperate weeks before the "Gate City's" surrender, state officials struggled to maintain a semblance of white authority in plantation regions. . . .

Emergency measures . . . did little to allay white concern over possible slave unrest. Throughout the war, visions of a Yankee-inspired racial uprising haunted the minds of Georgia planters, who saw their coercive power over blacks weakening while the danger of Northern invasion increased. . . . The Lincoln administration's September 1862 decision to support emancipation as a war measure raised new fears of black rebellion and caused Governor Brown to seek extra supplies of gunpowder for the Christmas holidays. No mass uprising took place, but in December three slaves were arrested in Chatham and McIntosh counties "with arms in their hands against their masters." As the new year began, an up-country planter stated flatly that "Lincoln's [Preliminary Emancipation] proclamation is well known by the negroes and is causing some trouble by the bad ones."

Most white Georgians either ignored or ridiculed Lincoln's official announcement of Negro freedom on January 1, 1863, but the presence of armed ex-slaves in Union regiments along the seaboard could not be so easily dismissed. The Savannah *Morning News* wrote ominously of Yankee efforts to "colonize" nearby Florida with black escapees who would plunge the state into a genocidal "war of races." The Georgia newspaper also reprinted articles from the New York *Tribune* advocating that Federal commanders invade South Carolina with a force of five thousand black troops and thereby "surprise the rebels, not with the phantom, but with the reality of servile insurrection." In May 1863 Governor Brown received copies of what purported to be captured military correspondence from North Carolina revealing elaborate plans for inciting slaves throughout the South to rise in rebellion on the night of August 1, 1863. The captured letter urged sympathetic Union officers to send reliable freedmen behind enemy lines to spread word of the revolt's date and purpose. At the appointed time blacks in each state were to "arm themselves with any and every kind of weapon" and "commence operations by burning all railroad and country bridges," tearing up tracks, and destroying telegraph lines. Eventually the slaves could retreat to swamp or mountain regions, emerging "as occasion may offer for provisions and for further depredations."

However implausible so grandiose a scheme may have been, there can be little doubt that Brown and other knowledgeable Georgians took the danger of an externally instigated insurrection seriously. . . .

By galvanizing public support for campaigns of racial vigilantism, insurrection scares temporarily shored up the structure of rural bondage. On the whole, plantation discipline grew more lax as the war progressed, but slaves received frequent reminders of the lengths to which local communities would go in defense of white supremacy. Even in areas not directly touched by the turmoil of anticipated uprisings, countless acts of violence and terrorism were directed at individual bondsmen. With depressing regularity black Georgians fell victim to the fury of enraged mobs in plantation regions. During a single three-month period of 1862, for example, a runaway slave was beaten to death by pursuers in Thomas County, a bondsman accused of stabbing his overseer was hanged by Washington County citizens who had "called a meeting to consider the case," and five Negroes accused of murdering their master were hanged and burned to death near Columbus.

Particular emotion surrounded the cases of black men accused of sexual offenses against white women. Punishment of alleged rapists was swift, often extralegal, and manifestly aimed at deterring other blacks from what most slaveowners considered the ultimate repudiation of white male authority. Death awaited nearly any male slave believed guilty of an interracial liaison, although the method of execution might vary. Sometimes public anger resulted in a sudden lynching like the one that occurred in Athens during July 1862 when a Clarke County bondsman was arrested for assaulting an overseer's wife. Despite the objections of prominent local citizens, a mob removed the prisoner from jail, marched him through town with a rope around his neck, and hanged him in a pine tree just outside the city limits. . . .

In areas of Georgia that escaped actual invasion, a combination of emergency police arrangements, harsh criminal sentences for black defendants, and intermittent acts of racial terrorism kept most plantations functioning until the war's end. Slaves, however, took frequent advantage of white absenteeism in order to lighten the burden of field work while stopping just short of the kind of open defiance that would result in violent reprisals.

As the war continued, more and more observers became convinced that the efficiency of black agricultural labor was declining. . . .

Whether they directed their criticism at negligent overseers or the conscript law itself, nearly all wartime commentators were in agreement upon one basic point: only white *men* could effectively control Georgia's black population. "Is it possible," asked one writer, "that Congress thinks . . . our women can control the slaves and oversee the farms? Do they suppose that our patriotic mothers, sisters and daughters can assume and discharge the active duties and drudgery of an overseer? Certainly not. They know better.". . .

Before dismissing such pronouncements as meaningless effusions of Southern male chauvinism and sexual anxiety, it is well to ask whether some shred of historical insight may not lie buried beneath the obvious hyperbole. An impressive body of surviving evidence confirms that Southern white women *did* encounter serious difficulties in controlling slaves during the war, and while much slave recalcitrance, theft, malingering, and absenteeism can be interpreted as a pragmatic exploitation of weakened institutional controls, there was frequently a dimension of black behavior which transcended simple opportunism. What took place on many remote plantations when husbands, sons, and overseers had gone to war was not, and logically could not be, wholly unrelated to the traditional status and role of women in Southern society.

Although Southern white women were never

the weak, submissive, dependent creatures depicted in cavalier mythology, they were in a very real sense prisoners of a male-dominated society. For better or worse they were products of a culture which reserved aggressive leadership roles for men and demanded that women maintain an outward posture of deferential acquiescence to males. Such a heritage left many women ill-prepared to take control of an isolated agricultural enterprise during the prolonged absence of a spouse. Even women who were psychologically equal to the challenge often found themselves hampered by lack of firsthand knowledge about the day-to-day details of farm work. . . .

Although knowledge concerning family structure and sex roles within the slave community remains incomplete, available evidence suggests that when monogamous family relationships existed in the quarters the tendency was toward some degree of male domination. It is, in any event, reasonable to suppose that black men were not unaffected by the overwhelmingly male orientation of white society and that they often defined their roles as husbands and fathers within a social framework somewhat similar to that of their white masters. In this regard, the significance of chattel slavery was doubly ironic, for while the slave system encouraged and reinforced a male-dominated, patriarchal family structure in white society, it acted to prevent the full development of corresponding sets of relationships in slave families by stripping black men of the capacity for autonomous action in domestic matters. At the same time, of course, slavery also placed all white women in a position of dominance over all black men.

With the coming of the war this situation changed appreciably in many remote rural areas. As institutional control and personal supervision of bondsmen lost its effectiveness, blacks experienced greater freedom of action in all areas, including their personal lives. The breakdown of the patrol system made it easier for black men to visit wives and children on other plantations and thus fulfill more effectively their husband and father roles. When white women were left to supervise agricultural units in their husbands' absence, black men often assumed actual control of daily farming operations. And if their role in this regard was something less than that of surrogate master, it was virtually or often literally that of full-fledged overseer. The assumption of these new roles and responsibilities must inevitably have contributed to what W.E.B. DuBois described some four decades ago as a "new undercurrent of independence" among bondsmen in the Confederacy. . . .

Much of the testimony on this subject is fragmentary and indirect, and offers only isolated glimpses of a process of gradual metamorphosis over time. However, numerous white women, whose extant wartime correspondence, if taken separately, consists of only a few disconnected letters, tell strikingly similar stories which suggest tentative outlines for a broader collective portrait of black responses to changing plantation realities. While the specific variations are endless, letters and diaries of Georgia's rural white women contain at least two common themes: personal feelings of inadequacy concerning practical plantation matters and increased reliance upon blacks for knowledge and assistance. The same documents attest to a pattern of growing assertiveness and independence among all blacks, but particularly among male field hands. . . .

. . . Even the most practical and strong-willed women usually experienced some doubts concerning their ability to maintain authority over bondsmen. Sarah A. Gilbert, who managed forty-two slaves on a plantation south of Macon, reported in late 1863, for example, that the slave George would not work without strict supervision and that she despaired "of ever doing anything with him here." Although she never directly analyzed the causes of slave discipline problems, Mrs. Gilbert clearly revealed her own uneasiness when deprived of an overseer and forced to rely upon the skills and knowledge of the blacks to accomplish important tasks about which she knew very little. "We are changing overseers & my hands are full," she wrote in December 1863. "Building is going on too . . . [including] a log kitchen which . . . I today have

Solomon & another boy daubing, after the most approved style, learnt by Sol up the country. You ought to see me overseeing the building & looking as if I knew something about it."

Some women, like Mary F. Akin, wife of Confederate Congressman Warren Akin, attempted to augment their limited farming knowledge by seeking detailed instructions by mail from absent husbands. Mrs. Akin went beyond purely agricultural matters, however, and attempted to use what might be termed a "correspondence" approach to slave discipline. After repeated problems with several male field hands whose work output had steadily declined as their open defiance of white authority increased, Mary Akin sought her husband's assistance. She complained especially about a slave named Bob who tended to be more blatant than most of the other blacks in disregarding her instructions. Congressman Akin's response revealed nothing so much as his own failure to comprehend the changes in black attitudes which had occurred during his absence. "I wish you to tell Bob," he solemnly instructed his wife from far-off Richmond, that

> *if he leaves the lot day or night, without your permission, I will certainly punish him if I live to get home.* Keep this letter and mark on it the day you tell him, and then keep an account of his going off, and give me this letter, and how often he has left without permission, after I return.

If, as the latter sentence indicates, Akin felt some misgivings over the potential effectiveness of threats conveyed by letter, his doubts in this regard were soon confirmed. Less than two weeks after issuing the instructions quoted above, he learned of further problems with Bob, who showed an increasing tendency to be "as mean as possible" about any work assigned him. Although Mrs. Akin never said so directly, her comments clearly reveal that Bob had been given somewhat greater responsibilities than his fellow bondsmen and that he acted as a sort of foreman. His duties included care of the livestock, including two valuable mules, for which purpose he was entrusted with the stable key. The mules were in "tolerably good order" and "if talking will make Bob curry them they will be well curried." Bob also made unsupervised trips with the mules and wagon to haul corn from a neighboring farm. This task, however, remained unfinished because "Bob was determined not to hurry himself before Christmas." He was equally unenthusiastic about hard physical labor like ploughing, and Mrs. Akin was reluctant even to rent new land since Bob "seems to think hauling wood is all he has to do this year." When informed of these and other difficulties, Congressman Akin could scarcely conceal his sense of frustration. Curtly (and rather unrealistically) he admonished his wife to rely on coercion instead of threats. "When you want Bob to do any thing don't *ask* him, but *order* him," Akin fumed. "That is the only way to do Bob. *Make* him do just what you want."

Selection 2

Lincoln and Emancipation

James Tackach

Abraham Lincoln, "The Great Emancipator," did not declare slaves free at the beginning of the Civil War. His initial policy was to prevent the secession of the slaveholding border states (Delaware, Maryland, West Virginia, Kentucky, and Missouri) and if possible to restore the Union by persuading the seceded states to return with slavery intact.

By the summer of 1862, with the Confederate armies holding off Union attacks, it became clear that Lincoln's policy was not working. Abolitionists demanded that he proclaim the slaves free, both because that was their committed goal and because, they claimed, it would deal the Confederacy a heavy blow. But traditionally racist northern Democrats bitterly opposed emancipation, which their working-class supporters feared would bring freedmen into northern cities in search of jobs. Lincoln was keenly aware of the extent of white northern racism, but he also knew that war-weariness would sap the Union cause unless something could be done to reverse battlefield losses.

Lincoln also realized that to announce a policy of emancipation while the North was losing battles would look like a move of desperation. But the bloody standoff at the battle of Antietam in September 1862 at least was

not a defeat, and he took this opportunity to announce that unless the Confederate states ceased their rebellion by January 1, 1863, he would proclaim the slaves in the seceded states "forever free." When, as expected, this day arrived with the Confederacy still fighting for its independence, he issued the Emancipation Proclamation, using his authority as commander-in-chief to use whatever means necessary to put down a rebellion.

The fate of emancipation ran parallel to the successes and failures of the Union army in the two years following Lincoln's proclamation. Northerners knew that the South would never accept the freedom of the slaves if the Union armies were unable to enforce the policy on the battlefield. Indeed, it was only the Union army's defeat of the Confederacy that ended American slavery. Writer James Tackach explores the difficulties Lincoln faced in convincing a war-weary North that the emancipation of the slaves was the road to reuniting the nation.

President Abraham Lincoln's Emancipation Proclamation, delivered on January 1, 1863, changed the purpose of the Civil War. The conflict had begun, in 1861, as a war to restore the Union, an effort to negate the votes of secession taken by eleven Southern states to protest Lincoln's election and to respond to the battle at Fort Sumter. When Lincoln freed the slaves in the rebellious states, however,

Reprinted by permission of Lucent Books from James Tackach, *The Emancipation Proclamation* (San Diego: Lucent Books, 1999).

his war aims changed. He had come to realize that peace between North and South could never be permanently established if the South returned to the Union with its 4 million slaves; with slavery still in place, the North and South, even if reunited, would continue bickering and eventually go to war again. As Lincoln had said in 1858 in his famous "House Divided" speech, his country could not permanently stand half slave and half free; it would eventually become all one or all the other. Now he was determined that it be reunited all free, with slavery forever forbidden. For the next two years, Lincoln, with his words and actions, would attempt to convince his country to embrace this goal.

The entire North did not immediately espouse Lincoln's change of purpose. Northern Democrats criticized Lincoln's Emancipation Proclamation and the subsequent shift in the goal of the war. Those loudly critical of Lincoln became known as copperheads because of their venomous attacks on the Lincoln administration's policies. One particularly vocal copperhead, Congressman Clement Vallandigham of Ohio, urged Northern soldiers to desert so that Lincoln could no longer wage his war to free the slaves. Vallandigham was ultimately arrested by the army and tried and convicted of treason.

But some Union troops listened to Vallandigham and other copperheads who urged them to abandon Lincoln's war. In one regiment from Lincoln's own state, the 128th Illinois, all but thirty-five men deserted, refusing to fight in a war to free the slaves. Moreover, the war was already two years old, with no victory in sight, and many soldiers, whether or not they supported Lincoln's Emancipation Proclamation, were ill, tired of fighting, and anxious to return home. Southern troops also deserted in large numbers.

Southern Victories

Two Southern battlefield victories, one at the end of 1862 and one in the spring of 1863, did little to lift the sagging spirits of Northern troops. On December 13, 1862, Yankee and Rebel troops clashed at Fredericksburg, a town on Virginia's Rappahannock River midway between Washington and Richmond. Union troops attacked a high ground outside of Fredericksburg called Marye's Heights that was solidly defended by General Robert E. Lee's infantry and artillery. Union Major General Ambrose Burnside sent wave after wave of Yankee regiments up the heights into the Rebel gunfire. Burnside's Yankees were cut to pieces; they never came within a hundred yards of the Confederate defenses. After a day of terrible fighting, dead and wounded Yankee troops were strewn on Marye's Heights. Some of the wounded men, left untended by overworked medical crews, froze and bled to death on the cold December night. Burnside lost 12,600 men, while Lee lost only 5,000.

The bitter Union defeat at Fredericksburg made some Northerners read Lincoln's forthcoming Emancipation Proclamation as an empty and meaningless document. If the North could not win on the battlefield, how would Lincoln's gesture of emancipation ever gain any force? Lincoln himself was depressed by the results from Fredericksburg. He began to wonder whether the Union could ever win this horrible war.

In April 1863, another Union defeat, at Chancellorsville, Virginia, further depressed Northern spirits. Having wintered in Virginia after the crushing December defeat at Fredericksburg, the Federal army regrouped and was reinforced for another campaign against General Lee's troops in the spring. The two armies clashed again at Fredericksburg and nearby Chancellorsville. Badly outnumbered, Lee nonetheless engineered a staggering defeat on the Union army. With only 60,000 men, Lee, commanding a series of brilliant offensive maneuvers and surprise attacks, sent a Union army of 130,000 men reeling into an embarrassing retreat.

Encouraged by his stunning victory at Chancellorsville, Lee decided that it was time for another invasion of the North. His earlier attempt to take the war to Northern soil ended when his army was checked at Antietam Creek, but his recent battlefield successes suggested that the Army of the Potomac, the main Northern army in the Virginia theater, was vulnerable. Lincoln had tried a handful of generals to command the Army of the Potomac, but none was successful. Lee convinced President Jefferson Davis of the Confederacy that a campaign into the North might result in a fatal blow to Lincoln's war effort.

In early June, Lee began to move his seventy-three-thousand-man Army of Northern Virginia out of its camp near Fredericksburg. He marched his troops north through the Blue Ridge Mountains into Maryland, a Union state. Unimpeded, Lee pressed his army into Pennsylvania. His target was the city of Harrisburg, where Lee could ready his troops for a siege of Philadelphia. If Lee could capture and hold a major Northern city like Philadelphia, he believed that he could bring Lincoln to the peace table. To stop Lee at that point, Lincoln would have to recognize the Confederacy's independence.

A large Union army consisting of 110,000 men under the command of Major General George Meade began to move northward with Lee. Meade kept his troops between Lee's army and Washington, D.C., to dissuade Lee from attacking the North's capital. As Lee moved north, the two opposing armies moved closer to each other. On July 1, they made contact near the small town of Gettysburg when Lee's men marched toward town to capture a shoe factory. After their long march from Virginia, many of Lee's men needed new shoes. Early in the morning on July 1, Yankee and Rebel battalions skirmished west of Gettysburg.

Victory at Gettysburg

Later on July 1, the two huge armies moved into position for a major confrontation. After the early fighting, Meade's men retreated southward to the high ground outside of the town of Gettysburg. They posted themselves on Cemetery Ridge, forcing Lee to fight uphill if he wanted to dislodge his enemy army. Lee's troops moved into town and positioned themselves east and southwest of town in the woods along Seminary Ridge.

On the second day of the battle, Lee ordered a major offensive on the Union left flank by troops under the command of Lieutenant General James Longstreet. After several hours of fierce fighting

around two hills named Little Round Top and Big Round Top, the Yankees held their position, mainly because of a heroic defensive stand taken by the 20th Maine Regiment. Longstreet's advance was thwarted, and the Federals also repulsed advances on their right flank.

After two days of fierce fighting, neither side had gained a significant advantage. Lee had come close to victory, but the Union army had held its ground. Both sides had endured staggering casualties. Unwilling to settle for a stalemate, Lee planned a major offensive on the Union position for the next day.

Abraham Lincoln

Early in the afternoon of July 3, Lee ordered a two-hour artillery bombardment on the center of the Union position on Cemetery Ridge. He hoped to soften the Union defenses for an all-out attack. At 3:00 P.M., Lee ordered thirteen thousand troops under the command of Major General George Pickett to advance on the Union center. His men marched out of their position in the woods across an open field. Sensing Pickett's attack, General Meade had massed his men on the center of his line. When Pickett's men were within firing range, hundreds of artillery pieces and thousands of rifles fired at once, blasting huge holes in the Rebel lines. The Confederates kept charging, but the Union guns cut them down before they could reach the Union position.

The Yankee line held. Confederates who reached it were quickly killed or captured in savage hand-to-hand fighting. Badly damaged, Pickett's men withdrew, limping across the open field over which they had just optimistically advanced. Half of Pickett's thirteen thousand men had been killed or wounded. The Union army had suffered staggering losses as well, but it was still firmly in position at the end of that day of terrible fighting.

Lee knew that he was beaten. In the epic three-day battle he had lost twenty-eight thousand men, while the Federal army had suffered twenty-three thousand casualties. Lee called off his invasion of the North. He retreated back into Virginia while the North celebrated a major victory. On the same day, July 3, General Ulysses Grant captured the important city of Vicksburg, Mississippi, on the Mississippi River, giving the North a double victory. Lee's advance in the East had been stopped, and Grant had gained control of the Mississippi River. These two great Northern victories changed the tide of the war.

The Enlistment of Black Troops

The two victories at Gettysburg and Vicksburg during the summer of 1863 uplifted Northern spirits. Further encouragement for the Northern cause that summer came from a new source of manpower: African American troops began to enlist in the Union army.

Lincoln's Emancipation Proclamation had announced a new War Department policy to allow blacks to enlist in the Union army and fight to end slavery. Encouraged by African American leaders like Frederick Douglass, thousands of young African American men, free Northern men and escaped slaves alike, joined the Union ranks during the next few months. At first, black soldiers performed only menial jobs—loading ammunition wagons, guarding camps and bridges, digging graves—but by the summer of 1863, they were ready for combat. In June, a black regiment saw action at a skirmish at Lilliken's Bend, Louisiana, and gave a good account of itself.

Two weeks after the great victory at Gettysburg, a black Union regiment, the 54th Massachusetts, led the Union charge on Fort Wagner in South Carolina. The attack against a strongly fortified Confederate position was not well planned, but the regiment impressed the entire North with its valor. Unflinchingly, the black troops, commanded by a white officer, Colonel Robert Gould Shaw of Massachusetts, marched into Confederate cannon and gunfire. The 54th Massachusetts suffered 40 percent casualties in the offensive, but no man failed in his duty, dispelling the notions of those who thought that black troops could not be disciplined and would not demonstrate courage on the battlefield.

Before the end of the war, more than 185,000 black soldiers would serve in the Union army. The influx of fresh troops, at a crucial moment in the war, helped put the North on the road toward victory.

Lincoln's Changing Attitude on Race

For Lincoln, the Civil War had begun as an endeavor to force the rebellious Southern states back into the Union. Though Lincoln personally opposed slavery, its abolition was not his most immediate war aim. Midway through the terrible conflict, however, he realized that freeing the slaves was a necessary war measure. First, Lincoln knew that it would deprive the South of much-needed manpower. Second, he fully realized that the Union could never be permanently restored if it remained half slave and half free. Hence, he issued the Emancipation Proclamation.

Lincoln's decision to change the war from a war over secession to a war over slavery also signaled a change in his attitude regarding issues of race. When Lincoln had run for the Senate in 1858, Senator Stephen Douglas had pressured Lincoln into stating that African Americans were inferior to whites, that they did not deserve the same rights of citizenship enjoyed by white Americans. During the harsh crucible of war, however, Lincoln discarded that concept. After realizing that abolishing slavery was the key to ending the conflict between North and South, and after recruiting black soldiers in the war and seeing them perform nobly on the field of battle, Lincoln finally fully comprehended that his nation must completely solve its racial problems. That would mean doing more than eliminating all forms of American slavery; it would mean extending the guarantees of liberty and equality articulated by Thomas Jefferson in the Declaration of Independence to all Americans, black and white.

Evidence of Lincoln's changing attitude appears in a wartime executive order delivered by Lincoln on July 30, 1863, less than a month after the Battle of Gettysburg. Lincoln had heard upsetting reports that Confederate officers had ordered captured African American troops to be sent into slavery or, worse, to be summarily executed. Lincoln was profoundly disturbed to hear these reports. He believed that all captives, regardless of race, should be treated as prisoners of war. In response to these reports, Lincoln issued an order of retaliation concerning the capture of soldiers on the battlefield.

Lincoln opened his order by asserting the fundamental equality of all citizens, including soldiers:

> It is the duty of every government to give protection to its citizens, of whatever class, color, or condition, and especially to those who are duly organized as soldiers in the public service. The laws of nations and the usages and customs of war as carried on by civilized powers, permit no distinction as to color in the treatment of prisoners of war as public enemies. To sell or enslave any captured person, on account of his color, and for no offense against the laws of war, is a relapse into barbarism and a crime against the civilization of the age.

Lincoln then informed the South that if its commanders executed any captured Union soldier, black or white, he would order a captured Confederate soldier executed in return. If any captured Union soldier were sent into slavery, "a rebel soldier shall be placed at hard labor on the public works and continued at such labor until the other shall be released and receive the treatment due a prisoner of war."

This order subtly reveals Lincoln's evolving attitude on race. He asserts that a government is duty-bound to protect all of its citizens, regardless of race, and he endorses the concept of equal treatment under law for all human beings. By asserting the dignity of all soldiers, Lincoln was making an affirmation about the basic equality of all human beings.

Lincoln at Gettysburg

Lincoln would make one of his most eloquent statements about race on the Gettysburg battlefield several months after the battle was fought. The occasion was the dedication of a national cemetery at Gettysburg to provide a proper burial place to those who died there during that fierce three-day battle in July. Lincoln was invited to offer a few words at the dedication ceremony, scheduled for November 19, 1863.

Myths surround Lincoln's Gettysburg Address—one being that he hurriedly wrote his speech on the back of an envelope while on the train to Gettysburg. Actually, Lincoln, a slow and careful writer, worked hard on the address. He wished to express his nation's appreciation for the men who fought and fell at Gettysburg. More importantly, perhaps, he wished to put into words the purpose of the terrible civil war in which his nation had been engaged for almost three years; he wished to give meaning to the awful conflict, to explain to Americans that the war was being fought for some worthwhile cause.

Lincoln was not the keynote speaker at Gettysburg. That honor belonged to Edward Everett, a nationally known orator. According to the ceremony's program, Lincoln was scheduled to offer only "Dedicatory Remarks" after Everett's oration. After Everett's speech, which lasted about two hours, Lincoln approached the podium and used about three minutes to convey to his audience, and to the nation, his newly realized meaning of the war.

Lincoln began by reminding his audience that only eighty-seven years ago America's Founding Fathers had established a new nation, "conceived in Liberty, and dedicated to the proposition that all men are created equal." He explained that that proposition was now being tested "in a great civil war"; he noted the purpose of the day's ceremony—to dedicate "a final resting place for those who here gave their lives that that nation might live." Lincoln assured his listeners that it was "altogether fitting and proper that we should do this."

Then Lincoln went on to examine the Battle

of Gettysburg "in a larger sense." He expressed his appreciation for what the men who died did at Gettysburg, and he urged his audience "to be dedicated here to the unfinished work which they who fought here have thus far so nobly advanced," that "from these honored dead we take increased devotion to that cause for which they gave the last full measure of devotion." He asserted that the dead at Gettysburg "shall not have died in vain" because their nation, under God, "shall have a new birth of freedom." He concluded with his hope that this American government "of the people, by the people, for the people, shall not perish from the earth."

Lincoln never used the words *slave* or *slavery;* he did not speak specifically of racial inequalities. But he clearly informed Americans of the meaning of their terrible war. It was a war about equality, a war that would determine whether every American would have equal opportunity—to work, to earn and save money, to live in peace, to be treated equally under the law. The Gettysburg Address was a logical extension of the Emancipation Proclamation. After Lincoln had freed the slaves and thereby changed the purpose of the war, he saw the struggle as a fundamental testing of the Declaration of Independence's assertion that all men are created equal. The soldiers at Gettysburg died to defend that proposition, not merely to restore the Union. As historian Garry Wills has stated, "In the crucible of the occasion, Lincoln distilled the meaning of the war, of the nation's purpose, of the remaining task, in a statement that is straightforward yet magical."

The Tide Changes

The Union victories at Gettysburg and Vicksburg did not end the war. The South fought on stubbornly. But the tide surely had changed. Early in 1864, Lincoln appointed General Ulysses Grant commander of the entire Northern army. Grant had essentially won the war in the Mississippi region, and he would come east to destroy General Lee's army.

In May and June 1864, Grant and Lee fought a series of brutal battles in Virginia that lasted six weeks. Grant could not completely destroy Lee, but he imposed staggering losses, and the Confederate army became short of men. In June, Grant commenced a long siege of Petersburg, a key city southeast of Richmond, the Confederate capital. Meanwhile, one of Grant's most talented lieutenants, General William Sherman, began an offensive in Tennessee with the goal of fighting his way to the strategic Southern city of Atlanta, Georgia. Sherman's campaign, later called "Sherman's March to the Sea," inflicted heavy damages on the Confederate army and the Southern landscape, thereby breaking the South's resolve.

The Election of 1864

In the middle of the terrible conflict, Lincoln had to run for reelection. His term in office would end in March 1865, and the election was set for November 1864. Some of Lincoln's advisers urged him, as commander-in-chief of the armed forces, to order a suspension of the election until the war ended. But Lincoln was determined that the proper democratic procedures take place, despite the war. As he asserted in a postelection address, "We cannot have free government without elections; and if the rebellion could force us to forgo, or postpone a national election, it might fairly claim to have already conquered and ruined us."

The Democrats nominated George McClellan, the Union general who had stopped Lee's advance at Antietam Creek two years earlier. Lincoln had dismissed McClellan from command of the Army of the Potomac because the general had not pursued Lee after the Battle of Antietam. The Democratic platform called for a truce with the South. McClellan did not energetically endorse that platform, but during the campaign he was sharply critical of Lincoln's handling of the war.

Fortunately for Lincoln, by the time the election came, the Northern armies had gained some victories on the battlefield. Sensing a change in the tide of the war, the American voters handed Lincoln a landslide victory. With the rebellious Southern states not voting, Lincoln received 55 percent of the popular vote and 212 electoral votes to McClellan's 21. As 1864 came to a close, Lincoln prepared for another four years in office.

The Second Inaugural Address

On March 4, 1865, Lincoln took his second oath of office. As is customary, he followed the oath with an inaugural address. Lincoln used this opportunity, as he had at the Gettysburg cemetery dedication, to explain to his fellow Americans the meaning and purpose of the dreadful war that had occupied their nation for almost four years. This Second Inaugural Address is much shorter than the speech delivered after his first inauguration, when he pleaded with the rebellious South to rejoin the Union and avoid a civil war.

Lincoln opened his address by reminding his audience of the situation four years earlier, when he was attempting to save the Union, while

> insurgent agents were in the city seeking to *destroy* it without war—seeking to dissolve the Union, and divide effects, by negotiation. Both parties deprecated war; but one of them would *make* war rather than let the nation survive; and the other would *accept* war rather than let it perish. And the war came.

Lincoln goes on to explain the reason for the conflict:

> One eighth of the whole population were colored slaves. . . . These slaves constituted a peculiar and powerful interest. All knew that this interest was, somehow, the cause of the war. To strengthen, perpetuate, and extend this interest was the object for which the insurgents would rend the Union, even by war; while the government claimed no right to do more than to restrict the territorial enlargement of it.

Here Lincoln clearly identifies slavery, not secession, as the essential cause of the war. Secession and the accompanying war were the inevitable effects of the nation's unresolvable debate over slavery.

Lincoln notes in his Second Inaugural Address that both North and South pray to the same God for victory on the battlefield, though he doubts that a just God could help a nation of

slaveholders: "It may seem strange that any men should dare to ask a just God's assistance in wringing their bread from the sweat of other men's faces." Lincoln then identifies American slavery as "one of those offenses which, in the providence of God, must needs come, but which, having continued through His appointed time, He now will to remove, and that He gives to both North and South, this terrible war, as the woe due to those by whom the offense came." Lincoln prays that "this scourge of war may speedily pass away." Yet he fears that the war will continue "until all the wealth piled by the bond-man's two hundred and fifty years of unrequited toil shall be sunk, and until every drop of blood drawn with the lash, shall be paid by another drawn with the sword."

Thus, Lincoln identifies slavery as a terrible sin for which God has sent a terrible war as due punishment. The sin was not the bickering between North and South that led to disunion; the sin was slavery itself, committed by the South but tolerated by the North to protect the Union. Now, as the thousands of dead on Civil War battlefields attest, both sides must pay in blood for committing this sin, until every drop of blood caused by the slave owner's whip is repaid with a drop of blood on the battlefield.

Lincoln concludes his address with words of healing, an olive branch of peace held out to the rebellious South:

> With malice toward none; with charity for all, with firmness in the right, as God gives us to see the right, let us strive on to finish the work we are in; to bind up the nation's wounds; to care for him who shall have borne the battle, and for his widow, and his orphan—to do all which may achieve and cherish a just, and a lasting peace, among ourselves, and with all nations.

Lincoln's Second Inaugural Address provides further explanation and justification for his Emancipation Proclamation. He informs his nation that he had to free the slaves. In Lincoln's view, as long as slave owners continued to demand from their slaves labor without pay, as long as they pushed their slaves by drawing blood with the whip, God would continue to require that blood be shed on the battlefield. Lincoln realized that he could not stop the bloodshed of war without ending the sin of slavery. After almost four years of death and carnage, Lincoln had firmly grasped the war's meaning.

President Abraham Lincoln set several important goals for his second term of office. First, and most important, he wished to conclude the war as quickly as possible. Once the war was over, Lincoln hoped to reconstruct his fragmented country, to bring the rebellious South back into the Union and to broker a lasting peace between the two warring regions of his country. To accomplish that goal, Lincoln knew that he would have to rid the nation of slavery forever. On January 1, 1863, in his Emancipation Proclamation, he had freed the slaves only in the states in rebellion. Lincoln fully realized that slavery's permanent abolition would have to be guaranteed in the U.S. Constitution so that it would vanish forever from American soil.

These were ambitious goals, but Lincoln was prepared for the hard work ahead. He had ushered his nation through the most difficult period in its history; he had held his country together during a bitter civil war, which was nearing its end as Lincoln began his second term in office. His reelection in 1864 proved that the people were behind him in his effort. Unfortunately, Lincoln would have only a very short time—barely six weeks—to accomplish these goals.

Winning the War

By the time Lincoln took his oath of office to begin his second term, the North's armies had gained a significant advantage on the battlefield. General William Sherman had taken the key cities of Atlanta and Savannah, Georgia, and he was pressing northward into South Carolina. In February, he had reached Columbia, South Carolina, the capital city of the first state that seceded from the Union in 1860. Sherman continued marching northward into North Carolina toward Virginia.

Meanwhile, General Ulysses Grant continued

his yearlong siege of Petersburg, Virginia, an important railroad junction only twenty miles from Richmond, the Confederate capital. The battle for Petersburg had begun the previous spring, when Grant had pressed his ninety-thousand-man army on the city hoping for a quick victory. But General Robert E. Lee's seasoned troops mounted a staunch defense of the key Southern city, and Grant began a long siege, posting his troops in long trenches outside and nearly surrounding the city. As the winter of 1864–1865 came, the Rebel soldiers and citizens of Petersburg suffered shortages of food, fuel, and clothing.

By the end of March, Lee knew that he could no longer defend Petersburg. On April 2, he removed his troops and moved northward across the Appomattox River, and Yankee soldiers occupied Petersburg. Lee's Army of Northern Virginia and another Confederate force battling General Sherman in North Carolina were the last significant Rebel armies between the North and complete victory. Sensing defeat, thousands of Confederate soldiers deserted and headed for home, hoping to bring neglected farms back into shape for spring planting. After Petersburg fell, the remaining Confederate soldiers defending Richmond abandoned that city, and President Jefferson Davis and his advisers fled Richmond as well. Yankee troops soon occupied the Confederate capital. The Southern cause was all but lost.

After occupying Petersburg, Grant's troops pursued Lee. The two armies clashed at Saylor's Creek, with Lee suffering heavy losses. Lee tried to retreat westward to escape Grant's pursuing army, but Lee's movement was blocked by a Union cavalry unit commanded by General Philip Sheridan. Trapped by Union armies and reduced now to less than thirty thousand men, Lee knew that further battle and bloodshed were senseless; he could never defeat Grant's larger and better-equipped force. Lee sent word to Grant that he was willing to discuss terms of surrender.

On April 9, the two great battle-weary generals met at Appomattox Courthouse to discuss surrender terms. Remembering the phrase "with malice toward none" from Lincoln's Second Inaugural Address, Grant imposed charitable terms of surrender upon Lee. Lee's troops would simply lay down their weapons and promise to go home and fight no more. Confederate soldiers could keep their horses and mules, which would be needed for spring plowing and planting. Lee's men were hungry, and Grant ordered rations for twenty-five thousand men to be sent to Lee's army.

The next day, Lee's men formally surrendered, laying down their weapons and battle flags before the victorious Union army. A few more Confederate regiments outside of Virginia fought on sporadically for a few weeks. But with Lee's surrender, the great civil war to restore the Union and end slavery was essentially over.

Reconstructing the Nation

More than 600,000 Americans lost their lives during the Civil War. Thousands more were permanently or partially disabled. Throughout the South, cities, towns, farms, homes, railroads, and roads were damaged and destroyed. The region's economy was in shambles. Without slave labor, the great Southern plantations would be unable to operate profitably. Moreover, even though the battle was over, the hostile feelings between Northerners and Southerners continued. When Lee surrendered to Grant at Appomattox Courthouse, the United States was still a house bitterly divided.

Lincoln knew that he faced a formidable task in reconstructing his fragmented nation. But even before Lee surrendered, Lincoln had been planning for the day when his nation would be fully restored. On April 11, 1865, Lincoln delivered a speech on reconstruction in Washington, D.C. He rejected the idea put forth by some Northerners that the rebellious Southern states should not be quickly readmitted to the Union. "Let us all join in doing the acts necessary to restoring the proper practical relations between these states and the Union," said Lincoln. He applauded the voters of Louisiana, who passed a resolution swearing allegiance to the Union and adopting a new state constitution that prohibited slavery.

Lincoln's plan to reconstruct the Union involved keeping Union armies in force in the South to maintain order and to protect the rights of newly freed slaves. Lincoln also planned to extend full citizenship rights to most Southerners, including those who served in the Confederate army, as long as they took an oath of allegiance to the Union. But Lincoln believed that those who had held high positions in the Confederate government and those who had served as officers in its army should not be able to vote or hold public office in the reconstructed United States. Most importantly, the state governments of the rebellious South must accept the Emancipation Proclamation. Slavery would have to be one of the casualties of the Civil War.

Lincoln also had formed a plan to deal with the hundreds of thousands of Southern slaves who had been liberated during the war. By the war's end, many were working for the U.S. government as soldiers or laborers. The federal government had begun to set up farms throughout the ravished South, and Lincoln hoped that freed slaves could work on these farms for fair wages. He also wanted to extend freed slaves the right to vote and hold public office.

Amending the Constitution

For Lincoln, permanently resolving the issue of slavery was the key to reconstructing the United States. He knew that his Emancipation Proclamation was solely a wartime measure advanced to cripple the South's ability to continue the war. Lincoln feared that sometime in the future the Supreme Court or Congress might invalidate the Emancipation, which Lincoln had sworn never to retract or modify. The only way to block a reversal of the Emancipation Proclamation was to draft a constitutional amendment to outlaw slavery forever.

As early as 1862, Republicans in Congress, with Lincoln's approval, began drafting a constitutional amendment to abolish slavery. In April 1864, the Thirteenth Amendment to the Constitution was formally introduced as a measure to be voted upon in the U.S. Senate. The Republican-dominated Senate passed the amendment by the required two-thirds vote, but to become law, the amendment would also have to be approved by two-thirds of the House of Representatives and three-quarters of the state legislatures as well. In June, the amendment abolishing slavery came to a vote in the House. House Democrats voted against the amendment, however, and it failed to garner the required two-thirds vote.

Republicans kept the issue alive. In the election of 1864, many Republican candidates campaigned on a platform that included ratification of the Thirteenth Amendment. Lincoln's reelection signaled that the amendment would eventually become law. The Republicans enjoyed some gains in the House of Representatives in the election, and these newly elected congressmen were anxious to kill slavery by making its prohibition part of the Constitution.

On January 31, 1865, even before the new congressmen took office, the Thirteenth Amendment again came to a vote in the House of Representatives. Lincoln had pressured Democratic congressmen who were leaving office to listen to the will of the American people and endorse the amendment. Some of these congressmen listened to Lincoln. This time, the measure attracted more than the required two-thirds of the vote.

Passage of the Thirteenth Amendment

Abolitionists cheered the House vote. Nonetheless, the Thirteenth Amendment was not yet a part of the Constitution. Having passed the Senate and House of Representatives, the Thirteenth Amendment still needed to be ratified by three-quarters of the individual state legislatures. Since Lincoln had maintained throughout the war that the South had never legally seceded from the Union, several Southern states would have to endorse the Thirteenth Amendment for it to achieve the required three-fourths of state legislatures.

The states began to act immediately. Within two months, the Thirteenth Amendment was approved by nineteen state legislatures, including Louisiana and Arkansas, which, near the end of the war, pledged allegiance to the Union and passed new state constitutions that outlawed

slavery. As of April 1865, however, the Thirteenth Amendment still needed to be ratified by three more states. The Civil War was over, but the slaves were not yet officially free. Their freedom depended on the untested legality of the Emancipation Proclamation; the abolition of slavery was not yet a part of the Constitution.

But Lincoln would not live to see the passage of the Thirteenth Amendment. In April 1865, just days after Lee's surrender to Grant marked the end of the Civil War, Lincoln himself became a casualty of that terrible four-year conflict.

A Theater Outing

On April 14, 1865, Lincoln was in good spirits. The war was virtually over. Several days earlier, Lincoln had visited Richmond. There, as he walked through the streets of the former capital of the Confederacy, freed black people had cheered him as their liberator. Lincoln had not only steered the North to victory, but he had expunged from his nation the great sin of slavery. In Richmond, he had seen firsthand the fruits of victory—the expressions of joy in the faces of free people who had once been slaves.

On the evening of April 14, Lincoln planned an evening of light entertainment with his wife, Mary, an opportunity to escape, for a few hours, the pain of war and the serious work of reconstructing the nation that lie ahead. The president and his wife had planned an outing to Ford's Theatre in Washington to see a performance of a British comedy, *Our American Cousin.* General and Mrs. Grant were supposed to accompany the Lincolns, but the Grants backed out at the last minute. Major Henry Rathbone and his fiancée, Clara Harris, a senator's daughter, attended instead.

The president's party arrived at Ford's Theatre a little late; the play had already begun when they entered the flag-draped presidential box in the theater balcony. When they were seated, the band struck "Hail to the Chief," and the audience applauded. Then the play continued. President and Mrs. Lincoln enjoyed the action on stage, and they laughed heartily at the play's many humorous lines.

The Assassin Arrives

Also arriving late for the start of the play that evening was an actor well known at Ford's Theatre, John Wilkes Booth. Booth had been a Virginia militiaman before the war; he had been among the guards stationed at the hanging of John Brown in 1859. When the Civil War began, Booth supported the Confederate cause, but he did not join the Confederate army. During the war, he made a good living as an actor. His father, Junius Brutus Booth, and his older brother, Edwin, were also accomplished actors. Lincoln had seen all three Booths perform on Washington's stages.

Booth had come to believe that Lincoln was mainly to blame for the South's troubles at the close of the war. Feeling guilty and cowardly for not having enlisted in the Rebel army, Booth vowed to take some other action to help the South's cause. At first, he planned to kidnap Lincoln and exchange him for several thousand Confederate prisoners of war. On March 17, 1865, Booth and a few accomplices actually attempted a kidnapping of Lincoln on the outskirts of Washington at Soldier's Home, where the Lincolns sometimes spent the night, but the Lincolns were not there that night.

When the war ended, Booth was determined to kill President Lincoln. He planned the assassination with four co-conspirators. In one night of terror, Booth hoped to murder Lincoln, Vice President Andrew Johnson, and Secretary of State William Seward. When Booth heard through one of the stagehands at Ford's Theatre that the Lincolns would be attending the performance of *Our American Cousin* on the evening of April 14, he launched his plan.

In the middle of the play, Booth entered the theater and climbed the stairs to the presidential box. The guard watching the rear door of the box was not at his post, and the door was unlocked. Booth was armed with a dagger and loaded derringer pistol. He waited for a moment when the theater audience erupted in laughter and applause, then he slipped into the president's box, fired his pistol at the back of Lincoln's head, and slashed at Colonel Rathbone with the dagger. Before anyone realized what had happened, Booth jumped from the balcony to the stage and shouted something to the audience. Some theatergoers thought he yelled *"Sic semper tyrannis!"*—Virginia's state motto, which meant "Thus be it ever to tyrants." Other witnesses claimed that Booth had shouted "The South is avenged!" With that, Booth quickly fled Ford's Theatre.

The crowd at Ford's Theatre was stunned. At first, they had no idea why the man wielding a long knife had jumped from the balcony to the stage. Soon, however, there were shouts from the presidential box. President Lincoln had been shot. A call went out for any doctors in the audience.

Two physicians hurried to Lincoln's side. His head was bleeding badly, and he was unconscious. The doctors applied mouth-to-mouth resuscitation to keep the president breathing, but they knew already that their efforts were useless. Booth's bullet had entered Lincoln's head behind his left ear and lodged in his brain behind his right eye. "His wound is mortal," said one of the physicians; "it is impossible for him to recover."

Lincoln was carried out of Ford's Theatre to a house across the street. Attendants placed him in a bed in a rear room. The news of the attempt on Lincoln's life quickly spread through the streets of Washington, and within minutes, Lincoln advisers were hurrying to the scene. Doctors could do nothing for the mortally wounded president; he lay in bed barely breathing. He had been shot on Good Friday. At 7:22 on Saturday morning, his breathing stopped. President Lincoln was dead.

Mourning the Slain President

The entire nation, North and South, was stunned by the assassination of Lincoln. Some bitter Southerners undoubtedly applauded Booth's murderous deed, but most Americans, even those who had criticized Lincoln's wartime policies, mourned his passing. They sensed that a great leader had been taken from them at a time when the war-torn nation needed strong leadership.

A short and simple funeral service was held for Lincoln at the White House on April 19. Then his coffin was transported by wagon to the Capitol building. Leading the funeral procession was a regiment of African American soldiers. The coffin was set in the Capitol's large rotunda room for two days so that visitors could pass through and pay their respects to their fallen president. Thousands of mourners entered the building and silently passed Lincoln's casket, offering prayers and shedding tears as they went by.

On April 21, Lincoln's coffin was loaded onto a train and transported for burial sixteen hundred miles away in Springfield, Illinois. All along the train route, mourners gathered to view the passing train. As the train passed through towns and cities, church bells tolled and soldiers and militiamen lined the tracks to salute their fallen commander.

Lincoln's body was laid to rest in Oak Ridge Cemetery, just outside of Springfield, on May 4. In a sense, he, too, had become a casualty of the great civil war to end slavery. In his Second Inaugural Address, he had predicted that God would not allow the war to end until the nation paid for the sin of slavery, until every drop of blood taken by the slave master's whip was repaid with a drop of blood on the battlefield. Early in his political career, Lincoln had tolerated slavery; in his First Inaugural Address, he had offered the rebellious Southern states the opportunity to return to the Union with slavery still in place. Now, as the war was coming to an end, Lincoln had shed his own blood so that slavery could be abolished.

The Thirteenth Amendment Becomes Law

At the time of Lincoln's death, the Thirteenth Amendment to the Constitution had not yet been ratified by three-quarters of the state legislatures. Final ratification of the amendment finally came on December 18, 1865, eight months after Lincoln's death.

The Thirteenth Amendment consists of two sections, each only one sentence long:

Section 1 Neither slavery nor involuntary servitude, except as a punishment for crime whereof the party shall have been duly con-

victed, shall exist within the United States, or any place subject to their jurisdiction.

Section 2 Congress shall have the power to enforce this article by appropriate legislation.

In simple language, the amendment gives the force of law to Lincoln's wartime Emancipation Proclamation. Slavery is prohibited throughout the United States and its territories. Only those convicted of crimes and serving prison terms can be made to work against their wills. Slavery was officially abolished from American soil; it would never again return.

The Civil War Amendments

The Constitution was twice more amended in the wake of the Civil War. The Thirteenth, Fourteenth, and Fifteenth Amendments to the Constitution are often called the "Civil War amendments" because they were passed as a result of the war. All three amendments concern the civil rights of African American citizens who were formerly slaves.

Soon after the passage of the Thirteenth Amendment, it became clear that the South's freed slaves were not totally free. They were legally free from their former owners, but they were not free to enjoy all the rights of American citizenship—the right to vote and hold public office, to serve on a jury, to live in the neighborhood of choice, to compete fairly in the job market, or to enjoy social amenities such as parks, restaurants, and hotels. Particularly in the South, freed slaves lived as second-class citizens, unable to enjoy the freedoms taken for granted by white Americans. Recognizing these conditions, Congress, in 1867, acted by proposing the Fourteenth Amendment to the Constitution.

The heart of the Fourteenth Amendment is the so-called equal protection clause in its first section. That section guarantees that all people born in the United States are citizens of the United States and citizens of the state in which they reside. It also guarantees that all citizens will be treated equally under the law:

No State shall make or enforce any law which shall abridge the privileges or immunities of citizens of the United States; nor shall any State deprive any person of life, liberty, or property, without due process of law; nor deny to any person within its jurisdiction the equal protection of the laws.

This amendment attempted to ensure that all American citizens, regardless of race, would enjoy all the rights and privileges of U.S. citizens. Thus, under the law, freed slaves and their children must receive fair and equal treatment.

The members of the Republican-controlled Congress knew that getting Southern states to ratify the Fourteenth Amendment would be difficult. Therefore, they refused to allow the states of the former Confederacy to seat their representatives in Congress until those states ratified the amendment. The amendment was eventually approved by both the Senate and House of Representatives and by three-quarters of the state legislatures. It became a part of the Constitution on July 28, 1868.

The Right to Vote

In 1870, Congress again acted on behalf of African American citizens when it became clear that Southern states were barring blacks from voting. In the South, laws were passed making it illegal for ex-slaves, their children, or grandchildren to vote. The Fifteenth Amendment was proposed to remedy this situation. Like the Thir-teenth Amendment, the Fifteenth contains two sections, each a single sentence in length:

Section 1 The right of citizens of the United States to vote shall not be denied or abridged by the United States or by any State on account of race, color, or previous condition of servitude.

Section 2 The Congress shall have power to enforce this article by appropriate legislation.

The Fifteenth Amendment became part of the Constitution on March 30, 1870.

The intent of the three Civil War amendments was to free the slaves forever and to guarantee to them and their descendants all the rights and privileges of American citizenship, including the right to vote. These measures, passed within five years of the end of the Civil War, were an attempt to prevent the United States from remaining a house divided along racial lines. By passing these three amendments, Congress and the state legislatures were certainly acting in accordance with Lincoln's wishes. At Gettysburg, he had predicted "a new birth of freedom" for his country, and in his Second Inaugural Address, he had hoped for "a just, and a lasting peace" for his war-torn nation. These Civil War amendments attempted to re-create the United States as a nation of free and equal citizens.

The Approach of the Yankee Army

Leon F. Litwack

How slaves reacted as the Union army over-ran the Confederacy in the late stages of the Civil War is a complex and fascinating story; it was not simply a matter of the "day of ju-bilee" bringing freedom. The "blue bellies" did not always treat the slaves well, and slaves did not automatically take the occasion to settle old scores with their masters with violence. The best way to characterize what happened is to say that slaves were generally cautious until they felt sure of what freedom really meant.

The last days of slavery are narrated in masterly fashion by historian Leon F. Litwack, a professor of history at the University of California, Berkeley, in this excerpt from his book Been in the Storm So Long: The Aftermath of Slavery.

"De war comes ter de great house an' ter de slave cabins jist alike," recalled Lucy Ann Dunn, a former slave on a North Carolina plantation. When the Yankees were reported to be approaching, even the less perceptive whites might have sensed the anxiousness,

the apprehension, the excitement that gripped the slave quarters. "Negroes doing no good," a Tennessee planter reported. "They seem to be restless not knowing what to do. At times I pity them at others I blame them much." The tension was by no means confined to the fields but entered the Big House and affected the demeanor of the servants, including some who had hitherto betrayed few if any emotions about the war. "I tole you de Nordern soldiers would come back; I tole you dose forts was no 'count," Aunt Polly, a Virginia house slave, exclaimed to the master's son. "Yes," he replied, obviously taken aback by her bluntness, "but you told me the Southern soldiers would come back, too, when father went away with them." "Dat because you cried," she explained, "and I wanted to keep up your spirits." With those words, Aunt Polly, a long-time family favorite for whose services her master said he could set no price, prepared to leave her "accustomed post" in the kitchen.

Although few slaves demonstrated such "impertinence" in the presence of the master's family, they did appear to be less circumspect in expressing their emotions. The pretenses were now lowered, if not dropped altogether. "The negroes seem very unwilling for the work," a young white woman confided to her journal; "some of their aside speeches very incendiary. Edward, the old coachman, is particularly sullen." On some plantations, the once clandestine prayer meetings were noticeably louder and more effusive, and there appeared to be fewer reasons to muffle the sounds before they reached the Big House. The singing in the slave quarters, Booker T. Washington remembered, "was bolder, had more ring, and lasted later into the night." They had sung these verses before but there was no longer any need to conceal what they meant by them; the words had not changed, only their immediacy, only the emphasis with which certain phrases were intoned. "Now they gradually threw off the mask," Washington recalled, "and were not afraid to let it be known that the 'freedom' in their songs meant freedom of the body in this world."

The mood of the slaves often defied the analysis of the master. On certain plantations, the slaves continued to act with an apparent indifference toward the war and the approaching Union troops, leaving their owners to speculate about what lay behind those bland countenances. . . .

Before the arrival of the Union Army, the roadsides were apt to be filled with the retreating columns of Confederate troops, their condition imparting most vividly and convincingly the visage of defeat. For many slaves, that sight alone confirmed what the "grapevine" and the demeanor of their "white folks" had earlier suggested, and the contrast with the initial predictions of ultimate victory could hardly have been more striking.

> I seen our 'Federates go off laughin' an' gay; full of life an' health. Dey was big an' strong, asingin' Dixie an' dey jus knowed dey was agoin' to win. I seen 'em come back skin an' bone, dere eyes all sad an' hollow, an' dere clothes all ragged. Dey was all lookin' sick. De sperrit dey lef' wid jus' been done whupped outen dem.

But even the anticipation of freedom did not necessarily prompt slaves to revel in the apparent military collapse of the Confederacy. Whether from loyalty to their "white folks," the need to act circumspectly, or fear of the Yankees, many slaves looked with dismay at the ragged columns of Confederate soldiers passing through the towns and plantations. For some, faithfulness may have been less important than simply pride in their homeland, now being ravaged by strangers who evinced little regard for the property and lives of Southerners, black or white.

The ambivalence that characterized the reaction of some slaves to the demise of the Confederacy reflected an understandable tension between attachment to their localities and the prospect of freedom. Three years after the war, an English visitor asked a Virginia freedman his opinion of Robert E. Lee. "He was a grand man, General Lee, sah," the ex-slave replied without hesitation. "You were sorry when he was defeated, I suppose?" the visitor then asked. "O no, sah," the freedman quickly retorted; "we were glad; we clapped our hands that day." If few slaves yearned for a Confederate victory, they did nevertheless view themselves as Southerners, they did sense that their lives and destinies were intricately bound with the white people of the South, and some even shared with whites the humiliation of defeat. "Dere was jes' too many of dem blue coats for us to lick," a former Alabama slave tried to explain. "Our 'Federates was de bes' fightin' men dat ever were. Dere warn't nobody lak our 'Federates."

When the unfamiliar roar of gunfire echoed in the distance, the emotions of individual slaves ranged from bewilderment and fear to unconcealed elation. In eastern Virginia, within earshot of the battle raging at Manassas, an elderly slave "mammy" preparing the Sunday dinner greeted each blast of the cannon with a subdued "Ride on, Massa Jesus." When the guns were heard near Charleston, a sixty-nine-year-old woman exclaimed, "Come, dear Jesus," and she later recalled having felt "nearer to Heaben den I ever feel before." The younger slaves were apt to be less certain about what was happening around them. The strange noise, the hasty preparations, the talk in the slave quarters were at the same time exciting and terrifying. Two young slaves who lived in different sections, Sam Mitchell of South Carolina and Annie Osborne of Louisiana, each heard what sounded like thunder when the

Yankees approached, and both of them sought an explanation. "Son," Sam's mother assured him, "dat ain't no t'under, dat Yankee come to gib you Freedom." When the cannons ceased booming, Annie's brother told her, "We's gwine be all freed from old Massa Tom's beatin's." No amount of time could dim those recollections, any more than Sarah Debro, who had been a slave in North Carolina, could forget the moment she asked her mistress to explain the thunder that had frightened her "near 'bout to death." Those were Yankee cannons killing "our men," the woman replied, before breaking down in tears. Alarmed by this unusual sight, Sarah ran to the kitchen, where Aunt Charity was cooking, and told her what had just happened. "She ain't cryin kaze de Yankees killin' de mens," the black woman declared, "she's doin' all dat cryin' kaze she skeered we's goin' to be sot free."

To perform the usual plantation routines under these conditions proved to be increasingly difficult. Although some planters and overseers tried to maintain business as usual, and some succeeded, the reported approach of the Union Army tended to undermine slave discipline and in some places it brought work to a complete standstill. . . .

The approach of the Union Army forced planters and slaves alike into a flurry of last-minute activity. "'Fore they come," a former Georgia slave recalled, "the white folks had all the niggers busy hidin' everything they could." On the assumption, which proved to be incorrect, that the Yankees would not disturb the slaves' possessions, many white families secreted their valuables in or under the slave cabins or on the very persons of the slaves. "Miss Gusta calls me and wrops my hair in front and puts her jewelry in under the plaits and pulls them back and pins them down so you couldn't see nothin'." With Union troops sighted nearby, a South Carolina planter moved some of his house furniture into the cabin belonging to Abram Brown, the driver and headman on the plantation, and told him to claim ownership if the Yankees asked any questions. To the Union soldiers, it must have looked like the best-furnished slave cabin in the South,

and they refused to believe Brown's story. Knowing the risks, some slaves simply refused to accept such responsibilities, using time-honored devices. "Mamma Maria was too nervous," her mistress wrote, "and cried too much to have any responsibility put on her."

During those tense, anxious days of waiting, there were slaves who provided whatever encouragement and support they could muster for their masters and mistresses. . . .

Not only did some slaves vow to protect their "white folks," as though the imminent arrival of the Yankees required a reaffirmation of loyalty, but they did what they could to ensure their safety. Preparing for the Union soldiers, a maid in Mary Chesnut's household urged her mistress to burn the diary she had been keeping lest it fall into the hands of the enemy. During the siege of Vicksburg, Mary Ann Loughborough, along with her daughter and servants, took refuge in a cave and remained there during the Yankee bombardment; one of the servants stood guard, gun in hand, assuring his mistress that anyone who entered "would have to go over his body first." No one had more experience in anticipating the changing moods of a master than did his slaves, and this valuable asset enabled some of them to save the lives of their masters. When the Yankees were sighted, Charley Bryant, a Texas slaveholder, ran into the house and grabbed his gun. But George Price, the head slave on the plantation, fearing for the safety of his volatile master, disarmed him and locked him in the smokehouse. "He ain't do dat to be mean," a former slave recalled, "but he want to keep old massa outten trouble. Old massa know dat, but he beat on de door and yell, but it ain't git open till dem Yankees done gone."

Anticipating the path of the Union Army, many planters had already removed the bulk of their slaves to safer areas. If that proved impractical, some attempted to hide them, along with the family jewels, money, and livestock, until the Yankees had passed through the neighborhood. Reversing traditional roles, the planter himself might seek refuge in the nearby woods or swamp, depending upon the slaves to supply him with food and not to betray his hiding place. . . . [But] appearances could . . . be deceptive. John S. Wise, the son of a prominent Virginian, recalled the abandonment of the family plantation near Norfolk and how Jim, the butler, had diligently assisted them. "Jim my father regarded as his man Friday. Nobody doubted that one so faithful and so long trusted would prove true in this emergency." But after helping to load the carriage with silverware and valuables, and just before they were to depart, Jim disappeared. "In vain we called and searched for him. We never saw him again. The prospect of freedom overcame a lifetime of love and loyalty.". . .

Before a master fled, he might entrust the plantation or town house to some responsible slave, usually the driver or house servants, in the hope that his property could be kept intact until his return. Such confidence in most instances was not betrayed, with the slaves demonstrating what few masters had willingly conceded them—the ability to look after themselves and the plantation without any whites to advise or direct them. . . .

When white families abandoning the plantations tried to take slaves with them, they often encountered the same resistance that had greeted earlier attempts to remove slaves to safer areas. The classic example occurred early in the war, when the sudden appearance of Union warships at the Sea Islands off the coast of South Carolina precipitated a mass exodus of planters and their families. Despite pleading, threats, and violence, however, the slaves stubbornly refused to accompany their owners to the mainland, many of them hiding in the swamps and fields rather than be taken. With freedom perhaps only a few hours or days away, this reluctance was not surprising. After being ordered to row his master to the mainland, Moses Mitchell, a carpenter and hoer, heeded his wife's suggestion to "go out dat back door and keep a-going." Equally determined, a slave named Susannah, valued as the family seamstress, refused to leave with her master and mistress despite their dire warnings about what would happen if she remained. Several days later, when her master's son returned

and ordered the slaves to destroy the cotton lest it fall into the hands of the Union Army, they refused to cooperate. "Why for we burn de cotton?" they asked. "Where we get money then for buy clo' and shoes and salt?" Rather than burn the cotton, the slaves took turns guarding it, "the women keeping watch and the men ready to defend it when the watchers gave the alarm." In some instances, however, slaves who resisted removal were shot down, even burned to death in the cotton houses. On Edisto Island, where a Confederate raiding party had tried to remove some blacks, "the women fought so violently when they were taking off the men," a white Charlestonian wrote, "that they were obliged to shoot some of them."

Not only did the areas of comparative safety within the Confederacy shrink with the advance of the Union Army but there were more compelling reasons why most slaveholding families chose not to flee. To stay was to try to save their homes and plantations from destruction and to preserve their slaves from the fearful epidemic whites diagnosed as "demoralization.". . .

Whether the master and mistress chose to stay or flee, they might lecture the slaves on how to behave when the Yankees arrived. . . . Rivana Boynton, who had been a house slave on a plantation near Savannah, remembered the day her mistress, Mollie Hoover, assembled the slaves and instructed them on what to tell the approaching Yankees. "If they ask you whether I've been good to you, you tell 'em 'yes.' If they ask you if we give you meat, you say 'yes.'" Most of the slaves did not get any meat, the former slave recalled, "but I did, 'cause I worked in the house. So I didn't tell a lie, for I did git meat." Most importantly, the white family warned the slaves not to divulge where the valuables had been hidden, no matter what the Yankees told them. "We knowed enough to keep our mouths shut," a former Georgia slave remarked. But a Tennessee slave, named Jule, who claimed not to fear the Union soldiers, had some different ideas. As the Yankees neared the plantation, the mistress commanded the slaves to remain loyal. "If they find that trunk o' money or silver plate," she asked Jule, "you'll say it's your'n, won't you?" The slave stood there, obviously unmoved by her mistress's plea. "Mistress," she replied, "I can't lie over that; you bo't that silver plate when you sole my three children."

When the Union Army was nearby, slaves were quick to discern any changes in the disposition of their owners. In some places, the frequency and the severity of punishments abated, and the masters—perhaps fearing slave retaliation—assumed a more benign attitude, prepared for the eventuality of free labor, and even offered to pay wages. After the Yankees had been sighted less than two miles away, a Tennessee planter who had beaten one of his slaves that morning apologized to him and begged him not to desert. But as slaves had learned so well, usually from bitter personal experience, the moods of their "white folks" were capable of violent fluctuations. If the wartime disruptions, privations, and casualties had earlier provoked fits of anger, the impending disaster they now faced and the knowledge that they were about to lose both the war and their slaves rendered even some usually self-possessed whites unable to contain their emotions. . . .

Not knowing what to expect of the invading army but fearing the worst, white families, in those final days and hours, often verged on panic and hysteria. At least that was how some of their slaves perceived them. In exasperation, masters were known to have lashed out at men and women who were too quick to celebrate their imminent release from bondage, while others refused to acknowledge either defeat or emancipation. After hearing of a new Confederate setback in the vicinity, Katie Rowe's master mounted his horse and rode out onto the plantation where the slaves were hoeing the corn. He instructed the overseer to assemble the hands around the lead row man—"dat my own uncle Sandy"—and what he told them on that occasion Katie Rowe could recall vividly many years later:

> You niggers been seeing de 'Federate soldiers coming by here looking purty raggedy and hurt and wore out, but dat no sign dey licked! Dem Yankees ain't gwin git dis fur, but iffen

dey do you all ain't gwin git free by 'em, 'cause I gwine free you befo' dat. When dey git here dey going find you already free 'cause I gwine line you up on de bank of Bois d'Arc Creek and free you wid my shotgun! Anybody miss jest one lick wid de hoe, or one step in de line, or one clap of dat bell, or one toot of de horn, and he gwine be free and talking to de debil long befo' he ever see a pair of blue britches!

Not long after that warning, the master was "blowed all to pieces" in a boiler explosion, "and dey jest find little bitsy chunks of his clothes and parts of him to bury." And when the Yankees finally arrived, the overseer who had previously terrorized them "git sweet as honey in de comb! Nobody git a whipping all de time de Yankees dar!"

Looking on with a growing sense of incredulity, slaves observed the desperation, the anguish, the helplessness that marked the faces and actions of their "white folks." A Tennessee slave recalled how her mistress, at the sight of Union gunboats, suddenly "got wild-like" and "was cryin' an' wringin' her han's," while at the same time she kept repeating to her slaves, "Now, 'member I brought you up!" Although the slaves shared much of the uncertainty that pervaded the Big House, the quality of their fears and the anticipation they felt were quite different. When Margaret Hughes, who had been a young slave in South Carolina, heard that the Union soldiers were coming, she ran to her aunt for comfort. Much to Margaret's surprise, she found her in the best of spirits and not at all dismayed by the news. "Child," she reassured her, "we going to have such a good time a settin' at de white folks' table, a eating off de white folks' table, and a rocking in de big rocking chair.". . .

The appearance of the first Yankee soldier symbolized far more than the humiliation of military defeat. No matter how certain they were of their own slaves, nearly every master and mistress sensed that the old loyalties and mutual dependencies were about to become irrelevant. "Negro slavery is about played out," John H. Bills, the Tennessee planter, observed, "we being deprived of that Control needful to make them happy and prosperous.". . .

Preparing to abandon the family plantation, as the Yankees approached, Eliza Andrews took time to note in her journal: "There is no telling what may happen before we come back; the Yankees may have put an end to our glorious old plantation life forever." That night, she paid a final visit to the slave quarters to bid her blacks farewell. "Poor things, I may never see any of them again, and even if I do, everything will be different. We all went to bed crying . . ." Four months later, returning to her home, she confided to her journal: "It is necessary to have some nickname to use when we talk before the servants, and to speak very carefully, even then, for every black man is a possible spy. Father says we must not even trust mammy too far."

Freedom: An Ex-Slave Remembers

Boston Blackwell

The ninety-eight-year-old former slave interviewed in this article begins his account by saying that he had been "borned" with his master's name, Pruitt, but that after emancipation he adopted Blackwell as his "freed name." Such name changes were fairly common as ex-slaves sought ways of establishing and testing their psychological and physical—as opposed to their legal—freedom. Many, for example, moved around, either in search of long-separated spouses, siblings, children, or parents or just to experience for themselves the ability to travel away from their plantation without feeling like a fugitive.

Blackwell says that in 1863, when the Union army approached the plantation, he

fled to the Yankees and joined in the fighting. His experience in the closing years of the Civil War was typical of the large numbers of former slaves who in many important ways helped the Union cause. So, unfortunately, was his failure to secure a military pension after the war. Blackwell was aware of the difficulties that slaves on outlying farms had in winning the freedom to which they were now entitled. His description of the Ku Klux Klan (one of the chief white terrorist organizations that tried to disrupt Reconstruction and intimidate the freedmen) rings true, and so does his bitter disappointment in being deprived of the right to vote by the Jim Crow laws. The dignity and insight with which Boston Blackwell spoke of his life as a slave, a soldier (if not a formally enlisted man), a free worker, and a citizen make his account a fitting way to conclude this account of the history of American slavery, and an intro-

Reprinted from Boston Blackwell, "Interview at North Little Rock, Arkansas," in *Life Under the "Peculiar Institution,"* edited by Norman R. Yetman. Copyright © 1970 Holt, Rinehart, Winston, Inc. Reprinted with permission from Dover Publications, Inc.

duction to the struggle of African Americans for their full rights.

? knows my age, good. Old Miss, she told me when I got sold—"Boss, you is thirteen—borned Christmas. Be sure to tell your new mistress and she put you down in her book." My borned name was Pruitt 'cause I got borned on Robert Pruitt's plantation in Georgia—Franklin County, Georgia. But Blackwell is my freed name. You see, after my mammy got sold down to Augusta—I wished I could tell you the man what brought her; I ain't never seed him since—I was sold to go to Arkansas, Jefferson County, Arkansas. Then was when Old Miss told me I am thirteen. It was before the Civil War I come here. The onliest auction of slaves I ever seed was in Memphis, coming on to Arkansas. I heerd a girl bid off for eight hundred

dollars. She was about fifteen, I reckon. I heerd a woman—a breeding woman—bid off for fifteen hundred dollars. They always brought good money. I'm telling you, it was when we was coming from Atlanta.

I'll tell you how I runned away and joined the Yankees. You know Abraham Lincoln declared freedom in '63, first day of January. In October '63, I runned away and went to Pine Bluff to get to the Yankees. I was on the Blackwell plantation south of Pine Bluff in '68. They was building a new house; I wanted to feel some putty in my hand. One early morning I climb a ladder to get a little chunk and the overseer man, he seed me. Here he come, yelling me to get down; he gwine whip me 'cause I's a thief, he say. He call a slave boy and tell him cut ten willer whips; he gwine wear every one out on me. When he's gone to eat breakfast, I runs to my cabin and tells

Former slaves who joined the Union army pose at a wharf in Alexandria, Virginia.
Freed slaves who fought for the Union were promised pensions, which often went unpaid.

my sister, "I'se leaving this here place for good." She cry and say, "Overseer man, he kill you." I says, "He kill me anyhow." The young boy what cut the whips—he named Jerry—he come along with me, and we wade the stream for long piece. Heerd the hounds a-howling, getting ready for to chase us. Then we hide in dark woods. It was cold, frosty weather. Two days and two nights we traveled. That boy, he so cold and hunngry, he want to fall out by the way, but I drug him on. When we gets to the Yankee camp all our troubles were over. We gets all the contraband we could eat. They was hundreds of runaways there. The Yankees feeds all them refugees on contraband. They made me a driver of a team in the quartermaster's department. I was always careful to do everything they telled me. They telled me I was free when I gets to the Yankee camp, but I couldn't go outside much. Iffen you could get to the Yankee's camp you was free right now.

That old story about forty acres and a mule, it make me laugh. They sure did tell us that, but I never knowed any person which got it. The officers telled us we would all get slave pension. That just exactly what they tell. They sure did tell me I would get a parcel of ground to farm. Nothing ever hatched out of that, neither.

When I got to Pine Bluff I stayed contraband. When the battle come, Captain Manly carried me down to the battleground and I stay there till the fighting was over. I was a soldier that day. I didn't shoot no gun nor cannon. I carried water from the river for to put out the fire in the cotton bales what made the breastworks. Every time the 'Federates shoot, the cotton, it come on fire. So after the battle, they transfer me back to quartermaster driver. Captain Dodridge was his name. I served in Little Rock until Captain Haskell. I was swored in for during the War. It was on the corner of Main and Markham Street in Little Rock I was swored in. Year of '64. I was 5 feet, 8 inches high. Living in the army was purty good. Iffen you obeyed them Yankee officers they treated you purty good, but iffen you didn't they sure went rough on you.

After the soldiers all go away, the first thing, I work on the railroad. They was just beginning to come here. I digged pits out, going along front of where the tracks was to go. I get one dollar a day. I felt like the richest man in the world! I boarded with a white family. Always I was a-watching for my slave pension to begin coming. Before I left the army my captain, he telled me to file. My file number, it is 1,115,857. After I keeped them paper for so many years, white and black folks both telled me it ain't never coming—my slave pension—and I reckon the children tored up the papers. That number for me is filed in Washington.

After the railroad I went steamboating. First one was a little one; they call her *Fort Smith* 'cause she go from Little Rock to Fort Smith. It was funny, too, her captain was name Smith. Captain Eugene Smith was his name. He was good, but the mate was sure rough. They's plenty to do on a riverboat. Never is no time for rest. Load, unload, scrub. Just you do whatever you is told to do and do it right now, and you'll keep outen trouble, on a steamboat, or a railroad, or in the army, or wherever you is. That's what I knows.

I reckon they was right smart old masters what didn't want to let they slaves go after freedom. They hated to turn them loose. Just tell them work on. Heap of them didn't know freedom come. I used to hear tell how the government had to send soldiers away down in the far back country to make them turn the slaves loose. I can't tell you how them free niggers was living; I was too busy looking out for myself. Heaps of them went to farming. They was sharecroppers.

Them Ku Kluxers was terrible—what they done to people. Oh, God, they was bad. They come sneaking up and runned you outen your house and take everything you had. They was rough on the women and children. People all wanted to stay close by where soldiers was. I sure knowed they was my friend.

After peace, I got with my sister. She's the onliest of all my people I ever seed again. She telled me she was scared all that day I runned away. She couldn't work, she shake so bad. She heerd overseer man getting ready to chase me and Jerry. He saddle his horse, take his gun and pistol, both. He gwine kill me on sight, but Jerry, he say he bring him back, dead or alive, tied to his horse's tail. But he didn't get us, Ha, Ha, Ha. Yankees got us.

Now you wants to know about this voting business. I voted for General Grant. Army men come around and registered you before voting time. It wasn't no trouble to vote them days; white and black all voted together. All you had to do was tell who you was vote for and they give you a colored ticket. All the men up had different colored tickets. Iffen you're voting for Grant, you get his color. It was easy. They was colored men in office, plenty. Colored legislators, and colored circuit clerks, and colored county clerks. They sure was some big officers colored in them times. They was all my friends. This here used to be a good county, but I tell you it sure is tough now. I think it's wrong—exactly wrong that we can't vote now. The Jim Crow law, it put us out. The Constitution of the United States, it give us the right to vote. It made us citizens, it did.

You just keeps on asking about me, lady. I ain't never been asked about myself in my *whole* life! Now you wants to know after railroading and steamboating what. They was still work the Yankee army wanted done. The War had been gone for long time. All over every place was bodies buried. They was bringing them to Little Rock to put in government graveyard. They sent me all over the state to help bring them here. Major Forsythe was my quartermaster then.

After that was done, they put me to work at St. John's hospital. The work I done there like to ruin me for life. I cleaned out the water closets. After a while I took down sick from the work—the scent, you know—but I keep on till I get so far gone I can't stay on my feets no more. A misery got me in the chest; right here, and it been with me all through life; it with me now.

I filed for a pension on this ailment. I never did get it. The government never took care of me like it did some soldiers. They said I was not an enlisted man, that I was a employed man, so I couldn't get no pension. I give me whole life to the government for many years. White and black both always telling me I should have a pension. I stood on the battlefield just like other soldiers. Iffen I could have had some help when I been sick, I might not be so no account now.

Appendix of Documents

Document 1: Slavery in Virginia, 1705

Robert Beverley, the English colonial official who wrote the first history of Virginia at the beginning of the eighteenth century, describes the advantages that the colony has gained by favoring slavery as the basis of its labor supply in the excerpt that follows.

Their Servants, they distinguish by the Names of Slaves for Life, and Servants for a time.

Slaves are the Negroes, and their Posterity, following the condition of the Mother, according to the Maxim, *partus sequitur ventrem* [status proceeds from the womb]. They are call'd Slaves, in respect of the time of their Servitude, because it is for Life.

Servants, are those which serve only for a few years, according to the time of their Indenture, or the Custom of the Country. The Custom of the Country takes place upon such as have no Indentures. The Law in this case is, that if such Servants be under Nineteen years of Age, they must be brought into Court, to have their Age adjudged; and from the Age they are judg'd to be of, they must serve until they reach four and twenty: But if they be adjudged upwards of Nineteen, they are then only to be Servants for the term of five Years.

The Male-Servants, and Slaves of both Sexes, and imployed together in Tilling and Manuring the Ground, in Sowing and Planting Tobacco, Corn, &c. Some Distinction indeed is made between them in their Cloaths, and Food; but the Work of both, is no other than what the Overseers, the Freemen, and the Planters themselves do.

Sufficient Distinction is also made between the Female-Servants, and Slaves; for a White woman is rarely or never put to work in the Ground, if she be good for any thing else: And to Discourage all Planters from using any Women so, their Law imposes the heaviest Taxes upon Female-Servants working in the Ground, while it suffers all other white Women to be absolutely exempted: Whereas on the other hand, it is a common thing to work a Woman Slave out of Doors; nor does the Law make any distinction in her Taxes, whether her Work be Abroad, or at Home.

Because I have heard how strangely cruel, and severe, the Service of this Country is represented in some parts of *England*; I can't forbear affirming, that the work of their Servants, and Slaves, is no other than what every common Freeman do's. Neither is any Servant requir'd to do more in a Day, than his Overseer. And I can assure you with a great deal of Truth, that generally their Slaves are not worked near so hard, nor so many Hours in a Day, as the Husbandmen, and Day-Labourers in *England*. An Overseer is a Man, that having served his time, has acquired the Skill and Character of an experienced Planter, and is therefore intrusted with the Direction of the Servants and Slaves.

But to compleat this account of Servants, I shall give you a short Relation of the care their Laws take, that they be used as tenderly as possible.

By the Laws of their Country.

1. All Servants whatsoever, have their Complaints heard without Fee, or Reward; but if the Master be found Faulty, the charge of the Complaint is cast upon him, otherwise the business is done *ex Officio.*

2. Any Justice of Peace may receive the Complaint of a Servant, and order every thing relating thereto, till the next County-Court, where it will be finally determin'd.

3. All Masters are under the Correction, and Censure of the County-Courts, to provide for their Servants, good and wholsome Diet, Clothing, and Lodging.

4. They are always to appear, upon the first Notice given of the Complaint of their Servants, otherwise to forfeit the Service of them, until they do appear.

5. All Servants Complaints are to be receiv'd at any time in Court, without Process, and shall not be delay'd for want of Form; but the Merits of the Complaint must be immediately inquir'd into by the Justices; and if the Master cause any delay therein, the Court may remove such Servants, if they see Cause, until the Master will come to Tryal.

6. If a Master shall at any time disobey an Order of Court, made upon any Complaint of a Servant; the Court is impower'd to remove such Servant forthwith to another Master, who will be kinder; Giving to the former Master the produce only, (after Fees deducted) of what such Servants shall be sold for by Publick Outcry.

7. If a Master should be so cruel, as to use his Servant ill, that is faln Sick, or Lame in his Service, and thereby render'd unfit for Labour, he must be remov'd by the Church-Wardens out of the way of such Cruelty, and boarded in some good Planters House, till the time of his Freedom, the charge of which must be laid before the next County-court, which has power to levy the same from time to time, upon the Goods and Chattels of the Master; After which, the charge of such Boarding is to come upon the Parish in General.

8. All hired Servants are intituled to these Priviledges.

9. No master of a Servant, can make a new Bargain for Service, or other Matter with his Servant, without the privity and consent of a Justice of Peace, to prevent the Master's Over-reaching, or scareing such Servant into an unreasonable Complyance.

10. The property of all Money and Goods sent over thither to Servants, or carry'd in with them; is reserv'd to themselves, and remain intirely at their disposal.

11. Each Servant at his Freedom, receives of his Master fifteen Bushels of Corn, (which is sufficient for a whole year) and two new Suits of Cloaths, both Linnen and Woollen; and then becomes as free in all respects, and as much entituled to the Liberties, and Priviledges of the Country, as any other of the Inhabitants or Natives are.

12. Each Servant has then also a Right to take up fifty Acres of Land, where he can find any unpatented: But that is no great Privilege, for any one may have as good a right for a piece of Eight.

This is what the Laws prescribe in favour of Servants, by which you may find, that the Cruelties and Severities imputed to that Country, are an unjust Reflection. For no People more abhor the thoughts of such Usage, than the *Virginians,* nor take more precaution to prevent it.

Major Problems in American Colonial History, ed. Karen Ordahl Kupperman (Lexington, Mass.: D.C. Heath & Co., 1993), pp. 98–100.

Document 2: The Treatment of Virginia Slaves: An Eighteenth-Century Planter's Account

Historians always treasure the personal papers of individuals who lived in societies of the past, even if they did not take a leading role in major historical events. Eighteenth-century Virginia produced a number of literate and highly articulate—indeed, verbose—planters whose correspondence and journals provide a revealing commentary on daily life in the colony. Naturally, such papers (like any historical source) must be read with a constant eye to the writer's bias.

One of the most prolific diary-keepers of the Virginia landed gentry was Colonel Landon Carter of Sabine Hall, a member of a family with enormous holdings of land and slaves that had emerged at the top of the colony's social hierarchy in the early eighteenth century. Landon Carter's journals, in which he made almost daily entries throughout the 1760s and early 1770s, are valuable to historians chiefly for what they reveal of a planter's everyday concerns: the weather, the price of tobacco, his own health and that of everyone around him, and maintaining correct discipline among his many slaves. Yet for all the paternalism that he felt called upon to exercise, Carter was primarily a businessman engaged in producing a cash crop for a distant market. Far from living a life of gracious ease in his handsome mansion, Colonel Carter never ceased to worry about his cash flow, about the rainy weather that seemed always to interfere with the proper cultivation or harvesting of his tobacco and corn, about the proper medicines with which to personally doctor everyone from his daughters to the slaves (in whom so much of his wealth was invested), and about having to get his unenthusiastic slaves to do routine tasks.

[February] 24. Wednesday . . .

It has rained pretty smartly in the night and till near 11 this mor[ning so t]hat Mortimer who was sent for to Mulatto Peter taken with a bleding at the nose off and on ever since this day sevennight cannot come.

To humour other people I have sent for [Dr.] Fauntleroy and [Dr.] Mortimer to this fellow although I have several times stopt the bleeding and really there is something in his case not regularly to be accounted for. It seems twice or thrice before in his life he has been subject to this bleeding but after every violent touch it has been stopt and left off. His state of health then nobody can give any account of but as to his present state till this bleeding we all can pronounce him a boy in great health and what should occasion such a bursting of the vessel of the nose without a fit of sickness or other visible cause is the difficulty. Had it been periodical I should have conjectured an intermittant and bleeding the crisis of it but it has been irregular in every bleeding of it and sometimes at 2 days' distance. I have kept him upon a low and cooling diet, given him cooling medicines, blooded him in the arm and foot a little at a time, Cupped him between the scapula [bo]th with and without scarification, have used warm baths to his feet for a delivation of the blood from his head besides many styptics of the shops and all the old women's methods of cold water to his head, to his privates, Vinegar cloths, and what not and all to no purpose. The evening before yesterday imagining it to be a divided state in the blood I administered 30 grains of the bark with 6 drops of Elixir Vitriol and have continued the use of this ever since with every now and then a cup of Comfrey decoction with saltpetre and gum Arabic in it in order to unite and thicken the blood. He has not bled to speak of since Monday 4 o'clock. Fauntleroy was here and seemed to think I gave too little bark, but sure I am small doses administered frequent have the best chance of entering the blood. I have not much expectation from such practitioners in such extraordinary cases for it must require a great length of practice to meet with such a one. However it is the duty of a Master and I have sent for them to satisfye that. . . .

[Tuesday, March 15, 1770]

Mr. Toney shall as certainly receive ample correction for his behaviour to me as that he and I live. The day before yesterday he began to pale in the garden and only fitted the rails to seven posts. When he began to put them up I was riding out and ordered him to leave the gateway into the garden as wide as the two piers next the gate on each side. Nay, I measured the ground off to him and showed him where the two concluding posts were to stand and the rest at 8 feet asunder from post to post to answer to the tenons of his rails and I asked him if he under stood me. He said he did and would do it so. I had been 2 hours out and when I came home nothing was done and he was gone about another jobb. I asked him why he served me so. He told me because it would not answer his design. The villain had so constantly interrupted my orders that I had given him about every jobb this year that I struck him upon the shoulders with my stick which having had ten year made out of hiccory so very dry and light had been long split and tied with packthread therefore shivered all to pieces and this morning, for that stroke which did not raise the least swelling nor prevent the idle dog from putting up the posts as I directed in which I convinced him that every thing answered, I say this morning he has laid himself up with a pain in the shoulder and will not even come out to take off a lock that he carried but 2 days agoe to Buckland's smith on purpose to get the spring mended which broke again this morning. I might as well give up every Negroe if I submit to this impudence.

[Friday, March 16, 1770] . . .

I do believe my old Carpenters intend to be my greatest rascals. Guy does not go about any jobb be it ever so trifling that he does not make three weeks or a month of it at least. The silling my Mudhouse, a jobb of not more than 3 days, he has already been above a fortnight about, and this morning when my people went to help to put the sills in, though he said he was ready for them, he had the rotten sills to cut out and because I told him he should certainly be called to account for it as I came back truly he was gone and no body knew where and had been gone for sometime but not about my house.

Mr. Tony, another rascal, pretends he is full of pain though he looks much better than any Negroe I have.

17. Saturday.

Tony came abroad and was well entertained for his impudence. Perhaps now he may think of working a little.

Guy actually run away. Outlawries are sent out against him for tomorrow's publication. . . .

[March] 22 [1770], Thursday. . . .

Guy came home yesterday and had his correction for run away in sight of the people. The 2 sarahs came up yesterday pretending to be violent ill with pains in their sides. They look very well, had no fever, and I ordered them down to their work upon pain of a whipping. They went, worked very well with no grunting about pain but one of them, to wit Manuel's sarah, taking the advantage of Lawson's ride to the fork, swore she would not work any longer and run away and is still out. There is a curiosity in this Creature. She worked none last year pretending to be with Child and this she was full 12 months before she was brought to bed. She has now the same pretence and thinks to pursue the same course but as I have full warning of her deceit, if I live, I will break her of that trick. I had two before of this turn. Wilmot of the fork whenever she was with Child always pretended to be too heavy to work and it cost me 12 months before I broke her. Criss of Mangorike fell into the same scheme and really carried it to a great length for at last she could not be dragged out. However by carrying a horse with traces the Lady took to her feet run away and when catched by a severe whipping has been a good slave ever since only a cursed thief in making her Children milk my Cows in the night. . . .

[March 30, 1770]

I think my man Tony is determined to struggle whether he shall not do as he pleases. He has with McGinis been 2 days only pailing in the dairy and henhouse yard with the posts ready hewed and morticed for him. I told him when I rode out this morning he would certainly get another whipping. He was ranging the pales at least one pannel above another full a foot pretending the ground was uneven. I asked him if he could not pare the ground away. He stoopt down like falling but I imagined it was the Negroe's foolish way of hearing better. I rode out. When I came home the pales were all laid slanting. I asked him why he did that. He still laid the fault on the ground and as his left shoulder was to me I gave him one small rap upon it. He went to breakfast afterwards and no complaint. This evening I walked there and then he pretended he could not drive a nail, his arm was so sore. I made Nassau strip his Cloaths off and examined the whole arm. Not the least swelling upon it and every now and then he would tremble. I asked him if I hit him upon the legs he said his stroke was in his bone which made all his body ach. At last, looking full upon him, I discovered the Gentleman completely drunk. This I have suspected a great while. I then locked him up for Monday morning's Chastisement for I cannot bear such a rascal. I thought this a truly religious fellow but have had occasion to think otherwise and that he is a hypocrite of the vilest kind. His first religion that broke out upon him was a new light and I believe it is from some inculcated doctrine of those rascals that the slaves in this Colony are grown so much worse. It behoves every man therefore to take care of his own. At least I am determined to do what I can. Mine shall be brought to their [p]iety though with as little severity as [possible]. . . .

[November 20, 1770]

I don't think Lawson has made the people work as they should have done. Indeed they are sickly every now and then.

Manuel a Villain, and must be whipped. He broke the Oxtree of the cart going with tobacco, by driving into the ditch. He has not halfe raised the tobacco house floor although he had been a week about it, and then truely he laid up sick; And was not plowing although then ready: pretending the grass roots were in his way. Whipped he shall be; and I saw Carpenter Jamy well laid with the Cowskin. . . .

[November] 21 [1770], Fryday

This morning we had a complaint about a butter pot's being taken from the dairy door where it was put to sweeten last night and that it was seen there after candle light. Unfortunately for the theif that night was a very particular one, everybody that was well or could move was sent down to hang a prodigeous cutting of tobacco on Scaffolds at the Mangorike tobacco house. So that it must be done near home. Owen had gone over the River at 12 o'clock with John Goldsby and did not come back till 2 in the night. So he could not say whether the Servants that lay in house had done it or not. How[ever] I sent Billy Beale to search all their holes and boxes; And in their loft it was found, but both of them solemnly deniing they knew anything of it. I have desired Colo. Brokenbrough to come here within these few days that I might pay those gentlemen for it. It seems such a theft was committed on two butter pots last year but nothing was said about them that I might not be angry; And I do suppose it was expected this would be past over in the same manner. . . .

I discovered this day what I never knew before, nay what I had positively forbid years ago, but negroes have the impudence of the devil. Last year the suckling wenches told the overseers that I allowed them to go in five times about that business; for which I had some of them whipt and reduced to half an hour before they went to work, half an hour before their breakfast; and half an hour before they go in at night. And Now they have made the simpletons believe I allow them to eat their morning's bit. So that a wench goes out to bake for that, then they must have time to eat it, then another bakes for their breakfast. But these things I have forbid upon their Peril. . . .

[March] 19 [1771], Thursday.

I should this day have made an observation on my poor little slave Charlotte, in this combined disorder of a bilious purging Joined with an unconquerable fund of worms, too many for her weak constitution I am affraid for either art or nature to carry off. But I don't care to do it yet awhile; because from a most surprizing circumstance hardly to be accounted for, and not to be remembered above 4 times in a very long life. Perhaps she may be under some invisible protection so assisting, her natural power as that she may be beginning to recover, as nothing is impossible with god. Yesterday a little after 3 o'clock I had, in order to tempt her to eat, directed some bread and beer to be boiled and sweetned. Whether the beer was sower I cannot tell; but upon taking but a Small spoonful she screamed out as Poor Eve had done who died before, complaining of her belly and immediately voided a stool of real excrement, with dead worms and maggots in it. Upon which her pulse intermitted and sunk, but being at home (a circumstance which was not in Eve's case, nor Nassau either) I ordered some mulled wine a little weak with water to be given every now and then and a little chamemile and Peppermint tea in Small quantities. The Pulse rose and abated of its intermission from to every 4th stroke to every 30th and then to every 60th when I went to bed, for I concluded if it was not a Cholic it was a rizer. She continued easy only complaining of sourness till 11 o'clock, which I had prevented by flannels dipped in hot chamemile tea, laid on hot and hot after being wrung drye. But a hasty stool or two coming one, and the night being really cool this encreased her rigor, by being imprudently taken up to do her occasions. A Clyster of starch with Syrrop Cacidium was thrown up; it stopped any more stools, but nothing could raise her pulse, and she grew cold in her extremes quite down and up to her stomach; and so she lay till breakfast time, easy but speechless, and sleeping without any emotion. So that the constant question was whether Charlotte was dead. But by 8 her pulse rose, her vital heat returned, she recovered her speech, and by the help of gruels she has with weak Mulled wine continued in a breathing moisture all over her and without any more stools at 1 o'clock. God only knows his own mercies, She may yet live and if she does how shall man account for such things but in the wisdom of the omnipotent? Otherwise I should say that this girl has explained the death of Eve after 4 days real recovery from her disorder. No Proper assistance near and Corrupted worms within must have brought on instant death.

Ferguson's daughter bravely recovered I thank God. His servant is diserous of releiving by his permission those distressed with sickness. Mr. Buckland taken ill. And 4 of Mr. Carter's People.

Killed a fine mutton this day; ordered some broth for the sick. Nassau tells me they are all mending. I hope in God they are; for though they can be no loss to such an advanced age, Yet they are human creatures and my soul I hope delighteth in releiving them.

A Scaffold fine tobacco hung last night.

At 11 o'clock Charlotte died. What a lightning before death as it is called was this? But god's will be done. It was a slave and as such or indeed as a human creature must be happier that it could be to have lived, for in innocence to die is to be sure to die happy.

20. Fryday.

It now evidently appears these children that have died have not been taken care of. My medicines have not been given; and by wrong accounts my attention to their worms was too soon left off or they might have been saved.

The Diary of Colonel Landon Carter of Sabine Hall, 1752–1778, ed. Jack P. Greene (Charlottesville: The University Press of Virginia, 1965), vol. 1, pp. 348–49, 369–70, 371–72, 378, 495–96; vol. 2, pp. 635–36.

Document 3: The Treatment of Virginia Slaves: An Eighteenth-Century Northern Observer's Account

In the early 1770s, as Colonel Landon Carter was commenting sourly in his diary about the vexations of running a large plantation, a young Princeton graduate named Philip Fithian was working as a tutor for the family of Carter's son, known as Robert Carter of Nomini Hall. Fithian also kept a diary. Being an outsider to Tidewater Virginia's society, Fithian took nothing for granted. The comments of this sharp-eyed young man provide historians with a gold mine of information about everything from dancing and dinner-table conversations to the treatment of slaves by their masters and overseers. In this extract from his diary, Fithian recorded what he had learned about the brutal, indeed sadistic, treatment that overseers were capable of meting out to slaves. Although colonial New Jersey was also a slaveholding society, what he heard and saw in Virginia plainly shocked him.

[Tuesday] December [23], 1773. . . . I then asked the young man what their allowance is? He told me that excepting some favourites about the table, their weekly allowance is a peck of Corn, & a pound of Meat a Head!—And Mr Carter is allow'd by all, & from what I have already seen of others, I make no Doubt at all but he is, by far the most humane to his Slaves of any in these parts! Good God! are these Christians?—When I am on the Subject, I will relate further, what I heard Mr George Lees Overseer, one Morgan, say the other day that he himself had often done to Negroes, and found it useful; He said that whipping of any kind does them no good, for they will laugh at your greatest Severity; But he told us he had invented two things, and by several experiments had proved their success.—For Sulleness, Obstinacy, or Idleness, says he, Take a Negro, strip him, tie him fast to a post; take then a sharp Curry-Comb, & curry him severely til he is well scrap'd; & call a Boy with some dry Hay, and make the Boy rub him down for several Minutes, then salt him, & unlose him. He will attend to his Business, (said the inhuman Infidel) afterwards!—But savage Cruelty does not exceed His next diabolical Invention—To get a Secret from a Negro, says he, take the following Method—Lay upon your Floor a large thick plank, having a peg about eighteen Inches long, of hard wood, & very Sharp, on the upper end, fixed fast in the plank—then strip the Negro, tie the Cord to a staple in the Ceiling, so as that his foot may just rest on the sharpened Peg, then turn him briskly round, and you would laugh (said our informer) at the Dexterity of the Negro, while he was releiving his Feet on the sharpen'd Peg!—I need say nothing of these seeing there is a righteous God, who will take vengeance on such Inventions! . . .

Fryday 24. . . .

The conversation at supper was on Nursing Children; I find it is common here for people of Fortune to have their young Children suckled by the Negroes! Dr Jones told us his first and only Child is now with such a Nurse; & Mrs Carter said that Wenches have suckled several of hers—Mrs Carter has had thirteen Children She told us to night and she has nine now living; of which seven are with me. Guns are fired this Evening in the Neighbourhood, and the Negroes seem to be inspired with new Life. . . .

Thursday [March] 24, [1774].

At Breakfast Mr Carter entertained us with an account of what he himself saw the other Day, which is a strong Representation of the cruelty & distress which many among the Negroes suffer in Virginia! Mr Carter dined at Squire Les some few Weeks ago; at the same place, that day, dined also Mr George Turburville & his Wife—As Mr Carter rode up he observed Mr Tuburvilles Coach-Man sitting on the Chariot-Box, the Horses off—After he had made his compliments in the House, He had Occasion soon after to go to the Door, when he saw the Coachman still sitting, & on examination found that he was there fast chained! The Fellow is inclined to run away, & this is the method which This Tyrant makes use of to keep him when abroad; & so soon as he goes home he is delivered into the pityless Hands of a bloody Overseer!—In the Language of a Heathen I query whether cunning old *Charon* will not refuse to transport this imperious, haughty Virginian Lord When he shall happen to die over the Styx to the Elysian Gardens; lest his Lordship in the passage should take affront at the treatment, & attempt to chain him also to the Stygean Galley for Life!—

Or, In the language of a Christian, I query whether he may be admitted into the peaceful Kingdom of Heaven where meekness, Holiness, & Brotherly-Love, are distinguishing Characteristicks?— . . .

[Monday] April 4,1774. . . .

After Supper I had a long conversation with Mrs Carter concerning Negroes in Virgina, & find that She esteems their value at no higher rate than I do. We both concluded, (& I am pretty certain that the conclusion is just) that if in Mr Carters, or in any Gentlemans Estate, all the Negroes should be sold, & the Money put to Interest in safe hands, & let the Lands which these Negroes now work lie wholly uncultivated, the bare Interest of the Price of the Negroes would be a much greater yearly income than what is now received from their working the Lands, making no allownace at all for the trouble & Risk of the Masters as to the Crops, & Negroes.—How Much greater then must be the value of an Estate here if these poor enslaved Africans were all in their native desired Country, & in their Room industrious Tenants, who being born in freedom, by a laudable care, would not only inrich their Landlords, but would raise a hardy Offspring to be the Strength & the honour of the Colony.

The Journal of Philip Vickers Fithian, A Plantation Tutor of the Old Dominion, 1773 & 1774, ed. Hunter Dickinson Farish (Williamsburg, VA: Colonial Williamsburg, 1943), pp. 51, 52, 113–14, 123.

Document 4: "He Has Waged Cruel War Against Human Nature Itself": Jefferson's First Draft for the Declaration of Independence Condemns the Slave Trade

Jefferson followed up his abstract assertion of human rights, as well as his justification of the people's right to rebel and institute new forms of government, by citing a long list of the colonists' grievances against the British government, personified by King George III. Most of this list the Continental Congress accepted when it adopted the Declaration of Independence on July 4, 1776. But a few grievances were edited out by the drafting committee. One of these was the statement, which appears here, that blamed the king of England for the Atlantic slave trade. By the time Jefferson drafted the Declaration, many Americans (including slave owners like Jefferson himself) were acutely embarrassed by slavery and especially by the horrors of the slave trade. They wished that somehow slavery could disappear (at minimal cost to themselves, of course), and they realized that fighting for their own independence while denying "inalienable rights" to their slaves was hypocritical. But the majority of the Congress obviously felt that it would be even more hypocritical to try to blame George III for American slavery.

He has waged cruel war against human nature itself, violating it's most sacred rights of life & liberty in the persons of a distant people who never offended him, captivating & carrying them into slavery in another hemisphere, or to incur miserable death in their transportation thither. This piratical warfare, the oppribrium of *infidel* powers, is a warfare of the CHRISTIAN king of Great Britain, determined to keep open a market where MEN should be bought and sold, he has prostituted his negative for suppressing every legislative attempt to prohibit or to restrain this execrable commerce: and that this assemblage of horrors might want no fact of distinguished die, he is now exciting those very people to rise in arms among us, and to purchase that liberty of which *he* has deprived them, by murdering the people upon whom he also obtruded them; thus paying off former crimes committed against the *liberties* of one people, with crimes which he urges them to commit against the *lives* of another.

The Spirit of Seventy-Six: The Story of the American Revolution As Told by Participants, ed. Henry Steele Commager and Richard B. Morris (New York: Harper & Row, 1967), pp. 316–17.

Document 5: The First Emancipation Proclamation: Lord Dunmore

Neither Thomas Jefferson nor George Washington nor the Continental Congress issued any proclamation freeing African American slaves during the American Revolution. That radical step instead was taken by the last royal governor of Virginia, the Earl of Dunmore. It was a move of desperation, taken as the pillars of British rule in Virginia were collapsing: Lord Dunmore issued it after he had fled to a British warship anchored off Norfolk. And it failed in its purpose.

As can be seen by studying this document, Dunmore hoped to rally a loyalist force that would include freed slaves willing to fight to restore British rule in the colony. Any slave who left his master and rallied to the British cause would be rewarded with freedom. Some slaves did hear of Dunmore's offer, and a few attempted to accept it. But the larger effect of Dunmore's proclamation was to convince wavering slave owners that the British authorities were willing to unleash a "servile insurrection" in order to maintain George III's rule in Virginia, and thus drove almost all of them into the camp of the patriot revolutionaries.

Proclamation by John, Earl of Dunmore

Off Norfolk, November 7, 1775

As I have ever entertained hopes that an accommodation might have taken place between Great Britain and this Colony, without being compelled by my duty to this most disagreeable, but now absolutely necessary step, rendered so by a body of armed men, unlawfully assembled, firing on His Majesty's Tenders; and the formation of an Army, and that Army now on their march to attack His Majesty's Troops, and destroy the well-disposed subjects of this Colony: To defeat such treasonable purposes, and that all such traitors and their abettors may be brought to justice, and that the peace and good order of this Colony may be again restored, which the ordinary course of the civil law is unable to effect, I have thought fit to issue this my Proclamation, hereby declaring, that until the aforesaid good purposes can be obtained, I do, in virtue of the power and authority to me given by His Majesty, determine to execute martial law, and cause the same to be executed throughout this Colony. And to the end that peace and good order may the sooner be re- stored, I do require every person capable of bearing arms to resort to His Majesty's standard, or be looked upon as traitors to His Majesty's crown and Government, and thereby become liable to the penalty the law inflicts upon such offences—such as forfeiture of life, confiscation of lands, etc., etc.: and I do hereby further declare all indented servants, Negroes or others, (apper- taining to Rebels) free, that are able and willing to bear arms, they joining His Majesty's Troops as soon as may be, for the more speedily reducing this Colony to a proper sense of their duty to His Majesty's crown and dignity. I do further order and require all His Majesty's liege subjects to retain their quit-rents, or any other taxes due, or that may become due, in their own cus- tody, till such time as peace may be again restored to this, at present, most unhappy Country, or demanded of them for their former salutary purposes, by officers properly authorized to receive the same.

Given under my hand, on board the ship *William*, off Norfolk, the 7th day of November, in the sixteenth year of His Majesty's reign.

DUNMORE

God Save the King!

The Spirit of Seventy-Six: The Story of the American Revolution as Told by Participants, ed. Henry Steele Commager and Richard B. Morris (New York: Harper & Row, 1967), p. 111.

Document 6: Thomas Jefferson Deplores Slavery, 1785

In 1785, while he was serving as American minister to France, Jefferson wrote the only book he ever published, Notes on the State of Virginia, *in which he responded to widespread expressions of curiosity about the new United States from educated Europeans. Among the topics Jefferson took up were his native state's natural features, wildlife, climate, agriculture, society, and Indians—and its race relations, including the problem of slavery. A wealthy slave owner, Jefferson fervently wished that slavery had never come to Virginia and hoped that some day it would go away, but he had no good ideas about how to accomplish this goal. As you read the following excerpt from Jefferson's book, ask yourself whether you feel that in 1785 he was ca- pable of developing a hopeful view of how to deal with slavery—or was he already tending toward implicitly justifying the institution?*

There must doubtless be an unhappy influence on the manners of our people produced by the existence of slavery among us. The whole commerce between master and slave is a perpetual exercise of the most boisterous passions, the most unremitting despotism on the one part, and degrading submissions on the other. Our children see this, and learn to imitate it; for man is an imitative animal. This quality is the germ of all education in him. From his cradle to his grave he is learning to do what he sees others do. If a parent could find no motive either in his philanthropy or his self-love, for restraining the intemperance of passion towards his slave, it should always be a sufficient one that his child is present. But generally it is not sufficient. The parent storms, the child looks on, catches the lineaments of wrath, puts on the same airs in the circle of smaller slaves, gives a loose to the worst of passions, and thus nursed, educated, and daily exercised in tyranny, cannot but be stamped by it with odious peculiarities. The man must be a prodigy who can retain his manners and morals undepraved by such circumstances. And with what execration should the statesman be loaded, who, permitting one half the citizens thus to trample on the rights of the other, transforms those into despots, and these into enemies, destroys the morals of the one part, and the *amor patriae* of the other. For if a slave can have a country in this world, it must be any other in preference to that in which he is born to live and labor for another; in which he must lock up the faculties of his nature, contribute as far as depends on his individual endeavors to the evanishment of the human race, or entail his own miserable condition on the endless generations proceeding from him. With the morals of the people, their industry also is destroyed. For in a warm climate, no man will labor for himself who can make another labor for him. This is so true, that of the proprietors of slaves a very small proportion indeed are ever seen to labor. And can the liberties of a nation be thought secure when we have removed their only firm basis, a conviction in the minds of the people that these liberties are of the gift of God? That they are not to be violated but with His wrath? Indeed I tremble for my country when I reflect that God is just; that his justice cannot sleep forever; that considering numbers, nature and natural means only, a revolution of the wheel of fortune, an exchange of situation is among possible events; that it may become probably by supernatural interference! The Almighty has no attribute which can take side with us in such a contest. But it is impossible to be temperate and to pursue this subject through the various considerations of policy, of morals, of history natural and civil. We must be contented to hope they will force their way into every one's mind. I think a change already perceptible, since the origin of the present revolution. The spirit of the master is abating, that of the slave rising from the dust, his condition mollifying, the way I hope preparing, under the auspices of heaven, for a total emancipation, and that this is disposed, in the order of events, to be with the consent of the masters, rather than by their extirpation.

Thomas Jefferson: Selected Writings, ed. Adrienne Koch (New York: Modern Library [Random House], 1944), pp. 277–79.

Document 7: "We Have the Wolf By the Ears": Jefferson on the Slave Owners' Dilemma, 1820

By 1820, long after he had retired from the presidency, and thirty-five years after he had written Notes on the State of Virginia, *Thomas Jefferson's thinking about slavery had grown more pessimistic. Deeply in debt (in part the result of his hobby of book-collecting and his constant, expensive rebuilding of Monticello), he saw no way of being able to free his own slaves while maintaining his standard of living. Moreover, the furious debate that had recently erupted in Congress between northern and southern states over admitting Missouri as a slave state threatened the very existence of the Union—and Jefferson, sympathizing with the southern side, saw the crisis as direct evidence that slavery was producing a grave sectional schism. Although there was still public discussion in Virginia about emancipating slaves and colonizing them outside the United States (see Chapter 6), Jefferson was skeptical about whether such schemes would work. Slavery, he was coming to think, was a "wolf" that southerners had "by the ears," fearful both to release it and to continue trying to grip it.*

These somber thoughts were conveyed in the following letter that Jefferson wrote to a friend in 1820, before the Missouri Compromise was agreed upon, temporarily ending the sectional crisis.

Monticello, April 22, 1820

I thank you, dear Sir, for the copy you have been so kind as to send me of the letter to your constituents on the Missouri question. It is a perfect justification to them. I had for a long time ceased to read newspapers, or pay any attention to public affairs, confident they were in good hands, and content to be a passenger in our bark to the shore from which I am not distant. But this momentous question, like a fire-bell in the night, awakened and filled me with terror. I considered it at once as the knell of the Union. It is hushed, indeed, for the moment. But this is a reprieve only, not a final sentence. A geographical line, coinciding with a marked principle, moral and political, once conceived and held up to the angry passions of men, will never be obliterated; and every new irritation will mark it deeper and deeper. I can say, with conscious truth, that there is not a man on earth who would sacrifice more than I would to relieve us from this heavy reproach, in any *practicable* way. The cession of that kind of property, for so it is misnamed, is a bagatelle which would not cost me a second thought, if, in that way, a general emancipation and *expatriation* could be effected; and, gradually, and with due sacrifices, I think it might be. But as it is, we have the wolf by the ears, and we can neither hold him, nor safely let him go. Justice is in one scale, and self-preservation in the other. Of one thing I am certain, that as the passage of slaves from one State to another, would not make a slave of a single human being who would not be so without it, so their diffusion over a greater surface would make them individually happier, and proportionally facilitate the accomplishment of their emancipation, by dividing the burden on a greater number of coadjutors. An abstinence too, from this act of power, would remove the jealousy excited by the undertaking of Congress to regulate the condition of the different descriptions of men composing a State. This certainly is the exclusive right of every State, which nothing in the Constitution has taken from them and given to the General Government. Could Congress, for example, say, that the non-freemen of Connecticut shall be freemen, or that they shall not emigrate into any other State?

I regret that I am now to die in the belief, that the useless sacrifice of themselves by the generation of 1776, to acquire self-government and happiness to their country, is to be thrown away by the unwise and unworthy passions of their sons, and that my only consolation is to be, that I live not to weep over it. If they would but dispassionately weigh the blessings they will throw away, against an abstract principle more likely to be effected by union than by scission, they would pause before they would perpetrate this act of suicide on themselves, and of treason against the hopes of the world. To yourself, as the faithful advocate of the Union, I tender the offering of my high esteem and respect.

Thomas Jefferson: Selected Writings, ed. Adrienne Koch (New York: Modern Library [Random House], 1944), pp. 698–99.

Document 8: Slavery in Georgia, 1838

Fanny Kemble (1809–1893) was one of the shrewdest and also one of the unlikeliest observers of nineteenth-century American slavery. She was one of the most celebrated English actresses of her time, a member of a large family of renowned theater people. After winning fame and critical respect in England, she twice toured the United States in 1832 and 1834, on the second occasion marrying a wealthy Georgian. She thereupon retired from the stage and settled on her husband's rice plantation in coastal Georgia. In 1838 and 1839 she kept a detailed diary in the form of a series of letters to an English friend. Her observations on slavery (to which she developed a deep aversion) today are an important source for historians of the "peculiar institution." Probably her growing distaste for slavery contributed to the deterioration of her marriage, for in 1848 she divorced her husband and resumed her career as a great Shakespearean actress. In early 1863 she published the second of her Journals, excerpted here, noting: "The slaves in whom I then had an unfortunate interest were sold some years ago. The islands themselves are at present in the power of the Northern troops. The record contained in the following pages is a picture of conditions of human existence which I hope and believe have passed away."

PREFACE

The following diary was kept in the winter and spring of 1838–9, on an estate consisting of rice and cotton plantations, in the islands at the entrance of the Altamaha, on the coast of Georgia.

The slaves in whom I then had an unfortunate interest were sold some years ago. The islands themselves are at present in the power of the Northern troops. The record contained in the following pages is a picture of conditions of human existence which I hope and believe have passed away.

London, *January* 16, 1863.

JOURNAL

Philadelphia, December, 1838.

My dear E—,—I return you Mr.—'s letter. I do not think it answers any of the questions debated in our last conversation at all satisfactorily: the *right* one man has to enslave another, he has not the hardihood to assert; but in the reasons he adduces to defend that act of injustice, the contradictory statements he makes appear to me to refute each other. He says, that to the Continental European protesting against the abstract iniquity of slavery, his answer would be, "The slaves are infinitely better off than half the Continental peasantry." To the Englishman, "They are happy compared with the miserable Irish." But supposing that this answered the question of original injustice, which it does not, it is not a true reply. Though the negroes are fed, clothed, and housed, and though the Irish peasant is starved, naked, and roofless, the bare name of freemen—the lordship over his own person, the power to choose and will— are blessings beyond food, raiment, or shelter; possessing which, the want of every comfort of life is yet more tolerable than their fullest enjoyment without them. Ask the thousands of ragged destitutes who yearly land upon these shores to seek the means of existence—ask the friendless, penniless foreign emigrant if he will give up his present misery, his future uncertainty, his doubtful and difficult struggle for life at once, for the secure, and, as it is called, fortunate dependence of the slave: the indignation with which he would spurn the offer will prove that he possesses one good beyond all others, and that his birthright as a man is more precious to him yet than the mess of pottage for which he is told to exchange it because he is starving.

Of course the reverse alternative can not be offered to the slaves, for at the very word the riches of those who own them would make themselves wings and flee away. But I do not admit the comparison between your slaves and even the lowest class of European free laborers, for the former are *allowed* the exercise of no faculties but those which they enjoy in common with the brutes that perish. The just comparison is between the slaves and the useful animals to whose level your laws reduce them; and I will acknowledge that the slaves of a kind owner may be as well cared for, and as happy, as the dogs and horses of a merciful master; but the latter condition—*i.e.*, that of happiness—must again depend upon the complete perfection of their moral and mental degradation. Mr.—, in his letter, maintains that they *are* an inferior race, and, compared with the whites, "*animals,* incapable of mental culture and moral improvement": to this I can only reply, that if they are incapable of profiting by instruction, I do not see the necessity for laws inflicting heavy penalties on those who offer it to them. If they really are brutish, witless, dull, and devoid of capacity for progress, where lies the *danger* which is constantly insisted upon of offering them that of which they are incapable. We have no laws forbidding us to teach our dogs and horses as much as they can comprehend; nobody is fined or imprisoned for reasoning upon knowledge and liberty to the beasts of the field, for they are incapable of such truths. But these themes are forbidden to slaves, not because they can not, but because they can and would seize on them with avidity—receive them gladly, comprehend them quickly; and the masters' power over them would be annihilated at once and forever. But I have more frequently heard not that they were incapable of receiving instruction, but something much nearer the truth—that knowledge only makes them miserable: the moment they are in any degree enlightened, they become unhappy. In the letter I return to you Mr.—says that the very slightest amount of education, merely teaching them to read, "impairs their value as slaves, for it instantly destroys their contentedness, and, since you do not contemplate changing their condition, it is surely doing them an ill service to destroy their acquiescence in it;" but this is a very different ground of argument from the other. The discontent they evince upon the mere dawn of an advance in intelligence proves not only that they can acquire, but combine ideas, a process to which it is very difficult to assign a limit; and there indeed the whole question lies, and there and nowhere else the shoe really pinches. A slave is ignorant; he eats, drinks, sleeps, labors, and is happy. He learns to read; he feels, thinks, reflects, and becomes miserable. He discovers himself to be one of a debased and degraded race, deprived of the elementary rights which God has granted to all men alike; every action is controlled, every word noted; he may not stir beyond his appointed bounds, to the right hand or to the left, at his own will, but at the will of another he may be sent miles and miles of weary journeying—tethered, yoked, collared, and fettered—away from whatever he may know as home, severed from all those ties of blood and affection which he alone of all human, of all living creatures on the face of the earth, may neither enjoy in peace nor defend when they are outraged. If he is well treated, if his master be tolerably humane or even understand his own interest tolerably, this is probably *all* he may have to endure: it is only to the consciousness of these evils that knowledge and reflection awaken him. But how is it if his master be severe, harsh, cruel—or even only careless—leaving his creatures to the delegated dominion of some overseer or agent, whose love of power, or other evil dispositions, are checked by no considerations of personal interest? Imagination shrinks from the possible result of such a state of things; nor must you, or Mr.—, tell me that the horrors thus suggested exist only in imagination. The Southern newspapers, with their advertisements of negro sales and personal descriptions of fugitive slaves, supply details of misery that it would be difficult for imagination to exceed. Scorn, derision, insult, menace,—the handcuff, the lash—the tearing away of children from parents, of husbands from wives—the weary trudging in droves along the common highways, the labor of body, the despair of mind, the sickness of heart—these are the realities which belong to the system, and form the rule, rather than the exception, in the slave's experience. And this system exists here in this country of yours, which boasts itself the asylum of the oppressed, the home of freedom, the one place in all the world where all men may find enfranchisement from all thraldoms of mind, soul, or body—the land elect of liberty.

Mr.—lays great stress, as a proof of the natural inferiority of the blacks, on the little comparative progress they have made in those states where they enjoy their freedom, and the fact that, whatever quickness of parts they may exhibit while very young, on attaining maturity they invariably sink again into inferiority, or at least mediocrity, and indolence. But surely there are other causes to account for this besides natural deficiency, which must, I think, be obvious to any unprejudiced person observing the condition of the free blacks in your Northern communities. If, in the early portion of their life, they escape the contempt and derision of their white associates—if the blessed unconsciousness and ignorance of childhood keeps them for a few years unaware of the conventional proscription under which their whole race is placed (and it is difficult to walk your streets, and mark the tone of insolent superiority assumed by even the gutter-urchins over their dusky contemporaries, and imagine this possible)—as soon as they acquire the first rudiments of knowledge, as soon as they begin to grow up and pass from infancy to youth, as soon as they cast the first observing glance upon the world by which they are surrounded, and the society of which they are members, they must become conscious that they are marked as the Hebrew lepers of old, and are condemned to sit, like those unfortunates, without the gates of every human and social sympathy. From their own sable color, a pall falls over the whole of God's universe to them, and they find themselves stamped with a badge of infamy of Nature's own devising, at sign of which all natural kindliness of man to man seems to recoil from them. They are not slaves indeed, but they are pariahs; debarred from all fellowship save with their own despised race—scorned by the lowest white ruffian in your streets, not tolerated as companions even by the foreign menials in your kitchen. They are free certainly, but they are also degraded, rejected, the offscum and the offscouring of the very dregs of your society; they are free from the chain, the whip, the enforced task and unpaid toil of slavery; but they are not the less under a ban. Their kinship with slaves forever bars them from a full share of the freeman's inheritance of equal rights, and equal consideration and respect. All hands are extended to thrust them out, all fingers point at their dusky skin, all tongues—the most vulgar, as well as the self-styled most refined—have learned to turn the very name of their race into an insult and a reproach. How, in the name of all that is natural, probable, possible, should the spirit and energy of any human creature support itself under such an accumulation of injustice and obloquy? Where shall any mass of men be found with power of character and mind sufficient to bear up against such a weight of prejudice? Why, if one individual rarely gifted by heaven were to raise himself out of such a slough of despond, he would be a miracle; and what would be his reward? Would he be admitted to an equal share in your political rights? would he ever be allowed to cross the threshold of your doors? would any of you give your daughter to his son, or your son to his daughter? would you, in any one particular, admit him to the footing of equality which any man with a white skin would claim, whose ability and worth had so raised him from the lower degrees of the social scale? You would turn from such propositions with abhorrence, and the servants in your kitchen and stable—the ignorant and boorish refuse of foreign populations, in whose countries no such prejudice exists, imbibing it with the very air they breathe here—would shrink from eating at the same table with such a man, or holding out the hand of common fellowship to him. Under the species of social proscription in which the blacks in your Northern cities exist, if they preserved energy of mind, enterprise of spirit, or any of the best attributes and powers of free men, they would prove themselves, instead of the lowest and least of human races, the highest and first, not only of all that do exist, but of all that ever have existed; for they alone would seek and cultivate knowledge, goodness, truth, science, art, refinement, and all improvement, purely for the sake of their own excellence, and without one of those incentives of honor, power, and fortune, which are found to be the chief, too often the only, inducements which lead white men to the pursuit of the same objects.

You know very well, dear E——, that in speaking of the free blacks of the North I here state nothing but what is true, and of daily experience. Only last week I heard in this very town of Philadelphia of a family of strict probity and honor, highly principled, intelligent, well-educated, and accomplished, and (to speak in the world's language) respectable in every way—i.e., *rich*. Upon an English lady's stating it to be her intention to visit these persons when she came to Philadelphia, she was told that if she did nobody else would visit *her*; and she probably would excite a malevolent feeling, which might find vent in some violent demonstration against this family. All that I have now said of course bears only upon the condition of the free colored population of the North, with which I am familiar enough to speak confidently of it. As for the slaves, and their capacity for progress, I can say nothing, for I have never been among them to judge what faculties their unhappy social position leaves to them unimpaired. But it seems to me that no experiment on a sufficiently large scale can have been tried for a sufficient length of time to determine the question of their incurable inferiority. Physiologists say that three successive generations appear to be necessary to produce an effectual change of constitution (bodily and mental), be it for health or disease. There are positive physical defects which produce positive mental ones; the diseases of the muscular and nervous systems descend from father to son. Upon the agency of one corporal power how much that is not corporal depends; from generation to generation internal disease and external deformity, vices, virtues, talents, and deficiencies are transmitted, and by the action of the same law it must be long indeed before the offspring of slaves—creatures begotten of a race debased and degraded to the lowest degree, themselves born in slavery, and whose progenitors have eaten the bread and drawn the breath of slavery for years—can be measured, with any show of justice, by even the least favored descendants of European nations, whose qualities have been for centuries developing themselves under the beneficent influences of freedom, and the progress it inspires.

I am rather surprised at the outbreak of violent disgust which Mr.——indulges in on the subject of amalgamation, as that formed no part of our discussion, and seems to me a curious subject for abstract argument. I should think the intermarrying between blacks and whites a matter to be as little insisted upon if repugnant, as prevented if agreeable to the majority of the two races. At the same time, I can not help being astonished at the furious and ungoverned execration which all reference to the possibility of a fusion of the races draws down upon those who suggest it, because nobody pretends to deny that, throughout the South, a large proportion of the population is the offspring of white men and colored women. In New Orleans, a class of unhappy females exists whose mingled blood does not prevent their being remarkable for their beauty, and with whom no man, no *gentleman,* in that city shrinks from associating; and while the slaveowners of the Southern States insist vehemently upon the mental and physical inferiority of the blacks, they are benevolently doing their best, in one way at least, to raise and improve the degraded race, and the bastard population which forms so ominous an element in the social safety of their cities certainly exhibit in their forms and features the benefit they derive from their white progenitors. It is hard to conceive that some mental improvement does not accompany this physical change. Already the finer forms of the European races are cast in these dusky moulds: the outward configuration can hardly thus improve without corresponding progress in the inward capacities. The white man's blood and bones have begotten this bronze race, and bequeathed to it, in some degree, qualities, tendencies, capabilities, such as are the inheritance of the highest order of human animals. Mr.—(and many others) speaks as if there were a natural repugnance in all whites to any alliance with the black race; and yet it is notorious, that almost every Southern planter has a family more or less numerous of illegitimate colored children. Most certainly, few people would like to assert that such connections are formed because it is the *interest* of these planters to increase the number of their human property, and that they add to their revenue by the closest intimacy with creatures that they loathe, in order to reckon among their wealth the children of their body. Surely that is a monstrous and unnatural supposition, and utterly unworthy of belief. That such connections exist commonly is a sufficient proof that they are not abhorrent to nature; but it seems, indeed, as if marriage (and not concubinage) was the horrible enormity which can not be tolerated, and against which, moreover, it has been deemed expedient to enact laws. Now it appears very evident that there is no law in the white man's nature which prevents him from making a colored woman the mother of his children, but there *is* a law on his statute-books forbidding him to make her his wife; and if we are to admit the theory that the mixing of the races is a monstrosity, it seems almost as curious that laws should be enacted to prevent men marrying women toward whom they have an invincible natural repugnance, as that education should by law be prohibited to creatures incapable of receiving it. As for the exhortation with which Mr.—closes his letter, that I will not "go down to my husband's plantation prejudiced against what I am to find there," I know not well how to answer it. Assuredly I *am* going prejudiced against slavery, for I am an Englishwoman, in whom the absence of such a prejudice would be disgraceful. Nevertheless, I go prepared to find many mitigations in the practice to the general injustice and cruelty of the system—much kindness on the part of the masters, much content on that of the slaves; and I feel very sure that you may rely upon the carefulness of my observation, and the accuracy of my report, of every detail of the working of the thing that comes under my notice; and certainly, on the plantation to which I am going, it will be more likely that I should some things extenuate, than set down aught in malice. Yours ever faithfully.

Frances (Fanny) Kemble, *Journal of a Residence on a Georgian Plantation* (New York: Harper & Sons, n.d. [ca. 1863]), pp. 8–16.

Document 9: The Emancipation Proclamation, January 1, 1863

The text of Lincoln's Emancipation Proclamation does not free the slaves in the border states that remained within the Union, nor in the parts of the seceded states that were then under Union military occupation. Lincoln wanted to persuade the border states to emancipate their slaves voluntarily (and with compensation to the slave owners), and in any case he could not order these slaves freed because the border states were not rebelling—the legal justification he claimed as commander-in-chief for proclaiming the freedom of slaves in the seceded states. Likewise, in the parts of Louisiana and Virginia that federal troops occupied on January 1, 1863, Lincoln hoped to create new unionist state governments, and negotiations over the future of slavery in these areas would have to include the question of what to do about slavery.

Whereas on the 22nd day of September, A.D. 1862, a proclamation was issued by the President of the United States, containing, among other things, the following, to wit:

"That on the 1st day of January, A.D. 1863, all persons held as slaves within any State or designated part of a State the people whereof shall then be in rebellion against the United States shall be then, thenceforward, and forever free; and the executive government of the United States, including the military and naval authority thereof, will recognize and maintain the freedom of such persons and will do no act or acts to repress such persons, or any of them, in any efforts they may make for their actual freedom.

"That the executive will on the 1st day of January aforesaid, by proclamation, designate the States and parts of States, if any, in which the people thereof, respectively, shall then be in rebellion against the United States; and the fact that any State or the people thereof shall on that day be in good faith represented in the Congress of the United States by members chosen thereto at elections wherein a majority of the qualified voters of such States shall have participated shall, in the absence of strong countervailing testimony, be deemed conclusive evidence that such State and the people thereof are not then in rebellion against the United States."

Now, therefore, I, Abraham Lincoln, President of the United States, by virtue of the power in me vested as Commander-In-Chief of the Army and Navy of the United States in time of actual armed rebellion against the authority and government of the United States, and as a fit and necessary war measure for supressing said rebellion, do, on this 1st day of January, A.D. 1863, and in accordance with my purpose so to do, publicly proclaimed for the full period of one hundred days from the first day above mentioned, order and designate as the States and parts of States wherein the people thereof, respectively, are this day in rebellion against the United States the following, to wit:

Arkansas, Texas, Louisiana (except the parishes of St. Bernard, Palquemines, Jefferson, St. John, St. Charles, St. James, Ascension, Assumption, Terrebone, Lafourche, St. Mary, St. Martin, and Orleans, including the city of New Orleans), Mississippi, Alabama, Florida, Georgia, South Carolina, North Carolina, and Virginia (except the forty-eight counties designated as West Virginia, and also the counties of Berkeley, Accomac, Northhampton,

Elizabeth City, York, Princess Anne, and Norfolk, including the cities of Norfolk and Portsmouth), and which excepted parts are for the present left precisely as if this proclamation were not issued.

And by virtue of the power and for the purpose aforesaid, I do order and declare that all persons held as slaves within said designated States and parts of States are, and henceforward shall be, free; and that the Executive Government of the United States, including the military and naval authorities thereof, will recognize and maintain the freedom of said persons.

And I hereby enjoin upon the people so declared to be free to abstain from all violence, unless in necessary self-defence; and I recommend to them that, in all case when allowed, they labor faithfully for reasonable wages.

And I further declare and make known that such persons of suitable condition will be received into the armed service of the United States to garrison forts, positions, stations, and other places, and to man vessels of all sorts in said service.

And upon this act, sincerely believed to be an act of justice, warranted by the Constitution upon military necessity, I invoke the considerate judgment of mankind and the gracious favor of Almighty God.

Reprinted from Abraham Lincoln, "Emancipation Proclamation," January 1, 1863.

Document 10: Robert E. Lee Urges the Confederacy to Enlist Slave Soldiers and Emancipate Them

One of the most ironic (and little-known) episodes in the history of American slavery occurred in late 1864 and early 1865, as the Confederate States of America reeled on the brink of defeat in the war it had begun in hopes of safeguarding slavery. As numerically superior Union armies, more than 10 percent of whose manpower was African American, thrust into the heart of the Confederacy and threatened its capital, Richmond, white southerners debated whether they should save their cause by arming their slaves, and on what terms. Many Confederate politicians and other influential leaders adamantly opposed trying to rely on blacks, logically pointing out that the whole rationale of slavery was black inferiority and that the South had seceded to protect its "peculiar institution"—all of which would be called into question if southern blacks were allowed to fight for the Confederacy. But Confederate president Jefferson Davis's administration realized that the South's cause would soon be lost unless large numbers of blacks were brought into the ranks. In February 1865, the Confederacy's revered military leader, Robert E. Lee, added his voice to the debate by writing an open letter in support of the administration's position to a Confederate congressman, excerpted here. Before the war, Lee had disliked slavery and had opposed secession, but when Virginia left the Union he had felt his first loyalty belonged to his native state rather than to the United States. Now he was speaking on behalf of a white southern nationalism that had come to value independence over maintaining slavery itself. Lee and President Davis well understood that to ask black men to die for the Confederacy meant that they must be assured of freedom.

Whether African Americans would have fought willingly for southern in-

dependence, and whether the Confederacy would have accepted a policy of emancipation, are questions that were never answered. By the time the first black Confederate troops were enlisted and given some rudimentary training, the South's defeat was at hand. The black units never went into combat. Lee surrendered his army on April 9, 1865, Davis tried unsuccessfully to flee, and the Confederacy and slavery were dead.

"HON. E. BARKSDALE, *House of Representatives, Richmond:*

"SIR: I have the honor to acknowledge the receipt of your letter of the 12th instant, with references to the employment of negroes as soldiers. I think the measure not only expedient but necessary. The enemy will certainly use them against us if he can get possession of them; and, as his present numerical superiority will enable him to penetrate many parts of the country, I cannot see the wisdom of the policy of holding them to await his arrival, when we may, by timely action and judicious management, use them to arrest his progress. I do not think that our white population can supply the necessities of a long war without overtaxing its capacity, and imposing great suffering upon our people; and I believe we should provide resources for a protracted struggle,—not merely for a battle or a campaign.

"In answer to your second question, I can only say that, in my opinion, the negroes, under proper circumstances, will make efficient soldiers. I think we could at least do as well with them as the enemy, and he attaches great importance to their assistance. Under good officers and good instructions, I do not see why they should not become soldiers. They possess all the physical qualifications, and their habits of obedience constitute a good foundation for discipline. They furnish a more promising material than many armies of which we read in history, which owed their efficiency to discipline alone. I think those who are employed should be freed. It would be neither just nor wise, in my opinion, to require them to serve as slaves. The best course to pursue, it seems to me, would be to call for such as are willing to come with the consent of their owners. An impressment or draft would not be likely to bring out the best class, and the use of coercion would make the measure distasteful to them and to their owners.

"I have no doubt that if Congress would authorize their reception into service, and empower the President to call upon individuals or States for such as they are willing to contribute, with the condition of emancipation to all enrolled, a sufficient number would be forthcoming to enable us to try the experiment. If it proved successful, most of the objections to the measure would disappear, and if individuals still remained unwilling to send their negroes to the army, the force of public opinion in the States would soon bring about such legislation as would remove all obstacles. I think the matter should be left, as far as possible, to the people and to the States, which alone can legislate as to the necessities of this particular service may require. As to the mode of organizing them, it should be left as free from restraint as possible. Experience will suggest the best course, and it would be inexpedient to trammel the subject with provisions that might, in the end, prevent the adoption of reforms suggested by actual trial.

With great respect, your obedient servant,
R.E. Lee, *General*."

James D. McCabe, Jr., *Life and Campaigns of General Robert E. Lee* (Atlanta: National Publishing Company, 1866), pp. 574–75 [out of copyright].

Document 11: Slaves Emancipate Themselves

The Reverend C.C. Jones was a white minister in the Old South, equally well known for his Scripture-based defense of slavery and for his efforts to persuade masters to see that their slaves were converted to Christianity. His daughter-in-law, Mary Jones, kept a diary during the Civil War. Her entries in January 1865, as the Union army under General William T. Sherman completed its destructive march across Georgia and prepared to turn northward into South Carolina testify to the slaves' awareness that emancipation was becoming a reality. The actions that she records her family's slaves as taking are an indication of how the bondspeople were taking charge of their lives in ways that accorded with their long-denied right to define their self-interest. Jones's letter to her daughter (also included here) in November 1865, after the war and slavery had ended, explains how former slaves were acting.

Mary Jones on the Concerns of Ex-Slaves, 1865
  Mary Jones in Her Journal, 1865
  Friday, January 6th. No enemy appeared here today, but we have heard firing around on different places.

The people are all idle on the plantations, most of them seeking their own pleasure. Many servants have proven faithful, others false and rebellious against all authority or restraint. Susan, a Virginia Negro and nurse to my little Mary Ruth, went off with Mac, her husband, to Arcadia the night after the first day the Yankees appeared, with whom she took every opportunity of conversing, informing them that the baby's father was Colonel Jones. She has acted a faithless part as soon as she could. Porter left three weeks since, and has never returned to give any report of Patience or himself or anyone at Arcadia. Little Andrew went to Flemington and returned. I sent him back to wait on our dear sister and family and to be with his own. I hope he will prove faithful. Gilbert, Flora, Tenah, Sue, Rosetta, Fanny, Little Gilbert, Charles, Milton and Elsie and Kate have been faithful to us. . . .

Tuesday, January 10th. We have been free from the presence of the enemy thus far today, although in great apprehension for several hours, as Sue came in at dinner time and advised us to hasten the meal, as she heard firing in the woods between this and White Oak, which is not much over a mile distant. It was reported they would return today with a large forage train of several hundred wagons going on to the Altamaha.

One thing is evident: they are now enlisting the Negroes here in their service. As one of the officers said to me, "We do not want your women, but we mean to take the able-bodied men to dredge out the river and harbor at Savannah, to hew timber, make roads, build bridges, and throw up batteries." They offer twelve dollars per month. Many are going off with them. Some few sensible ones calculate the value of twelve dollars per month in furnishing food, clothing, fuel, lodging, etc., etc. Up to this time none from this place has joined them. I have told some of those indisposed to help in any way and to wander off at pleasure that as they were perfectly useless here it would be best for me and for the good of their fellow servants if they would leave and go at once with the Yankees. They had seen what their conduct was to the black people—stealing from them, searching their houses, cursing and abusing and insulting their wives and daughters, and if they chose such for their masters to obey and follow, then the sooner they went with them the better; and I had quite a mind to send in a request that they be carried off. . . .

Thursday and Friday, January 12th and 13th. . . . Everything confirms the raid south. The enemy are in full possession of Savannah; Negroes in large numbers are flocking to them. . . .

Saturday Night, January 21st. On Thursday Mr. L.J. Mallard visited us. He is now with his family. Gave us various accounts of the enemy. They encamped near his house; at one time on his premises over a thousand. They entered his dwelling day and night. They were forced to obtain a guard from the commander of the post, who was stationed at Midway, to protect his family. The house was repeatedly fired into under pretense of shooting rebels, although they knew that none but defenseless women and children were within. And Mrs. Mallard, who is almost blind, was then in her confinement. They rifled the house of every article of food or clothing which they wished. Mr. Mallard had nothing left but the suit of clothes he wore. . . .

Kate, Daughter's servant who has been cooking for us, took herself off today—influenced, as we believe, by her father. Sent for Cook Kate to Arcadia; she refuses to come.

Their condition is one of perfect anarchy and rebellion. They have placed themselves in perfect antagonism to their owners and to all government and control. We dare not predict the end of all this, if the Lord in mercy does not restrain the hearts and wills of this deluded people. They are certainly prepared for any measures. What we are to do becomes daily more and more perplexing. It is evident if my dwelling is left unoccupied, everything within it will be sacrificed. Wherever owners have gone away, the Negroes have taken away all the furniture, bedding, and household articles.

Mary Jones to Her Daughter, Mary S. Mallard, November 17, 1865

As I wrote you, Sue had left. She is still at the Boro, and I am told has hired Elizabeth to work at Dr. Samuel Jones's. Flora is in a most unhappy and uncomfortable condition, doing very little, and that poorly. . . . I think Flora will certainly leave when she is ready. I overheard an amusing conversation between Cook Kate and herself: they are looking forward to gold watches and chains, bracelets, and *blue veils* and silk dresses! Jack has entered a boardinghouse in Savannah, where I presume he will practice attitudes and act the Congo gentleman to perfection. Porter and Patience will provide for themselves. I shall cease my anxieties for the race. My life long (I mean since I had a home) I have been laboring and caring for them, and since the war have labored with all my might to supply their wants, and expended everything I had upon their support, directly or indirectly; and this is their return.

You can have no conception of the condition of things. I understand Dr.

Harris and Mr. Varnedoe will rent their lands to the Negroes! The conduct of some of the citizens has been very injurious to the best interest of the community. At times my heart is so heavy I feel as if it would give way, and that I cannot remain. But I have no other home, and if I desert it, everything will go to ruin. Mr. Fennell has done all he could to protect my interest; but he is feeble physically, and I do not know that he has any special gift at management. I believe him to be an honest and excellent man. We planted only a half-crop of provisions here, and they did not work one-fourth of their time. Judge the results: not a pod of cotton planted, and all I had stolen, and the whole of that at Arcadia gone. You know I wished Little Andrew to return to Montevideo after Mr. Buttolph decided not to go to Baker, as he was our best plowman. He did not do so. Wanting help at this time in grinding cane, I wished him to come down. He did so, stayed part of a day, and walked off. I have not heard of him since. This is a specimen of their conduct. It is thought there will be a great many returning to the county; I do not believe so.

I have mentioned all the news I could collect in Aunty's letter, and refer you to that.

I hope Robert received your brother's letter in reference to the circulars. All we want at present is to obtain subscribers. The work probably cannot be published under a year. I have requested Joseph to confer with Mr. Rogers about the paper he so generously and kindly offered to give for printing the first edition. Do let him know where Mr. Rogers is.

I have just called Charles and asked if he had any messages. "He sends love to Lucy and Tenah, and begs to be remembered to you, and says he will make an opportunity to come and see them before long." This is the sum and substance of his message. It is impossible to get at any of their intentions, and it is useless to ask them. I see only a dark future for the whole race. . . . Do write me all about yourself and the dear children and Robert and the church. . . . Kiss my precious grandchildren. If they were here they should eat sugar cane all day and boil candy at night. . . . The Lord bless you, my dear child!

Ever your affectionate mother,
Mary Jones.

Major Problems in the History of the American South, vol. 1: *The Old South*, ed. Paul D. Escott and David R. Goldfield (Lexington, Mass.: D.C. Heath & Co., 1990), pp. 528–30.

Document 12: The Thirteenth, Fourteenth, and Fifteenth Amendments

The Emancipation Proclamation promised freedom only to those slaves who were beyond the reach of the federal government's power during the Civil War. In the parts of the Union that had not seceded or that the Union army had reconquered by the beginning of 1863, slavery did not end until the Thirteenth Amendment to the Constitution was ratified by those states that had remained within the Union. This ratification occurred in late 1865, and after the war had ended the former Confederate states were permitted to return to the Union only after their legislatures had ratified the Amendment.

Guaranteeing civil liberties to former slaves required two further constitutional amendments: the Fourteenth, ratified in 1868 (over strong objec-

tions from President Andrew Johnson, the successor to the assassinated Abraham Lincoln); and the Fifteenth, ratified in 1870, which forbade states to deny the vote to black males. Unfortunately, the North's decision to abandon support of the Reconstruction state governments in the former Confederacy meant that by the mid-1870s black civil liberties were drastically curtailed. Not until the "Second Reconstruction" of the 1960s were the promises extended by the Fourteenth and Fifteenth Amendments truly honored.

Article XIII

Section 1. Neither slavery nor involuntary servitude, except as a punishment for crime whereof the party shall have been duly convicted, shall exist within the United States, or any place subject to their jurisdiction.

Section 2. Congress shall have power to enforce this article by appropriate legislation.

Article XIV

Section 1. All persons born or naturalized in the United States, and subject to the jurisdiction thereof, are citizens of the United States and of the State wherein they reside. No State shall make or enforce any law which shall abridge the privileges or immunities of citizens of the United States; nor shall any State deprive any person of life, liberty, or property, without due process of law; nor deny to any person within its jurisdiction the equal protection of the laws.

Section 2. Representatives shall be apportioned among the several States according to their respective numbers, counting the whole number of persons in each State, excluding Indians not taxed. But when the right to vote at any election for the choice of Electors for President and Vice President of the United States, Representatives in Congress, the executive and judicial officers of a State, or the members of the legislature thereof, is denied to any of the male inhabitants of such State, being twenty-one years of age and citizens of the United States, or in any way abridged, except for participation in rebellion, or other crime, the basis of representation therein shall be reduced in the proportion which the number of such male citizens shall bear to the whole number of male citizens twenty-one years of age in such State.

Section 3. No person shall be a Senator or Representative in Congress or Elector of President and Vice President, or hold any office, civil or military, under the United States, or under any State, who, having previously taken an oath, as a member of Congress, or as an officer of the United States, or as a member of any State legislature, or as an executive or judicial officer of any State, to support the Constitution of the United States, shall have engaged in insurrection or rebellion against the same, or given aid and comfort to the enemies thereof. Congress may, by a vote of two-thirds of each house, remove such disability.

Section 4. The validity of the public debt of the United States, authorized by law, including debts incurred for payment of pensions and bounties for services in suppressing insurrection or rebellion, shall not be questioned. But neither the United States nor any State shall assume or pay any debt or obligation incurred in aid of insurrection or rebellion against the United States, or any claim for the loss or emancipation of any slave; but all such debts, obligations, and claims shall be held illegal and void.

Section 5. The Congress shall have the power to enforce, by appropriate legislation, the provisions of this article.

Article XV

Section 1. The right of citizens of the United States to vote shall not be denied or abridged by the United States or by any State on account of race, color, or previous condition of servitude.

Section 2. The Congress shall have power to enforce this article by appropriate legislation.

Reprinted from the Thirteenth, Fourteenth, and Fifteenth Amendments to the U.S. Constitution.

Chronology

Mid-1400s

Portuguese mariners explore the coast of West Africa and begin trading in black slaves; the first European slave-labor sugar plantations are established on islands off the West African coast and in the western Mediterranean.

1492

Christopher Columbus makes his first voyage to the New World.

1607

Virginia is established as an English colony.

1618

Tobacco is established as the primary staple crop in Virginia.

First Phase of American Slavery[1]

1619

The first Africans are imported into Virginia by a Dutch merchant vessel.

1620

English Pilgrims establish Plymouth colony.

1624–1640

The English establish colonies in the West Indies (St. Kitts, Barbados, Antigua, and other small islands).

1630

English Puritans begin to settle Massachusetts Bay colony.

1634

Maryland is established as an English colony.

1640–1660

A growing tendency to treat Africans and some Indians as lifelong slaves emerges in Virginia and Maryland.

---

1. As explained in the *Introduction*, these phases should be regarded as a general guide to conceptualizing the development of American slavery over time, not as rigid divisions.

1640–1670

The English establish thriving slave-labor plantations in the West Indies, especially in Barbados.

1655

England seizes Jamaica, which becomes another important sugar plantation colony.

1661

The Barbados slave code is enacted, the first such comprehensive legislation in an English colony, which eventually serves as a model for slave codes in mainland colonies; Maryland officially defines slavery as a lifelong, inheritable, and racially defined status.

1663

Carolina is chartered as an English colony.

1664

England conquers the Dutch colony of New Netherland, renaming it New York.

1670

The English settlement of what later becomes South Carolina begins; Virginia follows Maryland's lead by defining slavery as lifelong, inheritable, and racially defined.

1676

Bacon's Rebellion in Virginia; after its suppression, large planters apparently decide to favor African slavery rather than English indentured servitude to supply the colony's main labor force.

1685–1686

A large slave revolt occurs in Jamaica.

Second Phase of American Slavery

ca. 1690

Rice is established as a staple crop in Carolina; large-scale importation of slaves begins.

1696

Carolina enacts a slave code based on that of Barbados.

1712

A slave conspiracy in New York City is discovered; numerous slaves are executed, some by burning at the stake.

1720

South Carolina becomes a separate British royal colony; its population is now about two-thirds African.

1732

Georgia is chartered as a British colony with the intent of becoming a settlement for debtors, and with slavery and strong drink banned.

1739

The Stono River Rebellion erupts in South Carolina, the largest slave uprising in the history of North America.

1741

Another slave conspiracy is discovered in New York, and also punished with brutal severity.

1750

All restrictions against slavery (and strong drink) are abolished in Georgia; importation of slaves begins, soon making Georgia a thriving slave society.

Third Phase of American Slavery

1750s–1760s

The spread of Christianity among slaves begins, stimulated by the evangelical movement known as the First Great Awakening.

1760s

John Woolman urges his fellow Quakers to reject slavery and emancipate their slaves.

1776

The Declaration of Independence is written.

1777–1784

Slavery is abolished in Vermont, Pennsylvania, Massachusetts, Rhode Island, and Connecticut, mostly by provisions for gradual emancipation; slavery soon after dies out in New Hampshire without being officially abolished.

1779

Preparing to invade the southern colonies, British general Sir Henry Clinton issues the Philipsburg Proclamation, warning that blacks taken in "rebel" service will be sold but that slaves who desert to the British will be accorded favored treatment, perhaps including future freedom.

1787

Slavery is debated at the Constitutional Convention in Philadelphia, after which the Constitution, containing important compromises regarding slavery, is submitted for ratification by special state conventions.

1789

The U.S. Constitution goes into effect.

1790

The first Fugitive Slave Law is passed by Congress, but enforcement is weak.

1791

A slave rebellion begins in the French colony of Saint Domingue (today Haiti); French slave owners flee to the United States carrying stories of atrocities.

1794

The French Republic abolishes slavery in Saint Domingue.

1799

Slavery is abolished in New York by gradual emancipation.

1800

Gabriel's Insurrection in Virginia occurs, a widespread but unsuccessful conspiracy to launch a slave rebellion.

1801

Blacks begin a revolt against French attempts to restore white rule over Saint Domingue.

1804

Slavery is abolished in New Jersey by gradual emancipation; Haiti declares its independence as a black republic (but is not recognized by the United States until 1862).

1808

The legal right to import slaves into the United States ends (but slaves continue to be imported illegally).

1816

The American Colonization Society is established to resettle free blacks and emancipated slaves in West Africa.

1819–1820

The crisis over Missouri's application for admission as a slave state rocks the Union; it ends with the Missouri Compromise.

1820

Colonization of Liberia under the auspices of the American Colonization Society begins.

1822

Denmark Vesey's conspiracy to ignite a slave revolt is discovered in Charleston, South Carolina.

1829

David Walker publishes his *Appeal* in Boston.

Fourth Phase of American Slavery

1831

January 1 William Lloyd Garrison begins publishing *The Liberator* in Boston.
August Nat Turner's Rebellion erupts in Southampton County, Virginia, followed by Turner's trial and execution (in November).

1832

The Virginia state assembly debates but rejects the abolition of slavery.

1832–1833

The Nullification Crisis occurs, fueled by South Carolina's anxiety over potential federal interference with slavery.

1833

Parliament abolishes slavery in the British Empire. The American Anti-Slavery Society, headed by William Lloyd Garrison, is established to work for the abolition of slavery in the United States.

1835

Garrison is nearly lynched in Boston.

1837

February John C. Calhoun declares slavery "a positive good," reflecting a broad shift in attitude among slavery's defenders during the 1830s.
November Abolitionist Elijah Lovejoy is killed by a mob in Alton, Illinois.

1838

Frederick Douglass escapes from slavery and flees to the North, at first working in a Massachusetts shipyard.

1839

Amistad mutiny on the high seas; Theodore Weld and his wife Angelina Grimké publish *American Slavery As It Is*, documenting many abuses of slavery; the American Anti-Slavery Society splits into a radical faction (headed by Garrison) that denounces the Constitution as hopelessly compromised by toleration of slavery and supports the women's rights movement, and a moderate faction that looks to political action to end slavery.

1840

The Liberty Party is established by moderate abolitionists with the goal of ending slavery through political action; it nominates James G. Birney for the presidency.

1841

Frederick Douglass begins his public career as an abolitionist; the U.S. Supreme Court orders the release of the *Amistad* rebels and their return to Africa.

1843

Black abolitionist Henry Highland Garnet publicly calls for slaves to kill their masters if necessary to win freedom.

1845

The United States annexes Texas as a slave state; Frederick Douglass publishes his *Narrative*.

1846–1848

The Mexican War results in the U.S. annexation of the Southwest and California but precipitates a bitter sectional conflict over the spread of slavery.

1847

Douglass begins to publish the antislavery journal *The North Star* (later renamed *Frederick Douglass's Paper*); Liberia becomes an independent African republic.

1850

The Compromise of 1850 temporarily ends the sectional crisis; the compromise includes a stronger Fugitive Slave Law, admits California as a free state, and abolishes the slave trade in the District of Columbia.

1850–1851

Public anger over enforcement of the Fugitive Slave Law spreads through the North, fueling sectional conflict and antislavery sentiment.

1852

Harriet Beecher Stowe publishes *Uncle Tom's Cabin*.

1854

The passage of the Kansas-Nebraska Act rekindles the sectional political crisis.

1855–1857

Violence flares in "Bleeding Kansas" between proslavery and free-soil settlers.

1857

The Supreme Court issues its 7–2 decision in *Dred Scott v. Sandford,* keeping Scott a slave, denying African Americans citizenship, and voiding the Missouri Compromise.

1858

Lincoln and Douglas, running for the U.S. Senate in Illinois, debate the proper northern response to the slavery issue, attracting national attention.

1859

October John Brown's raid at Harpers Ferry, Virginia, attempts to initiate a slave revolt.
December Brown is tried and executed; his case intensifies sectional tensions.

1860

Abraham Lincoln is elected president on a platform of resistance to the territorial expansion of slavery; South Carolina secedes.

Fifth Phase of American Slavery

1861

Other southern states secede and form the Confederate States of America; Civil War begins.

1862

After the battle of Antietam on September 17, Lincoln issues the Preliminary Emancipation Proclamation, announcing his intention of freeing slaves in all rebellious states if they do not return to the Union by January 1, 1863.

1863

January 1 Lincoln issues the Emancipation Proclamation, abolishing slavery in all rebellious states (but not freeing slaves in loyal border states or in areas already occupied by the Union army).
July Black Union troops begin to serve in combat; the all-black 54th Massachusetts Regiment wins widespread admiration in the North with its heroic assault on Fort Wagner in South Carolina.

1864–early 1865

The advance of Union armies effectively frees slaves in the Confederacy; the Confederate government, in a desperate effort to avoid defeat, decides to emancipate slaves who volunteer for army service.

Postslavery Era

1865

April General Lee's surrender at Appomattox signals the final defeat of the Confederacy; Abraham Lincoln is assassinated.
December The Thirteenth Amendment is ratified, abolishing slavery everywhere in the United States.

1868

The ratification of the Fourteenth Amendment guarantees civil liberties to former slaves.

1870

The ratification of the Fifteenth Amendment guarantees the right to vote to all adult male citizens, including African Americans.

1877

The withdrawal of the last federal troops from former Confederate states marks the end of the Reconstruction period, the fall of the last radical Republican southern governments, and accelerating trends toward the intimidation and ultimate disfranchisement of southern black voters and the enactment of Jim Crow legislation.

Prominent People

Bacon, Nathaniel (1647–1676), Virginia planter and leader of Bacon's Rebellion. Unlike most Virginia planters, Bacon was a member of the English gentry. Soon after arriving in Virginia and buying several estates, Bacon joined the council of the royal governor, William Berkeley. Bacon took the side of Virginia's lesser planters in a political dispute with Berkeley. He advocated seizing more land from the Indians in order to provide estates for small planters and former indentured servants. In 1676, supported by these nonelite elements of the population, he rebelled against Berkeley and seized control of most of the colony. Then, suddenly, he died, a victim of Virginia's lethal climate that had claimed so many "unseasoned" European immigrants. His rebellion collapsed. But as a result of the scare his revolt had given to Virginia's elite, an implicit decision was made to build the colony's labor force with African slaves rather than English servants.

Bremer, Fredrika (1801–1865), Swedish writer and social reformer who traveled in the United States in the early 1850s. A strong critic of slavery, Bremer met some of the leading abolitionists and visited the South. Her remarks on slavery are of value to historians.

Brown, John (1800–1859), white abolitionist and would-be leader of a slave revolt. Trying to support his large family, Brown moved restlessly from one place to another in pre–Civil War America, but failed at everything: farming, tanning, shopkeeping, and land speculating. But when he settled in a community of ex-slaves in Elmira, New York, in 1849, his antislavery convictions blazed into a fierce determination to dedicate his life to abolition. A stern believer in predestination (the Calvinist doctrine that God had chosen everyone for a destiny of salvation or damnation), Brown came to see himself as the instrument of divine vengeance on slaveholders. He and his sons went to "Bleeding Kansas" in 1856 to fight for the antislavery cause, and there they murdered five proslavery men in cold blood by hacking them to death with broadswords—an act that he correctly expected would further inflame sectional passions. After leaving Kansas, in 1858 he developed plans to create a refuge in the mountains of western Virginia to which slaves could flee, arm themselves, and initiate a general revolt. His idea won a considerable amount of financial backing among New England abolitionists. As a first step in carrying out this plan, he seized the federal arsenal at Harpers Ferry. (For an account of the Harpers Ferry incident and Brown's subsequent trial and execution, see Chapter 15.)

Calhoun, John C. (1782–1850), U.S. senator from South Carolina and the most important defender of the South's sectional interests. Calhoun was educated at Yale University and began his political career as a nationalist and a Jeffersonian Republican, entering Congress in 1810 among the "War Hawks" who demanded war with Great Britain. Under President Monroe (1817–1825) he served as secretary of war and developed a consuming ambition for the presidency. Seeing the office as a stepping-stone to the White House, he served as vice president under both John Quincy Adams and Andrew Jackson (1825–1832).

During the 1820s, however, Calhoun also became an ardent advocate of states' rights and southern sectionalism. In this he reflected the South Carolina elite's growing anxiety about their state's stagnating economy and its large, restive slave population. He wrote an anonymous pamphlet in 1828, *The South Carolina Exposition and Protest,* which asserted the state legislature's right to "nullify" (render inoperative) any federal law that threatened its vital interests. In 1830 he broke with Jackson over this issue, and later he revealed his authorship of the *Exposition.* Resigning as vice president in 1832, he was soon elected to the U.S. Senate. During the Nullification Crisis (1832–1833), Jackson threatened to invade South Carolina and hang Calhoun, and he probably meant it. Faced with Jackson's wrath and not supported by the other southern states, Calhoun and South Carolina had to back down. Soon, together with Jackson's other bitter enemies, Daniel Webster and Henry Clay, Calhoun formed the Whig Party. But Calhoun had no sympathy for the northern Whigs' championing of business interests and moral reform. Instead, in 1837 he publicly called slavery a "positive good," not just a "necessary evil."

Throughout the 1840s Calhoun worked tirelessly for southern sectionalist interests, including annexing Texas as a slave state. In the aftermath of the Mexican War, he warned that the Union was doomed unless the South obtained a constitutional veto power over federal actions. He encouraged the slave states to hold a convention in 1850, at which secession was discussed.

Calhoun was that rarity, an intellectual in American politics. Highly intelligent and abstract in his thinking, he became obsessed with building for the South and slavery a bulwark against what he perceived was the rising threat of a North that was becoming more populous and more industrialized than the South. Intellectually a man of the late eighteenth century, he detested democracy and favored government by the elite. He always claimed to be a nationalist and a unionist, but as he grew older he insisted that the Union would survive only if the South got all the concessions that he demanded on its behalf.

Carter, Robert "King" (1663–1732), Virginia landowner and major importer of African slaves in the early eighteenth century. Carter was the son of a royalist who fled England in 1649 and settled in Virginia. By the 1690s the younger Carter had become a member of the colony's legislature (House of Burgesses) and of the governor's council. Building on the property his father had acquired, Robert Carter used his political connections to grow immensely rich. He was called "King" Carter by contemporaries who were annoyed with his arrogance and unprecedented wealth. He was the father of Colonel Landon Carter of Sabine Hall, the famous diarist, and the grandfather of Robert Carter of Nomini Hall. Among "King" Carter's other descendants were two presidents of the United States, six governors of Virginia, and Robert E. Lee.

Chase, Salmon P.   (1808–1873), important Ohio antislavery politician. Chase had strong free-soil convictions and as a young lawyer defended runaway slaves. Originally a Whig, he switched to the Liberty Party and later to the Free Soil Party, and in 1854 he helped found the Republican Party. Before the Civil War, he served in the U.S. Senate and as governor of Ohio, and he was a rival with Abraham Lincoln for the Republican presidential nomination in 1860. During the war he was secretary of the treasury, a position he filled with great ability while nursing a strong sense of intellectual superiority over Lincoln. In 1864 Lincoln maneuvered him out of the cabinet by naming him chief justice of the Supreme Court upon Roger B. Taney's death. After the Civil War he continued to seek the presidency. He tried to keep the Court from interpreting the Fourteenth and Fifteenth Amendments in ways unfavorable to ex-slaves.

Chesnut, Mary Boykin   (1823–1886), wife of the important South Carolina politician James Chesnut and author of a detailed diary that constitutes an important primary source on southern politics and daily life during the Civil War, including some insightful comments on slavery (which she hated) and race relations. She kept her *Diary from Dixie* with the intention of eventually publishing it, and after the war she reworked her text considerably, but died before finishing the job. It was not published until 1905.

Child, Lydia Maria   (1802–1880), leading Massachusetts abolitionist and writer of books for children and women during the pre–Civil War era. Her husband was often in business trouble, and her family depended on her publishing activity for financial support. In 1831 she met William Lloyd Garrison, who persuaded her to devote her life to abolitionism. Her *Appeal in Favor of That Class of Americans Called Africans* (1833), with its vigorous attack on white racism, caused her to be socially ostracized and caused her well-known children's magazine to fail. Suffering greatly from poverty, she continued to write and edit antislavery publications, which were effective in gaining converts to the abolitionist cause.

Clay, Henry   (1777–1852), one of the most important members of Congress, serving (with interruptions) from 1811 until his death. Together with Daniel Webster of Massachusetts and John C. Calhoun of South Carolina, Clay formed "the Great Triumvirate" of powerful, often rival senators. "Gallant Harry of the West," as he was also known, had countless admirers, including the young Abraham Lincoln, for whom Clay was a role model.

Born in Virginia, Clay moved to Kentucky in 1797 and quickly established a reputation as a lawyer, orator, and politician. As an admirer of Thomas Jefferson, he at first deplored slavery but later came to terms with it, and on his estate he raised hemp with slave labor. After the War of 1812 he developed a program ("the American System") aimed at developing the U.S. economy through a protective tariff, a national banking system, and federal subsidies for canals and roads. Highly ambitious, he clashed bitterly with Andrew Jackson and was one of the founders of the anti-Jacksonian Whig Party. The Whigs nominated him twice for the presidency (in 1832 and 1844), but both times he was defeated. As a Whig politician and strong nationalist, Clay generally opposed the territorial expansion of slavery, considering the issue politically divisive.

He was called "the Great Compromiser" for his leadership in bringing about the Missouri Compromise in 1820 and a settlement of the Nullification Crisis in 1833, as well as for his attempt to arrange the Compromise of 1850. Old and sick, Clay failed in his efforts in 1850, and concluding the deal fell to Illinois senator Stephen A. Douglas.

Clay was one of the leaders of the American Colonization Society, which promoted the resettlement of free blacks in Africa. He always regarded slavery as a "necessary evil," and in his will he freed all his slaves.

Crittenden, John J.   (1787–1863), U.S. senator from Kentucky who tried unsuccessfully to arrange a compromise in 1861 that would end the South's secession and preserve the Union. Crittenden generally shared the political outlook of Henry Clay, and his attempt at another compromise during the secession crisis was in the spirit of the earlier intersectional bargains over which Clay had presided. The compromise Crittenden proposed in 1861 would have given the South almost everything it wanted, including opening the entire West to slavery and amending the Constitution to bar any future federal action against slavery. The incoming president, Abraham Lincoln, rejected the compromise, feeling that a showdown with the secessionists should come sooner rather than later. Crittenden subsequently helped prevent Kentucky's secession. One of his sons served as a Union army officer, and the second as a Confederate officer.

Davis, David   (1815–1886), friend and political associate of Abraham Lincoln, whom Davis advised on policy matters until Lincoln appointed him to the U.S. Supreme Court in 1862. Holding moderate antislavery views, Davis did not agree with radical Republican demands for an all-out assault on slavery as a wartime measure.

De Bow, J.D.B.   (1820–1867), leading publisher in the Old South on the eve of the Civil War and staunch defender of slavery. Born in Charleston, South Carolina, he rose from impoverished origins to the editorship of a business-oriented magazine in New Orleans that he renamed *De Bow's Review*. He was a master of statistical analysis and was appointed superintendent of the 1850 U.S. census. De Bow admired John C. Calhoun and became an ever more impassioned defender of slavery in the course of the

1850s. "The negro," he wrote, "was created essentially to be a slave." De Bow promoted southern industry but expected agriculture to remain the South's economic mainstay.

Dew, Thomas Roderick   (1802–1846), Virginia economist generally credited with formulating the Old South's forthright defense of slavery. Dew began to teach at the College of William and Mary in 1827. In 1832 he published the pamphlet *Review of the Debate in the Virginia Legislature of 1831 and 1832,* analyzing the arguments made for and against emancipating the slaves in the wake of Nat Turner's Revolt. Dew's conclusion was that, from the standpoint of whites' security and prosperity, slavery could not safely be abolished. Moreover, he argued, attempting to deport the emancipated slaves out of Virginia would be prohibitively expensive and, if attempted, would devastate its economy. His pamphlet was reprinted several times before the Civil War under the title *The Proslavery Argument.* Dew became president of William and Mary in 1836 and built up its enrollment from as few as twenty students to about 140.

Douglas, Stephen A.   (1813–1861), powerful Democratic senator representing Illinois from 1846 until his death, best known for sponsoring the Kansas-Nebraska Act of 1854 and for debating with Abraham Lincoln during the senatorial election campaign of 1858.

Douglas shared the conviction of many of his constituents that slavery did not involve any important moral issue—a viewpoint that Lincoln strongly rejected. He was largely instrumental in pushing the Compromise of 1850 through Congress. Four years later, Douglas proposed the Kansas-Nebraska bill because he wanted to see a transcontinental railroad built westward from Chicago, in which he had large real estate investments; southern politicians' price for agreeing to this scheme was to set aside the Missouri Compromise, which barred slavery from the area of the original Louisiana Purchase. Douglas was confident that the Missouri Compromise prohibition was not necessary to preserve the region for free soil. Cotton and other plantation crops, he reasoned, could not be grown on the western plains. Instead, Douglas proposed that "popular sovereignty" should prevail—that the issue of whether a territory became a free or a slave state should be determined by a vote of the settlers. But by never making it clear when such a vote should take place, he helped bring about the violent conflict between settlers from different sections in "Bleeding Kansas" between 1855 and 1857.

As the sectional conflict worsened, Douglas moved toward the free-soil position that most Illinois voters found appealing. He broke with the pro-southern Buchanan administration and criticized the Supreme Court's *Dred Scott* decision in 1857. The famous Lincoln-Douglas debates of 1858 largely revolved around the two candidates' differing responses to *Dred Scott* and to how the West should be preserved for white settlement. In these debates, Douglas appealed crudely to voters' racism and tried to portray Lincoln as an abolitionist and an "amalgamator" (advocate of race mixing). At that time, senators were chosen by state legislatures rather than by popular vote, and Douglas won reelection because the Democrats gained more legislative seats than the Republicans, who were pledged to Lincoln.

In 1860 the national Democratic Party split into northern and southern wings. Douglas was nominated for the presidency by the northern Democrats. Lincoln, the Republican nominee, won the White House owing to this Democratic split. Douglas, always a strong nationalist and advocate of the Union, braved threats of assassination by barnstorming the South urging it to reject secession, and when the Civil War broke out he closed ranks with Lincoln. His death a few months later is generally attributed to his physical exertion in defense of the Union, as well as to his lifelong habits of overeating and overdrinking.

Douglass, Frederick   (1817–1895), the foremost black abolitionist, generally acknowledged as the greatest African American leader of the nineteenth century. (For a biographical sketch, see Chapter 14.)

Du Bois, W.E.B.   (1868–1963), brilliant black scholar and political leader whose career began in the late nineteenth century and spanned almost two-thirds of the twentieth century. He received a Ph.D. from Harvard in 1896 for a dissertation on the suppression of the slave trade, and later undertook important sociological investigations of black society and culture, including *The Souls of Black Folk* (1903). Teaching at historically black Fisk University, Du Bois vigorously defended African Americans against the racism in the white scholarship of the early twentieth century, and he laid the foundations for the more accurate and sympathetic treatment of black history that prevails today. He was one of the leaders in founding the National Association for the Advancement of Colored People between 1905 and 1909, and for many years he edited its magazine, *Crisis.* Du Bois also became a leader in the international Pan-Africanist movement, an attempt to unite the U.S. civil rights movement with anticolonialist movements in Africa. He became more radical in the 1930s, and his eventual decision in 1961 to join the American Communist Party caused him to be ostracized from the mainstream black movement. He died in Ghana, where he moved at the very end of his life and renounced American citizenship.

Dunmore, John, Lord   (1732–1809), last British governor of colonial Virginia. Dunmore belonged to the Scottish nobility and was appointed to his position in 1770. In Virginia he speculated in western lands, but as criticism of British rule mounted, he tended to overreact, causing him to lose power even more quickly. His last-ditch attempt to rally slaves to the British side, as well as to stir up the Indians against the rebels, had the opposite effect of uniting white Virginians behind the patriot leaders.

Emerson, Ralph Waldo   (1803–1882), one of the most important American men of letters in the nineteenth century. Emerson was the most prominent of the Transcendentalists, a group of New England writers and thinkers who attempted to redirect American intellectual life toward a more spiritual, less religiously dogmatic outlook. Like most other New England intellectuals, Emerson was strongly antislavery, though he may also have felt some personal prejudice against blacks. After John Brown's execution, he said that Brown had "made the gallows as glorious as the cross."

Equiano, Olaudah   (ca. 1745–1797), African-born slave who later wrote a moving account of his life, *The Interesting Narrative of the Life of Olaudah Equiano, or Gustavus Vassa, the African* (1789). Equiano was the first black slave who was able to tell his story to whites, and his book is a major source of our knowledge about eighteenth-century slavery and the experience of the Middle Passage. Equiano spent his last years tirelessly campaigning in Great Britain against slavery and the slave trade. (For a biographical sketch of Equiano, see Chapter 1.)

Fitzhugh, George   (1806–1881), Virginia proslavery writer. A lawyer who belonged to what he considered an aristocratic family descending from English nobility, Fitzhugh was a friend of J.D.B. De Bow. His books *Sociology for the South* (1854) and *Cannibals All! or, Slaves Without Masters* (1857) were among the most extreme of the pre–Civil War southern defenses of slavery.

Agreeing with mid-nineteenth-century socialists, Fitzhugh denounced capitalism as inherently exploitative and unjust. Unlike the socialists, however, he rejected political democracy and social reform, advocating instead that slavery be extended to the northern white working class. He believed that paternalistic slave owners would treat their human property, whether white or black, more justly than capitalistic factory owners. He also claimed that aristocratic southern white slave owners were racially superior to other whites, and should dominate the United States as a whole.

After the Civil War, Fitzhugh continued to practice law but faded into obscurity.

Frémont, John C.   (1813–1890), American explorer of the Far West, politician, and Civil War general. In the 1840s Frémont became famous as "the Pathfinder" who explored the Rocky Mountain area and took an important role in the American annexation of California. As the Republican Party's presidential nominee in 1856, he showed that the new party was capable of mounting a serious challenge to capture the White House. During the Civil War, Frémont commanded Union troops in Missouri, where in 1862 he attempted to emancipate the slaves on his own authority. His action was overruled by Abraham Lincoln, who insisted that as commander-in-chief the president alone had the power to issue such an order.

Gabriel   (ca. 1775–1800), also known as Gabriel Prosser, Virginia slave who led a widespread conspiracy intended to begin a slave rebellion. Gabriel was owned by Thomas H. Prosser, whose name is sometimes given as Gabriel's surname. The son of an African-born mother, Gabriel was deeply religious and became convinced that God had called him to deliver black people from bondage. In 1800, using an extensive network of contacts, Gabriel assembled an army of several thousand poorly armed black supporters with the intention of seizing Richmond, massacring all whites (except for Frenchmen, Methodists, and Quakers), and proclaiming himself the king of a black state, to which other insurgent slaves could rally. Exactly what role a French agent in Virginia may have played in this plot has never been clarified. A thunderstorm prevented the plan from being put into effect and gave the white authorities, who had been tipped off by a black informer, time to crush the would-be rebels. Gabriel and thirty-four of his closest associates were tried, convicted, and hanged. At his trial, Gabriel declared that, like George Washington, he had fought for the liberty of his people. His revolt so frightened Virginia whites that talk of emancipating slaves diminished rapidly.

Garnet, Henry Highland (1815–1882), important black abolitionist. Born a slave in Maryland, Garnet fled to New York in 1824. He was ordained a Presbyterian minister and became active in the American Anti-Slavery Society. In 1843 he publicly called on slaves to kill their masters, a radical stand that the black and white abolitionist groups did not endorse. Eventually overshadowed by Frederick Douglass, he turned his attention more to Presbyterian church affairs. During the Civil War he promoted the welfare of ex-slaves in Washington, D.C. Disgusted at the deteriorating position of blacks in the post-Reconstruction South, he advocated voluntary return to Africa. He moved to Liberia in 1882, but died soon after arriving.

Garrison, William Lloyd (1805–1879), major figure in the abolitionist movement. Born to a poor family in Massachusetts, Garrison grew up in an intensely religious atmosphere, and as a young man supported the American Colonization Society. He worked as a printer for the Quaker abolitionist editor Benjamin Lundy. By 1830, after taking alarm at the violent tone of David Walker's *Appeal*, he converted from gradualist emancipation to "immediatism," a slogan of the British antislavery movement indicating a demand for emancipation without any transitional period. *The Liberator,* the antislavery newspaper he began publishing in Boston in 1831, was uncompromisingly immediatist. Thereafter, Garrison always took the most radical positions against slavery, as well as in defense of women's rights. In 1840 he and a small group of supporters brought about a split in the abolitionist movement, and by 1844 he was advocating pacifism, nonparticipation in civic affairs (such as voting), and the North's secession from the slaveholding South. His influence declined in the 1850s, but during the Civil War he abandoned pacifism and strongly supported Abraham Lincoln's approach to emancipation. In 1865, with slavery dead, he attempted to dissolve the American Anti-Slavery Society, generally retired from public life, and declined to support activist efforts on behalf of ex-slaves' political rights.

Greeley, Horace (1811–1872), one of the most important newspaper editors of nineteenth-century America and a prominent antislavery advocate. A Whig, Greeley viewed political issues in strongly moralistic terms. In 1841 he founded the New York *Tribune,* which became known for the high quality of its news coverage and editorial writing. Greeley developed an intense political ambition in the 1850s and became one of the leaders of the new Republican Party, though he sometimes took eccentric political stands. He was uncompromisingly antislavery and generally supported the Radical Republicans during the Civil War. He opposed Abraham Lincoln's renomination in 1864 and in 1872 broke with President Ulysses S. Grant over the issue of political corruption to accept the presidential nomination of the Democratic Party (which he had spent his whole career denouncing), but he died soon after the election.

Grimké, Angelina (1805–1879), important abolitionist and women's rights advocate in the pre–Civil War era. Born into a wealthy, slaveholding family in Charleston, South Carolina, she and her sister Sarah developed an early dislike of slavery and were converted to Quakerism while they were visiting Philadelphia. After they publicly announced their approval for William Lloyd Garrison and his *Liberator* in 1835, they were informed by the authorities in Charleston that they would be imprisoned if they ever came back. The sisters began to speak in public at antislavery rallies attended by both men and women—at that time, a shocking thing for women to do—and the hostility that they encountered turned them into agitators for women's rights as well. Angelina Grimké married the prominent abolitionist Theodore Weld and did much of the work in compiling *American Slavery As It Is* (1839). Ill health later forced her to retire from the public view, but she continued her commitment to education and reform until her death.

Grimké, Sarah (1792–1873), elder sister of Angelina Grimké, whose views and activist stand against slavery and for women's rights she fully shared.

Hemings, Sally (1773–1835), long rumored and now widely believed to have been the enslaved mistress of Thomas Jefferson. Her father, John Wayles, was the Virginia slave owner whose legitimate daughter was Jefferson's wife, Martha Wayles Jefferson; as a young girl, Sally was Martha's personal servant. Although no portraits of her are known, she is said to have had a strong physical resemblance to Martha, including a light-skinned complexion. Martha died young, in 1782. In 1787, Jefferson, then serving as American minister to France, had Hemings (who was now his daughter's maid) and his young daughter sent to him. Hemings may have become Jefferson's mistress before he returned to the United States in 1789. She remained a slave at Monticello for the rest of her life, but she and her relatives enjoyed unusual privileges. DNA evidence shows that a male Jefferson—quite likely Thomas—was the father of her last child, conceived in 1808, and all of her known pregnancies coincided with times when she was with Jefferson in Paris or he was staying at Monticello. (For a biographical sketch of Hemings, see Chapter 5.)

Jacobs, Harriet Ann (1813–1897), escaped slave who, under the pen name of Linda Brent, published a book describing her experiences, *Incidents in the Life of a Slave Girl* (1861). Her book, some of whose sensational details have been corroborated by historians, gives a picture of sexual exploitation under slavery.

Jacobs was born in slavery in North Carolina. She had several children by a white lover, but, with the help of a sympathetic white family, she had to spend seven years in hiding (sometimes in an attic) to escape the sexual advances of her master. During this period of concealment she perfected her skills in needlework and taught herself to read and write. Eventually she was able to escape to New York, where she worked as a nursemaid and became active in the antislavery movement. There she met Harriet Beecher Stowe and told her some of her experiences, but not all the sexual details. When *Uncle Tom's Cabin* was published, however, Jacobs was angry because she thought Stowe had distorted what she had told her.

Jacobs wrote *Incidents* with the editorial assistance of Lydia Maria Child. Her intention was to make white women understand the sexually exploitative side of slavery and the parallels between slavery and certain aspects of marriage in contemporary white society. *Incidents* first appeared in serial form in Horace Greeley's *New York Tribune* in 1855 and in book form in 1861.

During the Civil War Jacobs worked as a nurse and teacher in Alexandria, Virginia, which was occupied by federal troops. After the war she lived in Washington, D.C., until her death.

Jay, John (1745–1829), New York lawyer and diplomat who served as the first chief justice of the U.S. Supreme Court. Although a slave owner, Jay was active in the movement for the gradual emancipation of slaves in New York State, which was accomplished by a law passed in 1799. He was also one of the coauthors (with James Madison and Alexander Hamilton) of *The Federalist* (1788), a collection of brilliant essays urging adoption of the U.S. Constitution. He was a conservative Federalist who wanted to see the powers of the national government consolidated. He became intensely unpopular when he negotiated Jay's Treaty in 1795, which was supposed to settle grievances between the United States and Great Britain but unavoidably made many concessions to British demands. After serving as governor of New York from 1795 to 1801, he retired from politics.

Jefferson, Thomas (1743–1826), principal author of the Declaration of Independence, leader of the American Revolution, diplomat, third president of the United States (1801–1809), and Virginia slave owner. His views and actions with regard to human bondage make him an important figure in the history of American slavery, especially in light of the evidence (which most historians now consider overwhelming) that he fathered at least one child by a woman who was both his slave and his deceased wife's half-sister.

In the Declaration of Independence and other public papers, Jefferson wrote ringing phrases in favor of human rights and self-determination, but today many historians debate the extent to which his criticism of slavery was sincere. Despite his expressed distaste for human bondage, he never emancipated the many slaves who served on his estates. As a retired statesman, in 1820 he admitted that ending slavery would be impractical, likening the institution to a wolf that slave owners were holding by the ears, afraid to let go. On that same occasion, he deplored northern states' attempts to raise the slavery issue in the growing sectional conflict over whether to admit Missouri as a slave state.

Las Casas, Bartolomé de   (1474–1566), Spanish friar who as a layman went to Santo Domingo (Hispaniola) in 1502 and took part in the exploitation of the Indians, but then, appalled at what was happening, became an outspoken defender of Indian rights. Las Casas incessantly preached to the Spanish that they were committing a grave sin by abusing the Indians, and he worked diligently to inform the government at home of the need for reform. At first he suggested that Africans be imported in order to spare the Native Americans from oppression, but after seeing the treatment meted out to slaves he condemned black slavery as well. He spent most of his very long life writing reports documenting the destruction of the native people of the West Indies and Central America—a catastrophe that resulted partly from exploitative behavior by the Spanish but mostly from the Indians' lack of immunities to the microbes that Europeans and Africans brought to the New World. Las Casas is remembered as the first great human rights crusader in the history of the Americas.

Lincoln, Abraham   (1809–1865), sixteenth president of the United States (1861–1865) who led the federal cause to victory in the Civil War, preserved the Union, and freed the slaves.

Lincoln was a gifted lawyer, a superb politician, and a man of immense moral sensitivity. Traveling down the Mississippi River on a flatboat as a young man gave him his first real look at slavery, which he learned to detest. But as a practical politician he had to acknowledge (and perhaps to some extent he shared) the racist feelings of his fellow whites. He sat in the Illinois state legislature and was elected to Congress as a Whig in 1846, but he served only one term. During that term he vigorously protested the Mexican War, which he thought was part of a southern plot to add more slave territory to the Union. Semiretired from politics after 1848, he became a successful lawyer representing business interests. In 1854, Illinois senator Stephen A. Douglas's sponsorship of the Kansas-Nebraska Act, which overturned the Missouri Compromise, gave Lincoln the target he needed to resume his political career. He helped organize the new Republican Party in Illinois and ran against Douglas for the U.S. Senate in 1858. By clarifying the political issues related to slavery expansion, Lincoln's debates with

Douglas made him a national figure, even though not enough Republican legislators were elected to name Lincoln the state's senator. In 1860 the Republicans nominated Lincoln for the presidency because he seemed more moderate (and therefore more electable) than better-known rivals like William Seward and Salmon P. Chase. Lincoln was elected as a result of the split between northern and southern Democrats, each of whom nominated their own presidential candidate. Southern states, fearing that despite his promises Lincoln would take steps to destroy slavery, began to secede even before Lincoln's inauguration.

Lincoln said that his paramount objective was to save the Union, not to free the slaves, and until early 1862 he resisted ardent antislavery leaders' calls for a policy of emancipation. Lincoln knew that keeping the loyalty of the slaveholding border states was essential to preserving the Union. But in the spring of 1862, when it became obvious that the Union army was going to have a difficult time defeating the Confederates, and that northern patience with the indecisive war was ebbing, he decided to use emancipation as a strategy for undermining the rebellion. The battle of Antietam (September 1862) gave him the opportunity to announce that, unless the seceding states returned to the Union by January 1, 1863, he would make the slaves in these states "forever free." This deadline was ignored, and he promulgated the Emancipation Proclamation on the first day of 1863. The "war between the states" now became a war of liberation against slavery, and Lincoln agreed that black troops should be enlisted in the Union army and sent into combat. By the end of the war, African American soldiers constituted about one-tenth of all federal forces and proved indispensable in achieving victory.

Lincoln's popularity with the northern public depended on the military situation. In November 1863, when he was riding the crest of surging popular support, he delivered his Gettysburg Address, pledging the nation to "a new birth of freedom." In the first half of 1864, amid another battlefield deadlock, complaints about Lincoln's effectiveness swelled, but he used his political wiles to ensure renomination. Then, in the fall, the military tide turned, giving him a landslide electoral victory. With the end of the war in sight, Lincoln revealed his true greatness by stressing the need not for vengeance but "to bind up the nation's wounds," as he put it in his Second Inaugural Address. Lincoln seemed to be moving toward granting black veterans and some other ex-slaves the right to vote and toward a reconstruction policy for the South that would bring together educated blacks and moderate whites. Whether this would have worked became forever unanswerable when, on April 15, 1865, Lincoln was assassinated by John Wilkes Booth, handing the presidency to the inept hands and racist prejudices of Vice President Andrew Johnson.

L'Ouverture, Toussaint. *See* **Toussaint L'Ouverture.**

Lovejoy, Elijah (1802–1837), abolitionist editor killed by a white mob in defending his right to print an unpopular newspaper. Lovejoy advocated a gradualist approach to emancipation. He originally published his paper in St. Louis, but under pressure from the community he moved across the Mississippi River to Alton, Illinois. There, mob violence several times caused the destruction of his printing presses, and in one riot in November 1837 Lovejoy lost his life. His death sent a wave of revulsion through the North and brought new recruits to the abolitionist cause. (See the biographical sketch of Lovejoy in Chapter 13.)

Lowell, James Russell   (1819–1891), American poet with strong antislavery convictions, which were especially evident in his *Biglow Papers* (1845–1848). In these poems, Lowell imitated the dialect of a shrewd Yankee farmer to denounce slavery and the Mexican War. Much of Lowell's poetry was concerned with other themes; he also published verses during the Civil War supporting the Union cause and justice for African Americans.

Lundy, Benjamin   (1789–1839), one of the first of the nineteenth-century abolitionists. Lundy, a Quaker, organized an antislavery society in Ohio in 1815 after witnessing the slave trade. He supported the American Colonization Society and at various places published a newspaper called *The Genius of Universal Emancipation;* William Lloyd Garrison worked on this paper as a printer in the late 1820s. Until his death, Lundy continued to look abroad for places where freed slaves could be resettled. He continued the abolitionist tradition begun by the Quaker John Woolman and was a transitional figure between the colonization movement and the "immediatist" abolitionists typified by Garrison.

Madison, James   (1751–1836), "Father of the Constitution" and fourth president of the United States (1809–1817). Madison, a man of superb intellect, was the guiding spirit of the 1787 Constitutional Convention in Philadelphia. As a member of the Virginia delegation, he worked out and presented at the beginning of the convention a plan for a greatly strengthened national (federal) government, replacing the loose structure created by the Articles of Confederation. With considerable modification to meet the demands of the smaller states, Madison's basic plan was embodied in the Constitution. His journal is an important source for analyzing the Convention's deliberations. During the ratification process, he was the principal author (with John Jay and Alexander Hamilton) of *The Federalist,* a penetrating explanation of the reasoning behind the Constitution and a groundbreaking work of political theory. After the Constitution went into force and the First Congress convened, Madison drafted the first ten amendments, which constitute the Bill of Rights. As president, Madison was much less effective. His administration blundered into the War of 1812, from which the United States barely emerged intact.

Madison was a slaveholder, much concerned with scientific farming. Like many leaders of Virginia in his generation, he deplored slavery but could not support its immediate abolition. On one occasion, when a slave escaped from his plantation but was recaptured, Madison emancipated and hired him.

McClellan, George B.   (1826–1885), Union general during the Civil War who organized a superbly equipped and trained fighting force, the Army of the Potomac, but was so cautious and indecisive in employing it that he failed to defeat the numerically inferior Confederate forces under Robert E. Lee. After the battle of Antietam (September 17, 1862), a bloody standoff in which the federal forces were unable to deal Lee's army a fatal blow, an exasperated President Lincoln relieved McClellan of his command. As a military professional, McClellan was contemptuous of Lincoln's strategic suggestions (which were often shrewd), and he kept the president ignorant of his own plans.

A strong opponent of emancipating the slaves, McClellan had close ties to the Democratic Party, which nominated him to run against Lincoln in 1864 on a platform of making peace with the Confederacy. As Union armies began winning a series of important battles in the fall of 1864, Democratic criticism of the president's conduct in the war lost credibility, and Lincoln won in a landslide. After the war, McClellan divided his time between military engineering, the railroad business, and politics.

Monroe, James   (1758–1831), governor of Virginia at the time of Gabriel's Insurrection (1800) and fifth president of the United States (1817–1825). Monroe was a Virginia slave owner and a participant in the American Revolution. He opposed ratification of the Constitution in 1788, but after its adoption he was elected to the U.S. Senate. A friend and political ally of Thomas Jefferson, Monroe favored keeping the federal government's power as limited as possible, a principle that he followed during his own lackluster administration. The Monroe Doctrine, which warned European governments that the United States would oppose any extension of their power into the Western Hemisphere, was largely the creation of Monroe's secretary of state, John Quincy Adams.

As governor of Virginia during Gabriel's Insurrection (1800), Monroe took vigorous action to suppress the rebellious blacks, and he approved of executing Gabriel and other leaders, yet he did what he could to prevent indiscriminate white retaliation.

Morris, Gouverneur   (1752–1816), New York banker, diplomat, and politician during the Revolutionary War and the early national period. As an expert on finance, Morris played a crucial part in trying to raise money for the American Revolution. At the Philadelphia Convention in 1787 he strongly criticized slavery. A Federalist, Morris advocated a strong central government and disliked democracy. He opposed the War of 1812 and favored separating New York and New England from the rest of the United States.

Parker, Theodore   (1810–1860), abolitionist Massachusetts minister and reformer. He was active in many social causes, including women's rights. He helped fugitive slaves to escape and was one of John Brown's important though secret backers before the Harpers Ferry fiasco.

Phillips, Wendell (1811–1884), abolitionist orator. Born to a wealthy Boston family, Phillips was trained in the law but dedicated his career and his considerable oratorical talents to the antislavery cause. He first made his mark by speaking at a Boston rally to protest the murder of abolitionist Elijah Lovejoy in 1837. Closely associated with William Lloyd Garrison, Phillips took an extremely militant stand against slavery. He was also one of John Brown's financial backers. During the Civil War, he assailed President Lincoln for not emancipating the slaves at once, and after the Emancipation Proclamation was issued he worked to ensure the freedmen's political rights. After the war he continued to speak out for women's rights, temperance, and other reform causes.

Pinckney, Charles (1757–1824), South Carolinian active in the American Revolution, and later governor of South Carolina. He contributed significantly to the work of the Constitutional Convention in 1787, including voicing demands on behalf of his slaveholding state that nothing be done to threaten slavery. In the early 1790s he switched from the Federalist to the Jeffersonian Republican camp, which favored limiting the power of the federal government. Late in life, he denounced the Missouri Compromise's ban on slavery expansion in the West.

Pinckney, Charles Cotesworth (1746–1825), South Carolinian Revolutionary War general and Federalist-era politician. He was the cousin of Charles Pinckney. Both men played important roles as leaders of the South Carolina delegation to the Constitutional Convention in 1787, opposing any provision that would weaken or threaten slavery. C.C. Pinckney remained a Federalist, took part in the abortive American mission to France in 1798 (in which the French demanded a huge bribe before beginning negotiations, the so-called XYZ Affair), ran unsuccessfully for vice president in 1800, and was the losing Federalist candidate for president in 1804 and 1808. With the collapse of the Federalist Party, he retired from politics.

Prosser, Gabriel. *See* **Gabriel.**

Remond, Charles Lenox (1810–1873), black abolitionist orator. A free black born in Massachusetts, Remond worked for the American Anti-Slavery Society. In 1840 the society sent him to London as a delegate to the World Anti-Slavery Congress, and he stayed abroad for a year and a half, lecturing in Germany, England, and Ireland. Later he was overshadowed by Frederick Douglass. During the Civil War he helped recruit blacks to serve in the famous 54th Massachusetts Regiment.

Scott, Dred (ca. 1800–1858), Missouri slave whose lawsuit demanding liberty on the grounds that he had been taken by his master to free territory precipitated a great sectional controversy on the road to the Civil War. (See Chapter 15 for a biographical sketch.)

Seward, William (1801–1872), antislavery New York politician who was Abraham Lincoln's chief Republican rival for the presidency, and who served under Lincoln as secretary of state. Seward was one of the founders of the Whig Party, served as governor of New York, and in 1849 was elected to the U.S. Senate. There he became famous (or notorious) for his provocative statement that when it came to slavery there was a "higher law"— God's law—than the Constitution. When the Whigs collapsed, Seward helped found the Republican Party, and he was considered its leading candidate for the presidential nomination in 1860. Lincoln wrested the nomination from him largely because Seward's "higher law" speech and his warning of an "irrepressible conflict" with the South made him appear too radical. Seward proved to be one of the nation's greatest secretaries of state.

Stowe, Harriet Beecher (1811–1896), American novelist whose *Uncle Tom's Cabin* had a tremendous effect in jolting northerners out of their previous indifference to slavery in the 1850s. She was the daughter of Lyman Beecher, a Connecticut minister who was one of the leading figures of the religiously oriented philanthropic movement in early nineteenth-century America known as the Benevolent Empire. Her brother Henry Ward Beecher and her sister Catharine Beecher were also notable figures in American public life. Harriet's husband, Ellis Stowe, an eminent biblical scholar, encouraged her to develop her literary talent. Before writing *Uncle Tom's Cabin*, she published other novels in the then-popular sentimental style. Her outrage over the Fugitive Slave Law of 1850 inspired her to begin *Uncle Tom's Cabin*, and upon its publication in 1852 the book garnered enormous sales in the United States and Great Britain. Dramatizations and serializations spread its message even farther. Stowe published other popular novels after *Uncle Tom's Cabin* and continued to advocate various social reforms.

Sumner, Charles (1811–1874), Massachusetts senator (1852–1874) who was a leading foe of slavery and advocate of black civil rights. Originally a Jacksonian Democrat, Sumner's antislavery convictions led him into the new Republican Party in the mid-1850s. His bitter 1856 speech denouncing "the crime against Kansas" allegedly committed by Stephen A. Douglas and by South Carolina senator Andrew Brooks (by opening the territory to advocates of slavery) caused him to be severely beaten with a cane in the U.S. Senate chamber by Brooks's nephew, Congressman Preston Brooks; Sumner was so badly injured that he could not return to the Senate for three years. During the Civil War, Sumner castigated President Lincoln for being slow in emancipating the slaves, and he opposed Lincoln's rather lenient terms for restoring the seceded states to the Union. During the Reconstruction period, Sumner was the leader of the Radical Republicans, who advocated severe treatment for the defeated South and voting and other civil rights for the ex-slaves. Sumner was one of the relatively few important U.S. politicians of the era who felt a genuine sympathy for African Americans, and who was free of racial prejudice.

Taney, Roger B. (1777–1864), chief justice of the U.S. Supreme Court whose decision in the *Dred Scott* case (1857) polarized the country. The son of a prominent Maryland slaveholding family, and a Roman Catholic, Taney was a Federalist before the War of 1812. He was a leading lawyer and eventually became a Jacksonian Democrat. President Jackson made him attorney general, and as a reward for his service named him as John Marshall's successor as chief justice in 1835. Taney left an important legacy on the Court by enlarging states' rights and by defining the legal status of corporations. All this has been overshadowed historically by his *Dred Scott* decision, in which he held that blacks were so inferior that they could not be citizens and that Congress had acted unconstitutionally by barring slavery from the West in the Missouri Compromise. Taney hoped that this decision would put to rest the sectional conflict, but it had the opposite effect. During the Civil War, he remained loyal to the Union and ruled against the Lincoln administration's attempts to jail citizens for opposing the war. Taney disliked slavery and freed the slaves he had inherited, but he opposed federal action with regard to slavery—an institution that he felt could be dealt with only by the states.

Tappan, Arthur (1786–1865), American businessman and, together with his brother Lewis, an important financial supporter of the antislavery cause. The Tappan brothers were drawn to the cause by their deep religious feelings, and they opposed William Lloyd Garrison's rejection of political action. Creating a new organization, the American and Foreign Anti-Slavery Society, they bankrolled the Liberty Party in its 1840 and 1844 elections. They became increasingly radical in the 1850s, encouraging resistance to the Fugitive Slave Law and helping runaway slaves escape.

Tappan, Lewis. *See* **Tappan, Arthur.**

Thoreau, Henry David (1817–1862), American essayist and antislavery writer, best known for *Walden* and for his civil disobedience against unjust government actions. Thoreau, a Harvard graduate, was befriended by Ralph Waldo Emerson, a fellow citizen of his hometown, Concord, Massachusetts. In 1854 he published *Walden,* a philosophical essay describing his earlier experience of living by Transcendentalist principles for two years in a simple woodland hut at Walden Pond, outside Concord. While living there, Thoreau put his principles to another test in 1846 by refusing to pay a small state tax that, he believed, would be used to support the Mexican War and the expansion of slavery. As a result, he spent a night in the town jail. Out of this came his pamphlet "Civil Disobedience" (1849), which eventually exerted a profound influence on such apostles of nonviolence as Mohandas Gandhi and Dr. Martin Luther King Jr. Thoreau, however, was not a pacifist, as is evident from his passionate defense of John Brown in 1859. At the time of his premature death from tuberculosis, Thoreau was directing his efforts toward the science of biology, a product of his lifelong nature studies and his interest in evolution provoked by studying Charles Darwin's *Origin of Species.*

Toussaint L'Ouverture (ca. 1743–1803), leader of the most successful slave revolt in the history of the Western Hemisphere. Toussaint (he added L'Ouverture to his name in 1793) was the son of an educated slave. His master favored him, gave him responsible managerial work, and in 1777 freed him. A fervent Catholic, Toussaint took from Christianity a burning hatred of slavery, and his magnetic, puritanical character made him a charismatic figure to all who met him. Joining the slave revolt that broke out in 1791, he helped his former master flee but then took part in the bloody vengeance that the rebels were inflicting on whites and mulattoes. (In the French Caribbean, mulattoes, or people of mixed ancestry, formed a distinct racial category, unlike in North America, where they were classified as blacks.) Toussaint displayed remarkable talent as a military strategist, repeatedly defeating the French troops and cooperating with the British and Spanish when they invaded Saint Domingue in 1793. However, the British and Spanish refusal to emancipate the slaves, coupled with the arrival of news that the French Republic had done so, caused Toussaint to go over to the side of the humbled French forces in 1794.

The French made him lieutenant governor of the colony, nominally under a French governor general, but actually Toussaint was the real ruler, and he defeated his former British and Spanish allies. Realizing that the island's ruined economy had to be rebuilt, he preached racial reconciliation, welcomed former owners back, and forced former slaves (now wage workers) to return to their tasks. In return for a promise not to attack the British West Indian colonies or the United States, he restored trade with these former commercial partners. He also eliminated his black rivals and forced out an atheistic and "immoral" French governor. In 1801, by now in complete control of the colony, he invaded Spanish Santo Domingo (the eastern two-thirds of the island), freed its slaves, and offered magnanimous terms to the whites if they would stay. Napoléon Bonaparte, then the ruler of France, recognized his power over the island, but Toussaint knew that Bonaparte hated blacks and planned to restore slavery. Other blacks, motivated by equally strong hatred of all whites, were coming to distrust Toussaint because of his wish for racial equality and his mysterious, occasionally brutal acts.

In 1802 a large French force landed, and most whites and mulattoes defected to it. Inviting Toussaint to a parley, the French general had him arrested and sent to a prison in France. He died there the next year. But meanwhile yellow fever was decimating the French troops, and the blacks rose in another massive revolt that culminated in the establishment of the black state of Haiti.

Truth, Sojourner (1797–1883), emancipated slave and crusader for abolition and women's rights. Sojourner Truth was the adopted name of Isabella Van Wagener. Born a slave to a Dutch-speaking family in New York, she learned Dutch before English. After abusive relationships with her early masters, she found refuge with Isaac Van Wegener, who emancipated her in 1827, shortly before she would have become legally free under New York law. A deeply religious Quaker, and inspired by what she believed were heavenly voices, she worked in New York City as a lay preacher while supporting herself by doing domestic labor.

She renamed herself Sojourner Truth in 1843 and became an itinerant preacher, as well as a powerful speaker on behalf of the antislavery and, after 1850, women's rights causes. During the Civil War she worked to supply black Union volunteers and was instrumental in integrating the streetcars of Washington, D.C. After the war she worked with the Freedmen's Bureau and encouraged former slaves to migrate to the West. (For a full biographical sketch of Sojourner Truth, see Chapter 14.)

Tubman, Harriet   (1820–1913), escaped slave who became a leading black abolitionist. In 1849 Tubman fled slavery in Maryland. Then, courageously, she returned to the South numerous times to help more than three hundred other slaves escape. In the North, she was befriended by the leading abolitionists, including John Brown. During the Civil War she worked as a nurse, laundress, and spy with the Union army in coastal South Carolina. In her poverty-stricken old age, she was honored for her wartime service with a government pension.

Turner, Nat   (1800–1831), Virginia slave who led the most important slave revolt of the nineteenth century. Turner's African-born mother taught him a passionate hatred of slavery and convinced him that he had supernatural gifts. Secretly learning to read deepened his religious faith, which was a mixture of Christianity and African tradition. Turner was trusted by his owners, who had no idea of what he was preaching to fellow slaves. In August 1831, an eclipse convinced him that the moment to strike had come. With some seventy-five followers he went on a murderous rampage, killing fifty-five whites, mostly with axes while they slept. He tried to reach the inaccessible Dismal Swamp, but a large force of whites managed to disperse his band, meanwhile massacring many blacks who had had nothing to do with the revolt. Turner himself was tracked down, tried, and hanged. Turner's revolt terrified southern whites and led to a more repressive treatment of slaves. It also helped end serious consideration of emancipation in Virginia. Blacks, however, revered "Old Nat" as a hero and martyr.

Vassa, Gustavus. *See* **Equiano, Olaudah.**

Vesey, Denmark   (ca. 1767–1822), South Carolina free black who organized an antislavery conspiracy in Charleston. Vesey was probably born in the Danish Virgin Islands and was sold to a sea trader, with whom he traveled extensively before settling in Charleston in 1783. Having won a lottery, in 1800 he was able to buy his freedom. He educated himself. Aware of the history of the Haitian revolution and able to read antislavery literature, he eventually decided to organize a slave uprising. As many as nine thousand slaves may have been involved in his plot to seize control of Charleston. The white authorities were warned by a black slave, and Vesey and about 130 others were arrested; he was one of thirty-five who were hanged.

Walker, David   (1785–1830), black abolitionist whose *Appeal . . . to the Colored Citizens of the World* (1829) sounded an impassioned call to struggle for liberation, violently if necessary. Walker, the son of a slave father and a free mother, was brought up free. He was largely self-taught. Able to travel extensively, he wound up living in Boston, where he supported himself as a secondhand clothes dealer. There he wrote and printed his *Appeal.* His occupation enabled him to slip antislavery literature to sailors, who smuggled it into southern ports. After this literature began turning up in the South, it was traced to Walker, but he refused suggestions that he flee to Canada. When he was found dead in his shop, poisoning was suspected but never proved. Walker's *Appeal,* with its apocalyptic tone and approval of violence, alarmed antislavery whites, among them William Lloyd Garrison; the urgency of Garrison's demand for an immediate end to slavery was in part driven by concerns that Walker's pamphlet had aroused.

Washington, Booker T.   (1856–1915), one of the two most important African American leaders of the late nineteenth and early twentieth centuries (the other being W.E.B. Du Bois). Washington was born in slavery in Virginia, and he moved with his family to West Virginia after emancipation. There he labored in a coal mine. Later he supported himself by working as a janitor while attending Hampton Institute, a black college in Virginia. After graduation, he joined the staff of Hampton. In 1881 he became head of Tuskegee Institute in Alabama, where he gained national fame for advocating vocational training and other forms of self-help for African Americans.

Washington saw self-help as essential for black people to enhance their dignity, their economic resources, and their inner strength. Outwardly claiming to accept African Americans' subordinate position in the Jim Crow era, he secretly did what he could to encourage resistance to segregation. Washington clashed with the more overtly militant Du Bois, but because he seemed to be more "moderate" and accommodating he became a great favorite of white progressives, including President Theodore Roosevelt, who received him at the White House despite vehement protests from racists.

Webster, Daniel   (1782–1852), U.S. senator from Massachusetts (1827–1841, 1845–1850), one of the dominant figures of pre–Civil War politics. Originally a Federalist and a defender of the New England states' claim to a right of nullification during the War of 1812, after the war he abandoned nullification and entered national politics as a National Republican. A strong anti-Jacksonian and defender of New England business interests, he became a Whig. He became famous for his 1831 speech during the Nullification Crisis in which he called for "Liberty *and* Union, now and forever, one and inseparable!" Together with Henry Clay, Webster spearheaded Whig opposition to Andrew Jackson and his successor, Martin Van Buren. Webster served as secretary of state from 1841 to 1843 and returned to the Senate. He was critical of the Mexican War. In 1850 he strongly supported the compromise in the face of strong opposition from his antislavery constituents. His speech of March 7, 1850, in defense of the compromise as Union-saving, is another classic of American oratory. From 1850 to 1852 he served again as secretary of state.

Weld, Theodore   (1803–1895), one of the leading white abolitionists. Weld trained for the ministry, but before he had graduated he became an agent for the American Anti-Slavery Society, recruiting new members. After he married Angelina Grimké, they worked together on *American Slavery As It Is* (1839), documenting the horrors of slavery. In the 1840s he lobbied Congress to get the gag rule lifted. He spent the rest of his life as an educator.

Welles, Gideon   (1802–1878), Connecticut politician and secretary of the navy under Abraham Lincoln. A man with strong antislavery convictions, Welles left the Democratic Party in 1854 to help found the Republican Party. He was highly effective as secretary of the navy, and Lincoln trusted his political advice.

Woolman, John   (1720–1772), American Quaker who was one of the earliest principled opponents of slavery. Humbly born and deeply religious, Woolman exemplified the Quaker reverence for the "inner light," the voice of conscience that Friends believed was God speaking directly to them in the quiet of contemplation. Woolman's "inner light" convinced him that slavery was morally evil. He traveled extensively in his native New Jersey and in Pennsylvania, Maryland, Virginia, and Rhode Island, visiting Quaker communities and urging individual Friends to free their slaves. His *Journal* is a valuable source not only for eighteenth-century slavery but also as the record of the thoughts of a man of conscience. Woolman died while in England, where he had gone as a Quaker missionary. Owing in significant measure to Woolman's influence, the American Quaker movement was moving toward abolitionism by 1770.

Old World Origins of Slavery in North America, 1690–1807

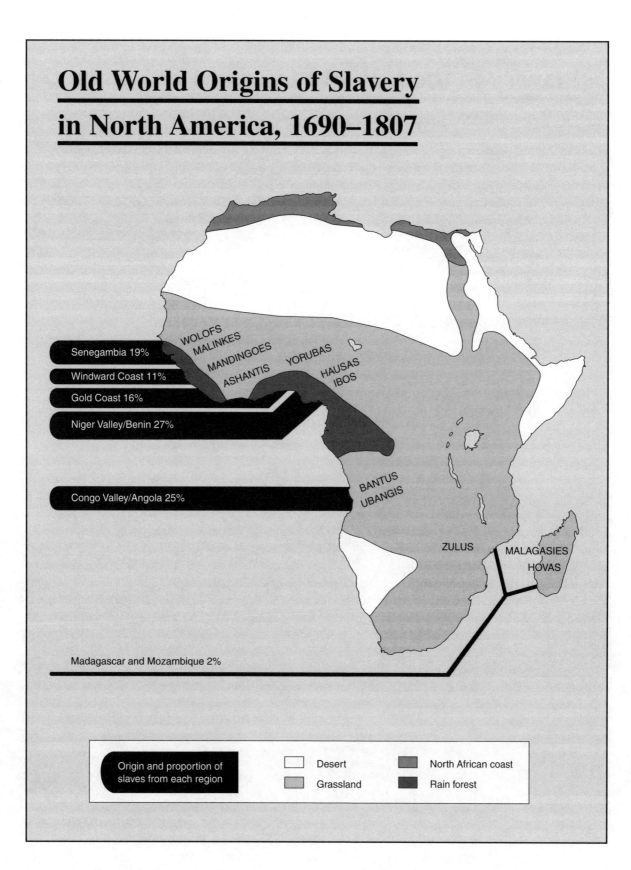

WOLOFS
MALINKES
MANDINGOES
ASHANTIS
YORUBAS
HAUSAS
IBOS
BANTUS
UBANGIS
ZULUS
MALAGASIES
HOVAS

Senegambia 19%

Windward Coast 11%

Gold Coast 16%

Niger Valley/Benin 27%

Congo Valley/Angola 25%

Madagascar and Mozambique 2%

Origin and proportion of slaves from each region

Desert

Grassland

North African coast

Rain forest

Slavery in the United States in 1790

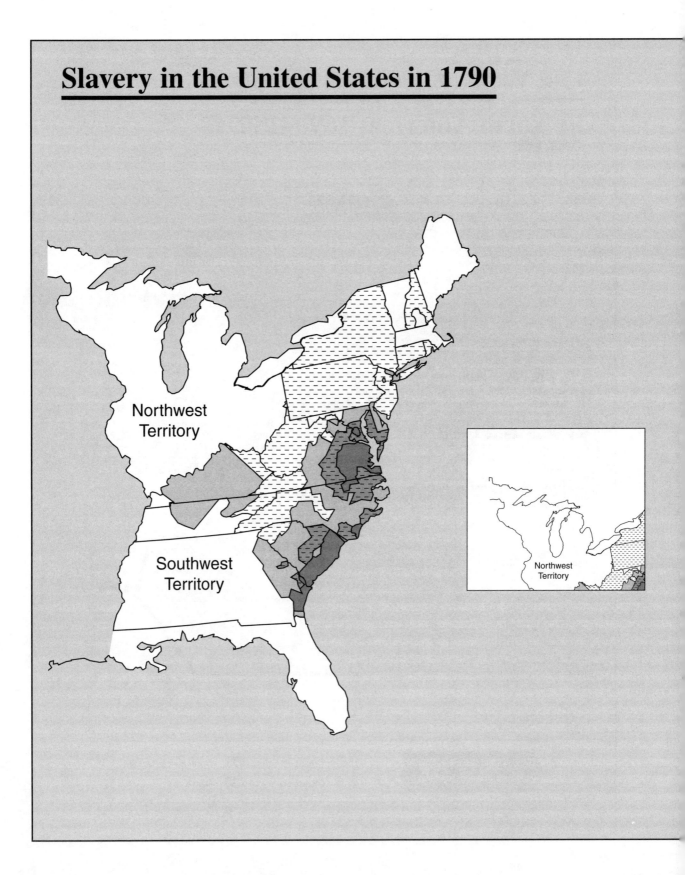

Slavery in the United States in 1860

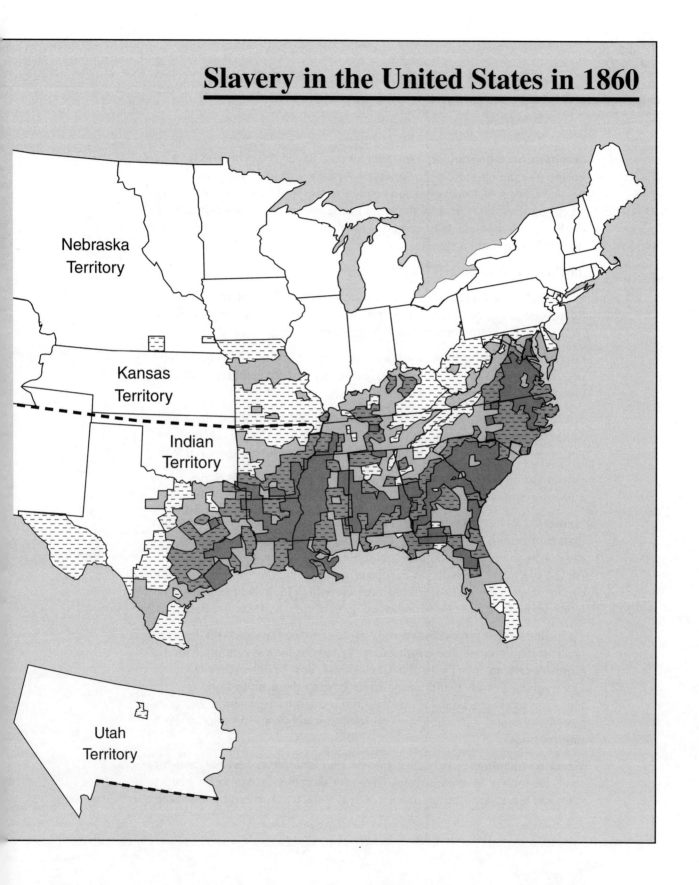

Nebraska
Territory

Kansas
Territory

Indian
Territory

Utah
Territory

Glossary of Terms

abolitionism; abolitionist: The demand that slavery be prohibited; an advocate of banning slavery. In American history, the antislavery movement began in the revolutionary era and resulted in the abolition of slavery everywhere north of Maryland by the early nineteenth century. Abolitionists included both "immediatists" and "gradualists," and they differed among themselves on many tactical issues.

antebellum: Before the [Civil] War.

Black Belt: The region of rich, dark (often black) soil in the interior of the South, stretching west across Georgia, Alabama, and Mississippi, that was well suited for cotton cultivation.

chattel: "Movable" personal property (as opposed to real estate), which a person can buy, sell, give away, lease, mortgage, bequeath, or inherit. By law, American slaves were chattel.

colonization: The policy of encouraging free blacks to leave the United States for resettlement overseas, especially in Liberia. Only a few thousand American blacks were ever induced to go to Liberia before the Civil War.

cotton gin: A simple, crank-driven machine devised by Eli Whitney in the 1790s for removing seeds from harvested cotton.

creole: A word of Spanish origin, meaning native-born American rather than European-born. Originally the term was confined to whites and reflected the greater political power and higher social prestige that the Spanish colonial system granted to European-born individuals. In the nineteenth century, especially in the Caribbean region (which included Louisiana), the word gradually came also to mean a person of racially mixed ancestry.

Fall Line: An imaginary line on the map connecting the rapids on the rivers (such as the Potomac, the Rappahannock, and the James) running from the North American interior to the Chesapeake Bay or the Atlantic Ocean. Ocean-going vessels could not navigate beyond these rapids, and thus the Fall Line marked a boundary in the Old South's transportation and commercial systems, separating the coastal Tidewater from the interior Piedmont regions.

Great Awakening: A period of intense religious fervor, revival, and turmoil. Historians identify several Great Awakenings in American history. The First Great Awakening, in the 1740s–1760s, was marked by a weaken-

610

ing of the formal authority of the established colonial churches (Congregationalist in New England, Anglican in the South) and by the rise of more emotional, less dogmatic forms of religious beliefs. Existing denominations (especially the Presbyterians) split, and new denominations (Methodists and Baptists) appeared, which often criticized slavery and the slave-owning elite. During the First Great Awakening, African Americans began to hear an emotional Christian message being preached, and large-scale conversions to Christianity began to occur among slaves. The Second Great Awakening, beginning about 1800 and carried forward in recurrent waves of religious emotion down to the Civil War, sparked the formation of a wide variety of reform movements directed against drinking and other forms of sinful behavior, and also against slavery and in favor of women's rights. Denominational diversity increased, and American Protestantism largely abandoned the Calvinistic tradition that had taught that everyone was predestined for salvation or damnation. Instead, salvation was held to be available to any sincere believer who wished to reform his or her life. Both whites and blacks were deeply affected by the Second Great Awakening: Slave owners and southern white clergy felt a need to find a religious justification for slavery, critics of slavery were sometimes inspired to demand the institution's abolition on moralistic grounds, and most blacks became deeply convinced Christians. During this era a distinctive African American form of Christianity took shape among slaves and free blacks alike, stressing God's mercy for those who found themselves in bondage and His promise of eventual liberty and salvation.

headrights: In seventeenth-century Virginia and Maryland, the practice of granting to a settler fifty acres of land for every additional person (whether free or unfree) whom that settler brought to the colony at his or her expense.

indentured servant: In the seventeenth and eighteenth centuries, a servant brought to the American colonies under a contract known as an "indenture." Such a servant agreed beforehand to work for his or her master for a term of years (usually five or seven), unpaid but receiving room and board. After the term had expired, the servant would regain personal liberty and would receive a modest grant of land. Until roughly the 1670s, indentured servants could include Africans as well as Europeans. The treatment of indentured servants was often very harsh—they subsisted on poor food, were overworked, suffered from brutal discipline and sexual abuse, and were subject to arbitrary extensions of the term of service as a punishment. All this misery was compounded by the high death rates that "unseasoned" Europeans and Africans suffered in the unhealthy Tidewater environment. As a result, historians believe that the odds were high that an indentured servant would not survive long enough to regain his or her freedom. Some did, of course, but after the 1670s, indentured servitude declined as a form of labor in Maryland and Virginia, giving way to African slavery.

Jim Crow: Blacks' name for the discriminatory laws that were enacted by white-dominated southern states in the post-Reconstruction period. These laws imposed rigid racial segregation and severely restricted blacks' civil rights, including the right to vote. Beginning in the late 1800s, the "Jim Crow" era lasted until the Civil Rights Revolution of the mid–twentieth century.

manumission: The legal act of voluntarily freeing a slave. Colonial and state laws governed the manner in which slaves could be freed, sometimes restricted the number of slaves who could be freed, and often required a freed slave to move away.

maroon: A community of runaway slaves, located in an isolated or protected place beyond the reach of slave owners. Maroons appeared in the slaveholding Portuguese and Spanish colonies, typically in remote forest or mountainous regions, but were uncommon in colonial North America. The most important North American maroons were in Florida, where local Spanish colonial officials encouraged slaves fleeing from the English colonies to form autonomous communities.

Mason-Dixon Line: The boundary between Maryland and Pennsylvania, surveyed in the eighteenth century. After slavery was abolished in Pennsylvania following the American Revolution, the Mason-Dixon Line became symbolic of the dividing line between free and slave states.

Middle Passage: Until the early nineteenth century, the routes of slave ships from West Africa to the Americas. Typically, the voyage was a harrowing experience for slaves who were "close packed" between decks, poorly fed, and brutalized, causing very high death rates.

mulatto: A person of mixed racial ancestry, and specifically half-white and half-black. Such distinctions (many others were also drawn) were typical of the Spanish and French, but not of the English, colonial societies. In the English colonies, and later in the United States, the tendency was to label anyone known to have even a small degree of African ancestry as "black."

overseer: A white man hired by the plantation owner to supervise the plantation's operations, including its slave labor force.

Old South: The southern states during the antebellum period.

patrol: See **slave patrol**.

"peculiar institution": Antebellum southerners' euphemism for slavery, "peculiar" in that it was what made the South a distinctive society within the United States.

Piedmont: The hilly interior of the South, separated by the Fall Line from the coastal Tidewater region and stretching west to the foot of the Appalachian Mountains.

plantation: In the seventeenth century, any unit of landed property held by a European settler ("planter"). By the eighteenth and nineteenth centuries, the term was generally reserved for a large, commercially oriented southern farming operation. *Plantation agriculture* is a modern term for commercially raising, in a colonial or semicolonial region, crops such as sugar, tobacco, or rice for shipment to an industrial center.

planter: See **plantation**.

Reconstruction: The post–Civil War period from 1865 to 1877, during which the former Confederate states were reintegrated into the Union, and the former slaves were accorded civil rights under varying degrees of federal military and political supervision. Reconstruction passed through several phases. First came the immediate postwar period (1865–1866), during which many ex-Confederates reasserted leadership of their shattered communities and plantation owners tried to force the ex-slaves—legally freed as a result of Lincoln's Emancipation Proclamation and by the adoption of the Thirteenth Amendment—to work for them under disadvantageous labor contracts. In the second phase, beginning about 1866 and extending in most states either to the late 1860s or the early 1870s, the defeated South was placed under federal military occupation and Congress supported the enfranchisement of former slaves. The Fourteenth and Fifteenth Amendments were added to the U.S. Constitution, guaranteeing blacks equal protection of the laws and black men the right to vote. During this phase, the southern states were governed by Republican administrations supported by black male voters. In the third phase of Reconstruction, beginning in the late 1860s and extending until 1877, white supremacist "redeemers" (drawn mainly from the old plantation elite) regained control of one southern state after another. The "redeemers" triumph owed much to the activities of the Ku Klux Klan and similar terrorist organizations, which intimidated blacks and the minority of pro-Reconstruction whites, and also to the growing indifference of northern public and Congressional opinion. Reconstruction ended in 1877 when the last federal occupation troops were withdrawn from the South and the last of the Republican state governments succumbed to the "redeemers." The Fourteenth and Fifteenth Amendments were not formally repealed, but federal and state courts increasingly ignored them while turning a blind eye toward the enforcement of black civil rights.

slave code: A system of laws or regulations officially defining the conditions and treatment of slaves.

slave driver: A slave whose job it was to "drive" the other slaves to work and to discipline those who failed to perform satisfactorily.

slave patrol: In the Old South, a group of local white men who had the legal obligation to "patrol" a rural community on the lookout for slaves who might be escaping from their plantations. Slaves could only move about the countryside if they carried a pass from their master authorizing their absence.

Slave Power: In antebellum America, the name that antislavery politicians and publicists applied to the alleged conspiracy of proslavery forces bent on controlling the U.S. government.

speculator: In the Old South, a slave trader.

spiritual: An African American song expressing strong religious faith, including a longing for both salvation and freedom.

Tidewater: The coastal regions of the Chesapeake Bay and of the Carolinas and Georgia.

triangle trade: A system of trade in the Atlantic region in the seventeenth and eighteenth centuries. Merchant ships sailed in a roughly triangular pattern between mainland North America, the Caribbean islands, and West Africa, buying and selling commodities at each point. For example, rum distilled in mainland North America was sold in Africa and the proceeds used to purchase slaves, who were sold in the West Indies; there, molasses was purchased for sale in mainland North America, where it was distilled into the rum destined to be marketed by traders who went to West Africa to buy slaves. Not all ships engaged in these voyages actually sailed in triangular patterns, however.

Underground Railroad: A system of routes and hiding places, complete with "stations," "conductors," and a "president," by which abolitionists aided slaves in escaping the South and finding refuge in the North or in Canada in the decades before the Civil War. Many historians now doubt whether any such organized system actually existed, arguing that the "Underground Railroad" was mainly a figment of the postwar imaginations of antislavery whites, who needed retroactively to magnify the degree to which they had acted as well as talked against slavery before the Civil War. However, there is no doubt that individual white and black abolitionists did offer important help to fleeing slaves, especially after the stringent Fugitive Slave Law of 1850 was passed. Probably most of the credit for helping slaves escape should go to free blacks, but there is little evidence that they maintained the kind of large regional networks that the legendary "Underground Railroad" implies.

For Further Reading

General and Reference Works

John B. Boles, *Black Southerners, 1619–1869.* Lexington: University Press of Kentucky, 1981.

John Hope Franklin, *From Slavery to Freedom: A History of Negro Americans.* 6th ed. New York: Vintage, 1980.

Lawrence B. Goodheart, Richard D. Brown, and Stephen G. Rabe, eds., *Slavery in American Society.* Lexington, MA: D.C. Heath, 1993.

Herbert Gutman, *The Black Family in Slavery and Freedom, 1759–1925.* New York: Pantheon, 1976.

Vincent Harding, *There Is a River: The Black Struggle for Freedom in America.* New York: Harcourt Brace Jovanovich, 1981.

Jacqueline Jones, *Labor of Love, Labor of Sorrow: Black Women, Work, and the Family from Slavery to the Present.* New York: Vintage, 1985.

Peter Kolchin, *American Slavery, 1619–1877.* New York: Hill and Wang, 1993.

Willie Rose Lee, ed., *A Documentary History of Slavery in North America.* New York: Oxford University Press, 1976.

Lawrence W. Levine, *Black Culture and Black Consciousness: Afro-American Folk Thought from Slavery to Freedom.* New York: Oxford University Press, 1977.

Randall M. Miller and John David Smith, eds., *Dictionary of Afro-American Slavery.* Westport, CT: Praeger, 1997.

Thomas D. Morris, *Southern Slavery and the Law, 1619–1860.* Chapel Hill: University of North Carolina Press, 1996.

Leslie H. Owens, *This Species of Property: Slave Life and Slave Culture in the Old South.* New York: Oxford University Press, 1976.

The Slave Trade and the Caribbean Background

Philip D. Curtin, *The Atlantic Slave Trade: A Census.* Madison: University of Wisconsin Press, 1969.

———, *The Rise and Fall of the Plantation Complex: Essays in Atlantic History.* New York: Cambridge University Press, 1990.

David Brion Davis, *The Problem of Slavery in Western Culture.* Ithaca, NY: Cornell University Press, 1965.

Richard S. Dunn, *Sugar and Slaves: The Rise of the Planter Class in the English West Indies, 1624–1713.* Chapel Hill: University of North Carolina Press, 1972.

Olaudah Equiano, *The Interesting Narrative of the Life of Olaudah Equiano or Gustavus Vassa, the African.* New York: Negro Universities Press, 1969.

Henry A. Gemery and Jan S. Hogendorn, eds., *The Uncommon Market: Essays in the Economic History of the Atlantic Slave Trade.* New York: Academic Press, 1979.

Alex Haley, *Roots.* Garden City, NY: Doubleday, 1976.

Joseph E. Inkiori and Stanley L. Engerman, eds., *The Atlantic Slave Trade: Effects on Economies, Societies, and Peoples in Africa, the Americas, and Europe.* Durham, NC: Duke University Press, 1992.

Herbert S. Kline, *The Middle Passage: Compar-*

ative Studies of the Atlantic Slave Trade. Princeton, NJ: Princeton University Press, 1978.

Robin Law, *The Slave Coast of West Africa, 1550–1750: The Impact of the Atlantic Slave Trade on an African Society*. New York: Oxford University Press, 1991.

Daniel C. Littlefield, *Rice and Slaves: Ethnicity and the Slave Trade in Colonial South Carolina*. Baton Rouge: Louisiana State University Press, 1981.

Paul E. Lovejoy, *Africans in Bondage: Studies in Slavery and the Slave Trade*. Madison: University of Wisconsin Press, 1986.

———, *Transformations in Slavery: A History of Slavery in Africa*. New York: Cambridge University Press, 1983.

James A. Rawley, *The Transatlantic Slave Trade: A History*. New York: W.W. Norton, 1981.

Richard B. Sheridan, *Sugar and Slavery: An Economic History of the British West Indies, 1623–1775*. Baltimore: Johns Hopkins University Press, 1973.

Barbara L. Solow, ed., *Slavery and the Rise of the Atlantic System*. New York: Cambridge University Press, 1991.

Colonial Slavery in Mainland North America

Timothy Breen and Stephen Innes, *"Myne Own Ground": Race and Freedom on Virginia's Eastern Shore*. New York: Oxford University Press, 1980.

Leland G. Ferguson, *Uncommon Ground: Archaeology and Early African America, 1650–1800*. Washington, DC: Smithsonian Institution Press, 1992.

Gwendolyn Midlo Hall, *Africans in Colonial Louisiana: The Development of Afro-Creole Culture in the Eighteenth Century*. Baton Rouge: Louisiana State University Press, 1992.

Winthrop D. Jordan, *The White Man's Burden: Historical Origins of Racism in the United States*. New York: Oxford University Press, 1974.

———, *White over Black: American Attitudes Toward the Negro, 1550–1812*. Harmondsworth, England: Penguin, 1968.

Marvin L. Michael Kay and Lorin Lee Cary, *Slavery in North Carolina, 1748–1775*. Chapel Hill: University of North Carolina Press, 1995.

Hugo Prosper Leaming, *Hidden Americans: Maroons of Virginia and the Carolinas*. New York: Garland, 1995.

Ronald L. Lewis, *Coal, Iron, and Slaves: Industrial Slavery in Maryland and Virginia, 1715–1865*. Westport, CT: Greenwood Press, 1979.

Edgar McManus, *Black Bondage in the North*. Syracuse, NY: Syracuse University Press, 1973.

Edmund Morgan, *American Slavery, American Freedom: The Ordeal of Colonial Virginia*. Chapel Hill: University of North Carolina Press, 1975.

Gerald W. Mullin, *Africa in America: Slave Acculturation and Resistance in the American South and the British Caribbean, 1736–1831*. New York: Oxford University Press, 1992.

———, *Flight and Rebellion: Slave Resistance in Eighteenth-Century Virginia*. New York: Oxford University Press, 1972.

Mechal Sobel, *The World They Made Together: Black and White Values in Eighteenth-Century Virginia*. Princeton, NJ: Princeton University Press, 1987.

Lorena S. Walsh, *From Calabar to Carter's Grove: The History of a Virginia Slave Community*. Charlottesville: University Press of Virginia, 1997.

Betty Wood, *The Origin of American Slavery: Freedom and Bondage in the American Colonies*. New York: Hill and Wang, 1997.

———, *Slavery in Colonial Georgia, 1730–1775*. Athens: University of Georgia Press, 1984.

Peter H. Wood, *Black Majority: Negroes in Colonial South Carolina from 1670 Through the Stono Rebellion.* Chapel Hill: University of North Carolina Press, 1974.

————, *Strange New Land: African Americans, 1607–1776.* New York: Oxford University Press, 1995.

The Revolutionary Era (1770–1830)

Ira Berlin and Ronald Hoffman, *Slavery and Freedom in the Age of the American Revolution.* Charlottesville: University Press of Virginia, 1983.

Fawn Brodie, *Thomas Jefferson: An Intimate History.* New York: W.W. Norton, 1974.

David Brion Davis, *The Problem of Slavery in the Age of Revolution, 1770–1823.* Ithaca, NY: Cornell University Press, 1975.

Douglas R. Egerton, *Gabriel's Rebellion: The Virginia Slave Conspiracies of 1800 and 1802.* Chapel Hill: University of North Carolina Press, 1993.

James Essig, *Bonds of Wickedness: American Evangelicals Against Slavery, 1770–1808.* Philadelphia: Temple University Press, 1982.

Paul Finkelman, *Slavery and the Founders: Race and Liberty in the Age of Jefferson.* Armonk, NY: M.E. Sharpe, 1996.

Sylvia Frey, *Water from the Rock: Black Resistance in a Revolutionary Age.* Princeton, NJ: Princeton University Press, 1991.

Annette Gordon-Reed, *Thomas Jefferson and Sally Hemings: An American Controversy.* Charlottesville: University Press of Virginia, 1997.

Alfred N. Hunt, *Haiti's Influence on Antebellum America: Slumbering Volcano in the Caribbean.* Baton Rouge: Louisiana State University Press, 1989.

Sidney Kaplan and Emma Nogrady Kaplan, *The Black Presence in the Era of the American Revolution.* Rev. ed. Amherst: University of Massachusetts Press, 1989.

Jan Ellen Lewis and Peter S. Onuf, eds., *Sally Hemings and Thomas Jefferson: History, Memory, and Civic Culture.* Charlottesville: University Press of Virginia, 1999.

Duncan J. Macleod, *Slavery, Race, and the American Revolution.* New York: Cambridge University Press, 1974.

Robert McColley, *Slavery and Jeffersonian Virginia.* 2nd ed. Urbana: University of Illinois Press, 1973.

John Chester Miller, *The Wolf by the Ears: Thomas Jefferson and Slavery.* Charlottesville: University Press of Virginia, 1991.

Benjamin Quarles, *The Negro in the American Revolution.* New York: W.W. Norton, 1961.

Donald L. Robinson, *Slavery in the Structure of American Politics, 1765–1820.* New York: Harcourt Brace Jovanovich, 1971.

Lucia Stanton, *Slavery at Monticello.* Charlottesville, VA: Thomas Jefferson Memorial Foundation, 1996.

Shane White, *Somewhat More Independent: The End of Slavery in New York City, 1770–1810.* Athens: University of Georgia Press, 1991.

Arthur Zilversmit, *The First Emancipation.* Chicago: University of Chicago Press, 1967.

Slavery, 1830–1860: Economic Aspects

Fred Bateman and Thomas Weiss, *A Deplorable Scarcity: The Failure of Industrialism in the Slave Economy.* Chapel Hill: University of North Carolina Press, 1981.

Charles B. Dew, *Bond of Iron: Master and Slave at Buffalo Forge.* New York: W.W. Norton, 1994.

Robert W. Fogel and Stanley L. Engerman, *Time on the Cross: The Economics of American Negro Slavery.* Boston: Little, Brown, 1974.

Eugene Genovese, *The Political Economy of Slavery.* New York: Vintage, 1965.

William K. Scarborough, *The Overseer: Plantation Management in the Old South.* Baton

Rouge: Louisiana State University Press, 1966.

Robert S. Starobin, *Industrial Slavery in the Old South*. New York: Oxford University Press, 1970.

Gavin Wright, *The Political Economy of the Cotton South*. New York: W.W. Norton, 1978.

Slavery, 1830–1860: The Experience of Enslavement

Ira Berlin, Marc Favreau, and Steven F. Miller, eds., *Remembering Slavery: African Americans Talk About Their Personal Experiences of Slavery and Freedom*. New York: New Press, 1998.

John Blassingame, ed., *Slave Testimony*. Baton Rouge: Louisiana State University Press, 1977.

Randolph B. Campbell, *An Empire for Slavery: The Peculiar Institution in Texas, 1821–1865*. Baton Rouge: Louisiana State University Press, 1989.

Frederick Douglass, *Narrative of the Life of Frederick Douglass, an American Slave* (1845). Numerous modern editions available.

Paul D. Escott, *Slavery Remembered*. Chapel Hill: University of North Carolina Press, 1979.

Barbara J. Fields, *Slavery and Freedom on the Middle Ground: Maryland During the Nineteenth Century*. New Haven, CT: Yale University Press, 1985.

Elizabeth Fox-Genovese, *Within the Plantation Household: Black and White Women of the Old South*. Chapel Hill: University of North Carolina Press, 1988.

Eugene D. Genovese, *Roll, Jordan, Roll: The World the Slaves Made*. New York: Vintage, 1974.

Wilma King, *Stolen Childhood: Slave Youth in Nineteenth-Century America*. Bloomington: Indiana University Press, 1995.

Ulrich B. Phillips, *American Negro Slavery*. New York: Appleton, 1918.

———, *Life and Labor in the Old South*. Boston: Little, Brown, 1929.

Kenneth M. Stampp, *The Peculiar Institution: Slavery in the Ante-Bellum South*. New York: Vintage, 1956.

William L. Van Deburg, *The Slave Drivers: Black Agricultural Supervisors in the Antebellum South*. Westport, CT: Greenwood Press, 1979.

Richard C. Wade, *Slavery in the Cities: The South, 1820–1860*. New York: Oxford University Press, 1964.

Deborah G. White, *Ar'nt I a Woman? Female Slaves in the Plantation South*. Rev. ed. New York: W.W. Norton, 1900.

Slavery, 1830–1860: Slave Communities and Culture

John W. Blassingame, *The Slave Community*. Rev. ed. New York: Oxford University Press, 1979.

Margaret Washington Creel, *"A Peculiar People": Slave Religion and Community-Culture Among the Gullahs*. New York: New York University Press, 1988.

Dena J. Epstein, *Sinful Tunes and Spirituals: Black Folk Music to the Civil War*. Urbana: University of Illinois Press, 1977.

Charles W. Joyner, *Down by the Riverside: A South Carolina Slave Community*. Urbana: University of Illinois Press, 1984.

Ann Patton Malone, *Sweet Chariot: Slavery, Family, and Household Structure in Nineteenth-Century Louisiana*. Chapel Hill: University of North Carolina Press, 1992.

Albert J. Raboteau, *Slave Religion: The "Invisible Institution" in the Antebellum South*. New York: Oxford University Press, 1978.

George P. Rawick, *From Sundown to Sunup: The Making of the Black Community*. Westport, CT: Greenwood Press, 1972.

Sterling Stuckey, *Slave Culture: Nationalist Theory and the Foundations of Black America*. New York: Oxford University Press, 1987.

Thomas L. Webber, *Deep Like Rivers: Education in the Slave Quarters, 1831–1865*. New York: W.W. Norton, 1978.

Slavery 1830–1860: Slave Owners and the Slave Society

David T. Bailey, *Shadow on the Church: Southwestern Evangelical Religion and the Issue of Slavery, 1783–1860*. Ithaca, NY: Cornell University Press, 1985.

Irving H. Bartlett, *Calhoun: A Biography*. New York: W.W. Norton, 1993.

Carol Blesser, ed., *Secret and Sacred: The Diaries of James Henry Hammond, a Southern Slaveholder*. New York: Oxford University Press, 1988.

Orville Vernon Burton, *In My Father's House Are Many Mansions: Family and Community in Edgefield, South Carolina*. Chapel Hill: University of North Carolina Press, 1985.

Catherine Clinton, *The Plantation Mistress: Women's World in the Old South*. New York: Pantheon, 1982.

William J. Cooper, *Liberty and Slavery: Southern Politics to 1860*. New York: Knopf, 1983.

———, *The South and the Politics of Slavery, 1829–1856*. Baton Rouge: Louisiana State University Press, 1978.

Drew Gilpin Faust, *James Henry Hammond and the Old South: A Design for Mastery*. Baton Rouge: Louisiana State University Press, 1982.

Drew Gilpin Faust, ed., *The Ideology of Slavery: Proslavery Thought in the Antebellum South, 1830–1860*. Baton Rouge: Louisiana State University Press, 1981.

George M. Fredrickson, *The Black Image in the White Mind: The Debate on Afro-American Character and Destiny, 1817–1914*. Middletown, CT: Wesleyan University Press, 1971.

Alison G. Freehling, *Drift Toward Dissolution: The Virginia Slavery Debate of 1831–1832*. Baton Rouge: Louisiana State University Press, 1982.

Eugene D. Genovese, *The World the Slaveholders Made*. New York: Pantheon, 1969.

Kenneth S. Greenberg, *Masters and Statesmen: The Political Culture of American Slavery*. Baltimore: Johns Hopkins University Press, 1985.

Michael P. Johnson and James F. Roark, *Black Masters: A Free Family of Color in the Old South*. New York: W.W. Norton, 1984.

Eric L. McKitrick, ed., *Slavery Defended: The Views of the Old South*. Englewood Cliffs, NJ: Prentice-Hall, 1963.

John R. McKivigan and Mitchell Snay, eds., *Religion and the Antebellum Debate over Slavery*. Athens: University of Georgia Press, 1999.

John Niven, *John C. Calhoun and the Price of Union: A Biography*. Baton Rouge: Louisiana State University Press, 1988.

James Oakes, *The Ruling Race: A History of American Slaveholders*. New York: W.W. Norton, 1982.

———, *Slavery and Freedom: An Interpretation of the Old South*. New York: W.W. Norton, 1990.

Robert V. Remini, *Henry Clay: Statesman for the Union*. New York: W.W. Norton, 1991.

Anne Firor Scott, *The Southern Lady: From Pedestal to Politics, 1830–1930*. Charlottesville: University Press of Virginia, 1970.

Steven M. Stowe, *Intimacy and Power in the Old South: Ritual in the Lives of the Planters*. Baltimore: Johns Hopkins University Press, 1987.

Michael Tadman, *Speculators and Slaves: Masters, Traders, and Slaves in the Old South*. Madison: University of Wisconsin Press, 1989.

Ronald Takaki, *A Pro-Slavery Crusade: The Agitation to Reopen the African Slave Trade.* New York: Free Press, 1971.

Larry Tise, *Proslavery: A History of the Defense of Slavery in America, 1701–1840.* Athens: University of Georgia Press, 1987.

Slave Resistance

Herbert Aptheker, *American Negro Slave Revolts.* 6th ed. New York: International Publishers, 1993.

John Hope Franklin and Loren Schweninger, *Runaway Slaves: Rebels on the Plantation.* New York: Oxford University Press, 1999.

Kenneth Greenberg, ed., *The Confessions of Nat Turner and Related Documents.* Boston: Bedford, 1996.

Helen Kromer, *Amistad: The Slave Uprising Aboard the Spanish Schooner.* Cleveland, OH: Pilgrim Press, 1997.

John Lofton, *Denmark Vesey's Revolt: The Slave Plot That Lit a Fuse to Fort Sumter.* Kent, OH: Kent State University Press, 1983.

Stephen B. Oates, *The Fires of Jubilee: Nat Turner's Fierce Rebellion.* New York: Harper & Row, 1975.

Abolitionism and Antislavery, Black and White

Robert H. Abzug, *Passionate Liberator: Theodore Dwight Weld and the Dilemma of Reform.* New York: Oxford University Press, 1980.

Eugene Berwanger, *The Frontier Against Slavery: Western Anti-Negro Prejudice in the Slavery Extension Controversy.* Urbana: University of Illinois Press, 1967.

James Bilotta, *Race and the Rise of the Republican Party, 1848–1865.* New York: Peter Lang, 1992.

R.J.M. Blackett, *Building an Antislavery Wall: Black Americans in the Atlantic Abolitionist Movement, 1830–1860.* Baton Rouge: Louisiana State University Press, 1983.

Stanley W. Campbell, *The Slave Catchers: Enforcement of the Fugitive Slave Law, 1850–1860.* Chapel Hill: University of North Carolina Press, 1968.

Lawrence J. Friedman, *Gregarious Saints: Self and Community in American Abolitionism, 1830–1870.* New York: Cambridge University Press, 1982.

Blanche Glassman Hersh, *The Slavery of Sex: Feminist-Abolitionists in America.* Urbana: University of Illinois Press, 1978.

Donald M. Jacobs, ed., *Courage and Conscience: Black and White Abolitionists in Boston.* Bloomington: Indiana University Press, 1993.

Aileen Kraditor, *Means and Ends in American Abolitionism: Garrison and His Critics on Strategy and Tactics, 1834–1850.* New York: Pantheon, 1970.

Gerda Lerner, *The Grimké Sisters from South Carolina: Rebels Against Slavery.* Boston: Houghton Mifflin, 1967.

Katharine Du Pré Lumpkin, *The Emancipation of Angelina Grimké.* Chapel Hill: University of North Carolina Press, 1974.

Henry Mayer, *All on Fire: William Lloyd Garrison and the Abolition of Slavery.* New York: St. Martin's, 1998.

Milton Meltzer, ed., *Frederick Douglass: In His Own Words.* San Diego: Harcourt Brace, 1995.

Stephen B. Oates, *To Purge This Land with Blood: A Biography of John Brown.* New York: Harper & Row, 1970.

Jane Pease and William H. Pease, *They Who Would Be Free: Blacks' Search for Freedom, 1830–1861.* New York: Atheneum, 1974.

Lewis Perry, *Radical Abolitionism: Anarchy and the Government of God in Antislavery Thought.* Knoxville: University of Tennessee Press, 1995.

Lewis Perry and Michael Feldman, eds., *Anti-Slavery Reconsidered: New Perspectives on the Abolitionists.* Baton Rouge: Louisiana

State University Press, 1979.

Benjamin Quarles, *Black Abolitionists*. New York: Da Capo Press, 1991.

Leonard L. Richards, *"Gentlemen of Property and Standing": Anti-Abolition Mobs in Jacksonian America*. New York: Oxford University Press, 1970.

Dorothy Sterling, *Ahead of Her Time: Abby Kelley and the Politics of Antislavery*. New York: W.W. Norton, 1991.

Harriet Beecher Stowe, *Uncle Tom's Cabin* (1852). Numerous modern editions available.

John L. Thomas, *The Liberator: William L. Garrison: A Biography*. Boston: Little, Brown, 1963.

John L. Thomas, ed., *Slavery Attacked: The Abolitionist Crusade*. Englewood Cliffs, NJ: Prentice-Hall, 1965.

Ronald G. Walters, *The Antislavery Appeal: American Abolitionists After 1830*. Baltimore: Johns Hopkins University Press, 1976.

Theodore Weld and Angelina Grimké Weld, *American Slavery As It Is: Testimony of a Thousand Witnesses*. Reprinted New York: Arno Books, 1968.

Bertram Wyatt-Brown, *Lewis Tappan and the Evangelical War Against Slavery*. Baton Rouge: Louisiana State University Press, 1969.

Jean Fagan Yellen and John C. Van Horne, eds., *The Abolitionist Sisterhood: Women's Political Culture in Antebellum America*. Ithaca, NY: Cornell University Press, 1994.

David Zarefsky, *Lincoln, Douglas, and Slavery: In the Crucible of Public Debate*. Chicago: University of Chicago Press, 1990.

Free Blacks in the South

Adele Logan Alexander, *Ambiguous Lives: Free Women of Color in Rural Georgia, 1789–1879*. Fayetteville: University of Arkansas Press, 1991.

Ira Berlin, *Slaves Without Masters: The Free Negro in the Antebellum South*. New York: Oxford University Press, 1974.

John Hope Franklin, *The Free Negro in North Carolina, 1790–1860*. Chapel Hill: University of North Carolina Press, 1967.

Michael P. Johnson and James L. Roark, eds., *No Chariot Let Down: Charleston's Free People of Color on the Eve of the Civil War*. Chapel Hill: University of North Carolina Press, 1984.

Suzanne Lebsock, *The Free Women of Petersburg: Status Culture in a Southern Town, 1784–1860*. New York: W.W. Norton, 1984.

Slavery and the Civil War

Ira Berlin et al., eds., *Freedom: A Documentary History of Emancipation*. New York: Cambridge University Press, 1990.

Dudley Cornish, *The Sable Arm: Negro Troops in the Union Army*. New York: W.W. Norton, 1966.

LaWanda Cox, *Lincoln and Black Freedom: A Study in Presidential Leadership*. Columbia: University of South Carolina Press, 1981.

Robert F. Durden, *The Gray and the Black: The Confederate Debate on Emancipation*. Baton Rouge: Louisiana State University Press, 1972.

Don E. Fehrenbacher, *The Dred Scott Case*. New York: Oxford University Press, 1978.

Paul Finkelman, ed., *Dred Scott v. Sandford: A Brief History with Documents*. Boston: Bedford, 1997.

John Hope Franklin, *The Emancipation Proclamation*. Garden City, NY: Doubleday, 1963.

William W. Freehling, *The Reintegration of American History: Slavery and the Civil War, 1780–1865*. New York: Oxford University Press, 1994.

Louis S. Gerteis, *From Contraband to Freedman: Federal Policy Toward Southern Blacks, 1861–1865*. Westport, CT: Greenwood Press, 1973.

Joseph T. Glatthaar, *Forged in Battle: The Civil War Alliance of Black Soldiers and White Officers.* New York: Free Press, 1990.

Janet Hermann, *The Pursuit of a Dream.* New York: Oxford University Press, 1981.

Thomas Wentworth Higginson, *Army Life in a Black Regiment.* 1867. Reprinted East Lansing: Michigan State University Press, 1960.

Victor B. Howard, *Black Liberation in Kentucky: Emancipation and Freedom, 1861–1884.* Lexington: University Press of Kentucky, 1983.

Peter Kolchin, *First Freedom: The Responses of Alabama's Blacks to Emancipation and Reconstruction.* Westport, CT: Greenwood Press, 1972.

Leon Litwack, *Been in the Storm So Long: The Aftermath of Slavery.* New York: Vintage, 1979.

James M. McPherson, ed., *The Negro's Civil War: How American Negroes Felt and Acted During the War for the Union.* Urbana: University of Illinois Press, 1982.

William F. Messner, *Freedom and the Ideology of Free Labor: Louisiana, 1862–1865.* Lafayette: Center for Louisiana Studies, 1978.

Clarence Mohr, *On the Threshold of Freedom: Masters and Slaves in Civil War Georgia.* Athens: University of Georgia Press, 1986.

Benjamin Quarles, *Lincoln and the Negro.* New York: Oxford University Press, 1962.

James Roark, *Masters Without Slaves: Southern Planters in the Civil War and Reconstruction.* New York: W.W. Norton, 1977.

Willie Lee Rose, *Rehearsal for Reconstruction: The Port Royal Experiment.* New York: Oxford University Press, 1964.

Bell I. Wiley, *Southern Negroes, 1861–1865.* New Haven, CT: Yale University Press, 1965.

Joel Williamson, *After Slavery: The Negro in South Carolina During Reconstruction, 1861–1877.* Chapel Hill: University of North Carolina Press, 1965.

C. Vann Woodward, *Mary Chesnut's Civil War.* New Haven, CT: Yale University Press, 1981.

Major Subject List

Index

Picture Credits

Archive Photos, 62, 71, 81, 192

Corbis, 224

Dover Publications, 278, 418

Library of Congress, 108, 159, 170, 262, 272, 350, 441, 449, 464

National Archives, 183, 332, 483, 509, 548

North Wind Picture Archives, 43, 88, 95, 119, 126, 135, 149, 202, 211, 231, 245, 252, 284, 297, 308, 322, 361, 369, 381, 397, 410, 427, 433, 459, 468, 496

Prints Old and Rare, 531

Stock Montage, 50